Trusts Law

Text and Materials

Fifth Edition

GRAHAM MOFFAT

Associate Professor in Law, University of Warwick

With

GERRY BEAN

Partner, DLA Phillips Fox, Melbourne

and

REBECCA PROBERT

Associate Professor in Law, University of Warwick

CAMBRIDGE
UNIVERSITY PRESS

CAMBRIDGE UNIVERSITY PRESS

Cambridge, New York, Melbourne, Madrid, Cape Town, Singapore, São Paulo,
Delhi, Dubai, Tokyo, Mexico City

Cambridge University Press
The Edinburgh Building, Cambridge CB2 8RU, UK

Published in the United States of America by Cambridge University Press, New York

www.cambridge.org
Information on this title: www.cambridge.org/9780521743822

First published by Butterworths 1988
Second edition first published by Butterworths 1994
Third edition first published by Butterworths LexisNexis 1999
Reprinted 2002
Re-issued by Cambridge University Press 2004
Fourth edition published by Cambridge University Press 2005
Reprinted 2006, 2007 and 2008
This edition published by Cambridge University Press 2009
Reprinted 2010

Printed in the United Kingdom at the University Press, Cambridge

A catalogue record for this publication is available from the British Library

Library of Congress Cataloguing in Publication data
Moffat, Graham.
Trusts law : text and materials / Graham Moffat, Gerry Bean, Rebecca Probert. – 5th ed.
  p.   cm. – (Law in context)
Includes bibliographical references and index.
Summary: "This fifth edition retains its hallmark combination of a contextualised approach and a
commercial focus. Recent developments, such as the Charities Act, are explored, the examination
of the law of trusts and taxation is restructured and comparative examples help students
understand the directions taken in the law of equity. Trusts Law brings a modern perspective to a
subject often perceived as traditional, with suggestions for further reading guiding the student to
contemporary debates" – Provided by publisher.
ISBN 978-0-521-76789-7
1. Trusts and trustees – Great Britain.   2. Trusts and trustees – Taxation – Great Britain.
I. Bean, Gerard M. D.   II. Probert, Rebecca.   III. Title.
KD1480.M64   2009
346.4105′9 – dc22   2009025027

ISBN 978-0-521-76789-7 hardback
ISBN 978-0-521-74382-2 paperback

Contents

8   The taxation of private trusts   371

9   An introduction to trustees and trusteeship   420

Preface to the fifth edition

This book seeks to present the law of trusts in a different way from conventional texts. The underlying premise is that an investigation of the social and legal contexts in which trusts commonly appear, and of the functions which trusts perform within these contexts, is an essential prerequisite to a proper understanding of trusts law. Developments that have occurred in the relevant social and legal contexts since the first edition of this book have confirmed our conviction in the value of this approach. The bulk of the book is therefore again divided into four parts: trusts and the preservation of family wealth (Chapters 3–11); trusts and family breakdown (Chapter 12); trusts and commerce (Chapters 13–16); and trusts and non-profit activity (Chapters 17–20). The new edition takes full account of the recent work of the Law Commission as well as statutory changes, including the Charities Act 2006, the Companies Act 2006 and those resulting from the Tax Law Rewrite Project, whilst the implications of the Perpetuities and Accumulations Bill 2009 are briefly introduced. Important cases, notably *Stack v Dowden* and *Barlow Clowes International Ltd (In Liquidation) v Eurotrust International Ltd*, together with an outpouring of academic literature, have all in their different ways contributed to a continuing debate about trusts law, particularly in its relationship to other areas of the common law. The effect of these influences is evident in all four parts of the book, as is the increasingly important international dimension of trusts law.

Our approach requires that, within each part of the book, relevant rules of trusts law are investigated usually only after the reasons why trusts are commonly created within the particular social and legal context – whether expressly by individuals or groups seeking to achieve particular purposes, or by court order – have first been studied. In the working out of this approach, express trusts and non-express trusts receive distinctly different treatment. Express trusts are depicted primarily as property-holding devices or 'institutions' which have been created, modified and refined by generations of practising lawyers in response to the particular purposes sought to be achieved by their clients. The law governing such trusts is presented as the judicial and, to a lesser degree, the legislative response to the aspirations of trusts lawyers and their clients (particularly as regards the rules determining whether novel forms of trust should be treated as valid) and to the numerous legal problems arising in the course of enforcement of valid trusts. The book shows how, in the main, this response has been supportive; otherwise English law would not include the highly sophisticated body of principles which we call trusts law. But circumstances in which judges or legislators have placed a check on the fulfilment of trust founders' objectives are also noted, along with the reasons why this should have occurred. In relation to non-express trusts, the focus of the book is chiefly on the relatively familiar theme that these contribute a quasi-remedial device for judicial innovation on grounds of 'equity'. But recourse to relevant contextual material paves the way for a discussion of how far 'equity' has in fact been achieved in specific social situations, and whether other express or implicit objectives – for example, legitimation of practices which might otherwise call for redress – are being pursued. The contexts in which these issues are most fully investigated are those of (1) family breakdown, where resulting and constructive trusts and proprietary estoppel have been prominent in a judicial search for some degree of 'equity' for non-earning (usually female) de facto spouses; and (2) commerce, where a battery of remedies, including a constructive trust, may be invoked in response to 'inequitable' behaviour by those in trust-like positions.

Although this way of classifying and analysing trusts law might seem to fragment the subject unduly, there is continued emphasis in the book on the unifying influence of the trust concept itself. The first chapter – 'Trusts introduced' – illustrates how the 'trust idea' in English law remains generally constant, despite having immense 'elasticity' (to quote Maitland), such as to render it useful in numerous social situations over several hundred years. This general proposition is reiterated later in the book. Nevertheless, there is a tension between fragmentation of the subject-matter of study and the notion of the 'trust idea' as a unifying feature. We suggest, however, that this reflects a source of tension within the subject itself, namely the competing influences on legal development of the claims of pure conceptual clarity as against pressures for pragmatic resolution of practical problems. An adequate understanding of trusts law requires that both these influences be taken into account by the student. Account also needs to be taken of one recent source of tension in the development of trusts law. A particular feature of our system of private law is the co-existence of overlapping jurisdictions. Circumstances can arise where the jurisdictions of the Law of Restitution, the Law of Trusts and even the Law of Tort can seem to overlap. It is at these points that tension can occur. We suggest that it is important to appreciate that efforts to minimise or remove any resulting dissonance may be a formative influence in current developments, particularly in the area of remedies for breach of trust or other 'inequitable' conduct.

In form the book is not an orthodox text, nor a set of cases and materials of a familiar type, but something in between. Textual commentary increasingly predominates, but extracts – sometimes quite long – from leading cases, statutes and relevant historical and empirical materials are also included. We assume that teachers using the book for a full-year undergraduate LL B course may want to indicate further cases and articles to be read. Many that are appropriate for this are mentioned in the text.

Many people have contributed to the production of this book. A change from the last edition is that John Dewar's increasing involvement in university management in Australia meant that he was unable to continue his contribution but, fortunately, Rebecca Probert agreed to step into the breach. As regards the division of labour in this edition therefore, Rebecca has contributed an almost completely rewritten Chapter 12 whilst Gerry Bean contributed Chapters 15 and 16. Graham Moffat bears responsibility for the remainder of the book. The intellectual debt owed to Michael Chesterman, the co-author of the first edition, is considerable, particularly in the areas of trust history and charity law, and is gratefully acknowledged. We are grateful to Sinéad Moloney and the publishing team at Cambridge University Press for their support and encouragement and for efficiently producing the index and tables of cases and statutes. The authors would also like to acknowledge the assistance of many trusts students, in responding over the years to ideas about trusts law put to them in the classroom and writing learned essays on trusts. Last and most important, as any writer knows, the gratitude owed to family tolerance cannot be overstated.

We have sought to take account of the law as at 1 April 2009.

Graham Moffat
Gerard Bean
Rebecca Probert

Acknowledgments

We are grateful to the following for allowing reproductions to be made from the publications indicated:

Basil Blackwell Ltd and R B M Cotterrell, *Journal of Law and Society*; Basil Blackwell Ltd and L Holcombe, *Wives and Property* (1983); Brookings Institution, R Barlow et al, *Economic Behaviour of the Affluent* (1966); Butterworths' Division of the Lexis-Nexis Group, The All England Law Reports; Canada Law Book Inc, Dominion Law Reports; *Cambridge Law Journal*; Foundation Publications, *American Bar Foundation Research Journal*; Council of Law Reporting for New South Wales, *New South Wales Law Reports*; Crown Copyright; Various Acts of Parliament; Incorporated Council of Law Reporting; Law Reports; Her Majesty's Stationery Office for the extracts from the Charity Commission Annual Reports; *Report of the Committee of Enquiry into the Public Trustee Office* (1972); *Report of the Insolvency Law Review Committee* (1982); Select Committee on a Wealth Tax (1975); CTT and Settled Property (1980); Law Commission, Law Commission No. 278, *Sharing Homes: A Discussion Paper* (2002); Consultation Paper No. 179, *Cohabitation: The Financial Consequences of Relationship Breakdown* (2006); Bernard Levin and Times Newspapers Ltd, *The Times*; C T Sandford, *Hidden Costs of Taxation* (1973); Little Brown & Co, R Pound (ed) *Perspectives of Law* (1964); Ministry of the Attorney-General of Ontario, *Ontario Law Reform Commission, Report on the Law of Trusts* (1984); *New York University Law Review*; Oxford University Press, *Oxford Journal of Legal Studies*; Pennsylvania Bar Association Quarterly; SLS Legal Publications, G W Keeton, *Modern Developments in the Law of Trusts* (1971); Thomson, Sweet and Maxwell for the extracts from J Edey and B Yamey (eds) *Debits, Credits, Finance and Profits* (1974); D J Hayton, *Commentary and Cases on the Law of Trusts and Equitable Remedies* (12th edn, 2005); A Oakley, *Parker and Mellows: The Modern Law of Trusts* (9th edn, 2008); G W Thomas, *Taxation and Trusts* (1981); Tolley Publishing Ltd, T Sherring, *Taxation of UK Trusts* (1990); *Conveyancer and Property Lawyer*; Fred B Rothman & Co, *University of Pennsylvania Law Review*; Consumers' Association, *Which?*; Yale Law Journal Company Inc, *Yale Law Journal*.

Abbreviations

Chesterman:	Chesterman *Charities, Trusts and Social Welfare* (1979)
Gardner:	Gardner *An Introduction to the Law of Trusts* (2nd edn, 2003)
Goff and Jones:	Goff and Jones *The Law of Restitution* (7th edn, 2007)
Hanbury and Martin:	Martin *Hanbury and Martin Modern Equity* (17th edn, 2005)
Hayton and Marshall:	Hayton and Mitchell *Commentary and Cases on the Law of Trusts and Equitable Remedies* (12th edn, 2005)
Parker and Mellows:	Oakley *Parker and Mellows: The Modern Law of Trusts* (9th edn, 2008)
Pettit:	Pettit *Equity and the Law of Trusts* (10th edn, 2006)
Snell:	McGhee (ed) *Snell's Equity* (31st edn, 2004)
Underhill and Hayton:	*Underhill and Hayton: Law Relating to Trustees* (17th edn, 2007)

Useful websites

None of us can ignore the vast range of internet sources now available and most students will have access to online resources such as Westlaw and/or Lexis. Other general websites that the reader may find useful are: www.bailii.org; www.austlii.org; www.wordlii.org; www.lawcom.gov.uk; and perhaps most useful of all is the invaluable 'hub' or 'gateway' maintained by the law librarian at Kent University: http://library.kent.ac.uk/library/lawlinks. Two specific websites relevant to Trusts Law are those of the Trust Law Committee (www.kcl.ac.uk/schools/law/research/tlc/) and the Charity Commission (www.charity-commission.gov.uk).

Table of statutes

Table of statutory instruments

Table of cases

1

Trusts introduced

1. Introduction

A 'trust' in English law is in some measure the translation into legal terms of the word 'trust' as used in ordinary speech. Its conceptual starting-point is 'a confidence reposed in some other' (this phrase is from the sixteenth-century legal commentaries of Lord Chief Justice Coke). The 'confidence' so reposed gives rise to moral obligations to which the courts, aided by the legislature, have purported to develop legal parallels. Inevitably, the moral weight given to trust and trusteeship in ordinary usage – to be 'in breach' of a 'sacred trust' is a serious matter, with repercussions possibly in the next world as well as this one – has had a significant impact on both the scope and the content of trusts law principles. There are still some contexts in which it may be difficult to say whether the word 'trust' is used in a legal or purely moral sense.

Yet this is by no means the whole story of trusts law. In the early twentieth century the historian and jurist F W Maitland praised the trust (see *Equity* (2nd edn, 1936) p 23 and *Selected Historical Essays* (1936) p 129); he regarded 'the development from century to century of the trust idea' as 'the greatest and most distinctive achievement performed by Englishmen in the field of jurisprudence'. But this was not because the trust embodied basic ethical principles but rather because of its versatility. It was, he said, '"an institute" of great elasticity and generality; as elastic, as general as contract'. The trust had in fact become a 'lawyers' device', used chiefly within the domain of private property transactions and institutions, and capable of serving a wide variety of purposes. In 1934, one finds a left-wing American commentator suggesting that, whatever the merits underlying the moral principle that a trust should not be breached, the versatility of this lawyers' device was exploited in at least one context – the preservation of private family wealth – in a manner which had little to do with ethics (M Franklin (1933–34) 19 Tul LR 473 at 475):

> The trust is an effort to escape from the ever-deepening and ever-recurrent crises in capitalism. It is the confession of the upper middle class – the class that has most used the trust – that the contradictions in capitalism cannot be resolved. The risks of capitalism, therefore, must be minimised as much as possible through the employ of an astute,

intelligent, ever-watchful class of professional managers of capital who are placed, because they are *élite*, beyond the control of the owner for consumption. But American lawyers do not have to be reminded that capitalism is so sick that even this device to protect the only class that benefits from capitalism has failed pathetically.

These generalisations reveal their origin in 1930s-Depression America (eg in the reference to capitalism's 'sickness'), but they illustrate well enough that, whatever its underlying moral base, the trust is by no means insulated from its social and political environment or from political controversy. The majority of those who consciously use the trust in a family context have been the minority of individuals and families who own capital to any significant extent. Moreover, the phrase 'professional managers of capital . . . beyond the control of the owner for consumption' suggests a significantly different role for trustees than is implicit in the phrase 'a confidence reposed in some other' or in other lawyers' descriptions of a trust (one of which is cited in the next section).

We refer in the previous sentence to 'description' of a trust because defining the trust, as opposed merely to describing it, has proved difficult. A sometimes overlooked facet of Maitland's assessment of the trust, that of development, highlights the difficulty. It was the process of trust development – more in response to pragmatism than principle – that so attracted him. This dynamic nature of the trust device necessarily makes attempts at definition, if by definition we mean stating the essence of a thing, a fraught exercise.

Paradoxically, however, at the very time Maitland was writing it appeared that the development process had reached a terminus. Although our understanding is inexact – the modern history of the trust has still to be fully documented – it does seem that the combined influence of the courts and treatise writers had, during the eighteenth and nineteenth centuries, completed the task of refining the family of concepts that constitute the trust. Accordingly what Maitland was holding up for inspection looked like a largely finished article with well-established features, though these features reflected the different functions that the trust had performed. However, the pace of fiscal, commercial and social change has quickened noticeably in the last half-century and, for reasons that will become apparent, 'development of the trust idea' is now firmly back on the agenda as attempts are again made to adapt the trust form to novel purposes.

Consequently, how far the principal subject of our study, the trust concept, can be said still to be in a process of development is a recurring theme in this book. At this stage, just one aspect of this need be introduced. We have just referred to 'the trust concept' but this singular notion may itself be misleading. If, with Maitland, we want to understand the process of development we need to consider whether in fact the 'trust concept' is but a collective term for describing a family tree of different trust ideas at various stages of development. Some branches will have grown to full maturity whereas others as yet have scarcely sprouted, and a process of incremental development, usually gentle but at times more dramatic, is still occurring. We should therefore be careful when meeting different types of trust not to assume that what is a central characteristic of one type of trust is a necessary element in all other types. Indeed we need to consider whether it is preferable to talk not of the law of trusts in the singular but of laws of trusts in the plural.

2. The nature of a trust in English law

One of the major traditional practitioners' texts on trusts law, *Lewin on Trusts*, gives the following description of a trust (18th edn, 2008) p 4:

> [The word 'trust'] refers to the duty or aggregate accumulation of obligations that rest upon a person described as trustee. The responsibilities are in relation to property held by him, or under his control. That property he will be compelled by a court in its equitable jurisdiction to administer in the manner lawfully prescribed by the trust instrument, or where there be no specific provision written or oral, or to the extent that such provision is invalid or lacking, in accordance with equitable principles. As a consequence the administration will be in such a manner that the consequential benefits and advantages accrue, not to the trustee, but to the persons called cestuis que trust, or beneficiaries, if there be any; if not, for some purpose which the law will recognise and enforce. A trustee may be a beneficiary, in which case advantages will accrue in his favour to the extent of his beneficial interest.

This is probably the most comprehensive of the 'definitions' of a trust to be found in standard legal works, derived incidentally from the judgment in an Australian case *Re Scott* [1948] SASR 193 at 196, but some additional comments must be made by way of elaboration.

(1) In most cases, a trust arises out of the conscious act or declaration of an individual or group of individuals. To this individual or group no single name is consistently applied: one finds 'founder', 'settlor', 'creator' and 'donor' (or their plurals, as the case may be). Where the trust is created by a will, 'testator' or 'testatrix' – being the words for describing the maker of a will, whether or not it contains a trust – acts as a substitute. A founder of a trust may be a trustee and/or a beneficiary under it (subject to point (3) below). Where a trust arises out of the conscious act or declaration of a 'founder' (as will be seen later, he or she need not actually use the word 'trust'), it is called an 'express trust'.

(2) Where there is no conscious act or declaration which creates the trust, it will owe its existence to legal rules (statutory and judge-made) which in certain defined situations impose trusts on individuals (so that they thereby become 'trustees') in respect of property owned by them or under their control. In such cases there is no founder of the trust, and the trust can be said to be an 'imputed' trust. 'Imputed' is not a recognised legal term in this context, but we will use it as a synonym for 'non-express'. As will

be explained later, there are more specific (though somewhat confusing) sub-classifications: 'statutory', 'implied', 'resulting' and 'constructive' trusts.

(3) A trust can have any number of beneficiaries or founders. The same applies to trustees, subject to practical considerations and to legal rules which insist in some cases that the number of trustees must not exceed four (Trustee Act 1925, s 34(1)). The same person (private individual or corporate body) may appear in any two or three of these roles, except that the law abhors the nonsense that a person should be sole trustee of property for himself or herself.

(4) The trust property may be any type of estate or interest recognised in property law, ranging from ownership of a car or a piece of land to 'intangible' property, such as a copyright.

(5) Although the Lewin definition refers to the property being 'held' by the trustee, 'or under his control', for practical purposes a trustee generally has legal title to the trust property. Where the trust property is an equitable proprietary interest – it may indeed be an interest under another trust – the trustee's title is equitable only.

(6) The 'consequential benefits and advantages' which accrue to beneficiaries may take the form of benefits in kind (eg occupation of land held on trust) or cash (eg income from shares). There is no rule that the entitlements of individual beneficiaries should be fixed in advance or that they should all receive benefit simultaneously; indeed, the allocation of benefits may be left to the trustee(s) (under a so-called 'discretionary trust') or to some third party, who may even have the power to exclude entirely beneficiaries listed or described in the trust deed. Furthermore it may be stipulated that interests arise only if a specified contingency is satisfied, and a trustee may have the duty or power to withhold all allocation of benefit within a specified period, ie to 'accumulate' income.

(7) In referring cryptically to 'some purpose which the law will recognise and enforce' the Lewin definition is speaking mainly of charitable trusts. Generally, a trust must have one or more persons as beneficiaries or potential beneficiaries, but if its terms require the trustee to administer the trust property for one or more purposes which fall within an artificial legal definition of 'charitable purposes', the trust may be valid even though it is expressed in terms of purposes rather than beneficiaries. There are some other narrowly defined situations where the failure to define beneficiaries is not fatal to a trust.

Most aspects of this general description of a trust will, of course, be further dealt with in the course of this book.

3. The trust's versatility

What aspects of the trust form give it the versatility so admired by Maitland, so that it has come to be employed for a wide variety of purposes over a long period of time? Very briefly, the secret of the trust's success is to be found in three things. First, in establishing a trust, a founder (or a court, in the case of 'imputed' trusts) can play a whole range of 'tricks' with three particular aspects of property ownership: nominal title, benefit and control. The founder (or the court) can juggle these around in a variety of ways. Second, the rights and obligations expressly created in a trust are fortified by effective equitable remedies and supplemented, so far as is necessary, by a substratum of detailed legal rules (as, indeed, is indicated in the Lewin definition). Third, in the areas where it is predominantly used, the trust performs its 'tricks' with property better, and has stronger legal reinforcement, than other competing legal institutions. We shall consider these factors under separate headings, giving some examples of trust dispositions under the first heading in order to illustrate what has been said so far and to show some of the common types of motive that underlie the present-day use of trusts.

4. Manipulating facets of ownership through trusts

(a) The trust's 'tricks'

The following are the most important of the trust's 'tricks' in this regard:

Trick no 1 Nominal ownership of property can be separated from benefit and the right of control.

Trick no 2 Benefits may be split amongst two or more beneficiaries, who may be entitled to shares, or successively, or contingently, according to the wishes of the founder of the trust (as set out in the trust) or any person(s) designated by him or her (which may include the trustees). In particular, where the trust property brings in income – such as rent or royalties or dividends – entitlement to income may be allocated separately from entitlement to capital (ie to the trust property itself). To have a 'contingent entitlement' means simply that the beneficiary must satisfy some requirement such as reaching a specified age before his or her interest will accrue to or 'vest' in him or her.

Trick no 3 Allocation of benefit may be put in suspense according to the wishes of the founder, or any person(s) designated by him (which may include the trustees).

Trick no 4 Some or all aspects of control and management of the trust property may be divorced from entitlement to benefit and reserved to the founder of the trust or conferred by him or her on the trustees or any other person.

Trick no 5 When trust property is 'converted' (eg land is sold, or money subject to the trust is invested in land or shares), the new property which is so acquired by the trustees is held by them subject to the trust.

Trick no 6   Where, for legal or practical reasons, the group of persons intended to benefit, directly or indirectly, from a disposition of property is too large to enable them to be constituted as co-owners holding legal title, the title can instead be transferred to an appropriately smaller number of trustees to be held on trust for the benefit of the intended beneficiaries, who still retain control.

The following examples illustrate how these 'tricks' can operate in practice (the principal relevant 'tricks' are referred to in parenthesis).

Example 1   (trick 1) Wisegirl completes a transfer of 10,000 £1 shares in Run Down plc in favour of Bear, Bull & Stag, her firm of brokers, instructing them to hold the shares as trustees (or 'nominees', as they are sometimes called in this context) for her son Whizz-kid. The shares will be registered in the company's share-register in the name of the brokers, but Whizz-kid is entitled to receive the dividends and any other benefits, and to instruct the brokers on all aspects of management, such as exercising the voting power attached to the shares and selling or otherwise dealing with the shares. He is 'the owner in all but name'.

Comment   The chief advantage of this arrangement as against a simple transfer of the shares from Wisegirl to Whizz-kid is that the latter may hope to conceal his 'beneficial ownership' of the shares from the company. He may want to do this if (for instance) he is a financial entrepreneur who is thinking of attempting a take-over. Note, however, that ss 793 and 820 of the Companies Act 2006 give UK companies the right to ask any registered nominee shareholder to disclose the beneficial owner of shares. It has been estimated that for most UK registered public companies at least 80% of their share register will comprise nominee names. It is thought that the rights under these sections are now used mainly by managements of companies which regard themselves as potential targets for a take-over bid (see Davies (ed) *Gower and Davies' Principles of Modern Company Law* (8th edn, 2008) paras 26–19; 28–49 to 28–51).

Example 2   (trick 1) The solicitors' firm of Addmore & Charge receives £50,000 from Credulous, a client, in order to pay for Credulous's purchase of a house. By law this money must go into a client's 'trust account' at the firm's bank. In general, the solicitors are only entitled to deal with the money on Credulous's instructions (eg they will pay it to the seller of the house when they have Credulous's instructions to settle). This type of trust is often called a 'bare trust'.

Comment   For practical reasons it is convenient to have the money lodged at the bank in the name of the solicitors, so that they can sign the necessary cheques, but for virtually all purposes it is still the client's money. In particular, if the solicitors go bankrupt, their creditors cannot get hold of the money to satisfy their claims: the client's claim prevails.

Example 3 (tricks 1, 2, 3 and 5) Stern provides in his will that Solemn and Sad, the executors and trustees thereof, should hold a house, 'Funfair', 32 Hootenanny Parade, Crazyville, on trust to permit his housekeeper Strict (if she should survive him) to occupy the same for the rest of her life and thereafter to sell the house and hold the proceeds thereof (with any income accruing thereto) on trust for his twin sons Serious and Sensible in equal shares when they attain the age of 25.

Comment Here benefit, in the form of actual occupation, and substantial control go first to Strict, but if on her death Serious and Sensible are not yet 25, there is a temporary suspension of benefit and a shift of control to the trustees, Solemn and Sad, in so far as they decide how to invest the proceeds of sale and whether to change the investments subsequently. In a sense, the 'dead hand' of Stern is also involved in control, because he has directed the retention and subsequent sale of the house and he may also have laid down stipulations as to the mode of investment of the proceeds, and other aspects of control. When the sons Serious and Sensible attain 25, they are entitled to require the benefit, which comprises both the trust investments and the income accumulated thereon since the proceeds of sale were first invested, to be transferred to them in equal shares. Ever since their acquisition, these investments have been held subject to the trust just as the land has, but the transfer to Serious and Sensible brings the trust to an end.

Overall, Stern has here provided for his dependants in a manner which he deems appropriate: his housekeeper has been assured of a place to live and his sons each receive a capital sum at an age when they are mature enough to make proper use of it and may well have an immediate need for it (eg in order to buy their own house). In the meantime, the trust investments have been competently managed.

Example 4 (tricks 1–5) In 1964, land and investments worth £1,000,000 are put into a 'Trust Fund' under a trust deed executed by Lucre, aged 56. He lists the following as the 'specified class': his mother (aged 80), his wife (aged 48), his three children (aged 25, 23 and 20) and his grandchildren, both existing (there is already one, aged three months) and to be born in the future. The trustees are his trusted and prudent friend Solomon and his solicitor Sheba. The key clause of the trust deed is as follows:

> The trustees shall stand possessed of the Trust Fund and the income thereof UPON TRUST for all or such one or more exclusively of the others or other of the members of the Specified Class if more than one in such shares and either absolutely or at such age or time or respective ages or times upon and with such limitations, conditions and restrictions and such trusts and powers (including discretionary trusts and powers over income and capital exercisable by any person or persons other than the Settlor or any Spouse of the

Settlor whether similar to the discretionary trusts and powers herein contained or otherwise) and with such provisions (including provisions for maintenance and advancement and the accumulation of income for any period or periods authorised by law and provisions for investment and management of any nature whatsoever and provisions for the appointment of separate trustees of any appointed fund) and generally in such manner as the Trustees (being not less than two in number or being a corporate trustee) shall in their absolute discretion from time to time by any deed or deeds revocable or irrevocable appoint.

Comment The significant feature of this 'discretionary trust' is that it is still a trust even though no one in the specified class is entitled under the trust deed to claim a specific share of the trust capital or income or even to insist at any specific time that all or any part of the capital or income should be distributed. The question of entitlement (as well as choice of investments and other aspects of control) is left entirely to the trustees subject only to any limits specified by Lucre. In the result, Lucre has provided for three generations of his family and ensured competent management of the trust property – as Stern did in the preceding example – but there are three further advantages to be gained from Lucre's trust:

(i) The trustees can allocate the benefit of the trust according to the *current* needs of the various beneficiaries. The comparative rigidity of Stern's will trust in example 3 could lead to anomalies; for example, if one of his sons becomes a millionaire pop star by the age of 25 while the other is unemployed, there is no provision in the will for giving all or substantially all of the trust fund to the latter. Furthermore, so long as Lucre is still alive, he can exercise de facto influence over his trustees (who may be wholly 'tame') to respect his views in this regard. (NB: For a salutary warning of the perils of behaving as a 'tame trustee' see *Turner v Turner* [1983] 2 All ER 745 and generally Chapter 11.)

(ii) If any of Lucre's beneficiaries go bankrupt, or are desperately trying to raise money to pay for the improvidence sometimes associated with the heirs of the wealthy, they have no ascertainable interest under the trust which their creditors can get hold of or which they themselves can sell or mortgage. To this extent, the trust remains immune from their creditors and acts as a 'caretaker' mechanism to protect them from their own improvidence or ill-luck.

(iii) According to the law, at the time of this trust's fictitious establishment in 1964, the trust had notable tax advantages. In particular, estate duty would not have been payable in respect of the creation of the trust, being an inter vivos disposition, provided Lucre lived for seven more years; and on the subsequent death of Lucre's mother or wife or indeed any of the beneficiaries, the existence of the trust would not have increased the estate duty payable on the deceased's estate because the deceased beneficiary would have had no fixed interest in the trust fund, but merely an expectation of benefit. (By contrast, the value of Stern's house would have been subject to estate duty twice, in his estate on his death, and in his housekeeper's estate on her death.) Taxation of transfers of capital has changed since 1964, and the discretionary trust is no longer such an outright tax-saver (see Chapter 8), but it represents a classic case of tax avoidance through the use of trusts and its importance in this regard over many years has had a significant impact on the law of trusts.

Example 5 (trick 6) Due to complex conveyancing rules, established initially by the 1925 property legislation, land cannot be held under any form of co-tenancy by more than four persons. If seven people wish to hold land in joint tenancy or tenancy in common, it must be vested in trustees in trust for them. If the conveyance simply names the seven individuals as transferees, the first four named will be treated as trustees (holding a joint tenancy) for all seven by virtue of a statutory 'imputed' trust. The changes introduced by the Trusts of Land and Appointment of Trustees Act 1996 have considerably simplified the rules relating to 'trusts of land' but have not affected this basic formal position on co-ownership. The statute substituted one form of trust – the trust of land – for the two types – trust for sale and strict settlement – that existed under the 1925 legislation. The powers conferred on trustees by the 1996 Act are significantly wider than those under the earlier legislation. These powers will be referred to only briefly at appropriate points in the text because trusts of land and the 1996 Act are more appropriately studied and discussed in the general context of land ownership and control.

Example 6 (tricks 5 and 6) The trust is a convenient vehicle whereby funds contributed or deposited by or on behalf of a large and possibly fluctuating number of people may be put into investments (usually stock exchange securities) for their collective benefit by a small group of trustees and managers. Three examples of this collective investment function of the trust are of particular importance:

(i) The *bond or debenture trust*, whereby a single company solicits loans at fixed interest from the public, arranging for a trustee (usually a corporate body) to act as a nominal lender of the total amount subscribed, a conduit-pipe for interest and principal payments from the company to the individual investor and a watchdog for the investors' interests. It would in theory be possible for the borrower to issue bonds or debenture stock direct to the lenders/investors. This would involve the disadvantage of the borrower dealing direct with hundreds, perhaps thousands, of the lenders/investors. Arguably this would be wholly impracticable in the case of a secured debenture issue since each lender would acquire a security interest in the assets of the borrower. The interposition of a trustee as an intermediary avoids these difficulties and provides the advantages referred to previously (see eg Duffet (1992) 1 JITCP 23–30; and generally Hayton et al (2002) 17(1) JIBFL 23).

(ii) The *unit trust*, whereby under close statutory regulation a corporate 'custodian trustee' holds a fund gathered from the public in return for the issue of 'units' of the fund, and a corporate managing trustee invests this fund in whatever stock market securities seem best at any given time. Dividends and capital gains earned from the investment accrue for the benefit of current unit-holders (see Fan Sin *The Legal Nature of the Unit Trust* (1998)).

(iii) The *private pension fund*, whereby money paid in on behalf of a company's employees by the company and, in most cases, by the employees themselves is invested by a small group of trustees (who may include one or more representatives from the employer's and the employees' respective 'sides') in order to provide pensions for the employees on their retirement (see Chapter 13).

Example 7 (Tricks 4 and 6) Where companies encounter trading difficulties and insolvency threatens it may be possible to refinance the business so as to keep it operating as a going concern. The claims of existing unsecured creditors will be of limited value to them in the event of insolvency. Those creditors may therefore be willing to subordinate their claims to the interests of potential later creditors such as banks who may then be willing to risk further injections of funds to keep the business afloat. A legal difficulty is that this runs counter to a principle of insolvency law that requires all unsecured creditors to be treated alike or 'pari passu' as it is known. Interposing a separate trustee between the company and the creditors can circumvent this problem by arranging that all of certain designated debts are owed to the trustee. The trust instrument, known as a 'subordination trust', can then specify the order in which the creditors will be able to claim in the event of the ultimate insolvency of the debtor company. The example described above is just one of many ways in which the trust can be employed as part of a commercial arrangement (see O'Hagan 'The Use of Trusts in Finance Structures' (2000) 8(2) JITCP 85; and the sources referred to under example 6(i)).

Example 8 (tricks 4 and 6) About three months after a coal-tip disaster at Aberfan, South Wales on 21 October 1966, in which 144 people, including 116 children, died, the massive fund collected by public appeals (it ultimately reached about £1,750,000) was transferred in the form of cash and investments to 14 trustees. Under the trust deed, it was to be held and applied by them in accordance with the directions of a management committee (which initially comprised six of the trustees and nine other representatives of the local community) on the following trusts:

(i) for the relief of all persons who have suffered as a result of the said disaster and are thereby in need; and

(ii) subject as aforesaid for any charitable purpose for the benefit of persons who are inhabitants of Aberfan and its immediate neighbourhood (hereinafter called 'the area of benefit') on the Twenty First day of October One Thousand Nine Hundred and Sixty Six or who now are or hereafter become inhabitants of the area of benefit and in particular (but without prejudice to the generality of the last foregoing trust) for any charitable purpose for the benefit of children who were on the Twenty First day of October One Thousand Nine Hundred and Sixty Six or who now are or hereafter may become resident in the area of benefit.

Comment This was a charitable trust: ie the purposes elaborated in the clause just quoted fall within the 'legal definition of charity', so the devoting of benefit to purposes instead of benefit to potentially ascertainable people did not invalidate the trust. It was unusual in that the trustees – the nominal owners – and the management committee – those with the right to control – were separate groups: in charitable trusts the trustees usually perform both these functions. But the role played by the trust in centralising nominal ownership and control of the large amount of money contributed whilst benefit could be spread out amongst a whole community (with particular attention to those who had suffered most from the collapse of the coal-tip) was evident enough, and typified the use of the trust for charitable activity.

Example 9 (trick 6) The Bunker Golf Club, having over 300 members, has its own golf course and a number of shares. These are formally vested in two trustees, Tee and Caddy, on trust to hold them for the benefit of the members of the club for the time being.

Comment A trust is used here not merely because of the rules of land law mentioned in example 5 but also because of the practical consideration that it would be grossly unwieldy to have all the members (who fluctuate from time to time) registered as legal owners of the land or the shares. Questions of control of this property are determined by the club's management body and membership in accordance with the constitution, to which all members have agreed to adhere when they joined the club (see Chapter 17).

Example 10 (tricks 1 and 5) X is the tenant under a lease of business premises on favourable terms. She asks Y, her estate agent, who negotiated the lease in the first place, to try to obtain a renewal for her. Y tells the lessors that X does not want a renewal, and manages, without telling X, to obtain a renewal for himself. X is entitled to claim that Y holds the lease as 'constructive trustee' for X, ie Y must treat X as the 'owner in all but name' and, if X so requires, must transfer the lease to her.

Comment This example falls within one of the categories of 'imputed' trusts. No one has consciously founded or created the trust, but in order to enforce the obligation binding Y, as X's agent, to act only in X's interests in negotiating the renewal, the law 'imputes' the trust in order to establish that Y's ownership of the renewed lease is nominal only, and the benefit and right of control belong wholly to X.

(b) Summary

This selected list of the trust's 'tricks' and the examples, fictitious and real, which illustrate them, give a general idea of the trust's versatility and of some of the common types of purpose which a trust's founder may have in establishing a trust. These purposes include concealing ownership, facilitating land conveyancing and other types of dealing in property, holding and controlling property for the sake of large groups of people (particularly in the fields of collective investment and charitable and other non-profit-orientated activity), providing for the founder's family in various ways over long periods of time (both before and after his or her death), protecting property from creditors and from the extravagance of individual members of the family, and cutting down tax liabilities, particularly on the transfer of private capital. In the case of 'imputed' trusts, the underlying purpose is to implement a judicial or legislative intent that, despite the absence of any express declaration of trust, a nominal owner of property should be treated in certain situations as holding the property for the benefit of someone else.

It will be observed that in some cases (eg examples 1 and 5), the trust is very short and simple; in others (especially 4, 6 and 7), a long and complex document, setting out detailed powers and duties, is required. Sometimes, the trust is 'embedded in', or very closely linked with, another legal concept or institution, such as a contract (9 – the Golf Club's rules take effect contractually), one or more 'powers' (4) or a will (3). At times, the trust seems to be no more than a mechanical common-form device, fitting in a gap left by technical rules of property law (5); in other cases (eg 4) it will be consciously and deliberately tailor-made to suit an individual founder's specific purposes. In other words, some founders of trusts have trusts thrust upon them, possibly without their realising it, others twist trusts to their own ends and yet others are somewhere in between.

The boundaries of the trust's areas of use are also somewhat random. Why, for instance, should it be prominent in collective investment and non-profit-making activity, but not in ordinary commercial enterprise? If one wants to put property in the name of another but enjoy the benefits secretly, would not a contract with that person be just as good as a trust? To answer questions such as these, one has to know something of the type of protection and reinforcement which the law gives to trusts and something of the type of 'tricks' that other legal institutions arising in the domain of private property can perform. In a broad sense only, these are the respective preoccupations of the next two sections of this chapter.

5. Equity's rules for enforcing trusts and supplementing their terms

The law of trusts consists chiefly of rules for the enforcement of obligations set out in trusts and rules which are designed to supplement these expressly imposed obligations. This does not cover the whole field of trusts law; there are also, for instance, rules for determining whether a valid trust has been properly created. At the risk of stating a commonplace, it must be emphasised that the ambit of the equitable rules that are briefly outlined below is not restricted to the enforcement of obligations associated with the trust. As will be seen at several points in this book, but particularly in Chapters 14 and 16, equitable rules and remedies have a much broader compass.

With regard to the rules concerning enforcement, a brief historical résumé is necessary here although we consider this topic more closely in Chapter 2. The rules were developed over a long period by a specific court, the Court of Chancery. This existed separately from the common law courts, in which, generally speaking, only common law titles to property were recognised. Chancery never formally denied such common law titles: it simply maintained that when owners of property under common law title held the property by virtue of a disposition which made them trustees thereof, they could be ordered by Chancery to exercise their rights of ownership for the benefit of those designated under the trust as beneficiaries. The development of this parasitic relationship of the trust notion to common law ownership explains why, generally speaking, a trustee is the legal owner of the trust property. The existence of a trust does not take this ownership away from the trustee, but renders it nominal by entitling the beneficiaries to invoke remedies granted by Chancery in order to secure such entitlement (in terms of benefit from the property and control of it) as the trust confers on them.

The remedies thus initially granted to trust beneficiaries took the form of claims against trustees deriving from the trustees' breach of confidence in failing to abide by the trust (cf the 'moral basis' of trusts referred to in the opening paragraphs of this chapter). In the course of time these remedies became quite extensive, so that nowadays trustees can be ordered (for example) to give accounts of their financial administration of the trust, to pay money out of their own pockets by way of compensation for damage to the trust or make restitution of profits which they have secretly made for themselves by virtue of their trusteeship, or to refrain from committing specified acts amounting to breach of trust. Concurrently, however, Chancery strengthened this arsenal of remedies by granting beneficiaries redress against third parties in appropriate circumstances. In particular, it developed the principle that, broadly speaking, any person who receives trust property from a trustee with 'notice' of the existence of the trust and/or without giving value for it should

be taken to hold the property subject to the pre-existing trust. Even though a bona fide purchaser without notice of the trust is *not* thus bound, this aspect of Chancery's protection of the beneficiary enabled the beneficiary's interest to be treated as akin to a right of property. The same effect has emerged from rules empowering beneficiaries to dispose of their entitlement under a trust like any other item of property: they can even transfer it on a further trust so as to create a 'sub-trust'. It has spread also to 'imputed' trusts: thus, for instance, where X holds property on 'constructive trust' (or any other form of trust) for Y, Y's rights to the property usually prevail over X's creditors.

Paradoxically, whereas the founders of trusts have wide discretions as to the terms of the trust, the sequence of events whereby Chancery developed trust remedies did not confer on them any general right to compel the trustees to observe the trust. To this extent, a transfer on trust operates to sever the founders from their former proprietary rights. But there are mechanisms whereby they can retain specific aspects of control: they may, for example, reserve to themselves a power to revoke the trust, or to determine beneficial entitlement, or to dismiss the trustees and appoint new ones.

The supplementing of an express trust by rules of equity chiefly takes the form of defining a trustee's administrative duties and powers where these have not been spelt out. Chancery and the legislature have been assiduous in this respect. For example, the Trustee Acts 1925 and 2000 confer on trustees a wide range of miscellaneous powers, including selling or mortgaging trust property, insuring it, compromising debts or other claims which the trust is entitled to make, maintaining minor beneficiaries out of trust income and applying to the Chancery Division for advice. The Trustee Act 2000 also contains provisions to facilitate the investment of trust funds and to stipulate the circumstances in which a statutory duty of care will apply to trustees. Most of these trusteeship powers and duties can, however, be abrogated, extended or modified in the trust instrument, and often are.

In the outcome, the extent to which a beneficiary's rights can be conceived as falling short of absolute ownership depends largely on two caveats:

(i) the extent to which powers of control and/or determination of beneficial entitlement are reserved to trustees or third parties; and

(ii) the importance to be attributed to the fact that a bona fide purchaser of the trust property for value and without notice may override the beneficiary, leaving him to pursue remedies against the trustee.

The first of these factors is very much at the discretion of the founder of the trust. The importance of the second factor depends largely on value judgement: given that in most situations purchasers are 'on notice' if they could reasonably have been expected to ascertain the trust's existence, its practical significance is probably not great. The degree of control left to founders after creation of the trust is a flexible matter, but specific powers which they reserve to themselves will receive legal protection. On top of all this, extensive trusteeship duties and powers are laid down by the law in the absence of express provision in the trust.

The sum total is an impressive barrage of rules ensuring that trustees cannot abuse with impunity their position as nominal owners, even though in formal terms at least their powers of management may be very wide. The state, chiefly through the Chancery offshoot of its judicial branch, has lavished plenty of care and attention on trusts.

6. When is a trust not a trust?

The opening chapter of a book on Trusts Law is not usually the place to come across Christmas cracker-like riddles. The reason for posing the riddle is to counter an impression that may be growing on the reader to the effect that there is no limit to the degree of separation of ownership, control and benefit that can be accomplished by use of a trust. The impression would be misleading. There must be some *genuine* separation of those features for a trust to be valid. Let us suppose my wife and I make a declaration of trust under which our house is to be held on trust for her and for my children. We continue to act as if we are absolute owners even to the extent of obtaining a loan from the bank on the security of the property to finance my business dealings. They turn out to be disastrous and the bank seeks to realise its security against 'my property'. With a flourish I produce the trust instrument, the existence of which I had omitted to inform the bank about, and which purports to show that I have no interest in the house at all. The bank will claim, probably successfully, that the declaration of trust is a 'sham' (see *Midland Bank v Wyatt* [1995] 1 FLR 696, discussed in Chapter 4 at p 164). Consequently the 'trust property' will still be beneficially owned by my wife and myself and available to some extent to meet the claims of my creditors. A more elaborate variant of a sham could arise where a settlor does genuinely transfer legal title in property to trustees but reserves to himself very extensive powers, for instance, to amend the terms of the trust, to appoint new trustees (including himself), to act as investment manager and to add or exclude beneficiaries and so on. If the trustees acquiesce in these arrangements and, in effect, act as a cipher for the settlor a court confronted with claims brought by creditors or by HMRC may decide that the trust is a sham. The outcome would be that the trustees hold the property on a bare trust for the settlor. And the answer to the riddle of course is: 'When it is a sham'.

7. The trust and 'competing' legal institutions

The material in the foregoing two sections shows that the trust – meaning here particularly the express trust – is potentially of use where it is desired to split the three facets of ownership referred to (nominal ownership, benefit and control) with the assurance that whatever arrangement is decided on will receive adequate protection from the courts. But English law also provides many other ways of permitting someone to deal with property for the benefit of another. When one then turns to ask whether the trust, in a given type of situation, is a *better* legal institution to use for this type of purpose than any other, a whole new range of issues is opened up. One has to consider the strengths and weaknesses of such other legal devices – contracts, bailments, conditions, etc – as appear to offer alternative means of reaching a similar result. These strengths and weaknesses reflect the different legal consequences that attach to each institution or, if you will, their different juridical natures. But in considering, as we do below, what aspects of their respective natures makes, for example, a contract or a trust better for a particular purpose, we should not lose sight of their functional similarities. To continue the contract-trust comparison, the origin of both is commonly a transaction between two persons, in the trust context settlor and trustee, and as Maitland acutely observed, it is impossible 'so to define a contract that the definition shall not cover at least three-quarters of all the trusts that are created' (*Equity* (2nd edn, 1936) p 54; Macnair 'The Conceptual Basis of Trusts in the 17th and 18th Centuries' in Helmholz and Zimmermann (eds) *Itinera Fiduciae* (1998) 207–236; see further Langbein 'The Contractarian Basis of the Law of Trusts' (1995) 105 Yale LJ 625 for an intriguing contemporary resurrection, not to say embellishment, of the 'trust as contract' idea).

We must therefore emphasise that a trap to be avoided is one of believing that certain transactions can be achieved *only* by means of a trust and others *only* by means of contract, etc. Indeed on occasions the one set of facts may permit more than one conclusion. For example, informal domestic arrangements concerning payments for alterations to a house may be construed as creating either a loan or a trust, as in *Hussey v Palmer* (see below, p 24). The situation is further complicated by the fact that the best way of achieving the desired result may be to use the trust in combination with other legal forms. Examples of this have already been given (see example 9 above).

This introductory section is no place to investigate these issues at length. But at this stage it is useful to consider what sort of factors may give the trust special prominence in particular types of property transaction, or alternatively may wholly or partly shut it out from use. This will be done by briefly comparing the trust with three other legal institutions – contracts, 'personal representation' with reference to a deceased's estate, and limited liability companies.

(a) Trust and contract

Let us consider the advantages and disadvantages of the trust and the contract in the 'secret ownership' situation illustrated in example 1 (p 6). If the arrangement is set up by contract alone – whether it be a contract between the brokers and Wisegirl, or the brokers and Whizz-kid, or all three – the major disadvantage from the point of view of Wisegirl and Whizz-kid is that, if the brokers were to sell or give the shares to a third party in breach of the contract, Whizz-kid's claim to the dividends, etc, would be overridden even though the third party knew all along about the contractual arrangement. One could evade this by dressing it up as a contract of agency between Whizz-kid (as principal) and the brokers (as agents), because if the brokers then gave the shares away or sold them to a third party who was on notice, Whizz-kid would have so-called rights of 'tracing' against the third party entitling him to claim the benefit of the shares. But, as we shall see, these rights only arise from a form of 'imputed' trust: in other words, agency smuggles the trust in by the back door. And there is the practical disadvantage that as Whizz-kid has to be made a party to the contract the simplicity of Wisegirl's transfer on trust is lost. The only possible advantage of using a contract is that Wisegirl herself (assuming she is a party) can easily sue the brokers if they play false, whereas the trust, it will be recalled, prima facie confers rights of action for breach of trust on the beneficiaries only. There are ways of combining the contract and the trust to achieve this result (eg the brokers could agree formally with Wisegirl to observe the trust in Whizz-kid's favour), but again the objective of simplicity has been lost.

If one alters the facts slightly, and makes Whizz-kid a bouncing baby or an unborn grandchild instead of a fast operator on the stock market, the trust's advantage over the contract is more obvious. Because Whizz-kid cannot contract with full capacity (if at all), no agency relationship will arise between the brokers and Whizz-kid, and in the absence of an express trust Whizz-kid has no claims in any circumstances against a third party who receives the shares.

This is not to say that every time the trust and the contract 'compete' to perform some property transaction, the trust always wins. Usually, in fact, it loses. The contract is adaptable to a far greater number of situations, simple and complex, than the trust and it permeates a considerably wider range of social situations than the property-holding milieu of the trust. But this example does show that, when it comes to making as watertight as possible an arrangement for separating facets of property ownership, the trust's special characteristics are likely to make it preferable.

(b) Trusteeship and 'personal representation'

The comparison of trusteeship with the position of 'personal representation' occupied by the executor or administrator of a deceased's estate raises a different issue. Put simply, the administration of a deceased's estate entails collecting all its assets, paying off its liabilities (in particular debts and inheritance tax) and distributing what remains to those entitled. Where the deceased has left a will which nominates someone to do this and this person accepts the office, he or she is an 'executor' or an 'executrix'; where the will makes no nomination, or there is no will, an 'administrator' or 'administratrix' is appointed by the court. The phrase 'legal personal representative' comprehends both these offices.

Clearly, personal representation has a good deal in common with trusteeship: the legal personal representative is a nominal owner of property who performs certain tasks in relation to it for the benefit of others – ie the beneficiaries under the will or the next of kin where there is no will. But, in contrast to the trust-contract comparison just described, one cannot consciously choose between trusteeship and personal representation with regard to property dissolution on death. This is because by law the tasks of administration fall wholly to legal personal representatives and are the only tasks required of them acting as such. In practice, the same individuals are often appointed to be executors and trustees: they act first as executors in administering the estate, then hold the remaining property as trustees of the trust(s) set out in the will (example 3 above – Stern's will – illustrates this process). Similarly, an administrator of an intestate estate becomes a trustee on 'statutory trusts' for the next of kin when administration is over. Thus, while personal representation and the trust are not alternative legal devices for achieving the same end, they have a similar fiduciary character, and are therefore assimilated by the law in a number of respects, for example, in having certain common powers and duties under the Trustee Acts 1925 and 2000. They are also closely associated in point of time. Indeed, fine legal distinctions have to be drawn to determine how the rules and practices to be followed by trustees and executors differ and when precisely an executor-cum-trustee exchanges an executor's hat for a trustee's hat (see generally Kerridge et al *Parry & Clark: The Law of Succession* (11th edn, 2002) pp 574–601). There is one significant distinction that needs to be mentioned and this relates to the interests of those entitled under the will or on intestacy, called legatees or devisees depending on the nature of the assets of the deceased's estate. It is generally accepted that they do not have any equitable ownership in the assets under the administration of the personal representative until the point of time when the personal representative changes hats (see *Stamp Duties Comr (Queensland) v Livingston* [1965] AC 694, where the issue of equitable ownership had implications for tax liability). Then they become beneficiaries with full equitable ownership. Until that time the equitable ownership can be said to be in suspense although, of course, legatees and devisees can call on the remedies that equity provides to ensure that the personal representatives comply with their fiduciary or 'trust-like' duties.

This brief comparison of trusteeship and personal representation helps to show that from a functional point of view the choice of alternatives when one is thinking about manipulating the distribution of one's property after death is between a will (which inevitably brings in administration) and an inter vivos trust (which virtually bypasses it so far as the property contained in it is concerned). But unless the mode of distribution is to be fairly simple, the will is likely to contain dispositions on trust, so it is not a matter of choosing between a will and a trust, but deciding whether or not to set up one's trust in a will. A comparison of examples 3 and 4 above (Stern's will trust and Lucre's inter vivos trust) illustrates this.

(c) Trust and company

We come now to the final comparison to be discussed in this chapter – trust and limited liability company. The similarity here is entirely at the level of function.

At the theoretical level, a company is a 'separate legal entity' whereas a trust is not: it follows that, whereas in company law the company is the legal entity liable for its debts, the liabilities claimed against a trust are in the first instance payable by the trustee(s). In practical terms a company differs from a trust in its personalities – shareholders, directors, etc – its constituent documents, its mode of coming into being (by formal incorporation at Companies House), and in numerous other ways. But a brief historical glance at the way in which these two legal forms have vied with each other in performing a number of functions relating to private property-holding gives useful insights into the sort of circumstances that can bring the trust into prominence or push it into eclipse.

When in the mid-nineteenth century the company with limited liability became freely available, necessitating only a simple registration procedure, the trust had already for about 100 years been an essential ingredient in a form of business association – the so-called 'deed of settlement' company – adopted by many medium- and large-scale industrial and commercial firms (see further Chapter 2). It was also essential to virtually all forms of charitable activity (whether in the form of the charitable trust per se or as part of the legal set-up of unincorporated charitable associations) and to many other forms of collective non-profit-making activity. It could also be used to avoid liability for debts, though the method was cumbersome. To summarise, the trust operated here as a means of association for economic and social purposes.

By about 1910, things had changed drastically. Despite the trust's possible use for avoiding debts, the company form had made a wholesale take-over of commercial and industrial activity (save amongst firms which were too small to have ever needed the trust form anyway). This occurred chiefly because the company offered straightforward limited liability, a separate 'corporate entity' which could hold property and enter into contracts in its own name without the need to appoint and re-appoint trustees, and a ready-made demarcation of shareholders and directors. Yet, while ousted from this area, the trust had embarked on a still persisting competition with companies in the field of collective investment on the stock market. The unit trust (described above) has a functional counterpart in the so-called 'investment trust', which, despite its name, is actually a company set up to perform a similar function. Furthermore, as twentieth-century rises in estate duty and other taxes made tax planning an increasingly absorbing occupation for the rich and their lawyers, the choice between vesting family assets in a trust or a private company was within certain wealth ranges a very fine one, depending on the particular circumstances of the family and the prevailing tax laws (see generally Ashton 'Does the Tax System Favour Incorporation?' [1987] BTR 256). With regard to charitable and other non-profit activity of a collective nature, the company limited by guarantee during all this period made inroads on the trust's dominance, though it is difficult to assess the extent of this.

Some of these developments will be referred to later in more detail, but this outline is enough to illustrate how the prominence of trust or company in a specific area often varies as a result of matters extraneous to trusts or company law, such as changes in tax law or even, in the case of the unit trust/investment trust 'competition', in investment experts' predictions of future stock market trends. Thus the trust-company comparison illustrates, better than any other similar comparisons, that the range of tasks assigned to trusts is very responsive to changes in its 'environment' – social, economic, legal – as well as to changes within trusts law itself, and that in this notion of a legal 'environment' one has to include the law governing other legal institutions having similar functions, such as companies. This is not to say that changes in trusts law itself are unimportant, and in the outcome it is the interaction of trusts law and its 'environment' that ultimately determines the shape of trusts and what they do. Tax considerations may even be such as to prompt the use of trust and company forms in harness, as with the emergence of the 'trading trust' in Australia (see eg Finn (ed) *Essays in Equity* (1985) ch 8; Ford and Hardingham 'Trading Trusts, Rights and Liabilities of Beneficiaries' in Finn (ed) *Equity and Commercial Relationships* (1987); *Jacob's Law of Trusts in Australia* (7th edn, 2006) paras 2042–2044; and Hayton 'Trading Trusts' in Glasson and Thomas (eds) *The International Trust* (2nd edn, 2006) ch 7).

The company-trust comparison also helps to show how far the character of a trust as a 'reposing of confidence' based on moral law has been transcended by its functions as an instrument of private capital within capitalist society (cf the opening paragraphs of this chapter). In so far as it can operate as a basis of association, a legal mechanism for aggregating, organising and preserving wealth at one remove from those who actually enjoy the benefits, it performs roles akin to those of the company, though in a manner less overtly linked with capitalism. The company's capitalist orientations are clearer, partly because it functions primarily within industry and commerce (which the trust does not) and partly because it has no underlying basis of 'confidence' and 'trust' (in the moral sense) to divert attention away from its capital-holding functions. This is not to say that the company operates free from any trust-like or 'fiduciary' obligations. Those who control corporate wealth have had such obligations superimposed upon their roles as managers, both through statute and the common law, and may even be enforced by the device of 'imputed trust'. With the trust the fiduciary concept came first and the rest later, but the end result is similar in important respects.

There are other comparisons that one can draw between trusts and similar legal institutions. One of these – the comparison of trusts and powers – is dealt with in some detail later as part of the discussion of discretionary trusts (Chapter 5). The interaction of these two ideas is too complex and technical to be covered in an introductory chapter. Another – the comparison of trust and debt – is considered in a commercial and consumer context in Chapter 15. To compare trusts with bailments, or conditions attached to a gift or bequest, or equitable charges is useful from the point of view of clarifying the precise legal nature of a trust, but bears little relation to the general themes of this chapter. Accordingly, these comparisons will be mentioned briefly at later points where they tie in with discussion of the trust in historical or contemporary contexts.

8. Internationalising the trust

As has been seen, the distinctive juridical nature of the trust offers attributes that can make it functionally efficient for carrying out all manner of tasks in our common law system. The term 'common law' is used here in contrast with civil law systems. But, as we have also seen, the trust is not constrained in its operation by national boundaries. Indeed it has been said that trusts and trust-like devices are spreading 'across the globe – both following and promoting the globalisation of business activities and wealth transfers' (Dyer (1999) 32 Vand J Transnat L 989 at 1007). This feature is relatively unproblematic as regards legal recognition where other jurisdictions are also common law systems. But our immediate European neighbours and trading partners do not share the same legal heritage. In particular the trust form as understood in the common law world has not, until recently, been adopted or even afforded recognition in civilian systems of law. To a degree this difference between legal systems provided some of the impetus for Maitland's writing on the subject of the trust. Today practical difficulties can arise as where property located within a civilian jurisdiction – let us say a Spanish holiday home – forms part of a deceased person's residuary estate held on trust for a surviving spouse. A difficulty then is that in principle under the civilian system the trustees would be viewed, applying trust law terminology, as the beneficial owners of the property. The fiscal consequences might be unwelcome.

It is to address some of the difficulties that can be posed by the absence of legal recognition of the trust that in 1984 'The Hague Trusts Convention', to give it its short title, was adopted and subsequently implemented in the UK by the Recognition of Trust Act 1987 (see generally Harris *The Hague Trusts Convention* (2002); Hayton (1987) 36 ICLQ 260; and Dyer, above). Broadly speaking the Convention serves two functions for those states that ratify it. It provides rules by which the courts of those states can determine whose laws apply in any given instance to a trust with an international dimension. Second, for states where the trust is unknown in domestic law, it provides a mechanism for dealing with trusts issues that might come before its courts. To do this there has to be some consensus about what a trust is and in that regard Article 2 of the Convention provides the following definition.

For the purposes of this Convention, the term 'trust' refers to the legal relationship created – inter vivos or on death - by a person, the settlor, when assets have been placed under the control of a trustee for the benefit of a beneficiary or for a specified purpose.

A trust has the following characteristics–

(a) the assets constitute a separate fund and are not a part of the trustee's own estate;
(b) title to the trust assets stands in the name of the trustee or in the name of another person on behalf of the trustee;
(c) the trustee has the power and the duty, in respect of which he is accountable, to manage, employ or dispose of the assets in accordance with the terms of the trust and the special duties imposed upon him by law.

The reservation by the settlor of certain rights and powers, and the fact that the trustee may himself have rights as a beneficiary, are not necessarily inconsistent with the existence of a trust. (Article 2)

This definition necessarily avoids any reference to the 'equitable jurisdiction of the court' (cf *Lewin* at p 3 above), a problematic concept for a civilian system. Equally there is no hint in the Articles of that elemental division in the common law trust between legal and equitable title. Consequently no attempt is made to define the nature of a beneficiary's interest, a wise omission given, as we shall see in Chapter 5, the difficulty of reaching a satisfactory conclusion on this issue even in a common law system.

The effects of the Convention must not be overstated. First, a state must choose to ratify the Convention but even then it does not affect the internal private law of the state. Second, the Convention does not introduce the trust into a legal system that does not have a trust concept but simply requires a signatory state to recognise trusts as a matter of private international law. The Convention does not therefore enable a settlor with assets in a civilian jurisdiction where there are so-called 'forced heirship' rules to avoid its laws on succession. Lastly, the Hague Convention applies only to trusts created voluntarily and evidenced in writing (Article 3). The Convention therefore has no purchase with the type of trust that we consider in section 9 below.

Recognition in the manner provided for in the Hague Convention constitutes in some sense just a passive acceptance of a quite narrowly defined version of the trust. What more is needed, it might be asked? There is no doubt, for instance, that under civil law systems a series of distinct legal arrangements – contract, agency, mandate – have been able to carry out many of the functions that a trust can perform *by itself* (see eg the chapters by Grundmann, Lupoi and Graziadei in Helmholz and Zimmermann (eds) *Itinera Fiduciae* (1998)). But there is a growing awareness within civilian jurisdictions that the functional efficacy of the trust, as demonstrated in the tricks described in this chapter, can carry a competitive advantage in certain commercial contexts. It is therefore not surprising that steps are being taken in some of those jurisdictions to introduce legal arrangements, some more trust-like than others, to counter the perceived functional advantages of the common law trust. A difficulty is that any move to introduce the trust *per se* can encounter significant doctrinal and legal cultural obstacles and policy objections (see Swann *Trust* (2009) for a possible model 'common European Law of Trusts' produced for the Study Group on a European Civil Code). Perhaps nowhere have these obstacles and objections been more profound than in France, yet in February 2007, under Law 2007–211, some 17 years in gestation, a novel legal institution, *la fiducie*, was introduced into the French legal system (see Matthews (2007) 21(1) TLI 17–42; Raffenne 'Trust, the Keepers of the Temple and the Merchants of Law: the Riddle of the Fiducie' (PhD Thesis, Warwick 2002)). Whilst *la fiducie* has some trust-like features it is not a trust as a common lawyer would understand it, partly because its scope has been determined by a legislative process. The introduction of a novel legal form by statute opens up for critical scrutiny some functions performed by the trust such as tax mitigation or creditor avoidance in a way that the modern development of the common law trust has largely avoided. It remains an open question whether legal institutions that are trust-like only in some ways can counter the functional flexibility and competitive advantage that the trust is claimed to offer.

9. Imputed trusts

The comparisons drawn between the trust and other legal forms refer principally to those circumstances where a conscious decision is taken about the choice of legal form – the 'trust-twisting' end of the spectrum. But, as previously indicated, the trust obligation can come into existence not only through the expression of an intention on the part of the trust founder(s) (an 'express trust'), but also where the law imputes or imposes a trust – an 'imputed trust'. It is necessary to explore a little further the distinctions between and within these different trust types even at this introductory stage. The reader should be aware that there is no unanimously accepted classification of trust types and, more importantly, that they do not divide into watertight, mutually exclusive compartments.

We need to refer first, if only briefly, to the express-imputed distinction. No possibility of confusion can arise in the overwhelming number of situations, the trust founder's intention being made quite explicit in writing. But express trusts can be created informally, an intention to do so being inferred from the actions of the trust founder. In such circumstances the distinction between inferring an intention to create a trust and the court imputing a trust can be a very fine one indeed, as we shall see when 'intention' is discussed in detail in Chapter 4.

Within the categories of imputed trusts themselves, a further sub-classification of one type of imputed trust, resulting trusts, into 'automatic' and 'presumed' resulting trusts has until recently been generally accepted. The first type arises where an express trust fails for some reason: the trustees cannot of course take the property for their own use and so, as the name implies, the beneficial interest in the property 'results', or goes back to, the trust founder. As we shall see in Chapter 4 where we look at the rationale of this trust,

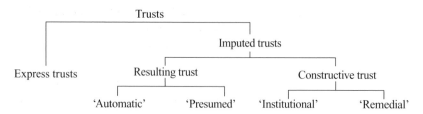

Figure 1.1 A Trust typology

reservations have been expressed about the appropriateness of the 'automatic' label; but for our immediate purposes, and in the absence of an accepted alternative, we will persevere with the present terminology. By way of contrast a 'presumed' resulting trust can arise where one person, A, gratuitously transfers property to another, B, in circumstances wherein equity adopts a rebuttable presumption that B then holds the property, not as beneficial owner, but on trust for A. This initially surprising presumption acquired a contemporary relevance in resolving property disputes where families break up, and the presumed resulting trust is discussed principally in that context (see Chapter 12). The second type of imputed trust, a constructive trust, is one imposed by operation of law irrespective (generally speaking) of the intention of the parties, and indeed quite possibly contrary to their intentions. Thus we have arrived at the classification set out in Figure 1.1.

Any impression of orderliness conveyed by this classification would be misleading for a number of reasons. We have not, for example, mentioned implied trusts. 'Implied trust' has been used, as we use imputed trust, as an umbrella term covering resulting trusts and constructive trusts. Indeed, in Chapter 12, reflecting recent judicial usage, we adopt 'implied trusts' as the umbrella term for resulting trusts and constructive trusts in the family home context. Unfortunately 'implied trust' has also been used to mean resulting trusts only, or presumed resulting trusts only, or even those express trusts where the intention has to be inferred from ambiguous language or conduct. Chapter 12 excepted, we therefore avoid using the term and can only reiterate that there is no authorised classification and that we restrict ourselves to the categories of constructive trusts, of which more shortly, and resulting trusts, the latter being subdivided for present purposes into 'automatic' and 'presumed' although this terminology will be reassessed in Chapter 4 (see p 193). A further reason why the appearance of an orderly structure would be misleading is that the linguistic confusion is in fact symptomatic of a more general conceptual uncertainty pervasive in imputed trusts. Two instances, one specific and one more general, illustrate the point.

Considering the specific example first, on occasions the courts have been less than scrupulous in distinguishing different forms of imputed trusts. In *Hussey v Palmer* [1972] 3 All ER 744, for example, the plaintiff, 'well over 70 and an old-age pensioner', paid £607 to a builder to erect an extra bedroom on a house belonging to her daughter and son-in-law for the plaintiff to live in. They quarrelled and the plaintiff left the house. Subsequently she sued to recover the £607. In the course of his judgment Lord Denning, the then Master of the Rolls, made the following observation (at 747):

> Although the plaintiff alleged that there was a resulting trust, I should have thought that the trust in this case, if there was one, was more in the nature of a constructive trust; but this is more a matter of words than anything else. The two run together. By whatever name it is described, it is a trust imposed by law whenever justice and good conscience require it. It is a liberal process, founded on large principles of equity, to be applied in cases where the defendant cannot conscientiously keep the property for himself alone, but ought to allow another to have the property or a share in it . . . [The trust] is an equitable remedy by which the court can enable an aggrieved party to obtain restitution.

Despite Lord Denning's view, it has conventionally been accepted until recently that whether a court imputes a 'presumed' resulting trust (as would have been the case in *Hussey v Palmer*) or, alternatively, a constructive trust, can have significant consequences. It was, for instance, thought to affect the proportion of 'the property or a share in it' that a successful plaintiff would be awarded as a remedy (see *Re Densham* [1975] 1 WLR 1519). Subsequent decisions of the courts, in particular those of the House of Lords in *Lloyds Bank plc v Rosset* [1991] 1 AC 107 and *Stack v Dowden* [2007] UKHL 17, have left us with a considerable degree of uncertainty about these matters (see generally Chapter 12 where they are explored in detail).

Our second instance of conceptual confusion concerns the circumstances in which a constructive trust will be imputed. The sweeping nature of the jurisdiction claimed by Lord Denning in *Hussey v Palmer*, for what he was to term elsewhere 'a constructive trust of a new model' (*Eves v Eves* [1975] 3 All ER 768 at 771), has been subject, perhaps unsurprisingly, to considerable academic and judicial criticism (see generally Chapter 12). Notions of 'justice and good conscience' can in the alternative be interpreted in terms of 'unpredictability and palm-tree justice'. Bagnall J in *Cowcher v Cowcher* [1972] 1 WLR 425, a case decided some six months before the hearing in *Hussey v Palmer*, captured the strong sense of unease in those who are uncomfortable with this sort of discretion being exercised in the area of property rights (at 430):

> I am convinced that in determining rights, particularly property rights, the only justice that can be attained by mortals, who are fallible and are not omniscient, is justice according to law; the justice which flows from the application of sure and settled principles to proved or admitted facts.

He went on to add that any developments in the law should be legitimate – 'by precedent out of principle' – 'since otherwise no lawyer could safely advise on his client's title and every quarrel would lead to a law suit'. The 'new model' was therefore sometimes contrasted unfavourably with the established or 'institutional' constructive trust whose incidence and consequences were thought to be more clearly defined. In *Westdeutsche Landesbank Girozentrale v Islington LBC* [1996] AC 669, Lord Browne-Wilkinson summarised the distinction in the following manner (at 714–715):

> Under an institutional constructive trust, the trust arises by operation of law as from the date of the circumstances which give rise to it: the function of the court is merely to declare that such trust has arisen in the past. The consequences that flow from such trust having arisen (including the possibly unfair consequences to third parties who in the interim have received the trust property) are also determined by rules of law, not under discretion. A remedial constructive trust, as I understand it, is different. It is a judicial remedy giving rise to an enforceable equitable obligation: the extent to which it operates retrospectively to the prejudice of third parties lies in the discretion of the court. Thus for the law of New York to hold that there is a remedial constructive trust . . . gives rise to different consequences from holding that an institutional constructive trust arises in English law.

An example of an 'institutional constructive trust', although not an example that is an everyday occurrence, is where A leaves property in her will ostensibly to B but on an understanding reached between them that B will pass it on to C. If B, having acquired legal title to the property under A's will, were to claim that the property was his rather than C's a court might say that B holds it on constructive trust for C. Of course we might say that since this complies with A's original intention, why do we not call it an express trust? We will have to address that question in Chapter 4 when we examine this arrangement – called a secret trust – in some detail since the classification of the trust is a matter of debate. Consider next the case of D, a company director of XYZ plc who instead of obtaining a contract with ABC plc on behalf of XYZ plc as is her duty as a director – called a fiduciary duty – acquires the contract for her own use. A court might say that D holds the benefit of the contract on constructive trust for XYZ plc although here also there is a marked lack of unanimity as to whether the imputing of a constructive trust is the appropriate remedy (see Chapter 16 at p 881). In both these instances we might equally say that it would be 'unconscionable' for B and D to assert their own rights under the will and contract respectively to the detriment of those of C and XYZ plc. But unconscionability used in this sense has a narrow meaning, being determined, as Lord Browne-Wilkinson points out, by rules of law rather than judicial discretion. The practical point to emphasise here is that the circumstances when the institutional constructive trust can be imposed are thought to be more predictable, some would claim more principled, than those applicable to a remedial constructive trust. In fact, as is implicit in the opinion of Lord Browne-Wilkinson, there are a number of well-established instances where a constructive trust may be imposed, and these constitute the heartland of the subject (see Oakley *Constructive Trusts* (3rd edn, 1997) for a detailed categorisation).

The converse perception that the new model or remedial constructive trust is uncertain in application clearly carries weight, and the consequences for the interests of third parties of imputing a trust in the manner envisaged by Lord Denning cannot be lightly dismissed. Nevertheless, legal systems tend to need some leeway to infuse elements of 'fairness' and to recognise novel claims of right. Indeed such notions can be thought of as important legitimating mechanisms for a legal system (see Chesterman 'Equity in the Law' in Troy (ed) *A Just Society* (1981)). In any event, criticism notwithstanding, Lord Denning's prototype, or at least the desirability of an equivalent, has exhibited some resilience and, in a modified form, has re-entered academic and juristic debate as a 'remedial constructive trust'. The principal area of operation of this type of trust remains that of family property disputes, although its presence has also been felt in some areas of commercial activity. Nevertheless it must be conceded that a jurisdiction of this nature remains contentious in the extreme and we will therefore revisit this issue briefly at the end of section 10 of this chapter. For the moment it is sufficient to note that depicting the circumstances in which a constructive trust, of whatever type, will be imposed, defining the nature of that trust and, as importantly, determining the appropriate remedy are proving to be elusive goals (but see eg Wright *The Remedial Constructive Trust* (1998) reviewed critically by Birks (1999) 115 LQR 681; Millett [1999] 14 Amicus Curiae 4; Millett (1998) 114 LQR 399; Rickett and Grantham [1999] LMCLQ 111; Rickett (1999) 18(3) NZULR 305; Birks 'Proprietary Rights as Remedies' in Birks (ed) *Frontiers of Liability* Vol II (1994) p 214; and Evans (2001) Sydney LR 463). It is worth noting, however, that uncertainty and disagreement about the scope for the constructive trust is not a phenomenon that first emerged with Lord Denning's 'new model constructive trust'. On the contrary it appears that the roots of the difference in approach adopted in English trusts law to this issue as compared with that of the US can be detected in contrasting analyses of this issue first evident in the mid-Victorian trusts law treatises (see Ibbetson *A Historical Introduction to the Law of Obligations* (1999) pp 281–284).

One problem in studying constructive trusts, therefore, is whether we can identify some unifying principle common, for example, to the trustee of an express trust who renews in his own favour a lease previously held for the trust, and to the 'secret trust' and to the company director who appropriates to herself a contract that she should have taken up on behalf of her company, other than a conclusion that constructive trusteeship may be imposed on all of them. A widely adopted approach is to examine in one chapter these and other circumstances in which a constructive trust has been imposed. This would certainly provide us with a mode of classification. It might also enable us to draw tentative conclusions about the nature of a constructive trust and to move towards identifying some common principle. This superficially attractive approach is, however, not without its dangers. It may provide an impression of coherence and certainty which one cannot confidently assert exists. Furthermore, if the categories as currently defined are construed as prescriptive rather than just descriptive, then devoting excessive deference to them may hinder our understanding of any incremental process of legal change.

This area of law remains in something of a ferment and there is controversy as to the direction and desirability of change, particularly when it occurs in a more overtly remedial fashion. However, as will be seen, notably in Chapter 12, various Commonwealth jurisdictions are developing different rationales for a 'remedial' form of constructive trust – unjust enrichment in Canada, versions of unconscionability in Australia and New Zealand, and estoppel as a juridical base in English law. We would suggest, however, that common to them all is an underlying problem that is intrinsic to this subject. Can the doctrines and practices of equity provide an adequate response to unconscionable conduct in a way that does not degenerate in the manner envisaged by Bagnall J in *Cowcher v Cowcher*? Although this book is predominantly concerned with the English law of trusts, at numerous points we refer to the different ways in which other Commonwealth jurisdictions are implicitly addressing that fundamental question. This is not comparison just for the sake of comparison; if, as some say, there is a cross-fertilisation of ideas between jurisdictions then we need to know something of what others do if we are to understand the responses of our own system and the processes of legal change.

This pattern of legal change returns us in a roundabout way to our family tree of trusts and to the emphasis that Maitland placed on the development of the trust idea and with which this introductory chapter began. The imputed trust branches are still developing and our preferred approach is therefore to forsake any claim to unity and instead fragment our treatment of imputed trusts in general and constructive trusts in particular. There are no chapters devoted specifically to resulting trusts or constructive trusts. Accordingly, whilst we still examine the constructive trust imposed on, for example, our trio of defaulting trustee, 'secret trustee' and disloyal company director described above, we do so in their respective family trust (Chapters 4 and 9), commercial (Chapters 14 and 16) and, if we add property relations between cohabiting partners to the equation, family breakdown contexts (Chapter 12).

We cannot quite leave the topic there, however. The brief discussion above about imputed trusts might create the impression of an area of trusts law hermetically sealed, divorced from other legal doctrines. At the boundaries this is emphatically not the case. Indeed, the use by Lord Denning of the term 'restitution' in *Hussey v Palmer* (see p 25) and our reference above to 'unjust enrichment' hint at the existence of broader horizons beyond the boundaries of trusts law, as conventionally defined.

10. Marking the boundaries

The broader horizons and some of the accompanying doctrinal tensions were succinctly summarised by Lord Goff in *Westdeutsche Landesbank Girozentrale v Islington London Borough Council* [1996] AC 669 at 685:

Ever since the law of restitution began, about the middle of this century, to be studied in depth, the role of equitable proprietary claims in the law of restitution has been found to be a matter of great difficulty. The legitimate ambition of restitution lawyers has been to establish a coherent law of restitution, founded upon the principle of unjust enrichment; and since certain equitable institutions, notably the constructive trust and the resulting trust have been perceived to have the functions of reversing unjust enrichment, they have sought to embrace those institutions within the law of restitution, if necessary moulding them to make them fit for that purpose. Equity lawyers, on the other hand, have displayed anxiety that in this process the equitable principles underlying these institutions may become illegitimately distorted; and though equity lawyers in this country are nowadays much more sympathetic than they have been in the past towards the need to develop a coherent law of restitution, and of identifying the proper role of the trust within the rubric of the law, they remain concerned that the trust concept should not be distorted, and also that the practical consequences of its imposition should be fully appreciated. There is therefore some tension between the aims and perceptions of these two groups of lawyers, which has manifested itself in relation to the matters under consideration in the present case.

This is not the place to explore in any great detail those 'matters under consideration' in the case nor the kaleidoscope of opinion and comment that the case has generated. Suffice to say here that the factual matrix was relatively straightforward. The council and the bank were engaged in a financial market arrangement termed a 'swap agreement' whereby in effect the council received capital (£2.5m) 'up front' in return for making staged repayments over several years. These contractual arrangements became almost commonplace during the stringent controls on local authority finance during the 1980s as they provided local authorities with a means of raising funds for expenditure without, it was thought, infringing statutory controls. Then in 1992 in *Hazell v Hammersmith and Fulham London Borough Council* [1992] 2 AC 1 the House of Lords held that such swap agreements were ultra vires the local authorities. Westdeutsche, which had been repaid about half the capital by Islington London Borough Council, sought to recover the balance. The bank succeeded in its claim; the ground of recovery need not concern us save to note that it was at common law. One issue was left outstanding: interest was payable on the amount to be repaid but was this to be calculated as simple interest or compound interest? The legal significance of this was that on a common law claim simple interest only could be awarded whereas in equity in certain circumstances compound interest could be awarded against a trustee or other person in a fiduciary capacity. And therein lay a problem for Westdeutsche. If their lordships were not prepared to align the criteria for awarding interest so that the claim for compound interest could be upheld on the alignment basis alone – and they were not – could the bank establish that the local authority held the capital as a trustee? The House of Lords decided unanimously that there was no fiduciary relationship and held by a 3:2 majority that the bank was not entitled to compound interest (the minority judges of whom Lord Goff was one considered that compound interest could be awarded on other grounds).

One source of the tension referred to by Lord Goff was to be found in one of the core arguments advanced on behalf of the bank and based on the law of restitution. Before considering the particular argument advanced in the case it is necessary to comment very briefly on the law of restitution. At its most straightforward and for present purposes it can be said to be concerned to a considerable extent but not exclusively with reversing the unjust enrichment gained by one person at the expense of another (see Birks *An Introduction to the Law of Restitution* (rev edn, 1989); *Unjust Enrichment* (2nd edn, 2005); Virgo *The Principles of the Law of Restitution* (2nd edn, 2006); but cf for a different perspective Jaffey *The Nature and Scope of Restitution* (2000)). As is apparent from the words of Lord Goff in *Westdeutsche*, the law of restitution is a relative latecomer to the English legal scene. Many of the restitutionary claims were initially seen as a somewhat miscellaneous collection lying outside the established categories of contract and tort, hence the search for some explanatory principle, and the ambition, in Lord Goff's words, 'to establish a coherent law of restitution'. (Lord Goff, with Gareth Jones, was the original author of the path-breaking English law text on this subject, now in its 7th edition, Goff and Jones *The Law of Restitution* (2007).) The outcome of the 'search for coherence' is that the English law of obligations now constitutes a triumvirate of contract, tort and restitution rather than contract, tort and 'a miscellany of other claims'. The search did not rest there but, again as Lord Goff points out, also potentially brought within the ambit of the law of restitution aspects of the law of trusts. It is that conjunction of ideas that was to provide that core argument for the bank in *Westdeutsche*. Based on an argument developed by Professor Peter Birks ('Restitution and Resulting Trusts' in Goldstein (ed) *Equity: Contemporary Legal Developments* (1992)) it was claimed where there was any voluntary transfer of legal title with no evidence of any intention to make a gift – as where money is paid under a mistake or on a condition which is not subsequently satisfied – then a resulting trust should be presumed to operate at once to reverse the enrichment of the recipient. Put simply, in the context of *Westdeutsche*, the gist of the argument was that there was a void contract, that the bank in those circumstances had clearly not intended to make a gift to Islington London Borough Council who therefore held the legal title on resulting trust for the bank. To reiterate, the point of making the argument in these terms was to establish a claim in equity; there was no doubt, as already indicated, that the bank was entitled to recover the capital and simple interest under a common law action. To accept the resulting trust argument would, in the view of the House of Lords, have involved an extension of the scope of resulting trusts – beyond that outlined above at p 23 – which would involve 'a distortion of trust principles' (per Lord Browne-Wilkinson at 715; see Birks [1996] 4 RLR 4 for an initial response to the judgment).

The core trust principle identified by Lord Browne-Wilkinson was that 'Equity operates on the conscience of the owner of the legal interest' and therefore '[that owner] cannot be a trustee of the property if and so long as he is ignorant of the facts alleged to affect his conscience, i.e. until he is aware that he is intended to hold the property for the benefit of others' (at 705, but cf Swadling in Birks and Rose (eds) *Lessons of the Swaps Litigation* (2000) 242 at 257–264 where reservations are expressed about the authority for and implications of the proposition, particularly as regards the centrality accorded to 'conscience'). It would be remiss to pretend that there were not other pragmatic considerations at work in the outcome of the *Westdeutsche* case. Lord Browne-Wilkinson specifically refers to a concern that any extension of proprietary interests in personal property in the manner argued for on behalf of the bank would be bound to produce commercial uncertainty (at 705):

> If the bank's arguments are correct, a businessman who has entered into transactions relating to or dependent upon property rights could find that assets which apparently belong to one person in fact belong to another; that there are 'off balance sheet' liabilities of which he cannot be aware; that these property rights and liabilities arise from circumstances unknown not only to himself but also to anyone else who has been involved in the transactions. A new area of unmanageable risk will be introduced into commercial dealings. If the due application of equitable principles forced a conclusion leading to these results, your Lordships would be presented with a formidable task in reconciling legal principle with commercial common sense. But in my judgment no such conflict occurs. The resulting trust for which the bank contends is inconsistent not only with the law as it stands but with any principled development of it.

Some of the other legal implications of *Westdeutsche* will be considered at various points in this book as will the significance attached to the commercial consequences of legal change. For the moment we are concerned simply with some more general implications for our understanding of contemporary developments in the law of trusts. First, the case highlights a particular feature of our system of private law; there are potentially overlapping jurisdictions. The law of restitution and the law of trusts can be conceived of as occupying two eccentric circles. It is where the borders overlap that friction can occur. The friction arises in part because the 'search for a coherent law of restitution' can elide into a more ambitious and wide-ranging agenda of reclassification of private law. This book is not the place to engage in an analysis of the pros and cons of the restitution enterprise, not least because the scholarship deployed in the considerable literature on the subject now embraces a diversity of views, some of which have changed as the scholarship develops (see eg Burrows *The Law of Restitution* (2nd edn, 2002); Birks *An Introduction to the Law of Restitution* (rev edn, 1989) and *Unjust Enrichment* (2nd edn, 2005); Virgo *The Principles of the Law of Restitution* (2nd edn, 2006); Jaffey *The Nature and Scope of Restitution* (2000); and the iconoclastic approach of Hedley *Restitution: Its Division and Ordering* (2001)). There is no unanimity, for instance, about the precise relationship between the law of restitution and the reversal of unjust enrichment nor indeed about whether there is or should be a distinct legal category of unjust enrichment. This does not mean that we ignore the insights that are provided by restitutionary analyses. These are discussed at various points in the book, primarily in Chapters 11, 14 and 16 where the remedies that might be invoked for breach of trust take centre stage. Consideration is also given, although to a lesser degree, to another boundary, that between trusts law and tort law, particularly where the competence and integrity of trustees and other fiduciaries is at issue. It is important in trying to understand the pace and direction of legal change that efforts to minimise or remove any dissonance resulting from these boundary conflicts may be a formative influence in current developments. More prosaically it may also be helpful to be aware that linguistic purity is not always present in this area. Thus a common complaint of restitution lawyers is that the term 'restitution' is on occasion used when what is meant is that a person is receiving compensation or what a common lawyer might call 'damages'. Restitution, in contrast, involves the surrendering up of a benefit gained from another person.

There remains one 'bit-part actor' on the *Westdeutsche* stage that we have not yet mentioned. One of the underlying themes in the case was how far it was appropriate for a more extensive proprietary restitutionary remedy to be developed using trusts law. On this point, Lord Browne-Wilkinson commented (at 716):

> Although the resulting trust is an unsuitable base for developing proprietary restitutionary remedies, the remedial constructive trust, if introduced into English law, may provide a more satisfactory road forward. The court by way of remedy might impose a constructive trust on a defendant who knowingly retains property of which the plaintiff has been unjustly deprived. Since the remedy can be tailored to the circumstances of the particular case, innocent third parties would not be prejudiced and restitutionary defences, such as change of position, are capable of being given effect. However, whether English law should follow the United States and Canada by adopting the remedial constructive trust will have to be decided in some future case when the point is directly in issue.

The glimmer of light for such hopeful claimants, often seeking priority over other claimants in an insolvency, indicated by Lord Browne-Wilkinson's comments in *Westdeutsche* was, however, quickly put out by the Court of Appeal in *Re Polly Peck International plc (No 2)* [1998] 3 All ER 812 (see Chapter 16 at p 845 where the remedial constructive trust is considered in a comparative and commercial context). Whether this rejection proves to be a temporary or permanent roadblock in English law is uncertain. A pragmatic objection to a remedial constructive trust is the possible consequences for the property interests of third parties, particularly creditors of a defendant. But, as Lord Browne-Wilkinson acknowledged in the extract above, in jurisdictions where the remedial constructive trust is employed as a response to unjust enrichment the courts have a wide discretion as to the remedy to be awarded. The interests of creditors can be taken into account. A more fundamental objection is encapsulated by the comments of Bagnall J in *Cowcher v Cowcher* (see above). That concern is the fear of unfettered discretion and accompanying lack of predictability of outcome or more prosaically 'palm tree justice'. Such concerns should not be discounted but, as we shall see at various points in the book, trusts law and equity are replete with concepts of an open-textured nature. We shall encounter inter alia the language of 'unconscionability', 'undue influence' and 'legitimate expectations'. None of these are any more susceptible to precise definition than, one might suggest, is the 'neighbour principle of negligence'. But nor does such terminology lead to the exercise of that unfettered discretion. One of our tasks is therefore to tease out the interpretation given to these terms in the different factual contexts in which they are deployed. We need not assume that the claims of 'unconscionability' will be treated with equal regard in such diverse contexts as family breakdown and corporate malfeasance. (See generally Birks (ed) *Frontiers of Liability* Vol 2 (1994) chs 13–17 for an excellent introduction to the remedial constructive trust.)

11. Focus on social contexts where trusts are used

Although, to repeat Maitland's words, the trust is a legal device 'of great elasticity and generality; as elastic, as general as contract', there are relatively few social contexts in which it has consistently been used to any significant degree. One may compare the position with contracts: the standard situations where these are commonly made are many and various. One thinks readily, for instance, of contracts of sale (relating to goods or land), contracts of hire or lease, contracts of employment, contracts of insurance, and the contract existing between members of a company or unincorporated association. There are many more categories of contract not on this list. By contrast, the contexts in which trusts, express or imputed, regularly make an appearance can be narrowed down to four, as follows:

(1) Preservation of family wealth   The aggregation and management of invested wealth, chiefly for the benefit of members of a family, and usually involving some element of transmission of wealth from one generation to the next.

(2) 'Family breakdown'   Imputed trusts are used to reach a just and fair result in the allocation of property between de facto partners on the break-up of their relationship. (Where the persons concerned have been married to each other, this aspect of their divorce is regulated by statute rather than trust principles.)

(3) Finance and commerce   The trust impinges on financial and commercial activity in three important ways. First, it provides a medium for collective

investment: examples are pension funds and unit trusts. Second, it is used on occasions as a device for securing commercial debt. Third, fiduciary law and doctrines of constructive trust form the basis for imposing standards of honesty and good faith on individuals engaged in business: in particular, on partners and company directors. (See Bryan 'Reflections on Some Commercial Applications of the Trust' in Ramsay (ed) *Key Developments in Corporate Law and Trusts Law* (2002); and in a US context Langbein 'The Secret Life of the Trust: The Trust as an Instrument of Commerce' (1997) 107 Yale LJ 165).

(4) 'Voluntary' activity　'Voluntary' – or, more precisely, non-profit – activity attracts the use of trusts where it is carried out *either* for welfare-oriented purposes which the law regards as 'charitable' *or* by an unincorporated association.

One further context where the trust plays a prominent part is in ownership of the family home. Where a home is in shared ownership, legal title is generally held, possibly to the puzzlement of the owners, on a statutory trust of land, now by virtue of the changes introduced in the Trusts of Land and Appointment of Trustees Act 1996. This arrangement is more usually and appropriately discussed in land law books (eg Gray *Elements of Land Law* (5th edn, 2009)).

The approach in this book is to examine the development and the present content of trusts law in conjunction with a study of each of the four contexts (1)–(4) above. The remainder of this book is accordingly divided into four parts.

The first of the four contexts – preservation of family wealth – has been in many respects the most important in terms of the development of trusts law. The trust notion was originally conceived and given legal recognition on account of the efforts of medieval conveyancers to protect the landholdings of their clients from certain forms of feudal taxation and to increase the range of dispositions of land which their clients could legally make on death. Most of the principles governing the creation, duration and administration of express trusts have been developed in this context of family wealth-holding. But each of the other contexts has provided an increasingly important basis for significant elaborations of trust doctrine.

2

The evolution of the private express trust

1. Introduction

As indicated at the end of Chapter 1, the trust concept originated in English law in medieval times, chiefly as a result of the efforts of conveyancers to preserve the landholdings of their clients from certain forms of feudal taxation and to increase the range of dispositions of land which their clients could legally make on death. The emergence of the trust concept at this time is intimately bound up with the assumption of jurisdiction in legal matters by the Lord Chancellor, on grounds of 'equity'. In time, as we will see, that jurisdiction became sufficiently pervasive and ordered so as to justify substituting an upper case 'E' in place of the lower case 'e'. The development of Equity in that manner involves matters that range far beyond those concerning the trust. Since it is the latter that is our prime concern, the roles are reversed here and Equity therefore appears in our story mostly as a member of the supporting cast only.

This chapter seeks to explain the development of major segments of trusts law – specifically, the law governing private express trusts – from these early beginnings until, approximately, the beginning of the twentieth century. It does so with particular reference to trust transactions which served, in various ways, to aggregate and safeguard privately held wealth for the benefit of members of a family and to ensure the smooth transmission of wealth from one generation of a family to the next. Towards the end of the chapter, some general comments are offered on the historical role of private family trusts. The chapter concludes by returning to the broader topic of the relationship between Equity and other areas of the common law, a topic that has of late been attracting close academic and judicial scrutiny.

First, however, a general note of caution needs to be aired about our capacity 'to explain'. In this chapter, and elsewhere in this book, we are concerned with change over time. But Milsom's words of warning are apposite here ('"Pollock and Maitland": A Lawyer's Retrospect' (1996) 89 *Proceedings of the British Academy* 243 at 251):

[s]ince it is almost a function of law to hide change, few developments other than those made by explicit legislation can be pinned down and dated. The same rule works differently.

> The same word changes its meaning. The same action is put to a fresh purpose. The same situation is analysed in a new way. It follows that there will be few conclusions that are securely established as one can establish a regular historical fact.

Whether or not one thinks that Milsom's general proposition about secure conclusions can be applied to the history of the trust, the elements of legal change that he identifies certainly have a compelling resonance in this context. There is, as we shall see, explicit legislation which, together with a hardening of doctrine, has at times imposed constraints on the 'efforts of conveyancers'. But there has also been scope to manipulate rules and language which, when the social and economic climate is right, stimulated inventiveness. One modest conclusion can be drawn: we are dealing with a process of creating law that has often operated 'from the bottom up'.

2. Medieval 'uses' of land

(For general discussion of the origins of uses, see eg Milsom *Historical Foundations of the Common Law* (2nd edn, 1981) ch 9; Bean *The Decline of English Feudalism 1215–1540* (1968); Biancalana 'Medieval Uses' in Helmholz and Zimmermann (eds) *Itinera Fiduciae* (1998) 111; Fratcher 'Uses of Uses' (1969) 34 Miss LR 39; Holmes *The Estates of the Higher Nobility in 14th Century England* (1957) pp 41–84; Barton 'The Medieval Use' (1965) 81 LQR 562.)

The medieval forerunner of the modern trust was not called a trust, but a 'use'. The term 'use' is a corruption of the Latin phrase '*ad opus*'. The background to its emergence in the thirteenth century was a common law system of landholding based on feudal conceptions. As reconstructed by modern historians, with some divergences of opinion, a tenant of land under post-Conquest feudalism had the legal right to possess the land (known as 'seisin') and to receive some degree of patronage and protection from the lord from whom the land was held. In return, he was bound to render due homage and various services and 'incidents' (ie material benefits of different kinds) to the lord and, in the case of tenants lower down the scale, to submit to the lord's jurisdiction in the manorial courts. The system was based on the idea that no one was the absolute owner of land. Instead, chains comprising these two-way relationships of tenure stretched downwards from the king, who was the ultimate overlord. The chain might have only one link, in which case the tenant, a so-called 'tenant-in-chief', held directly of the king. Or there might be several links, in which case the tenant with actual seisin was the 'tenant in demesne' and the intervening persons, each of whom was both a lord of the tenant below him and a tenant to the lord above him, were called 'mesne lords'.

Feudal landholding was thus a complex amalgam of personal relationships – manifested particularly in the subordination of tenant to lord through homage, services and incidents – and proprietary rights.

The rise of uses represents a form of response to the decline of the major ingredients of feudalism and feudal landholding coupled with the retention and, indeed, strengthening of the so-called 'incidents' such as 'relief' (a sum payable to the lord when a tenant succeeded to the land on the death of a former tenant), and wardship (the lord's right to guardianship of the 'body' of the heir and the lands themselves, including the profits arising from them, during the minority of a deceased tenant's heir).

The process of decline of feudalism was reflected in a number of important changes in the feudal landholding system. Most of these reflected the break-up of personal bonds between lords and tenants of land. For example, in certain tenures money payments were increasingly substituted for 'services' such as the provision of armies and the furnishing of produce of labour. Furthermore, some time during the twelfth and thirteenth centuries, feudal tenants acquired the right to pass land on to their heirs (usually the eldest son) and to alienate it inter vivos without needing the consent of the lord. The lord thus lost control over the identity of his tenants.

As regards the second factor underlying the development of uses – that is, the retention and strengthening of feudal 'incidents' – the main reason why these incidents survived whereas the services became increasingly less important was that the value of the incidents kept pace with the times. Because the late Middle Ages saw some periods of rapid inflation, the value of services commuted into fixed sums of money became negligible. Incidents, being geared to such things as the profits from the land, did not suffer in this way. Incidents thus emerged as something like a modern landlord's 'premium', or 'key money'. More significantly, they constituted for the king, the supreme landlord, a form of taxation based on landholding. In a period marked by foreign wars and substantial centralisation of royal authority, this was of considerable significance.

The 'use' was a product of these various social changes. As already stated, it became prominent in the thirteenth century, though instances have been traced back to about 1200. It had apparent predecessors in other systems of law. Links have been suggested, for instance, with the Roman law concept of *fideicommissum*; with a Germanic form of executor called the 'salman'; with the executor of a 'testament' of personal chattels recognised in the common law and ecclesiastical courts; and even with an Islamic legal concept called a 'waqf' (allegedly brought back to England by the Crusaders: see eg Avini (1996) 70 Tul LR 1139; Herman (1996) 70 Tul LR 2239).

Discarding ancient for modern terminology, the use was typically employed by medieval tenants of land as follows. A tenant P would convey his land to a group of trustees (say, Q, R and S) 'to the use of' himself as beneficiary, then to such uses as he should subsequently appoint. By his 'last will' (not to be confused with a will of chattels, which was then called a 'testament') or by prior instructions, he would indicate such uses. His eldest son might be designated the beneficiary as to most of his land, with the remainder being split up amongst his daughters, his younger sons, a monastery, parish or other church institution and (so far as necessary) creditors to whom he owed money at his death. This is no more than a typical example: in fact, the range of dispositions of benefit that a tenant could effect through uses was virtually unlimited. He could also give the trustees active duties; for example, ensuring that pecuniary legacies contained in his 'testament' were paid out of the rents and profits of his land.

This short description of the operation of the use is enough to show how closely it resembles the modern trust. It did, in fact, perform most of the same 'tricks' with land ownership as the trust now performs with ownership generally. In the historical context just described, these tricks served a number of different purposes.

First, and most significant politically, they brought about the evasion of feudal incidents. The incidents were all related to 'seisin', the common law right to possess. For example, it was when an heir acquired seisin by descent that a 'relief' could be exacted. Where uses were employed, seisin would be conferred upon the trustees. The number of these was kept at two or more, and the common law doctrine that on the death of a joint tenant his interest passes to the surviving joint tenant(s) was invoked with the result that the death of a sole tenant having seisin would scarcely ever occur. Thus, although the heir might still acquire some or all of the land on or after death, he did not do so by direct descent, but by transfer from the trustees.

Second, the range of dispositions available to a tenant increased considerably. In particular, he acquired a de facto power of devising – ie bequeathing – land to whomever he chose. Although feudalism had liberalised to the extent that a lord could not actively prevent the succession of an heir, this still meant that normally, on the death of a landowner, the eldest son was entitled at common law to take all the land. The landowner could only split up the land if he was prepared to alienate inter vivos. But uses gave the landowner the power to choose between strict primogeniture on his death, as required by the common law rules, or primogeniture modified as to provide for the rest of the family and for other purposes important to the tenant (as illustrated in the above example of a conveyance of uses) or indeed a total breakaway from primogeniture. If he wanted the land, or part of it, to pass to someone other than his heir, he did not have to make an out-and-out lifetime gift: instead, he had, in effect, a power of free disposition on death.

The remaining purposes to which uses were put can be briefly mentioned. Uses made secret conveyancing of land possible, whereas at common law a transfer of seisin had to take place by public act. They were employed to ensure that lands were looked after (ie by the trustees) while the tenant was fighting in the Crusades or in other wars, foreign or domestic. In so far as they were employed to confer the rents and profits of lands on Church institutions, they were, for a time, evading the policy of a statute purporting to prevent this. Finally, it was possible for a time to transfer land to trustees to one's own use in order to put the land out of the reach of creditors.

In short, it is difficult to dissent from the conclusion of Sir Edward Coke that there were 'two inventors of uses, fear and fraud; fear in times of troubles and civil wars to save their inheritances from being forfeited; and fraud to defeat due

debts, lawful actions, wards, escheats, mortmains, etc' (*Chudleigh*'s case (1594)
1 Co Rep 113b at 121b, as cited in Jones (1995) 54 CLJ 545).

The question now arises: how did these transactions involving uses come to
receive legal protection and support even though it was the trustees who had
title at common law to the fee simple or other estate conveyed at common law?
The answer lies in the early beginnings of Chancery jurisdiction.

The early history of the jurisdiction is somewhat obscure but one catalyst
in its development was the contemporary limitations of the common law.
During the fourteenth and fifteenth centuries the common law courts had for
a number of reasons – insufficient adaptability to new claims, limited range of
remedies, complexity of pleadings – proved inadequate. In particular, even if
the ingenuity of lawyers could have managed to squeeze the case of a defaulting
trustee into one of the specialised pleadings before the common law courts
the lack of specific performance as a remedy was a major disadvantage (see
Biancalana op cit at 148–149). The general remedy of statutory reform was not
seen as the answer. Instead, those aggrieved could petition the Chancellor, who
could order specific remedial measures on a variety of discretionary grounds
in order to achieve justice in individual 'hard cases'. Most early chancellors
were ecclesiastics and this may account for the prominence that notions of
'good faith' and 'conscience' claimed in Chancery jurisdiction (see generally
the essay by Helmholz 'The Early Enforcement of Uses' (1979) 79 Col LR 1503).
Indeed the 'decrees' of the Chancellor were specifically addressed to a person's
'conscience' – that is they sought to compel him to do what justice, or good
conscience, or 'equity' required of him. The following passage from a legal
history text fills out the picture as it applied to the trust (Baker *An Introduction
to the History of English Law* (4th edn, 2002) p 102):

> If someone granted land to others on trust to carry out his wishes, he would find that at
> law the grantees were absolute owners who could not be compelled to obey him. Now
> it was not that the common law held... that a promise or trust could be broken; such
> [a] proposition would have been dismissed as absurd. Yet those were the results that
> followed from observing strict rules of evidence, rules which might exclude the merits of
> the case from consideration but which could not be relaxed without destroying certainty
> and condoning carelessness. For a... promisee or trustee to take unfair advantage of those
> strict rules was without question wrong; but it was a matter for their consciences rather
> than for the common law.
>
> The Chancery worked differently. The Chancellor was free from the rigid procedures under
> which such injustices sheltered. His court was a court of conscience in which defendants
> could be coerced into doing whatever conscience required in the full circumstances of the
> case.

It seems that Chancery intervention, at the instance of beneficiaries, to order
trustees to abide by the terms of declared uses began about the end of the fourteenth century. This aspect of Chancery jurisdiction was firmly established by
the mid-fifteenth century. About this time a proprietary flavour was added to

the beneficiary's rights. It was decided, for instance, that a beneficiary's rights could be assigned. In addition, the Lord Chancellor was prepared to impute a use in several situations corresponding to modern imputed trusts. These developments were part of the integral change taking place in the Chancellor's jurisdiction whereby a form of equitable corrective, or gloss, upon the operations of a pre-existing common law system began to evolve into a separate collection of legal principles.

The chain of causation here is important for our understanding of the process by which the use was developed and ultimately recognised. Holdsworth's claim that the use was a 'product of the equitable jurisdiction of the Chancellor' does not tell the full story (*A History of English Law* (3rd edn, 1945) p 418). Indeed it has been said by Bean to put the proverbial cart before the horse (*The Decline of English Feudalism 1215–1540* (1968) p 129): 'The Chancellor's jurisdiction in uses arose from the fact that [uses] *already existed* and fraudulent feoffees were becoming a serious nuisance' (emphasis added). In short this is but one example of law, in this instance in the form of Equity, being shaped by the experience of practice or, we might say, malpractice.

The use as it finally emerged did not resemble the modern trust in all respects. In particular, the beneficiary's 'quasi-proprietary' protection was still defective in certain respects and the principles governing a trustee's powers and duties were still to be developed. But in the fifteenth century one can discern the foundations of modern trusts law.

One can also glimpse possible reasons why Chancery's intervention was (as it still is) in favour of beneficiaries only, rather than at the instance of the creators of uses. A transaction of the type outlined above (a transfer of land to trustees to the use of the transferee for life, thereafter to such uses as he shall appoint) was typical, because it achieved the desired effect of a testamentary devise. Remedies granted in the name of the beneficiary operated not only to protect the creator as long as he lived – because he himself was the beneficiary during this period – but also to ensure observance of the trust when the creator was no longer alive to take action himself. By contrast, to have treated the transmission solely as a contract between the creator and the trustees, enforceable only by these parties, would have left the ultimate beneficiaries without any remedy. In any event, there was in the fifteenth century no general doctrine of contract law under which the contractual element in the transaction between creator and trustees could be invoked as a basis for enforcement of the trustees' duties. (But cf Jones 'Uses, Trusts and a Path to Privity' (1997) 56 CLJ 175–200; and see generally Palmer *The Paths to Privity* (1992) who identifies 1500–1680 as the 'formative period' of the privity of contract doctrine.)

During the fourteenth and fifteenth centuries, the Crown made piecemeal attacks on uses and their enforcement. But uses were, on the whole, tolerated, and were given Chancery protection. This seems strange because they proliferated enormously – covering, it has been said, the 'greater part' of English land in the late fifteenth century – and were employed particularly by large landowners holding on knight service in order to evade the particularly valuable incidents of wardship and marriage. The explanation must be that, during this period – particularly during the Wars of the Roses, the power of the king was too precarious and too dependent on particular groups of nobles to enable him to confront the majority of them on an issue such as this.

To conclude this discussion of the medieval period, a few words should be said about dispositions in the nature of a trust relating to personal property. Such dispositions attracted much less attention and controversy than uses of land. This is chiefly because personalty accounted for far less wealth than land. The most common forms of valuable chattels in private hands were family heirlooms, jewellery and the like, but these were not income producing. The overall market value of such articles in a noble family was a good deal less than that of the landed estate.

3. The Statute of Uses

England's period of 'absolutist' rule under the Tudor monarchy was the occasion for a royal onslaught on the evasion of feudal incidents through uses. There was a brief return to 'fiscal feudalism'. Some limited efforts in this direction occurred during the reign of Henry VII, but the changes wrought by his successor were more dramatic and more fundamental. In 1535, Henry VIII pushed through Parliament the most important single statute in the history of the trust's development: the Statute of Uses. (See eg Brown (1979) 9 Manitoba LJ 409; Barton (1966) 82 LQR 215; Simpson *A History of the Land Law* (2nd edn, 1986) ch 8.) This sought to undermine the conceptual basis of the use rather than merely to impose piecemeal restrictions upon it. It provided that, with certain important exceptions which are outlined below, the creation of a use should operate not to give the beneficiary various rights against the trustees (and others deriving title from them) which Chancery would protect, but actually to confer seisin – ie legal title – on the beneficiary to the exclusion of the trustees. This conversion of the beneficiary's equitable rights under the use into legal title was called 'executing' the use.

The prime aim of the statute was to recapture lost feudal incidents for a monarchy which was heavily involved in wars for religious and mercantile purposes. Henry VIII also sought to achieve this aim by a number of administrative measures, notably the establishment of a Court of Wards in 1540.

Generally speaking, the frontal attack which the statute launched upon uses was effective in reviving 'fiscal feudalism'. Henceforth the death of a sole beneficiary attracted all the relevant feudal incidents in all circumstances. But the statute was taken also to abolish the power of devise: that is, it was thought (probably mistakenly) that since a landowner who transferred his land to trustees to his own use for life would now die seised of the legal estate, the common law rule prohibiting devises would apply to him, and he could not prevent the land passing to his heir. Whatever their views about the re-imposition of feudal incidents, the landowning aristocracy's reaction to this apparent re-introduction of compulsory primogeniture was so strongly manifested that in 1540 Henry had to compromise significantly with them. The Statute of Wills, passed in that year, dealt with the question by providing that at common law all lands held on non-military tenure and two-thirds of lands held on knight service should be freely devisable. In the case of lands so devised, however, the Crown could levy all the incidents that would be due if the land in question had passed to the heir, except only for wardship rights in lands held by knight service. These would only apply to the one-third of lands not devisable. The consequence is that the Statute of Wills became the 'prime defence' against threats to the revenues of the Crown (see Jones 'The Influence of Revenue Considerations upon the Remedial Practice of Chancery in Trust Cases, 1536–1660' in Lobban and Brooks (eds) *Communities and Courts in Britain 1150–1900* (1997) p 99).

In the present context, two points about the two statutes are of particular importance. First, the Statute of Uses, along with the Statute of Wills, introduced into common law land transactions a degree of flexibility previously only attainable by creating uses. This marked a major step in the emancipation of the common law of land from its feudal antecedents, and its adaptation to the post-feudal concept that ownership of an estate in land should confer a more or less unlimited power to dispose of it, irrespective of the feudal overlord's wishes. Flexibility in the common law forms of disposition, particularly on death, became much greater. This diminished pro tanto the role of the use. Indeed, the use's earlier function as a symptom of developing change in the objectives and ethos of land disposition had been brought to its resolution. The social changes to which it bore witness, first as an extra-legal mechanism, then under the aegis of a new jurisdiction developed by Chancery, were now reflected in the common law.

Second, the categories of use not executed by the Statute of Uses provided the starting-point for the development of the modern equitable trust. The exceptions to the Statute of Uses can be grouped under three heads:

(1) Uses declared on property other than freehold estates in land Because the statute used the word 'seised', which is a technical term referring to the rights at law of the owner of a freehold estate in land, any use relating to a property interest not within this description was not covered. Thus uses declared on copyholds, leases and personal property were not 'executed', and remained effective in equity. This seems to have been the case even where the 'use' was concealed, as where for political reasons no mention of the true beneficiary appeared on the documents so that the lease appeared to have been granted to a leaseholder for his own benefit (see Jones 'Trusts for Secrecy' (1995) 54 CLJ 545). A not uncommon political reason for concealment in the latter half of the sixteenth century would be the fear of religious persecution.

(2) 'Active' uses Any use under which the trustee had active duties to perform – for example, paying specific debts out of the land, or managing it during the original owner's absence – was held soon after the statute to be outside its scope. Various reasons have been put forward for this: for example, that 'execution' of the use, with the consequent exclusion of the trustee, was incompatible with the duties required of the trustee, and that the statute was assumed to relate to those uses which effectively gave the beneficiary a proprietary right, as opposed to rights significantly qualified by the conferment of active duties on the trustees.

(3) 'A use upon a use' After the Statute of Uses, the courts were confronted at times with dispositions (sometimes drafted in error) of the form 'to A to the use of B to the use of C'. At first, they simply said that the first use was executed by the Statute and the second, being repugnant to it, was void (*Tyrrel*'s case (1557), but cf the interpretation of the case in Jones (1993) 14 Legal History 75). How then are we to explain what appears to be the position, namely that the Chancellor was prepared to intervene to enforce the trust in the form of a use upon a use possibly as early as 1560 but almost certainly towards the end of the sixteenth century? (See eg the report of *Bertie (Dowager Duchess of Suffolk) v Herenden* published by Baker in (1977) 93 LQR 33; and the discussion in Jones 'Trusts in England after the Statute of Uses: A view from the 16th Century' in Helmholz and Zimmermann (eds) *Itinera Fiduciae* (1998) pp 173–205.) There are few reported cases although Baker suggests that by the time of James I (1603–1625) 'deliberately created trusts were commonplace' (*An Introduction to English Legal History* (4th edn, 2002) p 291 fn 56; and see *Sambach v Daston* (1635) in Baker and Milsom *Sources of English Legal History: Private Law to 1750* (1986) pp 126–127). This seems odd since it would appear that for the Chancellor to have treated B as 'seised', under an executed use, but subject to an equitable use in favour of C would have established a simple way to evade the fiscal policy of the Statute. But what if, as noted above, it was the Statute of Wills that offered the 'prime defence' against depletion of the revenue? Then it may well be, as Jones suggests, that the answer is to be found in a concern to enforce the terms of the Statute *only* where the use upon a use was a 'revenue evasion mechanism' as, for instance, where the purpose was to enable land to be bought in the name of another or to create trusts of long terms of years (above, pp 181–183). In other cases where the fiscal rationale for the Statute was not threatened there was no reason for the Chancellor not to exercise a jurisdiction still premised at that stage on the claims of conscience.

Judicial attitudes continued to change, particularly after the Civil War and the Restoration. In 1660 (regularising a position already existing in 1645), the Tenures Abolition Act abolished the burdensome incidents of military tenure. For all practical purposes, the feudal tenures and their incidents were dead. Not surprisingly, Chancery confirmed soon afterwards that, where a 'use upon a use' was created, the second use would be enforced in equity. It thus became possible to create in the trust form all the forms of interest in land which previously could only have existed as legal or 'executed' interests (see Yale [1957] CLJ 72). One did so by simply using the formula 'to A to the use of B to the use of C' or simply 'unto and to the use of B to the use of C'. In both these cases, B took as trustee for C.

In the next section we consider in closer detail the social and economic changes, in particular those of the eighteenth and nineteenth centuries, that helped shape the modern law of trusts. But first, reference must be made to a critical change that was to occur towards the end of the seventeenth century in the appointing of Chancellors, a change that in one particular instance was to have a lasting impact on the law of trusts. Prior to 1673, whilst it was by no means unknown for lawyers to be appointed as Chancellor, legal 'qualification' or experience was not a prerequisite for the post. This changed with the appointment of Lord Nottingham as Chancellor in 1673. Thereafter only lawyers have held the office of Lord Chancellor. But it is the contribution of Lord Nottingham during the relatively brief period of office – he died in 1682 – to Equity and to the embryonic law of trusts that is of particular significance here (see Yale (ed) *Prolegomena of Chancery and Equity* (1965)). He developed a classification of trusts, was responsible for the doctrine that there can be no 'clog on the equity of redemption' and is believed to have drafted the Statute of Frauds 1677, which in revised form still provides significant formalities requirements for the creation of express trusts or transfer of equitable interests. His influence was also instrumental in confirming the proprietary nature of the trust rather than it being merely a chose in action, a possible interpretation even in 1648 (see *R v Holland* (1648) Style 20 at 21 for a somewhat ambiguous view; and Smith 'Transfers' in Birks and Pretto (eds) *Breach of Trust* (2002) pp 119–124 on the significance for the 'proprietary right' of eventually extending protection to bind *innocent* recipients of trust property not just those who wrongfully received it). Moreover, however one may choose to analyse and interpret the reasons for the emergence of a 'rule against perpetuities' (see Chapter 6), it is evident that Lord Nottingham's role in formulating the rule in the *Duke of Norfolk's Case* (1683) 2 Swan 454 was decisive although it did subsequently require the House of Lords to confirm his formulation after his successor attempted to adopt a more restrictive rule in the case. There is also arguably a broader post-Restoration political significance to Lord Nottingham's tenure as Lord Chancellor in that the incorporation of the Chancery jurisdiction into the framework of a legal structure reflected a final break with the historical notion of it being part of monarchical authority. But it was the law of trusts as shaped primarily by Lord Nottingham and the further development of a more rigorous system of Equity by successor Chancellors such as Hardwicke and Eldon that was to provide a foundation on which practitioners could work to respond to the pressures for change to be discussed next.

4. The emergence of the modern trust

(a) The causes of change

Recognition of the three significant gaps in the operation of the Statute of Uses referred to above paved the way for the emergence of the modern trust concept and the further development of trusts principles within the context of family settlements. It appears that the word 'trust' came to be used during the sixteenth century to mean, in effect, unexecuted uses which Chancery would enforce. For economic and social reasons, rather than purely legal ones, it was this form of disposition, rather than executed uses or other categories of common law interest in land, that ultimately became predominant within family settlements.

The root cause of this process of change – which is observable in particular during the seventeenth, eighteenth and nineteenth centuries – was a fundamental alteration in the nature of wealth-holding. England passed from being a chiefly agricultural society, where the bulk of private wealth took the form of land, to a society in which mercantile, industrial and financial wealth came to predominate. The Tudor period had seen the growth of opportunities for investing in joint stock companies which were engaged, often with a monopoly obtained under licence from the Crown, in large-scale foreign trading ventures. Investment in government stocks and various emerging forms of production was increasingly important in the eighteenth century. From the mid-eighteenth century onwards, the Industrial Revolution brought about a further shift in wealth from land towards industrial production, trade and finance.

It became possible to participate in the ownership of these forms of enterprise, and indeed in landed wealth, in an indirect way – that is to say, through security interests such as stocks, shares, bonds and mortgages. Various legal forms of business organisation – the partnership, the 'deed of settlement' company, and the statutory company – furnished vehicles for making such investment. But it was the limited liability company, made freely available in the mid-nineteenth century, that enabled an individual's or family's funds to be channelled easily into and out of industry and trade (and their ancillary services such as banking and insurance) through the medium of the stock market. Accordingly, while the maintenance of a landed estate remained a preoccupation of many wealthy and noble families, the acquisition, aggregation and preservation of stocks, shares and other types of investment asset became an alternative, and increasingly important, form of family wealth-holding activity. This was equally the case, if not more so, for the new wealth-holders created by the Industrial Revolution (see Rubinstein (1992) 34 Business History 69 and Thompson (1990) 43 Economic History Review 40 for contrasting views on the relative importance of land and other forms of wealth to the new entrepreneurial class).

These new forms of family wealth-holding shared an important feature: unlike the landed estates of noble families, the assets acquired constituted 'investments' in the fullest sense of the word. They were acquired not only for the purpose of earning income, but also on the basis that, when the selling-price and the circumstances were appropriate, they might in due course be sold and the proceeds re-invested. This meant that the persons who owned and controlled such investments had an active, managerial role to perform – that of choosing investments to buy and watching over them and deciding whether and when they should be sold. By contrast, the trustees of a landed estate did not, as a matter of course, contemplate the sale of the estate. Retention of the family domain was instead the raison d'être of the settlement and it was only in extraordinary circumstances, such as impending bankruptcy, that a sale of the home or any significant portion of the land would occur.

The suitability of the equitable trust, as opposed to the various forms of common law interest for the acquisition and management of investment assets within wealthy families, and for the transmission of these from one generation to another, flows directly from the scope of two of the three exceptions to the Statute of Uses. As already explained, the Statute did not apply to dispositions of personal property – and most categories of investment asset (stocks, shares, bonds, etc) fell within this category. (In due course, even freehold interests in land itself, including mortgages of land, were deemed by equity to be personalty, not realty, if they were comprised in a trust disposition which provided for the sale of the assets comprised in it. This is the so-called doctrine of conversion.) Similarly, the Statute did not apply to active trusts – and the holding of invest-ment assets on terms that there might, in the ordinary course, be occasion to sell some or all of them and re-invest the proceeds obviously involves active, managerial functions.

One of the few academic lawyers to have described the emergence of trusts of investment assets summarises the process in these terms (Shattuck 'The Devel-opment of the Prudent Man Rule for Fiduciary Investment in the Twentieth Century' (1951) 12 Ohio State LJ 491 at 491–492):

> To be sure, a hundred or more years before the time of Victoria's death trusteeship had passed, somewhat nervously, from the concept of safe conduct of a specific *res* into the concept of maintenance of a stated set of values. During that transition the duty of the English trustee had transformed itself from the relatively restricted obligations related to care, custody and operation of family agricultural real estate and its appurtenances to the much more intricate task of trading in commercial and financial markets and to the attempted maintenance, through the life of the trust, of a value which had been stated to exist at the time of the opening inventory.

(For further discussion of this process of change, see Chesterman 'Family Set-tlements on Trust: Landowners and the Rising Bourgeoisie' in Rubin and Sugar-man (eds) *Law, Economy and Society, 1750–1914: Essays in the History of English Law* (1984) p 124 at pp 145–64. Much of the present section is based on this discussion. See too Anderson 'Law, Finance and Economic Growth in England: Some Long-Term Influences' in Ratcliffe (ed) *Britain and Her World 1750–1914* (1975) p 101.)

Little is known of the forms which trusts of investments took as they started to become common in the eighteenth and nineteenth centuries. In the absence of detailed studies, one can but conjecture that the majority are likely to have been testamentary trusts or marriage settlements, there being no fixed incentive to create other forms of inter vivos trust until the advent of high rates of income tax and estate duty in the twentieth century. Most testamentary trusts contained life-interests for a surviving spouse with remainders for children, or life interests for children (whether or not in addition to a surviving spouse) with remainders for grandchildren. Interests in favour of children often provided for accumulations of income (usually with an accompanying power of maintenance) until the child's attaining majority or marrying beneath that age. Two rather more sophisticated forms of disposition which were also used – the protective trust and the discretionary trust – will be described shortly.

The significance for trusts law of this shift in the nature of family wealth-holdings – that is, from land (predominantly) to investment assets as well as land – can scarcely be overstated. Hitherto, trustees of private trusts had primarily been passive, nominal owners of the land comprised in the trust, with the principal managerial decisions (eg as to farming the land or letting it out to tenant farmers) being taken by the beneficiary who was currently in possession. But as trustees increasingly assumed management responsibilities, a new set of legal principles regulating trust administration had to be developed by the Court of Chancery. In addition, the presumption in trusts of investment assets that some or all of the trust property might in the normal course of events be sold, with re-investment of the proceeds, had a significant impact on basic aspects of the creation and duration of trusts.

(b) The changes in trusts law and practice

The emergence of trusts of investment assets accordingly influenced the shape of modern trusts law and practice in a number of vital respects. The following examples of changes in trusts law and practice during the eighteenth and nineteenth centuries illustrate this (see also Stebbings *The Private Trustee in Victorian England* (2002)):

(1) Investment guidelines The managerial responsibilities associated with investment compelled Chancery to develop investment guidelines for trustees. The trading and industrial ventures of the time were often speculative, in that there was always a prospect of substantial loss and the standard of protection for investors was primitive. Chancery therefore took the view that, unless otherwise authorised, trustees should not invest any cash in hand in investments other than government stock or (according to some judges) first mortgages of land. This

laid the basis for a divergence between 'trustee investments', which comprise 'safe' securities within a range specified by the law, and the wider investment powers which are often expressly conferred upon trustees by a clause in the trust instrument in order that they should not be confined to 'trustee investments' only. (These developments and corresponding changes in the Trustee Act 2000 are reviewed more fully in Chapter 10.)

(2) Delegation   Rules regarding delegation by trustees to brokers or other professional agents had to be laid down. As investment possibilities became widened by statute in the nineteenth century, there was increasing pressure to ensure that, unless one or more of the trustees had legal or financial skills, tasks requiring expertise in these areas were duly delegated.

(3) Professional and corporate trustees   As an alternative to requiring continual reliance on professional agents, trustees possessing appropriate skills were often appointed. One modern historian, B L Anderson, places particular emphasis on the roles of solicitors in this regard. He describes these 'shadowy figures' as 'custodians of capital over a wide range of the population', since generally they were attorneys and financial intermediaries as well as trustees. In these capacities, they 'served the interests of "provident" rather than "pure" investors, the majority in a predominantly agrarian society; at the same time [they] were well placed to exploit the lengthening investment horizons of the 18th century' ((1969) 11 Business History 11 at 20). A further stage in this development was the emergence of corporate trustees, which started somewhat hesitantly in the mid-nineteenth century, but got under way more firmly early in the twentieth century. A corporate trustee offered the prospect of both professional expertise in trust management and a solid backing of assets if this expertise fell so far short of expectations that an action for negligence could be brought by a beneficiary. The increasing use of professional and corporate trustees is discussed further in Chapter 9.

(4) Standards of skill and care   The courts also had to reckon with the possibility that, in exercising their powers of management of the trust fund, trustees might cause serious losses through carelessness or incompetence. They might, for instance, lend out trust money on a mortgage where it was clear from the outset that the land mortgaged was of insufficient value to support the loan. Chancery developed the doctrine that trustees should be liable, at the instance of beneficiaries, to restore any losses suffered by the trust in such circumstances if they failed to 'conduct the business of the trust in the same manner that an ordinary man of business would conduct his own' (*Speight v Gaunt* (1883) 22 Ch D 727 at 739 per Jessell MR). In applying this objective standard of skill and care, the fact that the trustees were managing, not their own funds, but funds which, in the eyes of equity, belonged to other people, was taken into account, so as to rule out speculative transactions (*Re Whiteley* (1886) 33 Ch D 347 at 355 per Lindley LJ).

(5) Standards of good faith   It was recognised from the early days of enforcement of medieval uses that trustees were bound to act in a disinterested fashion. But it was not until the eighteenth century that the fiduciary character of executors or administrators holding the assets of a deceased's estate was established, or that unauthorised profits made by trustees or other fiduciaries through the use of their powers as such, or through opportunities becoming available to them because of their fiduciary office, could be claimed from them by the beneficiaries. Rulings to this effect – for example, the seminal decision of King LC in *Keech v Sandford* (1726) Sel Cas Ch 61 – were prompted by the consideration that trustees who were given the task of managing a changing 'fund' of investment assets were quite likely, on occasions, to encounter opportunities to make profits on the side. Although we cannot be certain – the judgment in *Keech v Sandford* is notable for its brevity of reasoning – it seems likely that the decision and others made by the Chancellor immediately prior to it were influenced by the size of losses incurred, following the South Sea Bubble of 1720, by opportunistic Chancery officials ('masters') who had speculated on the capital market with suitors' payments made and entrusted to the court (see Getzler 'Rumford Market and the Genesis of Fiduciary Obligations' in Burrows and Rodgers (eds) *Mapping the Law* (2006) 577 at 581–585).

(6) Premature termination of trusts   In a trust of investment assets, there was no presupposition that the trust property should be inalienable. This raised the question whether a trust of this nature should continue when its beneficiaries, being all ascertained and of full age and sound mind, wished it to come to an end. If, for example, a trust of securities gave a life interest to A, with a remainder to B on his attaining 25, and with accumulation of income between A's death and B's attaining 25, could the trust be terminated by A and B together once B turned 21? A and B might prefer to exchange their respective rights to present income and future capital for immediate shares in the capital, which they could dispose of freely.

In *Saunders v Vautier* (1841) 4 Beav 115, Chancery was confronted with this tug-of-war between a trust founder's power to control the future treatment of his property and a beneficiary's claim to have his entitlement treated as a disposable right of property. In a brief judgment on simple facts, Langdale MR held in favour of the beneficiary. In circumstances explained more fully below (Chapter 7), this ruling mushroomed into a broad principle that where all beneficiaries (however numerous) are sui juris and ascertained, they can terminate a trust notwithstanding the opposing wishes of the founder, as expressed in the trust.

(7) Discretionary and protective trusts   The notion that a beneficiary's primary entitlement under a trust of invested wealth was to monetary benefit only (instead of, or sometimes in addition to, occupation of land) paved the way for the development of discretionary trusts. In the early nineteenth century, the main function of these trusts seems to have been to act as a second limb in a trust device called the 'protective trust'. A 'principal beneficiary' – for example, the son of a rich merchant – was given a life interest in a trust fund, but this interest was expressed to be subject to premature termination if he tried to sell or mortgage it or if he went bankrupt. On such termination, a discretionary trust sprang up under which he and one or more specified persons (eg his wife and/or his children) were the beneficiaries. In the nineteenth century, recognition that this double-barrelled 'protective trust' was valid and effective to keep the beneficiary's life interest immune from prospective buyers, mortgagees and/or creditors, brought out some of the contradictions inherent in *Saunders v Vautier*. This time, the trust founder's 'caretaker' desire to exert his power of disposition so as to protect the life beneficiary from anticipated improvidence was upheld against the counter-argument that the beneficiary should be able to exercise his proprietary right of converting his interest under the trust into a capital sum which would then be used for 'active' entrepreneurial purposes. In the result, the beneficiary's interest under the trust obtained a degree of limited liability in respect of all his debts – whether incurred for business reasons or personal consumption or in any other circumstances – notwithstanding that limited liability, even for business debts, was not yet generally available.

Both protective trusts and discretionary trusts retain their potential for immunising family property from the creditors of its individual members (see Chapter 6). Furthermore, as explained in the next chapter, the function of the latter form of trust in the twentieth century was drastically altered and enhanced by the onset of inheritance taxation at high rates.

(8) Statutory intervention   Many of the changes in trusts law outlined here were the consequence of judicial decisions. But Parliament also took a hand. The first general statute on trusts was the Trustee Act 1850. This was concerned chiefly with technical aspects of the transfer of property held by trustees. Subsequently, enactments in 1859, 1860, 1888 and 1889 regulated trustee investment; the Conveyancing Act 1881 dealt with the appointment and removal of trustees and the nature and devolution of various trusteeship powers; and various aspects of beneficiaries' remedies against trustees and fellow beneficiaries were the subject of legislation in 1888 and 1896. The office of Public Trustee was established by the Public Trustee Act 1906.

The various statutory interventions were consolidated in the Trustee Act 1925 (replacing an earlier Act of 1893). A number of its provisions – for example, s 23 (power to employ agents) and s 33 (protective trusts) – directly reflect the historical developments in trusts law discussed in this section. The Trustee Act 2000 has modified and replaced several of the 1925 provisions – such as s 23 – but others – s 33 is one – remain in place. In addition it has introduced a statutory duty of care applicable to trustees and default provisions facilitating a broad discretion for investment of trust funds.

5. Strict settlements of land and married women's property rights

In the preceding section, the development of family trusts of investment assets during the seventeenth, eighteenth and nineteenth centuries was given prominence because this form of trust is still 'alive and well' and the legal developments associated with it are of major importance in the modern law. But this is not to say that the trust concept ceased to be significant in the context of settlements of landed estates during the same period. Its chief role was in filling gaps in a much-used form of disposition of land – the strict settlement – which took effect primarily through interests recognised at common law (including 'executory' interests). Furthermore the trust, during this period, was also employed by Chancery as a means of permitting married women to hold property in their own right. This was by way of mitigation of a common law rule that, once a woman was married, her husband was the sole owner of property that would otherwise be hers.

These two aspects of the history of trusts receive relatively limited attention here because the circumstances which rendered them important have ceased to exist. The Settled Land Act 1882 undermined the principal purpose of strict settlements – that is, retention of landed estates within successive generations of a family – by conferring a power to sell settled land on the current life-tenant. Estate duties in the twentieth century also provided a strong disincentive to any form of long-term settlement of land. Similarly, equity's intervention on behalf of married women became more or less redundant when married women's property legislation, commencing in 1870, abolished the common law prohibition of separate ownership. Some brief comments on these two aspects of trusts history are, however, desirable, as they provide insights into the nature of some modern equitable doctrines.

(a) Strict settlements

The phrase 'strict settlement' describes a form of settlement of landed estates which was widespread amongst wealthy families in England between the late seventeenth and late nineteenth centuries. (See generally Chesterman in Rubin and Sugarman (eds) *Law, Economy and Society* (1984) pp 127–145 and sources cited there.) The aims of the strict settlement have been much debated. Dynasticism was almost certainly a factor. From that perspective the principal aim was to inhibit to a significant degree, though not completely and irrevocably, any disposal of the family estates by the heirs or other immediate descendants of the settlor. But this was far from being the whole story. Habakkuk, for example, reminds us that 'the ambition of landowners to maintain the association between the male line and the ancestral estate was buttressed by the need to secure the fortunes of the wife and younger children' (*Marriage, Debt and the Estates System: English Landownership 1650–1950* (1994) p 64). He even concludes that 'In the long run . . . family provision proved a more durable support for the strict settlement than dynastic ambition'. What might be meant by 'family provision' is itself contentious. Spring, for instance, has argued that one purpose of the strict settlement was to subvert the more advantageous position under common law of heiresses and widows (*Land, Law and Family: Aristocratic Inheritance in England 1300–1800* (1993), but cf Cocks 'Unsettling Settlements' (1995) 16 J Legal History 210–217). However one assesses the aims of the strict settlement, one secure conclusion can be drawn. It was highly pervasive: as much as one-half of England may, according to one estimate, have been tied up in strict settlements around the middle of the eighteenth century.

A strict settlement operated by means of a complicated series of life estates, estates in remainder and other limited interests taking effect mostly at common law. It could be set up at any time, but the most common events precipitating the creation of a settlement would seem to have been the coming of age or the marriage of the eldest son (or, where no sons existed, the eldest daughter) of a landowner, or the landowner's death. Generally speaking, there had to be a resettlement once in every generation if the constraints on disposal of the land were to be maintained. But the *paterfamilias*, who was likely to favour this, was usually in a position to compel his children to co-operate in renewing the settlement.

Strict settlements made a significant contribution to the consolidation and preservation of both the wealth and the political power of the landowning aristocracy (see eg Stone *An Open Elite? England 1540–1880* (1986)). Yet the frequency with which they actually had sufficient legal force to restrain the sale of lands by a current life-tenant who was determined to sell is a matter of historical controversy. (The extensive debates and literature on this subject are best approached through the excellent introductory survey by English and Saville *Strict Settlement: A Guide for Historians* (1983).) The following rather graphic statement of a leading historian of the late nineteenth century, Sir Frederick Pollock, whilst probably overstating the efficacy of strict settlements in restraining alienation of land, does indicate their autonomous nature (*The Land Laws* (3rd edn, 1896) p 117):

> There is nothing, perhaps, in the institutions of modern Europe which comes so near to an *imperium in imperio* [an empire within an empire] as the settlement of a great English estate. The settlor is a kind of absolute lawgiver for two generations; his will suspends for that time the operation of the common law of the land, and substitutes for it an elaborate constitution of his own making.

Reference to the settlor as 'absolute lawgiver' and to 'his will' omits a central player from the cast. The settlor was usually very reliant on the advice and directions of his lawyer, advice which Habakkuk suggests was 'naturally enough, biased towards maintaining the family settlement' (op cit, p 69). The lawyer was often therefore much more than simply a translator of intentions. The 'kind of law' that emerged was therefore likely to reflect the conventions in Chancery and the creative practices of conveyancers (see also Cocks at 216).

(b) Strict settlements and trusts

Because strict settlements operated chiefly by means of legal interests, the role played by trusts was ancillary only. Trustees were commonly appointed, but, to quote Pollock again (p 117):

> The trustees of a family settlement are something like the constitutional safeguards of a complex political system; their presence is, in ordinary circumstances, hardly perceived, but they hold great powers in reserve, which may be used with effect on an emergency.

The following trust dispositions were commonly found within the lengthy, complex provisions of a strict settlement:

(1) A trust 'to preserve contingent remainders' This was a crucial conveyancing device. It was invented to get around technical legal rules whereby a life-tenant in possession who purported to sell the fee simple might destroy subsequent interests by the settlement so as to defeat its purpose completely.

(2) A trust to pay portions, debts etc out of rents and profits of specific lands This form of trust had predecessors amongst medieval uses declared to operate on the landowner's death. When a landowner established it during his lifetime, as a means of forced saving, it had a new function: that of protecting the landowner against his own imprudence.

(3) A trust to manage the estate in times of financial crisis Under this disposition, which was one of the 'safety-valves' for the pressures on liquidity exerted by the strict settlement, the trustees became managers of family capital, with important discretionary powers exercised independently of the creator and beneficiaries of the trust. This power to manage the family's landed wealth, even to the extent of telling the current 'head of the family' to limit his own personal expenditure, gave an important dimension to trusteeship of land. It was comparable, within the limited circumstances in which it operated, to the managerial role being increasingly adopted by trustees of investment assets.

(4) A trust to secure a separate income to a wife Because the creation of a strict settlement on the marriage of an heiress often involved an element of bargaining with her forthcoming inheritance, equity's recognition of separate property interests for married women was crucial in ensuring that the heiress herself, and other members of the family, did not completely lose the value of what they put into the settlement. But separate property rights for married women were also important in contexts other than strict settlement. They are accordingly given separate treatment in the next section.

This continuing association of trusts with a much-used and highly sophisticated form of common law settlement of land has left its mark on modern trusts law in two significant ways. These relate respectively to the question of remoteness of vesting of interests under trusts and the apportionment of benefit under trusts which differentiate between income beneficiaries and capital beneficiaries.

The validity of interests vesting at a future time – ie the issue of 'perpetuities' – was a crucial question for strict settlements. The courts accepted the strict settlement as valid in the late seventeenth century even though in the preceding decades many arrangements having a similar effect were struck down by the courts as 'tending to a perpetuity'. The eventual acceptance of the strict settlement may have been because the ties imposed by it were not wholly unbreakable; the process of resettlement that occurred once each generation allowed for some of the lands to be freed from the settlement. Alternatively, landowning Lord Chancellors and other rich lawyers may simply have followed an enhanced desire amongst most landowners to concentrate and preserve landholdings. In any event, a series of late seventeenth and early eighteenth century cases, notably Lord Nottingham's decision in the *Duke of Norfolk's* case (1683), laid down what came to be known as the 'modern rule against perpetuities'. It is to the following effect: 'no interest is good unless it *must* vest, if at all, not later than twenty one years after some life in being at the creation of the interest'. This rule did not endanger the strict settlement: indeed validation of the strict settlement probably influenced its precise formulation. But it now belongs within trusts law as a whole (subject to statutory modifications). It applies to family trusts of investment assets and to virtually all other forms of trust (though in the case of charitable trusts there are limited exceptions). The significance of this enlargement of the scope of operation of the rule against perpetuities is explored in Chapter 6.

Apportionment of benefit amongst income and capital beneficiaries (eg life tenants and remaindermen) depends substantially on what is meant by 'income' and 'capital'. Trusts law definitions of these have derived from a supposition underlying strict settlements, ie that the income-producing asset, the land, was not to be sold. The profits produced year by year from this immovable asset – comprising substantially the rents paid by tenant farmers – were naturally treated as 'income' for a settlement beneficiary, without any attention being paid to changes in the value of the asset itself. Further aspects of this question are discussed in Chapter 10.

(c) Trusts for married women

As already explained, the common law treated married women as having no capacity to hold property in their own right. Any property held by a woman on her marriage became the property of her husband. Her only solace under the common law was that, if she survived him, she became entitled to a proportion of his property as 'dower'.

The inroads on these principles made by the law of trusts between the seventeenth century and the late nineteenth century – at which point legislation intervened – are outlined in the following extracts from Holcombe's study of the origins and the enactment of the legislation (Holcombe *Wives and Property* (1983) pp 37–42, 46–47; cf Staves *Married Women's Separate Property in England 1660–1833* (1990), where the ideological dimensions of the law are considered):

Both the common law and equity proceeded upon the assumption that married women needed protection. The common law regarded a woman's husband as her guardian, under whose 'wing, protection and cover' she lived, moved, and had no legal being. But equity, generally considered to be 'the guardian of the weak and unprotected, such as married women, infants and lunatics', tended to view a woman's husband as 'the enemy', and against his 'exorbitant common-law rights the Court of Chancery waged constant war' (R H Graveson and F R Crane, *A Century of Family Law 1857–1957* (1957) p 140). As a result, the rules of equity relating to married women's property were diametrically opposed to the rules of the common law.

One might argue that if the common-law rules of the identity of husband and wife reflected the sacramental view of marriage held in medieval times, then the opposite view of husband and wife in equity resulted from the breakdown of the doctrines and power of the Church in the Reformation and post-Reformation ages....

A more persuasive argument as to the origin of the equitable assumptions respecting husband and wife is that, just as the common law reflected the economic and social realities of the medieval period during which it developed, so equity reflected the changed realities of a time when the structure of the medieval society and economy began to crumble. The common law had always recognized an owner's right to dispose of personal property, and as conditions of landholding changed, with the abrogation of military land tenure and the legal recognition of testation with respect to land, the general rule of the law came to be freedom of disposition of all property, real as well as personal. The landed classes were alarmed, for freedom to dispose of property implied the dangerous ability of both sons and daughters to squander the family wealth if their actions could not somehow be controlled. At the same time there had appeared important new classes of society whose wealth, derived not from land but from commerce and industry, did not fit comfortably within the legal categories of real and personal property. These classes, too, were concerned to find protection for their property to prevent its being wasted by sons and daughters alike. And both the old landed aristocracy and the new aristocracy of the business world felt acutely the special need to protect the property of their daughters from the common-law rights of husbands, and to ensure that if there were no children of a marriage the property would not pass to their daughters' husbands but would return to their own families. It was in these circumstances that the wealthy classes turned to equity for the protection of their property that they could not find under the common law....

In practice the Court of Chancery allowed the creation of a special category of property, the so-called separate property or separate estate of married women. At law a married woman could not own property, but in equity property could be settled upon her for her use under the management of a trustee who was responsible to the court for carrying out the terms of the trust. . . . The separate property created by the trust would be protected by the Court of Chancery against a woman's husband and all other persons according to the wishes of the donor. Interestingly, a married woman's separate property in equity existed only during her marriage, for its existence was due to the need to protect it against her husband's common-law rights.

. . .

The rights a married woman enjoyed with respect to her separate property varied, depending upon the way that property had been created. A written instrument settling property upon a woman often stated specifically what she could and could not do. For example, she might be expressly allowed to dispose during her lifetime of real property settled upon her or expressly barred from doing so, or she might be allowed or denied the right to dispose of her separate property by will, and so on.

To the feminists of Victorian times, the equitable rules relating to married women's property were naturally much more acceptable than were the rules of the common law. The law deprived married women of property, and thus deprived them of the rights and responsibilities of other citizens and subjected them to serious practical hardships. Equity allowed married women to have property, and thus ensured their independence and freedom of action. Under the law married women could have no legal existence separate from the husbands who controlled their property. In equity married women had an identity separate from their husbands because they controlled property.

At the same time feminists criticized the equitable rules applying to married women's property for two important reasons. First . . . equity did not recognize married women as having the same proprietary rights as other citizens, but accorded them special rights over certain property only. . . . The feminists' second major criticism of equity, and by far the more serious, was that . . . the relief it afforded from the provisions of the common law was not available to women who were not wealthy. The great majority of women in the country did not have property sufficient in amount and suitable in nature to be settled upon them as their separate property through the costly proceedings of the courts of equity. As A V Dicey summed up the situation (*Lectures on the Relation Between Law and Public Opinion in England During the 19th Century* (1920) p 383), 'There came . . . to be not in theory but in fact one law for the rich and another for the poor. The daughters of the rich enjoyed, for the most part, the considerate protection of equity, the daughters of the poor suffered under the severity and injustice of the common law.'

When feminists denounced the common law and criticized equity, and called for thoroughgoing reform of the married women's property law, they had a large and sympathetic audience. This was so not because most people agreed with feminist demands for equality for women, but because legal reform generally was the order of the day and the Victorian conscience was troubled by the sufferings of women under the law as it then existed.

The Married Women's Property Act 1870 (amended in 1874) took the first step towards entitling married women to enjoy legal as well as equitable ownership of property. This task was more or less fulfilled by the Married Women's Property Act 1882 (repealing the earlier legislation), though this scarcely constituted the total reformation of the law that feminists had sought and remnants of earlier doctrines remained in the law for many years afterwards (see eg Shanley *Feminism, Marriage and the Law in Victorian England 1850–1895* (1989)). As the right of married women to hold their own property became thus established by statute, the special significance of equity's intervention to protect their interests faded away.

6. The role of trusts in English law

In this review of trusts law and family settlement during a period of 500 or so years prior to 1900, some important aspects of the role played by the trust concept within the law have become apparent. It is useful to identify these here, before consideration (in the next chapter) of the transformation of trusts law and practice subsequently brought about by the onset of high rates of inheritance and income taxation.

A noted US authority on trusts drew attention some 85 years ago to the capacity of trusts to 'pave the way' for reform of property law. His thesis, put shortly, is that where trusts lead, statutory reform may eventually follow.

A W Scott (1922) 31 Yale LJ 457 at 457–458

It was chiefly by means of uses and trusts that the feudal system was undermined in England, that the law of conveyancing was revolutionized, that the economic position of married women was ameliorated, that family settlements have been effected, whereby daughter and younger sons of landed proprietors have been enabled modestly to participate in the family wealth, that unincorporated associations have found a measure of protection, that business enterprises of many kinds have been enabled to accomplish their purposes, that great sums of money have been devoted to charitable enterprises; and by employing the analogy of a trust, by the intervention of the so-called constructive trust, the courts have been enabled to give relief against all sorts of fraudulent schemes whereby scoundrels have sought to enrich themselves at the expense of other persons. Many of these reforms in the English law would doubtless have been brought about by other means; but the fact remains that it was the trust device which actually was chiefly instrumental in bringing them to pass.

Whether or not one endorses in its entirety Scott's sweeping claim for the pervasive influence of the trust device, it is clear that significant legal change has occurred. Moreover, it has long been recognised that as part of this process lawyers were not just ciphers in some inevitable onward march of legal logic, itself deducible from a pre-ordained system of rules (see eg John Reeves's explanation of the haphazard recognition of the use in his *History of English Law* (1787), cited in Lobban *The Common Law and English Jurisprudence 1760– 1850* (1991) at pp 50–56). On the contrary, they were frequently a creative force opportunistically fashioning developments in response to the perceived needs of their clients. Whilst we may see, in the long term, that the outcome has been major developments in the nature and form of the trust device itself or the stimulation of statutory reform, as with the Married Women's Property Acts, the process of legal change was, to adopt Anderson's phrase, one of 'controlled innovation' (*Lawyers and the Making of English Land Law 1832–1940* (1992) p 4), essentially practical and problem-solving in approach. But within this incrementalist method of legal change there lies another side to the picture of the trust as an agent of law reform. In Scott's words (pp 457–458):

> The trust has often served as a means of evading the law. Lord Bacon said that 'the special intent unlawful and covinous was the original of uses, though after it induced to the lawful intent general and permanent' *Reading on the Statute of Uses*, p 24. The line between evasion and reform is after all a difficult one to draw. The evasion which in the long run proves successful is usually a reform. Mr Justice Holmes, with characteristic discrimination, has said (*Bullen v Wisconsin* 240 US 635 (1916)):
>
> > 'We do not speak of evasion, because, when the law draws a line, a case is on one side of it or the other, and if on the safe side is none the worse legally that a party has availed himself to the full of what the law permits. When an act is condemned as an evasion what is meant is that it is on the wrong side of the line indicated by the policy if not by the mere letter of the law.'
>
> A trust is a device for enabling one to enjoy various rights, powers and privileges in respect to property greater than those enjoyed by owners of property, for enabling one to enjoy the benefits of ownership without subjection to all the duties and liabilities resulting from ownership. The question with which courts of equity have been compelled to struggle is how far it is possible to go without crossing the line which separates the legitimate use of the trust device from an illegal evasion of the letter or the policy of the law.

Thus Scott, whilst praising the trust for its reformist potential, also sounds a note of warning in this passage. He points out that the pressures for law reform through the use of the trust were often applied by property-owners who, with the help of their legal advisers, sought to avoid legal obligations, such as feudal 'incidents', or to escape the operation of restrictive legal rules, in each case with predominantly self-centred or family-centred motives. When 'reform' occurs on account of pressures such as these, the question to be asked is whether 'reform' is truly the right label.

There is a further proviso to be added here, not so much to challenge the broad sweep of the claim by Scott but to suggest that in some instances the influence claimed for the trust needs to be reappraised in the light of more recent research. Consider, for instance, the proposition that 'business enterprises of many kinds have been enabled to accomplish their purposes' by means of the trust. It is certainly the case that in the century before the mid-nineteenth century reforms in company law the trust was a key legal component of the unincorporated company. But it was not the only component. As Harris has illustrated in his account of the relationship between law, business organisation and the economy during early industrial capitalism, the unincorporated association was a complex legal phenomenon, developed in what he terms 'a learning-by-doing process' by attorneys and businessmen clients during the latter part of the eighteenth century (*Industrializing English Law* (2000) ch 6). It involved, apart from trusts law, the laws of agency, partnership and contract, the latter governing the contractual agreement between the members to form and regulate the company under a 'deed of settlement'. The trust potentially provided the means of compensating for the fact that the unincorporated company was not a legal entity. The property of the company would be vested in trustees who had standing to sue and be sued on behalf of the company and who were required to further the covenants set out in the deed of settlement (see also Cooke *Corporation, Trust and Company* (1950) pp 86–87).

Therein, as Harris persuasively argues, lay a number of difficulties relating both to the substance of trusts law at the time and to the procedures for its enforcement. The developments in trusts law described earlier in this chapter and concerning such matters as delegation, standards of skill and care, relieving trustees from liability mostly came about, or at least shifted from conjecture to certainty, in the latter half of the nineteenth century. These occurred too late to affect significantly the utility of the unincorporated company. Harris refers, for instance, to a popular trustees' guidebook from 1830 in which it is stated that 'carrying on trade or business for the object of a trust estate is a very hazardous expedient, for the trustee may easily make himself responsible for various losses' (Harding *Advice to Trustees*, pp 66–67, cited in Harris, above, at p 154). As Harris then pointedly emphasises: 'this is exactly what trustees of unincorporated companies were expected to do'. Moreover, perceived weaknesses in substantive trusts law were compounded by the high costs and delays that accompanied Chancery litigation. The conclusion drawn by Harris is that whereas the trust was able to provide a solution for some of the problems posed for the unincorporated company 'it was of no service in many other, more commercial and managerial aspects of [its] activities' (at p 159). Notwithstanding 'the industrious work of imaginative lawyers and businessmen' the disadvantages of the unincorporated corporation were manifest when compared with the advantages offered by the joint stock company (but cf the more positive assessment of the significance of the part played by the trust in Cooke op cit.)

This illustration of the limits of the trust in a particular context paradoxically does not invalidate Scott's argument. That a legal form such as the trust has acted as an agent for law reform can be seen on the one hand as a positive virtue whilst on the other hand the fact that reform is considered necessary should remind us of the reality that the trust has functional limitations as well as strengths (see also the discussion in Chapter 1 at pp 18–20). The paradox here is that to some extent it was the limitations of trusts law allied to the failings of Chancery procedure that was the catalyst for reform, contributing, along with other contingencies, to a perception that reform of the law affecting business organisation was necessary.

But there is yet another dimension to an analysis of the role played by the trust in English law, one less obviously laudatory than that expressed by Scott and one that can be perceived as a virtue or a vice depending on the standpoint adopted. The following extract from an article by Cotterrell that adopts a more sociological perspective argues that the chief contribution of the trust concept has, broadly speaking, been to help in masking the extent of inequality within society. It does so by obscuring the link between private property – a key source of power – and its ultimate owners. When property is held on trust, under a modern family settlement, the beneficiaries appear to be purely passive, because management of the property is vested in the trustees. But they still enjoy the material benefits conferred by the property, and their rights in this regard are legitimated, so the argument runs, through the use of the label 'trust', with all its moral overtones, to describe the obligations owed to them by the trustees.

R Cotterrell (1987) 14 Journal of Law and Society 77 at 83–88

As Maitland suggested long ago, it was, above all, the device of the trust which made it possible for English law to recognise many forms of property ownership by collectivities without attracting some of the technical difficulties and ideological conflicts centred on aspects of the doctrinal problem of corporate personality in continental civil law systems. Today, however, adopting a critical perspective on doctrine, we can see more clearly how this doctrinal device of the trust has served to extend the ideological utility of the property-form. The trust makes possible the maintenance of permanent, easily identifiable property-owners (explicitly recognised as such by law) in the form of replaceable trustees, together with an indefinite range of beneficially entitled individuals or collectivities (for example, groups of children or other issue, classes of discretionary beneficiaries, members of associations, organisations and interest groups of numerous kinds) who, having beneficial entitlements guaranteed in equity, can share in property-power but remain invisible to law as property-owners as such. The limitations which the property-form as an ideological form imposes on the nature of the property-owner (that is, basically, that such an owner should be a clearly identifiable 'person' and not an indefinite collectivity) are overcome. Equally, the trust makes possible the creation of enduring objects of property ('things', clusters of value) in the form of funds which can be invested in various ways to preserve and enhance their value. In this way the trust greatly facilitates the concentration and preservation of capital – and thereby helps guarantee the power and security which the property-form embodies. ... Only in certain (usually family) trusts, in which what is being provided for beneficiaries is security of use of real or personal property or the preservation of specific assets rather than power as such, is the asset held in trust important in itself. In other cases all that is fundamentally important is the maintenance of the value which currently held trust assets represent.

...

The major ideological significance of [the extension of the property-form which the trust allows] is the far greater flexibility in manipulation of property-power which is made possible by it, and a further 'disguising' in ideological forms of the nature of that power. An illustration of that disguising can easily be given. The trust form tends to disguise the actual nature of the power relationship between trustees and beneficiaries. The ideology of the trust is such that the legal owner (trustee) is the person who 'looks most like' an owner since she or he is the one who (usually) can carry out most of the ordinary legal transactions possible to an owner – sale, mortgage, lease, exchange, etc. The beneficiary under a trust is seen as passive. Typically the beneficiary cannot interfere in management of the trust property except by procuring the intervention of the courts (for example, in claiming breach of duty by the trustee). During the existence of the trust, control of capital typically rests with trustees. In discretionary and protective trusts, and in the exercise of powers of maintenance and advancement, the trustees may exert significant control over the situation of beneficiaries. Again, it is in some family trusts in which what is at stake is the property-security of dependants (the preservation of trust assets rather than use of the property-form as an instrument of power) that this control by trustees is often greatest!

This apparent power of trustees and passivity of beneficiaries is, however, misleading. It is the beneficiaries – often collectivities – unrecognised directly as legal owners who actually have access to the property-power embodied in the trust. This is ultimately admitted in, for example, the very strict rules governing trustees' duties with regard to investment, profit-taking by trustees and conflicts of duty and interest, and in the rule in *Saunders v Vautier*, which allows the trust device to be set aside if the beneficiaries so wish where all of them are identifiable persons having full legal capacity and hence easily recognisable as property owners within the orthodox commonsense conception. Yet the very fluidity of beneficial entitlements which the trust makes possible hides from view even more effectively than the property concept in its simple form the actual structure of power which private law guarantees and perfects.

How can this view of the ideological significance of property and trust help us to analyse trust law from a critical perspective? First, by looking at the trust in terms of its ideological significance in helping to exclude the element of power from recognition in legal doctrine we can begin to put the element of power back into our picture of law and its working. It is, indeed, impossible to understand law's relationship to power without analysing the way in which legal ideology is often able to exclude all recognition of private power . . .

A second reason for looking at the trust concept in terms of its ideological significance is that this emphasises that what appears as a highly technical and esoteric part of property law doctrine is actually a conception of wide influence in popular consciousness. The idea of fiduciary obligation of the trustee harnesses to legal doctrine a moral conception of great social significance and induces us to see the trust beneficiary not as the possessor of property-power but as a person meriting protection; a person to whom moral as well as legal obligations are owed. The trust-form, concentrating and guaranteeing property-power, not only fails to impose moral obligations on the powerful, but actually encourages us to think of *moral obligations owed to them* because of their beneficial entitlements.

On narrow technical grounds, it can be argued that this passage overstates the importance of the residuary powers of beneficiaries in controlling their trustees.

Termination of a trust under the rule in *Saunders v Vautier*, for instance, will often not be possible in practice particularly where the trust is a discretionary one with large numbers of beneficiaries spread over several generations. Similarly, challenging the investment decisions of trustees, even when they appear to be clearly misguided, is often very difficult, as where the investment power is conferred in wide discretionary terms by an express clause in the trust instrument. The reader may wish to consider these and other issues, which relate in broad terms to the 'balance of power' between trustees and beneficiaries, after reading the detailed treatment of them in the relevant chapters of this book (Chapters 9–11).

Turning to matters of ideology and power, whatever the present ideological significance of the trust device may be, its development has at times been marked by an ambivalent attitude on the part of the courts and the legislature towards the trust. Some nineteenth-century developments in rules about aspects of trust creation and management of trust property, suggest that 'fashionable considerations of economic liberalism and property rights' – the phrase is borrowed from Gardner's first edition of *An Introduction to the Law of Trusts* (1990) p 35 – may have tempered a facilitative presumption that people should be able to settle their property however they like. Yet it must also have been the case that many who endorsed laissez faire notions would have looked to the trust to provide security for their own families. Unfortunately the 'modern' history of trusts law is too undeveloped to allow anything other than tentative hypotheses to be advanced on these issues.

It is certainly the case that by 1900 the trust had become a flexible and highly sophisticated property-holding device which helped to maintain extensive private property ownership amongst wealthy classes. How far the moral concept of 'trust' in fact helped to legitimise the power attached to such ownership is, however, not easy to discern. This is in part because different modes of discourse are at work here. Gordon has suggested that 'despite the assiduous efforts of Marxist and legal realist critics, "property" is still to this day heard as univocally expressive of autonomy and liberty' ('Paradoxical Property' in Brewer and Staves (eds) *Early Modern Conceptions of Property* (1995) p 101). But we may need to distinguish here between the abstract appeal of 'property' as an idea and an everyman or everywoman appreciation of the trust as an everyday legal form. Of course it is conceivable, perhaps probable, that the notion of 'moral obligation owed to beneficiaries' and of a paternalist regard for the protection of them are constituents of a dominant discourse amongst the propertied and the legal fraternity. But a degree of scepticism may be called for as to whether the trust carries similar connotations for the propertyless or even the 'less-well-propertied'. Might we discover that 'the family trust' is inextricably harnessed in the public consciousness with 'tax avoidance' and, indeed, that that link engenders pejorative sentiments about the trust? (Although admittedly from a different context, consider the example of the NHS Trust where it is far from evident that deliberately attaching the label 'trust' rather than, let us say, 'corporation' to hospitals under the NHS reforms of various governments has had any significant effect on public perceptions of, and attitudes towards, those reforms.)

It is in the dimension of taxation that the effectiveness of the trust in these matters of legitimation now needs to be tested. During the eighteenth and nineteenth centuries, the chief danger to private ownership that family settlements – particularly, settlements of land – sought to avert was the break-up of family estates by the spendthrift conduct of heirs who wished to sell off assets to pay current debts. By the mid-twentieth century, as we shall see, the emphasis had shifted to one of securing protection from 'external' attack – ie the levies imposed by the Inland Revenue (now HMRC). But the trust, having been developed over several centuries through the artifice of conveyancers and given full effect by both judges and the legislature, was sufficiently well-established as a legitimate mode of wealth-holding to present a formidable challenge to the tax imperatives of the twentieth century. How successfully the trust has been adapted, whether by judicial or statutory change, to confront this new challenge is a recurring theme in the remainder of this section of the book. In particular it will be necessary to consider whether the framers of tax laws have been constrained by a perceived need to treat the established doctrines of trusts law as more or less sacrosanct, and therefore to tailor tax laws to fit with them. If this were to be so, it would indeed represent a considerable tribute to the entrenched status of trusts doctrine and the ideological power of the legal concept of 'trust'.

7. The jurisdiction of equity

(a) Equity and the common law

The principal focus of the chapter has been on the emergence, recognition and enforcement of the trust. At several points, however, mention has also been made of the development of Equity in general as a 'gloss' (Maitland *Equity* (2nd (Brunyate) edn, 1936) p 18) upon the operation of the common law system. But, it will be recalled, this was a gloss with teeth. While Equity might not have denied that a person held a legal title to property the Chancellor could order that person to deal with it for the benefit of the true owner in Equity. Failure to obey could constitute contempt of court for which the sanction of imprisonment might be imposed. Thus legal title was affirmed whilst, in effect, being subordinated to the interest of the owner in Equity by the imposition of a personal remedy against the holder of the legal title. As we have seen this became relatively non-contentious in the context of the recognition and enforcement of the trust or of 'other confidences reposed in some person'. None the less the potential for conflict between two parallel legal structures is evident. That conflict came to a head in the early years of the seventeenth century in the *Earl of Oxford's Case* (1615) 1 Ch Rep 1 ostensibly over a dispute about the validity of 'common injunctions' by which a party who had obtained judgment at common law could be restrained in Equity from enforcing it. The jurisdictional conflict was exacerbated by the fact that the two chief protagonists, Lord Ellesmere, the Lord Chancellor, and Sir Edward Coke, the Chief Justice of the common law courts, were personal and political rivals. Unsurprisingly the reiteration by Ellesmere in the *Earl of Oxford's Case* of the mantra that the role of the Court of Chancery was only 'to correct men's consciences . . . and to soften and mollify the extremity of the law' (at 6, 7) was unlikely to mollify Coke. He rightly recognised that even if formally the common law judgments were not impugned the effect of upholding the common injunction in the case would in substance undermine the indictment at common law issued by himself and, moreover, establish that where the jurisdictions conflicted Equity would prevail. The legal deadlock was referred to King James I. In 1616, acting on the advice of a legal panel including the influential Attorney General Francis Bacon but also consistent with his personal philosophy of royal prerogative and the role of Chancery as representing the King's conscience, James issued an order in favour of Equity and the Chancery Court (see Fortier 'Equity and Ideas: Coke, Ellesmere and James I' (1998) 51(4) Renaissance Quarterly 1255–1281). This effectively resolved the broader jurisdictional dispute although the demise of the two chief protagonists – through the death of the Chancellor Lord Ellesmere and the dismissal of the Chief Justice Coke – may also have been significant (see Getzler 'Patterns of Fusion' in Birks *The Classification of Obligations* (1997) 157 at 179–183; and Baker 'The Common Lawyers and the Chancery: 1616' in *The Legal Profession and the Common Law: Historical Essays* (1986)). The jurisdictional outcome was reaffirmed in the Judicature Act 1873, s 25(11), and re-stated in the Supreme Court Act 1981, s 49(1): 'wherever there is any conflict or variance between the rule of equity and the rules of the common law with reference to the same matter, the rules of equity shall prevail' (confirmed in eg *Walsh v Lonsdale* (1882) 21 Ch D 9).

   We must be clear about what supremacy for Equity came to mean. It did not leave each and every decision of the common law courts at the mercy of a discretionary intervention by the Chancellor, depending on his perception of what 'conscience' demanded. On the contrary, the importance of adhering to precedent became emphasised (see Winder (1941) 57 LQR 245–279). Consequently, from the latter part of the seventeenth century onwards, the content of the gloss was steadily refined in a manner that produced a body of more clearly defined equitable rules and principles. These in turn were to become almost as fixed and rigid as the rules of the common law, an outcome reflected in the much-quoted observation of Lord Eldon (*Gee v Pritchard* (1818) 2 Swan 402 at 414):

> The doctrines [of Equity] ought to be . . . made as uniform, almost, as those of the common law. . . . I cannot agree that the doctrines of this court are to be changed by every succeeding judge. Nothing would inflict on me greater pain in quitting this place than the recollection that I had done anything to justify the reproach that the equity of the court varies like the Chancellor's foot.

We should not overlook the use of the qualifying 'almost' in Lord Eldon's comments. It is possible to overstate the stance that Eldon took and it was not his intention that Equity should be consolidated in as rigid a manner as the common law was believed to be at the time (see eg Klinck 'Lord Eldon on "Equity"' (1999) 20(3) Legal History 51–74).

(b) The Judicature Acts 1873 and 1875

Almost contemporaneous with Eldon's periods as Chancellor (1801–1806, 1807–1827) reforms began to be introduced to the Court of Chancery in an attempt to counter the organisational weaknesses that had led to expense and delays and had on occasions resulted in injustice. By then it had become possible to perceive of Equity as a system, an incomplete system compared with the common law, but a system with its own court structure and defined rules and principles even though at every point it presupposed the existence of the common law (see Maitland, above, pp 16–17). The operation of two systems in separate courts with neither having the authority to grant the remedies of the other court was increasingly seen as tending to produce delay and confusion for the litigant. Despite further reforms which improved the position somewhat (eg Lord Cairns Act 1858 by which Chancery was given jurisdiction to award equitable damages where no other remedy was appropriate), pressure for wholesale restructuring increased. The outcome was the enactment of the Judicature Acts 1873 and 1875 by which the structure of the whole judicial system was finally reformed. These Acts abolished the previous individual courts and created a Supreme Court of Judicature but with separate divisions (originally five but now three comprising Chancery, Queen's Bench and Family Divisions). A key feature of the reforms was that under s 24 of the 1873 Act all judges were empowered, indeed placed under a duty, to give effect to both legal and equitable rights, obligations, liabilities, defences and remedies. In short the administration of the systems of law and equity became fused.

(c) Law and Equity: fusion or harmonisation?

Whilst the position as regards fusion of the administrative structure of the courts is clear, debate has subsequently developed as to whether there has been a *substantive* fusion of the common law and Equity. Certainly the contemporary perception was that fusion had occurred at the level of administration only. This was evident in parliamentary debate (*Hansard* 3rd Series, vol 216, 644–645, statement by the Attorney-General during the second reading of the Judicature Bill), in judicial statements (Jessell MR in *Salt v Cooper* (1880) 16 Ch D 544 at 549, but cf later ambiguous dictum in *Walsh v Lonsdale* (1882) 21 Ch D 9 at 14) and in Ashburner's famous metaphor: 'the two streams of jurisdiction, though they run in the same channel, run side by side, and do not mingle their waters' (*Principles of Equity* (2nd edn) p 18). This assessment is reinforced by the fact that the Judicature Acts were conceived as cautious measures, since previous parliamentary bills proposing a more thoroughgoing fusion of common law and equity had failed (Baker (1977) 93 LQR 529 at 530). It would be misleading, however, to give the impression that this outcome was achieved without controversy. The drafting of s 25(11) (see above) left sufficient uncertainty to permit a more radical interpretation of its meaning and intention, such that suspicion between the judges about the motives of some of their colleagues became evident. Baker refers, for instance, to the reported tension between Jessel MR, who was inclined to incorporate equitable doctrines into the common law, and his successor Lord Esher: '[He] is said to have complained openly that Jessel "had been sent to dragoon the Court of Appeal into substituting equity for Common Law, but that he (Esher) and his Common Law colleagues would not have it"' (*An Introduction to English Legal History* (4th edn, 2002) p 114, citing Underhill *Change and Decay* (1938) p 87).

A century later the controversy has re-emerged with the debate being conducted with even greater vigour. It cannot be denied that there is a significant line of authority that can be cited in support of a view that fusion has been more pervasive than was envisaged at the time of the Judicature Acts. A principal proponent of the idea of complete fusion was the late Lord Denning for whom the idea provided useful support to some of his efforts in law reform (see eg in *Errington v Errington and Woods* [1952] 1 KB 290 at 298; and extra-judicially in *Landmarks in the Law* p 86). Then in 1977 dicta in the House of Lords, in *United Scientific Holdings Ltd v Burnley Borough Council* [1978] AC 904, appeared to endorse the idea of complete fusion. A much quoted dictum of Lord Diplock can be seen as rejecting any distinctive existence for 'rules of equity': 'but to perpetuate a dichotomy between rules of equity and rules of common law which it was a major purpose of the Supreme Court of Judicature Act 1873 to do away with, is, in my view, conducive to erroneous conclusions as to the ways in which the law of England has developed in the last hundred years' (at 924). Lord Diplock proceeded to challenge directly the continuing relevance of Ashburner's metaphor (at 925):

> ... by 1977 this metaphor has in my view become both mischievous and deceptive. The innate conservatism of English lawyers may have made them slow to recognise that by the Supreme Court of Judicature Act 1873 the two systems of substantive and adjectival law formerly administered by the Courts of Law and Courts of Chancery ... were fused. ... If Professor Ashburner's fluvial metaphor is to be retained at all, the waters of the confluent streams of law and equity have surely mingled now.

It is tempting to respond to this proposition with the comment 'it all depends on what you mean by fusion'. On the one hand Lord Diplock's analysis of the purpose of the Judicature Acts seems clearly to be flawed, at least as measured against most contemporary opinion (see above). Moreover there are numerous continuing distinctions between common law and Equity. The distinction between legal and equitable interests forms the conceptual underpinning of our law of property and trusts; the common law and equitable rules for payment of interest are different (*Westdeutsche Landesbank Girozentrale v Islington London Borough Council* [1996] AC 669) as are, for the moment, those for tracing, equitable tracing being available only where an initial fiduciary relationship can be identified unlike tracing at common law (*Re Diplock* [1948] Ch 465). These constitute just a few of the examples that could be listed and it is scarcely likely that Lord Diplock was in complete ignorance of them. On the other hand, however, if we approach the 'fusion' issue from a standpoint which looks to the mingling of the systems, it is equally evident that there has been a degree of synthesis, a synthesis which admittedly has been taken further in some Commonwealth jurisdictions than in English law (see eg Mason (1994) 110 LQR 238; Capper (1994) 14 LS 313 at 315–317; Martin [1994] Conv 13).

It may appear at this point that the debate about 'fusion' is largely a matter of determining whether it is or is not accurate to *describe* common law and Equity as fused. But much more is involved than a terminological quibble. There is a *prescriptive* dimension to the debate whereby considerations of a 'should' or 'ought' nature come to the fore. We would therefore suggest that an important conclusion to be drawn from the fusion controversy is that the shadow of history as regards the origin of particular remedies and rights should not *of itself* be allowed to dictate the progress of any further synthesis. It is perhaps significant that both Sir Anthony Mason (former Chief Justice of Australia and a strong advocate of the distinctive contribution of Equity) and Sir Peter (now Lord) Millett have felt able to endorse the comments of Somers J in *Elders Pastoral Ltd v Bank of New Zealand* [1989] 2 NZLR 180 at 193 (see respectively (1994) 110 LQR 240 at 242 and (1995) 9 TLI 35):

> Neither law nor equity is now stifled by its origin and the fact that one Court administers both has inevitably meant that each has borrowed from the other in furthering the harmonious development of the law as a whole.

The notion of harmonious development incorporates two distinct dimensions both of which can be viewed as contributing towards what we might term a 'harmonisation' rather than a 'fusion' of the substantive elements of common law and equity. One dimension of harmonisation takes us back briefly and at a level of generality to the origins of equity jurisdiction and the notion of unconscionability that we touched on in the previous chapter. Drawing on analysis of a number of discrete examples Sir Anthony Mason has suggested that 'the underlying values of equity centred on good conscience will almost certainly continue to be a driving force in the shaping of the law unless the underlying values and expectations of society undergo a fairly radical alteration' ((1994) 110 LQR 240 at 258; see also various essays in Youdan (ed) *Equity, Fiduciaries and Trusts* (1989); and, confusingly, Waters (ed) *Equity, Fiduciaries and Trusts* (1993)). This theme of the role of unconscionability as a value and as a creative force, and how it is to be interpreted in particular contexts, will also be considered in greater detail in those contexts at several points in the book (see in particular Chapters 4, 12 and 16). But Sir Anthony Mason's comments on the significance of 'good conscience' serve another function. They alert us to the fact that considerations of conscience – and morality? – are no longer the sole preserve of the doctrines of Equity. Indeed Worthington, for example, reminds us that as early as 1760 Lord Mansfield was able to say that the gist of the common law action for the recovery of 'money had and received' was that 'the defendant, upon the circumstances of the case, is obliged by the ties of natural justice and equity to refund the money' (*Moses v Macferlan* (1760) 2 Burr 1005 at 1012; cited in 'Integrating Equity and the Common Law' (2002) 55 CLP 223 at 231–235).

A second dimension of the 'harmonisation' proposition draws directly on the idea that contemporary developments in deciding on an appropriate remedy in a given case should not depend entirely upon the historical origins of remedies. This may require us in some instances to challenge our conventional wisdom. In *A-G v Blake (Jonathan Cape Ltd, third party)* [2001] 1 AC 268, for example, the House of Lords by a 4:1 majority rejected the prevailing orthodoxy that damages in contract were restricted solely to recoupment of financial loss. Instead their lordships held that it is now possible in certain rare circumstances for the equitable remedy of an account of profits earned by the breaker of the contract to be awarded to the victim of a breach of contract (see Chapter 14 at p 791). As Lord Nicholls observed in *Blake* (at 278–280): 'In these choppy waters the common law and equity steered different course' with the consequence that 'the difference in remedial response appears to have arisen simply as an accident of history'. Conversely consider the principle that only equitable remedies can enforce purely equitable rights so that, for instance, common law damages cannot be awarded for breach of an equitable right. As we shall see in later chapters the rationale for this position has been challenged, most noticeably in the New Zealand Court of Appeal (see *Mouat v Clarke Boyce* [1992] 2 NZLR 559; *Aquaculture Corpn v New Zealand Green Mussel Co Ltd* [1990] 3 NZLR 299; *Day v Mead* [1987] 2 NZLR 443). In *Mouat v Clarke Boyce*, for instance, in a case concerning a claim for equitable compensation for breach of fiduciary duty, Sir Robin Cooke stated (at 566):

> For breach of these duties, now that common law and equity are mingled, the Court has available the full range of remedies, including damages or compensation and restitutionary remedies such as an account of profits. What is most appropriate to the particular facts may be granted.

A related question is whether common law concepts such as foreseeability and remoteness should apply equally to equitable compensation and common law damages (see *Canson Enterprises Ltd v Boughton & Co* (1991) 85 DLR (4th) 129). Whilst both at present share a causation requirement they may still differ, at least under English law, on these other points, a troubling matter to which we return in Chapter 11. It must therefore be emphasised that common law jurisdictions differ in their approaches to these matters. In particular New Zealand, as might be inferred from the words of Sir Robin Cooke, has shown greater liberality or, from a different standpoint, heresy in borrowing and adopting ideas from common law to equity and vice versa (but cf the comments of Sir Richard Scott VC in *Medforth v Blake* [2000] Ch 86 in holding that a receiver-manager appointed by a mortgagee was subject to an 'equitable duty of care' (at 102): 'I do not ... think it matters one jot whether the duty is expressed as a common law duty or as a duty in equity. The result is the same'). Thus, if following the New Zealand example with regard to remedies, 'common law' damages for mental distress might be recoverable for breach of fiduciary duty (*Mouat v Clarke Boyce*) and equitable compensation reduced on grounds of contributory negligence (*Day v Mead* [1987] 2 NZLR 443). Whether or not 'harmonisation' is desirable on any or all of these matters, and we do not *assume* that it is, is considered in more detail predominantly in the commercial contexts within which the issues have tended to arise (see Chapters 11, 14 and 16). What can be said here is that there is a siren attraction in aspects of the fusion debate. In particular who can reasonably resist the call that 'like cases should be treated alike'? As Burrows concludes in his important paper on this topic 'we should be able to say, at the start of the 21st century, "We do this at common law and we do the same in equity" rather than "We Do This at Common Law But That in Equity"' – the latter phrase being the title of his paper ((2002) 22(1) OJLS 1 at 16; see also by the same author *Hochelaga Lectures, Fusing Common Law and Equity: Remedies, Restitution and Reform* (2003)). Indeed to argue against 'treating like cases alike' could justifiably attract the charge of reasoning in an inequitable manner. As always, however, the devil is in the detail. Caution may therefore be needed in determining which instances are alike and furthermore how far, for instance, supposed rationales for the different common law and equitable remedies still carry persuasive weight (see eg Smith 'Fusion and Tradition' in Degeling and Edelman (eds) *Equity in Commercial Law* (2005) ch 2 and also the comprehensive and reasoned opinions from the New South Wales Court of Appeal in *Harris v Digital Pulse Pty Ltd* [2003] NSWCA 10). For that reason, to reiterate the point, consideration of some of these issues is deferred until the particular doctrines are considered at various points later in the book.

But there is one further and important point to emphasise about the pre-scriptive aspects of the fusion debate. The discussion above could convey the impression, to adopt a horticultural metaphor, that all that is required to resolve the 'fusion' debate is a relatively modest degree of pruning and perhaps some hoeing of straggling weeds that are restricting new growth. This conclusion would be misleading, although it has a certain seductive charm to 'tenta-tive fusionists' such as the writer of this chapter. There is a more ambitious prescriptive agenda, one that involves fundamental landscaping so as to achieve a complete integration of equity and common law doctrines, the 'endgame of duality' in Professor Birks's phrase (see (2004) 120 LQR 344 at 345 in his review of the 2004 edition of *Meagher, Gummow and Lehane's Equity Doctrines and Remedies*, the arch-opponents of such an approach). For some proponents the integration idea either is itself part of a more ambitious project to develop new principles of classification – a 'taxonomy' – of private law which would see a re-ordering of its categories or is seen as being likely to facilitate such a re-ordering as a necessary consequence of integration (see eg Worthington 'Integrating Equity and the Common Law' (2002) 55 CLP 223 and *Equity* (2nd edn, 2006); Burrows *Hochelaga Lectures, Fusing Common Law and Equity: Remedies, Restitution and Reform* (2003); and, amongst the many significant contributions of Professor Birks, 'Definition and Division' in Birks (ed) *The Classification of Obligations* (1997); 'Equity in the Modern Law; An Exercise in Taxonomy' (1996) 26 UWALR 1; and the classifications adopted in Burrows (ed) *English Private Law* (2nd edn, 2007) but cf Hedley in Degeling and Edelman ch 4 criticising the notion of any need for one dominant taxonomy).

It is beyond the scope of this book even to attempt an assessment of an ambitious project of that nature. What is of immediate conceptual interest is that it is envisaged that the trust – the express trust being in Worthington's words a 'hard case' for the integration project – would in some sense be dismantled, packaged up and parcelled off to different parts of the new landscape (see eg *Equity* ch 3 and pp 323–325). Three brief and somewhat random observations can be made about this proposition. First, as we saw in Chapter 1, the express trust is a somewhat strange conceptual hybrid of property and obligation. Doubtless it is possible from a conceptual standpoint to deconstruct the arrangement and relocate the various elements, some, for instance, into property law, others in contract and so on (cf Langbein 'The Contractarian Basis of the Law of Trusts' (1995) 105 Yale LJ 625 and the implications of the Contracts (Rights of Third Parties) Act 1999 enabling third parties to enforce contracts made for their benefit). What remain uncertain are the practical consequences of doing so. Would the functional flexibility offered by the trust be lost in the transformation? Should that worry us if, to ask a loaded question, tax avoidance arrangements were to be hampered (see eg Chapters 3 and 8)? The second observation is merely that at a time when civilian jurisdictions appear to be attracted to the trust concept it seems conceptually puzzling and economically questionable to discard a legal form in which legal practitioners in common law jurisdictions might be thought to have a competitive edge (see eg Hayton 'The Development of the Trust Concept in Civil Law Jurisdictions' (2000) 8 JTCP 159; Hayton (ed) *Modern International Developments in Trust Law* (1999) and the contributions by Dyer and Lupoi to a symposium on 'The International Trust' in (1999) 32 Vand J Transnat L at 967 and 989 respectively). Lastly, it is appropriate to return to the starting-point of the fusion debate, the Judicature Acts of 1873–75, not to refute the fusionist case but to confirm that its adherents have the correct target in their sights. Getzler succinctly sets out the problem in the following extract ('Patterns of Fusion' in Birks (ed) *The Classification of Obligations* (1997) 157 at p 158 – footnotes omitted):

> A final union of legal and equitable doctrine in one body of law may yet be impossible, simply because the historical and conceptual bases of legal and equitable actions are too distinct. The sticking point has always been the continued existence of the trust – indeed, it was regard for the trust that prevented full fusion being attempted when the Judicature Acts of 1873–75 were first drafted and debated.

Further comment is perhaps best avoided given the vested interest that this writer has in the status quo!

3

Taxation, wealth-holding and the private trust

1. Introduction

As Hubert Monroe lugubriously commented in a Hamlyn Lecture 'tax is scarcely a favourite topic' (*Intolerable Inquisition? Reflections on the Law of Tax* (1981) p 1). It is not difficult to endorse this sentiment particularly when applied to the taxation of trusts. In academic contexts the topic conventionally falls into a no-man's land between the separate domains of taxation and trusts. Yet even by the beginning of the twentieth century the incidence of taxation was influencing the development of the private express trust. Indeed, as will be seen later in this book, taxation or more appropriately the availability of relief from taxation, has exercised considerable influence on public types of trusts also – for example, pension funds and charities (see Chapters 13, 18 and 19). With respect to private trusts, however, it may be claimed that this influence has so increased that fiscal considerations now dominate trusts practice even if not directly the formal rules of trusts law. Whether trusts should be created, what types of trust should be adopted and where their administration should be located are all, in reality, decisions taken by property owners only after careful consideration of the fiscal implications.

The claim that these implications predominate will be probed later in this chapter (see p 75) but at the very least the taxpayer is unlikely to be satisfied with a tax lawyer or accountant who merely clarifies the probable size of the tax bill based on existing property arrangements. The taxpayer will also wish to know how to rearrange affairs so as to reduce that tax liability. It is at this stage that the 'tricks' the trust can perform with property interests come into consideration. The tax planner needs a thorough understanding of both tax and trusts law and the interaction between the two, if comprehensive and effective advice is to be given to the client. This chapter has no pretensions to providing the detailed knowledge of those areas that the tax planner needs. Indeed, the attainment of such skills would impose demands of time and space beyond the scope of trust courses or textbooks (see for excellent introductions to tax topics Tiley *Revenue Law* (6th edn, 2008); Lee (ed) *Revenue Law: Principles and Practice* (26th edn, 2008)). But this does not mean that the interrelation between tax and trusts can be left wholly unexplored.

An understanding of the tax landscape without necessarily knowing intimately the identity of each contour is useful for appreciating why a particular type of trust is used. Of comparable importance to this functional justification is the doctrinal consideration that certain major developments in trusts law may be explained best by reference to the stimulus of taxation. We have already seen in the context of pre-twentieth century family settlements how conveyancers, responding to the needs of settlors, gradually developed the trust concept and the developments were subsequently ratified by the courts. Out of this process emerged many of the detailed technical rules of trusts law. Since then settlors have continued to require the conveyancer to spin the intricate web of settlements to allocate property interests on the plane of time but now with a new dominant objective, the minimisation of tax. This has led to novel developments, particularly in the use of discretionary trusts (see Chapter 5), and the adaptation of existing concepts such as the power of advancement (see Chapter 7). These innovations have on occasion seemed to challenge firmly established rules of trusts law: sometimes the courts have responded rigidly, sometimes creatively. The underlying policy issue confronting the courts is what weight to attribute to the modernising demands posed by trust practice and the needs of trust users, as against the claims of apparently entrenched rules and doctrine. The connection between the tax influence and judicial pronouncement of a new rule is indirect and tenuous but none the less real. We must stress that the flexibility implicit in the developments being discussed here has a dual nature. The trust form with its capacity for fragmentation of ownership over time can facilitate flexible modes of property disposition. But as importantly trusts doctrine itself has a flexibility that has intermittently been demonstrated through judicial modification of technical legal rules and trusts concepts in response to new directions in trusts practice.

The conflict just referred to which emerges out of challenges to established rules takes essentially doctrinal form, although springing from practical considerations. There also exist conflicts more overtly about public policy which are equally deserving of the trust student's attention. One objective of taxation, particularly capital taxation, has at various times been to achieve some measure of wealth redistribution. One clear objective of the private express trust is to preserve wealth within the family. This potential conflict between a general aim of redistribution and a specific aim of wealth preservation causes difficulties for both fiscal policy formation and implementation. The challenge for fiscal policy formation is to achieve neutrality between outright and settled gifts. Is it possible for the parliamentary draftsman to resolve the problems posed, for example by the trust's fragmentation of property interests, without either favouring or penalising dispositions on trust? As regards attempts to implement policy decisions, these have inevitably involved the importation of property concepts into taxing statutes. What is not inevitable is that on occasion, as with the term 'interest in possession' in inheritance tax, no attempt is made to define the concept used. A problem of statutory interpretation for the courts therefore is whether to apply accepted property definitions or to identify a special meaning for the purposes of the tax statute. In deciding this apparently technical task of statutory interpretation do the courts consider the fiscal policy objectives, and indeed should they do so? As we shall see in subsequent chapters (eg Chapters 5 and 7) similar questions can be asked where courts are faced with pressures to modify trusts law.

Lastly, if fiscal policy concerning taxation of trusts is to be assessed adequately then the consequences of the use of the trust must be measured against the policy objectives. It is necessary to know in particular the extent to which disposition of property on trust has frustrated wealth redistribution by helping preserve wealth concentrations within families and free from the grasp of Her Majesty's Revenue and Customs (HMRC). This should be a simple task but it is complicated by a dearth of knowledge. Abel-Smith and Townsend writing in 1965 commented (*The Poor and the Poorest* p 9):

> Information about the rich is sparse. It has always been difficult to make scientific calculations of their true wealth and recent developments in tax laws and tax avoidance techniques have not made these calculations any easier.

The accuracy of this statement will be reviewed in the light of more recent data but it does highlight the twin functions of the trust. It is not only a key element of some tax avoidance techniques but it also operates to conceal concentrations of wealth. The lack of a precise measure of wealth concentration can itself contribute towards maintaining existing patterns of distribution by limiting awareness of wealth disparities and inhibiting pressure for change.

To summarise, the reasons for investigating the relationship between taxation and trusts are:

(1) The impact on trusts practice.
(2) The impact on trusts law, usually via the influence of trusts practice (see in particular Chapters 4, 5 and 7).
(3) The impact of the trust form on attempts to identify and counter tax avoidance.
(4) The impact of trusts concepts on interpretation of tax statutes (see Chapter 8).
(5) The combined impact of trusts and tax law on wealth distribution.

This chapter is primarily concerned with issues (1), (3) and (5) outlined above. Consideration of the detail of taxation of trusts is deferred until Chapter 8. By then we will have a closer familiarity with those elements of the trust which have provided such fertile ground for the tax planner.

Our initial approach to the subject has assumed that fiscal considerations predominate over any other motivation in trusts practice. But, as mentioned previously, the validity of this assumption needs to be examined.

2. Trust motivation and tax avoidance

(a) Trust founder's motives

An obsession with tax planning and the dominance of fiscal considerations has been sharply criticised by one North American writer who claims it is harmful and misrepresents the interests of those coming to lawyers seeking advice about their wills.

> Lawyers who deal with wills and so forth probably make a mistake when they let themselves be called estate planners. It is a fawning phrase, a piece of flattery for a man who is supposed to feel better when his mortgage and pension plan are called an estate. . . . There is deeper harm, too, beyond self-delusion – the harm that leaves us obsessed with manipulation and taxes, the professional fixation which diverts our observation from the here-and-now feelings of the men and women who consider death in the law office. . . . I don't believe that the rich only want to save taxes; I think that is what some lawyers and estate planners want them to want, for the same reason vacuum-cleaner manufacturers see the human condition in terms of dust and suction. (T L Shaffer *Death, Property and Lawyers* (1963) pp 1–2, 10)

The questioning of the assumption that fiscal factors dominate the thoughts of a trust founder is carried a stage further in the following extract where Friedman adopts a dual categorisation of trust types with the emphasis on non-fiscal motivations. As was demonstrated in Chapter 1, different trust types can achieve a variety of family purposes more efficiently than other available legal forms. The settlor's decision that the trust is the most appropriate property holding and transmission mechanism will not ignore tax implications, but the argument is that the choice is prompted first and foremost by family considerations.

Laurence M Friedman 'The Dynastic Trust' (1964) 73 Yale LJ 547 at 547–549

> Private express trusts can be conveniently divided into two polar types, corresponding to two underlying purposes. The first, the most common type, can be called the *caretaker trust.* Trusts for the benefit of minor children, or incompetents, or old people, or people with little or no business experience are all caretaker trusts. The caretaker trust is usually short-term, spanning one lifetime or less. It exists to protect and serve the interests or needs of one or more particular beneficiaries.
>
> Much less common is the *dynastic trust.* In its extreme form it is rare indeed. The dynastic trust, as the phrase is here used, is a trust set up primarily to perpetuate the trust estate for as long a period as possible . . .
>
> The psychology of the private dynastic trust is less obvious than that of the caretaker trust. Why should the settlor prefer unseen and unborn great-grandchildren to his closest blood relations? Most people would rather hold property outright than in trust, if only for

the right to control its ultimate disposition. Money is power; and principal more so than income. The settlor of the dynastic trust denies full power to his closest kin. But in so doing he extends his own power by projecting his wishes into a period that lasts long after his death, thus satisfying some sort of hunger for vicarious immortality.

The dynastic trust is apparently more common today than a century ago. The great increase in national wealth has made its growth possible, though national wealth does not fully explain the prevalence of this form of trust. Modern tax laws have also had a great influence on long-term trusts. A well-drafted testamentary trust lasting several generations is subject to only one estate tax, upon the death of the settlor. The intervening deaths of life beneficiaries do not constitute taxable events. But none of the tax savings accrues to the estate of the settlor himself. These savings redound to the benefit of later generations, while the immediate family gives up the right to enjoy unrestricted use of principal. In short, the dynastic trust saves taxes, but for itself, as an entity, rather than for the immediate income beneficiaries. It is commonplace to explain the modern long-term trust in terms of 'tax motives'; but these 'tax motives' are probably secondary, after the fact: the dynastic impulse comes first. (1)

Footnote 1

Frank H Detweiler has written: 'But how many times does a lawyer of our generation encounter a man with the supreme urge to keep his dead hand perpetually at the wheel of an existing or potential dynasty? . . . [M]ost of us would feel sure . . . that people of wealth in our day are far less likely than were their counterparts of a few generations ago to have their eyes fixed on providing a fortune for generations to come.' Detweiler sees a real 'decline of the dynastic impulse'. Long-term trusts are set up, he asserts, to avoid the crushing impact of taxes . . . Detweiler *The Owners' Control over Property Use and Disposition after his Death*, U Chi Law School Conf on Use and Disposition of Private Property 15, 21–22 (conference Series No 12, 1953). But Detweiler's reasoning is circular; long-term trusts are not set up for 'dynastic' reasons, but to save taxes in the long run. But why save taxes? It is probably more accurate to say that in addition to those who truly wish to found a dynasty (and of course this wish is not absent simply because a client does not articulate it baldly), there are many settlors today who, in the light of their financial circumstances, *prefer* having their estate pass relatively intact to grandchildren and great-grandchildren to seeing most of it go to the government, and that this preference is stronger than the desire to give financial autonomy (as opposed to security) to children.

The significance of Friedman's argument that tax motivations are irrelevant for caretaker trusts and only secondary for dynastic trusts is that our attitudes towards tax treatment of trusts may depend on whether tax avoidance motivations or pure trust motivations are perceived to predominate. The aura of benevolence and concern surrounding the idea of a caretaker motivation is a potent argument for encouraging a sympathetic approach from the tax legislator even to the extent of opening up loopholes in legislation. It is therefore important to assess the validity of Friedman's analysis which was based on the operation of the US federal tax system in 1964. A straightforward application to the UK context of his specific claims concerning tax motivations presents difficulties in three areas of taxation of transfer of property: life interests, discretionary trusts and inter vivos gifts (whether on trust or by outright gift).

Life estate In Friedman's example of the dynastic trust, dynastic motivations and tax advantages run parallel. Friedman recognises that 'a well-drafted testamentary trust lasting several generations is subject to only one estate tax, upon the death of the settlor. The intervening deaths of life beneficiaries do not constitute taxable events.' This favourable fiscal treatment on the death of the life tenant does not apply in England and, since the Tax Reform Act 1976, is no longer the position in the US. Instead, life estates are treated as if the property producing the income is owned by the life tenant. The capital is aggregated at death with other property owned absolutely by him and taxed accordingly. Contrary to the picture of trusts practice in the US portrayed by Friedman, a dynastic-style trust in England at a comparable time was becoming an endangered species. It had given way to alternative methods of transferring wealth including the discretionary trust.

Discretionary trust Friedman recognises that the terms 'caretaker' and 'dynastic' identify merely two polar types of motivation and that elements of both may be present in a complex mixture. A widely drawn discretionary trust such as that in *Example 4* in Chapter 1 is particularly difficult to categorise. Whereas the label 'caretaker' could justify the wide discretion given to trustees over allocation of benefit, it is less satisfactory in explaining the potential duration of the trust. On the other hand, dynasticism may explain duration but the abdication to trustees of control over beneficial entitlement scarcely ensures that the settlor 'extends his own power by projecting *his* wishes . . . thus satisfying some sort of hunger for vicarious immortality'. A widely drawn discretionary trust adopting a statutory perpetuity period of 80 years thus seems to defy a simple categorisation in terms of trust motivation. Furthermore, it is questionable whether Friedman's view that 'tax motives are probably secondary' can be sustained for such trusts.

Inter vivos gifts An omission from Friedman's analysis is that it deals with testamentary dispositions only. In the absence of an effective lifetime gifts tax, estate taxes at death can be avoided simply by transferring property inter vivos. An assessment of whether trust or tax avoidance motivations predominate therefore needs to account for the timing of transfer of property in addition to the form of transfer. A study of wealth transfer in the USA suggests that the timing of gifts is significantly influenced by fiscal considerations:

R Barlow, H Brayer and J Morgan *Economic Behaviour of the Affluent* (1966) p 104

What particular reasons did you have for making the gifts at that time?

Tax considerations were the most frequently reported reason, with the needs of the donees mentioned less than half as frequently. The importance of tax considerations rose only moderately with income. They were mentioned by 40 percent of donors with incomes of $10,000 to $15,000 and by 57 percent of those whose incomes exceeded $300,000. Tax factors persisted as the dominant motive irrespective of whether the donees were children, grandchildren, or other relatives. The relevance of tax considerations may perhaps best be illustrated in the words of the respondents themselves. For example, donors answered the above question as follows:

'Only one reason – to avoid inheritance taxes. [He then added, perhaps as an afterthought] My love for my children prompted it.'
'Estate taxation.'
'Part of a long-range program to avoid inheritance taxes.'
'Because of high inheritance taxes – because of high income taxes.'
'It's a personal thing. It seems like an appropriate time. I felt I'd better do it while the spirit moved me, and at the time the securities had appreciated greatly so there were large taxable gains on them. The recipients were not in the tax bracket that I was, so that was the time to do it.'

No comparable study into individual motivations has been carried out in this country although a survey of accountants involved in tax planning revealed that many of their clients did not in practice adopt the most tax-effective method of arranging their affairs.

Moral judgments, dislike of complexity, avarice, procrastination, unwillingness to spend, concern for public image, administrative complications, unpredictability of effects – all these militated against the adoption of tax avoidance schemes. (C T Sandford *Hidden Costs of Taxation* (1973) p 108)

The complexity of motivation suggested there lends some support to Friedman's sceptical approach. The extent to which financial self-interest predominates over other considerations in the attitudes of taxpayers towards their compliance with tax laws and, by inference, in their choice of legal form for their fiscal arrangements remains contentious (see generally Long and Swingen (1991) 25 Law and Society Review 637). Nevertheless Friedman may still be criticised for inadequately distinguishing between a motivation to achieve a particular family objective and one for adopting a particular legal form out of several alternatives for achieving that objective. His approach does remind us, however, of the heterogeneous nature of the trust and trust founder's motives. This should then alert us to the potential problems posed by this heterogeneity for the devising of a system for taxing trusts which is both fair and effective.

(b) Tax avoidance, tax evasion and creatures of a similar hue

(1) Defining avoidance: lawyer vs economist

In the previous section we suggested that one reason for establishing whether tax avoidance is the principal motivation for creating a trust is that this may affect attitudes towards treatment of trusts under a tax regime. Implicit assumptions behind this approach are that tax avoidance has a precise meaning and furthermore that it is undesirable. This section examines these interlinked assumptions. Unfortunately, however, the problem of disentangling various motivations is compounded by the absence of an accepted definition of tax avoidance.

Conventionally, a sharp distinction has usually been drawn between 'tax evasion' and 'tax avoidance'. What is called 'tax evasion' is illegal and involves non-payment of taxes which the taxpayer is obliged by law to pay, or would be had he disclosed all relevant facts about his finances to HMRC. Tax avoidance, in contrast, is lawful and involves the arrangement of a taxpayer's financial affairs so that tax liability is removed or reduced. As Professor Wheatcroft ((1955) 18 MLR 209) once bluntly put it: 'tax avoidance is the art of dodging tax without actually breaking the law'. The distinction is pointedly demonstrated by the following example (Tiley *Revenue Law* (6th edn, 2008) p 101):

> If two people marry in order to reduce their tax burden they are practising tax avoidance; if they tell the Inland Revenue that they are married, when they are not, they are guilty of tax evasion and may well be prosecuted.

Two important features of this distinction must be emphasised. First, the essence of the distinction is that evasion commonly involves non-disclosure of relevant facts: 'the concealment of material facts, leading to an under-assessment, marks the point at which avoidance crosses the borderline and becomes evasion' (Keith Committee *Report of the Committee on Enforcement Powers of the Revenue Departments* (Cmnd 8822, 1983) p 162). However, in some complex tax-planning arrangements (see below, p 87) what constitutes 'relevance' for the purposes of disclosure may itself be uncertain. Second, the distinction drawn here between avoidance and evasion is a legal one buttressed traditionally by a literalist approach to the interpretation of taxing statutes. A fundamental principle associated with literalism is that a taxpayer's liability to tax is decided solely by construing the language of the statute. As Rowlatt J said in *Cape Brandy Syndicate v IRC* [1921] 1 KB 64 at 71:

> ... in a taxing Act one has to look merely at what is clearly said. There is no room for any intendment. There is no equity about a tax. Nothing is to be read in, nothing is to be implied. One can only look fairly at the language used ...

In this approach, form not substance is the key to tax liability and the court stands apparently neutral between Crown and taxpayer, ignoring broad policy considerations and merits of individual cases alike. One consequence of this approach is that, in Lord Tomlin's words (*IRC v Duke of Westminster* [1936] AC 1 at 19):

Every man is entitled if he can to arrange his affairs so that the tax attaching under the appropriate Acts is less than it otherwise would be. If he succeeds in ordering them so as to secure that result, then, however unappreciative the Commissioners of Inland Revenue or his fellow taxpayers may be of his ingenuity, he cannot be compelled to pay an increased tax.

This statement represents the high-water mark of judicial acceptance of the literalist approach. Recent judicial developments, to be considered shortly, suggest that the statement now needs to be applied with considerable caution and perhaps even to be disregarded. A further consequence of these developments is that the evasion/avoidance dichotomy is, to put the point at its lowest, being refined. This is not to say, however, that the sentiments exhibited in the judicial statements above lack support. A robust and, of its time, representative defence not merely of a formalist stance towards interpretation but also of the taxpayer's moral right to use the legislation to best advantage was included in the 1982 edition of a student tax textbook:

Pinson on Revenue Law (15th edn, 1982) pp 685–686

Tax planning

Much nonsense is talked about tax avoidance. Politicians, unaware of its real nature, speak of it as a social evil to be legislated against. Others speak of avoidance as if it were a game of chess played annually with the Revenue. In fact, there is often more than one method of achieving a desired result in financial planning for business or the family and 'tax avoidance' is the result of selecting the method which is least costly in tax. Tax avoidance of this kind is not only unobjectionable: it is common sense. . . .

. . . 'avoidance' may be no more than the result of choosing one of two equally acceptable methods of achieving a desired result. In the world of commerce the transactions are often . . . complex and the range of alternative methods is much wider; if one method is used, the tax is £x, and for another it is £y (or even £ nil), and the terms 'tax avoidance' or 'tax planning' conveniently describe the techniques by which the lawyer and accountant can so arrange a client's affairs as to achieve a reduction in the amount of tax he would otherwise have to pay. This is an important function, for the burden of tax is nowadays so great that taxation must be regarded as one of the major costs of production; and enterprising and productive schemes are often made possible only by intelligent tax planning. In other cases legislation is so hasty and ill-conceived, essential reforms are so long delayed, or the consequences of legislation – unforeseen by ill-informed or non-commercially-minded legislators – are so immoral, that taxpayers have to rely on the concoction of highly artificial schemes to avoid what would otherwise be a manifestly unjust or even absurd result.

Reliance on a seemingly straightforward dichotomy between 'lawful' tax avoidance and 'illegal' tax evasion has increasingly been viewed as leaving some troublesome issues untouched. Should, for instance, the personal motivations of taxpayers or the consequences of their actions for fiscal policy be legitimate considerations for tax law to consider? If so, does what might be termed a traditional literalist approach to interpretation provide a sufficiently precise formula for evaluating those considerations? These and other questions are raised in the two following readings that focus on the complex financial arrangements of the Vestey family, outlined in rather sensationalist fashion in the *Sunday Times* extract. The readings are also evidence that disagreements about the meaning to be attributed to 'avoidance' are not confined to academic circles, but can fuel popular debate.

Philip Knightley 'Richest family in huge tax-dodge', *Sunday Times*, 5 October 1980

The Treasury is losing millions of pounds a year in unpaid income tax and surtax because of a major loophole in the tax law. The loophole's existence has been revealed in a sensational . . . tax case in the House of Lords involving the Vesteys, Britain's richest family. [*Vestey v IRC* [1980] AC 1148; see Sumption [1980] BTR 4; and Boyd [1980] BTR 442.] During the case it emerged that the Vesteys – peers of the realm, old Etonians, friends of the royal family, polo-players, deputy lieutenants of their county, pillars of the British establishment – have been exploiting this and other loopholes to avoid paying enormous amounts of income tax for more than 60 years.

The Vesteys, headed by Lord 'Sam' Vestey, 39, and his cousin Edmund, 48, run a worldwide empire in shipping, clothing, insurance, shops and meat – the Dewhurst chain of butcher shops is theirs. [*Note*: Dewhursts was put into receivership in 1995.] Inland Revenue decided that six members of the family, including Lord Vestey himself, were, over a four-year period, liable for income tax on £4.3 million and surtax on £7.3 million. But the Law Lords ruled – as they have done in the past in other Vestey cases – that the family need not pay a penny. [See eg *Vestey's Executors v IRC* [1949] 1 All ER 1108.]

The Vestey case, which covered 60 years of sophisticated tax-avoidance schemes, was extremely complicated. In brief: at one time a UK resident could transfer his assets to, say, Bermuda, and arrange for the income from those assets to be held by a trustee living there. He could further arrange that the trustee would pay him, out of the income, varying lump sums at irregular intervals. The lump sums would not be treated as income and so would not be liable for income tax.

Parliament plugged this loophole in 1936 with a new law which said: if a UK resident had the power to enjoy the income held by the trustee, then the Inland Revenue would consider that income to be the UK resident's and would tax him accordingly.

Tax-avoiders then got around this by arranging for the money to go, not to themselves, but to, say, their sons and daughters. But these 'passive beneficiaries', as the Inland Revenue calls them, were brought into the tax net by *Congreve v IRC* ([1948] 1 All ER 948). The House of Lords decided then that it did not matter who set up the tax-avoidance scheme in the first place, anyone who then benefited from it was liable for income tax.

The Law Lords' new decision has wrecked the 1948 one. They have decided that the law should apply only to the man who *originally* sought to avoid tax by transferring his assets

Table 3.1 Trusts distributions

Dates	Beneficiary	Amount
9 July 1962	Lord Vestey	£123,000
29 October 1962	R A Vestey	£215,000
1 January 1963	Edmund Vestey	£700,000
1 January 1963	Lord Vestey	£800,000
1 January 1963	Mark Vestey	£200,000
18 November 1964	R A Vestey	£150,000
2 May 1966	Mrs Payne	£100,000
2 May 1966	Mrs Baddeley	£100,000
18 November 1966	Edmund Vestey	£220,000
	Total	£2,608,000

abroad. His heirs, the passive beneficiaries, could collect the money free of income tax. Thus the Vesteys – and anyone else who is a passive beneficiary of an overseas trust – can go on receiving money in Britain free of tax.

The apparent gap revealed by the House of Lords decision in *Vestey v IRC* [1980] AC 1148 has subsequently been substantially closed (see now Income Tax Act 2007, Pt 13, Ch 2). Although doubtless complex in operation, the tax arrangements of the Vesteys were conceptually simple, yet provide a striking illustration of the potential of the trust form when linked to the attributes of the plane of time and of geographical location. The scheme used (i) separation of legal title to capital and income, (ii) the fragmentation of equitable title to capital and income among numerous beneficiaries in discretionary trusts, (iii) the location beyond the jurisdiction of HMRC of trustees and trust accounts, and thus legal title to trust assets and the income initially derived therefrom, and (iv) the plane of time to allow income to be accumulated within the trust fund and transmuted into capital. This last facet was particularly important for those beneficiaries resident in the UK: irregular receipt of capital sums would be likely to escape the UK income tax net. Therefore, as Knightley explains, 'the money . . . is allowed to accumulate until, when directed by the manager, the trustees make "occasional and discretionary payments" to beneficiaries: the Vesteys' (*Sunday Times*, 12 October 1980). The schedule of payments in Table 3.1 made between 1962 and 1966 illustrates the process.

Bernard Levin, *The Times*, 28 October 1980

'I am', says a Tom Stoppard character, 'a man of absolutely no convictions whatever. At least, I think I am.' You will, I am sure, realise that the character in question was not based on me: rarely am I obliged to say with Belloc that

> The question's very much too wide,
> And much too round and much too hollow,
> And learned men on either side
> Use arguments we cannot follow.

But in this strange position I find myself today anent the Affaire Vestey.... The principle at the heart of the uproar is comparatively simple; for decades on end the Vesteys have fiddled their taxes on a stupendous scale, paying something like fourpence-ha'penny a year on an annual income so large the noughts alone could hardly be accommodated in the width of a column of *Times* print. And, it is argued, such behaviour is reprehensible, and therefore ought to be stopped; it is also argued that the behaviour is not reprehensible and therefore ought not to be stopped, and for good measure that it is reprehensible but nevertheless ought to be allowed to continue. And I do not find a decision nearly so easy as many of those who have given tongue on the subject appear to do.

Before trying to sort out my ideas on the subject I must make it plain that when I say the Vesteys have fiddled their taxes I do not mean that they have done so in any way 'contrary to the law'. If they had, there would be no argument, at any rate of a moral kind. The reason that there is an argument is precisely that what they have been up to is legal; the law made it possible for them to set up trusts abroad and so to arrange matters that the money was not taxable, and they took advantage of the possibilities the law opened to them, and enjoyed the fruits thereof.

Now before we go any further, I must point out if you confine the argument to the statement of it I have just made, what the Vesteys have done is exactly what you and I do.... We do not break the tax laws, but we take advantage of the concessions they allow us; we deduct from our return of taxable income such sums as were expended wholly, necessarily and exclusively for business purposes, we claim similarly to be relieved of taxation on our mortgage interest, we do the same for legally ordered maintenance payment.... In short and the vernacular, we are damned if we will pay a penny more in tax than the law compels us to, and we so arrange matters that what the law compels us to pay is reduced as far as our time and our accountants' ingenuity can manage....

All this applies only if you accept the definition of tax-avoidance I offered in my last paragraph but one. What the Vesteys did takes the argument a step farther. They actively sought out, with the aid of a huge quantity of enormously expensive financial and legal advice, ways to get round the provisions of the tax laws without actually breaking them. And there is, obviously, some distinction between active and passive exploitation of the law, between deducting that which the law says plainly may legitimately be deducted, and finding ways to frustrate the intention of the law because the law is so constructed that it permits such frustration to be accomplished.

Here, of course, we are on marshy ground. What is 'the intention' of a law other than what it says? And who has ever heard of a law that did not have several ambiguities in it to keep the lawyers in fair round bells with good capon lined while the litigants wear a lean and hungry look? But to ask that question is not necessarily to admit that it has no answer. The law in this case ... was certainly not intended, for a start, to enable the Vesteys to get away with such an enormous quantity of swag.

We need waste no time on some of the peripheral arguments advanced. Of course the Vesteys were able to get away with it only because they were so filthy rich to start with that they could set up a scheme far beyond the pockets of other taxpayers, but that is hardly a matter of principle, and if you think it is kindly to say precisely what level of income should be the dividing line between those who should, and those who should not, be allowed to avoid their taxes. On the other hand, there is also nothing in the argument . . . that because the British tax laws are inequitable, damaging to our economy and largely based on a hatred of success, anybody ought to be allowed to get out of complying with them if he legally can. The cure for a bad law is its amendment or repeal . . .

At this point we must consider the argument that law is morally neutral, so that nothing which is lawful should be thought impermissible. This is liberalism (in the nineteenth-century sense) in its purest form, and it strikes me as drivel in its purest form. There is no law forbidding parents to treat their children, for years on end, with indifference and contempt, providing they do not actually beat them too hard; but I would withhold admiration from such parents, and rather hope that others would do likewise.

It is perfectly possible to think of the Vesteys as what Sellar and Yeatman called the Roundheads – Right but Repulsive (as opposed to the Cavaliers, who were Wrong but Wromantic). What kind of moral view should inform our attitude to those who, while obeying the law, behave in a manner which we find unacceptable?

Here, the ground becomes very marshy indeed. . . . [To] what extent should moral pressure ever be exerted against lawful behaviour? There are dangers, great dangers, in moral witch-hunts and moral lynch-law, and that is true even if the hunt and the lynching are conducted without any taint of hypocrisy, which is almost never the case . . .

Now perhaps you can see why I confessed at the outset that I do not find this argument at all easy to decide upon. My instinct from the start has been to find the Vesteys' behaviour disgusting, but I am not nearly so confident as some that my instinct is necessarily worth following. But I have, in the course of arguing the case here, happened upon a formula which may work. In deciding whether to judge a lawful action by a moral light, can we not ask ourselves whether it is possible for anyone seriously to admire the action? Never mind whether we do or do not do so, is it reasonably possible?

Even if, intuitively, one might have sympathy for Bernard Levin's criterion – 'not reasonably possible to admire the action' – it is not easy to see how it could be incorporated into a workable statutory formula for distinguishing unacceptable arrangements from those that are acceptable. Morality is not the only possible tool of analysis. If we adopt an economist's perspective two key criteria in any definition of 'avoidance' would be the motive for, and the end-result of, a particular transaction or arrangement.

C T Sandford *Hidden Costs of Taxation* (1973) pp 113–114

Defining and Minimising Avoidance
Amongst tax practitioners the generally accepted definition of avoidance . . . is any legal method by which a person can reduce his tax bill. But this definition can cover almost

anything – in fact anything that an economist would include in an analysis of 'effective incidence'. . . . I can reduce estate duty [now Inheritance Tax] by buying a farm, sharing my estate with my wife more than seven years before I die, or spending my wealth on a trip round the world. I can reduce my tax bill by buying sweets instead of cigarettes when the Chancellor increases the tax on tobacco. . . .

All these actions would come within the definition of avoidance yet they clearly cannot be treated on a par . . . We must surely make at least two categories of distinction, one relating to the taxpayer the other to the legislature. It is reasonable to confine 'avoidance' to action which results in the would-be avoider substantially achieving the objective to which the tax had become an obstacle. Let us give some examples. If a man ceases to buy cigarettes because of tobacco tax he has not achieved his pre-tax objective, ie to smoke. Buying sweets instead of cigarettes, therefore, is not avoidance. Again, if a taxpayer decides to use most of his wealth for a consumption spree because estate duty makes it not worth while saving for heirs, he is not 'avoiding' for he has abandoned his objective of passing property to heirs. On the other hand, if he reacts to estate duty by making inter vivos gifts (assuming he survives for seven years), this is avoidance; it has achieved, though by a more circuitous route, the objective of passing to heirs an intact property.

Let us turn to the second aspect of our definition, the conditions relating to the legislature. A government may have one of three attitudes to a particular 'avoidance' measure – using the wide definition of avoidance. It may welcome it; the government may have deliberately offered a tax concession to promote some objective, eg tax concessions on mortgage interest . . . in order to encourage owner-occupation. Second, without having sought positively to encourage a particular 'avoiding' action the government may find it entirely acceptable as when an income tax payer reduces his tax liability by taking a wife or having children; or when a person on retirement transfers savings from a building society to some other form of investment in order to reclaim income tax. Third, the government may deplore certain actions as contrary to its intentions; the action is in accord with the letter of the law but not its spirit. Only actions in this third category should rank as 'avoidance'.

We have reached the point in our argument where we have said that the term avoidance should be confined to actions by a taxpayer which enable him substantially to achieve the objective to which the tax had become an obstacle; and where the actions, while in accordance with the letter of the law were contrary to its intentions.

As an analytical tool the economist's approach as represented by Sandford has the initial attraction of restricting the term 'avoidance' to a more precise range of activity. However, as Sandford recognises, an approach which focuses on the intention of the legislature is itself problematic since 'the objective interpretation can only be found in the words the law uses' (p 114).

This does not, however, necessarily return us to the literalist stance on statutory interpretation as stated by Rowlatt J (see above, p 79). First, that approach must now be interpreted in the light of the decision in *Pepper v Hart* [1993] 1 All ER 42 that the court can look to parliamentary materials for guidance where (per Lord Browne-Wilkinson at 69):

(a) legislation is ambiguous or obscure, or leads to an absurdity; (b) the material relied on consists of one or more statements by a minister or other promoter of the bill together, if necessary, with such other parliamentary material as is necessary to understand such statements and their effect; (c) the statements relied on are clear.

There are circumstances, however, where reference to *Hansard* for guidance on interpretation of a statute may be unavailing. The point in issue may not have been foreseen or considered by the legislature and therefore no legislative intent may be discernible. In addition, as Robinson and Sandford have argued elsewhere (*Tax Policy-Making in the United Kingdom* (1983)), inadequate pre-parliamentary preparation of fiscal policy, the constraints of the parliamentary timetable governing the passage of annual Finance Acts, and the influence of pressure groups often combine to produce a taxing provision which may not only be obscure but also diverges sharply from the initial proposal (see also Shipwright (ed) *Tax Avoidance and the Law* (1997) pp xxxviii–xxxix, and 65).

The difficulties posed by the process of statutory interpretation and the possible absence of any coherent policy objective are therefore relevant to the applicability of the economist's criteria, as defined by Sandford, to tax treatment of trusts. Before considering this in more detail, reference must be made to recent judicial developments which it is tempting to suggest appear to narrow the gap between the strict literalist approach of the lawyer to statutory interpretation and the more policy-oriented approach of the economist. Unfortunately judicial disarray, particularly in the House of Lords, concerning the correct approach for the courts to adopt in interpreting tax statutes renders illusory any hope of arriving at firm conclusions.

(2) Judicial response[s]

Occasionally the tax-avoidance methods recommended by the tax-planning industry, often involving highly artificial schemes, take on a complexity beyond the comprehension of many of its customers. Tax consultants may create a scheme which seeks to utilise certain provisions in a taxing statute in a series of transactions usually carried out via a number of steps with the sole or predominant purpose of reducing the client's tax bill. The schemes vary in complexity but their general nature was entertainingly described by Templeman LJ in *W T Ramsay Ltd v IRC* [1979] 3 All ER 213 at 215:

The facts . . . demonstrate yet another circular game in which the taxpayer and a few hired performers act out a play; nothing happens save that the Houdini taxpayer appears to escape from the manacles of tax.

The game is recognisable by four rules. First, the play is devised and scripted prior to performance. Secondly, real money and real documents are circulated and exchanged. Thirdly, the money is returned by the end of the performance. Fourthly, the financial position of the actors is the same at the end as it was in the beginning save that the taxpayer in the course of the performance pays the hired actors for their services. The object of the performance is to create the illusion that something has happened, that Hamlet has been killed and that Bottom did don an ass's head so that tax advantages can be claimed as if something had happened.

The audience are informed that the actors reserve the right to walk out in the middle of the performance but in fact they are the creatures of the consultant who has sold and the taxpayer who has bought the play; the actors are never in a position to make a profit and there is no chance that they will go on strike. The critics are mistakenly informed that the play is based on a classic masterpiece called 'The Duke of Westminster', but in that piece the old retainer entered the theatre with his salary and left with a genuine entitlement to his salary and to an additional annuity.

The finer details of most of these schemes happily need not concern us beyond noting two particular points. First, although many of the schemes involve the use of trustees, frequently located 'offshore' in a tax haven such as the Isle of Man, there is rarely any intention that they be impressed with any continuing obligations. To adopt an analogy with an earlier era, the trustees' role is passive rather than active. Second, the 'finer details' can render problematic the disclosure obligation which, it will be recalled, marks the border between evasion and avoidance. As mentioned above, avoidance schemes are rarely simple and usually incorporate several distinct legal transactions involving the use of separate companies, trustees and, sometimes, jurisdictions. It is here that what has been termed 'non-disclosing disclosure' – 'disclosing the relevant facts but doing so in a way which makes it difficult . . . to recognise the presence or extent of a taxable transaction' – can be effective (McBarnett (1991) 42 British Journal of Sociology 323 at 331). A corollary of the complexity of schemes therefore is that HMRC may find it difficult to fit the parts of the jigsaw puzzle together and thereby discover the underlying legal and economic substance of the arrangement. In one recent important case on tax avoidance, *IRC v McGuckian* [1997] 1 WLR 991, Lord Browne-Wilkinson notes that the solicitor/tax consultant 'took every step to obfuscate what had happened and obstruct the Crown in discovering the true facts' (at 994). In short, taxpayers and their advisers can quite lawfully be economical with the truth.

The success of 'off-the-peg' schemes involving a series of self-cancelling or circular transactions has been transitory. The Inland Revenue took the offensive and in a series of cases, *W T Ramsay Ltd v IRC* [1981] 1 All ER 865; *IRC v Burmah Oil Co Ltd* [1982] STC 30; and later *Ensign Tankers (Leasing) Ltd v Stokes* [1992] 2 All ER 275, persuaded the House of Lords to neutralise such schemes. The outcome of these decisions is that where a scheme involves a series of separate legal transactions – in *Ensign* the scheme comprised 17 documents all dated 14 July 1980 – the scheme should be viewed as a whole, the consequence of each separate transaction ignored and the position of the taxpayer in real terms be compared at the start and at the finish.

The relatively straightforward facts of a leading case *Furniss v Dawson* [1984] 1 All ER 530 illustrate both the potential scope of the new judicial approach and why it has provoked judicial disarray. It seemed that the *Ramsay* principle, as it came to be known, could apply even to schemes where some 'loose ends' were left trailing, inadvertently or otherwise, provided that the following two essential ingredients were present: (i) a pre-ordained series of transactions and (ii) the insertion of steps with no commercial *purpose* other than the avoidance of liability to tax although they may have a business *effect*. The Dawsons (D) owned a UK private company which they agreed to sell to another company called Wood Bastow Holdings for £152,000. They (D) wished to *defer* a large capital gains tax bill which a direct sale would have incurred. To facilitate this they formed an Isle of Man company, Greenjacket, and transferred all the shares in the UK company to Greenjacket in exchange for shares in Greenjacket. This type of share-for-share exchange was exempt from capital gains tax (see now Taxation of Chargeable Gains Act 1992, s 135(1)). Greenjacket then sold the UK company shares to Wood Bastow for £152,000. Greenjacket retained the purchase money while the taxpayers (D) retained their shares in Greenjacket. However, although the purchase money had not been directly channelled to D by the time of assessment to tax, the Inland Revenue was still able to argue successfully in the House of Lords that Greenjacket's role in the transaction should be disregarded. When this is done, all that remains is a straight sale by the taxpayers (D) to Wood Bastow Holdings. The House of Lords concluded that the series of transactions in *Furniss* were pre-ordained and should therefore be viewed as one composite transaction. Lord Brightman concisely described the process (at 538):

> [It] was planned and executed with faultless precision. The meetings began at 12.45 pm on 20 December, at which time the shareholdings of the operating companies were still owned by the Dawsons unaffected by any contract of sale. They ended with the shareholdings in the ownership of Wood Bastow. The minutes do not disclose when the meeting ended, but perhaps it was all over in time for lunch.

The insertion of Greenjacket into the process constituted the necessary second ingredient. Again to quote Lord Brightman (at 543):

> that inserted step had no business purpose apart from the deferment of tax, although it had a business effect. If the sale had taken place in 1964 before capital gains tax was introduced, there would have been no Greenjacket.

The significance of the cases referred to above is that they contrast sharply with earlier judicial approaches to tax avoidance schemes. (See Wheatcroft (1955) 18 MLR 209; Flesch (1968) CLP 215; Stevens *Law and Politics* (1979) and *The English Judges* (2002); Millett (1982) 98 LQR 209). Indeed in *Ramsay*, counsel for the taxpayer had argued that the new approach marked a reversal of long-established principles of interpretation of taxing statutes. Lord Wilberforce responded (*W T Ramsay Ltd v IRC* [1981] 1 All ER 865 at 873):

> [The approach] does not introduce a new principle: it would be to apply to new and sophisticated legal devices the undoubted power and duty of the courts to determine their nature in law and to relate them to existing legislation. While the techniques of tax avoidance progress and are technically improved, the courts are not obliged to stand still. Such inability must result either in loss of tax to the prejudice of other taxpayers, or to Parliamentary congestion or (most likely) to both. To force the courts to adopt, in relation to closely integrated situations, a step by step, dissecting, approach which the parties themselves may have negated, would be a denial rather than an affirmation of the true judicial process.

In *Furniss v Dawson* [1984] 1 All ER 530, Lord Scarman acknowledged in a clear if controversial opinion that the courts were indeed developing new principles (at 532):

> I am aware, and the legal profession (and others) must understand, that the law in this area is in an early stage of development. Speeches in your Lordships' House and judgments in the appellate courts are concerned more to chart a way forward between principles accepted and not to be rejected than to attempt anything so ambitious as to determine finally the limit beyond which the safe channel of acceptable tax avoidance shelves into the dangerous shallows of unacceptable tax evasion [sic].
>
> The law will develop from case to case. Lord Wilberforce in *Ramsay's* case referred to 'the emerging principle' of the law. What has been established with certainty by the House in *Ramsay's* case is that the determination of what does, and what does not, constitute unacceptable tax evasion is a subject suited to development by judicial process. Difficult though the task may be for judges, it is one which is beyond the power of the blunt instruments of legislation. Whatever a statute may provide, it has to be interpreted and applied by the courts and ultimately it will prove to be in this area of judge-made law that our elusive journey's end will be found.

Where the boundaries of the new approach will finally be set remains uncertain but there are two points to be emphasised here. First, Lord Scarman's application of the term 'evasion' appears to blur the traditional distinction between avoidance and evasion based on criminality. But in fact it reflects a judicial rejection of the conventional avoidance-evasion dichotomy and a recasting of the traditional categories to recognise the existence of 'unacceptable tax avoidance'. In *Ensign Tankers (Leasing) Ltd v Stokes* [1992] 2 All ER 275, Lords Goff and Templeman indicated that in their view a distinction could be drawn between, on the one hand, acceptable 'tax mitigation' – whereby the taxpayer takes advantage of the law to plan her financial affairs so as to minimise tax – and, on the other hand, 'unacceptable tax avoidance' characterised by Lord Goff (at 295) as involving:

> ... the creation of complex artificial structures by which, as though by the wave of a magic wand, the taxpayer conjures out of the air a loss, or a gain, or expenditure, or whatever it may be, which otherwise would never have existed.

The second point to emphasise about the developing law is that post-*Furniss v Dawson* cases have done little to dispel a general air of uncertainty about both the scope of the *Ramsay* principle and current judicial attitudes to tax avoidance. *Furniss* left open such issues as the degree of certainty or timing necessary for a scheme to be pre-ordained, and whether the insertion of a step which is predominantly but not exclusively for tax purposes would fall within the scope of the *Ramsay* principle. These specific considerations have tended to shade into the broader issue of where to draw the line between acceptable 'strategic tax planning' or 'mitigation' and unacceptable tax avoidance.

Sharp divisions of opinion have emerged within the judiciary about these issues (see the extra-judicial comments of Lord Templeman in Shipwright (ed) *Tax Avoidance and the Law* (1997) ch 1; and cf Lord Oliver in Gammie and Shipwright (eds) *Striking the Balance: Tax Administration, Enforcement and Compliance in the 1990s* (1996)). The majority opinions of the House of Lords in *Craven v White* [1988] STC 476 and *Fitzwilliam v IRC* [1993] STC 502, decisions which favoured the taxpayer, seemed to reflect concern at the potential breadth and uncertain limits of the *Ramsay* principle as interpreted in *Furniss v Dawson*. Lord Oliver, with whom Lords Keith and Jauncey agreed in *Craven v White*, was at pains to reject a general proposition that 'any transaction which is effected for the purpose of avoiding tax on a contemplated subsequent transaction and is therefore "planned" is, for that reason, necessarily to be treated as one with that subsequent transaction and as having no independent effect' (at 503).

The pendulum continued its momentum, initially swinging back again seemingly in support of the Revenue position in the 5:0 defeat for the taxpayer in the House of Lords in *IRC v McGuckian* [1997] 1 WLR 991 (see Hoyle [1997] BTR 312; Tiley [1997] All ER Rev 465). All five Law Lords concurred in the result whereby an attempt to avoid a charge to income tax (and possible liability under a proposed wealth tax) by reconstituting income (a receipt of dividends) as a capital receipt failed. In the view of all the judges the arrangements fell clearly within the *Ramsay* principle. That much is uncontentious, the particular scheme carrying many of the hallmarks of the other 1970s arrangements so successfully challenged by the Inland Revenue.

Interestingly, however, the speeches of Lords Steyn and Cooke implicitly called into question the approach adopted in *Craven v White* ('a difficult case' per Lord Cooke at 1005). Lord Steyn, for instance, reviewed the history of statutory interpretation of taxing statutes and concluded that Lord Wilberforce's speech (see above, p 89) in *Ramsay* marked an intellectual breakthrough: 'The new development was ... founded on a broad *purposive interpretation*, giving effect to the intention of Parliament.... And in asserting the power to examine the substance of a composite transaction the House of Lords was simply rejecting formalism in fiscal matters and choosing a more realistic legal analysis' (at 1000, emphasis added). Both Lords Steyn and Cooke also emphasised that the law was still in the process of being developed: '[It] is wrong to regard the decisions of the House of Lords since the *Ramsay* case as necessarily marking the limit of the law on tax avoidance schemes' (per Lord Steyn ibid, Lord Cooke at 1005; and cf Lord Scarman in *Furniss*, see above, p 89). It is not surprising that an Inland Revenue Consultation Paper on the possible introduction of a statutory general anti-avoidance rule (GAAR) incorporated to a considerable degree the *Ramsay* principle as restated in *McGuckian* (see Inland Revenue *A General Anti-Avoidance Rule for Direct Taxes* (1998) and cf the critical response by the Tax Law Review Committee *A General Anti-Avoidance Rule for Direct Taxes: A Response* (1999)).

A further swing of the pendulum subsequently occurred in *MacNiven v Westmoreland Investments Ltd* [2003] 1 AC 311 where a unanimous House of Lords found in favour of the taxpayer (see Tiley [2001] BTR 153–158). The House accepted the proposition that it was necessary to adopt a purposive approach when construing taxation legislation but chose to draw the line at adopting what it regarded as a broader formulation of 'purposive interpretation' put forward by leading counsel for the Inland Revenue. Lord Hoffmann commented that it did not look like a principle of construction but more like 'an overriding legal principle, superimposed upon the whole of revenue law without regard to the language or purpose of any particular provision.... This cannot be called a principle of construction except in the sense of some paramount provision subject to which everything else must be read.... But the courts have no constitutional authority to impose such an overlay upon the tax legislation...' ([2003] AC 311 at 325).

It would be tempting to conclude that two decisions of the House of Lords, *Barclays Mercantile Business Finance Ltd v Mawsons* [2004] UKHL 51 and *IRC v Scottish Provident* [2004] UKHL 52, reached on the same day by an identical panel, have finally laid doubts to rest. Unfortunately that is not so, and not simply because of the contrasting outcomes of the appeals, the former being decided in favour of the taxpayer whereas in the latter the Inland Revenue were successful. The cases reiterate the position set out by Lord Steyn in *McGuckian* that the *Ramsay* approach was founded on adopting a 'purposive interpretation' of taxing statutes and that whilst the case 'liberated the construction of revenue statutes from being both literal and blinkered' it did not 'introduce a new doctrine operating within the special field of [those] statutes' (per Lord Nicholls in *Barclays Mercantile* at paras 29 and 33 respectively). But stating that revenue law is concerned with interpreting statutes and that they must be interpreted purposively and taking account of their context is the easy conceptual step. The tricky part comes with answering the question 'whether the relevant provision of the statute, upon its true construction, applies to the facts as found' (Lord Nicholls op cit para 32). Discouraging though it may be to the reader seeking certainty, it is difficult to dissent from the following conclusions of Tiley, commenting on the Barclays *Mercantile* and *Scottish Provident* cases ([(2005] BTR 273 at 273–274):

> There is less intellectual chaos since there is agreement on basic principles.... However, this does not produce certainty since it is in the nature of questions of construction that there will be borderline cases about which people will have different views. *MacNiven* showed that there was no general overriding judicial anti-avoidance rule of law (or doctrine) to be applied like a principle of EC law. *Barclays Mercantile* shows that there is no general overriding judicial anti-avoidance approach to construction. *Scottish Provident* shows that the House of Lords are not going to use their new approach to take us back to the 1960s and 1970s. The major case law beginning with *Ramsay* and ending earlier in 2004 is all upheld; ... The new era is not a haven for tax planners.

The general outcome, as Tiley goes on to note, is that 'the judges have recovered control of the whole process' (at 280). This is neither the place nor the book for detailed discussion of how the judges might exercise this control but some tentative observations, if not conclusions, can be offered (for initial indications see *Astall v Revenue and Customs Commissioners* [2008] EWHC 1471; *Drummond v Revenue and Customs Commissioners* [2007] STC 682). First, it may be that the search for 'a bright line rule' to distinguish the acceptable from the unacceptable was always likely to prove fruitless in this context. Moreover, and self-evidently, there remains some uncertainty as to where the borderline is to be drawn between strategic tax planning, or tax mitigation as it is sometimes called (see below), and unacceptable tax avoidance.

Second, it has to be conceded that at least in part the uncertainty is not solely the result of conceptual complexity or scholarly disagreements over juristic matters. As mentioned above, it also reflects acute differences of opinion amongst the judiciary both as to the extent of their law-making function and where the balance should be struck between competing interests of the individual taxpayer, HMRC and indeed the generality of taxpayers. Whether the purposive construction approach will 'lead back to those eras in which judges are seen as particularly inclined towards a hostile, neutral or benevolent view of avoidance remains to be seen' (Tiley op cit at 280; see generally in addition to the previously cited sources Lord Templeman (2001) 117 LQR 575–588; Lord Walker (2004) 120 LQR 412–427; and on the broader implications see Mumford *Taxing Culture* (2002) ch 7; McFarlane and Simpson 'Tackling Avoidance' in Getzler (ed) *Rationalizing Property, Equity and Trusts* (2003); and the contrasting approaches of Freedman [2004] BTR 332–357; (2007) 123 LQR 53 and Simpson [2004] BTR 358–374). Of course, a state of uncertainty may of itself have a deterrent effect and inhibit the future development of artificial schemes.

Lastly, it is questionable whether it is still possible to view the *Ramsay* principle, whatever form it may finally take, as marking a step towards incorporating into a judicial definition of 'unacceptable tax avoidance' the key elements of the economist's definition – individual motivation and government objectives.

Lord Nolan in *IRC v Willoughby* [1997] STC 995 referred to the distinction between 'tax avoidance' and 'tax mitigation' in the following terms (at 1003):

> [T]he hallmark of tax avoidance is that the taxpayer reduces his liability to tax without incurring the economic consequences that Parliament intended to be suffered by any taxpayer qualifying for such reduction in his tax liability. The hallmark of tax mitigation, on the other hand, is that the taxpayer takes advantage of a fiscally attractive option afforded to him by the tax legislation, and genuinely suffers the economic consequences that Parliament intended to be suffered by those taking advantage of the option.

By contrast Lord Hoffmann in *MacNiven v Westmoreland Investments Ltd* [2003] 1 AC 311 doubted the usefulness of the distinction between avoidance and mitigation (at 335; see further Hoffmann [2005] BTR 197): 'The fact that steps taken for the avoidance of tax are acceptable or unacceptable is the conclusion at which one arrives by applying the statutory language to the facts of the case. It is not a test for deciding whether it applies or not.' The distinction may be insufficiently subtle to capture the precise nature of what should and what should not be permissible given the difficulty at times in determining what Parliament did intend (see section (c) below and Lord Walker (2004) 120 LQR 412 at 419–424 for an alternative categorisation). On the other hand, the distinction does have the merit of exposing the flaws in an even more simplistic dichotomy, that of juxtaposing 'evasion' and 'avoidance'.

(c) Trusts and tax avoidance: a résumé

The applicability of the *Ramsay* principle, whatever its final form, or of those key elements in the economist's definition of tax avoidance to an analysis of trusts practice still presents difficulties. The uncertainties concerning settlors' motivations have already been commented on (see p 75), but also, as we have previously hinted, government objectives are not always clearly or easily identifiable. There is many a slip 'twixt party conference resolutions and Finance Acts. The possible objectives of the tax system as regards trusts will be examined in detail in the next section but a brief example demonstrates the scope for ambiguity that exists with specific legislation.

A distinct gap in the structure of estate duty, a form of death duty which existed in the UK up to 1974, was the absence of a tax on inter vivos – ie lifetime – gifts. Gifts made more than a certain period before death paid no estate duty. In addition, before the Finance Act 1969 estate duty was not usually chargeable on the value of property in a discretionary trust when one of the beneficiaries died (see Hawkins [1968] BTR 351). How, therefore, should we categorise the act of a settlor who placed property into a discretionary trust more than seven years before his death? The settlor avoided estate duty liability on both his own and beneficiaries' future deaths, thereby retaining the value of the property largely intact for future generations. This obviously seems to constitute highly successful tax avoidance if it is assumed that the policy objective of estate duty is being frustrated. But is the assumption justified? As regards inter vivos gifts Sandford reviews a range of possible explanations and concludes (*Hidden Costs of Taxation* (1973) p 116):

> A reasonable interpretation would be that the gifts *inter vivos* provision was intended to prevent as many gifts as possible from circumventing estate duty. But the logic of such a policy and the only way to close the avoidance loophole satisfactorily is to introduce a general gift tax. The only logical reason for not having a gift tax would seem to be the problems and cost of administering it.

What then of the discretionary trust aspect of our example? Did the failure of Parliament effectively to impose estate duty on the beneficiaries of discretionary trusts mean that governments were unaware of the practice, or could devise no effective method for assessing and imposing liability, or perhaps were neutral or were even covertly approving of the practice? Indeed, the estate duty regime may have involved what Simons (*Personal Income Taxation* (1938)), criticising the US income tax system, called (at p 219):

> ...a subtle kind of moral and political dishonesty. One senses here a grand scheme of deception whereby enormous surtaxes are voted in exchange for promises that they will not be made effective. Thus the politicians may point with pride to the rates, while quietly reminding their wealthy constituents of the loopholes.

A more prosaic explanation is evident in the following comment from Lord Walker, writing extra-judicially: 'Both in complex anti-avoidance provisions and in other more specific taxing provisions, parliament sometimes seems a bit inclined to throw in its hand, when it comes to the precise limits of their operation, and to leave that to the courts to work out' ((2004) 120 LQR 412 at 425). The difficulty of identifying clear government objectives may inhibit any extensive application of the economist's approach to legislative interpretation. But in any event the direct effect of the *Ramsay* principle, even as extended in *Furniss v Dawson*, is likely to be of limited application to trusts practice. The doctrine represents, in the trusts context, a judicial move to neutralise short-term manipulation of the division of legal and beneficial ownership as part of a series of transactions whose sole or, possibly, predominant motive is to avoid tax. Even where prompted by fiscal considerations, most examples of the use of the trust device seem likely to be viewed as tax mitigation rather than unacceptable avoidance (see eg the controversial decision of the House of Lords in *Fitzwilliam v IRC* [1993] STC 502). Attempts to reduce Inheritance Tax liability by setting up a series of small discretionary trusts (see Chapter 8) or by so-called 'channelling activities' between spouses involving a very limited function for trustees may yet be attacked by HMRC but, to reiterate, the direct impact of the doctrine on 'active' trusts is likely to be limited.

Of greater relevance is the possibility that the courts will be encouraged, where competing interpretations of statutory language exist, to take more account of the broad policy objectives of specific fiscal legislation than may have been the case under a literalist approach to statutory interpretation (see *Inglewood v IRC* [1983] 1 WLR 366, and Chapter 8).

We have referred to the impact of the *Ramsay* principle in clarifying the meaning of tax avoidance and to its implications for litigation specifically involving interpretation of taxing statutes. There is also a more remote and less tangible aspect which relates to changes in judicial attitudes past and present. These changes remind us to be conscious of the absence of consistently homogeneous judicial views, in particular when considering the connection between tax law, trusts practice, and the development of the law of trusts. The hypothesis to be borne in mind therefore is that certain strands of this development cannot be satisfactorily understood within the boundaries of conventional trusts law doctrines, and that the courts were willing to sanction with varying degrees of alacrity certain changes in the law as a response to the needs of the users of trusts. This is not to claim that courts consciously favoured the taxpayer, indeed there are occasions when the opposite was demonstrably true (see *Re Weston's Settlement* Chapter 7 below, but cf the comments of Venables QC on the surprising majority opinions in *Fitzwilliam*: 'Their Lordships clearly had enormous sympathy with a landed aristocratic family seeking to preserve its estates' in Shipwright (ed) *Tax Avoidance and the Law* (1997) p 62). Rather we should consider how far the processes of litigation and judicial decision-making in those cases where the Inland Revenue (now HMRC) is *not* a party to the dispute have enabled the trust's flexibility of form to be developed anew without regard to wider-ranging fiscal issues possibly affectxing the economy as a whole. The speculative question remaining, therefore, is whether a putative recognition of 'unacceptable tax avoidance' in the sphere of tax litigation will, or should, spill over into the narrower realms of private trust litigation.

3. Taxes and the policies underlying them

(a) Purposes of taxation

Sandford's definition of tax avoidance has two elements, the taxpayer's motivation and the intention of the legislature. If analysis of this intention is to develop beyond merely reiterating in mantra-like fashion 'the intention of the legislature is what the language of the statute says it is', it is necessary to be aware of the objectives of a tax system. Before describing them and, also, what are termed the principles of a tax system, a word of warning is appropriate. Government policy on taxation is the object of much pressure-group activity – those seeking an internally consistent tax system based on rational argument are likely to be disappointed.

What we might call the old but classical analysis is that the sole function of taxation was to raise revenue to meet government expenditure. A contemporary and modified restatement of this position would be that 'the main reason government levies taxation is to provide for collective wants without creating inflation' (Sandford *Economics of Public Finance* (4th edn, 1992) p 111; and see generally Devereux *The Economics of Tax Policy* (1996)). Whilst the raising of revenue is a necessary function of taxation, it does not constitute a complete explanation of the purposes of a tax system. Taxation is also an instrument of economic policy. A realisation grew that at any constant given level of government expenditure increases in taxation would tend to reduce private demand for goods and services and counteract inflationary trends while decreases in taxation would tend to have the opposite effect. The effectiveness of Keynesian-inspired demand-management policies and the weight to be attached to fiscal rather than monetary measures of control has been extensively debated among both economists and politicians (see eg Worswick 'Fiscal Policy and Stabilization in Britain' in Cairncross (ed) *Britain's Economic Prospects Reconsidered* (1971); *Monetary Policy: Third Report from the Treasury and Civil Service Committee* 163 HC Official Report (1980–81); and generally James and Nobes *The Economics of Taxation* (8th edn, 2008) part 1). Indeed it is sometimes argued that fiscal changes have been motivated more by electoral considerations than demand-management ones – the so-called 'political business cycle' (see Nordhaus (1975) 42 Review of Economic Studies 169; Cullis and Jones *Public Finance and Public Choice* (2nd edn, 1998) ch 10). Nevertheless it is widely accepted that one function of taxation is to attempt to stabilise fluctuations in the economy. It can still just be claimed that the annual budget process is viewed 'not as a simple balancing of tax receipts against expenditure but as a sophisticated process in which the instruments of taxation and expenditure are used to influence the course of the economy' (Plowden Report *Control of Public Expenditure* 1961 (Cmnd 1432) para 10). Indeed the financial market and economic crises of 2008 have seen governments and economists scurrying to restore Keynesian analyses to the centre of economic policy making.

A tax system may also be used to pursue specific social policy objectives some with moral overtones – for example, to discourage the consumption of commodities such as tobacco or alcohol, or to encourage the growth of small businesses or altruism through giving to charity or generally to act as a regulatory instrument (see eg Ogus (1998) 61(6) MLR 767–788). These economic, national accounting and 'public goods' objectives of taxation form the backcloth to our immediate concern which is with a subsidiary, and political although no longer politically fashionable, objective of a tax system, that of redistribution of wealth. By redistribution is meant the conscious effort to alter the present structure of wealth-holding rather than the automatic redistributive consequences that inevitably accompany the workings of any tax system where a taxpayer does not derive a benefit in collective goods and services equivalent to the tax paid.

(b) Principles of taxation

There exists a variety of taxes that can be selected to achieve any or all of these objectives. For example, to further a policy of redistributing wealth by directly taxing wealth-holdings a Chancellor of the Exchequer could impose a once-and-for-all capital levy on the net wealth of an individual or family; or impose an annual wealth tax; or tax only when property is transferred by the wealth-holder during life or on death, or indeed any permutation of these measures. The choice of method need not, however, be arbitrary. The decision about type and level of taxation and the appropriate fiscal treatment for trusts can be guided by established principles, dating back at least to Adam Smith's 'canons of taxation' first published in the *Wealth of Nations* (1776). Such principles are, however, capable of differing interpretations as the following cautionary comment by Sandford indicates (*Economics of Public Finance* (4th edn, 1992) p 112):

> It is impossible to postulate entirely satisfactory principles. Public finance is very much a part of *political* economy and political and ethical judgements cannot be wholly excluded from any statement of tax principles. Moreover, the principles themselves do not comprise a single mutually consistent system; they conflict with each other. Any tax system represents some sort of practical compromise.

The principles relevant to an assessment of wealth distribution and tax treatments of trusts are vertical equity ('ability to pay'), horizontal equity ('equality of treatment'), certainty and neutrality.

(1) Vertical equity

This principle concerns the way different people with different taxable capacity should be taxed. It is widely argued that vertical equity requires that taxes should be levied according to ability to pay, or as is occasionally and bluntly stated, that those with the broadest backs should carry the greatest burden. Unfortunately this simple formulation of the principle conceals considerable diversity of opinion. When comparing taxation of rich and poor, does vertical equity require proportional taxation, by which rich and poor pay the same proportion of their income or wealth in taxation? Alternatively does it require progressive taxation, by which the rich pay at a proportionately higher rate than the poor? Application, for example, of the law of diminishing marginal utility to the commodity of money provides support for a principle of progressive taxation. But even if one accepts the argument for progressive taxation, an unresolved issue is how steeply progressive the tax rates should be; how much more, proportionately, should the rich be taxed than the poor? If vertical equity implies progressivity this inevitably involves subjective value judgments about ability to pay and this element of subjectivity attracted the powerfully expressed criticism that 'the moment you abandon . . . the cardinal principle of exacting from all individuals the same proportion of their income or property, you are at sea without rudder or compass, and there is no amount of injustice or folly you may not commit' (McCulloch *A Treatise on the Principles and Practical Influence of Taxation and the Funding System* (1863) p 145).

The criticism is presumably reinforced by the subsequent emergence of redistribution as a conscious objective of the tax system.

(2) Horizontal equity

In contrast with vertical equity, horizontal equity has the appearance of objectivity. It requires that taxpayers who are equal in all relevant circumstances should pay equal amounts of tax. The objective simplicity is deceptive because in practice views differ about the basis of the relevant circumstances. Disputants may argue, for instance, about whether a tax should take account of household composition, or whether the individual or the family should constitute the tax unit. But there are circumstances where horizontal equity is clearly violated. Kay and King's study succinctly identifies them (*The British Tax System* (5th edn, 1990) p 41):

> In practice, horizontal equity is most frequently violated when administrative arrangements are unsatisfactory; when tax impinges heavily on some transactions but can be avoided on others; when tax is paid principally by the honest, or those without effective tax advisers or the readiness to reorganize their affairs so as to minimize their liabilities; when borderlines between activities . . . cannot be satisfactorily defined. . . . [Inequities of this kind] arose to a scandalous extent with the old estate duty and this has been true also of capital transfer tax and inheritance tax.

(3) Certainty

Certainty is a quality desired by both taxpayer and government. For the taxpayer the impact of any tax should not be arbitrary and the taxpayer's liability should be calculable in advance of any transaction. For the government certainty implies the ability to predict the probable revenue from taxes levied. Ideally simplicity should accompany certainty; a tax system should be sufficiently simple for a taxpayer not to need extensive legal or accounting advice. But the practice rarely measures up to the ideal. Criticism of the complexity and obscurity of tax statutes has a venerable pedigree (see Monroe *Intolerable Inquisition? Reflections on the Law of Tax* (1981) ch 2).

Complexity is not due to the perversity of parliamentary draftsmen but results from several influences. One already mentioned is that fiscal legislation is subject to special pleading from pressure groups. More fundamentally, the complexity reflects two interrelated features of our contemporary society with which those responsible for implementing policy objectives via taxation must cope. First, there is the ingenuity of tax avoiders which has invited a legislative response designed to render avoidance more difficult. The response, respecting the literalist method of interpretation historically adopted by the courts, has invariably been detailed which itself then encourages tax advisers to delve for further loopholes. The result of this continuous contest has not been intelligibility of taxing statutes. The second endemic feature and its consequence was identified by Gladstone as early as 1853 in a debate on the Finance Bill (127 Official Report (4th series) col 723, 27 May 1853): 'the nature of property in this country, and its very complicated forms, rendered it almost impossible to deal with it for the purpose of income tax in a very simple manner'. The comment is equally applicable to subsequent additions to the list of taxes such as estate duty and capital gains tax. The outcome appears to be that certainty of tax liability can only be purchased at the cost of considerable complexity.

Criticisms of complexity, both past and present, led in 1995 to the introduction of the Tax Law Rewrite Project to redraft statutes on direct taxation in a clearer, more simplified form but without necessarily changing the substance of the law (see Inland Revenue *The Path to Tax Simplification* (1995); and generally Salter (1997) 16 CJQ 294; (1998) 19 Statute LR 65). At present four pieces of rewritten legislation, all concerned with Income Tax, have been enacted, with a rewritten Corporation Tax act to follow. It remains to be seen how far certainty and simplicity have either been achieved or are achievable (see Kerridge [2003] BTR 257; James [2008] BTR 392).

(4) Neutrality

This principle, which can also be termed 'economic efficiency', is that taxes should as far as possible avoid distortions of the market. In the context of tax and trusts the decisions of taxpayers to place property, for example, into trusts for children rather than make outright gifts to them should not be influenced by the size of the respective tax bills.

Neutrality appears to conflict with one objective of a tax structure previously mentioned, that of influencing behaviour in a particular direction, thereby distorting the operation of the market. In fact the conflict is more apparent than real since neutrality can be interpreted simply as requiring that distortions of free choice should reflect a conscious legislative policy. The consequence, as Kay and King note (*The British Tax System* (5th edn, 1990)), is that 'the neutral tax system, in effect, provides a bench-mark against which non-neutralities, intentional or otherwise, can be judged'.

(c) Tax structure

This section briefly outlines the current UK tax structure, concentrating on the distinction between taxes on capital and income and their significance relative to the total annual tax revenue.

(1) The source of government revenue

The principles of taxation just referred to do not dictate that any specific tax structure be adopted. As the Meade Committee Report (*The Structure and Reform of Direct Taxation* (1978)) indicates, a range of possible tax structures

Table 3.2 Taxation receipts

	1978–79£m	2007–08£m
Taxes on income		
Personal income (including		
National Insurance contributions)	32,246 (63.2%)	247,734 (54.9%)
Company income	2,692 (5.3%)	46,383 (10.3%)
Stamp duties	433 (0.8%)	14,124 (3.1%)
Taxes on capital		
Capital Transfer Tax and Inheritance Tax	360	3,824
Capital Gains Tax	353	5,268
Total of taxes on capital	713 (1.5%)	9,092 (2.0%)
Taxes on expenditure (eg VAT;		
excise duties)	14,948 (29.3%)	133,717 (29.6%)
TOTAL	51,032	451,050

Sources: Financial statement and budget report 1979–80; *HMRC Statistics* (2008) table T 1.2

exists, all of which are potentially compatible with the basic principles. Thirty years on from Meade a new review is being undertaken by the Institute for Fiscal Studies under the chairmanship of Sir James Mirrlees to 'identify the characteristics of a good tax system for any open developed economy in the 21st century' and to assess the UK tax system against these 'ideals' and produce realistic recommendations for reform. The full report is to be published during 2009 (see www.ifs.org.uk/mirrleesreview/).

Taxes in the UK are formally categorised in terms of three tax bases: income, capital and expenditure. Table 3.2 identifies the source of tax revenue for the years 1978–79 and 2007–08.

Two points can be made about the figures (not adjusted for inflation) in Table 3.2. First, the apparent continuity in the proportions attributable to taxes on income and expenditure (also termed 'direct' and 'indirect' taxes respectively) is slightly misleading in that in the intervening period these have fluctuated with, for instance, the proportion attributable to taxes on expenditure reaching almost 40% at one point. This reflected, to some extent, the contrasting philosophies of different governments. Second, taxes on personal income and expenditure remain the predominant sources of revenue. In contrast, taxes on transfers of capital now provide only around one-fiftieth of total revenue and as such are of little consequence for the objectives of raising revenue or influencing the level of economic demand. The contribution from taxation on companies is, of course, particularly sensitive to the state of demand in the economy and its effect on corporate profits.

Despite their limited revenue importance, taxes on transfer of capital are of considerable significance to us for two reasons. First, they are the taxes levied on inter-generational transfers of wealth, and have influenced developments in trusts practice and law particularly since 1945. Second, the limited potential contribution of capital taxes to total tax revenue does not mean that they are similarly inconsequential for patterns of wealth distribution. The role of trusts practice in limiting the impact of these taxes and facilitating the continuing importance of inherited wealth is considered further below, p 108 et seq.

(2) Capital and income: a problem of definition

The terms 'income' and 'capital' do not have universally accepted definitions and, in particular, legal and economic definitions are at variance (see eg Holmes *The Concept of Income: A Multi-disciplinary Analysis* (2001)). As regards income, it has been said (*Kay and King* p 96) that:

> . . . it may seem too trite to observe that to operate an income tax it is necessary to have a clear definition of what constitutes 'income', but the sad truth is that no single definition of income commands universal assent.

There is, in fact, no statutory definition of income. The statutes enacted under the Tax Law Rewrite Project identify various sources and descriptions of sums of money to be taxed on an annual basis, but the sources are not exhaustive. Numerous examples of increases in a taxpayer's financial resources during a tax year fall outside the scope of the Act. Football pools, lottery or other gambling winnings are not classified as taxable income, nor are increases in the value of a taxpayer's capital assets such as shareholdings. The limited concept of income adopted for UK income tax contrasts with an economist's widely accepted definition of what is called 'comprehensive income'. Simons (*Personal Income Taxation* (1938) p 50) defined personal income as being:

> . . . the algebraic sum of (a) the market value of rights exercised in consumption and (b) the change in value of the store of property rights between the beginning and end of the period in question.

Severe administrative and valuation difficulties would hamper the use of this definition for tax assessment purposes (see Meade Committee *The Structure and Reform of Direct Taxation* (1978) ch 7), but the limited statutory definition also creates difficulties. It may become fiscally attractive to turn taxable investment income into non-taxable increases in the capital value of the income-producing assets. The problem is demonstrated by the following extremely simple example in the Meade Report (p 30):

> Consider two Government bonds both of which are issued at a price of £100, the difference being that on bond A the government undertakes to pay no interest but to redeem the bond at a price of £110 in a year's time, whereas on bond B the government undertakes to redeem the bond at its issue price of £100 in a year's time but meanwhile to pay £10 in interest on its borrowing. Is there no income but only gain in capital value on bond A, while there is income but no capital gain on bond B?

An attempt was made to counter this obvious gap in the tax structure and thereby to redress the balance between competing concepts of income by introducing a capital gains tax in 1965. In principle the object of this form of tax is to place on an equal footing assets such as A and B in the above example. A capital gains tax can be levied on an annual accrual basis, taxing the appreciation in asset values each year, or on a realisation basis, taxing the increase in value between the dates of acquisition and disposal. The UK version is a 'realisation' tax and stands on the borderline between income and capital taxation. Notwithstanding changes to tighten the scope of capital gains tax since 1965, there remain some circumstances where it is advantageous for the taxpayer to attempt to transmute income into capital (see eg *IRC v McGuckian* [1997] 1 WLR 991). Distinguishing between income and capital therefore still retains its importance for tax law, and also for trusts law because the conceptual confusion has left its imprint on the law governing trustees' duties of investment and impartiality (see Chapter 10).

Thus it is difficult to sustain a rigid distinction between concepts of income and capital, and even a tax on capital does not require that the tax be paid out of a stock of capital by disposing of assets. It merely indicates that the tax is assessed on the capital value of property. The tax itself may be paid out of the taxpayer's income, although a steeply progressive form of capital taxation based on the principle of vertical equity with wealth redistribution as its objective might well necessitate the disposal of capital assets.

Arguments based on vertical equity do not, however, provide the sole justification for capital taxes. A further consequence of the limited definition of income applicable to UK income tax is to strengthen a horizontal equity argument for capital taxation. As the then Chancellor Denis Healey expressed the point in the Green Paper on a proposed wealth tax (Cmnd 5704 (1974) p iii):

> ... income by itself is not an adequate measure of taxable capacity. The ownership of wealth, whether it produces income or not, adds to the economic resources of a taxpayer so that a person who has wealth as well as income of a given size necessarily has a greater taxable capacity than one who has only income of that size.

(3) Taxation of capital

The main possible forms of capital taxation are summarised in Figure 3.1 below (derived from figure 9.1 in Sandford *Economics of Public Finance* (4th edn, 1992) p 215).

In the UK at present there are no taxes on wealth stock, although proposals for an annual wealth tax have been considered (see *Select Committee on a Wealth Tax* (HC Paper (1975) no 696–1; see also Boadway et al *Taxation of Wealth and Wealth Transfers* (2009) (www.ifs.org.uk/mirrleesreview/reports/wealth_transfers.pdf)). A capital levy is usually perceived as being an occasional or, indeed, once-only measure.

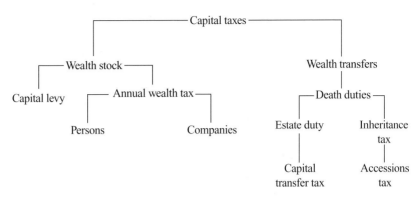

Figure 3.1 Capital taxes

In contrast, taxes on wealth transfer have a long lineage in the UK (see Chapter 2). Modern death duties have their origin in the Stamp Act 1694 and have an unbroken existence since. Death duties have proved a popular form of capital taxation with governments for essentially practical reasons. Valuation of assets is a major administrative difficulty for capital taxes but the problem is much reduced with death duties since only about 12 people in every 1,000 die each year. Valuation of the deceased person's assets is required in most circumstances for the administration of the deceased's estate. In addition to administrative convenience it can be argued that a death duty has a special attraction compared with other forms of capital taxation in that it taxes inherited wealth. The assumption is that there is less moral justification for inherited wealth than for that earned by an individual's own efforts. (Cf the contrasting views of Mumford 'Inheritance in Socio-Political Context' (2007) 34(4) JLS 567–593 and Bracewell-Milnes *Is Capital Taxation Fair?* (1974) and *Euthanasia for Death Duties: Putting Inheritance Tax out of its Misery* (2003).)

A duty imposed on death can be of a mutational or acquisitional character. A mutation duty, or estate duty, is in principle calculated according to the value of property changing hands on death irrespective of the destination of the property under the will or laws of intestacy. An acquisition duty or inheritance tax is calculated on the value of the benefit received by those entitled to the property on death irrespective of the size of the deceased's estate. A capital transfer tax and an accessions tax are respectively versions of estate duty and inheritance tax but incorporating lifetime gift taxes.

Before 1949 variants of both estate duty and inheritance taxes were to be found in the UK, but the latter were then repealed. In 1974 capital transfer tax (CTT) replaced estate duty. In 1986 substantial changes were introduced to CTT including renaming it, wholly misleadingly, as inheritance tax. It must be stressed that this inheritance tax is a form of estate duty (closely resembling the pre-1974 estate duty regime), and *not* an inheritance tax as described above.

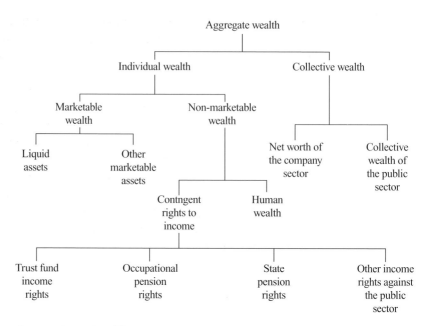

Figure 3.2 Forms of wealth

4. Taxation and redistribution

(a) Introduction

It is beyond the scope of this book to discuss whether existing wealth distribution is just or unjust and whether it should be altered. Instead it is accepted as a premise that redistribution on grounds of vertical equity has at various times, even if not now, been claimed to be a public policy objective. The more limited questions then to be assessed are how far large wealth-holdings are concentrated in trusts and whether the trust has been a significant contributing factor in frustrating redistributive policies. We do this in section 5 below. But to answer these questions adequately we need to know something about (1) the present concentration of wealth-holding and the persistence of inequality over time; and (2) the factors responsible for the persistence of inequality. We therefore consider these two issues in that order in this section. The process, however, is hampered by conceptual disagreements and statistical uncertainty. A particular difficulty to be confronted first is that the term 'wealth' permits a variety of definitions. There is, for instance, a distinction to be drawn between marketable and non-marketable wealth (see Figure 3.2 and for a detailed analysis see Royal Commission on Distribution of Income and Wealth (RCDIW) *Report No 5* (Cmnd 6999, 1977). Marketable wealth is usually considered as the most relevant measure for evaluating wealth distribution since it is closely linked to immediate command over economic resources. But it can be argued that even that measure fails to take account of all the potential benefits of wealth.

Hobhouse (in Gore (ed) *Property: Its Duties and Rights* (1913) p 10) claimed that ownership of property has two functions: 'the control of things, which gives freedom and security, and the control of persons through things which gives power to the owner'.

Property-power can take the form of corporate power through the ownership or control of stocks and shares, and political power through control of productive assets and employment strategies of companies. For trust users, however, the security associated with property interests is an equally compelling value. Security here extends beyond straightforward economic entitlement to income or capital, and can be claimed to incorporate notions of protection, protection, that is, against too easy an incursion by the state into property-based entitlement (see Cotterrell (1987) 14 J Law and Society 77 at 87–88). As will be seen in Chapter 8, the weight to be attached to perceptions of property as security may become important when tax statutes and property concepts intermingle. Inevitably, a quantitative analysis of wealth-holding can give no estimate of the benefits, if any, to be derived from such elusive properties as power and security.

(b) Wealth distribution and the importance of inherited wealth

Estimating wealth-holding in the UK is a complex statistical exercise producing somewhat uncertain results. A description of the basic method used, the estate multiplier method, and a review of criticisms of it are contained in a report by the RCDIW (*Report No 5* (Cmnd 6999, 1977) App C). Suffice to say here that there is no annual valuation of a taxpayer's wealth and that the main source for estimating wealth-holding is data collected by HMRC in administering inheritance tax.

Table 3.3 demonstrates historical trends in the distribution of marketable personal wealth. Different assumptions as to the appropriate definition of wealth would provide different wealth distribution statistics. For example in 1995 the estimated share of the top 1% of wealth-holders was 19% but if the values of occupational pension rights and state pension rights were to be included the figures would be reduced to 14% and 11% respectively. On the other hand if ownership of housing is excluded the results are even more skewed – for example, the shares of the most wealthy 1%, 5%, 10% and 25% increase to 33%, 58%, 72% and 86% respectively – suggesting that housing wealth is more evenly distributed.

Official Inland Revenue/HMRC estimates are only available for the period from 1960 onwards. For earlier years reference has been made to the study carried out by Atkinson and Harrison (1978). The basis for their figures is not wholly compatible with that for present HMRC estimates; consequently only general conclusions can be drawn about long-term trends. Despite this the main trend is striking. There occurred a substantial reduction in the share of total personal wealth of the top 1% of adult wealth-holders over the whole period, although until recently that share had remained almost constant for two

Table 3.3 Trends in the distribution of personal wealth of total adult population: selected years 1923–2003

	Top 1%	Top 5%	Top 10%	Top 20%
1923	60.9	82.0	89.1	94.2
1938	55.0	76.9	85.0	91.2
1950	47.2	74.3	–	–
1959	41.4	67.6	–	–
1960	33.9	59.4	71.5	83.1
1966	30.6	55.5	69.2	83.8
1972	31.7	56.0	70.4	84.9
1976	24.9	46.2	60.6	77.6
1979	20	37	50	–
1988	17	37	50	–
1995	19	38	50	73 (Top 25%)
2003	21	40	53	72 (Top 25%)

Sources: Atkinson and Harrison (1978); RCDIW *Report No 7* (Cmnd 7595, 1979) Tables 4.4 and 4.5; *HMRC Statistics* (2007) Table 13.5

decades. The apparent sharp reduction in wealth concentration between 1959 and 1960 is misleading and reflects a change in the method of collecting data from estates then.

Such statistical quirks apart, it is tempting to attribute the reduction in wealth concentration to high and effective rates of estate duty and income tax, but the inference to be drawn from the statistics is a subject of acute controversy (see Polanyi and Wood *How Much Inequality?* (1974); Atkinson and Harrison *Distribution of Personal Wealth in Britain* (1978); RCDIW *Report No 1: Selected Evidence* (Cmnd 6171, 1975)).

The decline in the share of the top 1% must inevitably be accompanied by a corresponding improvement in the shares of some groups lower down the wealth scale. But critics of the effectiveness of redistributive policies argue that, if housing is stripped out of the figures, the decline in inequality has been much less than a concentration on the share of the top 1% might suggest (see eg Harbury and Hitchens *Inheritance and Wealth Inequality in Britain* (1979); on the importance of investment in company securities for the top 1% of wealth-holders see Banks et al in Hill (ed) *New Inequalities* (1998) ch 13; Stark *A-Z of Income and Wealth* (1988)).

A 1973 RCDIW survey (*Report No 5*, Cmnd 6999) provides tentative support for the hypothesis that, despite an apparent trend towards greater equality in the distribution of wealth among individuals, distribution of wealth on a family basis has been largely untouched. The survey of a sample of estates valued in excess of £15,000 'confirms that inheritance operates primarily to retain wealth within the circle of relatives' (para 3.85).

But the fact that acquisition of wealth via inheritance is largely restricted to immediate family relationships tells us nothing about the value of inherited wealth relative to the value of personal wealth as a whole. The RCDIW survey estimated that total transmitted or inherited wealth accounted for about 25% of total wealth. Further support for the opinion that inheritance has played and continues to play the leading role in maintaining wealth inequalities comes from Harbury and Hitchens (*Inheritance and Wealth Inequality in Britain* (1979)). Their empirical study based on samples of rich males dying in 1956–57, 1965 and 1973 and rich women dying in 1973 cautiously concluded (at p 131) that:

> ... it is not too far from the truth that something between two-thirds and four-fifths of those who died rich in the third quarter of the present century owed their wealth to inheritances and the rest to entrepreneurship and luck.

They add (at p 136):

> ... it is difficult to avoid the conclusion that inheritance has been the most important single source of wealth inequality in the fairly recent past in twentieth-century Britain.

In the absence of firm data, it is not possible to advance any conclusions about the consequences of the uneven performance of the UK economy since the mid-1970s for the relative importance of inherited wealth. Whereas such familiar names as Branson, Sugar, Bowie and McCartney now feature in lists of the richest individuals in Britain, such evidence as does exist indicates that the impact of inheritance as a source of wealth remains unimpaired (see eg Dearden, Machin and Reed 'Intergenerational Mobility in Britain' (1997) 107 Economic Journal at 47–66; Rowlingson et al *Wealth in Britain: A Lifecycle Perspective* (1999)).

(c) Estate duty: a voluntary tax?

This importance of inherited wealth reflects the fact that estate duty, the tax apparently most directed towards breaking up concentrations of wealth, became extremely easy to avoid. Indeed 'whenever a particularly large estate is reported in the press with the duty paid representing between 60 per cent and 80 per cent of the value of the estate, the deceased is regarded as eccentric' (Revell *The Wealth of the Nation* (1967) p 110).

In fact, as the estate duty returns demonstrate and the Sandford survey of accountants suggests (see p 78), many taxpayers did not seek to avoid estate duty. At the same time there existed numerous methods for those who wished to avoid or mitigate the burden of the tax. Sandford (*Taxing Personal Wealth* (1971) pp 80–89), for instance, in a review of the principal methods of avoidance estimated that the duty forgone was at least 50% of the actual estate duty yield. (See also Horsman (1975) 85 Economic Journal 516.) Our interest lies in particular with a combination of two of those methods, the trust and the lifetime gift.

The most obvious and simple way of avoiding estate duty was to transfer property before death – by a gift inter vivos. To prevent the absurdity of death-bed transfers avoiding estate duty, tax law treated gifts made within a certain period before death as passing at death. The period, initially three months, was gradually extended up to seven years but provided the donor survived for that period no duty was payable. Assuming the donor still had a considerable life expectancy, the outside risk of estate duty liability could be countered by insuring the donor's life.

Outright gifts suffer from the disadvantage that control over the property is lost. One attraction of the trust is that the beneficiaries' control over income and capital can be restricted while, potentially, the settlor's influence can be indirectly retained. Under an inter vivos settlement the provisions for imposing estate duty on the settlor who failed to survive for the necessary period were the same as for outright gifts. The advantage of using the trust lay in the potential for minimising future incidence of estate duty liability. In general an interest in a trust fund attracted estate duty only when the person who was the beneficial owner of the interest died. Where, however, a beneficiary had no enforceable claim as an individual on the income or capital of the fund, as with a discretionary trust, then no definable interest passed on the death of a beneficiary and no estate duty could be levied. It was to counter the perceived weakness of estate duty as a counter-weight to wealth concentrations that the Labour Government in 1974 introduced capital transfer tax, a combination, it will be recalled, of a lifetime gifts tax and estate duty. Its decline and demise are considered further in Chapter 8.

5. Trusts and wealth concentration

(a) A statistical gap: identifying the numbers and size of trusts

Any attempt to assess the extent to which the trust was used to avoid estate duty is hampered by a lack of information about wealth held in non-dutiable trusts. Estate duty statistics relating to the 1940s and 1950s for example suggested a decline in the importance of settled property relative to total dutiable property. These statistics, however, referred to dutiable trusts only and omitted two potentially important forms of settled property, the discretionary trust and the surviving spouse settlement. One possible explanation therefore for the apparent decline in the importance of settled property is that there was a substantial movement out of dutiable settlements into exempt settlements such as discretionary trusts. Indeed this might seem a rational response by wealth-holders to sharp increases in the rates of estate duty that occurred during this period. There is, however, no firm statistical evidence to support this supposition. Indeed it is in the very nature of things that evidence about exempt settled property is hard to come by. As Revell noted ('Settled Property and Death Duties' [1961] BTR 177 at 180–181):

> *The practical problem*
> This mixture of statistical evidence and pure speculation is all that we have to go on in arriving at some estimate of the amount of settled property which is necessarily missing when one computes total wealth in the beneficial ownership of individual persons from the death duty statistics. Short of a complete census of all personal trusts it seems, indeed, that nobody can know the whole picture....

Little has changed at least as regards the property arrangements of the very wealthy. A survey conducted for HMRC in 2007 indicated that 'The complexity of their arrangements was seen as potentially militating against establishing reliable financial data' (Barnard et al *Researching the Very Wealthy* (2007) p 18). Nevertheless another study by Revell, based on a sample of corporate trustees and internal assessment by the Inland Revenue, attempted to remedy some of these deficiencies in information. His findings and other analyses which chart the rise in the popularity of trusts, in particular discretionary trusts, during the 1960s and early 1970s led the Inland Revenue to the following conclusion in its evidence to the Select Committee on the Wealth Tax ((1975) Evidence App 118 at para 15).

> There is firm evidence that the numbers of discretionary and accumulating trusts have increased very substantially in the period from 1960 to 1972, and what evidence exists on capital values, although subject to large margins of error, indicates a considerably faster growth than would be shown simply by the increases in market values. It can be concluded that but for the existence of such settlements there would have been a more marked reduction in the concentration of wealth.

According to later Inland Revenue estimates, by 1975 there existed some 310,000 non-discretionary trusts, or interest in possession trusts as they are now called, and 90,000 discretionary trusts with total capital values of £8.3 billion and £8.5 billion respectively, ie 6% of total personal wealth (Inland Revenue *CTT and Settled Property: A Consultation Document* (1980) App 1). However, if the hypothesis that users of trusts are sensitive to the prevailing fiscal climate is valid, then the introduction of CTT in 1974 could be expected to have resulted in a shift out of those trusts which were potentially most vulnerable to the new tax.

Subsequent studies, although still constrained by the statistical difficulty of identifying the number and value of trusts, indicate that the anticipated shift occurred. The most recent available detailed study, conducted by Robson and Timmins for the Inland Revenue, indicated that by 1988 the number of UK-resident discretionary trusts and interest in possession trusts had fallen to approximately 55,500 and 203,000 respectively (*Discretionary Trusts* (1988)). More recent estimates indicate a reversal in the relative popularity of different trust types, with the number of discretionary trusts increasing to an estimated 107,000 whereas the number of interest in possession trusts has fallen to 88,500 (*HMRC Statistics 2008*, Table 13.2). In addition, it was estimated by Robson and Timmins that there were some 7,000 overseas trusts potentially within the scope of UK tax laws, a development positively encouraged by the suspension of exchange control in 1979. The emphasis here is on 'potentially' as it is extremely difficult to determine the full extent of wealth held, often in trusts, offshore (see eg global estimates made by the Tax Justice Network *The Price of Offshore* (2005)).

The number of trusts tells us nothing about the value of assets held within them or the income accruing to those assets. As regards the latter, the total reported income of trusts liable to UK income tax in 2005–06 was £2.6 billion, £1.25 and £1.35 billion for respectively discretionary trusts and income in possession trusts. The data for assets is less certain, the latest recorded year for any data being 2001–02 and then only for discretionary trusts when the nominal value of assets was estimated at £21 billion (*Inland Revenue Statistics 2004* Table 13.3).

(b) Attributing beneficial ownership in trust funds

Estimating the number and total value of trusts, and discretionary trusts in particular, does not resolve all the statistical uncertainties. Two important problems remain: (1) the attribution of ownership of trust funds, and (2) their importance for top wealth-holders relative to other forms of property. The method adopted by the Inland Revenue in attributing beneficial ownership of property within discretionary trusts is described by Dunn and Hoffman:

'The Distribution of Personal Wealth' *Economic Trends* (1978) no 301 p 101 at 110–111

Allocation of excluded wealth

Discretionary trusts
These can be subdivided into:

a. Accumulation and maintenance trusts
b. Other discretionary trusts

The former are for the benefit of minors to whom they have been attributed. The treatment of other discretionary trusts is more difficult. The benefits of these trusts are allocated by the trustees at their discretion so that it is difficult to specify to whom they should be attributed. On the other hand, to adopt a 'legalistic' viewpoint and attribute them to nobody but simply to the personal sector as a whole would give a picture of the distribution of personal wealth which is scarcely realistic.

In order to add [the estimated figures on the numbers and size of these trusts] into the wealth estimates it is necessary to consider two sets of assumptions;

i. the average number of beneficiaries per settlement;
ii. the nature of the joint distribution of settled property and identified wealth.

It is crudely estimated that, on average, accumulation and maintenance trusts can be attributed to two beneficiaries and other discretionary trust property to four beneficiaries.

These assumptions were used to calculate two sets of estimates, labelled *a* and *b*. Of these, *a* implies that the beneficiaries have no other wealth – which assumption will minimise inequality of wealth – whilst *b* was chosen to maximise inequality by attributing the largest trusts, where possible, to the richest owners of free estate.

For accumulation and maintenance trusts the problem of making assumptions on basis *b* was simplified by the almost complete absence of large holdings of free estate by minors in the estimates of identified wealth.

The allocation of the property in other discretionary trusts is more difficult.

The allocation of holders of other discretionary trust property to the highest wealth ranges is again constrained by the relatively small numbers there. A third (and very extreme) assumption has been tested – that each trust benefited one person. But the effect of this was almost identical with that of basis *b*. The estimates shown in all relevant tables take the average of bases *a* and *b*.

The difficulty of drawing firm conclusions from the data is compounded by the fact that the statistics refer to individual rather than family wealth. Robson and Timmins, for instance, find that between one-quarter and one-third of discretionary trusts had beneficiaries in the second generation of a family (ie grandchildren) but none in the current or first succeeding generations. This is not surprising since the trust is an ideal vehicle for such 'generation-skipping' transfers, as they are termed, one consequence of which is to facilitate wealth redistribution although predominantly on an inter-generational family basis.

Nevertheless tentative conclusions can be drawn about the importance of trusts for individual wealth holdings. According to RCDIW *Report No 7* (App D) the value of discretionary and surviving spouse trusts was 3.9% of total personal marketable wealth in 1975. But the wealth held in those trusts, particularly in discretionary trusts, was concentrated among top wealth-holders. From the Inland Revenue data presented by Dunn and Hoffman, it is possible to estimate for 1975 the proportional significance of non-dutiable trusts for personal wealth (see Table 3.4).

The concentration is even more significant for those with personal marketable wealth in excess of £100,000 in 1975, then comfortably within the top 0.5% of wealth-holders. The figures for discretionary trusts, accumulation and maintenance trusts and surviving spouse settlements rise to 10.5%, 3.3% and

Table 3.4 'Non-dutiable trusts' as percentage of total personal wealth of top 1% of wealth holders in 1975

	Percentages	£ billion
Discretionary trusts	7.9	4.6
Accumulation and maintenance	2.5	1.5
Surviving spouse	6.4	3.8
Total	16.8	9.9

Source: Dunn and Hoffman *Economic Trends* (1978) no 301 tables A and B

9.8% (total 23.5%) respectively. It is simply not known whether these percentages or something near them are currently applicable. Robson and Timmins do not attempt to attribute beneficial ownership in the discretionary trusts covered by their 1988 research. Their study does demonstrate, however, that the distribution of trusts by asset value and income is, as with wealth-holding generally, highly skewed (*Discretionary Trusts* (1988) para 1.5). Thus 41% of the total income and 43% of the total assets of discretionary trusts were accounted for by slightly fewer than 3% of such trusts. This picture of a concentration of assets is broadly confirmed by Inland Revenue/HMRC data based on returns from trustees of discretionary trusts that are liable to a ten-yearly 'periodic charge' to Inheritance Tax (see Chapter 8). Thus for 2006–07, the latest year for which reasonably reliable statistics are available, 67.3% of assets were held in 16.7% of discretionary trusts (*HMRC Statistics 2008* Table 12.7).

6. Conclusion

The object of this chapter has been to introduce, in approximately equal measure, the motivations of those who create trusts, some interpretations of tax avoidance, basic principles and objectives of taxation and available statistical evidence on the impact of trusts on wealth distribution. The focus on wealth distribution has led us to emphasise the role of trusts in potentially countering the incidence of death duties and gift taxes. But it must not be overlooked that, for many, transferring property into trusts has had an equally important role historically in minimising their potential exposure to income tax liability (see eg the research by Stopforth [1990] BTR 225; [1991] BTR 86; [1992] BTR 88.

There is, however, a further dimension to the interplay between trusts and taxation which merits comment here, that is the role of lawyers. In both the previous and current chapters we have sought to emphasise the creative role of the lawyer in shaping the law from the bottom up, rather than just acting as a conduit for predetermined rules (see Lempert (1976) 2 Law and Society Review 173; Zemans (1983) 77 Am Pol Sci Rev 690). In the context of taxation, this role can involve more than passively acquainting clients with the fiscal consequences of a proposed course of action. In addition, lawyers, and indeed competing professionals such as accountants, can actively manipulate legal concepts, statutory language and rules of statutory interpretation in a fashion that operates within the letter but against the spirit of the law (see McBarnett (1991) 42 Br J Soc 323, and 'It's Not What You Do but the Way That You Do It' in Downes (ed) *Unravelling Criminal Justice* (1992)). The process of 'creative compliance', the term coined by McBarnett and her colleague Dr Whelan, is particularly apposite to an area such as tax law where, as we saw, certainty has since Adam Smith been regarded as a prime virtue. But certainty tends to encourage detailed prescriptive rules and, as McBarnett points out, 'creative compliance operates particularly effectively in the context of a rule-bound regime, where the words of the law can be treated as recipes for avoidance' ('When Compliance is not the Solution but the Problem' in Braithwaite (ed) *Taxing Democracy* (2003) pp 229–243 at p 230).

This perception of the nature of the lawyer's role in structuring the relationship between taxpayer and HMRC raises contentious issues. One issue, of course, is that schemes can 'go wrong'. Then creativity can turn out not to be risk free. In a controversial criminal prosecution, *R v Charlton* [1996] STC 1418, CA, a number of tax professionals were convicted – and imprisoned – on charges of producing false accounts to the Inland Revenue (criticised by Venables QC in Shipwright (ed) *Tax Avoidance and The Law* (1997) pp 23, 28–45; but for another view Bridges [1998] NLJ 118 at 185 and 219; see also Simser (2008) 11(2) JMLC 123–134 on the profits and perils for professionals involved in 'offshore schemes'). Yet here also 'creative compliance' by its very nature of purporting to comply with the letter of the law 'can claim to be "not illegal", to be quite distinct from non-compliance' (McBarnett in Braithwaite (ed), ibid, p 232). A related issue, although again only of indirect relevance to us, concerns the place of ethics in tax avoidance. In devising a tax avoidance scheme, or advising on its effectiveness, does the lawyer owe any obligation to anyone or any interest beyond that which is unquestionably owed to the client (see generally Cranston (ed) *Legal Ethics and Professional Responsibility* (1995) ch 1)? A more fundamental point, and one directly relevant to this chapter, concerns the implications of the creative role for the design and operation of the tax system. In particular it touches on the question as to whether the legislature should seek to provide for specificity in taxing statutes, with the possible opening up of a path to circumvention in the ways described earlier in this chapter, or opt for generality with a consequent reliance on judicial interpretation and HMRC practice to fill in the gaps.

One mode of generality that the government has decided not to pursue at least for the present is the enactment of comprehensive anti-avoidance legislation in the form of a General Anti-Avoidance Rule (GAAR). Instead an alternative measure to counter what the government perceives as tax avoidance rather than tax mitigation was introduced in the Finance Act 2004, ss 19 and 306–319, and to a large degree focuses on the professionals who devise and market tax avoidance schemes (see Fraser [2004] BTR 4 at 282–296 and [2004] BTR

5 at 454–459; and for further developments see Bland [2006] BTR 653; Oats and Salter [2008] BTR 505 and the Tax Avoidance Schemes Regulations, SI 2004/1863; SI 2004/1864; SI 2004/1865; SI 2006/1543). Radical new provisions have been put in place intended to elicit information about the arrangements taxpayers enter into that are designed to, or have the effect of, reducing their tax liabilities. The new rules require 'promoters' (s 307) of tax schemes to disclose to HMRC any arrangements where 'the main benefit, or one of the main benefits, that might be expected to arise from the arrangements' is the obtaining for their clients of a tax advantage, a term defined widely so as to incorporate relief or deferral of tax or the avoidance of any obligation to deduct or account for any tax (s 319). The new disclosure rules are designed to provide HMRC with advance information about potential tax avoidance schemes and arrangements so that, where appropriate, speedy anti-avoidance legislation can be implemented (see generally www.hmrc.gov.uk/avoidance/vision-strategy.htm for details of such measures introduced as a result of the operation of the new disclosure rules). It remains to be seen what effect this new approach allied to improved clarity and accuracy in tax statutes as a result of the Tax Law Rewrite Project will have on the tax avoidance industry.

Final conclusions, however, on all the above issues are better deferred until the more detailed examination of the taxation of trusts has been undertaken in Chapter 8. Here we simply pose for an interim assessment some problems suggested by the material.

(1) Why do people set up trusts?
(2) Is it misconceived to describe use of the discretionary trust under the estate duty regime as 'tax avoidance'? Consider this in particular in the context of the suggestion that 'the legislature in Great Britain has, possibly unconsciously, felt unable to close the loopholes in the tax structure since it was politically undesirable to reduce the rates' (Wheatcroft 'Proposals for a System of Estate and Gift Taxation – II' [1964] BTR 283 at 296).
(3) 'The claim that the trust has been a major force in frustrating redistributive policies rests largely on assertion and is not supported by the available evidence.' Do you agree? Does the evidence from the RCDIW and the data available to HMRC refute the further claim that the trust is an effective wealth-concealment mechanism? Would a 'complete census' of all private express trusts be desirable or practicable? (Eg what information would be required?)
(4) An issue that we do not address in this chapter is what unit of taxation (eg individual; + spouse; + children; + grandchildren) is most suitable either for measuring wealth distribution or for using as a tax base. As from 1991 the United Kingdom moved to a system of independent taxation for Income Tax. This is also broadly speaking the position for direct taxes on capital. Whatever the merits of independent taxation may be in terms of equality between men and women it is arguable that, in terms of

measuring wealth-holdings, calculations based on individual wealth rather than 'family wealth' convey a distorted picture of wealth concentration. Note that no such deference to independence is evident in Social Security legislation, where assets and income of partners (and indeed other family members) can be taken into account when deciding entitlement to benefit (see Cockfield in Shipwright (ed) *Tax Avoidance and the Law* (1997) pp 341–347). There is an extensive body of literature on the question of the appropriate tax base for a Wealth Tax; see eg the still valuable study by the Canadian Royal Commission on Taxation Study No 10 *Taxation of the Family* (1966); *Green Paper on a Wealth Tax* (Cmnd 5704, 1974) paras 8–10; Sandford et al *An Annual Wealth Tax* (1975) ch 11; and the forthcoming chapter by Boadway et al 'Taxation of Wealth and Wealth Transfers' in the Mirrlees Report (2009).

(5) Tiley, referring to the uncertainties engendered by the recent shifts in judicial attitudes to tax avoidance, comments: 'If practitioners do not like it, they have to face the no more attractive alternatives of either detailed and relentless (and occasionally retroactive) legislation or a general anti-avoidance rule' ((1997) All ER Rev 467). In response to an initiative by the then Chancellor of the Exchequer, Gordon Brown, the possibility of introducing a GAAR was the subject of a 1998 Consultation Document issued by the Inland Revenue. The document favoured the adoption of a widely drawn GAAR applicable to the corporate sector only (ie corporation tax, petroleum revenue tax and income tax payable by companies). Other areas would continue to be subject to the judicially developed anti-avoidance principles discussed earlier in this chapter. The proposal provoked a wide-ranging debate, much of it critical of the detail if not the general principle of a GAAR (see Tax Law Review Committee *A General Anti-Avoidance Rule* (1999); and see generally Masters [1994] BTR 647; Cooper (ed) *Tax Avoidance and the Rule of Law* (1997); and compare the contrasting positions of Freedman [2004] BTR 4 at 332–357 and Simpson [2004] BTR 4 at 358–374). It seems unlikely that any legislative initiative will be taken until the effectiveness or otherwise of the Finance Act 2004 disclosure requirements can be determined.

4

Creating the trust – I

1. Introduction

(a) The centrality of intention

When deciding how to give away property the owner of assets has a choice between outright gift or a gift in trust. Stripped to its essence the private trust, to reiterate a point made earlier, is a gift projected on the plane of time. However, the limited functional similarity of these two forms of gift, the absolute gift and the gift in trust, must not disguise the fact that they are conceptually distinct.

> Thus there are gifts, which are Legal, and, then again, there are trusts, which are Equitable. These are two distinct arrangements, not simply two types of benefaction, although it is not clear whether we treat them as distinct because we sharply distinguish wanting to make a gift to another, on the one hand, from wanting to make a trust for another, on the other hand, or because we pay attention to the historical distinction that gifts were creatures of Law, and trusts, creatures of Equity. But distinct they are, and so we think that there are separate requirements peculiar to each... (M Pickard 'The Goodness of Giving, The Justice of Gifts and Trusts' (1983) 33 U Toronto LJ 381)

In practice also there will usually be no difficulty in distinguishing the two forms since trusts are commonly created in writing, usually by deed, wherein the donor designates another person or group of persons as trustee(s). But neither writing nor the appointment of others as trustees is essential. There is a third method of making a gift: people can unilaterally and orally declare themselves to be trustees of property for the benefit of others. The absence of written evidence in such circumstances can lead to difficulty of interpretation in this area, particularly that of separating general intention from particular intention. By general intention is meant the intention on the part of the owner of assets to be a benefactor of some other person(s). Although both specific modes of giving, the outright gift and the declaration of oneself as trustee, do have as a common core that generalised intention to be a benefactor, the legal system discriminates between them. It purports to ignore the common generalised intention and concentrates instead on the particular intention, whether for instance to be a donor of an absolute gift or to be a trustee. And analytically these are very different.

> The giver means to be rid of his rights, the man who is intending to make himself a trustee intends to retain his rights but to come under an onerous obligation. The latter intention is far rarer then the former. Men often mean to give things to their kinsfolk, they do not often mean to constitute themselves trustees. An imperfect gift is no declaration of trust.
> (F W Maitland *Equity* (2nd edn, 1936) p 72)

As we shall see, it is the proposition contained in the final sentence that has tended to pose the problems of interpretation. The need to identify and respect a donor's particular intention is therefore central to much of the law and learning concerned with creating a valid trust. This approach assumes that a particular intention exists and can be discerned. But in some circumstances a donor may not advert to whether he intends to impose the obligations of trusteeship either on himself or others; rather he intends to benefit another with property, the method being at best a subsidiary consideration. Indeed the legal consequences of the method chosen may be unappreciated or even misunderstood.

Out of the resulting uncertainty can arise disputes, intra-family disputes over 'who gets what', and recourse must then be made to rules about trust creation in an attempt to divine what the donor intended. There may, for instance, be circumstances when it is important to know whether the donor intended the donee to be subject to a binding legal obligation or simply a moral one. But where the donor has failed to make this clear, then almost by definition the nature of the intention is problematic. Consequently, a number of general questions need to be kept in mind when analysing and evaluating the legal rules about creation of trusts. What tools of construction does a court use in such circumstances if called upon to decide what the particular intention is? How open-textured is the concept of intention: are, for instance, evaluative judgments about the merits of individual cases or the extent of the court's jurisdiction being invoked under the cloak of intention? More fundamentally, is there sound justification in principle and policy for sustaining the clear division described by Maitland in the quotation above, and consequently adhering to a principle that 'Equity will not perfect an imperfect gift'? This is not entirely an academic question since some recent controversial cases appear to indicate a softening both of the 'clear division' and of the underlying principle.

It is, however, important to retain a sense of perspective about the extent of the problems of interpretation outlined here. The pathological cases resulting from such disputes can give an impression that the creation of a trust is an act fraught with uncertainty. This is not so; some rules of trust creation, particularly those associated with formalities, are bedevilled by complexity but the overwhelming majority of trusts are created without difficulty. Indeed, it can be argued that most of the cases leave scarcely any imprint on trusts practice. The trite question which then applies with particular intensity to this complex area of trusts law, is 'Why study them?' The mountaineer's response – because they are there – will not suffice, nor perhaps for the student will the fact that some cases have prompted extensive academic debate. A more pragmatic justification is that the cases illustrate par excellence three particular facets of trusts litigation, which can on occasion overlap. First, there are the pathfinder cases, those where rules are changed and the boundaries of trusts law pushed outwards to accommodate new practical uses of the trust form. Even then, as we shall see here and also in Chapter 5 where they principally occur, each party to the litigation is likely to argue that its position truly respects the settlor's intention. Second, there are the pathological cases already referred to where, for example, lack of clarity on the part of a donor allied to flexibility of a concept such as intention may provide extensive leeway for the exercise of discretion by the courts. As always the challenge is how to provide for the discretion without creating excessive uncertainty. Third, another class of pathological cases arises where attempts are made by settlors or HMRC respectively to avoid or impose tax liability. Here both sides deploy the full complexity of rules concerning trusts creation, the public law issue of fiscal liability being fought out over the terrain of private trusts law.

The fiscal element returns us to the problematic nature of intention but at a wider level than that encapsulated by Maitland's dichotomy. We equated general intention with 'intention to be a benefactor' but it will be recalled from Chapter 3 that the choice of the mode of benefiting – gift in trust or absolute gift – is often influenced by tax-planning considerations. The final section of this chapter is, therefore, devoted to a case study – the *Vandervell* litigation – which illustrates inter alia both the problematic nature of these different levels of intention and how decisions may be influenced by which level is afforded most weight by a court.

(b) Maxims of Equity and trust creation

This is not primarily a book about Equity but the maxims or principles, such as 'Equity will not perfect an imperfect gift' referred to above, have directly influenced the development of the law concerning trust creation. Readers should consult one of the standard works on Equity such as *Snell's Equity* (McGhee (ed) 31st edn, 2005 – referred to hereafter as *Snell*) ch 3 for a detailed account of these maxims but brief reference is made here to those of particular relevance to this chapter. Other maxims will be considered at appropriate points in the book, as with 'Equality is Equity' in Chapter 5 and 'He who comes to Equity must come with clean hands' in Chapter 6.

(1) *Equity will not assist a volunteer.* The principle that 'Equity will not perfect an imperfect gift' is but one of two strands of the broader maxim 'Equity will not assist a volunteer'. The other strand is that Equity will not enforce gratuitous promises. But who then is this volunteer that Equity will not

assist? At its most straightforward we might say that just as in most instances making a gift to others or putting property into trust for them or declaring oneself as trustee of property for them is a voluntary act so the proposed recipients of your benevolence can be categorised as 'volunteers'. They have not provided you with anything in return, at least nothing that constitutes legal consideration – love, gratitude or affection for you will not suffice. This absence of consideration becomes relevant only if, for whatever reason, the 'giving' arrangement is not completed. If, for instance, you change your mind about making the gift the court will not usually compel you to complete the transaction. The volunteer cannot sue you at law for failing to do so nor will Equity offer its assistance. As Hackney pithily puts it, 'You cannot sue for presents in equity' (*Understanding Equity and Trusts* (1987) p 118). Nor, as already stated, will Equity transform an imperfect gift into a declaration of trust over the subject of the gift. But how, it may be said, can trust beneficiaries who are usually volunteers have enforceable rights against trustees? The simple answer is that when the transfer of property to trustees takes place the trust is completed or 'constituted' and the beneficiaries now have a species of property interest that can be enforced against the trustees. An unenforceable hope or expectation hardens into a property right at this point (see further p 136).

(2) *Equity looks to the intent rather than the form.* Equity is concerned with the substance of a transaction rather than the form. The intention of a person can therefore be respected by permitting a trust to be created even though the word 'trust' is not uttered and does not appear in any document. But caution is necessary here since an emphasis on substance does not mean that statutory formalities can readily be ignored. Moreover there is a negative aspect to this 'impatience with mere technicalities' (*Snell* p 39). The signing and sealing of a deed is seen as a mere technicality and does not constitute consideration for the promise in Equity. Consequently, if I promise in a deed to transfer £1,000 to trustees in favour of A but then either fail to do so or decide not to do so then the promise will not be enforceable in Equity by A unless she has provided 'legal' consideration for the promise. In these circumstances the promise is voluntary only and the beneficiary A is a volunteer and will fall victim to the maxim 'Equity will not assist a volunteer' (see further p 179 et seq).

(3) *Equity will not allow a statute to be used as an 'engine' or 'instrument' of fraud.* Equity will ignore a failure to comply with statutory formalities if to do otherwise would be to enable a person to achieve a fraudulent purpose by relying on that failure (see below, p 125).

(4) *Equity regards as done that which ought to be done.* This maxim is closely associated with the equitable remedy of specific performance. Thus where there is a contract or other obligation that can be specifically enforced then Equity treats the parties as being in the position that they would occupy upon completion of the obligation. An illustration from a land

law context is the well-known doctrine from the case of *Walsh v Lonsdale* (1882) 21 Ch D 9 whereby a specifically enforceable contract to grant a lease is treated as creating an equitable lease on the same terms. Similarly, and of more direct relevance to this chapter, a contract to sell land or 'unique' personal property is specifically enforceable, assuming that is that the contract to sell land complies with the formalities required by the Law of Property (Miscellaneous Provisions) Act 1989, s 2. The equitable maxim may then operate to transfer the equitable interest to the purchaser with the vendor being deemed to hold the legal title as constructive trustee pending completion of the contract. This is admittedly a somewhat unusual constructive trusteeship in that not only is there an absence of any element of improper conduct, but until the conveyance is completed the 'vendor-trustee' is fully entitled to protect his own interest in the property rather than that of the 'purchaser-beneficiary' (see Chambers and Swadling in Degeling and Edelman (eds) *Equity in Commercial Law* (2005) chs 17 and 18 respectively for sharply contrasting views on the explanation of and justification – or lack thereof – for the vendor–purchaser constructive trust). As will be seen (p 132) this process can become a weapon in the struggle between taxpayer and HMRC.

It must not, however, be overlooked that these and other so-called maxims of equity 'are not to be taken as positive laws of equity which will be applied literally and relentlessly in their full width but rather as trends or principles which can be discerned in many of the detailed rules which equity has established' (*Snell* p 27). There is a potential problem here. Which should prevail if, in a given fact situation, maxims clash or a maxim conflicts with a rule? Fortunately the siren-like attraction of the maxims is complemented by what Simon Gardner has described as 'a peculiarly Delphic quality' ('Two Maxims of Equity' (1995) 54(1) CLJ 60). In this they provide both a means by which the courts can exercise their discretion and a guide for interpreting that discretion.

2. Creating a trust: the requirements outlined

Our coverage of the requirements that must be satisfied for a valid express trust to be created is slightly unusual and so we provide below a brief but more conventional outline of those requirements as a reference point for the reader.

(a) Capacity to create a trust

In general the capacity to create a trust of property is co-extensive with the power to dispose of a legal or equitable interest in that property. Accordingly any person over the age of 18, unless suffering from mental incapacity, can create an express trust of any property which is capable of disposition (see *Hanbury and Martin* pp 78–79 for the consequences of mental abnormality on capacity to create a valid trust).

A minor cannot hold a legal estate in land (Law of Property Act (LPA) 1925, s 1(6)) and so cannot create a trust of land. As regards other property, including an equitable interest in land, a minor can create a trust but it is voidable; it can be repudiated on or shortly after attaining the age of majority, at present 18 (*Edwards v Carter* [1893] AC 360).

(b) The 'three certainties' must be present

These are usually stated to be 'certainty of words', 'certainty of subject-matter' and 'certainty of objects'. The authority commonly cited for the three-fold requirement is a dictum of Lord Langdale in *Knight v Knight* (1840) 3 Beav 148 at 173 (see also Lord Eldon in *Wright v Atkyns* (1823) Turn & R 143 at 157). As a broad description of the basic requirements, this categorisation is useful but it is misleading to think of it as identifying a set of precise principles (see Watkin 'Doubts and Certainties' (1979) 8 Anglo-American LR 123).

The expression 'certainty of words' is now more appropriately referred to as 'certainty of intention', which requires the existence of a specific intention to create a trust. This criterion in turn includes rules for determining whether a person intends to constitute himself as trustee, by conduct or otherwise; rules for determining whether 'precatory words' such as 'in full confidence' are intended to be legally rather than morally binding; and rules for deciding whether the use of the word 'trust' is decisive. In some commercial contexts the presence of an intention to create a trust may be particularly contentious (see Chapter 15).

Certainty of subject-matter also has an element of ambiguity since it refers to the requirement for certainty both of the particular property to be held on trust and the quantum of each beneficiary's interest in the trust (see Williams (1940) 4 MLR 20). It can even be argued that this category may extend to include rules as to whether certain kinds of property right are capable of being held on trust.

'Certainty of objects' referred originally to a requirement that the identity of beneficiaries should be stated with sufficient clarity, but now may extend to include the so-called beneficiary principle. This requires every valid non-charitable trust to have one or more beneficiaries and, consequently, trusts to achieve non-charitable purposes generally will be invalid.

The three groups of rules cannot be examined in complete isolation from each other. For example, in relation to certainty of words and certainty of subject-matter Sir Arthur Hobhouse in *Mussoorie Bank v Raynor* (1882) 7 App Cas 321 at 333 stated:

> Uncertainty in the subject of the gift has a reflex action upon the previous words, and throws doubt upon the intention of the testator, and seems to show that he could not possibly have intended his words of confidence, hope, or whatever they may be – his appeal to the conscience of the first taker – to be imperative words.

(c) The necessary formalities must be observed

'Now as regards the formalities necessary to the constitution of a trust, there is extremely little law – trusts have not been hedged about by formalities' (*Maitland* p 56). Recent case law prevents our wholeheartedly accepting this description but it is still correct to state that an inter vivos trust of personalty can be created 'without deed, without writing, without formality of any kind by mere word of mouth'. In contrast evidence in writing is necessary for the creation of a trust of land and the requirements of the Wills Act must be complied with for testamentary trusts.

(d) The trust must either be completely constituted or supported by valuable consideration

The most common way of creating a trust is for the settlor (S) to convey property – land, chattels, money, shares – to trustees to hold on trust. This simple statement conflates two separate elements, the declaration that a trust is intended and the transfer of property to trustees. Both elements must be present for a trust to be validly created and until the property is conveyed to trustees the trust remains incompletely constituted. While the trust is in this state it cannot be enforced by the beneficiaries, nor indeed can the trustees compel S to make the transfer, unless consideration of a type recognised by equity has been furnished by either the trustees or the beneficiaries. The rules defining such consideration are different from those defining consideration at common law. Of course, if S declares that he will himself in future hold certain of his own property as trustee no transfer of the property is necessary and the trust is immediately constituted.

(e) The trust must not infringe the rules relating to perpetuity, inalienability and accumulation (see Chapter 6)

(f) The trust must not be intended to defraud creditors or otherwise be contrary to public policy (see Chapter 6)

A brief note of explanation is necessary to explain the slightly idiosyncratic treatment of the above issues adopted in this book.

The topic of 'complete constitution' is fragmented. The part relating to the formal requirements for effectual transfer of property is dealt with alongside formalities for creation of trusts in section 3(b) (p 125) while declaration of oneself as trustee is considered along with certainty of intention in section 4(a) (p 160). Some cases concerning the enforceability of voluntary covenants made by settlors with trustees have excited sustained academic attention. In our view many of the legal and policy arguments are concerned essentially with whether a gratuitous promise should be enforceable, although the legal form the argument takes has frequently revolved around the degree of intention necessary or desirable to create a trust. Accordingly this aspect of complete constitution is also considered, albeit briefly, in the section dealing with certainty of intention (see 4(c), p 179).

The 'certainty of objects' criterion is separated from the other two certainties and becomes a central focus of Chapter 5. The cluster of rules gathered together under the umbrella of 'certainty of objects' were initially more dictated by and concerned with the court's ability ultimately to control and enforce the trust obligation than with the centrality to be accorded to the settlor's specific intention, which is the predominant focus of the present chapter. However, in Chapter 5 we consider whether the emphasis on enforceability has been gradually weakened by a judicial desire to respect the intentions of would-be settlors.

First, however, we consider what formalities are necessary to create a trust.

3. Formalities

(a) Foreword: creation of trusts and dealings in equitable interests

A by now familiar method of creating a trust is for a settlor (S), having absolute beneficial ownership of property, to transfer property to trustees (T1, T2) to hold on trust for B. The property is commonly the legal title to specified assets such as land or shares. But let us assume for a moment that S possesses an equitable interest such as a life interest in a trust fund consisting of pure personalty, the benefit of which it is intended to transfer to B. There are various methods of dealing with equitable interests to achieve this objective. One of these would be for S, as the owner of the equitable interest, to declare himself or herself a trustee of that interest for B, creating what is termed a 'sub-trust'. But if this declaration of trust is construed as a disposition of S's equitable interest, it will need to comply with the formalities specified for such dispositions in LPA 1925, s 53(1)(c) (see section 3(b)(2) below). The formalities to be considered thus include both those applying to the creation of trusts, that is bringing into existence equitable interests, and also those applying to the disposal of already existing equitable interests, those being the interests of beneficiaries under a trust.

As a brief guide, we outline here in general terms the different formalities requirements applicable to the two modes of trust creation – trust by declaration of oneself as trustee and trust by transfer of property (and declaration of some other person(s) as trustee(s)).

Trust by declaration of oneself as trustee   S, being owner of a relevant property interest, declares himself trustee for B:

(a) If the property is a legal interest, the only formal requirement is LPA 1925, s 53(1)(b) which concerns land or any interest in land (see section (b)(1) below).

(b) If it is an equitable interest, LPA 1925, s 53(1)(b) may apply, *but also* one must for the purposes of s 53(1)(c) scrutinise the transaction to see if *in substance* it is a 'disposition' rather than a 'sub-trust' (see section (b)(2) below).

Trust by transfer S transfers or takes steps to transfer the property interest to T1 and T2 as trustees for B. This transfer will usually be accompanied by a document stating – 'declaring' – the terms of the trust(s) on which T1 and T2 are to hold the property. In general, the formalities required are those prescribed by the rules governing the transfer of the relevant property interest (see 3(c) below: *Complete constitution of the inter vivos trust*). For example, transfers of shares in a company must be registered in accordance with the Stock Transfer Act 1963, s 1 and the company's articles.

The transfer must also comply, where appropriate, with the requirements of:

(i) Wills Act 1837, s 9 (see 3(d) below);
(ii) LPA 1925, s 53(1)(b);
(iii) LPA 1925, s 53(1)(c) applying to dispositions of equitable interests (see (b)(2) below).

Thus trusts by transfer, unlike trusts by declaration of oneself as trustee, can be created in two distinct temporal ways, one taking effect during the settlor's lifetime (an inter vivos trust), the other to come into effect on the death of the settlor (a testamentary trust).

The formalities required for the creation of trusts by transfer are best understood by considering separately their application to these two modes, inter vivos and testamentary. However, before considering the detail of the relevant rules in the order just described, a preliminary question must be addressed: what function are the rules intended to perform? The specific justification for these rules will be considered in their individual contexts, but it is appropriate to emphasise here a more general function of formalities, one which can generate a tension in this area of law. An obvious yet important function of the formalities is to maximise certainty about the creation of a trust and its terms. Where the rules require some form of writing not only will this guide trustees as to the extent of their obligations and powers but also it is likely at least to reduce the scope for disputes about a person's intentions as compared with, for instance, an oral disposition of property. As importantly the process of complying with requirements to commit one's intentions to writing may concentrate the mind wonderfully and reduce the scope for ambiguity.

However great may be the attraction of a strict application of the rules in the interests of certainty, of estate planning and, indeed, of minimising litigation costs, there is a countervailing driving force potentially at work behind developments of the law in this area. That is the wish to respect where possible people's clearly discernible intentions about the disposition of their property. The tension generated presents us with the questions of how courts do and should respond to transactions which fail to comply with the formalities requirements, yet where a specific intention is manifestly clear? Is the price of failure to comply to be invalidity? Does the answer differ depending on whether non-compliance is a conscious act or accidental?

These general considerations should be borne in mind in seeking to understand and evaluate the formal requirements set out in the following pages.

(b) Creation of trusts and disposition of equitable interests: inter vivos formalities

(1) Declaration of trust

Whilst most trusts are in practice declared in writing, whether with oneself or some other person(s) as trustee(s) there is no formality required where the property is pure personalty. Accordingly, a trust comprising such property may be declared by unsigned writing, orally, or by conduct.

On the other hand where the property is land or any interest in land, LPA 1925, s 53(1)(b) provides:

> a declaration of trust respecting any land or interest therein must be manifested and proved by some writing signed by some person who is able to declare such trust or by his will.

Writing is required only as evidence of the intention to declare a trust, the declaration itself need not be in writing. The signature to the writing must be that of the beneficial owner of the property not any agent of his. There are more rigorous writing requirements with regard to contracts to create a trust of any interest in land or to dispose of an equitable interest in land, now to be found in the Law of Property (Miscellaneous Provisions) Act 1989, s 2, repealing and replacing LPA 1925, s 40. Any such contract made after 26 September 1989 is now void unless *made in* writing (see Oakley (ed) *Megarry's Manual of the Law of Real Property* (8th edn, 2002) pp 148–154). The writing requirement in s 53(1)(b) applies to the creation of express trusts of land only since LPA 1925, s 53(2) provides that s 53 'does not affect the creation or operation of resulting, implied or constructive trusts'. Intriguingly s 53(1)(b) does not state any sanction for non-compliance and consequently it is generally assumed that the absence of signed writing renders the trust unenforceable not wholly void (see Youdan [1984] CLJ 306 at 320–322 for a concise discussion of this point).

The apparent mandatory nature of s 53(1)(b) is tempered by the existence of equitable doctrines, in particular the principle that 'Equity will not allow a statute to be used as an engine of fraud'. Section 53(1)(b) has its origins in the Statute of Frauds 1677 and the principle was developed subsequently to enable the courts to intervene where rigid application of the statute would promote the very fraud it was probably enacted to prevent. The principle was stated by Lindley LJ in the following terms in *Rochefoucauld v Boustead* [1897] 1 Ch 196 at 206:

> It is further established by a series of cases, the propriety of which cannot now be questioned, that the Statute of Frauds does not prevent the proof of a fraud; and that it is a fraud on the part of a person to whom land is conveyed as a trustee, and who knows it was so conveyed, to deny the trust and claim the land himself. Consequently, notwithstanding the statute, it is competent for a person claiming land conveyed to another to prove by parol evidence that it was so conveyed upon trust for the claimant, and that the grantee, knowing the facts, is denying the trust and relying upon the form of conveyance and the statute, in order to keep the land himself.

It is not necessary for the conveyance itself to be fraudulently obtained for the principle to apply: 'The fraud which brings the principle into play arises as soon as the absolute character of the conveyance is set up for the purpose of defeating the beneficial interest' (*Bannister v Bannister* [1948] 2 All ER 133 at 136). One minor issue of dispute is whether the doctrine simply permits the express trust to be enforced or, alternatively, gives rise to a constructive trust to implement the terms of the agreement. The Court of Appeal judgment in *Rochefoucauld v Boustead* was explicit: 'the trust which the plaintiff has established is clearly an express trust . . . one which the plaintiff and defendant intended to create. The case is not one in which an equitable obligation arises although there may have been no intention to create a trust' (at 208; and see Swadling in Birks (ed) *Resulting Trusts: Practical Issues* (1999) for a valuable discussion of those two cases). The trend in more recent cases, however, has been to favour the constructive trust conclusion (see eg *Re Densham* [1975] 3 All ER 726; *Allen v Snyder* [1977] 2 NSWLR 685; *Lyus v Prowsa Developments Ltd* [1982] 2 All ER 953; *Ashburn Anstalt v Arnold* [1989] Ch 1). This approach is more easily reconciled with s 53(1)(b) itself, from which constructive trusts are specifically excluded by s 53(2). Thus the impact, although not the formal requirement, of s 53(1)(b) is restricted to cases where the settlor declares himself trustee of his own land.

It must not be forgotten that a declaration of trust will not, by itself, be sufficient to complete a 'trust by transfer'. The property that is to be the subject matter of the trust must still be transferred to the trustees for the trust to be fully constituted and thereby enforceable.

(2) Disposition of equitable interests and creation of trusts

We have already noted that an existing equitable interest can be made the subject matter of a trust and that specific formality requirements may then apply. The basic modes of dealing with equitable interests in property were summarised by Romer LJ in *Timpson's Executors v Yerbury* [1936] 1 KB 645 at 664:

> Now the equitable interest in property in the hands of a trustee can be disposed of by the person entitled to it in favour of a third party in any one of four different ways. The person entitled to it: (1) can assign it to the third party directly; (2) can direct the trustees to hold the property in trust for the third party . . . ; (3) can contract for valuable consideration to assign the equitable interest to him; or (4) can declare himself to be a trustee for him of such interest.

The validity of any of these modes of dealing then depends, for purposes of compliance with formalities, on whether it also constitutes a disposition of an equitable interest under the following terms of LPA 1925, s 53(1)(c):

> A disposition of an equitable interest or trust subsisting at the time of the disposition, must be in writing signed by the person disposing of the same, or by his agent thereunto lawfully authorised in writing or by will.

In addition s 53(1)(b) will apply where a declaration of trust of an equitable interest in land is made.

Section 53(1)(c) did not spring fresh-born into existence in 1925 but has its antecedents, like s 53(1)(b), in the Statute of Frauds 1677. Its principal function, then as now, appears to be that of protecting trustees (but cf *Gardner* p 81). The notion, which has some judicial support (see *Vandervell v IRC* [1967] 2 AC 291 at 311) is simply that trustees need to be able to determine who the beneficiaries are. A requirement that any transfer of beneficial interests must be in writing will plainly assist the process, although somewhat surprisingly no obligation is imposed on the transferor or transferee to inform the trustees that a transfer has occurred.

Nevertheless, if the mere formality requirement were all that s 53(1)(c) effected then the scope of the section would possibly have remained unexplored. After all, accidental non-compliance would be rare in a transaction where lawyers are likely to have a formative hand and there is no incentive deliberately not to comply. However, fiscal considerations have intruded here also. Much of the case law concerning s 53(1)(c) is of recent vintage because, in Lord Wilberforce's words, 's 53(1)(c) . . . has recently received a new lease of life as an instrument in the hands of [HMRC (formerly the Inland Revenue)]. The subsection . . . is certainly not easy to apply to the varied transactions in equitable interests which now occur' (*Vandervell v IRC* [1967] 1 All ER 1 at 18).

Those varied transactions which attracted the Inland Revenue's attention included attempts to avoid stamp duty. Stamp duty is payable on instruments transferring property or an interest in property, not on the transaction itself, and is calculated ad valorem on the value of the interest transferred. The duty will thus be avoided if a transfer can be validly effected orally. But where this cannot be done and the writing requirements imposed by s 53(1)(c) are not complied with, the attempted transfer will be void. This provides an added incentive for HMRC to use the section: if the taxpayer has failed to divest himself of the

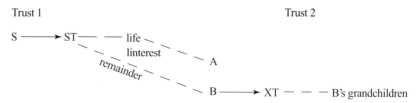

Figure 4.1 Equitable ownership

interest in the property he may become liable to assessment for income tax on any income accruing to the property. Two recent developments – one statutory, the other judicial – have combined, at least for fiscal purposes, to reduce the contemporary importance of the interpretation of s 53(1)(c). First, by virtue of the Finance Act 1985, s 82 transfers by way of gift are now subject to 50 pence duty only and not the ad valorem charge. Second, most stamp duty avoidance schemes of the type discussed here would now be likely to be caught by the *Ramsay* principle (see *Ingram v IRC* [1985] STC 835).

Before considering the various modes of dealing and their relationship to s 53(1)(c) two notes of warning are sounded. First, Romer LJ's classification is not exhaustive: recent cases have tended to produce ad hoc accretions to the basic categories. This cannot be said to have clarified the relationship between s 53(1)(c) and dealings in equitable interests. Second, it is important to consider, particularly for the purpose of applying s 53(1)(c), not simply the division between legal and equitable interests but the further sub-division between a 'bare' equitable interest and an equitable interest carrying beneficial rights.

The following example (see Figure 4.1), closely following that devised by Green (1984) 47 MLR 385 at 387, explains this distinction. Let us suppose that S, absolutely entitled to property, creates a trust by declaring herself trustee (ST) of the property for A for life remainder to B. The beneficial interest in the property will become distributed between A and B, reflecting the actuarial values of their respective equitable interests (Trust 1). Let us further suppose that B then assigns his equitable interest in remainder to XT as trustee for his (B's) grandchildren. XT will now hold B's original equitable interest, but with the *beneficial* interest extracted from it and transferred to the grandchildren as equitable interests in the new trust (Trust 2). B might equally have achieved the same outcome by declaring himself to be trustee of his equitable interest for the grandchildren. This 'sub-trust', as that last alternative form of transfer is called, has prompted some subtle nuances of analysis of the scope of s 53(1)(c).

With these cautionary reservations in mind, the various modes of dealing with equitable interests and their relationship to s 53(1)(c) can now be examined (see Figures 4.2.1 and 4.2.2):

Direct assignment of the equitable interest to a third party (Figure 4.2.1) Trustees T1 T2 hold property on trust for A absolutely who assigns the interest to B. This is plainly a disposition within s 53(1)(c) and is void unless in writing.

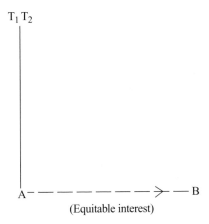

Figure 4.2.1 Assignment by A direct to B

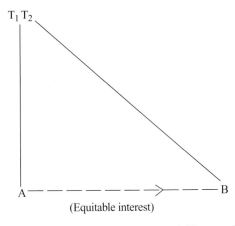

Figure 4.2.2 Direction by A to trustees to hold on trust for B

Direction to trustees to hold property on trust for a third party (Figure 4.2.2) T1
T2 hold property on trust for A absolutely and A directs T1 T2 that in future
they should hold the property in trust for B absolutely. This point arose in *Grey
v IRC* where the House of Lords unanimously held that there was a disposition,
with the consequence that the attempt to avoid stamp duty failed.

Grey v IRC [1959] 3 All ER 603 at 607

On 1 February 1955 Mr Hunter (H), the then outright owner of 18,000 shares,
transferred ownership of the shares to the appellant trustees (G) to hold as
nominees for himself.

On 18 February 1955 H orally and irrevocably directed the trustees to divide
the shares into six blocks of 3,000 shares each and to appropriate one block to
each of six pre-existing settlements created in favour of H's grandchildren.

On 25 March the trustees executed six deeds of declaration of trust – which
H also executed to testify to the earlier oral direction – declaring that they

had since 18 February held each block of shares on the trusts of the respective grandchildren's settlement.

The Revenue successfully argued (1) that the oral direction of 18 February was an attempted disposition of H's equitable interest which failed because it did not comply with s 53(1)(c), and (2) that therefore the written declaration in the deeds of 25 March constituted the disposition and the deeds were subject to stamp duty.

Lord Radcliffe: My Lords, if there is nothing more in this appeal than the short question whether the oral direction that Mr Hunter gave to his trustees on 18 Feb. 1955, amounted in any ordinary sense of the words to a 'disposition of an equitable interest or trust subsisting at the time of disposition', I do not feel any doubt as to my answer. I think that it did. Whether we describe what happened in technical or in more general terms, the full equitable interest in the eighteen thousand shares concerned, which at the time was his, was (subject to any statutory invalidity) diverted by his direction from his ownership into the beneficial ownership of the various equitable owners, present and future, entitled under his six existing settlements. But that is not the question which has led to difference of opinion in the courts below. Where opinions have differed is on the point whether his direction was a 'disposition' within the meaning of s 53(1)(c) of the Law of Property Act, 1925...

The trustees had argued that s 53(1)(c) should be construed as no more than a consolidation of three sections of the Statute of Frauds, s 3, s 7 and s 9, and that to be effective a declaration of trust of personalty did not require writing. Essentially the proposition advanced on behalf of the trustees was that a declaration of trust and a 'disposition of an equitable interest' were mutually exclusive modes of dealing with equitable interests under the Statute of Frauds and should remain so under s 53(1)(c). The House of Lords rejected the consolidation proposition and moreover Lord Radcliffe commented obiter that '... there is warrant for saying that a direction to his trustee by the equitable owner of trust property prescribing new trusts of that property was a declaration of trust. But it does not necessarily follow from that that such a direction, if the effect of it was to determine completely or pro tanto the subsisting equitable interest of the maker of the direction, was not also a grant or assignment for the purposes of s 9 and, therefore, required writing for its validity.' The apparent conflation of 'direction' and 'declaration' implicit in Lord Radcliffe's statement does not sit comfortably with Romer LJ's categorisation which distinguishes between them as being two different modes of disposing of an equitable interest in property. However, it is clear that whatever the descriptive label – be it 'direction' or 'declaration' – that is attached to an instruction such as that in *Grey*, there is a disposition for the purposes of s 53(1)(c).

The picture is much less clear where the 'declaration of trust' takes the form envisaged by Romer LJ's use of the term, ie where a person holding a legal or equitable interest declares herself to be a trustee of that interest (see following section).

Declaration by equitable owner of herself as trustee (sub-trust) Two separate forms of sub-trust fall to be considered here.

Assume that T1 and T2 hold property on trust for A absolutely. Consider first the position where A declares herself trustee of her equitable interest to hold for B for life, remainder to C, what for convenience we can call a type 1 sub-trust. This is a declaration of trust, which may be oral if the property is pure personalty, but must be evidenced in writing under s 53(1)(b) if the property subject to the interest is land. It is widely accepted that no disposition requiring writing under s 53(1)(c) occurs since A still retains her equitable interest – although now devoid of beneficial content which has shifted to the equitable interests of B and C. In addition it can be argued that, unlike the example that follows, this is more than a bare trust since A has taken on herself an active role.

The second form of sub-trust (type 2) arises where A declares herself trustee of her equitable interest for B absolutely. The position here as regards the writing requirement is uncertain. It is argued that what appears to be a declaration of trust results, in effect, in a disposition of A's entire equitable interest, which therefore requires writing within s 53(1)(c) whatever the nature of the property concerned: 'After all A is a simple bare trustee with no active duties to perform so that [s]he should drop out of the picture, [the original trustees] now holding for [B] instead of A: by A's action A's equitable interest has passed to [B]' (*Hayton and Mitchell* p 84 following Upjohn J in *Grey v IRC* [1958] Ch 375 at 382 who accepted the notion of a sub-trustee 'disappearing from the picture' on declaration of a bare sub-trust). It may be argued, however, that this analysis in effect transforms a declaration of a sub-trust into an assignment, which is not giving full effect to A's specific intention.

An alternative analysis therefore is akin to that applicable to the first form of sub-trust: the declaration of trust creates a sub-trust under which the original trustees owe their trust duties to A who herself continues to hold the equitable interest – but again one devoid of any beneficial interest – as a bare trustee only in favour of B. After all, unlikely though it may be, although possibly prudent to do so, there is presumably nothing to prevent the trustees still paying to A whatever she is entitled to under her equitable interest and leaving her to pay B. The implication of this alternative analysis would seem to be that no disposition of the equitable interest occurs under s 53(1)(c) (see eg Lord Cohen in *Oughtred v IRC* (below)).

In sharp contrast to any of the reasoning above, it has been argued that any declaration of either of the forms of a sub-trust necessarily involves a disposition of part of A's interest – the previously subsisting *beneficial* part of that interest – and should therefore fall within s 53(1)(c) (see Green (1984) 37 MLR 385 at 396–398). A necessary implication is that 'declaration' and 'disposition' are not mutually exclusive concepts and that dispositions of both 'equitable' and 'beneficial' interests are encompassed by s 53(1)(c).

Assuming, however, for the moment that s 53(1)(c) does not apply equally to the two forms of declaring a sub-trust, it is difficult to justify this excessively technical outcome either in terms of the underlying rationale of s 53(1)(c) outlined previously (see p 127) or because distinguishing an active sub-trust (type 1 above) from a bare sub-trust (type 2 above) is not always straightforward. Consequently in our view either neither form of sub-trust should require writing or, following Green's reasoning, both should. It is accepted, however, that neither of these views reflects received opinion.

Contract for valuable consideration to assign an equitable interest The application of trusts law principles to this mode of dealing and its relationship to s 53(1)(c) and s 53(2) has been beset with uncertainty although to some degree the Court of Appeal clarified the position in *Neville v Wilson* [1996] 3 All ER 171.

Consider the example whereby T1 and T2 hold property on trust for A absolutely. A contracts with B to transfer her (A's) equitable interest to B. Such a contract does not itself amount to a disposition although it might be thought that subsequent completion of a contract by assigning the equitable interest would constitute a disposition under s 53(1)(c). But is any subsequent formal assignment necessary to complete the transaction? Earlier in this chapter we saw that where there is a specifically enforceable contract – for example, to sell land or 'unique' personal property – the equitable maxim 'Equity regards as done that which ought to be done' operates to transfer the equitable interest to the purchaser with the vendor being deemed to hold the legal title as constructive trustee pending completion of the contract. Do these same principles apply where the property concerned is itself an equitable interest? Would the position now be: T1 and T2 hold on trust for A who now holds on constructive trust for B? Assuming that a constructive trust of a rather specialised nature (see above, p 120) is imposed, the question arises as to how A's equitable interest is transferred. Can the imposition of a constructive trust be viewed as bringing about an assignment? Furthermore is writing required under s 53(1)(c) or does s 53(2) apply, that subsection stating, it will be recalled, that s 53 'does not affect the creation or operation of resulting, implied or constructive trusts'?

These questions arose but were not fully resolved in *Oughtred v IRC* because the decision hinged on interpretation of the Stamp Act 1891.

Oughtred v IRC [1960] AC 206

Trustees held 200,000 shares in trust for Mrs Oughtred (O) for her life and then for her son Peter (P) absolutely. O also had absolute ownership of 72,700 shares in the same company. To ease potential estate duty liability on O's death, O and P *orally* agreed on 18 June 1956 that O would transfer to P her 72,700 shares in exchange for P's reversionary interest in the 200,000 shares.

On 26 June the agreement was implemented in three stages:

(1) O transferred her shares to P.
(2) A deed of release was executed by O, P and the trustees which recited the oral agreement that the shares were now held by the trustees in trust for O absolutely and that they were intended to be transferred to her.
(3) The trustees transferred the 200,000 shares to O absolutely.

The Revenue sought to levy ad valorem stamp duty in respect of the transaction which consisted of the sale of P's equitable reversionary interest. The document chosen as the appropriate instrument for assessing stamp duty was the transfer of the 200,000 shares at stage three. The taxpayers argued that this was a transfer of the bare legal title, and hence of nominal value and therefore liable only to a nominal duty of 50p. The beneficial ownership of the shares had, in their view, passed prior to the stage-three completion under the constructive trust which arose as a result of the specifically enforceable *oral* contract for the exchange of shares. At first instance Upjohn J accepted this argument.

But by a 3:2 majority (Lords Keith, Jenkins and Denning; Lords Radcliffe and Cohen dissenting) the House of Lords, affirming the Court of Appeal, upheld the assessment to ad valorem duty. On their view of the scope of the Stamp Act 1891, s 54, the question of whether an equitable interest in the settled shares had passed to O before stage three was immaterial. The majority did not therefore find it necessary to decide whether, under the oral agreement of 18 June, P became a constructive trustee of his reversionary interest in favour of O, and if so, whether that constructive trusteeship was exempt from the requirements of s 53(1)(c) by virtue of s 53(2). Lord Denning, commenting on the relationship between s 53(1)(c) and s 53(2), expressed the following opinion without giving reasons (at 233): 'But I may say that I do not think the oral agreement was effective to transfer Peter's reversionary interest to his mother. I should have thought that the wording of s 53(1)(c) of the Law of Property Act 1925 clearly made a writing necessary to effect a transfer; and s 53(2) does not do away with that necessity.'

Lord Radcliffe agreed with the reasoning of Upjohn J on the effect of s 53(2):

Lord Radcliffe (at 227): The reasoning of the whole matter, as I see it, is as follows: On June 18, 1956 the son owned an equitable reversionary interest in the settled shares; by his oral agreement of that date he created in his mother an equitable interest in his reversion, since the subject-matter of the agreement was property of which specific performance would normally be decreed by the court. He thus became a trustee for her of that interest sub modo; having regard to subsection (2) of section 53 Law of Property Act 1925, subsection (1) of that section did not operate to prevent that trusteeship arising by operation of law.

An alternative analysis of the arrangement is that the transaction was not formally completed and that the outcome of the 18 June and 26 June arrangements was to leave a bare equitable interest vested in Peter (P). P retained a mere shell, the kernel – the beneficial interest in the shares – having been extracted and transferred by the operation of a constructive trust. On this point Green has commented ((1984) 47 MLR 385 at 402):

> There would have been nothing unusual in this latter alternative prevailing. It is a common practice amongst those intent on avoiding *ad valorem* stamp duty to enter into a specifically enforceable agreement to transfer property which is left uncompleted: the promisee relying on his equitable proprietary right behind the bare trust thus established by his vendor. The documentary disadvantages of 'leaving the matter in contract' in this way are regularly seen as being outweighed by the stamp duty saving; and the purchaser always has the safety net of having a right to call for a conveyance if such becomes necessary at a later date.

Whether s 53(2) does or, as argued by Lord Denning, does not remove the requirement for writing under s 53(1)(c) has continued to prove controversial although with one exception subsequent cases have tended to follow the approach adopted by Lord Radcliffe (*Re Holt's Settlement* [1969] 1 Ch 100 (see below, p 342); *DHN Food Distributors Ltd v Tower Hamlets London Borough Council* [1976] 3 All ER 462; *Chinn v Collins* [1981] AC 533 at 548 per Lord Wilberforce but cf 'the exception' in dicta by Chadwick J in *United Bank of Kuwait plc v Sahib* [1997] Ch 107 at 129 who stated that he was 'far from persuaded' on the point). This trend was reaffirmed most recently by the Court of Appeal in *Neville v Wilson* [1996] 3 All ER 171. In that case shareholders of a private company JEN Ltd (J) claimed to have entered into individual *oral* agreements by which, inter alia, J's equitable interests in 120 shares in another private company (U Ltd) were to be distributed to the shareholders of J rateably according to their existing shareholdings. A key question before the Court of Appeal was whether the alleged oral agreements were ineffective because of the absence of writing required by s 53(1)(c). The court held that the effect of each individual agreement was to constitute the shareholder 'a constructive trustee for the other shareholders' (see Nolan (1996) 55 CLJ 436 and Milne (1997) 113 LQR 213 for critical comment on this conclusion but cf the decision of the High Court of Australia in *Halloran v Minister Administering National Parks and Wildlife Act 1974* [2006] HCA 3; [2006] Conv 390–397)). But did s 53(2) oust the writing requirement of s 53(1)(c)? The court reviewed the various opinions in *Oughtred* and concluded that it did (Nourse LJ at 182):

> Just as in *Oughtred v IRC* the son's oral agreement created a constructive trust in favour of the mother, so here each shareholder's oral or implied agreement created an implied or constructive trust in favour of the other shareholders. Why then should not sub-s (2) apply? No convincing reason was suggested in argument and none has occurred to us since. Moreover, to deny its application in this case would be to restrict the effect of general

> words when no restriction is called for, and to lay the ground for fine distinctions in the future. With all the respect which is due to those who have thought to the contrary [Lords Denning and Cohen in *Oughtred*], we hold that sub-s (2) applies to an agreement such as we have in this case.

There are four points to be made about this outcome. First, a consequence of the decision was to achieve the convenient result of avoiding an asset going to the Crown as *bona vacantia*. Second and relatedly, context may be a relevant consideration here and it is noticeable that most of the cases subsequent to *Oughtred* have not directly involved tax considerations. In the one case that did, *Chinn v Collins*, the consequence of adopting the constructive trust analysis was the defeat of a capital gains tax avoidance scheme. Third, as regards possible reasons for not applying s 53(2) to such 'constructive trusts' of equitable interests, it has been suggested that this provision 'was intended to embrace the kind of constructive trust which is imposed to prevent fraud [as in *Bannister v Bannister* [1948] 2 All ER 133] and did not envisage the anomalous constructive trust arising on a specifically enforceable contract for sale' (see *Hanbury and Martin* p 92). Our fourth point concerns reform: in 1979 one critic of the varying interpretations of s 53 commented: 'the complexity of the present position reflects no credit on the law and . . . the time has come for a long cool look' (Battersby (1979) 43 Conv 17 at 38). As part of its Seventh Programme of Reform the Law Commission proposed to initiate a review of the formality requirements for the creation of trusts. A Consultation Paper on the 'complex provision' was originally expected in 1999 but 'due to staffing shortages and the extent of the work that the team has had to do on other projects' the work has been delayed. Although it seems that a good deal of research has been undertaken there has been no further progress since 2001 and the Commission is currently concentrating its resources on the topics in the Ninth and Tenth Programmes of Reform (see Annual Report 2007–08 (Law Com No 310 (2008) paras 6.20–6.24; and Law Com No 259 (1999) pp 14–15).

A miscellany   The *Vandervell* litigation has teased out further difficulties for the application of s 53(1)(c) and s 53(2) and these are considered at p 197 et seq. But at the risk of some over-simplification the position reached by the cases can be summarised in the following proposition: if at the commencement of a transaction a person has a subsisting equitable interest and at the end no longer has that interest, then there has been a disposition within s 53(1)(c).

There are, however, two further modes of dealing with equitable interests which have been held not to require writing and that might be described as exceptions to the proposition. By way of conclusion to this section these are briefly outlined here. In *Re Danish Bacon Co Ltd Staff Pension Fund* [1971] 1 All ER 486, Megarry J very much doubted whether the section would apply to a nomination made under a staff pension fund where a member could nominate a person to receive moneys due in the case of death of the member before retirement. The reasoning here is that there was no subsisting equitable interest in property to come within s 53(1)(c) in that the employee was disposing of something that could never be his. Megarry J's opinion was approved in *Gold v Hill* [1999] 1 FLR 54 where the nomination took place under a life assurance policy. In similar vein s 53(1)(c) was held to be inapplicable to a disclaimer of an equitable interest. It was said that 'a disclaimer operates by way of avoidance and not by way of disposition' (*Re Paradise Motor Co Ltd* [1968] 1 WLR 1125 at 1143). There is no set form of words that constitutes a disclaimer and it is probably not essential to adopt the precise language employed by Mr Johns in the case: 'I have no **** shares. I want no**** shares and if I had any money to come of the bastard I wouldn't even take it' (at 1141). Finally on this topic, consideration of the applicability of s 53(1)(c) to variation of beneficial interests under the Variation of Trusts Act 1958 is deferred until Chapter 7 where the Act is examined in some detail.

(c) Complete constitution of the inter vivos trust

(1) Introduction

As stated previously, for an inter vivos trust by transfer of property to be perfectly created, it is necessary for the settlor both to state that the property is to be held on trust and to convey that property to the trustee. It is only when both these steps are implemented that the trust is completely constituted. If there is a failure to observe the formalities required to effect the transfer, the trust is incompletely constituted. This aspect of the requirement of complete constitution is, of course, unproblematic where a person declares themselves to be trustee of their own property. Legal title simply remains with the owner and no transfer is necessary.

The formalities necessary to transfer the legal interest in property to trustees will vary according to the nature of the property. So, for example, legal estates in land must be transferred by deed (LPA 1925, s 52), copyright by writing (Copyright, Designs and Patents Act 1988, s 90(3)), shares in private companies by the appropriate form of transfer (Stock Transfer Act 1963, s 1; Companies Act 2006, s 771) and personal chattels by delivery or deed of gift. Where the subject-matter of the intended trust is an equitable interest a correct transfer is also necessary and, as we have seen, a disposition of an equitable interest must be in writing (LPA 1925, s 53(1)(c)).

(2) *Milroy v Lord* and a 'bright line' rule

The classic statement of what is meant by complete constitution and of the primary consequences of incomplete constitution is contained in the judgment of Turner LJ in *Milroy v Lord* (1862) 4 De GF & J 264:

> I take the law of this Court to be well settled, that, in order to render a voluntary settlement valid and effectual, the settlor must have done everything which, according to the nature of the property comprised in the settlement, was necessary to be done in order to transfer the property and render the settlement binding upon him. He may of course do this by actually transferring the property to the persons for whom he intends to provide, and the provision will then be effectual, and it will be equally effectual if he transfers the property to a trustee for the purposes of the settlement, or declares that he himself holds it in trust for those purposes . . . but, in order to render the settlement binding, one or other of these modes must, as I understand the law of this Court, be resorted to, for there is no equity in this Court to perfect an imperfect gift. The cases I think go further to this extent, that if the settlement is intended to be effectuated by one of the modes to which I have referred, the Court will not give effect to it by applying another of those modes. If it is intended to take effect by transfer, the Court will not hold the intended transfer to operate as a declaration of trust, for then every imperfect instrument would be made effectual by being converted into a perfect trust.

This judgment clearly identifies the two methods of constituting a trust: effective transfer of property to trustees and self-declaration of trusteeship. Turner LJ also reaffirmed the principle (i) that outright transfers, transfers on trust and declarations of trust are separate and seemingly mutually exclusive modes of benefiting a person and, furthermore, (ii) that a failure to transfer property outright or to trustees cannot be remedied by construing the intended transfer as a self-declaration of trusteeship. The possibility that the existence of valuable consideration will 'rescue' the trust (see below, p 180) is not, however, mentioned.

(3) The 'rule' in *Re Rose*

Although the principles stated in Turner LJ's judgment in *Milroy v Lord* and indeed the decision itself appear to offer scant room for manoeuvre, subsequent cases (*Re Rose* [1949] Ch 78; confusingly *Re Rose* [1952] Ch 499; *Vandervell v IRC* [1967] 2 AC 291 but cf *Re Fry* [1946] Ch 312), again primarily involving transfer of shares, appear to have modified the rigid approach of *Milroy v Lord*. This modification is still more evident in two controversial recent cases, *T Choithram International SA v Pagarani* [2001] WLR 1 (PC) and *Pennington v Waine* [2002] 1 WLR 2075 (see further at p 141). The earlier decisions have themselves not gone uncriticised (see in particular McKay (1976) 40 Conv 139), the criticism focusing on subsequent interpretation of Turner LJ's stricture that 'the settlor must have done everything which, according to the nature of the property . . . was necessary to be done in order to transfer the property'. A particular difficulty arises out of the role of third parties in a transaction. This is best demonstrated by isolating the separate steps involved in share transfers of the type involved in the above cases:

  (i) the prescribed transfer form is signed by the transferor; and
  (ii) delivered by the transferor, with share certificates, to the transferee;

(iii) the transfer form is signed by the transferee and delivered, with the share
       certificates, to the company;
(iv) the company registers the transfer.

Step (iv) is not necessarily a mere technicality. A private company's articles of
association can provide directors with a power to refuse to register a transfer.
An additional complication specific to share transfers is that practice is not
consistent amongst companies. Thus whilst the articles of association of some
companies require the signatures of both transferor and transferee for the
transfer of *any* shares (see *Re Paradise Motor Co Ltd* [1968] 1 WLR 1125),
others may require this only where shares are not fully paid – the signature
of the transferor alone sufficing otherwise (see Companies Act Regulations
1985, SI 1985/805, Sch 1, Table A, para 23). Accordingly under company law
it is possible for a donor to transfer shares to an intended donee without
the latter playing any active role in the transaction. Moreover since 1996 the
position concerning documentation and share transfers is now quite different
for *public* limited companies registered on the London Stock Exchange. The
shares of these companies are now transferable by means of an electronic share-
dealing system known by the acronym CREST. The major change brought
about by the new transfer rules is that a share transfer is effected by a computer
instruction rather than by submission of a share certificate and a transfer form,
the assets consequently being held in a dematerialised form rather than as
physical share certificates (see Uncertificated Securities Regulations 2001 SI
2001/3755; Micheler [2002] JBL 358). Nevertheless, whether electronic transfer
or the paper method is employed the fact remains that *at law* legal title passes
only on registration (step (iv) above).

   It is therefore clear that a transfer will be incomplete in law until step (iv)
is completed. But, *Milroy v Lord* notwithstanding, could a transfer be valid *in
equity* after steps (i) and (ii), or after steps (i)–(iii) and thus a trust be completely
constituted? In reading *Re Rose* (below) consider in particular when the transfer
was deemed to have been complete and by what means. Consider also why the
issue was litigated and how a formalities requirement can become the means
for assessing liability to tax.

Re Rose [1952] Ch 499 at 510

The settlor (Rose) R died on 16 February 1947 and estate duty then became
payable on any inter vivos gift made subsequent to 10 April 1943. R had
by voluntary deed executed two transfers of shares in a private company
on 30 March 1943, one transfer being in favour of his wife beneficially, the
other to trustees. On the same date the transfer forms were handed with
the share certificates to the transferees. The directors of the company had
the power to refuse to register any transfer but the transfers were registered on
30 June 1943. The Revenue claimed estate duty on the shares, it being argued
that the legal title did not vest in the transferees until 30 June and hence the

shares were to be treated as being in the legal and beneficial ownership of R until that date.

Evershed MR (after quoting from Turner LJ's judgment in *Milroy v Lord*, see p 137) said:

> Those last few sentences form the gist of the Crown's argument and on it is founded the broad, general proposition that if a document is expressed as, and on the face of it intended to operate as, a transfer, it cannot in any respect take effect by way of trust... In my judgement, that statement is too broad and involves too great a simplification of the problem; and is not warranted by authority. I agree that if a man purporting to transfer property executes documents which are not apt to effect that purpose, the court cannot then extract from those documents some quite different transaction and say that they were intended merely to operate as a declaration of trust, which ex facie they were not; but if a document is apt and proper to transfer the property – is in truth the appropriate way in which the property must be transferred – then it does not seem to me to follow from the statement of Turner LJ that, as a result, either during some limited period or otherwise, a trust may not arise, for the purpose of giving effect to the transfer. The simplest case will, perhaps, provide an illustration. If a man executes a document transferring all his equitable interest, say, in shares, that document, operating, and intended to operate, as a transfer, will give rise to and take effect as a trust; for the assignor will then be a trustee of the legal estate in the shares for the person in whose favour he has made an assignment of his beneficial interest. And, for my part, I do not think that the case of *Milroy v Lord* is an authority which compels this court to hold that in this case – where, in the terms of Turner LJ's judgment, the settlor did everything which, according to the nature of the property comprised in the settlement, was necessary to be done by him in order to transfer the property, – the result necessarily negatives the conclusion that, pending registration, the settlor was a trustee of the legal interest for the transferee.

Evershed MR then referred to an earlier case of *Re Rose* [1949] Ch 78 – the same name being coincidental – and endorsed the following passage from Jenkins J commenting on *Milroy v Lord*:

> 'I was referred on that to the well known case of *Milroy v Lord* and also to the recent case of *Re Fry* [1946] Ch 312. Those cases, as I understand them, turn on the fact that the deceased donor had not done all in his power, according to the nature of the property given, to vest the legal interest in the property in the donee. In such circumstances it is, of course, well settled that there is no equity to complete the imperfect gift. If any act remained to be done by the donor to complete the gift at the date of the donor's death the court will not compel his personal representatives to do that act and the gift remains incomplete and fails. In *Milroy v Lord* the imperfection was due to the fact that the wrong form of transfer was used for the purpose of transferring certain bank shares. The document was not the appropriate document to pass any interest in the property at all.'

Having quoted from the judgment Evershed MR continued as follows:

> I venture respectfully to adopt the whole of the passage I have read which, in my judgment, is a correct statement of the law. If that be so, then it seems to me that it cannot be asserted on the authority of *Milroy v Lord*, and I venture to think it also cannot be asserted as a matter of logic and good sense or principle, that because, by the regulations of the company, there had to be a gap before Mrs Rose could, as between herself and the company, claim the rights which the shares gave her vis-à-vis the company, the deceased was not in the meantime a trustee for her of all his rights and benefits under the shares. That he intended to pass all those rights, as I have said, seems to me too plain for argument.

(The Court of Appeal confirmed that no estate duty was payable.)

The judgment supports the proposition that a trust will be completely constituted where a settlor has done everything within his own power to transfer property to the trustee. In the case of a share transfer this presumably arises after completion of steps (i) and (ii), although in *Re Rose* step (iii) had also been completed by the relevant date. The decision is not without its theoretical difficulties, however.

To establish that the transfer was valid in equity as from 30 March, the Court of Appeal was prepared to recognise that Rose held the shares as trustee for the period between delivery of the transfer and registration on 30 June. Did Rose intend to declare himself as trustee? If he did not, and it seems an unlikely eventuality, does the judgment necessitate a conclusion that an ineffective transfer was validated by treating it as a declaration of trust? Or is there a 'trust to complete the transfer'? (See Oakley *Constructive Trusts* (3rd edn, 1997) p 318 who suggests that these circumstances give rise to a constructive trust in the transferor; see also the different post hoc rationalisation by Lowrie and Todd (1998) 57 CLJ 46 drawing on the opinion of Lord Browne-Wilkinson in *Westdeutsche Landesbank Girozentrale v Islington London Borough Council* [1996] AC 669.) Whatever the theoretical difficulties presented by *Re Rose*, and the reasoning has been sharply criticised by McKay ((1976) 40 Conv 139) and Hackney ('an arbitrary deviation from principle' (*Understanding Equity and Trusts* (1987) p 94), the proposition it supports – now commonly heralded (paradoxically in view of its pragmatic origin) as a 'rule' or even 'principle' – has received widespread acceptance in other instances where some act of registration is required to complete a transfer (see *Brown & Root Technology Ltd v Sun Alliance and London Assurance Co Ltd* [1996] Ch 51 – assignment of a lease; and *Mascall v Mascall* (1984) 50 P&CR 119 – transfer of registered land).

Despite the criticisms the decision in *Re Rose* has been described (*Hanbury and Martin* p 125) as 'eminently sensible . . . in a context in which the liability to tax may be affected by the date on which the transfer is treated as being effective'. If the difference between the decision in a case such as *Re Rose* and the straightforward application of principle is to be attributed to the attitude of the court to the fiscal merits of the case then the justification is shaky indeed. It should be borne in mind that any form of estate duty which brings into charge to tax previous transfers within a specified period prior to death must necessarily have arbitrary results. Tax will not be paid by the estate of the person who dies immediately before the commencement of the period whereas the opposite will be the case for the person who dies immediately afterwards.

(4) A 'rule' or 'unconscionability': *Re Rose* revisited

The tension evident in *Re Rose* between responding to the perceived merits of the case and applying the basic underlying principle that equity will not come to the aid of a volunteer has resurfaced in two recent cases, *T Choithram International SA v Pagarani* [2001] WLR 1 (PC) and *Pennington v Waine* [2002] 1 WLR 2075. Both cases, invoking and possibly modifying further the rule in *Re Rose*, compel us to revisit that principle and cast still more doubts on the weight to be attached to the seemingly and oft-quoted bright line proposition first set down in *Milroy v Lord* by Turner LJ.

In *Choithram*, T Choithram Pagarani (TCP) a very successful and twice-married businessman, having provided financially for his first wife and children, had determined to leave the balance of his wealth to charity. The mechanism for achieving this was intended to be via a gift to the Choithram International Foundation, a charity established under a trust deed executed by TCP in February 1992 shortly before his death. TCP was named in the deed as one of the trustees. Immediately after signing the deed it is clear, although recollections amongst those present differed as to the precise terminology used, that TCP made an oral declaration stating that he was giving 'all his wealth to the foundation'. Now the Foundation was not incorporated and therefore had no legal personality as such with the consequence that any transfer of shares could only be valid if made to the trustees of the Foundation. Unfortunately by the time of his death just a month later TCP had not executed any transfer of shares to the Foundation nor seemingly had he declared himself to be the trustee of the property. The question for the court was whether TCP's gift to the Foundation had been completed or did the assets remain as part of his personal estate that would devolve to certain family members already generously provided for. The trial judge and the Court of Appeal of the British Virgin Islands, adopting the reasoning of *Milroy v Lord* that posited just two alternative ways of perfecting a gift, namely (a) by a transfer of the gifted asset to the donee, accompanied by an intention in the donor to make a gift; or (b) by the donor declaring himself to be a trustee of the gifted property for the donee. They concluded that TCP had intended to transfer the property to trustees but had failed to vest title to the assets in *all* the trustees. Moreover it was not possible to construe the language used by TCP as constituting a declaration of himself as trustee, thereby satisfying option (b). The Judicial Committee of the Privy Council allowed the appeal on behalf of, in effect, the Foundation. Lord Browne-Wilkinson, giving the judgment of the court, argued that the facts of the case were novel and that consequently it fell between the two common forms of gift-making outlined in *Milroy v Lord*. Lord Browne-Wilkinson stated that the language used by TCP – 'I give to the Foundation' – could have only one meaning in the particular context (at 12):

> The foundation has no legal existence apart from the trust declared by the foundation trust deed. Therefore the words 'I give to the foundation' can only mean 'I give to the trustees of the foundation trust deed to be held by them on the trusts of the foundation trust deed'. Although the words are apparently words of outright gift they are essentially words of gift on trust.

At first glance this conclusion does not really resolve matters since it is arguable that it should be immaterial whether the gift is an outright gift or a gift on trust – a transfer of legal title to the assets is still required. But at no point had TCP ever purported to vest legal title in the whole body of trustees. This difficulty is circumvented in the opinion of the Committee by the fact that TCP had appointed himself to be one of the trustees:

> There can in principle be no distinction between the case where the donor declares himself to be sole trustee for a donee or a purpose and the case where he declares himself to be one of the trustees for that donee or purpose. In both cases his conscience is affected and it would be unconscionable and contrary to the principles of equity to allow such a donor to resile from his gift. Say, in the present case, that TCP had survived and tried to change his mind by denying the gift. In their Lordships' view it is impossible to believe that he could validly deny that he was a trustee for the purposes of the foundation in the light of all the steps that he had taken to assert that position and to assert his trusteeship. In their Lordships' judgment in the absence of special factors where one out of a larger body of trustees has the trust property vested in him he is bound by the trust and must give effect to it by transferring the trust property into the name of all the trustees.

This reasoning rather leaves some points in the air (see Rickett [2001] 65 Conv 515 but cf Hopkins [2001] CLJ 483). First, whilst there is no doubt that TCP had declared himself to be a trustee, it is less evident how legal title in the assets was transferred to him *in that capacity*. A possible inference to be drawn from the judgment is that the case must be treated as one of a declaration by TCP of himself as trustee rather than one of transfer to trustees. A difficulty with this proposition is that it does not fit comfortably either with the language used by TCP or with the conclusion on the facts reached by the lower courts. Second, if this is the explanation then notwithstanding the view of their Lordships that this case falls between the two options available in *Milroy v Lord* it is difficult to see why this could not be construed as failed transfer being validated as a declaration of trust. An alternative interpretation adopting the unconscionability point is that the trust obligation to which TCP was subject prior to his death was a constructive trust 'imposed' to prevent TCP resiling from his obligation to transfer the assets to all the trustees. Notwithstanding these considerations there is little doubt that the judgment enabled the general intention of TCP to leave his wealth to the Foundation to be implemented. And therein lies the attraction and potentially the risk of the approach exhibited by the court. It is evident that their lordships in *Choithram* are turning their face against what may be seen as overly rigid application of rules. In explanation Lord Browne-Wilkinson offers us a qualification or modern gloss of the maxim 'equity will not assist a volunteer' by adding that '[equity] will not strive officiously to defeat a gift' (at 12).

The sentiment underpinning the modified maxim and the siren-like lure of 'unconscionability' are evident in a decision of the Court of Appeal in *Pennington v Waine* [2002] 1 WLR 2075. The case is yet another instance of litigation about the beneficial ownership of property arising on the death of a donor where purported transfer of legal title had not yet been completed. The donor Ada Crampton was the beneficial owner of 1,500 of 2,000 issued shares in a private family company. At a meeting on 30 September 1998 with Pennington (P), a partner in the company's auditors, Ada indicated that she wished to transfer immediately 400 of her shares to her nephew Harold (H), the company secretary, seemingly with the intention that H should become a director and eventually have a 51% shareholding in the company. P prepared a share transfer form that Ada signed and returned to him. The form was placed 'on the company's file' and no further action was taken with regard to it prior to Ada's death in November 1998. On 15 October 1998 P wrote to H (i) enclosing a form for H to sign giving his consent to become a director and (ii) informing Harold about the 'transfer' of 400 shares to him, adding that this transfer required no further action on H's part. H signed and Ada countersigned the director's consent form. Prior to her death Ada executed a will on 10 November leaving H 620 shares, which, together with the 400 shares, would constitute a 51% shareholding. The will made no mention of the 400 shares. The question posed for the court in litigation instigated by Ada's executors was whether those 400 shares formed part of the residuary estate or were to be held on trust by them for H absolutely. If the latter then how had this come about? Unlike *Choithram* there was no question in the case of there being a declaration of trust by Ada. Did then the purported gift satisfy the requirements of the principle in *Re Rose*? Had Ada done everything that she had to do so that in the words of Browne-Wilkinson LJ in *Mascall v Mascall* 'the donee [had] within his control all those things necessary to enable him to complete his title' ([1984] 50 P & CR 119 at 126). The Court of Appeal upheld the gift in equity notwithstanding its acceptance of the fact that Ada had *not* done everything in her power to transfer the shares to Harold, in that the transfer form had neither been sent to the company for registration nor delivered to H. Arden LJ, with whom Schieman LJ concurred, stated that there could be circumstances where delivery of, in this instance, the share transfer form would be unnecessary so far as the perfection of the gift in equity was concerned. The circumstances are those when it would be 'unconscionable' for the donor to purport to recall the gift and 'there can be no comprehensive list of

factors which make it unconscionable for the donor to change his or her mind:
it must depend on the court's evaluation of all the relevant considerations' (at
2090–2091). The relevant facts in this case, according to Arden LJ, were (ibid):

> [1] Ada made a gift of her own free will: . . . [2] She not only told Harold about the gift and
> signed a form of transfer which [3] she delivered to [P] to secure registration: [4] her agent
> also told Harold that he need take no action. [5] In addition Harold agreed to become a
> director of the Company without limit of time, which he could not do without shares being
> transferred to him.

Facts [1] to [3] merely establish that Ada had not complied with the *Re Rose*
requirements in that the form had not been delivered to H. The finding of
'unconscionability' must therefore rest on the addition of facts [4] and [5] to
the matrix but, as critics of the judgment have almost universally pointed out,
it is difficult to see why Ada's conscience should have been affected unless some
detriment had been suffered by Harold (see eg Doggett [2003] CLJ 263; Ford
[2002] 13(2) KCLJ 222; Ladds (2003) 17(1) TLI 35; Tijo and Yeo [2002] LMCLQ
296; Halliwell [2002] Conv 192). We are here moving close to the language of
estoppel but it is doubtful that either [4] or [5] would constitute the sort of
detrimental reliance associated with this concept (see below, p 191). Moreover
the judgments make no mention of estoppel, relying instead on a more general
and arguably vague notion of 'unconscionability'. As if sensitive to the possible
weaknesses of this position Arden LJ suggests in the alternative that a principle
of benevolent construction – in a sense adopting Lord Browne-Wilkinson's
dictum that 'equity should not strive officiously to defeat a gift' – could be
applied. The problem of non-delivery of the share transfers could thereby be
rectified by finding that the words used by P (constituting fact [4] above) should
be construed as meaning that Ada and P became agents for H for the purpose
of submitting the share transfer to the Company. On this reasoning delivery to
H's agent and therefore in effect to H had been completed, bringing the case
more closely within the letter of the rule in *Re Rose*.

A postscript to the case is that in subsequent litigation Ada's 'transfer' of
the shares to H was held to have been ineffective because it was in breach
of the articles of the private company which gave other shareholders a 'right
of pre-emption' to the shares (*Brian Hurst v Crampton Bros (Coopers) Ltd* [2003]
1 BCLC 304). Consequently H would be entitled to the shares only if the pre-
emption right was not exercised, his entitlement otherwise being only to the
price paid for the shares. The sub-text to the litigation is that it predominantly
concerned a family tussle for control of the company.

(5) Comment

In both *Choithram* and *Pennington v Waine* the judgments of the Privy Council
and Court of Appeal respectively involved a generous interpretation and application of the established equity doctrines or even as in *Choithram* a reformulation

of them. In practical terms in neither of the recent cases nor indeed in *Re Rose* was the court faced with an attempt by a donor to resile from an intended gift. Indeed in all the cases the hypothetical question – 'would equity have permitted the donor to revoke the gift?' – could be answered in the negative safe in the realisation that the court was enabling their arguably accurate perceptions of the deceased donor's intentions to be implemented. But it was suggested at the start of our discussion on this topic that invoking unconscionability as a ground for the decisions is a risky enterprise. This is particularly so in *Pennington v Waine* where the notion of unconscionability acted as the starter motor for imposing the obligation of constructive trusteeship on Ada and her executors. At least in *Choithram,* if one accepts the reasoning of their Lordships in the Privy Council, the element of unconscionability derives from the finding that the donor would have been in breach of a pre-existing obligation as trustee.

There is little doubt that the courts have moved a considerable distance from the position delineated in *Milroy v Lord.* From the *Re Rose* cases onwards, with their addition of the magical words 'within his [the settlor's] power' to the classic statement of Turner LJ in *Milroy v Lord,* there has been an incremental softening of the application of the criteria set out in that case. It remains to be seen whether 'unconscionability' is capable of providing an operable test for determining the circumstances when '[equity] will not strive officiously to defeat a gift' or simply leaves us in a position of uncertainty. The exercise of subjective perceptions of justice and good conscience leading to a lack of predictability of outcome would be an unwelcome consequence of *Pennington v Waine.* But whilst we should be wary of straying down that path, the notion of open-textured concepts, such as unconscionability, as organising or unifying themes is scarcely unknown to the law (see eg Halliwell *Equity and Good Conscience* (2nd edn, 2004); Delany and Ryan [2008] Conv 401–436 although critical of *Pennington v Waine*). What remains debatable in the immediate context, however, is whether one can identify appropriate and workable *objective* criteria that can guard against unconscionability dissolving into the exercise of unfettered discretion. A pragmatic if somewhat unprincipled response is that fears that claimants could readily invoke 'unconscionability' as a ground to prevent erstwhile donors from ever changing their minds are probably groundless unless the detriment hurdle to be overcome by claimants is lowered even further.

It only remains to emphasise that a corollary of the 'rule' in *Re Rose* is that once the transferor has done 'everything in his power' to transfer title in the property, it is too late to resile from the decision. Thus in *Mascall v Mascall* (1985) 49 P & CR 119, a father planning to transfer registered land to his son completed the relevant parts of the transfer form and handed it to him. Before the son had submitted the document to the Land Registry to acquire title, father and son unfortunately fell out. To the chagrin of the father, the transfer was declared effective, *Re Rose* being cited as authority. The father had done all that he needed to, as the son could make the application to the Land Registry.

(d) Creation of trusts and disposition of equitable interests: testamentary formalities

(1) Wills Act

The Wills Act 1837, s 9, as amended by the Administration of Justice Act 1982, s 17, specifies the strict formalities necessary for effective disposition of property – including creation of trusts – by will.

---

9. Signing and attestation of wills

No will shall be valid unless –

(a) it is in writing, and signed by the testator, or by some other person in his presence and by his direction; and

(b) it appears that the testator intended by his signature to give effect to the will; and

(c) the signature is made or acknowledged by the testator in the presence of two or more witnesses present at the same time; and

(d) each witness either –

    (i) attests and signs the will; or

    (ii) acknowledges his signature, in the presence of the testator (but not necessarily in the presence of any other witness), but no form of attestation shall be necessary.

Section 1 of the Act states that 'the word "will"' includes a testament . . . and any other testamentary disposition'. An attempt to create a testamentary trust by an instrument which does not comply with the requirements of s 9 will fail because the purported will itself is void. Furthermore, once a valid will is made any subsequent changes must also conform to the above requirements. Consequently, any provision, whether embodied in a will or incorporated into it by reference, purporting to reserve to the testator a power to alter the will without observing the necessary formalities is also void (*Re Edwards* [1948] Ch 440).

(2) Secret trusts

In view of the above it is initially puzzling to discover that if a testator (T) leaves property by his will perhaps to a trusted friend (A) absolutely and beneficially but T, while alive, has informed A that the property is to be held on specified trusts then, provided A accepts the trust, it is enforceable. Alternatively T may leave property to A with a direction in the will that it is to be held on trust, and details of the trust are not contained in the will but have been communicated to A before or at the time of the will. Here too the trust is enforceable.

These two methods of imposing a trust obligation, labelled secret trusts and half-secret trusts respectively, appear to conflict directly with s 9 of the Wills Act. Originally the existence of a conflict was implicitly accepted since the validity of secret trusts was initially based on an application of the maxim 'Equity will not permit a statute to be used as an instrument of fraud' (see *McCormick v Grogan* (1869) LR 4 HL 82 per Lord Hatherley LC and Lord Westbury). The modern analysis, as we shall see, is that there exists no conflict between s 9 and secret and half-secret trusts because such trusts are considered to operate outside the will: 'the whole basis of secret trusts . . . is that they operate outside the will, changing nothing that is written in it, and allowing it to operate according to its tenor, but then fastening a trust on to the property in the hands of the recipient' (per Megarry VC in *Re Snowden* [1979] 2 All ER 172 at 177). None the less it is difficult to deny that these trusts create a gap in the apparent stringency of the law concerning formalities for testamentary dispositions and are therefore in conflict with its policy. It is said (*Pettit* p 97) that 'it would be inappropriate and indeed misleading' to discuss the rules relating to secret and half-secret trusts in a section concerned with formalities. In our contrary view the recognition and operation of such trusts are best evaluated in the context of the policy considerations which require formalities to be observed.

Before identifying the requirements for secret and half-secret trusts it is worth reflecting on the reasons why testators should seek to rely on these devices. A will admitted to probate is a public document open to inspection by any member of the public. Such exposure will not necessarily appeal to some testators, who may therefore wish to keep their testamentary dispositions secret. In particular a testator may wish to keep a disposition secret from a narrower public, the other members of the family. And the classic historic reason for secrecy is said to be the wish of testators to provide for mistresses or illegitimate children or other persons or causes considered unwise to acknowledge publicly. This does not do full justice to the device which certainly in its sixteenth-century origins provided a means to protect property against the consequences of religious persecution (see eg *Bertie (Duchess of Suffolk) v Herenden* (1560) in Baker (1977) 93 LQR 33). These were trusts that depended on trust since, as Jones has pointed out: 'That they should come to litigation was unthinkable when they were created: . . . Should the trustees fail, unless the circumstances were changed which had given rise to the need for the trust in the first place, nothing could be done' ('Trusts in England after the Statute of Uses: A view from the 16th Century' in Helmholz and Zimmermann (eds) *Itinera Fiduciae* (1998) pp 173–205 at p 205). Understandably therefore there is a temptation to treat secret trusts as something of an historical anachronism. On the other hand the findings of recent research suggest that any sounding of the death knell of the secret trust may be premature. In a representative sample survey of probate practitioners conducted in 2001, 54% of respondents rejected the view that secret trusts were obsolete (Meager 'Secret Trusts – Do They Have a Future?' [2003] 67 Conv 203–214). Moreover 16% of the sample had been involved in the creation of fully secret trusts and a further 20% in half-secret trusts. Whilst, given the persistence of human frailty, the classic historical reason for creating secret trusts still exists the survey identifies a quite diverse range of other purposes including somewhat dubious attempts to conceal beneficial ownership from the state. The survey also tends to support the proposition that today it is more likely that the indecisive rather than secretive testator will use a secret trust. A will can be made leaving property to a trusted friend or a co-operative solicitor while retaining the ability to decide subsequently on the ultimate distribution of the property, thus avoiding compliance with the formalities required by the Wills Act. Whether this is a desirable policy to pursue will be considered below after examining the requirements for valid secret and half-secret trusts and their theoretical basis.

(3) Requirements for fully secret trusts

These were summarised by Brightman J in *Ottaway v Norman* [1971] 3 All ER 1325 at 1332:

> It will be convenient to call the person on whom such a trust is imposed the 'primary donee' and the beneficiary under that trust the 'secondary donee'. The essential elements which must be proved to exist are: (i) the intention of the testator to subject the primary donee to an obligation in favour of the secondary donee; (ii) communication of that intention to the primary donee; and (iii) the acceptance of that obligation by the primary donee either expressly or by acquiescence. It is immaterial whether these elements precede or succeed the will of the donor.

Communication to the secret trustee, which can be made through an authorised agent, must take place and the trust obligation be accepted during the lifetime of the testator although the acceptance can be either express or implied (*Wallgrave v Tebbs* (1855) 2 K & J 313, silence on the part of the trustee being construed as acceptance; *Moss v Cooper* (1861) 1 John & H 352). It follows that, where the proposed trustee does not learn of the existence of a proposed trust until after the testator's death, the trust is unenforceable and the trustee can retain full beneficial ownership of the property. A nice question is whether communication to, and acceptance of the obligation by, one or some only of two or more persons apparently beneficially entitled to property can bind them all. Perrins has persuasively argued ((1972) 88 LQR 225), contrary to orthodoxy (*Re Stead* [1900] 1 Ch 237), that the innocent recipient of an apparent gift should be bound by the secret trust only if the gift was induced by the promise of the knowing recipient.

Furthermore, the full details of the trust must be communicated. If a secret trustee is informed by the testator only that the property is to be held on trust but not advised of the terms of the trust, the property must then be held by the secret trustee on resulting trust for residuary devisees or legatees, if any, and otherwise, or if the trust property is residuary property, for those entitled on intestacy. It was accepted by Lord Wright MR in *Re Keen* [1937] Ch 236 that, by a quaint analogy with a ship sailing under sealed orders, there would be adequate communication and acceptance if the details of the trust were put in writing and placed in the trustee's possession in a sealed envelope even though marked 'Not to be opened until after my death'.

Secret trusts are not restricted to circumstances where, in reliance on a promise, the testator then makes a gift in favour of the secret trustee or leaves an existing disposition unrevoked. A secret trust can also arise where, in reliance on a promise to implement the trust by the person entitled on intestacy, no will is made (*Stickland v Aldridge* (1804) 9 Ves 516).

The usual method of implementing the secret trust is by the trustee making an inter vivos transfer of the trust property to the designated beneficiary, but it has been held (see *Ottaway v Norman* [1971] 3 All ER 1325 and *Re Young* [1951] Ch 344) that the doctrine can apply where the obligation on the secret trustee is to make a will leaving specified property to the intended beneficiary of the secret trust.

The description above from *Ottaway v Norman* of the 'essential elements' of a secret trust leave out of account the matter of 'constitution'. When does the trustee take the legal title to the property so that the trust is 'completely constituted'? The answer would seem to be that the property vests in the secret trustee – or legatee where the trust relies on the operation of the insolvency rules – only when the will or intestacy rules take effect on the death of the settlor. This analysis is certainly consistent with the position that the trust, like the will itself, can be revoked at any time before death (see eg *Re Cooper* [1939] Ch 811 and *Kasperbauer v Griffith* [2000] WTLR 333 per Peter Gibson LJ and Harman LJ). An implication of the analysis, one might have thought, is that if the secret beneficiary predeceases the settlor then the gift would lapse. Certainly in the case of a will itself if a legatee or devisee predeceases the testator the gift lapses and becomes part of the residuary estate. It is therefore surprising to discover that in *Re Gardner (No 2)* [1923] 2 Ch 230 Romer J held that the estate of a deceased beneficiary was entitled to the designated share of the trust property. The decision has been much criticised, Hayton, for instance, aptly commenting 'that the authority of *Re Gardener* [sic] is . . . very doubtful indeed' (*Hayton and Mitchell* at p 119; for a full discussion of this issue see Kincaid 'The Tangled Web: the relationship between a secret trust and the will' [2000] 64 Conv 420 at 431–434; Pawlowski and Brown [2004] Conv 388–398).

An obvious potential source of difficulty is proving the existence of a secret trust. The cautious testator will doubtless at least ensure both that the beneficiary is notified of the secret trust and that documentary evidence of the trust is available. 'A good practical precaution is for the testator to have a document signed by the intended trustee put into the possession of the secret beneficiaries' (*Hayton and Mitchell* p 105). The cautious trustee also may wish to have suitable evidence available. Thus in circumstances where a bequest is made to a solicitor on a secret trust it is advisable for solicitors to preserve the instructions from which the will was drawn and ensure that the terms of the secret trust are embodied in a written document, preferably signed or initialled by the testator.

If a dispute does arise the standard of proof is the ordinary civil standard of proof – the balance of probabilities – that is required to establish the existence of any ordinary trust (*Re Snowden* [1979] 2 All ER 172 at 179, but *contra Ottaway v Norman* [1971] 3 All ER 1325 at 1333). Where fraud is involved there is authority that a higher standard will be required (*Re Snowden*). But as Rickett has argued ((1979) 38 CLJ 260), if the real justification for the enforcement of secret trusts is that courts wish to carry out the revealed intentions of the testator, then fraud is irrelevant: 'What matters is the existence of a trust, and this is established by the ordinary method' (at 263). Debate about identifying the appropriate standard of proof therefore tends to obscure the point that the key question the court must face (as in *Re Snowden*) is whether the facts are sufficient to identify an intention to create a binding trust obligation or merely a more nebulous and unenforceable moral one. Yet where testators have failed to make their wishes legally precise one is again confronted with the problematic nature of intention and whether a specific intention can be divined by a sifting of the facts, no matter how scrupulous. From this perspective the secret trust represents simply a specialised forum for the application of certainty of intention rules. For this reason further consideration of *Re Snowden* and *Ottaway v Norman* is postponed until p 107 where these rules and their application are discussed.

(4) Requirements for half-secret trusts

It will be recalled that under a half-secret trust the will expressly states the existence of a trust but not the details of beneficial entitlement. Consequently, any conflict as to entitlement is not between the secret trustee and the prospective beneficiary of the trust since it is not possible for the trustee to claim property beneficially. Rather, where a half-secret trust fails, the trustee will still hold the property in trust, but on a resulting trust for the residuary devisees or legatees or for those entitled on intestacy.

As regards the requirements for validity, the principal distinction between fully secret and half-secret trusts lies in the criteria for communication and acceptance of the trust. The weight of judicial dicta now seems clearly to accept that communication and acceptance of a half-secret trust must occur before or at the time of the execution of the will (*Blackwell v Blackwell* [1929] AC 318; *Re Keen* [1937] Ch 236). Subsequent communication or acceptance even if during the testator's lifetime will therefore be ineffective. Indeed, most recently in *Re Bateman's Will Trusts* [1970] 3 All ER 817 Pennycuick VC accepted that 'it is really clear and not in dispute that once one must construe the direction (to trustees) as admitting of a future letter then the direction is invalid . . .'. The justification for this approach was stated by Viscount Sumner in *Blackwell v Blackwell* to be: 'to hold otherwise would indeed be to enable the testator to "give the go-by" to the requirements of the Wills Act'. The adequacy of this reasoning will be considered in the next section. Finally, a particular evidentiary distinction, inapplicable to fully secret trusts, is that evidence as to the alleged half-secret trust is inadmissible if it is inconsistent with the terms of the will (*Re Keen*).

(5) The theoretical basis of secret trusts

An historical justification, and one accepted by the House of Lords in 1869, for the enforcement of secret trusts is found in the doctrine of fraud: it would be a fraud on the part of the legatee to rely on the failure to comply with the statutory formalities necessary to create a testamentary trust and thus retain beneficial ownership of the property. This explanation was not without its difficulties as regards both the ultimate destination of trust property and the validity of half-secret trusts.

R H Maudsley 'Incompletely Constituted Trusts' in R Pound (ed) *Perspectives of Law* (1964) pp 254–256

Fraud would, no doubt, be a very adequate reason to prevent (the legatee) from taking beneficially, but the fact that [he] cannot take beneficially does not necessarily mean that the 'secret beneficiary' can take; unjust enrichment would be avoided by declaring a resulting trust for the estate. In this type of situation, however, both American and English courts hold that the beneficial interest goes forward to the intended beneficiary. This is so in England whether the question arises *inter vivos* or under a will, and little thought has been given to the question whether the beneficial interest goes forward to the beneficiary or back to the estate . . . [cf Hodge [1980] Conv 341 who argues against the resulting trust solution, on the basis that the fraud is on the secret beneficiary as well as the testator].

It has just been assumed that, once fraud prevents the legatee from taking, the beneficiary is entitled. We therefore seek some rational justification for projecting forward the beneficial interest. Such a situation makes interesting and relevant the theory that the trust is declared *inter vivos*, independently of the will and that, being incompletely constituted until the death, it is constituted by the vesting in the trustee of the ownership of the property.

In *Blackwell v Blackwell* [1929] AC 318 the House of Lords advanced the proposition that half-secret trusts are enforced on the same principles as fully secret trusts, both operating outside the will in the manner referred to by Maudsley, thus supposedly avoiding conflict with the Wills Act 1837. Some subsequent decisions of the courts are certainly consistent with this analysis. In *Re Young* [1951] Ch 344, for instance, a beneficial interest under a secret trust was upheld even though the beneficiary was a witness to the will. The normal rule (Wills Act 1837, s 15) that a witness to a will forfeits any beneficial interest arising under that will was held inapplicable by Danckwerts J (at 350):

[the person] does not take by virtue of the gift in the will, but by virtue of the secret trusts imposed upon the [trustee] who does in fact take under the will.

The reasoning in *Blackwell*, however, is not without its inconsistencies. The case concerns the validity of a half-secret trust created by a testator, John Blackwell, who wished to provide for a lady and her illegitimate son. The testator by a codicil gave £12,000 to five persons upon trust, the income to be applied 'for the purposes indicated by me to them'. The trust had been accepted prior to the execution of the codicil. The residuary legatees (including the testator's widow) claimed that no valid trust had been created on the basis principally that parol evidence was inadmissible to establish 'the purposes'. The House of Lords unanimously upheld the validity of the trust.

Viscount Sumner referred to a 'current of decisions' (including *Re Fleet-wood* (1880) 15 Ch D 594 and *Re Huxtable* [1902] 2 Ch 793) upholding half-secret trusts and then explained his reason for aligning the two forms of secret trust:

> Why should equity forbid an honest trustee to give effect to his promise, made to a deceased testator, and compel him to pay another legatee, about whom it is quite certain that the testator did not mean to make him the object of his bounty? In both [fully secret and half-secret] cases the testator's wishes are incompletely expressed in his will. Why should equity, over a mere matter of words, give effect to them in one case and frustrate them in the other? No doubt the words 'in trust' prevent the legatee from taking beneficially, whether they have simply been declared in conversation or written in the will, but the fraud, when the trustee, so called in the will, is also the residuary legatee, is the same as when he is only declared a trustee by word of mouth accepted by him. I recoil from interfering with decisions of long standing, which reject this anomaly, unless constrained by statute....

Viscount Sumner discussed the relationship between the equitable principle and the Wills Act, s 9, and concluded that:

> ... The effect, therefore, of a bequest being made in terms on trust, without any statement in the will to show what the trust is, remains to be decided by the law as laid down by the courts before and since the Act and does not depend on the Act itself.
>
> The limits, beyond which the rules as to unspecified trusts must not be carried, have often been discussed. A testator cannot reserve to himself a power of making future unwitnessed dispositions by merely naming a trustee and leaving the purposes of the trust to be supplied afterwards, nor can a legatee give testamentary validity to an unexecuted codicil by accepting an indefinite trust, never communicated to him in the testator's lifetime. To hold otherwise would indeed be to enable the testator to 'give the go-by' to the requirements of the Wills Act, because he did not choose to comply with them. It is communication of the purpose to the legatee, coupled with acquiescence or promise on his part, that removes the matter from the provision of the Wills Act and brings it within the law of trusts as applied in this instance to trustees, who happen also to be legatees ...

The decision in *Blackwell v Blackwell* does not equate secret and half-secret trusts for all purposes. Dicta in the judgment of Viscount Sumner indicate that communication of the details of a half-secret trust must take place before or at the time of the date of the will. This particular continuing distinction has been widely criticised (eg *Hayton and Mitchell* p 110; but cf Perrins [1985] Conv 248). It should be noted that the approach adopted to this matter by the English courts does not reflect universal practice, as is evidenced by the law in Ireland and many US jurisdictions (see Mee [1992] Conv 202). There is also Australian authority that communication of a half-secret trust need take place only before the death of the settlor rather than before the execution of the will (*Ledgerwood v Perpetual Trustee* [1997] 41 NSWLR 532).

Consider the following points:

(1) Viscount Sumner's explanation for the 'continuing distinction' – 'a testator cannot reserve to himself a power of making future unwitnessed dispositions by merely naming a trustee and leaving the purposes of the trust to be supplied afterwards' – does not seem consistent with his view that both secret and half-secret trusts operate outside the will and independently of the Wills Act. Moreover the very objective that he seeks to forestall, as set out in his explanation above, can be achieved by means of a fully secret trust. After all the terms of the trust there can be altered without legal formality after execution of the will. It is therefore difficult to see a policy rationale for retaining the 'continuing distinction' (but cf Wilde [1995] Conv 366 who suggests that stricter rules are appropriate for half-secret trusts since they are invariably drawn up by solicitors which process should involve awareness of the formal rules).

(2) It is not necessary when creating trusts, other than secret trusts, either that the trustees' consent to their appointment be sought or that details of the trust be communicated to them in advance. A person is, after all, free subsequently to decline the trusteeship, and such a refusal does not affect the validity of the trust itself; the principle that equity will not allow a trust to fail for want of a trustee would apply. Why, therefore, should communication and acceptance, at whatever stage, be deemed essential for a valid secret trust? Doubtless it is a commonsense precaution but a legal answer appears to reside, and is implicit in the language used by Viscount Sumner in *Blackwell*, in the notion of reliance on the promise of the trustee. This explanation then seems at least as consistent with a rationale for validating secret trusts based on prevention of fraud or unconscionable behaviour as on fulfilling a testator's expressed wishes. The picture, however, is clouded by residual uncertainty about the consequences of a disclaimer of the legacy or devise by the proposed trustee after the death of the testator. In *Re Maddock* [1902] 2 Ch 220 at 231 Cozens-Hardy LJ was of the view that the trust would fail in the case of a fully secret trust, seemingly on the basis that it depends upon the existence of a personal obligation binding 'the trustee'. On the other hand dicta of Lord Buckmaster in *Blackwell* suggests that the fully secret trust would be upheld in such circumstances (at 328): 'I entertain no doubt that the court having once admitted the evidence of the trust, would interfere to prevent its defeat.'

(3) We have seen that the *modern* justification for enforcing secret trusts is that they are not testamentary dispositions and that they operate outside the will in the sense that the communication and acceptance of the obligation occur inter vivos and all that the will does is to transfer legal title in the subject-matter of the trust to the secret trustee. Now it is arguable that this analysis represents an ex post facto rationalisation of their enforcement since there is authority that the original explanation was to prevent fraud by the 'trustee'. Moreover the modern explanation has not gone unchallenged. Let us accept (i) that testamentary gifts must comply with the formalities of the Wills Act, and (ii) that a proposed testamentary gift has two distinguishing features. These are that it is revocable at any time up until the death of the testator and that it remains undefined and ineffective ('ambulatory') until the testator's death, the effect being that the testator can still deal with his property as he wishes during his lifetime. Let us further accept that a secret trust is only completely constituted on the transfer of legal title to the 'trustee' on the testator's death, and is only intended to become operative from that time. Until then the trust is revocable, for instance by amendment to the will. The problem for the 'dehors (outside) the will' theory is to explain satisfactorily the position whereby secret trusts share at least some of the characteristics of testamentary gifts whilst not complying with the formalities of the Wills Act.

Critchley, for instance, argues that the 'dehors' theory is implausible ('Instruments of Fraud, Testamentary Dispositions, and the Doctrine of Secret Trusts' (1999) 115 LQR 631). She emphasises the point that the Wills Act, s 9 applies to *any* testamentary disposition and that secret trusts are testamentary dispositions because they exhibit the key indicia of such dispositions, namely they are revocable and, notwithstanding *Re Gardner No 2* [1923] 2 Ch 230, ambulatory. She therefore concludes (at 641): '[T]he *dehors* theory seems to be fatally flawed. In essence, the mistake is to confuse "outside the will" with "outside the *Wills Act*". The *dehors* theory needs – and fails – to demonstrate the truth of the latter and too often ends up resting merely upon the former, which is wholly inadequate as a justificatory argument.' Critchley persuasively identifies some difficulties with the dehors theory but, as she acknowledges and as we have already seen, an avoidance of fraud justification for enforcing secret trusts is also not compelling in every instance (see Maudsley above, p 151, and Critchley at 646–653). Whilst the fraud theory may support the enforcement of a fully secret trust where a trustee actively seeks to deny the trust and keep the property, it remains problematic, even in the more extensive formulation advocated by Critchley, in most other instances of fully secret or half-secret trusts.

(4) 'The conclusion (affirmed in *Blackwell v Blackwell*) that secret trusts operate outside the will is simply a pragmatic compromise that seeks unsatisfactorily to reconcile equitable principles, the policy of the Wills Act and professional practice.' Do you agree?

(6) Mutual wills, secret trusts and donatio mortis causa: a juridical conundrum

One issue left unresolved, indeed until recently almost untouched by the courts (see Burgess (1972) 23 NILQ 263; Sheridan (1951) 67 LQR 314), is the juridical nature of fully secret and half-secret trusts. The majority of textbook opinion (eg *Hanbury and Martin* – somewhat ambivalently – p 168; *Pettit* p 129; Oakley *Constructive Trusts* (3rd edn, 1997) p 130; and *Parker & Mellows* p 142; cf *Snell* p 559) leans towards treating fully secret and half-secret trusts as express trusts. The conclusion rests principally on the basis that the trust has been expressly declared by the initial communication to and acceptance by the trustee and is then constituted by the transfer of the property to the trustee and hence not imposed by the court. On the other hand, Sheridan ((1951) 67 LQR 314) has suggested that although half-secret trusts are express, fully secret trusts are constructive. There is a danger of circularity of reasoning here in so far as one's conclusion simply comes to reflect the prior analysis as to how secret trusts are enforced, ie on a 'fraud' or a 'dehors the will' theory.

In any event is the disagreement of any practical importance? It can be argued that the question is not merely reflective of an academic desire to pigeonhole secret trusts conceptually. If they are express trusts, is writing required under LPA 1925, s 53(1)(b) if the subject-matter of the trust is land? In contrast a constructive trust of land is exempt from the formalities requirements by virtue of LPA 1925, s 53(2). Yet even if secret trusts are express trusts it can be argued that secret trusts of land should still be enforced despite the absence of writing through application of the original explanation of their validity, prevention of fraud. The absence of writing to comply either with the Wills Act or LPA 1925, s 53(1)(b) would then be disregarded by application of the maxim that equity will not permit a statute to be used as an instrument of fraud (see above, p 126).

In *Ottaway v Norman* [1971] 3 All ER 1325, a fully secret trust of land was upheld without written evidence, but frustratingly there was no discussion either of the categorisation of secret trusts or of the relevance of any of the LPA requirements (see also *Brown v Pourau* [1995] 1 NZLR 352; discussed by Rickett [1996] Conv 302). Brightman J was content with the observation that 'the basis of the doctrine of secret trust is the obligation imposed on the conscience of the primary donee'. As Oakley points out (p 129), *Ottaway v Norman* 'might be thought to suggest, if only by virtue of the silence of the courts, that fully secret trusts are not express trusts'. But *Ottaway v Norman* cannot be conclusive. Dicta in a more recent judgment by Nourse J in *Re Cleaver* [1981] 2 All ER 1018, a case concerning mutual wills – a mode of property disposition analogous to secret trusts – advance a constructive trust conclusion. Whilst we do not discuss mutual wills in detail (see *Hanbury and Martin* pp 324–331; *Hayton and Mitchell* pp 121–126; Pearce and Stevens *The Law of Trusts and Equitable Obligations* (4th edn, 2006) pp 356–370) a brief note of explanation here should help point out both their similarities with and distinctions from secret trusts, and put Nourse J's analysis in perspective.

Mutual will The term 'mutual will' describes the arrangement whereby two people (usually (H)usband and (W)ife), having mutually agreed that they wish the same person(s) to have their property after they (H and W) are both dead, leave their respective properties to each other ('the mutual wills') – so that the survivor will benefit from all the property – with a remainder gift to the agreed ultimate beneficiaries. The fact that similar or even identical wills are made is a relevant but not decisive factor in establishing the existence of mutual wills: there must be evidence of a precise agreement to make and not to revoke the mutual wills (see *Re Goodchild* [1997] 1 WLR 1216, CA on the possible evidentiary difficulties in establishing that an agreement is to be legally and not just morally binding on the survivor). It is, however, not essential that the parties should leave the property the subject of the agreement to each other. The mutual wills doctrine has been applied in circumstances where the two testators had agreed to leave the property to particular beneficiaries rather than to each other (*Proctor v Dale* [1993] 4 All ER 129).

What clearly distinguishes a mutual will conceptually from a secret trust is that before the death of the first testator the agreement is a contractual one between two testators: 'without it the property of the second testator is not bound, whereas a secret trust concerns only the property of a person in the position of the first testator' (*Re Goodchild decd* at 1224 criticised by Harper [1997] Conv 182). The complication for the mutual wills agreement is that an existing will is always revocable either by specific act or, as in *Re Goodchild decd*, automatically on remarriage. Revocation would, of course, constitute a breach of the original agreement. If some such breach of the mutual wills agreement were to occur during the testators' joint lifetimes – for instance, by H revoking his will without informing W but then predeceasing her – one might expect W to seek a remedy, if such is available, in damages from H's executors for breach of contract (but cf *Bigg v Queensland Trustees Ltd* [1990] 2 Qd R 11; see generally Youdan (1979) 29 U Toronto LJ 390 and Rickett (1991) 54 MLR 581).

The problem that particularly concerns us here, however, occurs where the contractual arrangement is infringed by the survivor revoking his or her will and executing a new will with different terms and benefiting another beneficiary. It has been assumed that the privity rule prevents the original beneficiary obtaining a contractual remedy against the survivor or his or her estate. The impact of the Contracts (Rights of Third Parties) Act 1999 in these circumstances is yet to be determined but it may now be possible for the beneficiary to enforce the contract in his or her own right. If that is not so then it is here that the trust comes into the reckoning as an element of the mutual wills doctrine: the executors of the new will must hold the property, the subject-matter of the agreement, on a constructive trust for the original named beneficiary.

It is from this base that Nourse J attempted to build a broader statement of principle:

Re Cleaver [1981] 2 All ER 1018 at 1025

> ... these cases of mutual wills are only one example of a wider category of cases, for example secret trusts, in which a court of equity will intervene to impose a constructive trust... The principle of all these cases is that a court of equity will not permit a person to whom property is transferred by way of gift, but on the faith of an agreement or clear understanding that it is to be dealt with in a particular way for the benefit of a third person, to deal with that property inconsistently with that agreement or understanding. If he attempts to do so after having received the benefit of the gift equity will intervene by imposing a constructive trust on the property which is the subject matter of the agreement or understanding. I take that statement of principle, and much else which is of assistance in this case, from the judgment of Slade J in *Re Pearson Fund Trusts* (21 October 1977, unreported: the statement of principle is at p 52 of the official transcript). The judgment of Brightman J in *Ottaway v Norman* is to much the same effect.
>
> I would emphasise that the agreement or understanding must be such as to impose on the donee a legally binding obligation to deal with the property in the particular way and that the other two certainties, namely those as to the subject matter of the trust and the persons intended to benefit under it, are as essential to this species of trust as they are to any other.

No reasoning is advanced for extending a constructive trust conclusion to include secret trusts although subsequently the Court of Appeal have cited the opinion of Nourse J with approval (*Kasperbauer v Griffith* (1997) [2000] WTLR 333). Indeed, one might question whether a formal certainty of objects test, even in its modern very liberal form as applied to express trusts (see Chapter 5), would normally be seen as a requirement for the imposition of a constructive trust (see Rickett [1996] Conv 302)). The classification issue remains unresolved. Yet paradoxically *Re Cleaver* may lend even greater point to Burgess's comment that '... it is, perhaps, significant that the courts, when discussing secret trusts, have refrained from attempting to put them into any of the recognised categories of express or constructive trusts' ((1972) 23 NILQ 263 at 268). Notwithstanding Nourse J's constructive trust classification, the breadth of the principle he expounds is equally applicable to express *and* constructive trusts. Might we even hypothesise that the previous judicial unwillingness to categorise secret trusts into an express/constructive dichotomy was symptomatic of a broader reluctance to allow the formal categories deduced from basic principles of trusts law to constrain the courts' ability to 'do justice'? If this were the case, then an apparent conceptual vacuum would nevertheless provide flexibility to impose trust obligations through the most appropriate mechanism in individual cases.

We will return to this point at the end of section 4 of this chapter but some support for this interpretation might be gleaned from another legal institution *donatio mortis causa* or 'gift made in contemplation of death'.

Donatio mortis causa (DMC) A DMC does not fit comfortably either with the formalities requirements for testamentary gifts, or with the maxim that equity will not perfect an imperfect gift. Indeed the latter proposition can be turned on its head provided that the three essential requirements for a valid DMC are met. The requirements, as recently stated by Nourse LJ in *Sen v Headley* [1991] 2 All ER 636 at 639 (following the approach adopted in *Snell's Equity* (29th edn, 1990) pp 380–384) are as follows:

> First, the gift must be made in contemplation, although not necessarily in expectation, of impending death. Secondly, the gift must be made upon the condition that it is to be absolute and perfected only on the donor's death, being revocable until that event occurs and ineffective if it does not. Thirdly, there must be a delivery of the subject matter of the gift, or the essential indicia of title thereto, which amounts to a parting with dominion and not mere physical possession over the subject matter of the gift.

The bare facts of *Sen v Headley* pointedly illustrate both the nature of a DMC and the potentially competing policy considerations facing a court where its assistance is needed to complete the gift. The plaintiff Mrs Sen had had a close relationship with the deceased, Mr Hewett, for over 30 years. Three days before his death – he was terminally ill with inoperable cancer – he told the plaintiff that his house was to be hers adding: 'You have the keys. They are in your bag. The deeds are in the steel box.' The Court of Appeal accepted that possession of the sole key which provided access to the deeds satisfied the requirements for delivery of the essential *indicia* of title to the house. Mrs Sen's claim that a valid DMC had been made was contested by one of the deceased's relatives who would be entitled to the property under the intestacy rules. The Court of Appeal, contrary to previous authority which doubted whether land could be the subject-matter of a DMC (*Duffield v Elwes* (1827) 1 Bli NS 497, [1824–34] All ER 247 and *Bayliss v Public Trustee* (1988) 12 NSWLR 540), upheld Mrs Sen's claim, in effect imputing a constructive trust to perfect her full legal and equitable title.

The practical consequence of this controversial decision (see Sparkes (1992) 43 NILQ 35, cf Thorneley (1991) 50 CLJ 404 and Halliwell [1991] Conv 307), is that a death-bed gift of a house, reportedly worth in excess of £300,000, could apparently be validated by a few terse words and the placing of a key into the donee's handbag (see also 'the sterile appeal' in *Woodard v Woodard* [1996] 1 FLR 399, CA – a valid DMC of an Austin Metro by handing over a set of keys). But as Nourse LJ commented, in acknowledging the anomalous nature of the DMC doctrine, 'A *donatio mortis causa* of land is neither more nor less anomalous than any other. Every such gift is a circumvention of the Wills Act 1837' (at 647). There is, however, certainly nothing novel in legal systems disregarding strict application of formalities in such circumstances. Indeed as the name *donatio mortis causa* indicates the doctrine can trace its origins to Roman law.

In policy terms the examples of the doctrines of mutual wills and of DMC indicate respectively a willingness within the legal system, on the one hand, to counter fraud broadly defined and, on the other, to sidestep formalities in the interests of facilitating the wishes of donors. The question that remains is whether the policy rationales for these examples are equally applicable in the case of secret trusts.

(7) Secret trusts and the policy of the Wills Act

The judicial and dominant academic rationalisation for fully secret and half-secret trusts, that they operate outside the will, is unconvincing and leaves unresolved the apparent conflict with policy relating to testamentary dispositions. It may be as Friedman suggests ('The Law of the Living, the Law of the Dead: Property, Succession and Society' [1966] Wis LR 340) that 'the law of succession governs the orderly transfer of economic interests from generation to generation'. But, as Friedman points out, within the broad sweep of that objective the law regarding formalities may hope to perform a number of subsidiary functions (at 367):

> The formalities of executing a will are useful ones. They impress the testator with the solemnity of his acts; they ensure a standard written document; they eliminate most of the dangers of forgery and fraud; they encourage the use of middlemen (lawyers) who can help plan a rational, trouble-free disposition of assets.

What countervailing policy justification can there be for permitting what is potentially a significant gap in the operation of the law relating to testamentary dispositions (see generally for a discussion of the benefits and detriments of formality requirements, Critchley, 'Taking Formalities Seriously' in Bright and Dewar (eds) *Land Law: Themes and Perspectives* (1998))? Prevention of fraud can be advanced but this would be achieved negatively by merely preventing 'the secret trustee' from benefiting without enforcing the secret trust. It might even be argued that secret trusts generally are consistent with most of the functions identified by Friedman. After all non-compliance with a statutory formality does not mean that the transaction itself was entered into casually or informally. Yet Sheridan writing in 1951 had no doubts as to the merits of a more positive proposition ((1951) 67 LQR 314 at 328): 'the desire of a testator for secrecy is as much indulgeable as the desire of the State to ensure the existence of reasonable evidence of these dispositions. The trouble with the Wills Act is that it tries to provide for the evidence without making allowance for the secrecy.' The trouble with this explanation, as Gardner has pointed out (pp 92–93) is that there are other more efficient methods of achieving one's objective than a secret trust, such as setting up a bank account in the beneficiary's name. Meanwhile the plain fact remains that, unlike a *donatio mortis causa* or mutual wills, acceptance of secret trusts in principle allows any testator, not accidentally but in a deliberate and considered fashion, to circumvent the formalities of the Wills Act. But perhaps we should not be too alarmed. Although constituting a rather lame policy justification for continuing to recognise secret trusts, the probability is that few testators wish to rely on them and hence they do not constitute a serious threat to the practice of formal will-making (but cf Challinor [2005] Conv 492 who favours a more restrictive approach possibly incorporating abolition).

Even if an argument based fundamentally on freedom of testation is accepted as justifying secret trusts, it is not clear that it is adequate to support the present law in all its detail. For example, unlike half-secret trusts, details of a fully secret trust can validly be communicated to a secret trustee after the date of the execution of the will. The shakiness of the reasoning in *Blackwell v Blackwell* supporting this continuing distinction has already been referred to, and a considerable body of academic opinion supports the extension of the fully secret trust rule to half-secret trusts (see eg *Snell* at p 111 cited with approval obiter in *Gold v Hill* [1999] 1 FLR 54 at 63). The inappropriateness of the 'continuing distinction' is reinforced by the fact that it will not always be clear whether a secret or half-secret trust is intended (see eg a decisive difference of opinion in *Jankowski v Pelek Estate* (1996) 131 DLR (4th) 717 (Manitoba CA) as to whether a direction that the residuary estate be paid to 'my . . . Executor to deal with as he may in his discretion [sic] decide upon' constituted a fully secret (per Kroft and Helper JAs) or a half-secret trust (per Huband JA dissenting)). But alignment of rules can be achieved in two ways. It can be argued that the present fully secret trust rule on communication potentially encourages the indecisive rather than the secretive testator. Consequently, an alternative view is that the half-secret trust rule requiring communication before or at the time of the will should be extended to fully secret trusts. (See Watkin [1981] Conv 335 for a full discussion of the implications of this proposition; but cf Wilde [1995] Conv 366.)

4. Intention to create a binding trust obligation

(a) Certainty of intention

The hallmark of an express trust is the existence of an intention to create a binding trust obligation. To reiterate the point made previously, a generalised intention to benefit a person is in principle insufficient. There must be a specific intention to benefit by way of trust, ie to create a property interest having the attributes of a trust as conceived in equity. Hence the apparently straightforward requirement of certainty of intention. Where trusts are created in writing and based on legal advice there is unlikely to be any uncertainty as regards the obligation intended. But this clear picture becomes clouded where the maxim 'Equity looks to intent rather than the form' applies. No particular form of words is required for the creation of a trust, indeed 'a trust can be created by the most untechnical of words' (Maitland *Equity* (2nd edn, 1936) p 65) or may even be inferred from conduct. Conversely the use of the expression trust is not always conclusive evidence of a trust's existence (see *Stamp Duties Comr (Queensland) v Jolliffe* (1920) 28 CLR 178, including the dissenting judgment of Isaacs J on this point). In the remarkable 'Ocean Island Case', *Tito v Waddell (No 2)* [1977] 3 All ER 129, Megarry VC held that the expression 'trust' in documents and Mining Ordinances did not create a trust enforceable in the courts, but rather what he called a 'trust in the higher sense', meaning a non-enforceable government obligation.

Although a simple statement of principle concerning certainty of intention can be formulated, an obvious problem is the practical application of the stated requirement to varied fact situations. The problem is particularly pressing where those whose words or conduct are being analysed may be unsophisticated as far as knowledge of the principles of equity and the law of trusts is concerned. Indeed it is not unknown for professionally drafted wills, settlements and even commercial agreements to suffer from obscurity and ambiguities. A question that will then confront the courts is what sort of obligation, if any, was a particular transaction intended to impose?

In each case the court must examine the language used and, where admissible, extrinsic evidence to identify the relevant intention. Lord Upjohn in *Re Gulbenkian's Settlements* [1970] AC 508 aptly summarised the task of the court as being 'by the exercise of its judicial knowledge and experience . . . , innate common sense and desire to make sense of . . . expressed intentions, however obscure and ambiguous the language . . . , to give reasonable meaning to that language if it can do so without doing violence to it' (at 522). None the less positive identification of a specific intention may remain elusive. Can it then be argued that on occasion the court identifies the legal category most appropriate to achieving a 'desirable solution' and affirms the existence of an intention to achieve that objective? If so, the weight to be attached to particular language or conduct may depend on the circumstances in which the existence of a trust obligation is being pleaded. Thus a rigorous standard has been applied to one legally sophisticated constituency, The Law Society: 'It would, indeed, be surprising if a society of lawyers, who above all might be expected to make their intention clear in a document they compose, should have failed to express the existence of a trust, if that was what they intended to create' (*Swain v Law Society* [1982] 2 All ER 827 at 840 per Lord Brightman). Also a particular approach may be adopted where the context is commercial rather than familial, although even here the court may be faced with problems of interpretation. In *Don King Promotions Inc v Warren* [1998] 2 All ER 608 (aff'd [1999] 2 All ER 218, CA), the court took into account what the parties – the well-known boxing promoters Don King and Frank Warren – 'as a matter of business common sense [must] have intended to achieve' in deducing that they had intended the benefit of certain contractual arrangements to be held on trust for their, subsequently dissolved, partnership (see Tettenborn [1998] LMCLQ 498; and Chapter 15 on intention in other commercial contexts). In that case the court was driven somewhat surprisingly to rely on inferences drawn from agreements that 'though apparently professionally prepared . . . [are] by common consent badly drafted and replete with obscurities and inconsistencies' ([1998] 2 All ER 608 at 624).

Even within intra-family conflicts, however, the specific legal context in which doubts about intention surface may demand different emphases to be attached to similar language and conduct. Our study of certainty of intention is therefore subdivided here into (i) precatory words, (ii) declaration of trust and (iii) intention in the context of secret trusts.

(1) Precatory words ('Words in a will . . . expressing a desire that a thing be done', OED)

Problems over clarity of language have most often arisen with wills where a testator has used terms expressing confidence, wish, belief, hope or request that a legatee will use a gift in a particular way. It is widely agreed that in early cases courts readily held that such 'precatory words' imposed a trust obligation. It is now a fruitless exercise to attempt to categorise these cases, particularly as a change of attitude and approach occurred during the second half of the nineteenth century and the courts became more circumspect in identifying a trust obligation. As regards earlier cases, James LJ commented in *Lambe v Eames* (1871) 6 Ch App 597 at 599: 'in hearing case after case cited, I could not help feeling that the officious kindness of the Court of Chancery in interposing trusts where in many cases the father of the family never meant to create trusts, must have been a very cruel kindness indeed'.

The modern judicial approach, as evidenced in *Re Adams and the Kensington Vestry* (below), is to have regard to the language of the will as a whole to ascertain the testator's intention. Although in principle there is no presumption in favour of or against an intention to create a trust, the weight of decisions suggests a more sceptical approach to construing precatory words as exhibiting that intention.

Re Adams and Kensington Vestry (1884) 27 Ch D 394

The testator gave all his property to his wife 'in full confidence that she will do what is right as to the disposal thereof between my children, either in her lifetime or by will after her decease'. Cotton LJ (holding that the wife took the property absolutely) said (at 409):

> . . . it seems to me perfectly clear what the testator intended. He leaves his wife his property absolutely, but what was in his mind was this: 'I am the head of the family, and it is laid upon me to provide properly for the members of my family – my children: my widow will succeed me when I die, and I wish to put her in the position I occupied as the person who is to provide for my children.' Not that he entails upon her any trust so as to bind her, but he simply says, in giving her this, I express to her, and call to her attention, the moral obligation which I myself had and which I feel that she is going to discharge. The motive of the gift is, in my opinion, not a trust imposed upon her by the gift in the will. He leaves the property to her; he knows that she will do what is right, and carry out the moral obligation

> which he thought lay on him, and on her if she survived him, to provide for the children....
> I have no hesitation in saying myself, that I think some of the older authorities went a
> great deal too far in holding that some particular words appearing in a will were sufficient
> to create a trust.

The modern approach does not mean that precatory words can never be interpreted as creating a trust (see *Re Steele's Will Trusts* [1948] Ch 603). Indeed,
in apparent sharp contrast to *Re Adams and Kensington Vestry*, the House of
Lords (Lord Lindley dissenting) held in *Comiskey v Bowring-Hanbury* [1905]
AC 84 that there was no absolute gift where the will devised property to the
testator's wife 'in full confidence that she will make such use of it as I should
have made myself' and at her death 'devise it to such one or more of my nieces as
she may think fit'. An additional clause in mandatory terms – 'in default of any
disposition by her ... I hereby direct that all my estate and property acquired
by her under my will shall at her death be equally divided among my nieces' – is
significant, however, and confirms that it is the document as a whole that must
be construed to identify a specific intention.

Difficulties in determining in these cases whether an absolute gift to a spouse
or a trust in the form of a life interest is intended are most likely to occur
with home-made or 'kitchen table' wills. Recognising what it referred to as
the 'unintended life interest' problem the Law Reform Committee in its 19th
Report (*Interpretation of Wills* (1973 Cmnd 5301) paras 60–62) recommended
the adoption of a statutory rule of construction incorporating a presumption
to circumvent what it saw as a 'trap for unadvised testators'. Section 22 of the
Administration of Justice Act 1982 was enacted in response and provides:

> Except where a contrary intention is shown it shall be presumed that if a testator devises
> or bequeaths property to his spouse in terms which in themselves would give an absolute
> interest to the spouse, but by the same instrument purports to give his issue an interest in
> the same property, the gift to the spouse is absolute notwithstanding the purported gift to
> the issue.

Notwithstanding the reference to 'terms which in themselves would give an
absolute interest', Hart J in *Harrison v Gibson* [2006] 1 WLR 1212, the sole
reported case on the section, concluded that the court is still required to construe
words in the context of the will as a whole, in particular when determining
whether a 'contrary intention' is established. In the case itself a combination
of the words 'the bungalow I leave in trust to my wife' and a provision that
on her death it was to be sold and the proceeds divided equally between their
children meant either that the presumption did not apply or, even if it did, that
a contrary intention had been established and that the wife therefore had a life
interest only in the property.

This approach to construction reinforces the point made in *Mussoorie Bank Ltd v Raynor* (1882) 7 App Cas 321 (see above, p 121) as to the link between rules relating to certainty of intention and certainty of subject-matter.

(2) Certainty of intention or 'sham intention'?

As we have seen, precatory words cases are those where the language used, commonly in wills, is imprecise at least as regards any intention to impose a binding trust obligation. At the opposite end of the continuum are those instances of *lifetime* arrangements where the words used appear to create a trust but where it becomes evident that the 'settlor' had no real intention to create a trust of the property at all. In *Midland Bank plc v Wyatt* [1995] 1 FLR 697, for instance, a formally valid declaration of trust by Mr Wyatt (W) and his wife of the equity in their jointly owned family home in favour of, inter alia, two daughters was held to be a sham and therefore void and unenforceable. Shortly after executing the 'trust deed' W pledged the property to the bank as security for a loan for his business which subsequently failed and was put into receivership some three-and-a-half years later. The bank, though, was never informed of the existence of the 'trust deed' which, so the court found, 'was not to be acted upon but to be put in the safe for a rainy day' and that there was no intention on the part of Mr Wyatt when executing the trust deed 'of endowing his children with his interest in [the house]' (at 707).

A sham transaction is one where 'acts done or documents executed are intended to give to third parties or to the courts the appearance of creating between the parties legal rights and obligations different from the actual legal rights and obligations (if any) that the parties intend to create' (*Snook v London and West Riding Investments Ltd* [1967] 2 QBD 786 at 802 per Diplock LJ).

The *Wyatt* case was, in one sense, straightforward in that there were no separate trustees involved. There may, though, be more complex arrangements whereby, even though there is a transfer of legal title in property to trustees apparently for certain beneficiaries – and therefore arguably not a sham 'in form' as there is a real trust –, the settlor has no intention that the purported beneficiaries should actually benefit from the assets. On the contrary, the real intention is that the trustees should hold the assets for the settlor and that the trust is therefore a 'sham in substance' if not 'in form' or, as it is sometimes termed, a partial sham (see eg *Minwalla v Minwalla* [2005] 1 FLR 771 where a complex arrangement involved an offshore trust apparently to conceal beneficial ownership of assets in ancillary divorce proceedings). Although the matter is not beyond doubt in English law it seems that in such cases 'unless [the real intention] is from the outset shared by the trustee (or later becomes so shared)' the trust created will not be regarded as a sham (see *Shalson v Russo* [2005] Ch 281 at 342 following the approach of the Royal Court of Jersey in *In re Esteem Settlement* [2003] JLR 188; see generally on this topic Matthews (2007) 21(4) TLI 191–201; Conaglen (2008) 67(1) CLJ 176–207; Wadham (ed) *Willoughby's Misplaced Trust* (2nd edn, 2002); Mowbray [2000] PCB 1 at 28 and [2000] PCB 2 at 105).

(3) Declaration of trust

A person can create a trust by declaring himself trustee of property. Aside from the formal requirements where land or equitable interests are involved, no special form of words is required. The settlor 'need not use the words "I declare myself a trustee", but he must do something which is equivalent to it, and use expressions which have that meaning. . . . ' (*Richards v Delbridge* (1874) LR 18 Eq 11 at 14 per Jessel MR). It is even possible for the conduct of parties to indicate an intention to be bound by the trust obligation.

Paul v Constance [1977] 1 All ER 195

Constance (C) and his wife Bridgett (the defendant) separated in 1965. In 1967 C met the plaintiff Mrs Paul (P). From December 1967 they lived together as man and wife in the plaintiff's house until C's death in 1974. In 1969 C, who was a fitter, was injured at work and in 1973 was awarded £950 damages. C and P decided to pay the money into a bank deposit account. When C told the manager that he (C) and P were not married, the manager said: 'Well [the account] will be in your name only then?' C said: 'Yes'. Between then and C's death three small deposits of joint bingo winnings were made and the one withdrawal of £150 was divided between C and P after part of it had been used to buy Christmas presents and food. C died intestate and Bridgett, as administratrix of C's estate, closed the account. P commenced proceedings claiming that C had held the bank account on trust for himself and P jointly.

> **Scarman LJ:** A number of issues were canvassed at the trial, but the only point taken by the defendant on her appeal to this court goes to the question whether or not there was, in the circumstances of this case, an express declaration of trust. It is conceded that if there was the trust would be enforceable. . . . Counsel for the defendant has taken the court through the detailed evidence and submits that one cannot find anywhere in the history of events a declaration of trust in the sense of finding the deceased man, Mr Constance, saying: 'I am now disposing of my interest in this fund so that you, Mrs Paul, now have a beneficial interest in it.' Of course, the words which I have just used are stilted lawyers' language, and counsel for the plaintiff was right to remind the court that we are dealing with simple people, unaware of the subtleties of equity, but understanding very well indeed their own domestic situation. It is right that one should consider the various things that were said and done by the plaintiff and Mr Constance during their time together against their own background and in their own circumstances.
>
> Counsel for the defendant drew our attention to two cases, both of them well enough known (at any rate in Lincoln's Inn, since they have been in law reports for over 100 years), and he relies on them as showing that, though a man may say in clear and unmistakable terms that he intends to make a gift to some other person, for instance his child or some other members of his family, yet that does not necessarily disclose a declaration of trust; and, indeed, in the two cases to which we have been referred the court held that, though there was a plain intention to make a gift, it was not right to infer any intention to create a trust.

The first of the two cases is *Jones v Lock* ((1865) 1 Ch App 25). In that case Mr Jones, returning home from a business trip to Birmingham, was scolded for not having brought back anything for his baby son. He went upstairs and came down with a cheque made out in his own name for £900 and said, in the presence of his wife and nurse: 'Look you here, I give this to baby', and he then placed the cheque in the baby's hand. It was obvious that he was intending to make a gift of the cheque to his baby son but it was clear, as Lord Cranworth LC held, that there was no effective gift then and there made of the cheque; it was in his name and had not been endorsed over to the baby. Other evidence showed that he had in mind to go and see his solicitor, Mr Lock, to make proper provision for the baby boy, but unfortunately he died before he could do so. *Jones v Lock* was a classic case where the intention to make a gift failed because the gift was imperfect. So an attempt was made to say: 'Well, since the gift was imperfect, nevertheless, one can infer the existence of a trust.' But Lord Cranworth LC would have none of it.

In the other case to which counsel for the defendant referred us, *Richards v Delbridge* (1874) LR 18 Eq 11, the facts were that a Mr Richards, who employed a member of his family in his business, was minded to give the business to the young man. He evidenced his intention to make this gift by endorsing on the lease of the business premises a short memorandum to the effect that:

'This deed [ie the deed of leasehold] and all thereof belonging I give to Edward . . . [ie the boy] from this time forth with all the stock in trade.'

Jessel MR, who decided the case, said that there was in that case the intention to make a gift, but the gift failed because it was imperfect; and he refused from the circumstances of the imperfect gift to draw the inference of the existence of a declaration of trust or the intention to create one. The ratio decidendi appears clearly from the report. It is a short passage, and because of its importance I quote it . . .

Scarman LJ referred approvingly to the judgment of Turner LJ in *Milroy v Lord* on the different modes of 'rendering a settlement binding' and that an intended gift by transfer cannot operate as a declaration of trust (see above, p 137) and then concluded:

There is no suggestion of a gift by transfer in this case. The facts of those cases do not, therefore, very much help the submission of counsel for the defendant, but he was able to extract from them this principle: that there must be a clear declaration of trust, and that means there must be clear evidence from what is said or done of an intention to create a trust or, as counsel for the defendant put it, 'an intention to dispose of a property or a fund so that somebody else to the exclusion of the disponent acquires the beneficial interest in it'. He submitted that there was no such evidence.

When one looks to the detailed evidence to see whether it goes as far as that – and I think that the evidence does have to go as far as that – one finds that from the time that Mr Constance received his damages right up to his death he was saying, on occasions, that the money was as much the plaintiff's as his. When they discussed the damages, how to invest them or what to do with them, when they discussed the bank account, he would say to her: 'The money is as much yours as mine.' The judge, rightly treating the basic problem in the case as a question of fact, reached this conclusion. He said:

> 'I have read through my notes, and I am quite satisfied that it was the intention of [the plaintiff] and Mr Constance to create a trust in which both of them were interested.'

In this court the issue becomes: was there sufficient evidence to justify the judge reaching that conclusion of fact? In submitting that there was, counsel for the plaintiff draws attention first and foremost to the words used. When one bears in mind the unsophisticated character of Mr Constance and his relationship with the plaintiff during the last few years of his life, counsel for the plaintiff submits that the words that he did use on more than one occasion, namely 'This money is as much yours as mine', convey clearly a present declaration that the existing fund was as much the plaintiff's as his own. The judge accepted that conclusion. I think he was well justified in doing so and, indeed, I think he was right to do so. There are, as counsel for the plaintiff reminded us, other features in the history of the relationship between the plaintiff and Mr Constance which support the interpretation of those words as an express declaration of trust. I have already described the interview with the bank manager when the account was opened. I have mentioned also the putting of the 'bingo' winnings into the account, and the one withdrawal for the benefit of both of them.

It might, however, be thought that this was a borderline case, since it is not easy to pin-point a specific moment of declaration, and one must exclude from one's mind any case built on the existence of an implied or constructive trust; for this case was put forward at the trial and is now argued by the plaintiff as one of express declaration of trust. It was so pleaded, and it is only as such that it may be considered in this court. The question, therefore, is whether in all the circumstances the use of those words on numerous occasions as between Mr Constance and the plaintiff constituted an express declaration of trust. The judge found that they did. For myself, I think he was right so to find. I therefore would dismiss the appeal.

[Bridge, Cairns LJJ agreed.]

Disputes about the existence of the necessary intention to declare a trust are most likely to occur where an attempt is made to have an incomplete transfer of property construed as a declaration of trust. There was no doubt that Constance intended to benefit Mrs Paul but did the court construe a general intention to benefit as a specific intention to benefit by way of trust thereby blurring the distinction between gift and declaration of trust? Consider in particular the following criticism:

> Why was there 'no suggestion of a gift by transfer'? Surely C may have intended a gift to himself and P jointly. The result in *Jones v Lock* would probably have been the same if Jones had said 'This cheque is as much baby's as mine', instead of 'I give this to baby'. But is *Paul v Constance* distinguishable from that variation of *Jones v Lock*? (Heydon and Loughlan *Equity and Trusts* (5th edn, 1997 p 132)

It may be, as Gardner has argued (*An Introduction to the Law of Trusts* (2nd edn, 2003) pp 52–53), that the contrasting decisions in *Paul v Constance* and *Jones v Lock* are attributable to changing judicial attitudes towards discovering a declaration of trust in what Lord Cranworth LC in *Jones v Lock* labelled as 'loose conversations of this sort' ((1865) 1 Ch App 25 at 29). None the less, whereas in *Jones v Lock* there was no doubt that Jones 'really had the intention of settling something on the child', his *specific intention* was to implement this by altering his will. Doubtless he would have done so had he not died on the very day of his appointment with his solicitor. The fact remains, however, that wills are revocable and inter vivos trusts usually are not. Should this distinction have any relevance in cases such as these?

(4) Secret trusts

As with cases involving precatory words, the initial question where the existence of a secret trust is at issue may be whether the testator intended the legatee or devisee to be bound by a legal or a moral obligation. 'The real question is what did the testator intend should be the *sanction*? Was it to be the authority of a Court of Justice, or the conscience of the devisee?' (*McCormick v Grogan* (1867) IR 1 Eq 313 at 328 per Christian LJ cited in *Re Snowden* (see below)).

Two recent cases illustrate how contrasting approaches may affect the outcome.

Re Snowden [1979] 2 All ER 172

The testatrix (S), an elderly widow, by her final will made on 10 January 1974, six days before her death, left her residuary estate to her brother Bert absolutely. Six days after her death Bert also died, all his estate being bequeathed to his only son. There was evidence that the testatrix had been undecided about the final disposition of her estate among her nearest relatives, who, apart from her brother, were five nephews and nieces, and that she relied on her brother to implement her wishes as regards disposal of the residuary estate.

The evidence rested principally on four documents recording what was said on three separate occasions. First there was an attendance note of 31 August 1973 by S's solicitor recording the discussions that took place the previous day with S. The note stated that 'you weren't quite clear at the moment how you would deal with things, but you thought that the easiest way would be to leave legacies to the nephews and nieces, and then leave it to Bert to split up the remainder as he thought best'.

Second, there was a statement by the solicitor dated 22 February 1974 amplifying the attendance note:

> She thought the easiest way would be to leave legacies to her nephews and nieces and others of different amounts to suit their needs and her wishes for them, and for what was left to be divided between her nephews and nieces equally. She said she would like the

residue to be left to Bert and he could see everybody and look after the division for her. She turned to him and said 'You would see to it for me wouldn't you Bert.' He replied, 'Of course dear if you want me to.'

Finally, there were two affidavits by a solicitor and legal executive dated 21 November 1977 and 1 December 1977 recording what was said on 10 January 1974. These stated that the testatrix wanted 'to be fair to everyone', that her brother 'would know what to do', that he agreed 'to deal with everything for her' and 'that he was perfectly aware of how S wished him to distribute the money that would fall to him under the residuary gift when she died'.

After reviewing prior authority on standard of proof, Megarry VC concluded that 'in order to establish a secret trust where no question of fraud arises, the standard of proof is the ordinary civil standard of proof that is required to establish an ordinary trust'. The question to be decided therefore was whether Bert was bound by a secret trust, or whether he was subject to no more than a moral obligation.

> **Megarry VC:** Now it seems perfectly clear that the will was executed by the testatrix on the basis of some arrangement that was made between her and her brother regarding the gift of residue to him. The question is what that arrangement was. In particular, did it impose a trust, or did it amount to a mere moral or family obligation? If it was a trust, what were the terms of that trust? Although these questions are distinct, they are obviously interrelated to some degree. The more uncertain the terms of the obligation, the more likely it is to be a moral obligation rather than a trust: many a moral obligation is far too indefinite to be enforceable as a trust...
>
> I cannot say that there is no evidence from which it could be inferred that a secret trust was created. At the same time, that evidence is far from being overwhelming...

Megarry VC referred to the passage cited above from the judgment in *McCormick v Grogan* (1867) and summarised his conclusion on the facts as follows:

> The general picture which seems to me to emerge from the evidence is of a testatrix who for long had been worrying about how to divide her residue and who was still undecided. She had a brother whom she trusted implicitly and who knew her general views about her relations and her property. She therefore left her residue to him in the faith that he would, in due time and in accordance with her general wishes, make in her stead the detailed decisions about the distribution of her residue which had for so long troubled her and on which she was still undecided. He was her trusted brother, more wealthy than she, and a little older. There was thus no need to bind him by any legally enforceable trust; and I cannot see any real indication that she had any thought of doing this. Instead, she simply left him, as a matter of family confidence and probity, to do what he thought she would

> have done if she had ever finally made up her mind. In short, to revert to the language of Christian LJ, I cannot see any real evidence that she intended the sanction to be the authority of a court of justice and not merely the conscience of her brother. I therefore hold that her brother took the residue free from any trust.

Ottaway v Norman [1971] 3 All ER 1325

The testator Harry Ottaway (T) and his housekeeper Miss Hodges (H) had lived together as man and wife for over 30 years in T's bungalow. William Ottaway (O), T's son by his late wife, was a frequent visitor. The evidence of O, the plaintiff, was that on one of his early visits T told O in H's presence that if H survived him (T) she should have the bungalow for the rest of her life but that she should leave it to O on her death. H agreed to this. By his will made in 1960 T left the bungalow 'together with all furniture, fixtures and fittings' to H in fee simple. He also left H a legacy of £1,500 and the residuary estate he gave on trust to be divided equally between H and O. T died in October 1963. Immediately after T's death H made a will leaving all her property to O.

Subsequently H developed a close friendship with the defendant, a Mr Norman (N) and his wife, and made a new will in 1966 appointing N as executor but making no alteration to the beneficial dispositions. But in 1967, after disagreement between H and O over plans for alterations to the bungalow, H executed a new will by which she left the bungalow to N and his wife, and her residuary estate to O and N in equal shares. H died in 1968 and the plaintiff sought a declaration that N held the bungalow on a secret trust. The claim was subsequently amended to include money received by H under T's will.

> **Brightman J:** Counsel for the defendant invited me to reject the evidence of the plaintiffs that any such obligation as is alleged was imposed on Miss Hodges. He does not accuse the plaintiffs of deliberate lying but submits that their bitter disappointment at losing the bungalow has created in their mind an exaggerated picture of what really occurred; and that they have not discharged the heavy burden of proof which lies on them. Counsel further submitted that I ought to conclude that Mr Harry Ottaway merely indicated to Miss Hodges how he expected and hoped that she would dispose of the property, not how he required her to dispose of it. He pointed out to me a number of reasons for discounting the evidence of the plaintiffs. For example, it had on at least two occasions been brought to the notice of Harry Ottaway by his son that it would be possible for him to alter his will by creating an express trust to take effect on Miss Hodges's death. Why, therefore, should Harry Ottaway have relied on a secret trust? I believe that the suggestion of an express trust was not pursued because certainly Harry Ottaway, and I think also William Ottaway, had complete confidence that Miss Hodges would do what she had been told. Again it was said that the plaintiffs seemed remarkably uncertain as to the precise obligation imposed

on Miss Hodges. First the obligation was confined to the house: later it comprised also the contents and money.

... [I do not think] that there is much significance in the initial omission of any reference to the furniture and furnishings of the bungalow. In common parlance and in this sort of context they can readily go without saying.

... [H]aving heard the evidence I have no doubt in my mind that I have received an accurate account of all essential facts from Mr and Mrs Ottaway. I find as a fact that Harry Ottaway intended that Miss Hodges should be obliged to dispose of the bungalow in favour of the plaintiffs at her death, that he communicated that intention to Miss Hodges and that Miss Hodges accepted the obligation. I find the same facts in relation to the furniture, fixtures and fittings which passed to Miss Hodges under cl 4 of Harry Ottaway's will. I am not satisfied that any similar obligation was imposed and accepted as regards any contents of the bungalow which had not devolved on Miss Hodges under cl 4 of Harry Ottaway's will.

I turn to the question of money. In cross-examination William Ottaway said the trust extended to the house, furniture and money:

'Everything my father left to Miss Hodges was to be in the trust. The trust comprised the lot. She could use the money as she liked. She had to leave my wife and me whatever money was left.'

In cross-examination Mrs Ottaway said that her understanding was that Miss Hodges was bound to make a will giving her and her husband the bungalow, contents and any money she had left. 'She could please herself about the money. She did not have to save it for us. She was free to spend it.' It seems to me that two questions arise. First as a matter of fact what did the parties intend should be comprised in Miss Hodges's obligation? All money which Miss Hodges had at her death, including money which she had acquired before Harry's death and money she acquired after his death from all sources? Or, only money acquired under Harry's will? Secondly, if such an obligation existed would it as a matter of law create a valid trust? [On the second question see below, p 176 under 'certainty of subject-matter'.] I accept that the parties mentioned money on at least some occasions when they talked about Harry Ottaway's intentions for the future disposition of Ashcroft. I do not, however, find sufficient evidence that it was Harry Ottaway's intention that Miss Hodges should be compelled to leave all her money, from whatever source derived, to the plaintiffs. This would seem to preclude her giving even a small pecuniary legacy to any friend or relative. I do not think it is clear that Harry Ottaway intended to extract any such far-reaching undertaking from Miss Hodges or that she intended to accept such a wide obligation herself. Therefore the obligation, if any, is in my view to be confined to money derived under Harry Ottaway's will. If the obligation is confined to money derived under Harry Ottaway's will, the obligation is meaningless and unworkable unless it includes the requirements she shall keep such money separate and distinct from her own money. I am certain that no such requirement was ever discussed or intended. If she had the right to mingle her own money with that derived from Harry, there would be no ascertainable property on which the trust could bite at her death. This aspect distinguishes this case from *Re Gardner.*

> There is another difficulty. Does money in this context include only cash or cash and investments, or all moveable property of any description? The evidence is quite inconclusive. In my judgment the plaintiff's claim succeeds in relation to the bungalow and in relation to the furniture, fixtures and fittings which devolved under cl 4 of Harry Ottaway's will subject, of course, to normal wastage and fair wear and tear, but not to any other assets.

The absence of comment in *Ottaway v Norman* on the constructive trust/express trust debate about the status of secret trusts has already been referred to and aspects of the judgment have been criticised as being inconsistent with the requirement of certainty of subject-matter. But there is a more fundamental issue concerning intention, and *Re Snowden* and *Ottaway v Norman* can be usefully compared in this context.

Consider the following points:

(1) The statement that 'Harry Ottaway intended that Miss Hodges should be obliged to dispose of the bungalow . . . and that Miss Hodges accepted the obligation' does not necessarily resolve the matter of intention. The further question to be considered, but seemingly not addressed in the case, is whether the sanction was to be 'the authority of a Court of Justice, or the conscience of the devisee' (cf *Re Snowden* and see also *Brown v Pourau* [1995] 1 NZLR 352 where the obligation was described (at 373) as at best 'a familial or moral obligation'). With this point in mind, how satisfactory do you find Brightman J's treatment of the fact that Harry Ottaway rejected the advice to use an express trust to achieve his objective?

(2) 'Uncertainty in the subject of the gift has a reflex action upon the previous words, throwing doubt on the testator's intention' (*Mussoorie Bank Ltd v Raynor*). What should have been the relevance, if any, of this dictum to the facts in *Ottaway v Norman*?

(3) It is a nice question as to whether a stronger indication of an intention to benefit by way of trust was present in *Ottaway v Norman* than in *Re Snowden*, particularly since the standard of proof in *Ottaway* was pitched, in principle, at a higher level. Notwithstanding the decision in *Ottaway*, determining whether a trust-like obligation is intended is always likely to be a problem where informality is present. In *Gold v Hill* [1999] 1 FLR 54, for instance, in a situation described by Carnwath J as analogous to a secret trust, the nominee under an insurance policy on the life of one Gilbert was told by Gilbert 'over drinks before dinner' at a hotel: 'If anything happens to me you will have to sort things out – you know what to do – look after Carol and the kids. Don't let that bitch [Gilbert's wife] get anything.' The general intention was clear but was there a trust? Notwithstanding an apparent lack of clarity as to the terms of the trust, the court affirmed that the nominee was to hold the proceeds of the policy on trust for Carol for her 'to apply those monies for the benefit of herself and her children'.

(4) Do you think the judgment in *Re Snowden* would or should have been the same if the brother, Bert, had survived and asked for directions as to whether he was bound by a 'secret trust'?

(5) Although not decisive, evidence of changes of mind by a testator may be indicative of an intention that any obligation is to be of a morally binding nature rather than a legally enforceable one (see eg *Kasperbauer v Griffith* [2001] WTLR 333).

(b) Certainty of subject-matter

(1) Existing property (ie property existing at the time when the trust is intended to take effect)

A purported trust will be void if the property intended to form the subject-matter of the trust obligation cannot be clearly identified. Expressions such as 'the bulk of my residuary estate' (*Palmer v Simmonds* (1854) 2 Drew 221) are too uncertain. The other end of the uncertainty spectrum is to be found in *Boyce v Boyce* (1849) 16 Sim 476 where the property was certain but the individual entitlement was not. There a testator devised 'all my houses' – probably two but the report is ambiguous on the point – on trust to convey one to the eldest daughter Maria 'whichever she may think proper to choose' and the others to another daughter, Charlotte. Maria predeceased the testator without making any choice. The Vice-Chancellor held that the gift to Charlotte failed since there could be no certainty as to which house should be held on trust for her. Both properties were therefore held on resulting trust for the testator's heir, his grandson.

Boyce v Boyce might be thought to be a somewhat extreme case but it is the harbinger of a comparable contemporary problem. Consider the position where a company (G) invites investors to purchase gold bullion, for future delivery if and when required by them, but which in the meantime will be stored in safe-keeping as part of G's overall stock of bullion. Can there then be a valid trust if G purports to declare itself trustee of, let us say, 50 gold bars out of a total stock of 200 identical bars? Until G has segregated and appropriated 50 specific bars for B it seems that the trust will fail because it cannot be said with certainty which 50 gold bars are the subject-matter of the trust obligation (*Re Goldcorp Exchange Ltd* [1995] 1 AC 74, PC, discussed Birks [1995] RLR 83; see also *Re London Wine Co (Shippers) Ltd* [1986] PCC 121 'consignments of wine'). On the other hand if, in our example, G had declared that it held the bullion on trust for itself and B as tenants in common in their respective proportions (one-quarter and three-quarters), the trust would have been valid. The intention to hold 50 gold bars on trust for B is not the same as an intention to hold a one-quarter share of the *undivided* total and ascertained bullion. Litigation on this issue has tended to occur in the context of insolvency where prepaying purchasers of a particular quantity of goods from an identified bulk of those goods have sought, usually unsuccessfully, to achieve some measure of protection through establishing a proprietary interest in the goods (see Chapter 15, where these issues are considered more fully, and also the Sale of Goods (Amendment) Act 1995 which, in 'identified bulk' circumstances in an insolvency, now provides some protection for purchasers via the 'tenancy in common' mechanism; noted Burns [1996] MLR 260; Ulph [1996] LMCLQ 93).

In view of the above line of reasoning it is therefore somewhat surprising that the Court of Appeal in *Hunter v Moss* [1994] 1 WLR 452, confirming a decision of the High Court ([1993] 1 WLR 934), held that a declaration of trust of, in effect, 50 out of 950 shares in one company was not void for uncertainty of subject-matter – segregation or appropriation of particular shares being considered unnecessary as all the shares carried identical rights. But how is this case different from our gold bullion example? It must be said that the conceptual basis for the distinction is not very satisfactory and admittedly the case was argued and decided before the decision in *Goldcorp* was delivered on 25 May 1994 (see *Underhill and Hayton* p 104; Hayton (1994) 110 LQR 335, but cf Jones [1993] Conv 460; Martin [1996] Conv 223; and Clarke (1995) 48 CLP 117). In the High Court emphasis seems to be placed on the fact that *Hunter v Moss* is concerned with intangible assets – shares that were identical – whereas *Re London Wine* and earlier authorities involved tangible assets – chattels that may not necessarily be identical (see at 940 in *Hunter v Moss* where the judge provides as an illustration a consignment of the same wine and vintage but where some cases may have deteriorated and others not). This ground for distinguishing the authorities, although not explicitly endorsed in the Court of Appeal, has subsequently been adopted in another case concerning a trust of a particular number of shares (*Re Harvard Securities Ltd (in liquidation)* [1997] 2 BCLC 369 at 383; see Worthington [1999] JBL 1, Goode [2003] LMCLQ 379 and Eden (2000) 16 IL&P 134–137, 175–178; see also the judgment in Hong Kong of Yuen J in *Re C A Pacific Securities Ltd* [2000] 1 BCLC 494). In fact in the Court of Appeal Dillon LJ simply distinguished *Re London Wine* observing that it 'was a long way from the present case' in that '[it] involved the appropriation of chattels and when the property in chattels passes' and 'was not concerned with a declaration of trust' ([1994] 1 WLR 452 at 458). There is an alternative and pragmatic basis for the distinction. Unlike the cases cited in argument in *Hunter v Moss* there was, in that case, no question of unsecured creditors attempting to establish priority in an insolvency. It may be significant that in the absence of a third-party/creditor dimension, a key question in the High Court in *Hunter* seemed to be whether 'the court could, if asked, make an order for the execution of the purported trust' (at 945). In so far as criticism is directed at the reasoning rather than the outcome of *Hunter v Moss* it would not have been beyond the wit of the court to declare that Moss held the 950 shares on constructive trust for himself and Hunter as tenants in common in the proportions 18/19th and 1/19th respectively pending segregation of the

50 shares. This would mirror the approach now taken where the Sale of Goods (Amendment) Act 1995 applies to 'identified bulk' sales.

Lastly, it should be noted that a further practical consequence of the decision in *Hunter v Moss* was to prevent an employer, the defendant, from resiling from a 'promise' to provide the plaintiff employee with the shares the subject-matter of the dispute. One might therefore conclude that by discovering that there was an intention to create a trust and that the conceptual problems with certainty of subject-matter could be circumvented, the court was enabling the original intentions of the parties to the dispute to be implemented and the 'unjust' consequences of the subsequent 'falling out' that led to the litigation to be avoided.

The very different and much earlier case of *Sprange v Barnard* (1789) 2 Bro CC 585 illustrates another dimension of the certainty problem, yet also exhibits a concern with enforcement. A testatrix gave £300, invested in joint stock annuities, to her husband 'for his sole use and at his death the remaining part of what is left, that he does not want for his own wants and use to be divided between' a brother and sisters. No trust arose since it was uncertain what property would be left on the death of the husband who accordingly took the property absolutely. The potential uncertainty of subject-matter may have cast doubt on the intention of the testatrix, but *Sprange v Barnard* suggests a concern as much with enforcement – 'it appears to me to be a trust which would be impossible to be executed' – as with intention.

Sprange v Barnard and later cases appeared to establish firmly that if property were bequeathed essentially to X to pass on whatever was left at his death to Y, then this would normally be treated as an absolute gift to X, now statutorily presumed to be the outcome 'unless a contrary intention is shown' (see Administration of Justice Act 1982, s 22 and comparable provision in the Civil Partnership Act 2004, Sch 4 para 5). The apparent certainty of this stance, based fundamentally on enforceability, is challenged by the observations of Brightman J in *Ottaway v Norman* as regards the possibility of a secret trust of the money:

> I am content to assume for present purposes but without so deciding that if property is given to the primary donee on the understanding that the primary donee will dispose by his will of such assets, if any, as he may have at his command at his death in favour of the secondary donee, a valid trust is created in favour of the secondary donee which is in suspense during the lifetime of the primary donee, but attaches to the estate of the primary donee at the moment of the latter's death. There would seem to be at least some support for this proposition in an Australian case to which I was referred: *Birmingham v Renfrew*.

Birmingham v Renfrew (1937) 57 CLR 666 is a leading Australian authority on mutual wills. The purpose, and possibility, of a 'floating' or 'suspended' trust is explained in the judgment of Dixon J (at 689):

> The purpose of the arrangement for corresponding [ie mutual] wills must often be... to enable the survivor during his life to deal as absolute owner with the property passing under the will of the party first dying. That is to say, the object of the transaction is to put the survivor in a position to enjoy for his own benefit the full ownership so that, for instance, he may convert it and expend the proceeds if he chooses. But when he dies he is to bequeath what is left in the manner agreed upon. It is only by the special doctrines of equity that such a floating obligation, suspended, so to speak, during the lifetime of the survivor can descend upon the assets at his death and crystallise into a trust.

There is, however, one immediate and obvious practical problem with the ingenious solution. What can we identify as the obligations of the primary donee vis-à-vis the property during his or, usually, her own lifetime? Does the following observation of Dixon J satisfactorily resolve problems of enforceability?

> No doubt, gifts and settlements inter vivos, if calculated to defeat the intention of the compact, could not be made by the survivor and his right of disposition inter vivos is therefore not unqualified.

These words were adopted in *Re Cleaver* [1981] 2 All ER 1018 by Nourse J who added (at 1024): 'no objection could normally be taken to ordinary gifts of small value'. It is tempting to suggest that problems-a-plenty could lay in wait in determining whether the obligation undertaken has been breached, yet the absence of litigation on this aspect of mutual wills is striking (see eg Mitchell (1951) 14 MLR 140–142; Hodkinson [1982] Conv 228; and Oakley *Constructive Trusts* (3rd edn, 1997)). In conclusion, notwithstanding Nourse J's reaffirmation in *Re Cleaver* that the requirements of certainty of subject-matter are 'as essential to this species of trust as they are to any other' we suggest that it is not easy to reconcile the 'floating' or 'suspended' trust either with the conceptual requirement that the subject-matter of a trust must be certain or with the sort of practical concern with enforceability expressed in a case such as *Sprange v Barnard*. None the less the status of the trust is well established in the mutual wills context.

It only remains to add that if there is no identifiable property at all then there can be no subject-matter and therefore no trust. In *Hemmens v Wilson Browne (a firm)* [1995] Ch 223 a document purporting to give one party a right to call on the other party for a payment of £100,000 at any time did not create a trust because there was no identifiable fund from which to form the subject-matter of a trust (see also *MacJordan Construction Ltd v Brookmount Erostin Ltd (in receivership)* [1992] BCLC 350).

(2) Future property

'The scope of the trusts recognised in equity is unlimited. There can be a trust of a chattel, or of a right or obligation under an ordinary legal contract, just as much as a trust of land' (Lord Shaw in *Lord Strathcona Steamship Co Ltd v Dominion Coal Co Ltd* [1926] AC 108 at 124). A recent illustration of the breadth of this proposition is *Don King Productions Inc v Warren* [1998] 2 All ER 608 where Lightman J, specifically citing the dicta of Lord Shaw, held that even though a purported assignment of a contract involving the rendering of personal services would, by its nature, be ineffective at law this would not prevent a trust of the *benefit* of the contract being declared, assuming the intention to do so could be identified (affirmed by the Court of Appeal [2000] Ch 291 but cf Tettenborn [1999] LMCLQ 352). Indeed even where the contract prohibits assignment of the benefit this will not, unless explicitly excluded, prevent a party to the contract declaring a trust of the benefit in favour of a third party, a common practice in the commercial world (*Barbados Trust Co v Bank of Zambia* [2007] EWCA Civ 148; [2007] LMCLQ 278).

It is thus unquestionably correct that the subject-matter of a trust can be as varied as the range of property interests that exist. But 'exist' is a key word here. It is only existing property – for example, negotiable instruments, money, chattels, interests in land whether in possession or remainder – that can form the subject-matter of a trust. Future property, or 'mere expectancy', cannot, and a voluntary declaration of trust of future property will therefore be ineffective: 'As it is impossible for anyone to own something that does not exist, it is impossible for anyone to make a present gift of such a thing to another person, however sure he may be that it will come into existence and will then be his to give' (*Norman v Federal Comr of Taxation* (1963) 109 CLR 9 per Windeyer J). Often-quoted examples of future property are copyright in songs not yet written (*Performing Right Society v London Theatre of Varieties* [1924] AC 1), or the hope of inheriting under the will of a still living testator or on intestacy (*Re Lind* [1915] 2 Ch 345) or of acquiring book debts arising in a business (*Tailby v Official Receiver* (1888) 13 App Cas 523). Plainly, therefore, this is quantitatively a minor restriction on the scope of the trust. But it must not be overlooked that although a gift – a voluntary assignment – of future property is ineffective, an assignment for valuable consideration is treated as a contract to assign and therefore valid.

Circumstances can arise, however, where it is difficult to distinguish future property from existing vested or contingent rights to obtain property at some future time.

Williams v IRC [1965] NZLR 395 (New Zealand Court of Appeal)

Williams, the appellant, held a life-interest under a trust and was entitled to trust income. He executed a voluntary deed whereby he assigned 'to the assignee for the religious purposes of the Parish of the Holy Trinity for four years the first £500 of the net income which shall accrue to the assignor personally while he lives in each of the said four years from the [specified trust] . . .'. The Commissioner assessed Williams to income tax on the trust income, it being argued that the assignment was ineffective and Williams had failed to dispose of his interest in the £500. The New Zealand Court of Appeal rejected the appeal:

> **Turner J:** What then was it that the assignor [Williams] purported to assign? What he had was the life interest of a *cestui que trust* in a property or partnership adventure vested in or carried on by trustees for his benefit. Such a life interest exists in equity as soon as the deed of trust creating it is executed and delivered. Existing, it is capable of immediate assignment. We do not doubt that where it is possible to assign a right completely it is possible to assign an undivided interest in it. The learned Solicitor-General was therefore right, in our opinion, in conceding that if here, instead of purporting to assign 'the first £500 of the income', the assignor had purported to assign (say) an undivided one-fourth share in his life estate, then he would have assigned an existing right, and in the circumstances effectively.
>
> But in our view, as soon as he quantified the sum in the way here attempted, the assignment became one not of a share or a part of his right, but of moneys which should arise from it. Whether the sums mentioned were ever to come into existence in whole or in part could not at the date of assignment be certain. In any or all of the years designated the net income might conceivably be less than £500; in some or all of them the operations of the trust might indeed result in a loss. The first £500 of the net income, then, might or might not (judging the matter on the date of execution of the deed) in fact have any existence.
>
> We accordingly reject Mr Thorp's argument that what was here assigned was a part or share of the existing equitable right of the assignor. He did not assign part of his right to income; he assigned a right to a part of the income, a different thing. The £500 which was the subject of the purported assignment was £500 *out of the net income*. There could be no such income for any year until the operations of that year were complete, and it became apparent what debits were to be set off against the gross receipts. For these reasons we are of opinion that what was assigned here was money; and that was something which was not presently owned by the assignor. He had no more than an expectation of it, to arise, it is true, from an existing equitable interest – but that interest he did not purpose to assign...

Counsel for the appellants argued in the alternative that if the document were not effective as an assignment it was effective as a declaration of trust.

> ... [It] is useless to seek to use this device in the circumstances of the present case. Property which is not presently owned cannot presently be impressed with a trust any more than it can be effectively assigned; property which is not yet in existence may be the subject of a present agreement to impress it with a trust when it comes into the hands of the donor; but equity will not enforce such an agreement at the instances of the *cestui que trust* in the absence of consideration (*Ellison v Ellison* (1802) 6 Ves 656).

(3) Certainty of beneficial interest

The quantum of beneficial interest to be taken by a beneficiary must be certain. Although technically correct, this bald statement is potentially misleading because of two methods of remedying uncertainty. First is the discretionary trust: a settlor can confer a discretion on trustees to apply the trust fund among a class of persons, for example, on trust for such of my children and in such shares as my trustees shall in their absolute discretion decide. Second, in certain circumstances the court will assume that property is to be divided equally among beneficiaries, applying the maxim – 'Equality is equity' (but cf *Boyce v Boyce* above). Both these possibilities demonstrate the overlap between certainty of subject and certainty of object and are considered further in the next chapter.

Third, there may be circumstances where the language used permits a generous interpretation of what is meant by certainty. In *Re Golay's Will Trusts* [1965] 2 All ER 660, a testator's direction to executors 'to let Tussy . . . receive a reasonable income from my . . . properties' was somewhat surprisingly upheld. Ungoed-Thomas J decided that 'reasonable income' provided 'an effective determinant of what the testator intends'. He concluded that 'the court is constantly involved in making such objective assessments of what is reasonable and is not to be deterred from doing so because subjective influences can never be wholly excluded' (at 662).

(4) The residuary estate

For the avoidance of doubt it must be emphasised that a testamentary trust or gift of the residuary estate under a person's will *is not* uncertain for certainty of subject-matter purposes. It is true that we do not know precisely the content of the residuary estate until the personal representatives have completed their administration of the estate but at that point the residue – 'what is left' – will become certain.

(c) Incomplete constitution and the role of intention

(1) Incompletely constituted trusts, contracts and conceptual complexity

In this section we consider attempts that have been made to circumscribe the rule that incompletely constituted trusts are not enforceable. But the route to understanding has been obscured by the entanglement of two distinct concepts, those of common law contract and equitable trust. And the concepts are very different. Contract is a vehicle for the exchange of reciprocal obligations; it is a bargain which, under the common law system, by definition excludes a gift. In contrast the benefiting of a person by means of a trust is usually the equitable equivalent of a common law gift – transactions wholly voluntary as between settlor and beneficiary and donor and donee respectively. A consequence of its voluntary nature is that if a settlor agrees to create a trust but changes his mind between the making of the promise and delivery of property to trustees, the trust is incompletely constituted and in principle the beneficiary has no remedy against the settlor. The beneficiary is a volunteer and the maxim 'Equity will not assist a volunteer' applies. The long-standing rule was clearly expressed by Lord Eldon in *Ellison v Ellison* (1802) 6 Ves 656 at 662: 'If you want the assistance of the court to constitute you *cestui que trust*, and the instrument is voluntary, you shall not have that assistance' but he added that where the property is completely transferred to trustees 'though it is voluntary . . . the equitable interest will be enforced by this court'.

The entanglement referred to above begins where a transaction takes the following form: A contracts with B to the effect that B will do something for the benefit of C. C is not a party to the contract and since it has long been the common law rule that only the parties to a contract can sue on it, C is left helpless if B refuses to perform the contract and A is unable or unwilling to compel B to do so. As will be seen below the common law privity of contract doctrine has now been significantly modified by the Contracts (Rights of Third Parties) Act 1999. But, statutory reform aside, could a remedy be obtained by arguing that, expressly or impliedly, A and B had contracted on the basis that A was to be a trustee of the benefit of B's promise for C? C can then sue as a beneficiary of a completely constituted trust, the subject-matter of the trust being the benefit of the promise, a chose in action. This argument met with some initial success but the courts became increasingly reluctant to support this transparent device to evade the privity of contract doctrine and demanded clear evidence of what was, of course, rarely present, an intention to create a trust. By contrast in Australia the possibility and benefit of a trust solution, at least in the rather specialised context of insurance contracts, seems to be viewed more sympathetically (see eg the judgments, in particular Deane J, in *Trident General Insurance Co Ltd v McNiece Bros Pty Ltd* (1988) 80 ALR 574; and generally Dwyer (1995) U Tas LR 143; Jaconelli [1998] Conv 88)). None the less the prevailing approach in English law remains that clearly stated by du Parcq LJ in *Re Schebsman* [1944] Ch 83 at 104:

> Unless an intention to create a trust is clearly to be collected from the language used and the circumstances of the case, I think that the court ought not to be astute to discover indications of such an intention.

Although traces of the argument are to be found in the context of incomplete constitution, in this specific context the issue has now mostly decamped to the realm of contract law (see Treitel *Law of Contract* (12th edn, 2007) 14.082– 14.120; and the Law Commission Report No 242 *Privity of Contract: Contracts for the Benefit of Third Parties* (Cm 3329, 1996) implemented in the Contracts (Rights of Third Parties) Act 1999).

We have mentioned that a beneficiary has no remedy where a settlor changes his mind after the making of a promise to create a trust and decides not to transfer the property to trustees. But consider the position if A formally promises in a deed ('covenants') to transfer property to B to hold on trust for C but does not then perform the promise. The trust is not fully constituted but can it be argued that B holds the benefit of the covenant or the right of action on it on trust for C, so that A's promise can be enforced? If so this 'is a trust which plays the role of ensuring that the main trust is completely constituted' in the main trustees (Waters *The Law of Trusts in Canada* (3rd edn, 2005) p 77). There is a clear parallel with the contractual example given previously and, as we shall see in section (2) below, the legal form the argument takes also revolves around whether the requisite specific intention to create a trust is present. Furthermore, the parallel extends to the policy argument that is cloaked by the issue of intention: what we are essentially concerned with is whether a court should enable a promisee who has given no value for the promise to enforce it.

There is a further policy issue, one fundamental to the trust and with fiscal implications, but one which receives insufficient attention in the substantial academic debate surrounding incompletely constituted trusts. A significant attraction of the trust, as we saw in Chapter 3, is that its capacity to fragment ownership on the plane of time can facilitate extensive flexibility of property disposition. An underlying policy consideration that should therefore not be overlooked when reading the following sections is how far trusts law and principles of equity do or should encourage ever more abstract property forms.

Before considering the conceptual and policy problems posed by the enforceability of covenants to settle we can briefly note that the creation of an express trust, while usually a wholly voluntary transaction, can result from a bargain between the parties: A in return for some promise by B undertakes to transfer property to trustees (T1 and T2) on trust for B. What then is B's position if A subsequently declines to transfer the property to T1 and T2? The trust is incompletely constituted but there is a crucial difference from the voluntary arrangement. Now B has provided consideration and is not a volunteer and so can enforce the promise; equity will compel A to carry out the undertaking and transfer the property to T1 and T2. But what is 'consideration' in this context? The principle developed by equity is that *either* there must be valuable consideration in the common law sense, furnished by a trustee or a beneficiary, *or* the beneficiary must be able to bring himself or herself within what has been called the scope of marriage consideration. We have previously referred (see Chapter 2) to the role that marriage settlements, now rarely encountered, were intended to fulfil in the nineteenth century in protecting a wife and children from economic domination by the husband, and marriage was described as 'the most valuable consideration imaginable' (*A-G v Jacobs-Smith* [1895] 2 QB 341 at 354). A trust made before and in consideration of marriage, 'an antenuptial settlement', is regarded as being made for value as is a trust created after marriage if made in pursuance of an ante-nuptial agreement. Indeed, the courts, after considerable judicial toing and froing, extended the scope of consideration beyond the parties to the marriage to include the issue of the marriage, issue in this context including children and grandchildren. But there the courts drew the line. Next of kin were not within the marriage consideration and thus were 'volunteers' in the eyes of equity.

To summarise, an incompletely constituted trust can be enforced at the behest of beneficiaries as an agreement to create a trust provided that valuable or marriage consideration has been furnished.

(2) Covenants to settle and enforceability

It was common in marriage settlements for the promise with trustees to be made by covenant, ie promise in a deed under seal (under Law of Property (Miscellaneous Provisions) Act 1989, s 1, deeds no longer require a formal seal). But what difference if any does the addition of the formalities of a deed make to the promise to create a trust? It represents adequate consideration at common law, but not in equity. Can it assist the volunteer beneficiary, such as next of kin in a marriage settlement where there are no children? Or if not the volunteer beneficiary, can the trustee enforce the covenant? The following excellent account by *Hayton and Mitchell* succinctly summarises the possibilities at p 242.

> ### COVENANTS TO SETTLE OR TRANSFER PROPERTY
>
> If A covenants to pay £11,000 or transfer 1,000 ICI ordinary shares or transfer his unique fifth dynasty Ming vase to B, a volunteer, then B has a chose in action enforceable at law against A, the deed's formalities supplying the consideration. However, equity does not regard the deed's formalities as consideration and so treats B as a volunteer and 'equity will not assist a volunteer'. Thus B cannot obtain specific performance of the Ming vase covenant but will have to be satisfied with common law damages, as for the £11,000 covenant or the 1,000 ICI shares covenant, specific performance never being available in such cases where money compensation is itself adequate. Equity, however, will not frustrate a volunteer suing at law (*Cannon v Hartley* [1949] Ch 213) and so B may recover as damages £11,000 or the money equivalent of the shares or the Ming vase.
>
> Since B has a chose in action this is property that he himself as beneficial owner can settle on trusts whether declaring himself trustee of it, or assigning it to trustees on trusts, for C for life, remainder to D.
>
> If A covenants with B to transfer £60,000 to B as trustee with express or implied intent that B shall hold the benefit of the covenant upon trust for C and D if they attain 21 years of age, then A has created a completely constituted trust of the benefit of the covenant held by B as trustee, so this may be enforced by C and D, though volunteers, just as trusts are ordinarily enforceable by volunteers (*Fletcher v Fletcher* (1844) 4 Hare 67).

The formalising of a promise by means of a deed of covenant will therefore *not* assist enforcement by the volunteer beneficiary directly, unless it can be shown that a trust of the benefit of the covenant was intended. We have already seen that during the twentieth century the courts began to exhibit a sceptical attitude towards construing precatory words as being intended to impose obligations of trusteeship. In similar vein the courts have been reluctant to detect any implied intention to create a completely constituted trust of the benefit of a covenant. But we also mentioned previously the possibility of trustee enforcement and here the common law appears to offer a convenient escape from the conclusion that the covenant itself is otherwise unenforceable. Although, as Hayton points out, the equitable remedy of specific performance is not available to a covenantee, equity not regarding the deed's formalities as consideration, a common law action for damages can be pursued. Could not the trustees (B) with whom the covenant is made therefore sue the covenantor/settlor (A) for breach of covenant, recover substantial damages and hold them in trust for the volunteer beneficiaries (C and D)? There are difficulties with this solution. As Hayton points out (at p 253):

> [One] difficulty is that *ex hypothesi* B does not hold the covenant on trust for C [and D] so that he must either hold the covenant for his own benefit or by way of resulting trust for A and it is clear that he is not intended to hold the covenant beneficially. If, therefore, the covenant and the right to damages for breach of covenant are held on resulting trust for the settlor, A, then surely so must any damages for breach of covenant.

Assuming the conclusion that the resulting trust is unavoidable to be correct (cf Rickett (1979) 32 CLP 1 and (1981) 34 CLP 189) then patently it is a pointless exercise for B to sue A for damages which would then be held on resulting trust for A himself. A second difficulty with a solution premised upon enforcement by trustees is the weight of authority, admittedly at first instance, against it.

The case law on the issue (*Re Pryce* [1917] 1 Ch 234; *Re Kay's Settlement* [1939] Ch 329; *Re Cook's Settlement Trusts* [1965] Ch 902) is distinctly discouraging to trustees who may consider suing. It now seems clear that the courts will not support volunteers seeking to compel trustees to sue, and further, where the court's discretion is sought by trustees, will instruct them not to sue. The decisions and the specific reasoning (or lack thereof) in the cases have engendered an extensive academic debate (Elliott (1960) 76 LQR 100; Hornby (1962) 78 LWR 228; Barton (1975) 91 LQR 236; Meagher and Lehane (1976) 92 LQR 427: cf Davies [1967] ASCL 387; Lee (1969) 85 LQR 213). Although there is no direct authority were trustees, rather than seeking the court's direction, to attempt to bring an action, it seems doubtful that it would succeed (see *Re Ralli's Will Trust* [1964] Ch 288 at 301–303 'trustees might be constrained by the court not to do so' (cf Elliott (1960) 76 LQR 100)).

(3) Covenants of future property: a problem?

Nothing in the cases cited above necessarily undermines the proposition that if there exists a completely constituted trust of the *benefit* of the covenant this can be enforced by the trustees on behalf of the beneficiaries or by the beneficiaries themselves even if volunteers. But doubt, both judicial (*Re Cook's Settlement Trusts*) and academic (eg Lee (1969) 85 LQR 213 and Davies [1967] ASCL 387 at 392), has been expressed as to this possibility where the subject-matter of the covenant is 'after-acquired', or other future property (see also *Re Plumptre's*

Marriage Settlement [1910] 1 Ch 609; *Pullan v Koe* [1913] 1 Ch 9). In a marriage settlement it was usual for the parties to covenant to add to the settlement property which might subsequently come into their possession – hence 'after-acquired property'. It is certainly correct, as we have seen, that future property cannot be assigned or be the subject-matter of a trust (*Williams v IRC*). But it has been argued that 'a covenant to pay a sum to be ascertained in the future is just as good a chose in action as a covenant to pay a specified sum, and it creates legal property of value. The trust *res* is the benefit of the covenant, the chose in action; not the property which will be obtained by its performance' (*Hanbury and Martin* p 135; Barton (1975) 91 LQR 236 at 238; Meagher and Lehane (1976) 92 LQR 427 at 428).

If authority were needed to support this proposition it can be found in *Davenport v Bishopp* (1843) 2 Y & C Ch Cas 451, a case involving a covenant to transfer an unspecified sum at some future time. The academic affirmation of principle should be contrasted with the following judgment of Buckley J.

Re Cook's Settlement Trusts [1965] Ch 902

By an agreement made in 1933 between Sir Herbert Cook and his son, Sir Francis Cook, property including certain pictures from a very valuable collection became the absolute property of Sir Francis. The agreement provided that Sir Francis should resettle some of the property and covenant with the trustees of the settlement that in the event of certain pictures (including a Rembrandt) being sold 'during the lifetime of Sir Francis the net proceeds of sale shall be paid to the trustees' to be held on the resettlement trusts in favour of Sir Francis's children. Sir Herbert died in 1939. Sir Francis married several times and there were two living children. In 1962 Sir Francis gave the Rembrandt to his wife who wished to sell it. The trustees sought directions as to whether, if the Rembrandt were sold, they should seek to enforce the covenant.

> **Buckley J:** Counsel appearing for Sir Francis, has submitted, that, as a matter of law, the covenant is not enforceable against him by the trustees of the settlement; . . . counsel submits that the covenant was a voluntary and executory contract to make a settlement in a future event and was not a settlement of a covenant to pay a sum of money to the trustees. He further submits that, as regards the covenant, all the beneficiaries under the settlement are volunteers with the consequence that not only should the court not direct the trustees to take proceedings on the covenant but also that it should positively direct them not to take proceedings. He relies on *Re Pryce* [1917] 1 Ch 234, and *Re Kay's Settlement* [1939] Ch 329.
>
> Counsel for the second and third defendants [the children] have contended that, on the true view of the facts, there was an immediate settlement of the obligation created by the covenant, and not merely a covenant to settle something in the future. It was said, as counsel for the second defendant put it, that, by the agreement, Sir Herbert bought the rights arising under the covenant for the benefit of the *cestuis que trust* under the settlement

and that, the covenant being made in favour of the trustees, these rights became assets of the trust. He relied on *Fletcher v Fletcher*, (1844) 4 Hare 67; *Williamson v Codrington* (1750) 1 Ves Sen 511; and *Re Cavendish Browne's Settlement Trusts* (1916) 61 Sol Jo 27. I am not able to accept this argument. The covenant with which I am concerned did not, in my opinion, create a debt enforceable at law, that is to say, a property right, which, although to bear fruit only in the future and on a contingency, was capable of being made the subject of an immediate trust, as was held to be the case in *Fletcher v Fletcher*. Nor is this covenant associated with property which was the subject of an immediate trust, as in *Williamson v Codrington*. Nor did the covenant relate to property which then belonged to the covenantor, as in *Re Cavendish Browne's Settlement Trusts*. In contrast to all these cases, this covenant on its true construction is, in my opinion, an executory contract to settle a particular fund or particular funds of money which at the date of the covenant did not exist and which might never come into existence. It is analogous to a covenant to settle an expectation or to settle after-acquired property. The case, in my judgement, involves the law of contract, not the law of trusts.... Accordingly, the second and third defendants are not, in my judgement, entitled to require the trustees to take proceedings to enforce the covenant.

(The picture was subsequently sold for 760,000 guineas – *The Times* 20 March 1965, p 10.)

Unfortunately, for those seeking clear judicial guidance *Re Cook's Settlement Trust* is ambiguous. It is uncertain whether Buckley J held that the covenant was a 'mere expectancy' which could not form the subject-matter of a trust, or whether there was simply no intention to create a trust of the benefit of the covenant. Moreover *Davenport v Bishopp* was not cited in the judgment. Uncertainty, therefore, still surrounds the status of covenants to settle future property. But *Re Cook's Settlement Trusts* does not undermine the basic proposition that the benefit of a covenant to settle *existing property* can be the subject-matter of a trust where the necessary intention is present.

What remains more questionable is the identification of the necessary intention. In the early case of *Fletcher v Fletcher* (1844) 4 Hare 67, the often-cited authority for the basic proposition just referred to, evidence of intention was very thin, assuming that the intention in question is that of the covenantor and not the covenantee (see Maudsley in Pound (ed) *Perspectives of Law* (1964) and Feltham (1982) 98 LQR 17 for consideration of this latter point). It is significant that *Fletcher v Fletcher* was decided at a time when courts were quite eager to construe precatory words as revealing an intention to create a trust. This was also before the full development of privity of contract doctrine with the resulting sceptical approach to attempts to circumvent privity by invoking a 'trust of a promise'. It must be doubted whether a modern court would reach the same result about the relevant intention.

One question is whether it would even be necessary for a modern court to trouble itself with such matters in light of the enactment of the Contracts (Rights of Third Parties) Act 1999, a point considered in the next section.

(4) Enforceability and the Contracts (Rights of Third Parties) Act 1999

It must be emphasised at the outset that in the absence of any consideration, whether provided by potential trustees or beneficiaries, a promise to create a trust remains just that, a voluntary promise to act. The settlor retains the freedom to resile from the promise.

But to revert to our earlier example what if in the immediate context A covenants with B to transfer £10,000 to be held on trust for C and D who, not having provided any consideration, are 'volunteers' in the eyes of equity? Under the 1999 Act the position of any third party or beneficiary of any contract entered into on or after 11 May 2000 is fundamentally altered (see generally Andrews [2001] 60(2) CLJ 353–381; Merkin (ed) *Privity of Contract* (2000)). Section 1(1) provides that a third party – C or D in our case – will acquire a right to 'enforce a term of the contract' if either of two limbs of an 'intention' test are satisfied. Under s 1(1) this test will be satisfied (i) where A and B have expressly stated that the contract term is to be so enforceable (s 1(1)(a)) or (ii) where a term of the contract purports to confer a benefit on the third party unless 'on a proper construction of the contract it appears that the parties did not intend the term to be enforceable by the third party' (s1(1)(b), (2)). Unfortunately the meaning of the term 'enforce' is not elaborated on although under s 1(5) it is stated that '. . . there shall be available to the third party any remedy that would have been available to him in an action for breach of contract if he had been a party to the contract (and the rules relating to damages, injunctions, specific performance and other relief shall apply accordingly)'. In our example under the terms of the statute C and D would be treated as parties to the covenant and able to sue for damages. This largely replicates the position under the pre-existing case law whereby if a volunteer beneficiary was also a party to the deed she was able to sue upon it for common law damages (*Cannon v Hartley* [1949] Ch 213). But because the beneficiary in that case was a volunteer she would not have been able to obtain the equitable remedy of specific performance.

There is some doubt as to how far that equitable remedy is available under s 1(5). Leaving the example of a covenant to one side for the moment, s 1(5) would appear to mean that where a contract between A and B is supported by consideration then the third party can obtain the equitable remedy of specific performance of the contract in the circumstances where 'the rules . . . apply', for example, where the subject-matter is such that an award of damages would not be appropriate. After all under the terms of the legislation the volunteer third party is to be treated 'as if he had been a party to the contract'. This outcome does, however, depend on there being consideration to support the agreement. To this extent at least the legislation would seem to create an exception to the maxim that 'equity does not assist a volunteer'. But what then is the position of the volunteer beneficiary of a covenant since at equity a covenant is not regarded as satisfying the consideration requirement even though at common law the covenant does meet this requirement? It can be argued that all that the legislation does is to treat the volunteer beneficiary as if she were a party to the deed, enabling her to sue for damages but, by analogy with *Cannon v Hartley*, not to obtain specific performance of the covenant. An alternative starting-point for analysis is to ask whether there is a sound legal policy reason for adopting a position whereby the only third party who cannot seek specific performance of a contract or covenant is the volunteer beneficiary of the covenant. An answer may simply be that the 1999 Act deals essentially with the issue of privity and does not purport to alter, for instance, the requirement that a contract be supported by consideration nor what constitutes consideration under the rules of equity. The matter cannot be seen as settled, however, and the outcome may depend on how much weight should be given in the immediate context to the post-*Choithram* version of 'equity will not assist a volunteer'.

(5) Covenants, intention and legal policy

The question remains: 'Should the covenantor be made to implement his under-taking on behalf of the volunteers or not?' The response that this matter has been resolved by the Contracts (Rights of Third Parties) Act 1999 is tempting but possibly misleading. The 1999 Act is not retrospective and therefore does not affect pre-existing covenants and to that extent the previous learning has continuing relevance. More importantly there remain some uncertainties about the interpretation of the statute. Aside from those already discussed there is an argument that the law as represented by cases such as *Re Pryce* and *Re Kay's Settlement* is unaffected by the statutory change. Gardner, for instance, points out that the third party's right to enforce a covenant is only as strong as the right of the promisee or covenantee (s 1(5)) and also under s 3(2) the promisor or covenantor will have the same defence as would be available if 'the proceedings had been brought by the promisee' (*An Introduction to the Law of Trusts* (2nd edn, 2003) p 74). It will be recalled that under the old much-criticised law, as represented by cases such as *Re Pryce*, it was at the very least doubtful whether the court would permit a trustee-covenantee to enforce the covenant and obtain an award of damages where this would have the effect of sidestepping the 'equity will not assist a volunteer maxim' and thereby enable volunteer-beneficiaries to obtain by indirect means what they could not obtain by directly enforcing the covenant themselves. Gardner concludes that 'under the 1999 Act, the ben-eficiary should likewise be unable to enforce it'. Accepting this as a tenable if literalist interpretation of the Act, one might nevertheless question whether a purposive construction of the statute might not lead to a different conclusion. After all the whole tenor of the Act is to assist the volunteer third party and thereby undermine to some degree the equitable maxim. It would be strange therefore if the courts were to interpret the Act in a way that supported cases whose reasoning has been questioned and whose rationale is rendered almost otiose by the Act.

This indirectly returns us to the question of legal policy. A more liberal approach to voluntary covenants for the benefit of third parties is adopted in the US where the *Restatement of Trusts* (2nd edn) para 26n prescribes that 'in the absence of evidence of a different intention, the inference is that the promisee immediately becomes trustee of his rights under the promise' (also see Feltham (1982) 98 LQR 17 who supports this presumption).

But the acceptability of this or other presumptions depends, to reiterate the point, on what is perceived as desirable policy. This in turn depends on what justification if any can be advanced for enforcing gratuitous promises, where the intended beneficiary has suffered no detriment and placed no reliance on the promise. And judgment on this issue needs to take account of the form of the promise – the covenant.

Is the existence of a covenant a sufficient reason in itself for permitting enforcement by or at the behest of volunteers? Concentration on the form of the promise shifts the focus from the status of the third party as volunteer to the intention of the promisor. Does the act of formally promising in a covenant to settle property for volunteer third parties indicate an intention to be bound to them by that promise? On this it has been said, in relation to the no longer applicable requirement of a seal, that 'the affixing and impressing of a wax wafer – symbol in the popular mind of legalism and weightiness – was an excellent device for inducing the circumspective frame of mind appropriate in one pledging his future' (Fuller (1941) 41 Col LR 799 at 800). But the result of circumspection must be an intention to make an irrevocable promise if it is to be assumed that the benefit of a covenant is to be held by the promisee on trust for third parties. Are there circumstances in which a settlor who goes through the ritual of covenanting to settle property would wish to retain the choice whether or not subsequently to transfer the property? (See Feltham (1982) 98 LQR 17 at 18–19.)

Given this range of policy choices, it is initially surprising, and unfortunate for those seeking an articulation of policy premises, that the outcome of a dispute involving a covenant to settle property may depend on wholly fortuitous circumstances, as occurred in *Re Ralli's Will Trust* [1963] 3 All ER 940. In this case the testator, Ambrose Ralli, left his residuary estate on trust (the 1892 settlement) for his widow (W) for life with remainder to his two daughters Helen (H) and Irene (I) in equal shares. By a marriage settlement in 1924 H covenanted to assign her reversionary interest in the residuary estate of the 1892 settlement to the trustees of the settlement (the 1924 settlement) on trust, as events turned out, for I's children who were mere volunteers. H had not assigned the reversionary interest before her death in 1956. H pre-deceased W, who died in 1961, whereupon the reversionary interest fell into possession. The plaintiff (P), who was I's husband and the sole surviving trustee of the 1924 settlement, was also the sole surviving trustee of the 1892 settlement, having been appointed a trustee in 1946. Should then P as trustee of the 1892 settlement pay H's share of the residue to her personal representatives under her will or, as trustee of the 1924 settlement, retain it for the beneficiaries of that settlement, I's children? Had the trusts of the 1924 settlement become completely constituted by the chance acquisition of the *legal estate* by P in his capacity as trustee of the 1892 settlement? Buckley J, on the facts, was able to hold that H had made a prior effective declaration of trust of the reversionary interest but went on to consider the 'complete constitution' point (at 946–948).

Buckley J: In my judgement the circumstance that the plaintiff [P] holds the fund because he was appointed a trustee of the will is irrelevant. He is at law the owner of the fund and the means by which he became so have no effect on the quality of his legal ownership. The question is: for whom, if anyone, does he hold the fund in equity? In other words, who can successfully assert in equity against him disentitling him to stand on his legal right? It seems to me to be indisputable that Helen, if she were alive, could not do so, for she has solemnly covenanted under seal to assign the fund to the plaintiff and the defendants can stand in no better position....

Had someone other than the plaintiff been the trustee of the will and held the fund, the result of this part of the case would, in my judgement, have been different; and it may seem strange that the rights of the parties should depend on the appointment of the plaintiff as trustee of the will in 1946, which for present purposes may have been a quite fortuitous event. The result, however, in my judgment, flows – and flows, I think, quite rationally – from the consideration that the rules of equity derive from the tenderness of a court of equity for the consciences of the parties. There would have been nothing unconscientious in Helen or her personal representatives asserting her equitable interest under the trusts of the will against a trustee who was not a covenantee under cl 7 of the settlement, and it would have been unconscientious for such a trustee to disregard those interests. Having obtained a transfer of the fund, it would not have been unconscientious in Helen to refuse to honour her covenant, because the beneficiaries under her settlement were mere volunteers; nor seemingly would the court have regarded it as unconscientious in the plaintiff to have abstained from enforcing the covenant either specifically or in damages, for the reason, apparently that he would have been under no obligation to obtain for the volunteers indirectly what they could not obtain directly. In such circumstances Helen or her personal representatives could have got and retained the fund. In the circumstances of the present case, on the other hand, it is not unconscientious in the plaintiff to withhold from Helen's estate the fund which Helen covenanted that he should receive: on the contrary, it would have been unconscientious in Helen to seek to deprive the plaintiff of that fund, and her personal representatives can be in no better position. The inadequacy of the volunteers' equity against Helen and her estate consequently is irrelevant, for that equity does not come into play; but they have a good equity against the plaintiff, because it would be unconscientious in him to retain as against them any property which he holds in consequence of the provisions of the settlement.

For these reasons I am of opinion that in the events which have happened the plaintiff now holds the fund in question on the trusts of the marriage settlement, and I will so declare.

Just as a narrow, one might say fortuitous, event would have decided the case, had the issue discussed above been relevant, similarly a narrow meaning is attributed to conscience here. This is not conscience in any broad sense of 'fairness' but conscience in the precise sense that it would be 'unconscientious' for the personal representatives of H, standing in her place, to establish their claim by breaking the promise made to the covenantee/trustee. In short conscience follows legal form here.

Wherever the balance of policy argument concerning enforcement of voluntary covenants in general by third parties may lie, additional considerations arise where the subject-matter of the covenant is future property. Gardner, for instance, seeks to explain (pp 74–78) what he perceives to be the 'doctrinally dubious' decisions of the turn of the twentieth century (eg *Re D'Angibau* (1880) 15 Ch D 228; *Re Pryce* [1917] 1 Ch 234) in terms of a shift in judicial policy. He suggests that these are attributable to an emerging judicial scepticism towards the institution of marriage settlements, a scepticism reflecting, in Gardner's view, the influence of economic liberalism. Lee ((1969) 85 LQR 213) too has argued, although with a very different doctrinal analysis of the cases, that the recognition of marriage consideration in family settlements, thus permitting enforcement of covenants to settle after-acquired property, represented a breach with equitable principle explicable purely on contemporary public policy grounds. With the virtual disappearance of marriage settlements 'the reasons of public policy belong to a closed chapter of legal history' (at 227). Conversely it is said (Barton (1975) 91 LQR 236 at 246) that the restrictive approach evident in the later cases has imposed 'quite arbitrary limitations upon the employment of that very useful device, the trust'. Whereas these disagreements may reflect fundamental differences about the applicability of the relevant principles of equity and trusts law, they also, as we have previously suggested, have broader public policy implications. Acceptance of the enforceability of voluntary covenants to settle after-acquired property could materially increase the scope of the trust to facilitate dispositions of property rights over time. It is an open question whether the additional flexibility is necessary or desirable. (See eg Lindsay and Ziegler 'Trust of an Interest in a Discretionary Trust – Is it Possible?' (1986) 60 ALJ 387.)

(6) Exceptions to the maxim 'Equity will not assist a volunteer'

These are briefly summarised here for reference purposes only (cf *Hanbury and Martin* pp 141–147; *Pettit* pp 118–126, where the exceptions are considered at greater length):

(i) *The rule in Strong v Bird.* Where a donor (A) has attempted to make a gift inter vivos to the donee (B) but the gift is not completed through failure to comply with the necessary formalities, then, if B is subsequently appointed as A's executor or administrator the vesting of the legal title in B is treated as completing the gift. A gift can include, as indeed was the case in *Strong v Bird*, the release of a debt. For the rule to apply there must have been a continuing intention on the part of the donor to complete the gift during his lifetime. The consequence of the rule is that the claims of the beneficiaries under the will or on an intestacy are overridden. Whilst it is possible to view the rule as an illustration of the exceptions to the maxim, it would seem equally plausible to locate the rule alongside cases such as *Re Rose* (above, p 138) and *Re Ralli's Will Trust* as illustrations of 'widened circumstances in which equity is willing to find that a transfer has in fact been completed' however fortuitous or accidental that act of completion might be (see Pearce and Stevens *The Law of Trusts and Equitable Obligations* (4th edn, 2006) p 186). On this basis it can be argued that the 'rule' should also apply to perfect a trust. So if S makes an ineffective inter vivos transfer of existing property to T to hold on trust for C but T is appointed as S's executor then this should suffice to completely constitute the trust, assuming that S's intention to make the gift continues unchanged until death. If the 'outright gift to the executor' version of the rule is sufficient to override the claims of testamentary legatees there would seem no reason in principle why the claims of beneficiaries of S's intended trust should not equally prevail. But by contrast it should be noted that more restrictive approaches have been adopted in Canada (*Re Halley* (1959) 43 MPR 79) and most recently by the Supreme Court of New South Wales in *Blackett v Darcy* [2005] NSWSC 65 where *Strong v Bird* was seen as an anomaly which 'should not in this 21st century be extended at all' (para 35). As Jaconelli has pertinently observed, the question whether a 'trust form' of the rule in *Strong v Bird* is recognised may depend 'on the jurisdiction in which the question is posed' ([2006] Conv 432 at 444).

(ii) *Donatio mortis causa* (see above, p 157 and generally Borkowski *Deathbed Gifts – The Law of Donatio Mortis Causa* (1999)).

(iii) *Proprietary estoppel.* It is now well established that in circumstances where a promisor makes some promise to a volunteer promisee as to future rights over property and the promisee acts to their detriment in reliance on the promise, then the promisor will be prevented ('estopped') from going back on the promise. The approach taken by the courts to raising a 'proprietary estoppel' and awarding an appropriate remedy are examined in some detail in Chapter 12 since it is frequently in the context of property disputes between partners that the boundaries of the doctrine are being established. It is sufficient to note for the moment that it is yet another legal context in which all the elements of the doctrine are permeated by 'the fundamental principle that equity is concerned to prevent unconscionable conduct' (per Robert Walker LJ in *Gillett v Holt* [2001] Ch 210 at p 225).

(iv) There is a statutory exception to the maxim although here again it can equally be interpreted as a completion of an imperfect gift. We saw earlier in the chapter that a minor cannot hold a legal estate in land (LPA 1925, s 1(6)). An attempt to convey a legal estate in land to a minor operates as a declaration that the land is held in trust for the minor (Trusts of Land and Appointment of Trustees Act 1996, Sch 1, para 1 replacing Settled Land Act 1925, s 27).

(d) Intention to create a binding trust obligation: conclusion

We observed earlier that a feature distinguishing a gift by trust from an absolute gift, and one central to the concept of an express trust, is the intention to subject oneself to or impose on some other the obligations of trusteeship. Without this there is no express trust. Of course in the vast majority of cases settlors impose trusteeship on others or themselves because that is what they want to do. It might even be claimed that if courts were to permit third parties to enforce voluntary covenants they would be implementing the covenantor's implied intention previously frustrated by strict application of principles of equity. The technique adopted might involve what Lord Diplock has termed 'a juristic subterfuge' (in *Swain v Law Society* [1982] 2 All ER 827 at 832) construing the presence of a specific intention. Many of the rules we have been considering in this section are what might be labelled 'rules of construction' directed towards identifying the intention of the donor or settlor. Yet the borderline cases that arise are frequently just that because clear words of intention do not exist, and the uncertainties of behaviour and language open up leeway for the courts.

Where there is leeway there is temptation to use the vagueness generated by notions of intention to do justice by imposing trust obligations. The result is that some people might get trusts imposed not because they want them but because they 'deserve' them. Although *Paul v Constance* presents some difficulties for technical analysis, probably few would disagree that Mrs Constance's claim was lacking in merit. Similar sentiments might be expressed about the merits of discovering the requisite 'intention' in *Gold v Hill* (see p 172) or even in the commercial context of *Don King Productions Inc v Warren* [1998] 2 All ER 608 (see also *Rowe v Prance* [1999] 2 FLR 787 where on limited evidence the court 'identified' an intention to create an express trust of 'our houseboat'; criticised in Baughen [2000] Conv 58). But Hackney's warning on the temptation to do justice is apposite: 'encroachment on the proper sphere of moral regulation is a constant danger' ('The Politics of Chancery' (1981) 34 CLP 113). Thus the courts might easily slip into the assumption that the imposition and acceptance of obligations necessarily involves 'binding legal obligations'. *Ottaway v Norman* and *Re Snowden* plainly demand to be considered and contrasted in this light (see Hackney [1971] ASLC 384 at 384–385, for a critical assessment of the 'merits' in *Ottaway v Norman*). But leeway does not imply unfettered discretion. Consequently, although there are occasions where the borderlines between gift, promise to declare a trust and declaration of trust become blurred, there is scant evidence, *Paul v Constance* notwithstanding, that equity will yet perfect 'imperfect gifts' by construing them as 'declarations of trust', or readily recognise a 'voluntary covenant to create a trust' as implying a 'present declaration of trust' (but cf *Pennington v Waine* at p 143 and the uncertain ambit of unconscionability applied in that case).

One final point calls for speculation. Intention, we said earlier, is one of the hallmarks of an express trust; it is at the heart of the fundamental distinction between express trusts and constructive trusts imposed by the courts. In *Paul v Constance* Scarman LJ observed that 'one must exclude from one's mind any case built on the existence of an implied or constructive trust'. Possibly *Paul v Constance* was argued that way because the facts did not fit within any recognised category which would have supported the imposition of a constructive trust, although it is interesting to speculate on the consequences had the property in *Paul v Constance* been an owner-occupied house (cf Chapter 12, p 622). Irrespective of this the court was able to find the necessary intention and so, at a conceptual level, the fundamental distinction remains undisturbed. But is the flexibility provided by 'intention' such that on admittedly rare occasions, the distinction cannot be sustained in substance? Discovering 'intention' or deeming it to be present can then become one of the mechanisms by which the courts pursue the original jurisdiction of Chancery: doing justice in the interests of 'good conscience'.

5. Trusts creation and resulting trusts

A key performer in the *Vandervell* saga, which concludes this chapter, is a resulting trust. This point in the chapter therefore provides a convenient and appropriate forum for introducing the resulting trust in more detail, particularly as Megarry J subjected the concept to detailed analysis in the course of the *Vandervell* litigation. Subsequently doubt has been cast on elements of that analysis (see below) and debate about the theoretical basis for resulting trusts has proliferated. Nevertheless in our view the functional categorisation developed by Megarry J still has descriptive and analytical merit and provides an appropriate starting-point for understanding the nature of current controversies in this area of the law.

We have already briefly encountered two occasions when a resulting trust can occur: where the share of beneficial interests in a trust fund is uncertain and where an alleged half-secret trust is not established. In both cases, as the express trust fails and as the trustee plainly cannot take beneficially, the equitable interest in the property must reside somewhere and it goes back, or 'results back', to the transferor. Such a resulting trust can arise in a wide variety of circumstances. Further examples occur if there is a failure to dispose completely of the beneficial interest such as where A transfers property to trustees on trust for B for life but fails to dispose of the equitable remainder, or for B on attaining age 25 and B does not. These are all instances of trust failure and have been categorised as automatic resulting trusts – being imputed automatically to fill in the gap in beneficial ownership. Failure to create a trust effectively will not always bring about a resulting trust (see *Re Vandervell's Trusts (No 2)*, below). Accordingly, where in circumstances such as those in *Re Snowden* there is a failure of certainty of intention to impose a legally binding obligation of trusteeship the person in whom legal title to property is vested holds it for himself absolutely.

A second and distinct form of resulting trust, a 'presumed resulting trust', is briefly outlined below and examined in some detail in Chapter 12 (*Implied trusts and the family home*). It is in that context that the relevant presumption has been most clearly articulated and criticised. In principle the presumption is said to reflect the implied intention of the transferor (A) of property that the transferee should hold it on trust for A's benefit. As will be seen in Chapter 12 the presumption is rebuttable.

The rationale underpinning the automatic resulting trust could also be argued to be respect for presumed intention. It envisages the settlor saying 'I would like the property returned to me if for some unforeseen reason my original gift fails'. This may seem a safe and sensible assumption for the law to make and is now consistent with current judicial thinking although slightly at variance with that of Megarry J in *Re Vandervell's Trusts (No 2)*. Moreover in the context of tax law, as the *Vandervell* litigation demonstrates, a resulting trust is a cruel kindness and probably the least desirable result for the unfortunate, unwise or ill-advised settlor.

Re Vandervell's Trusts (No 2) [1974] 1 All ER 47 at 68

Megarry J: It seems to me that the relevant points on resulting trusts may be put in a series of propositions. . . .

(1) If a transaction fails to make any effective disposition of any interest it does nothing. This is so at law and in equity, and has nothing to do with resulting trusts.

(2) Normally the mere existence of some unexpressed intention in the breast of the owner of the property does nothing: there must at least be some expression of that intention before it can effect any result. To yearn is not to transfer.

(3) Before any doctrine of resulting trust can come into play, there must at least be some effective transaction which transfers or creates some interest in property.

(4) Where A effectually transfers to B (or creates in his favour) any interest in any property, whether legal or equitable, a resulting trust for A may arise in two distinct classes of cases . . .

    (a) The first case is where the transfer to B is not made on any trust. If, of course, it appears from the transfer that B is intended to hold on certain trusts, that will be decisive, and the case is not within this category; and similarly if it appears that B is intended to take beneficially. But in other cases there is a rebuttable presumption that B holds on a resulting trust for A. The question is not one of automatic consequences of a dispositive failure by A, but one of presumption: the property has been carried to B, and from the absence of consideration and any presumption of advancement B is presumed not only to hold the entire interest on trust, but also to hold the beneficial interest for A absolutely. The presumption thus establishes both that A is to take on trust and also what that trust is. Such resulting trusts may be called 'presumed resulting trusts'.

(b) The second class of case is where the transfer to B is made on trusts which leave some or all of the beneficial interest undisposed of. Here B automatically holds on a resulting trust for A to the extent that the beneficial interest has not been carried to him or others. The resulting trust here does not depend on any intentions or presumptions, but is the automatic consequence of A's failure to dispose of what is vested in him. Since ex hypothesi the transfer is on trust, the resulting trust does not establish the trust but merely carries back to A the beneficial interest that has not been disposed of. Such resulting trusts may be called 'automatic resulting trusts'.

This characterisation of the circumstances that can give rise to a resulting trust was broadly endorsed by Lord Browne-Wilkinson in *Westdeutsche Landesbank Girozentrale v Islington London Borough Council* [1996] 2 All ER 961 but with the addition of the following significant reservation about Megarry J's apparent dismissal of the role of 'intentions or presumptions' in 'automatic resulting trusts' (at 991):

Both types of resulting trust are traditionally regarded as examples of trusts giving effect to the common intention of the parties. A resulting trust is not imposed by law against the intentions of the trustee (as is a constructive trust) but gives effect to his presumed intention. Megarry J in *Re Vandervell's Trusts (No 2)* suggests that a resulting trust of type B [4(b) above] does not depend on intention but operates automatically. I am not convinced that this is right. If the settlor has expressly, or by necessary implication, abandoned any beneficial interest in the trust property, there is in my view no resulting trust: the undisposed-of equitable interest vests in the Crown as bona vacantia: see *Re West Sussex Constabulary's Widows, Children and Benevolent (1930) Fund Trusts* [1970] 1 All ER 544.

At first glance these comments, made obiter, do no more than provide a modest gloss to Megarry J's classification by emphasising that the rationale for the 'automatic' resulting trust is also rooted in what the law presumes the intention of the settlor to have been (see our comments above). Now this is, in our view, something of a fictional intention, not least because of the questionable inclusion of the trustee within the ambit of the 'intention', and it is difficult to escape from an analysis that functionally the law *is* imposing a trust almost in default to fill a gap in beneficial ownership. What the comments of Lord Browne-Wilkinson do emphasise, however, is that if the settlor has expressly or impliedly abandoned any beneficial interest in the trust property then the gap will be filled in a different manner, ie the bona vacantia option. We would suggest, however, that only on rare occasions will such an intention be revealed or discovered. The law does not readily assume abandonment of property. Consider, for instance, the recent case of *Air Jamaica Ltd v Charlton* [1999] 1 WLR 1399 where a clause in a pension trust deed stating that 'no moneys which at any time have been contributed by the Company . . . shall in any circumstances be repayable to the

Company' did not prevent the Privy Council from holding that a resulting trust should be imposed in relation to surplus funds arising when the trust was found to be void (the ownership of surplus funds is discussed further in Chapters 13 (pension schemes) and 17 (unincorporated associations)). The explanation provided in the case by Lord Millett for this conclusion has, however, placed the interpretation of 'intention' at the forefront of theoretical discussion about the rationale for the resulting trust (at 1412, emphasis added):

> Like a constructive trust, a resulting trust arises by operation of law, though unlike a constructive trust it gives effect to intention. But it arises whether or not the transferor intended to retain a beneficial interest – he almost always does not – since it responds to the *absence of intention on his part to pass a beneficial interest to the recipient*. It may arise even where the transferor positively wished to part with the beneficial interest as in *Vandervell v IRC* [1967] 2 AC 291.

In contrast to Lord Browne-Wilkinson's analysis in *Westdeutsche*, which appears to emphasise a *positive* role for intention, in Lord Millett's formulation 'intention' plays an almost *negative* role in that the focus is on the absence of intention to benefit the recipient or transferee. The onus is on that person to rebut the presumption that the transferor had no intention to benefit him or her. This formulation offers a practical advantage in that it comfortably encompasses the fact situations in both 'automatic' and 'presumed resulting' trusts and, more particularly, may provide a more compelling rationale for the type of resulting trust in *Vandervell v IRC*, where receiving a new equitable beneficial interest was certainly not what the settlor, Mr Vandervell, envisaged.

There are, however, difficulties associated with the 'absence of intention to benefit' approach. First, strictly speaking, the opinion of Lord Millett in *Air Jamaica*, being that of the Privy Council, is of persuasive authority only and in so far as it conflicts with that of Lord Browne-Wilkinson in *Westdeutsche*, the latter must be preferred. Second, the formulation has the capacity to be over-inclusive in the sense that it predicates a position whereby a resulting trust might be possible whenever the recipient of property was not intended to take it beneficially. But for some, on the other hand, this is a positive attribute that underpins the proposition that there is just one type of resulting trust, that which arises where property is transferred gratuitously in circumstances where 'the provider of property did not intend to benefit the recipient' (Chambers *Resulting Trusts* (1997) p 2). As importantly for its proponents this analysis also envisages a more extensive role for the resulting trust within the law of restitution whereby the law imposes a resulting trust to prevent the unjust enrichment of the recipient (see in particular *Chambers*; Birks 'Restitution and Resulting Trusts' in Goldstein (ed) *Equity and Contemporary Legal Developments* (1992); but cf Swadling (2008) 124 LQR 72–102, disputing the notion of a unifying theory whilst suggesting that the 'automatic' resulting trust 'defies legal analysis'; although see Piska [2008] Conv 441 at 448–450). As was mentioned briefly in Chapter 1 at p 30, concern at the practical implications of developing a more expansive role for the resulting trusts, particularly as regards creating a new class of secured creditors, underpinned its rejection by the majority in the House of Lords in *Westdeutsche*.

Where does this leave us? At the risk of over-simplification the basic proposition remains that resulting trusts arise by operation of law in the case of gifts – 'presumed resulting trusts' – and of trusts that fail but they may be displaced by evidence of a contrary intention on the part of the donor or settlor. Reverting back to the Megarry classification we are left with the following proposition: the classification still has descriptive value subject to the caveat, following Lord Browne-Wilkinson, that the label 'automatic resulting trust' is slightly misleading whilst reflecting what in most instances the law is in practice doing. There is one further point to note here concerning the weight to be attached to the analysis of Lord Browne-Wilkinson in *Westdeutsche*. Swadling persuasively points out that the twofold analysis of Megarry was foreshadowed in the opinions of Lords Wilberforce and Upjohn in *Vandervell v IRC* [1967] 2 AC 291 (at 313 and 329 respectively), the first stage of the *Vandervell* litigation (see 'Property' in Birks and Rose (eds) *Lessons of the Swaps Litigation* (2000) p 242 at pp 270–271). Lord Upjohn summarised the position this way (at 313, emphasis added):

> If A intends to give away all his beneficial interest in a piece of property and thinks he has done so but, by some mistake or accident or failure to comply with the requirements of the law, he has failed to do so, either wholly or partially, there will, *by operation of law*, be a resulting trust for him of the beneficial interest of which he had failed effectually to dispose.

This statement, arguably part of the ratio of the decision in the case, is, to put the point at its lowest, certainly more consistent with the Megarry classification of two types of resulting trust, one based on presumption and the other that operates irrespective of there being any intention, than that of Lord Browne-Wilkinson or indeed of Lord Millett. This reinforces our view that in the absence of a suitable alternative label – might 'default resulting trust' do? – we should continue with the Megarry nomenclature whilst recognising that it is a not wholly accurate label of convenience, particularly if one is applying the analysis of Lord Browne-Wilkinson (cf Rickett and Grantham (2000) 116 LQR 15 at 19 who propose that 'the resulting trust and its foundational presumptions operate . . . simply as a series of default rules').

6. The *Vandervell* saga

(a) The background

Mr Guy Anthony Vandervell (V) was chairman, managing director and principal shareholder of a successful engineering company, Vandervell Products Ltd

(VP). Almost all the voting shares in the company were owned by V and a fur-ther 100,000 non-voting shares in the company were held by NP Bank Ltd on a bare trust for V absolutely. The only other substantial shareholder was a private trustee company, Vandervell Trustees Ltd (VT) which acted as trustee (1) of a 1949 settlement for V's children and (2) of a retirement and profit-sharing fund for employees of VP.

In 1958 V decided to provide the Royal College of Surgeons (RCS) with £150,000 to fund a chair in pharmacology.

The method agreed upon was that V should arrange for the transfer of the 100,000 non-voting shares to RCS and that VP should declare dividends on these shares to provide the necessary money. As part of the arrangement it was agreed that RCS should grant an option to VT to repurchase the shares for £5,000. This method had the following advantages:

(i)   dividend income could be passed direct to RCS without being taxed in V's hands,

(ii) the RCS as a charity would probably be able to recover from the Inland Revenue income tax deducted at source from the dividends,

(iii) the declaration of dividends might help V to avoid a surtax assessment (an additional income tax levied then on high incomes) in respect of undistributed profits of VP which might have been deemed under the tax statutes to be part of V's income,

(iv) a saving of future estate duty liability otherwise payable if V had retained ownership of the shares, and

(v)   the inclusion of an option to repurchase the VPL shares would enable the shareholding to be returned to the control of the Vandervell family, thereby avoiding possible complications in the event of a planned public flotation of the private company being implemented.

The subsequent litigation that arose out of the straightforward (sic) exercise occupied 38 days in court and resulted in two trips to the House of Lords and a further final visit to the Court of Appeal. The cases provide in Lord Reid's words 'an illustration of the folly of entering into an important transaction of an unusual character without first obtaining expert advice regarding tax liabilities which it may create' (*Vandervell v IRC* [1967] 1 All ER 1 at 3). More pertinently the cases also involve discussion of several of the issues canvassed in this chapter: the requirements for a valid declaration of trust, the ambit of LPA 1925, s 53(1)(c) concerning the disposition of equitable interests, the circumstances in which an 'automatic' resulting trust will be imposed and the appropriateness of one possible rationale of that trust – that it is helping to achieve, or at least not frustrate, the settlor's intention.

The legal issues raised are best examined in two stages relating to the periods 1958–61 and 1961–65.

(b) Stage 1: 1958–1961

In 1958 V instructed NP Bank to transfer the 100,000 non-voting shares to RCS and, as agreed, RCS granted the option by deed to VT. Unfortunately for V, as it later transpired, there was nothing 'in the deed to indicate whether the shares to be acquired on the exercise of the option were to be held by [VT] beneficially or on trust, and, if so, what trust. It was, indeed, too short and too simple' (per Megarry J *Re Vandervell's Trusts (No 2)* [1974] 1 All ER 47 at 54). Between 1958 and October 1961 VP declared dividends amounting to approximately £157,000, net of income tax, on the shares now owned by RCS.

In September 1961 the Inland Revenue assessed V to surtax on the dividends claiming that he had not divested himself absolutely of all interest in the shares.

Vandervell v IRC [1967] 1 All ER 1, HL

The Inland Revenue supported the assessment on two separate grounds.

(1) *The formalities argument.* The Revenue argued that the transfer by NP Bank to RCS transferred only a bare legal title to the shares and that the beneficial ownership remained in V (Vandervell) because he had not effected a disposition of his equitable interest in the shares in writing as required by LPA 1925, s 53(1)(c). The House of Lords unanimously rejected this argument.

(2) *The resulting trust argument.* The Revenue claimed that because there had been no declaration of the trusts of the option (see above) VT must hold the option (*not* the shares) on resulting trust for V. Consequently under Income Taxes Act 1952, s 415 (repealed in 1971) V had failed to divest himself completely of all interest in the shares.

The House of Lords by a 3:2 majority (Lords Upjohn, Pearce and Wilberforce; Lords Reid and Donovan dissenting) upheld the resulting trust argument and consequently the assessment to tax.

Lord Upjohn (Lord Pearce concurring) (*on the formalities argument*): The object of the section [s 53(1)(c)], as was the object of the old Statute of Frauds, is to prevent hidden oral transactions in equitable interests in fraud of those truly entitled, and making it difficult if not impossible, for the trustees to ascertain who are in truth the beneficiaries. When the beneficial owner, however, owns the whole beneficial estate and is in a position to give directions to his bare trustee with regard to the legal as well as the equitable estate there can be no possible ground for invoking the section where the beneficial owner wants to deal with the legal estate as well as the equitable estate.

I cannot agree with Diplock LJ ([1966] Ch 261 at 287) that prima facie a transfer of the legal estate carries with it the absolute beneficial interest in the property transferred; this plainly is not so, eg, the transfer may be on a change of trustee; it is a matter of intention in each case. If, however, the intention of the beneficial owner in directing the trustee to transfer the legal estate to X is that X should be the beneficial owner, I can see no reason for any further document or further words in the document assigning the legal estate also expressly transferring the beneficial interest; the greater includes the less. X may be wise to secure some evidence that the beneficial owner intended him to take the beneficial interest in case his beneficial title is challenged at a later date but it certainly cannot, in my opinion, be a statutory requirement that to effect its passing there must be some writing under s 53(1)(c).

Counsel for the Crown admitted that where the legal and beneficial estate was vested in the legal owner and he desired to transfer the whole legal and beneficial estate to another he did not have to do more than transfer the legal estate and he did not have to comply with s 53(1)(c); and I can see no difference between that case and this.

As I have said, that section is, in my opinion, directed to cases where dealings with the equitable estate are divorced from the legal estate. . . . To hold the contrary would make assignments unnecessarily complicated; if there had to be assignments in express terms of both legal and equitable interest that would make the section more productive of injustice than the supposed evils it was intended to prevent.

[*on the resulting trust argument*] There are, as I see it, three possibilities. 1. That the trustee company was intended to take [the option] as trustee for the children's settlement of Dec 30, 1949. 2. That the trustee company should take beneficially, the taxpayer relying on his three friends and advisers, Messrs Robins, Green and Jobson, the directors and holders of all the shares in the trustee company, to carry out his wishes which from time to time should be intimated to them in the way of a gentleman's agreement, but having no power at law to enforce them. 3. That the trustee company should hold as trustee on such trusts as he or the trustee company should from time to time declare.

My Lords, this question is really one of inference from primary facts, but having regard to the way in which the matter has developed I should be reluctant to differ from the courts below . . .

I agree with the conclusions of the Court of Appeal [1966] Ch 261 and Plowman J that the intention was that the trustee company should hold on such trusts as might thereafter be declared.

That is sufficient to dispose of the appeal, but one question was debated in the Court of Appeal, though not before your lordships, and that is whether the option was held by the trustee company on such trusts as the trustee company in its discretion should declare or as the taxpayer should declare. Once it is established that the trustee company held solely as trustee that, as the Court of Appeal held, matters not. The taxpayer could at any time revoke that discretion, if he had vested it in the trustee company.

On the formalities argument the decision can be described as convenient since V could have required his nominees NP to transfer the legal title in the shares to himself and then transferred the then unified legal and equitable interests to RCS without any need to comply with s 53(1)(c). V simply took a short-cut. It does appear that in everyday practice where nominees hold shares or securities it is not unusual for instructions to be given orally or, nowadays, electronically. But the question remains: does this rationalisation adequately explain how V's separate equitable interest could be transferred outside s 53(1)(c)? (See further Jones (1966) 24 CLJ 19; Spencer (1967) 31 Conv 175; Strauss (1967) 30 MLR 461; and for a recent interpretation invoking the doctrine of overreaching see Nolan [2002] 61(1) CLJ 169, although the author concedes (at 172) that 'the concept was nowhere applied in the case').

On the resulting trust point, in the opinion of the majority the failure to specify for whom VT was to hold the benefit of the option led to the conclusion that 'possibility 3' (above) applied. The inevitable result then of the initial failure to identify the beneficiaries of the option was succinctly stated by Lord Wilberforce (at 329): 'But the equitable, or beneficial, interest cannot remain in the air: the consequence in law must be that it remains in the settlor...'

Lord Upjohn's suggestion that 'as the Court of Appeal held, it matters not' whether it was V or VT that could declare the trusts on which the option was to be held is not wholly accurate. The most that can be said is that neither Plowman J in the High Court nor the Court of Appeal took a view on 'whether the right to declare such new trusts in the future was retained by the settlor or had been vested in the discretion of the trustee company' ([1966] Ch 261 at 291 per Diplock LJ). It was unnecessary to do so because it was immaterial to the liability to tax for the two tax years concerned. A difficulty with Lord Upjohn's position is that a resulting trust is in essence a bare trust with, in this instance, VT holding the benefit of the option simply on trust for V. V therefore had power to terminate the trust of the option or to direct VT to hold the benefit of the option for the children's settlement or even for himself or anyone else. One would not normally expect the trustee – in this case VT – to have power itself to declare new trusts. Yet as we shall see the door left ajar for this possibility by Lord Upjohn was to prove significant in the next round of litigation.

(c) Stage 2: 1961–1965

In response to the assessment to tax, VT on 11 October 1961, with V's full oral agreement, exercised the option and paid RCS £5,000, the money being drawn from the funds of the children's settlement. Then on 2 November 1961 VT's solicitors informed the Revenue of the exercise of the option writing that 'consequently [the] shares [in VP] will henceforth be held by [VT] upon trusts of the children's settlement'. Between 1962 and 1964 V arranged for VP to declare dividends amounting to £769,580 net which were paid to VT as an addition to the children's settlement. On 19 January 1965 (the first day of the Court of Appeal hearing in *Vandervell v IRC*) V executed a deed of release by which he transferred to VT all 'rights, title, or interest (if any)' which he had retained in the option, the shares or the dividends, expressly declaring that the trustee company was to hold them on the trusts of the children's settlement.

V died on 10 March 1967 having made no provision in his will for his children, saying expressly that this was because he had already provided for them by the settlement. The bulk of his estate was left instead to his second wife, the children's stepmother.

Between July and October 1967 V's executors were assessed to surtax on the dividends declared between 1962 and 1964 on the grounds that V was beneficial owner of the shares until 19 January 1965. The executors, faced with a substantial tax bill, felt obliged to institute proceedings against VT, the trustees of the children's settlement, claiming that they (the executors) were entitled in effect to the dividends. An attempt to have the Inland Revenue joined as a party in the proceedings was unsuccessful (*Vandervell Trustees Ltd v White* [1970] 3 All ER 16, HL). One consequence is that, however inappropriately, the subsequent litigation could be portrayed as a family dispute between trustees seeking to safeguard the financial provision made for the children and a stepmother seeking to undermine it. The Inland Revenue of course had an interest in the outcome.

The litigation then proceeded, 'without the presence of the Revenue – whose claim . . . has caused all the trouble' (Lord Denning in *Re Vandervell's Trusts (No 2)*). Judgment for the executors would effectively result in the Inland Revenue's claim being upheld. The executors succeeded before Megarry J ([1974] Ch 269) on the basis that, following the exercise of the option, the shares were held on resulting trust for V absolutely subject only to a lien for £5,000 in favour of the children's settlement.

Megarry J explained his conclusion on this point as follows:

> That issue is, in essence, whether trustees who hold an option on trust for X will hold the shares obtained by exercising that option on trust for Y merely because they used Y's money in exercising the option. Authority apart, my answer would be an unhesitating no. The option belongs to X beneficially, and the money merely exercises rights which belong to X. Let the shares be worth £50,000 so then an option to purchase those shares for £5,000 is worth £45,000, and it will be seen at once what a monstrous result would be produced by allowing trustees to divert from their beneficiary X the benefits of what they hold for him merely because they used Y's money instead of X's.

The trustees' appeal against the decision was unanimously upheld – although with some hesitation on the part of Stephenson LJ – in the Court of Appeal (*Re Vandervell's Trusts (No 2)* [1974] Ch 269).

The judgments, which have been widely criticised (Clark (1974) 38 Conv 405; Hackney (1974) ASCL 528; Harris (1975) 38 MLR 557; Battersby (1979) 43 Conv 17; Green (1984) 47 MLR 385), present considerable difficulties of interpretation. We can only touch on a couple of the problems here – a close reading of the full judgments and criticisms of them is necessary for a more thorough understanding. Although there are distinct differences of emphasis in the judgments (cf Green above, who argues these are of substance), very broadly the Court of Appeal rejected the executors' claim because new trusts over the shares had been declared by VT (declaration of trust point) which displaced V's resulting equitable interest in the option without the need for compliance with s 53(1)(c) (the formalities point). Lord Denning MR and Lawton LJ were also prepared to hold that Vandervell was by his conduct estopped from denying the children's beneficial interest in the shares, but unfortunately they do not satisfactorily deal with the reasons given by Megarry J for rejecting the estoppel argument (see *Green* at p 418).

An indication of the conceptual difficulties associated with the formalities and declaration of trust points can be discerned in the following comments of Stephenson LJ:

> It is difficult to infer that [Mr Vandervell] intended to dispose or ever did dispose of something he did not know he had until the judgment of Plowman J in *Vandervell v IRC*, which led to the deed of 1965, enlightened him, or to find a disposition of it in the exercise by the trustee company in 1961 of its option to purchase the shares. And even if he had disposed of his interest, he did not dispose of it by any writing sufficient to comply with section 53(1)(c) of the Law of Property Act 1925.
>
> But Lord Denning MR and Lawton LJ are able to hold that no disposition is needed because (1) the option was held on such trusts as might thereafter be declared by the trustee company or Mr Vandervell himself, and (2) the trustee company has declared that it holds the shares in the children's settlement. I do not doubt the first, because it was apparently the view of the majority of the House of Lords in *Vandervell v IRC*. I should be more confident of the second if it had been pleaded or argued either here or below and we had had the benefit of the learned judge's views on it...I see, as perhaps did counsel, difficulties in the way of a limited company declaring a trust by parol or conduct and without a resolution of the board of directors, and difficulties also in the way of finding any declaration of trust by Mr Vandervell himself in October or November 1961, or any conduct then or later which would in law or equity estop him from denying that he made one.

(1) *Declaration of trust point.* The acts of VT deemed by Lord Denning in the Court of Appeal sufficient to constitute a declaration of trust were (i) the use of the children's settlement money, (ii) payment to the children's settlement of all the dividends received by VT, and (iii) trustees' notification to the Inland Revenue on 2 November 1961. It has been suggested that 'the second and third merely indicate what the trustees thought the position to be [ie no intention to declare a trust existed], while the first ignores [V's] beneficial ownership of the option' (*Hanbury and Martin* p 130; and see the judgment of Megarry J above). Moreover acts (ii) and (iii) occurred after the exercise of the option by the trustees. Trustees cannot usually declare a trust whether by conduct or otherwise but, as noted previously, the House of Lords had already indicated, whether erroneously or not, in *Vandervell (No 1)* that 'the option was held by the trustee company on such trusts as the trustee company in its discretion should declare or as the taxpayer should declare'. Assuming VT were able to declare trusts 'by conduct'

(as was arguably the case in *Paul v Constance*, see p 165) are the above criticisms valid?

(2) *Formalities point.* Lord Denning suggests that 'a resulting trust for the settlor is born and dies without any writing at all'. Under LPA 1925, s 53(2) writing is not required for 'creation or operation of resulting...trusts'. Can 'operation' be said to include 'termination' which seems almost the antithesis of 'creation or operation'?

Assume it is correct, as *Vandervell (No 2)* implies, that where trustees (eg VT) hold property on a resulting trust for a beneficiary (V) until V or VT declare new trusts then s 53(1)(c) does not apply to a declaration by VT. Would s 53(1)(c) have applied had the declaration been made by V and if not, on what basis could *Vandervell (No 2)* have been reconciled with *Grey v IRC* (above, p 129)?

(3) *The 'hard case' point.* When all the technical arguments have been thoroughly aired it is still apparent that the Court of Appeal in *Vandervell (No 2)* was influenced by the perceived merits of the case and that a 'hard case' be avoided if possible. Lord Denning put the point with characteristic vigour ([1974] Ch 269 at 320):

> If the law should be in danger of doing injustice, then equity should be called in to remedy it. Equity was introduced to mitigate the rigour of the law. But in the present case it has been prayed in aid to do injustice on a large scale - to defeat the intentions of a dead man - to deprive his children of the benefits he provided for them - and to expose his estate to the payment of tax of over £600,000. I am glad to find that we can overcome this most unjust result.

References to the lack of merit of the claims of Vandervell or his executors should not blind us to the fact that in substance it was the claim of the Inland Revenue that was being tested. In evaluating the 'hard case' argument consider the following questions: (i) What intention(s) did Vandervell have in deciding to transfer the shares from his own beneficial ownership? (ii) Why was the particular mode of transfer adopted? (iii) Are the merits of the Inland Revenue's case the same for both periods? If not, why not?

Finally, should the hardship of the case be a consideration if tax liability is in issue? (See generally Chapter 3, and see Hackney [1981] CLP 113 at 125.)

(d) Epilogue

One outcome of *Re Vandervell's Trusts (No 2)* was that the Revenue withdrew the assessment to surtax for the period 1962–64. En route the *Vandervell* saga provided an example of the perils of shaky advice – allegedly 'through an imperfect knowledge of the law of trusts' (per Lord Wilberforce, *Vandervell v IRC* [1967] 1 All ER 1 at 13) – a comprehensive analysis of the principles of resulting trusts, a further illustration of the flexibility of 'intention to create a trust' and an example of judicial pragmatism in the Court of Appeal judgment in *Re Vandervell's Trusts (No 2)* of which it has been said: 'it is improbable that the result would have survived the crueller scrutiny of the House of Lords' (Green (1984) 47 MLR 385 at 420). A lasting legacy is the addition of a further gloss on the accepted learning on dealings in equitable interests. Quite what the constituents of the gloss are is not easy to state. *Vandervell v IRC* clearly supports a proposition that LPA 1925, s 53(1)(c) does not apply where the beneficial owner (A) directs a bare trustee (T) to transfer the legal estate to a third party (B) with the intention that B will also acquire the beneficial interest. *Re Vandervell's Trusts (No 2)* is much more obscure and one commentator despairingly concluded (Harris (1975) 38 MLR 557 at 603) that 'a "hard case" may have been avoided; but as to what law the decision may have made, only clarification in future decisions will reveal'. Readers are invited to construct their own ratio!

5

Creating the trust – II

1. Introduction

On one level this chapter is simply concerned with completing the description of the necessary requirements for creating a valid express trust. This process provides a snapshot of the present rules relating to 'certainty of objects' and the 'beneficiary principle' whilst simultaneously identifying unresolved problems and teasing out inconsistencies. But as in other areas of law, the rules have not remained static and change here has been dramatic. Indeed during the last four decades the courts have so turned the world of 'certainty of objects' upside down that 'the forms and functions of settlements have changed to a degree which would have astonished Lord Eldon' (*Schmidt v Rosewood Trust Ltd* [2003] 2 AC 709 at para 34 per Lord Walker). This dynamic aspect of law-making also deserves attention. A second level of study, therefore, is to examine the shifts that have occurred and to understand the how and why of change.

However, the starting place for this study has to be traced back much further, to the decision in *Morice v Bishop of Durham* (1804) 9 Ves 399. There Sir W Grant summarised the court's approach as follows:

> There can be no trust, over the exercise of which this Court will not assume a control; for an uncontrollable power of disposition would be ownership, and not trust. If there be a clear trust, but for uncertain objects, the property, that is the subject of the trust, is undisposed of, and the benefit of such trust must result to those, to whom the law gives the ownership in default of disposition by the former owner. But this doctrine does not hold good with regard to trusts for charity. Every other trust must have a definite object. There must be somebody, in whose favour the Court can decree performance.

This statement laid a firm foundation both for a certainty of objects requirement – the beneficiaries of a trust must be capable of being ascertained – and for its offshoot the beneficiary principle – every non-charitable trust must have a human beneficiary. It also strongly suggests that the reason for the requirements is rooted in the ability of the court to control a trust. Lord Eldon LC reaffirmed this link between control and requirements for trust validity when *Morice v Bishop of Durham* was appealed ((1805) 10 Ves 522 at 539–540):

As it is a maxim, that the execution of a trust shall be under the control of the court, it must be of such a nature, that it can be under that control; so that the administration of it can be reviewed by the court; or, if the trustee dies, the court itself can execute the trust: a trust therefore, which, in case of maladministration could be reformed; and due administration directed; and then, unless the subject and the objects can be ascertained, upon principles, familiar in other cases, it must be decided, that the court can neither reform maladministration, nor direct a due administration.

The courts adopted a restrained view of their capacity to reform and administer a trust. It was not open to a court to act randomly or at its own discretion: any issue had to be justiciable. This in turn required the settlor to supply clear criteria by which the court, if called upon to do so, could execute the trust. From this requirement of enforceability based on justiciability, it seemed to follow logically that where trustees were given a discretion under a trust deed to choose who amongst the beneficiaries should benefit it would be inappropriate for a court to choose between competing claims or needs of those beneficiaries. Consequently if called upon to administer or enforce the trust, the court would rely on the maxim 'Equality is equity' and order that property be distributed accordingly (*Kemp v Kemp* (1795) 5 Ves 849). Equal distribution amongst all beneficiaries clearly demands that they are all identifiable. Accordingly, if it could be said at the inception of the trust that it would not be possible to draw up a complete list of the potential beneficiaries then the purported trust would be void for uncertainty.

Whereas this line of reasoning provides an explanation for the emergence of a particular certainty of objects criterion, it is less apparent that it does so for the beneficiary principle, which has fully evolved only more recently. In fact this principle did not achieve complete recognition by the courts until Roxburgh J's judgment in *Re Astor's Settlement Trusts* [1952] Ch 534. Although the primary justification for the beneficiary principle can be located in the perceived needs of enforceability as expressed in *Morice v Bishop of Durham*, its pedigree is uncertain. Indeed it has been suggested (McKay (1973) 27 Conv 420 and 421) that the statement cited above by Sir W Grant in *Morice v Bishop of Durham* 'was often construed as indicating that the objects must be certain, rather than certain *and* human'. And there exist a few cases, now usually categorised as anomalous and not to be followed, where trusts for non-charitable purposes have been upheld. These have chiefly to do with the upkeep of animals or of monuments (see below, p 258). Over time, however, a gloss to the reasoning emerged, the emphasis shifting to stress the absence of anyone who could *positively* enforce the trust. Indeed the seeds of this 'enforceability' proposition are actually in the last sentence of the quote from Sir W Grant in *Morice* (above). The point was summarised by the Privy Council in *Leahy v A-G for New South Wales* [1959] AC 457 at 478: 'A trust may be created for the benefit of persons as *cestuis que trust* but not for a purpose or object unless the purpose or object be charitable. For a purpose or object cannot sue, but, if it be charitable, the Attorney-General can sue to enforce it.' Because of the meritorious aspects of charitable trusts, the state, under long-established rules, supplies a 'nominal claimant' (in the person of the Attorney-General) to enforce them (see Chapter 20): no such benefit is conferred on non-charitable trusts.

At the start of this section we mentioned the element of change, and the lines of reasoning outlined above have not proved immutable. There has been a significant shift in the perception of the court's ability to enforce and control a trust, a shift that accompanied a radical change in the certainty of objects requirement. Consequently, today it is possible confidently to state that the degree of certainty required will depend on what the settlor wants the trustees to do: the obligations about whom to pay, when to pay and how much to pay are recognised as being different for fixed trusts and discretionary trusts. The shift in judicial perceptions raises important questions. What is the engine of this change and is its momentum exhausted? In one sense the driving-force is to be found in a judicial willingness, albeit not universal, to be innovative. But this trite conclusion begs the pre-existing questions as to how did the issues get litigated and why there has been pressure on seemingly firmly established rules.

The absence of empirical research in this area is striking but one hypothesis is to look for a simple market solution of demand and supply. Creative lawyers responded to their clients' commercial and fiscal needs by seeking out and applying new mechanisms. Resting quietly on the legal supermarket shelf was one rather old mechanism, the discretionary trust: its earlier use was chiefly in the context of protective trusts (see Chapter 6). Lawyers took it down, dusted it off and turned it to new uses. But, as it transpired, these new uses raised fundamental issues for the law of trusts. Consequently pressure from the bottom up produced a novel challenge to the established law on certainty of objects. Arguably the judicial responses to this challenge have generated a conceptual revolution that has in turn raised questions both about the legitimacy and appropriateness of the beneficiary principle, and about where the balance of power should lie between the court, trustees and beneficiaries in controlling a trust. This last aspect is touched on in this chapter but is considered further in Chapter 11.

The occasioning of legal change via judicial innovation, even over an extended period, necessarily involves a shift, in Milsom's revealing phrase (*Historical Foundations of the Common Law* (2nd edn, 1981) p 8), from 'eyes-down' application of existing rules to an 'eyes-raised' appreciation of the implications of change. But implications for whom and in relation to what? Legal change in this context does not merely concern the principles and practice of the law of trusts but also has consequences for the effectiveness of fiscal policy. Can conflict about the desirability and direction of change be categorised as falling solely within the realm of regulating intra-family property relations, and as being between established but questionable trusts law principles and a purposive response to the demands raised by trust users? If so, proponents of change may argue this is 'lawyers' law' peculiarly suitable for judicial development.

But what if those demands of trust users sprang from a desire to increase the flexibility of settlements, in the process requiring a relaxation of certainty of objects requirements, as a bulwark against increasing encroachment of Inland Revenue demands? Should not the broader fiscal policy implications of such legal development be a consideration? Or conversely can it be argued that it is not the function of the courts to allow the constraints of one public policy factor to 'hobble the common law in all classes of disputes' (per Lord Devlin in *Rookes v Barnard* [1964] AC 1129 at 1218 when considering a judicial innovation that out-flanked statutory protection afforded to strike organisers). The inference here is that if compensating adjustments in the interests of fiscal policy are considered necessary, then that is the function of legislation.

Yet we must be wary of any simple conclusion that a linear development can be traced between the post-1945 rise in the use of discretionary trusts for fiscal reasons and changes in certainty of objects requirements in trusts law. The relationship is both more complex and fluid, in part because the source of pressure for change was commercial as well as fiscal. The numbers of occupational pension schemes and employee benefit funds, of which discretionary trusts are frequently an integral element, sharply increased in the 1950s and 1960s, and prompted considerable litigation. The empirical question to be borne in mind therefore is how far a judicial decision arrived at in response to pressure in one sphere has provided the catalyst for possible unanticipated further development in the other sphere.

To understand and analyse the changes that have occurred in the rules concerning certainty of objects and the beneficiary principle, it is essential to appreciate that a settlement (or trust instrument) comprises a complex arrangement of trusts and what are termed powers. A digression into the nature of powers and the distinction between trusts and powers is therefore a necessary preliminary step to a study of those rules.

2. Trusts and powers

(a) Trusts and powers distinguished

A power is an authority to deal in certain ways with property where the person authorised does not own the property and indeed may not have any entitlement to it or proprietary interest in it. We shall meet powers at several points in this book. For instance, when the administration of trusts and the control of trustees are examined it will be seen that trustees are given – sometimes by statute, sometimes by the settlor – administrative powers such as powers of investment and delegation, power to appoint new trustees and others more mundane such as power to insure trust property.

In contrast there also exist powers of appointment, that is powers to select who are to be beneficial recipients of property or of benefits (such as income) accruing to property. It is these powers, which are equitable and must now operate behind a trust, that concern us here. The terminology applying to powers of appointment should be noted. The giver of a power is called the donor, the recipient the donee, and those who may (but not necessarily will) benefit from the exercise of the power are termed the objects of the power. When the power is exercised the donee becomes the appointor and those benefiting, the appointees. Where a donee dies without exercising a power of appointment the property will devolve to those persons named as taking 'in default of appointment'. As the label implies, they are simply the people designated in the trust instrument as being entitled to the property if no appointment is made by the donee of the power. Although certainly not necessary, it is quite possible for the objects of the power and the takers in default of appointment to be the same people (see Figure 5.1, example (2)).

Powers of appointment are classified as general, special and intermediate (or hybrid) powers. A general power is one exercisable in favour of anyone in the world including the donee. It follows that to give a donee a general power is tantamount to making an outright gift. But as Rudden and Lawson note, 'since there is no obvious advantage to be gained by giving a person a general power to appoint to an interest instead of giving him the interest itself, general powers are not often met with in practice' (*An Introduction to the Law of Property* (2nd edn, 1982) p 101). Much more common is a special power: this is exercisable among named individuals or a class such as one's own children or the employees of a company. The fact that the donee may also qualify as an object of the power does not affect its status. As the name implies an intermediate (or hybrid) power falls in between a general and a specific power. This means that it is exercisable in favour of anyone *except for* specified individuals or classes. An example would be a power to appoint to anyone in the world except the donor and the donor's spouse.

Powers of appointment will commonly be given to trustees. But this is not essential. For example a husband H may wish to leave property on trust for his widow W for life and then to their children A, B and C, but may equally wish to give to W the authority to decide upon the children's shares. H can give W a special power of appointment amongst A, B and C, coupled with a 'gift over' in default of appointment to A, B and C, in equal shares in case W should fail to exercise the power (Figure 5.1, example (2)). But equally the power could be given to the trustees T1 and T2 to exercise. Either variant of example (2) may be compared with example (3) in Figure 5.1, where H has already decided that the property should be held by T1 and T2 on trust for W for life with remainder to A, B and C in equal shares. The comparison highlights a key distinction between trusts and powers. A trust obligation is *imperative*; in example (3) T1 and T2 must distribute the property in the manner specified. The exercise of a power, however, is not mandatory – W is under no obligation to appoint in example (2) – and the existence of a gift over in default affords clear recognition of this. A gift over in default would be incompatible with the imperative duties imposed by a trust obligation. Regrettably, however, from the standpoint of ease

(1) T1 and T2 shall hold the trust fund upon the trusts of this settlement

(2)	(3)	(4)	(5)	(6)	(7)
£5,000, income therefrom to W for life, capital to such of A, B, C as W shall in her absolute discretion appoint. ... In default of appointment to A, B, C in equal shares.	£5,000, income therefrom to W for life, capital to A, B, C in equal shares.	£5,000, income therefrom to W for life, capital to such of A, B, C as W in her absolute discretion may appoint.	£5,000 to be distributed among such of A, B, C, and in such proportions as my trustees shall think fit.	(a) £10,000, the income therefrom to be accumulated for a period of 21 years. (b) T1 and T2 may pay income arising in any one year to such of groups A–E as they think fit. (c) Capital and accumulated income to X, Y, Z in equal shares.	(a) £10,000 to apply the income therefrom for a period of 21 years for such of groups A–E as T1 and T2 think fit. (b) T1 and T2 may accumulate income and add it to capital. (c) Capital and accumulated income to X, Y, Z in equal shares.
Life interest with special power of appointment over capital.	Life interest with fixed-interest trust of remainder.	as per (2) or a 'trust power'	Discretionary trust	(a) Trust to accumulate (b) + mere power of appointment (c) Fixed interest trust	(a) Discretionary trust to distribute (b) + power of accumulation (c) Fixed interest trust

Figure 5.1 Trusts and powers

of identification, the *absence* of a gift over is not decisive. The question whether there is a power or a trust is then one of construction of the language used, which may be ambiguous (see eg *Re Leek* [1967] Ch 1061). If there is no gift over and the disposition is construed as a power which has not been exercised, there will be a resulting trust of the property for the donor's estate (subject to the possibilities discussed in section (c) below).

There is one additional point of clarification about the classification of powers to be emphasised at this preliminary stage. Where trustees are the donees of a power of appointment, such as that in example (2) in the previous paragraph, then that power is termed a 'fiduciary power', whereas where the power is granted to some person other than a trustee then the power is commonly referred to as a 'mere' or 'bare' power.

The distinction is not simply one of language. The obligations attaching to a mere or bare power are significantly less than those of a fiduciary power. The donee of a mere power owes no duties to the objects of the power concerning its exercise. There is therefore no duty to exercise the power so as to appoint to an object of the power or even consider its exercise. The sole constraint is that if the donee of a mere power does wish to exercise it then unsurprisingly any appointment made must be within the terms of the power. If, for instance, the power of appointment is to decide who amongst A, B and C is to benefit then it constitutes what is termed a 'fraud on a power' to make an appointment to D (see further on 'fraud on a power' pp 547–548). On the other hand where the donee holds the power of appointment in a fiduciary capacity, most commonly but not exclusively as a trustee (see *Mettoy Pension Trustees v Evans* [1990] 1 WLR 1587), different considerations apply. Then, in contrast to a mere power, obligations to the objects of the power are imposed. Even though the exercise of the power by a trustee is discretionary, there being no obligation to make an appointment under it, the trustee must periodically consider whether to exercise the power. Moreover, before making any appointment the trustee should review or survey the range of possible objects of the power (see *Re Hay's Settlement Trusts* [1981] 3 All ER 786 at p 240).

But it is not the distinction between a mere power and a fiduciary power – a distinction focusing on the identity of the donee of the power – that has proved so significant for the development of trusts law. It is rather the problem of distinguishing whether the discretion granted to a trustee is in the nature of a 'trust' or a 'power' that has proved so troublesome and it is to that distinction and its implications that we turn next.

(b) Trusts and powers compared: discretionary trusts and powers of appointment

A similarity between trusts and powers appears, and confusion begins to creep in, where a settlor decides to give his trustees discretion as to the allocation of property vested in them. He might authorise them to allocate amongst some only of the specified objects (if they so wish), but with the intention that this discretion *must* be exercised. This constitutes a discretionary trust (see Figure 5.1, example (5)). As already mentioned the imperative nature of the trust obligation marks a sharp conceptual distinction between a discretionary trust and a power of appointment but their predominant feature – the exercising of a discretion in selection – is similar. Examples (2) and (5) in Figure 5.1 are linguistically and conceptually distinguishable but the language used is not always so clear (cf example (4) considered below, p 213). Then questions will arise as to whether the particular provision in the trust instrument confers a power on the trustees to allocate benefit or imposes a duty on them to do this.

The potential difficulties are amply demonstrated by the extensive litigation on this issue (see Harris (1971) 87 LQR 31 where the cases are listed under footnotes 2 and 3). Indeed in the leading case of *McPhail v Doulton* [1970] 2 All ER 228, the High Court and a majority of the Court of Appeal considered that the disputed provision constituted a power of appointment, whereas the House of Lords unanimously agreed that it was a trust. Lord Wilberforce commented (at 240):

> ... that what to one mind may appear as a power of distribution coupled with a trust to dispose of the undistributed surplus, by accumulation or otherwise, may to another appear as a trust for distribution coupled with a power to withhold a portion and accumulate or otherwise dispose of it. A layman and, I suspect, also a logician, would find it hard to understand what difference there is. [See Figure 5.1, examples (6) and (7).]

Why, then, if the distinction can be so obscure, does it matter? Whether a person is the object of a power held by trustees or the beneficiary of a discretionary trust makes little practical difference in terms of that person's entitlement to benefit; what, if anything, is received will depend on the exercise of someone else's discretion. There is, however, an essential difference. If a mere power is not exercised within the time stipulated (expressly or by implication) the property goes to those entitled in default of appointment. Their identity may be indicated by a gift over, as explained above, and may be wholly different from the objects of the power itself. On the other hand, if the benefits accruing under a discretionary trust are not allocated amongst the beneficiaries within the time and in the manner stipulated, the trustees are in breach of trust and the court can itself even take over the task of allocating benefit. Any such allocation will be amongst the stipulated class of beneficiaries. Furthermore, the distinction between a trust and power did have one particular practical consequence. The validity of an instrument could depend on whether the language created a trust or a power because the certainty of objects requirement was considered stricter for trusts than for powers.

Two similar cases, *Re Saxone Shoe Co Ltd's Trust Deed* [1962] 2 All ER 904 and *Re Sayer Trust* [1956] 3 All ER 600, demonstrate the problem. In both cases company benefit funds were established by trust deeds for, inter alia, 'employees and their dependants'. In *Re Sayer* the deed provided that 'the management committee is empowered to make payments' (a valid special power) whereas the deed in *Re Saxone* stated that 'the fund shall in the discretion of the directors be applicable...' (trust). The consequence was that the discretionary trust in *Re Saxone* was void under the then prevailing certainty of objects test for trusts, which required that all the possible beneficiaries be ascertainable. The inclusion of 'dependants' made this impossible. This 'list certainty' requirement, as it is called, did not extend to powers, a more liberal certainty of objects test being applied there. Where categorisation depends on such constructional niceties, arbitrariness is always a possible result. This outcome may be thought particularly unfortunate where both types of disposition are intended to achieve broadly the same objective. As Harris recognised:

> ...[such arrangements] are always in substance much more like one another (being complex settlements) than they are like either simple trusts to distribute property in equal shares immediately...or simple powers to appoint conferred on donees in whom the property is not vested...[(1971) 87 LQR 31 at 42].

Comparing examples (6) and (7) in Figure 5.1 with examples (2) and (3) illustrates this point. Furthermore a single will or settlement may contain a number of distinct dispositions – some trusts, some powers (see Figure 5.1) – which may be closely linked, as, for instance, in clauses (a), (b) and (c) in example (6). Yet, in analysing, each disposition must in general be taken separately.

As we shall see, the certainty tests for discretionary trusts and powers have been brought closer to each other by later decisions, so the implications of this question of characterisation are in practice less important.

(c) Trusts, powers and 'trust powers'

One fertile source of confusion, now also of limited practical significance, arose in the context of some family trust cases with a narrowly defined class of objects, such as children or other close relatives, amongst whom a selection was authorised to be made. Consider the position where property is held by T1 and T2 on trust for W for life then for such of A, B and C as W in her absolute discretion may appoint (Figure 5.1, example (4)). In practice the precise nature of W's discretion will be immaterial as long as it is exercised. But let us suppose that W dies without having exercised the discretion. There is no express gift over in default of appointment and the trustees, or the court if called upon, are therefore left to decide whether a trust or power was intended to be conferred on W. The consequences are different: if a trust, then some distribution amongst A, B and C must occur; if a power, then A, B and C are mere objects of a power who have no claim to the property, which will revert to the settlor's estate on a resulting trust. When faced with this conundrum the courts have on occasion resorted to what has been termed 'a trust power', in effect a trust in default of appointment, and authorised distribution of the property amongst the objects of the power.

Whilst some fine distinctions as to the nature of the 'trust' have been drawn in the cases (see in particular *Wilson v Duguid* (1883) 24 Ch D 244; and generally Unwin (1962) 26 Conv 92; Hopkins (1971) 29 CLJ 68; Bartlett and Stebbings [1984] Conv 227), it is clear that the courts infer the existence of a trust so as to implement the settlor's perceived general intention in favour of the specified class (see eg *Burrough v Philcox* (1840) 5 My & Cr 72 at 92). The inference of a trust power where there is no gift over in default expressed in the instrument is, however, a question of construction: there is no 'inflexible and artificial rule of construction' in favour of a trust power (*Re Combe* [1925] Ch 210 at 216, and see also *Re Weekes' Settlement* [1897] 1 Ch 289; and *Hopkins* at p 78). It may be that the courts have been more willing to imply a trust power where the objects are the settlor's children but the cases are not numerous. Where a trust power is imposed the courts generally apply the maxim 'Equality is equity' and order equal division amongst the objects.

It was this judicial preference for equal division and its corollary the 'list certainty' test of objects which proved so inappropriate for employee welfare trusts and the modern family discretionary trust, with a wide range of relations and other persons specified as beneficiaries. Such trusts, expressly or implicitly, authorise trustees to select *some only* of the beneficiaries (indeed, *one only* is possible) to receive benefit. In these circumstances equal distribution, as Lord Wilberforce recognised in *McPhail v Doulton* (see below), is probably the last thing the settlor wishes. Consequently, as will be seen, validating these new types of discretionary trust required a rejection of the claim that a court, if called upon to administer a discretionary trust, could do so only by authorising equal distribution amongst all the beneficiaries.

(d) Conclusion

Unfortunately one legacy of the 'trust power' referred to above has been to exacerbate a confusion of terminology that is rife in the cases and literature (see Bartlett and Stebbings [1984] Conv 227). What we have termed 'trust power' may also be called 'power in the nature of a trust' or 'power coupled with a duty'. To compound confusion it will be seen subsequently that in *McPhail v Doulton* [1970] 2 All ER 228 the term 'trust power' is treated as synonymous with 'discretionary trust'.

Clarity is not advanced by turning to powers of appointment. Whether special or intermediate, these are often labelled collectively as 'mere powers' or 'bare powers'. And when they are conferred on a trustee the expressions 'power collateral' or 'fiduciary power' *may* be encountered although quite commonly in the cases the term 'mere power' is employed even where the donee of the power is a trustee or other fiduciary.

In the text we attempt to simplify the position and use the term 'discretionary trust' to describe an *imperative* duty to exercise a discretion to allocate benefit, given to trustees by settlors; and 'mere powers' as the collective title for powers of appointment given to trustees or to other donees. But where relevant and necessary we will also distinguish between the situations where the mere power is held in a fiduciary capacity, when we will use the term 'fiduciary power', and those where 'mere powers' are held by other donees.

3. Certainty of objects

(a) The developing law: discretionary trusts and mere powers

(1) The re-emergence of the discretionary trust

The discretionary trust did not evolve specifically as a tax-effective means of holding family property. Settlements on discretionary trusts had been known to conveyancers for generations, particularly as a crucial element in what came to be termed a protective trust (see Chapter 6). The function of the discretionary trust in that context was to protect the capital and income of the fund and consequently the beneficiaries from the results of the latters' improvidence. This was achieved by the simple artifice of giving the trustees a discretion to decide on the allocation of the income, so that no beneficiary had any right to a specific share of the trust income. A bankrupt beneficiary's creditors could establish no better right to the income than the beneficiary himself. The potential effectiveness of the discretionary trust as a tax-avoidance mechanism was therefore plain. By keeping vague the rights of beneficiaries of a trust, those rights are made more difficult to tax. In addition the discretionary trust offered an appealing flexibility to provide for unexpected eventualities, be they familial or fiscal. Cozens-Hardy Horne writing in 1957 (BTR 256) could comment that 'under modern conditions the Inland Revenue has been substituted for the trustee in bankruptcy, in the minds of settlors and their advisers, as the villain whose evil designs must be thwarted'.

But the discretionary trust could also usefully be turned to the more specifically commercially based functions described in the Introduction to this chapter. Much subsequent litigation was to centre on the validity of such trusts when drafted as private discretionary trusts. Leading twentieth-century decisions on the definition of 'charitable purposes' (see Chapter 19) made it more difficult to achieve these aims through charitable trusts. Grbich aptly summarised these developments in the following way: 'practitioners were forced by revenue stimuli and the practical necessity of business reality into the flexible realms of discretionary trusts' ((1974) 37 MLR 643 at 656). A question to be resolved was whether the flexibility was compatible with the prevailing principles of trusts law, particularly the certainty of objects requirements.

(2) The breakthrough: *Re Gestetner Settlement* [1953] Ch 672 and 'mere powers'

The settlement in question 'made by one Sigmund Gestetner, a man of great wealth' (per Harman J at 681) on 4 April 1951, contained trusts of capital and income for such members of a 'specified class' as the trustees should think fit; and in default of appointment for a residuary class comprising the settlor's children. The latter were also members of the wide 'specified class'. In short there was a discretionary settlement comprising a mere power of appointment in favour of a wide class with a gift in default to a narrow class whose membership would at all times be ascertainable. The width of the specified class was striking: it comprised four named individuals; any person living or thereafter born who was a descendant of the settlor's father or uncle; any spouse, widow or widower of any such person; five charitable bodies; any former employee of the settlor or his wife or widow or widower of such employee; any director or employee of Gestetner Ltd, or of any company of which the directors of Gestetner Ltd were also directors. The last category was of potentially enormous width. As Harman J expressed it (at 683) 'any of the six directors of Gestetner Ltd.... may take on tomorrow a new directorship which brings in a new stream of possible objects of the trustees' bounty...'. It was, not surprisingly, accepted that the 'specified class' was not one which was ascertainable at any given time.

The litigation, which was to have considerable tax-planning significance, arose only indirectly as a result of Inland Revenue intervention. The trustees paid £262 10s to one of the named charities who then sought to recover from the Inland Revenue the tax deducted at source. The Inland Revenue rejected the claim contending that the trusts were void for uncertainty. The trustees then sought the direction of the court. Such direction was necessary because, as was pointed out by counsel for the settlor's children (at 680) and accepted by the learned judge (at 685), 'it is surprising that there is no authority in cases or in textbooks, on what is the duty of trustees who have a discretionary power of (this) kind'. There was, however, authority (*Re Park* [1932] 1 Ch 580 and *Re Jones* [1945] Ch 105) to support the proposition 'that a power may be good although it is exercisable in favour of an indefinite class' (per Harman J at 685). But the two supporting cases were those where the powers of appointment had been given to donees who were not trustees. The question for decision was therefore novel. Counsel for the Inland Revenue Commissioners who were represented at the hearing emphasised the importance of the decision, and argued that (at 681) 'it would be quite contrary to the principles of trust law to allow a vague trust of this kind to be valid'.

Harman J recognised that trustees, unlike other donees of powers, were under a duty (at 688) 'to consider at all times ... whether or no they are to distribute any and if so what part of the fund, and if so, to whom they should distribute it', but also considered that 'there is not any duty to distribute the whole of any income or capital'.

This distinction between 'duty to distribute' and 'duty to consider' was decisive in Harman J's opinion and, in the absence of clear authority, his approach was inclined towards respecting the settlor's intention if possible (at 688):

Harman J: The settlor had good reason, I have no doubt, to trust the persons whom he appointed trustees; but I cannot see here that there is such a duty as makes it essential for these trustees, before parting with any income or capital, to survey the whole field, and to consider whether A is more deserving of bounty than B. That is a task which was and which must have been known to the settlor to be impossible, having regard to the ramifications of the persons who might become members of this class.

If, therefore, there be no duty to distribute, but only a duty to consider, it does not seem to me that there is any authority binding on me to say that this whole trust [sic] is bad. In fact, there is no difficulty, as has been admitted, in ascertaining whether any given postulant is a member of the specified class. Of course, if that could not be ascertained the matter would be quite different, but of John Doe or Richard Roe it can be postulated easily enough whether he is or is not eligible to receive the settlor's bounty. There being no uncertainty in that sense, I am reluctant to introduce a notion of uncertainty in the other sense, by saying that the trustees must worry their heads to survey the world from China to Peru, when there are perfectly good objects of the class in England. Consequently, I am not minded to upset the scheme put forward by the settlor on the ground indicated, namely, that of uncertainty. There is no uncertainty in so far as it is quite certain whether particular individuals are objects of the power. What is not certain is how many objects there are; and it does not seem to me that such an uncertainty will invalidate a trust [sic] worded in this way. I accordingly declare the trust [sic] valid.

Note Harman J's description of the whole disposition as a 'trust'. On our terminology it would be a mere power of appointment vested in settlement trustees, coupled with a gift over on trust in default of appointment.

The creative aspect of this decision was quickly recognised: 'the case breaks entirely new ground on the relationship of powers, particularly hybrid powers, and trusts' ((1953) 17 Conv 240). Its considerable practical significance was also commented on in the periodical literature.

R E Megarry (1953) 69 LQR 309 at 310

The practical importance of the *Gestetner Case* is that in recent years there has been a marked movement away from settlements conferring defined interests on each beneficiary towards settlements which confer wide discretionary powers and powers of appointment. An important reason for this is that if a beneficiary dies, estate duty will normally be payable, whereas no estate duty is payable solely by reason of the death of one of the mere objects of a power or discretionary trust. For this and other reasons, such powers and trusts have been much favoured in recent years, although there has been one school of thought which has refused to countenance such devices on the ground that any uncertainty as to those

who constitute the objects may invalidate the entire scheme. The *Gestetner Case* may go
far towards meeting these objections.

It can be argued that the expectation of all involved in the operation of a
settlement such as that in *Gestetner* was that the default trust was unlikely ever
to become operative, but served primarily as a necessary formal requirement of
the settlement. The real intention was that the money, be it capital or income,
should be distributed amongst the objects of the power of appointment just as
much as if they were beneficiaries of a discretionary trust to distribute.

The practical importance of *Gestetner* was to be enhanced by a subsequent
Court of Appeal decision on the certainty test for discretionary trusts to distribute.

(3) The advance checked: the *Broadway Cottages* case

In the course of his judgment in *Re Gestetner Settlement* Harman J, drawing a
distinction between a discretionary trust to distribute and a mere power to do
so, observed, obiter, that: 'if it is the trustee's duty to distribute the fund among
a number of people, his task being to select which of those people shall be the
objects of his bounty, then . . . there is much to be said for the view that he must
be able to review the whole field in order to exercise his judgement properly'
(at 685).

An opportunity for the point to be settled followed shortly in *IRC v Broadway
Cottages Trust* [1955] Ch 20. By a settlement made in 1950 a settlor directed
a sum of £80,000 to be held on trusts, inter alia, to apply the income for the
benefit of all or any members of a wide class of beneficiaries including a charity,
Broadway Cottages Trust. Here again the validity of the trust was only brought
into question when the Inland Revenue refused to grant the charity exemption
from income tax on income received from the settlement. The instrument was
held by Wynn-Parry J at first instance to have created a trust for distribution
of the income which was void for uncertainty. This decision was upheld in the
Court of Appeal where it was conceded that it would be impossible at any given
time to obtain a complete list of the beneficiaries though the description was
sufficiently precise to say whether anyone was or was not within the description
(ie the test for mere powers advanced by Harman J in *Re Gestetner* would have
been satisfied).

Jenkins LJ, in giving the judgment of the Court of Appeal, based it squarely
on the policy and principle as stated by Lord Eldon in *Morice v Bishop of
Durham*. The taxpayers had pointed out that there was no practical difficulty
in executing the trust, but the court was not swayed, although it was agreed
that 'the argument had an attractive air of common sense'. Instead Jenkins LJ
specifically adopted the 'list certainty' test, formulated in an earlier case (*Re
Ogden* [1933] Ch 678), that 'a trust for such members of a given class of objects
as the trustees shall select is void for uncertainty unless the whole range of
objects eligible for selection is ascertained or capable of ascertainment'.

(4) Certainty unsatisfactory

The consequence of *Re Gestetner Settlement* [1953] Ch 672 and *IRC v Broadway Cottages Trust* [1955] Ch 20, was that different tests of certainty of objects were to be applied depending on whether, as a matter of construction, the particular disposition was held to fall either into the category of 'trusts' or into that of 'powers of appointment'. That its validity might depend on fine distinctions of language in frequently complex settlements containing a wide variety of 'trusts' and 'powers' was at the very least a pitfall for the unwary or ill-advised (though of course people establishing these settlements usually employ top-quality legal advice).

On the fiscal front this clearly posed an immediate danger since, if the certainty of objects requirement was not satisfied, a resulting trust might arise with potentially onerous income tax or estate duty consequences for the settlor. But from a tax-planning perspective there was potentially a further fiscal problem lurking below the horizon for those settlors who utilised a trust to distribute rather than rely on a power of appointment. Might the death of a beneficiary give rise to an estate duty liability? During the 1960s the House of Lords on two occasions mentioned this possibility (*Public Trustee v IRC* [1966] AC 520 and *Gartside v IRC* [1968] 1 All ER 121; see Hawkins [1968] BTR 351 for a detailed analysis of this question). As Lord Reid expressed it, 'you can say with absolute certainty that the individual rights of the beneficiaries when added up or taken together will extend to the whole income. You can have an equation $x + y + z = 100$, although you do not yet know the value of x or y or z. And that may lead to important results where the trust is of that character' (*Gartside v IRC* at 127). A doctrinal reason for the 'list certainty' requirement for discretionary trusts was thought to be linked to the function of the court: in default of distribution the court could not step in and exercise the trustees' discretion but would have to rely on the maxim 'Equality is equity'. The potential threat of the application of this maxim for estate duty liability was clear, as was the lesson to be drawn from it for tax planners. Maximum use should be made of powers of appointment and powers of accumulation.

The decision in *IRC v Broadway Cottages Trust* [1955] Ch 20 was also a minefield for benevolent fund trusts and pension schemes. In this commercial context the consequences of the 'fine distinction' in *Re Saxone* [1962] 2 All ER 904 and *Re Sayer Trust* [1956] 3 All ER 600 have already been referred to. But the potential seriousness of the problem went much wider than those individual cases which were litigated. The point was robustly expressed by W A Phillips, a pensions specialist ('Perils of Pension Scheme Trustees' (1967) 111 SJ 27 January 62):

> . . . hundreds of thousands of employed persons believe that their pension schemes provide a 'death in service' benefit, under a discretionary trust which, on examination, is found to be void for want of a completely ascertainable object because it includes 'dependants' among the possible beneficiaries without adequately, or at all, defining them.

> In a non-contributory scheme there is a resulting trust of the death benefit to the employer, who doubtless will pay out the money ex gratia to the intended beneficiary, incidentally avoiding estate duty... But an ex gratia payment, made at the employer's option, is not what the rules of the scheme purport to provide.
>
> In many schemes defective in this respect the trustees go on year after year gaily paying out the death benefit to the widow or the children, and it is not until a difficulty arises in locating anyone who the trustees feel comes within the discretion that legal advice is sought and the trustees learn to their dismay that they have repeatedly made payments *ultra vires.*

Almost from the time of confirmation of the 'list certainty' standard in *Broadway Cottages,* judicial misgivings were expressed about it. These misgivings increased (see Hopkins (1971) 29 CLJ 68 at 73, 83) as the courts were called upon to consider a series of cases centring on the discretionary trust-mere powers dichotomy and involving widely drawn classes of beneficiaries. Indeed, in the Court of Appeal itself, in 1961, Lord Evershed MR commented that 'the courts have quite plainly been... reluctant to hold (and if I may say so, naturally reluctant to hold) that a settlement which has been deliberately made is and was from the start invalid for uncertainty' (*Re Hain's Settlement* [1961] 1 WLR 440 at 447). Cross J subsequently endorsed this view, stating that he shared Lord Evershed's 'evident distaste... for the *Broadway Cottages* principle' (*Re Saxone* [1962] 2 All ER 904 at 914).

It is apparent with the benefit of hindsight that there existed fertile ground to support a change in the law. But when the opportunity arose sharp divisions in judicial opinions were exposed. Two judgments in the House of Lords in 1968 and 1970 concerning the trust deeds of Calouste Gulbenkian and Bertram Baden reshaped, and to some extent clarified, the certainty of objects requirements for mere powers and discretionary trusts respectively.

(b) Mere powers, certainty of objects and *Re Gulbenkian's Settlement Trusts*

The primary issue arising in *Gulbenkian* concerned the validity of an idiosyncratically drafted mere power containing among its objects 'persons with whom Nubar Gulbenkian may from time to time be employed or residing'. The power was similar in terms to one declared void for uncertainty in *Re Gresham's Settlement* [1956] 1 WLR 573. The trustees of the Gulbenkian settlement therefore took out a summons for direction in 1961. On a wider issue, doubt had emerged about the meaning to be attributed to the certainty criterion established in *Re Gestetner* [1953] Ch 672. Would a mere power be valid if it could be said with certainty that at least one person fell within the class of objects, or was it necessary to be able to say whether any given individual (not simply one) fell inside or outside the class?

The Court of Appeal held that the disputed clause in Calouste Gulbenkian's settlement was valid but in so doing Lord Denning MR and Winn LJ approved a 'one-person' certainty of objects criterion which required merely that, in Lord

Denning's words: 'if the trustees can say of any particular person that he is clearly within the category, the gift is good' ([1968] Ch 126 at 134). Moreover Lord Denning, obiter, added his voice to those critical of the *Broadway Cottages* 'list certainty' test, suggesting that for certainty of objects purposes discretionary trusts should be 'brought into line' with mere powers.

The House of Lords unanimously agreed with the Court of Appeal that the disputed clause was not void for uncertainty. Lord Upjohn, giving the principal judgment, accepted that although 'difficult and borderline cases' may occur in applying the description of the class to individual cases, the court if called upon could resolve them by reference to the language in the instrument and the surrounding circumstances. If this appeared to loosen the certainty test, their Lordships (Lord Donovan reserving his opinion) also tightened it by rejecting the 'one-person' test proposed by Lord Denning. In addition the latter's plea for alignment of the certainty tests for trusts and powers was firmly rejected. Four members of the House expressly approved obiter, the 'list certainty' test for trusts (Lord Reid dissenting). The reasoning of the majority with regard both to Lord Denning's 'one-person' test and his plea for alignment is expressed in the following extract from Lord Upjohn's judgment.

Re Gulbenkian's Settlement Trusts [1968] 3 All ER 785 at 792, HL

Lord Upjohn: I propose to make some general observations on this matter.

If a donor (be he a settlor or testator) directs trustees to make some specified provision for 'John Smith', then to give legal effect to that provision it must be possible to identify 'John Smith'. If the donor knows three John Smiths then by the most elementary principles of law neither the trustees nor the court in their place can give effect to that provision; neither the trustees nor the court can guess at it. It must fail for uncertainty unless of course admissible evidence is available to point to a particular John Smith as the object of the donor's bounty.

Then, taking it one stage further, suppose the donor directs that a fund, or the income of a fund, should be equally divided between members of a class. That class must be as defined as the individual; the court cannot guess at it. Suppose the donor directs that a fund be divided equally between 'my old friends', then unless there is some admissible evidence that the donor has given some special 'dictionary' meaning to that phrase which enables the trustees to identify the class with sufficient certainty, it is plainly bad as being too uncertain. Suppose that there appeared before the trustees (or the court) two or three individuals who plainly satisfied the test of being among 'my old friends' the trustees could not consistently with the donor's intentions accept them as claiming the whole or any defined part of the fund. They cannot claim the whole fund for they can show no title to it unless they prove they are the only members of the class, which of course they cannot do, and so, too, by parity of reasoning they cannot claim any defined part of the fund and there is no authority in the trustees or the court to make any distribution among a smaller class than that pointed out by the donor. The principle is, in my opinion, that the donor must make his intention sufficiently plain as to the objects of his trust and the court cannot give effect to it by misinterpreting his intention by dividing the fund merely among those present. Secondly, and perhaps it is the most hallowed principle, the Court of Chancery, which acts in default of trustees, must know with sufficient certainty the objects of the beneficence of the donor so as to execute the trust. Then, suppose the donor does not direct an equal division of his property among the class but gives a power of selection to his trustees among the class; exactly the same principles must apply. The trustees have a duty to select the donees of the donor's bounty from among the class designated by the donor; he has not entrusted them with any power to select the donees merely from among known claimants who are within the class, for that is constituting a narrower class and the donor has given them no power to do this.. . .

But when mere or bare powers are conferred on donees of the power (whether trustees or others) the matter is quite different. As I have already pointed out, the trustees have no duty to exercise it in the sense that they cannot be controlled in any way. If they fail to exercise it then those entitled in default of its exercise are entitled to the fund. Perhaps the contrast may be put forcibly in this way: in the first case it is a mere power to distribute with a gift over in default; in the second case it is a trust to distribute among the class defined by the donor with merely a power of selection within that class. The result is in the first case even if the class of appointees among whom the donees of the power may appoint is clear and ascertained and they are all of full age and sui juris, nevertheless they cannot compel the donees of the power to exercise it in their collective favour. If, however, it is a trust power, then those entitled are entitled (if they are of full age and sui juris) to compel the trustees to pay the fund over to them, unless the fund is income and the trustees have power to accumulate for the future.

Again the basic difference between a mere power and a trust power is that in the first case trustees owe no duty to exercise it and the relevant fund or income falls to be dealt with in accordance with the trusts in default of its exercise, whereas in the second case the trustees *must* exercise the power and in default the court will. It is briefly summarised in 30 Halsbury's Laws (3rd Edn), p 241, para 445:

'. . . the court will not . . . compel trustees to exercise a purely discretionary power given to them; but will restrain the trustees from exercising the power improperly, and if it is coupled with a duty . . . can compel the trustees to perform their duty'.

It is a matter of construction whether the power is a mere power or a trust power and the use of inappropriate language is not decisive (*Wilson v Turner* (1883) 22 Ch D 521 at 525).

So, with all respect to the contrary view, I cannot myself see how, consistently with principle, it is possible to apply to the execution of a trust power the principles applicable to the permissible exercise by the donees, even if the trustees of mere powers; that would defeat the intention of donors completely.

But with respect to mere powers, while the court cannot compel the trustees to exercise their powers, yet those entitled to the fund in default must clearly be entitled to restrain the trustees from exercising it save among those within the power. So the trustees, or the court, must be able to say with certainty who is within and who is without the power. It is for this reason that I find myself unable to accept the broader proposition advanced by Lord Denning MR and Winn LJ. . . .

The *Gulbenkian* judgment firmly establishes that the test for certainty of objects for mere powers is 'whether it can be said with certainty that any given individual is or is not a member of the class'. As we shall see shortly, interpreting this test has in turn created problems. As regards the certainty of objects requirement for discretionary trusts, Lord Upjohn's judgment can be interpreted as implying that the court could not execute a 'trust power', as he calls it, where all the beneficiaries were not ascertainable because to do so would flout the settlor's specific intention, and, possibly, because the exercise of the discretion was not a justiciable issue. Although obiter, his comments on the appropriate test for 'trust powers' might have been thought for practical purposes to have settled this point. This was not to be so, for little more than twelve months later the House of Lords gave its judgment on Bertram Baden's deed in *McPhail v Doulton* [1970] 2 All ER 228.

(c) Discretionary trusts, certainty of objects and *McPhail v Doulton*

Bertram Baden, Chairman and Managing Director of Matthew Hall and Company Ltd, with some 1,300 employees, had by deed established the Matthew Hall Staff Trust Fund.

Clause 9(a) of Bertram Baden's trust deed provided as follows: 'the trustees shall apply the net income of the fund in making at their absolute discretion grants to or for the benefit of any of the officers and employees or ex-officers or ex-employees of the company or to any relatives or dependants of such persons in such amounts at such times and on such conditions (if any) as they think fit'. The trustees were not obliged to exhaust the income of any year and there was provision for accumulation of undistributed income. Given the width of the class of objects, the validity of the trust appeared to depend on whether trustees were given a duty of discretionary distribution or a mere power of discretionary distribution. Mr Baden died in 1960 and a little over two years later, by which time the fund was worth £163,000, the executors challenged the validity of the trust deed. Accordingly the trustees then issued an originating summons to determine whether the deed was void for uncertainty. Goff J at first instance ([1967] 1 WLR 1457) held that the instrument created a mere power which was not void for uncertainty. Despite the apparent mandatory nature of 'shall apply' the Court of Appeal (Russell LJ dissenting) agreed with this. But to do so they adopted a constructional presumption to the effect that where competing interpretations of a provision are evenly balanced the court should prefer the one producing validity rather than invalidity (the doctrine of *ut res magis valeat quam pereat*). As to the distinction causing all the trouble, that between mere powers and discretionary trusts for purposes of certainty,

Harman LJ confessed that 'it . . . is an absurd and embarrassing result brought about by a line of cases in recent years stemming I am sorry to say from my own decision in *Re Gestetner . . .* ' (*Re Baden's Deed Trust* [1969] 2 Ch 388 at 397).

The executors appealed to the House of Lords. There were two changes in the panel from that hearing the *Gulbenkian* case. Lords Upjohn and Donovan were replaced by Viscount Dilhorne and Lord Wilberforce. The House unanimously reversed the Court of Appeal in holding that the disposition was a discretionary trust and not a mere power. But by a 3:2 majority (Lords Hodson and Guest dissenting, both of whom had concurred in Lord Upjohn's judgment in *Gulbenkian*) the House assimilated the certainty of objects test for discretionary trusts to that for mere powers.

McPhail v Doulton [1970] 2 All ER 228

What might be called the orthodox view was expressed as follows by Lord Hodson (dissenting):

> In my opinion a mere power is a different animal from a trust and the test of certainty in the case of trusts which stems from *Morice v Bishop of Durham* is valid and should not readily yield to the test which is sufficient in the case of mere powers.
>
> The unhappy results which may follow from incompetent drafting may be, in the case of an instrument held to impose a trust, that it is so much waste paper whereas in the case of an instrument differing perhaps on the face of it very little from the invalid trust instrument a good gift of a power to benefit objects may emerge. Thus it is said in order to avoid fine distinctions the test should be the same for both. One persuasive argument used is that, in applying the principle that where there is a trust the court must be in a position to exercise it, the court cannot exercise the trustees' discretion in the event of their failing to do so. The discretion being conferred on and exercisable by the trustees alone the court cannot do other than authorise a distribution in equal shares. This, in cases comparable with the present, must lead to a result tending towards absurdity and makes the strict test of certainty open to serious criticism. . . . For myself I do not deny that there is force in the argument based on the absurdity of an equal division especially as it has not always been accepted.

Lord Hodson referred to 17th and 18th century cases in which the court did exercise its own discretionary judgment against equal division but then continued:

> This practice, however, has fallen into desuetude and the modern, less flexible, practice has it appears been followed since 1801 when Sir Richard Aden MR in *Kemp v Kemp* (1795) 5 Ves 849 stated that the court now disclaims the right to execute a power and gives the fund equally. The basis of this change in policy appears to be that the court has not the same freedom of action as a trustee and must act judicially according to some principle or rule and not make a selection giving no reason as the trustees can. The court, it is said, is

driven in the end to the principle that equity is equality unless, as in the relations cases, the court finds something to aid it. Where there is no guide given the court, it is said, has no right to substitute its own discretion for that of the designated trustees. I regret that the court is driven to adopt a non possumus attitude in cases where trustees fail to exercise a trust power.... I have had the advantage of reading a speech which has been prepared by my noble and learned friend Lord Wilberforce whose opinion particularly on this topic is of very strong persuasive power. I cannot, however, bridge the gulf which still I think yawns between us. If one bases oneself, as I do, on the passage from Lord Eldon LC's judgment in *Morice v Bishop of Durham* as defining the features of a trust, it is, in my opinion, impermissible to sanction, in the case of an uncertain disposition in the sense of the passage quoted, the authorisation by the court of a scheme of distribution such as he suggests. I cannot accept that this is justified by stating that a wider range of enquiry is called for in the case of trust powers than in the case of powers (meaning 'mere' as opposed to 'trust powers'). To adopt this solution is I think to do the very thing which the court cannot do. As was pointed out by my noble and learned friend Lord Upjohn in the *Gulbenkian* case:

'The trustees have a duty to select the donees of the donor's bounty from among the class designated by the donor; he has not entrusted them with any power to select the donees merely from among claimants who are within the class, for that is constituting a narrower class and the donor has given them no power to do this.'

I have read and reread the speech of my noble and learned friend, Lord Wilberforce, with, I hope, a readiness to change my mind and to temper logic with convenience, but having given the best consideration I can to the problem, I still adhere to the view I have previously expressed in the *Broadway Cottages* case and in the *Gulbenkian* case as to the requirements for certainty in the case of the objects of a trust.

It was Lord Wilberforce (with whom Viscount Dilhorne and Lord Reid agreed) who broke new ground:

Lord Wilberforce: It is striking how narrow and in a sense artificial is the distinction, in cases such as the present, between trusts or, as the particular type of trust is called, trust powers, and powers. It is only necessary to read the learned judgments in the Court of Appeal to see that what to one mind may appear as a power of distribution coupled with a trust to dispose of the undistributed surplus, by accumulation or otherwise, may to another appear as a trust for distribution coupled with a power to withhold a portion and accumulate or otherwise dispose of it. A layman and, I suspect, also a logician, would find it hard to understand what difference there is.

It does not seem satisfactory that the entire validity of a disposition should depend on such delicate shading. And if one considers how in practice reasonable and competent trustees would act, and ought to act, in the two cases, surely a matter very relevant to the question of validity, the distinction appears even less significant. To say that there is no obligation to exercise a mere power and that no court will intervene to compel it, whereas a trust is mandatory and its execution may be compelled, may be legally correct enough, but the proposition does not contain an exhaustive comparison of the duties of persons who are trustees in the two cases. A trustee of an employees' benefit fund, whether given a power or a trust power, is still a trustee and he would surely consider in either case that he has a fiduciary duty; he is most likely to have been selected as a suitable person to administer it from his knowledge and experience, and would consider he has a responsibility to do so according to its purpose. It would be a complete misdescription of his position to say that, if what he has is a power unaccompanied by an imperative trust to distribute, he cannot be controlled by the court unless he exercised it capriciously, or outside the field permitted by the trust (cf *Farwell on Powers*, 3rd edn, p 524). Any trustee would surely make it his duty to know what is the permissible area of selection and then consider responsibly, in individual cases, whether a contemplated beneficiary was within the power and whether, in relation to other possible claimants, a particular grant was appropriate.

Correspondingly a trustee with a duty to distribute, particularly among a potentially very large class, would surely never require the preparation of a complete list of names, which anyhow would tell him little that he needs to know. He would examine the field, by class and category; might indeed make diligent and careful enquiries, depending on how much money he had to give away and the means at his disposal, as to the composition and needs of particular categories and of individuals within them; decide on certain priorities or proportions, and then select individuals according to their needs or qualifications. If he acts in this manner, can it really be said that he is not carrying out the trust?

Differences there certainly are between trusts (trust powers) and powers, but as regards validity should they be so great as that in one case complete, or practically complete ascertainment is needed, but not in the other? Such distinction as there is would seem to lie in the extent of the survey which the trustee is required to carry out; if he has to distribute the whole of a fund's income, he must necessarily make a wider and more systematic survey than if his duty is expressed in terms of a power to make grants. But just as, in the case of a power, it is possible to underestimate the fiduciary obligation of the trustee to whom it is given, so, in the case of a trust (trust power), the danger lies in overstating what the trustee requires to know or to enquire into before he can properly execute his trust. The difference may be one of degree rather than of principle; in the well-known words of Sir George Farwell (*Farwell on Powers*, 3rd edn, p 10) trusts and powers are often blended, and the mixture may vary in its ingredients.

Lord Wilberforce agreed that clause 9(a) constituted a trust and then considered what test of certainty was appropriate.

The respondents invited your Lordships to assimilate the validity test for trusts to that which applies to powers. Alternatively, they contended that in any event the test laid down in the *Broadway Cottages* case was too rigid, and that a trust should be upheld if there is sufficient practical certainty in its definition for it to be carried out, if necessary with the administrative

assistance of the court, according to the expressed intention of the settlor. I would agree with this, but this does not dispense from examination of the wider argument...

Assuming, as I am prepared to do for present purposes, that the test of validity is whether the trust can be executed by the court, it does not follow that execution is impossible unless there can be equal division. As a matter of reason, to hold that a principle of equal division applies to trusts such as the present is certainly paradoxical. Equal division is surely the last thing the settlor ever intended; equal division among all may, probably would, produce a result beneficial to none. Why suppose that the court would lend itself to a whimsical execution? And as regards authority, I do not find that the nature of the trust, and of the court's powers over trusts, calls for any such rigid rule. Equal division may be sensible and has been decreed, in cases of family trusts for a limited class, here there is life in the maxim 'equality is equity', but the cases provide numerous examples where this has not been so, and a different type of execution has been ordered, appropriate to the circumstances.

Lord Wilberforce then considered the cases referred to by Lord Hodson (above) but differed in the conclusion to be drawn, commenting that 'a discretionary trust *can*, in a suitable case, be executed according to its merits and otherwise than by equal division. I prefer not to suppose that the great masters of equity, if faced with the modern trust for employees, would have failed to adapt their creation to its practical and commercial character.' Lord Wilberforce then reviewed *Re Ogden* [1933] Ch 678 and *Re Gestetner* [1953] Ch 672, considered that neither case was strong authority against assimilating the tests, and continued:

So I come to *IRC v Broadway Cottages Trust*. This was certainly a case of trust, and it proceeded on the basis of an admission, in the words of the judgment, 'that the class of "beneficiaries" is incapable of ascertainment'. In addition to the discretionary trust of income, there was a trust of capital for all the beneficiaries living or existing at the terminal date. This necessarily involved equal division and it seems to have been accepted that it was void for uncertainty since there cannot be equal division among a class unless all the members of the class are known. The Court of Appeal applied this proposition to the discretionary trust of income, on the basis that execution by the court was only possible on the same basis of equal division. They rejected the argument that the trust could be executed by changing the trusteeship, and found the relations cases of no assistance as being in a class by themselves. The court could not create an arbitrarily restricted trust to take effect in default of distribution by the trustees. Finally they rejected the submission that the trust could take effect as a power; a valid power could not be spelt out of an invalid trust.

My Lords, it will have become apparent that there is much in this which I find out of line with principle and authority but, before I come to a conclusion on it, I must examine the decision of this House in *Re Gulbenkian's Trusts* on which the appellants placed much reliance as amounting to an endorsement of the *Broadway Cottages* case. But is this really so?... [As] a matter of decision, the question now before us did not arise or nearly arise.... Whatever dicta therefore the opinion [of the House in *Re Gulbenkian's Trusts*] were found to contain, I could not, in a case where a direct and fully argued attack has been made on the *Broadway Cottages* case, regard them as an endorsement of it and I am sure that my noble and learned friend [Lord Upjohn], had he been present here, would have regarded the case as at any rate open to review. In fact I doubt very much whether anything his Lordship said was really directed to the present problem. I read his remarks as dealing with the suggestion that trust powers ought to be entirely assimilated to conditions precedent and powers collateral.

Lord Wilberforce then referred to passages in Lord Upjohn's speech extracted above at p 221.

[Lord Upjohn's] reference to defeating 'the intention of donors completely' shows that what he is concerned with is to point to the contrast between powers and trusts which lies in the facultative nature of the one and the mandatory nature of the other, the conclusion being the rejection of the 'broader' proposition as to powers accepted by two members of the Court of Appeal. With this in mind it becomes clear that the sentence so much relied on by the appellants will not sustain the weight they put on it. This is:

'The trustees have a duty to select the donees of the donor's bounty from among the class designated by the donor; he has not entrusted them with any power to select the donees merely from among known claimants who are within the class, for that is constituting a narrower class and the donor has given them no power to do this.'

What this does say, and I respectfully agree, is that, in the case of a trust, the trustees must select from the class. What it does not say, as I read it, or imply, is that in order to carry out their duty of selection they must have before them, or be able to get, a complete list of all possible objects.

So I think that we are free to review the *Broadway Cottages* case. The conclusion which I would reach, implicit in the previous discussion, is that the wide distinction between the validity test for powers and that for trust powers, is unfortunate and wrong, that the rule recently fastened on the courts by the *Broadway Cottages* case ought to be discarded, and that the test for the validity of trust powers ought to be similar to that accepted by this House in *Re Gulbenkian's Settlements Trusts* for powers namely that the trust is valid if it can be said with certainty that any given individual is or is not a member of the class.

Assimilation of the validity test does not involve the complete assimilation of trust powers with powers. As to powers, I agree with my noble and learned friend Lord Upjohn in *Re Gulbenkian's Settlement* that although the trustees may, and normally will, be under a fiduciary duty to consider whether or in what way they should exercise their power, the court will not normally compel its exercise. It will intervene if the trustees exceed their powers, and possibly if they are proved to have exercised it capriciously. But in the case of a trust power, if the trustees do not exercise it, the court will; I respectfully adopt as to this the statement in Lord Upjohn's opinion. I would venture to amplify this by saying that the court, if called on to execute the trust power, will do so in the manner best calculated to give effect to the settlor's or testator's intentions. It may do so by appointing new trustees, or by authorising or directing representative persons of the classes of beneficiaries to prepare a scheme of distribution, or even, should the proper basis for distribution appear, by itself directing the trustees so to distribute. The books give many instances where this has been done and I see no reason in principle why they should not do so in the modern field of discretionary trusts (see *Brunsden v Woolredge* (1765) Amb 507; *Supple v Lowson* (1773) Amb 729; *Liley v Hey* (1842) 1 Hare 580, and *Lewin on Trusts* (16th edn, 1964, p 630)). Then, as to the trustees' duty of enquiry or ascertainment, in each case the trustees ought to make such a survey of the range of objects or possible beneficiaries as will enable them to carry out their fiduciary duty (cf *Liley v Hey*). A wider and more comprehensive range of enquiry is called for in the case of trust powers than in the case of powers.

Two final points: first, as to the question of certainty, I desire to emphasise the distinction clearly made and explained by Lord Upjohn, between linguistic or semantic uncertainty which, if unresolved by the court, renders the gift void, and the difficulty of ascertaining the existence or whereabouts of members of the class, a matter with which the court can appropriately deal on an application for directions. There may be a third case where the meaning of the words used is clear but the definition of beneficiaries is so hopelessly wide as not to form 'anything like a class' so that the trust is administratively unworkable or in Lord Eldon LC's words one that cannot be executed (*Morice v Bishop of Durham*). I hesitate to give examples for they may prejudice future cases, but perhaps 'all the residents of Greater London' will serve. I do not think that a discretionary trust for 'relatives' even of a living person falls within this category.

The case was remitted to the High Court to decide whether the deed satisfied the newly adopted test for certainty of objects.

Consider the following points:

(1) Both the majority and minority judgments (the latter citing Lord Upjohn's argument from *Gulbenkian*) stress the importance to be attached to the 'settlor's intention'. Whose interpretation of the meaning to be attributed to that intention do you find more compelling?

(2) Lord Wilberforce comments on Lord Upjohn's judgment in *Re Gulbenkian* as follows: 'I doubt very much whether anything his Lordship said was really directed to the present problem.' Do you agree?

(3) If the trustees of a discretionary trust of the type illustrated in *McPhail* fail to distribute the relevant funds as required, how should the court go about executing the trust? Given that the maxim 'Equality is equity' *cannot* be applied (because there is no 'list certainty') how far must the court go in (a) enquiring as to the identity of persons within the class of objects; (b) formulating guidelines for distribution; (c) determining who may properly be excluded from benefit? Are tasks such as these appropriate for a court? (See further section (d)(3) below.)

Whilst Lord Wilberforce's judgment assimilates the certainty of objects test for discretionary trusts ('trust powers') and mere powers it leaves outstanding a number of problems which are considered in the next section.

(d) Certainty of objects: some unresolved problems

(1) Certainty of objects and fixed trusts

One teasing academic question is whether the 'criterion certainty' test approved in *McPhail* extends to a fixed trust such as to T1 and T2 on trust for A, B, C, D and E in equal shares or some other fixed shares. The question is probably academic because it could arise only where the beneficiary class is one similar to that in *McPhail v Doulton*, and in practice it is unlikely in the extreme that a fixed-interest gift would be made to such a class.

The accepted view is that a fixed-interest trust will be void unless at inception it is clear that all the beneficiaries are ascertained or capable of being ascertained when the time for distribution of capital or income arrives. An orthodox explanation is 'that if trust property is to be divided among a class of beneficiaries in ... fixed shares, the trust cannot, in the nature of things, be administered unless the number and identity of beneficiaries are known' (*Hanbury and Martin* p 104). 'In the nature of things' must mean that the court, if called upon to administer the trust, must implement the settlor's specific intention and this can only be done if a complete list can be compiled at the appropriate time. The argument seems self-evident but it has been suggested that Lord Wilberforce intended the new test to apply to all trusts (see *Parker and Mellows* (5th edn, 1983) p 79 but note that the current editor shares the more generally accepted view set out above (9th edn, 2008) p 63). Whilst Lord Wilberforce does occasionally use the umbrella term 'trust' rather than the more precise 'trust power', the trust at issue in *McPhail v Doulton* was a discretionary trust and his Lordship's argument is directed towards this.

Nevertheless Lord Wilberforce did agree that 'a trust should be upheld if there is sufficient practical certainty in its definition for it to be carried out, if necessary with the administrative assistance of the court, according to the expressed intention of the settlor'. Bearing in mind the ambiguous nature of intention, does this statement support or reject a liberalisation of the 'list-certainty' test for fixed-interest trusts? (See Matthews [1984] Conv 22, for a view that list certainty is not required for fixed-interest trusts; cf Hayton and Martin [1984] Conv 307.)

(2) The test applied: *Re Baden (No 2)*

The test of certainty of objects for mere powers and discretionary trusts established in the two House of Lords' decisions is whether 'it can be said with certainty that any given individual is or is not a member of the class'. Unfortunately what at first glance appears a perfectly simple test has been shown to have unexpected nuances requiring clarification. One potential source of misunderstanding lies in what might be termed the different elements of the certainty requirement. It will be recalled that Lord Wilberforce endorsed the distinction, drawn by Lord Upjohn in *Re Gulbenkian* [1968] 3 All ER 785, between 'linguistic or semantic uncertainty which, if unresolved by the court, renders the gift void and the difficulty of ascertaining the existence or whereabouts of the members of the class'. The latter is usually termed 'evidential uncertainty' although, as Emery has emphasised, a further distinction can be drawn between 'evidential uncertainty' (the availability of evidence to identify a person as a member of the class) and 'ascertainability' (identifying the whereabouts or continued existence of persons *clearly* members of the class ((1982) 98 LQR 551 at 556–557; cf Matthews [1984] Conv 22 at 29, fn 61). Conceptual certainty (as linguistic or semantic certainty is usually termed) 'refers to the precision of language used by the settlor to define the classes of person whom he intends to benefit' (*Emery* p 552) and difficulties may arise where the draftsman uses vague language. Terms such as 'employees', 'my parents', 'my children' present no difficulty but moving along the continuum 'relatives', 'dependants', 'old friends', may be encountered. Are these expressions precise enough to satisfy the demands of 'conceptual certainty'?

The latent problems surfaced when Bertram Baden's Trust Deed was remitted to the High Court to decide on its validity. Brightman J held ([1972] Ch 607) that the disputed terms 'relatives' and 'dependants' were not too uncertain and upheld the deed. Undaunted the executors appealed. The case was by now taking on Vandervellian proportions, costs having amounted to £54,000 although the value of the fund had risen in the decade since the commencement of the litigation to £463,000, perhaps accounting for the executors' enthusiasm for the battle. The Court of Appeal unanimously agreed that the deed was valid, but differed about the meaning of the certainty test, in particular the relevance of the words 'or is not' in the phrase: 'the trust is valid if it can be said with certainty that any given individual is *or is not* a member of the class'. Megaw and Sachs LJJ, adopting a broad definition of relatives ('descendants of a common ancestor'), both held that it was immaterial that there might be a substantial number of persons of whom it was impossible to say whether they were within or without the class. Sachs LJ's view was that provided the class was conceptually certain, other difficulties were evidentiary only and could be resolved by the court. Megaw LJ held that the test would be satisfied provided a 'substantial' number of persons were clearly within the class. Stamp LJ was more troubled, however. He was of the opinion that it was necessary to be able to say positively of any given person that he was either within *or outside* the class. A category of 'Don't knows' was not permissible. Consequently Stamp LJ was only able to validate the trust by construing 'relatives' narrowly to mean 'next of kin'. All however agreed that the term 'dependants' was sufficiently certain in its context.

Re Baden's Deed Trusts (No 2) [1972] 2 All ER 1304

Sachs LJ: The [next] point as regards approach that requires consideration is the contention strongly pressed by counsel for the defendant executors, that the court must always be able to say whether any given postulant is *not* within the relevant class as well as being able to say whether he is within it. ... As counsel for the defendant executors himself rightly observed, 'the court is never defeated by evidential uncertainty', and it is in my judgment clear that it is conceptual certainty to which reference was made when the 'is or is not a member of the class' test was enunciated. (Conceptual uncertainty was in the course of argument conveniently exemplified, rightly or wrongly matters not, by the phrase 'someone under a moral obligation' and contrasted with the certainty of the words 'first cousins'.) Once the class of persons to be benefited is conceptually certain it then becomes a question of fact to be determined on evidence whether any postulant has on enquiry been proved to be within it; if he is not so proved then he is not in it. That position remains the same whether the class to be benefited happens to be small (such as 'first cousins') or large (such as 'members of the X Trade Union' or 'those who have served in the Royal Navy'). The suggestion that such trusts could be invalid because it might be impossible to prove of a given individual that he was *not* in the relevant class is wholly fallacious – and only the persuasiveness of counsel for the defendant executors has prevented me from saying that the contention is almost unarguable.

Megaw LJ: It is said that those words ['or is not'] have been used deliberately, and have only one possible meaning; and that, however startling or drastic or unsatisfactory the result may be – and counsel for the defendant executors does not shrink from saying that the consequence is drastic – this court is bound to give effect to the words used in the House of Lords' definition of the test. It would be quite impracticable for the trustees to ascertain in many cases whether a particular person was *not* a relative of an employee. The most that could be said is: 'There is no proof that he is a relative'. But there would still be no 'certainty' that such a person was not a relative. Hence, so it is said, the test laid down by the House of Lords is not satisfied, and the trust is void. For it cannot be said with certainty, in relation to any individual, that he is not a relative.

I do not think it was contemplated that the words 'or is not' would produce that result. It would, as I see it, involve an inconsistency with the latter part of the same sentence: 'does not fail simply because it is impossible to ascertain every member of the class'. The executors' contention, in substance and reality, is that it *does* fail 'simply because it is impossible to ascertain every member of the class'.

The same verbal difficulty, as I see it, emerges also when one considers the words of the suggested test which the House of Lords expressly rejected ... The rejected test was in these terms: ' ... it is said to be necessary ... that the whole range of objects ... shall be ascertained or capable of ascertainment'. Since that test was rejected, the resulting affirmative proposition, which by implication must have been accepted by their Lordships, is this: a trust for selection will not fail simply because the whole range of objects cannot be ascertained. In the present case, the trustees could ascertain, by investigation and evidence, many of the objects; as to many other theoretically possible claimants, they could not be certain. Is it to be said that the trust fails because it cannot be said with certainty that such persons are not members of the class? If so, is that not the application of the rejected test; the trust failing because 'the whole range of objects cannot be ascertained?'

In my judgment, much too great emphasis is placed in the executors' argument on the words 'or is not'. To my mind, the test is satisfied if, as regards at least a substantial number of objects, it can be said with certainty that they fall within the trust; even though, as regards a substantial number of other persons, if they ever for some fanciful reason fell to be considered, the answer would have to be, not 'they are outside the trust', but 'it is not proven whether they are in or out'. What is a 'substantial number' may well be a question of common sense and of degree in relation to the particular trust: particularly where, as here, it would be fantasy, to use a mild word, to suggest that any practical difficulty would arise in the fair, proper and sensible administration of this trust in respect of relatives and dependants.

. . . The essence of the decision of the House of Lords in the *Gulbenkian* case, as I see it, is *not* that it must be possible to show with certainty that any given person is or *is not* within the trust; but that it is not, or may not be, sufficient to be able to show that one individual person is within it. If it does not mean that, I do not know where the line is supposed to be drawn, having regard to the clarity and emphasis with which the House of Lords has laid down that the trust does not fail because the whole range of objects cannot be ascertained.

Stamp LJ: . . . There are . . . in my judgment serious difficulties in the way of a rejection of counsel for the executors' submission.

The first difficulty, as I see it, is that the rejection of counsel's submission involves holding that the trust is good if there are individuals – or even one – of whom you can say with certainty that he is a member of the class. . . . Clearly Lord Wilberforce in expressing the view that the test of validity of a discretionary trust ought to be similar to that accepted by the House of Lords in the *Gulbenkian* case did not take the view that it was sufficient that you could find individuals who were clearly members of the class; for he himself remarked, towards the end of his speech as to the trustees' duty of enquiring or ascertaining, that in each case the trustees ought to make such a survey of the range of objects or possible beneficiaries as will enable them to carry out their fiduciary duty. It is not enough that trustees should do nothing but distribute the fund among those objects of the trust who happen to be at hand or present themselves. Lord Wilberforce, after citing . . . from the speech of Lord Upjohn in the *Gulbenkian* case put it more succinctly by remarking that what this did say (and he agreed) was that the trustees must select from the class, but that passage did not mean (as had been contended) that they must be able to get a complete list of all possible objects. I have already called attention to Lord Wilberforce's opinion that the trustees ought to make such a survey of the range of objects or possible beneficiaries as will enable them to carry out their fiduciary duty, and I ought perhaps to add that he indicated that a wider and more comprehensive range of enquiry is called for in the case of what I have called discretionary trusts than in the case of fiduciary powers. But, as I understand it, having made the appropriate survey, it matters not that it is not complete or fails to yield a result enabling you to lay out a list or particulars of every single beneficiary. Having done the best they can, the trustees may proceed on the basis similar to that adopted by the court where all the beneficiaries cannot be ascertained and distributed on the footing that they have been: see, for example, *Re Benjamin* [1902] 1 Ch 723. What was referred to as 'the complete ascertainment test' laid down by this court in the *Broadway Cottages* case is rejected. So also is the test laid down by this court in the *Gulbenkian* case. Validity or invalidity is to depend on whether you can say of any individual – and the accent must be on that word 'any', for it is not simply the individual whose claim you are considering who is spoken of – that he 'is or is not a member of the class', for only thus can you make a survey of the range of objects or possible beneficiaries.

If the matter rested there it would in my judgment follow that, treating the word 'relatives' as meaning descendants from a common ancestor, a trust for distribution such as is here in question would not be valid. Any 'survey of the range of objects or possible beneficiaries' would certainly be incomplete, and I am able to discern no principle on which such a survey could be conducted or where it should start or finish. The most you could do, so far as regards relatives, would be to find individuals who are clearly members of the class – the test which was accepted in the Court of Appeal, but rejected in the House of Lords in the *Gulbenkian* case.

Stamp LJ construed relatives to mean 'nearest blood relatives' and upheld the trust on that basis.

The judgments of Megaw and Sachs LJJ can be said at the very least to support the narrow proposition that there is a presumption that if a candidate cannot positively establish that he is within the class, the application can automatically be placed in the reject tray. But not surprisingly, given the divergence of approach manifested in the Court of Appeal, the judgments have not gone uncriticised and have prompted further academic speculation on the meaning of the test. (See Hopkins [1973] CLJ 36 at 38; Hayton [1972] 36 Conv 351 at 354; *Underhill and Hayton* pp 114–117 but cf Emery (1982) 98 LQR 552 at 576–578.)

Consider the following points:

(1) It is suggested variously that Sachs LJ's 'robust, practical approach' fails to consider or, rather, sidesteps the problems of conceptual certainty; that Megaw LJ's judgment represents an attempt to reintroduce the test rejected by the House of Lords in *Gulbenkian* – that a mere power will be valid even if there is only one or a few persons who are within the class – and that his qualifying criterion of 'a substantial number' introduces uncertainty into the certainty of objects test.

Do these criticisms take adequate account of a possible tension between a literal interpretation of the 'criterion certainty' test and Lord Wilberforce's view mentioned previously that 'a trust should be upheld if there is sufficient practical certainty in its definition for it to be carried out . . . according to the expressed intention of the settlor'?

(2) '*Baden (No 2)* suggests that the courts will tolerate a degree of conceptual uncertainty in a discretionary trust to distribute; the degree of tolerance will increase with the width of the beneficial class.' Do you agree?

(3) Would Megaw LJ's approach enable a court to validate 'a trust . . . in the same language as that in *McPhail v Doulton* but to which there was added "any other person to whom I may be under a moral obligation . . . " which [phrase] is, let it be assumed, conceptually uncertain' (*Hanbury and Martin* p 114)? Questions of construction may be important here; if the clause is interpreted as creating one class rather than two or more distinct classes then it seems likely that the court will not uphold the gift (see *Re Wright's Will Trusts* (29 July 1982) reported in (1999) 13 TLI (1) 48–51). In that case the testatrix gave her residuary estate on trust 'to use as at [the trustees'] absolute discretion for such people and institutions they think have helped me or my late husband including among others [certain named ecclesiastical corporations and six charities including the Police Dependants Trust, the Donkey Sanctuary, and the RSPCA]'. It was accepted that there was no evidence that, for example, the Donkey Sanctuary or the Police Dependants Trust, had ever helped the testatrix or her husband. At first instance therefore, and notwithstanding the words 'including among others', the Vice-Chancellor treated the disposition as creating two distinct classes of beneficiaries, one uncertain – those who may have helped – and the other – the named institutions – certain. He upheld the gift as a valid discretionary trust among the named institutions. On appeal the Court of Appeal held that the testatrix had created one trust and one class of beneficiaries, that it was not possible to allocate any particular part of the fund to the named charities and that therefore the trust was void for uncertainty.

(4) What at first sight appears to be conceptual uncertainty may be remedied by the existence of a provision incorporating the opinion of a third party. For example, assuming the term 'Jewish faith' to be conceptually uncertain (see *Clayton v Ramsden* [1943] 1 All ER 16 but cf *Re Tuck's Settlement Trusts* [1978] 1 All ER 1047), a gift to 'persons of the Jewish faith' would be void whereas a gift to 'persons of the Jewish faith as defined by the Chief Rabbi' would be certain and valid. Where difficulty could arise is if such a gift is made to 'persons of the Jewish faith and if any doubt shall arise the decision of the Chief Rabbi shall be conclusive'. It may be argued that here the reference to Jewish faith is akin to the first example given above, and so is conceptually uncertain; and that, if conceptual uncertainty cannot be resolved by the court, a fortiori it cannot be resolved by reference to a third party (see *Underhill and Hayton* p 115). Whilst technically and logically correct, is it likely that a court operating in a post-*McPhail v Doulton* spirit would strain to draw this fine distinction and hence invalidate the gift? (See *Re Tuck's Settlement Trusts*, in particular the judgment of Eveleigh LJ; *Re Tepper's Will Trusts* [1987] 1 All ER 970; and Hackney (1976) ASCL pp 427–428 for an acute assessment of the probable limits of permissible uncertainty.) The rhetorical nature of that question may, however, be considered excessively complacent in view of the approach of the Court of Appeal in *Re Wright* (see above). Fox LJ states that:

'It is no use the trustees saying, "X in our view helped the testatrix". The problem is one does not know what the testatrix meant by "help".' It seems that *Re Tuck* was not cited to the court.

(5) Finally, there is one rather precarious surviving anomaly of the re-alignment of certainty of objects test. It will be recalled that in *Re Gulbenkian* the House of Lords (Lord Donovan dissenting) rejected the 'one person test' for certainty of objects for mere powers. It still survives in one particular context. Where there is a condition precedent or description attached to individual gifts (eg £1,000 to each of the sons of A who shall be an adherent of the doctrine of the Church of England), something akin to the individual certainty test seems to apply. The disposition is valid if one or more of A's sons clearly qualify even though there is difficulty in knowing whether other sons qualify (see *Re Barlow's Will Trusts* [1979] 1 All ER 296; but cf McKay [1980] Conv 263 and Emery (1982) 98 LQR 551 at 566–567).

(3) The duty to survey

The key to Stamp LJ's dissatisfaction in *Re Baden (No 2)* with his colleagues' acceptance of a widely defined class of 'relatives' lies in his assessment of the trustees' obligations in implementing the trust to distribute. Concern with this issue is understandable. Removal of 'list certainty' and the acceptance of 'criterion certainty' enhances the importance of the duty to survey the class. This was expressly recognised by Lord Wilberforce in *McPhail v Doulton* – 'a wider and more comprehensive range of inquiry is called for in the case of trusts... than in the case of powers'. But the content of this duty to survey is rather nebulous. Megarry VC attempted to expound the trustees' duties in *Re Hay's Settlement Trusts* ([1981] 3 All ER 786 at 793):

> The trustee must not simply proceed to exercise the power in favour of such of the objects as happen to be at hand or claim his attention. He must first consider what persons or classes of persons are objects of the power within the definition in the settlement or will. In doing this, there is no need to compile a complete list of the objects or even to make an accurate assessment of the number of them: what is needed is an appreciation of the width of field, and thus whether a selection is to be made merely from a dozen or, instead, from thousands or millions....
>
> Only when the trustee has applied his mind to the size of the problem should he then consider in individual cases whether, in relation to other possible claimants, a particular grant is appropriate. In doing this, no doubt he should not prefer the undeserving to the deserving; but he is not required to make an exact calculation whether, as between deserving claimants, A is more deserving than B.

As is to be expected, such guidelines leave a penumbra of doubt in between the extremes of surveying the whole field and making individual decisions. Should trustees of a benefit fund for present and past employees advertise for claimants? If so, where, how frequently and how widely? Can trustees rely on existing knowledge of the fund amongst employees? Could trustees be challenged if they merely asked the trade union representatives of employees to nominate deserving candidates, or alternatively if they restricted benefits to meeting education fees of the children of managerial employees? More generally, if the duty to survey is so nebulous is there any justification for retaining the theoretical distinction between discretionary trusts and powers on this point? (See Grbich (1974) 37 MLR 643 at 649–650.) Perhaps all that can be said about the practical operation of the new test is that, so far as the writers are aware, there are no cases of trustees being unable to operate within the new\break framework.

(4) Administrative unworkability: a continuing distinction between discretionary trusts and mere powers?

Lord Wilberforce provided a hostage to fortune at the very end of his judgment in *McPhail v Doulton* [1970] 2 All ER 228 at 247, when he appeared to reintroduce a distinction between discretionary trusts and mere powers in the shape of an 'administrative unworkability' criterion applying to the former, plainly separate from conceptual and evidential uncertainty:

> There may be a third case where the meaning of the words used is clear but the definition of beneficiaries is so hopelessly wide as not to form 'anything like a class' so that the trust is administratively unworkable or . . . one that cannot be executed. I hesitate to give examples . . . but perhaps 'all the residents of Greater London' will serve.

It is unclear whether 'administrative unworkability' was meant to refer to practical problems of surveying a wide class, or to administrative futility where a fund is deemed small in relation to the size of the class, or to undesirability of granting large numbers of people locus standi to enforce the trust (see generally Hardcastle [1990] Conv 24). Indeed the criterion has been strenuously criticised (see McKay (1974) 38 Conv 269) as resting on no satisfactory basis. Among the bases reviewed and rejected by McKay is one implied in Lord Wilberforce's words 'the ability of the court to execute the trust'. If trustees default or refuse to act or come to the court for directions the court must ultimately be able 'to execute the trust'. Amongst the various alternatives to equal distribution outlined by Lord Wilberforce (see above, p 230, and Hopkins (1971) 29 CLJ 68 at 92–101 for an extended analysis) was the possibility, 'should the proper basis for distribution appear', that the court could direct the trustees to distribute the fund (see *Re Locker's Settlement Trusts* [1978] 1 All ER 216 where, however, the trustees were permitted to exercise their discretion out of time). Can it therefore be argued that the exercise by the court of this residual yet fundamental function requires that there must be properly justiciable criteria to guide the court? Grbich argues that this is the rationale for the 'administrative unworkability' requirement ((1974) 37(6) MLR 643 at 652):

> The distinction is based on the quite discrete reason that the court cannot exercise the trust because the settlor has purported to impose an obligation but has failed to give the court enough objective criteria to enforce it. The court will execute a trust to exhaust a fund, and be very flexible in doing so, but it cannot write an instrument for the settlor. It may be that the instrument as a whole or admissible extrinsic evidence will give the court some criteria to appoint by. But if there are no such criteria, the exhaustive discretionary trust will be held void. It is void because there is not enough information to enable a court to frame an order which executes the obligation without resorting to guesswork.

If Lord Wilberforce's 'administrative unworkability' criterion is based on the court's residual function to execute the trust, the requirement can be seen as a judicial compromise, ie as an attempt to meet the criticisms of the dissenting minority in *McPhail v Doulton*.

In fact the criterion has been applied only once to invalidate a trust. In 1985, West Yorkshire Metropolitan County Council, threatened with abolition by the government, proposed to settle £400,000 on trust to spend the capital and income within two years 'for the purpose' of benefiting 'any or all or some of the inhabitants' of West Yorkshire (about two-and-a-half million people) by, inter alia: (i) assisting economic development within the county; (ii) providing assistance for youth, community and ethnic or other minority groups; and (iii) informing interested persons or bodies of the consequences of the proposed abolition of Metropolitan County Councils. The proposed trust was held administratively unworkable ostensibly because the class of beneficiaries was 'far too large' (*R v District Auditor, ex p West Yorkshire Metropolitan County Council* [1986] RVR 24; see Harpum (1986) 45 CLJ 392). Whilst the class of beneficiaries bears a superficial similarity to Lord Wilberforce's example – 'all the residents of Greater London' – the West Yorkshire local authority had, as the court accepted, every reason for wishing to benefit the inhabitants. Moreover, criteria were provided to guide the trustees in executing the trust. The case is an unsatisfactory authority because, as the court acknowledged, its decision was reached without the benefit of full argument on the academic comment and criticism of Lord Wilberforce's dictum. In the absence of that full argument on the administrative unworkability point, the rationale for the requirement remains obscure.

We have assumed so far that the requirement applies to discretionary trusts only, but Lord Wilberforce's rather guarded comment left the door fractionally open to the question: 'Might "administrative unworkability" also be a disqualifying factor for mere powers held by trustees?' The question has arisen in the context of settlors seeking to use widely drawn 'intermediate' powers to permit trustees to add persons to the primary class of beneficiaries. Such powers provide maximum flexibility for dealing with future tax changes or changes in personal circumstances. In *Blausten v IRC* [1972] Ch 256 a power to appoint anyone other than the settlor into a specified class of beneficiaries was validated by the Court of Appeal. But it was upheld only because the trustees' power to include any person was subject to the settlor's written consent, and so the settlor had put 'metes and bounds' on the exercise of the power. Yet subsequently in *Re Manisty's Settlement* [1973] 2 All ER 1203, Templeman J upheld a similar 'intermediate' power but one without the qualifying limitation regarded as necessary in *Blausten*. Templeman J expressed the view that a power cannot be invalid merely because it is wide in ambit but he did appear to accept that a 'special' power in favour of a class 'that negatives any sensible intention on the part of the settlor' (at 1211) would be void as being 'capricious' – 'the residents of Greater London' making a reappearance now as a capricious class.

The confused picture emerging from these conflicting views was examined in some detail in *Re Hay's Settlement Trusts* [1981] 3 All ER 786, where Megarry VC held valid an intermediate power to appoint to anyone in the world other than the settlor, her husband or the trustees. The purported exercise of the power in appointing to a discretionary sub-trust for that same class of objects was, however, held invalid as infringing a rule prohibiting unauthorised delegation of powers by a trustee. Megarry VC was also inclined obiter to hold the sub-trust void on grounds of administrative unworkability.

Re Hay's Settlement Trusts [1981] 3 All ER 786

Megarry VC: It is plain that if a power of appointment is given to a person who is not in a fiduciary position, there is nothing in the width of the power which invalidates it per se.... The difficulty comes when the power is given to trustees as such, in that the number of objects may interact with the fiduciary duties of the trustees and their control by the court.

The Vice-Chancellor reviewed the authorities on the duties of a trustee specific to a mere power and summarised them as follows:

...the duties of a trustee which are specific to a mere power seem to be threefold. Apart from the obvious duty of obeying the trust instrument, and in particular of making no appointment that is not authorised by it, the trustee must, first, consider periodically whether or not he should exercise the power; second, consider the range of objects of the power; and third, consider the appropriateness of individual appointments. I do not assert that this list is exhaustive....

On this footing, the question is thus whether there is something in the nature of an intermediate power which conflicts with these duties in such a way as to invalidate the power if it is vested in a trustee.

The Vice-Chancellor then considered *Blausten v IRC*:

It seems quite plain that Buckley LJ considered that the power was saved from invalidity only by the requirement for the consent of the settlor. The reason for saying that in the absence of such a requirement the power would have been invalid seems to be twofold. First, the class of persons to whose possible claims the trustees would be duty-bound to give consideration was so wide as not to form a true class, and this would make it impossible for the trustees to perform their duty of considering from time to time whether to exercise the power.

I feel considerable difficulty in accepting this view. First, I do not see how mere numbers can inhibit the trustees from considering whether or not to exercise the power, as distinct from deciding in whose favour to exercise it. Second, I cannot see how the requirement of the settlor's consent will result in any 'class' being narrowed from one that is too wide to one that is small enough. Such a requirement makes no difference whatever to the number of persons potentially included: the only exclusion is still the settlor. Third, in any case I cannot see how the requirement of the settlor's consent could make it possible to treat 'anyone in the world save X' as constituting any real sort of a 'class', as that term is usually understood.

The second ground of invalidity if there is no requirement for the settlor's consent seems to be that the power is so wide that it would be impossible for the trustees to consider in any sensible manner how to exercise it, and also impossible for the court to say whether or not they were properly exercising it. With respect, I do not see how that follows. If I have correctly stated the extent of the duties of trustees in whom a mere power is vested, I do not see what there is to prevent the trustees from performing these duties. It must be remembered that Buckley LJ, though speaking after *Re Gulbenkian's Settlement* and *Re Baden* had been decided, lacked the advantage of considering *Re Baden (No 2)*, which was not decided until some five months later. He thus did not have before him the explanation in that case of how the trustees should make a survey and consider individual appointments in cases where no complete list of objects could be compiled. . . .

From what I have said it will be seen that I cannot see any ground on which the power in question can be said to be void. Certainly it is not void for linguistic or semantic uncertainty; there is no room for doubt in the definition of those who are or are not objects of the power. Nor can I see that the power is administratively unworkable. The words of Lord Wilberforce in *Re Baden* are directed to discretionary trusts, not powers. Nor do I think that the power is void as being capricious. In *Re Manisty's Settlement* Templeman J appears to be suggesting that a power to benefit 'residents in Greater London' is void as being capricious 'because the terms of the power negative any sensible intention on the part of the settlor'. In saying that, I do not think that the judge had in mind a case in which the settlor was, for instance, a former chairman of the Greater London Council . . . [t]his consideration does not apply to intermediate powers, where no class which could be regarded as capricious has been laid down. Nor do I see how the power in the present case could be invalidated as being too vague, a possible ground of invalidity considered in *Re Manisty's Settlement*. Of course, if there is some real vice in a power, and there are real problems of administration or execution, the court may have to hold the power invalid: but I think that the court ought not to be astute to find grounds on which a power can be invalidated . . . a power should not be held void on a peradventure.

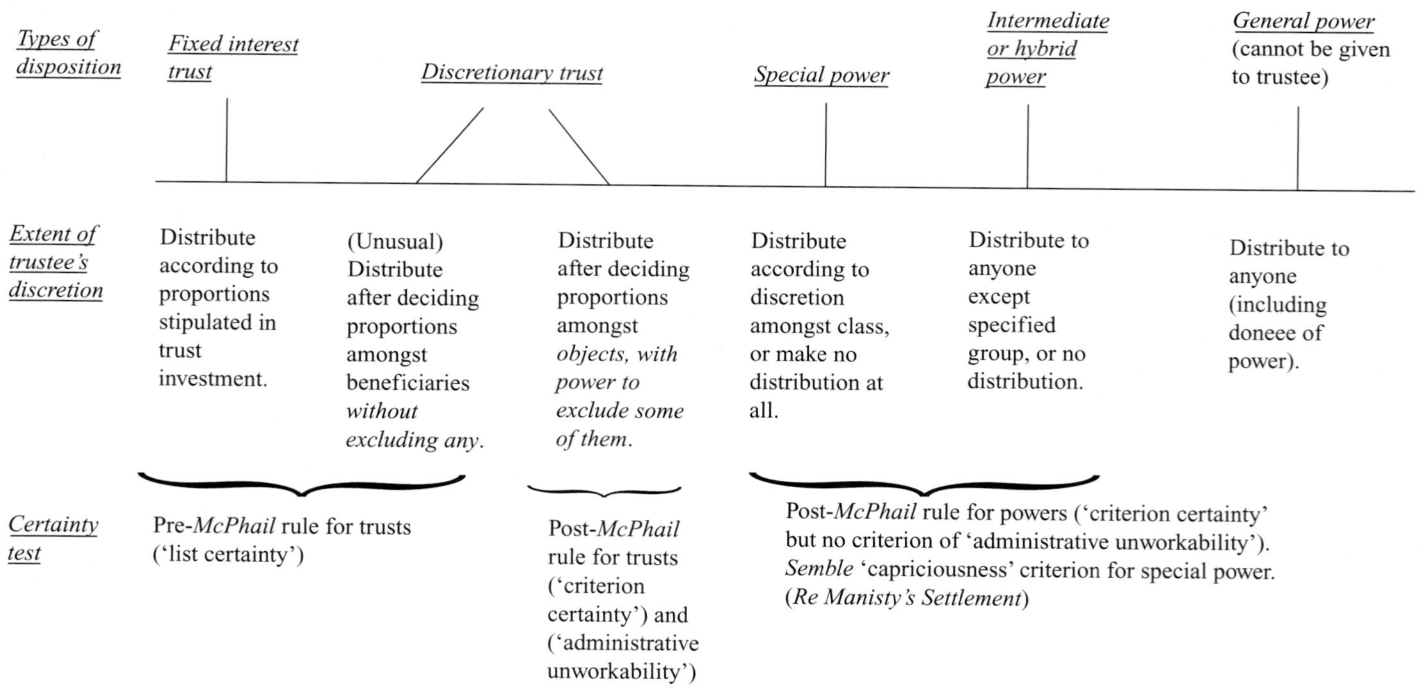

(Note: This figure which simplifies the propositions, must be read in conjunction with the text.)

Types of disposition	*Fixed interest trust*	*Discretionary trust*		*Special power*	*Intermediate or hybrid power*	*General power* (cannot be given to trustee)
Extent of trustee's discretion	Distribute according to proportions stipulated in trust investment.	(Unusual) Distribute after deciding proportions amongst beneficiaries *without excluding any*.	Distribute after deciding proportions amongst *objects, with power to exclude some of them*.	Distribute according to discretion amongst class, or make no distribution at all.	Distribute to anyone except specified group, or no distribution.	Distribute to anyone (including donee of power).
Certainty test	Pre-*McPhail* rule for trusts ('list certainty')	Post-*McPhail* rule for trusts ('criterion certainty') and ('administrative unworkability')		Post-*McPhail* rule for powers ('criterion certainty' but no criterion of 'administrative unworkability'). *Semble* 'capriciousness' criterion for special power. (*Re Manisty's Settlement*)		

Figure 5.2 Certainty of objects

Re Hay's Settlement Trusts does then lend tentative support to three propositions: (1) a criterion of administrative unworkability applies to discretionary trusts but not to mere powers; (2) there may be a criterion of 'capriciousness' that will invalidate 'special fiduciary powers' (ie special powers vested in trustees) but not 'intermediate fiduciary powers' (see Figure 5.2); (3) where the power of appointment is given to a person who is *not* in a fiduciary capacity the power will not be invalid on grounds of its width. If administrative unworkability is based on some notion of justiciability rather than the size of the class or administrative inconvenience, it is difficult to see how it differs from capriciousness, and both savour of being judicial 'safety nets' to cope with some unforeseen eventuality. One can only speculate as to whether the same safety-net concern explains the otherwise confusing and rather cryptic closing comments of Megarry VC alluding to 'real vice in a power' and 'real problems of administration or execution'.

(e) Conclusion

(1) *McPhail v Doulton*: an engine for change

From one perspective *McPhail v Doulton* can be seen simply as completing a tidying-up process in the rules concerning certainty of objects, by removing the 'narrow and artificial' distinction between discretionary trusts and mere powers. From another perspective *McPhail v Doulton* marks the culmination of a process of legal change initiated by the 'special powers' case of *Re Gestetner*, albeit requiring en route the reversal of a century-and-a-half of Chancery law and practice. The implications of this reversal are potentially far-reaching for trusts law and subsequent developments have demonstrated that the process of change is not exhausted.

On the one hand, at least in the commercial context of pension fund trusts, the 'narrow and artificial' distinction between discretionary trusts and mere powers has been somewhat elided. In *Mettoy Pension Trustees Ltd v Evans* [1990] 1 WLR 1587 (discussed in Chapter 13), Warner J accepted that there can exist powers of appointment which are 'fiduciary in the full sense' and under which the duties owed by the trustees to the objects of the power are essentially no different from those owed to the beneficiaries of a discretionary trust. It followed, and here Warner J broke new ground, that *all* the remedies identified in *McPhail v Doulton* as available to the court to control and enforce the administration of a discretionary trust should be equally available in the case of fully fiduciary powers of appointment. In *Mettoy*, for instance, the judge indicated that, if necessary, he would himself be able to decide on an appropriate scheme of distribution. This is a far cry indeed from Lord Upjohn's view in *Gulbenkian* as to the rights of the objects of a power of appointment and the remedies available to them. (Gardner (1991) 107 LQR 214 suggests that the assimilation of remedies might result in the 'administrative unworkability' criterion being applied to 'fiduciary powers'. But see below (and Chapter 13) on our doubts about the full applicability of propositions in pensions cases to the family trust context.) Further confirmation of the revolutionary nature of the changes initiated by the majority decision in *McPhail v Doulton* is to be found in the decision of the Privy Council in *Schmidt v Rosewood Trust Ltd* [2003] 2 AC 709. Their Lordships specifically endorsed Lord Wilberforce's view that 'differences . . . between trusts and powers are a good deal less significant than the similarities' and affirmed the right in principle of the claimant, Mr Schmidt, a *potential* beneficiary under a very widely drawn fiduciary power of appointment, to seek disclosure of information from trustees: 'there is . . . in their Lordships' view no reason to draw any bright dividing line . . . between the rights of an object of a discretionary trust and those of the object of a mere power (of a fiduciary character)' (at para 66).

On the other hand, Megarry VC's dicta in *Re Hay* simultaneously confirming and limiting the scope of the criteria of 'administrative unworkability' and 'capriciousness' are evidence of a gap existing between discretionary trusts and intermediate powers: indeed a 'narrow and artificial' distinction between the two is now re-appearing as a yawning chasm in terms of the breadth of discretion permitted by them. Yet this can also be seen as evidence of the discontinuous nature of legal change hinted at in the Introduction to this chapter. A criterion of 'administrative unworkability' might have been thought to impose limits on the flexibility of beneficial entitlement available to settlors. McKay, for instance, has argued ((1974) 38 Conv 269 at 284) that '[administrative unworkability] represents an unwarranted threat to settlors wishing to confer wide discretions upon their trustees' (cf Grubb [1982] Conv 432; and Grbich (1974) 37 MLR 643 at 651–654). But the new offshoot sprouting in the 'intermediate powers' cases of *Manisty* and *Blausten* initially reflecting a fiscal cum familial rather than commercial source of pressure for change, casts doubt on this proposition.

(2) Certainty uncertain and the 'black hole' trust

The new offshoot reaches its zenith in what has become known colloquially as 'black hole trusts' (see generally Hayton (1999) 7(2) JITCP 69; Matthews (2002) PCB (1) 42–54 and (2) 103–110). As their name implies one of the intentions of setting up such trusts is to exploit to the full one of the attributes of the trust form, namely concealment of beneficial ownership, not only from the world at large but even from 'the beneficiaries' themselves. In fact a feature of such a trust is that it will contain a class of named beneficiaries comprising just a limited number of legal persons only some of whom, or maybe even none of whom, are intended to benefit. In one Jersey case, for instance, *Re Gea Settlement* (1992) 13 TLI 188 the named beneficiaries were 'Save the Children Fund, RNLI, and RSPCA' who in theory would ultimately be entitled to the trust fund. In practice there is no intention in such cases that an outcome of that nature should arise. Instead trustees are likely to be given a discretion under an intermediate power of appointment, the exercise of which will often depend on the settlor's wishes as confidentially imparted to the trustees or to a 'protector' (see below, p 265). As a further cloak of concealment the identity of the true settlor in the sense of the person providing most of the trust fund may also be concealed behind some corporate figurehead who may have contributed only a nominal amount to the trust fund. With many, probably most, trusts of this sort the funds are held in offshore trusts usually in territories with which the settlor has no substantial connection. As Lord Walker noted in one such case *Schmidt v Rosewood Trust Limited* [2003] 2 AC 709 (PC), 'These territories . . . are chosen not for their geographical convenience . . . but because they are supposed to offer special advantages in terms of confidentiality and protection from fiscal demands (and sometimes from problems under the insolvency laws, or laws restricting freedom of testamentary disposition, in the country of the settlor's domicile)' (at para 1). This is not to say that such trusts are completely free of legal risk. The temptation for a settlor to remain in total control of the trust property is evident but can result in the trust being held to be a sham with the Vandervellian-type outcome that legal ownership may be deemed still to rest with the settlor (see eg *Rahman v Chase Bank (CI) Trust Co* (1991) JLR 103; and also Chapter 4 at p 163). If such temptations can be avoided and the trusts are valid then we have come a long way indeed from the argument of counsel for the Inland Revenue in *Re Gestetner* [1953] Ch 672 that 'it would be quite contrary to the principles of trust law to allow a vague trust of this kind to be valid' (at 681). This relatively recent offshore innovation raises in peculiarly acute form the new questions about a certainty of objects requirement in trusts law first posed by cases such as *Manisty* and *Blausten*.

(3) From 'certainty' to 'accountability and control'

On a purely practical level, the question must now be whether there exists any limit at all to the flexibility of beneficial entitlement that can be achieved in a settlement by a combination of trusts and intermediate powers. On the conceptual level the corollary of this question is whether a 'certainty of objects' test is now a misnomer: is it more appropriate to ask what degree of uncertainty will be tolerated by the courts? (See Watkin (1979) 8 Anglo-Am LR 123.) After *Baden (No 2)* the only substantive limits on this uncertainty are to be found in the residual disqualifying factors of 'administrative unworkability' and 'capriciousness' for discretionary trusts and special powers respectively. Moreover, if *Re Hay* is correct neither of these disqualifying factors apply to intermediate powers of appointment. Yet whilst both these requirements may operate in theory as disqualifying factors at inception, the current judicial approach leans towards upholding dispositions wherever possible, on the premise that this most closely reflects the settlor's wishes. Indeed, even the supposed principle of non-delegation of testamentary power, once seen as a potential curb on the scope of intermediate powers of appointment conferred by will, has recently been firmly and convincingly rejected by English courts as being 'a chimera, a shadow cast by the rule of certainty, having no independent existence' (*Re Beatty's Will Trusts* [1990] 3 All ER 844 at 849; [1991] 107 LQR 211–214). In that case the testatrix had granted her trustees a power to distribute, inter alia, £1.5m among 'such persons as they think fit' (with authority to include themselves) but with a gift over to the residuary estate if no distribution was made within two years (see also *Re Nicholls* (1987) 34 DLR (4th) 321 but cf the earlier decision of the High Court of Australia in *Re Tatham* (1951) 81 CLR 639).

Such control as exists must now, therefore, primarily be sought not at the creation of the instrument but when the discretion it confers is subsequently exercised. Yet almost any appointment by a trustee armed with intermediate powers of unlimited width will fall within the boundaries of the power and by definition cannot be attacked as an 'excessive execution of the power'. The autonomy of trustees is thus sharply increased; and an increase seeming to register the final victory for settlor's intention over enforceability as a guiding principle in this area of trusts law. But we have attempted in this chapter to stress the dynamic aspect of trusts law and, as Harris argued ((1971) 87 LQR 31 at 57) '[trustees] . . . are subject to rules of equity which will be developed to accommodate the new kinds of confidence which settlors, under changing social conditions, impose upon trustees'. One example of this dynamism is to be found in *McPhail v Doulton* itself where the majority rejected the constraints imposed by a narrow perception, derived from *Morice v Bishop of Durham*, of the court's ability to control and execute a trust. Another is the approach to 'enforceability and control' exemplified in cases such as *Mettoy*, although it may be premature to assume that such decisions will necessarily be applied to their fullest extent in the domain of the family trust (see Moffat (1993) 56 MLR 471, but cf Martin [1991] Conv 364 and Gravells (1992) 3 Canterbury LR 67). In any event, should we now expect to witness an emerging judicial willingness to invoke a more extensive jurisdiction to control the subsequent exercise of trustees' discretions? Will the courts be persuaded to intervene to control trustees, even under intermediate powers, who act 'capriciously, that is to say, act for reasons which . . . could be said to be irrational, perverse or irrelevant to any sensible expectation of the settlor' (per Templeman J in *Re Manisty's Settlement* [1973] 2 All ER 1203 at 1210). If so, an apparent loosening of judicial control via the broadening of a certainty of objects test may paradoxically result ultimately in an extension of that control. The decision of the Privy Council in *Schmidt v Rosewood* can be viewed from that standpoint. How far such a development would involve rewriting much of the law on trustees' powers and duties will be considered further in Chapter 11 where the Privy Council opinion is discussed in more detail.

If restructuring is to occur, the ripples from *McPhail v Doulton* will be spreading way beyond the boundaries of the certainty of objects test for discretionary trusts. It will support a contention that there has been a fundamental shift in the centre of gravity of trusts law with trustees' duties 'coming to take the place once reserved as sacred to equitable beneficial interests' (Davies [1970] ASCL 189). This in turn raises questions about the rationale of the beneficiary principle (see section 5 below). First, however, it is necessary to consider just what the nature of a beneficial interest now is.

4. The nature of a beneficiary's interest

(a) The 'great debate'

Analysing the nature of a beneficiary's interest under a trust is a vexatious question which something over half a century ago aroused acute controversy among leading legal scholars (see Waters (1967) 45 Can BR 219 for a review of the controversy). Our focus here, concentrating on the interest of a beneficiary under a discretionary trust, is much narrower for two reasons. One practical reason is that it is the very nature of this interest – an interest that in a material sense leaves the property ownerless – which stimulated the widespread adoption of the discretionary trust for tax planning. The second reason is that the requirement for a beneficial interest – a property interest – to exist provides an important conceptual prop to the beneficiary principle. An understanding of the nature of a beneficial interest at its most elusive, ie under a discretionary trust, may therefore help us to evaluate arguments about the need for a beneficiary principle. But to grasp the importance of recent developments an appreciation of the causes and consequences of that earlier debate are helpful.

The central issue then was whether a beneficiary's rights under a trust were better classified as *in rem* – a proprietary right enforceable against persons generally in respect of particular property – or *in personam* – usually understood as a right of action against a person, for example, a trustee. In fact the debate was founded on a premise that rights must be squeezed into one box or another. That premise and its consequences were sharply criticised in a comment that subsequently received judicial approval in *CSD v Livingstone* (1960) 107 CLR 411 at 449.

> It is a moot question whether the whole discussion raised by the arbitrary classifications borrowed from Roman law and distorted to fit in with new facts is not a mere academical tourney with no real bearing upon the practice of the law, and, being faulty in hypothesis and unsatisfactory in result, would be better abandoned altogether. (R W Turner *The Equity of Redemption* (1931) p 152)

Neither of the classifications is wholly appropriate. W W Cook's savage contemporary criticism (*Introduction to Hohfeld: Fundamental Legal Conceptions* (1923)) of the attempt to fit the range of 'legal rights, privileges, powers and immunities' into a dichotomous framework has if anything gained in strength over the intervening years:

> The analysis . . . has treated a very complex aggregate of legal relations as though it were a simple thing, a unit. The result is no more enlightening than it would be were a chemist to treat an extraordinary complex chemical compound as if it were an element.

That the debate occurred at all reflected the extent to which the idea of 'trust' had developed since its inception. Equity's initial view of a beneficiary's interest was that it amounted to nothing more than a right to compel the trustee to perform the trust or make good any loss arising from breach of trust – very much a right *in personam*. Subsequent developments extended the scope of this right to the extent that it became enforceable against everyone except the bona fide purchaser for value of legal title to the trust property.

A brief digression will help demonstrate how this simple personal right of enforcement has acquired a proprietary hue. Suppose a trustee T misappropriates trust property and sells it to P. With the proceeds T purchases shares in XYZ. According to principles developed comparatively early in the history of trusts law the beneficiary B has two remedies against T. B can sue T personally to require T to reimburse the trust fund or alternatively assert a proprietary right to follow, or 'trace' as it is called, the trust fund via the proceeds of sale into the shares and require that the shares be transferred into the trust fund. These two remedies will usually suffice but suppose further that T is insolvent and there is no property against which B's claim can be enforced. B may then, in certain circumstances, have recourse to a personal claim against P or a proprietary claim against the trust property in P's possession, except of course where P was a bona fide purchaser (see Chapter 14).

But developments went beyond this remedial stance and towards establishing a beneficial interest in the trust property itself. Under the rule in *Saunders v Vautier* (see Chapter 7) a beneficiary who is of full age, and sound mind and alone entitled to the trust fund can terminate the trust, thus obtaining the trust property. This development reached its apogee in *Baker v Archer-Shee* [1927] AC 844. Lady Archer-Shee's income tax liability as a UK resident depended in part on the nature of her life interest in a settled fund in New York. The trustees, after meeting local taxes and expenses, retained the balance of the income, obtained from dividends, in New York. The taxpayer was liable to tax only if she could be regarded as the beneficial owner of the dividends as they arose. It was argued to the contrary on her behalf that her only right as a beneficiary was to seek the court's assistance to compel the trustees to perform the trust. The House of Lords by a 3:2 majority, criticised by Hanbury (1928) 44 LQR 468 as being incompatible with equitable principle, rejected this argument. In Lord Wrenbury's words, '[Lady Archer Shee's] right is . . . an equitable right in possession to receive during her life the proceeds of the shares and stocks of which she is tenant for life. Her right is not to a balance sum, but to the dividends subject to deductions . . . ' (at 866). It is evident from the judgment that Lord Wrenbury was conscious of the fiscal implications of deciding the case differently.

In a previous edition of this book we prematurely asserted that the debate had been largely abandoned. It now shows signs of reinvigoration in a wholly different contemporary context, namely litigation about beneficial ownership of second homes in countries such as France and Spain. The primary issue is jurisdictional. Should cases be heard in England, often the domicile of one of the parties, or in the courts of the countries where the properties are located? Article 22(1) of Council Regulation (EC) No 44/2001, replacing Article 16(1) of the Brussels Convention on Jurisdiction and the Enforcement of Judgments in Civil and Commercial Matters 1968, confers exclusive jurisdiction 'in proceedings which have as their object rights *in rem* in immovable property' on the courts of the state in which the property is located. A key question then is whether a claim relating to a beneficial interest in land held under a trust is an action *in rem*. In *Webb v Webb* Case C-294/92 [1994] 3 WLR 801 a father who had purchased a flat in Antibes in his son's name sought (i) a declaration in the High Court that the son held the property as trustee under a resulting trust, and (ii) an order that legal ownership should be vested in the father. The European Court of Justice, to whom the case was referred, confirmed the High Court decision ([1992] 1 All ER 17) rejecting the argument on behalf of the son that the action was one *in rem* within the meaning of what is now Article 22(1). The ECJ emphasised that 'it is not sufficient, for the Article to apply, that a right *in rem* in immovable property be involved in the action or that the action have a link with immovable property: the action must be based on a right *in rem* and not on a right *in personam*' (para 14; see the critical comments by Birks (1994) 8 TLI no 4 at 99 but cf MacMillan [1996] Conv 125). In effect the father's claim was not viewed as asserting 'rights directly relating to the property which are enforceable against the whole world' (an action *in rem* on this analysis) but as one seeking 'only to assert rights as against the son', an action *in personam* within the meaning of Article 22(1) (at para 15). The opposite conclusion was arrived at by Rattie J in *Re Hayward (deceased)* [1996] 3 WLR 674, a case technically distinguishable in terms of the parties and the pleadings but one involving comparable substantive issues of beneficial ownership (see Stevens [1998] Conv 145; and further *Ashurst v Pollard* [2001] 2 All ER 75 and *Prazic v Prazic* [2006] EWCA Civ 497 where in both cases *Webb v Webb* was applied).

The position reached is hardly satisfactory but to some degree may reflect the difficulty of characterising, under a civilian system, the proprietary effect of equitable property interests. In a sense we are back to the problem of trying to squeeze into two inappropriate boxes an interest that is something more than *in personam* but is less than what a civilian would recognise as an ownership right *in rem* 'the holder of rights *erga omnes* that is to say rights effective against the whole world' (per Advocate-General Darmon in *Webb v Webb* at 816B). However indecisive it may seem, there is in our view still much to be said for the opinion that the interest of a beneficiary needs to be treated, at least for the purposes of this debate, as sui generis (see eg *Pettit* p 83) rather than attempting to force it into some inadequate straitjacket.

(b) Equitable ownership and the discretionary trust

Harris has tentatively suggested ((1971) 87 LQR 31 at 47) that what emerged from, inter alia, the developments in the certainty of objects rules described above was 'a distilled dogma of property law that equitable ownership is after all ownership and must be located somewhere'. A fixed-interest trust presents no difficulty for such a schema; a beneficiary's interest can easily be treated as having a proprietary character. But if it is thought necessary that legal ownership vested in trustees must be balanced by identifiable equitable ownership, then the discretionary trust presents problems. Where all the members of the class are identifiable then it is possible to posit that the class collectively owns the equitable interest and even that the class as a whole, if adult and under no disability, can terminate the trust (see *Re Smith* [1928] Ch 915). But the reasoning falters when faced with the permissible width of the beneficial class in a modern discretionary trust. Following *McPhail v Doulton*, this class may include persons who are not, nor ever will be, identifiable. Nevertheless, might one not argue that a class even of that nature in a sense possesses the whole of the equitable interest in the trust fund? Yet even if in a spirit of conceptualist consistency, or 'distilled dogma', one accepts the proposition it is difficult to see that it carries any practical consequences. This is particularly so given the rejection of the proposition in a tax context (see *Gartside v IRC* below).

We would suggest that the more pertinent question to be asked is: 'does a beneficiary of a discretionary trust have an "interest" in the trust property and, if so, what is the nature of that interest?'

(c) Cheese, the nature of the beneficiary's interest and discretionary trusts

It is essential at the outset to appreciate that the term 'interest' may encompass a variety of different meanings depending on the context. 'It is a fallacy to talk of an interest as if it were a piece of cheese' (Bagnall QC in *Re Holmden's Settlement Trusts* [1966] Ch 511 at 526). The following questions are in point:

(1) Can an individual object establish a right as against the trustee to any trust property or force the trustee to allocate?
(2) Can an individual object establish a right as against the rest of the world to any trust property?
(3) Has an individual object locus standi to ask the court to restrain the trustee, for example, from making an ultra vires appointment?
(4) If individual objects do not enjoy any of these rights, do they enjoy them collectively as a class?

The fact that a 'yes' answer may be given to some of these questions is not sufficient to establish a basis for assessing tax on the footing that the beneficiary has an interest. This was confirmed by Lord Wilberforce in *Gartside v IRC* [1968] 1 All ER 121 at 134 (a case of a 'non-exhaustive discretionary trust', ie income could be either distributed or accumulated):

> No doubt in a certain sense a beneficiary under a discretionary trust has an 'interest': the nature of it may, sufficiently for the purpose, be spelt out by saying that he has a right to be considered as a potential recipient of benefit by the trustees and a right to have his

interest protected by a court of equity.... But that does not mean that he has an interest which is capable of being taxed by reference to its extent in the trust fund's income: it may be a right with some degree of concreteness or solidity, one which attracts the protection of a court of equity, yet it may still lack the necessary quality of definable extent which must exist before it can be taxed.

The House of Lords in *Gartside* rejected the Revenue argument that as any one beneficiary might receive all the income, he or she should be treated as entitled to the whole income, and estate duty charged accordingly upon the whole of the undistributed capital of the fund on his or her death. Instead the House of Lords made it clear that such beneficiaries neither individually nor collectively have any 'interest' extending to the whole or any definable part of the income of the fund. The same proposition was subsequently confirmed in *Sainsbury v IRC* [1970] Ch 712, for 'exhaustive discretionary trusts' ie those where the trustees were obliged to distribute the whole of the income.

While these judgments firmly establish the negative proposition that a discretionary object's interest is insufficiently precise to be taxed, the positive rights attaching to a beneficiary's interest were not set out in any detail. More recently Walton J summarised these rights as they apply to objects of a mere power in *Vestey v IRC (No 2)* [1979] 2 All ER 225 at 235:

What 'rights' are ... conferred on any individual potential beneficiary? In my judgment, the only relevant rights which are conferred on such a beneficiary are: (i) the right to be considered by the person exercising the power when he comes to exercise it; (ii) the right to prevent certain kinds of conduct on the part of the person so exercising the power, e.g. by distributing part of the assets to persons not within the class; and (iii) the right to retain any sums properly paid to him by the trustees in exercise of their discretionary powers. But beyond that he has no relevant 'right' of any description.... Indeed, no individual has any power over any part of the income whatsoever. The most relevant right is, indeed, the third; but a right to retain what is properly paid to you is simply the negative right of being afforded a complete defence to any claim for repayment, and no more. Prior to actual payment, to which there is no right whatsoever, the recipient has no right to the money at all.

One may, indeed, contrast the situation in the present case with a situation where trustees are obliged to distribute income year by year under the terms of their trust deed among a certain class in such shares and proportions as they may think fit, a case in which each potential beneficiary is very much more likely in ordinary parlance to have power to enjoy the income than the present case. Even in such a case no individual potential beneficiary has any relevant right whatsoever, although collectively, they undoubtedly do have a right which, if they are all sui juris, they may collectively enforce.

The above description was specifically approved by the House of Lords on appeal ([1979] 3 All ER 976 at 983 per Lord Wilberforce). Where the disposition is a discretionary trust the trustees must distribute the relevant income or capital within a reasonable period after the time stipulated in the trust instrument. Although the duty to distribute can be enforced by a beneficiary this gives no greater entitlement to a definite portion of the income than that of the object of a mere power. This is not to say that legislation cannot ever attribute ownership or effective control to a beneficiary of a discretionary trust (see eg the application of Matrimonial Causes Act 1973, ss 23, 24 in *Browne v Browne* [1989] 1 FLR 291).

For the purposes of trusts law, however, the result, as Pettit with a fine sense of understatement has noted, is that 'it is very difficult to explain where the equitable interest lies in the case of discretionary trusts' (p 77; see also Everton [1982] Conv 118 at 119). There is a certain convenient attraction in Pettit's suggestion that 'perhaps the true view is that the beneficial interest is in suspense until the trustees exercise their discretion'. Yet this formula addresses only the proprietary element inherent in the notion of 'an interest'. There is no suggestion that any of the 'rights' described by Walton J are in suspense yet even here we may, as the next section hypothesises, be compelled to reassess the strength of even these rights.

(d) From 'equitable interest' to 'equitable right' and beyond

We have reached a position where we know that Equity came to recognise that a beneficiary under a trust possessed a form of property interest in the shape of equitable ownership. As with other species of property, that interest too is transmissible: it can be bought, sold, assigned, mortgaged, and bequeathed in a will. But as is evident in the analysis of Walton J in *Vestey v IRC (No 2)* these rights to dispose of or to alienate that one associates with property ownership become almost meaningless in any practical sense for the individual beneficiary in the context of the modern discretionary trust. The emphasis here has been on some search for a positive proprietary dimension to a beneficiary's interest. Yet, pending any allocation from the trust to a discretionary beneficiary by trustees, the adjective 'negative' provides more appropriate guidance in determining what a beneficiary's right encompasses. A right to prevent something being done with trust property in the way of misallocation or mismanagement of the trust therefore more accurately represents the position. Indeed Nolan, writing on a broader canvas than concerns us here and analysing how far a beneficary's interest under a trust can be described as 'proprietary', argues that 'a beneficary's core proprietary rights [sic] . . . consist in the beneficiary's primary, negative, right to exclude non-beneficiaries from the enjoyment of trust assets' ((2006) 122 LQR 232 at 233).

It is then no surprise that we are forced to turn the spotlight on to trustees' duties and the capacity of beneficiaries to hold them to account if we are to understand what equitable rights the beneficiary has. And our language has slipped from that of property – equitable ownership – to that of obligation –

enforcement of duties through the exercise of rights by beneficiaries. As we shall see in later chapters establishing exactly what rights the beneficiaries should be able to exercise to enforce accountability of trustees is a matter that is still attracting the courts' attention. There we could leave the matter albeit with the trite conclusion that although the property rights element of beneficiaries' interests – equitable ownership of a trust fund – may be difficult to attribute at any given time, it is possible to ascribe a raft of equitable rights to each and every beneficiary of a trust. Yet this conclusion may underestimate the extent to which settlors, with the assistance of their advisers, are able to exploit the flexibility of the trust form, and thereby pose new challenges for trusts doctrine.

It will be recalled that one of the aims of the 'black hole trust' is to minimise the transparency of the trust so as to render beneficial ownership opaque. Another aim might be to retain either directly or indirectly control over the administration and ultimate destination of the trust fund. One technique is to appoint a person known as a protector or enforcer. The title of 'enforcer' or more often 'protector' is usually given to persons who will commonly hold both negative powers – for example, requiring their consent to certain transactions – and positive powers – for example, to appoint or remove trustees – as well as the authority to enforce the trust almost as if a beneficiary. But beneficiaries, trustees or settlors they are not! The precise nature of their powers and duties in relation to the enforcement of express trusts is best considered alongside analysis of control and accountability in trusts for persons (see Chapter 11).

A still more ambitious tactic may be to relieve the trustee of any obligation to inform beneficiaries or possible objects of a power of the existence of their 'interest' and, almost as a corollary, to deny them rights to any information from the trustees. If we also decide that it would be desirable to place the right to hold trustees to account exclusively in the hands of an enforcer or protector we are entering some rather shoaly waters. Attempts to strip beneficiaries, or possibly also objects of powers, of the legal capacity to hold trustees to account raise fundamental questions about the nature of trusts. At present this would be a step too far. How can there be a trust if the trustees cannot be held to account by beneficiaries? As Millett LJ has said: 'If the beneficiaries have no rights enforceable against the trustees there are no trusts' (*Armitage v Nurse* [1998] Ch 241 at 253). In response, it may be contended that as long as there is some person – an enforcer or protector – who has the authority to hold trustees to account then the 'obligation' element of the trust is satisfied. It is unquestionably the case that the shift from an emphasis on the centrality of equitable ownership to one where 'enforceability' comes to the fore does pose difficulties for determining where, logically, one should draw the line in determining what is the irreducible core content of a trust. (See generally on this question Hayton (2001) 117 LQR 96; Hilliard (2003) 17(3) TLI 144; but cf Matthews in Hayton (ed) *Extending the Boundaries of Trusts and Similar Ring-Fenced Funds* (2002) p 203 and Parkinson [2002] 61(3) CLJ 657.) As will be seen in the next section the context in which debates about some of these matters has arisen is the present scope of and justification for one of the necessary requirements for the creation of a valid express trust, compliance with the beneficiary principle.

For the moment it is simply necessary to emphasise that many of the initiatives being outlined here are manifested predominantly in offshore jurisdictions with their own statutory framework and interpretations of trust law. The change of jurisdiction does not detract from the conceptual challenge but we need to appreciate that the response to the challenge may be influenced by the practical implications of the increasing internationalisation of trusts practice. We cannot assume that every jurisdiction will answer these fundamental questions with identical perceptions of conceptual purity. Nor can we assume that the conceptual framework of the English law of trusts will remain immune.

5. The beneficiary principle in modern trusts law

(a) Introduction

It will be recalled that one eventual product of *Morice v Bishop of Durham* was the beneficiary principle. Both the policy justification and the authority for the principle have come under scrutiny since *McPhail v Doulton*. In particular the recognition there of the remedies available to a court if called upon to execute a trust (eg by directing a scheme of distribution) questions the validity of any continuing narrow approach to those problems of enforceability which are at the heart of the beneficiary principle. Grbich, for instance, has claimed that *McPhail v Doulton* 'authoritatively extended [a] common sense remedial approach to discretionary trusts. It does not take much crystal-ball gazing to see the impact this extension will have on all the old sterile purpose trust and unincorporated association debates' (Grbich (1974) 37 MLR 643 at 656; see also Harris (1971) 87 LQR 31 and Everton [1982] Conv 118 at 121–125).

The 'sterile debates' revolve around two particular problems posed by the beneficiary principle. First, on the boundaries of the law of charitable trusts it may operate to invalidate a 'purpose trust' which falls outside the legal definition of charitable purpose thereby demarcating the border between private and public trusts; and, second, it can frustrate a donor's attempt to make a gift to a non-charitable unincorporated association. Some practical and conceptual consequences of these problems are considered further in Chapters 17 and 18, and also in Chapter 15 where the apparent departure from a strict application of the beneficiary principle in the commercial context of a 'Quistclose' trust is examined. Nevertheless, the beneficiary principle still stands as one of the formal requirements for the validity of a private express trust and it is convenient to consider here how firmly established it is in principle.

(b) The principle established

The student becomes accustomed to meeting rules and then immediately being introduced to the qualifying exceptions. However, it has been said that so great are the number of exceptions to the beneficiary principle that it was open to doubt as to which was the rule and which the exception (see Leigh (1955) 18 MLR 120 at 127), and the principle did experience only fluctuating recognition in the century following *Morice v Bishop of Durham*. It made a brief appearance in early editions of *Lewin on Trusts* but disappeared after its apparent firm rejection by North J in *Re Dean* (1889) 41 Ch D 552 – a case concerning a trust for the maintenance of horses and hounds. The modern line of authority began with dicta of Lord Parker in *Bowman v Secular Society Ltd* [1917] AC 406, received further support from Harman J in *Re Wood* [1949] Ch 498 and was then affirmed by Roxburgh J in *Re Astor's Settlement Trusts*, where the justifications for the rule were, for the first time since *Morice v Bishop of Durham*, fully considered.

In 1945 Viscount Astor and his son David settled substantially all the shares of Observer Ltd (proprietors of the *Observer* newspaper). The income of the settled fund was to be applied for a number of non-charitable purposes including: (i) the maintenance of good understanding between nations; (ii) the preservation of the independence and integrity of newspapers; and (iii) the protection of newspapers from being absorbed or controlled by combines.

Re Astor's Settlement Trusts [1952] Ch 534

Roxburgh J: Mr Jennings and Mr Buckley have submitted that [the trusts] are void on two grounds: (1) that they are not trusts for the benefit of individuals; (2) that they are void for uncertainty.

Lord Parker considered the first of these two questions in his speech in *Bowman v Secular Society Ltd* [1917] AC 406 and I will cite [the following] important passage . . . : 'A trust to be valid must be for the benefit of individuals, which this is certainly not, or must be in that class of gifts for the benefit of the public which the courts in this country recognise as charitable in the legal as opposed to the popular sense of that term.'

. . . I will first consider whether Lord Parker's propositions can be attacked from a base of principle.

The typical case of a trust is one in which the legal owner of property is constrained by a court of equity so to deal with it as to give effect to the equitable rights of another. These equitable rights have been hammered out in the process of litigation in which a claimant on equitable grounds has successfully asserted rights against a legal owner or other person in control of property. Prima facie, therefore, a trustee would not be expected to be subject to an equitable obligation unless there was somebody who could enforce a correlative equitable right, and the nature and extent of that obligation would be worked out in proceedings for enforcement. This is what I understand by Lord Parker's first proposition.

At an early stage, however, the courts were confronted with attempts to create trusts for charitable purposes which there was no equitable owner to enforce.

Roxburgh J explained the Attorney-General's role in enforcing charitable trusts.

But if the purposes are not charitable, great difficulties arise both in theory and in practice. In theory, because having regard to the historical origins of equity it is difficult to visualise the growth of equitable obligations which nobody can enforce, and in practice, because it is not possible to contemplate with equanimity the creation of large funds devoted to non-charitable purposes which no court and no department of state can control, or in the case of maladministration reform. Therefore, Lord Parker's . . . proposition would prima facie appear to be well founded. Moreover, it gains no little support from the practical consideration that . . . no case has been found in the reports in which the court has ever directly enforced a non-charitable purpose against a trustee. Indeed where, as in the present case, the only beneficiaries are purposes and an at present unascertainable person, it is difficult to see who could initiate such proceedings. If the purposes are valid trusts, the settlors have retained no beneficial interest and could not initiate them. It was suggested that the trustees might proceed ex parte to enforce the trusts against themselves. I doubt that, but at any rate nobody could enforce the trusts against them. This point, in my judgment, is of importance, because in most of the cases which are put forward to disprove Lord Parker's propositions the court had indirect means of enforcing the execution of the non-charitable purpose.

Roxburgh J then commented that 'on the one side' there is Lord Parker's proposition and continued:

On the other side is a group of cases relating to horses and dogs, graves and monuments – matters arising under wills and intimately connected with the deceased – in which the courts have found means of escape from these general propositions and also *Re Thompson* [1934] Ch 342 and *Re Price* [1943] Ch 422 which I have endeavoured to explain. *Re Price* belongs to another field. The rest may, I think, properly be regarded as anomalous and exceptional and in no way destructive of the proposition which traces descent from or through Sir William Grant through Lord Parker to Harman J. . . . I hold that the trusts here in question are void on the first of the grounds submitted by Mr Jennings and Mr Buckley.

The second ground upon which the relevant trusts are challenged is uncertainty. If (contrary to my view) an enumeration of purposes outside the realm of charities can take the place of an enumeration of beneficiaries, the purposes must, in my judgment, be stated in phrases which embody definite concepts and the means by which the trustees are to try to attain them must also be prescribed with a sufficient degree of certainty.

Roxburgh J held that many of the purposes were uncertain and concluded:

Accordingly, in my judgment, the trusts for the application of income during 'the specified period' are also void for uncertainty.

> But while I have reached my decision on two separate grounds, both, I think, have their origin in a single principle, namely, that a court of equity does not recognise as valid a trust which it cannot both enforce and control. This seems to me to be good equity and good sense.

The Court of Appeal in *Re Endacott* [1960] Ch 232 endorsed Roxburgh J's general approach and in particular his refusal to follow the 'anomalous and exceptional' cases. In Harman LJ's words these decisions were (at 250) 'perhaps merely occasions when Homer has nodded' and 'stand by themselves and ought not to be increased in number, nor indeed followed, except where the one is exactly like the other'.

The adequacy of a doctrinal analysis which portrays the anomalous and exceptional cases as representing a breach with an established beneficiary principle, remains open to question, however. Cotterell, for instance, suggests that *Re Dean* was consistent with the interpretation placed upon *Morice v Bishop of Durham* in other nineteenth-century cases ('Some Sociological Aspects of the Controversy Around the Legal Validity of Private Purposes Trusts' in Goldstein (ed) *Equity and Contemporary Legal Developments* (1992) p 302 at p 325; cf the classic conventional analysis of Gray (1902) 15 Harvard LR 509). On this view, it is the change of judicial approach evident in the modern cases that needs to be explained. It may simply be that a perceptible shift in the objects of purpose trusts, from their very limited scope in the early cases, towards purposes more contentious (*Bowman v Secular Society Ltd*), more abstract (*Re Astor*) and more eccentric (*Re Shaw* [1957] 1 WLR 729) engendered an intuitive judicial scepticism about the utility of facilitating a broad category of non-charitable purpose trusts.

In any event, since *Re Astor* the contemporary rationale for the principle is conventionally couched in terms of 'enforceability and control'. Indeed the so-called anomalous cases are usually termed 'trusts of imperfect obligation' because of doubts as to the trustees' duty to perform the trust. Such trusts, where upheld, must comply with perpetuity rules (see further Chapter 6). These trusts are conventionally classified in the following manner (Morris and Leach *The Rule Against Perpetuities* (2nd edn, 1962) p 310; and see generally *Hanbury and Martin* pp 374–379; *Parker and Mellows* pp 80–85):

(1) trusts for the erection or maintenance of monuments or graves;
(2) trusts for the saying of masses in private for the dead. Gifts for the saying of masses in public are charitable and therefore are not affected by perpetuity rules (see further Chapter 19);
(3) trusts for the maintenance of particular animals; and
(4) miscellaneous cases, once including trusts for the promotion and further-ance of fox-hunting, an activity now arguably illegal under the Hunting Act 2004.

Given our apparent 'human weakness' for the Rovers and Tinkerbells of this world it is not a surprise to discover that testamentary provision for the care of a particular animal, and also for the maintenance of graves, remains quite common (see the survey of probate practitioners in Brown [2007] Conv 148; see also Pawlowski and Summers [2007] Conv 440 on proposals for statutory reform in this area). The fact that an imperfect obligation trust or even an outright bequest to a legatee accompanied by a letter of wishes is unenforceable at law evidently does not dissuade people. And why should it? Our everyday trust in others does not always need the threat of legal sanction to ensure its being fulfilled, although the legal travails over the late Leona Helmsley's attempted gift of US$12m to her aptly named dog Trouble may serve as a cautionary tale (see *New York Times* 17 June 2008). Nevertheless, following *Re Endacott* it is clear that these 'concessions to human weakness or sentiment' will not be extended further and, subject to what is discussed in (c) below, trusts for non-charitable purposes are likely to fail unless contained within these narrow boundaries.

(c) The principle undermined?

Implicit in the beneficiary principle is the notion that non-charitable trusts can be divided into trusts for persons and trusts for purposes. This demarcation, however straightforward in theory, is not easy to apply where a combination of persons and purposes appears. Examples are a trust for the purpose of educating A's children or a trust to maintain two old ladies during their lives (see *Re Abbott Fund Trusts* [1900] 2 Ch 326). Are they trusts for purposes, with an indication of who is to benefit by the fulfilment of the purpose, or trusts for persons with the purpose merely signifying the motive for the gift? Should validity depend on whether there exists someone factually capable of enforcing the trust? These issues were confronted in *Re Denley's Trust Deed*, where land was conveyed to trustees by H H Martyn & Co Ltd 'to be maintained and used . . . for the purpose of a recreation or sports ground primarily for the benefit of employees . . . and secondarily for the benefit of such other . . . persons (if any) as the trustees may allow to use the same . . .' (Clause 2(c)). By clause 2(d) the employees were entitled to the use and enjoyment of the land.

Re Denley's Trust Deed [1969] 1 Ch 373 at 382

Goff J: Mr Mills has argued that the trust in clause 2(c) in the present case is either a trust for the benefit of individuals, in which case he argues that they are an unascertainable class and therefore the trust is void for uncertainty, or that it is a purpose trust, that is, a trust for providing recreation, which he submits is void on the beneficiary principle, or, alternatively, that it is something of a hybrid, having the vices of both kinds.

I think there may be a purpose or object trust, the carrying out of which would benefit an individual or individuals, where that benefit is so indirect or intangible or which is otherwise so framed as not to give those persons any locus standi to apply to the court to enforce the trust, in which case the beneficiary principle would, as it seems to me, apply to invalidate the trust, quite apart from any question of uncertainty or perpetuity. Such cases can be considered if and when they arise. The present is not, in my judgment, of that character, and it will be seen that clause 2(d) of the trust deed expressly states that, subject to any rules and regulations made by the trustees, the employees of the company shall be entitled to the use and enjoyment of the land. Apart from this possible exception, in my judgment the beneficiary principle of *Re Astor's Settlement Trusts*, which was approved in *Re Endacott* [1960] Ch 232 – see particularly by Harman LJ (at 250) – is confined to purpose or object trusts which are abstract or impersonal. The objection is not that the trust is for a purpose or object per se, but that there is no beneficiary or cestui que trust. The rule is so expressed in *Lewin on Trusts*, 16th ed (1964), p 17, and, in my judgment, with the possible exception I have mentioned, rightly so. In *Re Wood* [1949] Ch 498 Harman J said: '. . . a gift on trust must have a cestui que trust. . . .'

Again in *Leahy v A-G for New South Wales* [1959] AC 457 Viscount Simonds, delivering the judgment of the Privy Council, said (at 478):

'A gift can be made to persons (including a corporation) but it cannot be made to a purpose or to an object: so also,' – and these are the important words – 'a trust may be created for the benefit of persons as cestuis que trust but not for a purpose or object unless the purpose or object be charitable. For a purpose or object cannot sue, but, if it be charitable, the Attorney-General can sue to enforce it.'

Where, then, the trust, though expressed as a purpose, is directly or indirectly for the benefit of an individual or individuals, it seems to me that it is in general outside the mischief of the beneficiary principle.

Goff J referred to *Re Harpur's Will Trusts* [1962] Ch 78; *Re Aberconway's Settlement Trusts* [1953] Ch 647 and *Re Bowes* [1896] 1 Ch 507, all of which he considered supported his view.

The trust in the present case is limited in point of time so as to avoid any infringement of the rule against perpetuities and, for the reasons I have given, it does not offend against the beneficiary principle; and unless, therefore, it be void for uncertainty, it is a valid trust.

As it is a private trust and not a charitable one, it is clear that, however it be regarded, the individuals for whose benefit it is designed must be ascertained or capable of ascertainment at any given time: see *IRC v Broadway Cottages Trust.*

It was conceded that the class of employees was ascertainable and Goff J held that the provision as to 'other persons' constituted a power and was not void for uncertainty.

There is, however, one other aspect of uncertainty which has caused me some concern; that is, whether this is in its nature a trust which the court can control. . . .

Goff J quoted Lord Eldon's words from *Morice v Bishop of Durham* above, p 207.

> The difficulty I have felt is that there may well be times when some of the employees wish to use the sports club for one purpose while others desire to use it at the same time for some other purpose of such natures that the two cannot be carried on together. The trustees could, of course, control this by making rules and regulations under clause 2(d) of the trust deed, but they might not. In any case, the employees would probably agree amongst themselves, but I cannot assume that they would. If there were an impasse, the court could not resolve it, because it clearly could not either exercise the trustees' power to make rules or settle a scheme, this being a non-charitable trust: see *Re Astor's Settlement Trusts*.
>
> In my judgement, however, it would not be right to hold the trust void on this ground. The court can, as it seems to me, execute the trust both negatively by restraining any improper disposition or use of the land, and positively by ordering the trustees to allow the employees and such other persons (if any) as they may admit to use the land for the purpose of a recreation or sports ground....
>
> In my judgement, therefore, the provisions of clause 2(c) are valid.

Consider the following points:

(1) Goff J suggests that a trust such as that in *Re Denley* falls outside the 'mischief of the beneficiary principle'. What do you think that he considers the 'mischief' to be?

(2) Did Goff J consider that a factual interest in the carrying out of a trust was sufficient to provide the employees with locus standi to enforce the trust, or did he consider them to be 'licensees' under clause 2(d)? (See McKay (1973) 37 Conv (NS) 420 at 426–428.) Goff J indicates that even though (i) the beneficiary principle is satisfied, (ii) the class to be benefited is sufficiently certain, and (iii) there is no infringement of the rule against perpetuities, the trust may still be invalid if the court cannot control it – citing Lord Eldon's judgment from *Morice v Bishop of Durham* as authority. Assuming that there is a distinct class of 'persons/purposes' trusts (but see (3) below) is Goff J identifying an additional requirement for validity, analogous to that of 'administrative unworkability' subsequently adopted in *McPhail v Doulton*?

(3) Vinelott J commented on the *Denley* case in *Re Grant's Will Trusts* [1979] 3 All ER 359 at 368 (see generally Chapter 17) as follows:

> That case on a proper analysis . . . falls altogether outside the categories . . . of purpose trusts. I can see no distinction in principle between a trust to permit a class defined by reference to employment to use and enjoy land in accordance with rules to be made at the discretion of trustees on the one hand, and, on the other hand, a trust to distribute income at the discretion of trustees among a class, defined by reference to,

for example, relationship to the settlor. In both cases the benefit to be taken by any member of the class is at the discretion of the trustees, but any member of the class can apply to the court to compel the trustees to administer the trust in accordance with its terms.

This interpretation or explanation of *Re Denley* views the case as simply a trust for individuals and not a purpose trust at all. If one accepts the orthodoxy that there must always be a 'beneficiary' and not just some person with locus standi to act as an enforcer, then it would seem necessary to interpret *Re Denley* in that manner (see in particular the support for the analysis of Vinelott J by Matthews in Oakley (ed) *Trends in Contemporary Trust Law* (1996) 1 and Millett QC (as he then was) (1985) 101 LQR 269 at 281–282, but note the latter's puzzling reference to *Denley* as being concerned with 'the upkeep of a *garden* [emphasis added] for the use of employees'). It is, however, not easy to reconcile this interpretation of *Re Denley* with either the facts of the case or the judgment of Goff J. Moreover Vinelott J's observation that he can see no distinction between the 'two classes of cases' to which he refers is puzzling. One form of discretion is of an administrative nature – 'making rules for the use and enjoyment of land by all those employees able to benefit'– whereas the other – 'discretion to distribute income among a class' – is plainly dispositive.

This is not simply a dispute about labelling: if a mixed persons-purposes trust is recognised as something distinct from a trust for persons only, then whilst the enforcement powers of the members of the classes may be identical their beneficial entitlement may not be. In particular there would seem to be no reason for applying the rule in *Saunders v Vautier* (see Chapter 7) to such a trust. To do so could potentially allow the 'persons' if they were all agreed to defeat the purpose and claim the trust property. It is at least open to doubt whether that outcome would have been envisaged by Goff J as a corollary of his decision (see (4) below). On the other hand, using a widely drawn class of objects under the post-*McPhail v Doulton* certainty of objects test for discretionary trusts would (i) largely negate the likelihood of this outcome, and (ii) reinforce the possibility of an extremely flexible trust (but cf the failure on grounds of administrative unworkability of the trust in *R v District Auditor, ex p West Yorkshire Metropolitan County Council* [1986] RVR 24).

(4) It will be recalled that in *Re Denley's Trust Deed* Goff J referred to *Re Bowes*, a case that he submitted supported his conclusion. In *Re Bowes* money directed to be expended in the planting of trees on an estate part of settled land was held to belong to the owners of the estate absolutely. This is really an illustration of a principle of construction laid down in *Re Sanderson's Trusts* in the following terms: 'If a gross sum be given, or if the whole income of the property be given, and a special purpose be assigned

for that gift, the court always regards the gift as absolute, *and the purpose merely as the motive of the gift . . .*' (per Page Wood VC (1857) 3 K & J 497 at 503; emphasis added; see also *Re Andrew's Trust* [1905] 2 Ch 48 and *Re Osoba* [1979] 1 WLR 247). Whilst it may have been a useful case to pray in aid of the decision that Goff J wished to reach we would suggest that cases such as *Re Bowes*, on the face of it for a purpose but where the purpose is construed as a motive for the gift, are of a different order to *Re Denley*. In *Re Denley* in our view there was no question of the employees having any right to call for the trust property, even if they were all agreed on this.

(5)   In *Re Osoba* ([1978] 1 WLR 791; [1979] 1 WLR 247 CA; criticised by Rickett (1978) 37 CLJ 219) a residuary estate was bequeathed by the testator on trust 'for the maintenance [of my second wife] and for the training of my daughter [A] up to university grade and for the maintenance of my aged mother'. The testator's mother predeceased him and by the time the case came before the court his second wife had also died and A's university education had been completed. The purposes having been carried out, one question before the court was whether the residue was held on trust for the persons named or whether there was a partial intestacy, in which case the son from the testator's first marriage would have an entitlement. The Court of Appeal, applying *Re Sanderson*, held that the will created a trust for the benefit of the widow, the daughter and the mother absolutely as joint tenants, in effect for A as the sole survivor. But let us suppose someone in A's position had decided that university was not for her at the age of 18, that travelling the world would be more educational and consequently asked the trustees to pay the money over to her. If one assumes that a combination of the rule in *Saunders v Vautier* and a *Re Sanderson* 'purpose interpreted as motive' approach apply then there would seem to be no legal obstacle to the trust being terminated in this way and a world tour being undertaken. But this outcome would completely flout the *express* intention of the testator. Could, though, the courts if faced with such a case adopt a third option, namely the application of a *Re Denley*-like approach whereby as long as the purpose is capable of being furthered the trustees could resist any demand from the beneficiary to terminate the trust? In effect this would require the *Saunders v Vautier* rights of the beneficiary to be in suspense for an admittedly uncertain period. The testator might appreciate that there would be no practical way of preventing the trustees and the beneficiary from agreeing amongst themselves to terminate the trust should they choose to do so. Perhaps the testator would just have to trust the trustees. It only remains to add, for the avoidance of doubt, that not only is the 'problem' hypothetical but so also is the proffered solution, there being no authority for such a 'third option'.

(6)   *McPhail v Doulton* [1970] 2 All ER 228 may affect the rationale for the beneficiary principle that 'equity does not recognise a trust which it cannot

both enforce and control' (per Roxburgh J in *Re Astor*) in three further ways:

(i) Does the acceptance in *McPhail v Doulton* of a jurisdiction for the court to execute a trust more flexibly if called upon to do so suggest that a similar approach could be applied to a trust with purposes such as those in *Re Astor*?

(ii) If the beneficiary principle is based on the premise that 'a trustee would not be expected to be subject to an equitable obligation unless there was somebody who could enforce a correlative equitable right' (per Roxburgh J), to what extent does the difficulty of identifying the equitable ownership in a discretionary trust undermine the principle?

(iii) If a consequence of *McPhail v Doulton* was to elevate 'the effecting of a settlor's intention' over 'the demands of strict enforceability', could this preference equally justify a relaxation of the beneficiary principle (eg to permit enforcement by those with a factual interest in the performance of the trust)? (Cf Harris (1971) 87 LQR 31 at 56–57; and McKay (1973) 37 Conv 420 at 434–435.) One requirement of 'strict enforceability' is that there must be someone with a *positive* interest in enforcing the trust. It is not considered sufficient that there may exist some person, such as a residuary legatee or next-of-kin, who would be entitled to the trust property were the trust to fail. Such persons would certainly have standing to complain if the trust property were misapplied, but what incentive would they have if the remedy were to be, for instance, the appointment by the court of new trustees to carry out the purpose? Certainly in those anomalous trusts to maintain graves or animals for a limited period, those ultimately entitled to the property have a material interest in the trust *not* being performed. As Waters points out, there will be more for them to receive if they 'allow the grave to be overgrown with weeds or the animals to die of neglect' (*Law of Trusts in Canada* (3rd edn, 2005) p 633).

(7) In some jurisdictions the requirement for positive enforcement has been satisfied formally by creating a statutory enforcement mechanism (see (d) 'A "protector" postscript' below). Notwithstanding the absence of a statutory enforcement mechanism in this jurisdiction, it has been argued that private purpose trusts should be permitted so long as some person or persons is/are appointed by settlors to enforce the trust (Hayton [2001] 117 LQR 96 at 99–102). Assuming that such persons would not possess beneficial interests in the trust property there is no doubt that this notion of an 'enforcer principle' rather than a 'beneficiary principle' does not fit comfortably with established trusts law doctrines (see eg Matthews in Hayton (ed) *Extending the Boundaries of Trusts and Similar Ring-Fenced Funds* (2002) p 203). Nevertheless, as we have sought to emphasise in

discussions throughout this chapter, an important question is whether established principles should be regarded as immutable in light of the changes initiated by the decision of the House of Lords in *McPhail v Doulton*.

(8) Gardner has expressed scepticism about the merits of the enforceability principle (*An Introduction to the Law of Trusts* (2nd edn, 2003) pp 260–264). In the absence of legislation he propounds a more radical solution, suggesting that the arguments against recognising a category of valid though unenforceable trusts 'seems less supportable than the contrary view' (p 264). In effect this proposition places a premium on the integrity of trustees, but, as Gardner points out (p 263), 'compliant trustees regard their legal duties as such and try to perform them properly, irrespective of their enforceability' and 'most trustees seem to be compliant'. Assuming that Gardner's proposal deftly sidesteps the reasons advanced in *Re Astor* for the requirement of strict enforceability, would recognition of 'unenforceable trusts' nevertheless inevitably blur the conceptual distinction between trusts, powers and absolute ownership?

(9) Even if the courts were to be inclined to hold that an abstract purpose trust, such as that in *Re Astor*, could overcome or circumvent the requirements of enforceability, another obstacle to validity, one of policy, would still remain. It is improbable that the courts would be prepared to countenance *any* purpose trust no matter how eccentric. Instead the courts would be likely to exercise their discretion so as to invalidate trusts for 'useless' or 'capricious' purposes (as in *Brown v Burdett* (1882) 21 Ch D 667 – rooms of a house to be sealed up for 20 years; and the remarkable wills of the M'Caigs of Oban dedicated to constructing artistic towers and statuary on their estates, *M'Caig v University of Glasgow* 1907 SC 231 and *M'Caig's Trustees v Kirk-Session of United Free Church of Lismore* 1915 1 SLT 152). Indeed, a judicial reluctance to countenance non-charitable purpose trusts of a public nature (such as those in *Re Astor* or the *West Yorkshire* case) can be advanced as providing a plausible policy explanation for maintaining the beneficiary principle (see Harpum (1986) 45 CLJ 392). Contemporary liberalisation of the definition of charitable purposes (see Chapter 19) in the direction of recognising as charitable many, perhaps most, non-contentious purposes of a beneficial nature could paradoxically reinforce the adoption by the courts of a restrictive approach.

(10) In conclusion, write the Court of Appeal judgment if there had been an appeal in *R v District Auditor, ex p West Yorkshire Metropolitan County Council* (noted above, p 239 and see Harpum (1986) 45 CLJ 392).

Lest the speculative discussion above has tended to blur the 'is' and the 'ought', the result of *Re Astor's Settlement Trusts* [1952] Ch 534, supplemented by judgments of the Court of Appeal in *Re Endacott* [1960] Ch 232 and the Privy Council in *Leahy v A-G for New South Wales* [1959] AC 457, is that the beneficiary principle is firmly established and could only be overturned by legislation or the House of Lords.

Lastly there is a venerable body of literature (Ames (1892) 5 Harv LR 389; cf Gray (1902) 15 Harv LR 67; Scott (1945) 58 Harv LR 548), suggesting that an instrument purporting to create a purpose trust may sometimes be validated by construing the trust as a power. This possibility, however, seems effectively to have been frustrated by the Court of Appeal in *IRC v Broadway Cottages Trust* [1955] Ch 20 at 36: 'We do not think that a valid power is to be spelt out of an invalid trust' (followed in *Re Endacott* [1960] Ch 232).

(d) A 'protector' postscript

Reference is made above to the possibility of sidestepping by statutory means the limitations of the beneficiary principle. A pioneer in this regard was Bermuda with the Bermudan Trusts (Special Provisions) Act 1989 which facilitates the creation of purpose trusts. Bermuda is no longer a special case; the 1990s saw such a proliferation of statutory purpose trust regimes that settlors and their advisers can now choose from one of twenty or so different offshore locations if they wish to establish some form of purpose trust (see eg Baxendale-Walker *Purpose Trusts* (1999); Duckworth *STAR Trusts* (1998)). One feature common to almost all of these regimes is that specific provision is made for some person to enforce the trust. As we noted previously the title of 'enforcer' or more often 'protector' is usually given to such persons. Bermuda itself has taken one further step with the Trusts (Special Provisions) Amendment Act 1998. Under s 12B(2) the range of persons who can enforce the trust has been extended beyond 'the enforcer' to include 'any other person whom the court considers has sufficient interest in the enforcement of the trust' (see Anderson [1999] PCB 4 at 219).

Our immediate concern, however, is with the how and why of these contemporary developments. A principal objective of purpose trusts established under these regimes is to render beneficial ownership as remote and undetectable as possible. Not surprisingly such trusts with their attendant financial costs are not likely to be concerned with the erection of monuments or the maintenance of pets. Instead the belief is that they can be used to achieve a variety of purposes ranging from facilitating tax-efficient family provision to structuring commercial transactions through a purpose trust to achieve 'off balance sheet' arrangements, invisible to regulators, creditors and competitors alike (see eg Matthews 'The New Trust: Obligations Without Rights?' and Waters 'The Protector: New Wine in Old Bottles' in Oakley (ed) *Trends in Contemporary Trust Law* (1996) chs 1 and 4 respectively; and generally Baxendale-Walker, ch 10). As Matthews summarises the position: 'the offshore trusts jurisdictions saw that there was a need for a vehicle that could truly be said to belong to no one beneficially, and which could be slotted into complicated commercial transactions without difficulty' (at p 28).

Yet in a sense the reaction of the offshore jurisdictions represents simply the response of the market to the demand for a product. And there is nothing new in this development. An underpinning theme of this chapter has been the creativity of the practitioner responding to the perceived needs of the client. As stated earlier in this chapter, one illustration in our view was the re-emergence of the discretionary trust and its adaptation to tax-planning and commercial ends. In the example of the new 'purpose trusts' we see again a 'bottom-up' development, but this time incorporating the dimensions of geographical location and legal jurisdiction to complement the fragmentation of ownership and control. It remains to be seen whether the various statutory evasions of the beneficiary principle do succeed in subverting the conceptual purity of the notion that under any division of ownership it must be possible to locate both legal and equitable property ownership. It also remains to be seen whether this particular manifestation of globalising trends will prove to be inscrutable to national fiscal and regulatory regimes. (See generally the reservations expressed by Matthews (above) and his debate with Duckworth about the Cayman Islands Special Trusts (Alternative Regime) Law 1997 in Matthews (1997) 11(3) TLI at 67 and (1998) 12(2) TLI at 98 and Duckworth (1998) 12(1) TLI at 16 and (1999) 13 TLI 158.)

6

Trusts and public policy

1. Introduction

An express trust satisfying the requirements of formality, certainty and complete constitution will be valid unless it contravenes certain overriding limitations which stem broadly speaking from public policy considerations. These limitations can be grouped for convenience into three categories. One category is concerned with attempts to use the trust format to defeat the claims of the creditors of settlors or beneficiaries or even the claims of one's spouse or partner when relationships break down. A second category comprises a loose class of prohibitions which cluster under the umbrella of public policy but are primarily concerned not to undermine accepted notions of morality and family solidarity. Trusts which might tend to interfere with the sanctity of marriage, for example, will be held void. The final category of limitations concerns the plane of time: while the law may place few restraints on the types of interest a settlor can create and the conditions to which they may be subject, restrictions are imposed through rules of perpetuity, accumulations and inalienability on the duration of trusts.

These limitations and their respective policy justifications form the subject-matter of this chapter.

At first sight, however, it must seem rather odd to devote a chapter to trusts and public policy, when a recurrent theme in the book is to weigh the rules of trusts law against non-legal policy considerations and to assess how the development of those rules has been influenced by such considerations. And in a sense, as the description above implies, this is a chapter of convenience: as a focus of study, it assembles discrete issues about limits to the creation of trusts around an organising theme, namely the relationship of those issues to aspects of public policy. The term 'aspects', however, gives a clue to a further reason for the chapter, extending beyond convenience. Public policy is merely a shorthand term devoid of content unless we identify the particular policy under consideration (eg 'freedom of disposition' or 'protection of creditors'), the values inherent in it, and the interests that any particular policy advances. Indeed the rules discussed in this chapter do not reflect any one public policy. Public policy is a unifying theme only in so far as it prompts us in each of the discrete areas to consider, for instance, how closely the rules are aligned with a particular policy and which one amongst conflicting policies do the rules support. Furthermore, since policy is not immutable, are the legal rules responsive to change or do changes in economic and social circumstances leave us with a rule without a reason?

(a) Public policy and freedom of disposition

In concentrating on specific policy arguments it is also important to recognise that at the heart of a liberal property system lies a basic paradox that impinges in varying degrees on all the categories of limitations described above. The point may be put shortly, if rather simply, as follows. If in a pure liberal or market society the market is to carry out its function of allocation of resources amongst various uses, property must be freely alienable. This seems to require individual freedom of disposition of property, so a pure market society will require a system of property law designed to sustain freedom of disposition. But if freedom of disposition conferred on a person disposing of property means that he or she can regulate the circumstances in which, and the extent to which, the recipients can deal with the property, the recipients do *not* have freedom of disposition. In this sense unrestricted freedom of disposition cannot logically be permitted and fully maintained. The paradox can be summarised as follows: 'if the donor of a property interest tries to restrict the donee's freedom to dispose of that interest, the legal system in deciding whether to enforce or void that restriction, must resolve whose freedom it will protect, that of the donor or that of the donee' (Alexander 'The Dead Hand and the Law of Trusts in the Nineteenth Century' (1985) 37 Stanford LR 1189).

How the state resolves this conflict between competing 'freedoms' is a theme underlying much of the policy discussion in this chapter. It is as well to clarify here that references to 'resolution' of the conflict by the state do not imply that legal development faithfully reflects reasoned responses, whether in statute or common law. The influence of legal formalism, or more specifically in this context what has been pejoratively labelled as 'scholasticism', must also be considered, as the following section illustrates.

(b) Limitations in gifts, public policy and legal logic

(1) Conditions precedent and subsequent

A donor may wish not only to restrict a donee's freedom of disposition but also to influence the donee's behaviour in other ways by attaching conditions to the property interest. A brief digression is necessary to identify two of the types of condition that a donor may seek to impose; a condition precedent and a condition subsequent (see Oakley *Megarry's Manual of the Law of Real Property* (8th edn, 2002) pp 41–45 for a comprehensive account). An understanding of conditions and the criteria against which their validity is tested provides us with insights into a significant aspect of the interplay between formal legal reasoning and public policy in this area.

A condition precedent exists where A gives property to B but subject to a condition that the interest is not to commence (vest) until the occurrence of some event. An example is a transfer of property on trust for B if and when B qualifies as a civil engineer. In contrast a condition subsequent operates to terminate an already existing interest, for example, to cite a quaint example of Victoriana, property is held on trust for B so long as B does not marry a domestic servant (*Jenner v Turner* (1880) 16 Ch D 188). B's present enjoyment of the interest will be brought to a premature end if the condition is infringed. Both of the above illustrations involve dispositions on trust but this is not essential; a gift subject to a condition can be free-standing. Also the obligation imposed can be stated in positive terms. Thus, in more contemporary vein, an elderly parent might give a house or flat to, for instance, her daughter on condition that she looks after the parent in the premises (see eg *Ellis v Chief Adjudication Officer* [1998] 1 FLR 184). Here again if the condition is valid but is infringed, as for instance by evicting the hapless parent, the daughter's interest in the property would terminate.

The caveat about validity is important. There are limits on the conditions that can be imposed. One mentioned briefly in the previous chapter is that the condition must satisfy the requirement of certainty (*Re Barlow's Will Trusts* [1979] 1 All ER 296). In our 'aged parent' example the condition – 'that the daughter would look after the parent in the flat' – was held by the Court of Appeal in *Ellis* not to be too uncertain. Otton LJ interpreted it to mean that the parent was to remain in the home 'for so long as they both agreed or it was reasonably practicable to do so'. It should be noted, *Ellis* notwithstanding, that the certainty test for conditions subsequent has been stated to be stricter than that for conditions precedent (see *Re Tuck's Settlement Trusts* [1978] 1 All ER 1047; *Blathwayt v Baron Cawley* [1976] AC 397 at 425). This distinction is unfortunate as it is not always easy to distinguish between the two types of condition. Indeed Lord Denning was prompted in a typically robust statement in *Re Tuck's Settlement Trust* to deplore both the dichotomies on the grounds that 'they serve in every case to defeat the intention of the settlor' (at 1052). The way the settlor's intention is defeated is that the condition is void if uncertain. The consequence is that where a condition subsequent is void the interest becomes absolute and not subject to premature termination. In *Ellis*, for instance, had the condition been uncertain and therefore void, the daughter would have retained the flat leaving the mother to find alternative accommodation and reliant on Social Security. With conditions precedent a further distinction is drawn, that between realty and personalty (see *Re Elliott* [1952] Ch 217). Where realty is concerned the complete gift fails if the condition is void, whereas with personalty in contrast the gift normally takes effect, the condition being effectively ignored. Of course, conditions may also be void on grounds of immorality, illegality or being otherwise contrary to public policy.

A further ground for holding a condition subsequent, though not a condition precedent, void was if it purported to take away the freedom of alienation. The reason for this seems to have originated from a view that general restraints on alienation were seen as 'repugnant' to the nature of a fee simple, it being argued that one of the incidents of ownership is a right to sell or otherwise dispose of the property. In other words the condition would be void not because it was contrary to public policy but because alienability as a matter of legal logic could not be severed from the nature of the property interest. The incipient circularity of this doctrine and its underpinning reasoning was savaged by Glanville Williams ((1943) 59 LQR 343 at 346):

> The proposition is not one of empirical fact but one of law. Hence when one asserts that the power to alienate cannot be divorced from a fee simple *because* it is of the essence of a fee simple that it can be alienated, one is not really giving a reason for the rule, though appearing to do so; one is simply expressing the same rule over again by a different linguistic formula.

The point of Williams's criticism was that a criterion of repugnancy should be replaced by one of public policy. This would not necessarily result in different substantive decisions but spurious logic could be dispensed with and decisions opened up to informed scrutiny.

The concept of alienability as an inherent characteristic of property was not restricted, however, to the estate of a fee simple. Significantly for present purposes it was extended to other interests classified as proprietary. The outcome is that in a gift on trust to A for life, a condition subsequent that 'if A shall seek to charge or otherwise dispose of the interest or shall become bankrupt then A's interest will cease' will be void. A's interest will therefore not be subject to premature termination, an outcome that A might be expected to approve. But A's reaction would be premature since it overlooks the consequences of insolvency law. As will be seen in section 2 (Family Trusts and Creditors) below if A were to become bankrupt his creditors would be able to step into A's shoes and claim his interest in the trust fund.

Before considering further some legal and policy implications of this outcome it is necessary briefly to introduce a linguistic and logical curiosity.

(2) A conundrum for public policy? The determinable interest

We could leave the explanation of conditions precedent and subsequent there but for a difficulty that the existence of a species of property interest called a 'determinable interest' raises for an understanding of this area of legal logic. A determinable interest is one which will automatically terminate on the occurrence of some specified event. Such dispositions do not fall foul of the rule against 'repugnancy'. Accordingly a gift on trust for A for life or until A seeks to charge or otherwise dispose of the interest or becomes bankrupt, is a valid gift. A possesses a determinable interest that will cease on the occurrence of the determining event or 'limitation'.

But where, you may say, lies the difference between the example of the determinable interest and the previously mentioned condition subsequent? Such distinctions as exist are to be found in language and concept. Considering language first, 'the distinction is between a grant "to A *but if* he alienates then to B", (a condition)... and a grant "to A *until* he alienates, and then to B" (a limitation) where the gift to A comes to an end if he purports to alienate it' (*Williams* p 352).

The conceptual difference can be inferred from the linguistic: 'a limitation marks the bounds of the estate, a condition defeats the estate before it attains its boundary' (per Oakley *Megarry's Manual of the Law of Real Property* (8th edn, 2002) p 42). That different legal consequences in this context can follow from a wafer-thin linguistic distinction has prompted the criticism that it is 'little short of disgraceful to our jurisprudence that in reference to a rule professedly founded on considerations of public policy' such a verbal distinction can be admitted (*Re King's Trusts* (1892) 29 LR Ir 401 at 410), a sentiment endorsed by Pennycuick VC in *Re Sharp's Settlement Trusts* [1972] 3 All ER 151 at 156: but cf Rattie J in *Re Trusts of the Scientific Investment Pension Plan* [1998] 3 All ER 154 at 158: 'The distinction is not a particularly attractive one, being based *on form rather than substance*' [emphasis added]).

This well-established distinction would be of merely minor historical interest for our purposes but for two points of concern. One is that a determinable interest provides the basis of the protective trust, the device concerned with the protection of a beneficiary's income interest from creditors. This legal device, in essence just a particular form of express trust, is discussed in section 2(b) below. The other point of concern is that worrying reference to 'considerations of public policy'. Justification of the distinction on grounds of public policy does pose difficulties where the consequences that flow from deciding whether a clause imposes a condition subsequent or alternatively a limitation in the form of a determinable interest can be diametrically opposite. If, however, the distinction between the two is rooted in the 'scholasticism' or 'logic', spurious or otherwise, of the doctrine of repugnancy then it seems that a cornerstone of one area of the law ostensibly regulating competing claims of settlors, beneficiaries and creditors will have owed little to policy considerations.

2. Family trusts and creditors

(a) Trusts, insolvency and public policy

The arrival of an economic recession can be a harbinger of forthcoming financial disaster for individuals, families and companies. But the mutability of family fortunes does not rest solely on the crests and troughs of economic waves.

W B Yeats 'Meditations in Time of Civil War – My Descendants' *The Tower* (1928)

And what if my descendants lose the flower
Through natural declension of the soul,
Through too much business with the passing hour,
Through too much play, or marriage with a fool?
May this laborious stair and this stark tower
Become a roofless ruin that the owl
May build in the cracked masonry and cry
Her desolation to the desolate sky.

But might the mundane processes of law, in this context the trust, shield the property-owner and family from these uncertainties, economic or otherwise? If competence of descendants is a concern, placing property into trust to be invested and managed by trustees obviously reduces the autonomy of beneficiaries as compared with absolute ownership. Capital is thereby protected from destruction at the hands of present beneficiaries since the only property interest that the latter are likely to possess during the trust's existence is an entitlement to income. Supposition that the austere spectre portrayed by Yeats is an anachronism today has recently been confounded in the courts. In *Hambro v Duke of Marlborough* [1994] Ch 158 the 'unbusinesslike habits and the lack of responsibility' allegedly shown by the Marquis of Blandford, heir to the Marlborough Estates including Blenheim Palace, led the court to approve a resettlement whereby the interest of the Marquis was varied without his consent to a life interest only (see further Chapter 7 on variation of trusts).

Creating an interest in income rather than providing control over capital does not achieve full security. Where the beneficiary has a life interest this can be charged or otherwise disposed of. Indeed an interest can be sold on the auction market in London through specialist firms of auctioneers and valuers. In short, that interest is itself alienable. Consequently, in the event of a beneficiary's bankruptcy, that interest, because it is alienable, passes to the trustee in bankruptcy for the benefit of the beneficiary's creditors. It is here that the device of the protective trust can come into play by performing a 'now you see it, now you don't' conjuring trick. It provides for the beneficiary's entitlement to income to determine upon the happening of one of a number of contingencies, including bankruptcy. The income of the trust fund then ceases to belong to the beneficiary and is removed out of the direct reach of creditors, whilst at the same time being preserved for the family. It is notable that the resettlement in *Hambro v Duke of Marlborough* was in a form whereby the trust fund was to be held 'on protective trusts for the marquis for life'. The protective trust is examined in section (b) below.

If property-owners can so adapt the trust form to attempt to protect their accumulated capital and their successors from the consequences of the latter's improvidence, it may seem but a short step to using the trust to protect themselves also from economic misfortune. The attempts of settlors to defeat their own creditors are considered in section (c).

But as Keeton has pointed out, these twin desires of property-owners to conserve their wealth and to protect their successors from the consequences of improvidence 'run directly counter to the policy of practically all systems of law that property should be available for the satisfaction of its owners' liabilities' (Keeton *Modern Developments in the Law of Trusts* (1971) p 190). The policy of English law in relation to a bankrupt's assets is stated with stark simplicity in Halsbury's Laws of England (3(2) Halsbury's Laws (4th edn, 2002) para 390):

> The object of bankruptcy law is that all the property comprised in the bankrupt's estate should be realised by the trustee in bankruptcy and divided amongst the bankrupt's creditors.

In fact this statement is deceptive if taken at face value. Insolvency law is not designed to operate solely for the benefit of creditors, but is intended to strike a balance between their interests and those of debtors. Where the balance should be struck was one of the issues considered by the Insolvency Law Review Committee under the chairmanship of Sir Kenneth Cork ('The Cork Report').

Report of the Insolvency Law Review Committee (Cmnd 8558, 1982) paras 23–25

23. Society facilitates the creation of credit, and thereby multiplies the risk of insolvency. We consider that it is incumbent upon society to provide machinery which, in the event of insolvency, is adequate to ensure a fair distribution of the insolvent's assets amongst his creditors. While it will always remain essential to punish the dishonest or reckless insolvent, it is also important to devise a system of law to deal compassionately with the honest though unfortunate debtor who is often no more than a bewildered, ill-informed and overstretched consumer. The system must enable the insolvent to extract himself from a situation of hopeless debt as quickly and as cheaply and with as little fuss as possible.

24. In the complex world of credit, the legislature and, through the legislature, society has always striven hard to maintain a just balance between the creditor on the one hand and the debtor on the other. Over the centuries this balance has shifted first one way and then the other. In considering where it should be today, it must be remembered that it is the creditor who possesses the capital – which, in the aggregate, is the capital of society as a whole – to which the debtor seeks access for purposes beneficial first to himself, secondly to the creditor in providing him with a market for his capital and, thirdly, to society as a whole.

25. The economic and social implications of these relationships require a legal framework which gives the creditor confidence to extend credit, while at the same time does not encourage the potential debtor to act recklessly or irresponsibly.

The reference to 'society as a whole' suggests that insolvency policy should incorporate a dimension which reaches beyond just the interests of debtors and creditors. The conclusion arrived at in the Cork Report reflects this consideration:

THE BASIC OBJECTIVES OF INSOLVENCY LAW

192. The law of insolvency takes the form of a compact to which there are three parties: the debtor, his creditors and society. Society is concerned to relieve and protect the individual insolvent from the harassment of his creditors, and to enable him to regain financial stability and to make a fresh start. It accords him this relief in return for:

(a) Such contribution, not only from the realisation of his assets but also from his future earnings, as can reasonably be made by him without reducing him and his family to undue and socially unacceptable poverty and without depriving him of the incentive to succeed in his fresh start...

The Insolvency Act (IA) 1986 implemented many of the Cork Report recommendations. Some are relevant to issues discussed in this chapter whereas discussion of others will be considered in the Commerce and Family Breakdown parts of this book respectively.

The working of insolvency law and policy as reflected in the IA 1986 came under scrutiny in a quite wide-ranging review and consultation process conducted during 2000. The outcome was a Government White Paper published in 2001 that recommended only a shift in emphasis rather than any major change in the law of personal insolvency (Department of Trade and Industry *Insolvency – A Second Chance* (Cm 5234) paras 1.10–1.20). The objective, stated in language reminiscent of the Cork Report, was to enhance an individual's ability 'to make a fresh start'. The two principal proposals affecting personal insolvencies were to provide for the automatic discharge of most bankrupts after a maximum of 12 months rather than three years and to reduce the number of restrictions that are automatically imposed on bankrupts. These have now been enacted in Pt 10 of the Enterprise Act 2002 but the modifications to the legal framework do not in our view materially alter the terms of debate about the relationship between insolvency law and policy and trust law. To that extent the analysis set out in the Cork Report remains relevant and indeed arguably still provides the guidelines for government policy on personal insolvency.

One important question to be considered in the following pages, therefore, is how far the law of trusts can be said to operate in a fashion consistent with the policy objectives of insolvency law. But in our assessment of the appropriateness of the balance at present struck by the law of trusts, and by insolvency law so far as it impinges on the use of the trust, it is necessary to consider a fourth interest – respect for the settlor's or testator's wishes. Consequently in some circumstances the ground of debate about conflicts of interest shifts, as will be seen, from an emphasis on that between beneficiaries and their creditors, to that between settlor and beneficiaries' creditors.

First, however, we need to understand how the technique of the protective trust may operate to frustrate the claims of a beneficiary's creditors.

(b) Protective trusts

(1) The development of the protective trust

In 1811 Lord Eldon firmly established in *Brandon v Robinson* (1811) 18 Ves 429 that a condition restraining alienation could not validly be imposed on an equitable life interest. In this case one Thomas Goom was the beneficiary of an equitable life interest subject to a condition 'to the intent that the [dividends, interest and produce thereof] should not be grantable, transferable or otherwise assignable . . . '. Goom became bankrupt and his assignee claimed the benefit of the life interest. Lord Eldon ruled in favour of the assignee. The decision in effect carried over into the law of trusts the land law rules against restraints on alienability based on the doctrine of repugnancy. But the Lord Chancellor simultaneously firmly entrenched the determinable interest, which did not offend that doctrine, within the law of trusts (at 434):

> There is no doubt, that property may be given to a man, until he shall become bankrupt. It is equally clear, generally speaking, that if property is given to a man for his life, the donor cannot take away the incidents to a life estate: and, as I have observed, a disposition to a man, until he shall become bankrupt, and after his bankruptcy over, is quite different from an attempt to give to him for his life, with a proviso that he shall not sell or alien it. If that condition is so expressed as to amount to a limitation, reducing the interest short of a life estate, neither the man nor his assignees can have it beyond the period limited.

It has been suggested that 'the resulting parity between trust and property doctrines was a partial fulfilment of Eldon's objective more completely to assimilate equity and law' (Alexander (1985) 37 Stanford LR 1189 at 1199). In so far as the assimilation carried with it the repugnancy doctrine, which while striking down conditions subsequent restraining alienability did not invalidate determinable interests, it laid the foundations of the protective trust.

In the half-century following *Brandon v Robinson* there were numerous attempts to devise schemes for placing income and capital beyond the reach of creditors. Some failed because they were drafted as conditions rather than determinable interests, but the key to success was ultimately discovered in the granting of a dispositive discretion to trustees. By the mid-nineteenth century the device of adding a discretionary trust in favour of the beneficiary and his family to take effect on termination of the prior determinable interest was validated.

Why did the courts recognise a device which in practice clearly enabled a settlor to frustrate the claims of the beneficiary's creditors? Various possible explanations have been identified (see Chesterman 'Family Settlements on Trust: Landowners and the Rising Bourgeoisie' in Rubin and Sugarman (eds) *Law, Economy and Society* (1984) pp 156–157): forfeiture provisions represented a legitimate exercise of the settlor's or testator's *jus disponendi*; there were moral grounds for protecting widows and the young from their own improvidence or inexperience in financial matters; even, given the unpleasant nature of bankruptcy in mid-Victorian Britain, that fear of loss of income would be a deterrent to erstwhile spendthrifts. (See generally, McGregor *Social History and Law Reform* (1981) ch 5; Cohen (1982) 3 J Legal History 153; the factual background to a leading case *Rochford v Hackman* (1852) 9 Hare 475; and classically Charles Dickens *Little Dorrit* and *Pickwick Papers.*) In fact the search for an explanation couched in policy terms may be fruitless. As late as 1888, Kay J in *Re Dugdale* (1888) 38 Ch D 176 was stating (at 182) that 'the liability of an estate to be attached by creditors on a bankruptcy or judgment is an incident of the estate, and no attempt to deprive it of that incident by direct prohibition would be valid'. This is no more than a re-assertion of the repugnancy doctrine and the task for the draftsman 'was to discover what forms of indirect prohibition would not infringe this general principle' (Keeton *Modern Developments in the Law of Trusts* (1971) p 190). A determinable interest did not: it could not be attacked on formal legal grounds. In the event, whether through legal formalism or unarticulated policy considerations or both, the judiciary approved the combination of the determinable life interest followed by the discretionary trust.

What emerged therefore was a protective trust with a tripartite structure:

(i) a determinable interest;
(ii) a forfeiture provision specifying the determinable event; and
(iii) a discretionary trust springing up at forfeiture.

This became a standard conveyancing clause in widespread use and received statutory acceptance in the Trustee Act 1925 (TA), s 33, which provided a statutory formula for the protective trust.

(2) The Trustee Act 1925, s 33

Although settlors may still construct their own formulations if felt desirable, s 33 enables them to incorporate the statutory formula into a trust instrument by simply using the shorthand phrase 'on protective trusts for', for example, my daughter. The section will apply even where a different form of words is used, provided a settlor's intention is sufficiently clear. In *Re Wittke* [1944] Ch 166 a gift of income 'upon protective trusts for the benefit of my sister' was sufficient to incorporate s 33, it being inferred that the sister was intended to take a life interest (see also *Re Platt* [1950] CLY 4386; CLC 10917 ('for a protective life interest')). That it is a question of construction is apparent from a comparison of *Re Wittke* and *Re Trafford's Settlement* [1985] Ch 32. In the latter case the words 'upon protective trusts' were contained in a clause which also included a direction that the income should be held on an immediate discretionary trust during the life of the settlor. The latter cannot exist concurrently with a determinable life interest, so the court accepted that the reference to protective trusts was merely descriptive of the intention of the trust.

Trustee Act 1925, s 33

(1) Where any income, including an annuity or other periodical income payment, is directed to be held on protective trusts for the benefit of any person (in this section called 'the principal beneficiary') for the period of his life or for any less period, then, during that period (in this section called the 'trust period') the said income shall, without prejudice to any prior interest, be held on the following trusts, namely:

(i) Upon trust for the principal beneficiary during the trust period or until he, whether before or after the termination of any prior interest, does or attempts to do or suffers any act or thing, or until any event happens, other than an advance under any statutory or express power, whereby, if the said income were payable during that period, he would be deprived of the right to receive the same or any part thereof, in any of which cases, as well as on the termination of the trust period, whichever first happens, this trust of the said income shall fail or determine;

(ii) If the trust aforesaid fails or determines during the subsistence of the trust period, then, during the residue of that period, the said income shall be held upon trust for the application thereof for the maintenance or support, or otherwise for the benefit, of all or any one or more exclusively of the other or others of the following persons (that is to say) –

(a) the principal beneficiary and his or her wife or husband, if any, and his or her children or more remote issue, if any; or

(b) if there is no wife or husband or issue of the principal beneficiary in existence, the principal beneficiary and the persons who would, if he were actually dead, be entitled to the trust property or the income thereof or to the annuity fund, if any, or arrears of the annuity as the case may be;

as the trustees in their absolute discretion, without being liable to account for the exercise of such discretion, think fit.

(2) This section does not apply to trusts coming into operation before the commencement of this Act, and has effect subject to any variation of the implied trusts aforesaid contained in the instrument creating the trust.

(3) Nothing in this section operates to validate any trust which would, if contained in the instrument creating the trust, be liable to be set aside.

Several aspects of the structure of s 33 merit comment. First, it operates subject to any modifications that a settlor may impose (see s 33(2)) such as varying the class of persons entitled under the discretionary trust. Next, it is evident that a shorter period than a life interest can be selected (s 33(1) 'life or for any less period'). Accordingly it seems that a settlor can establish a series of protective trusts in favour of the same beneficiary. As Megarry points out ((1958) 74 LQR 182 at 184)

> [T]here may be advantages in setting up a series of protective trusts, eg one set until the beneficiary is twenty-five, another from twenty-five to thirty-five, a third from thirty-five to forty-five, and another for the rest of his life. The result would be that a youthful indiscretion at, say, twenty-two, would not irretrievably condemn the beneficiary to the mere hopes of a beneficiary under a discretionary trust, dependent upon the exercise of the trustees' discretion, but would give him a fresh start when he was twenty-five. Again, a bankruptcy at the age of thirty would not *per se* mean that when he was twice that age he would still have not an income as of right, but a mere hope of a well-exercised discretion.

The final point to note is the width of the forfeiture clause (s 33(1)(i)). This covers much more than bankruptcy or attempted assignment of the whole interest and includes any event which deprives the principal beneficiary of his right to receive any part of the income. The construction that the courts have imposed on this definition of forfeiture is considered briefly in the next section.

(3) Forfeiture

Bankruptcy of the principal beneficiary or attempted alienation of the life interest will obviously bring about a forfeiture under s 33. A plethora of other diverse circumstances has been held to cause a forfeiture, some in cases involving s 33, others in cases based on express provisions. Examples are a trustee impounding part of the income of the principal beneficiary to make good a breach of trust committed at the beneficiary's instigation (*Re Balfour's Settlement* [1938] Ch 928); an order for sequestration of income (*Re Baring's Settlement Trusts* [1940] Ch 737); and the bankruptcy of the principal beneficiary occurring before the trust came into operation (*Re Walker* [1939] Ch 974). On the other hand an authority to trustees to pay dividends on trust shareholdings to creditors for a period during which no dividend was declared did not bring about a forfeiture (*Re Longman* [1955] 1 All ER 455 – involving an express forfeiture clause more narrowly drawn than s 33). Other cases where no forfeiture occurred include *Re Greenwood* [1901] 1 Ch 887 'a garnishee order', and *Re Oppenheim's Will Trusts* [1950] Ch 633 'appointment of receiver where the life tenant was of unsound mind'.

Perhaps all that need be said is that in every case it is a question of construction of either s 33 or an express clause whether the particular occurrence should cause a forfeiture.

But cases most often get litigated because there is a penumbra of doubt. Is there any identifiable judicial preference as to the desirability of forfeiture where doubt exists? Russell LJ considered that 'where permissible, forfeiture clauses are to be narrowly construed' (*General Accident, Fire and Life Assurance Corpn Ltd v IRC* [1963] 3 All ER 259 at 265; for similar sentiments see *Re Greenwood* [1901] 1 Ch 887 at 891 and *Re Pozot's Settlement Trusts* [1952] 1 All ER 1107 at 1110). Considered as an abstract proposition, the consequence of forfeiture is to deprive a life tenant of a property right, an entitlement to the income of the fund, and replace it with an inferior claim, that of being merely one object of the trustees' discretion. It might therefore follow that the court should not lightly find a forfeiture to have occurred. But in reality, forfeiture may be precisely what settlor, life tenant and immediate family all desire. This will plainly be so where bankruptcy is the determining event. However, as we have seen, forfeiture is not restricted to the occurrence of bankruptcy, and there may be occasions when the principal beneficiary is opposed to forfeiture. Consider in particular the interests involved in two cases concerning the rearrangement of income entitlement upon divorce. In *General Accident, Fire and Life Assurance Corpn Ltd v IRC* [1963] 3 All ER 259 the Court of Appeal held that an order of the Divorce Court (see now Matrimonial Causes Act 1973, s 24(1)), altering a marriage settlement so as to redirect income from a husband's protected life interest to the wife, did not effect a forfeiture, the husband retaining entitlement to the balance of the income. This contrasts with the earlier case of *Re Richardson's Will Trusts* [1958] Ch 504, surprisingly not mentioned in the judgment, where an order made in the Divorce Court that the principal beneficiary's interest should be charged with an annual sum of £50 maintenance caused a forfeiture. The sequence of events in *Re Richardson* should be noted, however. The order was made on 3 June 1955, the principal beneficiary's interest was to become absolute on 24 October 1955, his thirty-fifth birthday, and he was adjudicated bankrupt on 27 August 1956. One consequence of forfeiture was to allow the discretionary trust to operate and thereby deprive the trustee in bankruptcy of both income and capital, an outcome not unwelcome to the principal beneficiary and consistent with the broad policy underlying s 33.

It is argued that the two cases can be reconciled on a narrow ground of construction of s 33 (see Crane (1962) 26 Conv 517) but there is a wider question to be considered. Should such court orders override the operation of s 33? In the *General Accident* case Donovan LJ said (at 262): '[Section 33] is intended as a protection to spendthrift or improvident or weak life tenants. But it can give . . . no protection against the effect of a court order such as was made here. Furthermore, if such an order involves a forfeiture much injustice could be done.' An analogy can be drawn between the consequences that flow from an order under s 24 of the Matrimonial Causes Act 1973 and one made under s 57 of TA 1925. This is an overriding section whose provisions are read into every trust and hence TA 1925, s 33 trusts are subject to the court's jurisdiction to make an order under TA 1925, s 57 (see p 329), no forfeiture thereby being caused (see *Re Mair* [1935] Ch 562). But it should also be noted: (1) that *Re Richardson* was specifically followed in *Edmonds v Edmonds* [1965] 1 All ER 379n (see also [1993] SJ 17 September p 919) where an attachment of earnings order to secure a maintenance payment brought about a forfeiture, the *General Accident* decision not being cited; and (2) one consequence had forfeiture occurred in the *General Accident* case would have been a reduction in estate duty liability.

(4) Applying the income

The effect of forfeiture is to activate the discretionary trust, and the trustees must then apply the income for the benefit of the discretionary class. 'Putting it in a negative way, [trustees] are not entitled, regardless of the needs of the beneficiaries, to retain in their hands the income of the trust estate' (*Re Gourju's Will Trusts* [1943] Ch 24 at 34 per Simonds J).

Given the requirement of prompt application of income how should the trustees exercise the discretion? Can they continue to pay income to the principal beneficiary? Can they use the income to buy goods or provide services for the principal beneficiary? To what extent, if at all, can payments to the principal beneficiary's spouse or children be claimed by an assignee or trustee in bankruptcy?

A series of cases (*Re Coleman* (1888) 39 Ch D 443; *Re Bullock* (1891) 64 LT 736; *Re Ashby* [1892] 1 QB 872) at the end of the nineteenth century established certain basic guidelines, and these were succinctly summarised in *Re Smith* [1928] Ch 915 at 919:

> **Romer J:** Where there is a trust to apply the whole or such part of a fund as trustees think fit to or for the benefit of A, and A has assigned his interest under the trust, or become bankrupt, although his assignee or his trustee in bankruptcy stand in no better position than he does and cannot demand that the fund shall be handed to them, yet they are in a position to say to A: 'Any money which the trustees do in the exercise of their discretion pay to you passes by the assignment or under the bankruptcy.' But they cannot say that in respect of any money which the trustees have not paid to A or invested in purchasing goods or other things for A, but which they apply for the benefit of A in such a way that no money or goods ever gets into the hands of A.

This statement requires some amplification. A distinction can be drawn between those rare cases where a beneficiary has assigned an interest without incurring a forfeiture and those where a forfeiture occurs. An example of the former is *Re Coleman* where one of four beneficiaries, JSC, assigned his interest under a discretionary trust. The Court of Appeal confirmed that where the trustees have notice of a valid assignment they must not pay money to or purchase goods for the principal beneficiary. If they do so, payment would have been made to the wrong person and the trustees would be liable to the assignee. Of course, as recognised in *Re Smith*, the assignees have no better claim to benefit from the trust than the assignor and the trustees need not pay them anything at all. On the other hand, where a forfeiture of the original interest occurs, there can be no objection in principle to the trustee making payments to the principal beneficiary but now as one of the class under the newly arisen discretionary trust. In practice, however, a trustee in bankruptcy might be able to claim the income from the beneficiary by virtue of statutory insolvency law (see (5) below).

The other point left uncertain by *Re Smith* is the extent to which trustees may exercise their discretion to apply income for the benefit of the principal beneficiary. Again there would seem to be no objection in principle under trusts law to a view expressed by Kekewich J in *Re Bullock* (1891) 64 LT 736 (at 738): 'I am unwilling to fetter the trustees' discretion which was intended to be and ought to be construed as large... [The trustees] certainly may... spend the whole or any part of the income in maintenance, using that word in its most general and widest sense;... the discretion is vested in them... and so long as they exercise it honestly – that is, as men of ordinary business habits and prudence, and with due regard to all the circumstances of the case – the court will not interfere with them.' No attention is paid here to the implications for the *creditors* of interpreting the trustees' power broadly.

(5) Assets, income and the Insolvency Act 1986

Where it is bankruptcy of the principal beneficiary that brings about a forfeiture, the above principles must be considered in the context of insolvency law. In particular, the property of a bankrupt divisible among his creditors includes not only property belonging to him at the commencement of the bankruptcy but also 'after-acquired property' – property which is acquired by or devolves upon the bankrupt between bankruptcy and discharge.

Of course the bankrupt is not left to face the world totally devoid of all income and property during this time. In reading the following extracts from the Cork Report and the relevant sections of the Insolvency Act 1986 (IA), consider in particular the resources that are permitted to be retained by the bankrupt to meet personal and family needs, the policy objectives of insolvency law and the relationship between TA 1925, s 33 and IA 1986.

Report of the Insolvency Law Review Committee (Cmnd 8558, 1982)

THE INSOLVENT'S SURPLUS INCOME

591. It has been almost the rule in the past to think in terms of 'selling up' the debtor and dividing the proceeds amongst the creditors as the main, if not the only, means of debt recovery. We believe that, in principle, far more emphasis should in future be placed on the prospect of the debtor's ability to pay his debts out of surplus future income. This is not to say that the existing assets are to be ignored or that a debtor's earning capacity is to be made available for payment until the debts are paid in full however long that may take; the debtor must in no circumstances become the slave of his creditors. This shift in emphasis should, nonetheless, enable a more realistic and a more humane attitude to be taken than previously regarding the position of the debtor and his family.

EXEMPT PROPERTY AND FAMILY ASSETS

1094. A primary aim of insolvency proceedings is the realisation of the debtor's property for the benefit of his creditors....

1096. A further aim of the bankruptcy code is to enable the individual debtor to achieve his rehabilitation as a useful and productive member of society. Certain assets necessary for this purpose are accordingly exempted from vesting in his trustee and are allowed, on the contrary, to be retained by the debtor.

The Committee recommended that a category of exempt property should include (i) tools and equipment, and (ii) clothing and furnishings, and this is reflected in the following sections of the IA 1986:

Insolvency Act 1986, s 283(1), (2), (3), (6); s 306; s 307(1), (2), 310(2)

283(1) . . . a bankrupt's estate for the purposes of any of this Group of Parts comprises –

(a) all property belonging to or vested in the bankrupt at the commencement of the bankruptcy.

(2) subsection (1) above does not apply to –

(a) such tools, books, vehicles and other items of equipment as are necessary to the bankrupt for use personally by him in his employment, business or vocation;
(b) such clothing, bedding, furniture, household equipment and provisions as are necessary for satisfying the basic domestic needs of the bankrupt and his family. . . .

(3) Subsection (1) does not apply to –

(a) property held by the bankrupt on trust for any other person . . .

(6) This section has effect subject to the provisions of any enactment not contained in this Act under which any property is to be excluded from a bankrupt's estate.

306(1) The bankrupt's estate shall vest in the trustee immediately on his appointment taking effect or, in the case of the official receiver, on his becoming trustee.
(2) Where any property which is, or is to be, comprised in the bankrupt's estate vests in the trustee (whether under this section or under any other provision of this Part), it shall so vest without any conveyance, assignment or transfer.

307(1) Subject to this section and s 309, the trustee may by notice in writing claim for the bankrupt's estate any property which has been acquired by, or has devolved upon, the bankrupt since the commencement of the bankruptcy.
(2) A notice under subsection (1) above shall not be served in respect of –

(a) any property falling within subsections (2) or (3) of section 283 above;
(b) any property which by virtue of any other enactment is excluded from the bankrupt's estate; or
(c) . . . any property which is acquired by, or devolves upon, the bankrupt after his discharge.

310(2) the court shall not make an income payments order, the effect of which would be to reduce the income of the bankrupt below what appears to the court to be necessary for meeting the reasonable domestic needs of the bankrupt and his family.

Working within this legislative framework the duty of the trustee in bankruptcy is to obtain title to the assets of the bankrupt and realise these for the benefit of creditors. As regards 'after acquired income' the trustee in bankruptcy can apply to the court under IA 1986, s 310 for an income payment order (IPO) under which a proportion of the bankrupt's income is also made available for creditors. Under the original terms of the IA 1986 IPOs ran only until the automatic discharge of the bankrupt, usually three years after the date of the bankruptcy order. The reduction of that period by the Enterprise Act 2002, s 279 from three years to 12 months for 'non-culpable bankrupts' has been accompanied by a change in the rules for IPOs. In the interests of keeping the balance between the position of creditors and the bankrupt person IPOs will last for a period of up to three years from the date of the IPO irrespective of the date of discharge of the bankrupt (s 259, amending IA 1986, s 310).

Consider the following points:

(1) The principle laid down in *Re Smith* suggests that if the trustees of a discretionary trust apply funds 'for the benefit of' a bankrupt beneficiary, the creditor has no recourse unless the beneficiary actually receives goods or property. This could pave the way for luxury benefits – for example, an extended holiday at the Ritz – well in excess of the limits implicit in s 283(2) and s 310(2). Cf the comment of Scott (*Law of Trusts* (4th edn, 1987) s 155(1), p 161): 'The distinction thus drawn between payments to the beneficiary and applying trust funds for his benefit seems to be arbitrary and without any sound basis in public policy.'

(2) Would it constitute a breach of trust for trustees to exercise their discretion under TA 1925, s 33(1)(ii) to provide income or goods to the bankrupt principal beneficiary in excess of the levels permitted by IA 1986, s 283(2), if the trustee in bankruptcy were successfully to claim any excess? In exercise of their discretion, could trustees pay income direct to the principal beneficiary's trustee in bankruptcy? Note, however, that in *Re Rayatt* [1998] 2 FLR 264, doubtless to the chagrin of creditors, private school fees of £844 per month were held to be reasonable expenditure under s 310(2) due in part to the disruption that would otherwise be caused to the child's education.

(3) The Ontario Law Reform Commission (*Report on the Law of Trusts* (1984)) recommended that draft clause 52 below be included in any new Trustee Act for the province.

> 52(1) Where property is held on trust for a person, in this section called 'the protected beneficiary', for an interest that is determinable on a claim being made by a creditor or trustee in bankruptcy against the income payable to the protected beneficiary, such a claimant may apply to the Court for payment of his claim, and the Court may order the payment of the claim out of income arising from the trust until the interest but for the determinability would have terminated.
>
> (2) If it is established to the satisfaction of the Court that any successive beneficiary, including any beneficiary of a discretionary trust, as to the income or capital of the trust, has derived any benefit from any debt incurred by the protected beneficiary, payment of which is being sought by the creditor, the Court may

> order that the whole or part of the capital of the trust be released from the trust to meet, in whole or in part, the claim of the creditor or trustee in bankruptcy of the protected beneficiary.

...

Note that the clause as it stands would affect only protective trusts. Presumably a suitably advised settlor could opt to use a discretionary trust to shelter property from the creditors of the beneficiaries. This possibility led one critic of the proposal, which was not adopted, to suggest that 'the settlor has been denied a risk management tool that was previously available to him without much else having been achieved' (Rossiter [1986] Estates and Trust Quarterly (3), 229–250 at 249). Would you recommend the modification of the TA 1925, s 33 along similar lines to those in Draft Clause 52?

(4) In principle, insolvency law treats the family as a unit for the purposes of assessing needs but does not aggregate the income or capital of individual members when measuring resources. This raises the question whether the assets of the bankrupt's spouse should be pooled with those of the bankrupt to meet the creditor's claims, and if so, whether in relation to (a) business debts, (b) consumption debts, or (c) both. The Cork Report robustly rejected a proposal that all the assets of the spouse should be pooled with those of the bankrupt and made available to meet the claims of creditors, in so far as they relate to trading or business debts:

> Para 1229. We reject this proposal as an unjustified interference with individual property rights, which would produce an unfair result in many cases, and which in many respects would be a reversion to outmoded concepts of matrimonial property which have long since been abandoned.... We regard the proposal as entirely out of line with modern attitudes to the proprietary rights of husband and wife.

Is this approach, based essentially on individual rights of property, consistent with:

(i) 'the protective trust which on forfeiture transmutes an individual property interest in income into a family property entitlement'; or

(ii) a conception of family life within which women are viewed increasingly as equal economic partners: 'married women are not single women. They live with and for their husbands in a unit known as the family, which it is the policy of the law to cherish and support' (Lord Scarman *Women and Equality before the Law* (1971) p 8; see also Chapter 12 and Freedman et al *Property and Marriage: An Integrated Approach* (1988) Institute for Fiscal Studies)?

(5) A TA 1925, s 33 protective trust is not the only statutory mechanism that can prevent a trustee in bankruptcy from gaining immediate title to a bankrupt's property under IA 1986, s 306. An accrued pension entitlement

is often a bankrupt's most valuable asset and has on occasion proved an attractive target for the trustee in bankruptcy. In *Kilvert v Flackett* [1998] 2 FLR 806, for instance, a lump sum pension payment of some £50,000 was successfully claimed by the trustee in bankruptcy under an IPO, although the case is arguably incorrectly decided in that it treats a capital payment – the lump sum – as if it were an income stream. The Pensions Act 1995, ss 91–95 provides that a person's entitlement to, or an accrued right in, an occupational pension does not form part of the bankrupt's estate for the purposes of the IA 1986. This protection has now been extended as from 29 May 2000 by the Welfare Reform and Pensions Act 1999, s 11 to include rights which a bankrupt may have under any HMRC approved pension, not just occupational schemes. In practice, even prior to the legislative initiatives, many pension trust deeds contained a forfeiture clause to the effect that the pension rights may be forfeited on bankruptcy leaving the trustees with discretion to pay any 'forfeited benefits' to the bankrupt, to his or her spouse, to a widow or widower or to any dependants. The analogy with the discretion under TA 1925, s 33 is evident.

But why should pension rights be relatively immune from the claims of creditors? Aside from the obvious riposte that might cite TA 1925, s 33 as justification, one possible rationale for the protection of accrued pension rights may lie in a policy argument that pensions are intended to provide financial security for pensioners and their families. We will return to this point when considering briefly the status of the family home in an insolvency (see below).

(6) In conclusion, would you agree that 'there is no incompatibility between the protective trust and insolvency law. Both are primarily directed towards enabling a debtor to regain financial stability and make a fresh start'?

(6) Insolvency and the family home

A full evaluation of a 'fresh start' policy and of the capacity of the trust form to put assets beyond the reach of a beneficiary's creditors would need to take account of the treatment under insolvency law of co-owned property, in particular the family home. Acute questions of policy and principle arise here. On the one hand, unpaid creditors will want to recoup their losses from what may well be the most valuable available asset. On the other hand, homelessness with its attendant consequences may be inflicted on possibly innocent family victims of the bankrupt's financial failure. Faced with this dilemma the Cork Report concluded that it would be 'consonant with present social attitudes to alleviate the personal hardship of those who are dependant on the debtor but not responsible for his insolvency, if this can be achieved by delaying for an acceptable time the sale of the family home' (para 1116). The present law of bankruptcy affords some recognition to these recommendations but it is debateable how far the provisions of IA 1986, s 335A, to be discussed shortly, 'delay for an acceptable time the sale of the family home'.

The questions raised by this issue run much wider than the specific focus adopted in this chapter (see eg Dewar in Bright and Dewar (eds) *Land Law Theories and Perspectives* (1998) pp 336–345), but the limited nature of legislative and judicial protection for the family home under insolvency law throws into sharp relief some conceptual and policy inconsistencies. In particular it is apparent that the interests of the family and, one may say, principles of property law are subordinated to the interests of creditors.

Under Trusts of Land and Appointment of Trustees Act (TOLATA) 1996, s 14 (replacing LPA 1925, s 30 as from 1 January 1997) 'any person who ... has an interest in property subject to a trust of land' can apply for an order to sell the land. The court has a wide-ranging discretion under s 14(2) as to the order it may make and, with one significant exception, s 15 sets out the criteria to govern the exercise of the discretion. It is the exception that concerns us here. It takes effect in a case where insolvency intervenes and the beneficial interest of a bankrupt spouse in the property vests in the trustee in bankruptcy who thereby becomes a 'person interested' for the purposes of s 14. Where the applicant under s 14 is a trustee in bankruptcy different considerations to those under s 15 apply. The court must then exercise its discretion applying criteria now contained in Insolvency Act 1986, s 335A (previously in s 336).

Section 335A(2) provides that where an application for a sale of property is made the court shall make such order as it thinks just and reasonable having regard to:

(a) the interests of the bankrupt's creditors;
(b) where the application is made in respect of land which includes a dwelling house which is or has been the home of the bankrupt or the bankrupt's spouse or former spouse,
   (i) the conduct of the spouse or former spouse, so far as contributing to the bankruptcy,
   (ii) the needs and financial resources of the spouse or former spouse, and
   (iii) the needs of any children; and
(c) all the circumstances of the case other than the needs of the bankrupt.

The omission of any reference in s 335A to 'the purposes for which the property is held' as a criterion for the court to consider (cf its inclusion in TOLATA 1996, s 15(1)(b)) seems to confirm that in a bankruptcy the interests of the creditors take clear precedence over fulfilling the purposes for which the property was purchased. Its omission effectively lays to rest the prospect of the court being able to take into account the 'collateral purpose' of the trust in the exercise of its discretion under s 335A (cf the Court of Appeal decision in *Abbey National plc v Moss* [1994] 1 FLR 307 under the LPA 1925, s 30 (Hopkins (1995) 11 LQR 72); Cretney [1994] Fam Law 255; Clarke [1994] Conv 331).

Of more significance is the sting in the tail of the section; s 335A(3) requires that where an application for sale is made after the end of the period of one year from the bankruptcy 'the court shall assume, unless the circumstances of the case are exceptional, that the interest of the bankrupt's creditors outweigh all other considerations'. Dicta in a Court of Appeal decision in *Re Citro* [1991] Ch 142 indicated that, in interpreting s 336(5) (the predecessor of s 335A), the courts were to apply the same test as had evolved in case law under LPA 1925, s 30. The legislative history of the requirement of 'exceptional circumstances' in s 336(5) leaves it unclear as to whether this was in fact the legislature's intention (see Cretney (1991) 107 LQR 177 and 'Insolvency and Family Law' in Rajak (ed) *Insolvency Law Theory and Practice* (1993) pp 71–82). The outcome, however, if the Court of Appeal decision in *Re Citro* is an accurate indication, is a stringent test indeed. At first instance in that case, which concerned the bankruptcy of two brothers who ran a garage business as partners, appreciation of the hardship that would be caused to the family, including educational difficulties for the children and an absence of suitable alternative accommodation, led Hoffmann J to order a postponement of sale until the youngest child in each family reached the age of 16 (the youngest then being twelve and ten respectively). By a majority, the Court of Appeal reversed the decision because the circumstances of the cases were not 'exceptional', substituting a postponement for six months only. As Nourse LJ reluctantly if resignedly accepted (at 157) '[such] circumstances, while engendering a natural sympathy in all who hear of them, cannot be described as exceptional. They are the melancholy consequences of debt and improvidence with which every civilised society has been familiar . . . ' (see also *(Trustees) Bowe v Bowe* [1998] 2 FLR 439 at 446 – 'disruption, unhappiness and possibly extreme inconvenience to the family' not to be treated as exceptional for the purposes of s 336(5)).

In the light of *Re Citro*, circumstances sufficiently 'exceptional' to justify postponement of sale seemed unlikely to be very common (cf *Re Holliday* [1981] Ch 405; *Re Gorman* [1990] 1 WLR 616; and see Hall [1991] CLJ 45). However, a number of more recent cases clarifying what constitutes 'exceptional circumstances' can be interpreted as representing a slight shift in emphasis from that evidenced in *Re Citro*. In *Judd v Brown* [1998] 2 FLR 360 a wife's serious illness – a sudden and serious attack of ovarian cancer requiring extensive surgery and chemotherapy – was held by Harman J to constitute 'an exceptional circumstance' which would have justified refusing to grant an order for possession and sale (the order was refused on other grounds). In *Re Raval* [1998] 2 FLR 718 the likely detrimental effect on the wife's health – a paranoid schizophrenic – of an immediate forced move amounted, inter alia, to exceptional circumstances that justified the suspension of an order for sale and possession for one year (see also *Claughton v Charalambous* [1999] 1 FLR 740 – the wife of the bankrupt was aged 60, suffered from, inter alia, chronic renal failure, had reduced life expectancy and the home was fitted with a chair-lift; and *Re Bremner* [1999] 1 FLR 912 where the exceptional circumstances were the emotional needs of the wife, aged 74, as sole carer of the 79-year-old bankrupt who was terminally ill with inoperable cancer; sale was postponed until three months after his death). Notwithstanding cases such as these it is still difficult to dissent from the view that the effect of the amended 1986 legislation, as one leading text suggests, 'is that the bankrupt's family will in practice be given one year's grace but in the absence of truly exceptional circumstances no more' (Masson et al *Principles of Family Law* (8th edn, 2008) p 173).

It is questionable, moreover, whether the outcome of 'exceptional circumstances' cases under s 335A will be materially altered by the Human Rights Act 1998. Article 8(1) of the European Convention states that 'everyone has the right to respect for his private and family life, his home and his correspondence'. These rights are qualified by para 2 which provides that: 'There shall be no interference by a public authority with the exercise of this right except such as is in accordance with the law and is necessary in a democratic society in the interests of . . . the protection of the rights and freedoms of others.' The rights and freedom of others clearly encompasses the rights of the creditors of the bankrupt. In that general sense the 'balancing of interests' under s 335A(2) is not inconsistent with Article 8 and indeed 'it might be contended that section 335A precisely captures what is required by [the Article]' (*Nicholls v Lan* [2007] 1 FLR 744 at [43]). Nevertheless, in *Barca v Mears* [2005] EWHC 2170 Strauss J, whilst accepting that in the general run of cases the creditor's interests will outweigh all other considerations (as they did in the case itself), suggested that a shift in emphasis in the interpretation of s 335A might be necessary to achieve full compatibility with the Convention rights (at 39): '[it is] questionable whether the narrow approach as to what may be "exceptional circumstances" adopted in *Re Citro* is consistent with the Convention' (see Dixon [2005] Conv 161–167 and, in the different context of the enforcement of actions for possession brought by local authorities under various statutes, see *Kay v Lambeth Borough Council* [2006] 2 AC 465; Hughes and Davis [2006] Conv 526).

The approach taken under English law is not the only one possible. Other jurisdictions (eg New Zealand, Canada, the US) have introduced legislation which seeks to strike a different balance between the legitimate commercial interests of creditors and the competing claims of families to residential security 'at a special time of crisis' (see the discussion in Gray *Elements of Land Law* (5th edn, 2009) pp 1016–1017 and Gravells (1985) 5 OJLS 132 at 140–143). By way of comparison with English law Gray points out that in New Zealand, for instance, legislation was enacted 'with the express object of promoting the stability and permanence of family life as a higher social end than that represented by commercial security for the creditor' (at 1017).

Leaving to one side the policy issue here, there remains a question about consistency of approach. Is insolvency law consistent in permitting a forced sale under s 335A of a jointly owned house, yet rejecting the pooling of family assets, let us assume including income available under a protective trust, to meet the claims of creditors (see Clarke 'Insolvent Families' in *Rajak* pp 83–92)?

(7) American and English approaches compared

Concluding his note on the series of protective trusts set up in *Re Richardson's Will Trusts* [1958] Ch 504, Megarry commented that 'England lacks the device of the spendthrift trust in the American sense, but it is far from clear that the fullest possible use is being made of the existing machinery of protective and discretionary trusts' ((1958) 78 LQR 182 at 184).

The spendthrift trust is the outcome of US law making a sharp conceptual break with English trusts law. In the USA two significant nineteenth-century decisions (*Nichols v Eaton* 91 US 716 (1875) and *Broadway National Bank v Adams* 133 Mass 170 (1882)) firmly established, contrary to Lord Eldon's view in *Brandon v Robinson* (1811) 18 Ves 429, that restraints on alienability of an equitable life estate were valid. A spendthrift trust is one that contains a restraint against both voluntary and involuntary alienation. Accordingly the trustees must pay the trust income to even a bankrupt beneficiary and in principle the beneficiary's creditors have no rights against the trust income or capital. In practice several states in the USA (see Bogert *Trusts and Trustees* (2008 update) ss 222–227; McCorkle *Validity of Spendthrift Trusts* 34 ALR 2d 1335) have moved towards allowing creditors some degree of statutory access to trust income. Indeed it has been suggested that the consequence of statutory reform is that 'in those American jurisdictions where there are statutory limits to the immunity of the beneficiary's interest from creditors' claims, the position of the creditor is substantially better than that of English creditors against a beneficiary under a protective trust' (Keeton *Modern Developments in the Law of Trusts* (1971) p 200). The very popularity of spendthrift trusts stimulated pressure for statutory intervention on behalf of creditors. It was estimated that in 1968, for instance, the capital value of spendthrift trusts totalled US$140 billion, with an annual protected income of US$5.6 billion (Bushman (1968) 47 *Oregon Law Review* 304; see also Chester *Inheritance, Wealth and Society* (1982) p 125). Apart from the statistical data, the continuing popularity in the US of spendthrift trusts and other asset protection trusts is exemplified by the existence of specialist journals and texts such as the *Asset Protection Journal* and Osborne and Schurig's four-volume 1995 treatise *Asset Protection: Domestic and International Law and Tactics* (see also the specialist practitioners' papers prepared by Tansill SH032 ALI-ABA 345 and Osborne and Catterall SH069 ALI-ABA 1713 for the American Law Institute-American Bar Association symposia in 2002 and 2003 respectively).

Consequently it is not surprising, given this pressure, that the public policy arguments about 'protecting spendthrifts' have historically been widely canvassed in the US (see Hirsch (1995) 73 Washington University LQ 1–93 for an overview that draws upon the disciplines of economics and cognitive psychology). At an early stage the banner of individualism and freedom of disposition was fulsomely flourished on both sides of the barricades. Miller J in *Nichols v Eaton* posed the rhetorical question (at 727): 'Why a parent ... who ... wishes to use his own property in securing the object of his own affection, as far as property can do it, from the ills of life, the vicissitudes of fortune, and even his own improvidence, or incapacity for self-protection, should not be permitted to do so, is not readily perceived.' But a robust early critic of the spendthrift trust, John Chipman Gray, castigated this sentiment as being opposed to the fundamental principles of common law, 'that it is against public policy that a man "should have an estate to live on, but not an estate to pay his debts with"', and continued 'it is not the function of the law to save the foolish and the vicious from the consequences of their own vice and folly. [The fundamental principle] is a wholesome doctrine, fit to produce a manly race, based on sound morality and wise philosophy' (*Restraints on the Alienation of Property* (1895) p 243).

Implicit in these conflicting views is the paradox mentioned at the start of this chapter (p 266). Recognising the irresolvable nature of this debate, Griswold, the writer of the classic work on spendthrift trusts, reasoned that 'there is no syllogistic basis for the spendthrift trust' (*Spendthrift Trusts* (1947) p 634) and therefore the justification had to be found in public policy.

> It is obvious that there are competing factors. There are situations in which spendthrift trusts admittedly serve a useful function. Where they are created of moderate amount for the benefit of widows or for people who are really unable to manage their own affairs there can be little reason to argue against them in a regime of private property. The difficulty comes not so much from the existence of spendthrift trusts as from their generally unrestrained extent. The arguments for and against such trusts may in a large measure be reconciled by legislation expressly authorising them of a fixed and moderate amount, while allowing creditors to reach all income in excess of the specified amount. (E Griswold *Spendthrift Trusts* (1947) p 639)

More recently the terms of the policy debate in the US have taken on renewed vigour with the focus shifting to challenge the maxim, most forcefully expressed in Scott's treatise (Scott and Fratcher *The Law of Trusts* (4th edn, 1987) § 156.2, at 176), that one cannot create a spendthrift trust for oneself (see Danforth (2002) 53 Hastings LJ 287, but cf Sterk (2000) 85 Corn LR 1035). Indeed Griswold had foreshadowed this development suggesting that '[W]e may well question the soundness of a rule which allows a man to hold the bounty of others free from the claims of his creditors, but denies the same immunity to his interest in property which he has accumulated by his own effort' (at 361).

Turning to the protective trust in England one looks in vain for any discussion of the policy implications for debtor-creditor or settlor-beneficiary relationships let alone the philosophical considerations. The Ontario Law Reform Commission (*Report on the Law of Trusts* (1984)), when considering and rejecting the introduction of a statutory protective trust into a revised Trustee Act, was forced to comment (p 363):

> In view of the long struggle in the United States over the spendthrift trust between those who believe the donor should be able to impose restrictions upon his donee as he pleases, and those who feel that creditors should be paid their just due, it is surprising that the protective trust, particularly where such trusts run in series, should never have been questioned in those jurisdictions that provide statutorily for this device.

The Cork Report followed this trend: the protective trust receives no mention. The 2001 White Paper – *Insolvency: A Second Chance* (Cm 5234) – continues in this tradition! It is tempting to conclude that this apparent policy lacuna exists because the trust is no longer used by settlors, or because if it is used it presents no practical problems for creditor-debtor relationships. It is to be hoped that the reason for its absence from discussion is not solely formal, ie the protective trust is irrelevant to considerations of a bankrupt's status since technically the bankrupt has no entitlement to income or capital once forfeiture has occurred.

There is, however, one legislative straw in the wind to be found in the protective trust's treatment under inheritance tax (IHT), which suggests that the device is in use and is still favourably regarded (see eg *Hambro v Duke of Marlborough* at p 270). Under the original intended legislation in the Finance Bill of 1975 there were no special provisions relating to protective trusts. This would have resulted in IHT becoming payable on forfeiture of the protected life interest (an interest in possession) and the then penal discretionary trust regime applying (see generally, Chapter 8). Accordingly changes were introduced during the passage of the Bill. For IHT purposes the discretionary trust is treated as 'transparent' and the principal beneficiary's interest is regarded as nominally still subsisting 'in possession' with the consequence that no IHT charge arises on forfeiture (IHTA 1984, s 88; *Cholmondeley v IRC* [1986] STC 384). This privileged treatment is equally available to non-statutory protective trusts provided they are 'of like effect' to TA 1925, s 33 trusts. (This indicates that attempts to adopt a wider discretionary class than that specified in the statute would have undesirable fiscal implications.) Such an amendment would not have been thought necessary if protective trusts were only rarely used.

Consider the following questions:

(1) To what extent are policy arguments about the spendthrift trust relevant to protective trusts?
(2) Do you agree with the following claim: 'The protective trust stands as a monument to the victory of legal formalism over substantive reality. What is more surprising is that legislators have also allowed themselves to be blinded by such formalism'?

(c) Attempts to safeguard property from the creditors of the trust founder

(1) Common law

It has long been recognised that property-owners might try to hinder or defeat their own actual or potential creditors by means of absolute gifts or by transferring property into trust, and statutory restraints have been imposed to nullify such attempts. The current provisions are to be found in the IA 1986 (see sections 3 and 4 below). But, where the statute is inapplicable, does the general law of trusts prevent settlors using trusts to protect themselves from creditors?

In general property cannot be put into protective trusts so as to protect settlors against the consequences of their own bankruptcy. The attempted limitation against bankruptcy will be void as against the trustee in bankruptcy (*Re Burroughs-Fowler* [1916] 2 Ch 251 is but one of many cases affirming this proposition). This does not mean, however, that the settlement itself is void or that the limitation will be ineffective against an *individual creditor* as opposed to the generality of creditors represented by a trustee in bankruptcy.

Re Detmold (1889) 40 Ch D 585

As part of a marriage settlement a husband's own property was held on trust to pay the income to him 'during his life, or till he shall become a bankrupt . . . or shall suffer something whereby the [income] . . . would through his own act, default or by operation of law . . . become . . . payable to some other person'. If the husband's determinable interest became forfeit the trustees were to pay the income to the wife during her life. An individual creditor obtained an order appointing himself receiver of the income due from the trust fund. Subsequently the husband was adjudicated bankrupt.

> **North J**: The question is, whether the life interest given by the settlement to the wife is now subsisting, or whether it is invalid as against the trustee in the bankruptcy of the husband.

North J held that the order appointing a receiver terminated the husband's life interest.

> The trustee in the bankruptcy is also bound by that order, because the bankruptcy did not commence until the 29th of July. Before that date the husband had done an act, had suffered something, by which the right to receive the income had become vested in another person, and, therefore, the gift over in favour of the wife had taken effect. It is said that a gift over of a man's own property in the event of his bankruptcy is void, and no doubt that is so. But it has been held that a gift over in the event of a voluntary assignment by him is valid. . . . In my opinion, [the] authorities show that the limitation of the life interest to the settlor was validly determined by the fact that, in consequence of the order appointing the receiver, he ceased to be entitled to receive the income. This took place before the commencement of the bankruptcy, and, therefore, the forfeiture is valid as against the trustee in the bankruptcy.

The common law position is preserved for statutory protective trusts by TA 1925, s 33(3); see p 277.

Despite *Re Detmold*, if property-owners wish to protect themselves effectively against the consequences of a bankruptcy a determinable interest will not suffice but in principle a discretionary trust will. While statutory anti-avoidance provisions for income tax now make that option less attractive fiscally (see Chapter 8), counsel in *Re Trafford's Settlement* [1985] Ch 32 could point to standard conveyancing works which showed that 'a settlor to protect his own income against loss under a future bankruptcy was advised to create an immediate discretionary trust' (at 36). In effect the settlor must omit the first stage of the protective trust, moving straight to the second stage discretionary trust, with the same consequences for the trustee in bankruptcy as previously described.

The remainder of this section is concerned with certain statutory restraints applying generally to transfers of property (not just transfers on trust) which may have been entered into so as to defeat claims by the transferor's creditors. But the basic principle still holds; where statute does not intrude, a discretionary trust can provide an effective means of protecting a person's property from creditors.

(2) The statutory provisions: a case for reform

Until 1986 the relevant provisions were LPA 1925, s 172, and Bankruptcy Act 1914, s 42. The former rendered voidable any disposition intended to defraud creditors. Where a debtor had been adjudged bankrupt, s 42 enabled certain voluntary dispositions entered into within a specified period prior to an act of bankruptcy, whether or not with intent to defraud, to be voided by the trustee in bankruptcy. In particular s 42 was intended to prevent assets being put into the hands of the debtor's family or associates in order to preserve them from the claims of the transferor's creditors. Whilst the provisions inevitably overlapped, their objectives were different. Section 172 was designed to protect creditors from fraud: 'The principle on which the statute . . . proceeds is this, that persons must be just before they are generous, and that debts must be paid before gifts can be made' (*Freeman v Pope* (1870) 5 Ch App 538 at 540 and see Cork Report para 1202).

The bankruptcy code, on the other hand, is intended to achieve a pari passu distribution of the bankrupt's assets between all the creditors, not just any who are the objects of an intent to defraud. The latter have no priority.

Whilst the Cork Report endorsed these basic objectives, certain aspects of the prevailing law were criticised and the Report recommended its replacement by a new statutory framework. The government broadly accepted these particular recommendations (*A Revised Framework for Insolvency Law* (Cmnd 9175, 1984)) and the old law was replaced by the IA 1986. The LPA 1925, s 172 provision is replaced largely by IA 1986, ss 423 and 424, whilst the bankruptcy provisions are now to be found principally in ss 339–342.

(3) Transactions 'with intent' to defeat creditors: Insolvency Act 1986, ss 423, 424

> 423(1) This section relates to transactions entered into at an undervalue; and a person enters into such a transaction with another person if –

(a) he makes a gift to the other person or he otherwise enters into a transaction with the other on terms that provide for him to receive no consideration;

(b) he enters into a transaction with the other in consideration of marriage; or

(c) he enters into a transaction with the other for a consideration the value of which, in money or money's worth, is significantly less than the value, in money or money's worth, of the consideration provided by himself.

(2) Where a person has entered into such a transaction, the court may, if satisfied under the next subsection, make such order as it thinks fit for –

(a) restoring the position to what it would have been if the transaction had not been entered into, and

(b) protecting the interests of persons who are victims of the transaction.

(3) In the case of a person entering into such a transaction, an order shall only be made if the court is satisfied that it was entered into by him for the purpose –

(a) of putting assets beyond the reach of a person who is making, or may at some time make, a claim against him, or

(b) of otherwise prejudicing the interests of such a person in relation to the claim which he is making or may make.

(4)...

(5) In relation to a transaction at an undervalue, references here and below to a victim of the transaction are to a person who is, or is capable of being, prejudiced by it; and in the following two sections the person entering into the transaction is referred to as 'the debtor'.

424(1) An application for an order under section 423 shall not be made in relation to a transaction except –

(a) in a case where the debtor has been adjudged bankrupt... by the official receiver, by the trustee of the bankrupt's estate or the liquidator... or (with the leave of the court) by a victim of the transaction;

...

(c) in any other case, by a victim of the transaction.

(2) An application made under any of the paragraphs of subsection (1) is to be treated as made on behalf of every victim of the transaction.

The Cork Committee's recommendations were directed principally towards clarifying and modernising the language of the law rather than substantially altering its structure. Regrettably clarification has not brought brevity but the increased length is in part a consequence of specifying in some detail (s 425) the wide discretionary remedies available to the court 'for restoring the position to what it would have been'. These include requiring any property transferred as part of the transaction to be vested in the applicant.

Before considering the substance and effect of s 423 the requirements as to locus standi (s 424(1)) should be noted. Whereas applications for an order will usually be made by a creditor or trustee in bankruptcy, the language of the section extends to include a person merely capable of being prejudiced by a transaction, thus resolving a previously unsettled point (see *Cadogan v Cadogan* [1977] 3 All ER 831, CA). Section 424(2) in effect introduces a species of imposed class action, in that any application made must be treated as made on behalf of every person who may be prejudiced by the transaction.

Any applicant wishing to attack a transaction must be able to establish that it satisfies the twin requirements of s 423 (see generally Stubbs (2008) 21(2) Insolvency Intelligence 17–25). It must constitute a transaction at an undervalue (s 423(1)) *and* have been entered into with the intent specified in s 423(3). Note that where a person has been adjudicated bankrupt, the trustee in bankruptcy will in most circumstances prefer to institute proceedings under IA 1986, ss 339–342 ('the bankruptcy provisions') since there is no need to establish intent under those provisions.

Transaction at an undervalue (s 423(1)) The concept of a 'transaction at an undervalue' is fundamental to the operation of both the 'intent to defeat creditor' jurisdiction and the bankruptcy provisions (see s 339, below, p 300). The definition adopted in both instances is substantially the same and includes both gifts on trust and outright gifts. General questions of interpretation are considered here whilst specific matters concerning bankruptcy are dealt with below at p 300.

As recommended by the Cork Report (para 1216), marriage is no longer treated as valuable consideration (s 423(1)(b)) and the latter concept is itself more closely restricted by s 423(1)(c). The key element in the definition of 'transaction at an undervalue' lies in sub-s (1)(c), particularly in the phrase 'significantly less than'. What is required is a comparison between the consideration provided by the transferor and that provided by the other party. And the object of the comparison is to prevent an outcome whereby insolvent persons can succeed in reducing their net assets to the detriment of their creditors: 'Such reduction is achieved by a mismatch between that which is disposed of and that which is received' (*Re Thoars* [2002] EWHC 2416 at [13]). The problem lies in the measuring, particularly where the transaction involves some repackaging of property interests.

In *Agricultural Mortgage Corpn plc v Woodward* [1996] 1 FLR 226 the defendant farmer mortgaged his land, worth £1m with vacant possession, to the claimant mortgagee as security for a loan of £700,000. He fell into arrears and just before the date set by the mortgagee for repaying some £850,000 the farmer granted a tenancy of the property to his wife at a fair market rent. The effect was to reduce the freehold value of the farm to less than £500,000. There was no doubt that the purpose of the transaction was to prevent the mortgagee obtaining the property with vacant possession. Yet the claimant's action to have the tenancy agreement set aside was dismissed at first instance on the grounds that the agreement did not involve a transfer at an undervalue. The Court of Appeal reversed the decision principally on the basis that, in addition to the benefit of the tenancy itself, there were the following valuable benefits or 'consequences' of the tenancy:

(i)   the safeguarding of the family home;
(ii) the acquisition of the farming business free from its previous creditors; and
(iii) the benefit of the surrender value of the tenancy.

The last named – a 'ransom position' – was seen as particularly significant since 'the plaintiff would have had to negotiate with and no doubt pay a high price to [the wife] before it could obtain vacant possession of the farm, and sell it for the purpose of enforcing its security...' (at 235). Sir Christopher Slade, giving the principal judgment of the Court, concluded (at 236):

> ...when the transactions are viewed as a whole the benefits which the first defendant thereby conferred on [Mrs Woodward] were significantly greater in value, far greater in value, in money or money's worth than the value of the consideration provided by her. To hold otherwise would seem to me to fly in the face of reality and common sense.

The reference to 'reality and common sense' is revealing. It is evident that the court in searching for a practical answer was not attracted by the possibility of the claims of a creditor-mortgagee being defeated and the purpose of s 423 being subverted in this manner (see also *Barclays Bank plc v Eustice* [1995] 1 WLR 1238 where comparable if more complex transactions, again involving a 'ransom position' and carried out with the benefit of legal advice, were held to constitute 'a strong prima facie case' of transactions at an undervalue). The calculation as to whether or not there has been a mismatch in value between what is disposed of and what is received is not made easier by the fact that the value of property transferred may fluctuate. In principle the valuation has to be made at the date of the transaction but in making the 'mismatch calculation' it is permissible to take into account to a limited degree *ex post facto* developments. The extent to which such developments must be 'certain' before they can be considered remains itself uncertain partly because it is a question of fact to be determined on the totality of the evidence in any given case (see eg *Phillips v Brewin Dolphin Bell* [2001] WLR 143, HL; *Re Thoars* [2002] EWHC 2416; Ho (2003) 8(2) JIBFL 43 and (2001) 6 JIBFL 263).

Intent: 'For the purpose of' (s 423(3))   The very essence of s 423(3) is to be found in the requirement that a transaction was entered into 'for *the* purpose of...' [emphasis added]. There is an immediate problem with that formulation. What if there is more than one purpose for making a 'transaction at an undervalue'? In *Chohan v Saggar* [1992] BCC 306 Evans-Lombe QC, following the opinion of Lord Oliver in *Brady v Brady* [1989] AC 755, stated that the word 'purpose' 'must be construed bearing in mind the mischief against which the section in which that word appears is aimed' (at 321). The judge then continued by concluding that in the context of s 423 'It would defeat [the] purpose [of s 423] if it were possible successfully to contend that if the owner was able to point to another purpose, such as the benefit of his family, friends or the advantage of business associates, the section could not be applied' (cited with approval by the Court of Appeal in *Royscott Spa Leasing Ltd v Lovett* [1994] NPC 146 and *Barclays Bank plc v Eustice* [1995] 1 WLR 1238). Where the transaction at an undervalue takes the form of a gift on trust then one might have to add 'estate planning' to the above list, there being no obvious reason why this particular purpose should be privileged (see in a context of corporate tax avoidance *Aiglon v Gau Shan* [1993] 1 Lloyd's Rep 164 and Miller [1998] Conv 362 at 373). But where more than one purpose is pleaded is it also necessary to establish which is the dominant purpose? In *Royscott Spa Leasing Ltd v Lovett* Sir Christopher Slade, obiter, rejected the 'dominant purpose' criterion preferring instead the proposition that what 'has to be established . . . is substantial purpose, rather than the stricter test of dominant purpose' (see Miller at 368–372 for a discussion of this point).

Although the authorities have been in some disarray on this issue the Court of Appeal in *Inland Revenue Comrs v Hashmi* [2002] WTLR 1027 has confirmed that the 'substantial purpose' criterion is to be preferred to those of 'sole purpose' or 'dominant purpose' (see Keay [2003] 67 Conv 272 who argues that any attempt to impose a qualifying epithet to the statutory language will work to the detriment of creditors in a way unwarranted by the wording of s 423(3)). In *Hashmi* Arden LJ added, however, that it is necessary to distinguish between a purpose and a consequence. She summarised the position as follows (at 1035):

> [Section 423] does not require the inquiry to be made whether the purpose was a dominant purpose. It is sufficient if the statutory purpose can be properly be described as a purpose and not merely as a consequence . . . [I]t will often be the case that the motive to defeat creditors and the motive to secure family protection will co-exist in such a way that even the transferor himself may be unable to say what was uppermost in his mind.

After using 'a homely example' based around posting letters and simultaneously walking one's dog to demonstrate the possible combinations of purposes and consequences Arden LJ concluded:

> [F]or something to be a purpose it must be a real substantial purpose; it is not sufficient to quote something which is a by-product of the transaction under consideration, or to show it was simply a result of it . . . or an element which made no contribution of importance to the debtor's purpose of carrying out the transaction under consideration. [T]rivial purposes must be excluded.

There remains one further matter to be resolved under s 423. Is the test for establishing the required 'intention' a subjective or an objective one? The meaning of 'intent to defraud' was extensively litigated under the old legislation, not least because it was rarely possible to prove the presence of intent by direct evidence. Reliance was inevitably placed on drawing inferences from the surrounding circumstances. Whether the inferences could then be said to amount to an irrebuttable presumption of intent to defraud caused sharp differences of judicial opinion (cf *Freeman v Pope* (1870) 5 Ch App 538 at 541, and *Re Wise* (1886) 17 QBD 290 at 298).

The Cork Report had urged that it be made clear that 'intent may be inferred whenever this is the natural and probable consequence of the debtor's actions, in the light of the financial circumstances of the debtor at the time, as known, or taken to have been known to him' (para 1215). Confusingly s 423 retains the subjective element of intent ('for the purpose of'), but sidesteps the issue of whether and in what circumstances inferences should be drawn. Arden LJ in *Inland Revenue Comrs v Hashmi* confirms that it is open to the court 'to draw inferences which are appropriate' but without further clarifying the point (see also *Beckenham MC Ltd v Centralex Ltd* [2004] 2 BCLC 764 applying *Hashmi*). It is probably correct to say that the mere fact that creditors have been defeated or prejudiced is not sufficient per se to establish intention. Beyond that, perhaps all that can usefully be said is that it is now, as it probably always was, a question of fact to be decided in the light of the circumstances. Furthermore, as was thought to be the position under LPA 1925, s 172, the surrounding circumstances are capable of establishing a presumption that the requisite purpose was present. The onus will then be on the transferor or settlor to satisfy the court that this was not so. (See *Moon v Franklin* (1990) *Independent*, 22 June, where the court was unpersuaded by the insolvent's claim that a gift of £65,000 to his wife was 'an expression of gratitude for all the help and support you have given me'.)

What are the surrounding circumstances? Little is to be gained now by a recital of earlier case law and the most relevant circumstances are likely to be the financial position of the settlor and the time of the transaction. Where a person owing debts but who is still solvent (ie assets exceed personal liabilities) transfers property at an undervalue with the result that 'what remains in the hands of the debtor barely if at all covers the debt' (per Schiemann LJ in *Barclays Bank plc v Eustice* op cit, at 1248) then the inference that the purpose of the transaction falls within s 423(3) is likely to be strong. The inference will be still stronger if the transfer takes place at a time when action by the creditor prejudiced is anticipated or even probable should certain events occur. In *Inland Revenue Comrs v Hashmi*, for instance, in setting aside a declaration of trust over an interest in freehold property the judge held that the settlor, at the time of declaring the trust, 'was sitting on a "potential financial bomb" although there was no inevitability that it would ever explode' (at 1033).

Matters may not always be quite so straightforward [sic]. Consider, for instance, the position of a person who is intending to set up in business and is solvent with no immediate probability of insolvency occurring, and who then settles property on a spouse or on discretionary trusts, but subsequently finds that the business venture fails.

Re Butterworth, ex p Russell (1882) 19 Ch D 588

Charles Butterworth (B) had for many years been a successful baker in Manchester. He proposed to purchase a grocery business, a trade in which he had no experience, but before doing so he settled most of his property on his family. The grocery business was unsuccessful but B sold it six months later for the same price he had paid for it. He continued with his baker's business but was declared bankrupt when this failed three years later. The Court of Appeal held that the settlement was made with 'intent to defraud' and could be set aside, albeit by the creditors of the previously successful bakery business.

> **Jessell MR** [at 598]: The principle of *Mackay v Douglas* ((1872) LR 14 Eq 106), and that line of cases, is this, that a man is not entitled to go into a hazardous business, and immediately before doing so settle all his property voluntarily, the object being this: 'If I succeed in business, I make a fortune for myself. If I fail, I leave my creditors unpaid. They will bear the loss.' That is the very thing which the statute of Elizabeth was meant to prevent. The object of the settlor was to put his property out of the reach of his future creditors. He contemplated engaging in this new trade and he wanted to preserve his property from his future creditors. That cannot be done by a voluntary settlement. That is, to my mind, a clear and satisfactory principle.

Consider the following points:

(1) The 'principle of *Mackay v Douglas*' as elaborated in *Re Butterworth* was applied in the context of s 423 in *Midland Bank plc v Wyatt* [1995] 1 FLR 697, where a purported declaration of trust of the equity in the family home in favour of, inter alia, two daughters was set aside. A proposition to the effect that the principle should apply 'only where the settlor is about to enter into a business involving a high degree of risk either as a sole practitioner or as a partner' was firmly rejected (cf *Law Society v Southall* [2002] BPIR 336: no evidence at the time of the gift that the donor was in financial difficulties or was conducting a risky business). In *Wyatt* the defendant's 'contemplated fabrics business' had good prospects and was set up as a limited liability company nine months after the purported declaration of trust. The company was put into receivership some three-and-a-half years later. Note, however, that at no time was the bank, or indeed a business partner, made aware of the purported declaration of trust over the property upon the security of which the bank had loaned money to

Wyatt. (See also ch 4 at p 164: an alternative ground for the decision of the court was that the trust declaration was 'a sham' and therefore void and unenforceable.)

(2) Is the 'principle of *Mackay v Douglas*' an anachronism, given the availability of limited liability status under the Companies Act 2006 (but consider: (i) the liability of wrongful trading under IA 1986, s 214; and (ii) erstwhile creditors may insist on personal guarantees of company debts)? Is the fact that a family's liabilities may extend to include consumption debts as well as business debts a relevant consideration?

(3) Section 423(3) speaks of 'putting assets beyond the reach of *a* person' rather than '*any* person' (as under the previous law in LPA 1925, s 172). Can it be argued that the new formulation is intended to restrict the scope of the section to an identifiable creditor, rather than 'any' potential creditor? The point was not raised in *Midland Bank plc v Wyatt*.

(4) One presumably unintended quirk of the enactment of s 423 deserves comment. A transaction for valuable and adequate consideration does not constitute a 'transaction at an undervalue' (s 423(1)(c)). One consequence is that on a strict interpretation of the sub-section such a transaction made *with the intent of* prejudicing the interests of creditors could now be valid even where the transferee has knowledge of the intent. Indeed, this was the outcome at first instance in *Agricultural Mortgage Corpn plc v Woodward* (see above) but would not have been so under LPA 1925, s 172 (see *Lloyds Bank Ltd v Marcan* ([1973] 3 All ER 754). The Court of Appeal in *Woodward* was able to sidestep this problem by finding that the transaction was, in fact, at an undervalue. Different considerations apply where an individual is adjudged bankrupt. Such a transaction may then be open to challenge as representing a 'fraudulent' or 'voidable' preference (see Cork Report paras 1241–1277; Insolvency Act 1986, s 340).

(5) Is there any inconsistency of philosophy in a system of law that permits s 423 to co-exist with the protective trust (TA 1925, s 33)?

(4) Bankruptcy and transactions at an undervalue: Insolvency Act 1986, ss 339, 341

339(1) Subject as follows in this section and sections 341 and 342, where an individual is adjudged bankrupt and he has at a relevant time (defined in section 341) entered into a transaction with any person at an undervalue, the trustee of the bankrupt's estate may apply to the court for an order under this section.

(2) The court shall on such an application, make such order as it thinks fit for restoring the position to what it would have been if that individual had not entered into that transaction.

(3) For the purposes of this section and sections 341 and 342, an individual enters into a transaction with a person at an undervalue if –

(a) he makes a gift to that person or he otherwise enters into a transaction with that person on terms that provide for him to receive no consideration,
(b) he enters into a transaction with that person in consideration of marriage, or
(c) he enters into a transaction with that person for a consideration the value of which, in money or money's worth, is significantly less than the value, in money or money's worth, of the consideration provided by the individual.

341(1) Subject as follows, the time at which an individual enters into a transaction at an undervalue . . . is a relevant time if the transaction is entered into . . .

(a) in the case of a transaction at an undervalue, at a time in the period of 5 years ending with the day of the presentation of the bankruptcy petition on which the individual is adjudged bankrupt,
(b) . . .
(c) . . .

(2) Where an individual enters into a transaction at an undervalue . . . at a time mentioned in paragraph (a) . . . of subsection (1) (not being, in the case of a transaction at an undervalue, a time less than 2 years before the end of the period mentioned in paragraph (a)), that time is not a relevant time for the purposes of section 339 . . . unless the individual –

(a) is insolvent at that time, or
(b) becomes insolvent in consequence of the transaction . . . ;
but the requirements of this subsection are presumed to be satisfied, unless the contrary is shown, in relation to any transaction at an undervalue which is entered into by an individual with a person who is an associate of his (otherwise than by reason only of being his employee).

(3) For the purposes of subsection (2), an individual is insolvent if –

(a) he is unable to pay his debts as they fall due, or
(b) the value of his assets is less than the amount of his liabilities, taking into account his contingent and prospective liabilities.

Section 339 removes many of the curiosities of language so criticised in the Cork Report and reaffirms the vulnerability of settlements created by a property-owner who is subsequently adjudicated bankrupt. A trustee in bankruptcy may in certain circumstances apply for an order, inter alia, to vest in the trustee (s 342(1)(a)) any property transferred in 'a transaction at an undervalue' which includes gifts on trust as well as outright gifts. The statute in effect preserves the pre-existing position that the settlement is not void from inception but merely liable to be upset at the aegis of the trustee in bankruptcy. This will be so irrespective of the settlor's intention when making the settlement.

For a settlement to be upset it must fall within the two requirements of ss 339 and 341. First, and a prerequisite, is that there must be a 'transaction at an undervalue' (s 339(3)), as there will almost always be in the case of a voluntary settlement. The second requirement concerns the time when the settlement is made. The effect of s 341 is to distinguish between the case where a settlor is adjudged bankrupt within two years of the date of the settlement, and that where the settlor becomes bankrupt between two and five years after the creation of the settlement (s 341(1)(a)). In the first instance the solvency of the settlor is an irrelevant consideration: the transaction may still be set aside. In the second instance, however, the settlement will be valid unless at the date of the settlement the settlor was insolvent, as defined by the extremely wide criteria of s 341(3).

Transactions at an undervalue   Gifts or transfers of property between family members are vulnerable to challenge by a trustee in bankruptcy. In particular where one spouse is adjudicated bankrupt, prior acquisition by the other spouse of an equitable share in the family home during the period specified under s 341(1), can be set aside to the extent that the share exceeds the value of his or her financial contribution to the acquisition (see *Re Densham* [1975] 1 WLR 1519, and generally Chapter 12). Indeed, even a transfer of property made in compliance with a property adjustment order under the Matrimonial Causes Act (MCA) 1973 provides no automatic protection against a subsequent application by the trustee in bankruptcy under s 339 (IA 1986, Sch 14 amending MCA 1973, s 39). There is a tension here between two statutory schemes, one for the protection of a former spouse and child, and the other for the protection of a bankrupt's creditors. Both are competing 'for shares in a fund which will always be incapable of satisfying both' (per Thorpe LJ in *Haines v Hill* [2007] 2 WLR 1250 at [43]). Nevertheless, as is recognised in that case, there is little chance of an MCA order failing to satisfy the 'consideration' requirements of s 339 where it results from 'a hard-fought trial', and assuming the absence of any vitiating factor such as fraud, mistake, or concealment of information.

But what of the position where the transfer of property is made under a compromise of a claim for a property adjustment order under MCA 1973, s 24? The Bankruptcy Act 1914, s 42(1), the predecessor of s 339, excluded from its scope 'any settlement . . . made in favour of a purchaser . . . in good faith and for valuable consideration'. In *Re Abbott* [1982] 3 All ER 181 the Divisional Court accepted that under a compromise which involved a payment of £9,000 from her subsequently bankrupt husband, 'there was no transfer of a proprietary interest by the wife to the husband as part of the bargain . . . there was a compromise of (a right) not measurable in money terms' (at 185). But neither of these elements was held to prevent the compromise from constituting valuable consideration under s 42(1).

Under IA 1986, s 339(3)(c), however, consideration is defined more stringently in that it (i) must not be 'significantly less than the value, in money or money's worth of the consideration provided' by the bankrupt, and (ii) must be capable of being measured in money or money's worth. Notwithstanding the changes in language and the introduction of the notion of 'significant

Table 6.1 IA 1986: ss 339 and 423 qualifying conditions

	S 339	S 423
1. Bankruptcy	Applies only where individual is adjudged bankrupt	Applies irrespective of bankruptcy
2. Locus standi	Only trustee in bankruptcy can apply	'Any person prejudiced'
3. Transaction = transfer at an undervalue	Yes	Yes
4. Intent of settlor	No need to establish intent	'Intent' is a prerequisite
5. Time of transaction	Distinguish between (i) transaction up to 2 years before bankruptcy *and* (ii) transaction between 2 and 5 years before bankruptcy	No retrospective statutory time limit

undervalue', it appears that *Re Abbott* is still applicable 'to the extent that it decides that a compromise of a claim to a provision in matrimonial proceedings is capable of being consideration in money or money's worth' (*per* Ferris J in *Re Kumar* [1993] 2 All ER 700 at 711). However, because under s 339, unlike the old law, the value of the consideration must be assessed, it is apparent that the terms of any compromise approved by a court order, in particular its financial credibility, remains open to scrutiny by the court in any subsequent bankruptcy proceedings in assessing whether the 'consideration' offered by the bankrupt's spouse was adequate (see generally *Haines v Hill* [2007] 2 WLR 1250; Capper (2008) 124 LQR 361; and *Re Kumar* at 712–716).

(5) Conclusion

The scope of the jurisdiction available under IA 1986, ss 339 and 423 overlaps to some extent and Table 6.1 summarises their relationship to five separate factors.

These statutory provisions and the common law restraint are, generally speaking, effective in favour of creditors of *settlors*. But creditors of *beneficiaries* are also potentially prejudiced by discretionary trusts and even more so by protective trusts. Provided the settlor remains solvent, the Insolvency Act provisions have nothing to 'bite on'. Consequently it can be claimed that trusts law provides its own form of 'limited liability' for beneficiaries' property and for their families. How far this outcome is attributable to the ideological appeal of 'caretaker motivations' or to perceptions about the aims of insolvency law or simply to the logical consequences of a narrow legal formalism, as described earlier in this chapter, is an issue suitable for speculation if probably incapable of resolution.

(6) 'Asset protection trusts' and offshore jurisdictions

At several points in this book we emphasise that the dimension of 'location' is one factor that can contribute to the attractions of the trust to its potential clientele. Fiscal advantages are not the only ones associated with offshore jurisdictions. It is possible at some expense to take advantage of favourable 'asset protection trust' legislation, which is drafted so as to provide more extensive protection to settlors than that available under domestic legislation such as the IA 1986 provisions (see Matthews (1995) 6 KCLJ 62 at 62–88; and generally O'Sullivan *Asset Protection Trusts* (2000); and Thomas in Glasson and Thomas (eds) *The International Trust* (2nd edn, 2006) ch 6). The features of the legislation vary but might (i) exclude future creditors thereby reversing the 'principle of *Mackay v Douglas*'; (ii) allow transactions to be set aside only within a short period of their being made (eg one year); and (iii) refuse to enforce judgments from other jurisdictions. In addition some jurisdictions may increase the burden of proof on claimants to show, for instance, 'beyond reasonable doubt' that the principal intent of the settlement was to defraud the claimant creditor and that the settlement rendered the settlor insolvent (see the Cook Islands legislation, International Trusts Act 1984, ss 13B and 13D; and Duckworth (1999) 32 Vand J Trans L 879 at 930–932). The attraction is evident but there are pitfalls. In the UK a bankrupt will be guilty of an offence (IA 1986, s 357) if in the five years before the bankruptcy he entered into certain defined transactions unless he can prove that he had no intent 'to defraud or conceal his state of affairs' (s 352) from creditors.

Asset protection trusts of this nature appeal to a wider constituency than the individual wealthy citizen. Comparable arrangements may be adopted by transnational corporations particularly where they are concerned about the possible implications of fiscal or political change (see Wiggin 'Asset Protection for Multinational Corporations' and Schoenblum 'The Adaptation of the Asset Protection Trust for Use by the Multinational Corporation: The American Perspective' in McKendrick (ed) *Commercial Aspects of Trusts and Fiduciary Obligations* (1992) at pp 195 and 217 respectively).

The emphasis here has been on the possibilities of using the offshore 'asset protection trust' to secure assets out of the reach of creditors. A further reason for placing assets in an offshore trust may be to attempt to prevent the assets being taken into account in proceedings for financial provision on divorce. In *Charman v Charman* [2007] EWCA Civ 503, for instance, in divorce proceedings before the English courts it was argued on behalf of Mr Charman, the settlor, that £68m held within an offshore trust (The Dragon Holdings Trust) with Bermudan trustees and whose governing law was that of Bermuda should not be regarded as 'financial resources . . . which he has or is likely to have in the foreseeable future' (MCA 1973, s 25(2)(a)) and was therefore not fit for inclusion at all in the computation of his assets. Whereas Mr Charman argued that the trust was a 'dynastic trust' with the assets set-aside for future generations of the family, the Court of Appeal upholding the High Court judgment concluded on the evidence that the trust was a self-settled discretionary trust of which Mr Charman was a potential beneficiary (Kleiner and Munro (2007) 21(3) TLI 117–124; Graham [2007] PCB 6, 450–456). The tenor of the following guidance from Sir Mark Potter, giving the judgment of the Court of Appeal, may give greater comfort to family lawyers than to trusts lawyers (at para 57):

[W]henever it is necessary to conduct an enquiry [as to the attributability of the assets in a trust] it is essential for the court to bring to it a judicious mixture of worldly realism and of respect for the legal effects of trusts, the legal duties of trustees and, in the case of off-shore trusts, the jurisdictions of off-shore courts. In the circumstances of the present case it would have been a shameful emasculation of the court's duty to be fair if the assets which the husband built up in Dragon during the marriage had not been attributed to him.

The reference to offshore courts reflects the fact that in these cases jurisdictional issues can come to the fore, such as whether those courts will be prepared to enforce court orders made under the Matrimonial Causes Act 1973 or indeed whether disclosure of information by trustees will be ordered. All that can be said here on this complex topic is that much may depend on the provisions of local trusts laws and whether there are reciprocal enforcement arrangements between the offshore jurisdiction and the United Kingdom. It is evident, however, that English courts will be wary of granting orders which are unlikely to be enforced (see eg Hoffmann [2008] PCB 3, 168–175; Renouf and Hanson [2006] PCB 5, 310–317).

3. Other purposes contrary to public policy

(a) General

When considering this 'loose class of prohibitions' a distinction needs to be drawn between those cases where the validity of a trust is itself in issue and those where a particular restriction, usually in the form of a condition precedent or subsequent, is challenged. The consequences of conditions precedent or subsequent being invalid have already been described (see p 268) and can be contrasted with the result where the whole trust is void on grounds of public policy. Then the property will be held on resulting trust for the settlor or, where the trust arises under a will, fall into the residuary estate of the testator. If by some chance the property is itself the residuary estate, or if there is no residuary gift, it will become property undisposed of by the will and devolve accordingly, ie broadly speaking in accordance with the provisions of the law on intestate succession (see Kerridge *Parry and Clark: The Law of Succession* (11th edn, 2002) ch 2).

We consider only briefly here the relation between public policy and certain restrictive conditions inserted in settlements, and consequently scarcely touch on the extensive case law that has accumulated in this general area (see eg *Pettit* pp 205–213 for a more extensive account). Where a condition fails for being too uncertain there is, of course, no need to take the further step of considering whether the condition is void as being contrary to public policy.

Public policy in this context has operated over a narrow area, arguably reflecting the prevailing social mores, family traditions and the economic realities of marriage, during the periods in which the rules emerged. The rules are directed primarily at discouraging attempts to undermine the institution of marriage and at protecting the interests of children. Accordingly conditions intended to prevent marriage altogether or to encourage separation or divorce are generally considered to be void. The simplicity of the picture is complicated a little by two refinements. The first involves our old friend the determinable interest. A determinable gift – to A until marriage to B – will be valid, it being construed as merely demonstrating an intention to provide support until marriage and, placing faith in love's disdain for things material, not to discourage marriage altogether (*Re Lovell* [1920] 1 Ch 122). Second, the tensions induced by the demands of freedom of disposition reappear since this also is a value prized by public policy. Accordingly, a compromise has been struck whereby partial restraints on marriage are prima facie valid, subject to the formal requirement that where the property is personal, there must be an express gift over if the condition is to be effective. Partial restraints have generally been directed towards discouraging marriage with particular individuals or persons of particular religious faith or nationality.

Where the interests of children are involved, public policy has intervened to invalidate conditions designed to interfere with the proper exercise of parental duties (*Re Sandbrook* [1912] 2 Ch 471). But here again the law draws back from too intrusive a stance. It was argued in *Blathwayt v Baron Cawley* [1975] 3 All ER 625 that a clause providing for the forfeiture of the interest of a child if he became a Roman Catholic should be void because it might undesirably influence his parents in bringing him up. This was firmly rejected by the House of Lords. In Lord Wilberforce's words (at 637): 'To say that any condition which in any way might affect or influence the way in which a child is brought up, or in which parental duties are exercised, [is invalid] seems to me to state far too wide a rule.'

(b) Racial and religious discrimination

One further area in which settlors and testators have attempted to exercise their freedom of disposition is religion. Conditions imposing restrictions on choice of religion have been the source of much litigation. These have never been held contrary to public policy although the strict requirement of certainty for conditions subsequent has on occasions proved fatal (*Clayton v Ramsden* [1943] AC 320). The most recent judicial pronouncement came in the final round of litigation on the will of Robert Blathwayt where the House of Lords commented obiter on the present function of public policy. (See *Re Morrison's Will Trusts* [1939] 4 All ER 332 and *Re Blathwayt's Will Trusts* [1950] 1 All ER 582 for the earlier reported contests.)

Blathwayt v Baron Cawley [1975] 3 All ER 625 at 634

Clause 9 of the testator's will, made in 1934, declared inter alia that 'if any person who under the trusts . . . shall become entitled . . . shall (a) Be or become a

Roman Catholic . . . then . . . the estate limited to him shall cease. . . . ' The House of Lords unanimously agreed that Clause 9 was not void for uncertainty nor as being contrary to public policy on the ground of impermissible discrimination, nor on the grounds that it might undesirably influence the child's parents as to the child's upbringing.

The case is extracted on the discrimination point only.

Lord Wilberforce: . . . it was said that the law of England was now set against discrimination on a number of grounds including religious grounds, and appeal was made to the Race Relations Act 1968 which does not refer to religion and to the European Convention of Human Rights of 1950 which refers to freedom of religion and to enjoyment of that freedom and other freedoms without discrimination on ground of religion. My Lords, I do not doubt that conceptions of public policy should move with the times and that widely accepted treaties and statutes may point the direction in which such conceptions, as applied by the courts, ought to move. It may well be that conditions such as this are, or at least are becoming, inconsistent with standards now widely accepted. But acceptance of this does not persuade me that we are justified, particularly in relation to a will which came into effect as long ago as 1936 and which has twice been the subject of judicial consideration, in introducing for the first time a rule which would go far beyond the mere avoidance of discrimination on religious grounds. To do so would bring about a substantial reduction of another freedom, firmly rooted in our law, namely that of testamentary disposition. Discrimination is not the same thing as choice: it operates over a larger and less personal area, and neither by express provision nor by implication has private selection yet become a matter of public policy.

Lord Cross: Turning to the question of public policy, it is true that it is widely thought nowadays that it is wrong for a government to treat some of its citizens less favourably than others because of differences in their religious beliefs; but it does not follow from that that it is against public policy for an adherent of one religion to distinguish in disposing of his property between adherents of his faith and those of another. So to hold would amount to saying that although it is in order for a man to have a mild preference for one religion as opposed to another it is disreputable for him to be convinced of the importance of holding true religious beliefs and of the fact that his religious beliefs are the true ones.

The race relations legislation referred to by Lord Wilberforce has been replaced by the Race Relations Act 1976 where racial discrimination is defined in the following manner:

Race Relations Act 1976, ss 1, 3

1. RACIAL DISCRIMINATION

(1) A person discriminates against another in any circumstances relevant for the purposes of any provision of this Act if –

(a) on racial grounds he treats that other less favourably than he treats or would treat other persons; . . .

3. Interpretation

(1) In this Act, unless the context otherwise requires –

'racial grounds' means any of the following grounds, namely colour, race, nationality or ethnic or national origins.

Broadly comparable provisions concerning discrimination on grounds of religion or belief are to be found in the Equality Act 2006, ss 44 and 45. Both statutes make 'discriminatory' behaviour unlawful only in certain specified situations such as employment, education and the provision of goods and services, ie broadly speaking in the public domain. It would therefore appear, subject to what follows, that the statutes do not apply to the creation of private express trusts.

Lord Wilberforce refers to the European Convention on Human Rights in his opinion in *Blathwayt v Baron Cawley*. Since that judgment the Human Rights Act 1998 has been passed and, in effect, incorporates most Convention rights into our law. As from 2 October 2000, the implementation date of the Act, it has been 'unlawful for a public authority to act in a way which is incompatible with a Convention right' (s 6(1)). Amongst the Convention rights are Article 8(1) – 'everyone has the right to respect for his private life and family life, his home and his correspondence' – and Article 9(1) – 'Everyone has the right to freedom of thought, conscience and religion; this right includes freedom to change his religion or belief and freedom . . . to manifest his belief in worship, teaching, practice and observance'. Both Articles are subject to qualifications in Articles 8(2) and 9(2) respectively which specify, inter alia, that the rights can be subject to such limitations as 'are necessary in a democratic society . . . for the protection of the rights and freedom of others'. Trustees of private trusts are not 'a public authority' and, formally at least, the Act does not appear to affect the rights of settlors to exercise their freedom of disposition in a manner such as that in *Blathwayt v Baron Cawley*. But courts are 'public authorities' for the purposes of the Act. Can it then be argued that courts should not recognise as valid clauses such as that in *Blathwayt* on the grounds that they are incompatible with a Convention right? There are a number of difficulties with the proposition. One is that it is premised on a highly contentious argument to the effect that the Act affects rights and remedies in private law disputes (see eg Hunt [1998] PL 423; Phillipson (1999) 62 MLR 824: Buxton LJ (2000) 116 LQR 48, but cf Wade (2000) 116 LQR 217). Second, it may be argued that such a clause in any event is protected by the qualifications referred to above concerning 'the protection of the rights and freedoms of others'. Finally it can be contended that an individual's freedom, for instance, 'to manifest one's religion or belief' is not prevented although it may be made more costly if it incurs, through the operation of a forfeiture clause, the loss of a financial benefit previously enjoyed. It might be argued that this last-named outcome infringes 'the right to peaceful enjoyment of possessions, free from unjustifiable interference by the state' (Article 1 of Protocol 1 of the ECHR) but this claim will encounter the countervailing proposition that an individual's right to designate his successors and on what terms is equally protected by the same provision.

Consider the following questions:

(1) Even if not directly prohibited under a statute or by a Convention right would a forfeiture clause inserted in a settlement made after 1976 seeking to prevent a beneficiary from *marrying* a person of either a specific religious or racial group be void on grounds of public policy? Consider whether such clauses would operate over the 'larger and less personal area' referred to by Lord Wilberforce.

(2) 'It is sophistry to argue that the creation of discriminatory forfeiture clauses is a valid exercise of private property rights but that their subsequent enforcement requires the active intervention of the state judicial machinery and this intervention (ie to enforce a claim) would be contrary to state public policy.' Do you agree?

(3) The opposing poles of valid or void need not be the only options for 'discriminatory forfeiture clauses'. Would it be both consistent with legal principle and a practical compromise for the courts to recognise a species of condition which is valid but unenforceable?

(4) The approach in *Blathwayt v Baron Cawley* can be compared with developments in Canadian law. In a 1995 case, *Re Murley*, the judge asserted – no reasoning was offered – that a provision 'which restricts the religious affiliation of any person is, in Canada, contrary to public policy' ((1995) 130 Nfld & PEIR 271 at 274). This invocation of public policy has been lent a firmer basis by dicta in subsequent cases suggesting that testamentary conditions in restraints of religion may infringe the Canadian Charter of Rights and Freedoms (see Grattan and Conway (2005) 50 McGill LJ 511–552; see further Reichman in Friedmann and Barak-Erez (eds) *Human Rights in Private Law* (2003) ch 11).

(c) A statutory limitation on freedom of testation

In principle English law, unlike many civil law systems, imposes no general restrictions on testators' freedom to bequeath their property as they wish. There are no specific statutory directions as to the proportion of property, for instance, that must be given to one's descendants. But we have seen that the freedom of settlors to attach restrictive conditions to gifts can occasionally be reined in by the courts. But a testator may wish to exercise testamentary freedom by adopting a still more radical option. What if a will makes no or inadequate provision for a testator's family or dependants? To protect their interests public policy has intervened here also, in the form of the Inheritance (Provision for Family and Dependants) Act 1975. The statute enables the court in its discretion to order that provision be made out of a deceased person's estate where, whether by will or on intestacy, 'reasonable financial provision' has not been made for the applicant (s 2(1), and see Sachs [1990] Conv 45). The court is given wide powers by the statute, similar to those in the Insolvency Act, to undo the effects of dispositions by the deceased up to six years before death, and made with the intention of defeating an application for financial provision under the statute (s 10(2)). In this instance the necessary intention, and it need not be the sole intention, is to be determined on the balance of probabilities (s 12(1)).

It is probable that the very existence of the jurisdiction influences the content of wills since advisers almost always inform clients of the risks of failing to make proper provision for the five categories of persons defined in s 1(1) (see eg Masson [1994] Conv 360 at 367–368). Most reported litigation centres around the fifth category, 'any person who immediately before the death of the deceased was being maintained, either wholly or partly, by the deceased' (see eg *Bishop v Plumley* [1991] 1 All ER 236; Bridge [1991] CLJ 42; and generally Miller [2000] PCB 5, 305–314). It has been common for cases here to involve cohabiting relationships but the legislation has been amended so that now cohabitees and civil partners (and same-sex cohabitees) who were living as the husband or wife or partner of the deceased in the same household in the two years preceding death can claim reasonable financial provision without having to establish dependency (Law Reform (Succession) Act 1995, s 2; Civil Partnership Act 2004, Sch 4, part 2; and see *Re Watson (dec'd)* [1999] 1 FLR 878 on the 'living together as man and wife' requirement).

(d) Statutory limitation on dispositions to defeat the claims of a spouse

An approach broadly comparable to that described above is adopted under the Matrimonial Causes Act (MCA)1973, s 37. This enables the court to set aside certain dispositions, including those made by trust, entered into with the intention of defeating a claim by a spouse for financial relief. Where the disposition was made within three years before the date of the application there is a rebuttable statutory presumption (s 37(5)) that the disposition was made with the necessary intent. Otherwise the intent to defeat the claim must be affirmatively proved.

4. Trusts, illegality and public policy: a case for reform?

Notwithstanding the existence of statutory provisions such as IA 1986, s 423 or MCA 1973, s 37 there remains a temptation for property-owners to attempt to safeguard their assets from the claims of others such as creditors or spouses. In the context of the insolvency provisions, for instance, an individual may transfer property to some other person, usually a family member, with the intention of recovering it once the threat from the creditors has passed (as in eg *Gascoigne v Gascoigne* [1918] 1 KB 223). If the transaction remains undiscovered by creditors and the parties to the transaction remain on good terms then the attempt may prove successful and the property be restored. But what if the parties fall out? Can the transferor lawfully recover the property?

One potential means of recovery will be for the transferor to claim that he or she retains an equitable interest in the transferred property under a presumed resulting trust. It will be recalled (see *Re Vandervell's Trusts (No 2)* [1974] 1 All ER 47; Chapter 4) that where A transfers property to B then, in the absence of any bargain, B is presumed to hold the property on resulting trust for A. This presumption is, not surprisingly, rebuttable by evidence, for instance, to the effect that A's intention was to make a gift to B (see eg *Tinker v Tinker* [1970] P 136). Moreover, the presumption may in some cases, primarily those where certain family relationships are present, be displaced by a competing presumption of advancement, ie the intent of A to make a gift to B is presumed. In English law the latter presumption is probably limited to gifts from (i) father to child, and (ii) husband to wife, but not vice versa. Nor is there any presumption of advancement between more remote family relationships or between cohabiting couples of whatever sexual orientation. A cautionary word is necessary about the scope of a presumed resulting trust following the 4:1 decision of the House of Lords in *Stack v Dowden* [2007] UKHL 17 to the effect that transfer of title in a family home into joint names and therefore joint *legal* ownership raises a very strong presumption of joint *equitable* ownership also, applying the maxim 'equity follows the law' (see also *Gibson v Revenue and Customs Prosecution Office* [2008] EWCA Civ 645 for a suggestion that where a home is purchased in joint names the 'presumption of joint beneficial ownership' now performs the function of the presumption of advancement (at [27]). The full implications of *Stack v Dowden* are discussed in Chapter 12 but it is questionable whether the 'very strong presumption' has any weight where title to assets is placed in *sole* legal ownership. Moreover Baroness Hale's observation in the case that 'context is everything' means that there may yet be scope for the presumptions of resulting trust and advancement to operate outside the 'purchase of a family home' context (see eg *Laskar v Laskar* [2008] EWCA Civ 347 'property purchased as investments').

How then should the courts respond to attempts to recover assets whether in the context of insolvency or otherwise (cf *Re Emery's Investments' Trusts* [1959] Ch 410 'tax evasion'; *Tinsley v Milligan* [1993] 3 All ER 65 'social security fraud'; *Lowson v Coombes* [1999] Ch 373 'avoidance of claims under Matrimonial Causes Act 1973, s 37'; *Khan v Ali* [2002] 5 ITELR 232 'alleged mortgage fraud')? What weight should be attached, for instance, to the presumptions of resulting trust or advancement? Should the outcome depend, for instance, on such factors as whether the illegal purpose has to any degree been carried out or whether the illegal purpose has to be relied upon to establish the claim? Should the deterrence of illegality be a consideration?

In *Tinsley v Milligan* the House of Lords by a bare majority decided that reliance could be placed upon doctrines of property law, including the competing presumptions of resulting trust and advancement, to enforce a claim. Unfortunately this 'reliance principle' approach is uncertain in scope and effect, a point illustrated by *Tinsley v Milligan* itself and by a subsequent case *Tribe v Tribe* [1996] Ch 107. In the former case a lesbian couple purchased a house together intending to share ownership of it. They agreed that legal title to the house should be put in the name of one of them, Tinsley (T), so that the other, Milligan (M), would be able to make various fraudulent social security claims. After some years the relationship broke down and T moved out of the residence. At about the same time M, as it was put, 'made her peace' with the DSS and continued to draw benefit, this time lawfully. The litigation arose when T sought an order for possession claiming ownership of the property. M counterclaimed that T held the property on a 'presumed' resulting trust for them in equal shares. In response T contended that an equitable maxim 'he [sic] who comes to equity must come with clean hands' should be strictly applied; the presence of the illegal scheme should therefore prevent M from establishing her equitable interest in the property. Lord Browne-Wilkinson (with whom Lords Jauncey and Lowry concurred) stated that a party to illegality could still seek to enforce an equitable interest as long as he or she could establish that interest without relying on his or her own illegality.

> **Lord Browne-Wilkinson** (at 87): Where the presumption of resulting trust applies, the plaintiff does not have to rely on the illegality. If he proves that the property is vested in the defendant alone but that the plaintiff provided part of the purchase money, or voluntarily transferred the property to the defendant, the plaintiff establishes his claim under a resulting trust unless either the contrary presumption of advancement displaces the presumption of resulting trust or the defendant leads evidence to rebut the presumption of resulting trust. Therefore, in cases where the presumption of advancement does not apply, a plaintiff can establish his equitable interest in the property without relying in any way on the underlying illegal transaction.

On the facts of the case, whereas M could without any need for further explanation point to her financial contribution to the purchase of the property to establish her equitable interest, it was T who had to rely in evidence on the illegal purpose to support her 'clean hands' contention.

One problem with the majority opinion in *Tinsley v Milligan* is that the outcome appeared to depend on the type of relationship between transferor and transferee. What if the relationship is such that the presumption of advancement would apply to a transfer of property? In those circumstances it seems likely that the transferor's claim to establish full ownership of or a share in the property would fail. As Lord Browne-Wilkinson explained (at 87): '[In] such a case, unlike the case where the presumption of resulting trust applies, in order to establish any claim the plaintiff has himself to lead evidence sufficient to rebut the presumption of gift and in so doing will normally have to plead, and give evidence of, the underlying illegal purpose' (see eg *Shephard v Cartwright* [1955] AC 431). It would seem to follow that if a father puts property in the name of a son to defraud creditors he will be unable to recover the property ('presumption of advancement') but if the roles were reversed the son could recover ('presumption of resulting trust').

The consequences of this distinction between the presumptions were at issue in *Tribe v Tribe* [1996] Ch 107. There the plaintiff, the father of the defendant and the majority shareholder in a family company, was himself the tenant on a full repairing lease of two shop premises that the company occupied. It seemed likely (i) that he would be obliged to meet the cost of major repairs to the properties, and (ii) that he would have to sell his shares to do so. The plaintiff therefore transferred his shareholding to his son with the intention of deceiving his creditors and thereby protecting his assets. In the event no repairs were carried out and the judge found as a fact that there was no evidence of any creditor(s) being deceived. The son subsequently refused to return the shares to the father. It was argued on the son's behalf that the presumption of advancement applied and that the father could only rebut this by relying on the evidence of the illegal purpose, which evidence, under the 'reliance principle' as stated in *Tinsley v Milligan*, had to be disregarded. The Court of Appeal whilst accepting that it was bound by that 'general rule' held that there was an exception to it – 'the withdrawal exception': 'In a property transfer case the exception applies if the illegal purpose has not been carried into effect in any way' (per Nourse LJ at 121, citing as support a decision of the High Court of Australia, *Perpetual Executors and Trustees Association of Australia Ltd v Wright* (1917) 23 CLR 185; cf *Collier v Collier* [2002] EWCA 1095 CA where the presumption of advancement from a father to daughter could not be rebutted because the father had carried through a transaction intended to defeat creditors). Nourse LJ added that it was no 'objection to the plaintiff's right to recover the shares that he did not demand their return until after the danger had passed and it was no longer necessary to conceal the transfer from creditors. All that matters is that no deception was practised on them' (at 122; cf Enonchong [1996] RLR 78; Rose (1996) 112 LQR 386; Virgo (1996) 55 CLJ 23).

Consider the following points:

(1) *Tribe v Tribe* does not alter the fact that in English law where property is transferred for an illegal purpose that is carried through (as in *Tinsley v Milligan*) the outcome of an application to regain the property will

depend significantly on the presumption applicable. This distinction is generally seen as being indefensible. (See generally Berg [1993] JBL 513; Cohen [1994] LMCLQ 163; Enonchong (1994) 14 OJLS 295; Goo (1994) 45 NILQ 378; Halliwell [1994] Conv 62; Stowe (1994) 57 MLR 441; Davies in Oakley (ed) *Trends in Contemporary Trust Law* (1996) ch 2). The Court of Appeal has consistently applied the decision of the majority in *Tinsley v Milligan*, as it is bound to do, but not without voicing its criticism of the formalistic and restrictive nature of what can be termed the 'property doctrine' approach. In *Lowson v Coombs* [1999] Ch 373 Robert Walker LJ was critical of the importance attached to the presumption of advancement 'cogently criticised as being out of date in modern social and economic conditions... and as being uncertain in its scope' (at 385; see also comments of Nourse LJ in *Silverwood v Silverwood* (1997) 74 P & CR 453 at 458–459 and Cotterill [1999] LMCLQ 465).

Note that in *Nelson v Nelson* (1995) 132 ALR 133 a majority of the High Court of Australia rejected a test of enforceability based on the 'reliance principle' approach applied in *Tinsley v Milligan* – 'wholly unjustifiable on any policy ground' (at 166 per Dawson J) – in favour of an approach that held that an equitable right would be unenforceable *only* where the policy of the statute being circumvented was infringed. In *Nelson* the court held that, unlike the position in English law, a presumption of advancement could arise between mother and daughter. It further held that this did not bar the mother from asserting an equitable interest in property transferred to her daughter for an illegal purpose that had been carried into effect (cf *Tribe v Tribe*). The majority of the court tempered this outcome by making recognition of the mother's interest conditional on her surrendering to the government an amount equal to the benefit that she had unlawfully acquired from it. (See Creighton (1997) 60 MLR 102; Maclean (1997) 71 ALJ 185; Phang (1996) 11 JCL 53.)

(2) In *Tinsley v Milligan* [1993] 3 All ER 65 Lord Goff (with whom Lord Keith concurred) would have held in favour of the plaintiff, Tinsley, by applying the maxim or principle that a court of equity will not assist a claimant who does not come to equity with 'clean hands' (see generally Pettit [1990] Conv 416). On this view the fact that Milligan had engaged in the transfer for an illegal purpose would mean that the court would refuse to assist her 'even though the claimant can prima facie establish [her] claim without recourse to the underlying fraudulent or illegal purpose' (at 75). The principal distinction between the majority and the minority opinions in the case concerned the question whether in the particular context – ie the enforcement of property interests acquired in pursuance of an illegal transaction – the application of the equitable principle had become aligned with the less rigid common law rules governing claims under an illegal contract. The reasons of legal policy underpinning the majority opinion are evident in the opinion of Lord Browne-Wilkinson (at 90–91):

> In my judgment . . . the fusion of the administration of law and equity has led the courts to adopt a single rule (applicable both at law and in equity) as to the circumstances in which the court will enforce property interests acquired in pursuance of an illegal transaction, viz the *Bowmaker* rule (see *Bowmakers Ltd v Barnet Instruments Ltd* [1945] KB 65). . . . I therefore reach the conclusion that . . . as the law has developed the equitable principle has become elided into the common law rule. . . . The time has come to decide clearly that the rule is the same whether a plaintiff founds himself on a legal or equitable title. . . .

Care is needed in interpreting references to 'fusion' in these observations. The alignment that emerges from *Tinsley v Milligan* can be seen as an illustration of what in Chapter 2 was referred to as a process of 'harmonisation' (see p 65). By this we mean that differences between law and equity, particularly as regards the nature and scope of remedies, seem likely to be increasingly subject to challenge where the justification for the difference appears to rest predominantly on historical origins. This proposition of course begs the question as to what might constitute justification and, as importantly, in what direction 'harmonisation' should take place (see eg the reasoning of Millett LJ in *Tribe v Tribe* [1996] Ch 107 at 134 which advances a unifying principle – difficult to reconcile with the *Tinsley v Milligan* majority – based on a distinction between executed and unexecuted illegal schemes and which would marginalise the importance of the presumptions of resulting trust and advancement).

(3) The Court of Appeal in *Tinsley v Milligan* (Ralph Gibson LJ dissenting) argued for the adoption of a flexible 'public conscience' test which could openly address policy considerations: 'the court must weigh, or balance, the adverse consequences of granting relief against the adverse consequences of refusing relief. The ultimate decision calls for a value judgment' ([1992] Ch 310 at 319). The House of Lords unanimously rejected that test but the Law Commission subsequently published a Consultation Paper in 1999 (*Illegal Transactions: The Effect of Illegality on Contracts and Trusts*; Consultation Paper No 154; see Enonchong [2000] RLR 82 and Buckley (2000) 20 LS 156). The provisional recommendation of the paper was that the existing 'technical and complex rules' should be replaced by a discretion given to the courts (para 1.19):

> In exercising its discretion a court should consider: (i) the seriousness of the illegality involved; (ii) the knowledge and intention of the party seeking to enforce the illegal transaction, seeking the recognition of legal or equitable rights under it, or seeking to recover benefits conferred under it; (iii) whether refusing to allow standard rights and remedies would deter illegality; (iv) whether refusing to allow standard rights and remedies would further the purpose of the rule which renders the transaction illegal; and (v) whether refusing to allow standard rights and remedies would be proportionate to the illegality involved.

Plainly in any given case not all these criteria will point towards the same outcome. A value judgement would then have to be made in deciding what weight to attach to each criterion. Which, if any, of the criteria do you regard as most important for a context in which, let it be assumed, it is public policy to deter illegality such as attempts to defeat the claims of creditors? Applying these criteria what decision would you have reached in *Tinsley v Milligan* and *Tribe v Tribe*, and on what basis?

The Commission has acknowledged the 'extreme difficulty' of making reforms in this area and is therefore now focusing its work solely on the circumstances where 'one party has used a trust to conceal the true ownership of property for a criminal purpose' (Annual Report 2007/08, HC 540, paras 4.15–4.17). The preferred solution remains the introduction of a 'structured discretion' for the court 'to achieve a just outcome' and a draft Bill to that effect is in preparation.

(4) There is one further minor puzzling matter to resolve. In *Tinker v Tinker* [1970] P 136 a husband bought a house and put it in his wife's name hoping to avoid any risk of the property being taken by creditors in case his business failed, although on the facts the business was not in financial difficulty. In *Tribe v Tribe* Millett LJ comments on *Tinker* as follows (at 131): 'It is, of course, perfectly legitimate for a person who is solvent to make a gift of his property . . . to his wife in order to protect her against the possibility of [his] future business failure. It was not, therefore, a case of illegality at all.' Whilst it may be correct that such a transaction is not of itself illegal it is surely misleading to claim that the transaction is 'perfectly legitimate'. At the very least a transaction such as that is difficult to reconcile with the principle of *Mackay v Douglas* and IA 1986, s 423 (see above, p 299).

5. Public policy and perpetuities

(a) Introduction

At the start of this chapter we referred to the fundamental paradox of freedom of disposition. In confronting this paradox it can be claimed that the rule against perpetuities has achieved a satisfactory practical compromise by balancing the competing claims of successive generations (see Morris and Barton Leach *The Rule against Perpetuities* (2nd edn, 1962)). In this part of the chapter we probe the merits of this claim and in doing so implicitly raise the question of the need for a rule against perpetuities. There is, however, a further paradox here: the paradox is that the topic has tended to be studied, if at all, in the context of land law where it has little contemporary relevance (Oakley *Megarry's Manual of the Law of Real Property* (8th edn, 2002) ch 6, but see *Parker and Mellows* pp 254–274 and Watt, *Trusts and Equity* (3rd edn, 2008) pp 185–194. The origins of the 'modern rule' are controversial particularly as regards any causal relationship to alienability of land (see in particular Simpson *A History of the Land Law* (2nd edn, 1986) ch 9; Haskins (1977) 126 U Pa LR 19 and (1983) 48 Miss LR 451 and references therein). But whether or not it was in fact concerned to further alienability of land, legislation commencing with the Settled Land Act 1882 has long since permitted land to be sold irrespective of the existence of future interests. These can now only exist behind a trust. Yet today there are other types of property rights, often arising in commercial transactions, such as options, right of first refusal and grants of future easements which were never within the original contemplation of the Rule but are now caught by it, often in an inconsistent manner. The Law Commission has consequently responded to the perceived practical difficulties that the rule poses for commercial transactions involving such rights by recommending that the rule should cease to apply either to them or to pension schemes (*The Rules Against Perpetuities and Excessive Accumulations* Report 251(HC 579, 1998) para 1.15 (hereafter 1998 Report)). It is therefore primarily in the context of testamentary and inter vivos trusts of, in principle, freely alienable mixed property that a justification for the continuing existence of the rule must now be found.

In the context of a chapter primarily concerned with public policy constraints on freedom of disposition our main focus is policy-orientated: 'Does the idea of an inter-generational compromise itself provide a satisfactory justification for the rule's application to modern trusts of mixed investments?' We therefore do no more here than briefly restate the outlines of the rule, the present defects of the common law rules and of the statutory modifications not being considered.

The rule is also of interest for a different although related reason, the ability of a rule to survive the disappearance of the social and economic pressures that dictated its formulation. As the Manitoba Law Reform Commission recognised (Report 49 *The Rules Against Accumulations and Perpetuities* (1982) p 22), this phenomenon need not occasion surprise:

Once the rule is adopted by the courts, the very inductive growth of the common law through stare decisis ensures that a rule's existence becomes indelible. Attention is focused on its operation and how property dispositions and transactions are to be affected by it. The conveyancer has no reason for considering why the rule should be, or should be as it is; his task is to know the rule so well that he can reduce to the smallest possible dimension its effects on his client's wishes. The judge also is rarely likely to be concerned with the policy behind such a rule at this; his task is to determine if, and how, it applies to the issue before him, given the precedents brought to his notice, and the emphasis on technique and logical deduction which, he finds, characterises those precedents. Not until two hundred years after its commencement did any legislature become interested in its existence, and then the only concern was to remove some obvious excesses or contemporary inconveniences of a rule, which was by then luxuriant in growth, complex to an extreme, and hallowed by time. Few in the legislatures understood it, there was a vague sense that on the whole something like it was probably necessary, and lawyers who worked with it would naturally think in terms of a 'tune up' as all that was required.

This portrayal of an insular process of legal development leads us therefore to the further question of whether the rule has become an instance of that phenomenon mentioned in the Introduction to this chapter, 'a rule without a reason'.

(b) The 'rules' outlined

(1) The rule against perpetuities   The very title of the rule arguably qualifies as a misdescription on two grounds. First, Simpson has rightly pointed out that 'the rule *against* perpetuities . . . must be understood as *permitting* them within limits' and thus 'the contemporary oddity of the rule lies not in what it prevents, but in how much it allows' ((1979) 24 Jur Rev 1 at 17). Second, the rule is concerned with the commencement of interests rather than their duration; the rule strikes at the remote vesting of property interests. The classic statement of the rule reflects these considerations: 'no interest is good unless it must vest, if at all, not later than twenty-one years after some life in being at the creation of the interest' (Gray *The Rule against Perpetuities* (4th edn) p 201). In substance it permits the testator 'to give life estates to his wife and children . . . (and) to provide for unborn grandchildren during their minority' (Simes (1954–5) 103 U Pa LR 707 at 729). A significant weakness of the common law rule was its emphasis on remote possibilities – if a contingent interest *might* vest outside the perpetuity period it was void even if the probability was that it would vest within the period. A statutory response to this problem came with the enactment in 1964 of the Perpetuities and Accumulations Act. The Act sought to deal with this problem in two ways: (i) it permitted the settlor to specify a perpetuity period not exceeding 80 years in preference to a 'life in being plus 21 years' perpetuity period (s 1); (ii) it introduced the system of 'wait and see' under which an interest would only be void where it became evident that it could not possibly vest within the perpetuity period (ss 2 and 3). The changes applied only to instruments creating future interests after 25 July 1964 which left the common law rule intact for earlier instruments.

The Law Commission in its 1998 Report recommended that there should in the future be one fixed perpetuity period of 125 years. This period was selected for two reasons: (i) it is seemingly consistent with the longest period that could be obtained under the present 'life in being plus 21 years' criterion; and (ii) it gives some recognition to the views of those who preferred abolition of the rule (*1998 Report* para 8.13; see generally Sparkes (1998) 12(3) TLI 148–157). Whilst the government in 2001 indicated its intention to implement the proposals in relation to perpetuities no time was found in the parliamentary timetable to facilitate this until 1 April 2009. Then the Perpetuities and Accumulations Bill was introduced in the House of Lords under a new procedure, approved by the House in April 2008, whereby a significant part of the legislative process in the Lords for uncontroversial Law Commission Bills can be taken in Committee off the floor of the House (Law Commission 42nd Annual Report (2007–08) para 3.33). If finally enacted the provisions will, subject to minor exceptions, apply only prospectively and only to estates, interests, rights and powers that exist under a trust.

(2) The rule against inalienability This companion rule, also known as the rule against perpetual trusts, is directed principally at non-charitable purpose trusts (see Chapters 5 and 17). If the capital fund must be kept intact (ie inalienable) so that the income produced can be used for specific purposes for longer than the perpetuity period, the trust will be void irrespective of the applicability of the beneficiary principle. The assets contained in the fund will of course be fully alienable, but the rule is directed at eventually freeing the fund for alternative uses. This rule is unaffected by the 1998 Law Commission Report.

(3) The rule against accumulations A feature common to many trusts is that trustees will be given a discretion to accumulate income for specified periods (see eg the disputed clauses in *McPhail v Doulton* in Chapter 5). At common law, income could be accumulated for a period not exceeding the perpetuity period. Statutory restrictions, provoked initially in response to a will by one Peter Thelluson, were first introduced in 1800 to counter what were regarded as excessive accumulations (Keeton *Modern Developments in the Law of Trusts* (1971) ch 17). The principal objection then and subsequently is said to be economic; during an accumulation period neither capital nor income can be spent on consumption (see Simes *Public Policy and the Dead Hand* (1955) p 99).

The rule as formulated has permitted accumulation only for the periods specified by LPA 1925, ss 164, 165 and the Perpetuities and Accumulation Act 1964, s 13. The broad effect of s 164 has been to limit accumulations to any one of four periods: the life of the settlor (obviously only for inter vivos settlements), 21 years from the death of the settlor or testator, and two alternative periods of certain specified minorities. These available periods created problems for tax-planning in inter vivos settlements. In particular the fact that an accumulation of income during a settlor's lifetime had to cease at his death meant that a passing of property occurred which attracted estate duty (*Re Bourne's Settlement* [1946] 1 All ER 411). Accordingly, the Perpetuities and Accumulations Act 1964, s 13 introduced two further periods of accumulation as recommended by the fourth report of the Law Reform Committee (*The Rule against Perpetuities* (Cmnd 18, 1956)): (i) 21 years from the date of the making of the disposition; (ii) the duration of the minority of a person in being at that date. (See also on the tax-planning considerations Law Reform Committee paras 5–9, 55–57; Hawkins [1968] BTR 351; and contemporary tax-planning sources, eg Potter and Monroe *Tax Planning with Precedents* (5th edn, 1966).)

The Law Commission recommended the abolition of the rule: 'we have been unable to find any coherent reason for limiting accumulations to some shorter period than the perpetuity period' (*1998 Report* para 10.12). In particular the

Commission contended (i) that there is no evidence that abolition will have any adverse impact, and (ii) there is little likelihood of settlors creating trusts with a 'duty' to accumulate income for the duration of the perpetuity period. Under the Perpetuities and Accumulations Bill 2009 it is proposed to repeal LPA 1925, ss 164 and 165 and section 13 of the 1964 Act. The effect will be that the full perpetuity period will also be the upper limit for accumulations, as was the case under the common law before 1800. The reform is extolled as being deregulatory in nature and as essentially increasing the freedom of settlors to dispose of their property as they wish.

Aligning the Rule against – should we now say 'of' – Accumulations with the remoteness of vesting rules assumes that these rules themselves can be justified, a point to which we now turn.

(c) The 'dead hand' and the rule against perpetuities: a rule without a reason?

In 1956 the Law Reform Committee considered (para 4) that: 'the necessity for placing some time limit on the vesting of future interests . . . (is) beyond argument', and consequently no justification for maintaining the rule, as opposed to reforming it, was advanced. Subsequently Morris and Barton Leach, both of whom were involved in the preparation of the Law Reform Committee Report (see para 2), reviewed the various justifications advanced for retaining a rule against remoteness of vesting (*The Rule against Perpetuities* (2nd edn, 1962) pp 13–18).

They consider and reject arguments that the rule prevents an undue concentration of wealth, that it prevents capricious dispositions, that it facilitates control of wealth by the living rather than the dead, or that it prevents a tying-up of capital. The authors are more persuaded, however, by a justification based on 'compromise'.

Morris and Leach *The Rule against Perpetuities* (2nd edn, 1962) pp 17–18

Another reason for the Rule suggested by Professor Simes seems to the present authors far more realistic. It is that 'the Rule against Perpetuities strikes a fair balance between the desires of members of the present generation, and similar desires of succeeding generations, to do what they wish with the property which they enjoy'. It is a natural human desire to provide for one's family in the foreseeable future. The difficulty is that if one generation is allowed to create unlimited future interests in property, succeeding generations will receive the property in a restricted state and thus be unable to indulge the same desire. The dilemma is thus precisely what it has been throughout the history of English law, namely, how to prevent the power of alienation from being used to its own destruction. In this idea of compromise between two competing policies – freedom of disposition by one generation and freedom of disposition by succeeding generations – the Rule against Perpetuities seems to the present authors to find its best justification. . . .

> The Rule against Perpetuities undoubtedly has produced many hard cases where some unskilled or unfortunate draftsman has inadvertently broken the Rule although no threat to the public interest can be shown to have existed. Still, the present authors conclude that on the whole the Rule does more good than harm, though the policy considerations underlying it are much weaker than they were 300 or 100 years ago.

The 'compromise' formula has subsequently been adopted by the Law Commission as the justification for retaining the Rule (1998 Report, paras 1.9 and 1.17). The Law Commission had concluded that an alternative justification of economic efficiency could not be relied upon because the lack of empirical evidence made the competing economic arguments too uncertain. Indeed it appears that even if retention of the Rule could be proved to have economic disadvantages the Commission would have recommended retention of the Rule on the basis that the claims of intergenerational justice were 'strong enough to outweigh any possible adverse economic effect' (para 2.32).

Consider the following points:

(1) Neither Morris and Leach nor Simes nor the Law Commission in the 1998 Report explain *why* the particular compromise that the rule strikes is 'fair' (see Gallanis (2000) 59(2) CLJ 284 for a critical assessment of the Commission's philosophy). What justification is there for that compromise (eg consider which succeeding generations in theory lose their freedom of disposition over property comprised in a settlement in circumstances where the period allowed by the rule – possibly up to 125 years – is exploited to the full)?

(2) Do Morris and Leach accept that the rule is *necessary* to achieve the approved 'compromise'?

(3) Maudsley (*The Modern Law of Perpetuities* (1979) p 221) appeared to accept that estate duty and Inheritance Tax had in practice deterred over-ambitious settlors but considered nevertheless that a rule should be retained: 'those who argue for its abolition would, I suggest, think again, if it became the practice to set up trusts for great-great-grandchildren, or more remote issue'. The evidence on the likelihood of this occurring is mixed. The Law Commission received indications from some firms of solicitors that there remain many wealthy people who would be happy to take advantage of an abolition of the rule (Law Commission Consultation Paper 133 *The Rules against Perpetuities and Excessive Accumulations* (1993) para 5.38). On the other hand evidence from Scotland, described as a 'perpetuities-free zone' by a leading Scots lawyer, is that 'in practice the maximum duration of trusts...was about 100 years' (1998 Report para 2.37). Is concern for possible, if unlikely, future attempts to set up dynastic trusts a satisfactory reason for retaining a rule against perpetuities? Should the rule be retained as a statement of principle about appropriate limits to

freedom of disposition even if it were shown to have no practical effect on the decisions of settlors?

The almost universal consensus (see *Maudsley* App D p 247) that reform and not abolition was the appropriate method for dealing with perpetuity problems, real or imaginary, was broken in 1983. A majority report of the Manitoba Law Reform Commission (Report 49 *The Rules against Accumulations and Perpetuities* (1982)) rejected reform and recommended abolition, a recommendation which was implemented in the Perpetuities and Accumulation Act 1983 (see Deech (1984) 4 OJLS 453; Glenn (1984) 62 Can BR 618). Whilst there is no evidence of other Canadian provinces rushing to follow the Manitoba example, at least 21 states in the United States have abolished the rule against perpetuities. What proponents of abolition may find disconcerting is that this development appears to be predominantly the results of a combination of fiscal advantages being made available for long-term trusts and jurisdictional competition for profitable trusts business. One rough estimate is that in 2003 $100 billion in trusts assets moved jurisdictions to take advantage of the Rule's abolition (see Sitkoff and Schanzenbach (2005) 115(2) Yale LJ 357–437 and (2006) 27(6) Cardozo LR 2465–2509).

The Manitoba report introduced an additional and apparently compelling reason for abolition. It concluded that even if the function of balancing the interests of successive generations is considered desirable, the rule is irrelevant to this. The reason is that the rule in *Saunders v Vautier* and variation of trusts legislation give the courts a wide discretion to break up existing trusts. Both these elements are considered in detail in Chapter 7, and the relationship between them and the justifications for a rule against perpetuities are briefly reviewed at p. 355.

7

Flexibility in relation to beneficial entitlement

1. Introduction

In the previous chapter we saw how the rule against perpetuities formally limits the time over which a settlor's freedom of disposition can be exercised. But it is implicit that, within that time and subject to the other public policy restraints mentioned in Chapter 6, a settlor is substantially free to dictate in the trust instrument both beneficial entitlement and the mode of trust administration. Plainly there would be little point in this freedom if the settlor's instructions could be ignored or altered at the whim of beneficiaries or trustees. Consequently, a fundamental principle of the law of trusts is that of fidelity to the settlor's intentions: trustees must faithfully implement that intention as identified through the trust instrument. The settlor is the law-maker, the trustees are the administrators of that law who must not deviate from the terms of the trust. In principle, therefore, the courts will not readily approve any deviation: 'As a rule, the court has no jurisdiction to give, and will not give, its sanction to the performance by trustees of acts with reference to the trust estate which are not, on the face of the instrument creating the trust, authorised by its terms' (*Re New* [1901] 2 Ch 534 at 544 per Romer LJ).

But neither settlors nor their advisers are imbued with the wisdom of Solomon, and they may fail to provide for unexpected developments such as unanticipated changes in investment patterns. A settlor conferring only restricted powers of investment on trustees may leave them ill-equipped to respond to economic change and unable to maintain the trust fund's value. A still more serious encroachment on a settlor's plans affecting beneficial entitlement may come from fiscal changes, such as occurred post-1945 with the sharply increased nominal burdens of income tax and estate duty (see Chapter 8). These latter changes spawned the rapid expansion in the 1950s and 1960s of the use of the discretionary trust, which proved such an elusive moving target for the Inland Revenue. But many trusts, most prominently but not exclusively those containing life interests, were stationary targets. Was it, however, possible for the trustees, beneficiaries or the court to reduce exposure to tax liability by rearranging the line of beneficial interests laid out by the settlor?

The challenge to trusts law was plain. Could established rules and concepts be adapted to promote the sought-after flexibility in beneficial entitlement? In certain circumstances (see p 325) beneficiaries can themselves terminate the trust and thereby indirectly achieve flexibility, but, in the absence of express authority in the trust instrument, trustees could do nothing. Moreover there existed persuasive authority, long predating the emergence of the dominant fiscal considerations, that rejected any general jurisdiction on the part of the court: 'I decline to accept any suggestion that the court has any inherent jurisdiction to alter a man's will because it thinks it beneficial. It seems to me that is quite impossible' (*Re Walker* [1901] 1 Ch 879 at 885 per Farwell J).

What therefore emerges is a further example of the tensions encountered previously between trust principles, based on respect for the settlors' intentions, and the pressures placed on those principles by practitioners responding, in this instance, to the threat posed to the financial interests of beneficiaries by changing fiscal conditions. There is one additional source of tension not necessarily related to fiscal considerations. Let us suppose that the beneficiaries of a will trust decide that they would prefer to distribute the estate in a manner that would be strongly disapproved of by the testator. Notwithstanding the above dictum from *Re Walker* there are circumstances where this variation of beneficial interests may be achieved with the consent of the courts who indirectly will then be faced, in yet another form, with resolving the competing property claims of successive generations (see generally Chapter 6). This chapter is concerned primarily with the resolution of these tensions through a mixture of judicial and statutory responses, and with the implications of those responses for the allocation of authority within the trust institution as between settlors, trustees, beneficiaries and the courts.

Whilst referring to tensions between 'retaining fidelity to settlor's intention' and 'responding to needs for change' it must not be overlooked that settlors, in addition to granting powers of appointment, have long been able to arm trustees with authority over income and capital by means of powers of 'maintenance' and 'advancement' respectively (Trustee Act 1925 (TA), ss 31 and 32). The exercise of these powers too can achieve some alterations of beneficial entitlement and accordingly we consider the scope of those powers in this chapter.

First, however, a brief digression is called for to explain the approach adopted in this chapter with particular regard to our study of trust variation. It will quickly become apparent that this chapter is not concerned exclusively with exposition of the current statutory and common law framework that facilitates the flexibility of beneficial entitlement. On the contrary there is in addition a specific historical focus, one that concentrates primarily on the doctrinal developments and legislative background to a remarkable statute, the Variation of Trusts Act 1958. The statute is remarkable in that it was enacted almost completely uncontentiously by a Private Members' Bill whilst at one and the same time offering potentially impressive benefits to settlors and beneficiaries of private trusts and incurring significant detriment to the Exchequer in terms of tax revenue forgone. The question is how to explain this phenomenon. The answer, as will be seen, is not straightforward. Claims of manipulation and self-interest are not compelling; indeed there is scant evidence of any overt manoeuvring of that ilk. Instead more subtle responses invoking the concerns of trust practice and practitioners, a particularistic interpretation of formal legal doctrine, a perception of an issue as being peculiarly 'lawyers' law' all jostle for position in this story. In post-modern parlance it is the nature of the discourse that is to be understood in seeking to explain how legal change was brought about.

Readers will decide for themselves whether, of itself, that perspective provides sufficient reason for what is, in some modest degree, a case study of events around half a century ago. But there is another rather more oblique reason for the approach adopted to our study of the Variation of Trusts Act 1958. The processes of change and reform in trusts law and the attempts to achieve ever greater flexibility of beneficial entitlement did not come to a halt in 1958. Indeed they have taken on an added urgency with the extension of trusts doctrines into ever more diverse areas of practice, many involving an international dimension. It is our contention that an understanding of the pressures for and the processes and consequences of the 1958 legislation can help provide insights into those current developments and contribute towards an analytical framework for interpreting them.

2. Premature termination of trusts

(a) The 'rule' in *Saunders v Vautier*

Under the rule in *Saunders v Vautier* (below) a beneficiary of full age (ie over 18) and sound mind and entitled to the entire equitable interest can require the trustees to transfer the trust property to him and thus terminate the trust.

Saunders v Vautier (1841) 4 Beav 115

A testator W bequeathed £2,000 East India stock on trust to accumulate the dividends until V should attain the age of 25, and then to transfer the capital and accumulated dividends to V. V attained 21 and claimed to have the whole fund transferred to him.

> **Lord Langdale MR:** I think that principle has been repeatedly acted upon; and where a legacy is directed to accumulate for a certain period, or where the payment is postponed, the legatee, if he has an absolute indefeasible interest in the legacy, is not bound to wait until the expiration of that period, but may require payment the moment he is competent to give a valid discharge.

On a subsequent hearing before the Lord Chancellor it was argued on behalf of W's residuary legatees that V's interest was contingent on his attaining 25. The

Lord Chancellor held that the interest was vested although the enjoyment was intended to be postponed, and he ordered the transfer.

The case itself stands for a quite narrow proposition which, as pointed out elsewhere (Chesterman in Rubin and Sugarman (eds) *Law, Economy and Society: Essays in the History of English Law 1750–1914* (1984) ch 1), derived directly from a principle in the law of wills and originating in the practice of the ecclesiastical courts. A rule of much wider application subsequently emerged during the nineteenth century. This extended to include cases, whether under testamentary or inter vivos trusts, with two or more beneficiaries, and also to beneficiaries entitled in succession. For instance, a testator bequeaths property on trust for his wife W for life then to their adult children X, Y and Z in equal shares. W and the three children may subsequently agree on a fair method of distribution of the capital and require the trustees to distribute it accordingly. The above example refers to fixed entitlements to income and capital but the rule has been further extended to include, it would seem, a discretionary trust under which all the beneficiaries can be listed.

Re Smith [1928] Ch 915

A fund was held by the Public Trustee on trust to pay at the trustee's discretion the whole or any part of the income or capital for the benefit of Mrs Aspinall (A). Any surplus income was to be accumulated and the accumulations and remainder were to pass on A's death to her three children in equal shares. All the children attained the age of majority. Subsequently A, her two surviving children and the legal representatives of a deceased child mortgaged their interests under the trusts to the Legal and General Assurance Company. The Public Trustee sought the court's discretion as to whether he was obliged to pay the whole of the income to the company until the mortgage was discharged.

> **Romer J:** Mrs Aspinall, the two surviving children and the representatives of the deceased child are between them entitled to the whole fund. In those circumstances it appears to me, notwithstanding the discretion which is reposed in the trustees, under which discretion they could select one or more of the [still living beneficiaries] as recipients of the income, and might apply part of the capital for the benefit of Mrs Aspinall and so take it away from the children, that the four of them, if they were all living, could come to the Court and say to the trustees: 'Hand over the fund to us'. It appears to me that that is in accordance with the decision of the Court of Appeal in a case of *Re Nelson* (1916 reported [1928] Ch 920n) and is in accordance with principle. What is the principle? As I understand it, it is this. Where there is a trust under which trustees have a discretion as to applying the whole or part of a fund to or for the benefit of a particular person, that particular person cannot come to the trustees, and demand the fund; for the whole fund has not been given to him but only so much as the trustees think fit to let him have. But when the trustees have no discretion as to the amount of the fund to be applied, the fact that the trustees have a discretion as to the method in which the whole of the fund shall be applied for the benefit

> of the particular person does not prevent that particular person from coming and saying: 'Hand over the fund to me'. That appears to be the result of the two cases which were cited to me: *Green v Spicer* (1830) 1 Russ & M 395; *Younghusband v Grisborne* (1844) 1 Coll 400.
>
> Now this third case arises. What is to happen where the trustees have a discretion whether they will apply the whole or only a portion of the fund for the benefit of one person, but are obliged to apply the rest of the fund, so far as not applied for the benefit of the first named person, to or for the benefit of a second named person? There, two people together are the sole objects of the discretionary trust and, between them, are entitled to have the whole fund applied to them or for their benefit. It has been laid down by the Court of Appeal in the case to which I have referred that, in such a case as that you treat all the people put together just as though they formed one person, for whose benefit the trustees were directed to apply the whole of a particular fund.

The court directed that the Public Trustee was bound to pay the income to the company during the lifetime of Mrs Aspinall, or until the mortgage was discharged.

Re Smith emphasises the collective rights of beneficiaries. An accompanying rule is that a single beneficiary entitled to an absolute interest in a fixed share of a trust fund consisting of divisible personalty, can, if *sui juris*, generally ask for outright transfer of his or her share of the property (see *Stephenson v Barclays Bank* [1975] 1 All ER 625). But, not surprisingly, the rights of the individual beneficiary are less extensive than, and may be subordinated to, the rights of the beneficial interest holders as a body. In *Lloyds Bank plc v Duker* [1987] 3 All ER 193, for instance, a beneficiary (W) was entitled to 46/80 of a testator's residuary estate, which included 999 out of 1,000 shares in a private company, W's notional shareholding therefore being 574. Possession of those shares, giving a majority shareholding, would be more valuable to W than receiving 46/80 of the proceeds of the sale of the 999 shares as a bloc. It was held, however, that the duty to maintain a fair balance between the interests of all beneficiaries took precedence. W could not, therefore, claim the 574 shares but had to be content with a proportionate share of the total proceeds of sale.

(b) The explanation for and limits of the rule

The Court of Appeal in *Re Nelson* [1928] Ch 920n commented that 'the principle . . . is that where there is what amounts to an absolute gift, that absolute gift cannot be fettered by prescribing a mode of enjoyment' (at 921). This reflects an opinion reiterated at greater length on numerous occasions (see eg *Gosling v Gosling* (1859) John 265 at 272 per Page Wood VC) and is in substance our old and somewhat dubious friend the repugnancy doctrine (see Chapter 6). This formalist justification for the rule in *Saunders v Vautier* also supported a more pragmatic explanation. If attempts to impose conditional restraints on alienation were ineffective as being repugnant to the nature of the interest, it followed that the beneficiary had a definable property interest that could prima facie be sold or assigned in return for a capital sum. This would in practice defeat, albeit indirectly, the particular aim of the trust-founder to postpone receipt of the benefit. The court was quick to recognise and acknowledge that this reality underlay the rule in *Saunders v Vautier* (see *Curtis v Lukin* (1842) 5 Beav 147 at 156). The decisions may also have been influenced by a nineteenth-century feeling that capital should be 'active', ie freely available for entrepreneurial use beyond the limits possible for trustee investment.

That the rule is the product of a doctrine of free alienability, and not a fundamental prerequisite of a law of trusts, is demonstrated by the diametrically opposite approach of the American courts. Their rejection of *Brandon v Robinson* (see Chapter 6), reflecting the pre-eminence of the settlor's property rights, ultimately also resulted in a rejection of the rule in *Saunders v Vautier*. What emerged instead was a 'material purpose' doctrine: where the terms of a trust revealed a particular purpose on the part of a settlor or testator there could be no termination of a trust where that would defeat the purpose. (*Claflin v Claflin* 20 NE 454 (1889) discussed in Friedman (1964) 73 Yale LJ 550 at 586–592. See also Third Restatement of the Law of Trusts: s 65 (2003); Alexander (1985) 37 Stanford LR 1189 at 1202–1204, and cf Matthews [2006] 122 LQR 266–294.)

If developments from the original rule in *Saunders v Vautier* had rested solely on the repugnancy doctrine, a rule of much narrower scope than that subsequently recognised in *Re Smith* would have resulted (see Cantlie (1986) 25 Manitoba LJ 135 at 153–154 for a view that there are really two distinct rules with different consequences for the validity of dispositions). There was, after all, no repugnancy in the nature of the interests being considered in *Re Smith*. The rule in *Saunders v Vautier* is therefore now conventionally explained as being based on the beneficiaries' equitable ownership of trust property – in Harris's telling phrase 'fidelity to the settlor's intention ends where equitable property begins' (*Variation of Trusts* (1975) p 2). But as the American developments of the spendthrift trust (see Chapter 6) and material purpose doctrine demonstrate, where equitable property begins is a question admitting various responses.

Nevertheless there is now no doubt that in English law the rule in *Saunders v Vautier* supports the proposition that beneficiaries if of full age and sound mind can dissolve a trust. But the limits to the rule must be noted. As Lord Maugham summarised the position in *Berry v Green* [1938] AC 575 at 582, 'the rule has no operation unless all the persons who have any present or contingent interest in the property are *sui juris* and consent'. Accordingly where there are beneficiaries who are under age, unborn or even whose identity is unknown then the rule cannot be used to terminate a trust. Two obvious examples where this would be the case are (1) where there are interests in succession and one of the remaindermen is under 18, and (2) a protective trust. A further illustration of the limits to the rule arises from the relaxation of the test for certainty of objects. A discretionary trust can now conceivably exist without it being possible to list, and therefore obtain the necessary consent of, all potential beneficiaries.

By way of conclusion to discussion of the rule it is emphasised that the search for its rationale is not solely a matter of historical concern. It is relevant to analysis of the statutory scope for varying trusts discussed in the following section. Moreover, we might also ask whether the rule can be assumed to apply to all forms of private trusts. Should it, for instance, apply to a *Re Denley*-type of mixed persons-purposes trust discussed in Chapter 5? (See Hackney *Understanding Equity and Trusts* (1987) pp 72–73.) To give a positive response could in effect mean that the rights of beneficiaries to enforce a purpose could be transformed into rights of immediate ownership. The consequence would be to frustrate the trust-founder's intentions and to render nugatory the conceptual development apparently envisaged in *Re Denley*.

3. Variation of trusts

(a) Introduction

In the present century the rule in *Saunders v Vautier* has become a route to success in minimising taxation of beneficial interests not only by direct use of the rule, but also because the existence of the rule has provided both a theoretical starting-point and a policy justification for the Variation of Trusts Act 1958 (VTA). Yet the practical reality was that the rule in *Saunders v Vautier* was available to be used by beneficiaries in only a small minority of trusts (see the limitations described in section 2 above and the Sixth Report of the Law Reform Committee *The Court's Power to Sanction Variation of Trusts* (Cmnd 310, 1957) paras 6 and 7, below, p 335). Thus the pre-1958 issue was how to remodel beneficial interests in other circumstances.

There existed certain elements both of a statutory and an inherent judicial jurisdiction to vary trusts. These are now of limited significance but we consider them briefly here because, in combination with the rule in *Saunders v Vautier*, they provided the springboard for arguments favouring the wider jurisdiction granted in the VTA 1958. These prior jurisdictions can be divided into those concerned with acts done in the administration of a trust and those relating to altering beneficial interests.

(b) Pre-1958 jurisdiction

(1) Administration

The court has long-established inherent jurisdictions known as 'conversion', 'salvage' and 'emergency', which enable the court to authorise departures from the trust instrument (see Harris *Variation of Trusts* (1975) pp 9–11). TA 1925, s 57(1) in effect subsumes these within a broad statutory jurisdiction which now enables the court to permit trusts to effect any transaction 'in the management or administration of any property vested in the trustees' where the transaction is 'in the opinion of the court expedient, but the same cannot be effected by the reason of the absence of any power for that purpose' in the trust instrument.

The purpose of s 57(1) has been said to be 'to ensure that trust property should be managed as advantageously as possible in the interests of the beneficiaries . . . but it was no part of the legislative aim to disturb the rule that a court will not re-write a trust . . .' (*Re Downshire Settled Estates* [1953] Ch 218 at 248 per Evershed MR). Indeed it is quite clear that the section is concerned with administration and does not permit the court to reshape beneficial interests under the trust.

As regards the problem posed by changing investment conditions, s 57 seems wide enough to have enabled the courts to enlarge investment powers but there is little reported evidence of their doing so. Until 1990 the jurisdiction seems to have been exercised only in favour of applications by charitable organisations (*Mason v Farbrother* [1983] 2 All ER 1078), but in *Anker-Petersen v Anker-Petersen* (1990) [2000] WTLR 581 the court held that it is appropriate to use s 57 to widen investment powers provided that the beneficial interests are not directly affected. With the introduction of very wide powers of investment both under the Trustee Act 2000 and under express investment clauses in trust deeds the need to apply to the court to enlarge investment powers is likely to be increasingly rare.

(2) Beneficial interests

Under the Settled Land Act 1925 (SLA), s 64(1), the court can authorise a tenant for life of settled land to effect any transaction concerning it which could be for the benefit of the settled land or the settlement's beneficiaries and which could have been validly effected by an absolute owner. Section 64(1) was presumed initially to be limited to administrative matters but s 64(2) defines 'transaction' in broad terms. Accordingly, the Court of Appeal in *Re Downshire Settled Estates* [1953] Ch 218 recognised 'transaction' to be a 'word of the widest import as is emphasised . . . by the terms of the second subsection which make the meaning of the word comprehend (*inter alia*) any application of capital money and any compromise or other dealing or arrangement' (at 252 per Evershed MR). The result, as Harris points out (p 21), 'was that s 64 enabled the court to authorise the tenant for life to make an arrangement with the trustees and with other adult beneficiaries under the settlement which completely remodelled the beneficial interests . . .' (see eg *Raikes v Lygon* [1988] 1 WLR 281). The immediate purpose of the remodelling in *Re Downshire* was to avoid a claim for estate duty on the settlement (comprising land valued at £400,000 and capital worth £700,000), which would have arisen on the life tenant's death. In *Hambro v Duke of Marlborough* [1994] Ch 158 (see Cooke [1994] Conv 492) the court adopted a novel and very broad interpretation of the jurisdiction when, inter alia, varying an adult beneficiary's interest against his will.

Whereas s 64(1) did provide a pre-1958 avenue for rearranging beneficial interests so as to avoid tax, it is limited in scope, applying only where the trust corpus includes settled land. This jurisdiction will gradually diminish even further in importance now that the creation of settlements under the SLA 1925 are prohibited by TOLATA 1996, s 2(1).

Maintenance   Where a settlor has directed that trust income be accumulated, the court has an inherent jurisdiction to allow the expenditure of that income on the maintenance of beneficiaries. The settlor's instructions are ignored, the court presuming that a settlor 'did not intend that children should be left unprovided for or in a state of such moderate means that they should not be educated properly...' (*Re Collins* (1886) 32 Ch D 229 at 232 per Pearson J). This jurisdiction of necessity involves a variation of beneficial entitlement but its practical importance is minimal since most trust deeds specify express powers of maintenance or incorporate the statutory formula (TA 1925, s 31). In addition a seemingly little used statutory power (TA 1925, s 53) enables the court to authorise disposal of property to which a minor beneficiary is entitled in order to provide funds for his 'maintenance, education or benefit'. Under this section the court has authorised the sale of an infant's reversionary interest to a life tenant, with the object of reducing estate duty, provided that the proceeds were resettled on the minor and not paid outright to him (*Re Meux* [1957] 2 All ER 630; cf *Re Heyworth's Contingent Reversionary Interest* [1956] 2 All ER 21).

Compromise   Settlements are not always drafted with complete clarity. Where disputes arise about the rights of beneficiaries the court has an inherent jurisdiction to approve a compromise on behalf of infant and unborn beneficiaries. It became the practice for judges of the Chancery Division to adopt an extended meaning of 'compromise' so as to approve arrangements varying beneficial interests usually with the aim of minimising tax liability. A genuine dispute was not considered necessary: all that was required was some suitable bargain between the beneficiaries. The practice was generally exercised in chambers, and thus rarely reported. But did the jurisdiction exist to permit the practice?

The issue came before the Court of Appeal in three consolidated appeals (*Re Downshire Settled Estates*; *Re Blackwell's Settlement Trusts* and *Re Chapman's Settlement Trusts* [1953] Ch 218). The Court of Appeal unanimously agreed that the *Blackwell* and *Downshire* schemes came within the definition of 'compromise'. But in the *Chapman* case the court divided over the definition. The majority, in disapproving the *Chapman* scheme, held that the inherent jurisdiction should be limited to 'compromise' but that 'the word compromise should not be narrowly construed so as to be confined to compromises of disputed rights' ([1953] 1 All ER 103 at 113). In characteristically robust fashion the minority judge Denning LJ accepted the argument for an unlimited inherent jurisdiction for the court to approve variations of beneficial interests on behalf of infant and unborn beneficiaries (at 132):

> He [that is Lord Hardwicke] proceeded on the broad principle that the court had power to deal with the property and interests of infants or other persons under disability in a manner not authorised by the trust whenever the court was satisfied that what was proposed was most advantageous for them provided, of course, that everyone of full age agreed to it. I hope to show that that is the true principle today.

The decision on the *Chapman* scheme was appealed. The House of Lords unanimously affirmed the Court of Appeal decision. However, in sharp contrast to both the above views, the majority of the House of Lords (Lord Cohen dissenting) held that the court had power to approve arrangements varying beneficial interests only where a 'genuine dispute' about rights of beneficiaries existed.

Chapman v Chapman [1954] 1 All ER 798 at 801, HL

> **Lord Simonds** (considering the argument for an unlimited jurisdiction):
>
> My Lords, I am unable to accept as accurate this [Denning LJ's] view of the origin, development and scope of the jurisdiction of the Court of Chancery....
>
> In my opinion, the true view that emerges from a consideration of this jurisdiction through the centuries is not that at some unknown date it appeared full-fledged and that from time to time timid judges have pulled out some of its feathers, but rather that it has been a creature of gradual growth, though with many set-backs, and that the range of its authority can only be determined by seeing what jurisdiction the great equity judges of the past assumed and how they justified that assumption. It is, in effect, in this way that the majority of the Court of Appeal in the present case have approached the problem, and, in my opinion, it is the right way. It may well be that the result is not logical and it may be asked why, if the jurisdiction of the court extended to this thing, it did not extend to that also. But, my Lords, that question is as vain in the sphere of jurisdiction as it is in the sphere of substantive law. We are as little justified in saying that a court has a certain jurisdiction, merely because we think it ought to have it, as we should be in declaring that the substantive law is something different from what it has always been declared to be, merely because we think it ought to be so. It is even possible that we are not wiser than our ancestors. It is for the legislature, which does not rest under that disability, to determine whether there should be a change in the law and what that change should be.

Lord Simonds then briefly outlined the inherent jurisdictions of 'conversion', 'maintenance' and 'salvage'.

> This brings me to the question which alone presents any difficulty in this case. It is whether this fourth category, which I may call the compromise category, should be extended to cover cases in which there is no real dispute as to rights and, therefore, no compromise, but it is sought by way of bargain between the beneficiaries to re-arrange the beneficial interests under the trust instrument and to bind infants and unborn persons to the bargain

by order of the court. My Lords, I find myself faced at once with a difficulty which I do not see my way to overcome. For though I am not, as a rule, impressed by an argument about the difficulty of drawing the line since I remember the answer of a great judge that, though he knew not when day ended and night began, he knew that midday was day and midnight was night, yet, in the present case, it appears to me that to accept this extension in any degree is to concede exactly what has been denied. It is the function of the court to execute a trust, to see that the trustees do their duty and to protect them if they do it, to direct them if they are in doubt, and, if they do wrong, to penalise them. It is not the function of the court to alter a trust because alteration is thought to be advantageous to an infant beneficiary. It was, I thought, significant that learned counsel was driven to the admission that, since the benefit of the infant was the test, the court had the power, though in its discretion it might not use it, to override the wishes of a living and expostulating settlor, if it assumed to know better than he what was beneficial for the infant. This would appear to me a strange way for a court of conscience to execute a trust. If, then, the court has not, as I hold it has not, power to alter or re-arrange the trusts of a trust instrument...I am unable to see how that jurisdiction can be conferred by pleading that the alteration is but a little one.

Lord Morton concurred, and concluded his judgment with the following comment:

I would add...that if the court had power to approve, and did approve, schemes such as the present scheme, the way would be open for a most undignified game of chess between the Chancery Division and the legislature. The alteration of one settlement for the purpose of avoiding taxation already imposed might well be followed by scores of successful applications for a similar purpose by beneficiaries under other settlements. The legislature might then counter this move by imposing fresh taxation on the settlements as thus altered. The beneficiaries would then troop back to the Chancery Division and say, 'Please alter the trusts again. You have the power, the adults desire it, and it is for the benefit of the infants to avoid this fresh taxation. The legislature may not move again.' So the game might go on, if the judges of the Chancery Division had the power which the appellants claim for them, and if they thought it right to make the first move. I would dismiss the appeal.

Chapman v Chapman powerfully re-affirmed the principle of respect for the intention of the settlor as expressed in the terms of the trust instrument. In fact the settlors in the case, both of whom were alive, favoured the scheme presented to the court for approval, but as Lord Morton pointed out (at 818) 'the wishes of the grandparents, as settlors, are entirely irrelevant on the question of jurisdiction. By settling the property on certain trusts they have put it out of their power to alter these trusts, however much they may wish to do so.' It was this gap between non-legal social fact and the limits of formal precedent-based doctrine that Denning LJ had attempted to bridge in the Court of Appeal. But *Chapman v Chapman* was decided at a time when, it has been argued by Robert

Stevens, judgments of the House of Lords were reflecting a tendency towards 'substantive formalism' (*Law and Politics* (1979) pp 341–354, 374–375, and see also Paterson *The Law Lords* (1982) pp 132–133). For example, there is scarcely a hint to be found in Lord Simonds's judgment that he personally favoured the unlimited jurisdiction being argued for (this appears from his comments at 210 HL Official Report (5th series) col 377, 30 June 1958). In contrast Lord Morton's doubts as to the appropriateness of 'undignified games of chess' are clear but his was a lone voice on the taxation issue in this judgment (see *Stevens* 374–375 on Morton's isolated position amongst his colleagues concerning judicial approaches in tax litigation).

The practical consequence of *Chapman v Chapman* was sharply to diminish the possibilities of varying or terminating trusts for tax-planning purposes. Three years on, in January 1957, the question of whether the powers of the court to sanction variations of trust should be altered was referred to the Law Reform Committee (LRC). The Committee Report was completed in November 1957 (Cmnd 310) and the principal recommendation was that the court be given the virtually unlimited jurisdiction to sanction changes which it in fact exercised before *Chapman v Chapman*. A private member's bill implementing the recommendation was introduced in December 1957 and enacted without opposition in July 1958 as the Variation of Trusts Act.

(c) The roads to 1958

(1) The Law Reform Committee Report

Before briefly examining the arguments advanced by the LRC, the general terms of reference of the Committee and its membership merit comment. The Lord Chancellor's Law Reform Committee, to give its full title, was appointed by Lord Simonds in 1952 with the following terms of reference:

> to consider, having regard especially to judicial decisions, what changes are desirable in such legal doctrines as the Lord Chancellor may from time to time refer to the Committee.

The Committee comprised judges (five), practising lawyers (seven) and academics (three) 'who meet, on average, once a month in the latter part of the afternoon, and have no full-time staff of their own' (Blair (1982) 1 Civil Justice Quarterly 71; the numbers in parentheses indicate the 1954 membership of the LRC).

The Court's Power to Sanction Variation of Trusts no 6 (Cmnd 310, 1958)

> 5. In the course of the last twenty years or so it has become increasingly clear that the traditional type of settlement has not the flexibility which modern conditions demand. The primary object of the old-fashioned settlement was to preserve the settled property for future generations. . . . If the capital can only be invested in trustee investments, heavy

losses may be suffered in a period of inflation; if all the income is payable to one beneficiary, it may be largely absorbed in tax; if capital cannot be paid to beneficiaries but must be retained until the death of a life tenant, it may be largely swallowed up in death duties while some member of the family who has urgent need of capital for some reasonable purpose cannot be paid it. Accordingly, a settlement today is generally drawn on much more flexible lines. There is usually an unlimited power of investment and the trustees are usually given power to make capital payments to beneficiaries at any time; sometimes, indeed, they are empowered to distribute the whole fund in this way and to vary the destination of income among a class of beneficiaries at their discretion.

6. As the disadvantages of the old type of settlement became apparent, it was natural that in some cases the beneficiaries under such settlements or their legal advisers should ask themselves whether their provision could not be varied for the advantage of all concerned. So far as the beneficiaries were adults they could, of course, make such arrangements as they chose, but *nearly always* [emphasis added] some beneficiaries are infants and other potential beneficiaries are unborn or unascertained. The only way, therefore, in which the trusts could be varied was to ask the Court to sanction on behalf of infants and potential beneficiaries some re-arrangement of the provisions of the settlement which was for their benefit as well as for the benefit of the adult beneficiaries and to which they would (if well advised) have agreed if they could. . . .

7. The circumstances which made such re-arrangements of beneficial interests desirable varied, of course, in different cases. But it is perhaps worth noting that a common reason for applications to the Court was the fact that under the settlement in question the life interests were 'protected'. Even if the remaindermen were ascertained and of full age, the possibility that the life interest might be forfeited and a discretionary trust come into existence, some of the objects of which would be unascertainable persons, prevented any dealing with the capital being carried out by agreement between the beneficiaries.

. . .

9. The decision in *Chapman v Chapman* has not, of course, stopped beneficiaries under old-fashioned settlements from wishing to have the trusts of their settlements varied. But it has created distinctions between cases in which the trusts can be varied and cases in which they cannot be varied which have nothing to do with the merits of the proposed variations.

The LRC refers in paras 10 and 11 to the inherent 'compromise' jurisdiction (as modified by *Chapman v Chapman*); TA 1925, s 57 and SLA 1925, s 64.

12. The position, therefore, today is that so far as the terms of the settlement in question are ambiguous or so far as it comprises land, whether settled or held on trust for sale, or the proceeds of sale of land held on trust for sale, the Court will probably be able to approve on behalf of infant or potential beneficiaries a variation of the trusts which is agreed to by the adult beneficiaries and which can be shown to be for the advantage of the infant or potential beneficiaries; but that, on the other hand, if the terms of the settlement in question are free from ambiguity and the settlement consists entirely of personalty (not

being proceeds of land held on trust for sale) the Court will have no power to approve a variation of the trusts, however desirable it may be in the interests of the infant and potential beneficiaries that they should be varied.

13. We think it is clear that the present situation is unsatisfactory. It cannot be right that the question whether the Court can sanction changes in trusts on behalf of infants or potential beneficiaries should depend on the entirely irrelevant considerations upon which it depends today. In our view the only satisfactory solution of the problem is to give the Court the unlimited jurisdiction to sanction such changes which it in fact exercised in the years immediately preceding the decision in *Chapman v Chapman*. . . . Logically, there is no satisfactory stopping place short of an unlimited jurisdiction.

14. Nor is the matter simply one of logic. Justice alone, in our view, demands that the Court should have an unlimited jurisdiction. In the case of lunatics the Court of Protection has jurisdiction to sanction any disposition of the patient's property which the Court considers that the patient, if of sound mind and well advised, would make himself, including dispositions designed to lessen fiscal burdens (see *Re CWM* [1951] 2 KB 714). Similarly, if a husband and wife are divorced, the Divorce Court can sanction variations in their marriage settlement which are designed to prevent the trust fund being diminished by taxes or death duties (see *Thomson v Thomson* [1954] P 384). Why should an infant whose parents are happily married be in a worse position than a lunatic, or an infant whose parents are divorced? Why should an infant who is interested in land be better off than one who is interested in personalty? Why should it not be possible to arrange the affairs of all infants to their best advantage? Why should anyone be prevented from arranging his affairs to his best advantage by reason of some potential beneficiary who (if he ever acquires an interest) would be equally benefited by the arrangement?

15. . . . If a settlor objected to a proposed variation of the trusts, he would nearly always have some good grounds for doing so which would almost certainly incline the Court to refuse to sanction the proposed scheme. If, on the other hand, the settlor's objections are merely captious, it is right that the Court should have power to override them. When he makes the settlement, the settlor parts with his beneficial interest in the property, and he ought not to retain any right to veto changes in his dispositions which the Court considers to be desirable in the interests of his beneficiaries. Nor is it likely that any Judge of the Chancery Division would give his sanction on behalf of infants or potential beneficiaries under a settlement to any scheme of a kind which, as a citizen and a taxpayer, he would not think it right to enter into with regard to his own property. The fact that some adults enter into tax avoidance schemes of questionable character is no ground for refusing the Court jurisdiction to sanction on behalf of infants dispositions of their property which are beneficial to them and are morally unobjectionable.

16. We would add that, so far as concerns those cases where the object of a variation is to lessen the impact of taxes or death duties, we can see no valid reason why the Court should not be able to do on behalf of persons who are not *sui juris* or are not ascertained what the law allows to be done by persons who are *sui juris*. It appears to us that the legislature,

> while taking great care to prevent anyone from escaping the payment of taxes or duties by methods of which it disapproves, has shown no intention of adopting a policy of preventing the freer circulation of money and its division between the members of a family rather than its concentration in the hands of a few, so long as this is done by methods which are not forbidden by statute.

(2) The Variation of Trusts Bill

The sponsors of the Variation of Trusts Bill relied almost exclusively on the arguments for change advanced by the LRC and these raised no controversy. The quite brief debates concentrated on drafting amendments and the appropriateness of hearing applications in open court. Although tax avoidance was specifically considered, an almost unanimous consensus (but see Sir L Ungoed-Thomas and Lord Simonds's views below) was that the LRC Report adequately dealt with any doubts about the tax avoidance consequences of varying trusts.

Mr F P Crowder, a practising barrister, surprisingly presented the measure as 'a dull Bill' and as being primarily a technical tidying-up measure (579 HC Official Report (5th series) col 773, 6 December 1957):

> Looked at generally by a layman, this is a short and simple Bill and amounts to nothing more or less than a tidying-up Bill. I can say, as the leading article of *The Times* said this morning [6 December], that it will be accepted by the whole of the legal profession, I imagine without opposition.

Mr Crowder referred to Lord Morton's reservations in *Chapman v Chapman* about the development of 'an undignified game of chess' but doubted that the latter's fears would be realised: '[Lord Morton] was placing too great a stress on something which might happen occasionally here and there and too great an exaggeration on how, with commonsense and fairness, these matters are likely to work out' (col 774).

In slight contrast the principal Labour opposition spokesman Sir L Ungoed-Thomas (a then practising member of the Chancery bar, subsequently appointed as a judge in the Chancery Division), whilst supporting the Bill, stressed that it should be recognised as being primarily concerned with tax avoidance. He emphasised that a consequence of enacting the Variation of Trusts Bill would be to place the courts in precisely the position contemplated by Lord Morton: 'We must not just pooh-pooh Lord Morton's objection, but face it quite squarely and say whether, in spite of his substantial objection, we are or are not in favour of the principle in the Bill' (col 793).

As a private member's bill its success depended in part on a sympathetic government attitude, particularly in view of the possible fiscal consequences (see generally Marsh and Read *Private Member's Bills* (1988)). The government position conveyed by the Solicitor-General, was that the Bill's advantages, as described in the LRC Report, overwhelmingly outweighed the disadvantage that there was a risk to the Revenue which might 'involve some Revenue loss'. He concluded (cols 799–800):

> I prefer not to indict this as a tax avoidance Bill but rather to call it a 'fair restrictions for all' Bill. It will place persons not *sui juris* in a parallel position as regards adult persons for the purpose of invoking the jurisdiction of the courts. The more we look at it, the more it is apparent that both justice and logic require that the law be changed in the way this Bill will change it ... and so the Government think that on balance, and despite its disadvantages, the Bill should be accepted by the House.

The Bill passed unopposed through all its stages in both Houses. One slight check to its smooth progress occurred in the House of Lords. Viscount Simonds (as he had since become) strongly supported the Bill – '[the avoidance of tax] is an object from which I, for one, do not dissent in any way' (210 HL Official Report (5th series) col 377 30 June 1958) but expressed concern that not all Chancery judges would have identical views about the propriety of schemes whose main purpose was tax avoidance. In the interests of clarity and certainty he urged that the Bill be amended to state that 'it shall not be an objection to the exercise [of the court's jurisdiction] that a main purpose or consequence of its exercise is . . . to avoid the exigibility of tax which would otherwise be exigible'. Although remaining unconvinced, Viscount Simonds did not press the amendment when the Lord Chancellor responded (cols 380–382) that there was no real uncertainty since Chancery judges would apply the reasoning described in the LRC Report paras 15 and 16 (see above, p 336).

The Bill was enacted as the VTA in July 1958 and its structure, which closely follows the recommendations of the LRC Report, and operation are examined in the next section.

Consider the following points:

(1) The LRC accepted the view that 'a compromise of disputed rights alters the rights of beneficiaries just as much as an alteration of undisputed rights' (para 13). Lord Morton had argued that 'where rights are in dispute and the court approves a compromise it is not altering the trusts, for the trusts are, ex hypothesi, still in doubt and unascertained'. Whose view do you find more persuasive?

(2) Does the LRC (para 15 above) deal adequately with Lord Morton's concern about 'an undignified game of chess'? (See Waters [1960] CLP 36 at 57–58 and Mitchell (1954) 17 MLR 473 at 474–475.) How convincing is the LRC's analysis of 'tax avoidance' and 'tax evasion' in paras 15 and 16 (cf the discussion in Chapter 3)?

(3) The LRC places considerable emphasis on the anomalies in the capacity of the courts to approve variations. It is evident, however, that there were 'nearly always' (para 6) minor or unascertained beneficiaries who could not legally consent, thereby preventing adult beneficiaries achieving, in

effect, a variation under the rule in *Saunders v Vautier*. The usual method of removing an anomaly is to bring it into line with the majority position. Does the LRC stand this methodology on its head? Does the LRC establish its claim that '*logically* [our emphasis] there is no satisfactory stopping place short of an unlimited jurisdiction' (para 13)?

(4) The LRC emphasises that compared with contemporary settlements, increasingly then in the form of discretionary trusts, 'traditional settlements' lacked flexibility. Should the VTA therefore have had retrospective effect *only*?

(5) Was the LRC primarily concerned with the interests of 'minor beneficiaries' or 'adult beneficiaries' or both equally?

(6) 'The general impression [of the work of the LRC] is one of modernisation by way of simplification and elimination of anomalies, rather than by the creation of fresh rights or adjustment of the whole thrust of a given field of law' (Blair (1982) 1 Civil Justice Quarterly 71 at 77). Does this description apply to the LRC Report on trust variation?

(7) Westergaard and Resler in their analysis of power in a capitalist society refer to the non-manipulative exercise of power, a process they label as 'non-decision making' (Westergaard and Resler *Class in a Capitalist Society* (1976) pp 147–149, 246–247; see also Lukes *Power: a Radical View* (1974) chs 3 and 7).

Westergaard and Resler *Class in a Capitalist Society* (1976) p 147

But more is involved [in 'non-decisions'] than the capacity of a well-placed group to 'mobilize bias' or 'pre-empt decisions'... by actively preventing particular policy alternatives from being considered. That description certainly applies, for example, when officials or executives without formal powers of policy making – civil servants, say, or middle-level managers in business – are in a position so to prepare the ground that they present their 'masters' with no choice, or only quite a limited choice, between different courses of action. This entails more or less direct and deliberate manipulation. It does not cover the situation of which the essential feature is common acceptance of certain basic premises, which nobody directly engaged in dispute, bargaining or advice considers it realistic to challenge and which automatically rule out a wide range of alternative policies. This is a foreclosure of options without manipulation. None is needed here, on or off stage, so long as the unspoken agreement about premises holds.

It is tempting to characterise the law reform process culminating in the VTA 1958 as an illustration of non-decision making in the sense portrayed by Westergaard and Resler. Yet might even this type of analysis overstate the extent to which any non-legal policy considerations could have been a *conscious* factor in the decision-making processes? By 'conscious factor' we mean conscious in the Westergaard and Resler sense of ruling out alternative policy solutions simply because of a 'common acceptance of certain basic premises' which nobody considered it 'realistic to challenge'. In the example of the VTA 1958 the proposition might be that the commonly accepted basic premise, evident in the terms of reference of the Law Reform Committee (see above, p 334), is that this was an area of legal doctrine and one that required 'tidying up' by a doctrinal response. In sum was this legal reform a matter of legal discourse alone where alternative policy solutions did not even enter peoples' consciousness let alone be rejected by common agreement as unrealistic? Even if one is persuaded to categorise the decision-making process along the lines just described this does not quite conclude matters. For erstwhile critics there remains a further issue on which to reflect: what 'range of alternative policies', if any, could have been countenanced by the Law Reform Committee?

(d) The Variation of Trusts Act 1958

1(1) Where property, whether real or personal, is held on trusts arising, whether before or after the passing of this Act, under any will, settlement or other disposition, the court may if it thinks fit by order approve on behalf of –

(a) any person having, directly or indirectly, an interest, whether vested or contingent, under the trusts who by reason of infancy or other incapacity is incapable of assenting, or

(b) any person (whether ascertained or not) who may become entitled, directly or indirectly, to an interest under the trusts as being at a future date or on the happening of a future event a person of any specified description or a member of any specified class of persons, so however that this paragraph shall not include any person who would be of that description, or a member of that class, as the case may be, if the said date had fallen or the said event had happened at the date of the application to the court, or

(c) any person unborn, or

(d) any person in respect of any discretionary interest of his under protective trusts where the interest of the principal beneficiary has not failed or determined,

any arrangement (by whomsoever proposed, and whether or not there is any other person beneficially interested who is capable of assenting thereto) varying or revoking all or any of the trusts, or enlarging the powers of the trustees of managing or administering any of the property subject to the trusts:

Provided that except by virtue of paragraph (d) of this subsection the court shall not approve an arrangement on behalf of any person unless the carrying out thereof would be for the benefit of that person.

(2) In the foregoing subsection 'protective trusts' means the trusts specified in paragraphs (i) and (ii) of subsection (1) of section thirty-three of the Trustee Act 1925, or any like trusts, 'the principal beneficiary' has the same meaning as in the said subsection (1) and 'discretionary interest' means an interest arising under the trust specified in paragraph (ii) of the said subsection (1) or any like trust.

[Subsections (3)–(6) omitted.] Applications are made by originating summons under RSC, Ord 93, r 6 (Civil Procedure Rules 1998, Sch 1 and see Chapman (ed) *Chancery Practice and Procedure* (2001) on parties to the application and procedure generally).

(1) The Act in outline

Essentially the Act confers on the court the de facto pre-*Chapman v Chapman* jurisdiction. It enables the court to approve arrangements varying or revoking trusts, or enlarging trustees' administrative powers on behalf of the classes specified in s 1(1). The jurisdiction provides a 'very wide and, indeed, revolutionary discretion' whether to approve an application in any particular case (*Re Steed's Will Trusts* [1960] Ch 407 at 421 per Evershed MR; cf the words of Farwell J in *Re Walker* above, p 324). The discretion is subject only to the proviso in s 1(1) that, where the application is made on behalf of any person within subsections (a), (b), and (c), the arrangement must be for the benefit of each individual person. The meaning of benefit is considered in detail in the next section.

The intention of the Act is to enable the court to approve arrangements on behalf of beneficiaries who cannot give their own consent, as is made clear for those who are unborn or who are minors or mentally disabled in sections 1(1)(c) and 1(1)(a) respectively. A more difficult task is to disentangle and interpret the scope of the proviso in s 1(1)(b). In particular what meanings are to be attributed (i) to the phrase 'any person who may become entitled . . . to an interest' and (ii) to the proviso commencing at 'so however . . .' (see generally *Harris* pp 33–41)? As regards the meaning of 'interest' the proposition that the term should be interpreted in a lay rather than in its technical legal sense was rejected in *Knocker v Youle* [1986] 2 All ER 914. The consequence is that those who already have an interest, whether vested or contingent and no matter how remote, do not come within the scope of the subsection. (Cf Riddall [1987] Conv 144 who argues that 'interest' should be interpreted as referring to vested interest only, hence those with a contingent interest would come within the class on whose behalf the court can give approval under s 1(1)(b).) In *Knocker v Youle*, for instance, the outcome was that adult cousins with very remote contingent interests under default clauses in the settlor's 1937 will and whose consent it was not practicable to obtain – some of them were living in Australia – did not come within s 1(1)(b). The court could not therefore consent to a variation on their behalf, although it could do so under s 1(1)(a) for any cousins who were minors.

Who then does fall within the scope of s 1(1)(b) and on whose behalf can the court give its consent? It must be emphasised that the subsection is concerned only with those who may have an *expectation* of obtaining some interest under the trust but have no interest, vested or contingent, at the time of the application being submitted to the court. Among the classes that can come within the subsection are therefore presumptive next-of-kin of a living person or a potential future spouse. But the effect of the proviso within s 1(1)(b) on any such person and the significance of the word 'if' must not be overlooked. The proviso is that the court cannot give its consent if the future event that could transform 'expectation' into 'entitlement' had, hypothetically, actually happened by the date of the application to the court even though, of course, it had not. In *Re Suffert's Settlement* [1961] Ch 1 a trust had been established for Elaine Suffert for life with a power to appoint the capital to such of her children as she might select and in default of appointment to, in effect, her next-of-kin. Miss Suffert, who was a 61-year-old spinster with no children and whose only relations were three adult cousins, submitted an application to vary the trust but with the consent of only one of the cousins, the consent of the other two not having been obtained. Buckley J held that the court could not give its consent under s 1(1)(b) on behalf of the latter two cousins. The reason was that if the future event under which they would have become entitled, the death of Miss Suffert, had actually occurred at the date of the application to the court, the cousins would, as next-of-kin, have been beneficiaries with an interest under the trust and hence outside the scope of s 1(1)(b). Their own consent would therefore have to be obtained. It is surprising though consistent with the language of s 1(1)(b) to discover that the court can consent on behalf of a person where not one but two contingencies have to be satisfied before that person's expectation can harden into entitlement. In *Re Moncrieff's Settlement Trusts* [1962] 1 WLR 1344, as in *Re Suffert*, there was a life interest for the applicant, a Mrs Parkin, then for such of her children as she might appoint with the possibility that in default of any appointment the fund would go to those entitled were she to die intestate. Mrs Parkin had an adopted son Alan who was a person 'who may become entitled' under s 1(1)(b) but in addition there were four infant grandchildren of a maternal aunt and they also came within that category. Buckley J held that he could *not* give the court's consent to the proposed variation on behalf of Alan because he was caught by the proviso as being someone who would have been entitled if, at the date of the application, Mrs Parkin had died. On the other hand, consent could be given on behalf of the four grandchildren since their 'expectation' would have become 'entitlement' only on the occurrence of a 'double contingency', ie had the death of both Mrs Parkin and Alan happened, and the contingency of two deaths being required was outwith the scope of the proviso in s 1(1)(b).

In short the VTA 1958 does not permit the court to dispense with the consent of persons, whether with vested or contingent interests, who are ascertained and sui juris. The sole exception arises under subsection (d); here the consent of even adult and ascertained beneficiaries with contingent discretionary interests under a protective trust is not required. Indeed the arrangement need not even be for their benefit. The wide VTA 1958 jurisdiction largely supersedes those jurisdictions mentioned earlier, although s 1(6) preserves the powers conferred in SLA 1925, s 64 and TA 1925, s 57. And in one respect s 57 is technically of wider scope than the VTA since a transaction can be approved under s 57 provided in the opinion of the court only that it is 'expedient', the consent of all beneficiaries not being required (see *Mason v Farbrother* [1983] 2 All ER 1078).

Apart from the meaning of 'benefit' – to be discussed shortly – and the complexities of s 1(1)(b), two other particular problems of interpretation are created by the statute. First, in applying the phrase 'varying or revoking' in s 1(1) does the court have the jurisdiction to approve what is in truth a complete resettlement? The short answer is 'no', Wilberforce J accepting in *Re T's Settlement Trusts* that where an arrangement 'though presented as a variation . . . is in truth a complete new resettlement . . . I do not think that the court can approve [it]' ([1964] Ch 158 at 162). There the proposed variation would have transferred an 'irresponsible' daughter's share of a trust fund (to which she was shortly to become absolutely entitled) to new trustees to be held on protective trusts for her life. Subsequently Megarry J (*Re Holt's Settlement* [1968] 1 All ER 470; *Re Ball's Settlement* [1968] 2 All ER 438) accepted that a dividing line should be drawn but proposed what has been termed a 'substratum' test for deciding whether an arrangement is a 'variation' or a 'resettlement'. In Megarry J's view 'where an arrangement does not change the substratum yet effectuates the purpose of the trust by other means, it may still be possible to regard that arrangement as merely varying the original trusts, even though the means employed are wholly different and even though the form is completely changed' (*Re Ball's Settlement* [1968] 2 All ER 438 at 442). Harris caustically comments 'that a resettlement by any other name smells more sweet' (*Variation of Trusts* (1975) p 67) and there is no evidence that this distinction has caused any practical difficulty. It is questionable whether this 'distinction without a difference' is warranted by the language or intent of the VTA (see generally *Harris* pp 63–68).

The second problem requiring brief comment concerns the way a variation takes effect. Does the order of the court or the arrangement that the order approves vary the trust? Dicta of Lord Reid in *Re Holmden's Settlement Trusts* [1968] 1 All ER 148 at 151 seem conclusive:

> Under the [VTA 1958], the court does not itself amend or vary the trusts of the original settlement. The beneficiaries are not bound by variations because the court has made the variation. Each beneficiary is bound because he has consented to the variation . . . the arrangement must be regarded as an arrangement made by the beneficiaries themselves. The court merely acted on behalf of or as representing those beneficiaries who were not in a position to give their own consent and approval.

Previous practice had been to treat the order of the court as varying the trust (*Re Hambleden's Will Trusts* [1960] 1 All ER 353n), it being assumed that this dispensed with the need for any other instrument in writing. But a conclusion that the court merely provided the approval on behalf of minor beneficiaries posed a problem of formalities. How could the equitable interests of consenting adult beneficiaries be disposed of without any instrument in writing as required by LPA 1925, s 53(1)(c) (see Chapter 4)? Were many of the variations made since 1958 therefore void? The effect of the section was considered at length by Megarry J in *Re Holt's Settlement* [1968] 1 All ER 470 at 474–476 (decided before *Re Holmden* was reported), who also decided that it was the arrangement not the court order which varied the trusts. What then of s 53(1)(c)? The explanations, advanced by counsel and accepted largely on grounds of convenience by Megarry J, are succinctly summarised by *Pettit* (p 512) as follows:

> First, that by conferring an express power on the court to do something by order, Parliament in the Act of 1958 had provided by necessary implication an exception to s 53(1)(c). Secondly that where, as on the facts [in *Re Holt*], the arrangement consisted of a specifically enforceable agreement made for valuable consideration, the beneficial interest would have passed to the respective purchasers on the making of the agreement. This would be a case of constructive trust excluded from the operation of s 53(1)(c) by sub-s (2).

The 'constructive trust' argument, adopting the reasoning of Lord Radcliffe in *Oughtred v IRC* [1959] 3 All ER 623, was not easily reconcilable with the majority decision in that case, Lord Radcliffe being a dissentient. The outcome and the reasoning in *Re Holt* seem less dubious in the light of the adoption by the Court of Appeal in *Neville v Wilson* [1996] 3 All ER 171 of Lord Radcliffe's dictum in *Oughtred* (see Chapter 4, p 132; and Harris (1969) 33 Conv 197–199).

(2) Meaning of 'benefit'

'The word benefit... is... plainly not confined to financial benefit, but may extend to social or moral benefit' (*Re Holt's Settlement* [1968] 1 All ER 470 at 479 per Megarry J). In that case Megarry J approved a variation postponing the absolute vesting of children's interests in income and capital from the age of 21 to 30 – technically a financial detriment – and concurred with the sentiment of their mother that 'children should be reasonably advanced in a career and settled in life before they are in receipt of an income sufficient to make them independent of the need to work' (at 479; and see *The Independent* 16 February 1999, vesting in possession of entitlement to £1m capital sum and annual income of £250,000 for the son – then aged 14 – of the Duke of Northumberland postponed from age 18 to 25). In fact the whole arrangement in *Re Holt* involved substantial savings of, inter alia, estate duty and the financial advantages of the arrangement were overwhelming, removing any need to balance financial detriment against moral or social benefits. Nevertheless financial benefit, while not a prerequisite (see *Re C L* [1968] 1 All ER 1104), has been the benefit most frequently, indeed almost universally, relied on in arrangements submitted for approval under the VTA 1958.

Although our concern here is with the meaning of 'benefit', s 1(1) in theory places a dual function on the court: it must decide where necessary that 'benefit' exists and then 'may if it thinks fit' approve the proposed arrangement. No indication is given in the statute as to what should influence the exercise of this 'residual' discretion but two factors in particular merit consideration: (i) the settlor's intention; and (ii) tax avoidance. (See *Harris*, ch 4 for a detailed analysis identifying separate factors.)

Settlor's intention In one early reported case, *Re Steed's Will Trusts* [1960] Ch 407, the Court of Appeal stated that in exercising its discretion the court should consider not only the person on whose behalf its consent was sought but 'is bound to look back at the scheme as a whole, and when it does so, to consider, as surely it must, what really was the intention of the benefactor' (at 421 per Evershed MR). In that case a testator had wished to provide for his housekeeper (G) but had apparently been concerned that there was a danger of her 'being, to use a common phrase, sponged upon by one of her brothers'. Accordingly he left the property to her upon protective trusts. G asked the court to remove the protective element from her life interest with the result that she would then, in effect, be absolutely entitled to the trust property. The application to the court was necessary as, although G was 53, unmarried and with no intention of marrying, its approval was required on behalf of any future husband, described as a 'spectral spouse', as a contingent discretionary beneficiary under s 1(1)(d). There is no requirement under sub-s (1)(d) for the court to consider the matter of benefit and the court refused to sanction the arrangement because to do so would undermine the 'intention and desire of the testator' that G should not be exposed to the risk of being 'sponged upon'.

What *Re Steed* does not resolve is how the balance might be struck when the settlor's intention appears to conflict with benefit for those on whose behalf the court's approval is sought. This issue came before the courts in *Re Remnant's Settlement Trusts* (1970) and in *Goulding v James* (1997).

Re Remnant's Settlement Trusts [1970] 2 All ER 554
The children of two sisters, Mrs Hooper ('Dawn') and Mrs Crosthwaite ('Merrial'), were contingent beneficiaries of a trust consisting of two funds valued at £39,000 and £23,000 respectively. The trust contained a forfeiture clause which would operate in respect of any of the children who practised Roman Catholicism or who were married to a Roman Catholic at the time of vesting, with an accruer provision in favour of the children of the other sister. Dawn's children were Protestant while Merrial's children were practising Catholics. Although Dawn's children stood a substantial chance of taking Merrial's children's share under the accruer clause, both sisters asked the court to approve an arrangement which (i) deleted the forfeiture clause, and (ii) provided for £10,000 to be set aside on accelerated trusts for each sister's children.

Pennycuick J: . . . [Leaving] other considerations apart, the deletion of the forfeiture provisions must be detrimental to [Mrs Hooper's children]. However, that is by no means the end of the matter. In the first place they are being given an accelerated interest in £10,000.

Then there are the non-financial considerations which seem to me to loom large in this matter. The three considerations set out by Mrs Crosthwaite, and elaborated by counsel, are these: first, that the forfeiture provisions represent a deterrent to each of the Hooper children from adopting the Roman Catholic faith should she be minded to do so; secondly, that they operate as a deterrent to each of the Hooper children in the selection of a husband when the time comes; and thirdly, that the forfeiture provisions represent a source of possible family dissension. I am not sure that there is very much weight in the first of those considerations because there is no reason to suppose that any of these children has any particular concern with the Roman Catholic faith. On the other hand, I do think that there is a very real weight in the second and in the third consideration. Obviously a forfeiture provision of this kind might well cause very serious dissension between the families of the two sisters. On the best consideration I can give it I think that the deletion of the forfeiture provisions on the terms contained in the arrangements including the provision for acceleration in £10,000, should be regarded as for the benefit of the three Hooper children.

I have not found this an easy point, but I think that I am entitled to take a broad view of what is meant by 'benefit', and so taking it, I think that this arrangement can fairly be said to be for their benefit.

It remains to consider whether the arrangement is a fair and proper one. As far as I can see, there is no reason for saying otherwise, except that the arrangement defeats this testator's intention. That is a serious but by no means conclusive consideration. I have reached the clear conclusion that these forfeiture provisions are undesirable in themselves in the circumstances of this case and that an arrangement involving their deletion is a fair and proper one.

Neither *Re Tinker's Settlement* [1960] 3 All ER 85n (see Cotterrell (1971) 34 MLR 98), where the position was strikingly similar to that in *Re Remnant* but with a different conclusion, nor *Re Steed's Will Trusts* (above) were cited in *Re Remnant* (criticised by McPherson J in *Re Christmas' Settlement Trusts* [1986] 1 Qd R 372 as extending the notion of benefit to an extent that could not be fairly justified).

The importance to be attached to the trust-founder's intention was reduced still further in *Goulding v James* [1997] 2 All ER 239 (see Luxton (1997) 60 MLR 719) where the court's approval to a variation was sought on behalf of certain minors (great-grandchildren of the testatrix). The testatrix (F) left her residuary estate to her daughter J (aged 59) for life with remainder to her (F's) grandson M (aged 32) contingent on his attaining the age of 40. Provision was made for the estate to devolve upon F's great-grandchildren should M predecease his mother (J) or die before attaining the age of 40. J and M proposed an arrangement whereby 10% of the residuary estate should be put into a trust fund for the great-grandchildren with the balance being split immediately into equal capital payments for J and M. The great-grandchildren's interest under the existing will was actuarially valued at 1.85% of the value of the residuary estate. There was therefore no question, unlike *Re Remnant*, of there being any element of financial detriment to any of the great-grandchildren.

At first instance Laddie J rejected the application principally because evidence produced to the court demonstrated that the proposed arrangement 'was the complete opposite of what was provided for in the will and the settled intention of [F]' ([1996] 4 All ER 865 at 870). It appeared that the testatrix distrusted her son-in-law (J's husband), and her grandson (M) had not 'settled down'. The Court of Appeal reversed the decision and approved the arrangement. Giving the leading judgment Mummery LJ emphasised that the discretion of the court to approve an arrangement is fettered only by the proviso in s 1(1) which prevents 'the court from approving an arrangement which is not for the benefit of the classes referred to in [s 1(1)](a), (b) or (c)' ([1997] 2 All ER 239 at 249). This does not mean that where there is financial benefit approval automatically follows; the arrangement as a whole has to be considered and this involves 'a practical and business-like consideration of the arrangement, including the total amount of the advantages which the various parties obtain, and their bargaining strength' (above, citing Ungoed-Thomas J in *Re Van Gruisen's Will Trusts* [1964] 1 All ER 843n at 844). Mummery LJ emphasised that the function of the court is to act almost as a 'statutory attorney' for the beneficiaries who cannot act for themselves and that the intentions and wishes of the testatrix in the case 'had little, if any, relevance or weight to the issue of approval on behalf of [those beneficiaries] whose interest in residue was multiplied five-fold under the proposed arrangement' (at 252).

Two particular questions arise. First, whatever the merits of the legal logic in *Goulding v James* may be, how is the case distinguishable from *Re Steed*? Mummery LJ pointed to the specific facts of the latter case 'that explained and justified the court's refusal of approval' – the protective trust and the reason for it, the opposition of the trustees to the application, the legal fact that no question of benefit falls to be considered under s 1(1)(d). One can but speculate as to the outcome had the life interest in *Goulding v James* been held on protective trusts. As to our second question, what considerations would persuade a court to exercise its discretion to withhold approval in a case where there is a financial benefit for those beneficiaries on whose behalf approval is sought? In *Goulding v James* Sir Ralph Gibson, concurring with Mummery LJ suggested that if the arrangement constituted 'a dishonest or inequitable or otherwise improper act' on behalf of the adult beneficiaries then such evidence would be relevant as to 'whether the court should "think fit" to approve it on behalf of minor or unborn persons' (at 252). That vague formula simply leads to another question: in what circumstances, if any, should a tax-saving motivation for a variation be a ground for a court refusing to approve the application?

Tax avoidance   In *Re Weston's Settlements* [1968] 3 All ER 338, the settlor, Stanley Weston, applied to the court for orders (i) under TA 1925, s 41 (see Chapter 11) appointing new trustees to two settlements created in 1964, and (ii) under VTA 1958 to have the settlements, each valued at about £400,000, transferred to Jersey thereby avoiding a liability to capital gains tax of about £163,000. The settlor claimed that his family (comprising himself, his wife, one son Robert aged 25, and his wife and their child aged two, and another son Alan aged 19, and still a minor), who had moved to Jersey in 1967, intended to make it their permanent home.

Stamp J refused to approve the applications stating that he was 'not persuaded that this application represents more than a cheap exercise in tax avoidance which I ought not to sanction, as distinct from a legitimate avoidance of liability to taxation' ([1968] 1 All ER 720 at 725; see Bretten (1968) 32 Conv 194). The subsequent appeal by the trustees was dismissed (see Harris (1969) 32 MLR 320; Baker (1969) 85 LQR 15; Crane (1968) 32 Conv 431).

Re Weston's Settlements [1968] 3 All ER 338 at 342

Lord Denning MR: The court has power to approve a variation or revocation of the trust, if it thinks fit, on behalf of infants or unborn persons. The statute gives no guide as to the way in which this discretion should be exercised. It provides: 'The court may *if it thinks fit* by order approve.' Likewise with the appointment of new trustees, the Trustee Act 1925 gives no guide. It simply says the court may appoint new trustees 'whenever it is expedient'. There being no guidance in the statutes, it remains for the court to do the best it can.

Two propositions are clear: (i) in exercising its discretion, the function of the court is to protect those who cannot protect themselves. It must do what is truly for their benefit; (ii) it can give its consent to a scheme to avoid death duties or other taxes. Nearly every variation that has come before the court has tax avoidance for its principal object: and no-one has ever suggested that this is undesirable or contrary to public policy.

I think it necessary, however, to add this third proposition: (iii) the court should not consider merely the financial benefit to the infants or unborn children, but also their educational and social benefit. There are many things in life more worthwhile than money. One of these things is to be brought up in this our England, which is still 'the envy of less happier lands'. I do not believe it is for the benefit of children to be uprooted from England and transported to another country simply to avoid tax. It was very different with the children of the Seale family, which Buckley J considered (see *Re Seale's Marriage Settlement* [1961] 3 All ER 136). That family had emigrated to Canada many years before, with no thought of tax avoidance, and had brought up the children there as Canadians. It was very proper that the trusts should be transferred to Canada. But here the family had only been in Jersey three months when they presented this scheme to the court. The inference is irresistible: the underlying purpose was to go there in order to avoid tax. I do not think that this will be all to the good for the children. I should imagine that, even if they had stayed in this country, they would have had a very considerable fortune at their disposal, even after paying tax. The only thing that Jersey can do for them is to give them an ever greater fortune. Many a child has been ruined by being given too much. The avoidance of tax may be lawful, but it is not yet a virtue. The Court of Chancery should not encourage or support it – it should not give its approval to it – if by so doing it would imperil the true welfare of the children, already born or yet to be born.

There is one thing more. I cannot help wondering how long these young people will stay in Jersey. It may be to their financial interest at present to make their home there permanently, but will they remain there once the capital gains are safely in hand, clear of tax? They may well change their minds and come back to enjoy their untaxed gains. Is such a prospect really for the benefit of the children? Are they to be wanderers over the face of the earth, moving from this country to that, according to where they can best avoid tax? I cannot believe that to be right. Children are like trees: they grow stronger with firm roots.

The long and short of it is, as the judge said, that the exodus of this family to Jersey is done to avoid English taxation. Having made great wealth here, they want to quit without paying the taxes and duties which are imposed on those who stay. So be it. If it really be for the benefit of the children, let it be done. Let them go, taking their money with them, but, if it be not truly for their benefit, the court should not countenance it. It should not give the scheme its blessing. The judge refused his approval. So would I. I would dismiss this appeal.

Harman LJ: Now, the linchpin of the scheme is not to be carried out under the Variation of Trusts Act, 1958, at all. It is essential that the court should exercise its powers under the Trustee Act, 1925, either by appointing new trustees out of the jurisdiction, or giving leave to the existing trustees to make the appointment. It is not suggested that the present trustees are unsuitable or that any difficulty has arisen in the administration of the trusts. The scheme is entirely conditioned by the wish to avoid the incidence of capital gains tax. For this purpose it is essential that the affairs of the trust should be administered from outside the United Kingdom and that this should be done by appointing two persons so resident as trustees. It is proposed that these trustees should then be empowered while still trustees of the English settlements to revoke the whole of the trusts of those instruments and to transfer the assets to themselves as trustees of two settlements framed, it is said, so as to conform with the Jersey law.

Now, this law has never had any experience of trusts and so far as appears, the courts of Jersey have never made an order executing the trusts of a settlement. There is not, it appears, any Trustee Act in Jersey at all, and the effect of this last transaction must, so far as I can see, having nothing to recommend it from a trust point of view.

Under the circumstances the judge was entitled to consider whether the court 'should think fit' to accede to the scheme. The judge professed himself unsatisfied, and I think he was entitled to take that view. It is true that he expressed some dislike of tax avoidance of this sort, and in that he may have been mistaken, but he was in my opinion well justified in not being satisfied that a transfer of the whole trust to Jersey is expedient...

These are English settlements and they should I think remain so unless some good reason connected with the trusts themselves can be put forward. I am of opinion, therefore, that the judge was entitled in the exercise of his discretion to say that to use the powers of the Trustee Act, 1925, in this way was not justified and I would dismiss the appeal.

Consider the following points:

(1) Was the application in *Re Weston* refused: (a) because the transfer was not for the benefit of the minor or unborn beneficiaries; or (b) because the appointment of trustees under TA 1925, s 41 was not expedient; or (c) as an exercise of a residual discretion under s 1(1) to counter 'illegitimate tax avoidance'?

(2) 'There is no legal justification for refusing to sanction a scheme under the VTA 1958 because the sole object of the scheme is to avoid UK taxation.' Does this statement accurately reflect the language of the statute and its purpose, assuming the latter can be discerned from the LRC Report and parliamentary debates?

(3) Lord Denning MR appears to suggest that a substantial financial gain can be outweighed by the alleged benefit of developing 'firm roots' in 'this our England, the "envy of less happier lands"'. Is the decision in *Re Weston*, and indeed that in *Re Remnant*, an undesirable example of judicial paternalism?

(4) The immediate tax saving in *Re Weston* would have been that of capital gains tax (CGT). Although the evidence is not wholly persuasive it is possible to view *Re Weston* as a precursor of the hostile judicial attitude towards artificial CGT-avoidance schemes that was to emerge a decade later. (Review Chapter 3, and see Flesch [1968] CLP 215, for a contemporary review of shifting judicial attitudes.)

Lastly, it must be stressed that benefit under the VTA 1958 is essentially a question of fact in every case. The overwhelming majority of applications have been trouble-free, with actuarial evidence providing the basis for an assessment of benefit, and insurance provision to cater for the element of risk where appropriate (see the example *Re Robinson's Settlement Trusts* [1976] 3 All ER 61). Seen from this vantage point *Re Remnant* and *Re Weston* appear as isolated cases, which nevertheless demonstrate that where competing benefits must be balanced there may be substance in the opinion of Cotterrell ((1971) 34 MLR 96 at 98) that 'the measure of [benefit] is simply what the court says it is'.

(3) A *Re Weston* postscript: trust exporting

Since *Re Weston* was decided the climate in the Channel Islands and in numerous other attractive offshore locations has been deemed more congenial for export-ing trusts. *Re Seale's Marriage Settlement* [1961] 3 All ER 136 (distinguished in *Re Weston*) has since been followed in *Re Windeatt's Will Trusts* [1969] 2 All ER 324 where a transfer of trust assets to Jersey was approved, the beneficia-ries having lived there for 19 years. The scope was extended further still in *Re Chamberlain* (unreported, but noted by Morcom 'Trust Exporting' (1976) 126 NLJ 1034) where approval was given to a transfer of a trust to Guernsey with a consequent CGT saving. The beneficiaries had long ceased to be domiciled in the UK, the principal beneficiaries and remaindermen being resident in France and Indonesia respectively. *Re Weston's Settlements* perhaps stands at least as a warning that applications under the VTA 1958 may be unsuccessful where beneficiaries are still resident in or only recently removed from the UK. Indeed in a more recent case, Millett J, commenting on circumstances where the court might be asked to exercise a discretion of its own in appointing foreign trustees, indicated that 'the court is unlikely to assist [applicants] where the scheme is nothing more than a device to avoid tax and has no other advantages of any kind' (*Richards v The Hon AB Mackay* (1987) reported in (1997) 11(1) TLI 22; noted in [1990] Offshore Tax Planning Review 1 by R Bramwell QC). The judge accepted, however, that where trustees were exercising their own discretion, as under TA 1925, s 36(1) (see Chapter 11) or under a power in the trust instrument and merely seeking the authorisation of the court for their own protection, the role of the court is a more limited one:

> [The court] is concerned to ensure that the proposed exercise of the trustees' power is lawful and within the power and that it does not infringe the trustees' duty to act as ordinary, reasonable and prudent trustees might act, but it requires only to be satisfied that the trustees can properly form the view that the proposed transaction is for the benefit of beneficiaries or the trust estate. In my judgment, where the trustees retain their discretion, as they do in the present case, the court should need to be satisfied only that the proposed transaction is not so inappropriate that no reasonable trustee could entertain it.

This view was subsequently endorsed by Vinelott J in *Re Beatty's Will Trusts (No 2)* (1991) (reported in (1997) 11(3) TLI 77). There, however, the specific reason for seeking a declaration similar to that in *Richards v The Hon AB Mackay* was the avoidance of future CGT tax liability that would arise when certain of the beneficiaries, one of whom was non-resident and another who was about to become so, obtained interests in possession in the trust fund. It is nevertheless difficult to see circumstances other than perhaps those peculiar to a case such as *Re Weston* where exporting a trust for fiscal reasons would ever constitute 'a transaction so inappropriate that no reasonable trustee could entertain it'. In any event in *Richards v The Hon AB Mackay* there was no immediate tax liability to cloud the picture and the reason given by the trustees for the new appointment of a capital sum to the Bermudan trustees was couched in more general terms. In the words of Millett J (at 24):

> The main object of the proposal is not to gain a tax advantage but to obtain greater flexibility and diversification, with the concomitant additional protection to the trust estate which would result from spreading the risks by hiving off up to 25% of the trust fund and causing it to be the subject of an overseas settlement.

Re Weston and the other cases cited above merely touch the fringes of trust exporting, which is widely believed to have expanded substantially after the suspension of exchange control on 24 October 1979. Indeed it is said that one of the most important reasons why some individuals resident in the UK have set up trusts offshore is to enable their assets to be free of the restrictions that might accompany any future re-introduction of exchange control, however unlikely that prospect may be (see eg Matthews *Trusts: Migration and Change of Proper Law* (1997) para 11.3). In *Richards v The Hon AB Mackay* itself the trustees specifically identify 'a change in economic conditions that required the introduction of exchange controls' as one of the risks to be guarded against and therefore one of the reasons for exporting the funds. One of the other possible risks to be guarded against, aside from the matter of exchange controls, is a change in the UK tax regime. Concern about avoidance of CGT, the tax at issue *sotto voce* in *Re Weston*, by means of exporting trusts prompted a legislative response. Finance Act 1991, ss 83–87 (now Taxation of Chargeable Gains Act 1992, ss 80–84) imposes an exit charge, based on a deemed disposal and reacquisition of the trust assets, whenever (after 19 March 1991) the trustees of a settlement cease to be ordinarily resident in the UK (see Chapter 8 and generally Venables *Non-Resident Trusts* (8th edn, 2000)). The trustees and the court in *Re Beatty's Will Trusts (No 2)* demonstrated a fine sense of timing in so far as judgment was given just 19 days before the implementation of the provisions in the Finance Act 1991.

Settlors who are not deterred either from exporting trusts or from setting up new trusts overseas will have received further encouragement from the unanimous adoption by member states at the Fifteenth Session of the Hague Conference on Private International Law in 1984 of a draft Convention on the Law Applicable to Trusts and on their Recognition (see now Recognition of Trusts Act 1987). This establishes common conflict of law principles with reference to trusts (see Chapter 1 at p 21). The effect will be to reduce the unpredictability of what may happen if the courts of signatory states, in particular those whose domestic law does not recognise the trust, become involved with trusts because, for example, trustees or beneficiaries are resident there, or trust funds are invested there (Hayton (1987) 36 ICLQ 260; Gaillard and Trautman (1987) 35 AJCL 307; Dyer (1999) 32 Vand J Transnat L 989; and see generally Hayton in Glasson and Thomas (eds) *The International Trust* (2nd edn, 2006) ch 3). In practice most transfers of assets are made to the many offshore jurisdictions who 'are falling over themselves to provide international trust services' (*Matthews* p xiii). The concern expressed in early cases about the risks associated with appointing trustees in jurisdictions with little experience of trusts law (cf Harman LJ in *Re Weston*) now carries much less weight.

(4) The VTA 1958 in use

The VTA 1958 has been described as 'that most generous of revenue give-aways' (Chesterman in *Rubin and Sugarman* (eds) p 155). But tax saving is not the only motive for varying trusts (cf *Re Steed's Will Trusts* [1960] Ch 407), and between 1958 and the enactment of the Trustee Investments Act 1961 the courts approved numerous applications seeking wider investment powers. (See eg *Practice Note* [1959] 2 All ER 47; Price [1960] BTR 42 at 43–47; *Trustees of the British Museum v A-G* [1984] 1 WLR 418 signalled a renaissance of this jurisdiction.) But as has been judicially acknowledged tax-saving has been the principal objective for most applications (see most recently *Gibbon v Mitchell* [1990] 1 WLR 1304 and McCall (1996) PCB 389–398). The full amount of tax saved is impossible to discover although exhaustive researches through Chancery records 'of a jurisdiction invoked thousands of times over forty years' (per Mummery LJ in *Goulding v James* [1997] 2 All ER 239 at 246) might prove revealing. The alternative is to rely on an eclectic group of sources ranging from *The Times* (11 April 1959) – most applications being either unreported or occasionally reported in *The Times* – and the writings of taxation specialists (eg Wheatcroft [1964] BTR 283 at 295–296) to the work of interested economists. Revell, for example, writing in 1961 (BTR 177) attributed the apparent decline of dutiable settled property in the 1950s, in part to the breaking of existing trusts (at 180):

> This is a point on which we have no definite information at all, but it is widely believed that one of the reactions to the post-war increases in the rates of death-duty was the breaking of dutiable trusts during the lives of the life-tenants. The breaking of trusts if it were sufficiently widespread, could give rise to sharp drops in the proportion of dutiable settled property such as that which occurred during the 1950s.

There is no doubt that the heyday of trust-breaking occurred under the old estate duty regime but it is an error to assume that the VTA 1958 has no contemporary relevance (see *Gibbon v Mitchell* [1990] 1 WLR 1304 at 1306 and McCall (1996) 6 PCB 389–398). As ever it is predominantly contemporary tax provisions that either encourage or deter variations. On the one hand, changes to inheritance tax (IHT) and CGT in the 1980s re-established variation – including even the traditional partition between tenant for life and remainderman – as a part of the tax-planner's armoury. In *Ridgwell v Ridgwell* [2008] STC 1883, for instance, following changes to the tax treatment of trusts introduced in the Finance Act 2006, the benefit of a very substantial saving of IHT, potentially in the region of £21m, was sufficient to outweigh any detriment arising from a deferment in the vesting of interests for children then aged seven, five and two. On the other hand, the more severe restrictions imposed in Finance Act 1989 on a particular form of relief from CGT – hold-over relief – may in some circumstances have discouraged premature termination of a trust.

Variation also has a useful role to play in rearranging a deceased's estate. It may be highly desirable for fiscal purposes to vary trusts taking effect on a person's death (see eg Owen [1999] PCB 237–244). Indeed this was the reason for the application to the court in *Goulding v James* and it is believed that the VTA 1958 jurisdiction is widely used for this purpose. Inheritance Tax Act 1984, ss 17 and 142 provides that where, within two years of a person's death whether testate or intestate, any disposition of the deceased's property is varied by an instrument in writing then the variation is not a transfer of value, and it takes effect as if it had been effected by the deceased (see also Taxation of Chargeable Gains Act 1992, s 62(6) whereby such a variation is not a disposal for CGT purposes).

(e) Conclusion

Harris has described the LRC Report and, impliedly, the VTA 1958 as representing 'a triumph for the doctrine of equitable property over the doctrine of fidelity to settlors' intentions' (*Variation of Trusts* (1975) p 5). This observation is correct both at a formal conceptual level – the settlor's specific intention as contained in the terms of the trust is defeated – and substantively, since the settlor has no right to veto changes which the court considers desirable in the interests of beneficiaries.

But can it be argued that applications under the VTA 1958 usually further rather than frustrate a general intention of the settlor to preserve family wealth? Posner (*Economic Analysis of Law* (6th edn, 2003)) states that the dilemma posed between enforcing the settlor's or testator's intention and modifying the terms of the instrument is a false one: 'A policy of rigid adherence to the letter of the donative instrument is likely to frustrate both the donor's purposes and the efficient use of resources' (p 519). He suggests further that:

> ... since no one can foresee the future, a rational donor knows that his intentions might eventually be thwarted by unpredictable circumstances and may therefore be presumed to accept implicitly a rule permitting modification of the terms of the bequest in the event that an unforeseen change frustrates his original intention.

This rationalisation cannot justify decisions such as *Re Remnant* [1970] 2 All ER 554 and *Goulding v James* [1997] 2 All ER 239, nor indeed the rule in *Saunders v Vautier*. Yet this only serves to illustrate the paradox of *Saunders v Vautier*. A rule which permits beneficiaries to defeat the settlor's express intention simultaneously provides an important theoretical prop to a statute which can be claimed to sustain the settlor's general purpose.

Finally, we return briefly to a consideration of the rule against perpetuities and its relation to the variation of trust jurisdiction. The Manitoba Law Reform Commission argued that an expansive variation of trusts jurisdiction would render the rule unnecessary. The English Law Commission commented on this possibility in Consultation Paper no 133 (1993) as follows:

> **para 5.27.** The courts have construed 'benefit' widely but nevertheless it seems unlikely that they would consent to a variation which would deprive a beneficiary of his interest where the purpose of the variation is only to ensure that certain interests under the trust vest forthwith or within a specified period. However, it is possible that if the rule against perpetuities were to be abolished the courts might take a less restrictive view of their duty, in the interests of the good administration of the trust.

Notwithstanding the possibility canvassed in that last sentence, it can be argued that a justification for retaining the rule against perpetuities is to set 'metes and bounds' to the range of beneficial interests for which the court must find some benefit if it is to authorise a variation in the terms of the trust. The scope of the VTA 1958 would otherwise be unduly restricted (see Deech (1984) 4 OJLS 454; Glenn (1984) 62 Can BR 618). This justification is truly paradoxical. A rule – the rule against perpetuities – supposedly justified on the grounds of allowing freedom of disposition to successive generations (see Chapter 6, p 320) in fact provides a key element in undermining the freedom of disposition of the original settlor or testator. In *Goulding v James* Mummery LJ observes that 'the nature of the jurisdiction under the 1958 Act is such that even the most carefully planned and meticulously drafted intentions of a settlor or testator are liable to be overridden by an arrangement agreed between sui juris beneficiaries and by sanction of the court' (at 251). This is a very different state of affairs from that envisaged by Farwell J in 1901 (see above, p 324).

4. Flexibility in relation to capital entitlement and the power of advancement

(a) Introduction

Consider the following two examples. Property is given to trustees to hold (1) for A for life with remainder to B; or (2) for B if she reaches 30 or marries before that date. B's interest in (1) is vested and in (2) contingent yet in neither example does B have any present entitlement to trust property, irrespective of her present financial needs. As a counter to this type of inflexibility it has long been the practice for settlors to empower trustees to apply a specified portion of the trust capital for the 'advancement', as it is termed, of beneficiaries in positions such as those in the above examples. Before 1926 flexibility would have been achieved by an express power but TA 1925, s 32 now provides a statutory power of advancement that applies automatically to every trust in so far as 'a contrary intention is not expressed in the instrument' (TA 1925, s 69(2)). The contrary intention may be expressly stated or be inferred from the terms of the trust instrument. (See *Re Evans' Settlement* [1967] 1 WLR 1294 – direction 'to advance up to £5,000' – and *IRC v Bernstein* [1961] Ch 399 – a direction 'to accumulate income during the settlor's lifetime'.)

(b) The statutory power of advancement

Trustee Act 1925, s 32

32(1) Trustees may at any time or times pay or apply any capital money subject to a trust, for the advancement or benefit, in such manner as they may, in their absolute discretion, think fit, of any person entitled to the capital of the trust property or of any share thereof, whether absolutely or contingently on his attaining any specified age or on the occurrence of any other event, or subject to a gift over on his death under any specified age or on the occurrence of any other event, and whether in possession or in remainder or reversion, and such payment or application may be made notwithstanding that the interest of such person is liable to be defeated by the exercise of a power of appointment or revocation, or to be diminished by the increase of the class to which he belongs:

Provided that –

(a) the money so paid or applied for the advancement or benefit of any person shall not exceed altogether in amount one-half of the presumptive or vested share or interest of that person in the trust property; and

(b) if that person is or becomes absolutely and indefeasibly entitled to a share in the trust property the money so paid or applied shall be brought into account as part of such share; and

(c) no such payment or application shall be made so as to prejudice any person entitled to any prior life or other interest, whether vested or contingent, in the money paid or applied unless such person is in existence and of full age and consents in writing to such payment or application.

The section does not apply to capital money under the Settled Land Act 1925 (s 32(2) as substituted by the Trusts of Land and Appointment of Trustees Act 1996, Sch 3 para 3(8)).

As is the case with mere powers of appointment (see Chapter 5), trustees are under no obligation to exercise the power of advancement. But as will be seen in more detail in Chapter 11 the reference to 'absolute discretion' (s 32(1)) does not mean that the power can be exercised in an irresponsible fashion. The trustees must consider whether in their opinion the advancement proposed is for the benefit of the beneficiary in question. In *Re Pauling's Settlement Trusts* [1964] Ch 303, CA on several occasions trustees advanced capital nominally to children, all of whom were over 21 and at their own request, but in full knowledge that the money would be used directly to benefit the parents – the improper purpose – not the children, as by buying a house for the father in the Isle of Man and reducing the mother's bank overdraft. Intriguingly the trustees had been advised by counsel that since, as far as the trustees were concerned, they were advancing the money to the children for their own absolute use then it was up to the children how they used the money. The members of the Court of Appeal were not impressed by this proposition. Willmer LJ put the point in the following manner (at 334):

[I]f the trustees make the advance for a particular purpose which they state, they can quite properly pay it over to the advancee if they reasonably think they can trust him or her to carry out the prescribed purpose. What they cannot do is prescribe a particular purpose, and then raise and pay the money over to the advancee leaving him or her entirely free, legally and morally, to apply it for that purpose or to spend it in any way he or she chooses without any responsibility on the trustees even to inquire as to its application.

It is unclear quite what the trustees are able to do if upon inquiry they discover that the money advanced is to be used or even has been used for a different purpose to that originally stated by the advancee. The Appeal Court expressly left open the question whether the trustees could seek to recover the 'misapplied' money. It may therefore be that the trustees are left with the exercise of moral persuasion alone.

Although the power may be regarded as being concerned with trust administration it is also capable of altering the quantum of beneficial entitlement as well as the timing of receipt of benefit. Consider the position where £30,000 is held on trust for such of A, B and C who attain the age of 30, and, if more than one, in equal shares, and the trustees advance £5,000 (ie one-half a presumptive share) to A aged 22 who subsequently dies before reaching 30. The exercise of the power effectively reduces the shares that B and C could have anticipated (£15,000 each) had no advancement been made by the date of A's death. Furthermore s 32 applies even where the interest in capital – the section does not apply where a beneficiary has only an interest in income – is defeasible by the exercise of powers of appointment or revocation or liable to be diminished by an increase in members of the class to be benefited (eg birth of an additional child).

The proviso in s 32(1) imposes two important limitations on the statutory power:

(i) The requirement that not more than half the presumptive share may be advanced. This has been interpreted as follows: where a complete half-share is advanced to A, no further advancement can be made from the balance of A's share of the fund even if the remaining capital fund subsequently appreciates in value (see *Re Marquess of Abergavenny's Estate Act Trusts* [1981] 2 All ER 643). The consequences of inflation are studiously ignored so that advancements are only brought into account (s 32(1)(b)) on a cash basis, although the Law Reform Committee (23rd Report *The Powers and Duties of Trustees* (Cmnd 8733, 1982)) recommended that an index-linked or fractional basis be adopted (paras 4.43–4.47).

(ii) The requirement of consent of persons with prior interests. But the consent of objects of a discretionary trust is not required (*Re Beckett's Settlement* [1940] Ch 279).

It should be noted, however, that the settlor may choose to extend the power of advancement, for example, by authorising the advance of the whole of the beneficiary's share or by excluding the requirement for consent. (But cf *Henley v Wardell* (1988) *Times*, 29 January, where a power in a will giving 'absolute and uncontrolled discretion' to advance all the capital was not in itself sufficient to override the requirement for the life tenant's consent.) There is also the possibility of applying to the court for an order under the VTA 1958 to authorise the trustees to exceed the 'one-half of presumptive share' restriction. In *D (a child) v O* [2004] 3 All ER 780 the court held that it was for the benefit of a 12-year-old child, who was solely entitled to her share of the fund, to release up to her full presumptive share to pay school fees. The report is silent on the question of whether there was any other person with primary responsibility for payment of the fees (see also *Fuller v Evans* [2000] 1 FCR 494 below at p 370).

(c) 'Advancement or benefit'

In *Pilkington v IRC* [1964] AC 612, HL, two settlements were the subject of litigation. Under Trust A, a testator left property on protective trust for his nephew Richard Godfrey Pilkington (RGP) for life. RGP had three children, one of whom, Penelope (P), was born in 1956. RGP held a power of appointment in favour of his children and remoter issue. In default of appointment the property would be held in trust for such of his children as attained 21 in equal shares. P's interest in the fund was therefore both contingent and defeasible.

Subsequently, RGP's father 'Guy', a trustee of trust A, proposed to create a trust (Trust B) in favour of P (then aged two). The trustees were to have power to apply the income for P's maintenance until she reached the age of 21 and to accumulate and capitalise any surplus income. If P attained 21 the trustees were to pay the income to her until the age of 30 when she would become absolutely entitled to the fund. If P were to die under 30 leaving children, then the fund was to be held on trust for such children at 21. There was a further family default trust. Under Trust B, P could not receive any capital entitlement unless and until she attained the age of 30.

Guy paid £10 to the trustees of Trust B. The trustees of Trust A then sought the directions of the court as to whether they could lawfully advance one-half of P's expectant share under Trust A (about £7,600) to the trustees of Trust B. The Inland Revenue was added as defendant by order of the Court of Appeal.

The application raised a number of difficult questions:

(1) It was not contested that substantial savings of estate duty and income tax could be anticipated, and that these constituted a 'benefit'. The Revenue argument was that this was not a benefit contemplated by s 32, and that although the language of s 32 was wide it did not permit trustees to postpone the vesting of an interest in capital. The Court of Appeal, in refusing to approve the application, in fact held that benefit had to be related to a beneficiary's 'own real or personal needs' ([1961] Ch 466 at 481).

(2) Whether, notwithstanding limited authority to the contrary, s 32 should be restricted so as to exclude a resettlement?

Pilkington v IRC [1964] AC 612, HL

Viscount Radcliffe (describing the origins of s 32): The word 'advancement' itself meant in this context the establishment in life of the beneficiary who was the object of the power or at any rate some step that would contribute to the furtherance of his establishment. Thus it was found in such phrases as 'preferment or advancement' (*Lowther v Bentinck* (1874) LR 19 Eq 166, 'business, profession, or employment or... advancement or preferment in the world' (*Roper-Curzon v Roper-Curzon* (1871) LR 11 Eq 452) and 'placing out or advancement in life' (*Re Breeds' Will* (1875) 1 Ch D 226). Typical instances of expenditure for such purposes under the social conditions of the nineteenth century were an apprenticeship or the purchase of a commission in the army or of an interest in business. In the case of a girl there could be advancement on marriage (*Lloyd v Cocker* (1860) 27 Beav 645). Advancement had, however, to some extent a limited range of meaning, since it was thought to convey the idea of some step in life of permanent significance, and accordingly, to prevent uncertainties about the permitted range of objects for which moneys could be raised and made available, such words as 'or otherwise for his or her benefit' were often added to the word 'advancement'. It was always recognised that these added words were 'large words' (see Jessel MR in *Re Breeds' Will*) and indeed in another case (*Lowther v Bentinck*) the same judge spoke of preferment and advancement as being 'both large words' but of 'benefit' as being the 'largest of all'....

So much for 'advancement', which I now use for brevity to cover the combined phrase 'advancement or benefit'. It means any use of the money which will improve the material situation of the beneficiary. It is important, however, not to confuse the idea of 'advancement' with the idea of advancing the money out of the beneficiary's expectant interest. The two things have only a casual connection with each other. The one refers to the operation of finding money by way of anticipation of an interest not yet absolutely vested in possession or, if so vested, belonging to an infant: the other refers to the status of the beneficiary and the improvement of his situation. The power to carry out the operation of anticipating an interest is not conferred by the word 'advancement' but by those other words of the section which expressly authorise the payment or application of capital money for the benefit of a person entitled....

I think, with all respect to the commissioners, a good deal of their argument is infected with some of this confusion. To say, for instance, that there cannot be a valid exercise of a power of advancement that results in a deferment of the vesting of the beneficiary's absolute title (Miss Penelope, it will be remembered, is to take at 30 under the proposed settlement instead of at 21 under the will) is in my opinion to play upon words. The element of anticipation consists in the raising of money for her now before she has any right to receive anything under the existing trusts: the advancement consists in the application of that money to form a trust fund, the provisions of which are thought to be for her benefit....

I have not been able to find in the words of section 32, to which I have now referred, anything which in terms or by implication restricts the width of the manner or purpose of advancement. It is true that, if this settlement is made, Miss Penelope's children, who are not objects of the power, are given a possible interest in the event of her dying under 30 leaving surviving issue. But if the disposition itself, by which I mean the whole provision made, is for her benefit, it is no objection to the exercise of the power that other persons benefit incidentally as a result of the exercise.

Viscount Radcliffe referred to *Lowther v Bentinck* and *Re Kershaw's Trusts* (1868) LR 6 Eq 322.

Nor in my opinion will it be bad merely because the moneys are to be tied up in the proposed settlement. If it could be said that the payment or application permitted by section 32 cannot take the form of a settlement in any form but must somehow pass direct into or through the hands of the object of the power, I could appreciate the principle upon which the commissioners' objection was founded. But can that principle be asserted? Anyone can see, I think, that there can be circumstances in which, while it is very desirable that some money should be raised at once for the benefit of an owner of an expectant or contingent interest, it would be very undesirable that the money should not be secured to him under some arrangement that will prevent him having the absolute disposition of it. I find it very difficult to think that there is something at the back of section 32 which makes such an advancement impossible. Certainly neither Danckwerts J nor the members of the Court of Appeal in this case took that view. Both Lord Evershed MR and Upjohn LJ [1961] Ch. 466, 481, 486, explicitly accepted the possibility of a settlement being made in exercise of a power of advancement.

Viscount Radcliffe referred to *Re Halsted's Will Trusts* [1937] 2 All ER 570 and *Re Ropner's Settlements Trusts* [1956] 1 WLR 902.

The truth is, I think, that the propriety of requiring a settlement of moneys found for advancement was recognised as long ago as 1871 in *Roper-Curzon v Roper-Curzon* ((1871) LR 11 Eq 452) and, so far as I know, it has not been impugned since....

I have not yet referred to the ground which was taken by the Court of Appeal as their reason for saying that the proposed settlement was not permissible. To put it shortly, they held that the statutory power of advancement could not be exercised unless the benefit to be conferred was 'personal to the person concerned', in the sense of being related to his or her own real or personal 'needs' ([1961] Ch 466, 481). Or, to use other words of the learned Master of the Rolls (Ibid 484), the exercise of the power 'must be an exercise done to meet the circumstances as they present themselves in regard to a person within the scope of the section, whose circumstances call for that to be done which the trustees think fit to do'. Upjohn LJ (Ibid 487) expressed himself in virtually the same terms.

My Lords, I differ with reluctance from the views of judges so learned and experienced in matters of this sort: but I do not find it possible to import such restrictions into the words of the statutory power which itself does not contain them. First, the suggested qualification, that the considerations or circumstances must be 'personal' to the beneficiary, seems to me uncontrollably vague as a guide to general administration. What distinguishes a personal

> need from any other need to which the trustees in their discretion think it right to attend in the beneficiary's interest? And, if the advantage of preserving the funds of a beneficiary from the incidence of death duty is not an advantage personal to that beneficiary, I do not see what is. Death duty is a present risk that attaches to the settled property in which Miss Penelope has her expectant interest, and even accepting the validity of the supposed limitation, I would not have supposed that there was anything either impersonal or unduly remote in the advantage to be conferred upon her of some exemption from that risk....
>
> To conclude, therefore, on this issue. I am of opinion that there is no maintainable reason for introducing into the statutory power of advancement a qualification that would exclude the exercise in the case now before us. It would not be candid to omit to say that, though I think that that is what the law required. I am uneasy at some of the possible applications of this liberty, when advancements are made for the purposes of settlement or on terms that there is to be a settlement.

Lords Hodson, Jenkins and Devlin concurred with Viscount Radcliffe's judgment.

Lord Reid confessed to being only reluctantly persuaded by Viscount Radcliffe's reasoning that s 32 could be applied:

> It may be that one is driven step by step to hold that the power conferred by section 32... must be interpreted as including power to resettle such money on an infant in such a way as will probably confer considerable financial benefit on her many years hence if she survives. But that certainly seems to me far removed from the apparent purpose of the section and considerably beyond anything which it has hitherto been held to cover.
>
> Nevertheless I am compelled to recognise that there is no logical stopping place short of that result. You cannot say that financial benefit from avoidance of taxation is not a benefit within the meaning of the section. Nor can you say that the section only authorises payments for some particular or immediate purpose or that the benefit must be immediate and certain and not future or problematical. And again you cannot say that the beneficiary must consent to the course which the trustees have decided is for his benefit for that would rule out all payments where the beneficiary is under age.
>
> I have more difficulty about the resettlement... But I think that the cases show that it is too late now to say that this power can never authorise trustees to convey funds to new trustees to hold for new trust purposes: to say that might endanger past transactions done on the faith of these authorities.
>
> I realise that this case opens a wide door and that many other trustees may seek to take advantage of it. But if it is thought that the power which Parliament has conferred is likely to be used in ways of which Parliament does not approve then it is for Parliament to devise appropriate restrictions of the power.

Their Lordships, however, all held that the intended advancement was analogous to the exercise of a special power of appointment and would be void as infringing the rule against remoteness of vesting. See Perpetuities and Accumulations Act 1964, s 3.

Pilkington v IRC establishes that 'benefit' in s 32 is a concept of enviable width. It has subsequently been decided in an admittedly most unusual case (*Re Clore's Settlement Trusts* [1966] 1 WLR 955) that even relieving the beneficiary of a self-confessed moral obligation to make payments to charity could constitute benefit. Subsequently in *X v A* [2006] 1 WLR 741 Hart J, whilst confirming that the power can be used to discharge a moral obligation held by a beneficiary, refused to sanction the proposed exercise in favour of a charitable foundation notwithstanding the principal beneficiary's very strongly held personal reasons, based on an antipathy to inherited wealth, for requesting the 'advancement'. The principal ground for refusing the application was the absence of even an 'indirect' *material* benefit to the principal beneficiary, a feature the judge considered, following *Pilkington*, to be a minimum prerequiste for the court's approval to be granted. In *Re Clore* by contrast it had been accepted that the obligation would have had to be met out of the beneficiary's own pocket if not paid from the trust fund.

The *Pilkington* case does therefore leave in its wake teasing analytical and comparative problems.

Consider in particular the following points:

(1) It is unresolved whether, in the absence of express authority in the trust instrument, the power of advancement can be used to settle property on discretionary trusts. Two potential obstacles are 'benefit' and 'delegation'.

> *Benefit* The question is whether the possibility of achieving a greater tax saving by settling on a discretionary trust, rather than a fixed interest trust, could compensate a beneficiary for the uncertainty as to whether the trustees would look kindly on him or her in determining how to exercise their discretion.

> *Delegation* Viscount Radcliffe in the *Pilkington* case rejected an argument that s 32 did not permit trustees to delegate their power of advancement (at 639):

> I think that the whole issue of delegation is here beside the mark. The law is not that trustees cannot delegate; it is that trustees cannot delegate unless they have authority to do so. If the power of advancement which they possess is so read as to allow them to raise money for the purpose of having it settled, then they do have the necessary authority to let the money pass out of the old settlement into the new trusts. No question of delegation of their powers or trusts arises. If, on the other hand, their power of advancement is read so as to exclude settled advances, *cadit quaestio.*

This is relevant to the discretionary trust point because advancement into a new settlement that includes discretionary trusts would appear to involve the delegation of dispositive discretion to the new trustees. But, as pointed out by *Hanbury and Martin* (p 597, quoting Kiralfy (1953) 17 Conv 285 at 289), it is generally assumed that 'dispositive (as opposed to administrative) discretions . . . cannot be delegated without express authority'. This point appears 'not to be covered by Lord Radcliffe's dictum'.

An alternative interpretation is that the dictum means that a power of advancement, whether statutory or express, can be construed as being sufficiently wide to authorise an advancement into a discretionary trust with even wide powers of appointment. Obviously this is a matter of interpretation upon which opinions can differ. The fact that it is possible for a valid advancement to be made where the beneficiary takes no *direct* benefit in the sum advanced, as in *Re Clore*, tends to support the proposition that an advancement into a discretionary trust can be a valid exercise of the power. On the other hand *Re Clore* is a somewhat unusual case and is less persuasive when compared with a purported advancement into a discretionary trust where the original beneficiary is, let us say, a member of a widely drawn class such as that in *McPhail v Doulton*. This beneficiary might in practice then not only never receive any *direct* benefit in the shape of payment from the trust but also, unlike *Re Clore*, there would be no evident *indirect* material benefit accruing.

To some extent one's conclusion on this issue may depend upon whether the power of advancement is viewed as being concerned with 'administrative' or 'dispositive' discretions.

(2) To what extent does the power of advancement provide an alternative method for varying trusts? Is there any similarity in the approaches adopted by the House of Lords in *Chapman v Chapman* and *Pilkington v IRC* to the issues raised in the respective cases? It is striking that no mention of the power of advancement appears in the LRC Report *The Court's Power to Sanction Variation of Trusts* (Cmnd 310, 1957). Would the expansive interpretation of 'advancement' eventually adopted in *Pilkington* have supported or subverted the reasoning of the LRC?

(3) E P Thompson ('The Grid of Inheritance: A Comment' in Goody et al *Family and Inheritance* (1976)) has argued that one function of eighteenth- and nineteenth-century inheritance practices – the 'grids of inheritance' – was '[to devise] rules and practices by which particular social groups project forwards provisions and (as they hope) guarantees of security for their children' (p 358). In particular he refers to a 'third, complementary, grid for the propertied classes: that of interest, preferment to office, purchase of commissions, reversions to sinecures, placings within the Church and so on. . . . Along this grid the lesser gentry sought to secure the future of their families'. In so far as the power of advancement is one of the 'rules and practices' referred to by Thompson, the interpretation of 'benefit' in

Pilkington can at first impression be seen as effecting a transformation in the application of that power as compared with its historical usage. Yet in terms of the function that the power might be said to fulfil – part of the grid of inheritance – has the interpretation of benefit merely ensured continuity, albeit reflecting the contemporary context of tax avoidance as a path to financial security?

(4) Does *Pilkington* sufficiently protect beneficiaries against advancements made just before their interest falls into possession but having the effect of postponing their entitlement for some significant period? Should there be some explicit restriction on this way of using powers of advancement?

5. Flexibility in relation to income entitlement and the power of maintenance

(a) Introduction

We referred previously (p 331) to the court's inherent maintenance jurisdiction as being based on the presumption that a settlor 'did not intend children should be left unprovided for . . . or not be educated properly . . . '. This paternal concern for infants also has an extensive statutory history. In 1860 Lord Cranworth's Act (23 and 24 Vict C 145) authorised payments for 'the maintenance or education' of infants. The modern formulation in TA 1925, s 31 (see below) now extends the purposes for which payment from trust income may be made to include the benefit of an infant. But, as with the power of advancement of capital, also characterised as being 'peculiarly for the assistance of an infant' (*Pilkington v IRC* [1964] AC 612 at 638), the paternal nature of the power of maintenance is now conjoined with tax considerations when settlors consider whether, and how, to incorporate it in the trust instrument. Indeed, the accumulation and maintenance settlement, until recently much favoured under inheritance tax (see Chapter 8), has been built principally around the statutory power (see Brown (1994) 8(2) TLI 49).

As with s 32, the statutory power in s 31 is read into every trust instrument unless a contrary intention is expressed in the instrument (TA 1925, s 69(2)). A contrary intention will be discerned if the application of s 31 'would be inconsistent with the purport of the instrument' (*IRC v Bernstein* [1961] 1 All ER 320 at 325). This will be the case with a direction to accumulate the income. Also, an express power of maintenance will exclude the statutory provision to the extent that they are inconsistent. In short, s 31 supplies 'a code of rules governing the disposal of income . . . where a settlor or testator has made dispositions of capital and either (a) being an unskilled draftsman has not thought about income, or (b) being a skilled draftsman, has been content to let the statutory code apply' (*Re Delamere's Settlement Trusts* [1984] 1 All ER 584 at 587 per Slade LJ). But, to reiterate the point, the pre-eminent rule is that the settlor's intention prevails.

(b) The statutory power of maintenance

Trustee Act 1925, s 31(1)

31(1) Where any property is held by trustees in trust for any person for any interest whatsoever, whether vested or contingent, then, subject to any prior interests or charges affecting that property –

(i) during the infancy of any such person, if his interest so long continues, the trustees may, at their sole discretion, pay to his parent or guardian, if any, or otherwise apply for or towards his maintenance, education, or benefit, the whole or such part, if any, of the income of that property as may, in all the circumstances, be reasonable, whether or not there is –

   (a) any other fund applicable to the same purpose; or

   (b) any person bound by law to provide for his maintenance or education; and

(ii) if such person on attaining the age of [18 years] has not a vested interest in such income, the trustees shall thenceforth pay the income of that property and of any accretion thereto under subsection (2) of this section to him, until he either attains a vested interest therein or dies, or until failure of his interest:

Provided that, in deciding whether the whole or any part of the income of the property is during a minority to be paid or applied for the purposes aforesaid, the trustees shall have regard to the age of the infant and his requirements and generally to the circumstances of the case, and in particular to what other income, if any, is applicable for the same purposes; and where trustees have notice that the income of more than one fund is applicable for those purposes, then, so far as practicable, unless the entire income of the funds is paid or applied as aforesaid or the court otherwise directs, a proportionate part only of the income of each fund shall be so paid or applied.

(2) During the infancy of any such person, if his interest so long continues, the trustees shall accumulate all the residue of that income [by investing it, and any profits from so investing it] from time to time in authorised investments, and shall hold those accumulations as follows:–

(i) If any such person –

   (a) attains the age of [18 years], or marries under that age, and his interest in such income during his infancy or until his marriage is a vested interest; or

   (b) on attaining the age of [18 years] or on marriage under that age becomes entitled to the property from which such income arose in fee simple, absolute or determinable, or absolutely, or for an entailed interest;

   the trustees shall hold the accumulations in trust for such person absolutely, but without prejudice to any provision with respect thereto contained in any settlement by him made under any statutory powers during his infancy, and so that the receipt of such person after marriage, and though still an infant, shall be a good discharge; and

(ii) In any other case the trustees shall, notwithstanding that such person had a vested interest in such income, hold the accumulations as an accretion to the capital of the property from which such accumulations arose, and as one fund with such capital for

> all purposes, and so that, if such property is settled land, such accumulations shall be held upon the same trusts as if the same were capital money arising therefrom;
>
> but the trustees may, at any time during the infancy of such person if his interest so long continues, apply those accumulations, or any part thereof, as if they were income arising in the then current year. [Subsections 3–5 omitted.]

The age of majority was reduced from 21 to 18 by the Family Law Reform Act 1969 for instruments made on or after 1 January 1970; see for the implications on existing settlements *Begg-MacBrearty v Stilwell* [1996] STC 413. The words in parentheses in s 31(2) were substituted by Trustee Act 2000, s 40(1), Sch 2, Pt II, para 25.

A preliminary point to be established is whether a 'person' has any entitlement to income out of which sums may be expended on maintenance. Where this entitlement exists, the 'code of rules' in s 31 regulates three distinct issues:

 (i) the application of income accruing to vested and contingent interests during a beneficiary's minority (s 31(1)(i));
 (ii) the application of income when a beneficiary attains the age of 18 (s 31(1)(ii)); and
 (iii) the destination of income not expended on maintenance but accumulated during a beneficiary's minority (s 31(2)).

The preliminary question as to entitlement will be considered first and then each of the three further issues will be considered in turn.

(1) Availability of income for maintenance

The apparent universality of s 31(1) – 'any property', 'any person', 'any interest whatsoever' – can be misleading. In particular the picture is complicated by the treatment of interests to which a contingency is attached. Section 31(1) applies to a contingent interest only if it 'carries the intermediate income of the property' (s 31(3)), ie where any income earned between the date of the gift and the time when the interest vests belongs to the beneficiary. The general position is that both vested gifts and inter vivos contingent gifts carry the 'intermediate income' unless a contrary intention appears (eg where the income is directed by the settlor to be paid to someone other than the donee of the gift). For instance, an inter vivos gift of shares on trust for A if she attains 18 will carry the intermediate income, so that any dividend on the shares will accrue to A's interest.

The complications emerge where 'deferred' (or 'future') and contingent testamentary gifts are involved. A deferred gift is one which is limited to take effect at a specified time, or on the occurrence of a specified event, and may be either vested – to A on the death of B – or contingent – to A five years after the death of B if A attains the age of 21.

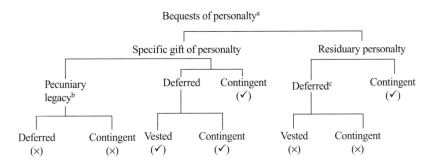

Figure 7.1 Bequests of personalty

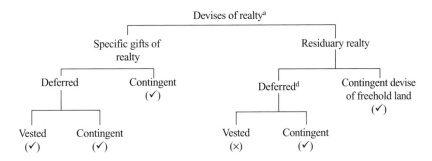

Figure 7.2 Devises of realty

Notes: (a) A devise is a gift of realty by will. A bequest is a gift of personalty by will.
(b) The proposition concerning contingent or deferred pecuniary legacies is subject to limited exceptions – in particular where the testator is a parent of the minor, or some person in loco parentis – when intermediate income will be carried. (See *Hanbury and Martin* p 596; *Pettit* p 475.)
(c) See *Re McGeorge* [1963] 1 All ER 519 at 522–523 for an explanation of the differential treatment of deferred specific gifts and deferred residuary gifts.
(d) See Snell p 768, for comment on the 'odd' treatment of deferred residuary devises.

Whether deferred or contingent testamentary gifts carry the intermediate income involves the application of complex rules, some based on case law and some on statute (LPA 1925, s 175). Regrettably the subject is excessively technical and almost wholly devoid of conceptual coherence (see *Re McGeorge* [1963] 1 All ER 519 per Cross J). Surprisingly, the LRC in its report, *The Powers and Duties of Trustees*, did not appear to consider whether any change in the law was desirable.

Figures 7.1 and 7.2 summarise the effects of the rules concerning testamentary *contingent* or *deferred* gifts only.($\checkmark$) signifies that the gift carries the intermediate income; ($\times$) that it does not.

(2) Applying the income

One notable aspect of the flexibility generated by the 'paternalist' nature of s 31(1) lies in the treatment of a minor's vested interest in income. In a trust for A (a minor) for life, with remainder to B, A's apparent absolute entitlement to income is transformed. The section not only gives the trustees discretion whether to apply income for the maintenance of A but places them under a duty (s 31(2)) to accumulate any income not so applied during a beneficiary's minority. (The application of the accumulated income when beneficiaries attain the age of 18 is considered in section 4 below.) Whether any income is applied for the maintenance of a minor beneficiary is a matter for the trustees' discretion which must be consciously and not automatically exercised. (See *Wilson v Turner* (1883) 22 Ch D 521 for the consequences of automatic payment to the parent of a minor.)

The proviso in s 31(1) lays out the criteria to be considered by the trustees and requires in particular that maintenance be drawn proportionately from different funds where more than one fund is available yet less than the total income is needed. The proviso is in practice frequently excluded but the LRC rejected suggestions that it be repealed, arguing that the principle of proportionality was sound and that it should be left to settlors to deviate from that by specific provision in the trust instrument (paras 4.38–4.40).

(3) Application of income arising after age 18

The statutory power to maintain is exercisable only in favour of a minor beneficiary. What then is to happen to the income of a beneficiary who attains the age of 18 but has only a contingent interest in the trust property (eg to A if she attains 25)? The section here works a further 'trick' with beneficial entitlement: s 31(1)(ii) intervenes to accelerate part of the beneficiary's interest by requiring the trustees to pay the whole of the income (arising from the trust property and the accumulations) to the beneficiary.

Contingent entitlement to the capital is unaltered, so that if the beneficiary fails to satisfy the contingency (eg A dies at age 21) the gift fails. But in the interim A will have benefited by receipt of the income.

The subsection does not apply where a person has a vested interest in income, even if liable to be divested (see *Re McGeorge* [1963] 1 All ER 519), or where a contrary intention is expressed as with a direction to accumulate (see *Re Turner's Will Trusts* [1937] Ch 15).

(4) The destination of accumulated income

Section 31(2) requires the trustees during the minority of a beneficiary to accumulate the residue of any income not expended on maintenance, although during this period the accumulations may still be applied as if they were income. What then is to happen to any surplus accumulation when the beneficiary attains 18?

A beneficiary who satisfies either of the conditions in s 31(2)(i) will be entitled to the accumulations. Not surprisingly, where a beneficiary had a vested life interest during her minority, she will satisfy the condition in s 31(2)(i)(a) and be entitled to the accumulation. This will also be the outcome under s 31(2)(i)(b) where a beneficiary becomes entitled to the capital from which the income was derived at age 18 or earlier marriage – obtaining a life interest will not suffice. The word 'absolutely' there applies to personalty only, and *Re Sharp's Settlement Trusts* [1972] 3 All ER 151 decides that where a vested interest in personalty is liable to be defeated by the exercise of a power of appointment, the entitlement is not 'absolute' (cf the position of a determinable interest in realty: see Hayton (1972) 36 Conv 436).

In every other case the accumulations are added to the capital. This will be so both for an interest in capital contingent on attaining an age greater than 18 (eg to A if she attains 21) – see s 31(2)(i)(a) – and for a life interest which does not vest until the age of 18 or later (eg to A for life if she attains 18) – see s 31(2)(i)(b).

The effect of s 31(1) on a minor's apparently vested interest in income has already been discussed (see section 2 above). Section 31(2) goes one step further. Where a minor has a vested interest in income (eg a life interest) and dies before attaining the age of 18 it would seem that any accumulations should form part of the beneficiary's estate, but this is not so (see TA 1925, s 31(4), however, regarding accumulated income from a vested annuity). Instead the accumulations accrue to the capital as if the interest were contingent on attaining age 18. In *Stanley v IRC* [1944] KB 255 the Court of Appeal held that under s 31(2) a beneficiary's rights over accumulated income 'are, whatever their technical description, precisely what they would have been if they had been expressly made contingent' (at 262). The effect of the section is to engraft 'on the vested interest originally conferred on the infant . . . a qualifying trust of a special nature which confers on the infant a title to the accumulations if and only if he attains [18] or marries' (at 261).

For all practical purposes during the beneficiary's minority a vested interest becomes a contingent interest, with considerable fiscal significance. The income is treated as that of the trust for income tax purposes and broadly no income accumulation can be attributed to the beneficiary or the settlor. Furthermore the accumulation when paid to the beneficiary on attaining 18 will take the form of capital not income. It is these features deriving from s 31 which have rendered an accumulation settlement so potentially attractive for tax purposes in the appropriate circumstances (see Chapter 8). Paternalism is attractively enhanced by fiscal advantage.

As with s 31 generally, the provisions of s 31(2) are also subject to any contrary intention expressed in the trust instrument. Whilst therefore the mere fact that there is a vested interest in income clearly cannot, consistently with s 31(2)(i)(a), demonstrate a contrary intention, an appointment by trustees of income to a minor beneficiary 'absolutely' has been held sufficient (see *Re Delamere's Settlement Trusts* [1984] 1 All ER 584, CA, criticised by Griffiths [1985] Conv 153).

(c) Conclusion

The power of maintenance supplied by TA 1925, s 31, initially seems merely to fulfil a limited auxiliary task of trust administration. It has the 'caretaker' purpose of ensuring that, subject to adequate trust income, minors may be maintained, educated or otherwise benefited. Yet in achieving this, considerable flexibility of beneficial entitlement is introduced. A beneficiary's contingent interest in capital may be supplemented at age 18 by a vested but defeasible interest in income, while a minor's vested interest in income under the terms of a trust is effectively converted into a contingent interest both as regards income and accumulations. Furthermore, concentration on the 'caretaker' quality of the power should not obscure the consideration that the adoption, omission or alteration of s 31 and the subsequent exercise of trustees' discretion to maintain will be influenced by income tax and inheritance tax implications. (See Chapter 8.)

Finally, although the power of maintenance is rooted in a paternal concern for minors, is the statutory power consistent with or in conflict with the legal obligation of parents to maintain their children? Section 31(1) is hardly a ringing endorsement of the latter and stands in sharp contrast to the words of Langdale MR in the early case of *Douglas v Andrews* (1849) 12 Beav 310 under the now almost redundant inherent jurisdiction: 'However large a child's fortune may be, whilst the father is of ability to maintain the child, he must perform his duty, and no part of the child's fortune is to be applied for that purpose' (at 311). There is some evidence that the apparent strictness of this prohibition tended to be mitigated in practice by taking account of particular family circumstances (see eg *Pettit* p 478 on the inconsistency of approach in early nineteenth-century cases). Moreover it must not be forgotten that both under s 31(1) and, usually also, specific maintenance powers in trust deeds, the decision to apply the income is at the 'sole discretion' of the trustees, a discretion with which the courts will be reluctant to interfere assuming it is exercised bona fide (see generally Chapter 11 on controlling trustee discretions). The recent case of *Fuller v Evans* [2000] 1 FCR 494 provides confirmation, if it were needed, that as long as trustees exercise their discretion in the best interests of the minor beneficiaries the fact that this may incidentally benefit, in that case, the settlor/parent is not a prohibiting factor. Lightman J held that the trustees were not precluded from exercising the power of maintenance to pay children's school fees (the children were aged 14 and 12) even though this would 'incidentally' relieve the father from the legal obligation under a consent order in divorce proceedings to pay such fees until the children were 17. That obligation was 'no more than a consideration to which due weight must be given' by the trustees (at 498). No mention is made in the case of the possibility, depending on whether s 31(2) applies, that if the income of the trust fund was accumulated – the settlement provided for an accumulation period of 21 years – rather than expended on school fees then on attaining the relevant age the accumulations could be 'held on trust for the beneficiary absolutely'. Perhaps all that need be said by way of conclusion is that, as with its interpretation under variation and advancement, the concept of 'benefit' is capable of demonstrating what our economist colleagues might term 'elasticity'.

8

The taxation of private trusts

1. Tax planning and the trust

What to the legislator and parliamentary draftsman can appear as a trust problem may simultaneously be to the tax adviser a means of achieving a tax planning objective. In this first section we re-emphasise the peculiar facets of the trust that create this situation.

The basis of the trust's attraction for tax planning is founded on the fundamental division of ownership between nominal title, benefit and control.

P A Lovell 'Reflections on a Unified Estate and Gift Tax Regime' [1974] BTR 141 at 157–158

> The trust as a device depends for its success on the correct interplay between three basic concepts: the ownership of property, the management of the same, and the beneficial interests therein and enjoyment thereof, . . .
>
> Discretionary trusts, . . . are . . . problematic for, whilst ownership and management are vested in the trustees, the property is, in a material way, ownerless; the interest in possession is absent and the distribution of the benefits accruing from the trust property are distributable, subject to any powers of accumulation extant, at the discretion of the trustees.
>
> . . . Even in those trusts where a beneficial interest in possession in income has been created, it may nevertheless be possible to combine such income enjoyment with an element of capital expectancy. Thus a beneficiary may be given a right to income at the same time as the trustees are given a power, should such be considered appropriate, to apply the capital, by outright transfer or otherwise, for the benefit of the same income beneficiary.

A threefold predicament is therefore presented to our hypothetical legislator. First, a taxable event must be identified but, having done this, two problems remain to be resolved. These are:

(i) what to tax (eg property in one trust, or aggregated with other settled property, or aggregated with property owned absolutely); and

(ii) against whom to assess tax (eg the settlor, the trustees or the beneficiaries).

Compounding these difficulties are two additional elements that contribute to the flexibility provided by the trust form. One is that the trust can facilitate the exploitation of the artificial division – artificial at least to the economist – that both tax law and trusts law draw between capital and income (see generally Chapter 10). But to accomplish the conjuring trick of turning income into capital and vice versa, a further dimension, that of time, is necessary. 'The private trust' in Lawson and Rudden's simple yet memorable description (*The Law of Property* (1982) p 55) 'is basically a gift projected on the plane of time and, meanwhile, in need of management.' That the plane of time is itself a valuable resource is a fact long recognised by both proponents and opponents of tax planning.

R Venables *Tax Planning Through Trusts* (1983) pp 125–126

The basic advice which should be given to anyone who is likely to amass wealth which he does not wish the state to inherit is to make gifts during his lifetime, to give early, to give regularly and to give assets away before they have risen in value.

One difficulty of implementing the foregoing advice is that there may be no suitable donees in existence to whom the donor may wish to make his gifts. He may as yet have no issue, or his issue may be of tender years. While his issue may be adult, he may not, for a variety of reasons, wish them to have the absolute ownership of property, nor even, perhaps, a secure, unearned income. Further, the donor may be prepared to divest himself of the right beneficially to enjoy gifted assets but may wish to retain the power which comes from the control of them... Subject only to certain limitations of perpetuity, certainty and legality, ownership of capital can be divorced from that of income, and the decision as to the ultimate beneficial ownership of the capital and income can be postponed for many years. The trust is the ideal mechanism for giving away property when one has no one in particular to whom to give it.

By divorcing control of the trust assets from beneficial ownership, the trust enables power to remain with the trustees, of whom the settlor may be one, or, indeed, the only one. Such power is, of course, responsible power, but need be no less wide than that of, say, the politician or the civil servant and equally gratifying to the person in whom it is reposed. Moreover, the ability in the due exercise of one's discretion to control the entitlement of beneficiaries to capital or income may bring a satisfaction scarcely less than that of an absolute owner to give or withhold at his caprice.

R Titmuss *Income, Distribution and Social Change* (1962) pp 68–69

...we now have to consider the relativities of time and kinship...The individuals who constitute [different classes] at different points in time have, in consequence and for various historical and cultural reasons, different sets of attitudes, behaviour and propensities in relation to getting, spending and hoarding. They are conditioned, as Keynes said, by different anticipations of the future and by 'all sorts of vague doubts and fluctuating states of confidence and courage' (*The Lessons of Monetary Experience* (1937) p 151).

> What we wish to underline are the possible effects on the income distribution statistics caused by different degrees of command over resources-in-time by different income classes. Any definition of 'resources' would, to be realistic, have to include much more than income actually received and statutorily recorded for a specified period. It would have to embrace the possession of stored wealth, command over certain other people's income-wealth, expectations of inheritance from the past and untaxed gains in the future, power to manipulate and use the critical educational, occupational and nuptial keys to wealth advancement, and much else besides.
>
> Here we are only concerned with a limited part of the wider notion of a *masse de manoeuvre* in command over resources-in-time. This we may conveniently describe as the power and opportunity to rearrange income-wealth over time . . .
>
> The degree to which individuals have the knowledge, the opportunity and the expertise to rearrange and spread their income over time varies greatly. These characteristics are much more likely to be found among those at the top of the conventional income distribution table than among those at the bottom . . . The one characteristic these rearrangements all have in common . . . is that they have their source in social relationships. Income-wealth is rearranged over time on a family or wider kinship basis. A different conspectus of time and a different view of economic man as a taxable unit are thus introduced to complicate the statistical problems of measuring inequality.

The advantage that time as a resource can confer is not dependent solely on the trust but, as Venables recognises, the trust is the mechanism par excellence for exploiting it.

The final element that needs to be mentioned is mobility. People can be geographically mobile and, more importantly, so can capital and its management. The relative ease or difficulty with which trust assets can be transferred abroad and held by trustees safe from the grasp of Her Majesty's Revenue and Customs (HMRC), while leaving settlor or beneficiaries still resident in the UK, is potentially crucial to the effectiveness of a tax regime. The advantage of mobility is greatly enhanced by the mobility of intangible property, particularly shares and other securities (excluding real property mortgages). Shares can be transferred by simply changing the registry at which they are held. Mobility was, as we saw in Chapter 3, the kernel of both the long-term tax planning of the Vesteys and the short-term, off-the-shelf capital gains tax avoidance schemes. Tax avoidance is not the only possible motive for seeking to move ownership of assets offshore. Some offshore jurisdictions permit types of purpose trust which are usually thought to be void under English law, although even here tax considerations can form part of the reason for seeking to create such trusts (see Chapter 5 at p 265). But in most instances it is the tax considerations that will predominate whether they are simply to avoid the impact of existing taxes or to protect against the consequences of any future possible tax changes.

A legislative counter-attack to mitigate the fiscal consequences of such initiatives involved the enactment of widely drawn anti-avoidance provisions and special rules for offshore trusts. We do not examine this aspect of taxation and trusts in any detail. (See generally Lee (ed) *Revenue Law: Principles and Practice* (26th edn, 2008) chs 18, 27 and 35; Clarke *Offshore Tax Planning* (14th edn, 2007).) Suffice it to say that a significant inhibition on the export of resident trusts – those where the settlor was a UK resident when the trust was created – was the pre-1979 requirement of Bank of England consent. The suspension of exchange controls in 1979 is widely believed to have stimulated the creation of new offshore trusts and the export of existing trusts. Concern about the extent of tax being avoided by this means eventually prompted a legislative response directed in particular at attempts to avoid Capital Gains Tax (CGT), a tax first introduced in 1965 (see further below at p 383). We saw in Chapter 7, for instance, that one of the motives behind the attempt in *Re Weston's Settlement* [1968] 3 All ER 338 to transfer the trust to Jersey was to avoid a charge to CGT. The various subsequent attempts to avoid this tax and the regular legislative responses that these have attracted at the behest of HMRC aptly illustrate the potential complexity of the problems involved. As with resident trusts it is necessary for taxpayers, their advisers and the legislator to take into account the possible taxation liability of the settlor, the trustees and the beneficiaries. But here it is the interplay of these relationships allied to the concepts of location and time – who is resident where and when? – that creates the opportunity for avoidance and the problem for the legislator. One response was that with effect from 19 March 1991 an 'export' charge to capital gains tax was levied on UK trusts where the trustees and trust administration are moved offshore (see Taxation of Chargeable Gains Act 1992 (TCGA), ss 80–84). Moreover as from 17 March 1998, in a further anti-avoidance measure, gains realised by overseas trustees have been made attributable to UK-resident beneficiaries irrespective of the domicile and residence of the settlor when the trust was set up (Finance Act 1998, s 130; see McCutcheon [1998] BTR 479). This measure was intended to bring into the tax net gains realised by trusts either exported or set up offshore before 1991. At the same time the reach of the CGT net was further widened by extending the definition of settlor-interested trusts, thereby increasing their liability to the tax. The introduction of anti-avoidance measures has continued unabated with further modifications in the Finance Acts of 2000, 2003 and 2005.

The outcome of these and other initiatives is that there are now four sets of special rules affecting the offshore dimension of settlements. The rules apply to: (i) the migration offshore of the trust; (ii) the disposal of a beneficial interest by a UK resident beneficiary under a non-resident trust – the disposal of a beneficial interest under a UK resident trust does not give rise to a charge to CGT; (iii) the example referred to above where gains realised by a non-resident trust can be attributed to UK beneficiaries – usually only the trustees are liable for CGT under a UK resident trust; and (iv) under very widely drawn provisions the attribution of gains under a non-resident trust to a settlor who has an interest under the trust and comes within certain domicile and residence requirements (TCGA 1992, s 86 and Sch 5). Almost needless to say the rules are complex and offer what Tiley describes as 'sophisticated responses to sophisticated schemes and so reinforce a climate in which sophistication can be attempted' (*Revenue Law* (6th edn, 2008) p 1199). It must not be overlooked that the 'sophistication' must also in practice take account of the two other principal relevant taxes, income tax and inheritance tax.

This simple outline of the flexibility offered by the trusts device merely hints at the complexity which manipulation of the various elements or resources described above can achieve.

2. The taxation of trusts: an introduction

In the previous section we surveyed those peculiar facets of the trust and its environment that pose such conceptual problems for the would-be tax legislator, and consequent drafting difficulties for the parliamentary draftsman. The response to the challenge posed by the trust has usually taken the form of extremely complex legislation. Our principal concerns are to review how the tax system copes with the trust and its accompanying tax-saving potential, and whether the principle of fiscal neutrality (see Chapter 3) is or can be respected. Consequently, we examine only selected aspects of tax law as it affects trusts. (For more detailed explanation of the taxation of trusts reference should be made to one or more of the texts on tax law such as Tiley *Revenue Law* (6th edn, 2008); Lee (ed) *Revenue Law: Principles and Practice* (26th edn, 2008); Chamberlain and Whitehouse *Trust Taxation* (2007); or for a less detailed overview Morse and Williams *Davies: Principles of Tax Law* (6th edn, 2008).)

Complexity may be an inevitable consequence of legislative attempts to counter tax-avoidance techniques but comprehensibility of legislation has not been made easy by the apparently piecemeal approach to it that has been applied. As the Meade Committee noted (*The Structure and Reform of Direct Taxation* (1978) p 401): 'as each new tax has been introduced, a system of taxing trusts has been invented without, it seems, very much thought about how the new tax would fit in with other taxes'. The terms 'settlement' and 'settled property', for example, are prominent in the structure of income tax (IT), capital gains tax (CGT) and inheritance tax (IHT) yet have until recently had a different meaning under each tax. Possible reforms, in particular the integration of IT and CGT treatment of trusts and their closer alignment with the taxation of individuals, were canvassed in an Inland Revenue consultative document, published in 1991 (*The Income Tax and Capital Gains Tax Treatment of UK Resident Trusts* (1991); see Venables (1992) 13 Fiscal Studies 106). The government of the day decided not to implement the principal proposals, apparently because of their differential impact on different classes of beneficiaries (see 221 HC Official Report (6th series) written answers col 326, 18 March 1993).

In December 2003, however, at the request of the government the Inland Revenue (now HMRC) initiated a consultation process with 'trust professionals' as a prelude to introducing a revised IT and CGT system for trusts. The government adopted as its premise that trusts have an important role to play in society. Unsurprisingly it also wants, if possible, 'a tax system for trusts that does not provide artificial incentives to set up a trust but, equally, avoids artificial obstacles to using trusts where they would bring significant non-tax benefits' (Inland Revenue *Modernising the Tax System for Trusts: A Consultation Document* (August 2004) p 4). As will be seen below, changes simplifying the taxation regime for trusts of small value and trusts for the vulnerable were introduced with effect from 6 April 2005. Moreover the type of definitional problem posed by the different meanings attached to the term 'settlement' has begun to be addressed by effectively aligning, as from 6 April 2006, what is treated as a 'settlement' for IT and CGT purposes and by introducing commonality of treatment for those trusts in which the settlor has either retained or is deemed to have retained an interest (Finance Act 2006, Schs 12 and 13).

The overall strategy appeared to be to simplify and harmonise the current regimes for the two taxes rather than attempt to introduce a completely new system. The government recognised, however, that some of the proposals might open up the possibility of fresh avenues for tax avoidance. The sting in the tail of the proposals therefore was the warning that those who seek to use trusts to avoid tax may find that new anti-avoidance provisions may turn out at least as rigorous and complex as under the then existing system. Whether the desire for simplicity can be married to effective anti-avoidance measures remains to be seen.

This introductory section would be incomplete without mention of the major changes contained in the Finance Act 2006 to the treatment of trusts under IHT. The whole structure of IHT taxation of trusts has been altered with the introduction of a less accommodating or, if one prefers, harsher regime. It is reasonably clear that the driving force was a determination to limit the use of trusts as a means to avoid or minimise the incidence of IHT. In so doing it is arguable that any attempt to achieve parity of treatment under IHT between the transfer of property outright and transfer on trust has been sacrificed (see p 408 et seq).

Notwithstanding the various changes referred to above, the starting-point for the tax legislator is deceptively simple; it is to decide which of two possible methods of taxing trusts to adopt. The Meade Committee labelled these as *personification* – taxing the trust itself as a separate entity – and *transparency* – taxing by reference to the circumstances of the beneficiary as if the trust did not exist. Consistency of approach, however, has rarely been achieved. In reading the following description of taxation of trusts under IT, CGT and IHT consider the factors that have until now inhibited the attaining of a common approach.

3. Income tax (IT)

(a) Taxation of the individual

Lord Macnaghten drolly but inaccurately stated that 'income tax, if I may be pardoned for saying so, is a tax on income' (*LCC v A-G* [1901] AC 26 at 35).

There is, however, no statutory definition of income. An obvious question is how can income be taxed if the subject-matter of the tax is nowhere defined. The somewhat strange answer is that income means any sum falling within the scope of statutes that are the product of the Tax Law Rewrite Project, these being the Income Tax (Earnings and Pensions) Act 2003 (ITEPA) and the Income Tax (Trading and Other Income) Act 2005 (ITTOIA). For the taxpayer to be assessed for IT on any sum of money HMRC must show that it falls within the scope of one of those statutes. But establishing that income is assessable to tax is only a first step. Income tax, *pace* Lord Macnaghten, is chargeable on taxable income, and that is not the same as total income. Reliefs and allowances (such as the single person's allowance, currently £6,475 (2009–10), and payments to approved pension schemes) may be deducted in arriving at taxable income. An individual is then taxed on that figure at the basic and higher rates of tax prescribed annually in the Finance Act (FA). At present (2009–10) tax is levied on an individual's taxable income at, with two exceptions, the following rates:

>20%   £1 − £37,400 (basic rate)
>40%   Excess over £37,400 (higher rate)

The first exception concerns income from savings. The exception is that there is a 10% starting rate of income tax on savings income up to a starting rate limit (£2,440 in 2009–10) unless the taxpayer has *savings income* in excess of that starting rate limit. In that case all the savings income will be taxed in the same way as other income, ie at the lower rate of 20% up to the basic rate limit and at the higher rate of 40% for income above the basic rate limit. The other exception is that the rates applicable to dividends paid by UK companies are 10% and 32.5% respectively. The lower rates reflect the fact that, in effect, both the company and the individual are paying tax on profits that are distributed as dividends.

(b) Taxation of the trust

Where income accrues to a trust the method of taxation is part personification and part transparency. Reflecting this hybrid approach income tax is imposed by a two-tier process, first on trustees and then, where appropriate, on beneficiaries. A modification to this structure was introduced by the Finance Act (FA) 2005 for trusts for the 'most vulnerable'. This category includes two types of trust, those set up for the benefit of individuals with a disability and those set up for minor children on the death of a parent (see Inland Revenue *Modernising the Tax System for Trusts: A Consultation Document* (August 2004) ch 1 and section (3) below). Subsequent changes have seen the introduction of a standard rate band for most trusts (FA 2005) and measures to bring the principal trust-related definitions for income tax and capital gains tax – such as 'settlement' – into line with each other (FA 2006), measures consistent with the trust modernisation agenda in the 2004 Consultation Document.

(1) Trustees

Each trust is initially personified for IT purposes. At this stage the identity of the beneficiary ultimately entitled to the income is irrelevant and the trust income is treated as that of the trustees. Of course, trustees are not entitled to the income beneficially but for the purposes of IT liability they are 'entitled' in the sense that they are able to sue and claim receipt of income. Moreover, although the trust is personified trustees are not 'technically individuals' for IT purposes but 'are together treated as if they were a single person (distinct from the persons who are trustees of the settlement from time to time' (Income Tax Act 2007 (ITA) s 474(1)). Thus the personal tax circumstances of the trustees themselves are irrelevant to the assessment to IT, as indeed at the initial stage of assessment are those of the beneficiaries unless they have a vested interest in the income or the income accrues directly to them (see (2) below). The method of taxation of trust income consequently differs from and, in most respects, is simpler than that applicable to individuals. In general, all the income arising from trust assets is taxable, there being no allowance for administrative expenses, nor are personal or other allowances applicable. A further consequence of trustees not technically being 'individuals' for IT purposes is that they are not liable to tax at the higher rate since this is applicable to individuals only. Therefore, whether trust income is £500 or £50,000, only the basic rate of tax (20% in 2009–10) is levied on income received by the trustees.

Where tax is deducted at source (10% for dividend income and 20% on other savings income) the amount deducted will be treated as satisfying the basic rate tax liability of the trustees and therefore no further tax charge is levied on that income. There is, however, one important exception, contained in ITA 2007, ss 479 and 480, to the tax position of trustees as set out above.

ITA 2007, ss 479 and 480

479 Trustees' accumulated or discretionary income to be charged at special rates:

(1) This section applies if –
   (a) accumulated or discretionary income arises to the trustees of a settlement, and
   (b) the income does not arise under a trust established for charitable purposes only....

480 Meaning of 'accumulated or discretionary income':

(1) Income is accumulated or discretionary income so far as –
   (a) it must be accumulated, or
   (b) it is payable at the discretion of the trustees or any other person, ...
(2) The cases covered by subsection (1)(b) include cases where the trustees have, or any other person has, any discretion over one or more of the following matters –
   (a) whether, or the extent to which, the income is to be accumulated,
   (b) the persons to whom the income is to be paid, and
   (c) how much of the income is to be paid to any person.

For trusts that come within the above sections – broadly speaking those where there is a trust to accumulate or where trustees have a discretion over disbursement of income – special rates of income tax (the trust rate and dividend rate) are charged on the income (net of certain administrative expenses) of those trusts. The effect (in 2009–10) is to increase the total rate of IT chargeable to trustees in these circumstances to 40% or to 32.5% on dividend income. The purpose of s 479 is to reduce the attractiveness of accumulation trusts and discretionary trusts as effective tax shelters where income can be generated and accumulated while being taxed at the trustees' rate only, rather than the rate appropriate to individual beneficiaries. But countering tax avoidance possibilities is not the only objective of the project to modernise the tax treatment of trusts. Another objective of the reforms is to reduce the burdens on smaller trusts. As one element of that policy and to mitigate the potential burden on small trusts to which the trust rate and dividend rate might otherwise apply a new basic rate band for all trusts liable to those rates was introduced from 6 April 2005 (see now ITA 2007, s 491). It applies to the first £1,000 of income taxable at the trust and dividend rates, the effect being to tax that tranche of income at the relevant basic rate only instead of those higher special rates. The overall consequence is that around one-third of trusts currently provisionally liable to the higher rates will no longer pay those rates on any of their income because their total income will fall below the £1,000 threshold (see Inland Revenue *Modernising the Tax System for Trusts: A Consultation Document* (August 2004) ch 2).

A source of tension in the tax treatment of trusts, previously referred to, lies in the relationship between general principles of trusts law and the language of taxing statutes. Expenses which are 'properly chargeable' to income by statute or case law, although not deductible against the trustees' liability to tax at the basic rate, may be deducted in arriving at the amount of income chargeable at the 'rate applicable to trusts' (ITA 2007, s 484(3)). The words 'properly chargeable' have prompted litigation which demonstrates how this interpretational problem can be accentuated by the capacity of settlors to modify the application of those general principles. Trusts law draws a distinction between trust expenses attributable to income and those attributable to capital. An example of the latter can be a premium paid on a life assurance policy. It is, however, within the power of a settlor to authorise trustees by the terms of the trust deed to pay income expenses out of capital or vice versa.

In *Carver v Duncan* [1985] 2 All ER 645, trustees had paid premiums on life assurance policies intended to cover possible IHT liability in the event of the early death of the settlor. The trustees were empowered to pay the premiums out of income and they did so. It could therefore be said that trustees 'properly' paid the premiums out of income in the sense of not being in breach of trust. But were the expenses 'properly chargeable' to income under s 686(2)(d) (the forerunner of ITA 2007, s 484)? Lord Diplock, the sole dissenting voice in the House of Lords, considered that they were. In contrast the reasoning of the majority, as reflected in the judgment of Lord Templeman (at 654), was that:

'although a settlor may provide that capital expenses shall or may be paid out of income, the settlor cannot alter the nature of those expenses'. In the opinion of the majority 'properly chargeable' in s 686(2)(d) refers to the position under the basic principles of trusts law, not the position as modified in the terms of a trust deed by a settlor (see further *Peter Clay Discretionary Trust Trustees v Revenue and Customs Commissioners* [2008] Ch 291).

(2) Beneficiaries

A beneficiary to whom trust income is distributed or who is entitled to trust income as it arises, whether distributed or not, will be subject to IT on it (*Baker v Archer-Shee* [1927] AC 844). The transparent approach is adopted to this second tier of income taxation of the trust, and therefore it is the tax status of the beneficiary that is decisive. Trust income will already have been taxed in the hands of trustees at the basic rate or, where relevant, the trust rate. Whether, therefore, more tax is payable, or, indeed, a refund allowable will depend on the beneficiary's income from other sources.

When submitting a tax return the beneficiary must account for both the income received and the tax already paid by the trustees, ie the amount to be declared is increased to the original gross figure. Thus, if the basic rate is 20%, a receipt of £800 will be 'grossed up' to £1,000. If the beneficiary's marginal rate of tax – the rate applicable to each additional pound of trust income – is higher than the basic rate then the beneficiary will be liable for the additional tax. A beneficiary entitled to the trust income whose marginal rate of tax is 40% would therefore be liable to pay £400 IT on grossed-up trust income of £1,000, against which can be credited the tax of £200 already paid by the trustees. On the other hand, a similar beneficiary whose rate of tax is nil will also receive a credit for the tax paid by the trustees and can therefore recover this amount from HMRC. The procedure is more complicated where trust administration expenses are involved. In effect the beneficiary will not be entitled to such proportion of the tax credit as is attributable to administration expenses incurred by the trustees (*Macfarlane v IRC* (1929) 14 TC 532).

Where beneficiaries have no entitlement to the trust income but merely a right to be considered, as in a discretionary trust, only income distributed to them is liable to tax in their hands. Here also, for the purposes of assessing liability, the net payment received by a beneficiary must be grossed-up but now at the trust rates. The tax credit received by a beneficiary is increased correspondingly. The effect of the higher rate applicable to income of accumulation or discretionary trusts is therefore to encourage trustees to distribute income to those with lower marginal rates of tax so that some or all of the tax paid by the trustees can be recovered by the beneficiary concerned.

(3) Trusts with vulnerable beneficiaries

When introducing the revised income tax structure in 2004 the government recognised that applying the special trust and dividend rates (40% and 32.5%

respectively) to trusts established for the 'most vulnerable beneficiaries' could prove detrimental. In particular it would be unusual and possibly undesirable to distribute the whole of the trust income to the beneficiary each year. Instead it may be preferable, indeed judicious, at times to accumulate the income, the consequence being that in the absence of any mitigating provision the higher rates would be charged on the income. Special provision was therefore made in the Finance Act 2005, Part 2 Chapter 4 whereby the trustees and the 'vulnerable' person can jointly and irrevocably elect for trust income to be taxed on the basis of the vulnerable beneficiary's individual circumstances. In effect a 'transparency' method of taxation is adopted.

(c) Anti-avoidance measures

The imposition of the additional rate of tax on accumulation and discretionary trusts is not the only anti-avoidance measure, and indeed it would be inadequate if it were so. Unless further restrictions were imposed it would be a simple matter for a wealthy taxpayer whose marginal rate of tax on income was 40% (and until as recently as 1988 could have been 60%) to place income-producing assets in a trust where the income would be taxed at only 20% or, until the increase in 2004–05 in the rate applicable to trusts to 40%, 34%. If that income were then to be paid to the settlor's spouse or children, or accumulated so as to be subsequently returned to the settlor or spouse as capital, a substantial reduction in income tax liability would have been achieved. As a consequence of these capital accumulation and income-splitting possibilities a series of anti-avoidance provisions was enacted over a period of some sixty years. This piecemeal development led to overlapping provisions and the rules were simplified in the Finance Act 1995. Some existing provisions were repealed and replaced by new anti-avoidance provisions. The rules are all now contained in ITTOIA 2005, Pt 5 Ch 5 and apply to all 'settlements'. Notwithstanding the continued use of the term 'settlement', so redolent of Jane Austen and the notions of estates, there is nothing very nineteenth century about its very wide-ranging definition. It includes 'any disposition, trust, covenant, agreement, arrangement or transfer of assets' (s 620). It should be noted, however, that whereas a settlement under trusts law can be established for consideration it seems that liability is not incurred under Part 5 unless some element of 'bounty' is present (see *Jones v Garnett* [2007] UKHL 35). To give just one example, an outright gift of a National Savings certificate to a child would be a 'transfer of an asset' and therefore within the definition of a settlement (*Thomas v Marshall* [1953] AC 543).

The statutory provisions cover three distinct areas:

(i) where the settlor or spouse or civil partner retains an interest in the settlement (ss 624–628);

(ii) where an unmarried minor child of the settlor receives a benefit from the settlement (s 629); and

(iii) where the settlor or spouse or civil partner or minor child has received a capital payment or benefit from the settlement (ss 633–643).

The anti-avoidance technique adopted is quite simple, even if the detailed implementation remains complex. The settlement is treated not so much as transparent as like a mirror. Thus under ITTOIA 2005, ss 624–628 all income arising under the settlement is deemed to be that of the settlor unless it can be shown that it arises from property in which the settlor has no interest. In deciding whether that exclusion is satisfied another deeming provision comes into play: a settlor is to be regarded as having an interest in property if that property or any derived property is, or will or may become, payable to or applicable for the benefit of the settlor or his spouse or his civil partner *in any circumstances whatsoever* (s 625). It seems that if the settlor is to avoid a charge to tax there must be no power of revocation which could benefit the settlor or spouse or civil partner, no discretion or power to benefit the settlor or spouse or civil partner and no reversionary interest to the settlor. A settlor, for instance, is treated as having an interest in settled property from which his or her spouse or civil partner is capable of benefiting unless the benefit derives from an outright gift to the spouse or civil partner (see also s 627(1) that provides an exception for certain settlements made by one party to a marriage to the other on the break-up of the marriage). The potentially sweeping nature of these anti-avoidance provisions is best illustrated by the fact that it was an earlier manifestation of the provisions that ensnared the hapless Mr Vandervell (see Chapter 4).

The same 'mirror' approach is adopted where property is settled in favour of the settlor's infant unmarried children – a definition extending to stepchildren and illegitimate children. Here also any income arising under the settlement and which is paid to or for the benefit of any unmarried minor child of the settlor will be treated as that of the settlor (s 629, but subject to a de minimis exception of £100). There is, however, one important and surprising exception to this. Where income is accumulated under a capital settlement in favour of the settlor's unmarried minor child, the income is not after all treated as that of the settlor. Instead the tax regime described above (section (b)(1)) applies, the trustees being liable to the trust rate of income tax. But if any income is distributed to the infant unmarried beneficiary or is used for the child's maintenance, education or benefit then the s 629 'mirror' takes effect. Furthermore, the possibility of trustees accumulating the income and then using it, for example, to pay the beneficiary's education fees has been countered. Section 631 provides that such a capital payment out of the settlement fund will be treated as the income of the settlor to the extent it can be matched against any available undistributed income in the fund (ie income left after payments to any other beneficiaries and payments of expenses properly charged to income).

It must be stressed that s 631 applies only where the settlor is the parent of the unmarried minor beneficiary. Consequently generation-skipping capital settlements by grandparents still provide income tax advantages, since distributed income will be treated as that of the beneficiaries, not of the parents. In addition the inheritance tax treatment of such settlements can be favourable.

The logic of the legislative purpose of s 631 remains obscure. The section, as was its predecessor, is designed to counter income-splitting and so prevent high-rate taxpayers maintaining their infant children partly at the expense of HMRC. But somewhat confusingly, as Williams and Morse once perceptively noted in relation to the accumulations provision (*Introduction to Revenue Law* (2nd edn, 1985) p 171): 'it seems that . . . the legislature is saying: "But we don't mind parents building up a nest-egg for the child's future."' The alignment of the rate applicable to trusts (40%) where income is retained in the trust and the higher rate of IT at 40% reduces, at least at current IT rates, the attractions for parents of this type of settlement.

The third occasion when the anti-avoidance measures come into play is where a capital sum is paid by trustees out of accumulated income to the settlor or spouse. That capital sum is to be treated as the income of the settlor (ITTOIA 2005, ss 633–643). The definition of capital sum is widely drawn, extending to include, for instance, loans to the settlor, payments to third parties and even payments made to the settlor or spouse in breach of trust.

4. Capital gains tax (CGT)

(a) General

CGT is an attempt to compensate for the inability of the limited definition of income adopted for IT purposes to tax increases in the capital value of assets. It seeks to charge tax to individuals on the disposal of 'chargeable assets', the tax being based, in principle, on the difference between the value at date of acquisition and value at date of disposal. The disposal can be by sale, gift, exchange or generally any method whereby the owner of an asset derives a capital sum from it. This could even include, for instance, insurance money paid for damage or destruction of an asset (TCGA 1992, s 22).

An early criticism of the tax was that no allowance was made for the consequences of inflation on asset values and CGT could be levied on paper as well as real gains. This criticism was countered by the introduction of an indexation allowance, whereby the original cost of an asset was notionally uprated in line with the increase in the Retail Price Index. The intention was that CGT should tax only non-inflationary gains. In 1998, however, the government decided to modify further the CGT system by progressively removing indexation and replacing it – for individuals, trustees and personal representatives although not companies – by a system of taper relief. The stated rationale for taper relief was to encourage longer-term holding of assets and thereby help investment. The relatively simple notion was that the longer one held an asset the greater would be the relief. Indeed taper relief on disposal of assets could at its maximum reduce the effective rate of CGT from, for instance, where the taxpayer's own marginal rate of income tax was 40% (the 'marginal rate' being the rate charged on each extra pound earned by the taxpayer) to either 10% on business assets or 24% on non-business assets. Unfortunately the simplicity of the idea proved less than simple in its implementation and led to what one leading tax text described as 'the most complex area of capital gains tax in relation to individuals partly because the rules changed in almost every year between 1998 and 2003' (Lee (ed) *Revenue Law: Principles and Practice* (26th edn 2008) p 492). It seems, however, that currently nothing is more certain for the tax adviser than that the arrangements for CGT will be 'reformed' at regular intervals. In the Finance Act 2008 taper relief, together with what remained of indexation, was abolished and in its stead a revised flat rate of 18% on all realised gains exceeding an annual threshold was introduced (FA 2008, s 8). This prompted vehement complaints from the business community that the withdrawal of taper relief had increased the effective rate of CGT on disposal of business assets from 10% to 18%. In response a new form of relief – 'entrepreneurial relief' – was hastily introduced, effectively reducing the CGT rate back to 10% on the first £1m of chargeable gains realised when a taxpayer disposes of a business (FA 2008, s 9 and Sch 3; [2008] BTR 417–421).

The method of charging tax was originally that an individual was taxed at a flat rate (30%) on the annual total of chargeable gains less allowable losses but in 1988 the then Chancellor (Nigel Lawson) introduced changes which sought to align the rates of income tax and CGT for each individual. But the changes in the FA 2008 have effectively returned the system to the pre-1988 basis of imposing a flat rate charge on realised capital gains although now at a rate of 18%, except where 'entrepreneurial relief' applies where, as indicated above, the effective rate is 10%. There remains, however, an annual exemption which in 2008–09 is £9,600 and therefore only realised gains in excess of this figure are taxable.

The structure of CGT has fluctuated considerably since its introduction in 1965. During the 1980s, for instance, it was possible to postpone the payment of CGT on lifetime gifts, usually until the asset was eventually sold or otherwise disposed of for value. The relief, termed 'hold-over relief', which was introduced in FA 1980, s 79, initially applied to disposals between individuals only but was subsequently extended to include disposals by or to trustees (FA 1981, s 78; FA 1982, s 82). One consequence of the availability of hold-over relief was that if a series of gifts of an asset occurred, the gains could be cumulatively held over. In 1989, s 79 was repealed on the ground that the relief was increasingly being used as a simple form of tax avoidance. Relief was, however, still available where property was transferred into a discretionary trust (TCGA 1992, s 260), or where business assets were settled on trust or disposed of by trustees, other than by an arm's-length sale (s 165). Following the changes to IHT treatment of trusts introduced in the FA 2006 whereby, with very limited exceptions, the IHT 'relevant property' regime for discretionary trusts became applicable to other types of trust, the scope of hold-over relief has been extended. Transfers into and out of such trusts will now also be eligible for hold-over relief (TCGA 1992, s 260(2)A).

(b) Trusts

(1) Introduction

Although there is no definition of settlement as such, settled property is defined as 'any property held in trust' (TCGA 1992, s 68). There are certain specified exceptions to this (s 60) including where trustees hold property for a beneficiary who is absolutely entitled to the property as against the trustees. Then, even though a bare trust exists (as in the example of Whizz-kid in Chapter 1), the property is not 'settled property' for CGT purposes and is treated as belonging to the beneficiary. In similar fashion trusts established for the most vulnerable can, on election by the trustees and the beneficiary, be treated for CGT purposes as if in effect the gains accrued directly to the beneficiary (FA 2005, s 31). Apart from these limiting exceptions trusts are personified under CGT. Transparency would require the attribution of gains to beneficiaries in circumstances where their identification might prove difficult and the actuarial valuation of their respective interests in trust capital a highly artificial exercise. Under the solution adopted for CGT, trustees are treated as a single body of persons, the retirement and appointment of individual trustees of a settlement therefore generally having no tax effect. As from 2008 the rate at which gains are taxed will revert to the flat rate of 18% whereas for the previous decade the relevant rate was the special trust rate of income tax (40%). The re-emergence of a differential between that trust rate and the flat rate of CGT (18%) might encourage attempts to revive the 'old game' of transforming income into capital gain. Aware of this possibility, HMRC have indicated that they will 'continue to monitor the CGT rules and reliefs to ensure they cannot be abused by those who wish to pay less than their fair share of tax'. Despite the alignment of the CGT rate for trustees with that for individual taxpayers the status of trustees is not, however, fully equated to that of individuals. Plainly if an equal annual exemption were allowed, tax avoidance by fragmenting capital into numerous trusts each gaining the benefit of an annual exemption would be possible. To counter this, an annual exemption of only half the rate applicable to individuals is provided (2008–09 one half of £9,600 = £4,800) and there are rules intended to prevent the same settlor getting the benefit of more than one trust exemption by setting up numerous trusts simultaneously (TCGA 1992, Sch 1). Finally, it should be noted that UK non-resident trusts – 'offshore trusts' – are subject to a different, and for UK settlors, potentially more severe CGT regime (see eg Chamberlain and Whitehouse *Trust Taxation* (2007) ch 10).

(2) The charge to CGT

A charge to CGT may arise:

(i) on the creation of a settlement;

(ii) on gains accruing to trustees as a result of actual disposal of chargeable assets; and

(iii) on gains arising where a deemed disposal takes place.

Creation of the settlement The creation of a settlement, whether revocable or irrevocable, is deemed to be a disposal of assets by the settlor (TCGA 1992, s 53) and a chargeable gain, or loss, will result. Liability for CGT lies with the settlor rather than the trustees. As mentioned previously, hold-over relief is available where assets are transferred to those trusts subject to the 'relevant property' IHT regime or more generally where the assets comprise business property.

Actual disposals by trustees Trustees are chargeable to CGT on gains accruing to the trust when they dispose of chargeable assets in the course of administering the trust. The charge to tax is calculated on the normal principles applicable to individuals but with the smaller annual exemption limit mentioned above. Trustees will most commonly incur CGT liability on actual disposals when switching the trust's investments.

Deemed disposals by trustees Deemed disposals occur on two principal occasions though only one of these will create a chargeable gain.

Where a life-interest in possession terminates on the death of the life-tenant but the property continues to be settled property – for example, to A for life remainder to B contingently on attaining 25 and A dies before B reaches 25 – there is a deemed disposal and re-acquisition of the assets of the trust fund by the trustees at the prevailing market value. But, consistent with normal CGT principles and with the treatment of a non-settled property on the death of an individual, no chargeable gain arises (TCGA 1992, s 72). There is therefore an uplift in the base value of the property but without incurring any charge to CGT.

The second category of deemed disposal occurs whenever a beneficiary becomes absolutely entitled to any portion of the settled property as against the trustee (TCGA 1992, s 71(1)). Whether there is an appointment of trust assets to a beneficiary, or the trustees retain the property as bare trustees under s 60, they are deemed by virtue of s 71 to have disposed of the assets of the fund and immediately re-acquired them at their market value. Any gain will be chargeable to CGT unless the deemed disposal was triggered by the death of a life-tenant. Then, as in the previous paragraph and consistent with CGT principles, there is no charge to CGT and an uplift occurs in the base value of the property for any future gain.

It is in the context of 'deemed disposals' that a conceptual difficulty associated with the interpretation of the phrase 'absolutely entitled as against the trustees' in TCGA 1992, s 71(1) has come under the spotlight. It is now clear that 'absolutely entitled' does not just mean 'absolutely and beneficially entitled'. On the contrary, where trustees appoint property to new trusts, under a power of advancement, for instance, the trustees of the new settlement (who may be the same persons as the trustees of the original settlement) *may* become absolutely entitled to that property as against the previous trustees and a deemed disposal arise under TCGA 1992, s 71(1), with a resultant charge to CGT (see *Hoare Trustees v Gardner* [1978] 1 All ER 791). The outcome will depend on whether the new trusts remain part of the existing main settlement, as sub-trusts, or constitute a new settlement, since only in the latter instance will a deemed disposal occur. Whether property has been made subject to the trusts of a new settlement is a question of fact which must apparently be answered 'according to the view which would be taken of the transaction by a person with knowledge of trusts who uses language in a practical and commonsense way' (per Hoffmann J in *Swires v Renton* [1991] STC 490 at 499; see also Lord Wilberforce in *Roome v Edwards* [1981] 1 All ER 736).

Exactly when a resettlement occurs for the purposes of s 71(1) remains uncertain, although the courts have indicated that this will not be the position unless the power exercised by the trustees expressly or implicitly authorises them to remove assets from the original settlement into a new settlement. In this connection a distinction was drawn in *Bond v Pickford* [1983] STC 517, CA between a power in the narrower form (such as a special power of appointment) and a power in the wider form (typically a power of advancement). The former type of power may allow trustees to define or vary the beneficial interests but it will not allow them to remove assets from the trust or delegate their powers and discretions. It is consequently 'difficult to imagine any appointment within the scope of [a narrow] power which could be construed as the creation of a new settlement' (per Hoffmann J in *Swires v Renton* at 499). Unfortunately it does not follow that every exercise of a power in the wider form to appoint property into new trusts will constitute a resettlement. An Inland Revenue Statement of Practice (SP 7/84), accurately summarising the present position, indicates that there will *not* be a resettlement if (i) the appointment is revocable, or (ii) the trusts declared are non-exhaustive (ie the assets could revert to the original settlement), or (iii) the trustees of the original settlement still have duties in relation to the assets in the new trusts. Beyond this guidance, all that can rather unhelpfully be said is that each case must depend on its facts and the intention of the parties, viewed objectively, will be an important consideration (see *Swires v Renton* [1991] STC 490; Inland Revenue *The Income Tax and Capital Gains Tax Treatment of UK Resident Trusts* (1991) ch 9; Walker [1991] BTR 129).

Lastly, as mentioned previously, since 19 March 1991 there is also a deemed disposal by the trustees where the trust is exported so that trustees cease to be resident in the UK (TCGA 1992, s 80(2)). The fiscal effect is similar to that which arises when a beneficiary becomes absolutely entitled to the whole or any part of the trust property (TCGA 1992, s 71(1)).

5. Inheritance tax (IHT)

(a) Introduction: estate duty to inheritance tax – a return journey?

Death duties have a long history in the UK but the last quarter of the twentieth century witnessed particularly sharp changes of direction in this form of capital taxation. Moreover, given the absence of any political consensus on the issue, the longevity of any particular tax structure seems doubtful. It is, therefore, both useful for purposes of comparison and necessary for an understanding of the present and possible future tax treatment of trusts to trace how the present framework of tax law regulating transfers of capital emerged (see Sandford *Taxing Personal Wealth* (1971) for an informative account of the history of death duties).

From 1894 to 1974 the main, and from 1949 the sole, death duty in the UK was estate duty. Two interlinking features dominated the history of estate duty during this period. These were the ever-increasing nominal burden of estate duty and the growth of avoidance.

From its inception estate duty incorporated a progressive rate structure, ie the rate of tax increased with the value of the estate. In 1894 the rates varied between 1% and 8%, and in future years the rate schedule consistently grew steeper. By 1914 the maximum rate had risen to 20%, by 1919 to 40%, by 1939 to 60% and by 1949 to 80%. The rates remained broadly at this high level thereafter. Furthermore the effects of continuous inflation increased the nominal burden of the tax after the Second World War. Under a progressive rate schedule, if no allowance is made for inflation by changing the rate structure of the tax, the result is to push the same real value of estates into ever higher tax brackets. Sandford has estimated, for instance, that an estate valued at £100,000 in 1949 and paying duty at 45% would have been equivalent to an estate valued at £195,000 in 1967, but the rate of duty on the latter would have been 55%. The absence of indexation increased the incentive to take advantage of the numerous loopholes and concessions. Attempts were made to nullify these, for example, by extending the length of the period before death within which gifts were made taxable. Also steps were taken in FA 1969 to counter the avoidance potential of discretionary trusts. Consequently, on the death of a beneficiary of a discretionary trust, a proportion of the value of that fund based on the beneficiary's share of the income of the fund in the seven preceding years, was attributed to the deceased's estate. The effectiveness of these responses to avoidance is questionable. They did nothing to still the criticisms of estate duty based on grounds both of horizontal equity ('fairness') and vertical equity ('ability to pay') (see Chapter 3).

A range of alternatives was extensively canvassed with opinion divided between the competing merits of inheritance-based or donor-based systems. (Amongst those favouring a donor-based system were Wheatcroft (ed) *Estate and Gift Taxation* (1965) and Prest *Public Finance* (1967). Those favouring an inheritance-based system included Meade *Efficiency, Equality and the Ownership of Property* (1964) and Sandford, Willis and Ironside *An Accession Tax* (1973).) Eventually in 1974 a Labour government introduced a donor-based lifetime gifts tax with the title 'capital transfer tax' (CTT). The distinguishing characteristic of CTT as compared with estate duty was the extension to include lifetime gifts on a cumulative basis, rather than to those made only within seven years of death. The principle of cumulation is simply that the rate of tax on any gift, or on an estate left at death, is determined by the amount of taxable transfers previously made during the cumulation period. When cumulation is added to a steeply progressive rate schedule the potential for a severely redistributive tax is apparent.

Yet it was soon claimed that CTT was even less effective than estate duty as an attack on inequality of wealth distribution. The reason in the opinion of one sharp critic (Sutherland 'Capital Transfer Tax: An Obituary' (1981) Fiscal Studies 51) is that 'CTT has become, as estate duty was, a voluntary tax'. This assessment depends on the assumption that wealth-holders would utilise fully the various concessions made available after the introduction of CTT (see Robinson and Sandford *Tax Policy-Making in the United Kingdom* (1983) for a detailed account of the policy process involved). Among the more important concessions were:

(i) the granting of business and agricultural property relief so that for tax purposes the value of the property transferred could be reduced by up to 50% (now 100% in some circumstances);

(ii) the increase in the tax threshold greater than that required to keep pace with the rise in the Retail Price Index; and

(iii) the abandonment in 1981 of the principle of lifetime cumulation and the substitution instead of a cumulation period of ten years.

In consequence it was theoretically possible at 1985–86 tax rates for a married couple – transfers of property between spouses generally being 'exempt transfers' – to pass on to heirs over an 11-year period £334,000 free of CTT. These figures take no account of the possible eligibility of the assets transferred for business or agricultural property relief. When it is appreciated that an individual with sufficient wealth to fund such a transfer would then have been among the top 1% of wealth-holders in the UK the limited nature of the revenue-raising and redistributive potential of CTT is apparent.

Then in 1986 further significant changes to the structure of CTT were introduced. To the chagrin of tax purists the title of the tax was misleadingly altered to inheritance tax (IHT), a name commonly associated with a receipt-based or accessions tax, whereas the result of the changes was in substance a return to a form of estate duty. Indeed the new structure is an unwieldy amalgam of estate duty and CTT rules. The major alteration to CTT is that the tax charge on lifetime gifts between individuals is abolished, as is a charge on gifts into certain trusts. But, as with estate duty, you must make sure you live for seven years after making the gift if tax is to be avoided altogether, since gifts made up to seven years before the transferor's death are chargeable. At that point, however, IHT breaks with estate duty by retaining the principle of cumulation, albeit in a modified form based on a seven-year cumulation period. Consequently, where a transferor dies within seven years of making a gift, that gift will be brought into the tax net *and* will, in some circumstances, itself be cumulated with certain other transfers made within the seven years previous to that particular gift. One further and important modification concerns the tax rate structure. Unlike the position under estate duty and CTT there is no longer any progressive rate structure.

As from 6 April 2009 IHT rates chargeable on estates at death are as follows:

Lower Limit (£)	Upper Limit (£)	Rate of tax (%)
0	325,000	Nil
325,001	–	40

Note that the rate of tax charged on chargeable lifetime transfers (eg into a discretionary trust) is half that applicable on death (ie 20% or, of course, 0% if the transfer is below the threshold).

None of the initial reforms to CTT or subsequent concessions related specifically to transfers of property into trusts or to the problems of taxing trusts under a gifts-tax regime. But CTT did introduce a radical scheme for taxing trusts, particularly discretionary trusts. As mentioned previously, the FA 2006 introduced major changes to IHT treatment of trusts so that, with very limited exceptions, the IHT 'relevant property' regime for discretionary trusts now applies to most other types of trust. The scope and adequacy of the existing approach is considered in section (c) below.

(b) Inheritance tax in outline

FA 1986 effected the change from CTT to IHT entirely by way of amendment to the Capital Transfer Tax Act 1984 – or Inheritance Tax Act (IHTA) 1984 as it is now called (FA 1986, s 100) – 'superimposing new complexities on old, without proper consolidation' as one critic caustically commented (*Financial Times*, 11 August 1986). We adopt the new title and refer throughout to IHT except where specific reference is being made to the situation under CTT. Our concern with complexities of the tax is kept to a minimum and we do no more here than sketch in the conceptual scheme, which remains substantially unamended from CTT (see generally the comprehensive treatment in Lee (ed) *Revenue Law: Principles and Practice* (26th edn, 2008) chs 28–36).

IHTA 1984, s 1, declares: 'IHT shall be charged on the value transferred by a chargeable transfer.' A chargeable transfer is 'a transfer of value which is made by an individual but is not an exempt transfer' (s 2(1)). The keys to understanding the structure of the tax lie in the terms 'value transferred', 'transfer of value' and 'exempt transfer'. To these three elements we must now add a new concept, 'the potentially exempt transfer' (PET). This is an inter vivos transfer of value made by an individual that either (i) constitutes a gift to another individual, or (ii) constituted, until 22 March 2006, a transfer into most trusts other than discretionary trusts. The position as regards trusts has now been almost completely reversed in that transfers only into certain very narrowly defined trusts – predominantly for the disabled – qualify as PETs. A PET, as the name implies, is essentially a gift in a state of limbo for tax purposes. If seven years elapse with the transferor still alive it becomes an 'exempt transfer', and it is only if the transferor dies within that period that the gift becomes a 'chargeable transfer' (IHTA 1984, s 3A(4)). As regards 'exempt transfers' in general, the most common exemptions are gifts up to £3,000 each year and transfers of property between spouses and, since 2005, civil partners although not cohabitees (IHTA 1984, Pt II). Gifts to charities and political parties are also exempt (IHTA 1984, ss 23 and 24 respectively).

The two remaining elements of the tax to be considered are 'transfers of value' and 'value transferred'.

IHTA 1984, s 3(1) defines a transfer of value as:

> a disposition made by a person as a result of which the value of his estate immediately after the disposition is less than it would be but for the disposition; and the amount by which it is less is the value transferred by the transfer.

IHT operates as a death duty by virtue of deeming a transfer of value to have been made immediately before a person's death, the value transferred being equal to the value of the estate (IHTA 1984, s 4(1)).

Central to an understanding of the operation of IHT is that it is the reduction in the value of the transferor's estate – the diminution principle – that represents the value transferred. This will often be the same as the value by which a transferee's estate is increased but need not necessarily be so, as for example where a transfer of 2% of a company's shares from A to B (A holding 51% and B 5%) results in a loss of control of the company by A but not the acquisition of control by B. The diminution principle becomes particularly important where the transferor rather than the transferee pays the tax. Then the tax itself becomes taxable because the transferor's estate is diminished not just by the value of the property transferred but also by what has to be paid to HMRC. The process is known as grossing-up and in principle operates as described previously in the context of income tax (see p 380). In short, if the transferor wishes to put

£100,000 into the hands of the transferee he must calculate what sum after deduction of tax will leave £100,000 clear.

One further consequence of a reversion towards an estate duty structure of taxation has been the re-introduction of 'reservation of benefit' rules (FA 1986, s 102 and Sch 20). These rules are intended to prevent a donor obtaining a tax advantage by making a gift as a PET, while effectively retaining an interest in the property given. The effect of the rules is that where a gift with reservation of benefit is made, the transfer has no immediate IHT consequences. Instead, the gifted property will be deemed to be a part of the donor's estate immediately before his death and taxed according to its value at that time (s 102(3)). The rules are closely based on earlier estate duty legislation and cases decided under that regime have, to some extent, provided relevant guidance. Thus it seems that a settlor, for instance, will be treated as having reserved a benefit if he is a remunerated trustee (*Oakes v Comr of Stamp Duties for New South Wales* [1953] 2 All ER 1563), or one of a class of objects of a discretionary trust, irrespective of whether he receives anything (*Gartside v IRC* [1968] 1 All ER 121).

The implementation of the rules provides yet another illustration of the ways in which property interests can be manipulated to exploit loopholes in the legislation which can in turn lead to unanticipated consequences. The Finance Act 1999 closed a loophole in s 102 whereby it was possible to dispose of property by gift whilst applying 'the highly sophisticated English land law' to retain a right to residence in the property (see Finance Act 1999, s 95, reversing the decision of the House of Lords in *Ingram v IRC* [1999] 1 All ER 297: 'Section 102 does not prevent people from deriving benefit from the object in which they have given away an interest. It applies only where they derive benefit from that interest' per Lord Hoffmann at 304). Undaunted, taxpayers, their advisers and promoters of avoidance schemes returned to the fray. They were no doubt encouraged by the fact that the rate of increase in the value of house prices outpaced the inflation-linked annual rise in the IHT threshold thereby enhancing the attractiveness of taking estates outside the scope of IHT. Vos aptly summarised the position: 'The attraction of saving 40% inheritance tax on the value of the house and so increasing the amount which they can pass on to their heirs is sufficient to persuade [taxpayers] to put aside their concerns and to enter into tax planning arrangements which can be complicated, inflexible, costly to implement and which may ultimately not succeed. Compared with the amount of tax at stake, however, these disadvantages can pale into insignificance' ([2003] PCB 6 379–390 at 379). A number of schemes were marketed mostly exploiting the fact that the 'gift with reservation' rules (Finance Act 1986, s 102(5)) do not apply to inter-spouse transfers. The schemes would commonly involve some combination of a trust creating a life or lesser interest for the settlor's spouse and one or more discretionary trusts with the settlor as one of the discretionary beneficiaries. The consequence was that although the settlor would de facto remain in occupation of the property the transfer of property was taken outside the scope of the gift with reservation rules in s 102 (see eg *IRC v Eversden* [2003] STC 822).

The Inland Revenue responded in the Finance Act 2003 to counter such schemes but this did not prevent still more novel schemes being marketed to clients – estimated at 30,000 by the Inland Revenue – to try to achieve the ends sought by the taxpayer. In 2004 the Inland Revenue sharply changed tack and in effect accepted that it was possible to give away assets yet still benefit from them without the assets entering the estate for IHT purposes. Instead an unexpected and controversial riposte from the Inland Revenue was to introduce with effect from 6 April 2005 a free-standing charge to income tax – a 'pre-owned assets tax' – on the deemed value of the benefit the taxpayer gains from enjoyment of the formerly owned assets (Finance Act 2004, Sch 15; see Chamberlain [2004] BTR 5 at 486–493; Whitehouse [2004] PCB 3 at 128). In the case of residential property, for instance, a 'market rent' will provide the basis for the valuation whilst for other assets a specified percentage of the capital value will be used. There is a de minimis threshold of £5,000 but above that a rate of 40% will be charged. Although the point scarcely needed stating in light of the measure proposed, the Paymaster General, Dawn Primarolo, in the Standing Committee on the Finance Bill emphasised that the government wanted 'to send a clear message that artificial avoidance of that kind is not acceptable. Those who devise and market such schemes and the people who take advantage of them, need to understand that and not assume that avoidance is risk-free' (18 May 2004, col 238).

(c) Settled property: a continuous revolution?

Prior to the Finance Act 2006 it was possible to view the IHT treatment of trusts as being reasonably settled and relatively benign to the taxpayer. This is not to say that matters were completely straightforward as there were in effect two separate IHT regimes. The approach adopted under IHT was to divide settled property broadly into two categories and tax them by different methods. The basic distinction drawn was between settled property where some person was beneficially entitled to an interest in possession (eg a life-interest) and settled property in which there was no interest in possession (eg a discretionary trust), or 'relevant property' as it was termed in the legislation. Under the interest in possession tax structure, the IHT approach was one of 'transparency' although predicated on the fiction of the trust fund itself, not merely the income entitlement, being 'owned' by the beneficiary. By contrast the approach to a 'relevant property' trust was 'personification', treating the trust itself as the taxable entity. This straightforward duality was then modified by the fact that out of the 'relevant property' category was carved one particular group of settlements that received favourable tax treatment, accumulation and maintenance trusts ('A and M trusts'), broadly meaning trusts for minors – eg grandchildren of a common grandparent – but where no beneficiary had an interest in possession. Where a trust fell within the conditions specified for 'A and M trusts' in IHTA 1984, s 71 it was relieved from the normal tax charges applicable to 'relevant property'. In short the 'A and M' trust provided many of the benefits of the discretionary trust without being taxed as one.

There is one further important feature to emphasise about the treatment of different trust types under IHT. Gifts into 'A and M' trusts or into interest in possession trusts were, like outright gifts, 'potentially exempt transfers' (PETs). In contrast gifts into 'relevant property' trusts were 'chargeable transfers'. The following simple and improbable example drawn from 2004–05 when the above provisions still applied illustrates the consequence of this differential approach:

(1) A makes a transfer of value of £273,000 into an 'A and M' trust. This is a PET and no IHT is payable unless A dies within seven years and the transfer does not enter the cumulative total.

(2) A makes a similar transfer into, for example, a discretionary trust which is a chargeable transfer that exceeds the nil rate threshold by £10,000 and IHT of £2,000 (at 2004–05 rates: 20% rather than the 40% payable on chargeable transfers at death) is immediately chargeable even if A should survive for seven years.

This overall structure that had remained largely unaltered for 20 years was, as briefly mentioned previously, turned upside down with the introduction of radical changes in the Finance Act 2006. One consequence of the changes is that there will for the foreseeable future be a new dual IHT regime for trusts, largely reflecting whether a trust was created pre-22 March 2006 or after that date. The 'radical change' means in effect that, with very limited exceptions (see p 406), all trusts created post-21 March 2006 will now be subject to the 'relevant property' IHT regime, one widely perceived to be less sympathetic to trusts. A consequence is that the lifetime ('inter vivos') creation of a trust will now generally be a chargeable transfer and not, as was previously the case for non-'relevant property trusts', a PET. The 'very limited' exceptions comprise (i) trusts for disabled persons; (ii) will trusts for bereaved minors; (iii) age 18–25 trusts; and (iv) immediate 'post-death interest in possession trusts' (see (g) below).

As with the treatment of trusts under the other taxes discussed in this chapter, our treatment of the detail of the tax arrangements is somewhat cursory. Our principal concern is with the principles underpinning the tax treatment of trusts, in particular the notion of 'fiscal parity' between property owned outright and that held in trusts. That was stated to be the underpinning principle at the inception of CTT in 1974: 'in general the charge to tax should be neither greater nor smaller than the charge on property held absolutely' (*White Paper on Capital Transfer Tax* (Cmnd 5705, 1974) para 17). Whilst the principle of parity has been broadly accepted by both Conservative and Labour governments, any attainment of parity has been rendered problematic in practice by the complexity and flexibility of beneficial ownership facilitated by the trust form. Whether present or past structures of IHT satisfy the parity principle or, indeed, whether parity is a realisable or desirable goal will be assessed after we have examined the IHT treatment of the different trust types. In addressing these considerations we will look first at the pre-22 March 2006 IHT rules and their application to key trust types (sections d–f), and then review some of the changes introduced by the FA 2006 (section g). Lastly (section h) we will return to the questions posed above about the appropriateness for and applicability of the parity principle to IHT. A subsidiary yet important focus in our coverage is to explore the interplay between the flexibility offered to trust users and their advisers by the trust form and the attempts of the tax legislator to accommodate or counter this flexibility.

(d) Pre-22 March 2006 rules: interest in possession trusts

(1) Interest in possession trusts: the charge to IHT

Where there is an interest in possession, the method of imposing IHT liability stems directly from that applicable to estate duty. The trust is regarded as transparent, the person entitled to the income being treated as beneficially owning the relevant portion of the trust capital (IHTA 1984, ss 49(1), 50(1)). This is, of course, a fiction since the life-tenant has no entitlement to capital. Nevertheless, if A is the tenant of a settled fund worth £100,000, for IHT purposes it is as if she owns the capital of the fund, and if A has an interest in half the fund, it is as if she owns half the capital and so on. Two important consequences flow from this method of attributing ownership. First, since the capital is regarded for IHT purposes as belonging to the life-tenant it therefore forms part of her total estate and when a chargeable event affecting the settled property occurs it is the rate applicable to the beneficiary (A) that determines the IHT payable. The second consequence is that no charge to IHT arises if capital is distributed to A, since she is receiving merely what she is already deemed to own, and there is no fall in the value of her total estate. It should also be noted that since life-tenants have the full value of the capital attributed to them, reversionary interests are generally excluded from the charge to IHT (see IHTA 1984, s 48(1) for exceptions to this rule). If holders of reversionary interests were treated as owning a proportion of the capital also, the total valuation would exceed 100% and an element of double taxation would arise.

Consistent with attempting to achieve parity with property owned absolutely, a charge to IHT can arise on the death of the deemed beneficial owner. On the other hand, prior to 22 March 2006, a termination or disposal of an interest in possession during the income beneficiary's lifetime (eg by surrendering or assigning the interest) would have been a PET provided that it was in favour of (F(No 2)A 1987, s 96):

(i) an individual, either absolutely or under a new interest in possession trust,
(ii) an accumulation and maintenance trust, or a trust for a disabled person.

A disposition into a discretionary trust was, however, not a PET and a charge to IHT might, therefore, have arisen immediately. This is now also the position for any post 21 March 2006 lifetime termination of an interest in possession unless, after termination, the property is owned outright by an individual or is held on trust for a disabled person. Transfers into a new interest in possession trust or an 'A and M' trust would now be chargeable transfers.

(2) The meaning of an 'interest in possession'

The concept of 'interest in possession' is one familiar in property and trusts law. It is also central to the working of the pre-22 March 2006 IHT regime for settled property and remains relevant, although to a much reduced extent, for some post-21 March 2006 settlements. Regrettably, however, the phrase 'beneficially entitled to an interest in possession' is nowhere defined in the legislation. Did this absence of definition therefore mean that the recognised property and trusts law interpretation of 'interest in possession' also applied for the purposes of IHT? The Inland Revenue's published view ([1976] BTR 418) was that:

> ... an interest in [possession in] settled property exists where the person having the interest has the *immediate entitlement* (subject to any prior claims by the trustees for expenses or other outgoings properly payable out of income) to *any income* produced by that property as the income arises; but ... a discretion or power, in whatever form, which can be exercised *after income arises so* as to withhold it from that person negatives the existence of an interest in possession. For this purpose a power to accumulate income is regarded as a power to withhold it, unless any accumulation must be held solely for the person having the interest or his personal representatives.
>
> On the other hand the existence of a mere power of revocation or appointment, the exercise of which would determine the interest wholly or in part (but which, so long as it remains unexercised, does not affect the beneficiary's immediate entitlement to income) does not ... [in the Board's view] prevent the interest from being an interest in possession.

The House of Lords considered the meaning of 'interest in possession' in *Pearson v IRC* [1980] 2 All ER 479 and by a 3:2 majority, reversing unanimous Court of Appeal and Chancery Division judgments, broadly endorsed the Inland Revenue view. Central to the case was the meaning of trusts law concepts and their applicability to the fiscal legislation.

The facts of *Pearson* are quite simple. The settlor, Sir Richard Pilkington, created a trust in 1964 primarily for the benefit of his three daughters, including one Fiona, on attaining the age of 21. By the end of February 1974 all were over 21 and both capital and income of the trust fund was then held for them in equal shares. Their entitlement, however, was subject to (i) a power of appointment in favour of a wider class, and (ii) a power to accumulate income for a maximum period of 21 years. The trustees who had regularly accumulated the income exercised the power of appointment in favour of Fiona to give her an irrevocable interest in £16,000. This clearly constituted an interest in possession. But the Inland Revenue, in line with its published stance, argued that no prior interest in possession had subsisted in the trust because of the existence of the power of accumulation, and therefore CTT (of £444.73) was assessed on the distribution.

Fox J ([1979] 1 All ER 273) and a unanimous Court of Appeal ([1979] 3 All ER 7) rejected the Inland Revenue's claim. Fox J defined an interest in possession as 'a present right to present enjoyment', an interpretation accepted by the Court of Appeal and by at least one of the majority judges, Viscount Dilhorne, in the House of Lords. Where the majority of their Lordships differed from all the other judges was in their application of the test.

Compare Fox J's and Lord Russell's analysis of the consequences of the power of accumulation with that of Viscount Dilhorne:

Pearson v IRC [1979] 1 All ER 273 at 281

Fox J: The position as to the trustees' power of accumulation, as I understand it, is this. The power is purely permissive. The trustees are not bound to exercise it. If they do exercise it, they must do so within a reasonable period after the income has arisen: see *Re Allen-Meyrick's Will Trusts* [1966] 1 All ER 740 and *Re Locker's Settlement Trusts* [1978] 1 All ER 216.

The result, it seems to me, is that the daughters would be entitled as of right to income of their shares in each of the following circumstances: (a) if the trustees decide not to accumulate that income; (b) if the trustees fail to agree as to whether they should accumulate or not; (c) if the trustees, having allowed a reasonable period to elapse after receipt of income, have reached no decision whether to accumulate or not. In each of those cases the daughter will be entitled to the income as of right. She will be entitled to it, not because the trustees have decided to give it to her (as would be the case of . . . the discretionary objects in *Gartside v IRC* [1968] 1 All ER 121) but because she is entitled to it in right of what is, beyond doubt, her interest in the trust fund. She is entitled to it by reason of her vested interest . . . In *Gartside v IRC* the beneficiaries got nothing unless the trustees decided to give it to them. In the present case the daughters are absolutely entitled to income unless the trustees decide to accumulate that income.

Pearson v IRC [1980] 2 All ER 479 (Viscount Dilhorne, Lords Keith and Lane; Lords Salmon and Russell dissenting)

Viscount Dilhorne: All we have to decide is whether, on reaching 21, Fiona and her sisters acquired interests in possession in settled property. In other words had they then a present right of present enjoyment of anything?

As to that, there are, it seems to me, two possible conclusions. The first is that, the power of appointment under cl 2 not having been exercised, the three sisters on reaching that age acquired interests in possession defeasible should the trustees decide to exercise their power to accumulate income. They were then entitled absolutely to the capital and income of the trust fund in equal shares subject to the exercise of that power. The second is that they never secured an interest in possession for they never acquired on reaching that age the right to the enjoyment of anything. Their enjoyment of any income from the trust fund depended on the trustees' decision as to the accumulation of income. They would only have a right to any income from the trust fund if the trustees decided it should not be accumulated or if they failed to agree that it should be or if they delayed a decision on this matter for so long that a decision then to accumulate and withhold income from the sisters would have been unreasonable.

As I read their judgments, the courts below took the first view. Reluctant as I am to differ from judges so experienced in the law relating to trusts, I find myself unable to agree with them. Fox J held that ([1979] 1 All ER 273 at 278):

'. . . the interest of a person who is entitled to the income of property subject only to a power in the trustees to accumulate is in possession . . . it is a present interest, giving a present right to *whatever is not accumulated*.' (My emphasis.)

In *Gartside v IRC* [1968] 1 All ER 121 at 128, an estate duty case, Lord Reid said:

'"In possession" must mean that your interest enables you to claim now whatever may be the subject of the interest. For instance, if it is the current income from a certain fund your claim may yield nothing if there is no income, but your claim is a valid claim, and if there is any income you are entitled to get it; but a right to require trustees to consider whether they will pay you something does not enable you to claim anything. If the trustees do decide to pay you something, you do not get it by reason of having the right to have your case considered; you get it only because the trustees have decided to give it to you.'

That case concerned a discretionary trust where payment was made to the beneficiaries at the discretion of the trustees. Here the three sisters' entitlement to income was subject to the trustees' power to accumulate. On reaching 21 they had no valid claim to anything. If there was any income from the settled property, they were not entitled to it. Their right to anything depended on what the trustees did or did not do and the receipt of income by them appears to me to have been just as much at the discretion of the trustees as was the receipt of income by the beneficiaries in the *Gartside* case.

It was recognised by the trustees that, if cl 3 had created a trust to accumulate subject to which the trust fund was to be held in trust for the three sisters absolutely on their attaining 21, they would not have secured an interest in possession on reaching that age. It makes all the difference, so it was said, that the trustees were not under a duty to accumulate but only had power to do so if they thought fit. I am not able to accept this for in neither case can it in my opinion be said that the sisters on attaining that age secured the right to the present enjoyment of anything.

Fox J in the course of his judgment distinguished... *Gartside v IRC* [1968] 1 All ER 121 from the present case on the ground that [there] 'the beneficiaries got nothing unless the trustees decided to give it to them' whereas in the present case the sisters 'were absolutely entitled to income unless the trustees decided to accumulate' ([1979] 1 All ER 273 at 281). I do not think that that is the case. I do not read the trust deed as providing that. Clause 3(a) gives the trustees power to accumulate as they think fit and the sisters' entitlement depends on whether that power is exercised. If it were the case that the deed did so provide, then I would agree that the sisters had a defeasible interest in possession. Such an interest may be terminated by the exercise of a power of revocation or of an overriding power of appointment such as that contained in cl 2 in this case. The existence of such a power does not prevent the holding of an interest in possession prior to the exercise of the power, and, until it is exercised, the holder of the interest has a present right of present enjoyment.

A distinction has in my opinion to be drawn between the exercise of a power to terminate a present right to present enjoyment and the exercise of a power which prevents a present right of present enjoyment arising.

Lord Russell (dissenting): The crucial question in my opinion, lies in the well-known distinction between a trust and a power, a distinction recognised by this House in *McPhail v Doulton* and there only regretted as a distinction which might lead in a given case to invalidity of the disposition. [This] is clearly a case of a mere power to accumulate, as distinct from a trust to accumulate unless and to the extent to which the trustees exercised a power to pay allowances to the sisters or any of them. The sisters were able to say that as income accrued on the £16,000 they were then entitled to that income, subject to the possibility that the trustees might *subsequently divert* it from them by a decision to accumulate it. (Indeed but for the cl 2 power of appointment, and the possibility until the death of the settlor in December 1976 of the birth of further children, they were notwithstanding the power of accumulation, entitled to claim transfer of the £16,000.)... The case is distinguishable from the case of a discretionary trust of income among a class, as in *Gartside v IRC.*

The reasoning of the majority judgment has been criticised in part as being purportedly based on misconceptions about principles of property law and the differences between trusts and powers. (See Thomas *Taxation and Trusts* (1981) pp 180–194; Tiley (1980) 39 CLJ 256; cf Murphy (1980) 43 MLR 712.) Yet, as Thomas conceded, a plausible explanation for the majority judgment is that it is a 'policy decision' plain and simple (at p 193):

Ultimately, perhaps all we can and need say about *Pearson* is that it is a straightforward 'policy decision'.

...Had *Pearson* been decided differently, it might have opened up the way for the rehabilitation of the discretionary trust in a new form and to other methods of tax avoidance. Trustees would have enjoyed not just the benefits of the interest in possession regime but also the flexibility of a discretionary trust as regards distribution of income. Moreover, accumulation of income would have been possible for beneficiaries over the age of 25 without endangering the 'interest in possession status' of the trust (which is only possible now for 'under 25s' under an accumulation and maintenance trust). Amending legislation would no doubt have followed. The majority of the House of Lords, however, simply refused to aid and abet in a decision which defeated legislative policy, despite the fact that the problem at issue had been manifest when CTT was introduced and that the government had simply refused to do anything about it.

The 'flexibility of a discretionary trust' would have been obtained by virtue of the combined effect of the power of accumulation and overriding power of appointment. As explained by Murphy ((1980) 43 MLR 712 at 715): 'The existence of the accumulation power means that the trustees can divert all of the trust income and capitalise it. Once capitalised, it is subject to the overriding power and thus can be appointed away from the daughters.'

Consider the following points:

(1) It might be said that the minority judges sought to apply principles of property and trusts law whereas the majority pragmatically considered only the practical consequences for IHT of the operation of those principles. Indeed it has been suggested ((1981) 97 LQR 3) that *Pearson* 'marks a significant departure from the normal approach to the taxation of settlements whereby the fiscal provisions are construed in the light of and superimposed on traditional concepts of trust and property law'. Does the division of settlements for IHT purposes into only two categories necessitate such a 'novel' approach? What inference, if any, as to the judicial approach to be adopted in defining an interest in possession should be drawn from the absence of a statutory definition of the concept?

(2) Thomas suggests (p 194) that 'the application of the trust/power distinction – which is, after all, fundamental to the law of trusts in general, defining as it does the extent and nature of a trustee's obligation and of the beneficiary's rights and interests – would have made for a more coherent and comprehensible conclusion'. Do you agree that, post-*McPhail v Doulton*, the trust/power distinction is 'fundamental' in this context? Which approach in *Pearson* do you consider to be more consistent with the reasoning of Lord Wilberforce in *McPhail v Doulton* (see Chapter 5) – that of the House of Lords majority or the minority (including Fox J)?

(3) If a power of accumulation prevented an interest in possession arising, should the existence of a power 'to apply income towards the payment of any taxes, or other costs or outgoings, which would otherwise be payable out of capital' have the same effect? The Inland Revenue contended that the *existence* of the power was a further reason why there was no interest in possession prior to the appointment in favour of Fiona. Viscount Dilhorne, drawing a distinction between administrative and dispositive powers, held obiter, without giving reasons, that such a power fell on the administrative

side of the line and hence would not have invalidated an interest in possession. Note, however, that the power could by its terms be used not just to pay trust management expenses (clearly 'administrative') but could also be applied to other expenses and taxes (eg CGT and IHT charges) which would normally be payable out of the capital of the fund (arguably 'dispositive'). In any event Viscount Dilhorne's observations were obiter and it seems that HMRC is still adhering to the position the Inland Revenue adopted in *Pearson*. Consequently such clauses are best avoided! (See *Thomas* pp 186–189; Jopling [1982] BTR 105 at 110–113; and *Miller v IRC* [1987] STC 108.)

(e) Pre-22 March 2006 rules: 'relevant property'

(1) The structure of the charging provisions

The term 'discretionary trust' does not appear in IHTA 1984. Instead the umbrella term used to identify settlements with no interest in possession is 'relevant property'. 'Relevant property' is defined in IHTA 1984, s 58(1) as 'settled property in which no qualifying interest in possession exists', other than those trusts specified in s 58 as receiving favoured treatment. The category of favoured settlements included, before 22 March 2006, 'A and M' trusts, but since the changes introduced in the FA 2006 this category is restricted to the much more limited types of trust described in section (g) below.

The method of taxing 'relevant property' contrasts sharply with the transparency approach adopted for settlements with an interest in possession. In general each settlement is personified, although settlements created before 27 March 1974 (pre-CTT settlements) are treated slightly differently from those created after that date. The basic principle for pre-CTT settlements is that each trust is treated as if it is a separate person with no record of previous chargeable transfers, ie all connection with the settlor is severed. For post-CTT settlements, however, the settlor's record of previous chargeable transfers at the commencement of the settlement is crucial in determining the rate of tax charged. This approach might be more aptly regarded as part personification and part mirror-image.

Personifying the trust, however, would not in itself be sufficient to solve the problem of identifying a taxable event in the life of a discretionary trust, the type of trust for which the 'relevant property' rules were primarily devised. For example, if the basis of the charge to tax were to be when capital is distributed from the trust it would be possible to postpone a charge until the termination of the trust at the end of the perpetuity period. This could be some eighty years or even longer if an appropriate 'lives in being' clause was selected. The premise underlying the approach eventually adopted is that property owned outright is charged to IHT once a generation, ie approximately every thirty years. In an attempt to achieve parity the solution therefore arrived at is (i) to impose a charge to IHT on the settlor when property is first settled; (ii) to impose a tax of 30% of a normal IHT charge at lifetime rates on the settled property every ten years (the periodic charge), and (iii) to impose a charge whenever property in the settlement ceases to be 'relevant property', usually termed an interim or exit charge. Hence if the trust terminates or property is distributed to beneficiaries or an interest in possession is appointed in any portion of the fund, an IHT charge will be imposed to the extent of the property ceasing to be held on discretionary trusts. But why, it might be wondered, opt for a ten-year periodic charge? The justification is apparently a pragmatic compromise (*CTT and Settled Property* (1980) para 4.4.4):

> The present system is in effect a compromise between imposing a full charge once a generation – which would be less equitable than the present system – and achieving maximum equity by a system of annual charges – which would produce considerably more work for both the Revenue and taxpayers. This compromise does not seem unreasonable.

The three key elements, therefore, in taxation under the 'relevant property' rules are the timing of the charge to tax, the property to be taxed and the rate of tax to be charged.

(2) The timing of the charge and the property to be taxed

The periodic charge is to be levied on the tenth anniversary of the commencement date of a settlement and on every subsequent ten-year anniversary. The charge is imposed on the value of 'relevant property' comprised in the settlement immediately before the anniversary date as illustrated in the following example (IHTA 1984, s 64).

Example 1

On 1 May 1999 A, having made previous chargeable transfers of £210,000, settles £50,000 on discretionary trusts. On 1 May 2009, the ten-year anniversary, the value of the fund is £200,000 and that is the amount chargeable to tax under the periodic charge.

Once the amount on which tax is chargeable is known, the next step is to discover the *rate* of tax applicable. The calculation is somewhat complex not least because it is based on a purely hypothetical transfer that takes into account both the cumulative chargeable transfers made by the settlor in the seven years preceding the creation of the settlement and chargeable transfers made out of the settlement (see Lee (ed) *Revenue Law: Principles and Practice* (26th edn 2008) pp 912–915 for a clear yet comprehensive example). For our purposes it is sufficient just to note that since the highest lifetime rate of IHT is 20% (half of 40%) the highest effective rate that could be charged would be 30% of the lifetime IHT rate 20%, ie 6%. Moreover, where the settlement comprises business property qualifying for 50% relief, this effective rate falls to 3% and assuming that the option to pay in instalments (see IHTA 1984, s 227) is exercised, the annual charge over the ten-year period becomes a mere 0.3%.

If the property qualifies for 100% business or agricultural property relief, there is no periodic IHT charge at all.

The other possible 'relevant property' IHT charge is the exit charge which is in general a proportion of the previous periodic charge. The exit charge is levied on the amount by which 'relevant property' is reduced by the chargeable event. This, in effect, follows basic IHT principles and consequently, unless the transferee pays IHT, the value will have to be grossed-up to calculate the tax.

Example 2

Taking the facts of Example 1, on 1 May 2010 a life-interest in £20,000 is appointed to a beneficiary who pays the tax. No grossing-up is necessary, so the amount chargeable to tax is £20,000. The relevant proportion of time for calculating the exit charge is the number of quarter years completed since the last ten-year charge, divided by the total number of quarters in a ten-year period, each ten-year period being conveniently divided into forty quarters. In our example the relevant proportion would be four-fortieths and that proportion is then applied to the rate charged on the preceding ten-year anniversary to determine the exit rate of tax to be charged. That rate of tax is then applied to the amount of £20,000.

(f) Pre-22 March 2006 rules: accumulation and maintenance trusts

Prior to 22 March 2006 some settlements in which there was no interest in possession were nevertheless excluded by IHTA 1984, s 58(1) from the definition of 'relevant property' and received favoured treatment for IHT purposes. The most important, conceptually and numerically, were accumulation and maintenance trusts ('A and M trusts') – broadly meaning trusts for minors where there is no interest in possession. Where a trust came within the conditions specified for 'A and M trusts' in IHTA 1984, s 71 it was relieved from the normal tax charges on 'relevant property'.

The creation of an 'A and M trust' was a PET and therefore did not usually incur an IHT charge. Thereafter, there was no periodic charge, and no exit charge when a beneficiary obtained an interest in possession or became absolutely entitled to the settled property (IHTA 1984, s 71(4)(a)). Furthermore, no charge was imposed on the death of a beneficiary before attaining the specified age (not exceeding twenty-five). In effect 'A and M trusts' were treated as transparent: once the trust had been created the settled property was thereafter treated as belonging to the beneficiary (or beneficiaries).

What explanation can be offered for the apparently favourable treatment offered to 'A and M' trusts? A clue can be found in one well-known guide to tax planning (*Potter and Monroe's Tax Planning* (9th edn, 1982), written before the shift from CTT to IHT, that explained the favoured treatment in terms of both social desirability and parity between gifts to adults and gifts on trust to infants (at pp 65–66):

It is usually thought undesirable to give minors property absolutely or even to give them a right to the income of the property. On the other hand, it is normally desirable that the income should be available to be used for their maintenance, if required. The most usual type of trust for minors or young persons is thus an accumulation and maintenance trust. This means, broadly, that the income is accumulated until the beneficiary attains a specified age...but the trustees are empowered to use the income (including the accumulated income) for the maintenance of the beneficiary. Until the beneficiary reaches the age at which he becomes entitled to income, there will clearly be no interest in possession. Unless a special provision were made for this type of trust, it would be liable to the periodic charge and to a further charge when the minor or young person became entitled to the settled property, either absolutely or for an interest in possession. Because of the undesirability of forcing settlors to give minors or young persons an interest in possession purely for fiscal reasons, the legislature has quite wisely conferred a special exemption on this type of trust...Of course, to prevent such trusts being abused they must comply with stringent conditions.

The 'stringent conditions' designed to counter avoidance attempts were specified in IHTA 1984, s 71(1) and (2). The intention was that the benefit of the 'A and M trust' should be restricted to the minors of one generation only. Section 71(2) therefore provided that if property was settled for the benefit of the settlor's children and grandchildren the trust could last for only 25 years as an 'A and M trust' (s 71(2)(a)). This restriction did not apply where there was a grandparent common to all the beneficiaries (s 72(1)(b)), a provision potentially advantageous for effective generation-skipping transfers of wealth. The conditions did not therefore prove so stringent as to prevent 'A and M' settlements being effective for tax purposes. In the words of the most recent edition of one prominent text: 'Accumulation and maintenance settlements which, correctly designed, may shelter capital from taxes as we know them for anything up to 80 years... (depending upon the longevity of the beneficiaries) have been understandably popular' (Hutton *Tolley's UK Taxation of Trusts* (16th edn, 2006) para 10.29).

The Finance Act 2006 brought an end to the privileged treatment of 'A and M' settlements. Although some special but more restrictive IHT provision is made for property settled on minors after 21 March 2006 (see eg IHTA 1984, s 71D, p 405), the practical consequence is that the creation of any trust that does not comply with the new provisions will no longer qualify as a PET and the trust will subsequently be liable for the periodic and exit charges under the 'relevant property' rules. But what of those many 'A and M' trusts already in existence at that time? These trust assets too will become subject to the 'relevant property' rules unless the terms of the trust provide for the assets to go to a beneficiary *absolutely* on their attaining age 25 (or earlier) or the terms were modified before 6 April 2008 to provide this (IHTA 1984, s 71D).

One key aspect of the qualifying conditions for an 'A and M' trust was the meaning to be attached to the phrase 'will...become beneficially entitled to [the property].' (IHTA 1984, s 71(1)(a)). This same phrase is retained (with the substitution of 'absolutely entitled' for 'beneficially entitled') in the new s 71D added by the FA 2006 as a qualifying condition for an '18–25' trust established under a parent's will. It is therefore convenient here to consider the dispute that arose about the meaning of 'will'. Plainly, absolute certainty is not possible since a beneficiary might die before reaching the age when entitlement becomes absolute. But if absolute certainty is not necessary, what degree of certainty will suffice? The context for this issue is provided by the capacity of the trust-form to be made almost infinitely flexible as regards certainty of beneficial entitlement. The use of appropriately worded powers of revocation and appointment could open up the possibility of creating what was in form an 'A and M trust' but in its operation might more closely have resembled a discretionary trust. Should, therefore, the inclusion in a trust of wide powers of revocation and re-appointment, possibly to benefit a person at an age exceeding 25, have prevented a trust from satisfying IHTA 1984, s 71(1)(a)? The competing interpretations are summarised together with respective policy justifications in the following extract from *CTT and Settled Property* (1980) para 4.8.7, and were the subject of litigation in *Inglewood v IRC* [1983] 1 WLR 366.

The Inland Revenue's view is that (with some exceptions) the word 'will' means that a person will *inevitably* become entitled. The alternative view is that the condition will be satisfied if the trusts operating at the time the test has to be applied provide that a person will become entitled – ie the conditions can be satisfied even though the trusts are revocable so that it is in fact uncertain who will benefit or when. It has been suggested that, whatever the correct interpretation of the present legislation, the second view gives a fairer result. But this seems open to question. The essence of the present relief is that it is available where there is a commitment for property to devolve on a person before he attains the age of 25. Under the alternative view the relief would be available in a case where, in the event, that never happened (and perhaps was never intended to happen).

Inglewood v IRC [1983] 1 WLR 366 (Oliver, Fox and Robert Goff LJJ)

Fox LJ (delivering the judgment of the court): . . . Suppose that property is held upon trust for A, a minor, absolutely upon attaining the age of 25 but subject to a power in the trustees to revoke that trust and to appoint the property to other persons in such manner as the trustees determine. Can it be said, having regard to the power of revocation, that A 'will' become entitled to the property on attaining 25? [Fox LJ outlined the changes wrought by the introduction of CTT, set out the terms of the trust deed including the power of revocation and re-appointment and then turned to consider the arguments advanced by counsel for the appellant trustees, including reference to a number of anomalous cases which, on the Inland Revenue's construction, fell outside the scope of s 71(1)(a).]

> ...[The] word 'will' may be capable of such a construction as the trustees put on it in the present case, and we think it necessary therefore to examine the implications of the rival constructions to see what light they throw upon the matter and whether what appears to us to be the clear prima facie meaning of the language used is displaced....
>
> We accept that these examples, and others which can be given, demonstrate the existence, on the Crown's construction, of hard cases. But this is often so in statutes which lay down conditions for the applicability of a section. Illogicalities and hardships may occasionally result...
>
> Looking at the whole matter more widely it appears to us unlikely that Parliament can have intended that a trust should have the benefit of [s 71(1)] if it was subject to a power of revocation which could be exercised for the benefit of other persons at ages exceeding 25. The Finance Act 1975 plainly continued and extended the policy of the Finance Act 1969 of reducing the fiscal advantages enjoyed by discretionary trusts. It did that by imposing the discretionary trust regime. That regime was burdensome on trusts for persons contingently upon attaining a specified age – which are necessarily very common because it is undesirable to give capital to persons absolutely at too early an age. [Section 71(1)] was enacted accordingly. Existing trusts could be converted into [section 71(1)] trusts at low rates of tax.... Parliament, having decided on assistance for contingent trusts, would, it seems to us, in the context of this legislation, be likely to confine it within fairly strict boundaries. In particular, it seems to us, highly unlikely that the benefit of [s 71(1)] was intended to be available to what were, in effect, discretionary trusts, by reason of the existence of wide powers of revocation and re-appointment, merely by the device of a primary trust for a person at 25 which could be revoked at any time.

The Court dismissed the appeal.

(g) Post-21 March 2006 rules

(1) Introduction

As mentioned previously, the whole structure of taxation of trusts under IHT was radically altered in the FA 2006 in two particularly significant respects. First, whereas before 22 March 2006 most trusts, other than discretionary trusts, created during the settlor's lifetime qualified as PETs in the same way as outright transfers into the absolute ownership of an individual, the position now is starkly different. After 21 March 2006 the only such trust that can qualify as a PET is an interest in possession trust in favour of a disabled person. The lifetime creation of any other trust will therefore now be a chargeable transfer and subject to IHT where it exceeds the current nil rate band (£325,000 in 2009–10). The other major change is that save for the few exceptions to be discussed shortly, one of which is the trust for a disabled person, any trust created after 21 March 2006 will be subject to the 'relevant property' regime that applied predominantly to discretionary trusts under the previous arrangements.

(2) Exceptional cases not subject to the 'relevant property' regime

Disabled person's trust (IHTA 1984, ss 89, 89A and B) This is a trust created in favour of a disabled person under which that person is treated for IHT purposes as the beneficial owner of the trust property and to which the pre-2006 rules for interest in possession (IIP) trusts (s 49) continue to apply. The definition of disability is widely drawn so as to include not just mental incapacity but also, for instance, eligibility to receive certain types of social security allowances for the disabled (see s 89(4)–(6)).

Immediate post-death interest trusts (IPDI) (IHTA 1984, s 49(1)A) These are interest in possession trusts that can be established only under a will. A common example would be a life interest trust of a testator's residuary estate for a spouse. As with a disabled person's trust, an IPDI trust will be subject to the established pre-2006 s 49 rules for an IIP trust.

Bereaved minor trusts (BMT) (IHTA 1984, s 71A) As the name implies, these are trusts that can be created only by will (or that arise on intestacy or, rarely, under the Criminal Injuries Compensation Scheme) and only to benefit a minor child of the testator. Also they must specify for the beneficiary to become absolutely entitled at 18 to the trust property and any income arising from it. Whilst the IHT treatment of these trusts is broadly similar to that for the no-longer-available 'A and M' trusts – eg no periodic or exit charges nor any charge on the premature death of the beneficiary – these qualifying conditions are significantly more restrictive than those that applied to those trusts (see above, p 403).

18-25 trusts (IHTA 1984, s 71D) Broadly speaking the same qualifying criteria apply to these trusts as have to be met by a BMT. A difference is that a special IHT charging regime (s 71F) operates for events, such as the death of a beneficiary, that might occur between the ages of 18 and 25.

(3) Finance Act 2006 and a policy conundrum

So, the curious reader might ask, do these changes indicate a change of policy towards the IHT treatment of trusts? Do they mean, for instance, that the premise – 'to put property into settlement is the appropriate way for providing for the next generation' (Inland Revenue *CTT and Settled Property* (1980) para 4.8) – can no longer be regarded as sustainable or, at least, must be subordinated to a policy of parity of treatment between property held in trust and property owned outright? The pages of Hansard do not always provide the clearest evidence on such matters but the Paymaster General, Dawn Primarolo, advanced the following explanation for the IHT changes during the Standing Committee Debate on the Finance (No 2) Bill on 13 June 2006 (cols 569–571):

The majority of people who have assets leave them to others outright when they die, but some choose to set up trusts as a way of passing on their wealth. Because trusts do not die, there is no natural occasion on which inheritance tax might be paid, so it disappears into a labyrinth. . . . The two types of trust that have, until now, been exempt from the [IHT discretionary trust] charges are accumulation and maintenance trusts and interest in possession trusts. There is no clear rationale for privileging those trusts in that way, and it has become clear that some wealthy individuals have taken advantage of that special treatment as a convenient way of sheltering their wealth from inheritance tax. That is clearly unfair . . . and contributes to the widely held notion . . . that IHT is optional, at least for the very rich.

The measure that was announced goes to the heart of the difference between money put into trusts and outright gifts. . . . It is somewhat simplistic to think that the two activities are identical just because they received the same inheritance tax treatment in the past. The recipient of a gift can do whatever they want with it. . . . Things are quite different for the beneficiary of a trust. The beneficiary will only get what the trustees decide to give them. . . . [S]omeone making a gift relinquishes control of whatever they are giving. Someone setting up a trust does the opposite. . . . By leaving instructions for the trustees, the control of those who set up trusts can linger long after they have died . . . There is no reason why money in trusts should continue to be treated as akin to an outright gift when it is clearly not. Since there is already a tax regime designed to properly capture IHT on trust assets, it seems entirely logical for A and M trusts and IIP trusts to come under these rules. We believe that there should be no artificial incentive for setting up trusts because they provide an opportunity for an unfair inheritance tax advantage. . . . The tax regime for trusts is being brought into line so that there will be more fairness in how and when the rules bite.

It is possible to present the changes introduced in the FA 2006, Sch 20 as no more than a technical alignment of the IHT treatment of different trusts (see HMRC Budget Note 25 (2006 Budget) *Aligning the Inheritance Tax Treatment for Trusts*). It is questionable whether this 'technical alignment' perception is wholly consistent with the tenor of the Paymaster General's comments that appear to be directed, at least in part, to countering the tax avoidance opportunities offered by the trust. The alternative perceptions – 'alignment' or 'anti-avoidance' – are not incompatible if one sees the changes as intended to further the goal of attaining parity of treatment or 'fairness' between property owned outright and property held in trust. This brings us back to the fundamental problem that has bedevilled the IHT treatment of trusts: is parity attainable or, indeed, desirable?

(h) Inheritance tax and trusts: conclusion

(1) Tax, time and trusts

CTT was the tax that was going to cause 'howls of anguish from the 80,000 rich people' (Denis Healey speaking at the 1973 Labour Party Annual Conference).

In fact any howls have been muted: the yield to the Inland Revenue from CTT/IHT, after adjustment for inflation, had fallen in the two decades following the introduction of the tax by between 50 and 65%. On the other hand, the anticipated IHT yield for 2007–08 is £3,824m, an increase in real terms of around 50% since 1998–99. Any 'howls of anguish' are not to be heard so much from the top 5% of wealth-holders but are more likely to be forthcoming from those who have seen the increase in value of their home bring them potentially within the scope of IHT. The decline in the impact of CTT/IHT on those at whom it was originally targeted in large part reflects the many changes the tax has undergone under both Labour and Conservative governments in its existence. Yet it is the possibility of such changes, whether resulting from pressure-group activity or a new government with a different fiscal philosophy, that reinforces the trust's value as a mechanism able to utilise the plane of time. The removal of a transfer tax on lifetime gifts to individuals or, even though temporary, into 'A and M trusts' and interest in possession trusts has provided an opportunity for substantial tax-free transfers of wealth to the next generation. The influence of the time element is also demonstrated by the fall and rise of the discretionary trust coincident with changes in the prevailing tax regime. The CTT provisions in the FA 1975 affecting discretionary trusts were seen as penal. Thomas (*Taxation and Trusts* (1981)), for example, concluded that (p 79):

> [the] complex and punitive provisions enacted in the Finance Act 1975 have imposed considerable disadvantages on the discretionary trust: its value as a method of tax avoidance has been severely curtailed; and a settlor attracted by the non-fiscal advantages of such a trust will now have to be prepared to suffer heavy tax penalties.

The severity of the regime was mitigated by generous transitional provisions (FA 1975, Sch 5, para 14) presumably intended to encourage the termination of existing discretionary trusts. But not all advisers considered that termination was necessarily the most prudent policy – inactivity was also a tenable option. Hepker and Whitehouse (*Capital Transfer Tax* (1975)) counselled against precipitate decisions for the following political and financial reasons (p 135):

> For one thing the wealth tax may well redress the balance to some extent by giving discretionary trusts favourable treatment. For another there is bound to be a General Election before October 1979. It may therefore be wise to leave pre-27 March 1974 discretionary trusts intact until the position is clearer. The schedule of transitional relief ranges from 90% down to 80% between 27 March 1974 and 31 March 1980 and then on 1 April 1980 disappears, so that a policy of wait-and-see will involve very little loss of relief.

The period of transitional relief was extended to 1 April 1982 by F(No 2)A 1979 and subsequently to 1 April 1983.

In fact, a substantial shift of property out of discretionary trusts, at least to the estimated value of £2 billion, did occur between 1975 and 1980, of which approximately half was transferred into 'A and M trusts' (*CTT and Settled Property* (1980) App 2). Although the total number of UK-resident discretionary trusts (which includes 'A and M trusts') fell from an estimated high of 90,000 in 1975 to 55,000 in 1988, more recent HMRC statistics indicate a resurgence in their popularity with their number increasing to an estimated 107,000 (*HMRC Statistics 2008* Table 13.2; and see Inland Revenue Consultation Document *The Income Tax and CGT Treatment of UK Resident Trusts* (1991) para 2.6; Robson and Timmins *Discretionary Trusts* (1988)). Initially, changes in the cumulation period and the IHT regime for discretionary trusts in FA 1981 and 1982 respectively gave a new lease of life to the discretionary trust, although it must be conceded that it can no longer perform the amazing vanishing tricks so effectively demonstrated on the estate duty stage. Whilst IHT now encourages outright transfers of property, one tax planning specialist was at pains to emphasise that the potential of the discretionary trust both as a tax shelter for assets with high growth prospects and as a value-splitting device has not completely disappeared:

> Particularly since the reforms introduced by the Thatcher government, the discretionary trust, properly tailored, can be a splendid vehicle for the preservation of wealth in the family for a century or more with no, or comparatively insignificant, liability to [IHT]. No beneficiary will have any right of any value in the settled property and thus no [IHT] will be exigible on his death. If a donor makes a series of discretionary trusts each of small initial value at a time when he has only a very modest history of chargeable transfers of value still liable to be cumulated in calculating the tax on a present gift, the level of tax on the trusts themselves can be entirely manageable. (R Venables *Tax Planning Through Trusts* (1983) p 127)

This capacity of the trust to shelter assets from tax by combining fragmentation of ownership and control with exploitation of the plane of time can prove particularly valuable for family companies. Yet even here the chameleon character of the trust is evident; in the hypothetical example below, caretaker, dynastic and tax mitigation purposes are all present.

M Hutton *Tolley's UK Taxation of Trusts* (16th edn, 2006) paras 15.21–15.22

FAMILY COMPANIES

15.21 The rules for the valuation of shares in family companies are of long standing. They date back to the invention of estate duty in 1894 and have remained virtually unchanged since. Therefore, it would seem reasonable to expect these rules to be the basis of fiscal valuation for some time to come. These rules favour small minority holdings, each owned by a different taxpayer as compared with influential holdings.

15.22 An entrepreneur aged 30 feels that he has financial responsibility not only for his wife and one-year old child, but also for his parents who live on social security and on gifts from him. He wishes to start a new company with £3,000. He has made no previous chargeable transfers and can give away £3,000 within his annual exemption. He makes six settlements each of £500 on discretionary trusts for his father, mother, wife, his present child and any further children born in the next 30 years. After his death, his widow can benefit. The trustees of the settlements subscribe the entire £3,000 share capital of his new company (which is denominated into 3,000 £1 nominal value shares). He dies at the age of 60 when IHT rates, etc are the same as in 2006–07 [ie IHT threshold of £285,000]. The company could be worth, say, £2,500,000 on a take-over. One-sixth of its shares, put on the market as a single parcel, would be worth, say, £200,000. Therefore the total settled shares are:

(a) worth £2,500,000, and
(b) valued at £1,200,000 (ie £200,000 × 6)

and each settlement can distribute its holdings, without tax as follows:

	£
Valuation of 500 shares	200,000
5 related settlements valued at commencement	2,500
Chargeable to inheritance tax	202,500
Inheritance tax is NIL.	

There will, in the meantime, have been three ten-year charges but there can have been no tax unless the valuations on those occasions exceeded £285,000. An equally satisfactory result could probably have been obtained by the use of accumulation and maintenance settlements had it not been for the desire to protect the older generation.

Although not relevant to the above example, the retention of hold-over relief for CGT purposes on gifts into discretionary trusts could further enhance their attraction as a medium for transferring property. The consequence of a combination of CGT hold-over relief and IHT reliefs for business and agricultural property is that, as Hutton puts it (para 15.32), 'entrepreneurial families now have an infinite variety of plans open to them to prevent death causing a financial crisis'. The overall effect of these various reliefs is to take most family businesses and farms outside the IHT tax net altogether. But there is no guarantee that this scale of relief will always be available. Here again the trust has a part to play: 'If it is feared that the new reliefs will be withdrawn by a future government, a gift of property on to flexible trusts under which the donor retains control as trustee should be considered' (Lee (ed) *Revenue Law: Principles and Practice* (26th edn , 2008) para 31.61).

The element of time is not without its dangers for tax planning: time is an asset resting on a potentially insecure foundation. Its value is dependent in part on the absence of retrospective tax charges. By retrospective charge is meant one that applies to events taking place before the date on which the tax change was announced. It is commonly asserted, however, that retrospective amendment of liability to tax is as reprehensible as retrospective criminalisation. If, for example, lifetime cumulation periods were to be re-introduced for IHT, the not unreasonable assumption of tax planners is that it would only apply prospectively. It is, though, a nice question whether the introduction of the income tax charge on 'pre-owned assets' to counter IHT avoidance – a 'retroactive' not a 'retrospective' change in the words of the Paymaster General – offends against the principle. Consider also the position where HMRC seeks to challenge in the courts an existing practice by taxpayers; the concept of retrospectivity becomes blurred. The development, for example, of the *Ramsay* doctrine by the House of Lords is self-confessedly the exercise of a law-reforming function (see Lord Roskill [1984] CLP 247; and generally Chapter 3). The de facto retrospective consequences for taxpayers who purchased 'off-the-peg' CGT avoidance schemes in the 1970s were drastic. The Inland Revenue expected eventually to recover at least £400m from the general body of the purchasers of the schemes overturned in *Chinn v Collins* [1981] AC 533 and *W T Ramsay Ltd v IRC* [1981] 1 All ER 865 alone (34 HC Official Report (6th series) written answers cols 18–19, 13 December 1982; see also Millett (1982) 98 LQR 209 who refers to unofficial estimates that the decisions would yield the Exchequer 'in excess of £1,000m in tax from pending cases alone' and Tutt *The Tax Raiders: The Rossminster Affair* (1985) ch 9). Had Parliament legislated to counter such avoidance schemes, it is unlikely that the legislation would have had retrospective effect.

In Chapter 3 we suggested that the *Ramsay* principle may have only limited impact on conventional trusts practice. Indeed, whether the doctrine applies at all to IHT has been doubted. In *Fitzwilliam v IRC* [1993] 3 All ER 184, where an IHT avoidance scheme – a close relative of the unsuccessful scheme in *Furniss v Dawson* – was surprisingly upheld, Lord Browne-Wilkinson reserved his opinion on this point. He emphasised, instead, the availability of what at first glance appears to be a catch-all 'associated operations' rule (now IHTA 1984, s 268). 'Associated operations' are defined by s 268 to include 'any two operations of which one is effected with reference to the other, or with a view to enabling the other to be effected or facilitating its being effected, and any further operation having a like relation to any of those two, and so on'. Lord Browne-Wilkinson commented obiter that this provision 'amounts to a statutory statement, *in much wider terms* [our emphasis], of the *Ramsay* principle which deals with transactions carried through by two or more operations which are interrelated' (at 221, and see *IRC v Macpherson* [1988] STC 362 where although upholding the Revenue's case the House of Lords set limits to the scope of the provision). The Inland Revenue may even have suspected a touch of irony in Lord Browne-Wilkinson's comments in *Fitzwilliam v IRC* since it had abandoned an argument based on s 268 at first instance in favour of a *Ramsay*-type proposition! There is thus some uncertainty about which, if either, of the anti-avoidance mechanisms might be applicable. Consider, for example, the IHT advantages of spouses making full use of their separate individual annual exemptions and nil rate of tax bands to transfer property: could the transfer of money from one spouse to another (an exempt transfer) knowing that it will subsequently be transferred into a waiting settlement be caught by the *Ramsay* principle or the statutory provision if HMRC decided to challenge the practice? To date it seems that the Inland Revenue/HMRC has chosen to attack inter-spouse transfers only in blatant tax-avoidance cases (see eg Tiley *Revenue Law* (6th edn, 2008) pp 1297–1301). Most straightforward use of the trust in medium- to long-term tax planning therefore seems unlikely to be affected by either of the anti-avoidance mechanisms referred to here.

This view is reinforced by the most recent decision on the meaning of the 'associated operations' provision that illustrates its limits and would appear to confirm the effectiveness of the type of arrangement described by Hutton (see above, p 408). In *Rysaffe Trustees Co (CI) Ltd v IRC* [2002] STC 872 the settlor had made five identical or 'mirror' discretionary settlements on separate days, each comprising an initial sum of £10 and with the same beneficiaries and trustees (see Wood [2003] BTR 275–283). Private company shares were subsequently added to each trust. The Revenue argued that together they constituted one settlement on the basis that the several transfers were associated operations and so amounted to a single disposition for tax purposes. In rejecting the Revenue's argument on this point Park J, whose judgment was upheld by the Court of Appeal ([2003] STC 536), commented that whilst the definition of associated operations is quite wide, 'the practical operation of the associated operations provision is comparatively limited. It is not some sort of catch-all anti-avoidance provision which can be invoked to nullify the effectiveness of any scheme or structure which can be said to have involved more than one operation and which was intended to avoid or reduce IHT' (at para 27). It is not easy to reconcile this interpretation with the comments, admittedly brief and obiter, of Lord Browne-Wilkinson in *Fitzwilliam v IRC*.

(2) Parity: an unrealisable goal?

We have already seen that it is questionable whether fiscal 'parity' between property owned absolutely and settled property has been achieved for the various trust types under IHT. A further question relevant is whether complete 'parity' is ever attainable (see generally Inland Revenue Consultation Document *The Income Tax and CGT Treatment of UK Resident Trusts* (1991)). Trusts give birth to forms of property-holding with no parallel amongst simple outright transfers. There will often be an element of value judgement in determining which situation of outright transfer most closely resembles any given transfer on trust, so as to decide what basis to select for achieving 'parity'. The history of the IHT treatment of discretionary trusts is evidence of this. The pre-1982 regime was widely criticised as being excessively penal. Indeed it was claimed (Sherring *Capital Transfer Tax* (1982) p 4) that 'virtually no such settlements were made from 1974 to 1982'. Whether the present revised structure, even with its hypothetical 30-year charge, has established parity is equally questionable.

Even the long-established pre-22 March 2006 approach to taxing interests in possession was criticised as providing a practical solution but not one that achieved parity. The criticism was that since the life-tenant was never the owner of the capital, nor did she control it during her lifetime, it was inequitable to tax the full value of the capital on the life-tenant's death. Instead, it was suggested that when an interest in possession changes hands, the value of the interest itself should be taxed rather than the value of the underlying capital. (See *CTT and Settled Property* (1980) para 3.2.2 for alternative suggestions of a somewhat similar nature.) However, as the Inland Revenue pointed out, there are valuation difficulties with this approach (above, para 3.2.3):

> First . . . the values of all the interests in a settlement do not add up to the value of the underlying capital. Second, the interests can be reduced to a minimal value by creating powers to override or terminate them. Third, a limited interest would in practice normally be taxable only when it ceased on its owner's death, at which time it would have no value. While it might be possible to overcome these difficulties, the resulting system would undoubtedly be far more complex than the present one.

In short, practical compromise was preferred to a probably unattainable parity, a conclusion reinforced by the application, post-21 March 2006, of the 'relevant property' IHT rules to most trusts.

6. Conclusion

In devising an appropriate tax regime for trusts our erstwhile legislator is exhorted to adhere to the principle of neutrality, usually interpreted as requiring parity of treatment between property owned absolutely and that held in trust. Furthermore, to satisfy the requirement fully, parity must be sustained across the complete range of taxes and over time – a monumental demand. In several instances in this chapter we have questioned whether parity has been achieved but a more pressing preliminary question must be asked. Is neutrality of treatment desirable? The reasons for adopting neutrality as the principal criterion are couched in terms of economic efficiency and horizontal equity. The economic justification is that individual taxpayers' decisions about how to hold or dispose of property should not be distorted by taxation. Whether neutrality then requires parity is a nice point. Where, for example, some non-fiscal benefit such as protection of a minor's property from their own or others' depredation is obtained by placing the property in trust, should a tax charge be proportionately higher than that on property owned absolutely by the minor which does not have the same protection? Alternatively, if such provision is considered socially desirable should not tax laws favour trust property as against property owned absolutely? In either case neutrality, in the sense of parity of treatment, would be infringed but by conscious choice rather than unconsidered accident.

A more fundamental attack on neutrality is implicit in the following comment by Sinfield on the value of time as a 'resource' ('Analysis in the Social Division of Welfare' (1978) 7 J Social Policy 129 at 150): 'to dismiss the effects of public policy as simply non-egalitarian, or at best neutral in effect and so irrelevant to the analysis of structural inequalities, is to miss the significance of the time dimension . . .'. The point of this criticism in relation to tax treatment of trusts is that neutrality assumes that a comparison can be drawn between property owned absolutely and that held in trust. The difficulty of achieving neutrality, given, for instance, the flexibility of beneficial entitlement provided by discretionary trusts, is extensively recognised but the criticism runs wider than this. To expand the point made in the previous section, the criticism is that, in practice, the trust provides a mode of disposition of property *over time* that has no comparable basis in absolute ownership. For example under CTT the combined use of the nil rate band, the ten-year cumulation period and the annual exemption was equally available for property placed into trust or distributed absolutely. But it was the availability of the trust as a wealth-holding medium which enhanced the attractiveness of those provisions and facilitated the gaining of maximum advantage from them. How useful for the donor would these have been in the absence of the trust? Venables' pithy comment precisely summarises the advantage: 'the trust is the ideal mechanism for giving away property when one has no one in particular to whom to give it' (*Tax Planning Through Trusts* (1983) p 126). Neutrality, however, is not the sole guide for the legislator. Simplicity and intelligibility are also to be commended. One naive MP once requested of Mr Gladstone that 'tax laws ought to be made intelligible to all persons who had not received a legal education'. Perhaps today we should be satisfied if such laws were intelligible to all who have received a legal education. But intelligibility and simplicity although closely related must not be confused. Intelligibility is primarily a matter of craftsmanship and is always to be hoped for, whereas simplicity of tax structure is likely to prove much more elusive. Although the Tax Law Rewrite Project is producing legislation rewritten in clearer terms this does not of itself lead to a more simplified structure of direct taxation. It remains to be seen whether the publication of the Mirrlees Review (see above, p 100), one of whose objectives is to 'produce realistic recommendations for reform', will encourage movement towards that more simplified structure. Some steps along the reform path have already been taken with the implementation of the HMRC modernisation agenda for taxation of trusts, as with, for instance, harmonising the definition of 'settlement' for IT and CGT purposes (see generally Inland Revenue *Modernising the Tax System for Trusts* (August 2004)).

But simplicity may only be purchased at a price. Doubtless as Thomas suggests (*Taxation and Trusts* (1981) p 199) 'a simple, straightforward, and consistent approach to the taxation of settlements may well be possible in theory' but the attainment of other objectives 'may lead inevitably to complexity and constant change'. The objective most likely to frustrate a search for simplicity is the wish to counter the tax avoidance potential of the trust (see eg *Inland Revenue* (1991) para 4.8; and *Inland Revenue* (August 2004) para 7.31). When to this is added the attaining of neutrality, complexity seems an inescapable consequence. In part this is because legislators have been constrained by, inter alia, three related factors: (1) the perceived predominance of a literalist approach to interpretation of taxing statutes; (2) the flexibility of modes of property dispositions made available by property concepts and so ably exploited by the ingenuity of tax avoiders and their advisers; and (3) the additional level of complexity created by the mobility of capital and the availability of fiscally sympathetic offshore jurisdictions. A fourth factor, that of 'support for the competitiveness of the UK economy', ought perhaps to be added to the list. It is specifically identified in the 2004 Consultation Document (p 5) as being a criterion by which any new measure should be evaluated although without further elaboration, of which there is none, its meaning in this context is obscure. Broadly, the legislative response has been to anticipate possible developments while subsequently blocking loopholes on an ad hoc basis when exposed. The public law of taxation has conventionally been adapted to the private ordering of property law (see eg the interpretation of the arrangements in *Ingram v IRC* [1999] 1 All ER 297). The task of anticipating developments has been eased by the introduction in the Finance Act 2004 of the obligation on those who devise and market tax avoidance schemes to give advance notification to the Inland Revenue (see Chapter 3 at p 114). Whether this will eventually facilitate the introduction of less detailed legislation is uncertain.

It is tempting to suggest that any view that complexity is inevitable may yet need reappraisal. The judicial development of the *Ramsay* principle implicitly questions the need for complex anti-avoidance legislation. In 1984, the then Chief Secretary to the Treasury, Peter Rees QC, MP – a case of poacher turned gamekeeper given his role in the 1970s tax avoidance schemes (see eg Tutt *The Tax Raiders* (1985); Gillard *In the Name of Charity* (1987)) – appeared to accept that some simplification of tax legislation might be possible (58 HC Official Report (6th series) col 254, 10 April 1984):

> Taken with the decision in *Ramsay*'s case, it is now clear that the widespread assumption based on the *Duke of Westminster*'s case in the 1930s – that the courts will always look at the form rather than the substance of a transaction or various transactions – is no longer valid... The principle in *Furniss v Dawson* should lead, in future, to greater simplicity in our tax system... and will, I hope, enable us in time to prune out provisions which owe their existence to the complexities of a high rate – some might say a confiscatory rate – tax system with a multiplicity of special reliefs.

In practice, simplicity may be difficult either to attain or sustain if it is understood to depend upon more open-ended legislation such as a 'general anti-avoidance rule' (GAAR) and the exercise of judicial discretion to distinguish economic substance from legal form. Such a development is likely to encounter vehement opposition (see eg McBarnett and Whelan 'The Elusive Spirit of the Law: Formalism, and the Struggle for Legal Control' (1991) 54 MLR 848). Moreover opinions differ about the effectiveness of a GAAR (see eg Freedman [2004] BTR 332–357; (2007) 123 LQR 53–90; and Simpson [2004] BTR 358–374; and generally Cooper (ed) *Tax Avoidance and the Rule of Law* (1997); Shipwright (ed) *Tax Avoidance and the Law* (1997). In any event, this issue is in our view only tangential to tax treatment of trusts and of secondary importance compared with the potential threat to trusts practice that an extension of the strategy apparently adopted for trusts under IHT might pose.

Thomas, in a critical comment on the House of Lords majority judgment in *Pearson v IRC*, suggests (p 193) that 'in truth the 1975 [Finance] Act attempted to force all settlements into (basically) two distinct categories, whereas the trust lawyer's world is more complicated than this. Hybrid trusts which partake of the nature of both types abound ... *Pearson* provided the House of Lords with the opportunity ... to bring home to the craftsman of the 1975 Act that every possible contingency had not been foreseen and catered for'.

Whether as a result of lack of foresight or by conscious design, the FA 1975 can be seen in retrospect as signalling the emergence of a new approach to the taxation of trusts. Under this approach those trusts that are to be encouraged or are more susceptible to equal treatment with property owned absolutely would be isolated within narrowly defined statutory guidelines – as with, until 2006, 'A and M trusts' in IHTA 1984, s 71, and, with effect from April 2005, trusts for the 'most vulnerable' (*Inland Revenue* (August 2004) ch 1). For those settlements not conforming to those guidelines any pretence at neutrality would be discarded and a penal regime imposed, effectively discouraging their use. This could ultimately encourage simplicity of tax structure – although the pre-1982 CTT provision for discretionary trusts stands as a monument to complexity – but at the cost of a considerable impact on trusts practice and the sacrifice of 'neutrality'. No longer would every possible contingency be catered for: trusts practice and ultimately the trust form would be subordinated to the demands of fiscal legislation. Whilst there is no suggestion of such an approach in the HMRC 2004 'modernisation' proposals concerning IT and CGT, the changes to the IHT rules for trusts introduced in the FA 2006, Sch 20 can be seen as a step in that direction.

If such a solution to the legislative problem posed by the trust were to be adopted it would have profound implications which range far beyond the merely technical level of identifying and implementing an effective method of taxing trusts. It would impinge directly on the conflict that lies at the heart of the tax-trusts conundrum, that between a redistributive function of tax law and the wealth preservation and concealment functions of the private family trust. There are deep ideological waters here. The trust can be portrayed as the embodiment of private property rights, incorporating, in particular, the notion of 'property as security – as a form of protection' (Cotterrell (1987) 14 J Law and Society 77 at 87). Indeed the history of the private trust could be interpreted as a struggle to achieve security for property in an otherwise insecure material world – one thinks here, for instance, of the use, the marriage settlement, the power of advancement. At a fundamental level therefore the proposed solution for taxing trusts could be seen to entail a substantial restriction in the exercise of private rights in property, by de facto limiting the range of dispositions that could be accomplished by using the trust. But this does not dispose of the question. What has to be considered is whether the solution strikes an appropriate balance between the competing claims of public law, in the sense of advancing goals of the state, and private law, in the role of preserving an area of autonomy for ordering private affairs. It is a nice question whether the introduction of the statutory disclosure obligation on promoters of tax avoidance schemes, potentially diminishing to some degree the wealth concealment function of the trust, should also be seen as interfering with the claims of personal autonomy.

Simmonds summarised the dilemma in his challenging discussion of the implications for doctrinal legal science of the tension between private and public law domains (*The Decline of Judicial Reason* (1984) p 127):

> If not taken away altogether, the owner's rights to use his property are increasingly restricted by public law. Some restriction is inevitable and proper within any society. But it is one thing to restrict the exercise of private rights in order to protect the rights of others, and another to restrict private rights so as to advance public goals, government plans, development programmes, and so forth. At the present day, private rights are treated as objects of administration, rather than as a frame within which public law must operate.

From one perspective, therefore, the institution of the private family trust is an instrument for frustrating any policy of wealth redistribution and a mere technical device suitable for restriction. A very different view, almost a celebratory paean, was trenchantly stated by Venables (*Tax Planning Through Trusts* (1983) p 126):

> [The trust's] flexibility is such that it can be adapted to meet the multifarious needs of a free society. It is ideal for a state in which it is conceived that the law is made for man and not man for the law. It must be the envy of poorer, continental systems of jurisprudence created by and for more authoritarian regimes than are tolerated in England.

Making due allowance for hyperbole in this statement, it is nevertheless at the more fundamental level of conflicting political theories that solutions to the trust-tax problem need ultimately to be tested.

Paradoxically, if private property rights associated with the trust are to be treated as objects of administration and subordinated to public policy goals, the influence that most stimulated twentieth-century developments in the private family trust – taxation – would also be responsible for its restriction and decline.

Consider the following points:

(1) 'The objective of achieving fiscal neutrality between settled property and property owned absolutely is as undesirable as it is unattainable.' Discuss.

(2) '*Inglewood v IRC* [1983] 1 WLR 366 exposes the difficulty of drafting a statute to counter the flexibility of disposition provided by the trust form. The Court of Appeal upheld the legislative intent but only through bypassing trust concepts rather than interpreting the statute to fit them.' Discuss. Do you agree with Fox LJ that, as regards the power of advancement, 'its purpose, like an administrative power, is to aid the beneficial trusts and not to destroy them'? (Cf *Pilkington v IRC* [1964] AC 612; see Chapter 7 at p 358.)

(3) Does FA 2006, Sch 20 represent 'a justified alignment of the IHT treatment of trusts' or 'an ill-judged IHT raid on trusts' or neither of these?

(4) A recent additional dimension to the contest between taxpayer and HMRC is that offered by the European Convention on Human Rights and the Human Rights Act 1998. (See eg *Burden and Burden v United Kingdom* (2007) 44 EHRR 51 and see also Salter et al *Revenue Law – Text and Materials* (2007) ch 4.)

(5) Note that at the time of writing the future of IHT is a matter much debated. Proposals range from those that suggest strengthening the redistributive scope of IHT to those advocating its abolition (see eg Patrick and Jacobs *Wealth's Fair Measure: The Reform of Inheritance Tax* (1999); Maxwell *Fair Dues: Towards a More Progressive Inheritance Tax* (2004); Conservative Tax Reform Commission *Tax Matters: Reforming Taxation* (2007)). Such proposals perhaps lend added weight to one of the themes of this chapter, the capacity of wealthy trust users to exploit the 'planes of time and place' to minimise the effectiveness of any form of inheritance taxation (see generally Lee (2007) 27(4) LS 678–708 for an assessment strongly critical of IHT).

9

An introduction to trustees and trusteeship

1. Introduction

One of the first decisions to be taken by a settlor or testator creating a trust concerns the selection of the trustees. Who should be appointed: the settlor himself or herself, a family friend, a professional person – probably an accountant or solicitor – or a corporate trustee such as a trust department or trust subsidiary of a bank, or indeed some combination of these? The decision is of the greatest importance. Not only may the trustees be empowered to decide beneficial entitlement but also they will be responsible for trust administration including preserving the value of the trust fund through effective investment. Decisions about whom to appoint assume the existence of people or organisations willing to serve as trustees. After all, people cannot be forced to become trustees of express trusts, and if appointed may immediately disclaim or subsequently retire (see Chapter 11). It may therefore be important that the law, in seeking to oversee the exercise of trusteeship, does not unduly discourage potential trustees.

This chapter and the next two are concerned predominantly with the benefits and burdens of trusteeship. First, this chapter focuses on the nature of trusteeship with particular reference to a possible source of tension created between, on the one hand, a concept of trusteeship rooted in moral obligation and, on the other, one which perceives trusteeship as a managerial function to be financially rewarded. In this context we concentrate in particular on the principle that trustees should not adopt a position where their personal interests, most notably in securing some financial reward for themselves, may conflict with their duties to the beneficiaries. Then in Chapter 10 some of the significant powers and duties respectively conferred and imposed upon trustees in the management of trust property are considered. Finally, in Chapter 11 the emphasis shifts to the issue of control: can the settlor, the court or beneficiaries effectively regulate the exercise by trustees of these powers and duties? What remedies are available to beneficiaries when things go wrong? Also in Chapter 11 we discuss the statutory and common law provisions relating to appointment and removal of trustees. Discussion of this topic, variously described as technical and dull, is deferred until then because the authority to appoint and/or remove trustees can provide a key mechanism in seeking to control the trust and hold trustees accountable. Before commencing the study of selected aspects of trust administration and control a preliminary step is to consider whether there exists an accepted model of trusteeship that guides the development of the relevant legal rules.

2. Trusteeship: moral obligation and a profit motive

(a) A model of trusteeship

The function or office of trustee is conventionally described as being an onerous one: 'there is much to be said about the duties and obligations of a trustee, little of his rights' (Law Reform Committee (LRC) 23rd Report *Powers and Duties of Trustees* (Cmnd 8733, 1982) para 1.2). A starting place for understanding why trusteeship should be described in this manner is the fact that trusteeship is a fiduciary relationship, arguably the fiduciary relationship par excellence. In *Bristol and West Building Society v Mothew* [1998] 1 Ch 1 Millett LJ, basing himself on the seminal work of Paul Finn (*Fiduciary Obligations* (1977)), offered the following description of the obligations attaching to a fiduciary relationship (at 18):

> A fiduciary is someone who has undertaken to act for or on behalf of another in a particular matter in circumstances that give rise to a relationship of trust and confidence. The distinguishing obligation of a fiduciary is the obligation of loyalty. The principal is entitled to the single-minded loyalty of his fiduciary. The core liability has several facets. A fiduciary must act in good faith; he must not make a profit out of his trust; he must not place himself in a position where his duty and his interest may conflict; he may not act for his own benefit or the benefit of a third person without the informed consent of his principal. This is not intended to be an exhaustive list, but it is sufficient to indicate the nature of fiduciary obligations.

But the allegedly onerous nature of trusteeship is not attributable solely to the fiduciary content of the obligation. To this we must add duties associated with competent and personal administration of the trust. In principle the fundamental obligation of the trustee as holder of property belonging beneficially to others is to administer it without financial reward solely for their benefit in accordance with the terms of the trust. Moreover it is axiomatic that a trustee should not deviate from the terms of the trust unless authorised. Donovan Waters has suggested (*Law of Trusts in Canada* (3rd edn, 2005) p 852) that this basic obligation of administering property for others has resulted in the courts imposing three 'substratum' duties on all trustees:

> First, no trustee may delegate his office to others; secondly [the fiduciary element], no trustee may profit personally from his dealings with the trust property, with the beneficiaries, or as a trustee; thirdly, a trustee must act honestly and with that level of skill and prudence which would be expected of the reasonable man of business administering his own affairs.

This description stands in need of some reconsideration in light of recent statutory changes but it is still a valid indicator of the type of conduct and level of competence to which in principle trustees are expected to aspire. With the exception of the standard of skill and prudence these strict duties with their unforgiving standards – Lord Chancellor Cottenham once deemed any man who would accept a trusteeship a second time fit only for a lunatic asylum (*Law Times* 17 June 1854, p 125) – were firmly settled by the Court of Chancery by the close of the eighteenth century.

The standard of skill and prudence is more an outcome of the full rise to prominence within trusts of the notion of a trust fund of investments. This change in the type of trust property prompted an extension of the trustees' functions. (See Chapter 2 and generally Chesterman 'Family Settlements on Trust: Landowners and the Rising Bourgeoisie' in Rubin and Sugarman (eds) *Law, Economy and Society* (1984).) In the nineteenth century well-advised sett-lors and testators began to confer ever-wider administrative powers on trustees. In particular, as a trust of investments did not presuppose the retention of par-ticular assets, the trustees needed powers to sell assets where appropriate and reinvest the proceeds, and this active managerial role called for legal controls. Guidelines had to be developed for determining, inter alia, the types of invest-ment that could legitimately be retained by trustees, or that could legitimately be bought by the trustees with the proceeds of any property sold by them or with any other cash coming into the trust funds. It was also necessary to deter-mine which aspects (if any) of the process of sale or reinvestment trustees could properly delegate to expert agents such as valuers, estate agents, solicitors and brokers, and what overall standards of skill and care should be required of the trustees in their handling of investments. In the last quarter of the nineteenth century the courts in a series of cases (in particular *Speight v Gaunt* (1883) 9 App Cas 1, *Learoyd v Whiteley* (1887) 12 App Cas 727, and *Rae v Meek* (1889) 14 App Cas 558) adopted standards which tested the competence of trustees' administration of a trust against the standard of that familiar legal creation, the reasonable man, or, as he came to be called in this context, the ordinary prudent man of business.

The image of trusteeship that emerges from this initial description of its basic duties is one of disinterested devotion to the gratuitous administration of a friend's or relative's property – and a burden undertaken usually out of a sense of obligation. But this is a one-dimensional picture only. To an increasing extent professional persons, such as solicitors or accountants, or trust corporations are appointed as trustees and will act only where express provision is made for their remuneration. This practical reality is now reflected in the Trustee Act 2000 whereby trust corporations and trustees 'who are acting in a professional capacity' are entitled to receive 'reasonable remuneration' for services provided to the trust (see section 4 below). Moreover they are likely to seek to limit or exclude any liability for negligent administration or investment. Seen from this perspective trusteeship is more akin to a contractual market-based relation: in

Mitchell Franklin's phrase (see Chapter 1, p 1) trustees appear as 'professional managers of capital' administering another's property in exchange for a fee. Thus there are various reasons that can explain the willingness of people to become trustees. Many act on grounds of friendship or loyalty whilst others do so for reward. The consequence is that 'human goodwill and the profit motive between them can be relied upon to produce a supply of people prima facie willing to become trustees' (Gardner *An Introduction to the Law of Trusts* (2nd edn, 2003) p 228).

(b) The influence of the traditional model

It is a commonplace to observe that there can exist a divergence between form, here the image of trusteeship, and reality. Whilst it is relevant to inquire as to the extent of the divergence – whether, for instance, substratum duties can be modified or excluded by settlors either voluntarily or at the insistence of trustees – it is equally germane to explore the continuing importance of that image of trusteeship. Does it, for instance, inhibit judicial or statutory responses to new problems revealed by contemporary trusts practice? Or, on the contrary, is the elegant structure of rules that has been erected on the foundations of the substratum duties, being eroded by those responses?

Speculative allusions to a clear distinction between 'trusteeship as onerous obligation' and 'trusteeship as market-oriented enterprise' must not, however, be taken to imply that all trust rules or indeed trusteeship in practice must fall neatly into one or other category. As Friedman has argued ((1964) 73 Yale LJ 547 at 592):

> Private non-charitable trusts . . . differ greatly in size, type, and function, and they run all the way from great dynastic estates to pitiful sums set aside for orphans. It is no more likely that there is one optimal policy for 'trusts' than that there is one such policy for 'corporations'.

The virtues and vices of the two images of trusteeship must therefore be measured against different trust types and the perceived needs of present and future trust users. One of our objectives here, as in earlier chapters, is to assess how trusts law has adapted to the changes we have outlined.

(c) The decline of gratuitous trusteeship

G W Keeton 'The Selection of Trustees' in *Modern Developments in the Law of Trusts* (1971) pp 13–14

> The typical trustee of the eighteenth century, it has been suggested, was the country landowner, who managed his estate thriftily, stood high in the estimation of the county,

and almost certainly took his place on the Bench at Quarter Sessions. If we think of Addison's Sir Roger de Coverley we shall not be far wrong. By the second half of the nineteenth century he has changed greatly. He has become a professional man, or a member of some well-established firm. He may sit upon one or two boards of directors, but if he does it will only be after a careful scrutiny of the company's business, and it will be with the intention of exercising the same vigilance in supervising the conduct of the company's affairs as he exercises in his own. Though he may be generous in his private affairs, he will be careful even to the point of parsimony in the expenditure of public money, and he will possess to a marked degree that nice and unheated judgment which, in the nineteenth century, was such a striking characteristic of the English upper middle class business man, with a public school background. In fact, if one wishes to see a full-length portrait of the ideal trustee of this period it is to be found in the pages of *The Forsyte Saga*, in Galsworthy's Man of Property, Soames Forsyte.

Keeton's portrait of an 'ideal-type' trustee can be seen as the mirror image of the model of disinterested trusteeship outlined previously. Yet by the end of the very period Keeton is describing, a number of factors – economic and social change, problems of trustee competence and availability, evidence of human frailty – were beginning to undermine both the model of trusteeship and type of trustee. As regards frailty, loss of trust funds through fraud, even if not prevalent, had become a matter for concern. A Select Committee on Trusts Administration, appointed at the behest of Sir Howard Vincent, a prominent campaigner for the creation of a Public Trustee, reported in 1895 that 'the evidence puts it beyond question that large sums of money are annually misappropriated by private trustees ... and those who suffer are chiefly the poorer and more helpless' ((1895) 99 LT 67; see Edmunds and Lowry in Birks and Pretto (eds) *Breach of Trust* (2002) ch 9). Contemporaneously with the demand for security of funds, a potential market for the services of trustees was expanding because of more widespread wealth-holding and use of wills (see Marsh *Corporate Trustees* (1952) pp 67–69). This was occurring, however, at the very time that the imposition of rigorous legal standards on trustees was seemingly discouraging private individuals from taking on the 'burden' of trusteeship. When to these developments is added the consideration that effective management of trust funds increasingly demanded specialist knowledge, the scope for the extension of professional and corporate trusteeship is apparent. Eventually a 20-year campaign, strenuously opposed initially by the solicitor side of the profession, culminated in the creation of the office of Public Trustee in 1906 (see Offer *Property and Politics* (1981) pp 54–55; and Polden (1989) J Legal History 228 at 231–234).

The subsequent general growth of corporate trusteeship is briefly summarised in the Report of the Committee of Enquiry into the Public Trustee Office (see also *Marsh* and the report of an earlier inquiry, Cmd 9755 (1956)).

Cmnd 4913, 1972 paras 5–6

5. 'The Office [of Public Trustee] was set up under the Public Trustee Act 1906, the Attorney General having given as its main raison d'être the difficulty of inducing private persons to accept the onerous responsibilities of a trustee, and the losses incurred by beneficiaries as a result of incompetence or dishonesty on the part of private trustees.

6. . . . in the early years of the Office the Public Trustee had very little competition. Although there existed before 1906 a number of companies whose memoranda and articles of association permitted them to undertake trust administration, they did so only to a negligible extent. After 1906 banks and insurance companies began to take on trust work but the Public Trustee suffered little at first from their competition. . . . From 1920 onwards, the competition of other corporate trustees . . . had an ever-increasing effect on the business of the Public Trustee. The Committee gave statistics showing that by 1949 the Public Trustee had 20,226 cases under administration; by 1955 this figure had fallen to 17,732. They concluded that the trustee facilities then offered by the banks and insurance companies, and the protection afforded by the Law Society against defalcations by solicitors, made up a very different picture from that which presented itself in 1906; had similar conditions existed at that time, there would have been little occasion for the creation of the Office of Public Trustee.

(d) Present demography of trusteeship

The enjoinder of one writer to 'take into account trusts as they are' and to 'count them and classify them, and study their nature' (Friedman (1964) 73 Yale LJ 547 at 592) is impossible to satisfy given present availability of information. This is particularly so where identity and type of trustee are at issue. The most that can be achieved here is to assemble the few available pieces of the jigsaw.

In 1980 The Association of Corporate Trustees (TACT) produced figures establishing that their members administered 103,048 trust funds with a total value of £4,955 million. (See Thomas *Taxation and Trusts* (1981) p 1; and the survey of three clearing banks conducted by Revell and Lovering *Exempt Settled Property* RCDIW Research Paper no 3 (1979) which broadly confirms this estimate.) These figures reflected the expansion of corporate trusteeship in the 1960s and 1970s into 'what one might loosely term the "mass market" of rather smaller trusts which used to be managed by [amateur] trustees before life became so complicated' *(Revell and Lovering* p 8). A more recent informal estimate derived from a questionnaire-based survey of some TACT members suggests that there has been a decline in the numbers of trusts administered by members to 36,190 trusts with an asset value of £4,015m (Frost 'Private Trusts – A Survey of the Market' (1997) 3 TACT). This decline has been offset by a significant expansion in their commercial trust work such as pension trusts and capital loan trusts (see a survey conducted for TACT by Europe Economics *Economic and Financial Analysis of Commercial and Private Trusts in the United*

Kingdom (2002). Clearly the estimates depend on the representative nature of the responses and, as Frost emphasises, the data need to be treated with some caution. Nevertheless the figures do give a general indication of the involvement of corporate trustees. To these figures we can add the gradually declining number of trusts administered by the Public Trustee Office. In 2003–2004 this stood at 1,386 with an estimated asset value of £271 million, representing almost a halving of the numbers since 1984 (*Annual Report of the Official Solicitor and Public Trustee Office 2003–2004*). The process of decline in the role of the Public Trustee Office has accelerated further since then. Following a recommendation from the National Audit Office that the work of the Public Trustee Office should be put out to tender a private sector corporate trustee, Capita Trust Company, has been appointed with effect from 1 April 2007 to administer some 500 cases where there are deemed to be 'no exceptional circumstances' that require a public sector trustee (www.officialsolicitor.gov.uk/estates/estates.htm). It is estimated that barely 200 existing trusts will remain with the Public Trustee Office.

This estimate of trusts administered by corporate trustees and the Public Trustee Office probably accounts for only 15–20% of all trusts. Of the remaining trusts it is at least probable that a substantial proportion have professional trustees appointed. Indeed the clearing banks surveyed by Revell and Lovering all agreed that very large trusts, discretionary trusts and trusts containing mainly agricultural estates or unlisted shares were more likely than other types of trusts to be administered by non-corporate professional trustees. The reason is thought to be that such trustees will be less inhibited in taking risks, perhaps even involving a breach of trust, in the interests of beneficiaries.

Broadly speaking, therefore, trusteeship in practice is still divided among the following three different types of trustee although there is a perceptible trend towards professionalisation:

(1) non-professional unpaid trustees of the 'family friend' type;
(2) paid, often professionally qualified, trustees such as solicitors or accountants; and
(3) corporate trustees such as specialist trust companies (eg the long-established Law Debenture Corporation) and trustee departments of banks or insurance companies who advertise themselves as such.

The types of trustee are not mutually exclusive: it is not uncommon for a combination of professional and non-professional trustees to be appointed so that the trust may benefit from professional expertise whilst retaining a family or friendship link.

(e) Trustee Act 2000: a summary

As mentioned above, and as will be discussed in more detail in section 6(2) below, the law on remuneration of trustees was significantly modified by the

Trustee Act 2000. But the scope of the Act runs much wider than that. The evolving social and economic role which trusts now fulfil allied to the changing nature of trusteeship all contributed to a growing awareness of the need to reform the law of trusts and the Act is the culmination of a long history of proposals in that direction. Several of the reforms in the Act were first considered in 1982 in the Twenty-third Report of the Law Reform Committee (LRC) *The Powers and Duties of Trustees*. No action was taken on their recommendations. Then in November 1995 the Law Commission embarked on a review of the powers and duties of trustees that led in June 1997 to the publication of a Consultation Paper *Trustees' Powers and Duties* (LCCP No 146). In the interim in May 1996 the Treasury published its own Consultation Document on the investment powers of trustees but attempts to modify the law on trustee investment by means of an order under the Deregulation and Contracting Out Act 1994 were frustrated when Parliament was dissolved in 1997. Subsequently in July 1999 the Law Commission and the Scottish Law Commission jointly published their report on *Trustees' Powers and Duties* (1999) Law Com No 260, Scot Law Com No 172. The outcome was the Trustee Act 2000, which came into force on 1 February 2001 and implements, with minor modification, the changes in relation to the law of England and Wales recommended in the Law Commission Report (see for overviews of the Act, Garton (2001) 15(1) TLI 34; and Panesar (2001) 12(5) ICCLR 151). The principal change is the creation of a new and wider statutory power of investment to replace the limited power under the Trustee Investments Act 1961. In addition to these measures relating to trust investment powers (ss 3–7) and those dealing with trustee remuneration (ss 28–33) the Act contains a range of 'new' powers largely replacing more limited ones in the Trustee Act 1925 for trustees to appoint nominees and custodians, to delegate certain of their functions and to insure trust property (ss 11–27). The new powers are intended to facilitate the better administration of trusts and are complemented by a new safeguard for beneficiaries in the form of a statutory duty of care (ss 1–2) which will apply to trustees in the exercise of their new wider powers under the Act. With the exception of trustee remuneration, which is discussed in this chapter, the principal new statutory powers are considered in detail in Chapter 10 in the context of our study of the management of the trust.

It only remains here to emphasise that in one key respect the law of trusts remains largely unaltered. It is still open to settlors and their advisers to write their own law in the trust instrument. In short statute law still remains primarily default law.

3. Trusteeship and trustees: an introduction

(a) Trustees: capacity and numbers

In principle any person able to hold property, including a limited company or other corporation, may be a trustee. Even an infant may become a trustee, for example under a resulting trust (eg *Re Vinogradoff* [1935] WN 68), but not by express appointment. The Law of Property Act (LPA) 1925, s 20 declares such an appointment void.

Similar latitude is exhibited with respect to the number of trustees. At present the general rule is that the number may be unlimited, one being sufficient and any greater number permissible. The sole exception is in most trusts of land where the Trustee Act (TA) 1925, s 34 (as amended by the Trusts of Land and Appointment of Trustees Act 1996) imposes a maximum of four (see s 34(3)(a) for the limited exceptions). The LRC in its 1982 Report recommended (para 2.2) that 'where the settlor makes no specific provision about numbers, the number of trustees should be limited to four regardless of the nature of the trust property, on the ground that when the number of trustees exceeds four, costs, administrative inconvenience and delays are increased'.

As regards the minimum number, whereas a single trustee is possible it is also undesirable (unless a corporate trustee) because maladministration or misappropriation of funds is made easier. Also, although there need be only one trustee to hold land, at least two trustees are needed to sell land (again unless the sole trustee is a corporate trustee) since this number is necessary to give a valid receipt for capital money (TA 1925, s 14(2)).

(b) Special types of trustee

(1) Public Trustee

The office of Public Trustee, 'the father-figure of the modern corporate trustee' (Sladen *Practical Trust Administration* (3rd edn, 1993) p 317), has experienced a chequered existence since its foundation in 1906. The need for the provision of a public body which could be considered by testators as a safe appointment as executor in a will or codicil, or as trustee of a trust, has over time been eroded by the availability of alternative suitably qualified professional help in the private sector. Its abolition was recommended by a Committee of Enquiry (Cmnd 4913) in 1972, and although subsequently reprieved the existence of the office as an independent administrative entity ended in 1986 with the passage of the Public Trustee and Administration of Funds Act 1986 (see Polden (1989) 10 J Legal History 228). The 1986 statute amalgamated the activities of the Public Trustee with, inter alia, those of the Court Funds Office and located them within the Lord Chancellor's Department, where, after July 1994, it operated with the status of an executive agency. In fact the principal areas of activity then undertaken by the Public Trust Office, as it was renamed, were those concerned with the property and affairs of mental patients. Indeed, it was largely in that connection that the overall financial performance of the Public Trust Office became the subject of two quite critical reports by the National Audit Office (*Looking After the Financial Affairs of People with Mental Incapacity* HC (Session 1993–94) 258; *Protecting the Financial Welfare of People with Mental Incapacity* HC (Session 1998–99) 206). Subsequently a quinquennial review of the Public

Trust Office was carried out in 1999 and led to substantial changes. A key change in jurisdiction was that the Mental Health functions were transferred to a new organisation, the Public Guardianship Office (PGO) sited within the Court of Protection. Organisationally the offices of Public Trustees and Official Solicitor to the Supreme Court were in effect merged as from April 2001 and one person now formally holds both offices. In practical terms the trust division of the Public Trust Office was merged with those parts of the office of the Official Solicitor which remained after the formation of the Children and Family Court Advisory and Support Service.

As regards the legal framework the Public Trustee is a corporation sole; he can act alone or jointly with others and may be appointed as an ordinary trustee, a custodian trustee or as a judicial trustee (see below, p 430). He may not act as the trustee of a religious or charitable trust (Public Trustee Act 1906, s 2(5)) and may only carry on a business owned by the trust for a time not exceeding 18 months for the purpose of winding it up (s 2(4) and Public Trustee Rules 1912, r 7)). The principal specialised function now is to act as a trustee of 'last resort', meaning broadly where there is no one else suitable, able or willing to act and an injustice would result if the Public Trustee did not accept the post. Whilst the Public Trustee may decline to accept business he may not, unlike any other corporate trustee, do so solely on the grounds 'of the small value of the trust property' (s 2(3)). Given this restrictive approach towards soliciting or accepting business it is not surprising, as noted in section 2(d) above, that the number of trusts administered by the Public Trustee is declining.

(2) Trust corporation

(See generally Keeton *Modern Developments in the Law of Trusts* (1971) pp 18–26, and the early study by Marsh *Corporate Trustees* (1952), still an unrivalled source on the development of corporate trusteeship.) The trust department of a bank or insurance company usually springs to mind when thinking of a trust corporation but the term has a wider meaning, extending to include any corporation appointed by the court or 'entitled by rules made under [s 4(3)] of the Public Trustee Act 1906 to act as a custodian trustee' (TA 1925, s 68(18)). Where a bank or insurance company wishes to act as trustee it must therefore fulfil certain now not very onerous conditions set out in the Public Trustee (Custodian Trustee) Rules 1975, SI 1975/1189). The key requirements are:

1. The company must be incorporated either in the UK or some other member state of the EU.
2. The company is authorised by its constitution to undertake the business of acting as a trustee, and of acting as a personal representative in England and Wales.
3. It must have an issued capital of not less than £250,000 (or its equivalent in the currency of the state of incorporation), of which not less than £100,000 must have been paid up in cash.

4. The company must have at least one place of business in the UK, no matter where it is incorporated.

The basic financial requirements in the third condition above, which were intended to provide a measure of protection to beneficiaries, are now totally inadequate to do so. The value of assets in any one trust may exceed by many times the amount of the minimum required paid up capital. Moreover the test is as to the amount of the issued share capital of the company, and not as to its asset value. Thus, if a company had issued shares to the extent of £250,000, it would still be eligible to be a trust corporation even if it had by improvidence lost all its shareholders' funds. In fact it is debatable whether onerous capital adequacy requirements are necessary for firms, including corporate trustees, involved in investment business. An alternative view is that a combination of insurance and strict separation of clients' accounts should provide adequate protection. (See Franks and Mayer *Risk Regulation and Investor Protection* (1989) for survey data and a summary of the debate.) In addition to the above requirements, if, as is likely, a corporate trustee also wishes to carry on in the UK the business of investing trust funds, it must be authorised to do so under the provisions of the Financial Services and Markets Act 2000 and comply with the regulations implementing the single European market in investment services (see Sabalot and Everett *The Financial Services and Markets Act 2000* (2004) ch 4).

Lastly, as regards fee-charging, a trust corporation will usually not agree to act unless it is able to charge fees, commonly on a fixed ad valorem scale, for its services. Where a trust instrument contains no express charging clause authorising such remuneration a trust corporation can now, under the terms of the Trustee Act 2000, s 29 (see below, p 442), charge 'reasonable remuneration' out of the trust funds for any services that it provides to or on behalf of any private trust.

(c) Special forms of trusteeship

(1) Custodian trustees

The concern for the security of trust funds that underlay the creation of the office of Public Trustee was carried a step further in s 4 of the Public Trustee Act 1906; it introduced the possibility of functionally dividing ordinary trusteeship between custodian and managing trustees. The relationship between the two is comprehensively defined in s 4(2) (see generally Maurice (1960) 24 Conv 196). As their respective titles imply, custodian trustees act as passive holders of trust property and related documents of title whilst the active management and exercise of all powers and discretions rests with managing trustees. Appointment to the statutory office of custodian trustee is not restricted to the Public Trustee but extends to include both trust corporations and, for limited purposes, a diversity of other corporate bodies (see Public Trustee (Custodian Trustee) Rules 1975, SI 1975/1189, as amended by SI 1976/836, SI 1981/358, SI 1984/109,

SI 1985/132 and SI 1994/2519). An advantage of the division of functions, in addition to that of enhanced security, is convenience. The title to trust property remains vested in the custodian trustee thus saving the trouble and expense of transferring title to property where changes occur, perhaps because of death or retirement from the trust, among managing trustees.

Despite these apparent advantages it seems that the scheme of custodian trusteeship is not in widespread use in family trusts. The converse is the case in the commercial area. For example, pension scheme trustees extensively use the services of custodian trustees. Indeed the practice of custodianship, or 'global custody' as it is known in the financial services sector, now constitutes an essential cog in the operations of investment fund management globally (see eg the annual survey of global custody in *Pensions Management*).

(2) Judicial trusteeship

A judicial trustee is some person or corporation appointed to act as trustee by the court under the provisions of the Judicial Trustee Act 1896. The object of the jurisdiction has been stated to be the provision of 'a middle course in cases where the administration of the estate by the ordinary trustees had broken down and it was not desired to put the estate to the expense of a full administration. In these circumstances, a solution was found in the appointment of a judicial trustee who acts in close concert with the court and under conditions enabling the court to supervise his transactions' (*Re Ridsdel* [1947] Ch 597 at 605 per Jenkins J).

Accordingly, the appointment is more likely to occur following an application from an existing trustee or beneficiary, although it can be made on the application of a person creating or intending to create a trust (see Judicial Trustee Rules 1983, SI 1983/370). The procedure has not been extensively used and is only likely to be invoked where there is excessively complex litigation (see *Re Diplock* [1948] Ch 465) or where gross mismanagement of the trust has occurred – 'trouble-shooting accountants are often appointed to sort out the muddled situation' (*Hayton and Mitchell* p 545, and see [1993] SJ 760 at 760–761 commenting on the appointment of judicial trustees in a pensions case *McDonald v Horn* (1993) *Times* 12 October, Ch D). When appointing a judicial trustee the court decides on an appropriate level of remuneration (see Judicial Trustee Rules 1983, r 11(1)(a); *Practice Direction* [2003] 3 All ER 974).

(3) Nominees and bare trusts

We saw in Chapter 1 that one of the tricks for which the trust's division of ownership between legal and equitable title can be used is to conceal beneficial ownership of a shareholding (see Example 1 at p 6). This was, of course, also the mechanism in *Vandervell v IRC* [1967] 1 All ER 1 by which National Provincial Bank held legal title to the shares in Vandervell Products on trust for Mr Vandervell absolutely (see Chapter 4, p 198). Whilst the 'nominee' or 'bare trustee' – for present purposes the titles are synonymous – will receive, for instance, the dividends and execute any transfer of title this will be done solely for the principal's benefit and in conformity with the latter's instructions. In short the beneficiary is owner in all but name. A corollary of this position is that a bare trustee has no active duties to perform. The overall position was summarised in an Australian case *Herdegen v Federal Comr of Taxation* (1988) 84 ALR 271 by Gummow J in the following manner (at 281): '[bare trustees] have no interest in the trust assets other than that existing by reason of the office and legal title as trustee and who never have had active duties to perform or who have ceased to have those duties, such that in either case the property awaits transfer to the beneficiaries or at their direction.'

It would be a mistake, however, to think of nominees solely in terms of tricks and subterfuge. An increasingly important functional use of nominees will be to act, in effect, as the delegates of trustees for the purpose of facilitating share dealings particularly as a dematerialised mode of share transfer takes over (Ford (1997) 11(1) TLI 18–19; and see generally Chapter 10).

4. Trustees' duties and powers: an outline

(a) Trustees' duties

We have previously referred to the three substratum duties imposed on trustees in administering a private express trust and to the possible modification of those duties through the new powers made available to trustees in the Trustee Act 2000. To these duties must be added those associated with each individual trust. Thus, for instance, where the retention of capital in the trust fund over a period of time is necessary, trustees must ensure that the trust fund is at all times in a proper state of investment (see Chapter 10). Also the trustees must act impartially where there are different classes of beneficiary, for example, those entitled to income and capital respectively, not favouring one against the other unless authorised to do so by the trust instrument (see Chapter 10). In addition there are a number of subsidiary but practically important duties associated with the acceptance and administration of the office of trusteeship. With one exception (a duty of disclosure of information: see Chapter 11) these are not significant for our purposes and a brief outline only is provided here.

On appointment trustees should familiarise themselves with the terms of the trust and ensure that the appointment was properly made. It would be both inconvenient and expensive for the trust if acts of administration were found to be invalid because of an improper appointment, or if a breach of trust, such as payment to the wrong beneficiary, were to occur because of ignorance of the trust terms. Therefore, to protect trust property trustees should bring it under their control by ensuring where appropriate that the legal title to the property is transferred to them. If appointed to an existing trust, a trustee should find out from the current trustees about the past and present business of the trust. In particular the new trustee must be alert to the possibility of an undetected previous breach of trust and be prepared to initiate action to remedy it. New trustees who fail to inquire are unwise as well as being in breach of duty. If loss is caused to the trust fund they risk being held liable, not for participating in the original breach of trust but for failing in their own duty of inquiry. However, 'a new trustee is not expected to act like a bloodhound straining to sniff out some breach of trust; in the absence of suspicious circumstances he may assume that the previous trustees have properly discharged their duties' (*Parker and Mellows* p 630, citing as authority *Ex parte Geave* (1856) 8 De GM & G 291 at 309 where Turner LJ makes the point rather less colourfully).

Once these initial duties have been complied with the trustees can turn their attention to the duties involved in the day-to-day administration of the trust. A number of express and statutory powers, such as those of maintenance and advancement (see Chapter 7), are usually conferred on trustees and provide the machinery for administering the trust. Here the duty of trustees, as with mere powers of appointment (see Chapter 5), is to consider whether to exercise any such powers. If they do decide to act, a further duty, except in the case of charitable trusts, is that they must act unanimously – the majority cannot bind the minority (see eg *Boardman v Phipps* [1967] 2 AC 46) – unless the terms of the trust instrument, or the court, otherwise direct (see *Cowan v Scargill* [1985] 1 Ch 270).

The detection of breaches of trust rests largely with the beneficiaries and as 'policemen' they will wish to be kept informed about the trust's administration. Not surprisingly, therefore, trustees are under a duty to keep proper financial accounts and records of the trust's administration, and, within limits, to make information available to the beneficiaries (see Chapter 11).

(b) Trustees' powers

In so far as trustees' administrative powers are intended to facilitate effective management of the trust, one of the most teasing decisions facing settlors concerns the width of the powers to be conferred on trustees. This is as true of the administrative discretions as it is of the dispositive discretions considered in Chapter 5. For instance, how much freedom in the choice of investments should settlors bestow on trustees? Should they seek to minimise risk by limiting the trustees' discretion to mere selection amongst secure investments, or should they grant a wide discretion to invest speculatively in the hope of greater financial return? In practice the development of the investment market during the last hundred years and more recent economic circumstances, in particular the effects at various times of inflation, have encouraged the conferment of extremely wide powers which, until the broadening of investment powers in the Trustee Act 2000, far exceeded those statutorily available to settlors (see generally Chapter 10). Prior to this legislative change the inclusion in trust deeds of broad powers of investment beyond those statutorily available constitutes merely one example of the tendency for the statutory powers automatically available to trustees to be supplemented or even replaced by express powers in the trust instrument. Nevertheless, the automatic statutory powers, first introduced to reduce the length and detail of trust instruments, still provide a common core of powers applicable to private express trusts.

In addition to the statutory powers of maintenance and advancement conferred on trustees by TA 1925, s 31 and s 32 respectively (see Chapter 7), Pt II of the statute confers other general powers of administration on trustees. These powers, which we do not consider in any detail, permit trustees to sell trust property at auction (s 12), to raise money by mortgaging or selling trust assets (s 16) and, inter alia, in s 15, to 'compromise, compound, abandon, submit to arbitration, or otherwise settle any debt, account, claim, or thing whatever relating to . . . the trust' (s 15(f)). Section 15 also exempts trustees from liability for any loss caused by an act done by them under the wide powers provided by the section so long as they have complied with the new statutory duty of care set out in TA 2000, s 1(1) and Sch 1. Previously trustees had been protected if they had merely acted 'in good faith'. The power for trustees to insure trust property against risks of loss or damage is contained in a revised s 19, as substituted by TA 2000, s 34(1). Formerly the power to insure had been limited but now the power to insure is unrestricted seemingly both as to the risks to be insured and the level of cover to be obtained (s 19(1)(a)). Section 19 is also subject to the statutory duty of care (TA 2000, Sch 1, para 5) and arguably a failure to insure adequately would be in breach of the duty.

Of far greater significance to the effective management of the trust are the new statutory powers to employ agents and, within certain parameters, to delegate the exercise of discretions (TA 2000, ss 11–27). These powers are mentioned here for the sake only of completing the overall picture as they are considered in detail in the context of trust management in Chapter 10.

(c) Duties and powers: a synthesis

The conceptual distinction between a duty and a power is clear: a duty is an obligation, a power an authority to act. But functionally in trust administration the two operate in harness. Consider, for example, the duty of trustees to ensure that the trust fund is maintained in a proper state of investment. This obligation is without content until the proper state of investment is identified by referring to the trustees' power of investment. But the exercise of that power must in principle then comply with the duties of trusteeship. Thus, to continue with the example, the authorisation provided by an apparently unlimited power of investment will be interpreted as being subject to, in Waters' words, the 'substratum' duties (see p 856). Consequently, the duty not to delegate requires that in principle a decision to sell or buy specific investments must be the trustees' own, not that of a third party no matter how expert (unless the power to delegate asset management duties has been exercised under TA 2000, s 15); the duty to avoid a conflict of interest requires that a trustee should not be a purchaser of trust property for himself; and the duty to display a reasonable level of skill and care means that trustees may be liable for loss caused by honest but foolish investment decisions.

This synthesis, however, is subject, as always, to the capacity of the settlor, or even in certain circumstances all the beneficiaries, to release the trustees from observance of the duties the courts have sought to impose on trustees for the protection of beneficiaries. The paramount nature of the law laid down by the settlor in the trust instrument must therefore never be overlooked.

5. Conflict of interest and duty

In enforcing the duties imposed on trustees courts have been seen at their strictest where a conflict may arise between trustees' personal interests and their position as trustees. This attitude can be traced back to the seminal case of *Keech v Sandford* (1726) Sel Cas Ch 61 (discussed in Chapter 16) but has been frequently asserted since then. Just one amongst the numerous judicial affirmations of a strict approach is Lord Herschell's statement in *Bray v Ford* [1896] AC 44 at 51 that it is 'an inflexible rule of a Court of Equity that a person in a fiduciary position . . . is not, unless otherwise expressly provided, entitled to make a profit; he is not allowed to put himself in a position where his interest and duty conflict'.

The reason for the rule is manifest. The trustees' obligation is to manage the trust solely for the benefit of the beneficiaries, and if the trustees' own interests conflict with theirs, then temptation exists. If, for example, trustees purchase property belonging to the trust or charge fees for carrying out the tasks of trusteeship then there may be a temptation to pay a less than market price or to charge exorbitant fees.

In this chapter we concentrate on how the courts have attempted to prevent such conflicts of interest occurring, or subsequently at least to control their outcome. To continue with the examples, an attractively simple response for a court determined to discourage the advancement of self-interest might be to say that any purchase of trust property should be set aside or that trustees must account to the trust for any fees paid. But profit for the trustees is not synonymous with loss for the trust. Let us suppose that the market price was paid or that the fees were reasonable. Should the court still apply those same remedies thus adopting an approach that exclusively emphasises a policy objective of deterrence?

The implications for a fiduciary of the strict approach are spelled out by Waters (*Law of Trusts in Canada* (3rd edn, 2005) p 879):

> whether the [fiduciary] was honest and well-intentioned or otherwise, whether or not he harmed the interests of his principal by his activities, and whether in the circumstances what he did was not unreasonable, are irrelevant issues. Once he is found . . . to be involved in activities which would result or have resulted in his own profit, and to have been so involved when he ought to have been in a position to give the exclusive benefit of his attentions to his principal, then he is in breach of the rule.

An alternative approach would be for the court merely to prevent any unfair gain from being retained by the fiduciary. The court would retrospectively assess, for instance, the fairness of the price paid or the level of fees charged, whereupon the good faith of the fiduciary and the absence of harm caused to the principal's interest would be relevant considerations.

The courts of equity in the nineteenth century, particularly under the early guiding influence of Lord Eldon, favoured the deterrent approach. This was in large measure because of concern over evidentiary difficulties facing a court in determining a trustee's motives where a possible conflict existed (*Ex p Lacey* (1802) 6 Ves 625; *Ex p James* (1803) 8 Ves 337, discussed in *Holder v Holder*: see below, p 452). But even then the strictness of the rule was mitigated where the nexus between the type of personal activity undertaken by a trustee and the interests of the trust was considered too remote. In this chapter we consider in particular the current variable application of the conflict of interest rule and which of two approaches, the prophylactic one placing priority on deterrence or the remedial one emphasising fairness and 'retrospective adjustment', can now be said to predominate in the approach of the courts.

The alert reader will have noted that Lord Herschell's statement (above) was not restricted to trustees but instead referred to 'a person in a fiduciary position'. Similarly Waters's comments were directed towards the implications of the conflict of interest rule for 'fiduciary agents'. It cannot be stressed too strongly that the category of 'fiduciary agents' extends beyond the confines of trustee-beneficiary to include well-recognised commercial relationships such as solicitor-client, company director-company, partner-co-partner. Indeed it has been said that the class of fiduciary relationships is never closed (*English v Dedham Vale Properties Ltd* [1978] 1 All ER 382 at 398 per Slade J, and see generally Finn 'The Fiduciary Principle' in Youdan (ed) *Equity, Fiduciaries and Trusts* (1989)). The determinants of when commercial relationships in particular are treated as fiduciary and how far the conflict of interest rule, with its origins in the trustee-beneficiary relationship, applies to them are considered at length in Chapter 16. It is sufficient at the moment to draw attention to the oft-quoted (eg Sealey [1962] CLJ 69 at 71) warning of Fletcher Moulton LJ in *Re Coomber* [1911] 1 Ch 723 at 728:

> Fiduciary relations are of many different types: . . . and the courts have again and again . . . interfered and set aside acts which, between persons in a wholly independent position, would have been perfectly valid. Thereupon in some minds there arises the idea that if there is any fiduciary relation whatever any of these types of interference is warranted by it. They conclude that every kind of fiduciary relation justifies every kind of interference. Of course that is absurd. The nature of the fiduciary relationship must be such that it justifies the interference.

The warning reflects the fact that, even if the restrictive bonds on trustees may now be loosening, the fiduciary relationship that has historically most justified interference is that of trustee-beneficiary. In Scott's memorable phrase, 'In some relations the fiduciary element is more intense than in others; it is peculiarly intense in the case of a trust' ('The Trustee's Duty of Loyalty' (1936) 49 Harv LR 521). To emphasise the point, it is the fiduciary element in the trust with which this chapter is concerned; consideration of the broader fiduciary context is deferred until Chapter 16.

The factual circumstances in which a conflict of interest may arise for a trustee are many and varied, but the following broad categories of activity can be identified for the purposes of analysing how the conflict principle operates in this particular context.

(1) Direct remuneration earned for acting as trustee (section 6).
(2) Indirect remuneration earned by virtue of trusteeship (section 7).
     – directors' fees
     – commission and analogous profits.
(3) Dealings with the trust property or beneficiaries (section 8).

However, just as there is no comprehensive definition of a fiduciary so there is no one accepted method of compartmentalising these various activities. This particular categorisation is adopted here partly because it enables us to concentrate on the 'bringing of trusteeship to the marketplace' but also because the fiduciary obligation in the several categories may be of varying 'intensity'.

6. Trustees and direct remuneration

(a) Introduction

Given the developments described in section 2 above, it is unsurprising that the fundamental rule, one element of Waters's second substratum duty, to the effect that a trustee is not entitled to receive payment for acting as trustee has come under increasing scrutiny and criticism. As recently as 1990 the rule's rigour was evident in the following statement from *Snell* (p 162):

> trustees . . . are generally entitled to no allowance for their care and trouble. This rule is so strict that even if a trustee or executor has sacrificed much time in carrying on a business as directed by the trust, he will usually be allowed nothing as compensation for his personal trouble or loss of time.

As already indicated, this fundamental rule is substantially modified by the Trustee Act 2000, ss 28, 29 whereby trust corporations and trustees 'who are acting in a professional capacity' are entitled to receive 'reasonable remuneration' for services provided to the trust (see section (b)(2) below). Even were this not the position the non-remuneration rule does not mean that trust administration is therefore cost-free. Trustees are statutorily empowered (TA 2000, s 11, and see further Chapter 10) to employ paid agents (eg stockbrokers, solicitors) to carry out specialist functions and the fees of such agents are chargeable to the trust fund not the trustees (TA 2000, s 32). Furthermore there is a well-established right, now confirmed in TA 2000, s 31(1), that trustees are entitled to be indemnified out of trust property against out-of-pocket expenses 'properly incurred when acting on behalf of the trust'. The entitlement will not normally extend to the payment of any interest on the expenditure incurred (see *Foster v Spencer* [1996] 2 All ER 672 where it was held that no interest was payable on 'ordinary costs and expenses accrued in a piecemeal fashion' (at 678)). 'Properly incurred' arguably reflects the position established under previous legislation and case law. The expenditure must therefore be reasonable and proper in the circumstances of the trust. Judicial scepticism can be expected to remain the prevailing attitude towards ingenious expenses claims such as those in *Malcolm v O'Callaghan* (1835) 3 Myl & Cr 52. In that case a trustee's efforts to reclaim the costs of several trips to Paris to attend a court hearing concerning the trust were unsuccessful since his attendance was not deemed necessary in a case turning on matters of French law alone. A trustee's right of indemnity is one against the trust estate and not normally against the beneficiaries (but see *Hardoon v Belilios* [1901] AC 118 – trustees as nominees – and generally Hughes (1990) 64 ALJ 567 for exceptions to this rule).

Notwithstanding these modifications what reasons are there for a general rule of non-remuneration? An oft-cited explanation is that advanced by Lord Talbot LC in *Robinson v Pett* (1734) 3 P Wms 249 at 251:

> a trustee, executor or administrator, shall have no allowance for his care and trouble: the reason for this seems to be . . . if allowed, the trust estate might be loaded, and rendered of little value. Besides, the great difficulty there might be in settling the quantum of such allowance, especially as one man's time may be more valuable than that of another; and there can be no hardship in this respect upon any trustee, who may choose whether he will accept the trust, or not.

As Bishop and Prentice have pointed out ((1983) 46 MLR 289 at 304) there are three separate justifications here. First, trustees may be tempted to undertake unnecessary work in administering the trust so as to earn more fees; second, valuing the trustee's services presents difficulties; and third, persons are free to refuse the office of trustee.

The current relevance of these justifications has been the subject of debate and doubt but the last named – ie the voluntary nature of the office – paradoxically indicates one reason why the rule is now almost the exception. Professional and corporate trustees will not agree to act unless provision is made for their remuneration.

In some other jurisdictions, for example, many states in the US, the non-remuneration rule is reversed and corporate trustees are statutorily authorised to receive remuneration at prescribed rates. It is therefore not surprising that this matter came under review by law reform bodies in the UK. In its 1982

Report the LRC considered and rejected a proposal to introduce a comparable (statutory) provision into English law (paras 3.46–3.47). The LRC considered that 'it would be difficult to frame a universally applicable provision which would not be open to abuse', that settlors or testators might be unaware of what they would be taken to 'have agreed to' and that a standard clause would 'encroach too far upon the general principle that a trustee should not profit from his trust'. These conclusions were criticised by Parry [1984] Conv 275 who concluded that the changed social and economic climate called for increased professionalism on the part of trustees and that 'if a professional is appointed to undertake this function, which the [LRC] itself describes as an "onerous one" then he should be entitled to reasonable remuneration for his services' (at 285). Subsequently the Law Commission returned to the issue in its review of the law on Trustees' Powers and Duties (Report No 260 (1999)). It concluded that the LRC approach was too cautious and that a combination of defects in the current law and practical considerations made it desirable to introduce a statutory default charging clause (paras 7.5–7.7), a recommendation implemented in the Trustee Act 2000.

We have mentioned previously that for descriptive purposes trustees can be placed into one or other of three categories: corporate trustees, other professional trustees and lay trustees. A similar type of categorisation is adopted for the purposes of charging provisions of the Trustee Act 2000. These distinguish between a trust corporation, a trustee acting in a professional capacity and a 'lay trustee'. The Act (s 39(1)) adopts as the definition of a trust corporation that contained in the Trustee Act 1925, s 68(18) (see section 3(b)(2), above, p 429). A 'lay trustee' is then defined under the Act in negative terms as being a person who 'is not a trust corporation and does not act in a professional capacity' (s 28(6)). The key definition in the Act for the purposes of the statutory charging provisions is therefore that of 'acting in a professional capacity' and is provided in s 28(5):

[A] trustee acts in a professional capacity if he acts in the course of a profession or business which consists of or includes the provision of services in connection with –

(a) the management or administration of trusts generally or a particular kind of trust, or
(b) any particular aspect of the management or administration of trusts generally or a particular kind of trust, and the services he provides to or on behalf of the trust fall within that description.

It should be noted that the emphasis is on the nature of the business undertaken as the defining element of 'professional capacity' for statutory purposes. On this definition a person who is a professional and takes on trusteeship not as part of their business but as an individual will be characterised as a lay trustee, irrespective of whether he or she is a Chancery barrister or a chartered accountant or a professional footballer. For this reason at least it seems likely that many trust deeds will continue to contain more widely drawn express charging clauses such as that set out in the next section.

Notwithstanding the statutory changes introduced by the Trustee Act 2000 the starting-point for discussion, and for the law, remains that a trustee is entitled to remuneration only where it can be established that the case falls within one of the following 'exceptions' to the general rule: (1) authorisation in the trust instrument; (2) authorisation by statute; (3) agreement with beneficiaries; (4) litigation work by solicitor-trustees; and (5) authorisation by the court. Each of these 'exceptions' will be considered in turn.

(b) Remuneration: the rules

(1) Authorisation in the trust instrument

A charging clause included in a trust instrument can authorise payment of remuneration to the trustees. Traditionally such clauses have been strictly construed against the trustee. Thus a solicitor-trustee who was authorised to charge for 'professional services' only was allowed no recompense for 'time and trouble' on work which could have been undertaken by someone other than a solicitor (see *Re Chalinder and Herington* [1907] 1 Ch 58). Now, where there is an express charging clause, TA 2000, s 28(2) provides for trustees, in the absence of any contrary indication in the trust instrument, 'to be treated as entitled' to receive payment even for 'services which are capable of being provided by a lay trustee'. The entitlement applies only where the trustee is a trust corporation or is 'acting in a professional capacity' as defined in the Act (see above). Thus s 28(2) does not purport to amend the common law position on strict construction that in principle would therefore still seem to apply where the trustee does not come within the scope of s 28. Consequently, more widely drawn charging clauses, similar to the following example, are still likely to be commonly inserted in trust instruments:

> Any Trustee being a solicitor accountant or other person engaged in any profession business or trade shall be entitled to be paid all usual professional or business or trade charges for business transacted time expended and acts done by him or any employee or partner of his in connection with the trusts hereof including acts which a trustee not being in any profession business or trade could have done personally.

Some early authorities tended to suggest that a widely drawn clause such as that cited here should only be adopted under the express instructions of a settlor fully informed as to its effect. This would not have seemed unreasonable where the non-remuneration rule so clearly held sway. It is at least questionable whether this view should be sustained given the approach in s 28(2) and in a context where default statutory charging clauses have been introduced (see (2) below). In practical terms, however, it is likely that the implications of such a clause would be fully explained to clients and indeed one text book suggests such clauses and their effects *should* be specifically drawn to the attention of the client (*Parker and Mellows* p 826; and see the delphic comments of Vinelott J in *Re Orwell's Will Trusts* [1982] 1 WLR 1337 at 1340: 'it has been said that a wider form of charging clause...ought not to be included except under express instructions given by the client himself with full knowledge of its effect'). The reference in a charging clause to 'usual...charges' imposes a limit on the trustee's freedom to decide on the level of charge although where the fees are those normally charged by the particular professional person it is likely that they will be treated as falling within the scope of a clause such as that set out above. In the case of a solicitor-trustee the beneficiaries can insist on having the charges assessed by a court official, a taxing master.

There are different methods for calculating the charge to be levied on the trust. A solicitor will normally charge at an hourly rate. Other professionals, corporate trustees and the Public Trustee charge fees, on a published ad valorem basis, subject in every case to the addition of Value Added Tax at the rate in force when the fee becomes due (17.5% with effect from 1 January 2010). The following example is of the fees currently charged (wef 1 April 2008) by the Public Trustee (Public Trustee (Fees) Order 2008 SI 2008/611):

Acceptance Fee

in respect of the first £50,000	1.25%
in respect of any excess over £50,000	0.5%

Administration Fee

This fee is due annually on 1 April on the capital value of funds under administration. The fee rates are as follows:

in respect of the first £30,000	5.00%
in respect of any excess over £30,000 up to £150,000	3.00%
in respect of any excess over £150,000 up to £375,000	2.00%
in respect of any excess over £375,000 up to £2,500,000	1.25%
in respect of any excess over £2,500,000 up to £3,000,000	0.60%
in respect of any excess over £3,000,000	0.30%
Minimum fee £375	

Other Activity Fees

An income collection of 7.5% is charged on the gross amount of income actually received by the Public Trustee. There is no fee on the income paid direct from source to a beneficiary.

A reasonable fee may be charged according to the work involved for various duties particularly those of an unusual, complex or exacting nature resulting in the normal fee charged being insufficient.

Withdrawal Fee

From 1 April 2007 no withdrawal fee is charged on the retirement of the Public Trustee in favour of new trustees. A withdrawal fee is payable on the distribution or withdrawal of trust property. It is calculated at a percentage rate on the gross capital value of the funds at the relevant time. In the case of retirement of the Public Trustee other than that just mentioned the percentage rate is the effective rate of the Administration or Management Fee due immediately prior to the retirement and in all other cases one half of the effective rate.

One further change introduced by the TA 2000 is to alter the presumption about the status of an express charging clause. Any payment to which a trustee is entitled under the clause in respect of services is, for two purposes, to be treated as remuneration for services and not as a gift (s 28(4)). One purpose is related to s 15 of the Wills Act 1837 whereby gifts to an attesting witness are void (s 28(4)(a)). Trustees can now undertake work in connection with testamentary trusts and be safe in the knowledge that they can be paid even where they witness the will under which the trust is created. The second purpose is also concerned with wills and their administration. In relation to the administration of an estate a trustee's charges are to be treated, for deaths occurring on or after 1 February 2001, as an expense of administering the estate and not as a pecuniary legacy as was the previous position. The practical effect of this change is to grant priority to the trustee's entitlement over the interests of the will beneficiaries and thereby reduce the risk that the trustees might be unable to obtain their fees in the event of some unanticipated claim on the estate. Both changes had been recommended by the Law Commission which stated that the reasons for treating professional charging clauses as 'a gift' were largely historical and 'closely related to the outmoded view of trustees as "gentlemen amateurs"' (Report No 260, para 7.19).

(2) Remuneration authorised by statute

The Trustee Act 2000 introduces new provisions concerning remuneration of trustees that apply only where there is no provision 'about entitlement to remuneration' in the trust instrument or in any other statutory provision (TA 2000, s 29(5)). This legislative approach therefore adopts the established practice in trusts law of providing statutory default provisions only. Under s 29(1) a trustee who is a trust corporation but is not a trustee of a charitable trust is entitled to receive 'reasonable remuneration out of the trust funds for any services' it provides to or on behalf of the trust. Similar provision giving entitlement to 'reasonable remuneration' is made in s 29(2) for 'a trustee who acts in a professional capacity' (s 29(2)(a)) but 'who is not a trust corporation, a trustee of a charitable trust or a sole trustee' (s 29(2)(b)). But s 29(2) contains a proviso not present in s 29(1) that the entitlement arises only 'if each other trustee has agreed in writing' that the trustee acting in a professional capacity 'may be remunerated for the services'.

There are several points to note about the new statutory provision. One is that the exclusion of trustees of charitable trusts from the scope of s 29 reflects the fact that other policy considerations are thought to be posed by such trusts (see the discussion in Chapter 20 at p 1076). The Secretary of State is nevertheless empowered to make regulations for the remuneration of such trustees (s 30) although at the time of writing no such regulations have been put before Parliament. A second and unsurprising point to note is that, as with the interpretation of charging clauses under s 28, a trustee under s 29 is to be entitled to remuneration even if the services in question are capable of being provided by a lay trustee. Third, the proviso in s 29(2) requiring the agreement in writing of other trustees to the remuneration is intended to act to some extent as a safeguard for beneficiaries. The Law Commission considered that as a matter of principle where there was no express charging clause 'trustees should actively consider whether one of their number should be remunerated' and 'whether this would be to the advantage of the trust' (see for a full review Report No 260 (1999) paras 7.10–7.12 and, for the reasons justifying the non-application of the proviso to trust corporations, see para 7.17). Lastly, a key issue to be addressed might be thought to be the meaning of 'reasonable remuneration'. This is defined not altogether helpfully in s 29(3) as meaning 'in relation to the provision of services by a trustee, such remuneration as is reasonable in the circumstances for the provision of those services' to or on behalf of the trust. It remains to be seen just how the courts will interpret this wording. It does though seem probable that trust corporations and trustees acting in a professional capacity are likely to insist on the inclusion of express charging clauses thereby, by virtue of s 29(5), avoiding disputes with beneficiaries as to what constitutes 'reasonable remuneration' coming before the courts.

In addition to the new statutory framework there remain some more long-standing statutory provisions whereby remuneration can be authorised. The Public Trustee, if appointed, is authorised to charge fees on a scale fixed by Treasury Order irrespective of any provision in the trust instrument (Public Trustee Act 1906, s 9, and see Public Trustee (Fees) Order 2008, SI 2008/611). Other statutory provisions are as follows: (i) TA 1925, s 42 which gives the court full discretion when appointing a corporation to be a trustee, usually as a replacement trustee, to authorise such remuneration as the court thinks fit; and (ii) Judicial Trustee Act 1896, s 1(5) enables the court to assign remuneration to a person it appoints as a judicial trustee.

(3) Remuneration agreed by contract with beneficiaries

Where all the beneficiaries are sui juris they can contract to pay the trustee. These contracts are not thought to be very common and if not 'fair and reasonable' will be viewed with suspicion by the courts and may be set aside (see also *Pettit* p 445 where the possibility of the contract being invalid on the ground of insufficiency of consideration is tentatively mooted).

(4) Remuneration for litigation work by solicitor-trustees

Even in the absence of an appropriate charging clause the 'curious exception . . . ' which is known as the rule in *Cradock v Piper* (1850) 1 Mac & G 664 (LRC, para 3.42) enables a solicitor-trustee, who has acted for *both* himself and a co-trustee, to charge costs for work done in an action or matter in court. The costs incurred for so acting must not, however, exceed the expense that would have been incurred if the solicitor-trustee had acted for the co-trustee only. (See Bishop and Prentice (1983) 46 MLR 289 at 306, on the rather dubious justification for the distinction between litigation and other work; see also Stebbings (1998) 19 Legal History (3) 189 and *The Private Trustee in Victorian England* (2002) pp 38–39 where it is argued that the limitation to litigation costs alone was 'a subsequent and theoretically unsound development' and one probably not anticipated by Lord Cottenham LC in the case itself.) Given the provision in the Trustee Act 2000, s 29 that, even in the absence of an express charging clause, a trustee acting in a professional capacity can claim reasonable remuneration, the scope for the curious exception to apply would seem to be limited. Indeed it would seem to be relevant only to the somewhat improbable circumstance of an express charging clause being interpreted as being too narrow to entitle a solicitor-trustee to pay himself for work done for the trust.

(5) Inherent jurisdiction and the non-remuneration rule

The court has an inherent jurisdiction to authorise remuneration although this seems potentially to conflict with the non-remuneration rule. The stricture that 'the jurisdiction should be exercised only sparingly and in exceptional circumstances' (per Upjohn J in *Re Worthington* [1954] 1 All ER 677 at 678) needs now to be considered in the light of the Court of Appeal judgment in *Re Duke of Norfolk's Settlement Trusts* (below).

Re Duke of Norfolk's Settlement Trusts [1981] 3 All ER 220, CA

Under the terms of a 1958 trust the Schroder Executor and Trustee Company (SETCO) was authorised to charge fees at its scale then in force. Subsequently SETCO claimed under the 'inherent jurisdiction' (i) extra remuneration (£25,000) for exceptional and unforeseen work involved in a central London property redevelopment scheme; (ii) similar sums for additional work in reorganising the trusts on the introduction of Capital Transfer Tax (CTT) in 1975; and (iii) to operate a revised scale of charges in the future, because the trust company's fees were low compared with those of similar institutions and SETCO was incurring a substantial and continuing financial loss. The adult beneficiaries did not oppose the application.

In the High Court ([1978] 3 All ER 907) Walton J approved the first claim but rejected that in relation to CTT as the work was not beyond the scope of any duty which the trustee could reasonably have been expected to perform. Walton J also held that there was no inherent jurisdiction to approve any revision in scale fees. The trustees appealed in respect of the scale fees point only. Fox LJ commented that both Brightman LJ and himself had the impression that since the early 1950s orders had been made in chambers under the inherent jurisdiction to authorise increases in remuneration beyond that stated in the trust instrument. Notwithstanding that this may have been the practice, Fox LJ addressed the issue 'as one of principle and on the reported cases' as follows:

> **Fox LJ**: If it be the law, as I think it clearly is, that the court has inherent jurisdiction on the appointment of a trustee to authorise payment of remuneration to him, is there any reason why the court should not have jurisdiction to increase the remuneration already allowed by the trust instrument?
>
> . . . [I]t is said that a trustee's right to remuneration under an express provision of the settlement is based on a contract between the settlor and the trustee which the trustee is not entitled to avoid, the benefit of that contract is to be regarded as settled by the trust instrument for the benefit of the beneficiaries. I find that analysis artificial. It may have some appearance of reality in relation to a trustee who, at the request of the settlor, agrees to act before the settlement is executed and approves the terms of the settlement. But very frequently executors and trustees of wills know nothing of the terms of the will until the testator is dead; sometimes in the case of corporate trustees such as banks, they have not even been asked by the testator whether they will act. It is difficult to see with whom, in such cases, the trustees are to be taken as contracting. The appointment of a trustee by the court also gives rise to problems as to the identity of the contracting party.
>
> The position, it seems to me, is this. Trust property is held by the trustees on the trusts and subject to the powers conferred by the trust instrument and by law. One of those powers is the power to the trustee to charge remuneration. That gives the trustee certain rights which equity will enforce in administering the trust. . . . But it seems to me to be quite unreal to regard them as contractual. So far as they derive from any order of the court they simply arise from the court's jurisdiction and so far as they derive from the trust instrument itself they derive from the settlor's power to direct how this property should be dealt with . . .

Fox LJ then rejected a proposition that the principles established in *Chapman v Chapman* [1954] AC 429 (see Chapter 7) on the limits of the court's inherent jurisdiction to vary beneficial interests were applicable in a context concerned with the 'ancient jurisdiction to secure the competent administration of the trust property'. The judge referred to *Bainbrigge v Blair* (1845) 8 Beav 588; *Re Masters* [1953] 1 All ER 19; and *Robinson v Pett* (1734) 3 P Wms 249 and said:

> I conclude that the court has an inherent jurisdiction to authorise the payment of remuneration of trustees and that that jurisdiction extends to increasing remuneration authorised by the trust instrument. In exercising that jurisdiction the court has to balance two influences which are to some extent in conflict. The first is that the office of trustee is, as such, gratuitous; the court will accordingly be careful to protect the interests of the beneficiaries against

claims by the trustees. The second is that it is of great importance to the beneficiaries that the trust should be well administered. If therefore the court concludes, having regard to the nature of the trust, to the experience and skill of a particular trustee and to the amounts which he seeks to charge when compared with what other trustees might require to be paid for their services and to all the other circumstances of the case, that it would be in the interests of the beneficiaries to increase the remuneration, then the court may properly do so . . .

I would allow the appeal . . .

Brightman and Cumming-Bruce LJJ concurred with Fox LJ's judgment. Brightman LJ pointed to what he saw as the illogicality of adopting a narrow version of inherent jurisdiction (at 231):

If the court has an inherent power to authorise a prospective trustee to take remuneration for future services, and has a similar power in relation to an unpaid trustee who has already accepted office and embarked on his fiduciary duties on a voluntary basis, I have some difficulty in appreciating the logic of the principle that the court has no power to increase or otherwise vary the future remuneration of a trustee who has already accepted office. It would mean that, if the remuneration specified in the trust instrument were lower than was acceptable to the incumbent trustee or any substitute who could be found, the court would have jurisdiction to authorise a substitute to charge an acceptable level of remuneration, but would have no jurisdiction to authorise the incumbent to charge precisely the same level of remuneration. Such a result appears to me bizarre, and to call in question the validity of the principle on which it is supposedly based.

It therefore seems that, in the appropriate circumstances, payment may be authorised under the inherent jurisdiction either prospectively or retrospectively, and the jurisdiction extends to increasing the level of remuneration beyond that authorised in the trust instrument. Consider, however, the following points:

(1) Should the court authorise an increase in remuneration to corporate trustees who appear to have made a bad bargain? (See Kenny (1982) 79 LS Gaz 217; Hodkinson [1982] Conv 231; Bishop and Prentice (1983) 46 MLR 289 at 307–309.) Consider, in particular (i) the significance of the professional charging clause cited at p 438 being, in effect, index-linked, unlike SETCO's fixed scale of fees, and (ii) whether TA 2000, s 29(3) – 'reasonable remuneration' – is or should be a material consideration.

(2) Can the courts under their inherent jurisdiction intervene to reduce a scale of fees which is higher than that charged by other corporate trustees (see Hodkinson [1982] Conv 231 at 234–235)?

(3) In a previous edition of this book we suggested that 'the decision in the *Duke of Norfolk*'s case establishes that there is now no logical stopping-place short of a presumption that professional trustees will always be entitled to

reasonable remuneration, unless the contrary is clearly expressed in the trust instrument'. This is the outcome broadly reflected in TA 2000, s 29. Note, however, that in the *Duke of Norfolk*'s case all sui juris beneficiaries had consented to the SETCO proposals. There is no corresponding statutory requirement in TA 2000, s 29. Should there have been? Should the prior agreement of all sui juris beneficiaries be a precondition to judicial approval of an increase in trustee remuneration under the inherent jurisdiction?

(4) Note that in some circumstances lay trustees may also be awarded remuneration. In *Foster v Spencer* [1996] 2 All ER 672 an application by lay trustees to be remunerated for work that 'was wholly outside their contemplation when appointed' and that made 'great demands' on their time and expertise was approved. The trustees had over a period of some twenty years managed to resolve difficulties associated with selling, on behalf of the members, a club cricket ground for development, eventually for £911,188. In addition to payment of accumulated out-of-pocket expenses amounting to £121,188, two trustees, one a chartered surveyor (F) and the other a managing director (S) of a local construction company, were awarded respectively £45,600, calculated as a commission of 5% on the sale price, and £50,000, based on an annual fee of £5,000, for their very different contributions as trustees. S's contribution apparently involved his having to deal over a ten-year period 'with the squatters, with the neighbours, with the local authority, with the police and with the press', not quite what we envisage as the everyday duties of trusteeship. On the other hand an application for future remuneration was refused even though the trustees indicated an unwillingness to continue unless remunerated. The court reaffirmed the underlying principle that remuneration would only be ordered where 'necessary for the good administration of the trusts' and that the remaining duties – 'to determine the beneficial interests by an originating summons to the court' – were neither onerous nor required special expertise on the part of the trustees (at 685).

(5) The inherent jurisdiction of the court to authorise remuneration can also be exercised in favour of fiduciaries other than trustees. Indeed, in the appropriate circumstances the court may even exercise its discretion so as to remunerate those who have committed some breach of trust. This extension of the inherent jurisdiction is considered further in Chapter 16 in the context of 'those appropriate circumstances' (see p 883).

7. Trusteeship and indirect remuneration

(a) Directors' fees

(1) The problem

It is not uncommon for trustees to find themselves holding blocks of shares which give them partial or even complete control of a company. Where the trust holds a majority shareholding, the trust instrument may authorise trustees to appoint themselves directors of the company and retain any fees paid to them in that capacity (*Re Llewellin's Will Trusts* [1949] Ch 225); a concise modern formulation is: 'The Trustees may make arrangements to remunerate themselves for work done for a company connected with the Trust Fund' (Kessler *Drafting Trusts and Will Trusts* (8th edn, 2007) p 327). But the trust instrument may be silent on this point. Can the trustees nevertheless use the voting rights that may attach to the shareholding to secure their own appointment as trustees, and if so to retain fees paid to them in their capacity as directors of the company?

(2) A rule

Contrasting views were expressed in two early cases. In *Re Francis* (1905) 92 LT 77, Kekewich J assumed, the point not being argued, that in the absence of express authorisation in the will, trustees were accountable to the trust for remuneration received as directors. *Re Francis* was then not cited in *Re Dover Coalfield Extension Ltd* [1908] 1 Ch 65, CA, where two directors of one company (A) were appointed as directors of another company (B), in which A held shares, in order to protect A's interests. Subsequently, so as to comply with the articles of B which required directors to acquire 1,000 shares within one month of appointment, A transferred the necessary shares to each of the two directors but to be held on trust for A. It was not disputed that dividends accruing to the shares became trust property but what of the directors' fees? It was held that the director-trustees could retain these. The decision has been explained (see *Re Gee* [1948] Ch 284 at 294 per Harman J) on the basis that the trustees there had become directors before they held any trust shares and, although they could only continue as directors by virtue of the shareholding, it was not by virtue of the use of the shares that they either became entitled or continued to earn their fees (see also *Re Orwell's Will Trusts* [1982] 1 WLR 1337). Yet dicta by Warrington J in *Re Dover Coalfield Extension Ltd* suggested a still more liberal approach. He doubted that a director's remuneration was 'profit' for which a trustee should be held accountable at all: 'it is payment for the work which the director does on behalf of the company of which he is a director, and the ratio between the value of the work and the amount of the remuneration is settled by the contract between those two parties' (at 83). This can be argued to represent an attempted modification of the rule in favour of one permitting reasonable remuneration, yet the modification, if that is what it was, was not followed in subsequent cases.

In *Re Macadam* [1946] Ch 73, under the articles of a company, trustees had power by virtue of their office to appoint two directors. They appointed themselves and were held liable to account for the remuneration they received. Cohen J summarised the position in the following way (at 82): 'the root of the matter really is: Did he acquire the position in respect of which he drew the remuneration by virtue of his position as trustee? . . . although the remuneration was remuneration for services as director of the company, the opportunity to receive that remuneration was gained as a result of the exercise of a discretion vested in the trustees, and they had put themselves in a position where their interest and duty conflicted.' The conflict which concerned Cohen J is clear enough. Where trustees are given a power to appoint directors, or can employ the voting power of the trust shareholding to the same end, their duty to the trust is to ensure that the best persons are appointed; their interest as potential recipients of remuneration is to choose themselves for the job.

Subsequently in *Re Gee* [1948] Ch 284 Harman J broadly followed Cohen J's approach, and indeed pointed out that it was not only positive use by trustees of their powers that was relevant but also that (at 295):

> A trustee who has the power, by the use of trust votes, to control his own appointment to a remunerative position, and refrains from using them with the result that he is elected to the position of profit, would also be accountable.

But Harman J is also at pains to emphasise the limits of the rule. It does not, for example, disentitle a trustee who owns shares beneficially from voting those shares in his own interest, nor does it disentitle directors who subsequently become trustees from continuing to receive their fees. Nor will it affect director-trustees where the terms of the trust authorise trustees to appoint themselves as directors. Nor it appears will it prevent a trustee from appointing a company that he controls to carry out work on behalf of the trust and then pay fees to it for doing so, provided that a charging clause can be construed as authorising the appointment, as was the case in *Re Orwell's Will Trusts* [1982] 1 WLR 1337. This approach concentrates essentially, in the absence of any express authorisation, on the independence of the appointment – did the trustees' acts or omissions materially affect the appointment – and represents a step away from a strict rule. But is the emphasis still unnecessarily prophylactic? A distinction based in effect on the trustee's use of the voting power attaching to the shares seems a reasonable one to draw but 'it clearly suffers from being a formula in an area where facts are infinitely variable' (Waters *Law of Trusts in Canada* (3rd edn 2005, p 906) a conclusion illustrated by the following hypothetical example drawn from a previous edition of *Waters*. A competent business person becomes a trustee of a trust with a considerable shareholding in a private company which is being poorly directed. She employs the voting power of the shares to acquire a directorship, and thereafter proceeds to make the company successful. She would be liable to surrender her fees as director. In another case an elderly trustee is invited by the board to become a director, the object being to placate trust beneficiaries. The trustee contributes little or nothing to board decisions. He would be entitled to retain his fee.

(3) A solution

The court, under an inherent jurisdiction of uncertain pedigree (see Green (1982) 45 MLR 211 at 213), is able to authorise a director-trustee to retain a director's fee even if strictly liable to account to the trust. The position was considered in *Re Keeler's Settlement Trusts* [1981] 1 All ER 888, where clause 4 of the settlement envisaged the appointment of trustees as directors of certain companies. However, the standard professional charging clause in the settlement did not indicate what was to happen to the fees of a director-trustee. The court reviewed the extent of its jurisdiction both to authorise the retention of fees already received and to empower director-trustees to retain fees in the future. On both points Goulding J closely followed the approach adopted by Walton J in *Re Duke of Norfolk's Settlement Trusts* [1978] 3 All ER 907 in concluding that the court has such a jurisdiction but subject to strict limits.

Re Keeler's Settlement Trusts [1981] 1 All ER 888 at 893

> **Goulding J**: I am accordingly of opinion that this must be treated as an exceptional juris-diction, to be exercised sparingly, and that the court will only exercise it (save perhaps in some wholly exceptional case) if satisfied that it is plainly expedient in the interests of the trust for the directorship in question to be held by a trustee, and that the additional duties imposed on the trustee are such that he cannot fairly be expected to undertake them without retaining an appropriate remuneration. The appropriate remuneration must be determined by the court in the interest of the trust; it will not necessarily be the whole of that paid by the company for the director's services . . .

Goulding J then turned to consider the question of remuneration already received:

> The test I have taken from the judgment of Walton J is whether any exceptional effort or skill was shown in acquiring the remuneration. That was his formulation in the *Duke of Norfolk*'s case [1978] 3 All ER 907 at 921–922. He paraphrased it by speaking (at 925) of –
>
> > 'those cases where the trustees are held to be accountable for profits which they have made out of the trust, but are in general allowed to keep that proportion of the profits so made (doubtless, in many cases, the whole) which results from their own exertions above and beyond those expected of a trustee . . .'
>
> I do not think that any and every effort or skill applied by a trustee in executing the office of a company director is to be regarded as exceptional or unexpected for this purpose, certainly not in the present case, where it is made perfectly clear by cl 4 of the settlement that a trustee may be proposed for appointment as a director of any company in which the trustees have an interest. The director-trustee, in my judgment, may in a proper case be allowed to retain reasonable remuneration for effort and skill applied by him in performing the duties of the directorship over and above the effort and skill ordinarily required of a director

> appointed to represent the interests of a substantial shareholder. The latter is something
> that a prudent man of business would in general undertake in the management of his own
> investments, and so in my view is in general an exertion reasonably expected of a trustee.

Consider the following points:

(1) *Re Keeler* was decided prior to the Court of Appeal judgment in the *Duke
     of Norfolk* case. What is the impact, if any, of the latter judgment on the
     criteria applied by Goulding J?

(2) Can it now be said that, even in the absence of authority in the trust
     instrument, director-trustees are *in effect* required to disgorge only those
     fees which are unreasonable in comparison with the work done? (See Green
     (1982) 45 MLR 211; Shindler [1981] Conv 237; Hodkinson [1982] Conv
     231 at 235; and for a comparative assessment of English and US approaches
     see Hughes (1980) 30 U Toronto LJ 151 at 171–178.)

(b) Commission and analogous profits

The opportunities for trustees to earn commissions or analogous profits are
numerous. A solicitor-trustee, for instance, may also hold an appointment as an
agent for an insurance company and receive commission on insurances placed
with that company. Can the solicitor insure trust property with the company
and retain the commission for himself or herself? Comparable opportunities
exist for corporate trustees. Banks possess savings departments and pay interest
on deposit accounts; they frequently manage in-house unit trusts which solicit
investments from the public at large. Can a bank trust department place trust
money in the bank's deposit account, or invest trust funds by purchasing bank-
managed units or even bank shares?

Prima facie both solicitor and bank would be making a profit directly by the
use of their position as trustees and a strict application of the rule prohibiting
a conflict of duty and interest would result in both being held accountable.
Whilst there is clear authority (*Williams v Barton* [1927] 2 Ch 9) supporting
the application of the strict approach the trust instrument can, and often does,
authorise trustees to retain commissions and banks to deposit trust funds with
itself as banker (see eg *Space Investments v Canadian Imperial Bank* [1986]
1 WLR 1072). As Lord Templeman pointed out in *Space Investments* specific
authority can modify the general rule: 'Although as a general rule, a trustee is
not allowed to derive a benefit from the trust property, that general rule may
be altered by the express terms of the trust instrument (at 1075; see also the
dictum of Lord Herschell in *Bray v Ford* above at 338; and Mowbray (1996)
10(2) TLI 49). In any event one consequence of the Financial Services Act 1986
(now the Financial Services and Markets Act 2000), and an additional check, is
that commission arrangements for many professional trustees will also have to
comply with such regulations as are promulgated by the relevant professional
body or regulatory organisation.

8. Dealings with the trust fund or beneficiaries

(a) Introduction: 'self-dealing' and 'fair-dealing' rules

In administering a trust there may be opportunities for a trustee to purchase either trust property or even a beneficiary's interest under the trust.
The temptation for the trustee is obvious. In either case the trustee's own interest in obtaining a good bargain could conflict with a duty to the trust or to the
beneficiary to obtain the best price. Equity has developed two rules to regulate the potential conflict – the 'self-dealing' rule and the 'fair-dealing rule' –
succinctly summarised by Megarry VC in *Tito v Waddell (No 2)* [1977] 3 All ER
129 at 241:

> The self-dealing rule is . . . that if a trustee sells the trust property to himself, the sale is
> voidable by any beneficiary ex debito justitiae, however fair the transaction. The fair-dealing
> rule is . . . that if a trustee purchases the beneficial interest of any of his beneficiaries, the
> transaction is not voidable ex debito justitiae, but can be set aside by the beneficiary unless
> the trustee can show that he has taken no advantage of his position and has made full
> disclosure to the beneficiary, and that the transaction is fair and honest.

In fact it is debatable whether the two rules are quite as distinct as might
be inferred from the words of Megarry VC, not least because, as the judge
himself pointed out, their common origin lies in the determination of equity to
prevent trustees from abusing their position or profiting from their trust: 'the
shepherd must not become a wolf'. Consequently whilst each rule is considered
separately below it should be borne in mind that both are manifestations of
a broader 'no conflict principle' which may in turn therefore influence the
practical interpretation and application of the rules in a particular factual
context. It only remains to add at this point the technical observation that
the summary of the rules by Megarry VC was obiter, there being no trust or
fiduciary obligation present in the case itself (see p 842).

(b) 'Self-dealing' rule and the purchase of trust property

The long-established rule was most forcibly stated by Lord Eldon in two leading
cases *Ex p Lacey* (1802) 6 Ves 625 and *Ex p James* (1803) 8 Ves 337. The strictness
of his approach and the rationale for it are apparent in the following passage
from *Ex p James* (at 344):

> This doctrine as to purchases by trustees, assignees, and persons having a confidential
> character, stands much more upon general principle than upon the circumstances of any
> individual case. It rests upon this, that the purchase is not permitted in any case, however

honest the circumstances, the general interests of justice requiring it to be destroyed in every instance; as no court is equal to the examination and ascertainment of the truth in much the greater number of cases.

Subsequent cases have confirmed that considerations such as the honesty of the trustee, the fairness of the price, the fact that the sale takes place at a public auction are all irrelevant (see in particular *Wright v Morgan* [1926] AC 788 and, in the context of a director and his company, *Aberdeen Rly Co v Blaikie Bros* (1854) 1 Macq 461). The purchase is voidable within a reasonable time at the option of a beneficiary. Not surprisingly the courts have been prepared to extend the rule to counter attempts at circumvention. The rule cannot therefore be evaded, for example, by a trustee selling to nominees, or to a partnership of which he is a member (*Re Thompson* [1985] 2 All ER 720), or to a company of which the trustee is a major shareholder (*Silkstone and Haigh Moor Coal Co v Edey* [1900] 1 Ch 167) or possibly even where the shareholding is sufficiently large to be capable of influencing the trustee's decision (*Movitex v Bulfield* [1988] BCLC 104 at 122 per Vinelott J). The self-dealing rule has also been held in *Kane v Radley-Kane* [1999] Ch 274 to apply to a personal representative. In that case the widow of the deceased, who was entitled to a statutory legacy of £125,000, transferred into her own name, without the sanction of the court or the consent of the beneficiaries – her three stepsons – shares then valued at £50,000 that had been part of her husband's intestate estate worth in total only £93,000. Some three years later she sold the shares for £1,131,438. At the request of one of the beneficiaries Sir Richard Scott VC held the transaction void: 'There is no doubt that, in appropriating . . . the shares to herself in or towards satisfaction of the £125,000 statutory legacy due to herself, Mrs Radley-Kane was effecting a transaction in which her duty [to the other beneficiaries in the intestate estate] and interest were in conflict' (at 280).

Where an improper sale has occurred there are a number of remedies available to the beneficiaries. In addition to a right to have a sale set aside – a right also effective against a subsequent purchaser from the trustee with notice of the circumstances – beneficiaries may opt instead to claim any profit where a trustee has subsequently resold at a profit. Alternatively if the property has not already been resold the beneficiaries may themselves prefer to have a resale ordered and to retain a higher price rather than have the property reconveyed. Whatever the preferred remedy, once beneficiaries become fully aware of the circumstances, they should not delay for an unreasonably long period in implementing proceedings or they will be deemed to have acquiesced in the purchase under the equitable doctrine of laches (see Chapter 11, p 602).

Part of the rationale for the rule, however, is that trustees should not *put* themselves in a position of conflict. Consequently, where they are placed in that position by a conscious decision of a settlor or testator the rule will not apply

(*Sargeant v National Westminster Bank plc* (1990) 61 P & CR 518, CA). Thus the trust instrument may expressly permit purchase by trustees, although they will still be subject to the fiduciary obligation to pay the best possible price. In addition, where all beneficiaries are sui juris and have full knowledge of all the facts, they also can authorise the transaction although, given the stringency of the equitable standards that apply to such a sale, there must be some doubt as to the future marketability of property purchased in this manner. For that reason any trustee wishing to purchase trust property is well advised to seek the prior approval of the court to the purchase. It seems, however, that this will not be granted where a beneficiary objects, unless all other avenues of selling the property have been exhausted (see *Tennant v Trenchard* (1869) 4 Ch App 537; and Heward *Chancery Practice* (1983) p 173).

Apart from these almost standard exceptions, it might be thought that the rule had been so firmly established by Lord Eldon's judgments, reinforced by the later authorities, as to be beyond serious question. But a dispute between two members of the Holder family over the purchase of two farms raised questions about the extent of the rule and its justification.

Holder v Holder [1968] 1 All ER 665

A testator appointed his widow, a daughter and a son, Victor, who was a tenant of two farms owned by the testator, as his executors. After the testator's death, Victor purported to renounce his executorship but not before he had performed some minor acts of administration which prevented the renunciation being effective. The two other executors put the two farms up for sale at an auction and Victor successfully bid for them through an agent. Another son sought to have the transaction set aside.

> **Harman LJ**: It was admitted at the Bar in the court below that the acts of ... [Victor] were enough to constitute intermeddling with the estate and that his renunciation was ineffective. On this footing he remained a personal representative even after probate had been granted to his co-executors and could have been obliged by a creditor or a beneficiary to re-assume the duties of an executor. The judge decided in favour of the plaintiff on this point because [Victor] at the time of the sale was himself still in a fiduciary position and, like any other trustee, could not purchase the trust property. I feel the force of this argument, but doubt its validity in the very special circumstances of this case. The reason for the rule is that a man may not be both vendor and purchaser, but [Victor] was never in that position here. ...
>
> Another reason lying behind the rule is that there must never be a conflict of duty and interest, but in fact there was none here in the case of [Victor], who made no secret throughout that he intended to buy. There is of course ample authority that a trustee cannot purchase.

Harman LJ cited, inter alia, the passage from Lord Eldon's judgment in *Ex p James* quoted above at p 452.

These are no doubt strong words, but it is to be observed that Lord Eldon was dealing with cases where the purchaser was at the time of sale acting for the vendors. In this case [Victor] was not so acting: his interference with the administration of the estate was of a minimal character, and the last cheque that he signed was in August before he executed the deed of renunciation. He took no part in the instructions for probate, nor in the valuations or fixing of the reserves. Everyone concerned knew of the renunciation and of the reason for it, namely that he wished to be a purchaser. Equally, everyone including the three firms of solicitors engaged assumed that the renunciation was effective and entitled [Victor] to bid. I feel great doubt whether the admission made at the Bar was correct, as did the judge, but assuming that it was right, the acts were only technically acts of intermeddling and I find no case where the circumstances are parallel. Of course, I feel the force of the judge's reasoning that if [Victor] remained an executor he is within the rule, but in a case where the reasons behind the rule do not exist I do not feel bound to apply it. My reasons are that the beneficiaries never looked to [Victor] to protect their interests. They all knew he was in the market as purchaser; that the price paid was a good one and probably higher than anyone not a sitting tenant would give. Further, the first two defendants alone acted as executors and sellers: they alone could convey: they were not influenced by the third defendant [Victor] in connexion with the sales.

I hold, therefore, that the rule does not apply in order to disentitle [Victor] to bid at the auction, as he did.

Danckwerts LJ: The principle that a trustee cannot purchase part of the trust estate goes back to the statement of it by Lord Eldon LC in 1802 in *Ex p Lacey*. Lord Eldon stated the principle in the most severe form. The reason given by Lord Eldon, that it is impossible to ascertain what knowledge the trustee may have seems less persuasive in the light of Bowen LJ's famous dictum that 'the state of a man's mind is as much a fact as the state of his digestion', and the almost daily experience of any judge engaged in ascertaining the knowledge and intentions of a party to proceedings.

Sachs LJ: It is moreover a matter which may well be open to argument whether the above rule is, in any event, nowadays quite as rigid as was postulated by counsel for the plaintiff. It is clear that the court has jurisdiction to allow a trustee to bid for trust property . . . and in addition it was conceded at the Bar that procedure exists by which a trustee or an executor can obtain the leave of the court in appropriate circumstances to purchase such property: and I understand that such leave has been given even where a beneficiary has objected.

Moreover I agree with Danckwerts LJ in his comments on that part of the foundation of the rule which stems from the alleged inability of a court to ascertain the state of mind of a trustee: and am inclined to the view that an irrebuttable presumption as to the state of his knowledge may no longer accord with the way in which the courts have now come to regard matters of this type. Thus the rigidity of the shackles imposed by the rule on the discretion of the court may perhaps before long be reconsidered as the courts tend to lean more and more against such rigidity of rules as can cause patent injustice – such as was done in *Cockerell v Cholmeley* (1830) I Russ & M 418. The rule, after all, appears on analysis to be one of practice as opposed to one going to the jurisdiction of the court.

The implications of the decision in *Holder v Holder* are assessed at the end of section (c).

(c) 'Fair-dealing' rule: dealings with a beneficiary including purchase of the beneficial interest

Here the less strict approach outlined by Megarry VC in *Tito v Waddell (No 2)* applies. Equity has recognised that a trustee may be in a position to exercise influence or to exploit professional skill or superior knowledge to strike a bargain advantageous to himself. Consequently any transaction between a beneficiary and a trustee is carefully scrutinised and a standard higher than the 'higgling of the market' is set. The onus is on the trustee to show in general that no advantage was taken of the position of trusteeship, and in particular that an adequate price was paid and that all available information was given to the beneficiary (see Lord Eldon in *Coles v Trecothick* (1804) 9 Ves 234 at 247). In short, only the fully informed consent of the beneficiary will suffice.

The contemporary application of both the self-dealing and the fair-dealing rule is most prevalent in fiduciary relationships other than that of trustee-beneficiary. The impact of equity's approach is apparent, for example, in the statutory provisions which now regulate dealings between company director and company and which place emphasis on full disclosure (see Companies Act 2006, ss 177 and 182; and *Movitex Ltd v Bulfield* [1988] BCLC 104; see also Chapter 13 for the relevance of the rules to trusteeship in pension schemes).

Consider the following points:

(1) In *Re Thompson's Settlement* [1985] 2 All ER 720 contracts for sale of two leases of farms, owned by a trust, to a company and to a partnership of which two trustees were respectively a majority shareholder (and managing director) and a partner were held unenforceable. Vinelott J, affirming the traditional approach, distinguished *Holder v Holder* in the following manner: 'The reason why, in the words of Harman LJ, the "self-dealing" rule did not apply [in *Holder v Holder*] was that Victor, though he might technically have been made an executor notwithstanding the purported renunciation, had never acted as executor in a way which could be taken to amount to acceptance of a duty to act in the interests of the beneficiaries under his father's will' (at 730). On this view *Holder v Holder* therefore either constitutes only a limited and technical exception to the 'self-dealing rule' or even, given the Court of Appeal's reservations about the 'intermeddling' concession made in the case, is more appropriately viewed as in substance a 'fair-dealing' case. If the latter, do you think that the Court of Appeal in *Holder v Holder* gave sufficient weight to the problems of detection and proof that might occur?

(2) 'The basic theoretical distinction between dealings with the "corpus" and dealings with the beneficiary is that, in the former, the fiduciary's power is one of control, while in the latter his power is one of influence.' (Shepherd *Law of Fiduciaries* (1981) p 156.) Are 'control' and 'influence' sufficiently different in practice to justify two distinct rules?

(3) Supposing that the decision in *Holder v Holder* were to represent a move towards aligning more closely the 'self-dealing' and 'fair-dealing' rules, should the payment of a 'fair market price' be a necessary but also a sufficient criterion for a transaction to be upheld? Conaglen, for instance, argues that whilst the two rules are just different applications of a common conflict of interest principle 'the substantive fairness of the transaction' is but one evidential element in establishing that 'fully informed consent' is present ((2006) 65(2) CLJ 366 at 396). It is the latter, on this view, that constitutes the fundamental concern of the courts in a 'fiduciary dealing transaction' whether categorised as 'fair-dealing' or 'self-dealing'.

(4) In cases where litigation occurs the facts are rarely sufficiently straightforward to fit neatly within the rules. In *Public Trustee v Cooper* [2001] WTLR 901, for instance, two of the trustees of trust funds and the funds themselves held substantial shareholdings in a brewery company, in the case of at least one of the funds primarily for the benefit of the company's employees. A take-over bid was received that was favourable from the standpoint of the shareholders but less so for the employees who consequently were opposed to the sale of the shareholdings of the trust funds. The trustees sought directions from the court on a number of points, one of which concerned the implications of the possible conflict of interest affecting the two trustees. The potential conflict was not one of 'self dealing' or 'fair dealing' but it was clearly in the personal interest of the trustees for the takeover to succeed whilst, on the facts, it was held to be also in the interests of the trust funds. But Hart J commented on the possible courses of action open to trustees in such situations (emphasis added):

> Where a trustee has such a private interest or competing duty, there are, as it seems to me, three possible ways in which the conflict can, in theory, *successfully be managed*. One is for the trustee concerned to resign.... Secondly, the nature of the conflict may be so pervasive throughout the trustee body that they, as a body, have no alternative but to surrender their discretion to the court. Thirdly, the trustees may honestly and reasonably believe that, notwithstanding a conflict affecting one or more of their number, they are nevertheless able fairly and reasonably to take the decision. In this third case, it will usually be prudent, if time allows, for the trustees to allow their proposed exercise of discretion to be scrutinised in advance by the court, in proceedings in which any opposing beneficial interests are properly represented, and for them not to proceed unless and until the court has authorised them to do so. If they do not do

> so, they run the risk of having to justify the exercise of their discretion in subsequent hostile litigation and then satisfy the court that their decision was not only one which any reasonable body of trustees might have taken but was also one that had not in fact been influenced by the conflict.

Although a different factual and legal context to either *Holder v Holder* or *Re Thompson's Settlement* the notion of 'managing' such conflicts is redolent more of the former than the latter. As Simpson, in a careful analysis of this area of conflicts of interest, has pointed out in relation to the third 'leg' of Hart J's analysis 'This amounts to an application of the "fair dealing" rule, but the consequences are imposed, not as an application of the "fair dealing" rule, but instead as the most appropriate manner in which to manage a conflict between duty and interest in the face of competing considerations...' ('Conflicts' in Birks and Pretto (eds) *Breach of Trust* (2002) pp 75–94 at p 87).

9. Conflicts of interest and duty: the wider picture

'The self-dealing rule is founded on and exemplifies the wider principle that "no one who has a duty to perform shall place himself in a situation to have his interests conflicting with that duty"' (per Vinelott J in *Movitex Ltd v Bulfield* [1988] BCLC 104 at 117, citing Lord Cranworth in *Broughton v Broughton* (1855) 5 De GM & G 160 at 164). Contemporary developments in corporate structures and in provision of financial services are increasing the situations in which such conflicts can occur. Even in the context of trusteeship itself, the potential for conflict has expanded in concert with the changing nature of and role for trustees. Consider, for instance, the position of a bank acting as trustee of a discretionary trust where one of its customers, whose account is overdrawn, is also a beneficiary of the trust. The temptation to favour that beneficiary unduly is obvious, as is the potential conflict between the bank's duties to the trust and its own financial interest. Yet there is some authority that such a potential conflict is not a decisive objection to a bank being appointed as trustee (*Re Northcliffe's Settlements* [1937] 3 All ER 804).

It is apparent, moreover, that the reach of the 'wider principle' stretches beyond the type of duty versus self-interest conflict just described (the 'no conflict' rule). Thus it is also often contended that a fiduciary should not place himself in a position where duties to one beneficiary can conflict with duties to another (the 'undivided loyalty' rule). In the same way that many illustrations of the application of the 'no conflict' rule occur in fiduciary relationships other than that of trustee-beneficiary, so also is this the position with the 'undivided loyalty' rule (eg being appointed a director for two competing companies or a firm of solicitors acting for both parties in litigation).

One consequence of the type of commercial and financial development referred to here is to raise afresh questions both about the nature and scope of fiduciary relationships in general, and about how contemporary conflicts of interest and duty can be either prevented or regulated. In addressing these questions, however, we need to be sensitive to a warning uttered by Lord Selborne in *Barnes v Addy* (1874) 9 Ch App 244 at 251: '[There is] no better mode of undermining the sound doctrines of equity than to make unreasonable and inequitable applications of them.' Much recent development in these doctrines and in the remedies applicable to breaches of duty has tended to occur in contexts other than that of trustee-beneficiary. It is our view that the developments are therefore better analysed within those usually commercial contexts, in particular Chapter 13 (Trusts in commerce: the regulation of occupational pension schemes) and Chapter 16 (Fiduciary relationships, commerce and constructive trusts). Only then will we be able to decide whether the 'fiduciary element' in the trustee-beneficiary relationship remains, to quote Scott again, 'peculiarly intense'.

10

Aspects of the management of trusts

1. Introduction

Management is a convenient umbrella term under which cluster a diversity of trustee tasks. In the case of those trusts not confined simply to the holding and retaining of legal title to designated property, the task dominating all others is that of protecting and indeed enhancing the value of the trust fund through effective investment. But trustees cannot just behave as individuals might with their own funds to invest. The courts of equity, in refining the obligations of trusteeship, have imposed a range of duties upon trustees, some of which impinge directly on the management of the trust fund. In this chapter we therefore consider, in addition to the duty of investment, the duties to act impartially between beneficiaries and not to delegate the trust. There is a complex interaction between these three topics. For example, on the one hand the variety of investments available to trustees suggests a need for expert help, and the process of investment-reinvestment itself necessarily involves some delegation of functions to intermediaries such as real estate valuers, stockbrokers, bankers and solicitors. On the other hand, in principle trustees have until recently been required to reserve to themselves the *exercise* of their discretions over investment decisions, especially with regard to the duty of impartiality. This long-held principle of non-delegation of discretions seemed increasingly to be at odds with a changing economic and social environment. In particular, fundamental changes in the way that investment business was being transacted contributed to a growing perception that there was a need to reform the law on trustees' powers and duties. Various proposals for reform were advanced from 1982 onwards (see Chapter 9 at p 426) and culminated in the Trustee Act 2000. As regards powers of investment and delegation conferred on trustees, the Trustee Act 2000 introduced important statutory modifications to the pre-existing common law and statutory framework. These broaden substantially the statutory default powers conferred on trustees to invest trust assets and in addition permit trustees to delegate more extensively the investment management function. These changes and the resulting legal framework are considered in sections 3 and 5 of this chapter. First, however, it is necessary to consider a major fundamental innovation in the Trustee Act 2000, the enactment in s 1 of a statutory duty of care applicable to, inter alia, the new default powers of investment and delegation.

2. Duty of care

(a) From the 'prudent man' to a statutory duty of care

(1) Introduction

There are two particular questions to be considered about the new statutory duty of care contained in Trustee Act 2000, s 1. What is the standard and why was it felt necessary to adopt a statutory duty? Interpretation of the standard will be considered in section (b) below (see p 463) but in our view that task requires some appreciation of the reasons why the pre-existing legal framework was considered in need of reform. After all the introduction of the statutory duty does not mean that before the commencement date of 1 February 2001 trustees enjoyed a carefree existence with no obligation to exercise skill and care in the management of the trust. Aside from the long-established fiduciary obligations, Chancery developed during the nineteenth century what came to be termed the 'prudent man of business standard', a commercial standard against which the competence and diligence of trustees was to be measured (see Chapter 2, p 48 and the detailed accounts in Stebbings *The Private Trustee in Victorian England* (2002) ch 5; and Getzler 'Duty of Care' in Birks and Pretto (eds) *Breach of Trust* (2002) ch 2). Trustees were expected to 'conduct the business of the trust in the same manner that an ordinary man of business would conduct his own' (*Speight v Gaunt* (1883) 22 Ch D 727 at 739 per Jessell MR). Did this then mean that there was one common standard applicable to all types of trustee and to all types of trust management activities? Unfortunately the answers to these questions became uncertain as the case law developed during the twentieth century.

(2) A variable 'prudent man' standard?

With regard to types of trustee the traditional view was that a common standard of skill and care applied to all trustees irrespective of whether they acted gratuitously or for payment (see *Jobson v Palmer* [1893] 1 Ch 71). This was first judicially doubted by Harman J in *Re Waterman's Will Trusts* [1952] 2 All ER 1054 at 1055: 'I do not forget that a paid trustee is expected to exercise a higher standard of diligence and knowledge than an unpaid trustee and that a bank which advertises itself largely in the public press as taking charge of administration is under a special duty.' This sentiment received firm endorsement from Brightman J in *Bartlett v Barclays Bank Trust Co Ltd* [1980] 1 All ER 139. He explained the reasons for the different standards in the following manner (at 152):

> I am of opinion that a higher duty of care is plainly due from someone like a trust corporation which carries on a specialised business of trust management. A trust corporation holds itself out in its advertising literature as being above ordinary mortals. With a specialist staff of trained trust officers and managers, with ready access to financial information and professional advice, dealing with and solving trust problems day after day, the trust corporation holds itself out, and rightly, as capable of providing an expertise which it would be unrealistic to expect and unjust to demand from the ordinary prudent man or woman who accepts, probably unpaid and sometimes reluctantly from a sense of family duty, the burdens of a trusteeship. Just as, under the law of contract, a professional person possessed of a particular skill is liable for breach of contract if he neglects to use the skill and experience which he professes, so I think that a professional corporate trustee is liable for breach of trust if loss is caused to the trust fund because it neglects to exercise the special care and skill which it professes to have.

This explanation left a number of points unexplained. First, what is the basis for imposing the higher standard? Is it the public professing of a specialist expertise, or that trust management is undertaken for a fee, or that a particular level of competence is to be expected from a professional trustee? The implications of these distinctions become clearer if we recall the threefold characterisation of trustees into unpaid amateur, paid professional – for example, solicitor – and corporate trustee. If the basis for liability is merely receipt of remuneration (must it be any level or a market rate?) then arguably there should be only two standards of skill and care – the amateur and the professional. But if professed or expected skill is relevant are professional non-corporate trustees something of a 'hybrid' (see Shindler (1980) 44 Conv 155 at 158)? Should a still different standard be applicable to them, and if so, what should it be? For instance, should a professional who proclaims no specialist trust expertise but assumes the administration of a trust, at a fee but merely to accommodate a client, be held to the same standard as a fellow professional specialising in estate and trust administration? There have even been suggestions (see Paling (1973) 37 Conv 48) that the ordinary prudent man of business standard was itself inappropriate for unpaid trustees and that they should be required to exercise only the degree of skill and care which they are accustomed to exercise in the management of their own affairs.

(3) Delegation, the duty of care and an agenda for reform

These uncertainties as to what the legal position was and, indeed, should be were compounded in the context of one particular managerial function, the exercise of the power of delegation. The specific difficulty arose over the matter of trustee liability for the acts or omissions of delegates in circumstances where trustees had exercised the limited statutory powers of collective delegation under the Trustee Act 1925. The relationship between s 23(1) and s 30(1), both now repealed by the Trustee Act 2000, became a matter of some uncertainty and debate, particularly as a consequence of a controversial judgment by Maugham J in *Re Vickery* [1931] 1 Ch 572 (see Potter (1931) 47 LQR 331; Holdsworth (1931) 47 LQR 463; Jones (1959) 22 MLR 381. In light of the long-standing academic controversy on this matter it was inevitable that the subject of the standard of skill and care and its material scope would form a necessary part of a review of trustees' powers and duties adopted in November 1995 as part of the Law Commission's Trust Law programme. Moreover it came as no surprise that the Law Commission felt able to conclude in its report that ss 23 and 30 did not form a coherent whole, were widely thought to be insufficiently demanding when compared with the common law and that it was 'necessary to replace them with a clearer and more appropriate duty of care that will apply to both the selection and supervision of agents by trustees' (*Trustees' Powers and Duties* (1999) Law Com No 260, Scot Law Com No 172, para 3.10). Significantly the Law Commission also decided to take the opportunity offered by the perceived need to replace the provisions to recommend 'that there should be a single statutory duty of care with which trustees must comply when carrying out certain prescribed functions'. Equally significantly the Law Commission decided to address any lingering uncertainty as to the standards applicable to different types of trustee by recommending that the statutory duty of care should expressly incorporate a subjective element. These recommendations were adopted and implemented in the Trustee Act 2000, s 1.

(b) A statutory duty of care: Trustee Act 2000, s 1

(1)(1) Whenever the duty under this subsection applies to a trustee, he must exercise such care and skill as is reasonable in the circumstances, having regard in particular –

(a) to any special knowledge or experience that he has or holds himself out as having, and

(b) if he acts as trustee in the course of a business or profession, to any special knowledge or experience that it is reasonable to expect of a person acting in the course of that kind of business or profession.

It should be noted that the new statutory duty of care applies *only* to the functions specified in Schedule 1 of the statute, irrespective of whether those functions arise under a default statutory provision or by a corresponding express clause in a trust instrument. The specified functions include: the exercising of *any* power of investment, including the new duties under Trustee Act 2000, ss 4 and 5 to review investments and obtain advice; the exercise of any power in relation to land, including the acquisition of land; the appointment and review of 'agents, nominees and custodians'; the power to insure; and the exercise of any powers of compromise. The statutory duty does not apply therefore to dispositive powers of trustees such as discretion to select from a class of beneficiaries, or even statutory powers of advancement and maintenance.

Furthermore the statutory duty of care applies only to the *exercise* of a power specified in the Schedule but not to the prior decision about whether or not to exercise it at all. There is no intention to alter what has historically been a more abstentionist role for the courts in this regard; in the words of the Law Commission 'the general rule is that the courts will not interfere in the absence of bad faith on the part of trustees, even though [the courts] may take the view that the trustees are not acting judiciously' (*Trustees' Powers and Duties* (1999) Law Com No 260, para 3.3. and see Chapter 11 at p 543 for a full discussion of judicial control of trustees' discretions).

The statutory formulation of the duty of care mirrors precisely the final recommendation of the Law Commission (para 3.25) and, with its reference to 'reasonable in the circumstances', is akin to the 'reasonableness' standard employed in the tort of negligence. This formula was not the only option. The Commission had set out a series of other possible standards in its 1997 Consultation Paper (Consultation Paper No 146, paras 6.45–6.55). In the subsequent 1999 Report two of the possible options – 'acting in good faith' and 'being vicariously liable for all acts and defaults of agents' – were rejected for being respectively too undemanding and too rigorous. A third possibility – listing a series of specified criteria – was viewed as impracticable given all the different managerial functions that were to be subject to the duty of care. The two further options considered by the Commission were the 'prudent person of business standard' – in effect the common law position – and the 'reasonable in the circumstances' standard now contained in s 1. The Commission noted that 'there may, in fact, be little difference between the two alternatives' because '[the prudent person test] may already recognise a gradation as to the standards expected according to whether the trustee is an unpaid layman, a paid professional, or a professional trustee who holds him or herself out as such' (*Trustees' Powers and Duties* (1999) Law Com No 260, para 3.24). Nevertheless the Commission considered that it was desirable for the avoidance of doubt '[to express] the subjective element of the test on the face of the statute' (above).

It is tempting to conclude that the new statutory duty of care is no more than a codification of the common law 'prudent man' standard. Regrettably the more detailed formulation of the duty of care in Trustee Act 2000, s 1 and Sch 1 still leave open some uncertainties of interpretation and application.

Consider the following points:

(1) There seems little doubt that the incorporation of the subjective element in the duty of care was intended by the Law Commission to reflect the opinion that 'the level of care and skill which is reasonable may *increase* if the trustee has special knowledge or skills . . . or if the trustee is acting in the course of a business or profession' (para 3.24, emphasis in the original text). Notwithstanding this view, can the fact that one of the 'circumstances' specified in s 1 refers to the personal qualities or characteristics of a particular trustee (see s 1(a)) support a proposition that 'it may be that the unintelligent or unworldly trustee owes a lower statutory duty of care . . . than that of

the prudent man of business under the pre-existing law?' (see *Parker and Mellows* p 640). We suggest that it is difficult to reconcile that proposition with either the tenor of the language used in s 1(a) – '*special* knowledge and experience' – or the fact that one of the options originally offered by the Law Commission containing the phrase 'the skills which the trustees actually have' was specifically rejected on grounds of excessive subjectivity (see para 3.24, footnote 51). Nevertheless the possibility cannot be completely ruled out that the phrase 'in all the circumstances' could lead to an outcome whereby a non-professional trustee who acts honestly but ineptly might be held to have satisfied the statutory test but not the prudent man threshold required by the common law test. We must also await clarification on the areas of uncertainty mentioned previously (see p 462) such as whether a professional who proclaims no specialist trust expertise but assumes the administration of a trust merely to accommodate a client will be held to the same standard as a fellow professional specialising in estate and trust administration. Also should the standard differ depending on whether or not a fee is charged, s 1 making no specific reference to remuneration although arguably this may be inferred from the reference to 'acting in the course of a business or profession'? By way of postscript it should be noted that under the previous common law test there was no concrete example where a difference in standards expected of lay and professional trustees was decisive. *Bartlett v Barclays Bank Trust Co Ltd (No 1)* [1980] 1 All ER 139 was the only reported case directly dealing with the issue and there Brightman J considered that (at 153) 'the bank failed in its duty whether it is judged by the standard of the prudent man of business or of the skilled trust corporation'. In both *Re Waterman's Will Trusts* [1952] 2 All ER 1054 and *Nestlé v National Westminster Bank plc* [1993] 1 WLR 260 the banks escaped liability.

(2) Any possible distinctions between the statutory duty of care and the common law test would be immaterial if the statutory duty had completely replaced the common law rule. That does not appear to be the position. The Explanatory Notes prepared by the Lord Chancellor's Department and published with the Act state that:

> The duty will take effect in addition to the existing fundamental duties of trustees (for example to act in the best interests of the beneficiaries and to comply with the terms of the trust) but will exclude any common law duty of care which might otherwise have applied (see para 10).

However, nowhere in the Trustee Act 2000 is there any provision purporting to abolish the common law rule as opposed to replacing it in the several functions specified in Sch 1. In principle where the statutory duty does not apply then presumably the common law prudent man test will still hold sway. That standard will therefore continue to apply in certain situations not specified in Sch 1 such as where the trustees are exercising a power under a trust deed to carry on a business. This may also be the case with the obligation to inquire into or intervene in the affairs of a company in which the trust has a controlling or majority interest in so far as not covered by the obligation under Trustee Act 2000, s 4(2) to keep the trust investments under review, an obligation caught by Sch 1 (see *Bartlett v Barclays Bank Trust Co Ltd (No 1)* [1980] 1 All ER 139; and *Re Luckings Will Trusts* [1968] 1 WLR 866). To reiterate, these distinctions between those powers specified in Sch 1 and those that are not will be immaterial if it transpires that there is no difference between the statutory duty and the common law duty of care.

(3) The underpinning philosophy of the Trustee Act 2000 can be viewed as one of liberalisation of the law to facilitate a more effective administration of trusts. To this end wider statutory powers, in particular of investment and delegation, have been conferred on trustees (see sections 3 and 5 of this chapter). As will be seen, each of these powers has specific safeguards attached to them in an effort to ensure that trustees act properly in exercising the powers in the sole interests of the beneficiaries. The general statutory duty of care in s 1 is intended to underpin and reinforce the specific safeguards. But as is the case with most other statutory provisions affecting trustees this is default law. The statutory duty of care may be modified or excluded 'in so far as it appears from the trust instrument that the duty was not meant to apply' (Trustee Act 2000, Sch 1, para 7).

Moreover the Trustee Act 2000 has nothing to say about trustee exemption clauses. Even where the statutory or common law duty of care is not complied with, the liability of a trustee for loss cannot be taken for granted as there is an important way of avoiding such liability. Corporate or professional trustees will often ensure that the instrument appointing them excludes liability arising from improper investment or limits it to cases of 'wilful default'. If valid to the full extent, such clauses may even have the effect of reversing the hierarchy of standards of skill and care so that the unpaid trustee may be subject to a higher standard than the paid professional. This important issue, now the subject of a Law Commission Report, goes to the heart of control of trusteeship and is discussed in that context in Chapter 11. Also discussed in Chapter 11 is the jurisdiction under Trustee Act 1925, s 61, whereby the court can relieve a trustee from liability if 'he has acted honestly and reasonably, and ought fairly to be excused'. Both of these features must be borne in mind when evaluating the impact on trusteeship of standards of skill and care.

3. Investment

(a) Introduction

It is a fundamental principle that trustees must invest trust funds under their control. Their investment policy can have a profound effect on the real benefit obtained from the trust by beneficiaries. One task for the law of trusts is therefore to provide legal rules to set a framework for trust investment policy, or at the very least to provide a mechanism to enforce a settlor's own prescribed investment plan. The rules need to take account of a number of special factors, which potentially differentiate the investment position of trustees from that of a private individual.

First and most obviously, trustees are not investing for themselves but on behalf of, probably, several beneficiaries. Individuals may be as reckless or as circumspect as they please in selecting their own investments. But in a leading nineteenth-century case Lindley LJ stressed that 'the duty of a trustee . . . is to take such care as an ordinary prudent man would take if he were minded to make an investment for the benefit of other people for whom he felt morally bound to provide' (*Re Whiteley* (1886) 33 Ch D 347 at 355, CA). The conclusion that a more cautious investment policy should therefore be adopted was most graphically stated by Lord Watson on appeal in the House of Lords (*Learoyd v Whiteley* (1887) 12 App Cas 727 at 733):

> Business men of ordinary prudence may, and frequently do, select investments which are more or less of a speculative character; but it is the duty of a trustee to confine himself to the class of investments which are permitted by the trust, and likewise to avoid all investments of that class which are attended with hazard.

Whilst the prudent man of business standard, like the 'reasonable man' of negligence, can appear timeless in its formulation, a question to be considered in this chapter is whether the liberalising provisions of the Trustee Act 2000 have rendered that prudent man standard irrelevant. It is certainly the case that contemporary investment practice, particularly the principles of portfolio investing, may require some reappraisal of what we understand by 'hazard'. Nevertheless it would be premature to assume that the new statutory power of investment under the Trustee Act 2000 permits trustees to disregard altogether matters of 'hazard' and the requirements of prudence.

A second distinctive feature of trustee investment is that trustees frequently have to consider the interests of both those beneficiaries entitled to income and those to capital. Because one duty of trustees is to deal fairly with both interests, trustees must remain conscious of the need to obtain a satisfactory income return, while not endangering the capital. This balancing consideration has led to the formation of a number of rules intended to enforce impartiality of treatment. These rules and proposals for their reform are considered in section 4 of this chapter.

Third, trustees must act exclusively in the best interests of the beneficiaries, best interests usually meaning 'their best financial interests' (per Megarry VC in *Cowan v Scargill* [1984] 2 All ER 750 at 760). Trustees are therefore generally not permitted, at least in the context of family trusts, to subordinate considerations of financial return to non-financial criteria, be they ethical or moral or political. The only significant, albeit limited, modification to the apparent strictness of this position is for charitable trusts: there it has been recognised that 'rare cases' can occur where trustees can decide, even at the risk of financial detriment, not to invest in a manner which might either conflict with the objects the charity is seeking to achieve – for example, a cancer or temperance charity refusing to invest in tobacco or brewery shares respectively – or alienate potential donors (*Harries v Church Comrs for England* [1992] 1 WLR 1241 at 1246–1247; see Nobles [1992] Conv 115). The nature of 'socially responsible investing', as the practice is sometimes called, and the rules of trusts law as they affect it are considered further in section b(5) below. Non-financial criteria are potentially of greater significance in the context of pension fund investment, and this issue is therefore also considered in that context in Chapter 13.

A fourth feature with which rules regulating trustee investment must be concerned is that of protection: protection of beneficiaries from unwise (or unscrupulous) trustees and of trustees from excessive liability for loss. Grosh outlines some possible implications for investment regulation ('Trustee Investment: English Law and the American Prudent Man Rule' (1974) 23(4) ICLQ 748):

> By legal limitation of acceptable trustee investments, the risk of unduly speculative investments and of self-dealing by the trustee can be reduced. To the extent that trustees in fact cannot be trusted, the beneficiaries may be protected by legal limitation on the investments which their trustees are permitted to make. This same sort of legal limitation can provide security from risk of liability for the trustee, who is given clear directions as to the propriety of his investments. There must be reasonably clear limitations on the trustee's liability for loss; and the trustee must have freedom from liability based solely on a loss in value of the investment. Few would wish to be trustees if they were held to be guarantors of the safety of the fund. Limits to trustee liability for loss can be set either by use of a list of investments which are proper, or by setting of standards for trustee conduct with regard to investment.

English trust law has historically favoured a statutory 'list system' albeit one reinforced by common law standards of prudence. That approach has been fundamentally altered by the new powers of investment given to trustees under the Trustee Act 2000.

Finally, to the list of factors can be added that of complexity of investment. The proliferation of available investments and development of techniques of analysis have transformed investment into a technical, even specialised, function. This specialisation then prompts us to appraise the rules of trusts law which determine how far and in what manner trustees are empowered to delegate investment decisions.

Before examining how the overall legal framework regulates investment by trustees, we first briefly consider the forms of investment potentially available and then the development of trust investment law (sections 3(b) and (c) respectively).

(b) The investment marketplace

(1) Types of investment

For present purposes investments can be broadly categorised into two types. The first is where the investor loans capital at a rate of interest; here there exist a variety of both borrowers and forms of loan. The other type of investment is where the investor through the purchase of shares obtains part-ownership of a company but more significantly seeks to participate in the profits: such investment has a greater risk-bearing element. An alternative categorisation is to classify investments into two polar types, those that primarily yield income and those that provide capital growth. However, some investments, such as equities, will be purchased in anticipation of achieving both. Whichever categorisation is adopted, investments can usefully be assessed in terms of the following characteristics which will be of concern to trustees:

(1) whether the income return is fixed or variable;
(2) whether the capital value is liable to fluctuation;
(3) the degree of security of investment capital; and
(4) whether the investment return is free of tax.

The following colloquial guide, revised and updated from one originally produced in 1986 in the Consumers' Association publication *Which?*, categorises the main types of investment available to trustees in terms of the above characteristics. (See generally, Brett *How to Read the Financial Pages* (5th edn, 2003) and Arnold *The Financial Times Guide to Investing* (2004) for excellent introductions to this subject. For more detailed reading, Rutterford *Introduction to Stock Exchange Investment* (3rd edn, 2007); Redhead *Introduction to Financial Investment* (1995); and Gleeson *People and their Money* (1981) provide contrasting approaches that are reasonably accessible to the non-numerate.)

GUIDE TO MAIN TYPES OF INVESTMENT

1. No risk of losing your capital, but rate of interest can change

Main investments. Most bank and building society investments, National Savings investment account, National Savings income Bonds [National Savings Guaranteed Equity Bonds].

How they work. The money you invest earns interest. The amount of capital you invest can't fall or rise. There are two risks; first, if inflation is greater than the rate of interest you can earn, the *real value* of your investment falls – ie it becomes worth less in terms of what you can actually buy with the money. Secondly, you get the going rate of interest. That's good if interest rates rise. But if interest rates fall, the return on your investment falls too . . .

2. No risk of losing your capital and interest rate fixed

Main investments. Bank term deposits, National Savings Certificates, Savings Bonds and Capital Bonds, local authority loans, insurance company income and growth bonds.

How they work. You usually invest for a fixed period of time and get a return which is guaranteed at the time you invest. The main risks are, first, that if inflation is higher than the return you can get, the real value (ie buying power) of your investment will fall; and, secondly, that you won't benefit from any increase in the general level of interest rates.

Comment. Notwithstanding the banking crises of 2008, references to 'no risk of losing your capital' still generally hold true although perhaps 'little' should be substituted for 'no' in the case of banks and building societies.

3. A choice of fixed or variable return (with fluctuating capital value)

Main investments. British government stocks (commonly called 'gilt-edged securities' or just 'gilts'), local authority stocks.

How they work. These are mostly fixed-interest investments (ie they pay a fixed amount of income), usually issued for a fixed period of time, although there are some undated stocks. If you hold a stock until the end of the fixed period, the government or local authority buys it back from you at a fixed price – so you know, at the time you invest, exactly what return you'll get. Used in this way, stocks can be regarded as a fairly safe investment, as long as you don't need your money back early. With undated stocks no redemption date is specified – as the borrower need never pay off the debt.

You don't have to hold the stocks for the fixed period, because you can buy and sell them on the Stock Exchange. As with shares, the prices of stocks fluctuate and so once you have bought some stock, the value of your investment can vary widely.

The prices at which you can buy and sell will determine the overall return you get. For stocks already issued, prices largely depend on the expectation that interest rates generally will change. If general interest rates are likely to rise, the price of the stocks will tend to fall. If general interest rates are likely to fall, the price will tend to rise. Stocks are issued for a wide range of periods. Traditionally, they are divided into short-dated (with a life of five years or less), medium-dated (with a life of more than five years up to 15 years) and long-dated (with a life of more than 15 years). The price of longer-dated stocks tends to fluctuate more widely than that of shorter-dated stocks.

One further distinction is that there are high-coupon stocks (the 'coupon' is the income the stock pays out annually) – [eg Treasury 9% 2004–8 will provide £9 per annum for £100 nominal investment] – and low-coupon stocks. The latter – [eg Treasury 4% 2004–09] – pay out a relatively small income so the return is made up largely of tax-free capital gain. [These differences in return are reflected in the purchase price of the stock. Thus at the time of writing the purchase price of 4% Treasury 2004–08 is £96.32 per £100 nominal value whereas Treasury 9% 2004–09 would cost £114.76 for the same nominal value of stock.] There's no guarantee with conventional stocks that your return will outpace inflation.

What they are suitable for. Stocks are extremely versatile investments which can be used in a number of ways:

- a guaranteed sum at a future date – if you hold the stock to the end of its life
- a regular income – choose stocks with a 'high coupon' (ie paying out a relatively large income)
- speculating for a capital gain – if you're willing to take a bit of a gamble on how their prices will change.

Note. The corporate equivalents of 'gilts' for the investor are debentures and preference shares. A debenture is a form of loan capital and in its simplest form, is an agreement to pay a fixed rate of interest and to repay the capital by a fixed date. Most debentures are secured by a charge against the assets of the company. Preference shares are shares in a commercial company which carry a fixed rate of interest. Being dependent on adequate profit levels (and since they are not secured by a charge on the company's assets) preference shares are a less secure investment than debentures.

As with gilts both debentures and preference shares can be traded on the Stock Exchange and so their capital values can fluctuate.

4. An inflation-proofed return

Main investments. Index-linked National Savings Certificates, index-linked British government stocks, index-linked corporate bonds.

How they work... These investments whose value is linked to changes in the Retail Price Index, largely protect your money against inflation. The main risk is that if interest rates are significantly higher than inflation, you'll miss out on the higher return you could have got from more conventional investments.

5. Going for growth in the value of your capital (with or without income)

Main investments. Shares, unit trusts, investment trusts, investment-type life insurance.

How they work and risks. The value of your capital can rise or fall. You invest in the hope that it will rise. Some of these investments provide a regular income as well.

Ordinary shares. When you buy a share you are buying a stake in the company which issued it. Over the long-term, share prices tend to reflect the expected future stream of profits of the company.

A company's share price will be influenced by things like profit forecasts, new product launches, strikes and so on. For the market as a whole, important factors include economic recessions and recoveries, Government policies, inflation expectations, interest rates, and so on. For companies relying on profits made abroad, the exchange rate will be particularly important. Note that share price movements try to anticipate events.

Unit trusts. Buying units in a unit trust gives you – along with many other investors – a stake in a large number of shares and other investments managed by the unit trust company. There are many unit trusts and they often specialise in particular types of investments or markets – eg UK shares, Japanese shares, recovery stocks and so on.

Investment trusts. These too invest in a range of different investments, so buying into an investment trust gives you a stake in a ready-made spread of shares. Like unit trusts, they offer a range of investment strategies with many specialising in particular markets. But investment trusts are themselves companies quoted on the Stock Exchange and you buy and sell shares in them just as you would with any other company.

OEICs. (Open Ended Investment Companies) are pooled investment vehicles, in company form and to that extent similar to investment trusts. They are the norm internationally and were introduced into the UK in May 1997. For most people, OEICs are easier to understand than either unit or investment trusts because they are quoted at a single price rather than with separate 'buy' and 'sell' prices.

What they are suitable for.

- Income – choose shares generally paying high dividends, or unit trusts, investment trusts, OEICs and insurance investments designed to provide an income.
- Capital growth – over the long-term, shares and investments linked to them have tended to produce good returns, and to beat inflation. But prices can fall, so direct investment in shares, and unit-linked investments, are not suitable if you can't face the risk, nor for money you need at short notice.

Whereas the above account describes the generally available range of investments, there are other types of investment, some highly speculative. Thus antiques, good wine or even land may be purchased with the object of achieving pure capital growth, ie with no expectation of income yield. Moreover, the progressive dismantling of regulation of the financial system from the 1980s onwards contributed to an explosive growth in new types of financial instruments such as derivatives – ie 'contracts' the value of which is supposedly related to the underlying value of, for instance, shares or commodities or currencies or even other derivatives (see Castagnino *Derivatives: the key principles* (2nd edn, 2004); Hudson, *The Law of Financial Derivatives* (3rd edn, 2002); and for an almost prophetic critique Bryan and Rafferty *Capitalism with Derivatives* (2006)). The practice of 'securitisation' – involving the provision of cash in exchange for a right to a future income stream from assets – and the employment of 'hedge funds' are other examples of this development. Whilst hedge funds bear some similarity to other forms of pooled investments such as OIECs and investment trusts, a distinctive feature is that hedge funds have been subject to little or no state regulation and hence have been able to engage in a variety of investment strategies not generally authorised for the regulated sectors. Their unregulated nature means that estimates of the number of funds and their value are necessarily imprecise but it is believed that the global hedge fund market doubled between 1999 and 2004, with asset values in 2007 approximating to US$1.3 trillion and accounting for 40%–50% of worldwide financial market trading activity (see eg Hurst 'Hedge Funds in the 21st Century' (2007) 28(8) Company Lawyer 228). The other uncertainty at the time of writing is to know the extent of the havoc wrought on those markets, in particular by

Table 10.1 Yearly average return from different investments where income tax has been payable at the basic rate

	Period of investment			
	End-1971 to end-1974 % per annum	mid-1970 to mid-1985 % per annum	mid-1980 to mid-1985 % per annum	1926–1985 % per annum
Return needed to match inflation	12.4	11.6	7.2	5.1
Bank deposit account	7.3	5.3	6.2	5.7
Building society ord. share account	6.4	7.3	9.3	Not available
UK shares	(−23.1)	14.7	20.1	11.0
British govt. stocks	(−10.0)	8.9	12.0	5.2
US shares valued in £s	(−7.0)	14.4	27.3	27.3

Sources: Financial Times 17 February 1986 (For a detailed analysis of the period 1919–1966 see Merrett and Sykes 'Return on Equities and Fixed-Interest Securities' (1966) *District Bank Review* June, p 29.)

the collapse in trading in derivatives, castigated by the prominent United States investment sage Warren Buffet in an oft-quoted phrase as 'financial weapons of mass destruction'.

Whatever the attractions and efficacy of these innovations in financial instruments may be for large institutional investors such as pension funds, for private family trusts these instruments would be difficult to reconcile with Lord Watson's injunction to avoid investments attended with hazard. After all, whilst the full extent of the costs of the current crisis in financial markets is unknown we do know that the collapse in 1998 in the US of the Long Term Capital Management hedge fund threatened to destabilise that country's banking system. Moreover it was trading in derivatives that led to the collapse in 1995 of Britain's oldest merchant bank, Barings, and bankrupted Orange County, California (see Crawford 'A Fiduciary Duty to Use Derivatives?' (1995) 1 Stan J L Bus & Fin 307 for the background to financial scandals in the US connected with trading in derivatives).

A very different and less high-risk innovation is the tracker fund that seeks to marry modern portfolio investment theory (see below, p 480) with advances in computer technology. Tracker funds, popularised by Richard Branson with his Virgin Tracker Fund, are unit trusts that aim to reproduce rather than beat the performance of a stock market index such as the FTSE 100 or the *Financial Times* All Share index. Tracker funds tend to have low running costs because management basically involves following a computer programme with a correspondingly reduced need to hire expensive investment experts to mull over the pros and cons of individual shares.

(2) Investment returns: the evidence

Investment is not restricted by national boundaries. There are counterparts to the conventional types of investment described above in many other countries and, as Table 10.1 illustrates, these can prove very rewarding. But Table 10.1 also

Table 10.2 Real investment returns by asset class (% per annum)

Investments	2007	2004	2002	Last 10 years	20 years	50 years	105 years
Equities	1	8.8	(−24.5)	5.0	7.2	6.3	5.1
Gilts	1.2	3.6	6.7	6.5	6.1	1.7	1.1
Corporate bonds	(−6)	3.3	6.6	8.5	–	–	–
Index-linked	1.4	4.9	5.1	5.3	4.1	–	–
Cash	1.8	1.1	1.1	3.0	4.2	1.9	1.0

Source: Barclays Capital Equity-Gilt Study 2003 and 2008

contains a salutary reminder that investment is not risk-free. Whereas the table demonstrates that in the short term (mid-1980 to mid-1985), in the medium term (mid-1970 to mid-1985) and in the long term (1926 to 1985), the average annual return on shares has generally exceeded the rate of inflation, it also shows that it is possible for sharp losses to be recorded (1971 to 1974). Indeed timing is all-important in investment. If, for instance, you had invested £1,000 in shares at the end of 1968, you would not have started to see a real return on your investment until 1983.

The roller-coaster ride of the UK economy since 1987 – from stock market crash in October 1987 via a major recession in 1990–91 to record share price levels in 1999 at the height of the dot.com boom followed by sharp reversals in 2001–02, recovery during the period 2003–07 and yet still steeper decline in share price levels since then – serves only to reinforce the note of caution implicit in Table 10.1. The consequence of this volatility in terms of investment returns to different types of investment is captured in Table 10.2. The data for the year ending 31 December 2008 were not available at the time of writing but there can be little doubt that return on equities would, as in 2002, show a negative figure, with the consequence that one's investments would have been worth substantially less at the end of the year than they were at the start.

One response to the particular set of figures in Tables 10.1 and 10.2 is to reassert the frequently made claim that in the long run investment in equities will always outperform gilts and corporate bonds. Well, it may but that very much depends on the timeframe chosen, the timing of acquisition and disposal of investments and on the questionable premise that the historically exceptional returns in the successful post-1975 periods will be the future norm (see eg Wachman *Observer Business* 6 July 2008 pp 4–5). In these matters trustees, at least of private trusts who must have regard to the terms of the trust instrument and the needs of the beneficiaries, may therefore have less flexibility than large financial institutional investors.

(c) Commerce, the courts and the development of trustee investment law

(1) Speculation vs security

The present principled stance of the law that investment should be characterised by some degree of prudence and that any return belongs to the beneficiaries is not the only possible one. Indeed, it only emerged following the traumas caused by the 'bursting' of the South Sea Bubble in 1720. (See generally for detailed accounts of this notorious share scam and the speculative mania that accompanied it Carswell *The South Sea Bubble* (1993); Balen *A Very English Deceit* (2002); and Harris *Industrializing English Law* (2006) ch 3.) Even Chancery masters had indulged in the orgy of investment speculation that preceded the crash, using funds which had been paid into court. In the sober aftermath, the Chancery court resolved to limit severely the range of investments to which funds paid into court could be committed (see Heward (1983) 4 J Legal History 46). In a step of major importance, it also insisted that, without express authorisation from the settlor, testator or beneficiaries, a trustee holding cash or other property with a duty or power (express or implied) to convert it and invest the proceeds was confined to the range of investments prescribed for funds paid into court. Even if an unprescribed investment was made in good faith and seemed safe, a trustee would be liable for any loss resulting from it (eg *Hancom v Allen* (1774) 2 Dick 498). There thus emerged the concept of 'authorised investments' to which trustees, if not otherwise authorised by the trust deed or the beneficiaries, must adhere in making trust investments if they are to avoid liability for loss.

Having determined by the late eighteenth century that (i) the yields on trust investment belonged to the trust, not the trustees, and (ii) that such investment was prima facie to be confined to categories prescribed by law, Chancery and the legislature had also, in dealing with the emergence of trusts of investments, to prescribe the contents of this list. For a considerable period the only form of investment unequivocally accepted by Chancery was government stock. Even first mortgages of land were thought by some judges to be unsuitable (*ex p Calthorpe* (1785) 1 Cox Eq Cas 182), and although there were dicta to the opposite effect (*Knight v Earl of Plymouth* (1747) 1 Dick 120 at 126; *Pocock v Reddington* (1801) 5 Ves 794 at 800), it was left to s 32 of the Law of Property Amendment Act 1859 to confirm that mortgages of land could be a legitimate form of trustee security. (See Offer *Property and Politics* (1981) p 144 on the extensive mortgage investment by trustees.) In the course of the nineteenth century, other limited categories of safe investment, such as local government stock, colonial stock, shares in a number of specified statutory public utility companies, and, under restrictive conditions, even debentures and preference shares of railway companies were added to the authorised list (see generally Stebbings *The Private Trustee in Victorian England* (2002) ch 5).

These authorised investments were consolidated in the Trustee Act (TA) 1925 and although there were some minor additions (see Keeton *Modern Development in the Law of Trusts* (1971) p 51) the list was not extended, as was being urged, to permit investment in company ordinary shares. Responding to criticism the Lord Chancellor appointed a committee in 1926 to consider whether any revision was necessary. Whilst the report (*Trustee Securities Committee* (Cmd 3107, 1928)) asserted that 'it cannot be suggested that there is any need felt by trustees for a wider range' (para 20), there seems little doubt that the committee was influenced by the government's determination to have trust money channelled in its direction and thus protect its programme of debt funding (see Marsh *Corporate Trustees* (1952) p 223; *Keeton* p 51).

Equity investment therefore remained unauthorised by statute until 1961, despite both clear evidence that those trusts restricted to the legal lists were substantially disadvantaged and dissatisfaction with the status quo. (See *The Committee on the Law and Practice relating to Charitable Trusts* (Cmd 8710, 1952) para 289; Latham (1954) 7 CLP 139 at 153; Law Reform Committee (LRC) 6th Report, *Court's Power to Sanction Variation of Trusts* (Cmnd 310, 1957) para 5.) A significant factor during part of this period was that equities provided greater protection than fixed-interest securities against the effects of inflation on capital and income. It has been estimated that the average net real return (measured by taxed dividends/interest and capital appreciation) for fixed-interest securities fell from 8.3% in the period 1919–1939 to a net yearly loss of –5.7% for 1946–66. In contrast the same average return for equities over the same periods fell only from 11.4% to 6.2% (see Briston *The Stock Exchange and Investment Analysis* (1975) p 174).

Concentration on the formal statutory structure to identify the manner of trustee investment can, however, provide a distorted picture for two reasons. First, a recurrent theme in the history of trustee investment is the evasion of the statutory lists by trustees, possibly through ignorance but also with the encouragement and consent of beneficiaries (see Chesterman 'Family Settlements on Trust: Landowners and the Rising Bourgeoisie' in Rubin and Sugarman (eds) *Law, Economy and Society* (1984) p 161; *Offer* p 112). Second, and most significant, is that the courts left the door ajar for the settlor or testator to authorise trustees to invest outside the statutory list. How prevalent the practice was is not known but by the end of the First World War widely drawn investment clauses permitting investment in equities were becoming more common. Thus Marsh, drawing on the experience of corporate trustees, could comment in 1952 that 'The tendency for increased powers of investment in trust instruments to counter the lack of flexibility in the legal lists has become more and more general since the [nineteen] thirties' (*Corporate Trustees* (1952) pp 226–227; see also *Keeton* ch 7; and Revell *The Wealth of the Nation* (1967) pp 135, 138–141 for statistical confirmation of the prevalence of the wide investment clauses). The irony is that the determination of the Chancery courts to channel trust funds into secure investments and the state's reluctance to extend the list of authorised investments contributed to the widespread use of clauses giving the broadest investment discretion to trustees.

In 1961 legislation appeared to catch up with the practice of conveyancers and the Trustee Investments Act (TIA) 1961 significantly widened the range of authorised investments. In so far as the pre-1961 statutory list of authorised investments reflected a risk-aversion strategy, the major criticism had been that it was based on nominal values of investments and ignored the corrosive effect of inflation on real capital value and income returns. As Table 10.1 illustrates, in the medium- and long-term investment in equities has tended to provide a more effective 'hedge' against inflation than fixed-interest securities, and the TIA 1961 represented a belated recognition of this proposition. The most significant feature of the TIA 1961 was that it empowered trustees to invest up to 75% of the trust fund in equities which satisfied certain requirements. (The proportion was increased in 1996 from 50% by Treasury Order.) But the TIA 1961 attempted to marry increased investment discretion for trustees with a continuing concern for security. Thus whilst the statute conferred a wider statutory power of investment on trustees, it also required them to obtain and consider advice and, as mentioned above, restricted the proportion of the trust fund that could be invested in more speculative investments.

Whatever may have been its merits in 1961, the TIA itself in due course became the target of criticism. Evidence submitted to the Law Reform Committee (LRC) 'made it clear that in the vast majority of cases the Act is either modified or wholly excluded in the trust instrument . . .' and that 'the frequent exclusion of the Act renders it largely irrelevant in current financial conditions' (23rd Report *The Powers and Duties of Trustees* (Cmnd 8733, 1982) paras 3.16–3.17). Indeed it was suggested that in practice the 1961 statute most commonly applied only to: (i) older trusts; (ii) trusts made without professional advice (eg trusts under home-made wills); and (iii) statutory trusts that arise on intestacy (see HM Treasury *Investment Powers of Trustees* (1996) p 4). The Law Commission in its 1999 report agreed with the criticisms that the need to conform to the Act's requirements increased 'administrative and dealing costs', that as a method of regulating the degree of exposure to risk the requirement to divide a trust fund into two parts – narrow range and wider range – was 'crude and administratively burdensome' (*Trustees' Powers and Duties* (1999) Law Com No 260, para 2.17), and that the definition of 'wider range' investments was itself unduly restrictive. As was seen in Chapter 7 it was possible to apply to the courts under the Variation of Trusts Act 1958 to grant wider investment powers but this was an expensive option. The consequence, so it was argued, was that the return to any trust employing a widely drawn power of investment would significantly exceed that of a trust of similar size encumbered by the statutory default provisions. Indeed the comparative performance of two such trust funds is cited as evidence of this proposition. One constrained by the TIA 1961 showed capital growth of 113% and 334% over ten and 20 years respectively whilst the comparable returns on the freely invested fund were 354% and 666% (para 2.18 and footnote 33). In our view such figures need to be treated with caution since, as was seen earlier in this chapter, the timing of acquisition and disposal of assets can quite dramatically affect the rate of return.

Nevertheless, in the light of the response to its Consultation Paper, it was not surprising that the Law Commission recommended that trustees should be given the very wide default powers of investment now contained in the Trustee Act 2000, s 3 (see below, p 490). It must not be overlooked, however,

that underpinning the new default power are the same twin concerns that have
exercised the courts and the legislature for at least the last half-century. Where
should the balance be struck between 'the desirability of conferring the widest
possible investment powers . . . appropriate for the trust' and 'the need to ensure
that trustees act prudently in safeguarding the capital of the trust' (para 2.19)?

(2) Express powers of investment (I): interpretation of investment clauses

It is trite law to observe that the meaning of an express investment clause is a
matter to be determined by construing its language. But it is arguable that over
the years interpretation has reflected prevailing judicial views on investment.
Consistent with the nineteenth-century judicial penchant favouring security
over speculation, express investment clauses were narrowly construed. In 1882
a clause authorising trustees to invest 'on such securities as they might think
fit' was interpreted without demur as merely giving a discretion to select from
among authorised securities (*Re Braithwaite* (1882) 21 Ch D 121; and for a clear
statement of a restrictive approach see *Re Maryon-Wilson's Estate* [1912] 1 Ch 55
at 66–67). But in an effort to circumvent restrictionism settlors and draftsmen
continued to devise, and trustees to accept, ever more explicitly worded and
widely drawn clauses.

A less restrictive judicial view was applied to such a clause in *Re Wragg*.

Re Wragg [1919] 2 Ch 58

The trustees sought the court's direction as to whether a clause in the testator's
will authorised the purchase of real estate as an investment.

> **Lawrence J**: Clause 10 of the will is relied upon as authorising the trustees to invest in the
> purchase of real estate. By that clause the testator authorises his trustees to invest any
> moneys forming part of the trust estate in or upon such investments 'of whatever nature
> and wheresoever' as his trustees should in their absolute and uncontrolled discretion think
> fit to the intent that they should have the same full and unrestricted powers of investing
> as if they were absolutely entitled to the trust moneys beneficially. It has been suggested
> that . . . the trustees in this case can only select such investments as are authorised by law
> for the investment of trust funds. . . . In my opinion it must depend in each case upon the
> construction of the particular instrument whether the investments authorised are confined
> to what are strictly trust investments or not . . . In my judgment if real estate can properly
> be called 'an investment' there cannot be any reasonable doubt that under the investment
> clause in this case the purchase of real estate is authorised. I can hardly conceive that any
> language could have been used which would have given a wider meaning to the word
> 'investments' then the language which the testator has used in this clause . . .

The more liberal approach to questions of construction was subsequently confirmed by Jenkins J in *Re Harari's Settlement Trusts* [1949] 1 All ER 430. After
considering 'a representative collection of the authorities', Jenkins J concluded
that he was left free 'to construe [the] settlement according to what I consider

to be the natural and proper meaning of the words used in their context, and, so construing the words "in or upon such investments as to them may see fit", I see no justification for implying any restriction' (at 434).

It is tempting to conclude that the introduction of the much wider default investment power in the Trustee Act 2000 has rendered redundant any discussion of express investment clauses and of the judicial approach to their interpretation. In fact it is probable that settlors and their advisers, particularly in inter vivos trusts, will continue to confer even more extensive unrestricted investment powers on trustees than those thought to be permitted by the Act. To some extent this preference for express investment clauses reflects a degree of uncertainty as to what meaning is to be attributed to the term 'investment'.

(3) Express powers of investment (II): meaning of investment

The interpretation of investment clauses also must be assessed in the context of the meaning applied to 'invest'. Those who buy works of art, or antique furniture or wine in anticipation of an increase in the value of the assets, might be said to be investing even though none of those assets produce income. The judicial definition of 'invest' in trusts law has been more limited. In *Re Wragg*, for instance, Lawrence J observed (at 64) that the word 'invest' includes 'as one of its meanings "to apply money in the purchase of some property from which interest or profit is expected and which property is purchased in order to be held for the sake of income which it will yield"'. Thus it is not surprising that an investment clause giving 'absolute discretion' to trustees was held not to authorise the lending of money where the only security was the personal promise of the borrower to repay (*Khoo Tek Keong v Ch'ng Joo Tuan Neoh* [1934] AC 529, PC). But if strictly applied, this 'definition' of income would, in the absence of express authorisation, prevent the purchase of a pure capital growth investment.

Furthermore, as a general rule trustees of personal property were not permitted to purchase land as an investment, unless the trust instrument so provided. Indeed, it was held that even under an express power to purchase land, purchase of a house not to produce income but solely for the purpose of conferring a benefit on a life-tenant by allowing her to occupy the house, would not be an investment (*Re Power* [1947] Ch 572; see also *Re Peczenik's Settlement Trusts* [1964] 1 WLR 720 at 723 – property acquired 'merely for use and enjoyment' not an investment). The Trustee Act 2000, s 8 has now statutorily reversed these general constraints on purchase of land. This in effect extends to all trustees the same powers regarding the purchase of land as are made available to trustees of land (including trustees of the proceeds of sale of land) under the Trusts of Land and Appointment of Trustees Act (TOLATA) 1996, ss 6 and 17. The statutory power in s 8 may be exercised to purchase land by way of investment, for occupation by a beneficiary, or for 'any other reason' (see below, p 490).

What the Trustee Act 2000 does not do, however, is to offer us a statutory definition of 'investment'. In this it follows the recommendation of the Law

Commission: 'The notion of what constitutes an investment is an evolving concept, to be interpreted by the courts' (*Trustees Powers and Duties* para 2.28, footnote 56). And the Law Commission is unquestionably correct when it observes that the criterion of 'profit' referred to in *Re Wragg* above can nowadays take the form of capital appreciation rather than just income yield. Judicial support for that stance can be found in *Harries v Church Commissioners* [1992] 1 WLR 1241 where Sir Donald Nicholls VC states (at 1246): 'Where property is held [as an investment], prima facie the purposes of the trust will be best served by the trustees seeking to obtain therefrom the maximum return, whether by way of income or capital growth, which is consistent with commercial prudence.' The fact remains that rather than rely on judicial interpretation of an evolving concept settlors and their advisers may wish to make explicit the breadth of the investment powers they wish to confer on trustees. It must be emphasised that decisions of the court do not establish that a settlor may not authorise trustees to 'invest' as he or she wishes; instead they set certain boundaries to the acceptable prima facie meaning of investment, and if settlors wish their trustees to venture further then the investment clause must give specific authority.

Consider how far the following model investment clause modifies the judicial restrictions on the meaning of 'investment':

> Money to be invested under the Trusts hereof may be applied or invested in the purchase of or at interest upon the security of such stocks funds shares securities or other investments or property of whatsoever nature and wherever situate (including the purchase or improvement of a freehold or leasehold dwelling-house situate in the United Kingdom or elsewhere and of any chattels for enjoyment *in specie* by any beneficiary hereunder who would be entitled to or to whom or to or for whose maintenance education or benefit the Trustees could for the time being pay appropriate or apply the net income, if any, thereof) and whether involving liabilities or not or upon such personal credit with or without security as the Trustees in their absolute discretion shall think fit and to the intent that the Trustees shall have the same powers in all respects as if they were absolute owners beneficially entitled.

Before we review the current default investment provisions in the Trustee Act 2000 it is necessary to consider the possible influence of two relatively recent additions to the agenda on trustee investment. Both may entail some reassessment of the meanings of 'investment' and 'duty of care'. Those two contrasting developments are the rise to prominence of the principles of portfolio investing and, from a less market-driven perspective, the pressure for trustees to take account of non-financial criteria when adopting an investment strategy.

(4) Trustee investment and modern portfolio theory

If pressed to capture in one phrase the spirit of the prudent man rule as traditionally understood we might respond with the oft-quoted words from an early Massachusetts decision: 'Do what you will, the capital is at hazard' (*Harvard College v Amory* (1830) 26 Mass (9 Pick) 446 at 461 per Putnam J).

A principal objective of modern portfolio theory is to minimise the degree of hazard. It seeks to achieve this by distinguishing between three different types of risk: market risk, industry risk and firm risk. Market or, as it is sometimes termed, systemic risk refers to those risks that are common to most securities. Thus the value of securities in the market might be particularly susceptible to political events or to aspects of the general economic climate such as changes in interest rate or the rate of inflation. By contrast, 'industry risk' is more limited in that it is specific to firms operating in a particular industry. A ban on smoking in all public places might be expected adversely to affect all tobacco companies. Still more specific is 'firm risk' where particular events impact on a single firm only. The contrast between 'industry' and 'firm' risks is exemplified in an example employed by John H Langbein: 'Thus if we take the international oils for example, we recall that all the producers suffered from the 1973 Arab oil embargo (industry risk), but only Exxon incurred the liabilities from the great Alaskan oil spill of March 1989 (firm risk)' ('The Uniform Prudent Investor Act and the Future of Trust Investing' [1996] 81 Iowa LR 641 at 647). Whilst not necessarily invalidating the theoretical model, the division between different categories of risk can become blurred. The example of the 1973 oil embargo – an 'industry' risk – is evidence of this in that one consequence of the embargo was a significant global economic downturn – a 'market' or 'systemic' risk – that contributed to the poor performance of the stock market in 1974 (see Table 10.1 at p 473).

This caveat aside, the basic proposition of modern portfolio theory is that an appropriately diversified portfolio of shares can minimise 'industry' and 'firm' risks. The following two extracts illustrate the basic framework of the theory (Pozen) and an important implication for trustee investment (Langbein).

R Pozen 'Money Managers and Securities Research' (1976) 51 NYULR 923 at 928, 940

Economists have developed an extensive body of portfolio theory and empirical evidence on the stock markets. According to portfolio theory, it is a reasonable approximation to characterise every investment by two measures - expected return and risk. Expected return is usually defined as the weighted average of all possible returns from an investment: Risk is usually defined as the average amount of variation among all the possible returns from an investment. As a general rule, risk and return are positively correlated. An investment with a low risk, like a United States savings bond, usually has a low return. An investment with a high risk, like a speculative stock, usually has a high return.

Portfolio theory generally assumes that investors are 'risk averse': they will avoid investments with increased risks unless compensated by appropriate increases in expected returns. This assumption of risk aversion is probably realistic for most investors ...

The basic principle of diversification is that the overall construction of the portfolio, rather than the selection of individual securities, should be the focus of investment decisions. To the extent that the individual securities in the portfolio react differently to the same future events, the aggregate risk of a portfolio of securities is lower than the average of the risks of the individual securities. To take a simplified example, suppose a portfolio consists of two shares of stock – one from Company A that manufactures oil heaters, the other from Company B that manufactures gas heaters. If only oil prices increase, the stock of Company A will decline but the stock of Company B will rise. Conversely if only gas prices increase, the stock of Company A will rise but the stock of Company B will decline. Since the price movement of each share of stock is offset by the price movement of the other share of stock, the aggregate risk of this portfolio will be lower than the average of the risks of both shares.

J H Langbein and R A Posner 'Market Funds and Trust – Investment Law' [1976] American Bar Foundation Research Journal 1 at 6

A. Portfolio Design
The trustee's investment decision involves two conceptually distinct steps. One is evaluating specific assets that might be included in the trust. The other is combining specific assets to form the trust's portfolio, the package of assets constituting the corpus of the trust. The great emphasis of the law of trusts has been on the first step; less attention has been paid to the design of the portfolio. Yet from the beneficiary's standpoint – which is, of course, the relevant standpoint – what counts is the performance of the portfolio rather than the performance of its individual components. If the value of the portfolio rises from $500,000 to $600,000, what does it matter to the beneficiary whether this increase resulted from a uniform 20 per cent increase in the value of all of the assets in the portfolio or from larger gains in a few of the assets partially offset by losses in others? Conversely, if the portfolio has declined in value, it is of small comfort to the beneficiary to know that one of the components did spectacularly well rather than that all had declined. From the beneficiary's standpoint, the portfolio is the relevant security.

There is little doubt that in at least two respects the prudent man standard as conventionally understood was incompatible with modern portfolio theory. One requirement of the prudent man standard was that trustees should avoid investments, even if within the authorised class, which in Lord Watson's words 'are attended with hazard'. Indeed in the leading case *Learoyd v Whiteley*, although a mortgage on a freehold brickfield was within the trustees' investment authority, because the particular property was a wasting asset the security was of a 'peculiarly hazardous nature' and investment in it therefore constituted a breach of trust. Second, the historic assumption of the prudent man rule was that each investment should be separately evaluated, rather than considered as part of a portfolio of investments. It is evident with the benefit of hindsight that there was an increasing disjuncture between those two aspects of the prudent man standard and the widespread acceptance of the tenets of portfolio investing amongst the investment community generally. When the opportunity arose through the pleadings in *Nestlé v National Westminster Bank plc* (29 June 1988), the court was prepared to modify the prudent man standard to reflect the basic 'diversification' tenet of portfolio theory ((1996) 10 TLI 113; see also Ford (1996) 10(4) TLI 102). Hoffmann J stated that 'modern trustees acting within their investment powers are entitled to be judged by the standards of current portfolio theory, which emphasises the risk level of the entire portfolio rather than the risk attaching to each investment taken in isolation'. Writing extra-judicially Lord Nicholls has endorsed this approach, at least in its application to a large fund although the reasoning behind his conclusions seem more generally applicable ((1995) 9(3) TLI 71 at 76):

> Traditional warnings against the need for trustees to avoid speculative or hazardous investments are not to be read as inhibiting trustees from maintaining portfolios of investments which contain a prudent and sensible mixture of low-risk and higher-risk securities. They are not to be so read, because they were not directed at a portfolio which is a balanced exercise in risk management.

There are two observations to be made here about this judicial recognition of the 'standards of current portfolio theory'. First, it would be unwise to assume that trustees now have carte blanche to ignore the hazardous nature of an individual investment. The distinction they must now draw 'is between a prudent degree of risk on the one hand, and hazard on the other' (*Bartlett v Barclays Bank Trust Co Ltd* [1980] 1 All ER 139 at 150). In *Bartlett* a speculative property-development project was considered too hazardous for trustees, although acceptable to the board of a wealthy company. Where the balance lies between 'prudence' and 'hazard' is likely to depend to some degree on the characteristics of the trust fund. In *Trustees of the British Museum v A-G* [1984] 1 All ER 337, Megarry VC, approving an application under the Variation of Trusts Act 1958 to widen the range of authorised investments, commented that a material consideration is the size of the fund: 'A fund that is very large may well justify a latitude of investment that would be denied to a more modest fund; for the spread of investments possible for a larger fund may justify the greater risks that wider powers will permit to be taken' (at 343). Whilst such comments fall short of endorsing speculative investments it may be inferred that whether an investment is labelled 'hazardous' is a reflection both of the characteristics of the individual investment and the size of the fund: the larger the fund, the greater the degree of risk that is considered reasonable in respect of a particular investment.

Our second observation concerns the practical implications for trustees of the judicial acceptance of the 'standards of current portfolio theory'. The use of the singular 'theory' here is potentially misleading. Whilst the basic 'diversification tenet of the theory' is uncontentious and comprehensible, its practical implementation has spawned a diversity of complex mathematically based models, few of which would, we suggest, be comprehensible to the average or even more financially sophisticated trustee (see for a general and quite basic overview Elton and Gruber in Longstreth, *Modern Investment Management and the Prudent Man Rule* (1986) Appendix A). The appropriate response of the reasonable trustee will be either to seek advice or to delegate the management of the trust fund (see below, p 516). But this is no panacea or guarantee of success. In the year 2008, for example, only three out of the 30 *Financial Times* categories of funds under professional investment portfolio management showed a positive return, with the overall performance varying from +10.34% to –40.44%. Of course 2008 was an exceptional year in financial markets. But even if we take a longer period – from the bear market caused in 2000 by the fallout from the dot.com boom, through a bull market starting in March 2003 to the bear market starting in July 2007 – only nine out of 177 actively managed investment funds in the UK All Companies sector throughout that time outperformed the FTSE All Share Index (Britton, *Financial Times* 12 December 2008). It would have needed a very astute or lucky investment adviser to have accurately identified in March 2000 those nine funds.

Some of the implications of the above two observations for accountability and liability of trustees are considered further at pp 495–6.

(5)　Investment and non-financial criteria

If trustees are to be expected to follow the tenets of modern portfolio theory in exercising their powers of investment then, at first glance, this would seem to exclude any consideration of non-financial criteria or, as it is more commonly termed, 'social investing'. Yet, as mentioned in the Introduction to this section of the chapter (see p 466), the appropriateness of a stance that would appear to exclude consideration of such criteria from the deliberations of trustees is not beyond question. (See generally Lord Nicholls (1995) 9 TLI 71; McCormack (1998) 19 Co Law (2) 39; Irish and Kent (1994) 8 TLI 10; Salisbury (ed) *Should Pension Assets be Managed for Social/Political Purposes?* (1980); and from a more critical standpoint Thornton (2008) 67(2) CLJ 396–422 and Langbein and Posner (1980) 79 Mich LR 72.) Before examining the legal response to 'social investing' it is necessary to clarify what is understood by that term and also the different ways in which trustees might employ non-financial criteria in decision-making. Whilst the following account is concerned with social investing in the context of pension schemes, the categorisation employed, if not all the implications, is equally applicable to other trust types.

J D Hutchinson and C G Cole 'Legal Standards Governing Investment of Pension Assets for Social and Political Goals' (1979–80) 128 U Pa LR 1344 at 1344–1345

The techniques for implementing a policy of social investing may also vary widely: from a policy of excluding future investments in particular companies, to the affirmative selection of certain preferred investments, to the divestiture of undesirable investments. In each of these situations, moreover, the relative weight given to economic and social factors may be different: social considerations may dictate investment policy, or they may be invoked only as a guide when all other characteristics are comparable.

Most of the diverse practices discussed in the context of 'social investing' can be classified within one of three basic categories: (1) totally neutral investment policies; (2) socially sensitive investment policies; or (3) socially dictated investment policies.

'Totally neutral investment policies' focus solely on the financial aspects of investment alternatives. Fiduciaries would analyse the traditional investment considerations, such as the plan characteristics (design, funding, etc), risk/return considerations, liquidity, and diversification. Within this frame of reference, it may be that labor-relations practices, compliance with environmental or safety standards, or other policies could affect the financial stability and profitability of a company whose securities are being analysed. If the fiduciary performing the financial analysis of the investment activity has a sound empirical basis for considering these factors, then their use is defensible on purely financial grounds. The fiduciary does not override basic financial investment considerations for the sake of a social objective, nor does he temper judgements on comparable alternatives by focusing on non-investment factors. The question of 'social investing' never arises in this setting, and we need not confuse the legal analysis applicable to 'social investing' by belabouring such practices.

'Socially sensitive investment policies' include those investment practices in which the investing fiduciary analyses traditional investment considerations such as plan character-istics, risk/return factors, liquidity, and diversification. Once this analysis is completed, however, the fiduciary then selects among financially comparable investment alternatives by considering other factors . . .

There remains the question, however, whether the investment is being undertaken 'solely in the interest' of plan participants and beneficiaries. It is at this point that certain 'socially sensitive' investment policies that consider non-financial factors may pass legal muster, while others may not . . . Certain policies that are intended to serve the interests of plan participants, in their capacity as participants, may be employed. On the other hand, policies that cannot be related in some plausible fashion to the primary interests of plan participants, but instead serve the interests of the employer, union, or third parties, may well violate this standard of loyalty.

'Socially dictated investment policies' are those investment practices and policies which either (1) permit the sacrifice of safety, return, diversification, or marketability; or (2) are undertaken to serve some objective that cannot be related to the interests of plan partici-pants and beneficiaries in their capacity as such. When a plan fiduciary sacrifices traditional investment quality, he faces the substantial risk of violating the prudence standard.

This issue was first litigated in the UK in *Cowan v Scargill* [1985] Ch 270, a case concerning the investment policy of the mineworkers' pension fund. The National Union of Mineworkers (NUM) and the National Coal Board each nominated half of the trustees. The investment strategy required the unanimous approval of trustees but the NUM nominees refused to agree to an investment plan submitted by a panel of investment advisers in so far as the plan conflicted with the stated policy of the union executive on the investment of the pension fund (see further Chapter 13 at p 688 where more detailed consideration is given to the relevance of non-financial criteria to pension fund investment). In particular the NUM and its nominees objected to new and continuing investments overseas and to investments in energy resources competing with coal.

The initial response of the court when faced with this issue seemed straight-forwardly premised on fundamental principles of trust law. Megarry VC sum-marised the position as follows (at 287–288):

> The starting point is the duty of trustees to exercise their powers in the best interests of the present and future beneficiaries of the trust, holding the scales impartially between different classes of beneficiaries. This duty of the trustees towards their beneficiaries is paramount. They must, of course, obey the law; but subject to that, they must put the interests of their beneficiaries first. When the purpose of the trust is to provide financial benefits for the beneficiaries, as is usually the case, the best interests of the beneficiaries are normally their best financial interests. In the case of a power of investment, as in the present case, the power must be exercised so as to yield the best return for the beneficiaries, judged in relation to the risks of the investments in question; and the prospects of the yield of income and capital appreciation both have to be considered in judging the return from the investment.
>
> This leads me to the second point, which is a corollary of the first. In considering what investments to make trustees must put on one side their own personal interests and views. Trustees may have strongly held social or political views. They may be firmly opposed to any investment in South Africa or other countries, or they may object to any form of investment in companies concerned with alcohol, tobacco, armaments or many other things. In the conduct of their own affairs, of course, they are free to abstain from making any such investments. Yet if under a trust investments of this type would be more beneficial to the beneficiaries than other investments, the trustees must not refrain from making the investments by reason of the views that they hold.

Megarry VC acknowledged that there might be rare instances when this stance might be modified even where the only object of the trust was to provide financial benefits. The somewhat unlikely scenario is posited of a trust where all the actual and potential beneficiaries are adults with very strict views on moral and social matters, condemning all forms of alcohol, tobacco and popular entertainment, as well as armaments. In these circumstances 'it might not be for the "benefit" of such beneficiaries to know that they are obtaining rather larger financial returns under the trust by reason of investments in those activities than they would have received if the trustees had invested the trust fund in other investments. The beneficiaries might well consider that it was far better to receive less than to receive more money from what they consider to be evil and tainted sources' (ibid).

There are two other instances where the apparent rigour of Megarry VC's approach may not apply. One, most obviously, is where the trust instrument itself requires, let us say, the trustees to avoid investments in armaments manufacturers. The other instance can occur in the context of charitable trusts where particular investments may be incompatible with the purpose of the charity. The facts of the case in which the latter issue was aired, *Harries v Church Commissioners for England* [1992] 1 WLR 1241, were rather atypical in that the purpose of the fund to be invested was to some extent closer to that of a pension fund. Almost 85% of the income of the fund was absorbed by stipends for serving clergy, pensions for retired clergy and much of the housing cost for both groups. In short it might be argued that the investment policy of the Church Commissioners should be driven by purely financial considerations. In contrast the then Bishop of Oxford and other clergy sought a declaration that the Commissioners should not select investments that would be incompatible with the purpose of 'the promotion of the Christian faith through the Church of England' even if this involved some risk of financial detriment. Sir Donald Nicholls VC declined to grant the remedy sought, holding that the Commissioners' policy was not erroneous in law in that they were only prepared to take non-financial considerations into account to the extent that they did not 'significantly jeopardise or interfere with accepted investment principles'. In short the Church Commissioners appeared to follow what, applying the Hutchinson and Cole categorisation, could be termed a 'socially sensitive' investment policy. Nevertheless, in the judgment the Vice-Chancellor considered whether there were any circumstances where financial criteria could be subordinated to other criteria (at 1246–1247):

> In most cases the best interests of the charity require that the trustees' choice of investments should be made solely on the basis of well-established investment criteria, having taken expert advice where appropriate and having due regard to such matters as the need to diversify, the need to balance income against capital growth, and the need to balance risk against return.
>
> In a minority of cases the position will not be so straightforward. There will be some cases, I suspect comparatively rare, when the objects of the charity are such that investments of a particular type would conflict with the aims of the charity. Much-cited examples are those of cancer research charities and tobacco shares, trustees of temperance charities and brewery and distillery shares, and trustees of charities of the Society of Friends and shares in companies engaged in production of armaments. If, as would be likely in those examples, trustees were satisfied that investing in a company engaged in a particular type of business would conflict with the very objects their charity is seeking to achieve, they should not so invest. Carried to its logical conclusion the trustees should take this course even if it would be likely to result in significant financial detriment to the charity. The logical conclusion, whilst sound as a matter of legal analysis, is unlikely to arise in practice. It is not easy to think of an instance where in practice the exclusion for this reason of one or more

companies or sectors from the whole range of investments open to trustees would be likely to leave them without an adequately wide range of investments from which to choose a properly diversified portfolio.

There will also be some cases, again I suspect comparatively rare, when trustees' holdings of particular investments might hamper a charity's work either by making potential recipients of aid unwilling to be helped because of the source of the charity's money, or by alienating some of those who support the charity financially. In these cases the trustees will need to balance the difficulties they would encounter, or likely financial loss they would sustain, if they were to hold the investments against the risk of financial detriment if those investments were excluded from their portfolio. The greater the risk of financial detriment, the more certain the trustees should be of countervailing disadvantages to the charity before they incur that risk.

Another circumstance where trustees would be entitled, or even required, to take into account non-financial criteria would be where the trust deed so provides.

No doubt there will be other cases where trustees are justified in departing from what should always be their starting point. The instances I have given are not comprehensive. But I must emphasise that of their very nature, and by definition, investments are held by trustees to aid the work of the charity in a particular way: by generating money. That is the purpose for which they are held. That is their raison d'être. Trustees cannot properly use assets held as an investment for other, viz non-investment, purposes. To the extent that they do they are not properly exercising their powers of investment.... I should mention one other particular situation. There will be instances today when those who support or benefit from a charity take widely different views on a particular type of investment, some saying that on moral grounds it conflicts with the aims of the charity, others saying the opposite. One example is the holding of arms industry shares by a religious charity. There is a real difficulty here. To many questions raising moral issues there are no certain answers. On moral questions widely differing views are held by well-meaning, responsible people. This is not always so. But frequently, when questions of the morality of conduct are being canvassed, there is no identifiable yardstick which can be applied to a set of facts so as to yield one answer which can be seen to be 'right' and the other 'wrong'. If that situation confronts trustees of a charity, the law does not require them to find an answer to the unanswerable. Trustees may, if they wish, accommodate the views of those who consider that on moral grounds a particular investment would be in conflict with the objects of the charity, so long as the trustees are satisfied that course would not involve a risk of significant financial detriment. But when they are not so satisfied trustees should not make investment decisions on the basis of preferring one view of whether on moral grounds an investment conflicts with the objects of the charity over another. This is so even when one view is more widely supported than the other.

Whilst the leading cases cited here appear to support a quite restrictive view of the acceptability of 'non-financial criteria' it is tempting to conclude that a more nuanced view can be detected at least as regards 'socially sensitive' investing. This is partly because the very breadth of investment opportunities in the market is so extensive as to enable trustees, as Lord Nicholls writing extra-judicially has noted, 'to give effect to moral considerations, either by positively preferring certain investments or negatively avoiding others, without thereby prejudicing beneficiaries' financial interests' ((1995) 9(3) TLI 71 at 75; see also Megarry VC in *Cowan v Scargill* [1985] 1 Ch 270 at 297: 'If the investment in fact made is equally beneficial to the beneficiaries, then criticism would be difficult to sustain in practice, whatever the position in theory'). More prosaically, as will be seen in section (e)(1) below, actually proving that a particular investment policy has caused a loss to the fund is far from a straightforward matter.

In any event it should not be assumed that an investment policy that satisfies social goals necessarily results in even short-term financial detriment. Although ethically managed unit trusts are of relatively recent vintage, having only been available in the UK since 1984, there is evidence of sustained performance producing financial returns roughly equivalent to the performance of the FTSE All-Shares index over a comparable period (see McCormack (1998) 19 Co Law (2) 39 at 48–49). For example if we select the period prior to the downturn in stock market values in 1999, the most longstanding ethical fund grew 933% between 1984 and 1998, compared to the average for the UK equity sector of 735%. The overall comparative performance of the sectors tends to endorse this assessment. In a report published in November 2002, UK stockbrokers West LB Panmure comment: 'Although the observation period is not long enough to be able to draw final conclusions, a simple performance comparison already shows that the frequently voiced hypothesis of a systematic return disadvantage of ethical/SRI is clearly not supported by the present data.' This positive performance of the ethical sector has continued even in the period of relative volatility in share values since 1999. In July 2001, the FTSE4Good Index series was launched to measure the performance of companies that meet globally recognised corporate responsibility standards, and to facilitate investment in those companies. Analysis of the performance of the FTSE4Good Global Index over the past five years when compared directly with the FTSE100 index of the UK's most highly capitalised shares shows the two indices moving in a fairly close relationship but also highlights past periods of outperformance by the ethical index and vice versa (see www.ftse.com/ftse4good, and generally www.ethicalinvestors.co.uk; and www.Eiris.org).

It must be emphasised, however, that the sums invested in ethical funds remain relatively modest – at £8.9 billion at the end of 2007 compared with approximately £400 billion in all UK retail funds – and this necessarily limits the weight to be attached to the empirical data. Indeed, for those who remain unpersuaded of either the virtue or the economic value of ethical investing solace might be found in a proposition based on analysis of a US index, the S & P 500. The proponent of the proposition, C Warder, argues that whilst vices such as alcohol, tobacco and gambling may be deemed socially irresponsible, in the investment world in a depressed market such as that operating since 1999 these stocks continue dramatically to outperform the S & P 500 (*The Wages of Sin* (2004)).

(d) Powers of investment and the Trustee Act 2000

(1) The scope of the statutory power

The Trustee Act 2000 (TA) confers on trustees the extensive statutory powers of investment recommended by the Law Commission. In particular s 3(1) provides that 'a trustee may make any kind of investment that he could make if he were absolutely entitled to the assets of the trust'. The 'general power of investment', as this new power is called (s 3(2)), is subject to the qualification that investments in land are not permitted other than by way of 'loans secured on land' (s 3(3)). This restriction is rendered more apparent than real by virtue of s 8(1) of the Act, which states that:

> 8(1) A trustee may acquire freehold or leasehold land in the United Kingdom –
>
> (a) as an investment,
> (b) for occupation by a beneficiary, or
> (c) for any other reason.

This initially confusing drafting arrangement involving ss 3 and 8 is attributable partly to the perceived need to give trustees powers to purchase land other than for investment reasons (s 8(1)(b) and (c)). It will be recalled that a weakness of the investment powers as interpreted in the cases was that the purchase of land for the purpose of providing property for occupation by a beneficiary, now provided in s 8(1)(b), did not qualify as an 'investment' (*Re Power* [1947] Ch 572). This restriction on the powers of trustees was removed by TOLATA 1996, s 6(3), but only for trusts of property that included land or the proceeds of sale of land. TA 2000, s 8 simply extends to all trusts, including those where the property is only personalty, those same powers in relation to the acquisition of land.

Subject to certain exceptions, the general power of investment applies to all trusts 'whether created before or after' the commencement of the Act (s 7(1)) and 'in addition to powers conferred on trustees otherwise than by [the Act]' most obviously by a trust instrument (s 6(1)(a)). The exceptions just referred to are those where a separate statutory regime applies. The general power of investment does not therefore apply to pension trusts, to unit trusts or to certain common investment or deposit schemes for charities (see TA 2000, ss 36–38). As is common with most other statutory powers conferred on trustees, the new power of investment is a default power. It is therefore subject to 'any restriction or exclusion imposed by the trust instrument' (s 6(1)(b)) whether created before or after the 2000 Act. It should, however, be noted that restrictions or exclusions contained in a trust instrument made *before* 3 August 1961, the commencement date of the TIA 1961, are to be ignored (TA 2000, s 7(2)). To do otherwise would in effect resurrect restrictions in the trust instrument that had been overcome by the now repealed s 1(3) of the TIA 1961.

Finally, on a point of interpretation, care will be needed in applying s 6(1)(a) and (b) to investment clauses drafted *after* 3 August 1961 and intended to grant wider powers than those available under the TIA 1961. How, for instance, should we construe a power in a trust instrument permitting trustees to 'invest in any shares quoted on the London Stock Exchange' – ie a power more extensive than that under the TIA 1961 but more restrictive than the TA 2000, s 3 power? Should this be interpreted as 'a restriction' on the general power of investment? To do so would not seem to be in keeping with the liberalising approach of the legislation. It therefore seems probable that any restriction or exclusion will need to be explicitly worded if it is to have effect. The Explanatory Notes accompanying the TA 2000 suggest that an express power 'to invest in shares quoted on the London Stock Exchange but not in shares of X plc' would take effect as the general power of investment subject *only* to the restriction on investing in X plc.

(2) Varying investment clauses

As was mentioned in Chapter 7, one of the purposes of applications to the court under the Variation of Trusts Act (VTA) 1958 was to amend restricted powers of investment. Indeed TIA 1961, s 15 expressly provided that the statute was not to affect the VTA jurisdiction. Nevertheless a line of cases commencing with *Re Kolb's Will Trusts* [1962] Ch 531 supported the opinion that the powers of investment in the 1961 Act should 'be taken to be prima facie sufficient and ought only to be extended if, on the particular facts, a special case for extending them can be made out' (at 540). Subsequently in several cases in the 1980s involving substantial trust funds the courts came to accept that the investment powers under the TIA 1961 had themselves become outdated (see eg *Mason v Farbrother* [1983] 2 All ER 1078; *Trustees of the British Museum v A-G* [1984] 1 All ER 337; *Steel v Wellcome Custodian Trustees Ltd* [1988] 1 WLR 167). Indeed in *Trustees of the British Museum v A-G* [1984] 1 All ER 337 Megarry VC viewed the *Re Kolb* rule as 'one that should no longer be followed since conditions have changed so greatly in the last 20 years' (at 342). But the Vice-Chancellor was also careful to leave open the way for resuscitation of the rule if the recommendations for reform of the TIA 1961 proposed in 1982 by the Law Reform Committee were enacted.

As we have just seen, by virtue of s 7(1) of the TA 2000 trustees' powers of investment have been generally widened even as regards trusts that were created before the Act came into force. It would seem to follow that the future demand to vary investment powers in a trust deed will be very limited. But what stance should the court take if presented with a request to vary the investment powers by, for instance, removing a restriction imposed by the settlor in the trust instrument? After all s 6(1)(b) specifically recognises the possibility of such restrictions. In such circumstances it is unclear when, if ever, the courts would consider it to be appropriate to vary the powers of investment. It may be that the courts would decide to resurrect the *Re Kolb* rule in some guise so that a 'special case' justifying the variation would have to be made out. We say 'in some guise' because strictly speaking the rule would not apply as trustees would not be seeking an extension of investment powers beyond the scope of the TA 2000 but rather the removal of an exclusion so as to give full rein to the statutory power. The wider the scope of the 'restriction or exclusion' the easier it may be to establish that its removal or modification would satisfy the 'benefit' requirement of the VTA 1958. As was the case prior to the TA 2000, the same criteria in evaluating any proposed alteration would apply whether the proposal is made under the VTA 1958 or TA 1925, s 57. Note that it has been suggested that on grounds of cost and convenience applications to vary investment powers should usually be submitted under s 57 (see *Anker-Petersen v Anker-Petersen* [1991] 16 LS Gaz R 32 (see also (1998) 12 TLI 166) referring, inter alia, to the fact that, unlike the VTA 1958, the consent of each adult beneficiary is not required and the court can consider the interests of each category of beneficiary collectively rather than individually).

(3) Safeguards and the duties of trustees: introduction

It will be recalled (see p 478) that the Law Commission accepted that statutory safeguards for the protection of beneficiaries should balance the introduction of wider statutory powers of investment. To that extent caution is necessary in interpreting the wording of TA 2000, s 3(1) that 'a trustee may make any kind of investment that he could make if he were absolutely entitled to the assets of the trust'. Absolute owners of property can be as reckless as they wish in determining what degree of risk to tolerate. But trustees are not absolutely entitled to the assets and are subject to certain constraints in the investment policy that they follow. First, it must not be overlooked that trustees remain subject to the general duties that the law imposes to act in the best interests of the beneficiaries and to avoid any conflict between their duties as trustees and their own personal interest. Trustees must also act impartially; hence an investment policy should seek to balance the interests of income and capital beneficiaries (see section 4 of this chapter). More specifically trustees remain subject to the statutory duty of care when exercising their powers of investment whether statutory or otherwise. In addition to these generic and pervasive duties the TA 2000 imposes two specific duties on trustees in the performance of their investment function – a duty to have regard to what is termed 'standard investment criteria' (s 4) and a duty to obtain and consider advice (s 5). But as the Law Commission acknowledged neither of these duties is new, the TIA 1961, s 6 providing a statutory precedent for both.

(4) Trustee Act 2000, s 4 and the 'standard investment criteria'

TA 2000, s 4(1) lays down that a trustee 'must have regard to the standard investment criteria' in two sets of circumstances. One is where the trustee is exercising *any* power of investment, whether arising under the statutory default power or otherwise. The other circumstance is where the trustee is carrying out the obligation imposed by s 4(2), that is 'from time to time to review the investments of the trust and consider whether . . . they should be varied'. The point here quite simply is that the investment duties of trustees do not end with the initial decision to invest: more is required than a strategy of 'buy and hold'. The fund must be managed and in the process the trustees must decide when to retain and when to realise investments. Section 4(2) is in effect a codification of the common law position as set out in *Nestle v National Westminster Bank plc (No 2)* [1993] 1 WLR 1260: '[A] trustee . . . must undertake periodic reviews of the investments held by the trust' (at 1282 per Leggatt LJ).

The standard investment criteria to which the trustee 'must have regard' are set out in s 4(3):

> (3) The standard investment criteria, in relation to a trust, are –
>
> (a) the suitability to the trust of investments of the same kind as any particular investment proposed to be made or retained and of that particular investment as an investment of that kind, and
>
> (b) the need for diversification of investments of the trust, in so far as is appropriate to the circumstances of the trust.

The precise relationship between the 'standard investment criteria' and the general duty of care in s 1 is not made explicit in the Act. It may be that in exercising their investment functions trustees will have to have regard to matters other than the criteria of s 4(3) but those criteria will be central to the process of investment decision-making.

The definition of the criteria is very similar to the requirements of TIA 1961, s 6(1) and raises similar issues of interpretation. What is clear is that the 'criteria' accord with the tenets of modern portfolio theory particularly as regards diversification. What is also clear is that references in s 4(3) to 'suitability' and 'circumstances of the trust' remind trustees that selection of the portfolio needs to take account of factors other than the risk/return calculus of the investments under consideration. Nevertheless whilst the language of s 4(3) is precise in directing the attention of trustees to particular issues it still leaves room to speculate on the meaning of 'suitability' or what are relevant 'circumstances of the trust'. It can be said with some confidence that a factor – a 'circumstance of the trust' – relevant to the need for diversification (s 4(3)(b)) will be the size of the trust fund. One can say with equal confidence that suitability includes consideration of both the type of investment – for example, fixed-interest securities or ordinary shares – and the specific investment of that type – for example, Tesco or Powergen shares. Beyond that the picture is less clear, although such matters as the expected duration of the trust, the probable timing of distribution of income or capital to specific beneficiaries and their tax position should all be relevant to the trustees' consideration of the suitability requirements in s 4(3)(a). A trustee who fails to take account of such matters could be argued to be in breach of the duty of care (see eg *Parker and Mellows* p 671).

(5) Exercising the power of investment: seeking advice

The other principal statutory safeguard for beneficiaries is the advice requirement contained in TA 2000, s 5:

> (5)(1) Before exercising any power of investment, whether arising under this Part or
> otherwise, a trustee must (unless the exception applies) obtain and consider proper advice
> about the way in which, having regard to the standard investment criteria, the power should
> be exercised.
>
> (2) When reviewing the investments of the trust, a trustee must (unless the exception
> applies) obtain and consider proper advice about whether, having regard to the standard
> investment criteria, the investments should be varied.
>
> (3) The exception is that a trustee need not obtain such advice if he reasonably concludes
> that in all the circumstances it is unnecessary or inappropriate to do so.
>
> (4) Proper advice is the advice of a person who is reasonably believed by the trustee
> to be qualified to give it by his ability in and practical experience of financial and other
> matters relating to the proposed investment.

Several points should be noted about the advice requirements in this section.

First, the section does not absolve a trustee from the obligation to exercise
independent judgment; the trustee must 'obtain and consider', not blindly
follow the advice. Nevertheless it will be difficult to establish a breach of trust
where a trustee bona fide acts on proper advice. The outcome may be different
where the trustees act against the advice given even if they do so in good faith.
This point was considered in the context of the common law prudent man
standard of care by Sir Robert Megarry VC in *Cowan v Scargill* [1984] 2 All ER
750 at 762:

> **Megarry VC**: That duty includes the duty to seek advice on matters which the trustee does
> not understand, such as the making of investments, and on receiving that advice to act
> with the same degree of prudence. This requirement is not discharged merely by showing
> that the trustee has acted in good faith and with sincerity. Honesty and sincerity are not
> the same as prudence and reasonableness.... Accordingly, although a trustee who takes
> advice on investments is not bound to accept and act on that advice, he is not entitled to
> reject it merely because he sincerely disagrees with it, unless in addition to being sincere
> he is acting as an ordinary prudent man would act.

Second, s 5(2) merely confirms that the advice requirement must also be
satisfied when complying with the obligation under s 4(2) to keep the investment
of the trust under review.

Third, as with the 'standard investment criteria' of s 4(3), the provisions
have their origins in and bear some similarity to those of the TIA 1961. The
new provisions are, however, more extensive yet also more flexible. Thus the
obligation to 'obtain and consider' advice is now unqualified in that it applies to
the exercise of any power of investment yet also provides for an exception where

the trustee 'reasonably concludes... that it is unnecessary or inappropriate to do so'. No statutory guidance is given as to when the exception applies but relevant considerations might be, for instance, (i) where the trust fund is small, so that fulfilling the advice requirement might be disproportionately costly or (ii) where one or more of the trustees might possess the appropriate skill or knowledge. Whilst there is no statutory requirement that any advice received should be in writing it would be a sensible precaution and arguably best practice for trustees to insist that any advice is put in writing.

Fourth, s 5(4), clarifying 'proper advice', must be read in the light of the Financial Services and Markets Act 2000. That Act prohibits (s 19) any person from carrying on an investment business – and this includes the giving of investment advice – unless duly authorised (s 31). The fact that a person is qualified to give financial advice does not necessarily mean that their expertise will be appropriate to the circumstances of the trust. If the trustees are proposing to invest in land they will need to consult an adviser with expertise in the valuation of land rather than an adviser whose specialist expertise is in the area of corporate bonds.

It is convenient to mention briefly here the repeal by the TA 2000 of TA 1925, ss 8 and 9 which contained broad guidelines for trustees investing in mortgages. Section 8 relieved trustees from charges of breach of trust where the terms of the section, which related broadly to the competence of advice and permissible size of loan, were complied with, whilst s 9 limited the quantum of liability where breach occurred. The nineteenth century was the heyday of investment by trustees in mortgages and this type of investment is much less common for trustees now, although still specifically authorised under TA 2000, s 3(3). Where trustees do wish to invest in mortgages the general guidelines regarding duty of care, standard investment criteria and advice will apply as with any other investment. It may, however, be advisable for cautious trustees to pay regard to the pre-1925 authorities with their suggested limitations on trustees' powers to invest in mortgages. It was, for instance, considered inadvisable although not impermissible for trustees to lend on the security of anything other than a first mortgage of freehold or leasehold land (see *Chapman v Browne* [1902] 1 Ch 785). The TA 2000 is silent on these matters but it may be difficult for trustees to argue that they have satisfied the duty of care if they invest in a second mortgage and the trust fund suffers a loss because, for instance, the first mortgagee exercises the power of sale leaving little or nothing for the second mortgagee.

(e) Investment management, risk and liability for loss

(1) Trustees as investors

Investment involves risk. The expectation of profit must be counterbalanced by the possibility of loss and, as experience shows (see p 473), the timing of decisions as to when to retain and when to realise investments can be a crucial factor in determining success or failure. The value both of classes of investment and of individual investments within the class will fluctuate. The inherent uncertainty of the outcome of the investment process poses difficult questions for the law on trustee investment. In what circumstances should trustees be held liable for losses that are incurred by a poor performing portfolio of investments? Should the answer depend not on the portfolio return itself but on whether appropriate processes were followed by trustees? Assuming that it can be shown that a breach of trust has caused a loss – and this may be a bold assumption in light of the decision in *Nestlé* (see below) – how should the quantum of the loss be established?

These questions are not new. In a leading nineteenth-century case the Court of Appeal had to consider in what circumstances trustees should be liable for a notional or realised loss through retaining an asset which is depreciating in value.

Re Chapman [1896] 2 Ch 763 at 774–776, CA

The plaintiffs claimed that the trustees were liable for a loss in the value of mortgage securities.

> **Lindley LJ:** . . . the mortgages are still unrealised; and it is now unfortunately true that, with one or two exceptions, they cannot be realised except at a great loss; and the real question is whether the trustees are liable for this loss. A mortgage security is unlike an ordinary investment, inasmuch as it consists of a debt which can be enforced by action, and also of a security which can be realised by sale or foreclosure. A trustee of a mortgage security is, therefore, liable for loss sustained by his wilful default in not obtaining payment in either of these ways. But a trustee is not a surety, nor is he an insurer; he is only liable for some wrong done by himself, and loss of trust money is not per se proof of such wrong.

Lindley LJ considered and rejected the argument that the trustees should either have sued the mortgagor for payment or foreclosed.

> There is no rule of law which compels the court to hold that an honest trustee is liable to make good loss sustained by retaining an authorised security in a falling market, if he did so honestly and prudently, in the belief that it was the best course to take in the interest of all parties. Trustees acting honestly, with ordinary prudence and within the limits of their trust, are not liable for mere errors of judgement. Any loss sustained by the trust estate under such circumstances falls upon and must be borne by the owners of the property – ie, the cestuis que trust – and cannot be thrown by them on their trustees, who have done no wrong, though the result may prove that they possibly might have done better.
>
> The case is an important one not only to the trustees of this particular will, but to trustees of mortgages generally. Owing to the great fall in the value of agricultural land trustees of mortgage securities have been placed in a position of great difficulty. To throw on the trustees the loss sustained by the fall in value of securities authorised by the trust, wilful default, which includes want of ordinary prudence on the part of the trustee, must be proved; but it is not proved in this case.

The judgments in *Re Chapman* display an acute awareness that the decline in the value of mortgages in that case merely reflected a general economic malaise affecting parts of the agricultural sector in the last quarter of the nineteenth century, which brought in its train lower profits, lower rents and lower capital values. (See Mathias *The First Industrial Nation* (1969) pp 397–398; and Saul *The Myth of the Great Depression 1873–1896* (2nd edn, 1985) pp 34–36.) A similar approach to trustee liability was applied by United States courts in the aftermath of the 1929 stock market crash. In Massachusetts, for instance, it seems that not a single trustee was held liable for losses so caused (see Grosh (1974) 23(4) ICLQ 748 at 758). The sentiments evident in *Re Chapman* and the American authorities were reiterated in *Jones v AMP Perpetual Trustee Company NZ Ltd* [1994] 1 NZLR 690. Thomas J reviewed the authorities and concluded (at 707) that it was 'not inherently negligent for a trustee to retain stock in a period of declining market values and that there was no "magic percentage" of decline which, when reached, necessitated a sale'.

Whether the protection offered by the principle in *Re Chapman* is equally available where the notional or realised loss on an investment runs counter to the general market trend is an unanswered question. Inevitably much must depend on individual circumstances, including nowadays the extent to which any such loss would be seen as reflecting a reasonable exposure to risk in an investment portfolio. But the reader may care to reflect on the hypothetical liability of trustees who held shares in any of those major UK companies which went into liquidation or experienced severe financial crises (eg, Polly Peck (1991); Ferranti (1993); GEC-Marconi (2000)) in the last two decades. At what stage in the decline of a previously secure company does a prudent investment become imprudent, and can the retention of an investment which is at present paying no dividend and showing a capital loss be justified by a belief in its eventual recovery? Here again an important consideration will be whether the trustees obtained and considered advice if appropriate, whether under TA 2000, s 5 or as part of the general statutory duty of care.

A variant of this problem, and a consequence of inflation, is whether a trustee is under any obligation to preserve the real value of the trust fund rather than merely seek to protect the nominal value of the fund through securing the safety of trust assets. The nineteenth-century cases do not comment on what was to become a twentieth-century problem. But in *Nestlé v National Westminster Bank plc* [1993] 1 WLR 1260, CA, the courts were confronted with a claim that the defendant bank had failed to meet the prudent man standard in its management of a trust fund over a period of more than sixty years. The plaintiff's claim was that a fund worth £269,000 in 1986, when she became solely entitled, should with proper investment management have been worth over £1m. Notwithstanding that the bank had (i) failed to seek advice on, and indeed had misunderstood, the terms of the investment clause, and (ii) had apparently omitted to conduct regular reviews at least between 1927 and 1959, the claim failed. To establish liability it was also necessary to prove that 'through one or other or both of those causes, the trustees made decisions they should not have made or failed to make decisions which they should have made' (per Staughton LJ at 1276). It is a formidably difficult burden to establish that 'no prudent trustee' (at 1281), if properly appraised as to the full scope of the clause, would over a period of sixty years have made the investment decisions complained of. Leggatt LJ concluded that 'by the undemanding standard of prudence the bank is not shown to have committed any breach of trust resulting in loss', adding, however, that 'no testator, in the light of this example, would choose this bank for the effective management of his investment' (at 1285).

Even a shorter time-span may not materially alter this position. Consider, for instance, the poor performance in the 1970s of trust funds managed by the Public Trustee for some thalidomide victims. In one case, for instance, £13,518 invested in 1971 in authorised investments produced total interest in the next seven years of £2,882, ie less than 3% per year. During the same period the Retail Price Index had risen by 147% and an investment even in building society shares would have produced some £10,000 in interest. The Lord Chancellor, who investigated newspaper complaints, concluded, following advice, that no action for breach of trust or negligence could be sustained in such circumstances. (See also the recent criticisms of the Public Trustee Office by the National Audit Office: *Protecting the Financial Welfare of People with Mental Incapacity* HC (Session 1998–99) 206.) It still remains to be determined, however, whether a comparable 'shortfall' resulting from speculative zeal as opposed to excessive caution would be similarly viewed.

The present state of the law was aptly summarised by Leggatt LJ in *Nestlé* (at 1284): '[Performance] is to be judged not so much by success, as by absence of proven default.' That summary by Leggatt LJ leaves outstanding one rather puzzling aspect of the *Nestlé* litigation. It might be argued that there was 'proven default'. One might be prepared generously to accept that the misunderstanding of the investment clause could be categorised, employing Lindley LJ's language from *Re Chapman*, as 'a mere error of judgment'. It is more difficult to see how a failure to conduct periodic reviews of the investments could be consistent with the 'prudent man of business' standard particularly given the opinion of Leggatt LJ in *Nestlé* that '[A] trustee . . . must undertake periodic reviews of the investments held by the trust' (at 1282; see now the specific statutory requirement in TA 2000, s 4(2)). It must be emphasised, however, that even if there were 'proven default' it would still have to be shown that, but for the particular breaches of trust, the losses would not have occurred (see the comments of Staughton LJ above).

(2) Trustees as shareholders

One conclusion that can be drawn from the litigation is that trustees who wish to avoid any risk of liability should ensure that adequate procedures for supervision of investments are put in place. In the normal course of supervision a periodic review only is required but this 'watching-brief' may be inadequate where the trust has a controlling shareholding as will often be the case in a private company. How active a role should trustees then be expected to adopt, assuming the shareholding is an expressly authorised investment?

In *Bartlett v Barclays Bank Trust Co Ltd* [1980] 1 All ER 139 the bank as trustee of the Bartlett family trust had a controlling interest in a private family company with assets in rented properties. The board of directors of the company wished to extend its activities into property development, partly to ensure ultimately a favourable public quotation. The bank indicated that it did not object to this policy provided the income position of the life-tenants was protected. The board then embarked on two development projects at sites at Guildford and the Old Bailey, London. However, planning permission was refused for the latter, and consequently the trust suffered a large loss as a result of depreciation in the company shares. The property development would have been too speculative for direct investment by trust fund moneys. But, applying the prudent man of business standard, what course should the trustees have adopted where their investment was a controlling interest in the company undertaking the development? Brightman J, holding the bank liable for the loss, rejected an argument that where the trustees believed the directors to be of high calibre they need 'probe only if and when alerted'.

> **Brightman J:** What the prudent man of business will not do is to content himself with the receipt of such information on the affairs of the company as a shareholder ordinarily receives at annual general meetings. Since he has the power to do so, he will go further and see that he has sufficient information to enable him to make a responsible decision from time to time either to let matters proceed as they are proceeding or to intervene if he is dissatisfied. This topic was considered by Cross J in *Re Lucking's Will Trusts* [1967] 3 All ER 726.

Cross J said (at 732–733) that the prudent man 'ensures that he is represented on the board' and that 'in the same way trustees holding a controlling interest ought to ensure so far as they can that they have such information as to the progress of the company's affairs as directors would have'.

> I do not understand Cross J to have been saying that in every case where trustees have a controlling interest in a company it is their duty to ensure that one of their number is a director or that they have a nominee on the board who will report from time to time on the affairs of the company. He was merely outlining convenient methods by which a prudent man of business (as also a trustee) with a controlling interest in a private company, can place himself in a position to make an informed decision whether any action is appropriate to be taken for the protection of his asset. Other methods may be equally satisfactory and convenient, depending on the circumstances of the individual case. Alternatives which spring to mind are the receipt of the copies of the agenda and minutes of board meetings if regularly held, the receipt of monthly management accounts in the case of a trading concern, or quarterly reports. Every case will depend on its own facts. The possibilities

are endless. It would be useless, indeed misleading, to seek to lay down a general rule. The purpose to be achieved is not that of monitoring every move of the directors, but of making it reasonably probable, so far as circumstances permit, that the trustees or (as in *Re Lucking's Will Trusts*) one of them will receive an adequate flow of information in time to enable the trustees to make use of their controlling interest should this be necessary for the protection of their trust asset, namely the shareholding. The obtaining of information is not an end in itself, but merely a means of enabling the trustees to safeguard the interests of their beneficiaries.

Having been put on notice, what safeguarding action would it be appropriate for trustees to take, bearing in mind that disposal of the shareholding will rarely be a desirable or practicable possibility? As Brightman J describes it (at 151), 'appropriate action will no doubt consist in the first instance of inquiry of and consultation with the directors, and in the last but most unlikely resort, the convening of a general meeting to replace one or more directors'.

The full sad tale of the failed development project is too lengthy to relate here (yet should be read to form an assessment of the trustees' conduct). Consider, however, in particular whether the interpretation of the prudent man of business standard in *Bartlett* (above) is imposing an unreasonable administrative burden on corporate or professional trustees. On this point it may be unwise, in any event, to assume that settlors would wish to have professional trustees or trust corporations represented on the board of a family company or taking a close interest in its affairs. There may therefore be a mutuality of interest in incorporating a clause in a trust deed which relaxes the obligations implicit in the *Bartlett* and *Lucking* cases. (See, for instance, the example in Kessler *Drafting Trusts and Will Trusts* (8th edn, 2007) p 105: 'The trustees are under no duty to inquire into the conduct of a company in which they are interested, unless they have knowledge of circumstances which call for inquiry'.) Note also that Brightman J's comments in *Bartlett* are made in the context of a case involving a corporate trustee, and it is uncertain how extensive the administrative burden should be for the unpaid trustee.

Finally, if trustees are appointed as directors of a company they may also be held liable (as trustees) for breach of trust for their conduct in the management of the company. In *Re Lucking's Will Trusts* [1967] 3 All ER 726 a trust held 70 per cent of a company's shares and one of the trustees (L), who was also a substantial shareholder, was a director while the managing director (D) was an 'old and trusted friend' of his. The latter (D) over a period of years improperly withdrew some £15,000 from the company's bank account, subsequently became bankrupt and the debt could not be recovered. In consequence, the value of the trust's shareholding was reduced. L had developed the practice as director of signing blank cheques for D – ironically because he trusted D completely. The practice continued even after it became apparent that D was overdrawing from the company's account. L was held liable for breach of trust involving a negligent failure to supervise D's drawings from the bank account.

(f) Investment and the Trustee Act 2000: a panacea for all ills?

(1) Trustee Act 2000 and 'the small family trust'

Over twenty years ago the Law Reform Committee (LRC) castigated the Trustee Investments Act 1961 as 'tiresome, cumbrous and expensive in operation with the result that its provisions are now seen to be inadequate' (23rd Report *The Powers and Duties of Trustees* (Cmnd 8733, 1982) para 3.17). For most modern trusts this criticism was immaterial, the trust instrument usually conferring wide investment discretion on the trustees. But, as the Law Commission was later to point out, such a discretion is seldom included in trusts and wills made without professional advice (*Trustees' Powers and Duties* (1999) Law Com No 260 at para 2.3). The response in the Trustee Act 2000, as we have seen, was to confer the widest possible investment powers on trustees coupled with safeguards. One of the safeguards was an obligation to 'obtain and consider' advice except where the trustee 'reasonably concludes... that it is unnecessary or inappropriate to do so'. In 1982 the LRC had taken a different stance on the question of advice. It recommended a reform agenda combining freedom with guidance. The guidance element was reflected in the LRC's recommendation that investments should be divided into those which could be made without advice – such as gilts, unit trusts and investment trusts – and those such as equity investments which should be made only with advice. The Committee explained its reasons in the following manner:

> 3.20 Although a general freedom to invest within the framework of what may loosely be described as a duty of care has its attractions and might reflect current practice where the present law is excluded, we think that such a solution would create considerable difficulties, particularly for smaller trust funds. Further we think that in any event the law should continue to provide some guidance and indeed protection for trustees.

In 1997 the Delegated Powers Scrutiny Committee of the House of Lords commenting on a Treasury proposal (the Draft Regulation (Trustee Investments) Order 1997) to introduce an advice requirement very similar to that now contained in TA 2000, s 5, noted that:

> 73. The Treasury argues that necessary protection for beneficiaries and trustees will be maintained under the proposal. As the explanatory memorandum states 'trustees of larger funds will tend to obtain advice as a matter of course. To require the trustees of smaller funds to seek advice regardless of circumstances would continue to require them to incur unnecessary costs to the detriment of beneficiaries.'

Whilst this may be a persuasive response to an argument advocating a compulsory advice requirement it is less convincing where the question of statutory guidance is concerned. Neither the Treasury proposal nor TA 2000, s 5 contains the guidance argued for by the LRC in 1982. It can be argued that in the absence of any statutory guidance as to the type of investment that may be safely selected without advice, prudent trustees might be well advised always to seek advice if only for their own protection. Indeed are there any circumstances now when an amateur trustee of a 'small trust' should exercise the power of investment without getting the benefit of professional advice (cf Latham (1994) 3 Nottingham LJ 95)? If this were to be the outcome then paradoxically one consequence of the new law might be to *increase* the administrative costs of trusts of small funds, unless the advice resulted in countervailing enhanced investment returns.

(2) The Trustee Act 2000, the 'prudent man of business' and modern portfolio theory: an interim conclusion

The objective 'prudent man of business standard' emerged at the end of the nineteenth century in the wake of concern about trustee defalcation and in an unstable economic climate. Its adoption can be seen as serving the twin functions of protecting beneficiaries from the idiosyncrasies of particular trustees and promoting higher standards of trustee conduct and competence (see Paling (1973) 37 Conv 48). In fact it is not easy to identify positively what the standard required. Indeed, at its adoption the formula attracted the sceptical stricture that 'the only rule really is what the courts think a prudent trustee ought to do' (Sir H Davey QC, counsel in *Learoyd v Whiteley* (1887) 12 App Cas 727 at 729). Nevertheless the standard, based initially on a concern to preserve the trust capital, inevitably resulted in an emphasis on security and the avoidance of risk. But investment conditions can change and the changes posed a challenge for the prudent man standard. Was it flexible enough to adjust to contemporary developments in investment theory and practice such as those described in this chapter? To an extent that question became redundant with the passage of the TA 2000 with its implicit acceptance of the major tenets of modern portfolio theory, namely the need to diversify and to evaluate risk and return in terms of the overall performance of the investment portfolio. There are, however, a number of questions posed for trustee investment law by the new statutory default regime that have yet to be resolved.

Consider the following points:

(1) There is now no doubt that, whether under the prudent man of business standard or the default statutory power of investment, trustees are authorised to balance 'risk of loss' against 'rate of return' within a total portfolio approach. In *Nestlé v National Westminster Bank plc* (29 June 1988, but not reported until (1996) 10 TLI 112), Hoffmann J comments that 'an investment which in isolation is too risky and therefore in breach of trust may be justified when held in conjunction with other investments' (at 115). In *Trustees of the British Museum v A-G* [1984] 1 All ER 337, Megarry VC, approving an application under the VTA 1958 to widen the range of authorised investments, commented that a material consideration in assessing the justification is the size of the fund: 'A fund that is very

large may well justify a latitude of investment that would be denied to a more modest fund' (at 343). These comments may mean that trustees need no longer be bound by the strictures of Lord Watson in the House of Lords in *Learoyd v Whiteley* (1887) 12 App Cas 727 to the effect that 'it is the duty of a trustee to confine himself to the class of investments which are permitted by the trust, and likewise *to avoid all investments of that class which are attended with hazard*' (at 733, emphasis added). They may equally mean, as suggested earlier in this chapter, that whether an investment is labelled 'hazardous' is a reflection both of the characteristics of the individual investment and the size of the fund: the larger the fund, the greater the degree of risk that is considered reasonable in respect of a particular investment. On the other hand, it is open to question whether such comments can be stretched so far as to endorse, at least for trustee investment, the view of portfolio theorists that few, if any, investments are imprudent per se. The only issue for the portfolio theorist is whether the investment makes the portfolio as a whole imprudent. It is possible that the implementation of modern portfolio theory to trustee investment will enhance the returns to beneficiaries. On the other hand, if we accept that prudence is to be measured only by the performance of the portfolio as a whole this may make the monitoring of performance more problematic both for beneficiaries and the courts. Determining whether a particular investment is per se speculative or hazardous may be relatively straightforward. The matter becomes more complex if the question is whether the specific investment makes the portfolio as a whole imprudent. Jeffrey Gordon, in exploring the implications of portfolio theory for the prudent man rules in the US, summarises the position in the following manner: '[The] portfolio theory model complicates the determination of prudence, both as a matter of theory among financial economists and as a matter of proof before a court. . . . Courts will be called upon to evaluate complicated strategies, not simply specific investments viewed in isolation. Instead of referring to a list of imprudent investments . . . courts will have to evaluate conflicting expert testimony. Courts may fear that portfolio theory will serve as a smokescreen for trustee incompetence' ((1987) 62 NYUL Rev 52 at 93). This evocation by Gordon of potential pitfalls returns us to a residual question that troubled the nineteenth-century courts and one that is left open by the relatively unconstrained default powers of investment now conferred on trustees. Can that grant of discretion be sufficiently monitored so that incompetent or faithless performance by trustees will be adequately deterred?

(2) In *Nestlé v National Westminster Bank plc* [1993] 1 WLR 1260, CA Leggatt LJ states that 'the importance of preservation of a trust fund will always outweigh success in its advancement. Inevitably a trustee in the bank's position wears a complacent air, because the virtue of safety will in practice put a premium on inactivity' (at 1284). How one interprets 'preservation' in an

investment context is crucial; in *Nestlé* the *nominal* value of the funds had increased approximately five-fold to £269,903 from 1922 to 1986 whereas it was argued that in real terms 'if the equity portion of the fund as it stood in 1922 (74%) had been invested so as to achieve no more than the index, the fund as a whole would have been worth over £1.8m' (at 1275). Is the approach suggested by Leggatt LJ compatible or incompatible with a portfolio theory of investment? Consider in particular whether a distinction should be drawn between pre- and post-*Nestlé* investment performance. After all, trustees are now on notice that a portfolio approach has received both judicial endorsement and implicit statutory acceptance. (See in particular the protracted and very expensive litigation instigated by Unilever Pension Fund in 2001 to recover compensation from Merrill Lynch Investment Managers for underperformance in the investment of the pension fund. The case was settled out of court and substantial compensation paid: *Financial Times* 7 December 2001.)

(3) Trustees cannot reduce their liability to make good losses arising from wrongful investment by 'setting off' a profit earned on one transaction against a loss made on another even if both are unauthorised. A fortiori unauthorised losses cannot be set off against authorised profits. The justification for the rule is clear: any gains made belong to the beneficiaries and are not the trustees' to set against their own personal liability. But the rule does not apply where the gain and loss are part of the same unauthorised transaction. The difficulty lies in deciding what constitutes a single transaction. (See *Hanbury and Martin* p 658 for a comparison of two leading nineteenth-century cases *Dimes v Scott* (1828) 4 Russ 195 and *Fletcher v Green* (1864) 33 Beav 426.) It will be recalled that in *Bartlett v Barclays Bank Trust Co Ltd* [1980] 1 All ER 139 there were two property-development projects, and although the Old Bailey project was a financial disaster, a substantial profit was made on the Guildford development. In allowing the bank's claim for 'set off', Brightman J commented on the rule as follows (at 155):

> The general rule as stated in all the textbooks, with some reservations, is that where a trustee is liable in respect of distinct breaches of trust, one of which has resulted in a loss and the other in a gain, he is not entitled to set off the gain against the loss, unless they arise in the same transaction. . . . The relevant cases are, however, not altogether easy to reconcile. All are centenarians and none is quite like the present. The Guildford development stemmed from exactly the same policy and (to a lesser degree because it proceeded less far) exemplified the same folly as the Old Bailey project. Part of the profit was in fact used to finance the Old Bailey disaster. By sheer luck the gamble paid off handsomely, on capital account. I think it would be unjust to deprive the bank of this element of salvage in the course of assessing the cost of the shipwreck.

At a minimum, these words endorse the proposition that individual gains or losses that emerge from unauthorised investments in pursuit of a common, but wrongful, investment policy can be set against each other in assessing trustee liability (see generally Chapter 11 on measuring trustee liability). How far the notion of a 'policy' can be stretched remains to be answered; would, for example, a set off be allowable where a policy of property development involved one hazardous project and one of 'reasonable risk'? In practice, however, acceptance of a portfolio approach (see (1) above) is likely further to limit the scope of any prohibition against set off. This consequence appears to have been recognised by Hoffmann J in *Nestlé* where in a footnote to the passage cited in (1) it is commented that 'this is not to say that losses on investments made in breach of trust can be set off against gains in the rest of the portfolio but only that an investment which in isolation is too risky and therefore in breach of trust may be justified when held in conjunction with other investments' ((1996) 10 TLI 112 at 124, footnote 3; see also Langbein (1994) 8(4) TLI 123 on the comparable US position).

(4) 'The prudent man of business standard as applied to authorised investments, can be criticised for merely setting minimum standards of performance, penalising only the grossly incompetent, and offering no inducement to seek a high financial return. Consequently it can be argued that "under modern conditions a settlor's best protection for the trust fund would seem to lie in the quality of persons he or she selects as trustees".' Are the criticism and the conclusion well founded? (See eg Watt and Stauch [1998] Conv 352 but cf *Re Mulligan (Deceased)* [1998] 1 NZLR 481.)

4. Impartiality and investment

(a) Introduction

We have previously referred in rather sweeping fashion to the principle that trustees must act impartially between beneficiaries in their dealings with trust affairs. In particular it has been suggested that, where there are successive beneficiaries, the trustees must not favour either the life-tenant or remainderman. In the immediate context of investment this should require that an investment portfolio be so balanced as to support the successive interests equally. But the duty of impartiality runs wider than merely investment, arising also in the context of trust expenses. There is, for example, a general rule that all outgoings of a recurrent nature (such as rates and income taxes) which relate broadly to property benefiting the income beneficiary should be met out of income, whilst those incurred for the benefit of the whole estate (such as obtaining investment advice or paying endowment assurance policy premiums) should be borne by the capital (see generally *Underhill and Hayton* pp 694–707). This is subject to the proviso that the trust instrument may itself indicate how trust expenses should be allocated (see *Carver v Duncan* [1985] AC 1082).

In fact any broad statement implying universal application of the principle of impartiality is potentially misleading for two reasons. First, and as always, a settlor or testator may choose to modify its application by providing that a disproportionate weight be attributed to the interests of different beneficiaries. Thus trustees may be instructed, for instance, to retain a high-income yielding security which suffers a capital depreciation, thus favouring the life-tenant as against the remainderman. It may even be the case that trustees can themselves make such judgments 'if they consider it would be fair to do so' (*Nestlé v National Westminster Bank plc* (1996) 10 TLI 112 at 115 per Hoffmann J). How far it is appropriate for the court to make this sort of judgment is a matter to which we will return (see below, p 517). Second, as will be seen below, the implementation of the general principle takes the form of specific rules which impinge only on certain aspects of investment practice whilst leaving others seemingly untouched. The rationale for such selective intervention rests on certain questionable assumptions about the settlor's or testator's implicit intentions.

It is clear, however, that when exercising their discretion in choosing investments trustees must not select with the intention of prejudicing an individual or class of beneficiary in order to benefit another (see *Raby v Ridehalgh* (1855) 7 De GM & G 104, as the classic authority). But trust property coming into the trustees' hands will not necessarily consist of cash which must then be invested to obtain an income return. On the contrary the settlor may place specific property (eg shares in a private company) into trust, or a testator may leave a residuary estate comprising various forms of personalty on trust. If the settlor has made clear an intention that the trust property should be converted and the proceeds re-invested then that intention will prevail. But if no such intention is expressed or can be inferred, then unless the specific rules just referred to apply, the law has seemed to be that trustees are placed under no duty to realise the trust property and reinvest the proceeds so as to balance competing interests of beneficiaries. Accordingly, where the rules do not apply it is axiomatic that the tenant for life receives merely the net income, however low or high it may be, while the remainderman is entitled eventually only to the capital irrespective of the degree of capital appreciation or depreciation that may occur to the particular investment.

The inevitability of this outcome needs to be reconsidered in the light both of the new approach to trustee investment envisaged by the TA 2000 and recent decisions such as that in *Nestlé*. Indeed, it might have been thought that the new Act would specifically address the appropriateness of the rules determining the duties of conversion and apportionment. In fact during the passage of the Bill the matter was raised indirectly in the course of debate concerning the implications for charitable endowments of the rigid distinction between capital and income receipts. Responding to the points raised the Lord Chancellor acknowledged that the law of apportionment was in 'some disarray' but suggested that the issues should be dealt with as a whole rather than 'in a piecemeal fashion' as an amendment to the Trustee Bill (*Hansard* (HL) 14 April 2000, vol 612, col 396). The outcome was a reference to the Law Commission to examine, inter alia, (i) the circumstances in which trustees may or must make apportionments between the income and capital of the trust fund, (ii) the circumstances in which trustees must convert and re-invest trust property, and (iii) the rules which determine whether money or other property received by the trustees is to be treated as income or capital. The Law Commission in July 2004 published a Consultation Paper *Capital and Income in Trusts: Classification and Apportionment* (No 175; see also the reform proposals from the Trust Law Committee *Capital and Income of Trusts* (1999) www.kcl.ac.uk/schools/law/research/tlc/consult.html). The consultation process was held in abeyance whilst priority was given to other matters but the Commission has now appointed an advisory group with which it will liaise during 2009 before finalising its report.

(b) The 'annual harvest' and some problems of capital and income

Before considering the scope and limitations of the rules implementing the principle of impartiality it should be appreciated that they are premised on a legal concept of capital and income whose relevance under modern investment conditions merits close consideration. The origin and elements of the legal concepts are highlighted in Flower's comparison of them with those of the economist.

J Flower 'A Note on Capital and Income in the Law of Trusts' in H C Edey and B S Yamey (eds) *Debits, Credits, Finance and Profits* (1974) pp 85–87

The courts developed a concept of capital which is fundamentally different from that used by the economist as exemplified by the famous definition of Hicks: 'Income is the maximum amount the individual can consume in a week and still expect to be as well off at the end of the week as he was at the beginning' (JR Hicks *Value and Capital* (1938) p 172).

Suppose that X's capital at the start of 1972 is £20,000; under the Hicksian definition he will have maintained his capital, as measured by disposable wealth, intact if he finishes the year with assets worth £20,000 (given constancy of the general price level). Any increase will be income. The composition of the assets is immaterial – only their total value is taken into account.

The lawyer's normal concept of capital in the context of a trust is different. To him, if X's capital at 1 January 1972 was 1,000 shares in a company, X will have maintained his capital intact if he finishes the year with the same 1,000 shares. If he sells some shares, the money that he receives in exchange is regarded as the equivalent capital asset. Any increase in the value of the assets whether realised or unrealised is not part of income. If a capital asset is sold for a value greater than its initial value, the extra value has indeed to be recorded, but it is called a 'capital gain' to differentiate it from income.

Lawyers have thus tended to regard a capital asset as a res or a 'thing'. Seltzer in a fascinating chapter has traced this concept to the practice of entailing landed estates in eighteenth-century England (L H Seltzer *The Nature and Tax Treatment of Capital Gains and Losses* (1951) ch 2). The person, to whom a life-interest in the estate was granted, was entitled to receive the income of the estate but had no right to spend the capital. The courts often had to decide what was in fact the income of the estate and therefore belonged to the life-tenant, as opposed to what was capital. Not unnaturally they took the view that the capital was the land itself and the income was the annual harvest. The life-tenant was entitled to the annual harvest, which could be disposed of without affecting the physical existence of the land.

Over the next two hundred years estates came to consist more and more of financial securities – shares, bonds, etc – but the courts applied the same principles to these assets as to land. The capital to be maintained was the bond itself, not its money value. A rise or fall in the market value of the bond did not change the physical character of the bond; it was not therefore regarded as an element of income. If the bond were sold, the entire proceeds of the sale retained the character of a capital asset as did any assets acquired with the money. Any surplus arising on the sale was of course capital; the life-tenant had no right to it. It was described as a capital gain to emphasise this point. Thus the practice developed of recording capital gains when they were 'realised', ie on the sale of the assets. Unrealised capital gains were ignored. The income of the bond was its annual 'harvest' – that 'which is periodically detached and periodically recurs', ie the annual interest payment.

The reason for the courts adopting the res principle seems to have been largely pragmatic. To have applied a Hicksian 'value' principle consistently and accurately would have required regular revaluations of all the assets of the estate. This would not only have entailed considerable extra work but would have provided endless opportunities for disputes between life-tenants and remaindermen....

There is clearly a world of difference between the lawyer's and the economist's concept. The lawyer's realised capital gain would be classified by an economist as income if it were expected; it would be a capital gain from the point of view of economic analysis only in so far as it was unexpected, and this concept, unlike the lawyer's, would have nothing to do with respective property rights. Many of the lawyer's capital gains can be clearly shown to be expected. A person who in December 1972 buys £100 of 3 per cent Savings Bonds at 89 which are due to be redeemed at 100 in 1975 is clearly expecting to make a gain on redemption of £11. The economist would regard this as income, the lawyer would call it a capital gain.

The gap identified by Flower between legal and economic concepts is theoretically narrowed in some cases, to be discussed shortly, where either trusts law or the trust instrument imposes a duty on trustees to convert trust property and reinvest in authorised investments. Where there is such a duty to convert, a companion set of rules require trustees to apportion between capital and income beneficiaries the gains of wealth derived from the original property pending conversion (see *Flower* pp 88–91 for detailed explanation and calculation).

The reservation implicit in 'theoretically narrowed' is necessary because the duty to apportion is in practice nearly always excluded (see below). But even were this not so the area of application of the rules is very limited, leaving numerous circumstances where the consequences of investment decisions by trustees can have a very significant effect on the respective entitlements of income and capital beneficiaries.

A still more fundamental objection to the way the established rules operate is that trustees do not always have control over the form in which profit is received by them. For instance, successful companies do not usually distribute all their profits annually. A company may therefore subsequently be able to choose under its articles of association whether to issue retained profits in the form of dividends (and hence 'income' to the trust fund) or alternatively to capitalise the profits by issuing additional ('bonus') shares to shareholders. If the latter course is adopted the general rule is that the new shares are to be treated by the trustees as an accretion to the capital of the trust fund, although the income beneficiary will of course benefit from any future dividends declared on those shares (*Bouch v Sproule* (1887) 12 App Cas 385; *Hill v Permanent Trustee Co of New South Wales Ltd* [1930] AC 720; *Re Outen's Will Trusts* [1963] Ch 291; Goodhart (1975) 39 Conv 355). A further complication is that no distinction is drawn in company law between the distribution of profits derived from current trading and those that accrue from a realisation of the company's capital assets. In both cases the profits are available for distribution to shareholders by way of dividend and hence as a receipt of income to the trust fund. Whilst for trust law purposes this is appropriate as regards trading profit, realisation of capital assets is more naturally considered as accruing to capital. Yet under trust law all dividend payments must be treated as income. Application of company law principles in this manner therefore fails to hold a fair balance between the interests of income and capital beneficiaries. Moreover, as the Law Commission notes, the courts will usually 'consider themselves to have no jurisdiction to order apportionment to remedy this imbalance' (*Capital and Income in Trusts: Classification and Apportionment* (No 175) para 2.44). In short trusts law is usually subordinated to company form.

The appropriateness of this approach becomes ever more difficult to sustain in novel fact situations where corporate practice and corporate law devise ever new ways of rearranging capital to achieve commercial or tax advantages. The problem posed by the rule in *Bouche v Sproule* was at the forefront of litigation arising out a demerger whereby ICI plc transferred its bioscience activities to a newly created holding company called Zeneca Group plc. The ICI shares formed part of the capital of the fund. The question was whether the Zeneca shares issued to ICI shareholders to compensate for the loss of part of the ICI undertaking should be treated as income or capital receipts. The authorities, following and developing the rule in *Bouche v Sproule*, pointed clearly in favour of treating the Zeneca shares as income. Sir Donald Nicholls VC felt that such a solution would not accord with the economic realities of the situation: 'No one would imagine that the Zeneca Group shares could sensibly be regarded as income' (*Sinclair v Lee* [1993] Ch 497 at 504). The Vice-Chancellor drew a somewhat formalistic distinction between a 'direct' demerger and an 'indirect' demerger – the latter being the situation in *Sinclair v Lee* – and was thereby able to avoid on narrow technical grounds applying the rule in *Bouche v Sproule*. It is evident, however, that this distinction was adopted solely to avoid what the Vice–Chancellor considered to be an otherwise unsatisfactory outcome: 'I am acutely conscious of the danger of doing more harm than good by the apparent departure from established principles so as to reach a fair conclusion in a particular case. Nevertheless, in my view an application of existing principles in their full width would produce a result in this case which would, frankly, be nothing short of absurd' (at 515; see comment in *The Lawyer*, 11 May 1993, p 10; see also Duffield (1995) 9 TLI 55).

One way of avoiding absurdity is to ignore a rule and the Law Commission suggest 'that in many cases trustees (especially those who are not legally advised) will, as a matter of practice, allocate in accordance with common sense rather than [in compliance with the strict rules]' (para 2.47). This is hardly a satisfactory position and one question is whether a general duty of impartiality may provide a more appropriate solution. Before considering this as a possible reform we need to consider more closely the present scope of the duty to act impartially.

(c) The scope of the duty to act impartially

(See generally Phillips (1977) 10 U Queensland LJ 83 at 88–94; Scane (1984) 62 Can BR 577.)

(1) The investment process

It must not be overlooked that investment is a two-step process. First, the decision to realise and convert existing investments must be taken and only then can the discretion to select from among the range of authorised alternative investments be exercised. There is no doubt that in taking the second step trustees must attempt to maintain an even hand between conflicting interests. But the general duty of impartiality is heavily qualified by the limited scope of the rules regulating the first step – the duties to convert and apportion. It must be emphasised that these rules are not only limited in formal scope but in practice are also commonly excluded. We therefore concentrate here on the principles involved rather than their detailed implementation (see generally *Hanbury and Martin* pp 562–569; *Parker and Mellows* pp 752–771).

(2) The rules of conversion and apportionment

Duty to convert A settlor or testator may expressly or impliedly impose in a settlement or will a duty to sell or to convert and reinvest, in which case the trustees' duty depends upon the precise terms of the trust. Otherwise such a duty arises only in the case of a bequest of residuary personalty for persons entitled in succession when the rule in *Howe v Earl of Dartmouth* (1802) 7 Ves 137 will apply. The rule is therefore of limited application. It does not apply (i) to property settled inter vivos; (ii) to devises of real estate, whether specific or residuary; nor (iii) to specific as opposed to residuary bequests (see Bailey (1943) 7 Conv 128 and 191).

The requirements of the rule were summarised in the 1982 Report of the Law Reform Committee (*The Powers and Duties of Trustees*, 23rd Report, Cmnd 8733) para 3.28):

> Where . . . [the rule] does apply, wasting investments (eg royalties in respect of copyright) which are not permanent and may be of reduced or no value at the death of the life-tenant, to the prejudice of the remainderman, and all hazardous or speculative investments, a term which covers all unauthorised investments, are directed to be converted to protect the interests of the remainderman. Reversionary or other non-income-producing property is directed to be converted into income-bearing investments in order to protect the tenant for life who might otherwise get nothing at all from those parts of the trust property. In all cases, however, the duty to convert is based upon an implied or presumed intention of the testator so that where he has indicated that the property should be enjoyed in kind the rule will not be applied. [*Macdonald v Irvine* (1878) 8 Ch D 101.]

One effect of wider investment powers conferred on trustees by TA 2000, s 3 is to extend the range of 'authorised' investments thereby significantly reducing the circumstances in which the rule has any application. This development therefore raises afresh questions about the appropriateness of the rule as a means of achieving its underlying objective of securing a fair balance between beneficiaries entitled to income and those entitled to capital.

A general duty of impartiality?   A note of caution must be sounded here about the apparent certainty of the statement that, in the absence of express instruction in the instrument and following *Howe v Earl of Dartmouth*, a duty to convert can never be applicable to inter vivos trusts. The rationale for not implying any such duty is that, in contrast to residuary gifts in wills, the settlor has intentionally appropriated the particular investments to the trust. There is some evidence, however, that this presumption may be losing its hold.

In the Canadian case of *Re Smith* [1971] 1 OR 584 (affd [1971] 2 OR 541), a corporate trustee of an inter vivos trust, in effect deferring to the wishes of the settlor who was also the remainderman, refused the life-tenant's request to sell low income-yielding authorised investments (paying 2% per annum compared with widely available rates of 7% to 10%) but with a high capital growth rate. Although the trust company was empowered by the trust instrument to retain the investments the court ordered its removal stating ([1971] 1 OR 584 at 589): 'Unless there is some provision in the trust agreement which prevents the trustee from [maintaining an even hand], it seems . . . inescapable that the trustee is in breach of his well-recognised duty' by refusing to exercise the power to invest in securities which would produce a reasonable return for the life-tenant. Cullity in a comment critical of the decision concluded ((1972) 50 Can BR 116 at 120):

> Although the finding is not altogether free from ambiguity it does appear to represent more than a decision that the trustee had failed to exercise its discretion: it appears rather as a finding that a conversion and reinvestment should have been made. The even-hand rule was thus treated as governing the way in which the discretion whether to convert or retain ought to have been exercised.

Somewhat intriguingly none of the judgments in *Re Smith* make reference to *Howe v Earl of Dartmouth* and the present status of the case as authority is debatable, even in Canada (see Ontario Law Reform Commission *Report on the Law of Trusts Volume I* (1984) pp 280–281 for a concise summary, and Scane (1984) 62 Can BR 577).

Duty to apportion　The duty to apportion pending conversion arises whether there is a duty to convert under an express trust for conversion (*Gibson v Bott* (1802) 7 Ves 89) or under the rule in *Howe v Earl of Dartmouth*. A series of somewhat elaborate rules exists governing apportionment 'which well-drafted trust instruments routinely exclude' (*Capital and Income in Trusts: Classification and Apportionment* (No 175) para 3.39).

The following is a brief summary of the objectives of the more important of the rules.

(i) Wasting, hazardous or unauthorised investments: the theoretical assumption is that such investments provide the life-tenants with a high income at the risk of capital loss. The object of apportioning the income is to ensure that they receive only a yield equivalent to that currently available from authorised investments (fixed in 1924 at a now unrealistic 4%) and that any surplus is added to the capital. The yield of 4% is not only unrealistic in most contemporary circumstances but also out of line with the interest rates applied by the courts in other contexts (see eg *Bartlett v Barclays Bank Trust Co Ltd (No 2)* [1980] Ch 515, but cf *Re Berry* [1962] Ch 97, the last reported case on this issue).

(ii) Future or reversionary property: This rule applies where that part of the trust fund governed by a duty to convert comprises a reversionary interest or other future property producing no income. When the property is sold – the trustees may have deferred sale in the interest of the trust as a whole – the proceeds must be apportioned, part to capital for the remainderman and part to income for the tenant for life (the rule in *Re Earl of Chesterfield's Trusts* (1883) 24 Ch D 643). This rule is intended to compensate the life-tenant for loss of income from the future property while it remains unconverted.

(iii) The rule in *Allhusen v Whittell* (1867) LR 4 Eq 295: the life-tenant under a will is entitled to the income earned after the testator's death. The testator may, however, leave debts which may not be paid immediately. In the meantime the life-tenant receives income from capital in fact required for the payment of those debts, whereas in fairness she should receive the income from the net estate only. The rule – intended to provide for the life-tenant's income to make a contribution – is complex, the calculations required cumbersome, and since in most cases only small sums of money are involved, it is invariably excluded in well-drafted wills.

(3) Summary

By way of recapitulation it can be said:

(i) subject now to the significant qualification posited by *Re Smith* there is no obligation to convert existing investments unless the rule in *Howe v Earl of Dartmouth* applies or there is an express duty to convert in the trust instrument usually in the form of a trust for sale – a power to sell not being sufficient;

(ii) where conversion takes place the trustee must attempt 'to be fair' when considering the choice of investments; and

(iii) the apportionment rules designed to achieve fairness between successive beneficiaries are frequently either expressly excluded or ignored in practice. This is because they are perceived both as unduly complex and more importantly largely irrelevant under modern investment conditions.

(d) Reform and the principle of impartiality

(1) The Law Commission Consultation Paper

As we have noted the reference to the Law Commission by the Lord Chancellor in 2000 is but the latest in a series of official and quasi-official reviews of the rules that have as their rationale the principle that trustees must be impartial in their management of the trust. The almost universal response of the several reviews has been that the rules are complicated, unsatisfactory in their impact and are frequently excluded or even ignored. To this catalogue of criticisms can now be added the further charge that the advancement of the cause of portfolio investment theory in the Trustee Act 2000 will be frustrated in so far as 'the current law as it appertains to classification and apportionment makes it impossible to realise all the potential benefits of that theory' (*Capital and Income in Trusts: Classification and Apportionment* (No 175) para 1.9). The argument is that the rules based on the traditional distinction drawn by trusts law between capital and income are preventing trustees from realising the larger economic returns that might have been achievable were the Hicksian or economist's definition of capital and income adopted.

In response to these various pressures for reform the Law Commission has advanced several key proposals for consultation. Unsurprisingly the Commission restates the centrality of the 'duty of impartiality' or, as it is sometimes called, the duty to 'keep a fair balance'. This duty to be even-handed in the treatment of different classes of beneficiaries therefore underpins the specific proposals.

As regards the equitable rules of apportionment the Law Commission proposals closely follow the earlier recommendation of the LRC to the effect that the existing rules should be abrogated (paras 5.83–5.88). Similarly the Commission proposes that the duty to convert trust property under the rule in *Howe v Earl of Dartmouth* should also be abrogated. On the other hand, where a settlor expressly creates a trust for sale (without a power to postpone sale) then the Commission proposal is that trustees should continue to be under a duty to convert the trust property and reinvest the proceeds (paras 5.89–5.91). But what of the position where there is an inter vivos settlement or the trust fund at its inception is comprised of authorised investments, or realty? Should the law still assume, as has been the case, that the settlor intended that such gifts were intended to be enjoyed in specie and that there is therefore no implied obligation to convert so as to achieve a 'fair balance'? The Commission proposes what is tantamount to a reversal of those assumptions and, it might be added, an endorsement of the result in *Re Smith* by suggesting that trustees should be subject to the duty to hold a fair balance except in so far as the settlor in the trust instrument expressly, or by necessary implication, excludes or modifies that duty (see paras 5.19–5.31).

In place of the 'old' rules, and as a necessary adjunct to the proposed duty to 'keep a fair balance' the Law Commission proposes the introduction of a statutory power of allocation for trustees. The proposed power would enable trustees to achieve the underlying objective of maintaining a balance between capital and income beneficiaries by empowering the trustees to allocate receipts or expenses between income and capital. The Commission also proposes a replacement of the existing rules on classification of distributions by corporate entities, based as they currently are on company law principles, by new rules deemed more appropriate for trustee-shareholders (see paras 5.3–5.18). Devising rules that can adjust to every new complexity in corporate manoeuvres to achieve commercial benefits is probably impossible and so the Commission has also proposed that any consequential problems of imbalance could be overcome by the proposed power of allocation. It is therefore evident that the content and scope of that proposed power is central to the reform agenda. It is not possible to explore all the ramifications of the Law Commission proposals here but three particular points merit brief comment. They are (i) the continuing relevance of a capital-income distinction; (ii) the scope of an obligation to act fairly; and (iii) the effectiveness of methods of enforcing a general duty of impartiality.

(2) Capital and income reconsidered

Empowering trustees to convert income into capital and vice versa enables them to hold an even hand more easily. It overcomes the limitations imposed on allocation of receipts and outgoings by the lawyer's concepts of capital and income. To an extent settlors are already able to achieve this by direction in the trust instrument. For example, a settlor concerned that the income produced for a life-tenant may prove inadequate can either direct trustees, or provide them with a discretion, to supplement income out of capital. There is an income tax pitfall here, however, in that payments of a recurrent nature will be treated as the income of the beneficiary (*Brodie's Will Trustees v IRC* (1933) 17 TC 432 at 438–439; *Lindus and Hortin v IRC* (1933) 17 TC 442; cf *Stevenson v Wishart* [1986] STC 74). However, the conferment of such a discretion interferes with the capital-income distinction at the allocation of receipts and outgoings stage only, and does not directly confront the more fundamental issue, that of the rigidity imposed on trustees' investment policy by that distinction.

A more radical proposal to sever investment decisions from the influence of the legal concepts of income and capital is the 'unitrust' or 'percentage trust'. In a unitrust trustees manage a single fund with the investment objective being an increase of the total fund. All receipts of whatever nature are paid into the one fund and all outgoings of whatever nature are paid out of the fund. Whether the source of the increase is income or capital appreciation is irrelevant since there is no separate allocation to capital or income. A method of calculation of the life-tenant's interest under a unitrust is described by one American proponent as follows:

E M David 'Principal and Income – Obsolete Concepts' [1972] Pennsylvania Bar Association Quarterly 247

Each year there would be distributed to the life-tenant an amount equal to a stipulated percentage of the current market value of the entire combined fund. The percentage would be one defined by the testator or grantor. It might be a fixed percentage or one related to economic factors, such as prime rate of interest. It would not be related to the purchasing power of the dollar, since hopefully that would be reflected in the current value of the combined fund. If a fixed percentage rate is stipulated, as would probably be most common, the rate should be determined by taking the projected income, adding the projected appreciation, deducting an amount to cover the estimated loss due to the decline in the value of the dollar through inflation and also deducting a reasonable reserve for possible principal losses. It might be suggested that this calculation involves a good deal of judgement if not actual guesswork. Nevertheless, it is surely better than giving the trustee the option of paying the life-tenant any amount between 1 per cent and 8 per cent with no guidance as to which figure he is to approach. It is better to pay a stated rate than to pay 'income' which now means little in terms of rate of return.

The capital beneficiary will of course receive the balance of the fund at the termination of the life-tenant's interest. The unitrust is not without its own difficulties, in particular those of liquidity of assets, cost and timing of valuation of assets and taxation treatment. Indeed a criticism of the unitrust voiced in the US is that 'it has little to offer except complexity of administration, since a draftsman can already achieve similar results by use of "invasion of capital" clauses and provision for interest-free loans'. (See 'The Trust Income Plan – A Solution for the Life-Tenant?' (1984) 190 The Accountant, 3 May, p 11; Wolf (1997) 32 Real Property Probate and Trust Journal 45; Dobris (1997) Real Property Probate and Trust Journal 255; Manns (1998) 28 VUWLR 611.)

The Law Commission in its Consultation Paper steers an agnostic path – it seeks views on the pros and cons of promoting such trusts – but identifies two potential problems. One is the lack both of awareness of and legal expertise in the percentage trust in England and Wales. The second difficulty lies in the current tax system for trusts which is based exclusively at present on the traditional concepts of capital and income. The alternative method of achieving a 'total return' investment approach, and one favoured by the Law Commission is, as indicated above, to confer on trustees a statutory power to allocate trust receipts and expenses between income and capital (paras 5.39–5.55).

(3) The duty to maintain a fair balance

The Law Commission proposes that a statutory power of allocation would be available to trustees only in so far as necessary to discharge the duty to maintain a fair balance. Any proposal invoking a notion of fairness inevitably invites the question: What criteria are we to employ in determining fairness? In *Nestlé v National Westminster Bank plc* ((1996) 10 TLI 112), for instance, Hoffmann J, responding to the argument that the investment policy of the trustee had unfairly favoured the life-tenant, comments (at 115):

> The trustees have in my judgement a wide discretion. They are for example entitled to take into account the income needs of the tenant for life or the fact that the tenant for life was a person known to the settlor and a primary object of the trust whereas the remainderman is a remoter relative or stranger. . . . It would be an inhuman law which required trustees to adhere to some mechanical rule for preserving the real value of the capital when the tenant for life was the testator's widow who had fallen upon hard times and the remainderman was young and well off.

Similar sentiments were expressed by Staughton LJ in *Nestlé* in the Court of Appeal ([1993] 1 WLR 1260 at 1279): 'If the life-tenant is living in penury and the remainderman already has ample wealth, common-sense suggests that a trustee should be able to take that into account, not necessarily by seeking the highest possible income at the expense of capital but by inclining in that direction.'

An appeal to common sense as an adjudicating factor is fraught with risk. Indeed the Law Commission, rejecting the notion that balance should be defined by reference to a statutory list of relevant factors, proposes instead that 'the meaning of "balance" should be a matter of common sense informed by the common law' (para 5.57). However, the Law Commission does *not* think that the personal circumstances of beneficiaries should be a relevant factor in the exercise of the statutory power of allocation.

Consider the following points:

(1) Which of the following statements (both drawn substantially from the Law Commission Consultation Paper) regarding the relevance of personal circumstances to the question of 'a fair balance' do you find more persuasive:

> The instinctive response of many trust lawyers [to the *Nestlé* approach is] that it would be unconscionable or inequitable not to shift the balance of the trust fund to reflect the personal circumstances of the beneficiaries. It is said that trustees should know about and take an interest in the beneficiaries' personal circumstances and that equity should do what is 'right' (para 5.73); *or*

> The *Nestlé* approach equates the idea of administering a trust fund 'impartially' with administering it 'fairly' (in the sense of meritoriously). Introducing the concept of fairness makes the beneficiaries' entitlements dependent upon a much wider range of moral considerations which otherwise have no place within a fixed interest trust. . . . If trustees are able to take into account personal circumstances, they would have a power akin to an indirect dispositive discretion for which the settlor has (possibly for good reason) made no provision in the terms of the trust (para 5.76).

(2) Under a trust for successive beneficiaries does the discretion given to trustees to select from a wide range of authorised investments in effect transform what appears as an administrative power to manage wealth into a significant dispositive power?

(4) Enforcing a general duty of impartiality

Adopting a statutory power of allocation in preference to clearly defined rules, even of limited application, so as to help satisfy a general duty of impartiality potentially poses a problem of control. Faced with a comparable issue in its 1982 Report the LRC proposed that trustees should not be liable for breach of the duty of impartiality if they acted in good faith. The Committee nevertheless recommended that 'any beneficiary should be entitled to apply to the court for an order directing the trustee either to make or adjust an apportionment' provided that the beneficiary could demonstrate that 'the trustees' exercise of their discretion had substantially prejudiced [the beneficiary's] interest' (23rd Report, *The Powers and Duties of Trustees* (Cmnd 8733, 1982) para 3.37). The LRC concluded that 'bearing in mind the vast choice of investments available to trustees, in practice it would be exceptional for [the court] to conclude that they had not held an even balance'. It would be surprising, as the Law Commission notes in its Consultation Paper, if a similarly wide margin of appreciation were not to be accorded to trustees exercising the proposed power of allocation before the courts would hold that trustees were in breach of their duty to maintain a balance. Consequently the Commission proposes simply that a statutory power of allocation should be subject to review by the courts on the same basis as any other discretionary power (*Capital and Income in Trusts: Classification and*

Apportionment (No 175) paras 5.80–5.82). It remains an open question whether either the recommendation of the LRC or the proposal of the Law Commission strikes an appropriate balance between the conflicting pressures of preserving a wide investment discretion for trustees, avoiding the imposition of unduly onerous accounting obligations on them and protecting the interests of the beneficiaries (cf the facts of *Nestlé v National Westminster Bank plc* [1993] 1 WLR 1260).

5. Delegation

(a) Introduction: from prohibition to the Trustee Act 2000

Where the office of trusteeship is described as one of personal confidence, this reflects the moral element of the obligation. The person creating the trust is in effect saying to the trustee, 'I trust you to implement my instruction' and where discretion is given, 'I trust you to decide matters'. Trusts law, recognising and seeking to enforce the personal nature of the obligation undertaken by a trustee, initially adopted a principle of non-delegation: 'trustees who take on themselves the management of property for the benefit of others have no right to shift their duty on other persons' whether third-party agents or co-trustees (per Langdale MR in *Turner v Corney* (1841) 5 Beav 515 at 517). Yet even when 'there was nothing in any way incongruous in expecting a member of the landowning class to devote considerable time and skill to the gratuitous administration of the property of a neighbour, and incur heavy liability if his judgment proved erroneous' (Keeton *Modern Developments in the Law of Trusts* (1971) p 11), there existed tasks which required specialised expertise. But any proposed retreat from a principle of non-delegation poses two questions. In what circumstances should a trustee be able to delegate? How far should a trustee be held personally liable for loss caused by the agent's errors or dishonesty?

One answer to the first question emerged as early as 1754 when the strict application of the non-delegation principle was tempered by the impact of conventional business practice. It was established by Lord Hardwicke LC in *ex p Belchier* (1754) Amb 218 that trustees could employ skilled agents to carry out specialised tasks – in that case the sale of tobacco by auction – on the ground of 'legal or moral necessity', the latter meaning in the normal course of affairs. Changes in the nature of trust property allied to increasing specialisation and professionalisation of business, financial and legal functions increased the pressures on trustees to delegate. Moreover, the courts recognised that 'in the administration of a trust a trustee cannot do everything for himself, he must to a certain extent make use of the arms, legs, eyes and hands of other persons' (per Bowen LJ in *Speight v Gaunt* (1883) 22 Ch D 727 at 762). The leading case, *Speight v Gaunt* (1883) 9 App Cas 1, HL in effect confirmed that the principle of non-delegation had been modified so that trustees could employ agents where a prudent man of business would do so. Subsequently the TA 1925, s 23(1) so widened the scope of delegation that the duty not to delegate became transmuted into a power to delegate. But despite these developments the influence of the 'personal confidence' standard remained and a distinction was still drawn between the employment of agents and the delegation of discretion. The position was concisely summarised in the 29th edition of Snell *Principles of Equity* (1990) p 267: 'a power to employ agents to do specified acts is not power to authorise agents to decide what acts to do'.

The distinction identified in that edition of *Snell* is increasingly difficult to justify and sustain in modern investment conditions. The scope of the power of delegation came under review by the Law Commission which concluded that fundamental changes in the way that investment business was being conducted established a strong case for reform (*Trustees' Powers and Duties* Consultation Paper No 146 (1997). In particular the Commission pointed to the increasingly complex range of investment opportunities available requiring specialist fund management expertise, to major changes in share dealing and settlement mechanisms on the London Stock Exchange and to the introduction (in 1996) of dematerialised holding and transfer of title to securities under the CREST system (a computer-based system for the electronic transfer of and settlement of trades in securities on the London Stock Exchange; see Consultation Paper No 146, paras 2.24–2.26). Indeed in its subsequent 1999 report the Commission went so far as to suggest that the then existing prohibitions 'far from promoting the more conscientious discharge of the obligations of trusteeship . . . may force trustees to commit breaches of trust in order to achieve the most effective administration of the trust' (*Trustees' Powers and Duties* (1999) Law Com No 260, para 4.6). These material reasons for recommending change were complemented by one of long-standing pedigree, ie a concern to minimise the administrative burdens of trusteeship so as not to deter potential trustees. It was therefore not surprising that in the 1999 Report the Commission recommended a major extension of the power to delegate administrative duties and discretions (Pt IV). It must be emphasised that the Law Commission was concerned with delegation of *administrative* duties and discretions and not the exercise by trustees of their *dispositive* discretions; as the Consultation Paper put it: 'The distribution of trust property is one of the most essential functions of trusteeship . . . trustees should be expected to perform it unless the settlor has provided to the contrary' (para 1.15).

Turning now to the second question – the extent of the trustee's liability for the acts and defaults of agents – the answer came also to reflect the prudent man of business standard. Where the appointment of an agent was justified, the trustee was held bound to display proper care in the selection of the agent – not employing an agent to act outside the scope of his business (*Fry v Tapson* (1884) 28 Ch D 268) – and in supervision of the agent's work (*Speight v Gaunt* (1883) 9 App Cas 1 per Earl of Selborne LC at 14–15). A statutory indemnity clause (Law of Property Amendment Act 1859, s 31) which relieved trustees from liability for loss arising out of an agent's acts or defaults unless the loss happened through the trustee's wilful default received a parallel interpretation: '[the clause] does not substantially alter the law as it was administered by Courts of Equity, but gives it the authority and force of statute law . . .' (*Re Brier* (1884) 26 Ch D 238 at 243 per Earl of Selborne LC). Subsequent interpretation of this clause (in the now repealed TA 1925, s 30(1)) and reconciling it with other sections of the TA 1925 created confusion as to both the standard of liability and the apparent symmetry of common law and statute law. As was discussed earlier in this chapter, the Law Commission recommended the introduction of a statutory duty of care and the position now is that a trustee's liability when delegating will be determined by the application of the new statutory duty of care in TA 2000, s 1.

(b) Trustees' powers of delegation and the Trustee Act 2000

(1) Introduction

The Law Commission recommendations concerning trustees' powers of delegation were implemented in the Trustee Act 2000, Pt IV. As with other default provisions of the 2000 reforms the new wide powers of delegation conferred on trustees apply to all trusts whenever created (TA 2000, s 27), are additional to any express powers to appoint agents and are subject to any restrictions or exclusions imposed by the trust instrument (TA 2000, s 26). The most significant feature of the new powers, unlike the position prior to the TA 2000, is that it is now possible for trustees to delegate their power of investment (ss 11–15). Another important innovation, linked to the objective of facilitating greater efficiency in trust administration, is to confer on trustees the powers to vest trust property in nominees and to employ custodians (ss 16–23). In a sense this innovation reverses the position at common law whereby trustees placing trust property in the hands of a third party when they have not been expressly empowered to do so would commit a breach of trust and be liable for any loss caused as a result. This new power is considered further in section (b)(4) below.

It is important to emphasise that the new statutory regime in Pt IV is concerned with delegation of functions by trustees as a collective body. There are important distinctions between this aspect of delegation and delegation of functions by an individual trustee. The latter jurisdiction, which is still governed by TA 1925, s 25 and Trustee Delegation Act 1999, s 1, is considered briefly at the end of this part of the chapter. There are also important distinctions between charitable trusts and private trusts as to the functions that can be delegated. Those aspects of the new default powers that relate solely to charitable trusts are therefore considered in the context of the regulation and administration of charitable trusts in Chapter 20.

(2) The scope of the power to appoint agents

The key questions confronting any reform of the law on delegation are what functions should be delegable, to whom and on what terms. The omission of the 'when can trustees delegate?' question from that agenda simply reflects the fact that there is no change from the previous position under now repealed TA 1925, s 23(1). Trustees can still appoint an agent to exercise 'any or all of their delegable functions' whether or not there is any necessity for them to do so even if they could readily have performed the function themselves.

Indeed it must be emphasised that the new Act says nothing about the duty of trustees in deciding whether or not to exercise the power to delegate. Trustees are therefore, with one exception, under no statutory duty of care at this stage of the delegation process. The sole exception is under TOLATA 1996, s 9A(1) where the statutory duty of care in the TA 2000 is stated to apply in relation to decisions by trustees of land as to whether to delegate to a beneficiary. That exception aside, it would appear that trustees do not need to demonstrate, for instance, that it is reasonably necessary to delegate a particular management function to agents. The Law Commission was of the view that any legal control over the trustees' decisions as to *whether* to exercise their discretions should be left to the inherent jurisdiction of the courts although, as the Commission note: '[the courts] will not generally interfere with a discretionary power if the trustees are unanimous as to its exercise' (para 3.3 and see further Chapter 11 of this book at pp 541–552). None of this may matter if it is a case of a lay trustee delegating certain management functions to professionals. But should a professional trustee be allowed to employ at the trust's expense an agent to do what, it may be argued, the trustee is already being paid to do? The Law Reform Committee (LRC) in its 1982 Report thought not; it recommended that the trust be charged *only* where the charges and expenses of delegation 'are reasonably incurred, taking into account the trustee's knowledge, qualifications and experience and the level of remuneration received by him' (23rd Report *The Powers and Duties of Trustees* (Cmnd 8733, 1982) para 4.6). Whether, as a longstop means of control, the court could or should invoke the generic duty of trustees 'to exercise their powers in the best interests of the beneficiaries' as a means of impugning an 'unreasonable' or 'unnecessary' appointment of an agent is a matter that may yet have to be addressed.

The delegable functions   What then are the delegable functions? The underlying rationale of the approach adopted by the Law Commission was that a distinction should be drawn between administrative powers that would be delegable and distributive (or dispositive) powers that would not. The Commission was concerned, however, that a straightforward unqualified statutory distinction between the two different types of power might have enabled trustees to delegate their powers under TA 1925, s 36 to appoint and remove trustees in certain circumstances (see Chapter 11 at p 537). Delegation of a power such as that was rightly considered to be inappropriate unless expressly authorised in the trust instrument. The method of implementing the desired distinction between those powers that should be delegable and those that should not is therefore to permit trustees to appoint an agent to exercise any or all of the trustees' delegable functions (TA 2000, s 11(1)). Those delegable functions are then defined in s 11(2) as 'any function other than' the following four exceptions listed in the subsection:

(a) any function relating to whether or in what way any assets of the trust should be distributed,
(b) any power to decide whether any fees or other payment due to be made out of the trust funds should be made out of income or capital,
(c) any power to appoint a person to be a trustee of the trust, or
(d) any power conferred by any other enactment or the trust instrument which permits the trustees to delegate any of their functions or to appoint a person to act as a nominee or custodian.

To give an obvious example of a power that cannot be delegated, trustees cannot delegate their discretion to appoint between the objects of a discretionary trust.

The agent As to who can be appointed as an agent, some guidance is provided by TA 2000, s 12. No beneficiary can be appointed as an agent thus avoiding possible conflicts of interest arising (s 12(3)). On the other hand, an existing trustee, assuming he or she is not also a beneficiary, can be appointed as agent (s 12(1)) as indeed can a nominee and/or custodian for the trustees (s 12(4)). The only other specific provision in the section is that two or more persons may not be authorised to exercise the same function unless they are to exercise the function jointly (s 12(2)). It must not be overlooked, however, that any exercise of the power to employ agents under s 11 is subject to the statutory duty of care in TA 2000, s 1.

The terms of appointment Turning next to the terms on which an agent may be appointed, s 14 (1) empowers the trustees to 'authorise a person to exercise functions as their agent on such terms as to remuneration and other matters' as they may determine. This sweeping discretion is qualified in three ways. First, remuneration of agents, nominees and custodians is regulated by TA 2000, s 32, which applies irrespective of whether the appointment is made under the statutory power or by a term of the trust instrument. Section 32(2) provides that where the appointment provides for remuneration (s 32(2)(a)), such remuneration can be paid out of the trust fund provided that 'the amount does not exceed such remuneration as is reasonable in the circumstances for the provision of those services' (s 32(2)(b)). In addition the trustees may reimburse out of the trust fund agents, nominees or custodians for expenses properly incurred in exercising the functions delegated to them (s 32(3)).

The second restriction to be considered here refers to what the statute categorises in s 13 as 'Linked functions etc.'. Where an agent is authorised to exercise a function to which specific duties or restrictions would apply if the trustees themselves were exercising the function, then those duties or restrictions will apply equally to the agent, regardless of the terms of the agency agreement (s 13(1)). Somewhat unusually s 13 itself contains an example in the following terms: 'a person who is authorised under section 11 to exercise the general power of investment is subject to the duties under [TA 2000] section 4 in relation to that power' those duties being the standard investment criteria (see above, p 492). There is a limitation within s 13 in that if the 'duty or restriction' referred to in s 13(1) relates to obtaining advice then the agent need not comply with this requirement 'if he is the kind of person from whom it would have been proper for the trustees . . . to obtain advice' (s 13(2)). There is one further specific qualification to the scope of s 13. An agent authorised under TA 2000, s 11 to exercise any function relating to land subject to the trust is *not* obliged to consult with and possibly give effect to the wishes of beneficiaries with interests in possession in that land, an obligation imposed on trustees by TOLATA 1996, s 11(1) (see s 13(3), (5)). Trustees may not exploit this dispensation and they therefore cannot appoint an agent on terms that would enable them to avoid their own obligations to carry out such consultations with the relevant beneficiaries (TA 2000, s 13(4)).

The third and potentially most contentious restriction on the terms of appointment is to be found in s 14 itself.

Trustee Act 2000, s 14(2), (3)

(2) The trustees may not authorise a person to exercise functions as their agent on any of the terms mentioned in subsection (3) unless it is reasonably necessary for them to do so.

(3) The terms are –
   (a) a term permitting the agent to appoint a substitute;
   (b) a term restricting the liability of the agent or his substitute to the trustees or any beneficiary;
   (c) a term permitting the agent to act in circumstances capable of giving rise to a conflict of interest.

The statute provides no assistance as to the meaning of reasonable necessity. The context in which the term is most likely to be subject to scrutiny is that of investment management and here the operation of the market is likely to be a significant factor. The Law Commission recognised that as regards all three terms – sub-delegation under s 14(3)(a), exclusion of liability (s 14(3)(b)) and conflicts of interest (s 14(3)(c)) – trustees may in practice have little option in the appointment of fund managers but to accede to their standard terms of appointment (see in particular *Trustees' Powers and Duties*, paras 4.25–4.29). The recommendations of the Commission reflected this analysis and are encapsulated in the 'reasonable necessity' approach adopted in s 14(3). The Explanatory Notes to the TA 2000 equally reflect this perception of the significance of the market place. Referring to the limitations of the pre-2000 law on sub-delegation and the modifications of s 14(3)(a) the Note suggests that '[t]his [limitation] is no longer appropriate in modern conditions where the appointment of a fund manager will often be essential to the efficient and effective management of the assets of the trust' (para 61). The Note on s 14 concludes with the following observation (para 61):

> As the standard terms of business of fund managers generally require limits on liability and the ability to act despite a conflict of interest, the ability to appoint a manager would amount to little in practice if trustees were unable to accept such terms.

The fact that trustees may have to accept such terms does not, we would suggest, obviate the need to survey the market for the best deal available. Trustees may well discover that all professional fund managers will incorporate exclusion clauses in their standard terms and conditions. Indeed this is quite probable since the Institute of Fund Managers standard terms of engagement produced prior to the TA 2000 included an exclusion clause as well as clauses permitting sub-delegation and conflicts of interest (see Wilson (2003) 2 PCB 91 at 94; and generally on agreements with investment managers Hayton (1990) 106 LQR 88–93). It does not necessarily follow that their scale fees will be identical or that their investment performance will be uniform. Might there be circumstances where trustees are required to demonstrate that notwithstanding their compliance with s 14(3) their selection of fund manager nevertheless satisfied the statutory duty of care requirement?

(3) Delegation and the asset management function

The Law Commission recognised that reliance solely on the duty of care and the reasonable necessity requirement of s 14(3) as safeguards for beneficiaries would not be satisfactory where what the Commission termed 'the asset management function' was to be delegated. Accordingly the Commission made specific recommendations for additional requirements to be imposed where trustees wished to delegate that function. These recommendations are implemented in s 15 of the Act and are principally directed at establishing what we might term 'a paper trail'.

Section 15(5) defines the asset management functions of trustees as comprising:

(a) the investment of assets subject to the trust,

(b) the acquisition of property which is to be subject to the trust, and

(c) managing property which is subject to the trust and disposing of, or creating or disposing of an interest in, such property.

This definition is clearly sufficiently broad to encompass the appointment of an agent to manage a portfolio of investments (s 15(5)(a)) but also extends to include such activities as appointing an agent to sell trust property (s 15(5)(c)). Section 15(1) provides that trustees may not authorise an agent to exercise any of the above asset management functions unless by an agreement in or evidenced in writing. Nowhere in s 15 is it stated that its provisions apply only to a delegation under the TA 2000 and the section would therefore seem to apply to any delegation of the asset management function whether under the Act or, for instance, under the terms of the trust instrument. A key part of the delegation process under s 15 is that trustees must prepare a policy statement that must itself be in writing or witnessed in writing (s 15(4)). The policy statement should give written guidance to the agent as to how the asset management functions should be exercised (s 15(2)(a)) and the guidance must be formulated 'with a view to ensuring that the asset management functions will be exercised in the best interests of the trust' (s 15(3)). The s 15(1) written agreement between the trustees and the agent must then include a term to the effect that the agent will comply with that policy statement or any subsequent revision of it. The origins of this requirement are to be found in a comparable arrangement imposed on trustees of pension schemes by s 35 of the Pensions Act 1995 (see Chapter 13 at p 684). The contents of any policy statement are likely to depend on the type of trust and size of the trust fund but would be expected to include reference to such matters as types of investment and the balance between capital growth and income yield, and whether certain types of investment should be excluded and on what grounds.

One question not addressed in the Act is whether professional trustees who are part of a financial conglomerate whose activities embrace a diverse range of financial roles should be permitted to delegate the investment management function of a trust to an associated investment management company. The convenience of doing so is obvious and the trust instrument may specifically permit it but otherwise it is arguable that there exists a potential conflict of interest (see generally McCormack (1999) 20 Co Law 1 at 3–13). The trustee company would be in a position where there might be a conflict between its duty to the trust to obtain the best terms and its financial interest, possibly indirect, in placing the business with its associated company. The matter has yet to come before the English courts but a decision in a Hong Kong case held that there is no absolute prohibition on a trustee delegating its investment management functions to a wholly owned subsidiary. The question to be determined in the view of the court was whether there was a 'real possibility of conflict arising' and if there was no such risk then delegation was permissible. The question of whether a risk exists was held to be one of fact and degree in any given case (see *HSBC (HK) Ltd v Secretary of Justice* (2000–01) 3 ITELR 763, and comment by Wilson [2003] PCB 2, 91 at 91–93).

(4) Nominees and custodians

At common law trustees have a duty to take such steps as are reasonable to secure and retain control of trust property. Thus, as mentioned previously (see above, p 520) trustees placing trust property in the hands of a third party when they have not been expressly empowered to do so would commit a breach of trust and be liable for any loss caused as a result. It therefore followed that in the absence of express authority trustees could neither vest legal title to property in nominees nor place trust documents in the custody of a custodian. To some degree these restrictions acted as a safeguard for beneficiaries, particularly against the risk of loss through fraud. Changes in the rules of the Stock Exchange regarding share dealing and the introduction of the electronic CREST system for the dematerialised holding and transfer of title to shares and securities posed problems for trustees. Could they both comply with the rules of trusts law and gain the benefits of the modern investment practices facilitated by the sort of changes to the system of dealing in shares and securities just described? The Law Commission was of the view that they could not. It therefore recommended that trustees should be given new statutory powers to employ nominees and custodians.

The TA 2000 now confers on trustees the power to appoint (i) a nominee in relation to such assets as the trustees may determine (s 16(1)) and (ii) a custodian again of such assets as the trustees may determine (s 17(1)). A custodian is defined as a person who 'undertakes the safe custody of the assets or of any documents or records concerning the assets' (s 17(2)). Where the assets of the trust include securities payable to a bearer, s 18(1) of the Act imposes a *duty* on the trustees to appoint a person to act as a custodian of the relevant securities unless the trust instrument or any enactment provides otherwise (s 18(2)). In all three of the above instances the appointment must be in or evidenced in writing. None of ss 16–18 applies where the trust already has a custodian trustee. The Act imposes certain limitations (s 19) on who may be appointed as nominees or custodians but in most instances this will not create problems, the appointee satisfying the requirements by virtue of being a 'person who carries on a business which consists of or includes acting as a nominee or custodian' (s 19(2)(a)). Section 20 of the Act governs the terms of appointment and remuneration of nominees and custodians. It is identical in all material respects to s 14 and the same considerations as affect the operation of that section will apply here also (see above, p 522).

(5) Delegation and the liability of trustees

It is important to emphasise at the outset that any obligations or responsibilities of trustees do not cease simply when an appointment is made under ss 11, 16, 17 or 18. While any agent, nominee or custodian continues to act for the trust, the trustees must keep the arrangement under review and consider whether there is any need to exercise any power of intervention that they might have, even to the extent of revoking the authorisation or appointment (s 22(1) and (4)). Here, as in other instances, this obligation is subject to any contrary intention in the trust instrument (s 21(3)). A similar review requirement applies to the delegation of asset management functions under s 15 of the Act (s 22(2) and (3)).

It is also important to emphasise that trustees' liability for their own acts or omissions in delegating functions to agents, nominees and custodians is determined exclusively by application of the statutory duty of care under TA 2000, s 1 and Sch 1 (see section 2 of this chapter for discussion of the duty of care). The duty of care applies to a trustee 'when entering into arrangements' under any of ss 11, 16, 17 or 18 to appoint any agent, nominee or custodian and also when carrying out any of the review duties under s 22. Under Sch 1, para 3 'entering into arrangements' is defined as including (a) selecting the person who is to act, (b) determining the terms of the delegation and (c) the preparation of a policy statement where the asset management function is delegated under s 15 of the Act.

An issue that was the subject of doubt and controversy under the pre-2000 law was whether and to what extent trustees could be held 'vicariously liable' for the acts or defaults of agents. The matter is now put beyond doubt. Section 23 of the Act states that 'a trustee is not liable for any act or default of any agent, nominee or custodian unless [the trustee] has failed to comply with the duty of care applicable to him under paragraph 3 of Schedule 1'. Trustees are therefore not to be held liable merely because the agent, nominee or custodian does some act that causes a loss to the trust. The liability of trustees, to reiterate the point, is determined by reference to their own conduct and the application of the duty of care to that conduct.

At the time of writing there had been no reported case law on the interpretation of the new statutory duty of care. But a key authority from a somewhat earlier era, *Fry v Tapson* (1884) 28 Ch D 268, illustrates the risk to which trustees are exposed if they employ an agent to carry out functions outside the scope of the agent's usual business. Trustees were considering investing trust money on a mortgage, as they were authorised to do. They in effect delegated to their solicitor the selection of a surveyor to value the land against which the mortgage was to be secured. Unfortunately not only did the nominated surveyor lack knowledge of the local area where the land was situated but also he was the agent of the potential mortgagor in that he would receive commission if the mortgage was granted. In fact he overvalued the property, the money was lent and a loss ensued when the mortgagor became bankrupt. The trustees were held liable to make good the loss suffered by the trust fund. The legal position was aptly summarised by Kay J: 'If the trustee employs an agent to do that which is not the ordinary business of such an agent, and he performs that unusual task improperly, and loss is thereby occasioned, the trustee would not be exonerated' (at 280). Whilst this case involved an early application of the prudent man of business standard there is no reason to think that similar conduct would not equally fall foul of the new statutory duty of care.

Finally, it should be noted that even if the trustees exceed their powers in the authorisation or appointment of a person as agent, nominee or custodian their failure in this regard does not invalidate the authorisation or appointment (TA 2000, s 24).

(6) Individual delegation

We have seen that initially the common law applied a principle of non-delegation in part because the office of trusteeship was viewed as being one of personal confidence. Whilst this position became modified as regards the delegation of administrative functions there was no break with the principle that the exercise of discretions could not be delegated. But guiding principles of trust law can in many instances be subordinated to the express wishes of settlors. The position therefore has never been that delegation of discretions is not possible: 'The law is not that trustees cannot delegate: it is that trustees cannot delegate unless they have authority to do so' (per Lord Radcliffe, *Pilkington v IRC* [1964] AC 612 at 639). In practice true delegation of trustees' discretions could be achieved either under authority bestowed by the settlor in the trust instrument or under TA 1925, s 25. The object of s 25 is to enable an individual trustee to delegate his or her trusts, where for some reason and for a relatively short period of time, he or she is unable to perform the trusts. Indeed at its inception the statutory power could be invoked only during the absence of a trustee overseas. Since then s 25 has been amended by the Powers of Attorney Act 1971 and more recently by the Trustee Delegation Act 1999, s 5. The overall effect has been to extend and clarify the scope of the jurisdiction.

Trustee Act 1925, s 25(1), (2), (3)

(1) Notwithstanding any rule of law or equity to the contrary, a trustee may, by power of attorney, delegate the execution or exercise of all or any of the trusts, powers and discretions vested in him as trustee either alone or jointly with any other person or persons.

(2) A delegation under this section –

. . .

(b) continues for a period of twelve months or any shorter period provided by the instrument creating the power

(3) The persons who may be donees of a power of attorney under this section include a trust corporation [*but not (unless a trust corporation) the only other co-trustee of the donor of the power*].

The italicised words in s 25(3) were removed by the Trustee Delegation Act 1999 with the consequence that there is now no statutory restriction as to who may be a donee of the power of attorney. The delegation must be made by deed and written notice of the delegation must be given to the other trustees and to any person entitled to appoint new trustees (s 25(4)). Section 25(4) makes clear, however, that failure to comply with those requirements will not prejudice the interests of any person dealing with the donee. Section 25 has its limitations, the principal one being that the trustee donor of the power of attorney 'shall be liable for the acts or defaults of the donee in the same manner as if they were the acts or defaults of the donor' (s 25(7)). As we have seen in the previous section, this automatic vicarious liability compares unfavourably with the position of trustees who employ agents under the powers of collective delegation provided by the TA 2000.

(7) Delegation: a miscellany

There are two particular contexts – pension scheme trusts and trusts of land – where alternative statutory arrangements have been introduced to facilitate delegation of certain powers.

The Pensions Act 1995, s 34 gives pension scheme trustees new powers of delegation in relation to investment. These are discussed in Chapter 13. Note, however, that other powers of delegation under the TA 2000 do apply to trustees of pension schemes although subject to certain modifications. For the protection of pension scheme members, pension trustees are expressly prohibited from delegating any function to the scheme employer (TA 2000, s 36(6)).

As regards trusts of land, the Trusts of Land and Appointment of Trustees Act 1996, s 9 empowers trustees of land to delegate any of their functions relating to land 'to any beneficiary or beneficiaries of full age and beneficially entitled to an interest in possession in the land' (s 9(1)). The limited class of persons to whom functions can be delegated primarily reflects the objective of allowing trustees of land, where that land is held for successive interests (the strict settlement under the 1925 legislation), to give the current life-tenant of the land control of its management. The Trustee Act 2000 instituted some changes to the provisions of the 1996 Act dealing with trustees' liability for any default of the beneficiary-delegate. A new section (9A) has been inserted in the 1996 Act to the effect that the duty of care under s 1 of the TA 2000 applies to trustees of land in deciding *whether* to delegate any of their functions under s 9 of the 1996 Act (see TA 2000, s 40(1), Sch 2, Pt II). Once the delegation has been made the duty of care is similar to that applicable to delegation by trustees more generally. Thus it applies equally to the trustees' obligation to keep the arrangement under review and to consider whether there is any need to exercise any power of intervention that they may have (s 9A(3) and (5)). This reverses what appeared to be the position under the now repealed s 9(8) of the 1996 Act whereby trustees of land were jointly and severally liable for any act or default of the 'beneficiary-delegate' in the exercise of the function delegated 'if, but only if, the trustees did not exercise reasonable care in decid-ing to delegate the function ... '. From this language it had seemed that once trustees had made the appointment they were under no further obligation to supervise the conduct of the delegate (see the critical comment by Kenny [1997] Conv 372).

(8) A postscript

In a previous edition of this book we suggested that trusts law as it affected the power of delegation by trustees had still to come to terms with the fact that trusteeship had developed from a quasi-managerial role in special situations (strict settlements) to a fully managerial role on a day-to-day basis (most trusts of investments) and even in some instances into mere director-like supervision of specialist management by others. The re-writing in the TA 2000 of the law on delegation and also on powers of investment compels a reappraisal of the claim. As the Law Commission pointed out in its Report the reforms were seen in part as a necessary response to the fundamental changes in the way that investment business was being transacted in a new era of liberalisation of the investment markets. And the underpinning philosophy of the TA 2000 can itself be interpreted as one of liberalisation of the law so as to facilitate a more effective administration of trusts and the generation of improved economic performance for the benefit of beneficiaries. The model of trust fund management implicit in the new legal framework is one of trustees delegating, one might even say sub-contracting, the management to investment specialists. The financial object might be said to minimise the risk of loss and increase the prospects of gain in the investment market. It can therefore be argued that trust law has now come to terms with a new model of trusteeship in the sense that the new Act has brought the law into line with much contemporary trusts practice.

There is little doubt that the reforms have been widely welcomed as was evidenced by the 'very positive response' from a large majority of those who responded to the Consultation Paper (*Trustees' Powers and Duties*, para 1.12 and Appendix D). It would be churlish not to acknowledge the numerous positive elements of the new legal framework as described in this chapter but equally it would be remiss not to raise some reservations about the appropriateness of certain aspects of the new default powers of delegation from a regulatory standpoint.

The question is whether the appropriate balance is struck between conferring greater freedom for trustees in their administration of the trust and securing adequate protection of the interests of beneficiaries. If one takes the standpoint of the Law Commission the very question is misconceived. In the Consultation Paper the Law Commission sought to emphasise that the purpose of the law was facilitative rather then regulatory: 'The reforms which we propose are intended to do no more than facilitate the administration of trusts by providing wider default powers for trustees. It is not our intention that they should in some sense be regulatory' (para 6.22). This is not to say that the Commission was unaware of the risks that accompany greater managerial freedom for trustees particularly where delegation of investment management functions to agents was concerned: 'We have also been very mindful of the tension between the advantages and the dangers of allowing trustees wide powers of delegation.' The danger being adverted to here is principally financial. There are costs involved with delegation. The process might involve higher transaction costs, such as agents' fees, and even at least theoretically an increase in the risk of loss through the acts or omissions or even fraudulent conduct of agents. The stance adopted by the Commission was that the weighting of the balance between advantages and dangers should in large degree be left to settlors (at para 6.23): 'It should be emphasised that we are recommending what the *default* powers of delegation should be. It would remain open to a settlor (as it is under the present law) to extend or restrict those powers.'

It might be argued that for trust funds of any significant size settlors initially and trustees subsequently should be allowed to be the best judges of what is best for the trust fund. But not all trusts have funds in the order of several millions, or even, billions, of pounds. There are many family trusts on a more modest scale and one suspects that it is trusts such as these that are quite likely to adopt the 'default regime'. What is a small or modest trust is necessarily a relative matter and data on private family trusts needs to be treated with caution. Nevertheless according to HMRC estimates of property held in discretionary trusts and derived from information submitted to the Revenue for the purposes of calculating the ten-year charge to IHT on such trusts, there were in 2006–07 51% of trusts with assets between £250,000 and £499,999 and 11% with assets less than £250,000 (*HMRC Statistics 2008*, Table 12.7). Whether the interests of beneficiaries in trusts such as these are best served by the light regulatory approach adopted in the default powers of the TA 2000 remains an open question.

11

Trusteeship, control and breach of trust

1. Introduction

In the previous two chapters we considered, inter alia, the relationship between trusts law and contemporary trusteeship, including the management of the trust and the powers and duties of trustees associated with that function. One emerging consideration was how far does or should the law seek to intervene to limit the autonomy that settlors might confer on trustees in their management of the trust? In this chapter we focus on the means of controlling trustees, the scope of beneficiaries' rights and the effectiveness of remedies available to them. The appointment and removal of trustees and the control over the exercise of their discretion, issues central to an assessment of trustee autonomy in managing the trust, are considered in sections 2 and 3, whilst the measure of trustee personal liability for breach of trust forms the subject-matter of section 4. Beneficiaries are not restricted to a reliance on the personal liability of trustees as a means of securing recompense for some breach of trust. There may be circumstances where beneficiaries wish to take advantage of the proprietary remedies that the law provides where some breach of trust has occurred. In section 5 we briefly introduce the proprietary remedies that may be available to a beneficiary where the personal remedy against trustees proves inadequate. The full range of the proprietary remedies that equity makes available in cases of breach of trust or where there is some breach of fiduciary duty are considered in detail in Chapter 14.

The by now familiar starting-point for our study is the changing nature of trusts practice. We have previously examined in some detail the responses of settlors and their advisers to twentieth-century commercial and fiscal pressures, and have emphasised the accelerating trend, particularly post-1945, in favour of enlarging trustees' discretions. This process became apparent in discretions over both the management of property (eg widely drawn investment clauses) and the allocation of benefit (eg the discretionary trust). But the willingness of the courts to countenance these developments and to uphold dispositions wherever possible (see eg *Re Hay's Settlement Trusts* [1981] 3 All ER 786) potentially opens a Pandora's Box of questions concerning control of trustees' behaviour. As we pointed out in Chapter 5 one consequence of these developments is that such control as exists must now primarily be sought not at the creation of the trust instrument but when the discretion it confers is subsequently exercised. At a general level, can the courts square the circle of simultaneously approving the formal minimisation of beneficiaries' individual interests in the trust corpus – until recently so necessary for tax-planning purposes – while providing adequate methods for enforcement of trustees' redefined obligations? To reiterate – and the point cannot be emphasised enough – it is the exercise of a discretion conferred by the trust instrument that may now be more susceptible to legal challenge. Specifically, how far, if at all, should the courts be prepared to develop trusts law so as to ensure closer monitoring of the exercise of trustees' discretions? Should they be prepared to advise uncertain trustees on how they may exercise those discretions?

In fact prior to the important Privy Council decision in *Schmidt v Rosewood Trust* [2003] 2 WLR 1442 concerning rights to disclosure of information from trustees recent litigation on these issues within the family trust has been sparse (although see *Re Locker's Settlement Trusts* [1978] 1 All ER 216; *Turner v Turner* [1983] 2 All ER 745; *Murphy v Murphy* [1999] 1 WLR 282). Indeed the introduction of inheritance tax prompted a move by settlors away from the use of discretionary trusts into accumulation and maintenance trusts or even outright gifts although discretionary trusts have taken on a fresh lease of life in offshore trusts. But these most recent practical shifts in trusts fashion represent changes in emphasis rather than direction and do not alter the fact that modern trustees still retain a substantial measure of administrative and dispositive discretion compared with their predecessors. Of course in one sense it is still accurate to state that the enforceability of the beneficiary's rights against the trustees represents the heart of the trust concept, retaining the conceptual link with the original moralistic basis of Chancery intervention – to protect the 'reposing of trust or confidence in some other'. But that trust or confidence now commonly passes substantial authority to trustees and we need to ask how autonomous this process has rendered them. Can, for instance, beneficiaries limit trustees' managerial discretion by directing them as to investment policy? Can a beneficiary effectively challenge the trustees' exercise of a dispositive discretion? Are trustees obliged to give even a hearing to a beneficiary or to give reasons for a decision? What information about the management of the trust's affairs are beneficiaries entitled to? These last two questions are of particular practical importance. If beneficiaries can be kept in ignorance about trust affairs, their ability to challenge trustees will be restricted.

When assessing the extent of trustee autonomy in the light of such questions, it must not be overlooked that where trustees are in breach of trust, as for instance by investing in a hazardous and speculative enterprise, the courts have extensive powers to impose liability on trustees and, incidentally, also to grant them relief where appropriate. Yet even this assertion of ultimate judicial control must be viewed in the contemporary context of widespread professional trusteeship. Clauses seeking to limit or exclude liability for loss to the trust fund are now commonplace. If they are valid to the full extent then this factor lends added weight to the description of trustees, advanced over half a century ago, as being 'professional managers of capital who are placed . . . beyond the control of the owner for consumption' (Franklin (1933–34) 8 Tul LR 473 at 475).

Before turning to examine the law in detail, there are several important qualifications to be made here about the substance of that law, as conventionally interpreted. First, it is in our view unwise to assume that some judicial decisions about the rights of beneficiaries and the obligations of trustees made in the commercial context of pension schemes (see Moffat (1993) 56 MLR 471; Hayton [2005] Conv 229 and generally Chapter 13) will necessarily apply in full force to family trusts, and, of course, vice versa. Support for a view that it may on occasion be necessary to distinguish family trusts from commercial trusts can be drawn from comments made obiter by Lord Browne-Wilkinson in *Target Holdings Ltd v Redferns* [1995] 3 WLR 352. In *Target Holdings*, a case involving a breach of trust occurring in the course of a somewhat suspect mortgage arrangement, Lord Browne-Wilkinson warned that 'it is . . . wrong to lift wholesale the detailed rules developed in the context of traditional trusts and then seek to apply them to trusts of a quite different kind' (at 362). He added that 'it is important, if the trust is not to be rendered commercially useless, to distinguish between the basic principles of trust law and those specialist rules developed in relation to traditional trusts which are applicable only to such trusts and the rationale of which has no application to trusts of quite a different kind' (ibid). As will be seen when we look more closely at the case (see below, p 573) this proposition has its critics and there is an alternative slant that can be placed on the comments of Lord Browne-Wilkinson. This is that it is necessary in applying the rules of trust law to distinguish between a bare trust, such as that applicable in *Target Holdings* itself, and a trust where the trustees have active duties of management and administration to perform. The decision in *Target Holdings* also raises another contemporary theme relevant to developing our understanding of the law. That theme concerns what we termed in Chapter 2 'harmonisation' of the common law and equity. In this chapter that theme occurs in the context of considering whether differences in criteria for assessing compensation for breach of trust and common law damages are being elided.

Our final prefatory comment again concerns a development first introduced in an earlier chapter (Chapter 5), ie the appointment of a 'protector' or 'enforcer' as a watchdog over the administration of a trust. Although mentioned there primarily in the context of purpose trusts, protectors can also be appointed in other trusts and be armed with extensive powers, for instance, to direct trustees in the exercise of their powers and discretions, both administrative and dispositive. The protector is also often given power to dismiss trustees, to appoint new trustees and even, for instance, to authorise breach of the self-dealing rule. In practice protectors are likely to be encountered principally, almost exclusively, in offshore trusts where, in many jurisdictions, specific statutory provision clarifying, modifying or regulating the powers of protectors are to be found (see eg Cook Islands International Trusts Act 1984 (as amended) Part IV). The emergence of what appears to be a relatively novel addition to the trusts ensemble potentially poses questions about the accountability of protectors to beneficiaries (see for an overview of the issues Waters 'The Protector: New Wine in Old Bottles?' in Oakley (ed) *Trends in Contemporary Trust Law* (1996) ch 4; Ham et al in Glasson and Thomas (eds) *The International Trust* (2nd edn, 2006) ch 4; Duckworth (2006) 20(3) TLI 180–195; 20(4) 235–261). We say 'appears to be' because it can be claimed with some justification that there is nothing very novel in certain powers in relation to trust property being held by persons other than trustees although the enlarged scope of the powers and extent of the practice accorded to protectors in those offshore jurisdictions arguably is novel (see Duckworth op cit at 180). As regards matters of accountability there are two points only to be made. One is simply that any thorough assessment of the powers and duties of protectors would need to take account of the various statutory provisions and their interpretation by the courts of the jurisdictions concerned, an exercise suitable for more specialist works. Second, the types of powers and duties granted to protectors suggests that English courts, if called upon, are likely to construe these as being fiduciary in nature and that therefore many of the decisions discussed in this chapter and elsewhere in the book would in principle be applicable to protectors.

2. Appointment and removal of trustees

However extensive the discretion formally granted to trustees may be, this would be largely illusory if the trustees could easily be removed at the whim of the settlor or beneficiaries, and more malleable persons appointed. First, we therefore consider the jurisdiction to appoint and remove trustees.

(a) The role of the settlor

A settlor or testator normally appoints the first trustees. Indeed, in an inter vivos trust the settlor may appoint himself, particularly as nowadays such an appointment does not appear to have any fiscal drawbacks. Thereafter, however, the trustees must act independently. They are not to be the settlor's cipher. In practice, trustees, when exercising their discretions, might be tempted to defer to the wishes of a settlor attempting to retain de facto control over property while surrendering beneficial ownership of it. But if the trustees do so they run the risk of being held in breach of trust.

Complexity may arise where a settlor seeks to reserve to himself a power in the trust instrument to appoint or remove trustees. The inclusion of a power of removal is seemingly not common, at least in UK trusts, and tends to be discouraged both on grounds of principle – being inconsistent with a trustee's independence – and for practical reasons (see Kessler *Drafting Trusts and Will*

Trusts (8th edn, 2007) para 7.30). Indeed, even if a settlor incorporates a power of removal in the trust instrument any attempt to remove trustees on the ground of failing to comply with the settlor's wishes is unlikely to be upheld by a court if challenged by the threatened trustees. The purported exercise would arguably constitute an invalid exercise of the power. It is, however, not unusual in an inter vivos settlement for a settlor to retain the right of appointment of future trustees during his lifetime, either by inserting an express power to that effect in the trust instrument or, more commonly, by nominating himself as the person to exercise the statutory power of appointment (Trustee Act (TA) 1925, s 36(1)(a), see below). Settlors may hope that such powers will help curtail the independent exercise of discretion by trustees, but in principle trustees' discretion must be exercised in the interests of beneficiaries *only*, not those of the settlor.

Formally, therefore, in the absence of any special provision the settlor retains no right to appoint or remove trustees once the trust has been created.

(b) Appointment of new or additional trustees

The TA 1925 and the Trusts of Land and Appointment of Trustees Act (TOLATA) 1996 provide a detailed, if complex, code of rules to facilitate the appointment, replacement and retirement of trustees.

(1) Trustee Act 1925, s 36

The statutory power of appointment, which applies unless a contrary intention appears in the trust instrument, is nowadays usually regarded as adequate by settlors. The section has a dual function. First, it enables an outgoing trustee to be replaced where the circumstances outlined in s 36(1) apply. Second, it empowers the appointment of additional trustees provided only that, following the appointment, the total number of trustees does not exceed four and that the appointor may not appoint himself – the subsection (s 36(6)) requiring the 'power to be exercised in favour of "another person or persons"' (cf s 36(1) below; see *Re Power's Settlement Trusts* [1951] Ch 1074). The Law Reform Committee (LRC) recommended the removal of this restriction (23rd Report *The Powers and Duties of Trustees* (Cmnd 8733, 1982) para 2.6).

Trustee Act 1925, s 36(1)

(1) Where a trustee, either original or substituted, and whether appointed by a court or otherwise, is dead, or remains out of the United Kingdom for more than twelve months, or desires to be discharged from all or any of the trusts or powers reposed in or conferred on him, or refuses or is unfit to act therein, or is incapable of acting therein, or is an infant, then subject to the restrictions imposed by this Act on the number of trustees –

(a) the person or persons nominated for the purpose of appointing new trustees by the instrument, if any, creating the trust; or

(b) if there is no such person, or no such person able or willing to act, then the surviving or continuing trustees or trustee for the time being, or the personal representatives of the last surviving or continuing trustee;

may, by writing, appoint one or more other persons (whether or not being the persons exercising the power) to be a trustee or trustees in the place of the trustee so deceased remaining out of the United Kingdom, desiring to be discharged, refusing, or being unfit or being incapable, or being an infant, as aforesaid.

The circumstances described in s 36(1) permitting replacement of trustees are largely self-explanatory. The exceptions are 'unfitness' and 'incapacity', there being little authority on the meaning to be attributed to those terms. A number of nineteenth-century decisions (see eg *Re Lemann's Trust* (1883) 22 Ch D 633) indicate that 'incapacity' refers to personal incapacity, such as physical or mental infirmity, whereas 'unfitness' appears to relate more to deficiencies commonly attributed to character. For instance bankruptcy is probably sufficient ground to constitute unfitness, although the position is not clear (see *Re Wheeler and De Rochow* [1896] 1 Ch 315), particularly where the bankrupt trustee is free from moral blame (*Re Bridgman* (1860) 1 Drew & Sm 164). Section 36(1)(a) and (b) establishes a hierarchy for exercising the statutory power. The person(s) nominated has (have) pre-eminence and the power devolves upon the classes named in s 36(1)(b) only where there is no express nominee or where the nominee is unable or unwilling to act.

Section 36(1) and the hierarchy established under it now have to be read subject to the jurisdiction introduced by TOLATA 1996, s 19. Section 19, which applies to trusts of personalty as well as to trusts of land, confers a power on beneficiaries to give a written direction to one or more trustees to retire and to direct the appointment of new trustees, subject to the statutory limitation on numbers of trustees not being exceeded (see Chapter 9 at p 428). The beneficiaries may give joint or separate directions but their directions must be unanimous both as to the trustee(s) to retire and as to the person(s) if any to be appointed as new trustee(s) (s 21). Moreover exercise of the jurisdiction is not limited to the circumstances specified in s 36 above. However, there are several reasons why the powers conferred on the beneficiaries under this jurisdiction may, in practice, prove to be less sweeping than at first glance appears. First, the power given is, in a sense, an extension of the rule in *Saunders v Vautier* (see Chapter 7) in so far as all the beneficiaries must be in agreement, of full age and capacity and collectively entitled to the trust property. The powers to direct retirement and/or appointment of trustee(s) therefore cannot be exercised where there is a minor beneficiary nor may they be exercised where the trust instrument expressly nominates a person for the purpose of appointing new trustees (s 19(1)(a)). Moreover the statutory powers can be excluded by settlors and testators if they do not wish beneficiaries to be able to exercise this degree of control (s 21(5)–(8)) and it is understood that this is commonly done.

(2) Appointment by the court: Trustee Act 1925, s 41

Section 41(1) provides, inter alia, that:

> The court may, whenever it is expedient to appoint a new trustee or new trustees, and it is found inexpedient, difficult or impracticable so to do without the assistance of the court, make an order appointing a new trustee or new trustees either in substitution for or in addition to any existing trustee or trustees, or although there is no existing trustee.

Despite the wide discretion it seems that the court will not act where the power provided by s 36(1) can be exercised. An application to the court is most likely where those with the power to appoint new trustees cannot agree, or where there is doubt about an issue such as 'unfitness' or 'incapacity'. Section 41 gives no indication as to the criteria the court should apply but some guiding principles emerged in *Re Tempest* (1866) 1 Ch App 485 at 487:

> **Turner LJ**: First, the court will have regard to the wishes of the persons by whom the trust has been created, if expressed in the instrument creating the trust, or clearly to be collected from it. I think this rule may be safely laid down, because if the author of the trust has in terms declared that a particular person, or a person filling a particular character, should not be a trustee of the instrument, there cannot, as I apprehend, be the least doubt that the court would not appoint to the office a person whose appointment was so prohibited . . .
>
> Another rule which may, I think, safely be laid down is this – that the court will not appoint a person to be trustee with a view to the interest of some of the persons interested under the trust, in opposition either to the wishes of the testator or to the interests of others of the cestuis que trusts. . . . Every trustee is in duty bound to look to the interests of all, and not of any particular member or class of members of his cestuis que trusts.
>
> A third rule which, I think, may safely be laid down is – that the court in appointing a trustee will have regard to the question, whether his appointment will promote or impede the execution of the trust, for the very purpose of the appointment is that the trust may be better carried into execution.

Turner LJ also referred to the difficulty where a proposed appointee is not wanted by existing trustees or further where they refuse to act with the person. He considered that the court ought not necessarily to refrain from appointing the person since to do so 'would be to give the continuing or surviving trustee a veto upon the appointment of the new trustee' (at 490). Instead the court should first see whether the existing trustees' objections were well founded. In contrast, and although s 41 is silent on the point, the court will not appoint a new trustee against the wishes of the persons who have statutory power to appoint, apparently even if requested to do so by a majority of the beneficiaries (*Re Higginbottom* [1892] 3 Ch 132).

Modern instances of the use of the court's jurisdiction under s 41 have involved the appointment of persons resident abroad as trustees. We have seen previously (Chapter 7 at p 350) that in some circumstances the courts might adopt a restrictive approach to requests to authorise such appointments under s 41. Thus in *Re Whitehead's Will Trusts* [1971] 1 WLR 833 the view was expressed that it would not generally be 'right or proper' for the court to use the statutory power unless the beneficiaries have a real and substantial connection with the country where the proposed trustees are resident (cf *Re Weston's Settlements* [1969] 1 Ch 223). The approach now seems to be much more liberal although it has been said that 'the court is unlikely to assist [applicants] where the scheme is nothing more than a device to avoid tax and has no other advantages of any kind' (*Richards v The Hon AB Mackay* (1987) reported in (1997) 11(1) TLI 22 per Millett J). However, where trustees are exercising their own discretion (eg as under TA 1925, s 36(1)), and are seeking only a declaratory authorisation from the court for their own protection, the position now is that authorisation will be withheld only where the proposed transaction is 'so inappropriate that no reasonable trustee could entertain it' (followed in *Re Beatty's WT (No 2)* (1997) reported in (1997) 1(3) TLI 77). A desire to avoid tax will seemingly not make it inappropriate.

(3) The position of the beneficiaries

The judgment in *Re Higginbottom* subordinated the wishes of the majority of beneficiaries to those of the trustee. But is this still the result if all the beneficiaries are sui juris and in agreement? There is no doubt that under the rule in *Saunders v Vautier* they can terminate the trust. Can they therefore also compel trustees, acting under s 36, to appoint as trustee the beneficiaries' own nominee? The answer at common law is clear; they cannot.

Re Brockbank [1948] Ch 206 at 208–209

Vaisey J: This case involves a question which is said to be novel. It is possible, I think, that the reason for the novelty is that the courage required for the raising of it has hitherto been lacking...

It is said that where all the beneficiaries concur, they may force a trustee to retire, compel his removal and direct the trustees, having the power to nominate their successors, to appoint as such successors such persons or person or corporation as may be indicated by the beneficiaries, and it is suggested that the trustees have no option but to comply.

I do not follow this. The power of nominating a new trustee is a discretionary power, and, in my opinion is no longer exercisable and, indeed, can no longer exist if it has become one of which the exercise can be dictated by others. But then it is said that the beneficiaries could direct the trustees to transfer the trust property either to themselves absolutely, or to any person or persons or corporation, upon trusts identical with or corresponding to the trusts of the testator's will. I agree, provided that the trustees are adequately protected against any possible claim for future death duties and are fully indemnified as regards their costs, charges and expenses...

It seems to me that the beneficiaries must choose between two alternatives. Either they must keep the trusts of the will on foot, in which case those trusts must continue to be executed by trustees duly appointed pursuant either to the original instrument or

> to the powers of s 36 of the Trustee Act, 1925 and not by trustees arbitrarily selected by themselves; or they must, by mutual agreement, extinguish and put an end to the trusts with [disadvantageous fiscal] consequences . . .
>
> The claim of the beneficiaries to control the exercise of the defendant's fiduciary power of making or compelling an appointment of the trustees is, in my judgment, untenable.

It is tempting, but would be slightly misleading, to state that TOLATA 1996, s 19 in effect reverses *Re Brockbank*. It does so but only where the limitations on the scope of s 19 (see above) do not apply, namely there must be no minor beneficiaries, no express power of nomination in the trust instrument and no exclusion of s 19.

Re Brockbank has a broader significance in that it appears to support the principle that beneficiaries cannot dictate how trustees shall exercise their discretionary powers (see below, p 544). However, the following comments of Romer LJ in *Butt v Kelson* [1952] 1 All ER 167 at 172, a case where the trust fund comprised shares in a private company of which the trustees were directors by virtue of the trust's shareholding, are difficult to reconcile with this principle:

> The beneficiaries are entitled to be treated as though they were the registered shareholders in respect of trust shares with the advantages and disadvantages (eg restrictions imposed by the articles) which would be involved in that position and that they could compel the trustee directors, if necessary, to use their votes as the beneficiaries - or as the court, if the beneficiaries themselves are not in agreement - should think proper . . .

It should be noted, however, that the point of principle was not in fact argued in the case, nor was *Re Brockbank* cited to the court (cf also *Re George Whichelow Ltd* [1954] 1 WLR 5 where the approach in *Butt v Kelson* was not followed, and *Holding and Management Ltd v Property Holding and Investment Trust plc* [1989] 1 WLR 1313 where *Re Brockbank* was affirmed obiter but without discussion).

There is one further section of TOLATA 1996 that to a limited degree can impinge on the direct relationship between trustees of land and beneficiaries. Section 11 of the Act requires trustees, in exercising any function in relation to land subject to the trust, to consult the beneficiaries of full age and beneficially entitled to an interest in possession in the land. Furthermore the trustees should, so far as is consistent with the 'general interest of the trust', give effect to the wishes of the beneficiaries or, if they cannot all agree, to the wishes of the majority calculated by the value of their respective interests. The obligation to consult can be excluded by the settlor (s 11(2)) and does not apply to any property other than land. Moreover it is clear that a purchaser or mortgagee of the land is under no obligation to see that the requirements of s 11(1) have been complied with (s 16(1)).

(c) Retirement and removal of trustees

(1) Retirement

There is no statutory retirement age for trustees. Nevertheless, if beneficiaries and a trustee are locked in disagreement the wretched trustee need not remain yoked in harness until death or trust termination brings blessed relief: trustees can no more be compelled to remain in office than they can be forced to become trustees in the first place. A trustee who wishes to be discharged from all or some of the duties under a trust can be replaced by a newly appointed trustee (TA 1925, s 36(1)). In addition TA 1925, s 39 enables a trustee to retire, without being replaced, where the following requirements are satisfied:

(i)   there remain two or more individual trustees or a trust corporation, and
(ii) the remaining trustees and anyone named in the trust instrument as having power to appoint new trustees consent to the retirement, and
(iii) the retirement is effected by deed.

Independently of statute a trustee can also retire (1) under an express power although the combined effect of ss 36 and 39 has rendered such powers unnecessary, or (2) by authority of the court exercising its inherent jurisdiction.

Retirement does not, however, provide escape from liability: trustees remain liable for breaches of trust committed during their trusteeship. Furthermore, they should exercise care in the manner of their departure. Trustees who retire knowing, or perhaps even only suspecting, that their retirement will facilitate a breach of trust by their successors or the continuing trustees, run the risk of being held jointly liable where loss occurs (*Head v Gould* [1898] 2 Ch 250, where Kekewich J observed (at 273) that 'you must shew . . . clearly . . . that the breach of trust . . . was contemplated by the former trustee').

(2) Removal of trustees

We have already seen that TOLATA 1996, s 19 introduced a novel jurisdiction whereby beneficiaries can direct a trustee or trustees to retire. The procedure for implementing the retirement follows closely that set out in TA 1925, s 39 (above). However, the jurisdiction under s 19 is potentially subject to a number of limitations (see above, p 537). A last resort, therefore, for beneficiaries dissatisfied with trustees but unable to use the s 19 power is to seek their removal by the court. As we have seen, TA 1925, s 36(1) permits the forcible removal of a trustee who remains out of the United Kingdom for more than twelve months, or who refuses to act or is unfit or incapable of acting. The court also has an inherent jurisdiction to remove trustees as part of the process of administering the trust. But what circumstances will justify removal? General, if extremely vague, guidelines were set out by Lord Blackburn in *Letterstedt v Broers* (1884) 9 App Cas 371 at 387, PC:

> In exercising so delicate a jurisdiction as that of removing trustees, their Lordships do not venture to lay down any general rule beyond the very broad principle... that their main guide must be the welfare of the beneficiaries. Probably it is not possible to lay down any more definite rule in a matter so essentially dependent on details often of great nicety.

Lord Blackburn had previously quoted from a contemporary treatise (Story's *Equity Jurisprudence*) to the effect that not every breach of trust warranted removal: 'But the acts or omissions must be such as to endanger the trust property or to shew a want of honesty, or a want of proper capacity to execute the duties, or a want of reasonable fidelity' (at 385). Subsequently in *Re Wrightson* [1908] 1 Ch 789, Warrington J declined to remove trustees even though they had invested in unauthorised investments and a minority of beneficiaries wished them to be removed. He observed (at 803) that:

> ... disagreement between the cestuis que trust and the trustees, or the disinclination on the part of the cestuis que trust to have the trust property remain in the hands of a particular individual is not a sufficient ground for the removal of the trustees. You must find something which induces the court to think either that the trust property will not be safe, or that the trust will not be properly executed in the interests of the beneficiaries.

In fact the trust in question had only a little time to run and replacement of trustees would have been uneconomical.

Whilst friction between beneficiary and trustee will not therefore usually provide sufficient ground for the court's intervention, hostility between trustees is likely to be viewed more seriously. Trustees are generally required to act unanimously and if they cannot agree to do so then the welfare of the beneficiaries would seem threatened (see *Re Consiglio Trusts* [1973] 3 OR 326 where all the trustees were removed and replaced by a trust corporation).

Finally, even where trustees act unanimously and in what they and the majority of beneficiaries consider to be the latter's best interests, this will not render them immune from challenge by a dissatisfied beneficiary if the acts are unlawful (*Clarke v Heathfield (No 2)* [1985] ICR 606). This trite proposition, a minor ripple of the 1984 National Union of Mineworkers' (NUM) strike, none the less illustrates the limits to trustee and beneficiary autonomy. The NUM rules required the trustees of the union's funds to obey 'the lawful orders and directions' of the union's National Executive Committee. The trustees, acting on instructions but as it transpired unlawfully, refused to repatriate union funds which had been sent abroad to frustrate a sequestration order. The court removed the trustees on the grounds, inter alia, of thwarting the orders of the court and endangering union funds.

There are special statutory provisions relating to suspension, disqualification and removal of trustees in pension schemes and in charitable trusts. These measures are discussed at the appropriate points in Chapters 13 and 20 respectively.

3. Controlling trustees' discretion

(a) Trusts, powers and discretions

We saw in Chapter 10 in the context of the exercise of the power to delegate that under the Trustee Act 2000 trustees do not need to demonstrate that it is reasonably necessary to delegate a particular management function to agents. Rather the Law Commission was of the view that any legal control over the trustees' decisions as to *whether* to exercise their discretions should be left to the inherent jurisdiction of the courts although, as the Commission note, '[the courts] will not generally interfere with a discretionary power if the trustees are unanimous as to its exercise' (Report No 260 *Trustees' Powers and Duties* (1999) para 3.3). Hanbury and Martin succinctly summarise the position as follows: 'The basic principle governing trustees is that, while duties must be discharged, the exercise of discretions needs only to be considered' (p 529). Accurate though this statement is, we need to probe a little more extensively into the relationship between duties and discretions in this context. In this section of the chapter we therefore consider whether and to what extent the courts are willing to intervene in the decisions of trustees as to the exercise of discretions conferred on them.

First, however, an overlap both in language and practice between trusts, powers and discretions needs to be disentangled. By definition a power, whether for example a mere power of appointment or a power of advancement or maintenance, confers a discretion on trustees. But equally the carrying out of trustees' duties may require the exercise of a discretion, as where an exhaustive discretionary trust imposes a duty on trustees to distribute income but with a discretion as to the selection of the persons to benefit. As Cullity has observed ([1976] Can BR 229 at 237): 'Exactly the same relationship will often exist between administrative duties and discretionary powers as, for example, in the common case of a trustee's duty to invest proceeds of sale in investment to be selected by him at his discretion.' But as was seen in Chapter 5, the fact that the execution of both trusts and mere powers may involve an element of discretion does not mean that both are subject to precisely the same degree of judicial control.

The continuing basic difference remains that where trustees have a duty imposed on them then they must exercise any discretion attached to it. Consequently if the discretion is not exercised, the court, if called upon, will enforce it (*Re Locker's Settlement Trusts* [1977] 1 WLR 1323 and (1978) 42 Conv 166). In contrast, trustees need only consider periodically whether or not to exercise a mere power, with the consequence that where, for example, the power relates to the distribution of income it will lapse after a reasonable period (see *Re Allen-Meyrick's Will Trusts* [1966] 1 WLR 499) and the income will devolve on those entitled in default of appointment. Furthermore, as we also saw in Chapter 5, a continuing distinction, albeit one of uncertain application, between discretionary trusts and mere powers of appointment is that in exercising the discretion 'a wider and more comprehensive range of inquiry is called for' in the former (*McPhail v Doulton* [1971] AC 424 at 457).

One further distinction to be mentioned is between those circumstances where the power is held in a personal capacity and where it is held in a fiduciary capacity. Where the power is held in a personal capacity, the donee need not consider whether to exercise the power at all and may even 'release' it. A decision by the donee of the power to release it may be taken for one of any number of reasons ranging from the familial to the fiscal. In *Re Mills* [1930] 1 Ch 654, for instance, the donee released the power of appointment so as to create an indefeasible interest in those entitled in default of appointment. Where, however, the power is held by the donee in a fiduciary capacity the donee cannot release the power unless authorised to do so in the trust instrument (see *Re Wills Trusts Deeds* [1964] Ch 219). Determining the capacity in which the power is held by a donee therefore has important implications. Thus in *Mettoy Pension Trustees Ltd v Evans* [1991] 2 All ER 513 a power held by a company not as trustee but as employer was nevertheless construed as being held in a fiduciary capacity, thereby enabling the court to intervene on behalf of the members of the pension scheme ('the beneficiaries'; see further Chapter 13 at p 698).

Moving beyond these distinctions it is the scope for challenging the exercise of a discretion whether under a trust or a power that concerns us here, although, as will be seen, the borderline between non-exercise of a discretion and its improper exercise may at times be difficult to discern.

There is one further consideration to mention. Trustees might exercise their discretion bona fide but either mistakenly or without appreciating the full implications of their decisions. The latter may be of particular concern where the tax position of the beneficiaries or the settlor is adversely affected. Of course the immediate response is to suggest that in such circumstances an action for negligent breach of trust may lie against the erring trustees. An alternative response, owing much to the ingenuity of practitioners, has been to plead the operation of a principle purported to have been established in the case of *Re Hastings-Bass* [1975] Ch 25. In effect the court is being asked in these circumstances, often at the behest of all the directly affected parties, to undo the error by declaring the decision void or voidable. Whether the court should be prepared to assist the trustees in such circumstances and by what means is a matter of some contention. The current position and the accompanying points of controversy are considered in section c below. First, however, we consider the extent to which beneficiaries can challenge the exercise of discretion by trustees other than under the still uncertain extent of the principle in *Hastings-Bass*.

(b) Exercising the discretion

Before considering whether a court can or should interfere in the exercise of a discretion, the perhaps trite point must be restated, subject to any uncertainty prompted by *Butt v Kelsen* (see p 538), that it is the trustees' discretion, not that of the settlor or beneficiary, that must be exercised. The point is illustrated in *Turner v Turner* [1983] 2 All ER 745, which also provides a good example of an attempt by a settlor to divest himself of property ownership for tax-planning purposes while retaining de facto control. There, a power of appointment was conferred on three trustees – the settlor's elderly father, sister-in-law and her husband – none of whom had, in the words of Mervyn Davies J, 'any experience or understanding of trust matters' (at 747). The settlor said in his evidence that he considered himself to be the 'captain of the ship' (at 750) and the trustees, not appreciating that even during the settlor's lifetime they still had a discretion to exercise, willingly signed deeds of appointment when requested to do so by the settlor. Not surprisingly when the trustees sought the court's directions the appointments were held invalid and set aside.

It is necessary to enter a note of caution here lest it be assumed too readily that the exercise of a discretion by trustees is for them and them alone. It is possible, indeed by no means uncommon in offshore trusts, for 'a protector' to be appointed in the trust deed. The protector can be given a variety of functions, one of which might be that the exercise of any powers of appointment held by trustees will be subject to the consent of the protector. In effect the protector has the power of veto over the decisions of the trustees. This development then potentially raises questions about the status of protectors – are they necessarily fiduciaries? – and the degree of accountability and control, if any, to which they are subject (see eg Waters in Oakley (ed) *Trends in Contemporary Trust Law* (1996) ch 4; Duckworth 'Protectors – Fish or Fowl?' (1996) PCB 169; Waters (2000) 8(4) ITCP 237). It is doubtful that a generic answer can be given to such questions. Much will depend as ever on the interpretation of the powers conferred on the protector by the trust instrument and on the law of the jurisdiction within which the administration of the trust is located.

But where trustees exercise their own discretion can the court interfere? The high-water mark of judicial non-interventionism is to be found in the nineteenth-century case of *Gisborne v Gisborne* (1877) 2 App Cas 300, HL, where a testator had conferred on trustees 'uncontrollable authority' over subsequent disposition of income. The consequence in Lord Cairns's view was that, 'Their discretion and authority always supposing that there is no mala fides with regard to its exercise, is to be without any check or control from any superior tribunal' (at 305).

The subsequent application of this approach to an administrative discretion was demonstrated in *Tempest v Lord Camoys* (below), although the language of the judgment indicates a potentially greater scope for judicial intervention than that in *Gisborne v Gisborne*. Trustees were given an absolute discretion to sell and buy land, and also to raise money by mortgage for the purchase of land. One trustee wished to exercise the discretion to purchase property but the co-trustee would not agree and the court refused to order him to do so.

Tempest v Lord Camoys (1882) 21 Ch D 571 at 578, CA

Jessell MR: It is very important that the law of the Court on this subject should be understood. It is settled law that when a testator has given a pure discretion to trustees as to the exercise of a power, the Court does not enforce the exercise of the power against the wish of the trustees, but it does prevent them from exercising it improperly. The Court says that the power, if exercised at all, is to be properly exercised . . .

But in all cases where there is a trust or duty coupled with the power the Court will then compel the trustees to carry it out in a proper manner and within a reasonable time. In the present case there was a power which amounts to a trust to invest the fund in question in the purchase of land. The trustees would not be allowed by the Court to disregard that trust, and if Mr Fleming had refused to invest the money in land at all the Court would have found no difficulty in interfering. But that is a very different thing from saying that the Court ought to take from the trustees their uncontrolled discretion as to the particular time for the investment and the particular property which should be purchased. In this particular case it appears to me that the testator in his will has carefully distinguished between what is to be at the discretion of his trustees and what is obligatory on them.

Brett and Cotton LJJ delivered concurring judgments, the latter however rather elliptically observing (at 580):

No doubt [the Court] will prevent trustees from exercising their discretion in any way which is wrong or unreasonable. But that is very different from putting a control upon the exercise of the discretion which the testator has left to them.

A similar approach was manifested towards a duty of selection in the earlier case of *Re Beloved Wilkes' Charity* (1851) 3 Mac & G 440. Trustees had a duty to select a boy from only certain named parishes to be educated to be a minister of the Church of England, provided that a suitable candidate could be found there. In fact the trustees selected a boy (C) from another parish apparently after C's brother, himself a minister, had approached one of the trustees on C's behalf. The trustees refused to give any reasons for their choice but stated that they had considered the candidates impartially. The Lord Chancellor refused a request to set aside the selection and appoint instead a boy from one of the named parishes. He summarised the court's jurisdiction as follows (at 448):

The duty of supervision on the part of this Court will thus be confined to the question of the honesty, integrity, and fairness with which the deliberation has been conducted, and will not be extended to the accuracy of the conclusion arrived at, except in particular cases. If, however, . . . trustees think fit to state a reason, and the reason is one which does not justify their conclusion, then the Court may say that they have acted by mistake and in error, and that it will correct their decision; but if, without entering into details, they simply state, as in many cases it would be most prudent and judicious for them to do, that they have met and considered and come to a conclusion, the Court has then no means of saying that they have failed in their duty, or to consider the accuracy of their conclusion.

Although the courts resolutely refused to intervene in the above cases, the outlines of a residual judicial discretion can be identified. What, for example, will constitute an 'improper' exercise of a power and when will trustees' deliberations be deemed 'unfairly' conducted? In *Klug v Klug* [1918] 2 Ch 67, a refusal by one trustee, the beneficiary's mother, to approve the exercise of a power of advancement (trustee unanimity being required for the valid exercise of a power) was overruled because, in Neville J's words, 'she has not exercised her discretion at all' (at 71). In fact the mother's refusal to approve the capital advance had apparently been motivated by displeasure at her daughter's marrying without her consent. It is not a large step to recharacterise the court's intervention here as being on the grounds that the trustee was exercising a discretion (ie deciding not to advance capital) but doing so by taking irrelevant considerations into account. In similar vein one can point to the principle in *Re Hastings-Bass* [1975] Ch 25 concerning the effect of a mistaken exercise of discretion and which is discussed in section c below. Another circumstance analogous to the improper motive or irrelevant consideration of *Klug v Klug* is where trustees exercise a discretion for an improper purpose, as in *Re Pauling's Settlement Trusts* [1964] Ch 303, CA, a case also involving the power of advancement (see also *Re Smith* [1971] 1 OR 584). There, on several occasions trustees advanced capital nominally to children, all of whom were over 21 and at their own request, but in full knowledge that the money would be used directly to benefit the parents – the improper purpose – not the children, as by buying a house for the father in the Isle of Man and reducing the mother's bank overdraft.

The concept of improper purposes must logically also apply to trustees' pure dispositive discretions if only because of the restraint imposed by the doctrine of 'fraud on a power'. This doctrine, which we briefly outline here for the purposes of clarification and comparison only, applies to mere powers of appointment whether or not held by trustees (see generally Thomas *Powers* (1998) paras 9.21–9.48; Matthews [2007] PCB 131 and 191). The word 'fraud' needs to be treated with caution here: 'The equitable doctrine of "fraud on a power" has little, if anything, to do with fraud' (*Medforth v Blake* [2000] Ch 86 at 103 per Sir Richard Scott VC). It means no more than an improper use of the power. The exercise of a power will always be invalid if it exceeds the limits imposed by the donor (eg by appointing to D when A, B and C are the only objects). But the 'fraud' referred to also includes circumstances where the appointment is prima facie sound but is made for an improper motive. In the words of one of the many strict formulations of the doctrine: 'a party must fairly and honestly execute [the power] without having any ulterior object to be accomplished. He cannot carry into execution any indirect object or acquire any benefit for himself, directly or indirectly' (Lord St Leonard in *Duke of Portland v Lady Topham* (1864) 11 HL Cas 32 at 55).

A distinction is drawn, however, between purpose and effect. The mere fact that someone other than an object of a power benefits indirectly from its exercise does not invalidate the appointment; there must also be an *intent* to benefit that person. In the modern context litigation has usually occurred where, as part of an attempted arrangement to vary trusts for fiscal reasons, a life-tenant holder of a power of appointment wishes to appoint to certain beneficiaries so that the property can subsequently be divided amongst both parties. A strict application of the doctrine intended to protect the objects would be likely to invalidate the appointment, perhaps to the financial detriment of some of the objects of the power. But whether the ulterior purpose is present is a question of fact or inference and examples both of strict and benevolent interpretation can be found in modern cases. (See *Re Brook's Settlement* [1968] 1 WLR 1661; cf *Re Wallace's Settlements* [1968] 1 WLR 711; see also Cretney (1969) 32 MLR 317; Grbich (1977) 3 Monash U LR 210; and for a somewhat surprising valid use of a power in the context of a divorce settlement *Netherton v Netherton* [2000] WTLR 1171, but cf *Wong v Burt* [2004] NZCA 174 and the costly outcome of an attempt to circumvent the unanticipated consequences of a beneficiary's premature demise.)

To summarise: a failure by trustees to consider whether to exercise a discretion will be a breach of trust, and we have identified in addition several overlapping reasons which can enable a court to intervene to control trustees' positive exercise of their discretions. Even where a discretion is couched in the widest terms, as in *Gisborne v Gisborne*, its exercise can be attacked on grounds of mala fides. And, in so far as not included within the 'notoriously elastic' meaning of that term (see Cullity (1975) 25 U Toronto LJ 99 at 103), exercise for an improper purpose or based on improper or irrelevant considerations will be equally invalid. But although these limitations modify trustee autonomy they do not obviously ascribe to the court any jurisdiction to intervene merely because the court considers the trustees' particular decision injudicious. Can then the courts intervene, whether or not a discretion is described as 'uncontrollable', where they consider trustees to have acted honestly but unreasonably?

We already know that 'capricious' exercise of a dispositive discretion would be improper (see *McPhail v Doulton* [1971] AC 424 at 456, and *Re Manisty's Settlement* [1974] Ch 17 where it was described as meaning 'irrational, perverse or irrelevant to any sensible expectation of the settlor' (at 26)). Turning to administrative discretions such as those concerned with powers of investment, the reservations expressed by Cotton LJ in *Tempest v Lord Camoys* (above) have subsequently been interpreted by Slade LJ as meaning: 'even a power expressed in terms that it should be exercisable at the trustee's absolute discretion, was subject to the implicit restriction that it should be exercised properly within the limits of the general law' (*Bishop v Bonham* [1988] 1 WLR 742 at 753). The implication is that widely drawn clauses conferring absolute discretion on trustees will not *in themselves* be effective to exclude, for instance, the fundamental duties of prudence and impartiality (see *Boe v Alexander* (1988) 41 DLR (4th) 520 at 527; but see below, p 593 on clauses purporting to limit or exclude liability).

More tenuously a majority of the House of Lords in a Scottish appeal, although reserving their opinion on the appropriateness of the test, did consider whether trustees had 'acted in a manner that no reasonable trustee acting within the bounds of the duty laid on him by the testator could possibly act' (*Dundee General Hospitals Board of Management v Walker* [1952] 1 All ER 896). A more cautious exposition of the circumstances where a court might intervene to control the exercise of a discretion was given in that case by Lord Reid (at 905):

> If it can be shown that the trustees considered the wrong question, or that, although they purported to consider the right question they did not really apply their minds to it or perversely shut their eyes to the facts or that they did not act honestly or in good faith, then there was no true decision and the court will intervene.

We use the word 'tenuous' about the implications of the judgment because (i) counsel for the respondents conceded that 'reasonableness' was the appropriate test, and (ii) the propositions in the case would not necessarily apply to the English law of trusts. Nevertheless in *Scott v National Trust* [1998] 2 All ER 705 at 717 Robert Walker J specifically adopted Lord Reid's words as representing a clear statement of the principle to be applied even where trustees are expressed as having an absolute discretion, although in that case in the context of charity law (see also Chapter 20). The Court of Appeal affirmed that this approach was equally applicable to the exercise of a discretion by pension fund trustees (*Edge v Pensions Ombudsman* [2000] Ch 602 at 627). However clear the language used by Lord Reid may be, we are now moving even further into realms of uncertainty with terminology and concepts redolent of judicial review in administrative law. As with that area of the law, the key question is not 'Can the court intervene?' but 'In what circumstances will the court consider it appropriate to do so?' To that question must be added in the present context the further one 'What form would that intervention take?'

(c) The rule or principle in *Re Hastings-Bass (dec'd)*

Questions such as those just posed have come to the fore as a consequence of the recent rise to prominence of what is now more commonly referred to as the principle in *Re Hastings-Bass (dec'd)* [1975] Ch 25 – the less grand descriptor of 'rule' being increasingly displaced in the literature. At issue in the case was the validity of the exercise in 1958 of a power of advancement to set up a sub-trust comprising a life interest and remainders over, all with the overall intention of reducing estate duty liability. It became apparent following the decision of the House of Lords in *Pilkington v IRC* [1964] AC 12 (see Chapter 7) that the remainders over were void for infringing the rule against perpetuities, but was the life-interest valid? If so, the saving of estate duty sought would be achieved. Intriguingly, in view of the subsequent use to which the rule has been put, it was counsel for the Inland Revenue in *Re Hastings-Bass* who advanced the proposition that the exercise of the power of advancement by the trustees should be void because of their mistaken view as to the effect of the rule against perpetuities. It was in response to this proposition that Buckley LJ set out, in a negative formulation, what has become known as the principle in *Re Hastings-Bass* (at 41):

> Where by the terms of a trust...a trustee is given a discretion as to some matter under which he acts in good faith, the court should not interfere with his action notwithstanding that it does not have the full effect that he intended, unless...it is clear that he would not have acted as he did (a) had he not taken into account considerations which he should not have taken into account, or (b) had he not failed to take into account considerations which he ought to have taken into account.

As will be seen shortly, various formulations of the principle have subsequently been advanced, although in all of them the terminology is analogous to the previously mentioned dicta of Lord Reid in *Dundee General Hospitals Board of Management v Walker* [1952] 1 All ER 896 which is itself analogous to the language of 'Wednesbury unreasonableness' or 'irrationality' by which administrative decisions of public bodies may be challenged. Notwithstanding these conceptual and linguistic similarities the circumstances in which reliance is now sought to be placed on the principle tend to be somewhat different from those where beneficiaries are seeking to challenge the exercise of a discretion or power by trustees with which they disagree. On the contrary in recent cases it is commonly trustees, beneficiaries and, indeed, settlors who wish to seek the court's approval to undo a decision made in good faith by trustees yet misunderstanding the *consequences* of their decision.

The door left ajar by the Court of Appeal in *Re Hastings-Bass* was initially pushed further open in the context of pensions litigation (*Mettoy Pension Trustees Ltd v Evans* [1990] 1 WLR 1587; *Stannard v Fisons Pension Trust Ltd* [1991] PLR 225; *AMP (UK) plc v Barker* [2000] 3 ITELR 414). Here, for reasons explored in greater detail in Chapter 13 but reflecting a perception of the special nature of the right of pension scheme members to hold trustees to account, the courts demonstrated a willingness to review trustees' decisions arguably more extensively than had been thought to be the case in a family trust context. Thus Lawrence Collins J in *AMP (UK) plc v Barker*, following the earlier Court of Appeal decision in the Court of Appeal in *Stannard v Fisons Pension Trust*, confirmed that the test to be applied in determining when the court could interfere was whether the trustees *might* not have acted as they did rather than they *would* not have acted as they did (at [90]).

It is, however, predominantly in a few key cases where tax consequences have been either misunderstood or not foreseen that practitioners have sought to take advantage of the opportunity offered by the principle and in so doing extend its scope (see *Green v Cobham* [2000] WTLR 1101; *Abacus Trust Company (Isle of Man) v NSPCC* [2001] WTLR 953; *Breadner v Granville-Grossman* [2001] Ch 523; *Abacus Trust Company (Isle of Man) v Barr* [2003] Ch 409; *Burrell v Burrell* [2005] STC 569; *Sieff v Fox* [2005] 3 All ER 693). Decisions in these cases at first instance have not been consistent. Indeed Sir Robert Walker, as he then was, suggested in a lecture in 2002 that the law 'is in considerable doubt and disarray' ((2002) 13 KCLJ 173 at 183). It is a sentiment with which even several years later it is difficult to disagree.

To gain a full appreciation of recent developments and of the inconsistent reception given to the principle in *Re Hastings-Bass* would require a detailed examination of the key cases. Here we can do no more than outline the cause of the disarray and the contentious issues raised by current use of the principle (for more detailed analysis see Walker (2002) 13 KCLJ 173–185; Hilliard (2002) 16(4) TLI 202–213 and [2004] Conv 208–223; Nugee (2003) PCB 3 at 178–187; Hayton (2008) 22(2) TLI 81 at 86–90). There are three principal issues to consider. These are (i) the nature and seriousness of the mistake that brings the principle into consideration, (ii) whether, where the principle applies, the decision of the trustees is void or voidable and (iii) whether the principle should be applied and interpreted differently depending on whether the context is one involving family trusts or pensions trusts.

The first issue concerns the nature and seriousness of the error required to prompt the court's intervention. In two cases, *Green v Cobham* and *Abacus Trust Company (Isle of Man) v NSPCC*, the exercise of the powers had the direct legal *effect* intended – respectively the appointment of new trustees and the appointment of an interest to a charity – but also brought about the unforeseen and unwanted *consequence* of a capital gains tax liability. In *Abacus* the power of appointment had been exercised too early thereby wrecking the tax avoidance arrangement whilst in *Green v Cobham* the number of non-resident trustees was reduced with potential capital gains tax consequences described by counsel as 'catastrophic'. In both cases the principle was applied – there is little doubt that in those cases had the trustees realised the *consequences* of their decisions they 'would' have acted differently. On the other hand, in *Breadner v Granville-Grossman* [2001] Ch 523 Park J declined to adopt a 'natural and logical development' of the principle so as to enable the court to make *positive* decisions in the sense of holding 'that a trust takes effect as if the trustees had done something which they never did at all' (at 543). But the judge also commented more generally about the development of the principle. Whilst not directly criticising the decision in *Green v Cobham*, Park J stated that 'there must be limits to how far the courts will allow the principle in *In Re Hastings-Bass* to rescue trustees from the consequences of their tax-planning misjudgements' (at 553).

One possible limitation emerged in *Abacus Trust Company (Isle of Man) v Barr* [2003] Ch 409 where Lightman J held that the principle applied only where the exercise of the discretion involved a breach of the trustees' fiduciary duty to consider properly how to exercise their discretion. The potential restriction on the scope of the principle was clear: 'In the absence of any such breach of duty the [principle] does not afford the right to the trustee or any beneficiary to have a decision declared invalid because the trustee's decision was in some way mistaken or has unforeseen and unpalatable consequences' (at [24]). It was against this background of inconsistent decisions and academic and judicial disquiet at the ease with which the principle may enable courts to set aside what at first glance appear to be valid exercises of trustees' discretions that Lloyd LJ, sitting as a judge in the Chancery Division, conducted a thorough review of the competing authorities in *Sieff v Fox* [2005] 3 All ER 693 ((2006) 122 LQR 35; (2006) 65(1) CLJ 15; [2006] Conv 91). In the case itself trustees to the Duke of Bedford, acting on what turned out to be incorrect legal advice, had exercised a discretionary power of appointment to transfer property from one settlement to a second settlement so as to prevent a significant charge to inheritance tax arising. Unfortunately the trustees and their advisers failed to appreciate that the appointment would bring about a charge to capital gains tax estimated at £1m whereas an alternative formulation would have avoided the charge. The judge unsurprisingly concluded that if the correct advice as to the tax liability had been given to the trustees the appointment *would not* have been made and he therefore approved their request to have the appointment set aside. Lloyd LJ acknowledged that this 'problematic and developing area of law' had been the subject of a great deal of debate both inside and outside the court but accepted that he could not 'resolve the outstanding issues as a matter of decision; that is a task which remains to the Court of Appeal . . .'. Nevertheless, drawing on his review of the authorities Lloyd LJ produced the following reformulation of the principle (at para 119, emphasis added):

> Where trustees act under a discretion given to them by the terms of the trust, in circumstances in which they are *free to decide* whether or not to exercise that discretion, but the effect of the exercise is different from that which they intended, the court will interfere with their action if it is clear that they *would not* have acted as they did had they not failed to take into account considerations which they ought to have taken into account, or taken into account considerations which they ought not to have taken into account.

Drawing on this version of the principle and its application by Lloyd LJ in *Sieff* the following tentative comments on the prerequisite for the principle to apply can be offered. It would seem to follow that the 'effect of the exercise' encompasses not just the direct effect – eg whether the immediate legal effect was that intended, as will often be the case – but also the consequences that flow from it, most often unanticipated and expensive fiscal consequences. Moreover Lloyd LJ, differing from Lightman J, doubted that the principle should apply only in cases where some breach of duty had occurred. On the other hand, Lloyd LJ seemingly imposed a more stringent requirement by emphasising that in circumstances where the trustees are 'free to decide' whether or not to exercise their discretion then an application invoking the principle should succeed only where it can be shown that the trustees 'would', not 'might', have acted differently. This enabled Lloyd LJ rather deftly to distinguish those pensions cases involving the principle, a point we return to shortly.

On the second of our contentious issues – does the application of the principle in *Hastings-Bass* render the decision void or voidable? – Lloyd LJ was again faced in *Sieff* with a divergence of view in the cases. In *AMP (UK) plc v Barker* and in *Abacus Trust Company (Isle of Man) v NSPCC* the view was taken that the application of the principle renders the exercise of the discretion by trustees void. If this is the position then formidable difficulties may be posed where a lengthy period has elapsed between the exercise of the discretion and the application to the court – 22 years in *Breadner v Granville-Grossman* where, however, Park J declined to apply the principle, commenting that 'it would be . . . unacceptable . . . to upset some action by trustees . . . on the basis of which many intervening decisions and actions have been taken (at 553). On the other hand, Lightman J in *Abacus Trust Company (Isle of Man) v Barr* reached the opposite conclusion, holding that the appointment made some ten years before the application to court was voidable. Faced with these alternatives Lloyd LJ stated that he found the voidable option 'attractive' partly because it would give the court discretion to take account of the sort of considerations referred to by Park J. Yet it must be recognised that, however desirable, the consequence of applying the principle in *Re Hastings-Bass* in this way differs from other situations where a power or discretion is exercised improperly such as under the doctrine of fraud on a power. There the exercise of the power is declared void. It is therefore understandable, in light of the conflicting authorities and in a case where nothing turned on the distinction, that Lloyd LJ felt it was inappropriate and unnecessary to express any conclusive view on the issue. If it is to be the case that the exercise of a discretion, rather than being void, is to be voidable under the principle in *Re Hastings-Bass* then it has to be recognised that there is as yet very little guidance from the cases as to what criteria the court should apply in deciding what order, if any, to make so as to rectify the decision of the trustees.

The third contentious aspect of the principle takes us back to what can be interpreted as a twin-track process of development by way of, on the one hand, pensions cases and, on the other hand, private family trust litigation. The dilemma is whether interpretation and/or application of the principle in *Re Hastings-Bass* should vary depending on the context and if so in what direction. We have already referred to Lloyd LJ's deft distinguishing of pensions cases such as *Kerr v British Leyland (Staff) Trustees Ltd* [2001] WTLR 1071 and *Stannard v Fisons Pension Trust Ltd* [1991] PLR 225 involving the principle in *Hastings-Bass*. He agreed that the distinguishing features of those cases were (i) that 'the rights of the members or beneficiaries arose in the context of the contract of employment' and not from the bounty of a settlor and (ii) that consequently 'the trustees were under a duty to act . . . not merely a duty to consider from time to time whether to act' as was commonly the case in family trust cases (para 56). In the pensions cases, often involving scheme members' demands for review of the exercise of a discretion by trustees, Lloyd LJ agreed that the relatively low threshold of relevance ('might' rather than 'would') was appropriate to determine whether members should, in effect, have their cases reconsidered. It remains to be determined, notwithstanding *Sieff v Fox*, whether the lower threshold will also come to be adopted in the family trust context. To do so would broaden the jurisdiction of the court to 'interfere' with the trustees' decisions, although in the tax context in family trusts 'facilitate a variation of a decision' might often be a more appropriate phrase. The underlying legal and policy question remains one of whether some limit should be placed on the use of the principle to, in Park J's words, 'rescue trustees from the consequences of their tax-planning misjudgements'. (See Walker (2002) 13 KCLJ 173–185; Wu (2007) 21(2) TLI 62–79; and compare the contrasting views of Nugee (2003) PCB 3 at 178–187 and Hilliard (2002) 16(4) TLI 202–213; and [2004] Conv 208–223.) In similar vein Lloyd LJ in *Sieff* commented that 'the application of the principle is of potentially worrying breadth if it cannot be confined or controlled' (at para 81).

It only remains to mention the 'hound that did not bark', the hound in this case being Her Majesty's Revenue and Customs (HMRC), who on several occasions declined to be joined in proceedings despite, one might have thought, having a strong interest in the outcome. It now appears that this stance is to change because of 'our increasing concern that the principle as currently formulated is too wide in its scope' (Hutton (2006) PCB 5, 293 at 295). HMRC will now give 'active consideration' to intervening where large amounts of tax are at stake and 'will be particularly ready to intervene in cases where there would otherwise be no party in whose interest it would be to argue against the application of the principle' (ibid). It should be noted that HMRC 'tentatively suggest' that the principle in *Hastings-Bass* should be assimilated with the general principles of law by which the exercise of discretion by trustees may be impugned (see above, p 544) or, where appropriate, with the criteria whereby the court can set aside written instruments for mistake. In short there may be no need for a separate *Hastings-Bass* principle at all!

By way of summary here one can therefore only reiterate that, pending further consideration at appellate level, the law remains, in Lord Walker's words, 'in considerable doubt and disarray'.

(d) Beneficiaries' access to information

(1) Introduction

There is a fundamental conceptual and practical obstacle confronting an aggrieved beneficiary who wishes to challenge the decisions of trustees. A beneficiary is unlikely to be fully informed of the reasons for trustees' decisions or of the process of decision-making. Moreover where, for instance, the trustees' decision involves the exercise of a discretion they seemingly cannot be compelled to give the reasons for their decision, although if they volunteer the reasons the court can examine their adequacy (see *Re Londonderry's Settlement* [1965] Ch 918; *Wilson v The Law Debenture Trust Corpn plc* [1995] 2 All ER 337; *Karger v Paul* [1984] VR 161; and dicta in *Hartigan Nominees Pty Ltd v Rydge* (1992) 29 NSWLR 405 and (1993) 67 ALJ 703). Given this apparent constraint, what information are beneficiaries entitled to if they suspect that trustees have been negligent or indulged in fraud or other improper conduct?

We have seen previously that a fundamental obligation of trusteeship is the duty of the trustees to account to the beneficiaries for their (the trustees') stewardship of the trust. The recent Privy Council decision in *Schmidt v Rosewood* [2003] 2 WLR 1442 has thrown fresh light on two issues central to the accountability of trustees and the right of beneficiaries to seek access to information about the stewardship of the trust. One issue concerns the scope of the obligation – 'To whom is it owed by the trustees?' – whilst the other is about the nature of the right to information – 'Is it a proprietary right of beneficiaries or merely an aspect of the court's inherent jurisdiction to supervise the administration of trusts?' Both of these matters are considered below as are the criteria that the court may apply in determining what information should be disclosed.

It is convenient first, however, to outline briefly a basic building block of the obligation of trustees to account for their stewardship of the trust, the duty of trustees to keep accounts and records.

(2) Duty to keep accounts and records

Trustees are under a duty to keep accurate accounts of trust property and on request to allow a beneficiary or her solicitor to inspect the accounts and supporting documents. This obligation includes providing details of investments and allowing access to title deeds, share certificates or other documents concerning trust property. A beneficiary is not, however, entitled to free copies of documents, although it is accepted practice, certainly for professional trustees, to provide a copy of the accounts without charge (see Sladen *Practical Trust Administration* (3rd edn, 1993) p 240). Whilst there is no duty to have accounts audited, trustees have a statutory power to have an audit conducted by an independent accountant provided it is not more than once in every three years, unless the nature of the trust or any special dealings with trust property make a more frequent audit reasonable (TA 1925, s 22(4)). Rights such as these would be rendered meaningless if the identity and location of the trustees could be concealed and the court therefore has a discretion to authorise disclosure of this information to beneficiaries (*Murphy v Murphy* [1999] 1 WLR 282).

Furthermore, under a rarely used jurisdiction a beneficiary can insist on accounts being investigated or audited by any solicitor or accountant acceptable to the trustees, or, if agreement cannot be reached, by the Public Trustee, but not within twelve months of a previous investigation unless the court approves (Public Trustee Act 1906, s 13(1), (5)).

So that trustees can comply with the duty to provide information to beneficiaries about matters affecting the trust and trust property, it is advisable, indeed usual, for them to keep a trust diary or minute book. Decisions taken in administration of the trust and possibly minutes of trustees' meetings are recorded although, as we see in the next section, trustees may wisely choose to be selective in the information minuted.

(3) The right to seek disclosure
To whom is the obligation owed? *McPhail v Doulton* revisited

Schmidt v Rosewood [2003] 2 WLR 1442 brought to the forefront of debate questions about control of trustees that, since the path-breaking majority decision of the House of Lords in *McPhail v Doulton* [1971] AC 424, had lain largely dormant, at least as far as family trusts were concerned (cf in the context of the rights of members of pension schemes *Mettoy Pension Trustees v Evans* [1990] 1 WLR 1587). It may be recalled that the majority of their Lordships in *McPhail v Doulton* rejected the constraints imposed by a narrow perception, derived from *Morice v Bishop of Durham* (1805) 10 Ves 522, of the court's ability to control and execute a trust. Subsequently, partly for tax reasons and partly because of residual uncertainty as to the validity in discretionary trusts of expressions such as 'relatives' and 'dependants', settlors conferred on trustees ever wider dispositive discretions based commonly on a combination of discretionary trusts (or trust powers) and mere powers of appointment, often in the form of an intermediate (or hybrid) power. It must be borne in mind that one object of this exercise was to make the ultimate beneficial ownership in a trust as diffuse and difficult to ascertain as possible. This expanding scope of dispositive discretions granted to trustees does not mean that they are left bereft of any indication as to who amongst the widely drawn class of potential beneficiaries is to benefit from the settlor's bounty. It is increasingly common for settlors to provide trustees with confidential 'letters of wishes' which are non-binding but are designed to indicate what matters the trustees should take into account in exercising their discretions. They provide a medium 'for the written expression of facts, beliefs, expectations, concerns and (occasionally) prejudices about the beneficiaries which it would or might be hurtful, impolitic or simply undesirable for [the settlor] to include in a document which the beneficiaries had a right to inspect' (per Briggs J in *Breakspear v Ackland* [2008] WLR 698 at para 6). The nub of the 'largely dormant' issue therefore is what rights of information from and enforcement against trustees, if any, are available not just to beneficiaries but as importantly to the objects of a mere power.

The two 'similar but not identical' trust instruments at issue in *Schmidt v Rosewood* reflected the influences and traits referred to above, with the added dimension of the trusts being administered from the Isle of Man and their provenance being not altogether clear. The trust instruments contained a number of errors and omissions, to the extent that the Privy Council accepted counsel's submission that the settlement had been 'cobbled together' (at [18]). The appellant, who was seeking access to trust accounts and other information from the trustees, was Vadim Schmidt the son of Vitali Schmidt who appeared to be, at least in substance (the matter was in some doubt), a co-settlor of the two trusts, the Angora Trust and the Everest Trust set up in 1992 and 1995 respectively. Vitali, who died unexpectedly and intestate in 1997, was at the time a senior executive director of Lukoil, the largest oil company in Russia. Vitali was also the initial named 'protector' in the 1992 trust. The trustee at the time of the litigation was Rosewood Trust Ltd, an Isle of Man-registered corporate trustee. The named default beneficiaries in both trusts were a charity, the Royal National Lifeboat Institution, and, inter alia, Vitali Schmidt and other senior executives of Lukoil. In both trusts there was an overriding power of appointment, exercisable with the written consent of the protector. In addition the 1995 trust contained an intermediate power to add to the class of beneficiaries anyone in the world apart from a very small class of excluded persons, a clause similar to that upheld in *Re Manisty's Settlement* [1974] Ch 17.

In respect of both trusts the father had written letters to the trustees indicating that in the event of his death prior to the termination of the trust his 'share' or 'portion' was to be held on trust for his son Vadim. The trustees maintained that the letters were no more than the expression of wishes and therefore devoid of legal effect. Consequently, on this view, no actual interest in either trust ever vested in Vadim. Indeed under the 1995 trust Vadim was no more than the object of the intermediate power of appointment and, the trustees argued, as such had no rights to the disclosure of the trust information that he was seeking. The Court of Appeal in the Isle of Man supported this view and firmly rejected the proposition advanced by the appellant Vadim that there was no distinction to be drawn in this area between the rights of 'beneficiaries' and those of the objects of a power (*Rosewood Trust v Schmidt* [2001] WTLR 1081). Reversing that decision, the Privy Council accepted the proposition advanced on behalf of the appellant, at least for the purposes of disclosure of information. Lord Walker, giving the judgment of the Privy Council, referred extensively to the reasoning of Lord Wilberforce in *McPhail v Doulton* and also to the fiscal and conceptual influences on the widespread adoption of intermediate powers, and stated (at [66]; and see the perceptive case comment of Davies (2004) 120 LQR 1–7):

> There is therefore in their Lordships' view no reason to draw any bright dividing-line either between transmissible and non-transmissible (that is, discretionary) interests, or between the rights of an object [sic] of a discretionary trust and those of the object of a mere power (of a fiduciary character). The differences in this context between trusts and powers are (as Lord Wilberforce demonstrated in *McPhail v Doulton*) a good deal less significant than are the similarities.

Disclosure of information: 'proprietary right' or 'inherent jurisdiction'?

The appearance of the word 'therefore' in the above extract is significant. In reaching their conclusion the Privy Council had to address the central proposition in the argument of counsel for the trustees to the effect that 'no object of a mere power could have any right or claim to disclosure, because he had no proprietary interest in the trust property' (at [43]). Arguably that proposition reflected the long-established leading authority in the English case law *O'Rourke v Darbishire* [1920] AC 581 where Lord Wrenbury stated (at 626):

> If the plaintiff is right in saying that he is a beneficiary, and if the documents are documents belonging to the executors as executors, he has a right to access to the documents which he desires to inspect upon what has been called in the judgments in this case a proprietary right. The beneficiary is entitled to see all the trust documents because they are trust documents and because he is a beneficiary. They are in a sense his own.

The Committee of the Privy Council preferred to adopt the approach emerging from more recent Commonwealth case law that saw the matter as part of the court's inherent jurisdiction to supervise trusts (see *Hartigan Nominees Pty Ltd v Rydge* (1992) 29 NSWLR 405; *Attorney-General of Ontario v Stavro* (1994) 119 DLR (4th) 750; and also Hayton in Oakley (ed) *Trends in Contemporary Trust Law* (1996) p 52). Lord Walker summarised the opinion of the Committee as follows (at [50]–[51]):

> Lord Wrenbury's observations . . . are a vivid expression of the basic distinction between the right of a beneficiary arising under the law of trusts (which most would regard as part of the law of property) and the right of a litigant to disclosure of his opponent's documents (which is part of the law of procedure and evidence). But the [Committee] cannot regard it as a reasoned or binding decision that a beneficiary's right or claim to disclosure of trust documents or information must always have the proprietary basis of a transmissible interest in trust property. . . . Their Lordships consider that the more principled and correct approach is to regard the right to seek disclosure of trust documents as one aspect of the court's inherent jurisdiction to supervise, and if necessary to intervene in, the administration of trusts. The right to seek the court's intervention does not depend on entitlement to a fixed and transmissible beneficial interest.

Having established the right in principle of the appellant to seek disclosure the case was referred back to the Isle of Man court for the decision to be applied. The subtle way in which the Committee deals with the earlier and seemingly conflicting English authorities (in particular *Re Cowin* (1886) 33 Ch D 179; *O'Rourke v Darbishire* [1920] AC 581; and *Re Londonderry's Settlement* [1965] Ch 918) is probably sufficient to ensure that *Schmidt v Rosewood*, although a decision of the Privy Council and not strictly binding, will be followed in the English courts (see also *Daraydan Holdings v Solland International* [2004] EWHC 622 where Lawrence Collins J held that the High Court and Court of

Appeal can follow Privy Council decisions even where they depart from previous Court of Appeal decisions). Nothing, however, can disguise the fact that a quite radical shift has taken place, particularly in view of Lord Walker's comment that 'no beneficiary (and least of all a discretionary object) has any entitlement as of right to disclosure of anything which can plausibly be described as a trust document' (at [67]; and see Pollard (2003) 17(2) TLI 90; McCall [2003] PCB 5 at 358; Wilson [2004] PCB 3 at 161; and Lightman J [2004] PCB 1 at 23–40). Essentially a proprietary right to disclosure, admittedly of uncertain dimensions, has been supplanted with a right contingent on the exercise of judicial discretion. It is necessary, however, to consider just how much difference this shift will make to the practice of trustees and the courts. One immediate effect is that the debate that exercised the court and commentators as to whether or not a particular document was a trust document and therefore trust property can be discarded (see eg *Re Londonderry's Settlement*; and Megarry (1965) 81 LQR 192). The removal of the proprietary right basis for disclosure renders the issue largely redundant.

Disclosure of information and 'inherent jurisdiction': some practical implications

Whilst *Schmidt v Rosewood* has significantly rewritten the law on the right to seek disclosure from trustees, it must not be overlooked that the fundamental obligation of the trustees is unaltered, that is to account to the beneficiaries for their stewardship of the trust. It would be strange therefore if a judgment essentially concerned with extending to the objects of a mere power the right to seek disclosure were to lead to an outcome whereby a court would refuse, for instance, to permit a beneficiary with a transmissible interest – such as a life tenant – to inspect trust accounts. Notwithstanding Lord Walker's comment rejecting any notion of 'entitlement as of right', one might expect the court at least to start from a presumption in such a case that documents should be made available unless there is some good reason for refusing access (see eg *Foreman v Kingstone* [2005] WTLR 823 HC; Griffiths [2005] Conv 93).

On the other hand an area where the court's discretion is most likely to come to the fore is where an order for disclosure is sought by the object of a mere power or by a beneficiary of a discretionary trust. Then the court will have to undertake a balancing exercise. An important element in this assessment will be whether the claimant can establish a likelihood that at some stage they have a reasonable chance of obtaining some part of the trust property. In *Schmidt v Rosewood* itself, for instance, Lord Walker stated that although the appellant was 'a possible object of a very wide power ... [he is] an object who may be regarded (especially in view of the letter [from his father]) as having exceptionally strong claims to be considered' (at [69]). In *Schmidt v Rosewood* the appellant was seeking full disclosure of trust accounts and information as to the whereabouts of assets in excess of US$105m received by the two settlements between their creation and 1998. In somewhat similar vein a beneficiary of a discretionary trust who was one of four children of the settlor and where the number of potential beneficiaries was 'pretty limited' was granted an order against his father, the defendant, that the names and addresses of trustees should be disclosed (*Murphy v Murphy* [1999] 1 WLR 282; see Mitchell (1999) 115 LQR 206). It is noteworthy, however, that in respect of some other discretionary trusts where the class of beneficiaries was much wider and the plaintiff's claims to any share correspondingly weaker, disclosure was refused by the judge.

(4) Disclosure of information and the decision-making process of trustees

In neither *Schmidt v Rosewood* nor *Murphy v Murphy* were the claimants seeking information to satisfy idle curiosity or even simply to ensure that the trustees were handling the trust affairs competently, although in *Schmidt v Rosewood* there is a suggestion that alleged overcharging by trustees may be at issue. The information sought was in essence a first step towards attempting to establish that they [the claimants] should benefit personally from the trusts to a greater degree. In other words at some point the claimants might wish to challenge the decisions of the trustees. It is at this point that the 'right' to seek disclosure may on occasion conflict with the principle that trustees are not obliged to give reasons for the exercise of their discretions. Where trust correspondence or records (eg a trust diary) indicate the reasons, is the obligation of trustees to disclose or not? Whilst this issue is of considerable practical significance to aggrieved beneficiaries, it is also the paradigmatic case for assessing where power resides in the trustee-beneficiary relationship. Whilst much of the argument before the Court of Appeal in the leading case of *Re Londonderry's Settlement* revolved around the now disapproved 'proprietary right' to disclosure and its relationship to a definition of trust documents, the judgments do explore in some detail the problems posed by the conflict between accountability of trustees and their autonomy of decision-making.

Re Londonderry's Settlement [1965] Ch 918, CA

The settlor's daughter, Lady Walsh (W) was, in default of appointment, an income beneficiary under a discretionary trust and also a member of a class amongst whom trustees had power to appoint capital subject to the consent of certain other persons known as 'appointors'. In 1962 the trustees decided to terminate the trust by distributing the capital but W objected to the amount that the trustees proposed to give her. W asked the trustees to provide her with copies of various documents but they supplied only copies of (1) previous appointments of capital and (2) trust accounts. W remained dissatisfied and the trustees sought the court's directions as to which, if any, of the following documents they were bound to disclose:

> (a) the minutes of the meetings of the trustees...; (b) agenda and other documents (if any) prepared for the purposes of the meetings of the...trustees or otherwise for the[ir] consideration...; (c) correspondence relating to the administration of the trust property or otherwise to the execution of the trusts of the settlement and passing between

(i) the individuals for the time being holding office as trustees of or appointors under the settlement; (ii) the trustees and appointors on the one hand and the solicitors to the trustees on the other hand; (iii) the trustees and appointors on the one hand and the beneficiaries on the other hand.

Plowman J ordered disclosure and the trustees appealed. The appeal was substantially upheld, the Court of Appeal restricting the disclosure obligation to: (i) under (b) to any aide-memoire from the trustees' solicitor summarising the state of the fund or of the family or of any distributions from the fund; and (ii) under (c) the letters of the trustees' solicitors to the trustees. All the judges in the Court of Appeal rested their opinions largely on the overriding principle that trustees' deliberations on the exercise of discretions were confidential and each explained the rationale underpinning this approach:

Harman LJ: [As] the defendant beneficiary admits, trustees exercising a discretionary power are not bound to disclose to their beneficiaries the reasons actuating them in coming to a decision. This is a long-standing principle and rests largely, I think, on the view that nobody could be called on to accept a trusteeship involving the exercise of a discretion unless, in the absence of bad faith, he were not liable to have his motives or his reasons called in question either by the beneficiaries or by the court. To this there is added a rider, namely that if trustees do give reasons, the court can consider their soundness.

It would seem on the face of it that there is no reason why this principle should be confined to decisions orally arrived at and should not extend to a case, like the present, where, owing to the complexity of the trust and the large sums involved, the trustees, who act subject to the consent of another body called the appointors, have brought into existence various written documents including, in particular, agenda for and minutes of their meetings from time to time held in order to consider distributions made of the fund and its income.

. . .

Salmon LJ: . . . The settlement gave the absolute discretion to appoint to the trustees and not to the courts. So long as the trustees exercise this power with the consent of persons called appointors under the settlement, and exercise it bona fide with no improper motive, their exercise of the power cannot be challenged in the courts – and their reasons for acting as they did are accordingly immaterial. This is one of the grounds for the rule that trustees are not obliged to disclose to beneficiaries their reasons for exercising a discretionary power. Another ground for this rule is that it would not be for the good of the beneficiaries as a whole, and yet another that it might make the lives of trustees intolerable should such an obligation rest on them: . . . Nothing would be more likely to embitter family feelings and the relationship between the trustees and members of the family than that the trustees should be obliged to state their reasons for the exercise of the powers entrusted to them. It might indeed well be difficult to persuade any persons to act as trustees were a duty to disclose their reasons, with all the embarrassment, arguments and quarrels that might ensue, added to their present not inconsiderable burdens . . .

Similarly Danckwerts LJ (agreeing with Harman LJ) also laid emphasis on the consideration that disclosure of certain documents might 'cause infinite trouble in the family'. In a subsequent note ((1965) 81 LQR 192) Megarry prophetically commented (at 196), 'It seems safe to say that the last of *Re Londonderry's Settlement* has not been heard' and the case left several issues in an unsatisfactory state, not all of which have yet been resolved.

First, reconciling the decision with the rules of court procedure governing pre-trial discovery of documents is potentially problematic (see generally Taube (2005) PCB 5, 280–291). Indeed the final order of the court in the case was made 'without prejudice to any right of the defendant to discovery in separate proceedings' against the trustees. Can the beneficiary use litigation as a 'fishing expedition' by alleging bad faith or some other improper conduct on the part of the trustee and obtain discovery of documents, whether trust documents or not? The court's dilemma is clearly set out by Megarry:

> Will the courts permit the bonds of secrecy to be invaded by the simple process of commencing hostile litigation against the trustees? It is not easy to see how the courts can prevent this. True, questions of relevance may obviously arise; but on discovery the test of relevance is wide. The classical statement is that of Brett LJ: an applicant is entitled to discovery of any document 'which may fairly lead him to a train of inquiry' that may 'either directly or indirectly enable the party requiring the affidavit either to advance his own case or to damage the case of his adversary' (*Compagnie Financière et Commerciale du Pacifique v Peruvian Guano Co* (1882) 11 QBD 55 at 63; see now CPR 31.6 and 16).

If the decision in *Re Londonderry* is in part based on a principle of confidentiality, it seems inconsistent to allow that principle to be overridden by an order for discovery where some improper conduct is alleged but not where a beneficiary is making preliminary inquiries to find out whether such conduct has occurred. Indeed dicta of Mahoney JA in the New South Wales Court of Appeal in *Hartigan Nominees Pty Ltd v Rydge* (1992) 29 NSWLR 405 suggest that the principle that reasons should not be disclosed takes precedence and should not be circumvented by an order for discovery (at 437). On the other hand in *Scott v National Trust* [1998] 2 All ER 705 Robert Walker J confirmed obiter that if a decision of the trustees is directly attacked '[they] may be compelled either legally (through discovery or subpoena) or practically (in order to avoid adverse inferences being drawn) to disclose the substance of the reasons for their decision' (at 719; on the drawing of adverse inferences see *Taylor v Midland Bank Trust Co Ltd* [2002] WTLR 95 CA). Do the different contexts – actual litigation and pre-litigation manoeuvres – justify different approaches?

Notwithstanding these uncertainties and a certain shakiness of reasoning, the decision in *Re Londonderry* was broadly welcomed by commentators and approved as 'according with principle and common sense' by a majority of the New South Wales Court of Appeal in *Hartigan Nominees Pty Ltd v Rydge* (see

Lehane [1994] 3 JIP 60). Indeed a contrary decision might have resulted in the proposition that a beneficiary could learn the reasons for trustees' exercise of discretion where documented but not otherwise. And the argument for confidentiality rests substantially on the proposition that trustees need not give reasons. But to invoke this justification invites the further question of why should trustees be protected from a requirement to give reasons? The rules discouraging disclosure of reasons were formulated in a context where trustees were just as likely to be pressed to explain investment decisions as those of a dispositive nature. Stebbings astutely identifies the problem in the relationship between trustees and beneficiaries: 'Demanding, strong-willed and educated beneficiaries made formidable advocates of particular investment policies' (*The Private Trustee in Victorian England* (2002) p 81). The recommended response for trustees is to be found in advice tendered to them in a contemporary work: '[N]ever argue or reply to arguments, but barricade yourself behind your will or your [trust] deed and whilst profoundly regretting your inability to oblige, refuse to budge a foot' (Birrell *The Duties and Liabilities of Trustees* (1897) p 23, cited in Stebbings, above).

Turning to the various explanations advanced in *Re Londonderry* (see in particular Salmon LJ's judgment) these fall broadly into two overlapping categories – protection of trustees and of family harmony. As to the former, the notion seems to be that people would be deterred from becoming trustees if their every decision were to be potentially subject to question. On this point one critic (Samuels (1965) 28 MLR 220) trenchantly suggested that it is irrelevant in the context of modern, frequently professional, trusteeship, and concluded (at 223): '*Re Londonderry* will certainly relieve timorous trustees fearful lest their decisions might have to be publicly supported; but it will hardly create confidence in the office of trustee to further the interests of beneficiaries. What is more important: the susceptibilities of trustees or the welfare of beneficiaries?' Whether or not Samuels's criticism is convincing (not all trustees are professionals), the juxtaposition of the two interests is ironic since it is the welfare of beneficiaries as a class – avoiding the embitterment of family feelings – that provides an alternative justification. Yet, as Gardner points out, any unpleasantness, whether between beneficiaries themselves or between them and the trustees, is likely to derive from the decision itself, the results of which 'would be discoverable from the accounts, which [trustees] do have to disclose' (*An Introduction to the Law of Trusts* (2nd edn, 2003) pp 236–238). Moreover, even on the ground of welfare of beneficiaries as a class, the Court of Appeal judgments display inconsistency. Criticism was voiced of the trustees' decision to appeal against the order of Plowman J to disclose the documents (per Harman and Danckwerts LJJ; cf Salmon LJ who considered the trustees to be fully justified in appealing). In acting under the order of the Divisional Court the position of the trustees would have been protected, but they would then have been acting contrary to what they considered (rightly as it turned out) to be the best interest of the beneficiaries.

Lastly, one reason advanced by Salmon LJ for preserving confidence was that the trustees' reasons are immaterial since the courts will not interfere with a bona fide exercise of discretion. This reason is unsatisfactory because disclosure of reasons might reveal whether the discretion had indeed been exercised bona fide. It also rests fundamentally on a non-interventionist approach to control of trustees' discretion. We now return to that general issue.

(e) Conclusion

Drawing on our previous discussion it is tempting to advance three firm propositions about existing law: (1) trustees need not give reasons for the exercise of discretions; (2) beneficiaries have no direct right of access to documents or parts of documents which record those reasons; and (3) without clear evidence of improper motive or behaviour or, notwithstanding its uncertain ambit, unless the principle in *Re Hastings-Bass* applies it will be extremely difficult to persuade a court to interfere with the exercise of trustees' discretions.

A small note of reservation as to the universality of these propositions is, however, appropriate. *Re Londonderry*, for example, refers to a pure dispositive discretion in a trust where the only beneficiaries were a family group. Can it be assumed that the strictures as to non-disclosure of reasons or documents apply with equal force to the modern pension scheme trust, or to the dispositive-administrative borderline powers of advancement and maintenance, or to the exercise of wholly administrative discretions, for example, on investment? As regards the last mentioned, a non-interventionist approach can hardly be reconciled with enforcing the standards of skill and care, and the duty of impartiality, discussed in Chapter 10 (see Cullity (1975) 25 U Toronto LJ 99 at 118–119). Still more contentious, in our view, is the endorsement in *Wilson v The Law Debenture Trust Corpn* of a view that the principle of *Re Londonderry* applies to disclosure of reasons in pension scheme trusts (see Chapter 13, p 702 for a full consideration of the issues raised by the case).

Although a relatively recent case, *Re Londonderry* is close in tone to nineteenth-century decisions such as *Re Beloved Wilkes' Charity* (1851) 3 Mac & G 440, and *Gisborne v Gisborne* (1877) 2 App Cas 300. Furthermore, as was recognised in *Schmidt v Rosewood* [2003] 2 WLR 1442, it predates the conceptual developments triggered by *McPhail v Doulton* [1971] AC 424 (see Chapter 5) and the more extensive scope of judicial supervision envisaged there. If in response, therefore, to the broadening of trustees' dispositive and administrative discretions the courts were to re-assert a measure of control via a more robust interventionist approach, the *Re Londonderry* approach to disclosure of reasons or documents might be more susceptible to challenge (but cf *Karger v Paul* [1984] VR 161 where the court approved a non-interventionist approach, rejecting also an argument based on natural justice that beneficiaries must be given a fair opportunity to make representations to trustees).

If the principle underpinning *Re Londonderry* – that trustees need not give reasons for the exercise of discretions – is wrong or is to be qualified, little time need be lost on a search for an alternative linguistic formula facilitating intervention. Displaying admirable economy of judicial thought and language, some judgments in trusts law have adopted concepts similar to those of administrative law governing judicial review (see eg *Re Hastings-Bass (dec'd)* [1975] Ch 25; *Re Hay's Settlement Trusts* [1981] 3 All ER 786; and *Re Manisty's Settlement* [1974] Ch 17). It is linguistically a short step to the adoption of the type of test propounded by Lord Greene MR for reviewing the actions of local authorities: 'it may still be possible to say that, although the local authority have kept within the four corners of the matters which they ought to consider, they have nevertheless come to a conclusion, so unreasonable that no reasonable authority could ever have come to it' (*Associated Provincial Picture Houses Ltd v Wednesbury Corpn* [1948] 1 KB 223 at 233; see generally Gordon *Judicial Review in the New Millennium* (2003); Lewis *Judicial Remedies in Public Law* (2nd edn, 2000); but cf *Dundee General Hospitals Board of Management v Walker* [1952] 1 All ER 896 at 905 and Parry [1989] Conv 244 at 249). And even this test is something of an empty vessel and gives little indication of how courts might intervene. Just as application of the *Wednesbury* test in administrative law is not axiomatic and unchanging, so in trusts law the courts could apply contemporary judicial views of a band of reasonable behaviour within which trustees could freely operate. The proposition that the principles underpinning judicial review of administrative decisions in the public realm may be crossing the boundary into the area of decision-making by trustees gains added weight from the suggestion by Robert Walker J in *Scott v National Trust* [1998] 2 All ER 705 that 'legitimate expectation may have some part to play in trust law as well as in judicial review cases' (at 718). The somewhat improbable example he gives is of an elderly impoverished beneficiary to whom the trustees have for the last ten years paid £1,000 per quarter. The judge, whilst accepting that the beneficiary would have no legal or equitable right to continued payment, comments that 'it seems at least arguable that no reasonable body of trustees would discontinue the payment, without any warning, and without giving the beneficiary the opportunity of trying to persuade the trustees to continue the payment, at least temporarily. . . . [He] or she has an expectation' (ibid; but cf the sceptical views expressed in *Hayton and Mitchell* at pp 656–657 and Davern 'Impeaching the Exercise of Trustees' Distributive Discretions' in Hayton (ed) *Extending the Boundaries of Trusts and Similar Ring-Fenced Funds* (2002) on the importation of a 'Wednesbury irrationality' test; see further Chapter 13 for discussion of the notion of 'reasonable expectations' of beneficiaries in the context of pension schemes).

It is worth emphasising that adopting the language of the public law concept of judicial review does not necessarily entail an assimilation of doctrine. Trustees are different from public authorities and so is their decision-making. It therefore does not follow that any extension of the jurisdiction to review the exercise of discretion by trustees must bring in its train the same considerations and remedies as apply to a review of the decisions of public authorities. At its simplest what is at issue is the extent to which – post *McPhail v Doulton* and now *Schmidt v Rosewood* – trustee autonomy in decision-making should be subjected to the scrutiny of the courts. Acceptance of a view that judicial intervention depends on this essentially judicial policy ground – as indeed is implicit in *Re Londonderry* – does not necessarily indicate that a presumption favouring an extensive area for trustee autonomy should not continue to apply. On a practical level, perhaps trustees do need to be protected in a family context from insistent questioning about their decisions, and the courts from having to adjudicate on intra-family disputes. Perhaps trustees would raise fees to compensate for any increased administration costs associated with greater accountability (cf the discussion in Bishop and Prentice (1983) 46 MLR 289). Above all a non-interventionist approach can be interpreted as simultaneously respecting the primacy of the settlor's intention and reinforcing a strong notion of trusting (see eg Templeman J in *Re Manisty's Settlement* [1973] 2 All ER 1203 at 1210: 'the settlor has no doubt good reason in trusting the persons whom he appoints trustees').

Consider the following points:

(1) A potentially powerful deterrent discouraging a beneficiary from challenging the exercise of discretion by trustees could be the presence of a 'no contest' forfeiture clause in the trust deed. Such clauses, seemingly increasingly common in offshore inter vivos trusts, seek to exclude beneficiaries from receiving any benefit if they seek to contest the validity of any exercise of discretion by the trustees. Should such clauses be upheld as a legitimate exercise of the settlor's property power or declared void as being inconsistent with the right of beneficiaries to enforce the trust or should validity depend on the 'reasonableness' or 'justifiability' of the beneficiary's action? (See eg *AN v Barclays Private Bank and Trust (Cayman) Ltd* [2007] WTLR 565; [2008] PCB 1, 23–29; cf *Nathan v Leonard* [2003] 1 WLR 827 (testamentary 'no contest' clause).

(2) 'Letters of wishes' provide a particularly acute context for analysing the treatment of the contrasting claims of confidentiality and accountability under the court's inherent jurisdiction post-*Schmidt v Rosewood* (see eg *Breakspear v Ackland* [2008] 3 WLR 698 ((2008) 67(2) CLJ 252); *Countess Bathurst v Kleinwort Benson (Channel Islands) Trustees Ltd* [2007] WTLR 959; and cf the earlier powerful dissenting judgment of Kirby P in *Hartigan Nominees Pty Ltd v Rydge* [1992] 29 NSWLR 405 at 419–422). Whilst there is evidence of the court authorising a degree of disclosure, although not necessarily to beneficiaries themselves, the presumption clearly still favours confidentiality, as evident in the following extract from the judgment of Briggs J in *Breakspear v Ackland* (at para 58):

> It seems to me axiomatic that a document [a wish letter] brought into existence for the sole or predominant purpose of being used in furtherance of an inherently confidential process is itself properly to be regarded as confidential, to substantially the same extent and effect as the process which it is intended to serve.

(3) In *Murphy v Murphy* [1999] 1 WLR 282 Neuberger J, in refusing to order disclosure of the names and addresses of certain trustees to the plaintiff, commented (at 293): 'It would be most undesirable for this court to make orders which would be likely to result in trustees of discretionary private trusts being badgered with claims by many beneficiaries for consideration to be given to their claims for trust moneys, or for accounts as to how trust moneys have been spent: the duties of a trustee are, it may fairly be said, quite onerous enough without such added problems.' Does this observation apply with equal force to amateur and professional trustees? To what extent, if at all, do the widespread powers of delegation now conferred on trustees by the Trustee Act 2000 undermine the proposition advanced by Neuberger J?

(4) Assuming a willingness on the part of the court to intervene in circumstances of 'bad faith', 'irrelevant considerations' or even 'unreasonableness', to control the exercise of a discretion, what remedy should be imposed? The court's intervention is normally of a negative nature in that the trustees' decision will be set aside or their future conduct of affairs restricted (see *Klug v Klug* where the court authorised the advancement although in compliance with the wishes of the corporate trustee, and *Re Lofthouse* (1885) 29 Ch D 921, discussed in Gardner *An Introduction to the Law of Trusts* (2nd edn, 2003) pp 213–214). In addition, in the case of a dispositive discretion the court can plainly take the positive steps envisaged by Lord Wilberforce in *McPhail v Doulton* [1971] AC 424 of 'appointing new trustees or . . . authorising representative persons of the classes of beneficiaries to prepare a scheme for distribution' (at 457). In what circumstances, if any, should the court take the further step of itself making the decision as to the exercise of the discretion? Should it make any difference whether the discretion is in the form of a power or a trust? (See *Mettoy Pension Trustees Ltd v Evans* [1990] 1 WLR 1587; cf Gardner (1991) 107 LQR 214 and Martin [1991] Conv (NS) 364; and see also Mr Justice Young (1999) 73 Australia LJ 175–176 reviewing decisions in Australian pensions cases.)

(5) One way of analysing the rule in *Re Hastings-Bass* is to assess its consequences for trustee conduct. It may be argued that a narrow interpretation of the rule – namely, one that limits the scope for intervention by the court – will encourage trustees to aspire to a high level of competence otherwise they run the risk of being sued for negligence. On the other hand, if a broad interpretation of the rule is adopted, one that facilitates the court's intervention to correct mistakes, the rule acts to protect trustees

from successful claims for negligence (see Dawson [2002] Conv 67 at 71). A difficulty with this analysis is that frequently a trust instrument will contain a clause exonerating the trustee from liability for negligence. An alternative analysis therefore is that the rule really operates to protect beneficiaries from the consequences of trustees' negligence by enabling their decisions to be unpicked and corrected. As Hilliard succinctly puts the point: '[The rule] prevents [beneficiaries] losing out, not the trustees' (2002) 16(4) TLI 202 at 212). Do you find either of these 'justifications' for the rule persuasive?

(6) Perhaps the last word on the principle in *Hastings-Bass* should be to ask whether the principle is needed at all. The HMRC provisional view, referred to earlier, is that any provision for rectifying mistakes of trustees should be assimilated with the general principles of common law developed by the courts for setting aside voluntary transactions or written instruments for mistake. This would ensure that beneficiaries who consent to arrangements would be placed in no better position than an outright legal owner of property who wishes to unpick a transaction which turns out to have unforeseen fiscal consequences. Whether those consequences do or even should justify rectification for mistake at all is another matter altogether (see eg Tang (2004) 20 JCL 1; and (2007) 21(2) TLI 62).

4. Pursuing a remedy

(a) Introduction to trustee liability

Possible breaches of trust that can be committed by trustees are many and various. As Millett LJ observed in *Armitage v Nurse* [1997] 2 All ER 705 at 710:

> A breach of trust may be deliberate or inadvertent; it may consist of an actual misappropriation or misapplication of the trust property or merely of an investment or other dealing which is outside the trustees' powers; it may consist of a failure to carry out a positive obligation of the trustees or merely of a want of skill and care on their part in the management of the trust property; it may be injurious to the interests of the beneficiaries or be actually to their benefit.

We therefore examine more closely in section (b) below the different categories of breach that can be committed and their implications for the form of money remedies that may be obtainable by disgruntled beneficiaries.

First, however, we set out here a brief overview of the several forms of redress that the law provides, some of which are considered in greater depth in the pages that follow and others elsewhere in the book. Where a beneficiary can establish that some breach of duty has occurred strong remedies are available. It may be sufficient just to have the duty properly performed and the court can order this to be done. After all the basic right of the beneficiary is to have the trust properly administered. But what if financial loss has been caused? Then trustees can be held personally liable for all loss caused by the breach of trust directly or indirectly to the trust property. This is probably so irrespective of whether the loss arose as a result of the trustees' fraud or their incompetence, or even when acting innocently for the benefit of the trust and unaware that the conduct is in breach of trust (but see TA 1925, s 61; p 595). But not every breach of trust brings with it liability. There may be cases where the breach gives no right to compensation. In *Target Holdings Ltd v Redferns (a firm)* [1996] AC 421 (see below) Lord Browne-Wilkinson gives as an example the trustee who commits a judicious breach of trust by investing in an unauthorised investment which proves to be very profitable to the trust. A 'carping' beneficiary could insist that the unauthorised investments be sold and the proceeds invested in authorised investments; but the trustee would be under no liability to pay compensation either to the trust fund or to the beneficiary because the breach would have caused no loss to the trust fund.

However, compensation for loss is not the only remedy and indeed may not always be the appropriate one. There may be occasions where a breach of trust has resulted in trustees making an unauthorised profit for themselves, as in a share transaction by using confidential information gained solely in their capacity as trustees. If the beneficiaries have not even suffered any direct loss there appears to be no room for compensation. In these circumstances, however, the trustees may be held 'liable to account' to the trust fund for the profits made.

Moreover, suing a trustee personally does not exhaust the remedies available to a beneficiary. Where, for example, a trustee is insolvent the personal remedy may be inadequate. The beneficiary then may either have recourse to a personal remedy against third parties who have wrongfully received trust property, or may be able to invoke a proprietary claim to the trust property itself or its replacement. These further remedies are rarely necessary in the family trust context and detailed consideration is given to them in Chapters 14–16 in the context of their contemporary application to commercial environments.

Lastly, and just as in civil actions generally, a plaintiff alleging breach of trust can apply for an interlocutory order from the High Court. Thus, for instance, the full range of injunctive relief is potentially available to an aggrieved beneficiary (see Chapter 14; and generally Spry *The Principle of Equitable Remedies* (7th edn, 2007).

(b) Breach of trust and compensation claims: a classification

Until this point in the chapter the term 'breach of trust' has been employed in a manner which might be taken to suggest that in providing a remedy the law does not distinguish between the 'many and various' breaches of trust mentioned above. It is therefore important to emphasise that different types of breach may attract different responses from the law. In particular it is necessary to distinguish between those breaches that involve a misapplication of trust money through, for instance, an investment or a distribution of trust income unauthorised by the terms of the trust instrument – let us call that a Type 1 breach of trust – and other breaches that do not involve a failure to comply with those terms – let us call that a Type 2 breach. The most obvious example of the latter type of breach would be where the trustee fails to demonstrate the necessary standard of care as, for instance, in negligently making authorised investments or supervising authorised agents. A Type 1 breach involves the trustee doing something that he or she must not do. The wrongful act may be innocent – such as the trustee making a mistaken payment – or it may be fraudulent but in either case liability is strict. In a sense a Type 2 breach also involves a wrongful act but here, as Birks explains, 'the wrong act consists of doing badly something that the [trustee] is entitled to do' such as investing the trust fund but doing it in a careless manner (Birks and Pretto *Breach of Trust* (2002) p ix).

The principal significance of the distinction between the different types of breach lies in the fact that identifying the type of breach that has occurred is an important step in determining the type of claim to be made and the remedy to be sought. To explain this further it is necessary to take a step back and recall that a fundamental obligation of trustees is to maintain a record of their stewardship of the trust and, where called upon, to provide accounts of the trust to the beneficiaries. If a beneficiary was dissatisfied with the trustees' administration of the trust the traditional route to a remedy was through the mediation of Chancery's accounting procedure. The right of a beneficiary where some breach of trust is suspected is then said to be to have the 'accounts' reviewed, and to 'falsify the accounts' (Type 1 breach) or 'surcharge the account' (Type 2 breach). These are terms of art and do not readily translate into our everyday use of the words 'surcharge' and 'falsify'. Lord Millett, writing extra-judicially, has sought to explain the terms and their significance for the remedies for breach of trust. As regards what we have termed a Type 1 breach, Millett LJ, as he then was, writes as follows ((1998) 114 LQR 214 at 226):

> Where the beneficiary complains that the trustee has misapplied trust money, he [the beneficiary] falsifies the account, that is to say, he asks for the disbursement to be disallowed. If, for example, the trustee lays out trust money in an unauthorised investment that falls in value, the beneficiary will falsify the account by asking the court to disallow both the disbursement and the corresponding asset on the other side of the account. The unauthorised investment will then be treated as having been bought with the trustee's own money and on his own behalf. He will be required to account to the trust estate for the full amount of the disbursement – *not* for the amount of the loss. That is what is meant by saying that the trustee is liable to restore the trust property; and why common law rules of damage and remoteness are out of place.

As Millett LJ emphasised, this process is not, strictly speaking, seeking compensation for loss; it is rather requiring the trustee to perform the primary obligation to 'render an account of the fund' and, again strictly speaking, this obligation is enforceable whether or not there has been a breach of trust. The underpinning explanation for this approach, at first sight a puzzling one for the reader, is that equity takes a generous view of our defaulting trustee; it disregards the wrongful act and makes the trustee account as if he had behaved properly all along. In short, equity does not treat the trustee as a wrongdoer. As regards a 'remedy' there may be circumstances where the trustee will be required to 'restore' the original trust property and is able to do so. More often this will not be possible, the property perhaps having been sold to a bona fide purchaser, and the trustee will then be personally liable to 'restore' the trust by a money payment equivalent to the value of the misapplied trust property. Of course if the trustee has entered into an unauthorised transaction that proves profitable the beneficiaries can accept or 'adopt' the transaction in preference to 'falsifying' the account.

What then of the circumstances where the beneficiary seeks to surcharge the account as, for instance, when the trustees fail to obtain all that they should have done for the benefit of the trust, what we have termed a Type 2 breach? Again to quote Millett LJ: 'The trustee is made to account not only for what he has in fact received, but also for what he might with due diligence have received' (above). Historically the 'surcharge' was assessed by reference to what was termed an 'account on the footing of wilful default' or in contemporary parlance by reference to the loss caused by the trustee's failure to exercise skill and care. And here we encounter the significance of distinguishing between the different types of breach of trust. Where the breach is one of the type just described then, unlike the position with a Type 1 breach, there is now clear although not unanimous support for the view that common law rules of damage and remoteness, or at least a very close analogy to them, do have a role to play. In *Bristol and West Building Society v Mothew* [1998] Ch 1, for instance, Millett LJ comments as follows (at 17):

> Although the remedy which equity makes available for breach of the equitable duty of skill and care is equitable compensation rather than damages, this is merely the product of history and in this context is in my opinion a distinction without a difference. Equitable compensation for breach of the duty of skill and care resembles common law damages in that it is awarded by way of compensation to the plaintiff for his loss. There is no reason in principle why the common law rules of causation, remoteness of damage and measure of damages should not be applied by analogy in such a case. It should not be confused with equitable compensation for breach of fiduciary duty, which may be awarded in lieu of rescission or specific restitution.

Two comments can be made about this statement. First, notwithstanding the remarks of Millett LJ, the extent to which remoteness criteria are relevant even to Type 2 breaches of trust remains a contested issue, and one we return to in section (c)(3) below (see p 583). Second, the last sentence in the extract from Millett LJ's judgment points us towards one further distinction to be drawn to complete this preliminary step in the analysis of breach of trust. That distinction is between a breach of fiduciary duty and a breach of trust of either of the types described above. A trustee is a fiduciary and is therefore subject to the obligation of loyalty. As we noted in Chapter 9 this obligation means, inter alia, that a trustee must not place himself in a position where his duty and his interest may conflict; he may not act for his own benefit or the benefit of a third person without the informed consent of his principal (the beneficiaries) or unless authorised by the trust instrument. But as we have already seen trustees are also subject to other duties, such as a duty of care in several facets of trust administration. These two duties are distinct: one can be loyal and therefore not in breach of one's fiduciary duty but simultaneously be careless and thus in breach of trust. Indeed, if confirmation were needed, in *Bristol and West Building Society v Mothew* Millett LJ specifically indorsed the following comment of Ipp J in *Permanent Building Society (in liq) v Wheeler* (1994) 14 ACSR 109 at 157:

> It is essential to bear in mind that the existence of a fiduciary relationship does not mean that every duty owed by a fiduciary to the beneficiary is a fiduciary duty. In particular, a trustee's duty to exercise reasonable care, though equitable, is not specifically a fiduciary duty . . .

Conversely, one can comply with a duty of care but still be accountable for breach of fiduciary duty – as might be the position where trustees carefully invested trust money in authorised investments but in a way that earned them an unauthorised secret commission. It cannot be emphasised too strongly that for the purposes of deciding the relief to be granted it is necessary to determine the type of breach that has been committed and by whom.

At this point a word of warning of a similar nature to that offered in Chapter 5 is appropriate. We noted there that a source of potential confusion and misunderstanding was the tendency of the courts and also academic commentators to apply differing descriptive terms to powers of appointment conferred on trustees. It is as well to be aware of a comparable problem in the modern terminology surrounding the use of the term 'equitable compensation' to describe the money remedy employed by the courts where a trustee, or indeed other fiduciary, is held personally liable for breach of trust.

As is apparent from the comparison drawn by Millett LJ in *Bristol and West Building Society v Mothew*, the term equitable compensation can be used to describe remedies of distinctly different types. Indeed, apart from the contexts mentioned in the extract, the term may also be used in a Type 1 breach of trust where it is not possible to restore the original trust property but where instead the trustee is required to reconstitute or restore the trust fund by means of a payment of money. This indiscriminate use of equitable compensation as a label to describe the money remedy both for specific types of breach of trust and of fiduciary duty but also as a generic descriptive term for any money remedy against trustees is unfortunate to say the least. The linguistic ambiguity can engender conceptual uncertainty. In that regard the more precise and differentiated descriptive terminology and analysis proposed by Edelman and Elliott is particularly attractive (see eg (2004) 18(3) TLI 116–131). They persuasively argue, for example, that the term 'equitable compensation' should be avoided altogether. In its place, at least in so far as their analysis can be related to the three different types of breach outlined here, they suggest that the labels 'substitutive compensation' (Type 1 breach), 'compensatory damages' or 'reparative compensation' (Type 2 breach) and disgorgement damages be used (in preference to 'account of profits' for breach of fiduciary duty). This is not just a matter of labelling. Implicit in their nomenclature, in particular the use of 'damages', is a view of the direction in which the law should be developed (see further section (c)(3) below).

(c) The measure of liability

(1) The principle

'This talk of breach and liability is all very well, but what do I get?' is the likely plea of the disgruntled beneficiary. We outline below (section (c)(2)) a number of specific rules guiding any response but first there is a prior question to be addressed. It is necessary to consider matters of causation and what would at common law be termed remoteness or foreseeability of loss. In short what link must be established between breach and loss for liability to be imposed? In particular, if there has been some breach of trust does our disgruntled beneficiary have to prove in every instance that the breach caused the loss, even if the breach has occurred in circumstances where an order for the 'account to be falsified' might be made? The answer offered by the House of Lords in *Target Holdings Ltd v Redferns (a firm)* (see below) appears to be 'yes'! The reader should be aware that the reasoning in Lord Browne-Wilkinson's opinion in *Target*, concurred in by all their Lordships, does not appear to draw any distinction between the 'substitutive' and 'compensatory or reparative' categories referred to above. The implications of the adoption of the 'but for' causation test for breach of trust promulgated in the case are considered in comments on the judgment (at p 576).

Causation

The law in this area was reviewed in *Target Holdings Ltd v Redferns (a firm)* [1996] AC 421 (see Ulph (1995) 9 TLI 86; Rickett (1996) 112 LQR 27; Nolan [1996] LMCLQ 161; Capper [1997] Conv 14). In *Target*, the plaintiff Target (T) agreed to lend £1,525,000 to Crowngate Ltd (C) on security of commercial properties to be purchased by C from Mirage Properties Ltd and valued by an estate agent firm at £2m. In fact unbeknown to T the arrangement was more complex. Mirage had agreed to sell the property to C but by a circuitous route whereby the property would be sold to P Ltd for £775,000, which would then sell to K Ltd for £1,250,000, which in turn would sell to C for £2m. The loan money was paid to the defendant firm of solicitors Redferns (R), who were acting for both T and C and also, seemingly unbeknown to T, for P and K, to hold as bare trustee with instructions not to pay the money over to C before receipt of the executed conveyances and completion of mortgages in favour of T. However, R, in breach of trust, released £1.25m of the money to the account of the intermediate purchasers (P and K) before all the documents were executed. Subsequently C defaulted on the mortgages. T then sold the properties to recover its security but the sale realised only £500,000. It transpired that both C and the estate agent firm were in liquidation. T therefore sued R to recover the loss. R claimed that only a technical breach of trust had occurred and that T would have suffered the same loss even if the money had been paid to C at the agreed time. This is because the plaintiffs (T) did actually receive the mortgage securities which it had instructed the defendants (R) to obtain, although admittedly only some time after the release of the funds. In short T advanced the same amount of money, obtained the same security and received the same amount on the realisation of the security as it would have done had the transaction been completed correctly. It was, however, common ground before the court that there was a triable issue as to whether, if it had not been for the breach, the transaction would in fact have gone through. At first instance R was given leave to defend the claim subject to making a payment into court of £1m. R appealed against the payment into court stipulation whilst T cross-appealed, claiming that final judgment should have been given in its favour. The Court of Appeal [1994] 2 All ER 337 (Ralph Gibson LJ dissenting) found in favour of T. In the opinion of the majority 'the cause of action is constituted simply by the payment away of Target's moneys in breach of trust and the loss is quantified in the amount of those moneys, subject to Target giving credit for the realisation of the security it received' (at 353 per Peter Gibson LJ). In effect this sees the claim as one for 'substitutive compensation' with questions of causation being immaterial. On appeal the House of Lords restored the order of the first instance judge, Warner J. The only fully reasoned opinion was given by Lord Browne-Wilkinson.

Target Holdings Ltd v Redferns (a firm) [1996] AC 421 at 432

Lord Browne-Wilkinson: At common law there are two principles fundamental to the award of damages. First that the defendant's wrongful act must cause the damage complained of. Second, that the plaintiff is to be put 'in the same position as he would have been had he not sustained the wrong for which he is now getting his compensation or reparation'... Although... in many ways equity approaches liability for making good a breach of trust from a different starting-point, in my judgment those two principles are applicable as much in equity as at common law. Under both systems liability is fault based: the defendant is only liable for the consequences of the legal wrong he has done to the plaintiff and to make good the damage caused by such wrong. He is not responsible for damage not caused by his wrong or to pay by way of compensation more than the loss suffered from such wrong. The detailed rules of equity as to causation and the quantification of loss differ, at

> least ostensibly, from those applicable at common law. But the principles underlying both systems are the same. . . .

Lord Browne-Wilkinson rejected the argument that found favour with the Court of Appeal, namely that the quantum of compensation was to be fixed at the date of the claimed breach of trust (ie at the time the money was released by Redferns):

> The key point in the reasoning of the Court of Appeal is that where moneys are paid away to a stranger in breach of trust, an immediate loss is suffered by the trust estate: as a result, subsequent events reducing that loss are irrelevant. They drew a distinction between the case in which the breach of trust consisted of some failure in the administration of the trust and the case where a trustee has actually paid away trust moneys to a stranger. There is no doubt that in the former case, one waits to see what loss is in fact suffered by reason of the breach, ie the restitution or compensation payable is assessed at the date of trial, not of breach. However, the Court of Appeal considered that where the breach consisted of paying away the trust moneys to a stranger it made no sense to wait: it seemed to Peter Gibson LJ [1994] 2 All ER 337 at 351 obvious that in such a case 'there is an immediate loss placing the trustee under an immediate duty to restore the moneys to the trust fund'. The majority of the Court of Appeal therefore considered that subsequent events which diminished the loss in fact suffered were irrelevant, save for imposing on the compensated beneficiary an obligation to give credit for any benefit he subsequently received. In effect, in the view of the Court of Appeal one 'stops the clock' at the date the moneys are paid away: events which occur between the date of breach and the date of trial are irrelevant in assessing the loss suffered by reason of the breach.
>
> A trustee who wrongly pays away trust money, like a trustee who makes an unauthorised investment, commits a breach of trust and comes under an immediate duty to remedy such breach. If immediate proceedings are brought, the court will make an immediate order requiring restoration to the trust fund of the assets wrongly distributed or, in the case of an unauthorised investment, will order the sale of the unauthorised investment and the payment of compensation for any loss suffered. But the fact that there is an accrued cause of action as soon as the breach is committed does not in my judgment mean that the quantum of the compensation payable is ultimately fixed as at the date when the breach occurred. The quantum is fixed at the date of judgment at which date, according to the circumstances then pertaining, the compensation is assessed at the figure then necessary to put the trust estate or the beneficiary back into the position it would have been in had there been no breach. I can see no justification for 'stopping the clock' immediately in some cases but not in others: to do so may, as in this case, lead to compensating the trust estate or the beneficiary for a loss which, on the facts known at trial, it has never suffered.

Remoteness of loss

If it can be established that 'but for' the breach no loss would have occurred, does this then mean that every loss suffered, however remote, is to be recoverable?

Lord Browne-Wilkinson summarised what he considered to be the relevant principles in the following manner (at 434, sources cited are omitted):

> In relation to a traditional trust where the fund is held in trust for a number of beneficiaries having different, usually successive, equitable interests, (e.g. A for life with remainder to B), the right of each beneficiary is to have the whole fund vested in the trustees so as to be available to satisfy his equitable interest when, and if, it falls into possession.... The equitable rules of compensation for breach of trust [involving the wrongful paying away of trust assets] have been largely developed in relation to such traditional trusts, where the only way in which all the beneficiaries' rights can be protected is to restore to the trust fund what ought to be there. In such a case the basic rule is that a trustee in breach of trust must restore or pay to the trust estate either the assets which have been lost to the estate by reason of the breach or compensation for such loss.... If specific restitution of the trust property is not possible, then the liability of the trustee is to pay sufficient compensation to the trust estate to put it back to what it would have been had the breach not been committed.... Even if the immediate cause of the loss is the dishonesty or failure of a third party, the trustee is liable to make good that loss to the trust estate if, but for the breach, such loss would not have occurred.... Thus the common law rules of remoteness of damage and causation do not apply.

It is possible to construe these words in one of two ways (see the discussion by Elliott ((2002) 65 MLR 588). The final sentence might be taken to mean that, although common law rules of remoteness do not apply, the question of whether distinct equitable rules should be developed to perform a function similar to that performed by those rules in tort and contract is left open. An alternative and one might say less forgiving view is expressed by the authors of the most recent edition of *Lewin* (Mowbray et al *Lewin on Trusts* (18th edn, 2008) ch 39, para 3):

> If a trustee has been guilty of misconduct, and loss follows that would not have occurred apart from the breach, the court does not acquit the trustee because it is more immediately caused by some event wholly beyond the trustee's control, even if the immediate cause of the loss is the dishonesty or failure of a third party. The trustee is liable for the whole loss, however unexpected the result, however little likely to arise from the course adopted, and however free such conduct may be from improper motive.

Whether remoteness criteria should be a material consideration is a matter we return to in section (c)(3) below where we also revisit the possible importance of distinguishing between the different types of breach that can be committed. First, however, we describe some of the current differences between the common law and equitable approaches and how the rules on liability for breach apply to certain specific circumstances.

Causation and foreseeability: summary

On matters of both causation and foreseeability Lord Browne-Wilkinson cited, as 'an illuminating exposition of the rules' the judgment of McLachlin J from the Canadian Supreme Court case of *Canson Enterprises Ltd v Broughton & Co* (1991) 85 DLR (4th) 129. The case concerned the extent of a solicitor's obligation for breach of fiduciary duty in failing to disclose that a third party was making a secret profit, which it shared with the defendant solicitors, out of the purchase of development land by the plaintiffs (Canson). The vendors thought that the purchase price was $410,000 whilst the purchasers Canson thought it was $525,000. The difference provided the 'secret profit'. But the profit was not the subject of the litigation. The plaintiffs built a warehouse on the land it had purchased but because of the negligence of an engineer and a construction firm the building suffered extensive damage. The plaintiffs failed to recover from the negligent parties the full loss suffered and sued the defendant law firm for the balance of losses incurred. The Supreme Court unanimously held that the loss was too remote, although following different routes to the destination. In the case McLachlin J had said, inter alia, that 'losses are to be assessed at the time of trial using the full benefit of hindsight' (at 162), and emphasised that '[f]oreseeability is not a concern in assessing compensation but it is essential that the losses made good are only those which, on a common-sense view of causation, were caused by the breach' (at 163).

In similar vein Lord Browne-Wilkinson in *Target Holdings* concluded (at 439): 'In my view this is good law. Equitable compensation for breach of trust is designed to achieve exactly what the word compensation suggests: to make good a loss in fact suffered by the beneficiaries and which, using hindsight and commonsense, can be said to have been caused by the breach . . .'

Some of the implications of the decision and reasoning in *Target* are looked at below but two cases, cited with approval in *Target*, illustrate some of the differences, in practice, that can emerge from a continuing distinction between common law damages and equitable compensation.

In *Re Dawson* [1966] 2 NSWR 211 trustees paid away NZ£4,700 to a stranger who absconded with the money. At the time the Australian and New Zealand currencies were at par. As events happened Street J had to decide whether the liability of the trustees to compensate the estate should be satisfied by buying sufficient Australian £s to restore the NZ£4,700 as calculated at the date of breach or at the date of the judgment. In the intervening period between the dates the purchasing power of the Australian £ had depreciated against the New Zealand currency with the consequence that, at the date of the judgment, the trustees would have had to expend more than Australian £4,700 to restore the estate to the value that it would have had as measured in New Zealand currency. Street J affirmed that 'considerations of causation, foreseeability and remoteness do not readily enter into the matter' (at 214) and held that the rate of exchange should be taken as at the date of judgment. It must be borne in mind that *Re Dawson* is a case of misapplication of trust property and a claim for 'substitutive compensation', not one involving a breach such as a breach of duty of care. Street J's comments concerning 'foreseeability and remoteness' cannot therefore be taken as determinative of the relevance of these considerations where the breach of trust does not involve misapplication of trust property.

The judgment was cited with approval in *Target* as was the judgment of Brightman J in *Bartlett v Barclays Bank Trust Co Ltd (No 2)* [1980] 2 All ER 92, a case involving what we have called a Type 2 breach and a claim for reparative compensation. The case, which specifically approved (at 95) Street J's analysis from *Re Dawson*, concerned the measure of compensation payable by the bank. Brightman J commented that the equitable compensation sought by the beneficiaries was distinguishable from damages only 'with the aid of a powerful legal microscope'. It will be recalled that the losses had arisen from breaches of trust whereby the bank had permitted a company, in which as trustee it had a controlling interest, to engage in hazardous property speculation (see Chapter 10). The bank sought, inter alia, to apply by analogy the principle of *British Transport Commission v Gourley* [1956] AC 185 that damages for loss of earnings should take account of tax that would have been payable. The bank's point was that had no breach of trust occurred then larger dividends would have been declared with a consequently greater distribution to beneficiaries who would therefore have incurred larger tax liabilities.

> **Brightman J:** The so-called restitution which the bank must now make to the plaintiffs, and to the settled shares, is in reality compensation for the loss suffered by the plaintiffs and the settled shares, not readily distinguishable from damages except with the aid of a powerful legal microscope.
>
> In such circumstances there is, in my view, at least a plausible argument for taking tax into account in assessing the compensation. With some hesitation, I have reached the conclusion that the bank's submission is wrong and that tax ought not to be taken into account. My reasoning is this: the obligation of a trustee who is held liable for breach of trust is fundamentally different from the obligation of a contractual or tortious wrongdoer. The trustee's obligation is to restore to the trust estate the assets of which he has deprived it. The tax liability of individual beneficiaries, who have claims qua beneficiaries to the capital and income of the trust estate, does not enter into the picture because it arises not at the point of restitution to the trust estate but at the point of distribution of capital or income out of the trust estate. These are different stages . . .
>
> I think that this may produce a somewhat unjust bias against the fiduciary wrongdoer as compared with the contractual or tortious wrongdoer in a case such as the present, where the breach of trust has not enriched the defaulting trustee; but I do not feel that the established principles on which equitable relief is granted enable me to apply the *Gourley* principles to this case (*Bartlett v Barclays Bank Trust Co Ltd (No 2)* [1980] 2 All ER 92 at 96).

Consider the following points:

(1) Redfern's success in the House of Lords in *Target Holdings Ltd v Redferns (a firm)* [1996] AC 421 was, in a sense, procedural and possibly pyrrhic. The

overall transaction was, in the words of Lord Browne-Wilkinson, 'redolent of fraud and negligence' and there was a 'high probability' that at a full hearing it would emerge that 'the use of Target's [T] money to pay for the purchase from Mirage . . . was a vital feature of the transaction. If the moneys made available by Redfern's [R] breach of trust were essential to enable the transaction to go through, but for [R's] breach of trust Target would not have advanced any money'. It was therefore arguable that it would be established at trial that a breach of duty by R caused the loss, but a different breach – the omission, whether negligent or fraudulent, to inform T of the web of transactions. Had T known of this it seems improbable that the mortgage advance would have been made. Target would therefore be able to establish its claim for compensation. It is understood that the claim was settled on the basis that Target received the £1m (see *Parker and Mellows* at p 871).

(2) Is causation a concept that is susceptible to 'a commonsense view'? (See Vos (2001) 60(2) CLJ 337–352 for a discussion of some of the implications of different approaches to causation questions in equity and at common law.)

(3) We have referred previously to the claim that the term 'equitable compensation' is potentially misleading in that it has been employed to describe remedies of distinctly different types. In *Target Holdings* is the term used by Lord Browne-Wilkinson to describe a claim for, adopting the terminology of Edelman and Elliott ((2004) 18(3) TLI 116), 'substitutive compensation' or 'reparative compensation' (see the discussion in Rickett (2003) 25 Syd L R 31 at 40–45)?

(4) In *Target Holdings* Lord Browne-Wilkinson sought to warn against lifting 'wholesale the detailed rules developed in the context of traditional trusts and then seek to apply them to trusts of quite a different kind' adding that 'in the modern world the trust has become a valuable device in commercial and financial dealings'. On this view, although the fundamental principles of equity must be applied 'it is important, if the trust is not to be rendered commercially useless, to distinguish between the basic principles of trust law and those specialist rules developed in relation to traditional trusts which are applicable only to such trusts and the rationale of which has no application to trusts of quite a different kind' (at 435). Lord Browne-Wilkinson is here referring to and marginalising the traditional rules relating to 'falsifying the account' and 'substitutive compensation'. He draws a distinction between bare commercial trusts – *Target* being an example – and 'traditional trusts where the trusts are still subsisting' with, for instance, beneficiaries of different classes and entitlements (eg to A for life, remainder to ABC etc). On his Lordship's view only in the latter type of case should the 'traditional rules' apply. It is clear that in Target the depositing of the money with Redferns was but one aspect of a commercial conveyancing transaction and that once the transaction was completed 'to import into

such a trust an obligation to restore the trust fund would be entirely artificial'.

(5) An alternative analysis of *Target Holdings* has been advanced extra-judicially by Lord Millett ((1998) 114 LQR 214 at 226–227; and ch 12 in Degeling and Edelman (eds) *Equity in Commercial Law* (2005) at pp 309–312), one which sees the case as an example of what we earlier termed a Type 1 breach of trust for which a remedy is for the claimant to falsify the account. In *Target* the solicitor (R) paid away the money entrusted to it by the plaintiff firm (T) without obtaining an executed mortgage and the documents of title. This was an unauthorised application of trust money that entitled the plaintiff to falsify the account. At that stage, had T been aware of all the facts which of course it was not, then T could have sought to have the account 'falsified' so that the disbursement would be disallowed and the solicitor (R) treated as accountable as if the money were still in his client account and available to be paid out in the manner directed. As matters transpired R subsequently did what they were authorised to do, namely obtain the mortgage securities. Lord Millett summarised the resulting position as follows:

> The plaintiff could not object to the acquisition of the mortgage or the disbursement by which it was obtained; it was an authorised application of what must be treated as trust money notionally restored to the trust estate on the taking of the account. To put the point another way; the trustee's obligation to restore the trust property is not an obligation to restore it in the very form in which he disbursed it, but an obligation to restore it in any form authorised by the trust.

Three points can briefly be made about this analysis. First the suggested outcome would not have differed from that reached by the reasoning of Lord Browne-Wilkinson. But second, as Lord Millett has sought to emphasise, 'no question of causation would arise' (in *Degeling and Edelman* p 311). The third point is that Lord Millett's analysis would appear to be equally applicable to traditional trusts and to bare trusts whether of a commercial or family nature. The relevance of the distinction drawn by Lord Browne-Wilkinson between family and commercial trusts therefore remains somewhat uncertain at least in this particular context although in our view it has substance in relation to other contexts such as pension scheme trusts (see Chapter 13).

(6) The decision and reasoning in *Target Holdings* has been applied in cases where 'equitable compensation' was sought for a breach of fiduciary duty. In *Swindle v Harrison* [1997] 4 All ER 705, CA a solicitor, the unfortunately named Mr Swindle, offered his client Mrs Harrison a bridging loan in connection with the purchase of a hotel business to be secured by a first charge on the hotel. He failed to disclose (i) details of hidden profits that his firm would make from arranging the loan and (ii) that an anticipated

loan from a third party, which would enable H to pay off the bridging loan, was unlikely to be forthcoming. The business venture failed. In a separate transaction H had previously borrowed £80,000 from NHL on the security of her house to help finance the hotel business. She defaulted on the mortgage and NHL repossessed her house. She therefore sought to claim compensation for the loss of the value of the equity in the house, alleging breach of fiduciary duty by S. H's claim failed because although the Court of Appeal found that a breach of duty had occurred the court was unanimous in finding that 'she would have accepted the [bridging] loan and completed the purchase [of the hotel], even if full disclosure had been made to her' (at 718 per Evans LJ). She would have lost her house in any event and thus could not demonstrate that the loss was caused by the breach of fiduciary duty.

There remains some uncertainty as to the position where the breach of fiduciary duty complained of is 'the equivalent of fraud' (at 717). Evans LJ was of the view that in these circumstances the measure of compensation should be to restore the beneficiary to the position applying before the breach occurred *irrespective* of what the beneficiary would have done had there been no breach: '[Mrs Harrison] cannot recover damages or compensation for the loss [of the value of the equity in her home] except on proof *either* that the [solicitor firm] acted fraudulently *or* in a manner equivalent to fraud or that she would not have completed the purchase if full disclosure had been made i.e. if the breach of duty had not occurred' (at 718). Doubts have been expressed about this dictum, not least because it was not endorsed by the other members of the Court of Appeal (see Tijo and Yeo (1998) 114 LQR 181 at 183; Elliott [1998] RLR 135; Ho (1997) 11 TLI 72; see also *Nationwide Building Society v Various Solicitors (No 3)* [1999] PNLR 606 where Blackburn J indicated that if fiduciaries act dishonestly or in bad faith, the court might find them responsible for all losses which arise, but cf *Gwembe Valley Development Co Ltd v Koshy* [2004] 1 BCLC 131 at [139]).

(7) Circumstances may arise where a breach of duty by a trustee or other fiduciary results in a profit being made by the fiduciary whilst the claimant simultaneously suffers loss, for instance, by being deprived of the opportunity to gain benefit from the property in question. In principle there are two alternative and inconsistent remedies available to the beneficiary/principal – an account of profits and equitable compensation for loss. It would be unfair to the defendant if the claimant were able to 'adopt' the defendant's act for the purpose of claiming a profit and simultaneously disallow the same act for the purpose of proving a loss. In these circumstances 'the plaintiff must choose or elect between them, he cannot have both . . .' (*Tang Man Sit (Personal Representatives) v Capacious Investments Ltd* [1996] 1 All ER 193 at 197, PC per Lord Nicholls; Law Commission Report No 247 *Aggravated, Exemplary and Restitutionary Damages* (1997)

paras 3.64–3.76; but cf Birks (1996) 112 LQR 375; Stevens [1996] RLR 117). It would be difficult for a claimant to elect before a full picture as to the respective profit and loss is known. The basic principle therefore is that the claimant must make his choice when, but not before, judgment is given in his favour.

(2) The measure of liability: the practice

There are many different circumstances in which the principles just described may be applied. The following are some selective illustrations where the principles are mediated through subsidiary rules:

(i)   Where trustees make an unauthorised investment they are liable for all losses incurred when the investment is realised. This is so even where the sale is ordered by the court and, had the investments been retained, they would have shown a profit for the trust because of a rise in value after the date of the sale ordered by the court (*Knott v Cottee* (1852) 16 Beav 77). Beneficiaries may, if sui juris, validly opt to retain the investment.

(ii) Where trustees improperly retain unauthorised investments they are liable for the difference between the price for which the property could have been sold at the proper time and the actual selling price (see eg *Grayburn v Clarkson* (1868) 3 Ch App 605; and for the difficulties posed where the proper time constitutes a period of time during which price fluctuations occur see *Fales v Canada Permanent Trustee Co* (1976) 70 DLR (3d) 257 at 274; Waters (1977) 55 Can BR 342 at 353–356).

(iii) Where an authorised investment is improperly sold the beneficiaries can require the trustee either to repurchase the investment or to pay the difference between the proceeds of sale and the value of the investment or its equivalent, as calculated at the appropriate time ('appropriate time' post-*Target* must be taken to be the date of the court judgment; see also *Re Bell's Indenture* [1980] 3 All ER 425 and cf the approach in *Jaffray v Marshall* [1993] 1 WLR 1285 specifically overruled in *Target*).

(iv) Where trustees have a discretion to choose from a range of investments (as will usually be the case) but make no investment at all, it is impossible to say which investments might have been chosen and so calculate the loss accordingly. Early authorities indicated that beneficiaries were entitled only to recover the trust fund with interest (*Shepherd v Moulis* (1845) 4 Hare 500). A contemporary view, however, is that the beneficiaries should be entitled to the difference between the actual value of the trust fund and the value which a prudent trustee would be likely to have achieved by reference to the average performance of ordinary shares during the relevant period (*Nestlé v National Westminster Bank plc* [1993] 1 WLR 1260 at 1280 per Staughton LJ). In the New Zealand case of *Re Mulligan* [1998] 1 NZLR 481 a similar approach was adopted although the court allowed only 75% of the increase achieved by an appropriate index of equities. The 25% discount was made to take account of dealing costs and the assumption that the relatively small size of the fund to invest would have made it unlikely that any reasonable trustee would have been able to match the performance of the index.

Many of the specific compensation rules are drawn from nineteenth-century cases and a word of caution is appropriate when considering their application to contemporary investment practice and general economic circumstances (see eg *Re Bell's Indenture* and *Nestlé* (above)). This is most apparent where calculation of 'interest' is necessary. If trustees are required to replace a loss to the trust fund they will also usually be liable to pay interest. The rate historically charged was 4%. But in *Bartlett v Barclays Bank Trust Co Ltd (No 2)* [1980] 2 All ER 92 Brightman J considered it would be unrealistic to abide 'by the modest rate of interest which was current in the stable times of our forefathers' (at 98) and that in the absence of special circumstances, the appropriate rate should be that of the court's short-term investment account which is generally in line with that of the National Savings Bank (see Administration of Justice Act 1965, s 6(1)). 'Special circumstances' can include unauthorised use of trust money for the trustee's own purposes, and here the rate to be charged is currently 1% above the London clearing banks' base rate in force at the time (eg *O'Sullivan v Management Agency and Music Ltd* [1985] QB 428). Ultimately the determination of the appropriate rate is a matter for the discretion of the court, as is the decision whether simple interest or compound interest should be paid. Lastly, it can be argued that the interpretation of the set-off rule in *Bartlett v Barclays Bank Trust Co Ltd* [1980] 1 All ER 139 (discussed in Chapter 10), although not explicitly a consequence of changed investment theory and practice, represents a relaxation of previously applied strict standards.

(3) Breaches of trust and the measure of liability: a case for realignment?

Reference was made earlier to the linguistic ambiguity that surrounds the use of the term equitable compensation. If this were just a matter of inconsistent use of terminology then we should not waste much time or effort discussing it. But more is involved here than a debate about whether or not the language of damages should be substituted for that of equitable compensation. The more fundamental issue is whether there should be a realignment of the rules of equity on money remedies for breach of trust with common law rules on damages.

We noted that in *Target Holdings* Lord Browne-Wilkinson stated that 'the common law rules of remoteness of damage and causation do not apply'. By way of contrast in *Bristol and West Building Society v Mothew* [1998] Ch 1 Millett LJ saw no reason 'why the common law rules of causation, remoteness of damage and measure of damages should not be applied by analogy' in a case where breach of the equitable duty of skill and care was at issue (at 17). These contrasting propositions can be reconciled on the basis that the cases involve different types of breach of trust. Arguably *Target Holdings* was, on our typology, a Type 1 breach for which 'substitutive (equitable) compensation' is the appropriate money remedy whereas *Mothew* was a Type 2 breach, the money remedy for which is 'restorative (equitable) compensation'. In *Mothew*, Millett LJ sought also to emphasise that the existence of the separate categories of equitable compensation and common law damages was the product of history and a 'distinction without a difference' (see also the opinion of Tipping J in *Bank of New Zealand v The New Zealand Guardian Trust Co Ltd* [1999] 1 NZLR 664 at 681).

Underpinning this reasoning, and perhaps even a necessary adjunct to it, was the separation by Millett LJ in *Mothew* of the prescriptive duties of 'due diligence and prudence in management' from the proscriptive duties of loyalty, retaining the more stringent rules and equitable remedies for the latter only. The proposition then is that a remedy for breach of the prescriptive duties should be found, in effect, in the common law rules on negligence. Should we then infer that there is no reason for having the rules on causation and remoteness in equitable negligence claims pitched at a standard more generous to beneficiaries than those for claimants at common law alleging breach of a tortious duty of care? Strong support for this position is to be found in Hayton's contribution to Birks and Pretto (eds) *Breach of Trust* (2002) at p 387 (see also Hayton in *Degeling and Edelman* ch 11):

> While the nature of the fundamental trustee-beneficiary obligation requires strict liability if the trustee acts beyond the powers possessed *qua* trustee or breaches proscriptive fiduciary duties, it is the negligent failure to act as a prudent trustee should have done that is now regarded as the crucial dimension, the trustee-beneficiary relationship being regarded only as an incidental factor. Thus why should negligent trustees be treated any differently from negligent lawyers, accountants or doctors?

Notwithstanding the rhetorical nature of the question posed by Hayton there are other voices that doubt both the appropriateness of severing the equitable duty of care from the category of fiduciary duties as propounded in *Mothew* and the proposed assimilation of the common law and equitable rules on breach of duty of care (see eg Getzler in *Birks and Pretto* ch 2; and both Justice Heydon and Getzler in *Degeling and Edelman* chs 9 and 10 respectively).

However, whilst historical accident may not of itself provide a good reason to *retain* a separate set of rules for remedies more favourable to beneficiaries, this does not mean that assimilation of the equitable and common law rules should necessarily be assumed to be appropriate either. What is involved here is in some degree the working-out of a process of 'fusion' or, as we referred to it in Chapter 2, 'harmonisation' although pragmatic considerations are equally evident. A particular problem in the last decade or so is that the possibilities offered by stricter standards of liability for breach of fiduciary duties has encouraged attempts to impose liability for 'negligent' wrongdoing on professionals where common law tortious liability might not 'do the trick' (see eg *Henderson v Merrett Syndicates Ltd* [1995] 2 AC 145; and the analysis by Getzler in Birks and Rose (eds) *Restitution and Equity: Volume 1 Resulting Trusts and Equitable*

Compensation (2000) ch 13; and generally on the leading House of Lords cases, Robertson, *Judicial Discretion in the House of Lords* (1998) pp 187–234). If successful such attempts would tend to undermine not just tort law but also the assumptions of the parties about allocation of business risks based on the law. Getzler argues that a judicial response to this trend has been to 'develop techniques to strangle any emergent concurrent liability or overlap between equitable and common-law compensatory regimes' (above at p 253). Thus in *Henderson v Merrett Syndicates Ltd (No 1)* [1995] 2 AC 145 we find Lord Browne-Wilkinson stating as 'misconceived' a proposition that the defendants were under a fiduciary duty to conduct an insurance underwriting business with reasonable skill equivalent to a duty of care in tort (at 205; but cf the critical comments of Heydon in (1995) 111 LQR 1–8):

> The liability of a fiduciary for the negligent transaction of his duties is not a separate head of liability but the paradigm of the general duty to act with care imposed by law on those who take it upon themselves to act for or advise others. Although the historical development of the rules of law and equity have, in the past, caused different labels to be stuck on different manifestations of the duty, in truth the duty of care imposed on bailees, carriers, trustees, directors, agents and others is the same duty: it arises from the circumstances in which the defendants were acting, not from their status or description. It is the fact that they have all assumed responsibility for the property or affairs of others which renders them liable for the careless performance of what they have undertaken to do, not the description of the trade or position which they hold.

As we have seen, the proposition then is that a remedy for breach of the prescriptive duties by a trustee or other fiduciaries should be found, in effect, in the common law rules on negligence. Consider, however, the reservations expressed by McLachlin J in *Canson Enterprises Ltd v Broughton & Co* (1991) 85 DLR (4th) 129, disagreeing with the approach adopted by the majority of her colleagues (at 154):

> My first concern with proceeding by analogy with tort is that it overlooks the unique foundation and goals of equity. The basis of the fiduciary obligation and the rationale for equitable compensation are distinct from the tort of negligence and contract. In negligence and contract the parties are taken to be independent and equal actors, concerned primarily with their own self-interest. Consequently the law seeks a balance between enforcing obligations by awarding compensation and preserving optimum freedom for those involved in the relationship in question, communal or otherwise. The essence of a fiduciary relationship, by contrast, is that one party pledges herself to act in the best interest of the other. The fiduciary relationship has trust, not self-interest, at its core, and when breach occurs, the balance favours the person wronged. The freedom of the fiduciary is diminished by the nature of the obligation he or she has undertaken – an obligation which 'betokens loyalty, good faith and avoidance of a conflict of duty and self-interest'. In short, equity is concerned, not only to compensate the plaintiff, but also to enforce the trust which is at its heart.

Two brief points, one specific and the other in the nature of a more general observation, can be made with reference to the reservations expressed by McLachlin J. First, her comments are directed towards the 'proscriptive duties' and so do not of themselves, with one exception, undercut the proposition advanced in *Mothew* and obiter by Lord Browne-Wilkinson in *Henderson v Merrett Syndicates* and echoed by Hayton concerning liability of the fiduciary for negligence – 'the trustee–beneficiary relationship being regarded as only an incidental factor'. Second, the one exception and the specific point referred to above concerns contributory negligence. Here it may be necessary to draw upon the distinction between the bare trust and the traditional trust as portrayed by Lord Browne-Wilkinson in *Target Holdings*. As regards bare trusts, if one is persuaded by the proposition that in cases of negligence the label attached to the particular relationship is immaterial it would seem consistent to allow for the possibility of offsetting the liability of a trustee or other fiduciary where the conduct of the beneficiary may have contributed to the loss. On the other hand, for trusts of the traditional type trusts law already provides its own protection for trustees where beneficiaries instigate or acquiesce in some breach of trust, such as persuading trustees to invest in a hazardous project such as that in *Bartlett v Barclays Bank Trust Co Ltd* [1980] 1 All ER 139 (see section (e)(2) below on consent by beneficiaries). Whilst life is fully capable of throwing up factual situations beyond the imagination of textbook writers it is nevertheless difficult to see any appropriate role for contributory negligence being applicable to beneficiaries in the traditional trust where the trustees have brought about a loss through failure to act in a prudent manner.

But negligent failure to act as a prudent trustee or other fiduciary is the easy case! It is the proscriptive duties that present the difficulty. Should it be possible to hold a beneficiary partly liable for loss where the loss would not have occurred but for some breach by the fiduciary of those duties 'of loyalty, good faith and avoidance of conflict of interest'? The more straightforward case is where the breach involves dishonesty or is in some other way the equivalent of fraud. In those circumstances, 'the fiduciary is disabled from asserting that the other contributed, by his own want of care for his own interests, to the loss' (*Nationwide Building Society v Various Solicitors (No 3)* [1999] Lloyd's Rep PN 606 at 677, but cf *Collins v Brebner* [2000] Lloyd's Rep PN 587). The same can be said where the breach, although not fraudulent, is consciously disloyal, although as was recognised by Blackburn J in *Nationwide Building Society* the subject is 'highly contentious' (see amongst the competing references cited by the judge Davies 'Equitable Compensation: "Causation, Foreseeability and Remoteness"' in Waters (ed) *Equity, Fiduciaries and Trusts* (1993) pp 297–324; and cf Gummow J 'Equitable Damages for Breach of Fiduciary Duty' in Youdan (ed) *Equity, Fiduciaries and Trusts* (1989) pp 57–91; see also Rickett 'Compensating for Loss in Equity' in Birks and Rose (eds) *Restitution and Equity Volume 1: Resulting Trusts and Equitable Compensation* (2000) pp 173–191). Blackburn J was, however, of the opinion that in the latter type of case – conscious disloyalty not amounting to fraud or dishonesty – the conduct of the person to whom the fiduciary duty is owed can be relevant on the remoteness question, namely in determining whether the loss is too remote from the breach of duty. But the appropriateness of applying remoteness criteria to cases of conscious disloyalty also remains contentious. It does appear that the courts are looking for guidance to the criteria applicable to claims under the tort of deceit for recovery for losses. This is understandable in view of the type of policy considerations identified by Lord Steyn in *Smith New Court Securities Ltd v Citibank NA* [1997] AC 254 as being applicable to cases where deceit is alleged (at 279–280, emphasis added):

> [A] policy of imposing more stringent remedies on an intentional wrongdoer serves two purposes. First it serves a deterrent purpose in discouraging fraud. . . . Secondly, as between the fraudster and the innocent party, moral considerations militate in favour of requiring the fraudster to bear the risk of misfortunes *directly* caused by his fraud.

The analogy with policy considerations pertaining to intentional breaches of the fiduciary duty of loyalty is evident. This leads Elliott, for instance, to suggest that the concerns raised by fiduciary disloyalty are sufficiently similar to justify an approach whereby in claims for compensation for loss 'unforeseeable losses should be recoverable so long as they are the direct result of the breach' ((2002) 65 MLR 588 at 597). The normative aspect of the proposition stands in direct contrast to the more restrictive view expressed in *Lewin on Trusts* on the relevance of foreseeability considerations at all to breaches of duty such as those under consideration here (see above, p 574). One might harbour the suspicion that even if questions of remoteness were to be formally excluded from calculations of loss, they might in practice creep in through the back door, perhaps by applying the 'hindsight and common-sense' approach to causation suggested by Lord Browne-Wilkinson in *Target* (see above, p 577).

The 'highly contentious' nature of subjects such as foreseeability leads us to the more general point that is raised by the opinion of McLachlin J in *Canson Enterprises Ltd v Broughton & Co* (1991) 85 DLR (4th) 129. She has a number of practical objections to the appropriateness of drawing analogies with compensation under tort law, whilst accepting comparison may on occasion be fruitful: 'I readily concede that we may take wisdom where we find it, and accept such insights offered by the law of tort, in particular deceit, as may prove useful' (at 154). The more fundamental objection goes to what are seen as the different objectives pursued by tort law and fiduciary law. At its simplest we might say that tort law requires us not to harm others whilst fiduciary law requires us to act for the benefit of others. Of course matters are more complex than this on both sides of the equation.

But the very fact that they are more complex is, we would suggest, a reason for caution in the analogies that we might draw with tort law. After all it is not as if the functions of tort law are themselves beyond controversy (see eg Cane *The Anatomy of Tort Law* (1997)). Indeed in a tantalising conclusion Cane suggests that 'we should cease to think of tort law as a category with juridical significance. Rather we should analyse private law causes of action in terms of protected interests, sanctioned conduct, and sanctions' (p 238). This looks like a path leading us back towards the 'fusion debate' and even a reconsideration of the categories of private law. The modest even trite conclusion to be drawn here therefore is simply that careful consideration of the objectives of particular rules and doctrines of tort law and of the function they perform is advisable if with McLachlin 'we are to find wisdom' there.

(d) Liability of trustees: personal or collective?

The fact that co-trusteeship is common and that the different trustees may have varying levels of expertise poses a compelling question: 'Who is personally liable and for what?' In the present context 'personally liable' refers to equity's long-established recognition (*Townley v Sherborn* (1634) J Bridg 35) that a trustee is liable only for his own breaches of trust, not for those of co-trustees. But too much reliance cannot be placed on this limitation since a trustee may in some respects find himself at fault, even where a co-trustee causes the breach of trust. The circumstances are conventionally categorised as: (1) leaving a matter in the hands of a co-trustee without inquiry; (2) doing nothing whilst a breach of trust of which he is aware is being committed; (3) allowing trust funds to remain in the sole control of a co-trustee; (4) failing to take steps to obtain redress on becoming aware of a breach of trust committed or contemplated by a co-trustee. When to this is added the rule of equity that trustees (other than trustees of a charitable trust) must act unanimously in the exercise of their powers it is apparent that the notion of a 'sleeping trustee' receives short shrift in trusts law (see Bogert (1920–21) 34 Harv LR 483 at 501–507 for a classic discussion of principle; and for a contemporary illustration in the context of a co-director of a corporate trustee see *Bishopsgate Investment Management Ltd v Maxwell (No 2)* [1994] 1 All ER 261).

Until recently this liability in relation to the acts of co-trustees was modified by the statutory indemnity clause (Trustee Act 1925, s 30(1)). That section stated that a trustee (A) would be liable only for his own acts, neglects and defaults, and not for loss caused by those of a co-trustee, 'unless the same happens through his own (A's) wilful default'. It is debatable how far, if at all, the statutory indemnity clause widened the protection afforded to passive trustees (but see *Dalrymple v Melville* (1932) 32 SRNSW 596 applying the NSW equivalent of s 30(1)). In any event s 30(1) was repealed by the Trustee Act 2000 with the effect that a passive trustee may now be liable if he or she fails to act in accordance with the duty of care (see generally Chapter 10 on the duty of care). The illustrations in the previous paragraph of circumstances where liability may be imposed could all be categorised as a failure to satisfy the duty of care.

There are a few rare instances where a trustee is entitled to an indemnity from a co-trustee against his own liability, as where one trustee with special qualifications, for example, a solicitor, exercises a controlling influence on the other (see eg *Re Partington* (1887) 57 LT 654). On the other hand, it was held in *Head v Gould* [1898] 2 Ch 250 that there was no right to an indemnity from a solicitor where 'the co-trustee was an active participator in the breach of trust complained of, and is not proved to have participated merely in consequence of the advice and control of the solicitor' (at 265 per Kekewich J; see also *Re Mulligan* [1998] 1 NZLR 481 where the lay trustee and life-tenant, Mrs Mulligan, was refused an indemnity from her co-trustee, a corporate trustee, in circumstances where she was herself a person of some business acumen who disregarded the advice of her co-trustee to diversify the trust's investments, choosing instead investments to benefit her life-interest to the detriment of the remainder beneficiaries). Another instance when indemnity may arise is where a trustee is also a beneficiary and has benefited by the breach of trust. In those circumstances the beneficiary is liable to indemnify co-trustees up to the extent of 'his interest in the trust fund, and not merely to the extent of the benefit which he has received' (*Chillingworth v Chambers* [1896] 1 Ch 685 at 707 per Kay J; see generally the comprehensive discussion by Mitchell 'Apportioning Liability for Trust Losses' in Birks and Rose (eds) *Restitution and Equity Volume 1: Resulting Trusts and Equitable Compensation* (2000) ch 12).

Where more than one trustee is liable for a breach of trust, liability is joint and several, ie the beneficiary can claim the complete loss from any one trustee separately or from all or several of them jointly. As this option could operate harshly against such trustees as have the personal assets to satisfy the beneficiaries' claim, equity developed a rule that as between themselves trustees were equally responsible. Therefore a trustee compelled to pay more than an equal share of the loss was entitled to equal contribution from other trustees (see eg *Bahin v Hughes* (1886) 31 Ch D 390). The Civil Liability (Contribution) Act 1978 which applies, inter alia, to trustees (s 6(1)) has superseded the equitable rule and gives the court the broadest discretion to fix the level of contribution at 'such [amount] as may be ... just and equitable' (s 2(1)), even to the extent of a complete indemnity (s 2(2)). The general tendency, prior to the 1978 Act, was to avoid trustees being treated unequally not least because the sanction of equal liability could act as a warning against any temptation to be a 'sleeping trustee'. It is, though, questionable whether 'an equality of misery' approach should apply where lay trustees reasonably place reliance on professional trustees.

(e) Relief of trustees

(1) Limitations on scope of liability: introduction

The most secure policy for trustees is to avoid liability arising in the first place. Therefore a feature of considerable practical importance for trustees who are uncertain how to act or cannot agree, is the advisory and directive functions of the court. They can seek directions from the court regarding, for instance, the scope or interpretation of a discretion conferred on them or even on their proposed exercise of the discretion (RSC 1998, Civil Procedure Rules, Sch 1, Ord 85, r 2) 'and so be relieved of the agony of decision and the responsibility for the result' (Megarry (1966) 82 LQR 306). It should be noted, however, that there is a difference of approach between those cases where the trustees seek the court's approval of a proposed *exercise* by the trustees of their discretion and those where the trustees wish to *surrender* their discretion to the court. In *RSPCA v Attorney General* [2002] 1 WLR 448 Lightman J summarised the difference as follows (at 462):

> In cases where there is a surrender, the court starts with a clean sheet and has an unfettered discretion to decide what it considers should be done in the best interests of the trust. In cases where there is no surrender, the primary focus of the court's attention must be on the views of the trustees and the exercise of the discretion proposed by the trustees. Though not fettered by those views, the court is bound to lend weight to them unless tested and found wanting and it will not, without good reason, substitute its own view for those of the trustees.

It should be noted, however, that the court will be reluctant to accept a surrender of the exercise of the discretion unless there is a good reason. The most obvious good reasons are those either where 'the trustees are deadlocked (but honestly deadlocked, so that the question cannot be resolved by removing one trustee rather than another) or because the trustees are disabled as a result of a conflict of interest' (per Hart J in *Public Trustee v Cooper* [2001] WTLR 901, citing an unreported opinion of Walker J given in chambers). Moreover the court will not accept a general surrender of trustees' continuing discretion in future matters (*Re Allen-Meyrick's Will Trusts* [1966] 1 WLR 499).

Even where trustees fail to seek prospective protection for their actions, there are other grounds on which a trustee may be relieved from liability. First, the trust instrument may by its specific terms modify the trustees' duties (see eg *Hayim v Citibank NA* [1987] AC 730 at 744; and Hayton in Oakley (ed) *Trends in Contemporary Trust Law* (1996) 47 at 54–55). 'Duty modification' clauses in trust deeds can be appropriate in various circumstances such as, for instance, where a settlor wishes shares in a family company to be retained and incorporates a clause excluding the 'duty to diversify the trust investments'. There may also be a clause relieving trustees from liability for loss unless caused eg as a result of individual fraud. Beyond that the beneficiaries may have agreed to or concurred in a breach of trust. Finally the court may be prepared to relieve a trustee from liability under the discretion provided in TA 1925, s 61.

(2) Relief and the acts of beneficiaries

During argument in *Perrins v Bellamy* (1899) 1 Ch 797 Lindley MR commented that 'My old master the late Lord Justice Selwyn, used to say, "the main duty of a trustee is to commit *judicious* breaches of trust'" (at p 798; Lord Lindley subsequently modified 'main duty' to 'great use' in *National Trustees Co of Australasia v General Finance Co* [1905] AC 373 at 375; see also Lord Browne-Wilkinson in *Target Holdings Ltd v Redferns (a firm)* [1996] AC 421 at 433: 'say, as often occurs, a trustee commits a judicious breach of trust . . .'). Implicit in these statements is recognition that a particular course of action technically involving a breach of trust, far from invoking a challenge from beneficiaries, may be acquiesced in or welcomed by them. Indeed they may even have instigated the act. It is just not known how common agreed breaches of trust have been, although there is some evidence of their occurrence in the area of investment. Revell's 'balance sheet' of personal trusts in 1961 (see Revell *The Wealth of the Nation* (1967) p 139 (Table 6.2)) indicated that, a bare six months after the Trustee Investments Act 1961 significantly widened the range of authorised investments, about 85 per cent of the value of the trust assets surveyed by Revell were represented by assets not previously authorised. It is improbable that this figure was the result of a headlong rush to invoke the 1961 Act; rather, as Revell suggests (at p 135), it is to be explained by the presence of prior wider investment authority either in the original trust deed or – the important point for present purposes – obtained by agreement of the beneficiaries.

These practical realities have long been recognised by the courts. Consequently a sui juris beneficiary who consents to or acquiesces in a breach of trust will not subsequently be able to succeed in an action against trustees in respect of the breach (see Payne 'Consent' in Birks and Pretto (eds) *Breach of Trust* (2002) ch 10). Whether consent or acquiescence exists is a factual question but the two key elements are: the trustee must establish (1) that the beneficiary was fully informed of all the relevant facts, and (2) that the beneficiary was exercising independent judgment. As regards the second element – freedom from 'undue influence' – the Court of Appeal in *Re Pauling's Settlement Trusts* [1963] 3 All ER 1 considered that a trustee may be liable only 'if he knew, or ought to have known, that the beneficiary was acting under the undue influence of another, or may be presumed to have done so' (at 11). *Re Pauling*, the facts of which make rewarding reading for students and trustees alike, is a salutary warning of the perils of acting on the formal assumption that beneficiaries once over 18 are necessarily free from parental influence.

As regards the knowledge requirement, where trustees know that what they propose is unauthorised, the beneficiaries must be informed of this fact or the defence will not be available. But not all breaches of trust are deliberate. Therefore where trustees do not appreciate that the proposed act is unauthorised, it is not a prerequisite to the defence that the beneficiary must know that he is consenting to a breach of trust. *Holder v Holder* [1968] 1 All ER 665 illustrates this. There, an attempt was made to set aside a sale on the grounds that the defendant purchaser (D) was disqualified from bidding. D argued, inter alia, that the plaintiff (P) had acquiesced by affirming the sale, accepting his share of the purchase money and allowing D further to increase his financial liability to complete the purchase. Only subsequently had P discovered that the sale might have been in breach of trust, but the court nevertheless considered that P had consented to the sale. The Court of Appeal (at 673) approved Wilberforce J's statement in *Re Pauling's Settlement* [1961] 3 All ER 713 at 730 as representing the proper approach for the court:

> The result of these authorities appears to me to be that the court has to consider all the circumstances in which the concurrence of the cestui que trust was given with a view to seeing whether it is fair and equitable that, having given his concurrence, he should afterwards turn round and sue the trustees: that, subject to this, it is not necessary that he should know that what he is concurring in is a breach of trust, provided that he fully understands what he is concurring in, and that it is not necessary that he should himself have directly benefited by the breach of trust.

The consent of one or more beneficiaries to a breach of trust will not affect the rights of those who have not consented. The trustees are therefore still liable to be sued but may be able to offset their personal liability. Under its inherent jurisdiction the court could order the trustee to be indemnified out of the interest of any beneficiary who 'instigated', 'requested' or 'concurred' in a breach of trust, provided that, if the beneficiary had merely concurred, the trustees' right only applied if a personal benefit had accrued to the beneficiary from the breach of trust. A formally more extensive statutory jurisdiction was provided by statute (Trustee Act 1888, s 6). It now appears in Trustee Act 1925, s 62(1):

> (1) Where a trustee commits a breach of trust at the instigation or request or with the consent in writing of a beneficiary, the court may, if it thinks fit, make such order as to the court seems just, for impounding all or any part of the interest of the beneficiary in the trust estate by way of indemnity to the trustee or persons claiming through him.

The section does not mention motive or benefit although they are factors that a court would probably take account of in exercising the discretion. It is not necessary under s 62(1) for the trustee to show that the beneficiary knew that what he was 'instigating', 'requesting' or 'consenting to' was a breach of trust, but merely that the beneficiary had full knowledge of the facts (see generally *Re Somerset* [1894] 1 Ch 231).

(3) Relief and the acts of settlors: exemption clauses

As mentioned previously, it is possible to include in a trust instrument a 'duty modification' clause negating a duty so that no liability for breach of that duty can arise (*Hayim v Citibank NA* [1987] AC 730). A further step is to exempt or exonerate trustees from liability should a breach of trust occur. Clauses such as the one below are in widespread use, particularly where professional trustees are appointed (see *Butterworth's Encyclopaedia of Forms and Precedents* (2007) vol 40(1), Part 5, para 225):

> No trustee shall be liable for any loss or damage which may happen to the Trust Fund or any part thereof or the income thereof at any time or from any cause whatsoever unless such loss or damage shall be caused by his own actual fraud.

If exemption clauses in this extreme form are valid, the protection afforded to beneficiaries by trusts law will be sharply reduced. But are they always valid to their full extent? Prior to the Court of Appeal decision in *Armitage v Nurse* [1997] 2 All ER 705 it could be argued on the basis of some tenuous authority that such a clause would not be effective to exempt a trustee from liability for gross negligence. (See *Wilkins v Hogg* (1861) 31 LJ Ch 41 (concerning exclusion of duty rather than exemption from liability); *Rae v Meek* (1889) 14 App Cas 558 (a Scottish case); *Boe v Alexander* (1987) 41 DLR (4th) 520 at 527; and see generally Matthews [1989] Conv 42.)

But in *Armitage v Nurse* [1997] 2 All ER 705 a clause almost identical to the one quoted above was upheld as valid (see McBride [1998] CLJ 33; McCormack [1998] Conv 100; Nobles (1996) 10(3) TLI 66). On behalf of the claimant beneficiary it was argued that 'fraud' included 'equitable fraud', in other words any breach of duty which would attract the sanction of equity. This contention was rejected by the Court of Appeal, fraud being construed as excluding equitable and constructive fraud and instead simply connoting dishonesty. In its turn dishonesty was then defined in the following terms (at 711): 'If [a trustee] acts in a way which he does not honestly believe is in [the beneficiaries'] interests then he is acting dishonestly . . . and is not the less dishonest because he does not intend to benefit himself.' If clarification were needed Millett LJ seemed to put the position beyond doubt when he added with blunt frankness (at 711): 'In my judgment Clause 15 exempts the trustee from liability for loss or damage to the trust property no matter how indolent, imprudent, lacking in diligence, negligent or wilful he may have been, so long as he has not acted dishonestly.' The only saving grace for a disgruntled beneficiary was that Millett LJ accepted that fraud could include the situation where trustees pursued a course of action 'being recklessly indifferent whether it was contrary to the [beneficiaries'] interests or not'.

Subsequently the Court of Appeal added a gloss to the definition of dishonesty in *Walker v Stones* [2000] 4 All ER 412 where the trust instrument contained a clause purporting to exempt, in this case, a solicitor-trustee from liability for loss unless caused by 'wilful fraud or dishonesty'. Sir Christopher Slade held that the clause would not exempt the trustees from liability for breaches of trust 'even if committed in the genuine belief that the course taken by them was in the interests of the beneficiaries, if such belief was so unreasonable that no reasonable solicitor-trustee could have held that belief' (at 446; and see also the discussion of 'dishonesty' in the context of 'dishonest assistance' in Chapter 14 at p 758).

It was argued in *Armitage v Nurse* that a clause such as that at issue in the case was void either on grounds of repugnancy or as being contrary to public policy.

Both propositions were rejected by the court. On repugnancy Millett LJ, whilst conceding that there is an irreducible core of obligation owed by trustees to the beneficiaries and enforceable by them which is fundamental to the concept of a trust, did not agree that 'these core obligations include the duties of skill and care, prudence and diligence' (at 713). On the contrary, he concluded that the core obligation was limited to a duty 'to perform the trusts honestly and in good faith for the benefit of the beneficiaries' adding that that duty 'is the minimum necessary to give substance to the trusts, but in my opinion it is sufficient (at 713). The dichotomy seems almost too straightforward. Can we say that a trustee is acting 'in good faith' if he exhibits no care at all in the administration of the trust? It must therefore be emphasised that Millett LJ's observations on the content of 'irreducible core of obligation' are dicta with which not everyone would necessarily concur. (See generally on this issue Hayton in Oakley (ed) *Trends in Contemporary Trust Law* (1996) ch 3; and more specifically Penner 'Exemptions' in Birks and Pretto (eds) *Breach of Trust* (2002) ch 8 for a thought-provoking and provocative critique of the law on exemption clauses located within a conceptual analysis drawing on contrasting – some might argue complementary – 'obligational' and 'proprietary' aspects of the trust.) As regards the public policy point neither the judge nor, come to that, counsel could find any authority – including, inter alia, the cases cited above – supporting the proposition. It only remains to add on matters of interpretation that *Armitage v Nurse* does not alter the position that clauses need to be clear and unambiguous if they are to be successful (see eg *Wight v Olswang (No 2)* (1999/2000) 2 ITELR 684).

Assuming clauses such as that in *Armitage v Nurse* to be both enforceable and prevalent where professional trustees are appointed, their de facto effect is to lower the standard required from the professional to a point below that of the amateur trustee. In *Armitage v Nurse* Millett LJ acknowledged that there was a view that 'these clauses have gone too far' but saw reform, if it was desirable, as a matter for 'Parliament which will have the advantage of wide consultation with interested bodies . . .' (at 715). The statutory route has been followed in, for instance, Jersey and, to a limited extent, in pensions and company and financial services legislation here (Trusts (Jersey) Law 1984, art 26(9); Pensions Act 1995, s 33; Companies Act 2006, s 780(1) (trustees of debentures); and Financial Services and Markets Act 2000, s 253 (unit trust schemes) respectively).

In response to concerns raised in the House of Lords during the passage of the Trustee Act 2000 about the omission of any provision on exclusion clauses in the legislation, the Lord Chancellor agreed to refer the matter formally to the Law Commission (see *Hansard* (HL) 14 April 2000, vol 612, col 383). This was done in 2001 and the Law Commission published a Consultation Paper in 2003 followed by the Final Report in 2006 (Law Commission Report No 301 Trustee Exemption Clauses (Cm 6874); Reed [2007] PCB 3, 196). In the Consultation Paper the Law Commission rejected any absolute prohibition on all trustee exemption clauses but did make several provisional proposals for a statutory framework, in particular that professional trustees should not be able to rely on clauses which exclude their liability for breach of trust arising from negligence (see for comment on the Consultation Paper, Morris [2003] PCB 3 at 188–198; Groves and Hingham [2003] PCB 6 at 404–413).

Whilst the Commission accepted the proposition that there was a strong case for some regulation of trustee exemption clauses as a counter to 'unfair outcomes' it also recognised that an insistence by professional trustees on the inclusion of a clause similar to that on p 593 could represent a rational economic calculation on the degree of risk to be undertaken in a particular transaction. If the scope of exemption clauses were to be statutorily restricted, trustees might then respond to changes in the level of possible liability in various ways: increasing fees to compensate for the larger risk or the increased cost of insurance protection; behaving more cautiously, for example, by investing in secure investments only, perhaps leading to lower returns for beneficiaries; transfer of trusts to jurisdictions where no or fewer restrictions are placed on the use of exemption clauses or even withdrawing from trust business altogether. It could not therefore be assumed that an increase in the formal level of liability of trustees would necessarily be in the best interests of beneficiaries in general (see the Law Commission Report, Part 5; see also Revell and Lovering *Exempt Settled Property* RCDIW Research Paper no 3 (1979) pp 10–11 for a previous negative reaction by clearing banks to increases in operating costs of trust business). Moreover, a potential practical difficulty that came to the fore during the consultation process was that of avoidance of, or perhaps more aptly 'creative compliance' with, legislation through the use of 'duty modification' and 'expanded powers' clauses. The Report summarised the difficulty as follows (para 5.47):

> Narrow definitions of duty and wide definitions of powers both therefore have the potential to make it considerably more difficult for a beneficiary to establish that a trustee has committed a breach of trust (whether by breach of duty, or by acting *ultra vires*). Clauses of this kind can therefore be employed by trustees in an attempt to undermine regulation of clauses expressly excluding liability.

The outcome of the extensive consultation process (see Law Commission Report, Part 1 and Appendices F and H) was a conclusion that there were significant disadvantages associated with any comprehensive legislation. The Commission opted instead for a 'practice-based approach' intended to bring about reform of the conduct of trustees by emphasising the obligation to make full disclosure to settlors. The adoption by regulatory bodies such as the Law Society and STEP (Society of Trust and Estate Practitioners) of a 'rule of practice' incorporating the following elements was therefore recommended (para 1.22; and Appendix G for the STEP rule of practice):

> Any paid trustee who causes a settlor to include a clause in a trust instrument which has the effect of excluding or limiting liability for negligence must before the creation of the trust take such steps as are reasonable to ensure that the settlor is aware of the meaning and effect of the clause.

It is not the intention that such a rule should apply where statutory regulation is already in place (see above, p 594) nor, in general, to commercial trusts where settlors and trustees are both acting in the course of a business. And the sanction for failing to comply where a 'rule of practice' is applicable? Subject to any subsequent modification of the position set out in the judgment of Millett LJ in *Armitage v Nurse*, breach of the 'rule of practice' would not give rise in itself to liability in damages but would render the trustee open to disciplinary measures by the relevant governing body such as the Law Society in the case of solicitors.

Consider the following points:

(1) There is no evidence of any judicial support for the proposition, occasionally advanced, that the arrangement between settlor and trustee can be analysed in contractual terms and that therefore exemption clauses could be subjected to the reasonableness test in the Unfair Contract Terms Act 1977 (see eg *Baker v J E Clark & Co (Transport) UK Ltd* [2006] EWCA Civ 464 (CA) per Tuckey LJ paras 18–22; and for rejection of an 'artificial contractual analysis' *Re Duke of Norfolk's Settlement Trusts* [1982] Ch 61 at 76).

(2) The view of Millett LJ in *Armitage v Nurse*, expressed obiter, that the 'irreducible core of obligation' necessary for a trust to exist does not extend to include a duty of skill and care has its critics (see eg Heydon in Degeling and Edelman (eds) *Equity in Commercial Law* (2005) ch 9). At first glance it would seem a strange proposition to suggest that such a duty could be excluded altogether so that trustees could deal with trust property as carelessly as they thought fit. Of course, as we have seen, trustees can be exonerated for negligent breach of that duty but that is a different proposition from stating that the duty itself can be excluded. A countervailing proposition is that it is for settlors to decide what managerial obligations they wish to impose on trustees. Indeed, in this regard para 7 of Sch 1 to the Trustee Act 2000 states: 'The duty of care does not apply if or in so far as it appears from the trust instrument that the duty is not meant to apply.' Moreover, in some commercial contexts the combination of the trust form with contractual arrangements can lead to outcomes where the obligations of trusteeship are significantly circumscribed by the predominant contractual provisions (see eg *Citibank NA v MBIA Assurance SA* [2006] EWHC 3215 (Ch); Trukhtanov (2007) 123 LQR 342).

(3) 'It is a bold submission that a clause taken from one standard precedent book and to the same effect as a clause found in another, included in a settlement drawn by Chancery counsel acting for an infant settlor and approved by the court on her behalf, should be so repugnant or contrary to public policy that it is liable to be set aside at her suit' (per Millett LJ

in *Armitage v Nurse* [1997] 2 All ER 705 at 713). How important should current drafting practices be as a guide to decision-making by the courts?

(4) Trustee responsibility and the role of the court

Whether or not there is any exemption clause, the court has a statutory discretion (originating in the Judicial Trustees Act 1896, s 3) retrospectively to relieve a trustee from personal liability for breach of trust.

Trustee Act 1925, s 61

> 61. If it appears to the court that a trustee . . . is or may be personally liable for any breach of trust . . . but has acted honestly and reasonably, and ought fairly to be excused for the breach of trust and for omitting to obtain the directions of the court in the matter in which he committed such breach, then the court may relieve him either wholly or partly from personal liability for the same.

The key to this ample discretion lies in the trilogy of 'honesty', 'reasonableness' and 'fairness'. The most thorough discussion of the relationship between these criteria is still to be found in *Perrins v Bellamy*, although of course in respect of s 3 of the 1896 Act.

Perrins v Bellamy [1898] 2 Ch 521 (Kekewich J); affd [1899] 1 Ch 797

A solicitor incorrectly informed trustees that they had a power of sale over certain trust property. On receipt of advice from a surveyor that it was undesirable to keep the properties, they sold them and thus committed a breach of trust. The beneficiaries claimed that the trustees should not be relieved, as they had failed to seek the directions of the court.

> **Kekewich J:** The Legislature has made the absence of all dishonesty a condition precedent to the relief of the trustee from liability. But that is not the grit of the section. The grit is in the words 'reasonably, and ought fairly to be excused for the breach of trust'. . . . I venture . . . to think that, in general and in the absence of special circumstances, a trustee who has acted 'reasonably' ought to be relieved, and that it is not incumbent on the court to consider whether he ought 'fairly' to be excused, unless there is evidence of a special character shewing that the provisions of the section ought not to be applied in his favour. . . . The question, and the only question, is whether they acted 'reasonably'. In saying that, I am not unmindful of the words of the section which follow, and which require that it should be shewn that the trustee ought 'fairly' to be excused, not only 'for the breach of trust' but also 'for omitting to obtain the directions of the court in the matter in which he committed such breach'. I find it difficult to follow that. I do not see how the trustee can be excused for the breach of trust without being also excused for the omission referred to, or how he can be excused for the omission without also being excused for the breach of trust. If I am at liberty to guess, I should suppose that these words were added by way of amendment, and crept into the statute without due regard being had to the meaning of the context.

Although s 61 and its predecessor have since its inception spawned considerable litigation, most commonly in connection with unauthorised investments and the 'reasonableness' of relief (unsuccessfully pleaded in *Bartlett v Barclays Bank Trust Co Ltd* [1980] 1 All ER 139), a number of judges have observed that each case must depend on its own circumstances (see eg Byrne J in *Re Turner* [1897] 1 Ch 536 at 542). General guidelines are therefore elusive although losses arising from technical breaches of trust, as with the mistake of law in *Perrins v Bellamy*, are likely to be viewed sympathetically (see Sheridan (1955) 19 Conv 420 for a critical discussion of the cases). Reliance on professional advice, such as that of a solicitor, will be a material factor (*Re Allsop* [1914] 1 Ch 1). Relief will not be automatic even then, however, and the standing of the adviser in relation to the value of the trust fund will be a relevant consideration (see *Marsden v Regan* [1954] 1 All ER 475 at 482, per Evershed MR). Indeed reliance on legal advice can be a double-edged sword since the court may refuse to excuse a trustee who has failed to sue the adviser to recover the loss (see eg *National Trustees Co of Australasia v General Finance Co* [1905] AC 373 at 381–382). Beneficiaries themselves may, however, sue the adviser on behalf of the trust if the trustees unreasonably refuse to sue (*Parker-Tweedale v Dunbar Bank plc* [1991] Ch 12 but cf *Bradstock Trustee Services Ltd v Nabarro Nathanson* [1995] 1 WLR 1405 and see generally McCormack (1997) 11(3) TLI 60).

Providing guidance on the interpretation of s 61 is not assisted by the fact that only on rare occasions is it pleaded nowadays. The most recent case *Re Evans (dec'd)* [1999] 2 All ER 777 if anything simply confirms the discretionary nature of the relief. The defendant trustee was an unpaid lay person who had administered the modest estate of her father who had died intestate. The estate was to be held on the statutory trusts for herself and her brother in equal shares. In fact she had not heard from her brother for over thirty years and assumed he was dead. On legal advice she took out a 'missing beneficiary' insurance policy to cover approximately the value of half the capital assets of the estate and then distributed the entire estate in favour of herself. As in all the best mystery plots some four years later the missing brother reappeared to claim his share of the estate. He received the benefit of the insurance policy but sued for breach of trust partly on the basis that the policy was inadequate in not providing for the accrual of interest for the period after he had become entitled to his share. The defendant was held liable to account for the interest but was granted partial relief under s 61. As with earlier authorities account was taken of all the circumstances surrounding the technical breach of trust, including the size of the estate – a fact that justified not applying to the court for directions – the lay status of the trustee and the fact that she had sought and relied on her solicitor's advice.

Technical breaches of trust apart, any discussion of a 'relieving jurisdiction' cannot properly be divorced from a consideration of the standards of behaviour to which a trustee must aspire to avoid a breach of trust. Paling has argued that the enactment of the section in 1896, following the recommendation of a Select Committee Report on Trust Administration, was an admission that the standard of skill and care imposed on the volunteer amateur trustee – the prudent man of business standard – was too high ((1973) 37 Conv 48 at 53, nn 22 and 23). Indeed considerable concern was expressed in evidence to the Select Committee that lay persons were being discouraged from acting as executors or trustees because of the perceived threat of extensive liability for breach of trust (see Select Committee on Trusts Administration PP 1895(248) XIII; Stebbings *The Private Trustee in Victorian England* (2002) ch 6; and Lowry and Edmunds in Birks and Pretto (eds) *Breach of Trust* (2002) ch 9). One implication of this explanation for the legislation, subsequently confirmed in practice, is that a court will be much less likely to grant relief to a professional than an amateur trustee (see *National Trustees Co of Australasia v General Finance Co* and *Re Pauling's Settlement Trusts* [1964] Ch 303 at 338, CA where partial relief was granted).

It may be argued that if the claimant beneficiary's case at general law requires proof of lack of ordinary prudence, then if this is established it necessarily constitutes 'unreasonable' behaviour, and therefore s 61 cannot apply in those circumstances. If, however, the explanation offered by Paling is to be accepted, what level of competence is the amateur trustee expected to attain for s 61 to apply? Presumably something less than the prudent man of business standard would be acceptable but, if pure subjectivity is to be avoided, something more than just the standard a trustee exercises in the management of his or her own affairs. It is tempting to suggest that the introduction of the statutory duty of care in the Trustee Act 2000 has resolved these difficulties. Unfortunately the standard of care to be expected of the lay trustee (see Chapter 10, p 461) remains a matter of debate and, in any event the statutory duty will not necessarily apply to the breach for which relief is sought (see eg *Re Pauling's Settlement Trusts* [1964] Ch 303; *Re Evans (dec'd)* [1999] 2 All ER 777).

The desirability of leaving the question of liability so indeterminate and subject to wide judicial discretion has long been questioned (see Maugham (1898) 14 LQR 159). An alternative approach, rejected by the LRC in 1982 and made still less likely in view of the TA 2000 changes, would be to specify agreed standards in a statute, it usually being inferred that the standard for the amateur trustee should be lower (see Paling, (1973) 37 Conv 548; Sheridan [1955] Conv 420; LRC (23rd Report *The Powers and Duties of Trustees* (Cmnd 8733, 1982) paras 2.14–2.16; *Ontario Law Reform Committee* pp 35–39). Perhaps we should simply recognise that s 61 is, in effect, a little-used but still useful house of last resort whereby the court can give relief in a hard case 'if it thinks fit'.

(f) Protection of time

(1) Limitation of actions

For the trustee, final escape from the clutches of the beneficiary's claim may come with the passage of time (see Limitations Act 1980). The general rule (s 21(3)), in common with time limits for most actions founded on tort (s 2) and contract (s 5), is that a beneficiary must commence an action for breach of trust within six years of the breach being committed. This is so whether the beneficiary was aware of the breach or not although no right of action can accrue to any beneficiary who is entitled to a future interest in trust property until that interest has fallen into possession (s 23(1)). This means, for instance, that where there is a gift to A for life remainder to B and some breach of trust occurs during A's life, the time limit does not start to run against B until the remainder interest vests in B's possession on A's death. The statutory period of limitation does not apply where trustees have been in breach of their fiduciary duty of loyalty by contravening the self-dealing or fair-dealing rules (*Tito v Waddell (No 2)* [1977] Ch 106 at 249; and see generally Chapter 9 at p 452). Moreover s 23(1) is subject to the generic restriction in s 32(1)(b) that where there has been deliberate concealment of 'any fact relevant to the [claimant's] action' the period of limitation does not begin to run until the claimant has discovered the concealment or 'could with reasonable diligence have discovered it'. In the circumstances where s 23(1) does not apply the trustee may still get protection by the operation of the equitable doctrine of laches (see below). Other circumstances where no time limit is applied are set out in s 21(1):

21(1) No period of limitation prescribed by this Act shall apply to an action by a beneficiary under a trust, being an action –

(a) in respect of any fraud or fraudulent breach of trust to which the trustee was a party or privy; or
(b) to recover from the trustee trust property or the proceeds of trust property in the possession of the trustee, or previously received by the trustee and converted to his use.

Section 21(1)(b) confirms what has always been the position, namely that there is no statutory limitation period where beneficiaries seek to enforce their rights to trust property or its proceeds in possession of the trustee. 'Property or its proceeds' can extend to include 'notional proceeds' as in *Re Howlett* [1949] Ch 767 where it was held to apply to rent that the trustee should have paid for trust property that he was occupying. In the words of Dankwerts J '[the trustee] must be considered as having [the rent] in his own pocket at the material date' (at 778).

By contrast interpretation of s 21(1)(a) has proved more problematic. This is particularly so with regard to the relationship of the subsection to the limitation period applicable to actions for damages for fraud at common law. In contradistinction to s 21(1)(a) such an action is statute barred after six years. There is an obvious temptation for a claimant to exploit what may be seen as a loophole by pleading one's action in a way that is not caught by the statutory limitation periods, whereas if pleaded in an alternative manner it would be so caught. The potential opportunity to succumb to the temptation resides in the definition in the Act of 'trust' and 'trustee' which includes within it 'constructive trusts' and 'constructive trusteeship' (s 38). This has raised the question whether the exception in s 21(1)(a) should be applicable to persons who become liable as constructive trustees where the 'trusteeship' arises only as a result of some unlawful transaction. In *Paragon Finance v D B Thakerar & Co* [1999] 1 All ER 400 Millett LJ sought to distinguish between two entirely different situations of constructive trusteeship. On the one hand, there were 'those cases . . . where the defendant although not expressly appointed as trustee, has assumed the duties of trustee by a lawful transaction which was independent of and preceded the breach of trust and is not impeached by the plaintiff' whilst, on the other hand, there were 'those cases where the trust obligation arises as a direct consequence of the unlawful transaction which is impeached by the plaintiff . . .' (at 408). The exception in s 21(1)(a) in the view of the Court of Appeal was not applicable to the latter situation. In *Paragon Finance* itself, where more than six years had elapsed since the unlawful transaction, the court declined to allow the plaintiff mortgage lender to amend its pleadings so as to sue the defendant firm of solicitors, who acted both for the plaintiff and the borrower, for fraudulent breach of trust and intentional breach of fiduciary duty. The reasoning behind the approach of the court was stated quite explicitly by Millett LJ (at 414):

> There is a case for treating fraudulent breach of trust differently from other frauds, but only if what is involved really is a breach of trust. There is no case for distinguishing between an action for damages for fraud at common law and its counterpart in equity based on the same facts merely because equity employs the formula of constructive trust to justify the exercise of the equitable jurisdiction.

This overall jurisdiction is thus providing yet one more focus of a sensitivity to the effects on litigation of differences between the approaches of equity and the common law. (See also *Coulthard v Disco Mix Club Ltd* [1999] 2 All ER 457; *Cia de Seguros Imperio v Health (REBX) Ltd* [2001] 1 WLR 112 – claim for equitable compensation for 'breach of fiduciary duty' held 'analogous' (s 36(1)) to a claim for damages at common law and subject to same limitation period).

A remaining area of uncertainty is whether the s 23(1) limitation period or alternatively s 21(1)(a) applies to those liable for the equitable wrongs of 'dishonest assistance' and 'knowing receipt' (see generally Chapter 14). The authorities are inconsistent although it would not be surprising if reasoning analogous to that of Millett LJ in *Paragon Finance* were to prevail (cf *Cattley v Pollard* [2007] 3 WLR 317 and *Statek Corp v Alford* [2008] BCC 266; Mitchell [2008] Conv 226).

(2) Laches

Unlike the position with common law claims where it is statute alone that dictates when a claim is time barred, equity developed a doctrine of laches which may be invoked by a defendant to bar an action where the statutory limitation does not apply. The doctrine can therefore now apply only to the breaches of trust referred to in the s 21(1) exceptions and also to situations involving an infringement of the rules regarding self-dealing and fair-dealing.

(For a comprehensive and critical overview of the doctrine and associated aspects of civil procedure see Watt in Birks and Pretto (eds) *Breach of Trust* (2002) ch 12.) At its broadest laches can be viewed as a doctrine intended to prevent a claimant from unconscionably asserting a right against a defendant. Given this objective it is not surprising to encounter judicial statements to the effect that 'each case has to be decided on its facts applying the broad approach' (per Aldous LJ in *Frawley v Neill* [2000] CP Rep 20). Amongst the factors that the court will take into account is the period of delay in bringing the action and the reasons for it – did the claimant acquiesce in the breach, the extent to which the defendant's position has been prejudiced by the delay and whether that prejudice was caused by the acts of the claimant (see Laddie J in *Nelson v Rye* [1996] 1 WLR 1378 at 1382; see also *Patel v Shah* [2005] EWCA Civ 157 where the commercial context in which the trusts arose was regarded as a relevant factor in applying the doctrine; noted in Watt [2005] Conv 174–180).

(3) Conclusion

The admittedly rather confusing and unsatisfactory statutory limitation regime has been the subject of a Report by the Law Commission (Law Commission Report No 270 *Limitation of Actions* (2001)). The Report recommends sweeping reforms of the law including the introduction of a single core limitation regime applicable to all claims, including claims for breach of trust, claims to recover trust property and claims for breach of fiduciary duty (see paras 2.39–2.45, 4.94–4.119). Consistent with the view expressed recently by the courts in cases such as *Paragon Finance* a guiding principle adopted by the Commission is that no distinction should be drawn between broadly comparable claims at common law and in equity. The Report recommends the adoption of a 'core' limitation regime comprising (i) a primary limitation period of three years starting from the date on which the claimant knew or ought to have known certain key facts about the claim or (ii) a long-stop limitation period of ten years from the date when the cause of action first arose. At the time of writing there is no indication as to whether or when the recommendations will be implemented in legislation. It only remains to add that, if implemented as recommended by the Law Commission, the new Limitations Act would significantly limit the circumstances in which the doctrine of laches might be invoked (see Watt in *Birks and Pretto* at pp 364–367).

5. Proprietary remedies

(a) Tracing: an introduction

It would be wrong to leave the discussion of a beneficiary's remedies for breach of trust there. As previously indicated a personal claim against a trustee may not always provide an adequate remedy. Most obviously this will be so where, for example, the trust fund has been misappropriated and the trustee is insolvent. In these circumstances the beneficiary is not reduced solely to a personal claim and to standing in line with the insolvent trustee's other unsecured creditors. Instead the beneficiary may be able to invoke a proprietary remedy, by which we mean a claim against a particular fund or item of property. Broadly speaking the law has provided a set of rules under which the beneficiary can attempt 'to trace' the route taken by the trust property so as to establish a claim against it or its exchange product. 'Tracing' can be applied to trustees and to third parties who intermeddle with trust property (see Chapter 14 for an explanation of this term and of an intermeddler's personal liability in the context of commercial wrongdoing), and even to an innocent volunteer, ie someone, not being a purchaser, receiving trust property but with no actual or constructive notice of the trust. Two short examples may help illustrate the process.

(1) A trustee (T) sells trust property to a bona fide purchaser for value of the legal estate without notice, a 'bona fide purchaser', who, as usual, takes good title. With the proceeds T purchases for himself, in breach of trust, a different investment. Whereas the original property is irrecoverable by the beneficiary (B), she can 'trace' the proceeds of the sale into the new investment and indeed into any further change of investment made by T. In equity this property – the 'exchange product' – is as much B's as if T had actually purchased it as trustee, and is therefore immune from the claims of T's creditors. Even if T is not insolvent, B may opt to keep the investment in preference to a personal claim against T, where for instance the investment has increased in value.

(2) In breach of trust T transfers trust property to X who receives it with actual or constructive notice of the breach. The beneficiary (B) can 'trace' the property into the hands of X and indeed into those of any subsequent transferee unless a 'bona fide purchaser'. Again, as in the previous example, this process can be applied to the exchange product.

In both these straightforward examples it is assumed that the property in its original or converted form has been kept separate and is therefore readily identifiable. But this may not be so. Our defaulting trustee may have mixed his own and trust money in the same bank account, or even intermingled funds from two or three separate trusts in the one account. The innocent volunteer recipient of trust money may have spent it on improving her house. How far can tracing assist an aggrieved beneficiary in these sorts of circumstances? A number of technical rules, developed somewhat haphazardly, now mark out most of the boundary lines, although gaps and inconsistencies remain. Notwithstanding our reference to an 'aggrieved beneficiary' the gaps and inconsistencies are increasingly being addressed in a variety of contemporary commercial rather than family contexts. In our judgement therefore full consideration of the rules and practices of tracing, along with other equitable remedies, is best deferred to Chapters 14 and 15.

12

Implied trusts and the family home

1. Introduction

This chapter is concerned with the role played by implied trusts in resolving disputes over the ownership of the family home. It should be noted at the outset that the term 'family property' has no specialist meaning in English law: there is no special regime applicable to assets owned by a married couple or civil partners (save when they separate) or to those owned by cohabiting couples and other family members. The situations in which issues of ownership may fall to be determined were set out by the Law Commission in its discussion paper *Sharing Homes* (Law Commission No 278 (2002)) paras 1.10–1.12:

> 1.10 Over the last thirty years or so, a recurring question encountered by litigants before the courts in England and Wales has concerned the property entitlements of persons who are sharing, or have shared, homes together. The question arises in various contexts, and the many ways in which it has been answered have emphasised the lack of clear principle in this vital area of the law.
>
> 1.11 There are four principal circumstances in which the determination of the ownership of the shared home is highly material and to which we will return throughout this paper: They are as follows:
>
> (1) The persons (two or more) who share a home cease to do so. Typically, one leaves. It may be that this follows the breakdown of a relationship between the sharers. It may be that the living arrangement is no longer convenient to the person who leaves, as they have obtained employment elsewhere. The question arises of whether the person who leaves is entitled to receive payment of a capital sum representing their share of the property, or indeed, in the event of no satisfaction being obtained, whether that person can force a sale thereof.
>
> (2) One of the persons who has been sharing the home dies. The question arises whether that person had an interest in the property, and, if so, what therefore is now to happen to it.
>
> (3) The home is subject to a mortgage securing a loan negotiated by its owner or owners to facilitate the acquisition of the property or to provide funds for other purposes. The borrower defaults on the mortgage, and the mortgagee seeks possession in order to

realise its security by sale of the property. The question arises whether any of those living in the home can assert an interest in that property against the mortgagee, and whether they can successfully defend the proceedings for repossession.

(4) A creditor whose debt is not secured over the property by way of mortgage seeks to have the property sold so that the demand can be satisfied. The question arises whether any person who has been sharing with the debtor can successfully hold out against the creditor's claim.

1.12 The resolution of these questions is no easy matter. 'Who owns what?' may be very simple to ask, but in a short time the enquirers will find themselves immersed in the off-putting, and sometimes obscure, terminology of the law of trusts and estoppel. It may then be necessary to address potentially difficult issues of priority which may themselves depend on proper and timely registration of interests.

There are a number of reasons why such disputes have attained such prominence in the past thirty or so years. The first is the increase in home ownership: between 1981 and 2005 the number of owner-occupied dwellings increased by 48%, and they now comprise about three-quarters of all dwellings (ONS *Social Trends 37* (2007), fig 10.5). Following on from this is the fact that the family home is more likely to be the subject of a dispute over ownership than other family assets. The home is usually the most significant asset, and the substantial (if not always steady) increase in house prices over the second half of the twentieth century (*Social Trends 37*, p 69) meant that it was increasingly seen as worth litigating over issues of ownership. Moreover, the claimant's sense of entitlement to an interest in the shared family home may well be more acute – on account of the emotional link with the property – than would be the case in relation to items of personal property, or the other party's pension. A further reason for litigation to focus on the family home is the seeming tendency of family members to leave their property entitlements informally expressed rather than encapsulated in a legally binding document such as a conveyance or declaration of trust; not that family members are any more likely to make such formal arrangements in relation to their personal property, but the creation of trusts over personal property requires far fewer formalities (see Chapter 4 at p 123). Gaps in the procedures and remedies of family law – in particular in relation to cohabiting couples – have forced the court to articulate the consequences of this informality in terms of the rules of implied trusts.

This chapter also provides a further illustration of the theme, pursued elsewhere in this book, of the adaptability of ancient trust-forms to new functions. The origins of the implied trust (in the shape of the 'resulting use') can be traced back to the latter half of the fifteenth century (see Baker *An Introduction to English Legal History* (4th edn, 2002) p 251). In turn, the adaptation of the implied trust to the context of disputes over the family home has acted, and continues to act, as a stimulus to its conceptual development. In order to trace this development, we first need to consider the doctrinal origin and content of the category of implied trust; and then to understand why the implied trust has come to assume a significant (but not exclusive) role in resolving certain disputes over family property.

2. Legal starting-points

Before going any further, it will be helpful to restate some important distinctions as a way of clearing some conceptual ground: first, that between implied and express trusts; and second, that between different types of implied trust, and especially between resulting and constructive trusts.

(a) Express and implied trusts

There are two different ways in which we might distinguish these categories.

We could begin, first, with a *functional* distinction. We have seen in earlier chapters that the express trust may be employed as a means to advance private planning by families who wish to transmit wealth from one generation to the next in a secure and (usually) tax-efficient manner. The implied trust is not a planning device in this sense, but a way of resolving disputes over ownership or entitlement in circumstances where property has been acquired or transferred with no formal understanding as to whom it belongs, or where strict reliance on paper entitlements would be unfair. In short, the implied trust does not exploit the 'plane of time' in the same way that the express trust does – it is a retrospective 'once and for all' method of determining issues of entitlement, even though that entitlement may have accrued over a period of time.

Indeed, one of the key points of debate in this area is the extent to which implied trusts are based on the parties' intentions: are implied trusts a means of giving effect to the parties' informally expressed intentions, to their shared but unexpressed intentions, or to the intentions presumed from their conduct, or is it the role of the court to attribute an intention to the parties on the basis of what they might have intended had they given the matter any thought? As we shall see, the courts have answered this question in different ways at different times.

Second, a *formal* distinction can be drawn. Compliance with certain formalities of writing is a precondition of the creation of a valid express trust of land (LPA 1925, s 53(1)(b)). 'Implied, resulting or constructive' trusts, however, are unaffected by these requirements or operate as exceptions to them (s 53(2)). Since our principal concern is with disputes over *land* (ie the owner-occupied family home), this 'formal' legal distinction between implied and express trusts of land is of prime importance. The significance of the formality requirements applicable to land is well illustrated by *Rowe v Prance* [1999] 2 FLR 787, where a man encouraged his cohabitant to live with him on a yacht (an item of personal property), and referred to it as 'our boat'. As a result she was entitled to a half-share, but had the 'home' been on dry land, such an informal express declaration of trust would have had no effect.

The implied trust is just one example of a number of equitable doctrines that operate to qualify or modify rules of formality (see Chapter 4); and, of these, it has probably witnessed the most judicial activity in recent years, through the statutory gateway provided by s 53(2) of the LPA 1925. Of course, it is open to couples to put the question of ownership beyond doubt by creating an express trust in compliance with the formal requirements; but many couples, for whatever reason, do not do so, and the implied trust has been relied on heavily to fill the vacuum this creates.

It is debatable whether all of the examples of implied trust we shall be exploring in this chapter should properly be regarded as 'exceptions' to these requirements of formality, or as trusts which were never intended to be caught by the formality requirement in the first place (eg the 'presumed' resulting trust). Others, though, are more obviously exceptions in the sense that they arise in circumstances in which the formality requirement says they should not. Express oral declarations of trusts of land are a prime example. Here, the statute stipulates that, to be enforceable, the declaration must be in writing – yet, as we shall see, one effect of certain types of implied trust being enforced is that oral declarations of trusts of land are given effect, in defiance of the formality requirement. The reason they are enforced is that something has happened to justify enforcement. Precisely what that 'something' might be is the focus of much of this chapter (and see Gardner (2008) 124 LQR 422). As we shall see, judges have relied heavily on the idea that what they are doing is giving effect to the parties' common intentions, and have relied on specific indicators in searching for that intention; however, this conceptual basis for implied trusts has been heavily criticised, and has been abandoned in comparable jurisdictions.

(b) Resulting and constructive trusts

The category of 'implied trusts' may, for present purposes, be taken to refer to 'resulting' and 'constructive' trusts. In the last three decades of the twentieth century there was a tendency to blur these categories (see eg *Gissing v Gissing* [1971] AC 886); however, both resulting and constructive trusts have a separate history and it would now appear that there is a renewed appreciation of the different principles that underpin each of them (see eg *Curley v Parkes* [2004] EWCA Civ 1515). The orthodoxy that a resulting trust arises only where there has been a direct and contemporaneous contribution to the purchase price was firmly restated in that case; this rule has a long history, as an early summary by Eyre CB makes clear (*Dyer v Dyer* (1788) 2 Cox Eq Cas 92 at 93):

> The clear result of all the cases, without a single exception, is that the trust of a legal estate whether freehold, copyhold, or leasehold, whether taken in the names of the purchaser and others jointly, or in the name of others without that of the purchaser, whether in

> one name or several, whether jointly or successive, results to the man who advances the purchase money; and it goes on a strict analogy to the rule of the common law, that where a feoffment is made without consideration the use results to the feoffer.

By contrast, the modern constructive trust, as applied in the context of the family home, bears little relationship to the constructive trust that had been developed in the commercial sphere to require fiduciaries to surrender or return property acquired in breach of their fiduciary duty (see further Chapter 16, and note the comments by Etherton (2008) 67(2) CLJ 265). The idea of unconscionability is present in both, but is not a free-standing justification for imposing a constructive trust; according to Lord Diplock in *Gissing v Gissing* [1971] AC 886 at 905 such a trust:

> is created by a transaction between trustee and the cestui que trust in connection with the acquisition by the trustee of a legal estate in land, whenever the trustee has so conducted himself that it would be inequitable to allow him to deny to the cestui que trust a beneficial interest in the land acquired. And he will be held so to have conducted himself if by his words or conduct he has induced the cestui que trust to act to his own detriment in the reasonable belief that by so acting he was acquiring a beneficial interest in the land.

This statement laid the foundation for the subsequent law; it also laid the foundation for much subsequent confusion, as Lord Diplock did not distinguish between constructive, resulting *or* implied trusts, stating airily that 'it is unnecessary for present purposes to distinguish between the three classes of trust'. For our purposes, however, such taxonomic distinctions are necessary, since it is now established that the three requirements of belief, reliance and detriment are necessary for a constructive trust but have no relevance to the resulting trust.

3. Implied trusts and family property law

The implied trust plays a residual or default role in family property disputes: that is, it fills the vacuum left by the absence of other remedies, procedures or techniques. This means that the implied trust can only be properly understood in the context of the broader law applicable to spouses, civil partners and cohabitants in relation to which it has played this important gap-filling role. In particular, how and why have the gaps currently filled by the implied trust arisen?

The English law relating to family property is extremely complex, not least because it comprises an amalgam of rules derived from the general land-law framework, from family-law statutes, from insolvency law and from the law of trusts (see Dewar 'Land, Law and the Family Home' in Bright and Dewar (eds) *Land Law: Themes and Perspectives* (1998) ch 13, for an overview). The law thus supplies a number of ways of resolving ownership questions, whether through the exercise by a judge of a statutory discretion or the use of formal conveyances and declarations of trust; yet there is no comprehensive law of matrimonial or family property in English law. One effect of this has been that there have been, and remain, numerous gaps to be filled. A brief history will explain where these gaps lie.

(a) The common law

Like continental civilian legal systems, the common law imposed on married couples a special legal regime governing the ownership of matrimonial property. But whereas the civil law established a 'community of property' regime between spouses, vesting ownership of family property equally in both, the common law gave most of the wife's real property, and all of her income and personal property, to the husband's ownership and control. As was seen in Chapter 2, from the seventeenth century onwards the hardship of the common law rules was alleviated to an extent through the device of the wife's separate equitable estate and by other forms of private ordering (see also Staves *Married Women's Separate Property in England, 1660–1833* (1990)). But such devices were available only to the propertied and mercantile classes, and were concerned as much to protect the wealth of the wife's family or kinship group as with emancipating the wife herself. It was not until the late nineteenth century that calls for reform finally led Parliament to act.

(b) Statutory reform: the Married Women's Property Act 1882

The reform adopted by Parliament was to introduce the principle of separate property, enabling each spouse to acquire and control property independently of the other. This extended the principle of the equitable separate estate to all married women without the need for trustees, with the effect that all wives were capable of acquiring and owning their own property free from their husbands' control. However, important restrictions on women's contractual and testamentary capacity with respect to their property survived this legislation, and lingered into the twentieth century. As Shanley has put it, Parliament 'sought a way to give married women greater control of their property without conceding that they stood in the same relationship to their property as men stood in relation to theirs' (*Feminism, Marriage and the Law in Victorian England 1850–1895* (1989) p 129).

Even with respect to property acquisition, the Act achieved only the most formal degree of legal equality and did nothing to enhance the capacity of women to acquire property in legally recognised ways. As Kahn-Freund has pointed out, it was 'the connection at common law between inequality of status and the combination of both spouses' property in the hands of the husband' which meant that 'the idea of separation of property became in the minds of people, lawyers and laymen, interwoven with that of equality with which intrinsically it has very little to do' ('Matrimonial Property Law in England' in Friedmann (ed) *Matrimonial Property Law* (1955) at p 278). The law of family property continues to operate very much within this legacy of separation: many of the statutory reforms to family property law have been motivated by a desire to curb its worst excesses. As we shall see, there have been some notable judicial attempts to deploy the implied trust to the same end.

(c) Section 17: signs of community?

A significant feature of the 1882 Act was that under s 17 the courts were empowered to hear and resolve disputes as to the possession and ownership of matrimonial property, and to make such order as they 'thought fit'. Section 17 assumed a unique importance in resolving the property consequences of divorce, because until 1970 there was virtually no other statutory power enabling the courts to redistribute matrimonial assets on divorce (see below). The need for a redistributive power arose from the tendency for the matrimonial home to be owned and paid for by the husband. Thus, the effect of conveyancing practice, when combined with the principle of separation of property, was that most wives would have had no formal legal claim to a share in the ownership but for the operation of this section.

There was judicial debate over the scope of the jurisdiction conferred by s 17, and the principles to be applied under it. Some judges wished to treat it as creating a cloak for the introduction of communitarian principles, sometimes called the 'family assets' doctrine. Thus, in *Fribance v Fribance* [1957] 1 WLR 384, Denning LJ was able to dispose of a case brought under s 17 on the basis that 'the whole of [the spouses'] resources were expended for their joint benefit – either in food and clothes and living expenses for which there was nothing to see or in the house and furniture which are family assets – and the product should belong to them jointly. It belongs to them in equal shares' (at 387).

Others, however, regarded s 17 as merely procedural, as a way of clarifying what the parties' rights were under the general law, and not as entitling the judges to depart from strict property rights; and they took a narrower view of what those rights were. It was this latter, stricter, view of the scope of s 17 and the principles to be applied under it that prevailed in the House of Lords in the landmark cases of *Pettitt* and *Gissing*.

(d) The House of Lords' rules: *Pettitt and Gissing*

The House of Lords' decisions in *Pettitt v Pettitt* [1970] AC 777 and *Gissing v Gissing* [1971] AC 886 still provide the starting-point for any discussion of the contemporary law of implied trusts, even though the House of Lords has since restated the relevant principles (see below). Both were cases brought under s 17 by, respectively, a husband and a wife; in each case, a claim was made to a share in the equity value of the family home by a spouse who had no formal legal entitlement to a share; and in each case the claim was unsuccessful.

Between them, these cases established a number of important principles. The first was that s 17 was a procedural section only and enabled a court only to declare existing rights and not to vary or adjust those rights. The second concerned the central importance of the implied trust in disputes over family property in those cases where legal title is vested in only one spouse and no formal arrangements to share ownership have been made. In *Gissing*, Lord Diplock (with whom Lords Reid and Dilhorne agreed), made it clear that claims to ownership in such cases were based in trust, either express or implied.

The third point established by these cases concerned the basis on which the courts would be prepared to find a trust in favour of a claimant. At its simplest, the House of Lords held that a claim to a beneficial share under an implied trust (of whatever sort) would only be successful where the claimant was able to point to evidence of an agreement, or a 'common intention', that the claimant should have a share. This agreement could either be express but informal, or inferred from the parties' conduct. It was not open to a judge to invent it, or impute it to the parties. Although it emerges in different ways from the various judgments, the conduct necessary before the courts will infer the necessary intention is the making by the claimant of some financial contribution referable to the acquisition of the property in question (although there has been some dispute as to how 'referable' such contributions have to be: see further below).

At any rate, it was clear that mere acquisition for joint use or for a joint purpose would not be sufficient to disturb ownership based on payment: the 'family assets' doctrine was dead, and with it any immediate prospect of smuggling community principles through the back door of implied trust doctrine (see Tiley [1970] CLJ 210).

(e) Family law reformed

The contemporary significance of these House of Lords rulings can perhaps be appreciated when we remember that there were very few adjustive powers available to the courts in divorce cases at the time these decisions were handed down (see Law Commission *Matrimonial and Related Proceedings – Financial Relief* (Working Paper No 9, 1967), paras 78–85). Those powers that did exist were considered inadequate, especially in the context of the liberalised divorce law introduced by the Divorce Reform Act 1969. The decisions in *Pettitt* and *Gissing* offered little prospect of amelioration of the severe consequences of the principle of separation and helped to intensify pressure for an expansion of the courts' powers. This came with the Matrimonial Proceedings and Property Act 1970 (now Matrimonial Causes Act 1973, as amended), which conferred wide-ranging powers on the divorce court to reallocate a married couple's assets on divorce (see Masson, Bailey-Harris and Probert, *Cretney's Principles of*

Family Law (8th edn, 2008) ch 13). So, just as *Pettitt* and *Gissing* confirmed the centrality of the implied trust, the 1970 Act removed any role that the implied trust may have had in determining the ownership or allocation of property for married couples on divorce.

Indeed, recent decisions of the House of Lords have reduced the residual relevance of ownership still further, in holding that it is not only possible for the court to reallocate assets between the parties, but that sharing of assets is one of the key principles that underpins this jurisdiction (see eg *White v White* [2001] 2 FLR 981; *Miller v Miller, McFarlane v McFarlane* [2006] UKHL 17). Fundamental to this is the valuing (without precise evaluation) of the respective contributions of the parties. As Lord Nicholls stated in *White v White* (at 989):

> In seeking to achieve a fair outcome, there is no place for discrimination between husband and wife and their respective roles. Typically, a husband and wife share the activities of earning money, running their home and caring for their children. Traditionally, the husband earned the money, and the wife looked after the home and the children. This traditional division of labour is no longer the order of the day. Frequently both parents work. Sometimes it is the wife who is the money-earner, and the husband runs the home and cares for the children during the day. But whatever the division of labour chosen by the husband and wife, or forced upon them by circumstances, fairness requires that this should not prejudice or advantage either party when considering paragraph (f) [of the Matrimonial Causes Act 1973, s 25(2)], relating to the parties' contributions. . . . If, in their different spheres, each contributed equally to the family, then in principle it matters not which of them earned the money and built up the assets. There should be no bias in favour of the money-earner and against the home-maker and the child-carer.

As we shall see, these decisions have had the effect of widening the distinction between formal and informal relationships still further.

Other statutory family-law reforms have further reduced the relevance of legal or equitable ownership for spouses. For example, the Matrimonial Homes Act 1967 (now incorporated into the Family Law Act 1996) conferred on spouses an automatic right of occupation in the matrimonial home *qua* spouse; and the Inheritance (Provision for Family and Dependants) Act 1938 (now 1975) gave the courts wide powers to make reasonable provision for family members out of a deceased person's estate. And upon the passage of the Civil Partnership Act in 2004, all the rights enjoyed by spouses were extended to same-sex couples who had registered a civil partnership.

(f) Matrimonial property law and the ongoing marriage

Yet the reform of matrimonial property law has not been comprehensive. One area which has remained stubbornly resistant to reform is the owner-ship of matrimonial property *during* marriage (see Cooke, 'Community of Property, Joint Ownership and the Family Home' in Dixon and Griffiths (eds)

Contemporary Perspectives on Property, Equity and Trusts Law (2007) for reasons why this might be so). This has not been for want of effort. The Law Commission has on numerous occasions made elaborate proposals for automatic joint ownership of the matrimonial property during marriage (see Law Commission Reports Nos 52 (1973), 86 (1978), 115 (1982) and 175 (1988)). The need for reform, in the Commission's view, stems from the 'arbitrary, uncertain and unfair' state of the current law and from the view that it is not a sufficient answer to the problem of marital property to provide an adjustive jurisdiction available only when the marriage comes to an end (see Law Com No 175, para 1.4).

The proposals met with much criticism. It was suggested variously that they were unnecessary because (i) conveyancing practice increasingly ensures that both spouses appear on the legal title, thereby conferring on both an effective control over dealings, and (ii) the occupational protection accorded by ordinary land-law principles to equitable interests in land is sufficient. The proposals were also attacked as a matter of principle: it was wrong to single out married couples in this way; it was wrong to give spouses 'something for nothing'; and in any case, the proposals were more concerned with protecting the interests of mortgage lenders than with the protection of spouses (see Zuckerman (1978) 94 LQR 28; Murphy and Rawlings [1980] Fam Law 136; Murphy (1983) 46 MLR 330). The Law Commission eventually abandoned its proposals for automatic co-ownership of matrimonial property and turned its attention, also unsuccessfully, to devising rules for ownership of matrimonial property other than land.

More recently, the Law Commission has considered, at great length, the wider issues of ownership of land by 'homesharers', a term that includes all those who occupy land together. In spite of years of deliberation, the Commission concluded the project with no recommendations for reform of the law, arguing that it was 'not possible to devise a statutory scheme for the determination of shares in the shared home which can operate fairly and evenly across all the diverse circumstances which are now to be encountered' (Law Commission No 278, *Sharing Homes: A Discussion Paper* (2002) para 15; see further below). Statutory reform of the general law of property thus seems as remote as automatic co-ownership of the matrimonial home.

(g) Unmarried couples

The adjustive regime applicable on divorce applies, by definition, to married couples only. Although there has been some limited statutory recognition of non-marital relationships for some purposes (eg under Pt IV of the Family Law Act 1996, and under the Inheritance (Provision for Family and Dependants) Act 1975, as amended by the Law Reform (Succession) Act 1995), this has not so far included the power to reallocate property when such a relationship breaks down. The growth in cohabitation since the 1970s (Kiernan (2004)

26 Law and Policy 33), combined with the lack of any tailor-made statutory solution for cohabitants, has meant that cohabitants account for the majority of cases determining rights in the family home (see Law Commission CP No 179, *Cohabitation: The Financial Consequences of Relationship Breakdown* (2006) p 47).

Where there are children of an unmarried relationship, legislation provides for the division of property under Sch 1 to the Children Act 1989. The court has wide-ranging powers to make orders for periodic payments, lump sums and property transfers to or in favour of children (see Masson, Bailey-Harris and Probert *Cretney's Principles of Family Law* (8th edn, 2008) pp 477–484). Yet there are two reasons why this is not a complete solution to the issue of cohabitants' property rights. The first is that the powers are available only in respect of children, so that they will be irrelevant where the relationship is childless. Second, the purpose of the legislation is to provide for the child, not for the adult carer. This means that while it is not an obstacle to making an order (eg for the transfer of a house or a tenancy) that the adult carer will benefit from it, the order made should not benefit the child beyond the age of majority (see *A v A (Minor) (Financial Provision)* [1994] 1 FLR 657). In the case of freehold property, this will usually mean that the property will be settled to secure a right of occupation for the child and its carer for a limited or fixed period of time. Property rights thus remain a far more important factor on relationship breakdown in the context of a cohabiting relationship than if the parties have formalised their relationship.

(h) Other family relationships

There are even fewer specific rules governing the property entitlements of parents and adult children, or wider kin, who share or purchase a home together. Even under the Family Law Act 1996 their entitlement to occupy the home in question is dependent on their property rights. This lack of regulation to some extent reflects the fact that it is relatively rare for relatives to purchase a home for joint occupation; however, there are still contexts in which disputes over ownership may arise. Adult children may be remaining under the parental roof for longer (ONS *Social Trends 37* (2007) table 2.8), but any financial contribution they make to the running of the household is likely to be construed as rent rather than as a contribution to the purchase price. More difficult problems are posed by elderly parents who sell their homes and move in with their adult children: whether they acquire any interest in the home will depend on the shared expectations of the parties and the contributions made. One study of such arrangements found that the move was often precipitated by the illness of the parent with little time to consider its implications (Healy and Yarrow *Family Matters: Parents Living with Children in Old Age* (1997)); hardly conducive to clear discussions about ownership, especially given the vulnerability of the parent in such cases. A number of cases have also arisen out of cross-generational property purchases, the typical situation involving a parent with limited means who had been a tenant of social-sector housing for some years and acquired the right to buy it at a substantial discount, and an adult child who provided the means to fund the purchase (either by raising a mortgage or by direct contributions: see eg *Crossley v Crossley* [2005] EWCA Civ 1581; *Ritchie v Ritchie* [2007] EW Misc 5 (EWCC); *Laskar v Laskar* [2008] EWCA Civ 347). The expansion of home ownership in the 1980s as a result of the exercise of the right to buy has thus influenced both the number and the type of disputes over the family home.

We can now turn to the way in which ownership of the family home is determined under the law of trusts, distinguishing between those homes that are in joint names and those that are in the name of just one of the parties.

4. The family home in joint legal ownership

As the following extract explains, economic factors may be shaping the decision to purchase a home in joint names:

Douglas, Pearce and Woodward [2008] Conv 365 at 367–368

The average price paid by first-time buyers rose by 204 per cent between 1995 and 2005, as compared to their average incomes which rose by 92 per cent. The increase in property prices relative to net incomes means that fewer individuals can afford to buy on their own. The alternatives for would-be home owners include buying property jointly with another – some perhaps feeling under pressure to do so at an earlier stage in an intimate relationship than might previously have been likely – and seeking financial help from other family members. This has led to an increasingly complex mix of joint ownership arrangements and domestic situations including married couples, cohabitants, family members and unrelated friends or associates. Increases in the divorce rate may also have led to a higher proportion of properties being subject to charge-back arrangements whereby realisation of the ex-spouse's share is triggered by the occupier's cohabitation or remarriage. Divorcees, who may also be single parents, are often not in a position to buy out their ex-spouse without the financial help of their new partner, and a transfer into joint names along with re-mortgaging arrangements is sometimes seen as an answer to this predicament...The combination of these social and demographic changes highlights the importance of devising joint ownership arrangements which are appropriate for an increasingly complex variety of domestic situations.

Difficulties arise because joint legal ownership of the family home does not automatically connote shared ownership of the beneficial interest. The first question that must be asked to determine the beneficial ownership of the property is whether the parties have made any formal arrangements regarding their property.

(a) Express declarations

An express declaration of the parties' respective beneficial interests in the property is conclusive in the absence of fraud or mistake (*Goodman v Gallant* [1986] 1 FLR 513), regardless of the parties' later contributions (*Clarke v Harlowe* [2005] EWHC 3062 (Ch)). But how likely is it that there will be an express declaration of this kind? The legal background was set out by Baroness Hale in *Stack v Dowden* [2007] UKHL 17:

> [49]. In the olden days, before registration of title on certain events, including a conveyance on sale, became compulsory all over England and Wales, conveyances of unregistered land into joint names would in practice declare the purchasers' beneficial as well as their legal interests....
>
> 50. The question with which we are concerned has become apparent with the spread of registration of title. The formalities required for the transfer of registered land were designed to meet the concerns of the Land Registry rather than the parties. The Land Registry is not concerned with the equities. It is concerned with whether the registered proprietor or proprietors can give a good title to a later transferee. This is entirely consistent with the simplification of conveyancing in the 1925 property legislation, which was designed to allow the legal owners of land to pass a good title to bona fide purchasers for value without notice of the equities existing behind the legal title. But it meant that the form of transfer prescribed by the Land Registry did not require, or even give an obvious opportunity to, the transferees to state their beneficial interests as well as their legal title....
>
> [52]. The Land Registry form has since changed. Form TR1, in use from 1 April 1998, provides a box for the transferees to declare whether they are to hold the property on trust for themselves as joint tenants, or on trust for themselves as tenants in common in equal shares, or on some other trusts which are inserted on the form. If this is invariably complied with, the problem confronting us here will eventually disappear. Unfortunately, however, the transfer will be valid whether or not this part of the form is completed.... So there may still be transfers of registered land into joint names in which there is no express declaration of the beneficial interests. However desirable such a declaration may be, it is unrealistic, in the consumer context, to expect that it will be executed independently of the forms required to acquire the legal estate. Not only do solicitors and licensed conveyancers compete on price, but more and more people are emboldened to do their own conveyancing...

Thus it is possible, although less likely, that even some post-1997 conveyances will not contain an express declaration of the parties' beneficial interests (see further [2007] Conv 364).

A consultation document issued by the Land Registry (*Review of the Land Registration Rules 2003 and the Commonhold (Land Registration) Rules 2004* (2007)) asked whether completion of a declaration of trust should be made compulsory; 78.6% of respondents replied in the affirmative (*Review of the Land Registration Rules 2003: Report on Consultation* (2008) p 60). However,

69% also thought that a further option should be included for those who did not wish to commit themselves to an express declaration. In the light of the reservations expressed by the Law Society and the Association of Property Support Lawyers, the Land Registry decided that the issues required a separate review and announced that a working party would be appointed to this end (see also [2008] Conv 355, 356).

Given the binding nature of such a declaration, once made, considerable significance attaches to the box that is ticked when the property is purchased. But there is evidence that many couples are not making fully informed choices, as one recent empirical study demonstrates:

Douglas, Pearce and Woodward, [2007] Fam Law 36 at 38

Respondents were very hazy about the legal advice they had obtained at the time they purchased their properties. Most were vague about their mode of joint ownership and needed to be reminded by us of the different options. The advice that had stuck in their minds was about the right of survivorship which flows from a joint tenancy. Many were seemingly unaware that a joint tenancy also implied equal ownership, regardless of past or future contributions. It was clear that the half of the sample whose property was bought since the TR1 came into operation had not understood the full implications of the form . . . The conveyancers whom we interviewed perceived cohabiting purchasers as being simply keen to get into their new properties and not interested or focused on advice as to ownership options.

Thus, while the conclusive effect of an express declaration provides certainty, it may create injustice where the parties did not appreciate its effect (see further below). If a declaration of trust is made compulsory, the need for more detailed advice at the time of purchase is clear (see Douglas, Pearce and Woodward [2008] Conv 365 at 377–379).

Consider the following points:

(1) It was objected by the Law Society that making a declaration of trust mandatory might lead to applications being rejected and therefore to 'costs and delay' (*Review of the Land Registration Rules 2003: Report on Consultation* (2008) p 61). How do such costs compare to those that may be incurred disputing the beneficial ownership of the home?
(2) Is there any merit in allowing couples the option of expressly not making a declaration?

(b) No express declarations

What if two people purchase a home in joint names without making any declaration as to their beneficial interests? The starting-point is that equity follows the law, and so a legal joint tenancy is taken to indicate a beneficial joint tenancy. Until recently this was a starting-point from which the court could swiftly depart upon proof of unequal financial contributions (see eg *McKenzie v McKenzie* [2003] 2 P & CR DG6); however, the decision of the House of Lords in *Stack v Dowden* [2007] UKHL 17 held that a different approach was appropriate in the domestic context.

The facts of the case were relatively simple. It involved a cohabiting couple whose relationship had been lengthy – they had been in a relationship since 1975, and began to live together in a house purchased by Ms Dowden in 1983. This house was conveyed into Ms Dowden's sole name, and it was clear that it was she who had raised the majority, if not all, of the purchase price of this house. Four children were born to the couple over the next few years, and in 1993 the family moved to a new home. This was conveyed into joint names, but there was no indication as to the beneficial ownership of the property other than the declaration on the land registry form that the survivor of the parties could give a good receipt for capital moneys arising from a disposition of all or part of the property. Both Mr Stack and Ms Dowden assumed liability for the mortgage, and both made repayments under it. When the relationship finally broke down in 2002, Mr Stack claimed an interest in the home. The issue for the court was the extent of that interest: should he be entitled to half of the equity or, as Ms Dowden contended, no more than 35%, in recognition of her greater financial contribution?

The majority of the House of Lords took the view that it would be very difficult to show that the shares of the parties were not equal. Lord Walker emphasised that 'there will be a heavy burden in establishing . . . that an intention to keep a sort of balance-sheet of contributions actually existed, or should be inferred, or imputed to the parties. The presumption will be that equity follows the law' (at [33]). Baroness Hale (with whom Lord Hoffmann agreed) put it even more strongly, stating that 'cases in which the joint legal owners are to be taken to have intended that their beneficial interests should be different from their legal interests will be very unusual' (at [69]). And she identified a number of sound policy reasons for taking such an approach in the domestic context:

> [68] The burden will . . . be on the person seeking to show that the parties did intend their beneficial interests to be different from their legal interests, and in what way. This is not a task to be lightly embarked upon. In family disputes, strong feelings are aroused when couples split up. These often lead the parties, honestly but mistakenly, to reinterpret the past in self-exculpatory or vengeful terms. They also lead people to spend far more on the legal battle than is warranted by the sums actually at stake. A full examination of the facts is likely to involve disproportionate costs. In joint names cases it is also unlikely to lead to a different result unless the facts are very unusual. Nor may disputes be confined to the parties themselves. People with an interest in the deceased's estate may well wish to assert that he had a beneficial tenancy in common. It cannot be the case that all the hundreds of thousands, if not millions, of transfers into joint names using the old forms are vulnerable

to challenge in the courts simply because it is likely that the owners contributed unequally to their purchase.

So, a transfer of the legal title into joint names – of necessity under a joint tenancy – will create a presumption that the parties held the property on trust for themselves as beneficial joint tenants. But a presumption may be rebutted, and so the next question must be, what evidence will be sufficient to show that the parties had a different intention? Would the mere fact that the parties had made unequal financial contributions be sufficient to rebut the presumption? Not according to Baroness Hale:

[69] In law, 'context is everything' and the domestic context is very different from the commercial world. Each case will turn on its own facts. Many more factors than financial contributions may be relevant to divining the parties' true intentions. These include: any advice or discussions at the time of the transfer which cast light upon their intentions then; the reasons why the home was acquired in their joint names; the reasons why (if it be the case) the survivor was authorised to give a receipt for the capital moneys; the purpose for which the home was acquired; the nature of the parties' relationship; whether they had children for whom they both had responsibility to provide a home; how the purchase was financed, both initially and subsequently; how the parties arranged their finances, whether separately or together or a bit of both; how they discharged the outgoings on the property and their other household expenses. When a couple are joint owners of the home and jointly liable for the mortgage, the inferences to be drawn from who pays for what may be very different from the inferences to be drawn when only one is owner of the home. The arithmetical calculation of how much was paid by each is also likely to be less important. It will be easier to draw the inference that they intended that each should contribute as much to the household as they reasonably could and that they would share the eventual benefit or burden equally. The parties' individual characters and personalities may also be a factor in deciding where their true intentions lay. In the cohabitation context, mercenary considerations may be more to the fore than they would be in marriage, but it should not be assumed that they always take pride of place over natural love and affection. At the end of the day, having taken all this into account, cases in which the joint legal owners are to be taken to have intended that their beneficial interests should be different from their legal interests will be very unusual.

Two points should be noted. First, unequal financial contributions may justify an inference that the parties intended that their shares would also be unequal, but only when viewed in the context of the parties' relationship as a whole. Secondly, this broad-ranging exercise is aimed simply at quantifying the *extent* of the parties' respective interests; since the starting-point is that there is a beneficial joint tenancy, the question as to whether each has an interest under a trust has already been answered (although see Mee [2007] Conv 14 for the argument that a claimant attempting to establish a larger share in the property can only do so if the requirements for a constructive (or, presumably, resulting) trust are satisfied).

The approach of Baroness Hale found favour with the majority of the House of Lords. But there was a powerful dissent from Lord Neuberger, arguing that the starting-point that equity follows the law should be departed from if the parties had made unequal contributions (giving rise to a resulting trust in proportion to their contributions) or if there was further evidence as to the parties' intentions giving rise to a constructive trust. Imposing equality on parties who held the legal title jointly, regardless of their contributions, was, in his view, 'almost a resurrection of the "family assets" hypothesis disposed of in *Pettitt*' (at [112]). In addition:

[113] There are also practical reasons for rejecting equality and supporting the resulting trust solution. The property may be bought in joint names for reasons which cast no light on the parties' intentions with regard to beneficial ownership. It may be the solicitor's decision or assumption, the lender's preference for the security of two borrowers, or the happenstance of how the initial contact with the solicitor was made. As the survey mentioned by Baroness Hale in paragraph 45 of her opinion indicates, parties in a loving relationship are often not anxious to discuss how they should divide the beneficial interest in the home they are about to buy. They would have to debate what should happen if their relationship broke down (the most likely circumstance, albeit not the only one, in which the question would arise). While in some cases they may assume equal ownership, in others they may not. In many cases the point may not even occur to them, and if it does, they may be happy to rely on the law to provide the answer if the need arises. If they are happy with an equal split at the beginning, one might expect them to say so. The fact that they do not do so may be more consistent with the view that they (or at any rate the bigger contributor) would not be happy with that outcome for the very reason that their contributions differed.

[114] There is also an important point about consistency of approach with a case where the purchase of a home is in the name of one of the parties. As Baroness Hale observes, where there is no evidence of contributions, joint legal ownership is reflected in a presumption of joint beneficial ownership just as sole legal ownership is reflected in a presumption of sole beneficial ownership. Where there is evidence of the parties' respective contributions to the purchase price (and no other relevant evidence) and one of the parties has contributed X%, the fact that the purchase is in the sole name of the other does not prevent the former owning X% of the beneficial interest on a resulting trust basis. Indeed, it is because of the resulting trust presumption that such ownership arises. It seems to me that consistency suggests that the party who contributed X% of the purchase price should be entitled to X% (no more and no less) of the beneficial interest in the same way if he is a co-purchaser. The resulting trust presumption arises because it is assumed that neither party intended a gift of any part of his own contribution to the other party. That would seem to me to apply to contributions irrespective of the name or names in which the property concerned is acquired and held, as a matter of both principle and logic.

Yet Lord Neuberger did accept that the presumption of resulting trust could itself be rebutted if there was other relevant evidence of the parties' intentions – either at the time that the property was acquired or at a later date – giving rise to a constructive trust. And this in turn might lead to equal beneficial ownership, even if the parties had not made equal financial contributions (just as it might where the property was in the name of only one of the parties, as discussed further below). While his analysis of the role of the resulting trust in cases where there is no other evidence as to the parties' intentions is impeccable, the obvious objection to its application in the context of the shared family home is that in this context there will *always* be other evidence as to the parties' intentions, in the form of the respective contributions of the parties throughout their relationship (see also George (2008) 30 JSWFL 49).

Subsequent cases have confirmed the truth of Baroness Hale's observation that 'context is everything'. The presumption that legal joint tenants are also beneficial joint tenants does not apply to a property that has been purchased as an investment rather than as a home, even if the purchasers are related to one another (see *Laskar v Laskar* [2008] EWCA Civ 347), and is easier to displace where the parties are not living together as a couple (see eg *Ritchie v Ritchie* [2007] EW Misc 5 (EWCC)). Each of these cases involved a mother who had acquired the right to buy her property at a discount and an adult child who had assisted in the purchase. A similar result was reached in the earlier case of *Carlton v Goodman* [2002] EWCA Civ 545 in which the fact that the claimant had facilitated the purchase by lending her name to the mortgage did not give her an interest in the property, as this was not the intention of the parties. In such cases the resulting trust still has a role to play, in the absence of any express discussions or other contributions casting light upon the parties' intentions (see *Laskar v Laskar* [2008] EWCA Civ 347, at [21], per Lord Neuberger).

By contrast, in post-*Stack* cases involving couples, joint legal ownership has been reflected in joint beneficial ownership. In some cases the facts were such that this would have been the likely outcome even before the decision in *Stack* (see eg *Shah v Baverstock* [2008] 1 P & CR DG3). More dramatically, in *Gibson v Revenue and Customs Prosecution Office* [2008] EWCA Civ 645, the presumption of joint beneficial ownership was held to apply even where the mortgage repayments had been made by the husband with money that had been obtained from his criminal activities. The court refused to impute to the parties an intention that Mrs Gibson should not benefit from money obtained illegally: as May LJ pointed out 'it seems to me quite impossible for the law, in the guise of public policy, to attribute to Mr and Mrs Gibson an intention which they plainly did not have and would never have assented to' (at [18]).

Of more relevance to the typical dispute over the family home is *Fowler v Barron* [2008] EWCA Civ 377. Here the court found that the presumption of equal shares had not been rebutted even where the female cohabitant had made no financial contribution to the purchase of the property. As Arden LJ explained:

[41] . . . the decision in *Stack* shows that the critical factor is not necessarily the amount of the parties' contributions: the court has to have regard to all the circumstances which may throw light on the parties' intentions as respects ownership of the property. In this case, the judge found that Miss Fowler paid a number of expenses . . . He went on to hold that 'it was completely understood and accepted [by Miss Fowler] that her money was hers to spend as she chose when she wanted'. With respect to the judge, this makes it sound as if her income was no more than old-fashioned 'pin money'. The reality was that she spent much of her income and the child benefits principally on herself and her children and meeting what the judge termed 'optional expenditure' such as gifts, school clubs and trips, personal clothing, holidays and special occasions. In my judgment, the proper inference is that, with the exception of clothing for herself, these payments were her contributions to household expenses for which both parties were responsible. As I see it, the correct finding is that Mr Barron paid some items properly described as household expenses, such as the council tax and the utilities bills, whereas she paid other such items. The division was perfectly logical if, as I assume, she did most of the shopping for the children. The further inference that in my judgment it is appropriate to draw is that the parties intended that it should make no difference to their interests in the property which party paid for what expense. Those payments also throw light on their intentions in this respect. There was no prior agreement as to who would pay what. The inference from this, especially when taken with the evidence as to mutual wills . . . was that the parties simply did not care about the respective size of each other's contributions.

Given the clear message in *Stack v Dowden* that it would be very difficult for the parties to show that their beneficial interests were different from their legal interests, it may come as something of a surprise that the proceeds of sale were not divided equally in that case. The decision that Ms Dowden was entitled to 65 per cent of the proceeds reflected her greater financial contribution, but the inference that the parties did not intend to share the beneficial interest was based on the parties' whole course of dealing rather than simply the fact that one had made a greater contribution than the other. Considerable weight was attached to the fact that the parties had kept their savings and investments separate and that Ms Dowden had been responsible for all regular financial commitments other than those relating to the mortgage. In the conclusion of Baroness Hale:

[92]. This is, therefore, a very unusual case. There cannot be many unmarried couples who have lived together for as long as this, who have had four children together, and whose affairs have been kept as rigidly separate as this couple's affairs were kept. This is all strongly indicative that they did not intend their shares, even in the property which was put into both their names, to be equal (still less that they intended a beneficial joint tenancy with the right of survivorship should one of them die before it was severed). Before the Court of Appeal, Ms Dowden contended for a 65% share and in my view she has made good her case for that.

It should however be noted that it is far from unusual for cohabiting couples to keep separate bank accounts; moreover, empirical research shows that notionally separate bank accounts may be treated in practice as a joint pool (see eg the studies cited in Probert (2007) 15 Feminist Legal Studies 341; George (2008) 30 JSWFL 49). Such research suggests the need for caution in drawing inferences about couples' intentions from certain aspects of their behaviour. In addition, unequal financial contributions may in practice be offset by the parties' respective *non*-financial contributions. Fairness, certainty and the desirability of avoiding litigation thus all point in favour of a strong presumption in favour of joint beneficial ownership in the context of the jointly owned family home.

This is not to say that it cannot be displaced, even in this context. One situation in which it may be appropriate for the presumption to be displaced is where the decision to transfer a home previously owned by one party into the names of both is made at the instigation of a mortgage company upon the property being remortgaged. A recent empirical study by Douglas, Pearce and Woodward (*A Failure of Trusts: Resolving Property Disputes on Cohabitation Breakdown* (2007), Cardiff Law School Research Paper No 1) found examples of this practice (at p 138):

> This was generally done where a woman had been the sole owner, perhaps as a result of a prior divorce settlement. This meant that the value of the property became shared equally, with no recognition of the partner's prior ownership, effectively resulting in an inadvertent half share to the partner.

A final point of interest relates to the differential impact of *Stack* on different types of relationships. Both patterns of tenure and of ownership vary between married couples and cohabitants: one recent survey found that 74% of couples who had been married were home owners, and 92% of them had owned the home in joint names; by contrast, only 42% of cohabitants owned their home and only 46% of them were joint legal owners (Arthur et al *Settling Up* (2002) p 13; see also Cooke, Barlow and Callus *Community of Property: A Regime for England and Wales* (2006), p 22; Haskey, 'Cohabiting Couples in Great Britain: Accommodation Sharing, Tenure and Property Ownership' (2001) 103 Population Trends 26 at 33). Most cohabitants, therefore, will not benefit from the decision in *Stack v Dowden* and will need to establish an interest in the family home under a trust.

Consider the following points:

(1) Is it appropriate for a different approach to be adopted when ascertaining the rights of the parties in a domestic context, or should, as Lord Neuberger contended in *Stack*, the same principles be applied whether the parties are in 'a sexual, platonic, familial, amicable or commercial relationship' (at [107])? If the former, what relationships should be regarded as domestic in nature?

(2) The cases decided in the wake of *Stack* suggest that a distinction will be drawn between couples and other family members. Is there any basis for this distinction? (See also the discussion in the Law Commission's paper *Sharing Homes*, considered below at p 663.)

(3) Given the evidence that many of those who tick the box to state that they are joint tenants do not appreciate the significance of so doing, is it appropriate for the courts to infer that those who have *not* done so intended to hold the property as joint tenants?

(4) It was noted by Baroness Hale that 'the parties may not intend survivorship even if they do intend that their shares shall be equal' (at [57]). If the claimant has been unable to establish that unequal shares were intended, in what circumstances might he or she be able to show that the parties intended a tenancy in common in equal shares rather than a joint tenancy?

5. The family home in sole legal ownership

Again, the starting-point is to ask whether any formal declaration of trust has been made, either at the time of the purchase or at a later date. However, as the Law Commission has pointed out (Consultation Paper 179 (2006) para 1.13):

> ... [I]t is unlikely that a declaration of trust will have been made if the property was not jointly purchased. There is no obvious reason why legal advice would be sought where one person owns a house into which another comes to live. Even if a house is purchased at a time when the couple are living together, the Land Registry does not require the respective shares of the parties to be declared if the legal title is transferred into the name of one party only. In either circumstances, the non-owning party who wishes to claim a share in the property must resort to the doctrines of implied trust and proprietary estoppel ...

(a) Resulting trusts

As noted above, a resulting trust arises where, and only where, there has been a direct financial contribution to the initial purchase price. Such a contribution gives rise to a presumption that the person making the contribution is entitled to an interest in the property proportionate to the amount of the contribution.

The precise role attributed to the intentions of the parties in this scenario has been a matter of much debate. Academics have attempted to find a principled explanation that fits both the 'presumed' resulting trust that arises from a contribution to the purchase price and the 'automatic' resulting trust that comes into play where there has been an express declaration of trust and a failure to dispose of the entire beneficial interest in property (see Chapter 4). Chambers, for example, suggests that the unifying principle is that 'the provider of property did not intend to benefit the recipient' (Chambers *Resulting Trusts* (1997) p 2). The possibility of any such unifying theory is challenged by Swadling, who notes that what is being presumed in the case of a financial contribution or voluntary transfer is that the transferor is declaring a trust in his own favour; the 'automatic' resulting trust, however, 'defies legal analysis' (Swadling (2008) LQR 72 at 102; although see Piska [2008] Conv 441). We shall return to the issue of intention when considering the respective roles of the resulting and constructive trusts.

The presumption of resulting trust can be rebutted by the competing presumptions of 'advancement' (see Chapter 6, p 310). These are, in effect, presumptions that a gift is intended in certain cases, for example where a father purchases property in the name of a child of his, or otherwise transfers it to that child without consideration. A similar presumption applies to voluntary transfers by husbands to wives, and by fiancés to fiancées (but not vice versa). The effect of the presumption, where it operates, is to rebut or negate the presumption of resulting trust, since its underlying assumption is that the transferor intended to make a gift of the property in these particular contexts. However, the strength of the presumption of advancement is much weakened nowadays, and it can be rebutted by 'comparatively slight evidence' (see eg *McGrath v Wallis* [1995] 2 FLR 114 and *Ledger-Beadell v Peach* [2006] EWHC 2940 (Ch); *Laskar v Laskar* [2008] EWCA Civ 347). It should be noted, however, that where a home is purchased in joint names a similar effect may be produced by the presumption of joint beneficial ownership laid down in *Stack v Dowden*: in *Gibson v Revenue and Customs Prosecution Office* [2008] EWCA Civ 645 it was suggested that the latter now performs the function of the presumption of advancement (at [27]). The differences between the two should, however, be borne in mind: if the property in question was purchased by the husband, and conveyed into joint names, the presumption of advancement would yield the same result as the presumption of joint beneficial ownership; however, if the property in question was purchased by the wife (or by a cohabitant of either sex) and conveyed into joint names, the presumption of advancement would have no application. The point made in *Gibson* is nonetheless useful in reminding us of the fact that the law has long made assumptions about the intentions of home-owners on the basis of their family situation: *Stack v Dowden* could be seen as the presumption of advancement updated to meet the realities of twenty-first century families.

The difficulty in applying the presumption of resulting trust to the context of the family home lies in the fact that it focuses solely on direct financial contributions to the initial purchase price of the property. The first problem is one of application. It is only rarely that an individual can purchase a house outright with cash. Most people will require some form of mortgage finance to cover the lion's share of the purchase price. A mortgage loan is repaid over a period of time, often 25 years, and usually consists of a combination of capital repayments and interest. This means that for most people repaying a mortgage is the commonest way of acquiring a home. Yet, on a strict analysis, this is not how mortgage repayments are perceived in law: instead, they are merely the discharge of a debt incurred to finance a purchase that has already taken place. As such, they will not trigger a resulting trust in its conventional form (see *Calverley v Green* (1984) 155 CLR 242, per Mason and Brennan JJ). There is also a question as to whether the assumption of liability for that debt at the time of acquisition should be treated in the same way as a cash contribution to the purchase. The issue was reviewed by Lord Neuberger in *Stack v Dowden*:

> [117] . . . There is attraction in the notion that liability under a mortgage should be equivalent to a cash contribution. On that basis, if a property is acquired for £300,000, which is made up of one party's contribution of £100,000, and both parties taking on joint liability for a £200,000 mortgage, the beneficial interest would be two-thirds owned by the party who made the contribution, and one-third by the other. If one party then repays more of the mortgage advance, equitable accounting might be invoked to adjust the beneficial ownerships at least in a suitable case. Such an adjustment would be consistent with the resulting trust analysis, as repayments of mortgage capital may be seen as retrospective contributions towards the cost of acquisition, or as payments which increase the value of the equity of redemption.
>
> [118] However, there is an argument that taking on liability under a mortgage should not be equivalent to a cash payment. The cash contribution is effectively equity, whereas the mortgage liability arises in relation to a secured loan. If the value of the property in the example just given had fallen by 25% when it came to be sold, the party who made the cash contribution would lose £75,000 of his £100,000, whereas the other party would lose nothing (unless he would be liable to pay £25,000 to the former, which seems intuitively improbable).

Despite his reluctance to decide between the two approaches, in *Laskar v Laskar* [2008] EWCA Civ 347 Lord Neuberger subsequently held that in that case it was appropriate to treat the assumption of liability for the mortgage as a contribution from each of the parties. A key factor in that case, however, was that the mortgage had been paid out of the rental income from the property; it does not, therefore, establish how the assumption of liability for the mortgage should be treated in the more usual domestic case. In any case, if the actual mortgage repayments are to 'count' towards a share (and there is every reason why they should), then some other conceptual vehicle needs to be found to ensure that they do.

The second problem of the resulting trust lies in the potential unfairness in the family context of a rule that ignores other contributions made by family members at a later date – for example mortgage repayments, the payment of other household bills and non-financial contributions. As we shall see, this limitation has led to the development of the constructive trust as a more flexible mechanism for dealing with the ownership of the family home.

It was for these reasons that reliance on the resulting trust was becoming rarer even before the decision of the House of Lords in *Stack v Dowden* [2007] UKHL 17. Some commentators have seen *Stack* as effectively 'abolishing' the resulting trust in the domestic context (see eg Swadling (2007) 123 LQR 511). It is clear that the presumption that the parties intended their shares to be proportionate to their financial contributions has been displaced in favour of a presumption of joint beneficial ownership in the context of the jointly owned family home, but, as *Laskar* shows, once that presumption has been displaced the resulting trust may still have a role to play. It would thus be more appropriate to say that the presumption of resulting trust no longer holds sway (see eg Lord Walker in *Stack v Dowden* at [31]) because it no longer fits the facts. As Piska has pointed out, 'in the family-home context the presumption of declaration of trust is no longer the most likely inference from common experience . . . [T]he average home purchaser . . . will not have heard of a trust, let alone understand and intend to create one' ([2008] Conv 441 at 449).

For all these reasons, as Baroness Hale noted in *Abbott v Abbott* [2007] UKPC 53, 'the constructive trust is generally the more appropriate tool of analysis in most matrimonial cases' (at [5]).

(b) Constructive trusts

Before embarking on a consideration of the circumstances in which a constructive trust will arise, it is first necessary to consider whether such specific criteria have been abandoned in favour of a holistic analysis akin to that adopted in *Stack v Dowden* when quantifying the parties' interests. A number of commentators have adopted the latter view (see eg Dixon [2007] Conv 456; Gardner (2008) 124 LQR 422), drawing on a case decided in the wake of *Stack v Dowden*, the Privy Council case of *Abbott v Abbott* [2007] UKPC 53.

The case involved a divorcing husband and wife from Antigua, a jurisdiction which had no system for reallocating assets between the parties upon divorce. The matrimonial home was in the husband's sole name, but it had been built on land given by the husband's mother after the marriage. A loan had been taken out to fund the construction of the home, secured by a charge over the property: while the husband, as legal owner, had of necessity been the one who executed the charge, the wife had made herself jointly and severally liable for the repayment of the principal and interest. At first instance the judge had found that the parties each had an equal beneficial share in the property on the basis that the land had been a gift to them both, and also because of the wife's assumption of liability under the loan. The Eastern Caribbean Court of Appeal had allowed the husband's appeal, and held that the wife's share should be only 8.31%, based on her direct contributions to the mortgage payments. The Privy Council, by contrast, held that the Court of Appeal should not have interfered with the findings of the judge.

The part of the case that has led to confusion is Baroness Hale's statement that '[t]he parties' whole course of conduct in relation to the property must be taken into account in determining their shared intentions as to its ownership' (at [19]). However, this statement was made in the context of the *quantification* of the interest, not whether an interest had arisen, the husband having accepted that his wife did have some beneficial interest in the property (see also Lee (2008) 124 LQR 209). Other cases decided in the wake of *Stack v Dowden* indicate that the courts still regard themselves as constrained by the need to find that the requirements of a constructive trust are satisfied. We therefore need to turn to consider these requirements, and the logical starting-point for analysis of the modern law is the House of Lords' decision in *Lloyds Bank v Rosset* [1991] 1 AC 107.

(1) *Lloyds Bank v Rosset*

The pre-*Rosset* case law had suggested two distinct lines of development. The first recognised the existence of an implied trust only where the claimant had made some financial contribution to the acquisition of the property in question. The size of the share awarded was, in theory, governed by the size of the qualifying contribution. This type of implied trust seemed to be closely linked to the classic presumption of resulting trust. The second, exemplified by *Eves v Eves* ([1975] 1 WLR 1338) and *Grant v Edwards* ([1986] Ch 638), suggested that an implied trust would arise where (i) the defendant had explicitly promised the plaintiff a share in the beneficial ownership, or had acknowledged that the plaintiff was in some way entitled to such a share, and (ii) where the plaintiff had then relied on that promise to his or her detriment. In such cases, the courts seemed to exercise some discretion in fixing the size of the plaintiff's share. This second type of implied trust had been called 'constructive' in *Eves* and *Grant*. In *Rosset*, Lord Bridge purported to accommodate both of these approaches in his rationalisation of the modern law. How accurate his summary was is a matter of debate, but its influence on the subsequent case law cannot be doubted.

Unusually for litigation turning on implied trusts, *Rosset* was a case involving a wife rather than an unmarried cohabitant. The case concerned a matrimonial home which had been bought in the husband's sole name with money from a family trust. The wife had made no direct financial contribution to the purchase, but had carried out some renovations to the property and had supervised building works. Unknown to the wife, the husband had charged the house to the plaintiff bank as security for an overdraft of his. About a year after the purchase, the husband left the home following a breakdown in the marriage relationship. Following a failure to meet the bank's demand to repay the overdraft, the bank sought an order for possession and sale of the property. The wife resisted the bank's claim on the ground that she had an equitable interest in the property under an implied trust; and that this entitled her to assert a right of occupation of the property which took priority over the bank's charge.

Mrs Rosset lost at first instance, but won in the Court of Appeal. She lost again in the House of Lords, on the ground that she had acquired no interest in the house under an implied trust. In the course of reaching this conclusion, Lord Bridge summarised the law as follows (at 132–133):

> The first and fundamental question which must always be resolved is whether . . . there has at any time prior to acquisition, or exceptionally at some later date, been any agreement, arrangement or understanding reached between them that the property is to be shared beneficially. The finding of an agreement or an arrangement to share in this sense can only, I think, be based on evidence of express discussions, however imperfectly remembered and however imprecise their terms may have been. Once a finding to this effect is made it will only be necessary for the partner asserting a claim to a beneficial interest against the partner entitled to the legal estate to show that he or she has acted to his or her detriment or significantly altered his or her legal position in reliance on the agreement in order to give rise to a constructive trust or proprietary estoppel.
>
> In sharp contrast with this situation is the very different one where there is no evidence to support a finding of an agreement or arrangement to share, however reasonable it might have been for the parties to reach such an arrangement if they had applied their minds to the question, and where the court must rely entirely on the conduct of the parties both as the basis from which to infer a common intention to share the property beneficially and as the conduct relied on to give rise to a constructive trust. In this situation direct contributions to the purchase price by the partner who is not the legal owner, whether initially or by payment of mortgage instalments, will readily justify the inference necessary to the creation of a constructive trust. But, as I read the authorities, it is at least extremely doubtful whether anything less will do.

In *Rosset* itself, Lord Bridge held that there was insufficient evidence of any 'agreement, arrangement or understanding' between the spouses that Mrs Rosset should have a share, under the principles outlined in the first paragraph; nor had Mrs Rosset made any 'direct financial contribution' to qualify under principles contained in the second. The bank was accordingly granted the order it sought.

In his formulation, Lord Bridge refers throughout to the 'constructive trust'. One assumes that this usage was deliberate, and was intended to suggest that this sort of trust is indeed distinct from a resulting trust. We have seen how the traditional resulting trust relies on intention in only a negative sense, ie it raises a presumption about ownership that can be rebutted by contrary evidence of actual intention. Here, however, Lord Bridge (consistently with the authorities, especially *Pettitt* and *Gissing*) accords intention a more positive function. In his formulation, intention is either express but informal, or to be inferred from conduct (albeit a very limited type of conduct); and in both cases this intention forms the rationale for the existence of the trust. The proper name for this, it seems, is now 'constructive' rather than 'resulting' trust. Lord Bridge also describes his second category as giving rise to a 'constructive trust *or* proprietary estoppel'. Again, the purpose behind this use of terminology is unclear; but it raises conceptual and practical issues that will be discussed later in this chapter.

We now turn to consider the two alternative routes to establishing an implied trust set out by Lord Bridge.

(2) Express but informal agreements

Lord Bridge cited two cases as 'outstanding examples' of the principles he had in mind in describing his first category of case: *Eves v Eves* [1975] 1 WLR 1338 and *Grant v Edwards* [1986] Ch 638.

In *Eves*, the plaintiff, Janet Eves, and the defendant, Stuart Eves, had cohabited for four years, during which time a house had been paid for by, and conveyed into the sole name of, Stuart. Stuart told Janet that the conveyance would have been in joint names but for the fact that at the time Janet had been under 21. Janet accepted this explanation, and she did a good deal of work on the house and garden, including breaking up an area of concrete covering the front garden with a 14-pound sledgehammer and preparing the front garden for turfing; she also reared two children and performed the role of housewife. Janet later moved out of the house with the children and married another man. She claimed a share in the house, the value of which had risen from £5,600 in 1968 to £13,000 in 1973, leaving an equity value in excess of £10,000. The Court of Appeal awarded Janet a quarter share.

In *Grant v Edwards*, Linda Grant and George Edwards lived together for eleven years, from 1969 to 1980. They bought a house that was transferred jointly into George's name and that of his brother, Arthur. George told Linda that he would have put it jointly in his and her names but for the fact that it would prejudice her financial claims against her ex-husband. During the course of the relationship, Linda gave birth to two children. She made substantial financial contributions out of earnings to household expenses, and in the process succeeded in paying off one of two mortgages that had been secured on the property. Basing herself on her financial and domestic contributions, Linda claimed a share of the equity under an implied trust. On appeal, the Court of Appeal awarded Linda a half share.

In order to draw out the principles at work here, we shall consider these cases in stages. First, what do these cases tell us about the requirement that there be 'an agreement, arrangement or understanding' between the parties? Second, what is the link required between the agreement and the acts of detrimental reliance by the claimant? Third (and linked to the second), what acts by the claimant will count as detrimental reliance on the agreement? Fourth, how are shares valued under this type of trust? Finally, what are the implications of Lord Bridge's statement that a successful claim under this head gives rise to a 'constructive trust *or* a proprietary estoppel' (emphasis added)?

(i) Is there an 'agreement, arrangement or understanding'?

The first step under this head is to show that there was some 'agreement, arrangement or understanding' between the parties over the question of own-ership before the date of acquisition (or, in 'exceptional cases', later). In both *Eves* and *Grant*, the necessary 'agreement' was successfully established. But of what did it consist?

In both of these cases the man found an 'excuse' for not putting the property in joint names: in the former, that the woman was under 21 years of age, in the latter, that joint ownership might prejudice the woman's position in divorce proceedings in which she was involved. The Court of Appeal found in both cases that if there had not been a joint intention, there would have been no need for an excuse. But, with respect, is this necessarily so? I am about to move into a new house with my girlfriend. She wants to have a share in the property: I do not want her to have a share. I find some 'excuse' which fobs her off. Surely this is not agreement: it is disagreement. If I had agreed with her that there would be a joint holding of the property, I would not have found an excuse to fob her off in the first place. If an agreement, arrangement or intention is being found here, it is surely converting the intention of one party – albeit on these facts the innocent one – into an agreement. (P Clarke 'The Family Home: Intention and Agreement' [1992] Fam Law 72)

In a similar vein, Gardner ((1993) 109 LQR 263 at 265) has commented on the 'fallacious reasoning' in the cases. Mee, however, has defended the reasoning on the basis that an excuse that relates to the *legal* title may well create expectations relating to the *beneficial* interest.

Gardner does not appear to advert to the possibility that the woman in each case reasonably understood from her partner's representations that, while it was agreed between the parties that (beneficial) ownership was to be shared, there was some technical obstacle which prevented her being given legal ownership of the property. (Mee *The Property Rights of Cohabitees* (1999) p 123)

Both sets of arguments have force. On the one hand, it is clear that there was no real agreement or meeting of minds between the parties. But a mutual *understanding* can be discerned: it is credible that Janet Eves and Linda Grant did believe that they would be entitled to *some* interest in the property (although less so that they would conceptualise it in the way Mee suggests); it is also likely that this was the effect intended and understood by their respective partners (else they could have simply refused to put their respective partners on the legal title without resorting to any excuse).

Cases like *Eves* and *Grant* might lead one to assume that it is relatively easy to establish an agreement (see also *Hammond v Mitchell* [1991] 1 WLR 1127). However, two points should be noted. The first is the practical problem of proof. As Waite J pointed out in *Hammond v Mitchell* [1991] 1 WLR 1127 (at 1139):

The primary emphasis accorded by the law in cases of this kind to express discussions between the parties ('however imperfectly remembered and however imprecise their terms') means that the tenderest exchanges of a common law [sic] courtship may assume an unforeseen significance many years later when they are brought under equity's microscope.

Often there will be a conflict of evidence between the parties as to whether the relevant words were ever spoken. In such cases the issue becomes one of the credibility of the respective parties. The context of the case will of course be relevant in assessing the likelihood of the alleged words being spoken (see eg *Buggs v Buggs* [2003] EWHC 1538). In *Cox v Jones* [2004] EWHC 1486 (Ch), for example, the judge preferred the woman's evidence that there had been discussions about joint ownership:

> [67]...That explains Miss Cox's involvement in the house-hunting process...She was doing it because she thought she was contributing to something which would be a home for them, in which she would have an interest, and the reason that she believed that is because that was the basis of discussions between them – the property was to be not merely their home, but their jointly owned property. It is in this context that the nature and closeness of the relationship becomes a very important part of the background. Since it was one with long-term commitments potentially close at hand, it was one in which it is more likely that representations about joint ownership of property would be made.

The emphasis in that passage on the intention that the property was to be jointly owned, rather than 'merely' a home, leads on to the second point. A significant restriction on the scope of an agreement, arrangement or understanding is that it must relate to the ownership, rather than merely the enjoyment, of the property. In *Rosset* itself Lord Bridge overturned the finding of both the lower courts that Mr and Mrs Rosset had reached an arrangement as to ownership. The judge at first instance was convinced that Mrs Rosset 'genuinely believed that [the husband] would hold the property in his name as something which was a joint venture, to be shared between them as the family home' but that 'as so often happens the [husband and wife] did not pursue their discussions to the extent of defining precisely what their respective interests in the property should be'. It was this lack of precision that Lord Bridge took to be fatal to the wife's claim. He outlined the problem in the following terms (at 127–128):

> Spouses living in amity will not normally think it necessary to formulate or define their respective interests in property in any precise way. The expectation of parties to every happy marriage is that they will share the practical benefits of occupying the matrimonial home whoever owns it. But this is something quite distinct from sharing the beneficial interest in the property asset which the matrimonial home represents. These considerations give rise to special difficulties for judges who are called on to resolve a dispute between spouses who have parted and are at arm's length as to what their common intention or understanding with respect to interests in property was at the time when they were still living as a united family and acquiring a matrimonial home in the expectation of living in it indefinitely.

Thus expectations concerning joint use during marriage or cohabitation will not translate into an agreement as to ownership at its termination: something more specific is required.

The common pattern to emerge from these cases, then, is that a plaintiff must be able to point to a specific statement about ownership having been made. It does not matter that the statement in question is deceitful or mere trickery, or that the person making the statement did not 'really' mean what was said. The fact of it having been made in clear terms will be enough, assuming that the claimant understood it in those terms (as Mee has pointed out, while it is not fatal to a claim that the *defendant* did not subjectively share the alleged common intention generated by his or her words, it must be fatal to a claim if the *claimant* did not believe the assurances made: [2007] Conv 14 at 21). Equally, it will *not* be enough to point to an assumed but unarticulated common assumption about ownership. The formula 'agreement, arrangement or understanding' may therefore be inapt.

Consider the following points:

(1) Is it possible that the House of Lords in *Rosset* was influenced by the fact that the respondent to the wife's claim was not a matrimonial or cohabiting partner, but a creditor?

(2) Is it realistic to think that couples think of their home in terms of ownership versus use? Should references to 'our house' be sufficient grounding for an agreement, arrangement or understanding?

(3) Bottomley has suggested that the requirement, evident from the case law, that there should be something more specific than a mere expectation of ownership generated by joint use of property or cohabitation 'is not only a requirement of a certain jurisprudential approach but also a mode of reasoning and language which is more conducive to men than to women'. She further argues that 'women too often read silence as positive assent and lack of specificity as covering a number of issues with equal firmness rather than evading a particular issue' ((1993) 20 J Law and Society 56 at 62). Is one implication of Bottomley's argument that men and women may have different ideas of what it takes to make an agreement *at all*?

(ii) Detrimental reliance

On its own, an oral agreement (or, more accurately perhaps, an oral declaration) concerning equitable ownership of the family home amounts to no more than an ineffective attempt to create an express trust of land (LPA 1925, s 53(1)(b)). The claimant must go further and prove that he or she has acted to his or her detriment, in *reliance* on the agreement (per Lord Bridge in *Rosset* at 132), so as to bring the case within the statutory exception to the formality requirements for trusts of land (LPA 1925, s 53(2)). This raises two related but separate questions: first, what relationship must exist between the agreement on the one hand and the acts of detrimental reliance on the other? This is the question of reliance, or 'linkage'. Second, what acts will count as detrimental reliance at all?

The question of linkage received extensive, but divergent, treatment by the Court of Appeal in *Grant v Edwards* [1986] Ch 638. Mustill LJ seemed to envisage a contractual analysis: the plaintiff's activities must in some way be related to the bargain struck between the parties at the time of acquisition. This may involve the court in (re)constructing the terms of the agreement. As Mustill LJ put it (at 652), 'the proprietor promises the claimant an interest in the property on the basis that the claimant will do something in return. The parties do not themselves make explicit what the claimant is to do. The court therefore has to complete the bargain for them by means of implication.' Nourse LJ, on the other hand, seemed to have a causal test in mind. For him, the question was whether the plaintiff would have done what s/he did *but for* the agreement with the defendant: 'she could reasonably be expected to go and live with her lover, but not, for example, to wield a 14lb sledge hammer in the front garden' (at 648).

Browne-Wilkinson VC suggested, obiter, yet another approach (at 657):

> . . . it is impossible to say whether or not the claimant would have done the acts relied on as a detriment even if she thought she had no interest in the house. Setting up house together, having a baby, making payments to general housekeeping expenses (not strictly necessary to enable the mortgage to be repaid) may all be referable to the mutual love and affection of the parties and not specifically referable to the claimant's belief that she has an interest in the house . . . [O]nce it has been shown that there was a common intention that the claimant should have an interest in the house, any act done by her to her detriment relating to the joint lives of the parties is . . . sufficient detriment to qualify.

The differences between these three approaches may, however, be more apparent than real. It is clear that it is not necessary for the court to find that there was a bargain between the parties (see eg *Parris v Williams* [2008] EWCA Civ 1147), and in the absence of any explicit bargain, the process of implying what the claimant was to do to complete the bargain is likely to take into account what the claimant did do, and whether he or she would have acted in the same way but for the agreement. Similarly, the potential generosity of 'any act' being sufficient to qualify – in Browne-Wilkinson's account – is immediately qualified by the requirement that it must be to the claimant's detriment: again, the implication is that this is something that the claimant would not otherwise have done. Further support for the argument that reliance can only be established by claimants showing that they have done something that they would not have done 'but for' the agreement is provided by the speech of Lord Bridge in *Lloyds Bank v Rosset*, which referred to a trust arising where the claimant had 'altered her position in reliance on the agreement' (at 129).

It is not enough for claimants to show that they have relied on an agreement or declaration; they must go on to show that they have altered their position to their detriment. What counts as detriment is obviously related to the question of reliance, just discussed: the manner in which we define the link between the agreement, etc, and the reliance of the plaintiff, will affect the type of activities that will count as detriment. A 'causal test' leaves the way open to value judgements about what men and women can and cannot reasonably be expected to do 'normally' in the course of a domestic relationship. Women will find it difficult to point to domestic labour as detriment for these purposes, since they may be met by a judicial view that they would have done it anyway and that the agreement in question was not their sole or even dominant motivation. Such was the approach taken in *James v Thomas* [2007] EWCA Civ 1212. According to Chadwick LJ ((at [36]; see also *Morris v Morris* [2008] EWCA Civ 257):

> The true position, as it seems to me, is that she worked in the business, and contributed her labour to the improvements to the property, because she and Mr Thomas were making their life together as man and wife... It is a mistake to think that the motives which lead parties in such a relationship to act as they do are necessarily attributable to pecuniary self-interest.

A 'bargain-based test' leaves the matter more in the hands of the parties, so that conduct that may have failed the 'but for' test may nevertheless qualify if the defendant specifically requested it; however, it will be relatively rare for the parties to spell out a bargain in this way.

Despite this close dependence of the two concepts, there is a distinction to be drawn between reliance and detriment, although this may be more fully developed in the context of proprietary estoppel than in the current law relating to implied trusts (see Gray and Gray *Elements of Land Law* (5th edn, 2008) pp 1221–1234; and see Lawson (1996) 16 LS 218 for a critical discussion of the case law on detrimental reliance for constructive trust purposes).

The practical question posed, however, is how far have the courts felt able to exploit the notion of detriment in implied trust cases so as to move away from the 'solid tug of money' evident in traditional resulting trust doctrine? A mixed picture emerges from the cases. In *Grant v Edwards*, the detriment consisted of Linda Grant's substantial contribution to household expenses. These were not made directly towards the acquisition costs of the house, but nevertheless they were held to be sufficient to qualify her for a share. In *Eves*, Janet was rewarded for out-of-the-ordinary labour in the home. Although not directly a money contribution, one can see how it might be characterised as having worth in money: it was the sort of labour that might otherwise have to be paid for. Similar considerations applied to the female cohabitant's assistance in refurbishing the property in *Cox v Jones* [2004] EWHC 1486 (Ch). As the judge noted, '[i]n doing so she was doing something that either Mr Jones would have had to have done himself (but which he had insufficient time to do) or it would have had to have been done by a professional (who would have charged for it)' (at [73]).

Such non-financial contribution must be substantial: in *Rosset* itself, Lord Bridge was dismissive of Mrs Rosset's activities of supervising the building works and undertaking some of the redecoration of the property. Thus even if he had found an agreement between the parties, the requirement of detrimental reliance would not have been satisfied. 'On any view the monetary value of Mrs Rosset's work expressed as a contribution to a property acquired at a cost exceeding £70,000 must have been so trifling as to be de minimis' (at 131).

The broadest view is implied by the obiter passage from the judgment of Browne-Wilkinson VC quoted above, in which it appears that he would be willing to accept purely domestic activities as detriment. However, over two decades have passed without any judge following this lead, despite the fact that one could argue that the reasoning in *Cox v Jones* – that the other partner would either have had to do the work or pay someone else to do it – applies equally to domestic chores (see Probert [2005] Conv 168).

Consider the following:

(1) Do you agree with Browne-Wilkinson VC (above) that it is difficult to generalise about what motivates people when making domestic contributions of one sort or another? If so, is it fair to assume that *any* acts relating to the joint lives of the parties have been motivated by reliance on a proven assurance of ownership?

(2) It has been suggested that in determining what counts as detrimental reliance, judges have acted on expectations based on gender, especially concerning women. All the examples cited in the following extract are taken from case law:

> It is not [thought] reasonable to expect women acting out of love and affection to wield 14lb sledgehammers, to demolish or construct buildings, or to work awkward cement mixers. On the other hand, it does appear to be thought reasonable to expect such motives to prompt them to move in with their lovers, abandon their marriages, bear and bring up their lover's babies and generally perform 'all wifely duties'. Women acting out of love for their partners, together with the desire to live comfortably, are also expected to wallpaper and generally decorate and design their lovers' houses and to organise builders working on those same houses, even when this includes the purchase and delivery of the building materials. These preconceptions reflect traditional stereotypes of women and women's work. (Lawson, above at 225; see also Bottomley (1993) 20 J Law and Society 56.)

If the claimant has made a valuable contribution to the household economy, should it matter whether or not he or she would have made the same contributions even in the absence of any expectation of an interest in the property?

(iii) Outcome: quantifying shares

A claimant who successfully establishes all of the elements just discussed will be entitled to a share in the equity value of the property in question under a constructive trust. But by what criteria should that share be measured?

Early cases such as *Eves* and *Grant* adopted a discretionary approach to quantification (Janet Eves being awarded a one-quarter share and Linda Grant one half). In such cases the precise weight accorded to the parties' contributions or intentions was unclear. The appropriate approach has now been clarified by the House of Lords in *Stack v Dowden* [2007] UKHL 17. Two competing formulations were considered: first, the suggestion by Chadwick LJ in *Oxley v Hiscock* [2004] EWCA Civ 546, [69] that 'each is entitled to that share which the court considers fair having regard to the whole course of dealing between them in relation to the property'; secondly, the belief expressed by the Law Commission in *Sharing Homes* that 'there is much to be said for adopting what has been called a "holistic approach" to quantification, undertaking a survey of the whole course of dealing between the parties and taking account of all conduct which throws light on the question what shares were intended' (para 4.27). Of these, the second was thought by Baroness Hale in *Stack v Dowden* to be

[61]...the preferable way of expressing what is essentially the same thought, for two reasons. First, it emphasises that the search is still for the result which reflects what the parties must, in the light of their conduct, be taken to have intended. Second, therefore, it does not enable the court to abandon that search in favour of the result which the court itself considers fair. For the court to impose its own view of what is fair upon the situation in which the parties find themselves would be to return to the days before *Pettitt v Pettitt* [1970] AC 777 without even the fig leaf of section 17 of the 1882 Act.

Since the task of the court is to ascertain what shares were intended, any express discussions between the parties as to the quantum of their respective interests are obviously highly relevant (see eg *Clough v Killey* (1996) 72 P&CR D22; *Mortgage Corporation v Shaire* [2001] Ch 743). Explicit statements to third parties such as creditors may also be taken into account (see eg *Hurst v Supperstone* [2005] EWHC 1309 (Ch)). In the absence of any such agreement, a wide range of factors are to be taken into account in ascertaining the parties' intentions, as set out by Baroness Hale in *Stack v Dowden* (above, p 619).

Consider the following points:

(1) If domestic contributions are relevant when ascertaining the parties' intentions as to how their shares should be quantified, why are they not relevant when deciding whether the claimant has relied upon an expectation of an interest in the property to his or her detriment?

(2) How should the court go about inferring intentions from conduct? Should it examine empirical evidence as to the actual intentions of individuals in similar situations? Should it adopt certain presumptions? And is the process of inferring intentions from conduct likely to lead to a result different from that which would have been reached applying the test in *Oxley v Hiscock*?

(3) Should the court give effect to the parties' intentions if that would be unfair in the light of their contributions?

(iv) Constructive trust or estoppel?

In *Rosset* Lord Bridge suggested the elements of agreement, reliance and detriment give rise to a 'constructive trust *or proprietary estoppel*' (emphasis added). This comment raises some interesting questions. For example, does it entail the conceptual assimilation of constructive trusts of this sort with proprietary estoppel? Are they, in other words, to be treated as expressive of the same underlying principle? If so, what is that underlying principle, and does it recognise a wider range of contributions than implied trusts in general?

There are indeed strong similarities between constructive trusts (at least of the 'express but informal agreement' type) and proprietary estoppel: the requirements of an agreement, arrangement or understanding that has been relied on to the claimant's detriment are mirrored in the requirements of assurance, reliance and detriment necessary for estoppel (see Gray and Gray ch 10).

Some differences between the two may still be observed, however. For example, it is said that, conventionally, there is no discretion in constructive-trust cases in awarding shares. The claimant either gets what was promised or agreed, or gets nothing. In estoppel, by contrast, the courts have a complete discretion as to outcome, but are primarily concerned with the 'minimum necessary to do justice' to the claimant (per Scarman LJ in *Crabb v Arun District Council* [1976] Ch 179 at 198). The remedy awarded may range from the transfer of the legal title (eg *Pascoe v Turner* [1979] 1 WLR 431), through the securing of an amount of money by way of a charge on property (*Campbell v Griffin* [2001] EWCA Civ 990) to the grant of mere rights of occupation (eg *Greasley v Cooke* [1980] 1 WLR 1306; *Matharu v Matharu* [1994] 2 FLR 597), a monetary award reflecting the value of that accommodation (eg *Baker v Baker* (1993) 25 HLR 408) or even nothing at all (eg *Sledmore v Dalby* (1996) 72 P&CR 196; see the analysis by Gardner (1999) 115 LQR 438).

Related to this is the fact that a constructive trust interest arises as soon as the conditions for its creation are satisfied, whereas an estoppel interest is inchoate until declared by a court. In addition, it has been said that a constructive trust requires a common intention between the parties, some subjective meeting of minds; whereas, for estoppel, only unilateral conduct leading to an expectation of a property-interest is required (see Hayton [1990] Conv 370 at 371–372). There may also be differences in the test for detrimental reliance. In *Wayling v Jones* (1993) 69 P&CR 170, a case involving an estoppel claim against a deceased's estate, the Court of Appeal held that once a promise as to ownership has been made, then the onus of proof shifts to the defendant to show that the plaintiff did not rely on those promises. This contrasts with the 'but for' test espoused in *Grant v Edwards*, above, which appears to place a heavier onus on the plaintiff; and Browne-Wilkinson VC in *Grant* also appears to assume that the threshold of detrimental reliance is lower in estoppel than constructive trust (and see Lawson (1996) 16 LS 218).

However, it will be evident from the discussion so far that the constructive trust has become more estoppel-like in some of these respects. We have seen that in practice there is no requirement of a full consensus between the parties – some specific assurance, even a lie, is all that is necessary. We have also seen that the quantification of shares under implied trusts is already a largely discretionary exercise, even though the discretion is confined to valuation of shares rather than whether to award a remedy other than a share of the equity.

The desirability of assimilation has been urged by a number of judges and academic commentators over the years (see eg Browne-Wilkinson VC in *Grant v Edwards* [1986] Ch 638 at 656; Nourse LJ in *Stokes v Anderson* [1991] 1 FLR 391 at 399; Chadwick LJ in *Oxley v Hiscock* [2004] EWCA Civ 546; Hayton [1990] Conv 370; Gardner (1993) 109 LQR 263). But it is not a view held by all (see eg Lord Walker in *Stack v Dowden* at [37], resiling from his earlier suggestion in *Yaxley v Gotts* [2000] Ch 162 at 177; Ferguson (1993) 109 LQR 114).

According to Hayton, the virtue of linking constructive trusts to estoppel is that it would enable the courts to be more generous to claimants, possibly by taking domestic labour and child care into account (see below), while at the same time reducing the dangers to 'third parties', such as mortgage lenders, that this entails. Yet both sides of this argument are open to question. On the one hand, the fact that the claim is framed as one based on proprietary estoppel does not necessarily guarantee that the court will take a more generous approach to domestic contributions (see eg *Coombes v Smith* [1986] 1 WLR 808, *Lissimore v Downing* [2003] 2 FLR 308). It is true that in *Ottey v Grundy* [2003] EWCA Civ 1176 reliance was established on the basis that the claimant had given up her career to care for her partner, but the court opined that her conduct went beyond what could be expected of her as a girlfriend, thus implicitly endorsing the idea that actions performed in the course of an ordinary relationship would not be sufficient. On the other hand, the circumstances in which an equitable interest is capable of binding a third party have already been limited to a considerable extent (see eg *Bristol and West Building Society v Henning* [1985] 1 WLR 778, *Equity and Law Home Loans v Prestidge* [1992] 1 WLR 137 and *Abbey National Building Society v Cann* [1991] 1 AC 56; for discussion see Dewar 'Land, Law and the Family Home', op cit).

Nor would the assimilation of constructive trusts and proprietary estoppel necessarily lead to greater intellectual clarity. The principles underpinning the law of estoppel have been a matter of debate for many years (for an analysis in terms of unconscionability, see Finn 'Equitable Estoppel' in Finn (ed) *Essays in Equity* (1985) ch 4; Hayton [1990] Conv 370; and the judgment of Oliver J in *Taylor Fashions Ltd v Liverpool Victoria Trustees* [1982] QB 133n; for the argument that estoppel is concerned with protecting reliance interests only, see Robertson (1997) 19 Syd LR 32; and for the view that estoppel is concerned to protect expectations, see Cooke (1997) 17 LS 258 and *The Modern Law of Estoppel* (2000) pp 150–158; Gardner (1999) 115 LQR 438).

The argument so far assumes that assimilation entails the constructive trust becoming more like proprietary estoppel; the alternative, of course, is that proprietary estoppel may come to resemble the constructive trust. In *Yeoman's Row Management Limited and another v Cobbe* [2008] UKHL 55, Lord Scott, in reviewing the various claims that could be made, drew clear parallels between the constructive trust and proprietary estoppel (at [4]):

> First, both the proprietary estoppel claim and the constructive trust claim are claims to a proprietary interest in the property. The other remedies do not require proprietary claims but follow upon *in personam* claims for compensation or restitution. Second, a proprietary estoppel claim and a constructive trust claim would constitute, if successful, a means whereby B could obtain a remedy providing him with a benefit more or less equivalent to the benefit he expected to obtain from the oral and inchoate agreement; in effect a benefit based on the value of his non-contractual expectation. By way of contrast, an unjust enrichment remedy, a *quantum meruit* remedy and a consideration that has wholly failed remedy are essentially restitutionary in character, concentrating not at all on the value of the expected benefit of which B has been deprived but, as the case may be, on the extent of A's enrichment at B's expense, on the value of B's services or on the amount or value of the consideration provided by B to A.

Yet there remain good reasons for distinguishing between the constructive trust and proprietary estoppel. As noted above, an express common intention constructive trust requires that there be some understanding between the parties regarding the *current ownership* of the property. By contrast, an estoppel may also arise where there is an expectation regarding the *future* ownership of the property – for example, an expectation that the legal owner will leave the property to the claimant by way of a will (see eg *Gillett v Holt* [2000] 2 FLR 266; *Jennings v Rice* [2002] EWCA Civ 159; *Thorner v Curtis* [2007] EWHC 2422 (Ch)), or will otherwise transfer it to the claimant. It may also arise where the expectations of the parties relate to the *occupation*, rather than the ownership, of the property. Thus the advantage of proprietary estoppel is not merely its greater remedial flexibility, but rather the fact that it can respond to a wider range of situations. Whatever the terminology adopted, it is clear that the law needs to provide a remedy that accommodates these different scenarios.

Consider the following points:

(1) In *Yeoman's Row Management Limited and another v Cobbe* [2008] UKHL 55, Lord Walker of Gestingthorpe emphasised the need for certainty when applying estoppel principles: '[e]quitable estoppel is a flexible doctrine which the Court can use, in appropriate circumstances, to prevent injustice caused by the vagaries and inconstancy of human nature. But it is not a sort of joker or wild card to be used whenever the Court disapproves of the conduct of a litigant who seems to have the law on his side. Flexible though it is, the doctrine must be formulated and applied in a disciplined and principled way. Certainty is important in property transactions' (at [46]). Should unconscionable behaviour be a sufficient justification for the court

to act, or should its intervention be limited to cases where unconscionability takes a certain form?

(2) The courts have emphasised that general assurances of financial support will not be sufficient to give rise to an estoppel (see eg *Layton v Martin* [1986] 2 FLR 227; *Negus v Bahouse* [2007] EWHC 2628 (Ch)). Is it logical to draw a distinction between an expectation on the part of the claimant that he or she will be supported in the future and an expectation that he or she will own certain (unspecified) property?

(3) Is it more unconscionable to fail to make a will giving effect to one's promises than to fail to fulfil promises of support upon relationship breakdown?

(3) Inferred common intention and direct financial contributions

The second type of implied trust outlined by Lord Bridge in *Rosset* arises where (unlike the cases just discussed) there is no evidence of an express but informal arrangement between the parties, but where 'the court must rely entirely on the conduct of the parties both as the basis from which to infer a common intention to share the property beneficially and as the conduct relied on to give rise to a constructive trust' (at 132–133). The conduct of the parties thus plays the dual role of establishing both what their intention was, and that the claimant has relied on it. As Lord Bridge said in *Rosset*, the sort of conduct that would suffice for this purpose would be 'direct contributions to the purchase price by the partner who is not the legal owner, whether initially or by payment of mortgage instalments'; however, he was 'extremely doubtful whether anything less will do'. A number of commentators have in turn doubted whether this represented an accurate understanding of the authorities, and there are indications of a shift away from direct contributions in more recent cases.

This category raises a number of questions. First, what type of trust is this? Second, what contributions raise the inference of an intention to share the beneficial interest? Finally, how are shares quantified under this head?

(i) What type of trust?

It has been suggested that in emphasising direct financial contributions to acquisition, Lord Bridge was close to describing the traditional resulting trust. After all, the emphasis on money contributions in determining the existence (and, perhaps, the quantum) of an equity share suggests a return to the 'solid tug of money' characteristic of traditional resulting trust doctrine. However, Lord Bridge himself describes this trust as 'constructive'; and, notionally at least, intention plays a more positive role in this sort of trust than with conventional resulting trusts. Intention forms the rationale for the trust, rather than (as with conventional resulting trusts) merely a means of rebutting it once it has arisen (for a critical view of the role played by common intention in this context, see Hovius and Youdan *The Law of Family Property* (1991) pp 98–109; Glover and Todd [1995] 5 Web JCLI). Moreover, since *Rosset*, the description of this form of trust as 'constructive' has itself led to further developments, as we shall see.

(ii) What contributions are relevant?

As noted above, one reason for developing the constructive trust in this context is the modern method of financing the acquisition of owner-occupied property. The development of the constructive trust has enabled a return to a more purist approach to the resulting trust whereby the shares of the parties crystallise at the time of purchase (see eg *Curley v Parkes* [2004] EWCA Civ 1515). But the fact that the constructive trust is capable of taking account of financial contributions made *after* the initial purchase raises a further question: why should the court's inquiry be limited to the parties' direct financial contributions to the purchase price? Is it not possible for an intention to share the beneficial interest to be inferred from other types of contributions? After all, to exclude such contributions may lead to arbitrary results. Where both parties are earning, and are both capable of paying the instalments, it may be a matter of convenience as to who pays for what. To attribute ownership to the party who happens to meet the mortgage repayments is to place undue weight on what may be no more than an accidental feature of family finances. Also, the person paying the mortgage may not be able to afford to pay other household outgoings as well, so that the other partner's financial assistance is vital. In such cases, there is a strong case for regarding payments to general household expenses as equivalent to a contribution to the mortgage itself.

In *Le Foe v Le Foe and Woolwich plc* [2001] 2 FLR 970 (Pawlowski [2002] Fam Law 190) it was suggested that prior to *Rosset* it had in fact been understood that indirect financial contributions *could* be taken into account (at 973):

> The next question is whether an indirect contribution to the mortgage will suffice to draw the necessary inference. I do not believe that in using the words 'direct contributions' Lord Bridge of Harwich meant to exclude the situation which obtains here. In *Gissing v Gissing* [1971] AC 886 Lord Diplock referred to just such a case. He said (at 910–911): 'There is no suggestion that the wife's efforts or her earnings made it possible for the husband to raise the initial loan or the mortgage or that the relieving of the husband from the expense of buying clothing for herself and for their son was undertaken in order to enable him the better to meet the mortgage instalments or to repay the loan.' . . . I believe that Lord Diplock is saying quite clearly that if that was the situation, which I find to be the case here, then such would suffice to draw the necessary inference.
>
> The same point was addressed by May LJ in *Burns v Burns* [1984] Ch 317 . . . I agree that May LJ does not directly address the position that we have here; namely where there was no initial cash contribution but only an indirect contribution to the mortgage. But I believe that a fair reading of his judgment is that such a state of affairs should suffice to enable the necessary inference to be drawn. Otherwise these cases would be decided by reference to mere accidents of fortune, being the arbitrary allocation of financial responsibility as between the parties.

And it would appear that the interpretation adopted in *Le Foe* – whereby an indirect contribution that is referable to the purchase price will be sufficient evidence from which to infer that the parties intended to share the beneficial interest – has the approval of the House of Lords:

> 26. Lord Bridge's extreme doubt 'whether anything less will do' was certainly consistent with many first-instance and Court of Appeal decisions, but I respectfully doubt whether it took full account of the views (conflicting though they were) expressed in *Gissing* (see especially Lord Reid [1971] AC 886 at 896G–897B and Lord Diplock at 909 D-H). It has attracted some trenchant criticism from scholars as potentially productive of injustice (see Gray & Gray [*Elements of Land Law*], paras 10.132 to 10.137, the last paragraph being headed 'A More Optimistic Future'). Whether or not Lord Bridge's observation was justified in 1990, in my opinion the law has moved on, and your Lordships should move it a little more in the same direction … (*Stack v Dowden* [2007] UKHL 17 at [27], per Lord Walker; see also Baroness Hale at [61]; for commentary see Pawlowski [2007] Conv 354 at 360–361; [2007] Fam Law 606 at 609).

The Privy Council decision in *Abbott v Abbott* [2007] UKPC 53 likewise sends a clear message as to the desirability of the law being moved on to take account of indirect contributions.

It should however be noted that the potential for indirect contributions to give rise to an inference that the parties intended to share the beneficial ownership has also been limited by the concept of 'referability', as explained by Fox LJ in *Burns v Burns* [1984] Ch 317 (at 329):

> a payment could be said to be referable to the acquisition of the house if, for example, the payer either (a) pays part of the purchase price or (b) contributes regularly to the mortgage instalments or (c) pays off part of the mortgage or (d) makes a substantial financial contribution to the family expenses so as to enable the mortgage instalments to be paid.

On this basis, if the legal owner was capable of paying the mortgage instalments without the other's contributions – as would clearly be the case if he or she had been doing so for some time before the other moved in – then it could not be said that the contributions made by that other were referable to the purchase price. In *Stack*, however, Lord Walker suggested that a broader approach was appropriate (at [31]):

> 'Referable' is a word of wide and uncertain meaning. It would not assist the development of the law to go back to the sort of difficulties that arose in connection with the doctrine of part performance, where the act of part performance relied on had to be 'uniquely referable' to a contract of the sort alleged (see *Steadman v Steadman* [1976] AC 536). Now that almost all houses and flats are bought with mortgage finance, and the average period of ownership of a residence is a great deal shorter than the contractual term of the mortgage secured on it, the process of buying a house does very often continue, in a real sense, throughout the period of its ownership. The law should recognise that by taking a wide view of what is capable of counting as a contribution towards the acquisition of a residence,

> while remaining sceptical of the value of alleged improvements that are really insignificant, or elaborate arguments (suggestive of creative accounting) as to how the family finances were arranged.

Yet it would seem from *James v Thomas* [2007] EWCA Civ 1212 that it is still difficult for the claimant to establish an interest in a property that was purchased by the other party before the relationship began: although Chadwick LJ accepted the possibility that a constructive trust could arise on the basis of events that occurred after the property had been purchased, he warned that 'in the absence of an express post-acquisition agreement, a court will be slow to infer from conduct alone that parties intended to vary existing beneficial interests established at the time of acquisition' (at [24]; see also *Morris v Morris* [2008] EWCA Civ 257). It might seem irrational that the same contribution might result in a different result depending on whether the contributor was living in the property from the date of acquisition or not, yet it should be borne in mind that the constructive trust is not based purely on the contributions of the parties, but on their intentions (see further *Lightfoot v Lightfoot-Brown* [2005] EWCA Civ 201), and that the intentions of the parties may well differ according to whether they were together or not at the time of the purchase.

That said, the court in *James v Thomas* arguably set the bar too high in refusing to infer an intention to share the property beneficially in that case. Account could have been taken of the suggestion by the House of Lords in *Stack v Dowden* that substantial improvements to the property might be sufficient to raise the inference that the parties intended to share the beneficial interest (see eg Lord Hope at [12], Lord Walker at [36] and Baroness Hale at [70]).

Such a move would enable the inferred-intention constructive trust to provide a remedy in a wider range of cases (see eg *Thomas v Fuller-Brown* [1988] 1 FLR 237). But while this is to be welcomed, it should be noted that the types of improvements contemplated – major improvements to the fabric of the property – tend to be gender-specific. Men are more likely to carry out the DIY tasks that improve the property (Summerfield and Babb (eds) *Social Trends 33* (2003), table 13.3), while women are more likely to undertake the day-to-day domestic work. But just as the courts have tended not to regard domestic contributions as establishing detrimental reliance, so too they have overlooked the fact that it is arguable that domestic labour is also linked to property acquisition – 'The cock can feather his nest only because he does not spend his time sitting on it' (Sir Jocelyn Simon *With All My Worldly Goods* (1964) Holdsworth Club, Presidential Address). Purely domestic contributions are not regarded as sufficiently probative of the necessary 'intention'.

The injustice that this may cause is illustrated by the case of *Burns v Burns* [1984] Ch 317. Here, the parties had begun to live together in 1961, and a house was purchased in the name of the male partner in 1963. He was responsible for the mortgage repayments; she was responsible for looking after the house and their two children. After she took up paid work in 1975 she used her earnings to pay bills and purchase items of personal property. But when the relationship broke down, it was held that she had no interest in the property that had been her home for the previous 17 years. Her expenditure was not referable to the purchase of the house, and her domestic contributions raised no inference of any intention that the beneficial interest should be shared. According to Fox LJ (at 331): '[T]he mere fact that parties live together and do the ordinary domestic tasks is, in my view, no indication at all that they thereby intended to alter the existing property rights of either of them.'

(iii) Inference and imputation

What is the distinction between *inferring* the intentions of the parties from their conduct and *imputing* an intention to the parties? A succinct answer to this question was provided by Lord Neuberger in *Stack v Dowden*:

> [126] An inferred intention is one which is objectively deduced to be the subjective actual intention of the parties, in the light of their actions and statements. An imputed intention is one which is attributed to the parties, even though no such actual intention can be deduced from their actions and statements, and even though they had no such intention. Imputation involves concluding what the parties would have intended, whereas inference involves concluding what they did intend.

He went on to explain why the court should not impute an intention to the parties:

> [127] To impute an intention would not only be wrong in principle and a departure from two decisions of your Lordships' House in this very area, but it also would involve a judge in an exercise which was difficult, subjective and uncertain. . . . It would be difficult because the judge would be constructing an intention where none existed at the time, and where the parties may well not have been able to agree. It would be subjective for obvious reasons. It would be uncertain because it is unclear whether one considers a hypothetical negotiation between the actual parties, or what reasonable parties would have agreed. The former is more logical, but would redound to the advantage of an unreasonable party. The latter is more attractive, but is inconsistent with the principle, identified by Baroness Hale at paragraph 61, that the court's view of fairness is not the correct yardstick for determining the parties' shares (and see *Pettitt* at 801C–F, 809C–G and 826C).

At first sight it might appear that the other members of the House of Lords disagreed and were willing to contemplate imputing intentions to the parties. Baroness Hale, with whom the others agreed, noted that '[t]he search is to ascertain the parties' shared intentions, actual, inferred or *imputed*, with respect to the property in the light of their whole course of conduct in relation to it' (at [60], emphasis added). Yet it would be inappropriate to read too much into this, given that she explicitly rejected the idea that the court should quantify the shares of the parties according to what was deemed fair in the circumstances. Similarly, although Lord Walker's review of the authorities might appear to suggest that Lord Diplock had smuggled the possibility of imputing an intention into the law under the guise of inference, the process he describes would, according to Lord Neuberger's criteria, indeed be appropriately described as inference.

The point is that once the courts are willing to accept that a constructive trust may arise even when the intentions of the parties have not been expressly articulated, then the process of reconstructing the intentions of the parties is inevitably a difficult one. As Piska has pointed out, '[s]ubjective intentions can never be accessed directly, so the court must always direct itself to a consideration of the parties' objective intentions through a careful consideration of the relevant facts' ((2008) 71 MLR 120 at 127). It is thus only if the courts *ignore* the conduct of the individual parties when determining their intentions that they could be said to be imputing an intention to them.

Of course, the real test of the boundary between inferring and imputing an intention to the parties occurs where there is evidence that the parties had no common intention (rather than, as in the majority of cases, an absence of evidence that they had an explicit common intention). The case law suggests that the court is not willing to ascribe a common intention to the parties in such a case. For example, in *Lightfoot v Lightfoot-Brown* [2005] EWCA Civ 201, the ex-husband's direct financial contributions did not justify the inference of a constructive trust as the wife was unaware of them.

It has been suggested, however, that in *Midland Bank v Cooke* [1995] 2 FLR 915 the court crossed the line between inferring and imputing an agreement. The statement by Waite LJ to the effect that '[i]t would be anomalous to create a range of home-buyers who were beyond the pale of equity's assistance in formulating a fair presumed basis for the sharing of beneficial title, simply because they had been honest enough to admit that they never gave ownership a thought or reached any agreement about it' (at 927) would indeed seem to indicate that the court was here imputing an intention in the face of evidence that the parties had no such intention. Yet although the parties in the case did expressly state that there had not been any discussions as to the ownership of the property, there was evidence from which a *tacit* common intention could have been deduced; it was clear that the possibility of the property being conveyed to both parties had been contemplated, and that it was the attitude of the mortgage company (Mrs Cooke being at the relevant time a student with no income), rather than the parties themselves, that led to it being conveyed into the sole name of Mr Cooke.

The appropriate interpretation of the authorities would be that the court may infer an agreement even if the parties never communicated their respective intentions, but may not impute an agreement where the evidence is that the parties could not have had any common intention.

(iv) Quantifying shares

Before *Rosset*, a direct contribution to the purchase price would yield a proportionate interest in the property, in line with the mode of quantification under the resulting trust. In the immediate wake of *Rosset* it was assumed that the same method would continue to apply to the re-labelled constructive trust. However, a different approach was employed by the Court of Appeal in *Midland Bank v Cooke* [1995] 4 All ER 562. *Cooke* was similar to *Rosset* in the sense that it involved a married couple, and that the issue arose not between the spouses, but between the wife and a third party with a security interest in the matrimonial home. On appeal, the issue was whether the wife had a beneficial interest in the property and, if so, its size. There was no evidence that the parties had reached an express understanding about ownership, so the matter was argued as a case of direct financial contribution. The wife was found to have made such a contribution by virtue of a wedding gift made to the parties by the husband's parents. This had been used as part of the initial cash contribution to the purchase, and the wife's half share in this amount represented 6.47% of the purchase price. Sixteen years later, the bank sought possession of the house under the terms of a mortgage executed to secure the husband's business debts. During the intervening period, both parties had worked and the wife had been the primary carer of the parties' three children.

In assessing the value of Mrs Cooke's share in the property at half, the Court of Appeal explicitly abandoned any trace of an arithmetical approach. Citing *Grant v Edwards* and Lord Diplock in *Gissing*, Waite LJ held that the court was not bound to attribute shares in direct proportion to the parties' contributions, but was free 'to attribute to the parties an intention to share the beneficial interest in some different proportions' (at 574). In 'attributing' that intention:

> the duty of the judge is to undertake a survey of the whole course of dealing between the parties relevant to their ownership and occupation of the property and their sharing of its burdens and advantages. That scrutiny will not confine itself to the limited range of acts of direct contribution of the sort that are needed to found a beneficial interest in the first place. It will take into consideration all conduct which throws light on the question what shares were intended. Only if that search proves inconclusive does the court fall back on the maxim 'equality is equity'.

Waite LJ distinguished earlier authorities such as *Springette v Defoe* and *Huntingford v Hobbs* – which had adopted a more arithmetical approach – on the basis that the context of the cases was different. Of *Springette*, he said (at 575):

> [the judgments] need to be read in the context of a decision relating to the part-pooling of resources by a middle-aged couple already established in life whose house-purchasing arrangements were clearly regarded by the court as having the same formality as if they had been the subject of a joint venture or commercial partnership.

By contrast, *Cooke* was a case in which (at 576):

> one could hardly have a clearer example of a couple who had agreed to share everything equally . . . [and] when to all that there is added the additional commitment which marriage involves, the conclusion becomes inescapable that their presumed intention was to share the property beneficially in equal shares.

Lest it be thought that this approach is inherently more difficult to apply than the earlier arithmetic approach, consideration should be given to the appropriate treatment of mortgage payments. Should an arithmetical approach focus on (1) the parties' formal liability under the mortgage; (2) an agreement between the parties as to who would make the payments under the mortgage; (3) the actual cash payments made by each of the parties; or (4) the extent to which the repayments related to the capital rather than merely to the interest or (in the case of an endowment mortgage) the endowment policy premiums? (See the earlier case of *Huntingford v Hobbs* [1993] 1 FLR 736 for an example of the different results that these different approaches may produce.)

It is therefore clear that an inferred-intention constructive trust is distinct from the orthodox resulting trust, and that interests under both types of constructive trust – whether based on express discussions or inferred from conduct – are to be quantified in the same way, ie by reference to the parties' intentions, as explained in *Stack v Dowden*. But if a direct contribution is capable of giving rise to a constructive trust, quantified according to the intentions of the parties, and also a resulting trust, quantified according to the financial contributions of the parties, how is the court to determine which type of trust is appropriate in any given case?

The answer will depend on the circumstances of the case. If the only evidence before the court relates to the initial financial contributions of the parties to the purchase price, then a resulting trust will be the appropriate solution (see eg *Laskar v Laskar* [2008] EWCA Civ 347). But, as noted above, almost inevitably in domestic cases there will be further evidence to take into account – for example the division of financial and other responsibilities during the relationship. In such cases a constructive trust based on the parties' intentions is the appropriate course. Of course, the court may decide that it was the intention of the parties that their interests should reflect their financial contributions, but this is a very different exercise from an arithmetical approach under which the parties' shares are inevitably proportionate to their contributions. The resulting trust thus has a minimal role to play in the context of the modern family home, and will usually only be relevant where the parties have not shared a home.

Consider the following points:

(1) If the intentions of the parties as to the precise extent of their shares are to be ascertained by reference to all the circumstances of the case, why should

this approach not be adopted when determining whether they intended to share the beneficial interest in the first place?

(2) Consider the following extract:

> [I]t seems highly unlikely that the real incidence of common intentions is demarcated along different forms of activity . . . An agreement to share the ownership of the home seems no more or less likely between a woman who works outside the home and her partner than between one who works solely in the home and her partner. But if we are to remain faithful to the facts, as the law demands, the oddity lies not in the non-discovery of an agreement where the woman works solely in the home . . . The oddity actually arises in the case of direct financial contribution. There may very well be no agreement truly to be found here either, yet one is routinely discovered – that is to say, invented, in disregard of the prohibition. (Gardner (1993) 109 LQR 263 at 264)

Do you share the author's scepticism of the courts' reliance on intention inferred from contributions, and of the evidence relied on to infer it?

(3) Compare Mrs Cooke, whose contribution totalled 6.47%, with that of a hypothetical claimant who has made no direct financial contribution, but has otherwise engaged in the shared life described by Waite LJ. Even after Cooke, such a claimant would receive nothing, compared to Mrs Cooke's half share. Is that rational?

6. The rules in context

In evaluating the law, it is necessary to understand the social context in which these rules are being applied. As noted in the introduction, these rules are applicable to all kinds of family relationships, but the lack of alternative remedies available when a cohabiting relationship breaks down means that their operation is of particular relevance to cohabiting couples. Given the move away from legal marriage – 2 million cohabiting couples were recorded in the 2001 Census and it has been predicted that by 2031 the number will have risen to 3.8 million, or one-quarter of all couples (Government Actuary's Department *Marital Status Projections for England and Wales* (2005)) – it is clear that an increasing number of couples will be unprotected by the reallocative regime created to deal with assets on divorce or dissolution and will be forced to rely on the law of trusts.

One answer to this problem would be to encourage couples to make express agreements or declarations of trust in relation to their assets. The difficulty is that many cohabiting couples do not appreciate the need to make such arrangements. Surveys have demonstrated that the majority of such couples mistakenly believe that there is such a thing as 'common-law marriage' that confers legal rights on cohabitants after a period of time (see Barlow et al *Cohabitation, Marriage and the Law: Social Change and Legal Reform in the 21st*

Century (2005)). And even those who are aware of their lack of legal rights do not necessarily take any action to secure their position: in a follow-up study of a number of cohabiting individuals who had accessed an information website, it was discovered that none of them had even arranged to see a solicitor. The reasons for failing to take action included the cost and perceived complexity of the legal issues, the difficulty in talking about the possibility of separation and of persuading their partner that legal action was necessary, and an 'optimism bias' that led the respondents to assume that even if the relationship did break down, both parties would behave reasonably (Barlow, Burgoyne and Smithson *The Living Together Campaign – An Investigation of its Impact on Legally Aware Cohabitants* (2007) pp 32–38). Thus it cannot be assumed that simply supplying couples with the necessary information will have the desired effect, and reliance will continue to be placed on implied trusts.

The limitations of the current law in dealing with cohabiting couples were highlighted by the Law Commission in its 2006 consultation paper (No 179):

> 4.6 The claimed unfairness of the current law is the result of:
>
> (1) its dependence upon criteria and distinctions that appear arbitrary in the context of everyday domestic life, particularly in relation to domestic financial management;
> (2) its failure to respond meaningfully or adequately to parties' interdependence, particularly the impact of their contributions to the relationship, and associated sacrifices, on each party's economic position at the point of separation; and
> (3) its focus on the acquisition of individual assets, rather than a holistic review of the parties' economic positions; and its associated lack of remedial flexibility, which prevents it from responding constructively to cases involving modest assets.

One concern that has been expressed by a number of commentators is that the current rules operate to the disadvantage of women. It still remains true that men are more likely than women to be owner-occupiers: in 2006 over three-quarters of men either owned their home outright or were purchasing it with the assistance of a mortgage, as compared to three-fifths of women (ONS *Focus on Gender* (2008)). And there are a number of factors that affect women's ability to acquire an interest in the family home. First, the position of women in the labour market remains distinctive. Abbot and Wallace (*An Introduction to Sociology: Feminist Perspectives* (1997)) make the point succinctly (p 218):

> [T]he labour market is segmented horizontally and vertically. Women tend to be concentrated in lowly paid, low-status occupations and into work done only by women [Horizontal segregation]. Within each occupational stratum women also tend to be concentrated at the lower levels [Vertical segregation]. Furthermore, the work that women do is less likely to be classified as skilled than the work men do. The gender pay gap has not narrowed significantly in the last ten years; while some women have secured employment in the

higher-paid professional employment categories, women are still over-represented in lowly paid jobs.

A further distinction between the work patterns of men and women is that women are far more likely to work part-time than are men: according to the 2008 Labour Force Survey 38% of women with dependent children worked part-time, compared to 4% of men. The equivalent figures for those without children were 22% and 7%. These several differences in labour market participation are then reflected in the respective earnings from work. Average *hourly* earnings for women working full-time are 12.6% lower and for women working part-time 39.1% lower than for men working full-time (ONS *Annual Survey of Hours and Earnings 2007*). The disparity would be greater if weekly earnings are compared, men generally having greater access, for instance, to enhanced overtime pay rates.

The result is that women are not usually in a position to make an equal contribution to the household finances:

men still earn about two thirds of couples' joint earnings across all age groups, varying from 64 per cent in their late 20s and late 50s to more than 72 per cent in their early 40s. The late 20s represents the most equal period in the lives of men and women – before gender pay gaps are much in evidence and before many women have begun having children – although even at this stage women are not equal earners, providing on average only a third of joint earnings. The late 50s is likely to represent a time of early or semi-retirement for men while their (often younger) partners are still working, possibly full-time, as children are likely to have grown up or left home; at this stage women make their highest mean contribution, of just over 40 per cent. Between these ages, however, women's contributions dip, to less than 30 per cent in their late thirties. (Price 'Pension Accumulation and Gendered Household Structures: What are the Implications of Changes in Family Formation for Future Financial Inequality?' in Miles and Probert (eds) *Sharing Lives, Dividing Assets* (2009), p 262).

Structural constraints may also explain the division of responsibilities within the family home (although the direction of influence has been debated). It is still the case that women are more likely to perform most of the unpaid work within the home, and, in particular, to assume responsibility for those tasks that need to be done at a particular time of day (such as cooking the evening meal) and which therefore interfere with participation in the labour market (Bryan and Sanz 'Does Housework Lower Wages and Why? Evidence for Britain', ISER Working Paper (2008)). A comparison of the time spent by men and women on paid employment and unpaid work within the home reveals that there is a rough parity between these different types of contributions (see eg Harkness 'The Household Division of Labour: Changes in Families' Allocation of Paid and Unpaid Work' in Scott, Dex and Joshi (eds) *Changing Patterns of Women's Employment Over 25 Years* (2008)). This illustrates the injustice inherent in focusing too closely on financial contributions, and provides a justification for the broader approach endorsed in *Stack v Dowden*.

But, as we have seen, the scope for the court to take such contributions into account is limited to the stage at which the parties' interests are quantified. In order to get to this stage, it will be necessary to establish either an express agreement plus detrimental reliance or a financial contribution. Women's earnings are no longer regarded as 'pin money', to be used for the purchase of luxuries: indeed, the increase in house prices means that often two incomes will be necessary to acquire and sustain a mortgage. While most women will be in a position to make a financial contribution to the household (even if not an equal one), whether that contribution is direct or indirect will depend on the way in which that couple have chosen to organise their finances. The complexity of financial arrangements within couple relationships (see eg Vogler, Lyonette and Wiggins (2008) 56 Sociological Review 117) is a strong argument in favour of accepting indirect contributions to give rise to an interest in the property, to avoid the parties' entitlements depending on the arbitrary allocation of funds. As one recent survey found (Tennant, Taylor and Lewis *Separating from Cohabitation* (2006) p 27):

> The payment of the mortgage did not always reflect the ownership of the property. For instance, where the home was jointly owned, both parties usually contributed although not if only one was working. Where the home was in the sole name of one partner, sometimes only they paid the mortgage, though in other cases the other partner contributed whether directly, via a joint bank account, or indirectly, as part of a regular payment for 'keep'.

To the extent that the current law is now capable of accommodating indirect contributions, and taking non-financial contributions into account in quantifying the parties' shares, the force of the argument that it is unjust to women has been lessened. But the current law remains incapable of providing redress where one party has devoted themselves to providing care for others and has made no financial contribution. Douglas et al (2007) found a number of cases reminiscent of *Burns v Burns* [1984] Ch 317 in their recent study, noting that (at p 138):

> The disadvantaged partner was always the woman and after a long cohabitation in which she had cared for the children, she had no right to a share in the home which was held in the sole name of her partner, because she had made no financial contribution to its acquisition.

Such cases will no doubt continue to occur, but perhaps in smaller numbers, given the evidence from one small-scale empirical study of a generational difference in the behaviour of cohabiting couples (Barlow, Burgoyne and Smithson, op cit, p 28):

The younger couples in this study were far more likely to have mutually discussed their financial and legal situation, and found it easier to decide together how to regulate their affairs. There was more unease about talking about legal issues or financial concerns among the older cohabitants. The younger couples were far more likely to have bought a house in joint names, and were also more likely to view themselves as mutually independent in the case of relationship breakdown. Older couples were more likely to have considerable assets already, were more likely to have separate accounts, as well as houses owned in one person's name. The older women in particular were more likely to be in a situation of living in a partner's house which was owned in their partner's name, and of most of the household assets being in the man's name.

One final factor to bear in mind is that there is evidence that individuals are not always taking advantage of the rights that the law does confer. Perhaps the articles that periodically appear in the media exploding the common-law marriage myth have had an impact on some couples: such articles often go too far in asserting that cohabiting couples have no legal rights, with the result that such couples may assume that this is the case. Arthur et al found that only 26% of ex-cohabitants had consulted a solicitor about the legal aspects of the separation (Settling Up (2002) p 75). And a further study of separating cohabitants found that their property tended to be divided in accordance with the legal title (Tennant et al, op cit, p 77):

By far the most obvious influence on people's arrangements was ownership: whose name an asset (especially a house) was held in, who had bought it or whose side of the relationship it had originated from. What was meant here was legal title, rather than beneficial ownership – that is, registered ownership rather than any rights that might arise under a trust. This dominant motif applied to homes, bank accounts, debts, savings and assets of all types. In some cases, the non-owning partner had made no financial contributions and this was seen to reinforce the entitlement of the owner. But there were also instances where contributions had been made but were overridden by notions of ownership. This was most obvious in relation to the house. There were instances where the home was owned in one partner's name, and the fact that the other partner had contributed to the deposit, the mortgage, or to substantial material improvements was not seen to be significant in the face of registered title. This was often a source of shock, disappointment and upset to the other partner.

The dominance of the legal title in this context is particularly important given the relatively low levels of joint ownership within cohabiting relationships (see above, p 649).

Consider the following point:

(1) A policy issue underlying the law of family property, of which the implied trust now forms an integral (albeit residual) part, is how far strict questions of ownership, and the rigours of separation of property, should be modified

by the fact that family property has been acquired by and for family members. As the above extracts suggest, family life affects an individual's ability to acquire property in legally recognised ways (either by enhancing it or decreasing it). How far is it appropriate for the law of implied trusts to take the relationship of the parties into account in determining their intentions vis-à-vis the property? Or is the matter one for legislative intervention, as a number of judges and other commentators have argued?

7. New directions?

The implied trust has been made to bear a heavy burden in resolving disputes over family property, albeit in a residual context. In the continued absence of statutory intervention, the judges have had to steer a middle course between the two poles of allowing the economic gains and losses of a domestic relationship to lie where they fall on the one hand, and imposing joint ownership of assets purchased by joint efforts for joint use on the other. It is apparent from a review of the authorities that different judges differ over what counts as a qualifying contribution, and over the relationship between those qualifying contributions and the claimant's eventual share. These differences of approach appear within, as well as between, the two categories laid down by Lord Bridge in *Rosset*. Yet rarely are the issues addressed except in terms of doctrine. Difficult questions of justice and policy are usually given scant attention within the restricted conceptual framework of resulting and constructive trusts.

In recent years, however, there have been a number of important developments. In 2002 the Law Commission considered and rejected the idea of a statutory trust arising in prescribed circumstances, suggesting that there should instead be incremental development of the law. The House of Lords responded to the challenge in *Stack v Dowden*, although its ability to address the deficiencies of the current law was of course constrained by the issue before it. Furthermore, the Law Commission, having suggested in its earlier discussion paper that a new adjustive regime might be appropriate in the context of the family home, was invited to formulate a scheme on which such a regime might be based, and published its recommendations in 2007.

Yet even if Parliament does choose to legislate for an adjustive regime – an issue which at the time of writing remains uncertain – there will still be cases involving other family members, and couples who do not fall within the statutory scheme, where reliance will still need to be placed on the law of trusts. It is therefore appropriate to consider alternative methods of dealing with the family home within this framework. Comparisons will be made with other jurisdictions that have faced the same problem of determining whether, and if so how, the law should accommodate modern family life.

(a) Underlying policy issues

As Swadling ((2007) 123 LQR 511 at 518) has recently commented, 'we still need to know to what category of event this trust responds'. This reflects the fact that, although we know (more or less) when a constructive trust will arise, there has been little judicial discussion of *why* it arises. In this context, developments elsewhere provide some interesting answers.

(1) Unjust enrichment: Canada

According to the majority of the Canadian Supreme Court in *Pettkus v Becker* (1980) 117 DLR (3d) 257, '[t]he principle of unjust enrichment lies at the heart of the constructive trust'. The case involved an unmarried couple who, through joint efforts, had acquired several farm properties and had built up a bee-keeping business. Legal titles to all the properties were in the man's name, and all business receipts went to his bank account. The first farm had been bought out of the man's savings, but he had only been able to make these because the plaintiff, Rosa Becker, had paid all their living expenses. She had also contributed to the second farm, which was otherwise paid for out of business profits (as was the third). On the termination of the relationship, the plaintiff claimed a half share of the farms and of all other jointly acquired assets.

Dickson J (with whom Estey, McIntyre, Chouinard and Lamer JJ concurred; Marland and Beetz JJ dissenting) noted the flexible and malleable nature of principles of equity, which could be shaped 'so as to accommodate the changing needs and mores of society, in order to achieve justice'.

> How then does one approach the question of unjust enrichment in matrimonial cases? In *Rathwell* [(1978) 83 DLR (3d) 289 (SCC)] I ventured to suggest there are three requirements to be satisfied before an unjust enrichment can be said to exist: an enrichment, a corresponding deprivation and absence of any juristic reason for the enrichment. This approach, it seems to me, is supported by general principles of equity that have been fashioned by the courts for centuries, though, admittedly, not in the context of matrimonial property controversies.
>
> . . . It is not enough for the court simply to determine that one spouse has benefited at the hands of another and then to require restitution. It must, in addition, be evident that the retention of the benefit would be 'unjust' in the circumstances of the case . . .
>
> Miss Becker supported Mr Pettkus for five years. She then worked on the farm for about fourteen years. The compelling inference from the facts is that she believed she had some interest in the farm and that that expectation was reasonable in the circumstances. Mr Pettkus would seem to have recognised in Miss Becker some property-interest, through the payment to her of compensation, however modest. There is no evidence to indicate that he ever informed her that all her work performed over the nineteen years was being performed on a gratuitous basis. He freely accepted the benefits conferred upon him through her financial support and her labour.
>
> On these facts, the first two requirements laid down in *Rathwell* have clearly been satisfied: Mr Pettkus has had the benefit of nineteen years' unpaid labour, while Miss Becker has received little or nothing in return. As for the third requirement, I hold that where one person in a relationship tantamount to spousal prejudices herself in the reasonable expectation of receiving an interest in property and the other person in the relationship freely accepts benefits conferred by the first person in circumstances where he knows or

ought to have known of that reasonable expectation it would be unjust to allow the recipient of the benefit to retain it . . .

Causal connection

. . . The matter of 'causal connection' was also raised in defence of Miss Becker's claim, but does not present any great difficulty. There is a clear link between the contribution and the disputed assets. The contribution of Miss Becker was such as enabled, or assisted in enabling, Mr Pettkus to acquire the assets in contention. For the unjust enrichment principle to apply it is obvious that some connection must be shown between the acquisition of property and corresponding deprivation. On the facts of this case, that test was met. The indirect contribution of money and the direct contribution of labour is clearly linked to the acquisition of property, the beneficial ownership of which is in dispute . . .

Within this framework the role of the constructive trust is simply that of a remedy for unjust enrichment; it is, therefore, remedial rather than institutional. Analysing claims to an interest in the property within the framework of unjust enrichment removes the requirement to consider the intentions of the parties; it also refocuses attention on the enrichment of the legal owner rather than the reasons for the claimant's contributions. Dickson J regarded it as obvious that Rosa Becker's work was an enrichment to Mr Pettkus, and subsequent cases have both clarified and extended the jurisdiction. In *Sorochan v Sorochan* ((1986) 29 DLR (4th) 1), for example, the principle established in *Pettkus* was extended to unpaid work on a farm which contributed to the maintenance of its value, rather than contributing to its acquisition. More strikingly, in *Peter v Beblow* ((1993) 101 DLR (4th) 621) the Canadian Supreme Court further extended the principle to include the provision of services by the plaintiff in that case as 'housekeeper, homemaker and step-mother' and ordered that the family home (originally in the man's name) be transferred to the woman plaintiff under a constructive trust. The court found that the provision of domestic services by the woman was an enrichment to the man, from which it was assumed to follow (almost automatically) that there was a corresponding deprivation to the woman. This flows from the fact that, in the context of a close and long-term cohabiting relationship, there is (according to Cory J) 'a strong presumption that the services provided by one party will not be used solely to enrich the other. Both the reasonable expectations of the parties and equity will require that upon the termination of the relationship, the parties will receive an appropriate compensation based on the contribution each has made to the relationship' (at 633).

Cory J continued:

In today's society it is unreasonable to assume that the presence of love automatically implies a gift of one party's services to another. Nor is it unreasonable for the party providing the domestic labour required to create a home to expect to share in the property of the parties when the relationship is terminated. Women are no longer expected to work exclusively in the home. It must be recognised that when they do so, women forgo outside employment to provide domestic services and child-care. The granting of relief... should adequately reflect the fact the income-earning capacity and the ability to acquire assets by one party has been enhanced by the unpaid domestic services of the other.

Applying the test set out by Dickson J in *Pettkus*, the court also found that there was an 'absence of juristic reason for the enrichment': here, viewed objectively, the plaintiff had a reasonable expectation of sharing in the family assets at the end of the relationship and voluntarily provided her domestic labour on that basis, which was freely accepted by the respondent. As to the appropriate remedy, the court awarded the woman the house that had formerly been the family home, on the ground that this represented a fair approximation of the value of the woman's efforts as reflected in the family assets. The court also held that, while it was not confined to providing a remedy by way of constructive trust (it could, for example, award merely monetary compensation to reverse the enrichment), it was appropriate to do so in this case, largely because the house in dispute was the respondent's only significant asset (other than the houseboat in which he was living). Although there was some difference of opinion over when, in general terms, a constructive trust would be an appropriate remedy (in particular over the necessity for a direct link between the plaintiff's services and the property claimed), the court was unanimous that the measure of recovery for unjust enrichment, either by way of constructive trust or monetary compensation, could reflect either the 'value received' by the respondent (as in, for example, a *quantum meruit* claim) or the 'value surviving' in the respondent's hands.

Peter v Beblow is a striking example of the potential scope of unjust enrichment in this context (although some have doubted whether it can properly be analysed in terms of unjust enrichment: see Birks 'Proprietary Rights as Remedies' in Birks (ed) *The Frontiers of Liability, Vol 2* (1994) ch 16 at pp 219–220). It also shows strong judicial support for the notion that purely domestic labour can be placed on an equal footing with direct financial contributions: arguments which, as we have seen, have yet to penetrate the English law of implied trusts.

(2) Unjust enrichment: England

It has been argued that English law should develop the concept of unjust enrichment in the context of the family home (see eg Gardner (1993) 109 LQR 263). More recently, it has been suggested that *Stack v Dowden* constitutes 'a radical departure from previous authority in its use of the constructive trust as proprietary restitutionary relief for unjust enrichment rather than the declaration of a pre-existing trust on traditional lines' (Etherton (2008) 67(2) CLJ 265 at 266). The latter argument rests on the assumption that *Stack* introduced a more discretionary approach to the first stage of finding whether a trust had arisen (as opposed to the second stage of quantifying a trust that had already arisen), an interpretation that has been questioned above. For now, however, a more interesting question is what the consequences of adopting a restitutionary approach would be.

Etherton, for example, suggests that the result in *Stack* can be justified as a response to unjust enrichment: Mr Stack 'acted unconscionably since the intimate nature of their relationship was both the cause of Ms Dowden's contributions and the reason why she never sought or acted on legal advice in relation to them to protect her interests' (at 281). On this reasoning it is the very intimacy of the parties' relationship that makes it appropriate for Ms Dowden to recover a larger share of the assets in recognition of her greater financial contribution. It could, however, be argued that it is the intimacy of cohabiting relationships that justifies the inference that the parties intended to share their assets (see eg *Fowler v Barron*, above).

The values of 'trust and collaboration' are also central to Gardner's analysis ((1993) 109 LQR 263). These values, in his view, reduce the perceived conceptual problems of (i) characterising non-financial contributions as enrichments, and (ii) regarding such an enrichment as unjust. His reasoning is that a man who receives the benefit of services provided by one with whom he is in a relationship of trust and collaboration cannot claim that those services have no value to him. Nor can he retain the benefit of them without acting unjustly: the context of the relationship in which the services are offered supplies the necessary framework of expectation without more needing to be shown (see also Hovius and Youdan *The Law of Family Property* (1991) pp 98–109).

The elements of 'trust and collaboration' are thus seen as justifying a modified form of unjust enrichment; in appropriate cases, moreover, they suggest a more radical idea, that of 'communality' whereby assets are shared. The very fact that Gardner puts this forward as an alternative more suited to married couples (whereas the modified restitutionary approach would generally be more suitable for cohabitants) illustrates the limitations of even a modified restitutionary approach. A restitutionary analysis is simply concerned with reversing the enrichment of one party by the other and as such focuses more on the contributions made than the nature of the relationship. In addition, there remain doubts as to whether an unjust enrichment claim can be met by a proprietary remedy (see Gardner (2008) 124 LQR 422 at 439; although contrast Etherton (2008) 67(2) CLJ 265). It therefore seems unlikely that the adoption of a restitutionary approach in England and Wales would yield results equivalent to those in Canada.

(3) Unconscionability: Australia

By way of contrast, the High Court of Australia has adopted the concept of unconscionability as the key analytical tool in these cases. *Baumgartner v Baumgartner* (1987) 164 CLR 137 was a case in which an unmarried couple pooled their incomes in order to meet their living expenses. They lived first in a property owned by the man, Leo, which they sold in order to buy a house that was registered in his sole name. All household outgoings were paid from the parties' pooled income, of which the woman, Frances, contributed 45% over the four-year period of their relationship. There was one child of the relationship. After four years, Frances left, taking the child and most of the furniture. She claimed a half share of the house.

As in *Pettkus*, there was no evidence to support a finding of a common intention that Frances should have a share under a trust (although the matter had been discussed frequently by the parties). However, the High Court went on to consider the possibility of a constructive trust, the foundation of which 'is that a refusal to recognise the existence of the equitable interest amounts to unconscionable conduct and that the trust is imposed as a remedy to circumvent that unconscionable conduct'. This formula may be thought to beg the question of when the equitable interest will be held to exist: it implies, in effect, that a constructive trust will be imposed only where it would be unfair not to impose one, which in itself is hardly a useful principle. So of what does the unfairness or unconscionability consist? By way of clarification, the High Court cited the principle of joint endeavour, taken from the judgment of Deane J in *Muschinski v Dodds* (1985) 160 CLR 583, which (at 620):

> ... operates in a case where the substratum of a joint relationship or endeavour is removed without attributable blame and where the benefit of money or other property contributed by one party on the basis and for the purposes of the relationship or endeavour would otherwise be enjoyed by the other party in circumstances in which it was not specifically intended or specially provided that that other party should so enjoy it. The content of the principle is that, in such a case, equity will not permit that other party to assert or retain the benefit of the relevant property to the extent that it would be unconscionable for him to do so.

It was this principle that the High Court applied in *Baumgartner*, in circumstances where the parties had pooled their earnings 'for the purposes of their joint relationship, one of the purposes of that relationship being to secure accommodation for themselves and their child'. The court therefore held that (at 149):

> In this situation [Leo's] assertion, after the relationship had failed, that the [house], which was financed in part through the pooled funds, is his sole property ... amounts to unconscionable conduct which attracts the intervention of equity and the imposition of a constructive trust at the suit of the respondent.

The court went on to hold that Frances's share should be governed by the proportion of the pooled income she had contributed, that is, 45%. A number of adjustments were then made, entitling Leo to repayment of the amount in cash he had contributed to the purchase and an amount equivalent to the mortgage repayments he had made since Frances left, less an amount representing occupation rent.

The key concept here is that of a joint relationship or endeavour which has failed in circumstances where the parties would not have intended the gains and losses of that failure to lie where they fall. There is, therefore, at least a vestigial remnant of the concept of intention, although intention is much less to the fore than in the English cases. But perhaps the most ambiguous aspect of the case, and one which the High Court did little to elucidate, is the concept of 'joint relationship or endeavour' itself. Is this something that will be found simply by virtue of cohabitation? Or must there be some active economic contribution by both parties? For example, will it be unconscionable for a partner to retain the benefit of domestic labour by the other? (This echoes the question, posed above, of whether such services will amount to an 'enrichment' for the purposes of restitutionary analysis.)

Muschinski had been a case in which the dealings between the parties had formed part of a wider business project. In *Baumgartner*, the joint endeavour requirement appeared to be satisfied by the fact that the parties pooled their income. Subsequent cases went still further in finding a joint endeavour on the basis that the parties intended to share their lives in some way, as evidenced by child-rearing, a conventional sexual division of labour and a long and close relationship (eg *Hibberson v George* (1988) 12 Fam LR 735; *Parij v Parij* (1998) DFC 95–196; although cf *Brown v George* (1998) 24 Fam LR 59).

The flexibility of the implied trust, and its capacity to adapt itself to the contours of each relationship, has been made possible by the conceptual break from common intention. It permits the outcome of a case to be informed by the nature of the parties' relationship as evidenced by their own intentions, the reasonable expectations attaching to relationships of a particular type and the flow of gains and losses during it.

(4) Unconscionability: England

The concept of unconscionability is a familiar one within English law. Two distinct approaches can be discerned: first, a broad approach which holds unconscionability alone to be sufficient justification for the court to impose a constructive trust; secondly, an approach that regards certain specific forms of behaviour as unconscionable.

The first is best illustrated by Lord Denning's 'new model constructive trust' developed in the wake of *Pettitt* and *Gissing* in *Hussey v Palmer* [1972] 1 WLR 1286 at 1289–1290 (see also Chapter 1 at p 24):

> By whatever name it is described, it is a trust imposed by law whenever justice and good conscience require it. It is a liberal process, founded upon large principles of equity, to be applied in cases where the legal owner cannot conscientiously keep the property for himself alone but ought to allow another to have the property or the benefit of it or a share in it.

The problems with such an approach have been cogently summarised by Mee (*The Property Rights of Cohabitees* (1999) pp 178–180):

> The first objection to the 'new model constructive trust' relates to the manner of its develop-
> ment. There was virtually no authority for Lord Denning's views . . . A second objection lies
> in the nature of the doctrine itself. . . . The notion of a judge basing his or her decision on his
> or her own perceptions of justice and good conscience has conjured up in the minds of some
> commentators the image of a potentate stretched out under a palm-tree, dispensing justice
> to his subjects upon the whim of the moment . . . A final point militating against this use of
> the constructive trust to achieve justice *inter partes* is the possible injustice to third parties.

While the new model constructive trust did not survive the retirement of Lord Denning, the concept of unconscionability does underpin the key passage in Lord Diplock's judgment in *Gissing* in which he sets out the circumstances in which it will be inequitable for the legal owner to deny the claimant an interest in the land. Thus identifying the concept of unconscionability as the underpinning policy factor for the constructive trust would either do too much (in removing any objective criteria) or too little (in that the law already recognises that it is unconscionable for the legal owner to renege on an agreement on which the claimant has relied to his or her detriment).

(5) Reasonable expectations: New Zealand

In the case of *Gillies v Keogh* [1989] 2 NZLR 327, the New Zealand Court of Appeal purported to draw together the various strands of Commonwealth authority and to reveal an element common to all of them: the concept of reasonable expectations.

The case concerned a married couple who began their cohabitation in a house purchased in the name of, and paid for by, the woman. The parties later pooled their incomes, from which they paid all the outgoings. The man worked on improving and extending the house and garden. The first house was later sold and the proceeds used to purchase another house, which was also conveyed into the woman's sole name. Two monthly payments of principal on the mortgage were made from the parties' joint account. The parties separated shortly thereafter. The man claimed a share in the house. There was evidence that throughout their relationship the woman had told the man that she regarded the house as exclusively hers. Largely for this reason, the court found against the man. Nevertheless, the court used the opportunity to restate the principles underlying this area of law.

According to Cooke P (at 333):

> Whether one speaks in terms of reasonable expectations or unjust enrichment or any other
> objective test, it is plain that in grey area cases certain factors have to be weighed. The
> practical position now reached in de facto union cases by all the various routes appears to
> me to be that the courts have regard to the reasonable expectations of persons in the shoes
> of the respective parties, giving particular weight to the following factors . . .

As the factors, he lists, first, 'the degree of sacrifice by the claimant', which may include 'other opportunities forgone', and is usually 'a guide to the measure of any unjust enrichment of the other'. Second is 'the value of the broadly measurable contributions of the claimant by comparison with the broadly measurable value of the benefits received'. Thus, 'contributions to household expenses . . . may amount to no more than fair payment for board and lodging'. Finally, there is the importance of allowing parties to contract out of the reasonable expectations that would otherwise apply: 'a claimant cannot succeed if a reasonable person in his or her shoes would have understood that throughout the relationship the other party had positively declined to acquiesce in property sharing or any other right'. It was on the basis of this last factor that the man lost.

Richardson J, who delivered the other main judgment, arrived at the same conclusion but by the more conventional route of estoppel. However, he was willing to infer that cohabitation per se would be sufficient to generate expectations concerning property-ownership: 'social attitudes in New Zealand readily lead to expectations, by those within apparently stable and enduring de facto relationships, that family assets are ordinarily shared, not the exclusive property of one or the other, unless it is agreed otherwise or made plain' (at 347). Thus, even within the framework of estoppel Richardson J's judgment evinces a willingness to allow widely held social expectations to inform the reasonable expectations to be imputed to the parties as a matter of law. The parties can contract out of the consequences of this, but only expressly. This suggests a full turning of the circle: expressed intention is the way out of, not the way into, the implied trust.

Matters have been further clarified in *Lankow v Rose* [1995] 1 NZLR 277. Here, Tipping J held that the following four elements were necessary to establish a claim: (a) contributions, direct or indirect, to the property in question; (b) the expectation of an interest therein; (c) that such expectation is a reasonable one; and (d) that the defendant should reasonably expect to yield the claimant an interest (at 294). If these four elements are established, then 'equity will regard as unconscionable the defendant's denial of the claimant's interest and will impose a constructive trust accordingly'. He confirmed that the issue of expectation for the purposes of (c) and (d) was to be judged objectively ('any reasonable person in . . . the . . . circumstances' (at 300)). This suggests that, provided the relationship is one that a reasonable person would regard as generating expectations of sharing of ownership, almost all activities relating to the parties' joint lives will result in a proportionate share of the equity (see also *McMahon v McMahon* [1996] 3 NZLR 334).

(6) Reasonable expectations: England

The decision in *Gillies v Keogh* is helpful in illuminating the distinction between an intention that is imputed to parties in a particular situation – in that case, couples living together in an intimate relationship – and one which is inferred from the actions of the particular individuals. Putting the onus on the legal owner to show that there was no intention to share the property would lead to a different approach in those cases where the property rights of the parties were not expressly discussed. We have seen in this chapter, however, that the courts have been wary of imputing intentions to those who share a home, despite the abundant empirical evidence that many cohabitants do assume that they have legal entitlements as a result of their relationship (see Barlow et al, op cit). Rephrasing 'imputed intentions' as 'reasonable expectations' is unlikely to change that reluctance. In any case, questions inevitably arise about the scope of the doctrine, and the types of relationships within which reasonable expectations might arise: legislative reform may be a preferable means of giving effect to the expectations of cohabiting couples.

Consider the following points:

(1) Do the concepts of enrichment, joint endeavour or contribution generating a reasonable expectation sacrifice certainty to remedial flexibility? Which should be the priority for the law of trusts?

(2) One feature that is common to these different doctrinal formulations is that there is less emphasis on subjective agreements made between the parties, or inferred from their actions. Instead, the focus is on objective factors, of what is 'reasonable', which may have little to do with 'the parties' thinking' as such. It has more to do with justice and fairness in the particular circumstances of a relationship, and with commonly held expectations about entitlements in these circumstances. Are these judgements that should by made by the courts, or by the legislature?

(7) Contributions: *Sharing Homes*

A further attempt to move the constructive trust away from its reliance on intention was made in *Sharing Homes*. The Law Commission considered whether it would be appropriate to create a statutory trust that would arise if parties shared a home in property owned by one of them, and the other contributed to its acquisition, and where there was no express arrangement dealing with ownership. In trying to formulate the basis for such a trust, it was 'an underlying objective of the scheme that it would apply irrespective of the nature of the relationship between those who were sharing a home' (para 10).

The statutory trust envisaged by the Law Commission was to arise on the basis of the contributions – whether financial or non-financial – made by parties who had shared a home together. But the combination of a wide range of relationships and the elimination of intention from the scheme posed a problem, as the Commission illustrated by postulating two different kinds of home-sharing scenarios. In the first, an adult son had moved back into his parents' home and had remained there for ten years; in the second, a man and a woman had lived together for ten years and had had a child together. Both claimants had made financial contributions, but not directly to the acquisition of the house. According to the Commission:

3.71 There can be little doubt that a court would instinctively have greater sympathy for the unmarried mother... than for the child of elderly parents... But when it comes to characterising their respective claims, it is not really possible to articulate the differences without reference either to the probable intentions of the parties or to the nature of the relationship from which the claim has arisen.

It is easy to share the Commission's 'instinctive' feeling that these situations are different. But *why* are they different? Is it simply because the parties have different expectations in each case? After all, an adult son probably does not envisage remaining under the parental roof, while cohabiting partners are likely to hope that their relationship will be life-long. But does this explain why it is appropriate for the one but not the other to acquire an interest in the property once co-residence comes to an end? Nor do the differing intentions of the parties really indicate why different treatment might be appropriate: in each case the legal owner(s) may well have intended that the other should not acquire an interest in the property, but our perceptions of the reasonableness of that intention are likely to vary according to the context. This is implicit in the Commission's suggestion that the claim of the adult son would 'have the effect of eroding the accrued rights of his parents' and 'bristles with human rights implications' (para 3.67), whereas no such deference is shown to the accrued rights of the male cohabitant. But before we conclude that any difference must be due to the relationship status of the parties, it is worth bearing in mind that the Law Commission's example does not in fact compare like with like. It contrasts an adult male who has not, as far as we are told, made any sacrifices or changes as a result of living with his parents, and whose earning capacity is unimpaired, with a woman in a very different position, whose life course will be fundamentally different as a result of the relationship and caring for the parties' child.

The fact that the Commission was unable to formulate a simple scheme that was capable of addressing the variety of different home-sharing situations that might arise does not mean that the law of trusts is incapable of development, although the limitations of property law in this context should be recognised (see further Miles (2003) 23 LS 624). But the focus of debate has since moved on to the possibility of a different kind of reform, one focused specifically on cohabiting couples.

(b) A reallocative scheme

A number of other jurisdictions have already created statutory schemes to redistribute property at the termination of a cohabiting relationship (including Australia and New Zealand, with the result that the need to rely on concepts of unconscionability and reasonable expectations has been reduced). Most recently, and closer to home, the Family Law (Scotland) Act 2006 provides remedies for cohabitants whose relationship ends as a result of breakdown or death. Some jurisdictions have also enacted statutory schemes that extend to a wider range of family relationships (see eg Wong (2004) 26 JSWFL 361).

In the wake of *Sharing Homes*, one group of cohabitants was given the chance of opting in to a new legal regime. The Civil Partnership Act 2004 allowed same-sex couples to register a civil partnership and thereby acquire almost all the same rights and responsibilities as married couples. This in turn led to a renewed focus on the lack of rights accorded to couples – of the same or opposite sex – who had not formalised their relationship, and the Law Commission was asked to consider undertaking a review of the financial consequences of the termination of a cohabiting relationship (whether by separation or death). Work began in 2005, with a consultation paper being published in 2006 and a report in the summer of 2007 (for discussion see Bridge [2007] Fam Law 911, 998, 1076).

The project was thus narrower in scope than the earlier home-sharing project – in that it focused on only one type of relationship – but also more extensive, in that it was not limited to the acquisition of property interests in the family home. In outline, the key features of the recommended scheme were as follows:

> 8.1 We recommend that legislation should create a scheme of general application, whereby cohabiting couples would be entitled to apply for financial relief on separation:
>
> (1) provided they satisfy statutory eligibility criteria;
> (2) but not where they had reached an agreement disapplying the statutory scheme ('an opt-out agreement'), in which case the parties' own financial arrangements (if any) would apply.

'Cohabitants' would be defined as those who are 'living together as a couple in a joint household' without being parties to a legally recognised marriage or civil partnership (para 3.13); eligibility, however, would depend on the parties having had a child together (para 3.31) or on the parties having lived together for a minimum specified period (somewhere between two and five years being suggested as the appropriate minimum: para 3.63).

The scheme applicable to eligible cohabitants was described as a 'principled discretion' (para 4.15) within which guidance as to the aims of the scheme would be given and certain criteria would have to be satisfied.

> 4.32 We recommend that financial relief on separation should be granted in accordance with a statutory scheme based upon the economic impact of cohabitation, to the following effect.
>
> 4.33 An eligible cohabitant applying for relief following separation ('the applicant') must prove that:

(1) the respondent has a retained benefit; or

(2) the applicant has an economic disadvantage

as a result of the qualifying contributions the applicant has made.

4.34 A qualifying contribution is any contribution arising from the cohabiting relationship which is made to the parties' shared lives or to the welfare of members of their families. Contributions are not limited to financial contributions, and include future contributions, in particular to the care of the parties' children following separation.

4.35 A retained benefit may take the form of capital, income or earning capacity that has been acquired, retained or enhanced.

4.36 An economic disadvantage is a present or future loss. It may include a diminution in current savings as a result of expenditure or of earnings lost during the relationship, lost future earnings, or the future cost of paid childcare.

4.37 The court may make an order to adjust the retained benefit, if any, by reversing it in so far as that is reasonable and practicable having regard to the discretionary factors listed below. If, after the reversal of any retained benefit, the applicant would still bear an economic disadvantage, the court may make an order sharing that loss equally between the parties, in so far as it is reasonable and practicable to do so, having regard to the discretionary factors.

4.38 The discretionary factors are:

(1) the welfare while a minor of any child of both parties who has not attained the age of eighteen;

(2) the financial needs and obligations of both parties;

(3) the extent and nature of the financial resources which each party has or is likely to have in the foreseeable future;

(4) the welfare of any children who live with, or might reasonably be expected to live with, either party; and

(5) the conduct of each party, defined restrictively but so as to include cases where a qualifying contribution can be shown to have been made despite the express disagreement of the other party.

Of these discretionary factors, item (1) above shall be the court's first consideration.

It is clear that this scheme allows account to be taken of contributions and sacrifices currently ignored by the law of trusts (although it is interesting to note that the Commission envisaged that domestic contributions would usually give rise to a claim of economic disadvantage, rather than a claim of retained benefit, on the basis of the difficulty of making the link between such contributions and specific items of property). The process of enquiry to be carried out in ascertaining whether there is a retained benefit is similar to that employed under the current law when inferring a trust, and the difficulties to which that gives rise have been discussed above. However, the concept of economic disadvantage differs significantly from the law of trusts in that it is forward-looking rather than retrospective, being designed to address the ongoing impact of the relationship rather than simply the contributions made by the parties while it was subsisting. And, unlike the law of trusts, it is explicitly discretionary. Even though the judicial discretion is to be bounded and constrained by the concepts of retained benefit and economic disadvantage, it is envisaged that the judge can and will exercise a discretion in shaping the ultimate award.

Since the Law Commission's recommended scheme belongs within the province of family law rather than property law in terms of the techniques used, further analysis of its merits and potential flaws lies outside the scope of this work (for analysis see eg Probert (2007) 41 Family Law Quarterly 521; Hughes, Davis and Jacklin [2008] Conv 197). At the time of writing, the future of the Law Commission's recommendations for an adjustive regime is uncertain. The Government has indicated that it intends to examine the operation of similar principles in Scotland before deciding whether the scheme should be introduced in England and Wales. But even if it, or something similar, is enacted, there remains the question as to how the law should treat those couples who do not fall within the scheme's eligibility criteria and other home-sharers who are not in a couple relationship. For the time being, therefore, reliance will continue to be placed on the law of trusts in the context of the family home.

8. Conclusion

As will be clear from this chapter, *Stack v Dowden* has provoked much debate among academic commentators, not just as to the merits of the decision, but also as to what it actually decided. Some have criticised the House of Lords for articulating principles that were not relevant to the facts of the particular case (Dixon [2007] Conv 352); others have bemoaned the fact that there was not a fundamental review of the subject (Swadling (2007) 123 LQR 511). Neither criticism is entirely fair (as might be evident from the fact that both can be made): the case *does* provide a fundamental review of one particular type of case, that involving joint ownership of the family home. It seems highly improbable that the House of Lords intended to abolish the criteria for establishing a common-intention constructive trust in the context of sole-ownership cases (and inconceivable that such an act of abolition could be achieved by omitting to mention those criteria). Whether common intention should continue to be the theoretical basis for the constructive trust in this area is another matter: it is unarguable that the courts' search for a common intention has caused difficulties, but it is equally clear from *Sharing Homes* that it is difficult to dispense with intention altogether. It does seem evident, however, both from Baroness Hale's use of empirical data in *Stack v Dowden*, and from the Law Commission's extensive review of the demographic and social background in *Cohabitation: The Financial Consequences of Relationship Breakdown* (2007), that the context of these disputes will play an increasingly important role in shaping an appropriate solution.

13

Trusts in commerce I: occupational pension schemes

1. Introduction

(a) Commerce and the trust

The focus in this book has so far been on the use or imposition of the trust in various family contexts. It was often in response to problems posed in these contexts in particular that many of the basic rules of trusts law evolved. Some rules, for example, those relating to duties concerning investment and delegation, indirectly provide guidelines for commercial decisions to be taken during administration of a trust. But the trust concept has today also penetrated more directly into many and varied areas of commercial and financial activity (see Chapter 1 at p 9). In this chapter our focus shifts to one of those areas where the trust retains a significant role, namely collective saving for retirement via occupational pension provision. This is not to say that the trust does not feature significantly in other areas of commerce and finance. In the form of the 'unit trust', a hybrid creation comprising a complex amalgam of the concepts of common law contract and equitable trust, it provides a medium of collective investment for investors who wish to spread their risks over a wide range of securities (see Chapter 1). Recent estimates put the total number of unit trusts at closer to 1,800 with a market value in the region of £350 billion (thousand million) (*Financial Statistics* no 561, January 2009, Table 5.3D). Whilst the general body of law relating to the duties of trustees applies in principle to trustees of unit trusts, this is heavily qualified in practice by the fact that many aspects of the creation and operation of unit trusts are subject to statutory regulation and administrative control by the Financial Services Authority (see Financial Services and Markets Act 2000). That regulatory framework necessarily leaves a considerably diminished role for the general law of trusts. This position has contrasted sharply with the case of collective saving for retirement in occupational pension schemes, the principal focus of study in this chapter. Here statute law has in the past played a lesser role although it has been given greater prominence now, particularly via the Pensions Acts 1995, 2004 and 2008. Nevertheless the general law of trusts still has a significant role to play. Key questions for our purposes are whether the new statutory framework has affected the nature of the trust that underpins these collective savings schemes; and if it has, how? For instance, are the rules of trusts law as outlined in previous chapters compatible with the commercial nature of dealings to which it is now sought to apply them? To be effective – effective, that is, from the perspective of the persons seeking to employ the trust – must the rules be modified? If so, how far can these rules be stretched whilst remaining broadly consistent with some recognisable concept of the trust?

(b) Trusts law and occupational pension schemes: introduction

Most pension schemes are established and administered under trust. Pension contributions are paid into a trust fund by the employer sponsoring the scheme and, generally, by its members, who must be employees of the relevant employer. The fund is invested so that investment returns can increase its value and so supplement the contributions made by employer and members. The powers and duties of the trustees responsible for the administration and management of the fund are principally those laid down in the trust deed, supplemented by the general law of trusts, just as it is for ordinary family trusts. However, although the content of the duties governing trustees under the general law is also similar to those governing other trustees, the legal framework within which the occupational pension trust (OPT) operates has changed significantly since the early 1990s – certainly compared to that governing the private family trust. There is now, for example, a statute-based regulatory structure that overlays the system of governance otherwise provided by trusts law. What makes the OPT particularly interesting from our perspective, however, is the non-legal contexts in which it exists and the extent to which trusts law can accommodate and reconcile any or all of these other agendas.

First and foremost, as may be inferred from their title, OPTs are creatures of the employment relationship. Consequently the scope and terms of the pension arrangement can potentially become one of the objects of consultation and negotiation in industrial relations. Yet this possibility does not sit comfortably with the conventional approach of trusts law. We have seen in previous chapters that within the family context the flexibility of the rules and concepts of trusts law could be perceived as an attribute, one that provided settlors with considerable freedom to decide, for instance, on the balance of power between themselves, trustees, beneficiaries and the courts. In the current context this freedom is commonly reflected in the way in which the employer in the capacity of 'settlor' reserves powers to itself under the OPT. The employer buttresses this exercise of power with the argument that, as it provides the majority of the funding for the OPT, then it should have the final say on any matters of contention. However, those who perceive an industrial relations dimension of OPTs may disagree with the employer's analysis. The law's response to the possible conflicts of interest engendered here has been to bring employment law principles into the governance of the scheme; this in turn can raise questions about the nature of the trust itself.

A related issue arises from the welfare role occupied by the OPT. In 1998 the Labour government confirmed in a Green Paper that it regards OPTs as an essential part of pension provision in the UK, a view reiterated in another Green Paper in 2002 (see *A New Partnership for Welfare: Partnership in Pensions* (Cm 4179, 1998); *Simplicity, Security and Choice: Working and Saving for Retirement* (Cm 5677, 2002). OPTs may thus be regarded as a significant part of the welfare package provided for those citizens who are members of schemes. If this is the case, it poses a number of issues about the legal framework for OPTs. On the one hand it may be contended that it would not be appropriate to allow employers complete freedom of choice about when to wind up schemes or what kind of benefits to provide or even how far to pursue legitimate self-interest in administering schemes. On the other hand, those who sponsor schemes can argue in response that, as sponsors, they are commercial enterprises where costs matter and that an over-emphasis on regulation with its associated financial costs might force employers to review their decision to provide OPTs at all. Here again we will need to consider how satisfactorily a resolution of the possible tension between competing welfare and commercial objectives so evident here can be achieved within the four corners of a trusts law framework without subverting the fundamental nature of the trust. Indeed it is that very tension that has contributed to many employers seeking to minimise their exposure to financial risk by encouraging a shift in the type of occupational schemes from a 'defined benefit' to a 'defined contribution' basis over the last decade (see below, p 674 for further details).

One further feature of OPTs to mention here is that the investment policy pursued by these very large trust funds has important macro-economic and social policy implications. There are, for example, those who argue that this economic power should be used in a socially or ethically responsible way or with a view to the long-term interests of the UK economy. However, the law has tended towards the view that the funds must be invested in the best interests of the members, which interests are defined in financial terms only.

Before we look more closely at any of the legal issues posed by the contexts briefly outlined above, we need to examine further the characteristics of OPTs and the environments within which they operate. We can then see the ways by which pension fund trusts might be differentiated, *in fact*, from other trusts and so, in turn, the extent to which they are, or should be, treated differently in law. We examine the welfare aspects of pension provision, the size and source of funding of pension schemes, their economic significance, and the employment context. We will also look briefly at how forces operating within these different contexts have contributed to a process of legal change which, nevertheless, has left the role of the trust largely intact. Whether it has also left trusts law untouched is, as we shall see, a more troublesome question.

At the outset it is important to appreciate that, as with private trusts, there is enormous diversity in the size of OPTs. In 2007, for instance, schemes with at least 5,000 members accounted for just 1% of the total number of schemes whereas 82% of schemes had only between 2 and 12 members

(Office of National Statistics *Occupational Pensions Schemes Annual Report 2007* Table 2.2).

2. Significance of occupational pension provision

(a) The welfare significance of occupational pension schemes

OPTs are not the sole or even the principal source of pension provision in the UK. There is a complex and not wholly coherent set of arrangements in place, of which OPTs are a part. First there is state provision, currently comprising a two-tier system, on top of which sits a third tier of private pension provision. The first tier consists of a contributory basic pension but with the possibility of a means-tested top-up. The basic state pension (BSP: from April 2009, £95.25 a week for a single person) is payable in practice to everyone who has paid or been credited with National Insurance contributions for nine-tenths of their notional working lives (that is, 44 years for men and 39 years for women, although for anyone reaching pension age after April 2010 the qualifying number of years is being reduced to 30). The top-up arrangement, the Pensions Credit, is a benefit paid if the pensioner's income from other sources, including the BSP, does not reach a specified minimum level (from April 2009 £130.00 per week). Because the system is means-tested, benefit has to be claimed and it is estimated that between 20% and 30% of those entitled do not claim or take up their entitlement. The second tier of state provision operates on a contributory basis and is intended to provide a further tranche of pension for employees more closely related to their earnings level. There have been two principal schemes, the State Earnings Related Pension Scheme (SERPS: 1978–2002) and the State Second Pension (S2P: from April 2002). Significant pensions under S2P have yet to accrue but it should be noted that the main aim is to target resources at the lower paid. The maximum SERPS and S2P pension payable to someone retiring in 2009 is estimated to be around £150 per week (Pensions Policy Institute (June 2008) p 8). Employers who set up occupational schemes which satisfy certain minimum contribution requirements are allowed to contract-out employees from state second-tier provision; in return both employer and employee pay a reduced rate of National Insurance contribution. This facility will be available only to defined benefit schemes after April 2012.

The third tier of pensions provision comprises a variety of voluntary pension arrangements, including OPTs, that are not *directly* funded by the state although they do benefit from substantial tax reliefs. One source of this 'third tier' is provided by two types of individual pension arrangements; these are personal pensions and, as from 2001, Stakeholder pensions (see below). Personal pensions (PP) are generally funded by member contributions only. The contributions are invested on the capital markets by providers; the funds resulting from investment can then be used to buy an annuity on retirement. It will be noted that the PP does not therefore provide any guaranteed level of income on retirement. The sale of PPs was encouraged by the government in the 1980s, partly in an effort to shift some of the burden of pension provision from the state and partly because the dominant political culture then placed a premium on individual responsibility and freedom. The notorious misselling of PPs by the financial services sector discouraged people from investing in them to the extent that 'very few individual personal pensions are now sold to employees on average earnings or below' (First Report of the Pensions Commission *Pensions Challenges and Choices* (2004) p 90; see generally on 'misselling' Black and Nobles (1998) 61 MLR 789; Milner (1998) 12 TLI 130). Indeed the membership of personal pension schemes declined from approximately 10 million in 2002 to about 7 million by April 2008 (*HMRC Statistics 2008* Table 7.4).

In the wake of consumer concern about PPs, the Labour government introduced a new form of 'third-tier' private pension (Welfare Reform and Pensions Act 1999, Pt I). Employers who were not otherwise making available to employees a certain level of occupational pension provision were required to introduce a Stakeholder scheme with effect from 8 October 2001. The obligation on the employer was just to make a scheme available, either directly or through a pension provider such as an insurance company, and to enable an employee's contributions to be deducted from their remuneration. The initiative has had limited impact: 'The vast majority of small company Stakeholder schemes are empty shells with no contributing members' (Pensions Commission, above at p 92 and Figure 3.39). Moreover the employer is under no obligation to make any contribution and only between 4% and 10% of companies with fewer than 50 employees do so. The outcome is that by the end of April 2008 there were just 950,000 members of employer-sponsored schemes with annual contributions of just £1,800m (*HMRC Statistics* Table 7.5).

The OPT fits into this general scheme of pension provision by providing a source of 'third-tier' pension income to the approximately 60% of pensioners who have acquired this entitlement. There are approximately 27 million members of occupational pension schemes of whom 9.6 million employees are active members whilst 9.0 million have a deferred pension entitlement and another 8.5 million are currently in receipt of a pension. Occupational schemes currently provide about 27% of all pensioner income (Department of Work and Pensions (DWP) *The Pensioner Incomes Series 2006–2007* (2008) Table 2.1). In 2006–07 the average (mean) weekly payment received from an OPT was £156 (DWP Table 3.7; note, however, that the median payment was £98). The outcome for some current recipients is that their pensions may be sufficient to lift them slightly above social security thresholds, although scarcely into affluence. There is, however, little doubt that the value of an occupational pension has made pension entitlement a significant benefit to many employees. Indeed the value of membership of a OPT is reflected in the fact that the comparable mean and median payments for those in receipt of personal pensions income, some 12% of all pensioners, are more modest at £97 and £38 respectively. Another factor which supports the picture of the OPT as a welfare-related phenomenon is its tax treatment. It has since 1921 qualified for substantial tax relief: in 2007–08 tax relief in the amount of £18.9 billion was granted on employer and employee contributions and on the investment income of pension funds (*HMRC Statistics 2008* Table 7.9; Finance Act 2004, Part 4, ch 4).

Occupational pension provision has been almost a standard part of a remuneration package for larger employers: 90% of employers with over 100 employees provided pension schemes in 1994 (Casey, Hales and Millward *Employers' Pension Provision* DSS Research Report No 58 (1996)). This probably remains the position for most employers of this size but there is evidence of a decline since 2000 in the number of 'open' pension schemes (that is those that remain open to new members) and a corresponding increase in 'closed' schemes (see *Occupational Pensions* November 2008 pp 7–8). These shifts in provision predominantly reflect a decline in the willingness of employers to maintain what until recently was the most common type of scheme, that is the earnings-related (or defined benefit) schemes, so called because the pension was usually based on a fixed proportion of the member's salary at or close to retirement or the date of leaving the scheme if earlier. In most schemes of this nature, benefit accrued at a rate of 1/60th or 1/80th of final salary for each year of membership. Thus a person retiring at age 60 on a salary of £24,000 after 40 years' membership of the scheme could be entitled to a pension of 40/60ths of that salary, ie £16,000 per year. It is usually possible to take a proportion of the entitlement (up to 150% of 'final salary') as a tax-free lump sum on retirement. In practice matters are more complex as it is increasingly rare for people to remain with a single employer for so long, the average number of employers during a working life being six for a man and five for a woman (see Bone et al *Retirement and Retirement Plans* (1992): note the establishment in 1991 of a Pensions Registry so that holders of deferred pensions earned with a previous employer can trace their former schemes).

An alternative method of provision increasingly adopted by employers in the private sector in the last decade is a defined contribution or 'money purchase' scheme, whereby benefits are calculated by reference to contributions paid into the scheme in respect of that member, usually increased by an amount based on the investment return on those contributions. There is therefore no necessary relationship between salary level and pension paid. Instead at retirement the scheme member will have accrued an entitlement to a lump sum from which an annuity must be purchased to provide the pension. How good or bad the pension is will therefore depend on the past investment performance of the notional 'sub-fund' of the member and the annuity rates on offer at the time of retirement. Because this shift in the mode of provision is quite recent its significance to scheme membership and entitlement will not become fully apparent for some time.

Various factors do, however, counter the extent to which reliance can be placed in welfare terms on this private sector phenomenon. First, the pension eventually received may not ultimately match a member's pension expectations.

This potential shortfall can be attributed to two factors in particular, which can be termed the 'early leaver' and the 'pension in payment' problems. Employees leaving the company voluntarily, made redundant or otherwise dismissed before pension age – 'early leavers' – are potentially at a disadvantage in any scheme because their ability to accrue further years' entitlement to a pension within the scheme ends as their employment with the employer is terminated. They may still be entitled to a pension payable at pension age but, in a defined benefit scheme, one based only on accrued service and salary level at the date of termination. There is now a statutory obligation to increase this 'deferred pension', as it is called, until the date of payment but only in line with movement in prices (up to a maximum of 5%) not with average earnings (Pension Schemes Act (PSA) 1993, Pt IV; and Occupational Pension Schemes (Preservation of Benefit) Regulations 1991, SI 1991/167; the revaluation percentage of 5% is to be reduced to 2.5% from a date to be determined (Pensions Act 2008, Sch 2)). The outcome is that where the rate of increase in average earnings outstrips that of prices, as it consistently has, the real value of the deferred pension is subject to erosion, and the member's pension expectation is partially defeated. The 'pensions in payment' problem is also a product of inflation, but here primarily price inflation. The expectation of a stable standard of living in retirement will not be met if the real value of a pension in payment is allowed to decline. Most public sector pension schemes in practice increase pensions in line with the retail price index (RPI). For private sector schemes, indexation was introduced by the Pensions Act 1995, s 51 but subject to a statutory ceiling of 5% subsequently reduced with effect from April 2005 to 2.5% for benefits earned after that date (Pensions Act 2004, s 278).

Other factors also affect the contribution to welfare that OPTs make: for example, employers generally retain the discretion to wind up schemes. Although as we shall see shortly this is not an uncontrolled discretion, the controls that do currently operate on its exercise are to do with the employer's relationship with the members as employees, rather than as future potentially needy pensioners. Nevertheless, given the modest size of state pension provision and the otherwise slightly patchy pattern of private pension provision in the UK, OPTs do make a significant contribution to retirement welfare.

The future extent of that contribution is, however, a matter of some uncertainty. As many as 60% of defined benefit (DB) schemes are believed to have been closed to new members in the past decade and replaced by defined contribution (DC) schemes. The reasons are complex but include the consequences of increased regulation, our propensity to live longer, a decline in the returns on equity investments from the wholly exceptional and unsustainable boom of the 1980s and 1990s and a reduction in the tax relief on fund investment (Pensions Commission, above, pp 85–88). These all contributed to what the Pensions Commission concludes was 'an irrational exuberance which made improved promises appear costless' (see for a detailed review the Pensions Commission, above ch 3 Annex). The economic and welfare significance of this change is that the average level of contributions for retirement provision is markedly lower for DC schemes – around 7–11% (4–7% employer and 3–4% employee) – compared with DB schemes – 16–20% (11–14% employer and 5–6% employee).

(b) A financial profile of pension schemes

Large sums of money are paid into OPTs by way of contributions: for example, total contributions paid into funded pension schemes in 2006 amounted to £42,100m (ONS Blue Book, July 2007). The contribution rate of an employer can, and does, fluctuate since in a defined benefit scheme the employer normally contributes whatever additional sum the actuary advising the scheme considers necessary to fund the benefits promised (hence the term 'balance of cost' scheme).

The outcome of this very high level of contractual saving can be seen in the net assets held by pension funds, which totalled almost £1,010 billion at the end of 2006 (*Financial Statistics 561*, January 2009, Table 5.1B). To that figure can be added the long-term investment funds of life assurance companies, valued at £1,226 billion in 2006 (*Financial Statistics* op cit Table 5.1A), a significant proportion of which also represents pensions business. To put the figures into some sort of perspective, the total value of the combined assets constitutes approximately 40% of the total financial assets of the personal sector.

This channelling of personal savings into financial institutions has also led to a significant volume of ownership of company ordinary shares in their hands. The 2006 Share Register Survey showed that around 30% of UK ordinary shares are beneficially owned by insurance companies and pension funds compared, for instance, with 21% in 1975, and that overall ownership of shares by UK financial institutions is 41%, investors from outside the UK owning a further 40% (ONS *Share Ownership 2006*). Consequently, and notwithstanding the 1980s de-mutualisation and privatisation-induced increase in numbers of individuals owning shares, the decline in the proportion of shares held by those individuals has only been slowed not reversed: in 2006 UK-resident individuals owned only an estimated 13% compared with 37.5% in 1975.

Given the size of the assets invested by financial institutions it should not surprise us that the direction of that investment within capital markets has at regular intervals prompted criticism. Debates in this area have tended to focus on whether financial institutions adopt an unduly short-term view for assessing investment returns, thereby allegedly inhibiting business from long-term planning. These debates raise issues about economic policy, corporate governance and the role of institutional shareholders that go much wider than is required for our immediate purposes (see eg Davies 'The Role of the Institutional Shareholder' in Prentice and Holland (eds) *Contemporary Issues in Corporate Governance* (1993) ch 5; and generally Wheeler *Corporations and the Third Way* (2001); Dean *Directing Public Companies: Company Law and the Stakeholder Society* (2001); and the annual reports on shareholder voting published by PIRC, www.pirc.co.uk). Nevertheless those broad economic and financial market considerations do raise subsidiary yet important questions: how far are pension scheme members or member-nominated trustees able to influence investment policy of pension funds? What criteria should they seek to apply in that process? What level of expertise should trustees of pension schemes be expected to demonstrate? These questions were lent a sharper focus by the Myners Report on *Institutional Investment in the UK* (2001) that produced several important recommendations concerning the role of trustees and we touch on all these questions below (see p 685 et seq). On the specific matter of voting rights attaching to shareholdings it should be noted that the Companies Act 2006, s 1277 confers extensive powers on the government to make regulations requiring certain categories of institutional investors to provide information about the exercise of their voting rights. It appears that the powers will be acted upon only if disclosure on a voluntary basis proves ineffective.

(c) Occupational pension schemes and industrial relations

Occupational pensions are for most workers a relatively recent development. Some employers paid pensions before 1914 and the practice spread slowly between the two world wars, but rapid growth in pension provision only really began after 1945. In 1936, only 2.6 million employees (approximately 13% of the workforce) belonged to pension schemes, but total coverage had increased to 6.2 million by 1953 and to a peak of 12.2 million by 1967, since when, as seen above, the number of active scheme members has been in decline. (see generally Goode Report, ch 2; Hannah *Inventing Retirement* (1986)).

What prompted this considerable expansion in occupational pension provision? It is apparent that most schemes were initiated by employers, and not as a consequence of workforce or social pressures. Whereas generous tax treatment of pension contributions and pension fund profits may have had an effect, it has been argued that the two predominant considerations for employers were a tradition of paternalist benevolence linked to a desire to exercise control over the workforce (see Green 'Occupational Pension Schemes and British Capitalism' (1982) Cambridge Journal of Economics vol 6, 267–283). This combination of motives is apparent in a preamble to the printed flysheet announcing the Distillers Company's pension scheme in July 1919 (quoted in *Hannah* p 23):

IN ORDER TO PROMOTE

1. The well-being and contentment of their workpeople;
2. The length and improvement of service;
3. The removal of friction between employers and employed;
4. The encouragement of thrift among their Employees,

The Directors . . . submit for their workpeople's consideration and acceptance the following proposals . . .

Whatever the motives of employers may originally have been, once occupational pension provision became widespread, labour market considerations could not be ignored. Thus a firm may consider it necessary to offer a pension in order to recruit and retain staff (although its final decision may also be influenced by the tax position). In addition, the opportunity to use pension schemes to fund down-sizing in the labour market has not been ignored: the shock of redundancy can be mitigated by an enhanced early retirement pension. Neither employers nor unions have over-looked the implications of this: one example where controversy over such funding can continue well after negotiations are apparently complete can be seen in the case of *National Grid Co plc v Mayes* [2001] 1 WLR 864.

In any event, many trade unions were initially either hostile or indifferent to occupational pensions, preferring to concentrate on campaigning for better state pensions (see Hyman and Schuller (1984) 22 BJIR 289 at 291–292). It was only in the 1970s that attitudes of trade unions generally and the Trades Union Congress (TUC) began to change. A considerable stimulus was provided to the status of pension provision as a collective bargaining issue by the exemption of pension scheme benefits from incomes policies between 1972 and 1974, and between 1975 and 1978. Subsequently, interest has extended beyond the issue of benefit and contribution levels to that of participation in the management of pension schemes. A controversial White Paper published by the Labour government in 1976 (*Occupational Pension Schemes: The Role of Members in the Running of Schemes* Cmnd 6514) recommended that employee representatives should be entitled to 50% of the membership of any controlling board of an occupational pension scheme, and further that those representatives should be selected through trade union channels only. These proposals were never enacted, although the activities of Robert Maxwell, ironically, have achieved a similar outcome, though for different reasons.

(d) Maxwell and legal change

We have seen that occupational pensions are the product of many different forces. Employers will be concerned about the financial and certain industrial relations aspects of provision; members and unions will be concerned with the negotiation of benefits as well as the possible involvement of the membership in management-related issues and the continued health of the relevant company or industry. Government will use the tax and National Insurance systems to try to maximise the welfare potential of the schemes and thereby minimise the future role of the state in pension provision. All of the parties are likely to be aware of the economic influence exercised by the large agglomerations of capital assets held in the pension funds. Given all these factors, it is perhaps inevitable that concern has focused on the appropriate form of governance of such schemes and, in particular, with fund security.

There have in the past been several calls for the replacement of trusts law with a comprehensive statutory framework to govern occupational schemes (see eg

Committee to Review the Functioning of Financial Institutions Report (Cmnd 7937, 1980)). Others, in contrast, have expressed confidence in continuing reliance on trusts law. Thus the OPB in 1989, in an apparent volte-face from an earlier view, accepted that 'trust law should continue as the legal basis for pension schemes' (*Protecting Pensions* (Cm 573) para 8.14; see also Hayton [1993] Conv 283; Chatterton (1993) 7 TLI 91).

There the issue might have rested had it not been for the collapse of the business empire of the late Robert Maxwell and the subsequent revelation that some £420m had been removed unlawfully from the pension schemes of companies controlled by Maxwell. On the recommendation of the House of Commons Select Committee on Social Security (*Second Report* HC Paper (1991–92) 61 – the operation of pension funds), a committee of inquiry, the Pensions Law Review Committee, was appointed under the chairmanship of Professor Goode QC with a wide-ranging brief to review the legal framework within which occupational pension schemes operate. A key recommendation in the Committee's comprehensive report (*Pension Law Reform* (Cm 2342, 1993), 'Goode Report') was that 'trust law should continue to provide the foundation for interests, rights and duties arising in connection with occupational pension schemes but should be reinforced by a Pensions Act administered by a Pensions Regulator' (para 1.1.13). Following publication of the Goode Report, the Pensions Act (PA) 1995 was passed. Subsequent events including the Myners Report, and renewed concern about the threat to pension entitlement where schemes were found to be in deficit on a winding-up, have prompted further legislative intervention in the form of the Pensions Acts 2004 and 2008.

Both statutes introduce significant changes to the governance of occupational pensions. But the basic structure of reliance on the trust form is maintained. In the remainder of this chapter, we will look at the extent to which the trust can cope with the different demands put on it by the different interest groups, and what effect, if any, the response has had on the underlying trust concept.

3. The legal framework of occupational pension schemes

(a) The use of trusts for pension provision

Several explanations may be given for the continued use of the trust as the framework for pension provision (even though, for example, a contract between employer and employee could in principle equally well be used). One of the most important explanations concerns security of assets. Legal ownership of the trust fund is nominally separated from the employer's business, thereby, it is hoped, placing the fund beyond the reach of the employer's creditors in the event of the latter's insolvency. It should be noted however that security of neither pension entitlement nor expectation is guaranteed by this situation, for two reasons. First, as was discovered post-Maxwell, no system of law can prevent a determined fraudster. Second, as regards employer solvency generally, the security of the members' entitlement will depend on scheme solvency. This in turn depends on the accuracy of actuarial assessments about the timing and level of contributions necessary to ensure that the fund is adequate to fulfil the scheme's pension obligations. A statutory Minimum Funding Requirement, first introduced by the PA 1995, s 56, was replaced as from 30 December 2005 with scheme-specific funding requirements intended to allow schemes greater flexibility (Pensions Act 2004, Pt 3; Occupational Pension Schemes (Scheme Funding) Regulations SI 2005/3377). Trustees are required to agree various matters relating to funding with the employer and in the event of a failure to agree the matter must be referred to the Pension Regulator who has power to resolve matters (see below, p 707). Maxwell aside, the image of the OPT providing a secure pension entitlement was dealt a damaging blow by the evidence of companies becoming insolvent but with insufficient funds in their pension schemes to meet the accrued rights of scheme members. To address this problem a pension protection fund (PPF) has been established (with effect from April 2005), financed by a levy paid by DB pension schemes (Pensions Act 2004, s 173; see generally DWP *Working and Saving for Retirement* (Cm 5835) and *Simplicity, Security and Choice* (Cm 6111)). The protection was not retrospective and in response to pressure a government-funded Financial Assistance Scheme – £400m over 20 years – was introduced to offer help to some people who lost out on their occupational pension because their scheme was underfunded when it wound up and their employer had been unable to make up the deficit (Pensions Act 2004, s 286).

Another powerful reason for the continued use of the trust was the requirement that the scheme had to be established by means of 'an irrevocable trust' if it was to qualify for maximum tax reliefs. The explanation for this initially puzzling requirement is that historically it has been insisted upon as a means to counter possible corporate use of trust funds for tax avoidance purposes. Paradoxically we have the trust, which we have previously portrayed as a means of avoiding tax, now being cast in the role of an anti-avoidance tool. In the view of at least one writer, however, it was not fiscal advantages that first made the trust attractive as a vehicle for pension provision: 'the concept of a "trust" had emotional appeal for those who were trying to create more harmonious relations between masters and men' (*Hannah* p 19). Perhaps more important was the fact that the trust was a cheap and flexible vehicle: 'creative lawyers could draw up a trust deed with virtually any characteristic the employer chose. Those who wished to retain control of the funds themselves found, for example, that they could do so de facto by appointing all the trustees themselves, and many schemes of this nature were founded' (op cit and see generally Nobles *Pensions, Employment and the Law* (1993)). Fiscal incentives and the inherent attributes of the trust have therefore made a persuasive combination.

Whatever the reason for it, the trust has endured and is well established as the primary legal basis for the pension scheme. It has, for example, been judicially asserted that, as regards the obligations of trustees, there is 'no reason for holding that different principles apply to pension fund trusts from those which apply to other trusts' (per Megarry VC in *Cowan v Scargill* [1984] 2 All ER 750 at 763, and see the judge's clarification extra-judicially in Youdan (ed) *Equity, Fiduciaries and Trusts* (1989) 155). But this does not describe the whole legal picture. The OPT, like all trusts, will have within it a number of powers and discretions granted either to the trustees of the scheme or its relevant employer. In deciding how these powers and discretions are to be exercised, scope has been given for other legal principles to become relevant. For example, in general, the provisions of a scheme are to be interpreted against its commercial background (see *Re Courage Group's Pension Schemes* [1987] 1 All ER 528). More specifically, we will see that although the employer does have powers over the assets and funding mechanism – and the continued existence – of a scheme, those powers are subject to controls imposed by principles borrowed from employment law. The extent to which this mechanism gives *adequate* recognition to the employment context is one question to be addressed; but in any event, it is one of the factors pulling the OPT away from any real comparison with the private family trust.

Other such factors are many. Although early perceptions of occupational pension provision were that it was essentially a voluntary act by employers, mirrored by a legal framework which initially imposed few obligations or restrictions on them (see generally *Nobles* ch 3) statute did early on begin to make incursions into this freedom. There were restrictions on level of benefits imposed by the Inland Revenue under the Finance Acts, again principally to prevent the use of pension schemes for tax avoidance. Even before the PA 1995, provisions were introduced imposing minimum standards for vesting and preservation of occupational pension benefits (see now generally Pension Schemes Act (PSA) 1993). Moreover, significant obligations with regard to equal pay and equal treatment for men and women have been imposed under European Community law (see now PA 1995, s 65) and, as from May 2000, pension scheme rules have had to be amended to permit pension sharing on divorce (see now Matrimonial Causes Act 1973, s 24B).

(b) Trusteeship and conflicts of interest in the OPT: a prologue

A further important consideration shaping the legal framework is that, because the employer has more influence and interest in the running of the scheme than the settlor in most private family trust arrangements, the role of the trustees in safeguarding the rights and interests of members becomes particularly significant. This obligation is accentuated by the extremely technical and complex nature of the legal and financial issues involved. But trustees may also be faced with conflicts of interest, more acute than those that occur in family trusts, arising between employer and member as well as between different classes of member. The specific contexts in which conflicts can arise are many and various but include issues such as setting contribution rates, determining investment policy (including self-investment), deciding responses to corporate merger proposals and negotiating on scheme-funding deficits or, less commonly today, surpluses.

At worst, the failure to respond to such conflicts can even result in the wholesale fraud that was apparent in the *Maxwell* case. Less dramatically, it can create industrial relations tensions and the potential for members to lodge claims about inappropriate behaviour by the employer or against the decisions of trustees where these may be seen as 'favouring' one class of scheme members as against another. To counteract these tensions, and in accordance with trusts law, trustees must act prudently, conscientiously, honestly and, above all, independently in the sole interests of members. The trustees may not, however, be wholly free agents, particularly where nominated by the employer. Although the Maxwell story is an extreme example, the difficulty that can arise in practice is illustrated by the following extract from the 1992 report of the House of Commons Social Security Committee into the Maxwell affair (HC Paper (1991–92) no 61 (the operation of pension funds)):

> Para 48. Although we were told that all of the trustees were very much aware of their responsibilities, and the trustees acted with great faith and took their duties very seriously, as Captain Jackson [a trustee] told the Committee:
>
> > '...ultimately in a vote, if a vote was called, Mr Maxwell had the casting vote and he had used it in the past so we tried not to throw things to the vote, but ultimately the power of hire and fire was in his hands, as [it was] for all the scheme's advisers'.

There are therefore acknowledged dangers in relying too heavily on the personal office of trustee as adequate protection for members. One of the Goode Committee's recommendations on this was that some trustees should be nominated to the trust board by the membership. As a result, under PA 1995, ss 16–21 one-third of each trustee board was now to be member-nominated and the total number of such trustees should not be less than two (or one if the scheme has less than 100 members – see s 16(6)). The mechanisms by which these changes were to be introduced proved complex, costly to implement and included a well-used employer opt-out. Under the Pensions Act 2004, s 241 the 'opt-out' was removed (with effect from April 2006) and s 243(1) empowers the Secretary of State to increase the proportion of member-nominated trustees to one-half, although this has yet to be acted upon. It is important to note that member involvement on trustee boards implies neither trade union involvement nor equality of representation of the workforce. Indeed, those nominated as trustees are just that: trustees. They are 'nominated' by the membership rather than 'representative' of them and are subject to the same duties as other trustees. Their appointment was not recommended by the Goode Committee in order to pursue any goal of an increased employee control, but (in part) to ensure that their interests were kept clearly in mind in any trustee decision-making – which has a different emphasis. Some of the ways in which the potential conflicts of interests have been addressed are considered further at p 698.

The applicability and effectiveness of trusts law in general, with its presumption of independent trustees acting solely in the best interests of the beneficiaries, and subject to the fundamental or 'substratum' duties imposed by the general law of trusts – honesty and good faith, impartiality and prudence – in particular, is considered next. Three specific issues will be examined: investment policy, including delegation and trustee liability; 'beneficial ownership and control' of the fund; and trust governance, particularly in light of changes brought about by the PAs 1995 and 2004.

4. The administration of the pension scheme

(a) Investment policy and practice

(1) General position

We have now seen that pension trusts look different from most private trusts. The assets of even relatively modest self-administered pension funds far outstrip those of the overwhelming majority of private trusts. Two consequences in particular flow from this factual difference. The first relates to the delegation of investment management. It soon became impractical to expect all appointed trustees to deal with the financial markets as effectively as would experienced and professional fund managers; and given the size of funds, the best interests of the beneficiaries of such funds might anyway be better served by professionals. As we discover below, whilst the Pensions Act 1995 seeks to address this issue the widespread engagement of professional fund managers has raised fresh questions about the role and responsibilities of trustees in investment policy.

The second consequence is that the investment portfolio carried by the pension trust is capable of supporting a greater degree of diversity than ordinary family trusts, including investments such as works of art, options contracts in foreign currencies and futures contracts all of which might still be considered too speculative for most private trusts. Indeed, in *Trustees of the British Museum v A-G* [1984] 1 All ER 337 (see Chapter 10), Sir Robert Megarry VC implicitly recognised the idea that, in large funds, wide diversification is justified and risky investment more necessary where considerable capital growth is required (see also *Steel v Wellcome Custodian Trustees Ltd* [1988] 1 WLR 167). It would seem self-evident that this approach to investment should apply in full force to pension funds. But what if the members do not necessarily benefit directly from the higher returns associated with greater risk? As will be seen below in the context of ownership of pension funds this is a possible outcome. Paradoxically it may therefore be open to question whether trustees of pension funds should necessarily pursue an investment policy which emphasises risk-taking to achieve high returns (see generally Arthur and Randall 'Actuaries, Pension Funds and Investment' (1993) 43 Transactions of Faculty of Actuaries 125).

A key question and a starting-point for legal analysis then is whether the general principles of trusts law that govern trustee actions in private family trusts in relation to investment apply in equal measure to occupational pension trusts. In what is still a leading case, *Cowan v Scargill* [1985] 1 Ch 270, Sir Robert Megarry VC was in no doubt (at 289–290):

> ...there is the question whether the principles that I have been stating apply, with or without modification, to trusts of pension funds. Counsel for the plaintiffs asserted that they applied without modification, and that it made no difference that some of the funds came from the members of the pension scheme, or that the funds were often of a very substantial size. Mr Scargill did not in terms assert the contrary. He merely said that this was one of the questions to be decided, and that pension funds may be subject to different rules. I was somewhat unsuccessful in my attempts to find out from him why this was so, and what the differences were. What it came down to, I think, was that the rules for trusts had been laid down for private and family trusts and wills a long time ago; that pension funds were very large and affected large numbers of people; that in the present case the well-being of all within the coal industry was affected, and that there was no authority on the point except *Evans v London Co-operative Society Ltd* (1976) Times, 6 July, and certain overseas cases.
>
> I...consider the question of principle first. I can see no reason for holding that different principles apply to pension fund trusts from those which apply to other trusts. Of course, there are many provisions in pension schemes which are not to be found in private trusts, and to these the general law of trusts will be subordinated. But subject to that, I think that the trusts of pension funds are subject to the same rules as other trusts...

More will be said later on this potentially wide-ranging general statement of principle by the Vice Chancellor but first we consider the modifications to the statutory framework that have been put in place since *Cowan v Scargill*.

(2) Pensions Act 1995: investment and delegation

PA 1995, ss 34–36 now confers on trustees of OPTs very broad powers of investment and of delegating investment discretions. These provisions are unaffected by the Trustee Act 2000, which does not apply in these matters to pension schemes.

Investment Policy   Under PA 1995, s 35, the trustees of an OPT must secure that a written statement setting out the principles governing the investment policy of the fund is prepared, maintained and revised from time to time (the 'Statement of Investment Principles'). It has to set out the trustees' policy about, inter alia, the kinds of investments to be held; the balance between different investments; risk; the expected return on investments; and the realisation of investments (s 35(3)). Whilst preparing this statement, trustees are enjoined by s 35(5) to obtain and consider the written advice of a person who is reasonably believed by the trustees to be suitably qualified in terms of his ability and experience in financial matters; and to consult with the employer sponsoring the scheme. Revised regulations introduced in 2005 set out in some detail how their investment discretion is to be exercised (Occupational Pension Schemes (Investment) Regulations SI 2005/3378). Unsurprisingly it is stated that the assets must be invested 'in the best interests of members and beneficiaries' and, moreover, 'in their *sole* interest' in the event of a conflict of interest arising between their interests and that of the employer (Regulation 2; emphasis added). The same regulations also implement the requirements of the European Pensions Directive (2003/41/EC) and the Directive on Markets in Financial Instruments (2004/39/EC) whereby investments in 'risky instruments' such as derivatives may be made only in so far as they 'contribute to a reduction in risk' or 'facilitate efficient portfolio management' (Regulation 8; see Sims (2007) 21(4) TLI 165–176).

Delegation of discretions   Under PA 1995, s 34(1), subject to scheme rules to the contrary and the requirements of the statutory regulations, trustees may invest 'as if they are absolutely entitled to the assets of the scheme'. Of possibly greater legal significance is s 34(2) which allows any discretion regarding investment to be delegated fully to an investment manager, provided that the manager falls within the provisions of s 19 of the Financial Services and Markets Act 2000 and is authorised to carry out 'investment business'. Trustees can also delegate some discretion to a fund manager who is not authorised under the financial services legislation, provided that what is delegated is not 'investment business' within the terms of the 2000 Act. As the powers of trustees to delegate have been enlarged, so has attention been given to clarifying their supervisory responsibilities. Thus trustees are not to be liable for the acts or defaults of fund managers to whom discretions are delegated (s 34(4)), *provided* that the trustees have taken reasonable steps to satisfy themselves that the fund manager has the 'appropriate knowledge and experience for managing the investments of the scheme', is 'carrying out his work competently', and is complying with the investment guidelines as prescribed in s 36 (above). Note, however, that subject to those specific exemptions from vicarious liability, trustees *cannot* exempt themselves generally from liability for breach of their duties of care and skill in relation to their investment functions (s 33(1)).

One outcome of these changes is that the trustees' role has shifted from that of ever-watchful managers of capital to ever-watchful supervisors of investment managers. Whether trustees possess the expertise necessary to fulfil these tasks is uncertain, a point that came under scrutiny in a report in 2001 by Paul Myners, appointed by the Chancellor of the Exchequer to review institutional investment in the UK (*Institutional Investment in the United Kingdom: a Review* (March 2001); see Davis *The Regulation of Funded Pensions* Financial Services Authority Occasional Paper Series 15 (2001)). Myners interpreted this brief widely and in relation to trustees concluded, inter alia, that (i) trustees are often asked to take crucial investment decisions without either appropriate resources or expertise to make informed judgments; (ii) trustees therefore tend to rely heavily on a small number of investment consulting firms, whose advice and performance they are not sufficiently expert to examine critically, or evaluate; (iii) there is unnecessary emphasis placed on achieving short-term results because of lack of clarity about the timescales over which fund managers' performance is to be judged; and (iv) both fund managers and trustees appear unnecessarily reluctant to engage with companies in relation to corporate underperformance despite the possible benefits this might have for their clients.

Myners produced a number of recommendations that *potentially* affected the legal framework governing trustees of OPTs. In particular he concluded that in the interests of improved investment decision-making trustees should *voluntarily* adopt on a 'comply or explain' basis, a series of principles codifying best practice for decision-making in relation to investment, the object of which was to counter the perceived weaknesses just mentioned. The government adopted, with minor amendments, both the principles and the voluntarist approach (*Myners Principles for Institutional Investment Decision-making: A Review of Progress* (December 2004)). A review of the Myners principles was conducted during 2007–08, the outcome being that a smaller number of 'higher level principles' is to be developed by a joint government and pensions industry Investment Governance Group, all within a voluntary framework and with the intention of providing more flexibility for schemes of different sizes (see HM Treasury *Updating the Myners Principles* (October 2008)). The one legislative change to emerge from this process was the imposition, as from April 2006, of a statutory duty on trustees (i) to be 'conversant' with their scheme's trust deed and rules, statement of investment principles under PA 1995, s 35 and other scheme documentation (Pensions Act 2004, s 247(3)); and (ii) to 'have knowledge and understanding of the law relating to pensions and trusts' and of the principles relating to funding and investment of the scheme (s 247(4)). It is arguable that this is no more than declaratory of the existing common law duty, subject perhaps to that alarming reference to the law of trusts.

It remains to be seen whether the intention to strengthen the controls exercisable by trustees over the investment process in the manner envisaged by Myners is reconcilable with the understandable wish simultaneously to enhance the role of MNTs on boards of trustees. Might it be that diligence is the most that can realistically be expected from those that are lay people? Whilst a valuable role is to be performed by them – the virtues of common sense and a capacity to challenge accepted wisdom are often cited – it may be more unreasonable to assume knowledge of high finance amongst MNTs than it is amongst some employer-appointed trustees whose other functions might include, say, a post of finance director. Much will depend on the willingness of all parties to support an extensive training function for trustees.

Majority decision-making   PA 1995, s 34(5) empowers a trustee board to delegate any two of their number to exercise the board's power to make investment decisions (unless the trust deed indicates that this would not be appropriate). Given that one of the most significant changes introduced by the PA was the MNT, it is interesting to note that s 34(5) in effect gives trustee boards the power to exclude MNTs from investment decision-making. Thomas and Dowrick in *Blackstone's Guide to the Pensions Act 1995* (1995) point out that this runs counter to the spirit of s 16 of the Pensions Act, which specifically states that MNTs should be treated the same as the other trustees on the board (at p 57).

Differences of fact between private family trusts and OPTs have thus led to certain legal differences in the treatment of pension trusts although in the area of investment management the changes introduced in the Trustee Act 2000 have elided the legal differences. The basic duty of care in relation to investment decisions appears, however, to have remained unchanged. This situation may not be entirely satisfactory. The size of pension trust funds mean that the investment policy of those funds can have enormous impact on the financial markets; yet the law insists that trustees cannot easily take this into account when making investment decisions, a point we turn to next in the context of social investing.

Social investment   The delegation of fund management and diversification of investments have arisen as issues partly as a product of the size of pension funds. Size itself does not necessarily support any further modification of trusts law in its application to the investment policy of trustees. Nevertheless, in the context of what has been termed 'social' or 'divergent' investing, there is debate about the application of rules derived from the realm of the family private trust. We considered this issue in general terms in Chapter 10 (see p 484 et seq). But are there circumstances in which the investment of pension funds should diverge from the traditional investment goals of maximising investment returns at an appropriate level of risk, in order to pursue other goals?

This issue came to the fore in *Cowan v Scargill* [1985] 1 Ch 270, a case concerning the investment policy of the Mineworkers' Pension Scheme, which was set up under the Coal Industry Nationalisation Act 1946 (see Farrar and Maxton (1986) 102 LQR 32; Nobles (1984) 13 ILJ 167; Pearce and Samuels [1985] Conv (NS) 52).

The pension scheme provided for the payment of pensions to mineworkers employed by the National Coal Board (NCB) on retirement, on injury and on contracting certain diseases and also for payments to their widows and children. The funds of the scheme were provided by contributions from mineworkers, by payments made by the NCB and by profits from investment. There were ten trustees of the scheme, five appointed by the NCB, and five by the mineworkers' union. The trustees had very wide powers of investment. From 1976 onwards, investment decisions were taken by the investment manager in accordance with a general strategy laid out in four-year plans. In 1982 a plan amending the

1980 plan was put to the trustees for approval. The union-appointed trustees refused to approve the plan unless it was amended (i) to prohibit any increase in overseas investment, (ii) to provide for withdrawal from existing overseas investment at an opportune time, and (iii) to prohibit investment in energy industries which were in direct competition with coal.

The plaintiffs, the five trustees appointed by the board, applied to the court for directions that the defendants, the union-appointed trustees, were in breach of their fiduciary duties as trustees in refusing to concur in the adoption of the 1982 plan. Mr Scargill represented the union-appointed trustees. In the case, as we saw in Chapter 10 (at p 486) Sir Robert Megarry VC described the relevant duties of trustees as being (i) 'to exercise their powers in the best interests of the present and future beneficiaries of the trust, holding the scales impartially between different classes of beneficiaries' and (ii) 'under a trust for the provision of financial benefits, the paramount duty of the trustees is to provide the greatest financial benefits for the present and future beneficiaries' (at 287–288). In response to the proposition that different considerations should apply to the application of those duties in the context of large pension funds the judge commented as follows (at 290):

> The large size of pension funds emphasises the need for diversification, rather than lessening it, and the fact that much of the fund has been contributed by members of the scheme seems to me to make it even more important that the trustees should exercise their powers in the best interests of the beneficiaries. In a private trust, most, if not all, of the beneficiaries are the recipients of the bounty of the settlor, whereas under the trusts of a pension fund many (though not all) of the beneficiaries are those who, as members, contributed to the funds so that in due time they would receive pensions. It is thus all the more important that the interests of the beneficiaries should be paramount, so that they may receive the benefits which in part they have paid for. I can see no justification for holding that the benefits to them should run the risk of being lessened because the trustees were pursuing an investment policy intended to assist the industry that the pensioners have left, or their Union.

The judge reviewed the three authorities cited to him (*Evans v London Co-operative Society Ltd* (1976), *Times* 6 July; *Blankenship v Boyle* 329 F Supp 1089 (1971); *Withers v Teachers' Retirement System of the City of New York* 444 F Supp 1248 (1978)) and concluded:

> I can see no escape from the conclusion that the NUM trustees were attempting to impose the prohibitions in order to carry out union policy; and mere assertions that their sole consideration was the benefit of the beneficiaries do not alter that conclusion.

Two notable features of the case were that the NUM-appointed trustees (i) sought an absolute prohibition on certain forms of investment, and (ii) did not attempt to produce evidence from professional advisers to support their stance. It may therefore be contended that where the probable return from two investments, A and B, is equivalent it is defensible to follow an investment policy whereby A is selected in preference to B on social grounds, ie a 'socially sensitive' rather than 'socially dictated' investment policy. Extra-judicially Nicholls VC, now Lord Nicholls, has expanded on this theme, suggesting that even where the trust's objective is solely to provide financial benefits 'in most cases trustees may adopt an ethical investment policy' ((1995) 9 TLI 71 at 75). The rationale for this statement is that the range of available investments is so extensive that 'very frequently there is scope for trustees to give effect to moral considerations, either by positively preferring certain investments or negatively avoiding others, without thereby prejudicing beneficiaries' financial interests' (at 75). Interestingly Lord Nicholls specifically suggests that there is no objection in trusts law principles to this approach: 'the ordinary prudent person would surely feel no inhibitions in this situation, where the beneficiaries are not required to pay financial price' (at 75; see also Watchman et al (2005) 19(3) TLI 127–148 but cf Thornton (2008) 67(2) CLJ 396–422; and generally Chapter 10 at p 482).

Consider the following points.

(1) In 1999 the government imposed a duty on pension scheme trustees to disclose in their Statements of Investment Principle under PA 1995, s 35(3) 'the extent (if at all) to which social, environmental or ethical considerations are taken into account in the selection, retention and realisation of investments' (Occupational Pension Schemes (Investment) Regulations, SI 2005/3378, reg 2(3)(b)(vi)). The regulations clearly do not require trustees to undertake social investing nor do they purport to alter the current legal position as established by the common law in this area.

(2) Notwithstanding the reasoning in *Cowan v Scargill* it cannot be assumed that the benefits of a successful investment policy will necessarily accrue directly to the members of the pension scheme (see generally Nobles *Pensions, Employment and the Law* (1993) chs 6 and 8). Where the funding of a DB scheme is on a balance of cost basis an investment policy that produces a higher than anticipated rate of return may reduce the contribution that the employer has to make into the pension scheme. This poses a potential conflict of interest for trustees who are also directors or senior executives of the sponsoring company – so-called 'insider trustees'. There is some empirical evidence that these trustees 'act in the interest of shareholders of the sponsoring company, and not necessarily plan members' in that they place greater emphasis on a high rate of return than on security thereby allowing firms 'to make lower contributions into the plan' (see Cocco and Volpin *CEPR Discussion Paper 4932: The Corporate Governance of Defined-Benefit Pension Plans* (2005) p 3). In so far as this practice increases the profitability of the company this can be argued as being of *indirect* benefit to the employee scheme members.

(3) To the employer, one disadvantage of providing pensions by means of a trust fund is that it requires the alienation of capital from the business. This

disadvantage is alleviated in part by the tax advantages gained when an employer makes contributions to its pension fund. However, the argument can arise that the loss of capital can be further alleviated if the trustees invest a proportion of the fund in the sponsoring business itself. Self-investment has been used in the past, for example, to provide the business with loan capital at preferential rates or to provide a controlled sharehold-ing as a bulwark against an unwelcome take-over bid (see eg *Financial Times* 27 January 1987, p 1 in relation to a take-over bid by English China Clays for Bryant Holdings). But a consequence of self-investment is that those assets cease to be segregated from the employer. Any subsequent failure of the company therefore potentially places a double jeopardy on the active members of the scheme, since both their job prospects and their pension benefits may be endangered. In response to mounting pressure, accentu-ated by various cases where self-investment went wrong (such as those involving the Burlington International Group and the Lewis Group), reg-ulations were introduced in 1992 to restrict self-investment to 5% of the pension fund's resources. The position is now governed by PA 1995, s 40 and the Occupational Pension Schemes (Investment) Regulations 2005, SI 2005/3378. These make the additional provision that none of the scheme's resources may at any time be invested in any employer-related loan (Reg 12). There are also now penalties for trustees who fail to comply with the regulations.

(b) The occupational pension scheme: ownership, entitlement and control

(1) Introduction

A combination of better than anticipated investment returns and reduced lia-bilities, principally reflecting the large number of redundancy-induced 'early leavers' in the 1980s, created a position whereby substantial notional surpluses were revealed within many pension schemes. It should be noted as a prelimi-nary point, however, that unless treated with caution, the very word 'surplus', or indeed 'deficit', is apt to mislead. Both are abstractions derived from an actu-arial valuation of the assets and liabilities of a pension scheme. An actuarial surplus therefore represents 'the excess of the actuarial value of assets over the actuarial value of liabilities on the basis of the valuation method used' (Pensions Research Accountants Group *Pension Fund Surpluses* (1988) para 2.2). There are two points to emphasise about this definition. First, there are various meth-ods of valuing assets and liabilities, each of which can generate widely differing contribution rates, levels of funding and, therefore, size of surplus or deficit. Second, even a modest variation in an assumption, eg about future invest-ment returns, can markedly alter the valuation of a fund (see *London Regional Transport Pension Fund Trustee Co Ltd v Hatt* [1993] PLR 227, where it was estimated that a 0.5% reduction in dividend growth would reduce the surplus by 35% from £469m to £293m). The warning implicit in *Hatt* was prescient.

The consequence of the sharp decline in share prices between 1999 and 2002 (see above, p 474) combined with an increase in future liabilities of pension schemes was in many instances to convert surpluses into deficits. Since then the financial status of schemes has undergone a roller-coaster ride reflecting the vagaries of investment returns and the volatility in world stock markets over the last decade but also increases in future liabilities of schemes. A 2004 study, for instance, estimated that as of 31 December 2003, the FTSE 350 companies had an estimated aggregate deficit of £64 billion, equivalent to around 5% of market capitalisation (Keogh *Financial Significance of Deficits* (Mercer HR Consulting, September 2004)). Three years later, by contrast, a survey of the FTSE 100 companies conducted by Aon Consulting revealed aggregate surpluses of £33 billion (*Occupational Pensions* February 2008, p 2). By July 2008 the financial position of the FTSE 100 company schemes had so deteriorated that that they were showing estimated aggregate deficits of £41 billion (LCP *Accounting for Pensions 2008*). Notwithstanding these extreme fluctuations in scheme valuations, it has been in the context of debates about 'ownership' of surpluses that legal analysis of the respective rights and duties of employers, scheme members and trustees has been honed and remains significant for our understanding of the development and distinctiveness of pensions trusts law (see generally Goode Report, ch 4.3; Nobles *Pensions, Employment and the Law* (1993) ch 7; Moffat (1993) 56 MLR 471; Hayton [2005] Conv 229; cf Davis (2001) 15(3) TLI 130).

Disputes over attributing entitlement to a surplus can arise: (i) where an employer seeks in one of several possible ways to take a repayment of all or part of a surplus in the fund; (ii) where a take-over bid is made; or (iii) where a surplus is revealed on the winding-up of a scheme. The debate about entitlement intensified after statutory intervention in 1986. The government introduced measures designed to ensure that pension schemes would suffer partial loss of tax relief unless surpluses deemed excessive on a statutorily prescribed basis were reduced to an acceptable figure over a maximum period of five years (see Pension Scheme Surpluses (Valuation) Regulations 1987, SI 1987/412). Although the statutory restriction rendered inactivity in the face of a surplus an expensive option, it did not purport to resolve the controversy over entitlement. The statute simply indicates that, subject to the rules of the scheme, surpluses may be reduced: by improving benefits; reducing contribution rates – a 'contribution holiday' – for a specified period; making a refund to the employer; or by a combination of these methods.

The translation of a claim to 'convert' part of a surplus into extra cash in the weekly pension or to apply additional sums for the company has, however, meant in part that the debate about entitlement has used the language of 'property'. Each 'side' will discuss who 'owns' the surplus, despite the fact that, as we have seen, in an ongoing scheme at least, it is a term that refers to an actuarial construct rather than a specific 'pot of money'. The use of language of ownership, however, adds potency to the arguments. Many commentators have written about how 'property' and 'ownership' can be understood, and it has been noted that using the phrase 'it's mine' is one of the most powerful that people use (see Gray [1994] CLP 157 at 157–161). We saw in Chapter 2 how Cotterrell argued that the ideological significance of notions of trust and beneficial ownership was that it encourages us to think of moral obligations owed to beneficiaries because of their beneficial entitlement (see p 60). Nobles, in turn, has sought to apply this argument to the claims of pension scheme members ([1994] LS 345 at 351 et seq):

> This claim operates, [Cotterrell] argues, as a claim to exercise power, without having to justify that power. If one is the owner of a thing, one may exercise power represented by that thing, without further justification in terms of needs, deserts, etc. Thus in the context of pension schemes, to the extent that members can establish themselves as the owners of the pension fund, they should expect to exercise the power represented by that fund, without the need for further justifications. As the beneficiaries of a trust, the members should not ordinarily expect to exercise that power directly. But they may expect the power to be exercised on their behalf, again, not because they are in need, or deserve such protection, but simply because it is their property. . . . [T]he ideological conception of property identified by Cotterrell presents itself as a form of moral argument which can, and is, used to justify legal decisions.

It was unsurprising that discussion in the pensions context about the distribution of surplus would begin to incorporate arguments about ownership. Quite apart from the legal environment, which involves trusts and therefore property, the employment setting of the OPT also contributed to the debate. On the one hand it may be claimed that an occupational pension is a form of 'deferred pay', earned through service with the employer. There is for example some empirical evidence that downwards adjustment to wages is made to compensate for an employer's pensions contribution (Committee of Inquiry into the Value of Pensions Report (Cmnd 8147, 1981) paras 12–13; cf Morgan *Choice in Pensions* (1984) pp 65–6). Moreover, the courts have accepted in a variety of contexts that both employers' contributions and pension benefits do represent a form of deferred pay (see *Parry v Cleaver* [1969] 1 All ER 555 at 560 per Lord Reid, followed by Brandon J in *The Halcyon Skies* [1976] 1 All ER 856 at 863 – with respect to employers' contributions and, inter alia, *Barber v Guardian Royal Exchange Assurance Group* [1990] IRLR 240 with respect to pension benefits).

To conclude, however, that pension surpluses should belong to scheme members is, it may be claimed, to make 2 + 2 = 5. This is because employers also have powerful ownership claims. The employer's obligation under most scheme rules is to pay only sufficient contributions to meet scheme liabilities, which, it can be argued, are determined by reference to the benefit levels defined in the scheme rules. If it is subsequently discovered that the employer has paid in more than was needed to secure those benefits, then the 'over-payment' should, so the argument runs, rightfully revert to the employer and not be used to provide otherwise fortuitous benefit improvements to members. Employers gain support for this argument from the fact that, if the OPT goes into deficit, then it is the employer's obligation to make up the difference. Thus employers have both a property-based argument: the surplus is 'theirs' because it was created out of over-payments by them; and a justice argument: they have to bear the burden when times are hard, so why should they not reap the rewards when times are good?

These points may found the basis of claims to property-type ownership in OPTs. But however powerful the arguments may appear as claims, if they are to have *legal* significance they must have influence on the legal context (the trust) within which OPTs exist. The terms of the trust deed are paramount, since the realisation and allocation of a surplus will involve the exercise of a discretion, usually in the form of a power contained in the deed. The nature of the power will vary according to the context in which the claim to surplus arises. For example, if a scheme is being wound up, trustees may be required by the deed to decide whether to dispose of any surplus by making a repayment to the sponsoring company. If the scheme is ongoing then the deed may give options as to how the surplus can be reduced. If no express powers are given, then the employer may wish to introduce an appropriate provision by seeking to have the scheme's terms amended. The trustees may then have a pivotal role if the discretion to amend is for them to exercise. But it must be emphasised that it is not the *existence* but the *exercise* of the *discretion* that is relevant. And here the courts have emphasised that trustees should normally only use their powers to promote the main purpose of the pension scheme: 'a pension scheme is established, not for the benefit of a particular company, but for the benefit of those employed in a commercial undertaking' (per Millett J in *Re Courage Group's Pension Schemes* [1987] 1 All ER 528 at 541); and then only in terms of providing retirement benefits.

This is not to say, however, that the deferred pay or over-contribution arguments outlined above are without effect. For example, consider the following comments of Warner J in *Mettoy Pension Trustees Ltd v Evans* [1991] 2 All ER 513 at 537:

> [The members'] rights have contractual and commercial origins. They are derived from the contracts of employment of the members. The benefits . . . have been earned by the service of the members under those contracts and, where the scheme is contributory, pro tanto by their contributions.

The courts do appear to have been influenced by the perception that members of pension schemes are not volunteers in the equitable sense, as their rights spring from a source different to that of beneficiaries of the private family trust. On the other hand, consider the following.

Millett J in *Re Courage Group's Pension Schemes* [1987] 1 All ER 528 at 545 (obiter)

Such surpluses arise from what, with hindsight, can be recognised as past overfunding. Prima facie, if returnable and not used to increase benefits, they ought to be returned to those who contributed to them. In a contributory scheme, this might be thought to mean the employer and the employees in proportion to their respective contributions. That, however, is not necessarily, or even usually, the case. In the case of most pension schemes, and certainly in the case of these schemes, the position is different. Employees are obliged to contribute a fixed proportion of their salaries or such lesser sum as the employer may from time to time determine. They cannot be required to pay more, even if the fund is in deficit; and they cannot demand a reduction or suspension of their own contributions if it is in surplus. The employer, by way of contrast, is obliged only to make such contributions if any as may be required to meet the liabilities of the scheme. If the fund is in deficit, the employer is bound to make it good; if it is in surplus, the employer has no obligation to pay anything. Employees have no right to complain if, while the fund is in surplus, the employer should require them to continue their contributions while itself contributing nothing. If the employer chooses to reduce or suspend their contributions, it does so ex gratia and in the interests of maintaining good industrial relations.

From this, two consequences follow. First, employees have no legal right to 'a contributions holiday'. Second, any surplus arises from past overfunding not by the employer and the employees pro rata to their respective contributions but by the employer alone to the full extent of its past contributions and only subject thereto by the employees.

We therefore seem to arrive at a position where we have two potentially competing propositions from which to derive an opinion about who in law should receive what from a pension scheme surplus.

The point is perhaps that neither of these lines of reasoning *alone* establishes entitlement to a surplus. They may simply be brought to bear when deciding how trustees may properly exercise a particular discretion or power granted within a scheme. Placing the debate into the discourse of ownership may therefore not always be helpful, let alone decisive. In adjudicating these matters, however, the courts do appear to have begun to analyse the nature of the rights and duties of each party involved.

(2) Rights and duties of employers

Remember that in classic trusts law theory, the employer is the settlor of the trust. As such, it may reserve certain conditions to itself when setting up the trust. In OPT terms, this equates to the retention of powers within the trust deed to, for example, give or refuse consent to increases in pensions in payment, or to wind up the scheme, or to modify the terms of the scheme (although the latter is often only with trustee consent). Powers like these can affect the use of surplus as much as a direct power to take a surplus repayment. For example, an employer might choose to use the power to make increases to pensions in payment in order to use up a surplus in an ongoing scheme. There are now certain statutory controls on such powers: under PA 1995, s 37 (as modified by PA 2004, s 250) where there is a power under the scheme to pay surplus to an employer, that power is only exercisable by the trustees. The courts also began in the context of surpluses to develop limits on how employers can use any retained powers. This is graphically illustrated in *Imperial Group Pension Trust Ltd v Imperial Tobacco Ltd* [1991] 2 All ER 597.

The Imperial Tobacco Company pension scheme had a surplus of at least £130m, to which the company had no right under the scheme rules. Following a successful take-over bid, Hanson Trust plc sought to encourage the members to transfer their rights and assets to a new scheme, under the rules of which any ultimate surplus would be returnable to Hanson. A feature of Hanson's attempt to persuade members to transfer was its apparent refusal, in contrast with previous practice, to consider any future discretionary increase to pensions in payment in the old scheme. Such increases could be implemented only by the exercise of a power of amendment which, under the rules, required the consent of the company. What, though, was the nature of the company's obligation in relation to the exercise of the power? Browne-Wilkinson VC rejected a suggestion that it was fiduciary in nature. He did, however, accept that pension trusts were of a different nature to traditional trusts, since the trust deed should be interpreted in the context of an employment relationship and therefore concluded that the power could only be exercised in accordance with 'the implied obligation of good faith' (at 607), a standard drawn from an implied duty of mutual trust and confidence imposed on employers under the contract of employment (see eg *Woods v WM Car Services (Peterborough) Ltd* [1981] ICR 666 at 670). According to the Vice-Chancellor, that obligation in the context of pensions requires that the employer exercise its rights with a view to 'the efficient running of the scheme' and 'not for the collateral purpose of forcing the members to give up their accrued rights in the existing fund' (at 607), neither of which criteria Hanson was able to satisfy on the evidence before the court. The Vice-Chancellor also held, however, that an employer was entitled to take its own interests, financial and otherwise, into account in making its decision.

The line of reasoning is of some significance in interpreting, some might say 'adapting', trust law in the pensions context. First, unlike the settlor of a private family trust, the employer in an OPT does not have unrestricted freedom of action over dealing with 'his own assets', even where the relevant discretion was reserved to the employer in setting up the scheme in the first place. This modification of the pure trusts law position appears to have arisen as a result of the employment context in which OPTs exist and the claims to 'respectful treatment', rather than in recognition of claims to ownership by the membership. As we shall see below, comparable claims have in turn resurfaced in the guise of 'reasonable expectations'. Nevertheless the position remains that where powers are reserved to the employer qua employer the courts will *tend* to recognise and enforce the freedom of action of the employer as a commercial entity, despite the claims of the membership. The outcome therefore seems to be that on the one hand the employer-settlor of the OPT is less free in the exercise of powers reserved to itself than the settlor of the traditional private trust. On the other hand, the employer has greater freedom to pursue its own interests than if it were bound by a fiduciary power.

There is an important caveat to note here arising from a restriction, introduced by PA 1995, s 67, on the exercise of a power of amendment by an employer where this might adversely affect a member's subsisting rights. In most circumstances any amendment would have had to be subject to the member's consent. Amendments to s 67 introduced by PA 2004, s 262 have liberalised the position somewhat; the position now is broadly that certain amendments affecting the accrued rights of a scheme member can be made without member consent provided that the scheme actuary can certify that actuarially equivalent rights are being conferred on the member (see Occupational Pension Schemes (Modification of Schemes) Regulations SI 2006/759; and *Code of Practice No 10* (2007) issued by The Pensions Regulator).

On a more limited compass there may be circumstances where it can be claimed that the scheme rules do not reflect the true intentions of the parties to the trust deeds. Notwithstanding statutory limitations and restrictions in scheme rules to any retrospective amendments could employers and/or trustees seek to invoke the principle in *Hastings-Bass* (see Chapter 11 at p 550) and gain the court's approval to, in effect, rectify the scheme rules? In *Smithson v Hamilton* [2008] 1 WLR 1453 the court rejected such an application, Sir Andrew Park stating, inter alia, that the rule applies only to acts of trustees in certain restricted circumstances and that in any event the rule could not be used to rectify or change a particular rule but only to nullify it. It therefore seems doubtful that the principle in *Hastings-Bass* can be used to achieve what the judge termed 'rectification by the back door' (paras 61–80).

(3) The duties of the trustees of OPTs

The trustees of OPTs are in principle subject to the same kinds of duties as trustees of other types of trust. They are fiduciaries and so must act with undivided loyalty in the best interests of the beneficiaries; further, they must administer the scheme in accordance with the terms of the trust deed. Moreover, any powers granted to them must be used for the purposes for which the power is conferred and not for any other collateral reason (the 'fraud on a power' doctrine; see Chapter 11 p 547 and, in the present context, *Re Courage Group's Pension Scheme* (see below); applied by the Privy Council in *Bank of New Zealand v Board of Management of the Bank of New Zealand Officers' Provident Association* [2003] PC 73). However, the application of these rules tends to reflect the practical implications of the pensions context. For example, we have already seen from *Cowan v Scargill* that a beneficiary's 'best interests' are defined, in legal terms, as best financial interests. Nevertheless, even when acting to pursue these interests, employer-retained powers in the trust deed governing the scheme mean that trustees might sometimes agree to deal with the pension fund in ways that may not secure for members as much *financial* benefit from the scheme as appears to be available. So, for example, a trust deed may contain powers of amendment that can be exercised by the employer but only with trustee approval. Where an employer then wishes to amend scheme rules to facilitate a repayment of surplus, then although the membership might feel that they have the right to the whole of the scheme fund, the trustees' duty might be translated into a duty to consult and negotiate with the employer for a share of that surplus.

Re Courage Group's Pension Scheme v Imperial Brewing & Leisure Ltd [1987] 1 WLR 495 at 515G–515H

It will . . . only be in rare cases that the employer will have any legal right to repayment of any part of the surplus . . . Repayment will . . . normally require amendment to the scheme, and thus co-operation between the employer and the trustees or committee of management. Where the employer seeks repayment, the trustees or committee can be expected to press for generous treatment of employees and pensioners, and the employer to be influenced by a desire to maintain good industrial relations with its workforce. It is, therefore, precisely in relation to a surplus that the relationship between 'the company' as the employer and the members as its present or past employees can be seen to be an essential feature of a pension scheme . . . while [members] have no legal right to participate in the surpluses in the existing schemes, they are entitled to have them dealt with by consultation and negotiation between their employers . . . and the [trustees] . . . and not to be irrevocably parted from these surpluses by the unilateral decision of a take-over raider with only a transitory interest in the share capital of the companies which employ them.

At first glance this interpretation of acting in the 'best interests of the members' seems at odds with the approach required by *Cowan v Scargill*. It can though be argued as necessary to accommodate: (i) the commercial; and (ii) the industrial relations contexts within which the employer seeks to amend scheme rules. (See generally Nugee (1998) 12 TLI 216; and see also the facts of *Edge v Pensions Ombudsman* (below, p. 697) and the comments at first instance of Sir Richard Scott VC ([1998] Ch 512 at 537): '[T]he proposition that the trustees were not entitled, when deciding how to reduce the £29.9 million surplus, to take account of the position of the employers is one with which I emphatically disagree. . . . It seems to me obvious that the continued viability of the respective employers was something that, in the interests of the Pension Scheme and its members as a whole, the trustees were entitled to promote.')

Schemes in winding-up When a pension scheme is wound up because of employer insolvency or otherwise, both the assets and the liabilities of the scheme crystallise and must be dealt with in accordance with the specific scheme rules but subject to certain priorities established by the PA 1995, ss 73–74. Commonly, if any surplus is discovered after basic liabilities have been met, the winding-up rule will contain a power enabling benefits to be increased – a power to augment as it is called – at least up to HMRC permitted maxima. There may in addition be a gift over of those assets in favour of the employer or (in effect) to creditors, where the winding-up is a consequence of employer insolvency. This power may be held by the trustees alone, by the employer as employer or as sole trustee, or by employer and trustees jointly. Two questions particularly concern us here. (i) What entitlement, if any, to the surplus can the members claim in these circumstances? (ii) What obligations, if any, do the holders of a power to augment owe to the members?

These questions were addressed, but not finally resolved, in *Mettoy Pension Trustees Ltd v Evans* [1991] 2 All ER 513, an insolvency case where the trustees were left with a surplus of about £9m after the cost of the mandatory benefits (but without any augmentation) had been determined. The power to augment was conferred on the employer in the following terms:

> Any surplus in the trust fund…may at the absolute discretion of the employer be applied to secure further benefits within the limits stated [by the Inland Revenue], and any further balance thereafter remaining…shall be paid to [the employers] in cash.

Notwithstanding the language of the clause, Warner J held (i) that the power was fiduciary; (ii) that the members of the scheme therefore had 'a right to be considered for discretionary benefits' (at 550–551); and (iii) that the liquidator (in the shoes of the insolvent employer) could not exercise the power because his fiduciary duty to act solely in the best interests of the members would conflict with his duty to the creditors.

A 'right to be considered' does not necessarily lead to any benefit improvements for the members. Under traditional trusts law doctrine the donee of a power has no duty to exercise it and the members would have no remedy if the power were not exercised in their favour. Here, however, Warner J broke new ground. He decided that there was no obstacle on grounds either of principle or authority to aligning the remedies available to objects of powers with those available to beneficiaries of discretionary trusts. As regards the latter, the judge maintained that it was open to the court to adopt whichever of the methods laid down in *McPhail v Doulton* ([1971] AC 424 at 457; see Chapter 5) by Lord Wilberforce was most appropriate. In the absence of any alternative proposal from the parties, Warner J accepted that the court could itself give directions as to the proper exercise of the discretion (cf Gardner (1991) 107 LQR 214 at 219 where reservations are expressed about Warner J's treatment of the authorities). The judge then called for further submissions as to the form that the court's final declaration should take. He did, however, firmly reject counsel's proposition, building on Millett J's acceptance in *Re Courage* of the balance of cost analysis, that any surplus 'belongs in principle to the employer' (at 551):

> One cannot, in my opinion, in construing a provision in the rules of a 'balance of cost' pension scheme relating to surplus, start from an assumption that any surplus belongs morally to the employer.

Consider the following points.

(1) Do you think that the approach adopted in *Mettoy* to the exercise of a fiduciary power gives courts a more interventionist role and members of pension schemes greater rights than would be the case under the conventional discretionary trust? (See Martin [1991] Conv (NS) 364; Gardner (1991) 107 LQR 214; Nobles (1990) 19 ILJ 204; and cf *Schmidt v Rosewood* [2003] 2 WLR 1442 (above, p 557).)

(2) In *Mettoy* Warner J wanted further evidence as to the extent to which the surplus could be attributed proportionately either (i) to successful investment of the trust fund, and/or (ii) to a reduction in the workforce, with reference in particular to the fact that 'departing employees received only "early-leaver benefits" . . . instead of benefits based on their projected final salaries for which the scheme had been funded, though not to the full extent'. This may in practice be difficult to calculate and, in the event, the case was settled with the surplus being divided between members and the employer in the proportion 2:1. (See also *Thrells Ltd (in liquidation) v Lomas* [1993] 2 All ER 546 where the actuary was able to attribute only two-thirds of the surplus to specific sources (at 556).)

(3) Where there is a scheme deficit on winding up then the employer can be required under PA 1995, s 75 to make up the deficit, the amount required having the status of a statutory debt owed to the trustees. There is scope for disagreement between trustees and employer as to the appropriate investment assumptions to adopt in calculating the amount payable (see eg *Pitman Trustees v Telecommunications Group plc* [2004] EWHC 181 (Ch)).

(4) Trustees and conflicts of interest

As mentioned previously, there is considerable scope for trustees of OPTs to be placed in a position where they may be faced with conflicts of interest (see p 681). One such conflict can arise where trustees are faced with making decisions that may have a differential impact on, for instance, employee scheme members and retired members. In *Cowan v Scargill* Sir Robert Megarry made a passing reference to ' . . . the duty of trustees to exercise their powers in the best interests of the trust, holding the scales impartially between different classes of beneficiaries' (at 287). But what precisely does this duty of impartiality entail? Does it, for example, mean that each class of beneficiary must always receive equal consideration (say, in financial terms) from trustees when exercising a discretion under the scheme rules? We have seen that in *Cowan v Scargill* the problem of how to assess the 'best interest of the trust' was resolved by conceptualising it in financial terms, since other forms of interest are subjective and therefore more difficult to compare. But should this always be the case? In other circumstances, trustees are empowered to make decisions which affect different classes of beneficiary in quite different ways, even to the financial detriment of one of those classes; that is, in the exercise of dispositive powers.

This point was addressed in *Edge v Pensions Ombudsman* [2000] Ch 602, CA (see Simpson 'Conflicts' in Birks and Pretto (eds) *Breach of Trust* (2002) p 75). The case concerned a pension scheme that in 1993 was in substantial surplus. The trustees therefore amended its terms so that active members paid reduced contributions and received enhanced benefits, whereas the pensioners received no enhancements. It emerged that the main purposes of the trustees' policy were to maintain the viability of the funds in the face of falling membership; to help the employer to retain staff; and to plan budgets by reducing the contributions made by the employer. Under the rules of the scheme, employer contributions could not be reduced below the level of employee contributions; hence the reduction in the latter also. In addition, it appeared that the pensioners had received benefit improvements whilst in service, that pensions were already index-linked and that pension increases were above average for comparable schemes.

The pensioners nevertheless complained to the Pensions Ombudsman, who determined that the trustees' amendments were made in breach of trust and were invalid, because the decision 'breached their duty of impartiality . . . [the trustees] did not act in the best interest of all the beneficiaries, and . . . [they] exercised their power for an improper purpose'. On appeal the decision of the Ombudsman was reversed, Chadwick LJ commenting on the impartiality point as follows (at 627):

> Properly understood, the so-called duty to act impartially – on which the ombudsman placed such reliance – is no more than the ordinary duty which the law imposes on a person who is entrusted with the exercise of a discretionary power: that he exercises the power for the purpose for which it is given, giving proper consideration to the matters which are relevant and excluding from consideration matters which are irrelevant. If pension fund trustees do that, they cannot be criticised if they reach a decision which appears to prefer the claims of one interest – whether that of employers, current employees or pensioners – over others.

Thus, as the Pensions Ombudsman also recognised, the duty to act impartially does not equate with a duty to exercise their discretion on all occasions in such a way as to produce equal benefits of equal value to all beneficiaries; or require that all beneficiaries receive some benefit from an exercise of discretion. In short the trustees are 'entitled to be partial', at least when exercising dispositive powers.

The other significant feature of *Edge* is that it lends support to a proposition that trustees may, unless prevented by scheme rules or statute from doing so, take account of the interests of the employer at least in circumstances where it may be argued that this may provide some benefit, even if indirect, to scheme members. In the High Court in *Edge*, for instance, Sir Richard Scott VC was in no doubt on the point ([1998] Ch 512 at 537): '[T]he proposition that the trustees were not entitled, when deciding how to reduce the £29.9 million surplus, to take account of the position of the employers is one with which I emphatically disagree. . . . It seems to me obvious that the continued viability of the respective employers was something that, in the interests of the Pension Scheme and its members as a whole, the trustees were entitled to promote.'

A basic conflicts of interest principle of trusts law is that trustees cannot act as such if they find themselves in a position where their own personal interest may conflict with their duty as trustees, unless expressly authorised to do so. The dangers of inappropriate, some might say incorrect, application of trust law principles in a pensions context were illustrated by a controversial decision that member trustees would be unable to benefit, as members, from an arrangement whereby the trustees were to distribute a surplus on winding up of the scheme (see eg *Re William Makin & Sons Ltd* [1993] OPLR 171 at 179 and *British Coal Corpn v British Coal Staff Superannuation Scheme Trustees Ltd* [1994] OPLR 51 at 62; criticised by Mowbray (1996) 10 TLI 49 and distinguished by Lindsay J in *Re Drexel Burnham Lambert UK Pension* [1995] 1 WLR 32 at 42). Subsequently Scott VC in *Edge v Pensions Ombudsman* [1998] Ch 512 described 'the notion as . . . quite simply ridiculous' (at 539). The position has in any event been reversed by PA 1995, s 39 (see Milner (1996) 10 TLI 15 on the uncertain position of the 'representative beneficiary').

(5) The rights of the members of occupational pension schemes

We have already looked at some of the duties that are owed to members as beneficiaries of this type of trust in sections 1–4 above. From the point of view of the members, these duties give correlative rights for certain matters to be *considered* when a decision is being taken, rather than *guaranteeing* a certain outcome on the basis of the existence of a given set of facts. In this sense, they may be classified as 'procedural' rather than 'substantive'. Since this section began with a discussion about the potential 'ownership' rights of members in the surplus assets of the fund, a member of an OPT might feel a little cheated at this. The courts have given some thought to the substantive rights of members of schemes to surplus assets. Indeed, in some ways the development of case law in this area has been favourable to the member, because on occasion the courts have been more inclined to hear their claims to entitlement than previously.

Apart from the rights already referred to, there is now a duty to consider the position and expectations of members. In *Stannard v Fisons Pension Trust Ltd* [1992] IRLR 27, a case concerning a sale by Fisons (F) to NHF and involving the transfer of nearly 40% of F's workforce, the trustees were to approve the transfer of 'such amount [of the pension fund] as the Trustees, after consulting the Actuary, consider to be just and equitable'. The amount to be transferred did not take account of a substantial increase in the notional value of the fund between the date of the last actuarial valuation (1979) and the date of the transfer (31 December 1982). The Court of Appeal concluded that the trustees had failed to give properly informed consideration to the exercise of their powers. Staughton LJ saw entitlement to the surplus as a key issue (at 32):

> At the heart of this case...lies the question whether the employees of a company have any legitimate interest in a surplus which exists in the company's pension fund. Perhaps 'legitimate' is not the right word to use, for it is not suggested that the employees have a legal right to participate directly in the surplus. More accurately, in deciding what is just and equitable upon a division of the pension fund, should one have regard to, and evaluate, the possibility that all or part of the surplus will one day prove to be a benefit for the employers [sic]?...
>
> It...seems to me that, as at December 1982, there was some degree of likelihood that the Fisons fund would continue to be in surplus for the foreseeable future; and there was some degree of likelihood that the existing employees and pensioners would receive some benefit from that surplus in the future, in the form of increased pensions or other benefits. When the trustees came to consider what was just and equitable upon a division of the fund..., they ought to have borne those points in mind and made some evaluation of them.

Millett J had spoken in terms of members' 'expectations' in *Courage* (at 514) in the following terms: '[Hanson's] proposals would have had the effect of reducing or extinguishing the present expectation of employees of the Courage group of companies of a continued suspension of their contributions.' The conceptualisation of members' claims to surplus as 'expectations' was further followed up in *London Regional Transport v Hatt* [1993] PLR 227 (at para 157 et seq). This case concerned the merger of two pension schemes. The issue, in brief, was the validity of the deeds setting up the new amalgamated scheme. It was agreed in this regard that the employer could not remove any 'vested property rights', which brought up the question of what those rights were, as far as the members were concerned. Amongst the rights listed by the court was 'the *expectations which members might quite legitimately harbour* that discretions will be exercised in their favour where no such breach of a duty of good faith by the employer or abuse of a fiduciary power is involved in the non exercise of the discretion' (emphasis added). The court considered a typical situation as that: 'where there is a surplus discerned by the actuary to the fund and one possibility is for pensions to be increased. No doubt the larger the surplus the livelier the expectation, but in the great majority of pension funds it remains an expectation rather than a right.' This expectation can have positive effects: it may be a matter to be taken into account in a process of apportioning a pension fund between continuing and ongoing members (eg *Stannard v Fisons*). Similarly, on a winding-up, a trustee could not decline to exercise a power to use surplus to increase benefits solely on the ground that the employer was under no legal obligation to provide the surplus in a balance of costs scheme (*Thrells v Lomas* [1993] 2 All ER 546 at 556–557).

Note that in *Hatt*, the court had a clear opportunity to classify the interests of beneficiaries in property and ownership terms, but carefully avoided doing so. It appeared to prefer to adopt the 'procedural rights' route: giving members rights to be considered in a certain way. Similarly, the Court of Appeal in *National Grid* stated that 'the language used by Knox J . . . in the *LRT* case must not be elevated into a general proposition that members of a contributory pension scheme have interests in the application of surplus equivalent to rights of property. They do not' (*National Grid Co plc v Laws* [1999] PLR 37 at para 46).

Consider the following points:

(1) The Pensions Regulator has power (previously vested in the Occupational Pensions Regulatory Authority (OPRA) – see further below), where the scheme rules do not otherwise permit, to modify them so as to allow a return of surplus to the employer (see PA 1995, s 69 et seq). The accompanying regulations require, inter alia, that any proposal must be approved by HMRC and that the trustees must be satisfied that the proposal is in the interests of the beneficiaries. (Occupational Pension Schemes (Payments to Employers) Regulations 1996, SI 1996/2156).

The number of employers taking refunds from schemes has, in practice, been relatively low: over the period from 1987–88 to 2002–03, 293 took refunds, at a value of £1.3 billion. By contrast a common phenomenon, consistent with the 'balance of cost' provisions in most trust deeds, has been for schemes to suspend or temporarily to reduce employers' contributions and, less commonly, employees' contributions. Over the same period, 2,997 schemes reported a reduction or suspension of employer contributions, whereas just 190 schemes introduced comparable reductions for employees, although in a further 1,867 schemes increases in benefits were introduced (*Inland Revenue Statistics 2004*, Table 7.8). In view of the substantial scheme deficits currently being reported it should be noted that the total reduction in surpluses during this period via the various methods was £29.7 billion.

(2) In *Thrells Ltd (in liquidation) v Lomas* [1993] 2 All ER 546, the pension scheme of the company, which had become insolvent in 1984, had a surplus of £505,000 from which no repayment had been made to the employer before 17 August 1990. Sir Donald Nicholls VC decided that where there was a power to augment, albeit in the case only in favour of deferred pensioners, (i) the fact that a surplus might be attributed to overpayment by the employer was not, per se, sufficient reason to refuse to exercise the power, and (ii) that 'members have a reasonable expectation that if the scheme funds permit . . . the trustee will exercise that power to the extent that it is fair and equitable in all the circumstances, having particular regard to the purpose for which the power was conferred' (at 557). The scheme had been wound up in 1984, prior to the introduction of the statutory protection for deferred pensioners in 1986 (see now PSA 1993, Pt IV).

The Vice-Chancellor authorised an increase in benefits which provided the deferred pensioners with an equivalent level of protection. The outcome was that the surplus was divided approximately equally between deferred pensioners and the unsecured creditors of the company. Note also that the court held that a power of alteration in the trust deed could not be exercised once winding-up had commenced.

What guidance would you give members of a scheme where the trustees state that, after full consideration, they have decided not to exercise a 'power to augment', with the consequence that the surplus will go to the creditors? (Cf *Icarus (Hertford) Ltd v Driscoll* [1990] PLR 1 and *Mettoy Pension Trustees Ltd v Evans* [1991] 2 All ER 513; Nobles (1990) 53 MLR 377). The questionable dicta in *Davis v Richards and Wallington Industries* [1991] 2 All ER 563 at 589–593 (criticised by Nobles (1990) 19 ILJ 204) cannot really stand given the clear disapproval expressed by the Privy Council in *Air Jamaica Ltd v Charlton* [1999] 1 WLR 1399 (see Chapter 17 where the cases are considered in the context of the destination of surplus funds of unincorporated associations at p 906).

(3) Note that the rights of the members under the terms of the trust can be affected by a term of the contract of employment. In *South West Trains v Wightman* [1998] PLR 113 the court accepted that the terms of an agreement between employees and the company that, contrary to the scheme rules, a pay increase was not to be fully pensionable was nevertheless binding on the trustees.

(c) Governance: members' rights and remedies

The conflicts of interest that can arise in the management of pension funds should by now be apparent. Even the advisers to an OPT have come under scrutiny in terms of how they too can assist in keeping the assets of the OPT secure; scheme employers as well as actuaries and auditors now owe a duty to report any irregularities to the Pensions Regulator in the exercise of any duties relevant to the administration of the scheme (PA 2004, s 70). In the following section, we look briefly at the courses of action that are available when a member suspects trustee or employer wrongdoing.

(1) Information

In 1982 the OPB rejected proposals to prescribe statutory minimum levels of funding in favour of 'freedom with disclosure'. It sought to strengthen membership control by recommending a statutory obligation of disclosure. The general principle of disclosure has now been further reinforced by the PA 1995 and regulations made thereunder (see the Occupational Pension Schemes (Disclosure of Information) Regulations 1996, SI 1996/1655, as amended). One of the major changes introduced was the power vested in OPRA, now the Pensions

Regulator, to impose fines if trustees fail to comply with the regulations. Otherwise the information that should be made available to members includes scheme details, annual individual benefit statements, trustees' annual reports, the audited accounts and any actuarial valuation report.

The original intention of disclosure was that the regulations should be 'sufficient to enable an expert pension adviser to form a complete picture of the scheme and its financial soundness' (DHSS *Greater Security for the Rights and Expectations of Members of Occupational Pension Schemes* (1984) App B). However, as has been discovered in other areas of consumer protection (such as, for example, financial services regulation), the mere existence and accessibility of relevant information alone is not a sufficient safeguard for members. The Goode Report found even before statutory intervention in the PA 1995 that the problem was to find the 'right balance between comprehensive and comprehensible information' (para 4.12.18). Members and their advisers may receive too much information, which is difficult to interpret but yet does not give a complete picture. In that regard, can members who may wish to question the decision of the trustees discover why that decision was taken or will they find that the decision in *Re Londonderry's Settlement* [1965] Ch 918 places an insurmountable obstacle in their path? As we saw in Chapter 11, the effect of the decision in that case is that beneficiaries are not entitled, broadly speaking, to have access to documents that disclose the reasons for the exercise of the trustees' discretion, in the absence of evidence of improper motive or irrelevant influencing factors. Whether *Re Londonderry* applies equally to OPTs is uncertain notwithstanding the decision of the High Court in *Wilson v Law Debenture Corpn* [1995] OPLR 103 (noted Schaffer (1994) 8 TLI 118) appearing to affirm that that is the position.

Consider the following.

(1) In *Wilson v Law Debenture*, the discretion under scrutiny related to the determination by the trustee as to what proportion of the funds of one scheme should be transferred to another scheme, in order to support the accrued pension entitlement of employees who were being transferred from one employer to another. In the event, the amount that the trustees agreed to transfer effectively excluded the transferring employees from a share of a surplus that had arisen in the fund. Two of these employees, members of the fund, wanted to find out why this decision had been taken. Rattee J held that general trust rules applied and that there was moreover 'sound reason for the parties to the trust instrument . . . [to confer] such a discretion on the trustees in the hope of minimising the potential for dispute . . .' (at 111). Aside from a practical concern for 'smooth administration' of the trust, the judge concluded that it would be wrong in principle, even in the pensions context, and possibly unfair to the trustees, to disapply 'long-established principles of trust law'. Writing extra-judicially Sir Robert

Walker has suggested (i) that the conclusion reached by Rattee J in *Wilson* 'seems, with great respect, to treat *Re Londonderry* as a rather more precise and definitive statement of principle than it may be' and (ii) that 'there are strong arguments that [pension fund] trustees should be ready to justify their decisions to those whose interests they represent, subject to protection for what is truly confidential' (in Oakley (ed) *Trends in Contemporary Trust Law* (1996) pp 130–131; see in similar vein Lord Browne-Wilkinson (1992) 6 TLI 119 at 125; cf Pollard (1997) 11(1) TLI 11). The tenor of the judgment of the Privy Council in *Schmidt v Rosewood Trust Ltd* [2003] 2 AC 709, given by Lord Walker, that sees disclosure of information matters as but one aspect of the 'court's inherent jurisdiction to supervise, and if necessary to intervene in, the administration of trusts' (at [51]) suggests that the tide may be running against any continuing rigid application of *Re Londonderry* (see generally Chapter 11 at p 560 et seq).

(2) As a practical matter trustees may be unwise to place complete reliance on the *Re Londonderry* principle, whether in relation to their administrative or dispositive discretions. The Pensions Ombudsman (see further below) has been willing to limit the scope of *Re Londonderry* and *Wilson v Law Debenture* by treating a failure of trustees to provide 'reasons for their decisions to those with a legitimate interest in the matter' at issue as 'maladministration' (see in particular Determination L00370 *Allen and TKM Group Pension Scheme* (25 April 2002)). Moreover, the implicit risk in failure to give reasons is evident in the following obiter comments of the Court of Appeal in *Edge v Pensions Ombudsman* [2000] Ch 602 at 633: 'That is not . . . to say that the court, or the [Pensions] Ombudsman, cannot draw appropriate inferences from any failure of the trustees to give an explanation when an explanation is called for . . .' (at 633 per Chadwick LJ).

The disclosure of relevant information is only a step towards adequate control. Several further options are also open for members who feel that they not being protected adequately: they can pursue the dispute internally, approach one of three external agencies, or seek legal advice and go to court. We address each of these, briefly, in turn.

(2) Internal Dispute Resolution (IDR)

The Pensions Act 1995, ss 50, 50A–B, requires the trustees or managers of OPTs to make and implement provisions for some system for resolving disputes internally. If a dispute arises, a wide range of people (including all classes of member and dependants, as well as the trustees and managers of the scheme) can apply for the dispute to be heard and if an application is made, then an individual must be nominated to hear it (see eg Code of Practice No 11 (2008) issued by the Pensions Regulator).

(3) The Pensions Advisory Service (TPAS)

TPAS is an independent advisory and conciliation service which investigates and seeks to resolve complaints from pension scheme members via a network of volunteer advisers. It also handles complaints about both personal pension arrangements and state pension provision. Its incoming complaints caseload in 2007 was 7,026, approximately one-third of which concerned OPTs (TPAS Annual Report 2007–08). Notwithstanding the introduction of IDR, TPAS remains for many members the first source of redress outside the scheme itself.

If unhappy about the outcome of a TPAS investigation, a pension scheme member can refer the complaint to the Ombudsman.

(4) The Pensions Ombudsman

The Pensions Ombudsman was established in 1990 (see PSA 1993, ss 145–152) and provides a forum for members which is (in theory) speedier and cheaper than court action. The Ombudsman can only hear matters within his statutory jurisdiction (note that they do not have to be referred from TPAS). However, this jurisdiction was expanded by the PA 1995 to include complaints about the maladministration of the scheme from either actual or potential beneficiaries against the trustees/managers or the relevant employer, or from trustees against each other or the employer. In addition, the Ombudsman can hear any dispute of fact or law arising between the trustees of a scheme and those of another scheme; or as between trustees of the same scheme (see PSA 1993, s 146(1)–(4)). Cases taken and determined by the Ombudsman may be appealed to the High Court (PSA 1993, s 151(4)). (See *Legal & General Assurance Society Ltd v CCA Stationery Ltd* [2003] EWHC 2989 where Laddie J expressed the view that the Ombudsman could not make an order of a kind which a court could not make, but cf the doubts expressed by the Ombudsman in the Annual Report 2003–4 as to the legal basis for this view; see also Farrand (2000) 14 TLI 146.) The future of the Pensions Ombudsman as a separate entity is uncertain as there are government plans to merge it with the Financial Ombudsman Scheme, although it is not anticipated that this would limit its powers in any way (see *Occupational Pensions* July 2007).

(5) The Pensions Regulator (formerly Occupational Pensions Regulatory Authority (OPRA))

The PA 1995 introduced a whole new public regulatory system, one which now exists alongside that represented by the trust. Under the Pensions Act 2004 a new regulator – The Pensions Regulator or TPR – replaced OPRA from 6 April 2005. TPR's principal statutory objectives are to protect the benefits of members of occupational pension and personal pension schemes and, significantly, 'to reduce the risk of situations arising which may lead to compensation being payable from the Pension Protection Fund (PPF)' (s 5(1)(a)–(c)). TPR also has a more general educational-cum-advisory objective 'to promote . . . the good administration of work-based pension schemes' (s 5(1)(d)). But central to TPR's role is the requirement to ensure that pension schemes are adequately funded, thereby protecting both scheme members and the PPF (see TPR Code of Practice No 3 *Funding Defined Benefits*). In this regard it has extensive powers of intervention under PA 2004, Part 3, ranging from a power to impose contribution rates where employers and trustees cannot agree (s 121) to an authority to 'freeze schemes' under investigation (s 23) and even, where a scheme cannot be financially rescued, to wind it up (s 154). In addition, amongst a raft of other powers, TPR has responsibility to ensure that IDR procedures are set up and that MNTs are appointed (see TPR Code of Practice No 8).

From our point of view, however, an equally significant aspect of TPR's activities is its jurisdiction to supervise the trustees of OPTs. TPR has wide powers to prohibit a person from being a trustee, and to suspend or remove a person as trustee (PA 1995, ss 3, 4). There is also provision for the appointment by TPR of a replacement trustee should an individual be removed or suspended (PA 1995, s 7). Indeed, if an individual persists in acting as a trustee in the face of a removal or suspension order, then criminal charges can be preferred. These powers are complemented by PA 1995, s 29 which, for the first time in the context of pension schemes, introduced a statutory disqualification for certain persons from acting as trustees (cf the statutory disqualification under the Charities Act 1993 applicable to charity trustees: see p 1062). In short TPR has a specific responsibility to oversee the carrying out of trust duties.

(6) Going to court

Despite alternative means of redress that have been created, the most controversial disputes between the membership, or sections of it, and the trustees or employer are likely to revert to the courts for final determination. To some extent this simply reflects the possibility of appeal from decisions of the Ombudsman. Over these matters the law of trusts and the courts still hold sway. The threat of court action may discourage imminent breaches of trust, but this means of redress is likely to be drawn-out – and costly. It is well established that trustees involved in litigation can apply for a 'Beddoes Order'; that is, an order to the effect that their costs can be paid out of the trust fund (see *Re Beddoe, Downes v Cottam* [1893] 1 Ch 547). However, such orders are not available to members who bring their own actions. The case of *Evans v London Co-operative Society Ltd* (1976) *Times* 6 July, initiated by Robert Evans, a retired London milkman, is hardly encouraging to potential litigants even though the plaintiff succeeded. The time involved – the case took almost ten years to come to court – and the financial cost the plaintiff incurred (he was not legally aided) for little personal reward provide more of a warning than an incentive to vigilant scheme members. (The case was settled in 1977 when the defendant company paid £1.4m into its pension fund. The direct benefit for Mr Evans was an increase of £1.81 in his weekly pension: *Guardian* 17 November 1977; cf the cost of litigation in

Stannard v Fisons Pension Trust Ltd [1990] PLR 179, estimated even before the Court of Appeal hearing at £1.5m: Ellison *Pensions: Law and Practice* (1992) para 8.024.)

This unappealing situation was mitigated to an extent by the decision in *McDonald v Horn* [1995] 1 All ER 961, CA; affirming the High Court judgment of Vinelott J. In this case, members of the Melton Medes Pension Fund sued the trustees for breach of trust on the grounds that the trustees had allegedly made loans to the employer and exercised the power of investment for its benefit rather than bona fide in the interests of the members of the scheme. In addition, the plaintiffs successfully sought the replacement of the trustees by judicial trustees. The plaintiffs' trade union had been able to fund the preliminary stages of the action. In the High Court, Vinelott J granted a so-called 'pre-emptive costs order' on behalf of the beneficiaries which, in effect, allowed the action to be continued at the expense of the pension fund, until discovery (with an opportunity for further application at that stage). He identified four criteria to be considered in deciding whether to grant the order: (i) prospect of success for the action; (ii) likelihood of an order for costs; (iii) the court's perception of the justice of the case; and (iv) other special factors (see Hand [1993] SJ 760). As regards the two last-named criteria, Vinelott J commented as follows:

> No beneficiary can be expected to have the resources to pursue major litigation of this kind and there is no real possibility that any fighting fund could be financed out of their joint resources. If the litigation is not pursued, serious claims will never be investigated...
>
> In the case of a pension fund, unlike a conventional trust fund, the beneficiaries have themselves contributed both in cash and in service to the employer. They are entitled to be satisfied that the trust fund to which they have contributed is administered in a way which reflects their legitimate expectations by trustees in which they have full confidence.

It remains to be seen whether the range of measures now open to members of occupational pension schemes will provide an appropriate structure for the good governance of the OPT. It also remains to be seen how effectively the pensions governance structure will mesh with the industrial relations structures that seek to provide for the regulation of terms and conditions of employment in general.

5. Conclusion

Whilst the Pensions Acts 1995 and 2004 have brought in major changes in the governance of the OPT, they have not undermined the central role of trusts law. Of course some of the changes introduced have shifted boundaries within the trust to an unfamiliar degree. The introduction of MNTs has brought members more centre-stage in terms of trust management (see Milner [1997] Conv 89). In addition, the balance of power between employer and member as beneficiary has become more delicate – not something that is generally of much concern or influence in, say, the traditional family trust. Finally, the 'public' elements of the OPT have grown: both trustees and employers are subject to public accountability through the activities of TPR whilst statistics about the biggest schemes are matters of public record (see eg ONS, Occupational Pension Schemes Annual Reports). These developments do highlight two underlying themes in this chapter. Does the trust still provide a satisfactory legal framework for pension provision? To what extent is it still appropriate in interpreting the rights and liabilities of the parties in the OPT to look for guidance to trusts law as developed by the courts in the context of the traditional family trust?

At the heart of the pension trust, as the Goode Report put it (para 4.2.1), is 'the pension promise, that is the collection of undertakings given to scheme members about the provision of benefits on or before retirement'. What is needed is a legal framework that provides for security of the fund and the fulfilment of the pension promise. Two key safeguards for attaining these goals are (i) that the pension fund should be separate from the employer's business, and (ii) that the primary duty of those managing the scheme should be to secure the rights and interests of members. Notwithstanding the all too many recent examples of fund shortfalls being revealed on employer insolvency the trust still satisfies both requirements to a certain extent. Although, as we have seen, the courts refused to recognise property-based arguments for members in surplus disputes, they nevertheless raised the profile of the claims of members, via the notion of 'reasonable expectations', to a larger degree than may have been envisaged a decade or so ago. But entitlement and protection come at a price. And the fact remains that both the creation and continuation of a pension scheme are voluntary acts by an employer, in the sense that no legal compulsion to do so has existed. Thus an employer faced with what it perceives as excessive demands in terms of benefits or with unacceptable interference in scheme administration or with rising funding costs can as a last resort terminate the scheme or shift the risk exposure on to scheme members by switching from a defined benefit scheme to a defined contribution one (see the prescient article by Pollard in (2003) 17(1) TLI 2; and NAPF *Pension Provision and the Economic Crisis* (2009) for ominous predictions about the future for defined benefit schemes in the private, although not yet the public, sector).

Indeed recognition of these social and economic realities underpinned the approach to reform advocated by the Goode Committee:

> Para 1.16. In carrying out our review we have had regard both to the level of concern expressed about the security of pension funds, the rights and interests of members in those funds, and the need to avoid measures which will discourage employers from continuing to provide good pension schemes...

In the event, as we saw earlier in this chapter, the Goode Report concluded that the framework provided by trust law was 'broadly satisfactory' (para 4.1.14).

But before one decides whether or not to endorse this view it is as well to be clear what is understood here by the term 'trust law'. We suggest that by 'trust law' is meant 'trust law as at present interpreted in the context of pension schemes'. The point here is that the regulation of OPTs and the financial and commercial reasons for their creation locate them closer to the commercial rather than the family end of a continuum of trust types. The hypothesis then is simply that the judicial forays into law-making described at several points in this chapter can be interpreted as contributing towards a distinctive law of pension trusts rather than marking the cutting-edge of developments in an organic law of trusts (see Moffat (1993) 56 MLR 471; Hayton [2005] Conv 229; see generally Sir Robert Walker in Oakley (ed) *Trends in Contemporary Trust Law* (1996) 123 and also dicta of Lord Browne-Wilkinson in *Target Holdings v Redferns* [1996] AC 421 (see Chapter 11) and writing extra-judicially (1992) 6 TLI 119, but cf Lord Millett (2000) 14(2) TLI 66). The conceptual distinction may in practice be unimportant unless future developments become constrained by judgments that seek to apply trust principles without any differentiation to all non-charitable express trusts, be they family or pension or other commercial trusts.

But does acceptance of a distinctive 'pension trust' mean that one is undermining the conceptual coherence of the trust? We would suggest not. If the heart of the trust is (still) the notion of (separate) fiduciary ownership supported by appropriate remedies, enforceable at the behest of the beneficiaries, then the OPT is still a pure trust form despite the different emphases required by commercial considerations such as the freedom of action of the employer. If anything, the OPT example merely reinforces the concept of the trust as the paradigmatic flexible legal mechanism where more than two parties or sets of interests are involved. At the purely functional level the trust may even be claimed to represent one way of managing the tensions that arise out of the employment relations context: both the employer's and the members' collective interests are represented in the trust-form (whether the law represents adequately the different and competing agendas that might be at play here is another question). The flexibility necessary to adapt the trust to the change of environment from family to commerce is one of the strengths of the trust-form; but also perhaps its weakness. The form lacks certainty: it does not give any definitive answers to questions such as entitlement to surplus; decisions here are, and are likely to remain, highly contentious. It might even appear odd that within a legal form often associated with a 'law of private property relations' such decisions are left to fair 'decision-making' and not to 'ownership' principles. But this also is the nature of the trust.

It would be remiss to end this chapter without any reference to the latest statutory development in the 'continuous revolution' of pensions law, the Pensions Act 2008. Concern that many millions of workers are failing to make sufficient or even any private financial provision for retirement has prompted the government to require employers from 2012 to offer a workplace pension scheme to workers, all of whom must be automatically enrolled in the scheme. It will, in addition, be compulsory for both employer and worker to make contributions, the total minimum being 8% of a specified band of earnings of which at least 3% must come from the employer. What effect these arrangements will have for the OPT is uncertain. The possibility that this new statutory 'floor' of pension arrangements will become the norm for much employer provision should not be discounted.

14

Trusts in commerce II: commerce and equitable remedies

1. Introduction

The last decade of the twentieth century witnessed a fascinating resurgence of interest in, commentary on and litigation about equitable remedies. There are many reasons for this trend that has continued unabated but a prominent one is the presence of fraud. In litigation the aftermath of the collapses of BCCI and Asil Nadir's Polly Peck company, the Maxwell saga and mortgage fraud all made their contribution. One consequence 'is that courts are increasingly concerned with attempts by the victims of fraud to trace their money and recover it, not from the fraudsters or their confederates, who have usually disappeared, but from those through whose hands it has passed' (Millett QC (now Lord Millett) 'Tracing the Proceeds of Fraud' (1991) 107 LQR 71). Frequently the passage of money has involved sophisticated exercises in money laundering, often through bank accounts in several countries. Put simply money laundering is the process by which the proceeds of fraud or some other criminal activity are converted into assets which appear to have a legitimate origin, the purpose of the process being that the assets can then be retained permanently or even possibly recycled to finance further crimes. The process of tracing and the legal remedies by which the proceeds of fraud may be recovered have involved to some degree the processes and remedies provided by equity, and it is broadly within this commercial context that our study of equitable remedies is located.

But the attempts at recovery have also involved resort to common law processes and remedies. What these attempts then highlighted were some of the uncertainties and inconsistencies in our legal rules in this area: 'There is no lack of rules; no want of authority. It is their abundance that causes the difficulty.... No two judges...are agreed on the correct classifications of the various different situations that can arise, let alone on the requirements for recovery in each' (Millett, ibid). As might be inferred from these comments, the relationship between the common law and equitable systems and the search for a coherent response to the practical problems of recovery has exercised a growing influence on academic debate and, arguably, on litigation also. Space does not permit any extensive study of these important matters or indeed of the common law remedies but this issue – loosely labelled as 'harmonisation' in

Chapter 2 – does constitute an important conceptual backdrop to the material studied in this chapter and will be referred to at appropriate points (see generally the excellent essays in Degeling and Edelman (eds) *Equity in Commercial Law* (2006)).

Just as the contemporary litigation about equitable remedies has tended to arise in a commercial context, often but not exclusively from malpractice, so arguably, have the responses taken account of commercial considerations. In *Westdeutsche Landesbank Girozentrale v Islington London Borough Council* [1996] 2 All ER 961, for instance, one of the considerations seemingly militating against adopting a broad version of resulting trust doctrine (see Chapter 1 p 28) was a concern at 'the consequential commercial uncertainty which any extension of proprietary interests in personal property is bound to produce' (per Lord Browne-Wilkinson at 992). This consequentialist element is a further factor to be kept in mind when seeking to interpret and understand the developing scope and nature of equitable remedies. The position is therefore reached where an often practitioner-driven search for a remedy for commercial clients raises sometimes new, sometimes long-dormant, conceptual problems whose resolution in turn may depend on a weighing of the implications for commercial practices and standards of behaviour.

The 'equitable remedies' we are referring to here are those remedies historically the product of the courts of equity and which were developed to supplement the perceived limitations of the then available common law remedies. The equitable remedies can be awarded to enforce both equitable rights and those rights that are exclusively legal. In some cases of fraud, for instance, the principles of equity may be invoked to provide a remedy to a defrauded victim in the same way as they might assist a wronged beneficiary of a trust (see eg *Dubai Aluminium Co Ltd v Salaam* [2003] 2 AC 366; and *Papamichael v National Westminster Bank plc* [2003] 1 Lloyd's Rep 341). The distinctive although not universal features of equitable remedies are that they are discretionary, operate in personam and are not awarded where common law remedies are adequate (see generally Chapter 2 p 65). The notion that equitable remedies are discretionary needs to be treated with some caution. Lord Hoffmann, for instance, commenting on the equitable remedy of specific performance, stated that whilst 'there are no binding rules' there are 'settled principles . . . which do not have to be re-examined in every case, but which the courts will apply in all but exceptional circumstances' (*Co-operative Insurance Society Ltd v Argyll Stores (Holdings) Ltd* [1998] AC 1 at 16). On the other hand, common law remedies have conventionally been held to be available as of right although only to enforce common law rights.

Almost as a corollary of the nature and scope of equitable remedies is the fact that they can affect a diversity of legal relations, ranging far beyond the concerns of this chapter and indeed of this book. Our coverage is largely dictated by the particular focus of this chapter and is therefore somewhat functional and selective. Thus rescission and rectification of contracts, for instance, are largely irrelevant to our purposes and, in any event, tend to find their home in courses concerned with contractual relations. The same can be said for the decree of specific performance and we discuss this topic only to the extent necessary to establish its link to other equitable remedies covered in this chapter. By contrast, the equitable remedy of an injunction is more pervasive altogether and in its various forms can provide a powerful weapon against fraudsters and others who may contemplate inducing or participating in breaches of trust. For that reason and also because its most recent manifestations (the 'Mareva Injunction' or 'Freezing Order' and the 'Anton Piller Order' or 'Search Order') illustrate the continuing creative potential of equity doctrines in the hands of the courts, our coverage is more comprehensive. To complete the picture, tracing and a particular species of constructive trusteeship, although not strictly speaking remedies, are directly relevant to the concerns of this chapter and are considered at some length in sections 2 and 4 respectively.

It may be helpful at this point, and in relation to that species of constructive trusteeship just mentioned, to revert back to the issue of classification mentioned by Sir Peter Millett. Let us assume circumstances whereby bank B permits a solicitor, S, of whose penchant for heavy gambling it is aware, to withdraw large sums of money from the clients' account of his firm, F. S loses the money at a casino (P) and is declared bankrupt. F seeks to recover the amount from B. Now one of the ways in which F might seek to plead its case is to argue that B should be liable as a constructive trustee for 'dishonestly assisting in a breach of trust' and/or that P should be similarly liable for what has been termed 'knowing receipt'. It is immaterial for the moment whether or not these claims might succeed – they form the subject-matter of section 4 of this chapter – for there appears to be an immediate problem with this analysis as far as B's possible liability is concerned. There does not appear to be any property held by B which can form the subject-matter of the trust (cf the constructive trust discussed in Chapter 12).

One would not usually expect a person to be a trustee unless there is property which is, or can be required to be, vested in him or her. Indeed there is clear and long-standing authority for this proposition (see eg *Re Barney* [1892] 2 Ch 265 at 272 per Kekewich J). One consequence of property being held on trust is that this can provide the basis for a proprietary claim with its attendant advantages for the claimant, as, for example, where a defaulting trustee becomes insolvent. Then the particular item of property or, as we shall see in section 2 below, its substitute does not form part of the insolvent estate and therefore is not available to the trustee's creditors. But trustees and, come to that other fiduciaries, can also be made subject to a personal liability to compensate for loss (see generally Chapter 11). Similarly it is also only a personal form of liability which seems to arise when the label 'constructive trustee' is used to describe a person who has dishonestly assisted in some breach of trust or other fiduciary relationship but without ever having actually received or controlled the trust property. Thus we seem to have an example of 'constructive trusteeship without trust property' – in other words a personal liability to account. The constructive trust here is aptly described as nothing more than 'a formula for equitable relief' (per Ungoed-Thomas J *Selangor United Rubber Estates Ltd v Cradock (No 3)* [1968] 2 All ER 1073 at 1097). It is therefore not surprising that the use of the term 'constructive trustee' in this manner has been widely and frequently criticised (see eg Birks in McKendrick (ed) *Commercial Aspects of Trusts and Fiduciary Obligations* (1992) ch 8; Millett (1998) 114 LQR 399).

It should also not surprise us that in his judicial guise Lord Millett has sought to correct what critics view as both linguistic anomaly and conceptual confusion. In *Dubai Aluminium Company Ltd v Salaam* [2003] 2 AC 366, for example, Lord Millett explicitly addresses the issue (at [141]–[142]):

> The claim against [the defendant] is simply that he participated in a fraud. Equity gives relief against fraud by making any person sufficiently implicated in the fraud accountable in equity. In such a case he is traditionally (and I have suggested unfortunately [in *Paragon Finance v D B Thakerar & Co* [1999] 1 All ER 400 at 409]) described as a 'constructive trustee' and is said to be 'liable to account as a constructive trustee'. But he is not in fact a trustee at all, even though he may be liable to account as if he were. He never claims to assume the position of trustee on behalf of others, and he may be liable without ever receiving or handling the trust property. If he receives the trust property at all he receives it adversely to the claimant and by an unlawful transaction which is impugned by the claimant. He is not a fiduciary or subject to fiduciary obligations; and he could plead the Limitation Acts as a defence to the claim. In this . . . class of case the expressions 'constructive trust' and 'constructive trustee' create a trap. [Lord Millett endorsed the comments of Ungoed-Thomas J (above) and concludes:] I think that we should now discard the words 'accountable as constructive trustee' in this context and substitute the words 'accountable in equity'.

Even if this reclassification is adopted and is appropriate for the liability imposed on a stranger who 'dishonestly assists' in a breach of trust, it remains open to debate whether the same can be said of the personal liability imposed on a stranger – the casino P in our example – who may have knowingly received or handled misapplied trust property (see Martin [1998] Conv 13; and section 4 below).

There is, however, a preliminary yet important matter to be addressed before the detail of the remedies is explored. Tracing provides the starting-point for our study since, as will be seen, it is this process that can establish a basis from which both proprietary and personal claims can be made and for which some of the equitable remedies discussed in this chapter can be awarded.

2. Tracing

(a) Tracing: an introduction

In Chapter 11 we briefly summarised why in certain circumstances a personal claim against a trustee may not always produce an adequate remedy for a beneficiary. This would most obviously be the case where the trust fund has been misappropriated and the trustee is insolvent. Then, we suggested (see p 603), a beneficiary might seek to follow or trace the misappropriated trust property itself so as to establish a proprietary claim over it or its exchange product or indeed a personal claim of the type described above. 'Following' and 'tracing' tend nowadays to be interpreted not as synonyms but rather as representing distinct steps in the process of identifying what has happened to the claimant's property. Lord Millett in *Foskett v McKeown* [2001] AC 102, adopting the distinction formulated by Smith in *The Law of Tracing* (1997) pp 6–15, defined the two concepts in the following way (at p 127):

> The process of ascertaining what happened to the plaintiffs' money involves both tracing and following. These are both exercises in locating assets which are or may be taken to represent an asset belonging to the plaintiffs and to which they assert ownership. The processes of following and tracing are, however, distinct. Following is the process of following the same asset as it moves from hand to hand. Tracing is the process of identifying a new asset as the substitute for the old. Where one asset is exchanged for another, a claimant can elect whether to follow the original asset into the hands of the new owner or to trace its value into the new asset in the hands of the same owner. In practice his choice is often dictated by the circumstances.

Of course in the type of example referred to above, commonly termed a 'clean substitution', matters can be relatively straightforward even if en route there has occurred, for example, a transfer of money from person A to person B followed by a substitution of that money by shares in a company. There is usually no obstacle to tracing a property into its substitute product. But consider the following circumstances: the investment manager of company EA is bribed by C into buying worthless shares with EA's money; C then channels the funds obtained by the share purchase through several bank accounts in various jurisdictions and ultimately uses the funds to buy a share in a property development project on behalf of a company (D) located in England. En route the original funds may even have been mixed with other funds belonging to or fraudulently acquired by C. Two particular questions are posed by this much more complex example. Does EA, like our beneficiary in the simple example above, have a right to trace? If so, can its money be traced through all the different accounts so as to establish a proprietary claim over some portion of the shares in the property development project? Of course in our example a personal claim will probably lie against C but may well be unenforceable or worthless. Questions might also arise as to the possible personal liability of D but those do not concern us for the moment.

In one sense to pose, as we have done, the question 'can its money be traced?' is misleading as Lord Millett points out in his analysis of the tracing process in *Foskett v McKeown* (at 128):

We speak of tracing money into and out of the account, but there is no money in the account. There is merely a single debt of an amount equal to the final balance standing to the credit of the account holder. No money passes from paying bank to receiving bank or through the clearing system (where the money flows may be in the opposite direction). There is simply a series of debits and credits which are causally and transactionally linked. We also speak of tracing one asset into another, but this too is inaccurate. The original asset still exists in the hands of the new owner, or it may have become untraceable. The claimant claims the new asset because it was acquired in whole or in part with the original asset. What he traces, therefore, is not the physical asset itself but the value inherent in it.

Reverting to our two questions posed above, and taking the second question first, a number of technical rules, developed somewhat haphazardly, now mark out most of the boundary lines delineating the circumstances in which property can be traced through these more complicated transactions (so-called 'mixed substitutions'), although some gaps and inconsistencies remain. These rules and their limits as regards tracing and claiming in equity are explained more extensively in sections (c) and (d) below. Tracing and claiming can also be undertaken at common law by those holding legal title to assets and the relevant rules are considered in section (b).

Our immediate concern, however, is with the first question we posed as to whether in our example EA had any right to trace in equity. It is now well established that equitable tracing is not restricted to the trustee–beneficiary relationship but is available wherever there is an equitable proprietary interest derived from a fiduciary relationship. The point was firmly established in *Re Hallett* (1880) 13 Ch D 696: 'Has it ever been suggested, until very recently, that there is any distinction between an express trustee or an agent, or a bailee, or a collector of rents, or anybody else in a fiduciary position? . . . the moment you establish the fiduciary relation the modern rules of equity as regards following trust money apply' (per Jessell MR at 709, 710). But this extension of the right to trace beyond trust situations to include other fiduciaries can be seen from another perspective as too restrictive. If the basis for equitable tracing is rooted in some notion of unconscionability, then the formal requirements, derived from equity's historical jurisdiction, that there must exist a fiduciary relationship and an equitable proprietary interest, can be criticised as imposing unwarranted limitations on the availability of equitable tracing (see Smith *The Law of Tracing* (1997) pp 123–130; Birks *Introduction to the Law of Restitution* (1989) pp 377–385; Maudsley (1959) 75 LQR 234; Pearce (1976) 40 Conv 277). In fact the last sentence in the above quote from *Re Hallett* is capable of being construed as meaning simply that the existence of a fiduciary relationship is *sufficient* to enable the rules of equitable tracing to apply rather than that relationship being a *necessary* prerequisite (see eg *Smith* pp 124–125). Nevertheless, in the light of recent decisions of the courts and notwithstanding criticism on grounds of principle and authority, it seems that for the present a prerequisite for the right to trace in equity is the existence of an initial fiduciary relationship and an equitable proprietary interest in the claimant, legal ownership being insufficient (see *Re Diplock* [1948] Ch 465; *Agip (Africa) Ltd v Jackson* [1992] 4 All ER 451 at 466 per Fox LJ; *Boscawen v Bajwa* [1995] 4 All ER 769 at 777 per Millett LJ; and *Westdeutche Landesbank Girozentrale v Islington London Borough Council* [1996] 2 All ER 961: '. . . your lordships should not be taken to be casting any doubt on the principles of tracing as established in *Re Diplock*' (at 996 per Lord Browne-Wilkinson), but cf Birks 'The Necessity of a Unitary Law of Tracing' in Cranston (ed) *Making Commercial Law* (1997) p 240, footnotes 11 and 12 and accompanying text).

Paradoxically, judicial practice has in some degree simultaneously confirmed and undermined the criticisms of these requirements. Thus it has seemed that on occasion where the court thinks justice will best be served by providing a right to equitable tracing, it has been willing to strain the concept of fiduciary relationship to the limit to achieve this (eg *Chase Manhattan Bank NA v Israel-British Bank (London) Ltd* [1981] Ch 105; see Chapter 16, p 841 et seq where fiduciary relationships and their associated duties and reservations about the reasoning in the case if not its outcome are discussed). In an analogous development Lord Browne-Wilkinson has held that stolen money is traceable in equity on the grounds that a constructive trust is imposed on the fraudulent recipient (*Westdeutsche Landesbank Girozentrale v Islington London Borough Council* [1996] 2 All ER 961 at 998; see also Lord Templeman in *Lipkin Gorman v Karpnale Ltd* [1991] 2 AC 548 at 565–566). This establishes the necessary equitable interest for the purposes of tracing in equity. Thus, whilst the requirements of fiduciary relationship and equitable interest are functionally less of an obstacle to equitable tracing than might be thought, this outcome is only gained at the cost of reducing the fiduciary element at times almost to the status of a fiction. It is notable that Millett J felt able to comment in *Agip (Africa) Ltd v Jackson* [1992] 4 All ER 385 that the fiduciary requirement is 'readily satisfied in most cases of commercial fraud, since the embezzlement of a company's funds almost invariably involves a breach of fiduciary duty on the part of one of the company's employees or agents' (at 402). To revert to our original example, the investment manager of EA would be likely to have been held to be in breach of a fiduciary duty of loyalty to the employer thereby giving it the right to invoke the 'tracing process' in equity.

We have used the term 'tracing process' in preference to 'tracing remedy' since it is strongly arguable that tracing is not itself strictly a remedy at all. It is a process whereby assets are identified against which an appropriate claim can be made and a remedy sought. It is the means to the end although, as will be seen, there are occasions when it might be said that ends and means become indistinguishable. The distinction between 'process', 'claim' and 'remedy' is clearly stated in the following extract from a judgment of Millett LJ (*Boscawen v Bajwa* [1995] 4 All ER 769 at 776):

Equity lawyers habitually use the expressions 'the tracing claim' and 'the tracing remedy' to describe the proprietary claim and the proprietary remedy which equity makes available to the beneficial owner who seeks to recover his property in specie from those into whose hands it has come. Tracing properly so-called, however, is neither a claim nor a remedy but a process. Moreover, it is not confined to the case where the plaintiff seeks a proprietary remedy; it is equally necessary where he seeks a personal remedy against the knowing recipient or [dishonest] assistant. It is the process by which the plaintiff traces what has happened to his property, identifies the persons who have handled or received it, and justifies his claim that the money which they handled or received (and if necessary which they still retain) can properly be regarded as representing his property.

These distinctions were subsequently restated extra-judicially by Lord Millett ((1998) 110 LQR 399 at 408) and re-affirmed in *Foskett v McKeown* ([2001] 1 AC 102 at 128) and are now widely accepted. Nevertheless it is necessary to bear in mind that these linguistic and conceptual distinctions will not have been drawn in most earlier cases nor, come to that, in contemporary academic writing where instead the omnibus term 'tracing' will commonly have been used. One virtue of drawing a distinction between 'process' and 'claim' is to remind us that tracing can lead to either a proprietary or a personal claim, a point emphasised by Millett LJ in the above extract. That said, the principal attraction for the claimant seeking to invoke the tracing rules is usually the hope that it will establish the basis for the more advantageous proprietary claim.

Where, by virtue of the rules that shape the tracing process, assets can be identified, then equity traditionally has provided two principal proprietary remedies or forms of relief: either (i) an order to restore an unmixed sum of money (or its exchange product) to the trust fund, or (ii) where the asset is a mixed fund (or property acquired by a mixed fund) a lien or declaration of equitable charge over it. A lien or equitable charge is a form of proprietary security interest which confers on the claimant a right for his claim to be met out of the proceeds of sale of the property to which the lien attaches. The security element is critical to the operation of the lien in that, as a proprietary interest in the property it gives priority to the claimant's interest over the interests of the defendant's other creditors, whether secured or unsecured.

Our discussion so far has concentrated on *equitable* tracing and its prerequisites but, as mentioned above, the processes of following and tracing are also available at common law to the legal owners of assets, including of course trustees who may wish to seek a common law remedy where property has been misapplied. In which case one might reasonably ask: 'Why in our example did not EA as legal owner of the misappropriated funds simply seek to trace at common law and recover "its property" from the ultimate recipient?' To answer this question we need to know something about the limits of common law tracing as compared with tracing in equity.

(b) Tracing and claiming at common law

At common law circumstances can arise where the owner in law of an asset may have an action for conversion (in the case of chattels) or for 'money had and received' (in the case of money) against the recipient of the asset. Can the legal owner use the tracing process to identify the chattel (or its substitute) or money (or its product) as belonging to him or her and thereby assert a proprietary claim at common law? Answering 'Yes' to that question encounters the problem that historically the common law generally provided only personal remedies for either of these actions although the court did have a discretionary power to order specific recovery of a chattel (see now Tort (Interference with Goods) Act 1977, s 3). Personal actions are, as a general rule, of limited value where the recipient, or indeed, the transgressor is bankrupt. Moreover a 'Yes' answer would encounter the further problem that the tracing process at common law might be ineffective because of the limitations of the rules on common law tracing.

Some recent developments have clarified, some might say developed, the scope of tracing at common law in a way that has improved the prospects of being able to offer at least a qualified 'Yes' answer (see generally Smith *The Law of Tracing* (1997) pp 320–329; Oakley (1995) 54 CLJ 377; and Matthews in Birks (ed) *Laundering and Tracing* (1995)). In *Lipkin Gorman v Karpnale Ltd* [1991] 2 AC 548, a solicitor Cass (C) embezzled some £323,222 from his firm's client account, held at Lloyds Bank, of which around £100,313 was repaid. Cass who was imprisoned for three years, had devoted most of the stolen money to gambling at the tables of the Playboy Club, unfortunately losing more than he won. The firm (Lipkin Gorman) sought to recover the shortfall of £222,908 from Karpnale Ltd (Playboy) under, inter alia, a common law action for money had and received. But what exactly was the asset of which the firm could claim legal ownership and which it could seek to trace? It could not, for instance, establish legal title to the money withdrawn by Cass from the bank account. The firm did not 'own' the cash in the bank account. Indeed, on withdrawal of the cash from the account C became owner at common law of the money. However, the plaintiff firm did have a species of property, a chose in action in the form of a debt owed to it by the bank and 'since the debt was enforceable at common law, the chose in action was legal property belonging to the solicitors at common law' (per Lord Goff at 574). The House of Lords affirmed that common law tracing principles would enable the firm to trace the chose in action into its product – the money withdrawn – and thence into the hands of the volunteer recipient (Playboy). The firm was therefore able to establish a *proprietary claim* – that the money in Playboy's hands belonged to it [the firm] at common law – which enabled it to seek the *personal remedy* against the club for 'money had and received'.

The broader significance of the decision in *Lipkin Gorman* is the acknowledgment by the House of Lords that the action for 'money had and received' is a species of a restitutionary action to reverse an unjust enrichment: '[T]he law imposes an obligation on the recipient of stolen money to pay an equivalent sum to the victim if the recipient has been 'unjustly enriched' at the expense of the true owner' (at 559 per Lord Templeman). But had the club been unjustly enriched? Certainly the club had been enriched at the plaintiff firm's expense but were the circumstances unjust? The judgments do not clearly identify the 'unjust factor' in the case. The club after all had provided a lawful gambling service or facility in exchange for the money. But a defence based on Playboy having given consideration in good faith to C failed as the gambling contracts were void under s 18 of the Gaming Act 1845. However, in a landmark judgment, the House held that the doctrine of 'change of position' should be recognised as a defence to the common law claim (see further p 730). The proposition advanced by counsel for the respondent club (Playboy) was that recovery should be denied to the plaintiff firm Lipkin Gorman because of the change in position of the respondents, who acted in good faith throughout. Lord Goff summarised the position as follows (at 580):

> Whether change of position is, or should be, recognised as a defence to claims in restitution is a subject which has been much debated in the books. It is however a matter on which there is a remarkable unanimity of view, the consensus being to the effect that such a defence should be recognised in English law. I myself am under no doubt that this is right. [Lord Goff then referred to the recognition of the defence in the USA, Canada, New Zealand and several Australian States and concluded:] The time for its recognition in this country is, in my opinion, long overdue.

In *Lipkin Gorman* it was held that the paying out of winnings to C in good faith by Playboy constituted a change of position by the club. The plaintiff firm was therefore entitled to recover only Playboy's net winnings of £154,695 rather than the complete shortfall claimed by the firm (see Watts (1991) 107 LQR 521; McKendrick (1992) 55 MLR 377; and the trenchant criticism by Halliwell [1992] Conv 124).

In *F C Jones & Sons (Trustee) v Jones* [1997] Ch 159 a further step was taken in extending the scope of tracing at common law. The plaintiff, the trustee in bankruptcy (T), was enabled to trace property not only into the exchange product but also to claim profits made from it. One of the partners of a bankrupt firm F C Jones & Sons drew cheques in favour of his wife (J) to the value of £11,700. The money was profitably invested within an account that J had opened with a firm of commodity brokers. J received cheques from the brokers to the value of £50,760 which she then deposited into another account that she had opened with R bank. J conceded that T was entitled to the original £11,700 under a personal action for money had and received but not to the profit since liability in that action crystallises at the moment of receipt and it would be irrelevant what the defendant had done with the money after she received it. In fact T did not argue the case on the 'money had and received' ground – what we would now categorise as unjust enrichment – and indeed was not suing J at all.

T had brought an action in debt against the bank when it declined to pay the money in the account to T. The bank, in the unenviable position of being faced with two claims against the one account, interpleaded, joining J as defendant, and paid the money in the account into court. Only at this stage was the issue joined between T and J as to who had title to the assets. The Court of Appeal (Millett and Beldam LJJ) held (i) that no title ever passed to J in law or in equity but under statutory insolvency law remained in T; (ii) that T, as legal owner, could follow the chose in action (under the partnership bank account) through its various substitutions (via cheques, broker's account, more cheques and eventually to the account with R) and claim the balance of £49,860 (£900 had been withdrawn) in the account with R. As Lord Millett was to put it, commenting later on the case: '[T] claimed the money from the bank because it belonged to him or represented profits made by the use of the money which belonged to him. This was a question of title, not unjust enrichment' (in Burrows and Rodger (eds) *Mapping the Law: Essays in Memory of Peter Birks* (2006) ch 14 at 268; cf Smith *The Law of Tracing* at 328–330; Birks (1997) 11(1) TLI 2 at 6–9 on the contentious analysis that J at no time obtained any title, legal or equitable, to the cheques or the account balance at the brokers). The particular significance of the case, therefore, is that it recognises that there are circumstances, probably rare, where tracing through a clean substitution can give rise to a proprietary claim at common law incorporating profits made en route. A criticism of the outcome of the case, however, is that the result was unfair to J in that T, and J's creditors, benefited from the skill or luck which accompanied J's investment of the money whilst J received no recognition for this. Lord Millett has subsequently suggested that in such circumstances and assuming the defendant to be an innocent party, the law might be developed so as to provide, as can be done in equity, an allowance for skill and effort (op cit at 269).

An important feature in *Jones* – a case of tracing through clean substitutions – is that at no stage did the funds become mixed in a bank account with other funds, whether those of J or some other person. Had this happened then at common law tracing would not have been possible, it being generally presumed – though the presumption has been strongly challenged – that the common law right to trace is defeated where money of the claimant is mixed with other money in a bank account prior to it being paid into the defendant's bank account. In *Agip (Africa) Ltd v Jackson* [1990] Ch 265 Millett J summarised the position at common law as follows (at 285 and cf Scott (1966) 7 U West Australia LR 463; Goode (1976) 92 LQR 360):

> [I]t can be no defence [to an action for money had and received] for the defendant to show that he has so mixed [the plaintiff's money] with his own money that he cannot tell whether he still has it or not. Mixing by the defendant himself must, therefore, be distinguished from mixing by a prior recipient. The former is irrelevant, but the latter will destroy the claim, for it will prevent proof that the money received by the defendant was the money paid by the plaintiff.

Moreover the paucity of common law remedies, in particular the absence of the 'far-reaching remedy of a declaration of charge' (*Re Diplock* [1948] Ch 465 at 520), prevents recovery in such circumstances. A further possible constraint of considerable practical importance today is the proposition that at common law only a physical asset such as a cheque can be followed and not money transferred electronically (see Millett in *Agip (Africa) Ltd v Jackson* [1990] Ch 265 at 286; and (1991) 107 LQR 71 at 74; (1995) 9 TLI 35 at 39; *Bank Tejarat v Hong Kong and Shanghai Banking Corpn (CI) Ltd* [1995] 1 Lloyd's Rep 239, but cf Oakley (1995) 54 CLJ 377; Birks (1995) 9 TLI 91; and Fox LJ in the Court of Appeal in *Agip* [1991] Ch 547 at 565 who thought the absence of a cheque was immaterial). The practical significance of this limitation, if persisted with, is evident once it is appreciated that in the UK under the Clearing House Automated Payment System (CHAPS) payments worth over £52,000 billion were transferred in, for instance, 2001, the maximum figure in any one day being £319 billion (www.apacs.org.uk, cited in Thomas 'Electronic Funds Transfer and Fiduciary Fraud' [2005] JBL 48–69 at footnote 1).

In contrast to the position at common law, the metaphysical approach of equity 'found no difficulty in regarding a composite fund as an amalgam constituted by the mixture of two or more funds...' and 'capable, in proper circumstances, of being resolved into its component parts' (*Re Diplock* at 520). But it must not be assumed that common law tracing, although usually now of less practical relevance, is in all respects inferior. For example, it does not depend, unlike its equitable counterpart, on the presence of a fiduciary relationship. Nevertheless, doubts about the adequacy of common law remedies and uncertainty as to the extent of its right to trace have combined to give greater practical significance to the equitable version.

The existence of separate qualifying criteria and rules for common law and equitable tracing has been widely criticised (see eg Birks in Cranston (ed) *Making Commercial Law* (1997) ch 9; Smith *The Law of Tracing* (1997) pp 120–130; Millett LJ in *Jones* at 169: 'there is no merit in having distinct and different tracing rules at law and in equity'; and Walker LJ extrajudicially in [2000] RLR 573). Notwithstanding a reiteration by Lords Steyn and Millett in *Foskett v McKeown* ([2001] 1 AC 102 at 113 and 129 respectively) of dissatisfaction with different rules for tracing at law and in equity (but cf the reservations of Lord Browne-Wilkinson), their comments are obiter and therefore the position described above remains the law for the present although in a distinctly fragile condition (but cf *Shalson v Russo* [2005] Ch 281 where Rimer J reviews the cautious dicta in *Foskett v McKeown* and concludes: 'it cannot be said that *Foskett* has swept away the long recognised difference between common law and equitable tracing' (at [104]) and the contrary view expressed obiter in *Bracken Partners v Gutteridge* [2003] EWHC 1064 at para 31).

The need for a reconsideration and arguably a synthesis of the doctrines remains unabated.

(c) Tracing and claiming in Equity

In contrast to the still relatively restrictive rules of tracing at common law, more flexible rules have been developed by the courts under the aegis of equitable tracing. These are most evident where mixing of products or of money takes place. The position where mixing of goods takes place in a manufacturing process is considered further in Chapter 15. Here, we are primarily concerned with the consequences where trust property is converted into or takes the form of money and is mixed with (1) the trustee's own money, or (2) money belonging to another trust or to an innocent volunteer.

In the following straightforward examples, which are intended merely to give an indication of the principles applicable, the terms trustee and beneficiary are used as shorthand for the parties to fiduciary relationships generally, to whom the same principles apply.

(1) Mixing of trust property with trustee's own property

The basic principle   The basic principle is that beneficiaries have a first charge over the mixed fund or any property which is purchased from it, to the extent necessary to satisfy their claim. Indeed, in principle 'the beneficiary will be entitled to every portion of the blended property which the trustee cannot prove to be his own' (per Ungoed-Thomas J in *Re Tilley's Will Trusts* [1967] Ch 1179 at 1182, citing *Lewin on Trusts* (16th edn, 1964) p 273). But mixing most commonly occurs in a banking account and here special rules have evolved. Where the beneficiaries seek to claim against the balance in the account, the rule in *Re Hallett's Estate* (1880) 13 Ch D 696 applies. Under this rule the trustee is assumed to exhaust his own money first, irrespective of the order in which money was paid into the account.

To illustrate the effect of this rule let us suppose the following circumstances: on 1 April a trustee, T, pays £1,000 of his own money into a bank account, followed on 1 May by £3,000 of trust money and 1 June by a further £1,000 of his own money. On 1 July T withdraws £2,000 and spends it on a holiday cruise with C plc. Under the rule in *Re Hallett* T is assumed to have spent his own £2,000 first, leaving the balance in the account of £3,000 as trust property. Contrast this result with the common law position applicable to transactions between banker and customer in an active banking account. Under the rule in Clayton's case (1816) 1 Mer 572, debits and credits are set against each other on a 'first-in, first-out' basis: withdrawals from an account are presumed to be made in the same order as payments in. The different approach in *Re Hallett* is conventionally attributed to the court applying a presumption of honesty to acts of the trustee. More precisely, the wrongful act is not allowed to be used as a shield; the rule prevents the trustee or any person claiming through him 'to say against the person entitled to the property that [the trustee] has done [the act] wrongfully' (*Re Hallett's Estate* (1880) 13 Ch D 696 at 727).

The rule in *Re Hallet* is relevant only where a claim is made against a balance in an active bank account. In contrast, consider our original example of the payments of £5,000 into the account but now with T first purchasing shares for himself worth £2,000 and then dissipating £2,000 on that holiday leaving a balance of £1,000. It is not possible to trace into the money spent on the holiday and no action can lie against C plc whom, it is assumed, sold the holiday to T in good faith. A strict application of the *Re Hallett* rule would here work to the disadvantage of the beneficiaries (B) since T would be deemed to have purchased the shares with his own £2,000 leaving B with merely a charge against the £1,000 balance. In fact the rule is subordinated to the basic principle mentioned at the start of this section that a beneficiary is entitled to a first charge on property purchased out of a mixed fund. In the example, B would therefore have, in addition to a charge against the £1,000 balance, a charge against the shares for £2,000 (*Re Oatway* [1903] 2 Ch 356).

The emphasis here, however, is on choice. If the asset has depreciated in value so that B would be better served by electing to rely on a charge on the balance of the fund in the account, then she can opt for that alternative (*Re Tilley's Will Trust*). To put the point more prosaically, the beneficiary is in the enviable position of saying 'Heads I win, Tails you lose'.

Left unexplained by these examples is whether, where shares are purchased and then increase in value, the charge is limited to the amount of trust money laid out in the purchase. Dicta in two leading cases suggested that this was indeed the position (*Re Hallett's Estate* (1880) 13 Ch D 696 at 709 per Jessell MR and *Sinclair v Brougham* [1914] AC 398 at 442 per Lord Parker). But this would mean that the trustee (T) would keep all the profit and would have benefited by virtue of a breach of trust – a surprising proposition. The dicta were subsequently distinguished by Ungoed-Thomas J in *Re Tilley's Will Trusts* [1967] Ch 1179, and it was conceded that the charge should be for a proportionate share (*Scott v Scott* (1963) 109 CLR 649 provides strong support for this position).

The matter has now been put beyond doubt by a majority 3:2 decision of the House of Lords in *Foskett v Mckeown* [2001] 1 AC 102, a somewhat unusual case although one categorised by Lord Millett, one of the majority judges, as 'a textbook example of tracing through mixed substitutions' (at 126; see Stevens [2001] Conv 65; Grantham and Rickett (2000) 63 MLR 905; Jaffey (2000) 14 TLI 194; Rotherham (2000) 59 CLJ 440; Fox [2001] LMCLQ 1; Walker [2000] RLR 573; Wu (2001) MULR 295). A textbook example maybe, but unusual in one particular feature highlighted by Lord Browne-Wilkinson – also one of the majority judges but who conceded that he had changed his mind only after reading the speech of Lord Millett (at 106): '[T]here are many cases in which the court has to decide which of two innocent parties is to suffer from the activities of a fraudster. This case, unusually, raises the converse question: which of two innocent parties is to benefit from the activities of the fraudster.' In the case a trustee (M) of funds provided to him by depositors for investment in a property development scheme in Portugal had in 1986 effected a life assurance policy on his own life at an annual premium of £10,220. In March 1989 M divested himself of any beneficial interest in the policy which thereafter was to be held on trust principally for his children. M paid the premiums for 1986 and 1987 with his own money. The origin of the 1988 premium was disputed but the 1989 and 1990 premiums were paid, in breach of trust, out of the fund held on trust for the depositors. The funds were dissipated and in 1991 M committed suicide whereupon the insurers paid the death benefit of £1m due under the life assurance policy to the defendant trustees of the children's trust. A particular factual difficulty in the case was that a combination of the time frame of events and the terms of the policy meant that the premiums paid from the trust fund had been unnecessary to ensure the payment of the £1m sum assured. This was one of the issues about which the opinions of the majority in the House differed from those of the minority. The investors brought an action claiming the proceeds of the policy. At first instance Laddie J held that the claimants were entitled to a lien on the proceeds for a pro rata share reflecting their contribution to the policy premiums (53.46%). By contrast, the majority of the Court of Appeal, [1998] Ch 265 CA (Morritt LJ dissenting), held that the claimants were entitled only to recover the premiums paid out of their moneys. (See generally on the Court of Appeal case Stevens [1998] Conv 406; McCormack (1998) 19 Co Law 80; Smith (1997) 113 LQR 552; Mitchell [1998] LMCLQ 465.)

On appeal the majority of the House of Lords agreed that the depositors' equitable ownership of the money in the trust account could be traced into the premiums paid in 1989 and 1990, thence into the chose in action constituted by the policy and then ultimately into the death benefit proceeds of the policy in the proportion declared by Laddie J at first instance (ie 53.46%). Lord Millett commented as follows on Jessell MR's dictum and the 'rule' in *Re Hallett* (at 131–132):

> In my view the time has come to state unequivocally that English law has no such rule. It conflicts with the rule that a trustee must not benefit from his trust. I agree . . . that the beneficiary's right to elect to have a proportionate share of a mixed substitution necessarily follows once one accepts, as English law does, (i) that a claimant can trace in equity into a mixed fund and (ii) that he can trace unmixed money into its proceeds and assert ownership of the proceeds. Accordingly, I would state the basic rule as follows. Where a trustee wrongfully uses trust money to provide part of the cost of acquiring an asset, the beneficiary is entitled *at his option* either to claim a proportionate share of the asset or to enforce a lien upon it to secure his personal claim against the trustee for the amount of the misapplied money. It does not matter whether the trustee mixed the trust money with his own in a single fund before using it to acquire the asset, or made separate payments (whether simultaneously or sequentially) out of the differently owned funds to acquire a single asset. Two observations are necessary at this point. First, there is a mixed substitution (with the results already described) whenever the claimant's property has contributed in

part only towards the acquisition of the new asset. It is not necessary for the claimant to show in addition that his property has contributed to any increase in the *value* of the new asset. This is because, as I have already pointed out, this branch of the law is concerned with vindicating rights of property and not with reversing unjust enrichment. Secondly, the beneficiary's right to claim a lien is available only against a wrongdoer and those deriving title under him otherwise than for value. It is not available against competing contributors who are innocent of any wrongdoing. . . . As against the wrongdoer and his successors, the beneficiary is entitled to locate his contribution in any part of the mixture and to subordinate their claims to share in the mixture until his own contribution has been satisfied. This has the effect of giving the beneficiary a lien for his contribution if the mixture is deficient.

But is even this outcome being too generous to a defaulting trustee? If the profit could only have been earned by using trust money, no matter how small the proportion, ought not the trustee to be restricted to recovering just the initial outlay, ie all profit should accrue to the beneficiary (see Berg (2001) 117 LQR 366)? An obvious point of comparison here is with the common law tracing case of *F C Jones & Sons (Trustee) v Jones* [1997] Ch 159. There, it will be recalled (see above) the trustee in bankruptcy was entitled to claim the fruits of the successful investment, although of course in the context of a case where no mixing of funds had occurred. On the other hand, where a defaulting trustee is insolvent an outcome where the claimant beneficiaries recover all the profit – a windfall to them – might seem hard on other creditors who may feel entitled to claim against that proportion of the profit attributable to the trustee's original contribution.

The 'lowest intermediate balance' rule

The outcome provided by the rule in *Re Hallett* – that our defaulting trustee (T) exhausts his own assets first – may be equitable as between T and a beneficiary (B), but what if T has other creditors? In their interests the presumption of honesty on the part of the trustee is subject to one important modification. Once trust money has been drawn upon by T (ie the balance outstanding falls below the original value of the trust money mixed in the account) that part of the trust money is deemed to have been spent. Subsequent payments by T into the account are not treated as replacing the trust money unless it is clear that the subsequent payments into the account are specifically intended to replenish the trust fund (*Roscoe v Winder* [1915] 1 Ch 62). To revert to our earlier example, if we assume that T withdrew the £2,000 on 2 May (and not 2 July) to spend on a holiday, the then existing balance of £2,000 would be treated as trust property but not the subsequent deposit of £1,000 on 1 June. As to the shortfall, B is left to a personal action against T for breach of trust, and must take her place in the line with T's other creditors. This 'lowest intermediate balance' rule, as it is known, was reaffirmed in *Bishopsgate Investment Management Ltd ('BIM') v Homan* [1995] Ch 211, a case arising out of the Maxwell saga. The case involved improper transfer of assets from funds belonging to BIM (trustees of certain pension schemes) into an overdrawn bank account of Maxwell Communication Corporation plc (MCC). The Court of Appeal confirmed the orthodoxy that tracing did not extend through an overdrawn bank account, whether overdrawn at the time of payment in of the money or subsequently (see Smith (1994) 8 TLI 102; Gullifer [1996] LMCLQ 446; Jones [1995] Conv 490 and [1996] Conv 129).

Backward tracing? A question left open by the judgments in *BIM v Homan* is whether it is possible to trace misappropriated funds into assets acquired by the defendant with moneys drawn from an overdrawn bank account *before* the misappropriated funds were paid into the account. Dillon LJ, agreeing with the view expressed by Vinelott J at first instance, stated that it was 'at least arguable . . . that there ought to be an equitable charge . . . on the asset' (at 217) where it was the intention *either* that the 'borrowed money' – ie the money drawn from the overdrawn account – should be repaid into the bank account by use of the misappropriated money *or* where the misappropriated money was used to reduce an overdraft so as to make finance available within the overdraft limit to purchase the particular asset. By way of contrast Leggatt LJ firmly rejected the notion (at 221): [T]here can be no equitable remedy against an asset acquired *before* misappropriation of money takes place, since ex hypothesi it cannot be followed into something which existed and so had been acquired before the money was received and therefore without its aid. The concept of a composite transaction is in my judgment fallacious' (Henry J agreed with both judgments! For a view supportive of Dillon LJ see dicta of Scott VC in *Foskett v McKeown* [1998] Ch 265 at 283–284: 'I regard the point as still open'; Millett (1995–96) 6 KCLJ 1; but cf Oakley [1995] CLJ 377; and see generally *Smith* pp 146–152 and 353–356).

(2) Mixing of two trust funds or of trust fund and money of an innocent volunteer

Where the funds of two or more trusts have been mixed together by a trustee, or where the same has happened with trust property and that of an innocent volunteer, none has priority over the others: they share pari passu (ie proportionately) in the mixed fund or in any property purchased from it. Lord Millett reaffirmed the position in *Foskett v McKeown* ([2001] 1 AC 102 at 132):

> Where the beneficiary's claim is in competition with the claims of other innocent contributors, there is no basis upon which any of the claims can be subordinated to any of the others. Where the fund is deficient, the beneficiary is not entitled to enforce a lien for his contributions; all must share rateably in the fund. The primary rule in regard to a mixed fund, therefore, is that gains and losses are borne by the contributors rateably.

But does this primary rule apply where, as will often be the case, mixing takes place in an active banking account? Then the 'first-in, first-out' rule in Clayton's case (1816) 1 Mer 572 has been applied (see eg *Re Diplock* [1948] Ch 465 at 554). It is questionable, however, whether this promotes a fair outcome. Consider the position, for instance, where T is trustee of three separate trust funds (A, B, C) of £1,000 each and on successive days pays each fund into her own account in the order A, B, C. T then withdraws £1,500, which she loses on a slow horse. Applying the rule in Clayton's case, fund A has disappeared, fund B has been reduced to £500, while fund C remains intact. Not surprisingly the application of this common law rule has been criticised, both on practical grounds as leading to arbitrary and inconvenient results and conceptually as being irrelevant to weighing equitable property rights between beneficiaries (see McConville (1963) 79 LQR 388). Indeed, in *Re British Red Cross Balkan Fund* [1914] 2 Ch 419 Astbury J declined to apply the rule calling it 'a mere rule of evidence not an invariable rule of law'. On the other hand, practical convenience may also be claimed as a virtue of the rule, particularly in a more complex setting, for instance, with multiple transactions and clients over a long period, than the simple illustration used above (see eg the argument of the applicant in *Re Winsor and Bajaj* (1990) 75 DLR (4th) 198).

Notwithstanding criticisms of the rule, the Court of Appeal has accepted that it still applies to cases where the moneys of beneficiaries have been mixed in a bank account by a third party. But the court also held that the rule should *not* apply where its application would be either contrary to the express or implied intention of the claimants, or be impractical or cause injustice (*Barlow Clowes International Ltd v Vaughan* [1992] 4 All ER 22, noted by Martin [1993] Conv 370; applied in *Commerzbank Aktiengesellschaft v IMB Morgan plc* [2005] 1 Lloyd's Rep 298 paras 42–50). In *Barlow Clowes* the court ordered a pari passu distribution in preference both to the rule in *Clayton's* case and to a third alternative, originating in North America, a 'rolling charge' whereby each withdrawal from a fund is attributed proportionately to all beneficiaries having money in the fund at the date of withdrawal (considered in *Re Ontario Securities Commission* (1986) 30 DLR (4th) 1; affd (1988) 52 DLR (4th) 767n). The rule in *Clayton's* case again came under consideration in *Russell-Cooke Trust Co v Prentis* [2003] 2 All ER 478 (see (2005) 64(1) CLJ 45). The judgment seems to confirm that the court will strive where possible to displace a rule, described in the case as 'arbitrary' by Lindsay J, as long as there is some circumstance or factor to justify disapplying it. The case concerned a shortfall revealed in a solicitor's client account, set up as part of a scheme to acquire somewhat risky mortgage investments for clients, that was closed following intervention by the Law Society in its regulatory role. The particular circumstance justifying the displacement of the rule was that the pattern of payments out of the account prior to its closure seemingly bore no relation to the patterns of payments in. The shortfall that had arisen in the fund was therefore allocated on a pari passu basis as being the 'least unfair' method, Lindsay J describing the alternative offered by the American system as being 'complicated and ... expensive to apply' (at 495, para 57).

It remains to be seen whether the exceptions will ultimately swallow the rule, so that the outcome will be decided by the sometimes uncomfortable bedfellows of convenience and fairness (cf Lord Atkin in *General Medical Council v Spackman* [1943] AC 627 at 638, 'Convenience and justice are often not on speaking terms').

(d) The limits to equitable tracing and equitable proprietary claims

(1) Introduction

Even equitable tracing is not unlimited in its scope. As usual the rights of bona fide purchasers for value without notice remain paramount. Whilst it is theoretically possible to trace property into their hands, the bona fide purchasers take ownership of that property free from the claims of the beneficiaries. The latter are therefore left to pursue either the proceeds of sale in the trustee's hands or a personal action against the trustee or possibly even against someone who 'knowingly received' trust property but who no longer has the property or its proceeds. What constitutes 'notice' in the context of the bona fide purchaser defence and 'knowledge' for the purpose of establishing 'knowing receipt' or, as it may be termed, 'recipient liability' is discussed at p 745 et seq.

There are two further instances where the tracing process reaches its limits and no equitable proprietary claim can be sustained. One such instance is where the property or its exchange product ceases to be ascertainable whilst in the other instance it would be inequitable for the proprietary claim to be enforced.

(2) The limits to ascertainability

Property ceases to be ascertainable when it has been dissipated by the trustee (T), for instance on a holiday, or where it can no longer be traced through T's bank account under the rules outlined above. The personal action of the beneficiary (B) against T remains intact but may be worthless where T is insolvent.

But, as may often be the case, a bank might be the trustee. Let us then suppose that the bank deposits trust moneys with itself as banker but subsequently becomes insolvent. Can the beneficiaries trace the trust moneys into the assets of the bank? Leaving conceptual sophistication to one side for the moment, it is difficult to see how, in practical terms, the beneficiaries would be able to identify the trust funds within the general assets of the bank. In *Space Investments Ltd v Canadian Imperial Bank of Commerce Trust Co (Bahamas) Ltd* [1986] 1 WLR 1072, PC, a case where the deposit of the trust moneys by the defendant trustee bank with itself had been authorised by the trust instrument, the Privy Council confirmed that this was so. Lord Templeman explained the reasoning as follows (at 1074):

A bank in fact uses all deposit moneys for the general purposes of the bank. Whether a bank trustee lawfully receives deposits or wrongfully treats trust money as on deposit from trusts, all the moneys are in fact dealt with and expended by the bank for the general purposes of the bank. In these circumstances it is impossible for the beneficiaries interested in trust money to trace their money to any particular asset belonging to the trustee bank.

Lord Templeman went on to consider the position where a bank might have dissipated trust money through unlawful mixing with other moneys of the bank and suggested obiter: '... equity allows the beneficiaries ... to trace the trust money to all the assets of the bank and to recover the trust money by the exercise of an equitable charge over all the assets of the bank' (ibid). One consequence of imposing a charge granting priority to the interests of the beneficiaries is to benefit them at the expense of the bank's general creditors. Lord Templeman's view has been criticised as being contrary both to the policy and principle of insolvency law (see eg Goode (1987) 103 LQR 433) and was not followed in *Bishopsgate Investment Management Ltd ('BIM') v Homan* [1995] Ch 211, where, as we have seen, the Court of Appeal in effect reasserted the orthodox view that money paid into an overdrawn account ceases to be ascertainable (see also the cautious comments of Lord Mustill in *In Re Goldcorp Exchange* [1995] 1 AC 74 at 104; and Birks (1995) 9 TLI 43 to the effect that the dicta 'are now as good as dead' (at 45)). It should be noted, however, that in neither of the cases just mentioned was a view expressed about the situation specifically identified by Lord Templeman, that is of a trustee bank depositing with itself trust funds that can therefore no longer be identified and where the deposit was *unauthorised*.

The controversy cannot, however, obscure the fact that ascertainability appears to be dictated on occasion by a perceived need to provide an effective legal, or in this instance equitable, response to the creativity of fraudsters. Consider, for instance, our earlier illustration, drawn from *El Ajou v Dollar Land Holdings (DLH)* [1993] 3 All ER 717, where funds of Mr El Ajou were misappropriated and 'laundered' through bank accounts in different offshore jurisdictions – some of them civilian systems – before apparently resurfacing in a London property development undertaken by the fraudsters in conjunction with the defendant company DLH. Whilst it was possible to some degree to trace the misappropriated moneys by means of matching corresponding debits and credits at various links in the chain, there came a point when the trail 'went cold' in the sense that the precise route taken by the moneys could not be identified with any certainty. Undaunted, Millett J was prepared to hold that this difficulty could be sidestepped by means of invoking an equitable charge (at 735–736):

The victims of a fraud can follow their money in equity through bank accounts where it has been mixed with other moneys because equity treats the money in such accounts as charged with the repayment of their money. If the money in the account subject to such a

> charge is afterwards paid out of the account and into a number of different accounts, the victim can claim a similar charge over each of the recipient accounts. They are not bound to choose between them. Whatever may be the position as between the victims inter se, as against the wrongdoer his victims are not required to appropriate debits to credits in order to identify the particular account into which their money has been paid. Equity's power to charge a mixed fund with the repayment of trust moneys (a power not shared by the common law) enables the claimant to follow the money, not because it is theirs, but because it is derived from a fund which is to be treated as if it were subject to a charge in their favour.

But what, it may be said, of the fact that money had passed through the hands of recipients in civil law jurisdictions where neither the concept of equitable ownership nor that of an equitable charge on an account within that jurisdiction were recognised? The judge's response to the proposition was simply to assert that the defendant DLH's obligation to restore to their rightful owner assets which it received in England is governed exclusively by English law, including equitable tracing rules, and that the efficacy of the equitable charge is not negated by 'the temporary repose of the assets in a civil law country nor their receipt by intermediate recipients outside the jurisdiction' (at 737).

As will be seen later in this chapter, *El Ajou* was reversed on appeal – the principal issue concerning questions of knowledge under a 'knowing receipt' claim – but Hoffmann LJ appeared to endorse the equitable charge analysis of Millett J ([1994] 2 All ER 685 at 701). There are three points to emphasise about that analysis. First, the analysis, as Millett J points out, concerns the position as between a wrongdoer and his victim and not that between two or more innocent victims when different considerations may apply. Second, the analysis has an obvious practical benefit in so far as it eases the task of victims and of the courts in identifying the proceeds of fraud when faced with complex money-laundering exercises. Third, and more fundamentally, does it provide a more precise, and perhaps more controllable, means of achieving a limited version of the equitable charge outlined by Lord Templeman in *Space Investments*? (See generally Oliver (1995) 9 TLI 78; and Moriarty in Birks (ed) *Laundering and Tracing* (1995)).

(3) Inequitability and 'change of position'

The perception that 'ascertainability' is a somewhat uncertain criterion with imprecise boundaries is reinforced when consideration is given to the circumstances where it would be deemed inequitable for a claimant beneficiary to maintain an equitable proprietary claim. Consider, for instance, the position where an innocent donee of a fund mixes it with his own funds to improve his immovable property. 'In such a case has the traced fund "gone" or is it merely inequitable to impose a charge or mortgage upon the real estate of an innocent person?' (Waters *Law of Trusts in Canada* (3rd edn, 2005) p 1284). The Court of Appeal in *Re Diplock* [1948] Ch 465 decided that the right to impose a charge was lost in those very circumstances, the innocent donees being charities who had spent the plaintiff's money on improvements and alterations to their own land. It was held that no charge should be imposed because a charge is enforceable by sale which could have produced an outcome whereby the innocent donees would have had to sell their own land. Notwithstanding *Re Diplock* the defence of 'inequitability' was narrowly applied in English law.

The apparently limited scope of the 'inequitability' defence to an equitable proprietary claim now needs to be reappraised in the light of the decision of the House of Lords in 1991 to accept the proposition that a broader defence of 'change of position', long established in the US, should be generally available in restitution actions (*Lipkin Gorman v Karpnale Ltd* [1991] 2 AC 548, and see generally Nolan in Birks (ed) *Laundering and Tracing* (1995) ch 6; Goff and Jones *The Law of Restitution* (7th edn, 2007)).

The Restatement of Restitution defines the defence in the following terms (para 142(1)):

> The right of a person to restitution from another because of a benefit received is terminated or diminished if, after the receipt of the benefit, circumstances have so changed that it would be inequitable to require the other to make full restitution.

The immediate question here is whether a 'change of position' defence should be available to an equitable proprietary claim. The point was not at issue in *Lipkin Gorman*, which was not a case about equitable tracing, but was nevertheless touched on by Lord Goff (at 581):

> The defence of change of position is akin to the defence of bona fide purchase; but we cannot simply say that bona fide purchase is a species of change of position. This is because change of position will only avail a defendant to the extent that his position has been changed; whereas, where bona fide purchase is invoked, no inquiry is made (in most cases) into the adequacy of the consideration. Even so, the recognition of change of position as a defence should be doubly beneficial. It will enable a more generous approach to be taken to the recognition of the right to restitution, in the knowledge that the defence is, in appropriate cases, available; and while recognising the different functions of property at law and in equity, there may also in due course develop a more consistent approach to tracing claims, in which common defences are recognised as available to such claims, whether advanced at law or in equity.

It is possible to infer that Lord Goff envisaged that the defences of bona fide purchaser for value and change of position should both be available in the case of equitable proprietary claims. On the other hand, comments by Lord Millett in *Foskett v McKeown* [2001] AC 102, in the context of rejecting the view that a proprietary equitable tracing claim is a species of restitutionary action to prevent unjust enrichment, distinguished between the two defences. Notwithstanding previous comments to the contrary in *Boscawen v Bajwa* [1996] 1 WLR 328 (at 334–335) Lord Millett seemed to imply that only the bona fide purchaser defence was applicable to equitable proprietary claims (at 129): 'A claim in unjust enrichment is subject to a change of position defence, which usually operates by reducing or extinguishing the element of enrichment. A [proprietary tracing claim] is subject to the bona fide purchaser for value defence, which operates to clear the defendant's title.'

It remains to be seen in which direction this uncertainty will be resolved in the context of *proprietary* claims. On the other hand where a *personal* claim is brought, as for instance under recipient liability (see below, p 743), there seems a greater likelihood of a change of position defence being available as part of the developing law in this area.

What is then left to be determined here is the extent of a change of position defence. In *Lipkin Gorman v Karpnale Ltd* [1991] 2 AC 548 Lord Goff observed that the change of position defence to actions for restitution would have to develop on a case-by-case basis. Subsequent developments indicate that there must be some causal link between receipt of the claimant's property and the subsequent change of position by the defendant. This seems entirely consistent with Lord Goff's admonition that 'the mere fact that the defendant has spent the money, in whole or in part, does not of itself render it inequitable that he should be called upon to repay, because the expenditure might in any event have been incurred by him in the ordinary course of things' (at 581). It is clear that in most instances therefore defendants will seek to establish the defence by demonstrating that they have been 'disenriched' in some degree by reference to some explicit item of expenditure that would not have occurred *but for* the receipt of the misapplied assets. The defence was interpreted more widely in *Phillip Collins Ltd v Davis* [2000] 3 All ER 808 where two defendant musicians were entitled to royalties for their contribution to recordings by Phil Collins but by mistake were overpaid to the tune of $300,000 over a seven-year period. The judge accepted that even though they could not point to a specific expense incurred in reliance upon the payments, they had tailored their lifestyle to fit their means. He therefore allowed the defence to the extent of 50% of the claim against them. Subsequent authorities suggest that the defence *may* even be established where there is no 'direct disenrichment' as such but where, for instance, a defendant forgoes an opportunity to earn income or acquire assets (*Dextra Bank & Trust Co Ltd v Bank of Jamaica* [2002] 1 All ER (Comm) 193, PC) or even decides not to seek better paid employment (*Jones v Commerzbank AG* [2003] EWCA Civ 1663; see Birks (2004) 120 LQR 373–378).

Aside from the factual matter of establishing some change of position there remains the fundamental requirement of good faith: 'It is, of course, plain that the defence is not open to one who has changed his position in bad faith, as where the defendant has paid away the money with knowledge of the facts entitling the plaintiff to restitution; and it is commonly accepted that the defence should not be open to a wrongdoer' (Lord Goff in *Lipkin Gorman v Karpnale Ltd* at 580). Understanding what constitutes 'good faith' poses problems analogous to those that concern the meaning of 'knowledge' in the context of the liability of strangers for 'knowing receipt'. Discussion is therefore best deferred until that subject has been considered (see below, p 746).

(4) A restitutionary postscript

One of the points that separated the minority and majority opinions in *Foskett v McKeown* [2001] AC 102 was how to categorise the tracing process and the claim flowing from it. In this regard Lord Millett commented that 'this branch of the law is concerned with vindicating rights of property and not with reversing unjust enrichment'. This comment was also partly in respect of another point on which the majority and the minority judges disagreed: what implication was to be drawn from the fact that the premiums paid from the trust fund had, as events turned out, been unnecessary to ensure the payment of the £1m sum assured? It was this peculiarity of the facts that provided the basis for an argument put before the House couched in terms of the justice of the case and what would be a fair outcome in terms of entitlement to the £1m. This specific line of argument implicitly reflects a broader proposition developed predominantly in academic commentary that it is misleading to view the law on tracing either wholly or predominantly as part of the law of property. Instead, so the argument might run, a more coherent and logical approach to the law will be facilitated if we view the rules of tracing as a means to determine whether or not a defendant has been unjustly enriched at the claimant's expense. In short tracing is essentially part of the law of restitution (see eg Birks (1992) 45 (2) CLP 69; Birks (1997) 11(1) TLI 2; [2002] CLP 231; Burrows (2002) 117 LQR 412). From this perspective one virtue in separating the element of 'tracing' from that of 'claiming' is that it strips away or undermines what are claimed to be artificial or fictional presumptions about the transmission of title from the original misappropriated asset to its substitute(s).

Professor Burrows, an advocate of one mode of restitutionary analysis, argues that it is fictional in the case of a substitution of one asset for another to maintain that a claimant P's ownership of the original asset continues through to ownership of the substitute traced property simply because of P's ownership of that original asset. On the contrary Burrows argues that: 'the truth is that P is given a new title to reverse [the defendant] D's unjust enrichment at P's expense' ('Proprietary Restitution: Unmasking Unjust Enrichment' (2001) 117 LQR 412 at 418; see also a similar analysis in terms of unjust enrichment deployed by Birks 'Mixing and Tracing' (1992) 45(2) CLP 69; and 'Receipt' in Birks and Pretto (eds) *Breach of Trust* (2002) pp 215–220 at p 213 but cf the distinctive and contrasting views of Virgo whose analysis found an echo in the majority opinions in *Foskett v McKeown The Principles of the Law of Restitution* (1999) pp 11–16 and 'Vindicating Vindication' in Hudson (ed) *New Perspectives on Property Law, Obligations and Restitution* (2003) pp 203–222). Burrows accepts that P can have a *pure* proprietary claim to the original asset but not to the substitute and illustrates his argument with the following examples (ibid; footnotes omitted):

> If I own land, I own the oil under it. But this cannot, without invoking fiction, be extended to tracing through to substitutes. Ownership of a pig can explain ownership of the piglets but does not explain why P can be said to own the horse that D has obtained in substitution for the pig stolen from P. To reason from one to the other is to apply a very tempting but, in truth, fictional notion of property. Some added explanation is needed. Unjust enrichment supplies the explanation. The defendant has been enriched by the horse. The enrichment was at the claimant's expense in that the claimant could trace from his pig to the horse.

Where the enrichment is unjust then, so the argument runs, the original owner of the asset is given a title to the substitute asset under the law of unjust enrichment so as to reverse the enrichment. Whether the enrichment was or was not unjust, and therefore whether the original owner of the asset will obtain a title to the substitute asset in the way Burrows suggests, will depend on the circumstances. In the example the fact that the pig was stolen would indicate that D would be unable to rebut P's claim that the enrichment was unjust.

In response to the general proposition two brief comments only can be made here, brief because it is not possible to do full justice to the competing conceptual frameworks at this point and, moreover as will be seen below, the majority opinions in *Foskett v McKeown* specifically endorse a 'property law' analysis of the tracing process. First, it is not immediately clear why the boundaries of ownership should be drawn at the point of substitution. There is, in the above example, for instance, no *necessary* reason why the oil, or the piglets, should belong to the owners of the land or the pig respectively and not to the parish or the state or the Crown (cf eg the discussion of feudalism in Chapter 2). Ownership of the oil, or come to that the piglets, is therefore itself an artificial or fictional construct, albeit one firmly established by long-held rules of property law. In similar vein whilst one might concede that attributing ownership of the substituted asset is fictional in some degree, it is a fiction that is supported by equally well-established rules of property law. A second observation in response to the unjust enrichment analysis is that it might be argued that the 'unjust' element in the doctrine of unjust enrichment is itself as much a fictional construct as is the concept of property rights recognised in law. This is not to say that the current rules of tracing and their implications for proprietary claims should not be subject to debate and perhaps change. There is though a clear absence of consensus on the merits of doing so, as evidenced by the division of opinion in the House of Lords in *Foskett v McKeown*.

It will be recalled that each of the majority opinions in the House in that case expressly stated that they were applying rules of property. From this standpoint it was not necessary to decide the unjust enrichment issue of whether giving the claimants – the purchasers of the land from the deceased trustee Murphy – a rateable share of the life assurance policy moneys would not be to reverse an unjust enrichment in the hands of the beneficiaries of the policy – the innocent volunteer children – but instead to give the claimants a wholly unwarranted windfall. This unjust enrichment line of argument was firmly rejected by the majority judges in the House of Lords, Lord Browne-Wilkinson stating that: 'This case does not depend on whether it is fair, just and reasonable to give the purchasers an interest as a result of which the court in its discretion provides a remedy. It is a case of hard-nosed property rights. . . . [T]his windfall is enjoyed because of the rights which the purchasers enjoy under the law of property' (at 109). Lord Millett, with whom Lord Hoffmann agreed, explained his conclusion on this point as follows (at 127):

> The transmission of a claimant's property rights from one asset to its traceable proceeds is part of our law of property, not of the law of unjust enrichment. There is no 'unjust factor' to justify restitution (unless 'want of title' be one, which makes the point). The claimant succeeds if at all by virtue of his own title, not to reverse unjust enrichment. Property rights are determined by fixed rules and settled principles. They are not discretionary. They do not depend upon ideas of what is 'fair, just and reasonable'. Such concepts, which in reality mask decisions of legal policy, have no place in the law of property.

(e) The personal claim in equity

It is convenient to mention here that where the proprietary remedy against an innocent volunteer fails for one of the reasons given above, there *may* still remain the possibility of a personal action in equity against him. In *Re Diplock* [1948] Ch 465, as we have seen, executors mistakenly distributed large sums of money to numerous charities under the terms of a residuary bequest subsequently held invalid. In the context of the administration of an estate the House of Lords (*Ministry of Health v Simpson* [1951] AC 251) expressly affirmed the decision of the Court of Appeal that the next of kin, the rightful owners, had the right to bring *personal* actions against the innocent recipients of the property. It did not matter that the assets had been spent (cf the limits to the proprietary claim) or that the overpayment arose from a mistake of law by the personal representatives, or that the defendants, as innocent volunteers, were unaware of the mistake: 'it is prima facie at least a sufficient circumstance that the defendant . . . has received some share of the estate to which he was not entitled' (at [1948] Ch 465 at 503 per Lord Greene). The sole saving grace from the standpoint of the innocent recipients is that the Court of Appeal held that they should be liable only to the extent that the moneys paid in error could not be recovered from the personal representatives who were responsible for the mistake. In *Re Diplock* itself the claims against the personal representatives had been compromised and the amounts recovered from the individual charities were therefore proportionately reduced to reflect the amount paid by the executors under the terms of the compromise agreement. It follows, however, that there may be other circumstances where nothing can be recovered from personal representatives because of their insolvency or where they acted under the protection of an order of the court. Then the recipients will be liable for the whole of the payment wrongfully made.

We emphasise here only the possibility of such a personal action because it has been thought to be open to question whether the right is available where the mistake, whether of fact or of law, arises in the course of the administration of a trust, as opposed to the administration of the estate of a deceased person (see *Ministry of Health v Simpson* at 265–266 per Lord Simonds). However, the recognition of the 'change of position' defence by the House of Lords in *Lipkin Gorman v Karpnale Ltd* [1991] 2 AC 548 would seem to open up the possibility of the defence being available to a personal claim such as that in *Re Diplock*. If so, this would seem to remove one objection to the further development of the personal action. More significantly and, it must be emphasised, controversially, it may also pave the way for extending *Diplock* personal liability, as we might call it, to replace the current fault-based personal liability of a person who has 'knowingly received' misappropriated trust property (see below, p 746 et seq).

Consider the following points:

(1) 'When the route taken by the money or property is clearly visible and leads to its dissipation, the notion that the claimant's proprietary rights are then replaced by a new equitable charge over the defendant's free assets at the expense of his unsecured creditors surely cannot be countenanced either in principle or in policy, for their infusion of funds against a defeated expectation is as much a contribution to the swelling of the debtor's estate as the infusion of the tracing claimant' (Goode (1987) 103 LQR 433 at 447). This criticism is directed at Lord Templeman's comments, obiter, in *Space Investments* (above, p 732). (See also Jones (1988) King's Counsel 15, and *Liggett v Kensington* [1993] 1 NZLR 257.) The same criticism might conceivably be made of the flexible *El Ajou* charge or of 'backwards tracing'. Do you agree, contrary to the premise adopted by Professor Goode, that a claimant whose assets are held in trust by the defendant and are subsequently wrongfully dissipated, did not accept the same risk of loss as that taken by the general body of the insolvent defendant's creditors? If so, should that be a relevant consideration in deciding whether an equitable charge is justifiable?

(2) The Law Commission decides to review the present status of the rule in Clayton's case. Prepare a position paper (i) briefly summarising the current scope of the rule, and (ii) outlining the strengths and weaknesses of other options. (See Insolvency Law Review Committee (Cmnd 8558, 1982) paras 1076–1080; British Columbia Law Reform Commission *Report of Competing Rights to Mingled Property* (1983).)

(3) 'Whether equitable tracing is analysed as a remedy or alternatively as a process of asset identification is a matter of semantics. Its boundaries are dictated by the court's view of the merits of the plaintiff's claim; the court order – "the remedy" – is just formal confirmation of this, as the reasoning

in *El Ajou v Dollar Land Holdings (DLH)* [1993] 3 All ER 717 confirms.'
Discuss.

(4) Notwithstanding the proprietary nature of the remedies that accompany
equitable tracing, it cannot be assumed that 'trust property' is wholly
secured in the event of the insolvency of the trustee. Consider, for instance,
the position where before the trust property can be realised, it proves
necessary for a liquidator to carry out essential work of administration so
as to separate trust property from the insolvent's own property. Who should
bear this cost – the beneficiaries or the unsecured creditors of the insolvent
trustee? One answer is that the court *may,* under its inherent jurisdiction
to award remuneration, order that an allowance be made for the costs
incurred and skill and labour expended in administering the property.
The outcome may involve a sharing of the cost. Do you regard this as an
equitable outcome? (See *Berkeley Applegate (Investment Consultants) Ltd*
[1989] Ch 32, and *(No 3)* (1989) 5 BCC 803; *Re Local London Residential
Ltd (Liquidator's Costs)* [2004] 2 BCLC 72; and generally Anderson in
McKendrick (ed) *Commercial Aspects of Trusts and Fiduciary Obligations*
(1992) ch 9.)

(5) A statutory process of tracing has been incorporated in criminal law to
facilitate the recovery of property obtained through unlawful conduct (see
Proceeds of Crime Act 2002, ss 304–310).

3. Subrogation

If a negligently driven motor car damages my bicycle and myself, I may expect
to recover my loss from my insurers. They in turn will be entitled, in effect, to
step into my shoes and seek to recover their outlay from the tortious wrongdoer.
In short they will be 'subrogated' to my existing rights against the third party.
This is a remedy with an element of proprietary protection. If, for instance,
the insurers pay me but before they can bring an action against the wrongdoer
I recover damages from him, then the insurers will be entitled to assert an
equitable lien over the damages, a matter of some importance if I am insolvent
(see *Napier and Ettrick (Lord) v Hunter* [1993] AC 713; Jones [1993] Conv 391).

It is important for our purposes to distinguish that form of subrogation –
so-called 'simple subrogation' (see Mitchell and Watterson *Subrogation Law
and Practice* (2007)) – from the equitable remedy of subrogation that may arise
as a consequence of tracing. It will be recalled that in *Re Diplock* [1948] Ch 465
the administrators had in error paid to several charities moneys that were the
property of the next of kin. The charities had in turn used the moneys to pay
off debts both secured and unsecured. Could then the next of kin claim to
be subrogated to the rights of the creditors, who had been paid off with the
next of kin's money, against the charities – 'reviving subrogation' in Mitchell's
terminology? The Court of Appeal in *Re Diplock* held that debts which had
been extinguished could not be revived. We might say that as a consequence the

charities could have been, in a sense, unjustly enriched – by having those debts extinguished – at the expense of the next of kin. It is this position and the role of unjust enrichment 'as a remedy not a cause of action' which was reviewed by Millett LJ giving the judgment of the court in *Boscawen v Bajwa* ([1995] 4 All ER 769 at 777).

> [Subrogation] is available in a wide variety of different factual situations in which it is required in order to reverse the defendant's unjust enrichment. Equity lawyers speak of a right of subrogation, or of an equity of subrogation, but this merely reflects the fact that it is not a remedy which the court has a general discretion to impose whenever it thinks it just to do so. The equity arises from the conduct of the parties on well-settled principles and in defined circumstances which make it unconscionable for the defendant to deny the proprietary interest claimed by the plaintiff. A constructive trust arises in the same way. Once the equity is established the court satisfies it by declaring that the property in question is subject to a charge by way of subrogation in the one case or a constructive trust in the other.

In the somewhat complicated circumstances of *Boscawen v Bajwa*, money from building society A (Abbey National) was advanced to refinance the purchase of property from B and to redeem a legal charge held by building society H (Halifax) on that property. A intended for itself to have a charge on the property but the purchase fell through. In the event the property-owner B or to be more precise his judgment creditors – he was by now bankrupt – was in the position of having had the legal charge redeemed by A without its obtaining any charge on the property as security. In the proceedings the judgment creditors, of whom Boscawen was one, sought enforcement of a charging order absolute over the property which had been sold and the proceeds of £105,311.83 paid into court. The Abbey National (A) counterclaimed that it had priority over the judgment creditors because its moneys could be traced into the payment to H and it was therefore entitled to be subrogated to H's legal charge over the property. Judgment was given for A in the High Court and the judgment creditors appealed. In the following extract Millett LJ neatly summarises the gist of Abbey National's claim and emphasises the distinction to be drawn between tracing and subrogation (at 777):

> Tracing was the process by which the Abbey National sought to establish that its money was applied in the discharge of the Halifax's charge; subrogation was the remedy which it sought in order to deprive Mr Bajwa (through whom the appellants claim) of the unjust enrichment which he would thereby otherwise obtain at the Abbey National's expense.

The Court of Appeal, perhaps unsurprisingly with hindsight, held in favour of Abbey National, affirming in the process that a party claiming to be subrogated to a creditor's security did not have to prove (i) that it intended that its money should be used to discharge the security in question, or (ii) that it intended to obtain the benefit of the security by subrogation (see Birks (1995) 9(4) TLI 124; Andrews (1996) 65 CLJ 199; Oakley [1997] Conv 1). The superfluity of intention as a prerequisite was restated by Lord Hoffmann in *Banque Financière de la Cité v Parc (Battersea) Ltd* [1998] 1 All ER 737 where he also affirmed the distinctive nature of equitable subrogation as a remedy to prevent unjust enrichment (at 747):

> I think that it should be recognised that one here is concerned with a restitutionary remedy and that the appropriate questions are therefore, first, whether the defendant would be enriched at the plaintiff's expense; secondly, whether such enrichment would be unjust and thirdly, whether there are nevertheless reasons of policy for denying a remedy.

And there, save for one troubling question, we might leave subrogation, simply noting the re-emergence of a discretionary remedy seemingly located firmly within the firmament of restitution. What now is the status of *Re Diplock*? After all, following *Boscawen v Bajwa* and the endorsement of its reasoning in *Banque Financière de la Cité v Parc (Battersea) Ltd*, it would seem that even where a creditor's security or even an unsecured personal right (*Philby v Mortgage Express (No 2) Ltd* [2004] EWCA Civ 759) has been discharged the remedy of subrogation is available to a claimant/lender so as to *in effect* revive or resurrect the original creditor's security or even an unsecured personal right for the benefit of the lender. In *Boscawen v Bajwa* Millett LJ went to some length to suggest that the denial of a remedy to the next of kin in *Re Diplock* may need to be reviewed; he suggested that the emergence of a change of position defence (see above, p 730) meant that the sort of considerations of fairness that influenced the court in *Re Diplock* 'today . . . would be regarded as relevant to a change of position defence rather than as going to liability' (at 783). The inference to be drawn is that this approach would enable both a proper regard to be had to the respective positions of the parties and a flexible remedial approach to be adopted (see eg the hypothetical solution to *Re Diplock* posited by Millett LJ (ibid) and the innovative remedy awarded by the House of Lords in *Banque Financière de la Cité v Parc (Battersea) Ltd*; see Mitchell [1998] RLR 144).

4. 'Strangers', equitable personal liability, 'constructive trusteeship' and commercial considerations

(a) Introduction: the two categories of 'constructive trusteeship' or 'equitable personal liability'

In the introduction to this chapter we mentioned that in some circumstances third parties, or 'strangers', to the trustee-beneficiary or fiduciary-principal relationship may incur a *personal* liability to compensate for a loss caused to the beneficiary or principal. We also mentioned that such persons are somewhat misleadingly referred to as constructive trustees even though the trust in such circumstances is a strange creature – a propertyless phenomenon. The classic statement of the circumstances in which a constructive trusteeship will be so imposed on third parties, together with a warning about the unwelcome commercial consequences of over-extending its scope, is to be found in the judgment of Lord Selborne in *Barnes v Addy* (1874) 9 Ch App 244 at 251–252:

> Strangers are not to be made constructive trustees merely because they act as the agents of trustees in transactions within their legal powers, transactions, perhaps of which a Court of Equity may disapprove, unless those agents receive and become chargeable with some part of the trust property, or unless they assist with knowledge in a dishonest and fraudulent design on the part of the trustees.... If those principles were disregarded, I know not how anyone could, in transactions admitting of doubt as to the view which a Court of Equity might take of them, safely discharge the office of solicitor, of banker, or of agent of any sort to trustees. But, on the other hand, if persons dealing honestly as agents are at liberty to rely on the legal power of the trustees, and are not to have the character of trustees constructively imposed upon them, then the transactions of mankind can safely be carried through...

Lord Selborne's judgment is the source from which subsequent decisions of the courts developed two separate categories whereby constructive trusteeship may be imposed on a 'stranger'. The two categories have until recently been termed (1) 'knowing receipt' of, and dealing with, trust property and (2) 'knowing assistance' in a fraudulent design. A combination of recent decisions in the courts and academic criticism has rendered this terminology increasingly inappropriate. In its stead the terms 'recipient liability' and 'accessory liability' or 'dishonest assistance' are now becoming common currency (see eg Lord Nicholls in Cornish et al (eds) *Restitution: Past, Present and Future* (1998) ch 15). As we noted earlier in this chapter the terminology of 'constructive trusteeship' has also come under critical scrutiny. In *Dubai Aluminium Company Ltd v Salaam* [2003] 2 AC 366, Lord Millett sought to correct what he saw as both linguistic anomaly and conceptual confusion in the employment of the term 'constructive trustee' in these contexts, preferring instead to substitute the words 'accountable in equity'. However apposite the new phrase may be for 'accessory liability' it can be argued that the previous terminology of 'liable to account as a constructive trustee' remains relevant in the circumstances where a defendant received or handled misapplied trust property. Whatever terminology is employed, and the language of constructive trusteeship is inevitably prominent in many of the cases and much of the literature, the key factor to keep in mind is that it has to do only with a personal claim against the recipient or accessory.

As regards 'accessory liability' the change of name reflects an important shift in the law as a result of the decisions of the Privy Council in *Royal Brunei Airlines Sdn Bhd v Tan* [1995] 2 AC 378 and *Barlow Clowes International Ltd v Eurotrust International Ltd* [2006] 1 WLR 1476 and of the House of Lords in *Twinsectra v Yardley* [2002] 2 AC 164. Suffice to say for the moment that 'accessory liability' of the stranger depends on his lack of honesty but no longer requires the existence of some 'dishonest and fraudulent design on the part of the trustees' – mere breach of trust will suffice. What constitutes dishonesty for this purpose is itself a contentious matter (see below, p 760).

There is one further introductory, albeit fundamental, matter to mention at this point and which is implicit in the change in terminology. Influential academic and judicial voices have urged that recipient liability *should become* recognised as restitution-based in the sense that the stranger, irrespective of any wrongdoing on its part, who receives misdirected trust property should be held strictly liable to make restitution to the trust subject to there being a change of position defence for the innocent recipient. Lord Nicholls, for instance, writing extra-judicially and regretting that no case on recipient liability has reached the House of Lords for many years, has revealingly commented: ' . . . nothing is more important for the future rational development of "knowing receipt" than that its role within restitution is fully appreciated and examined by the judiciary' (in Cornish et al (eds) *Restitution: Past, Present and Future* (1998) at pp 234–235, citing with approval Burrows *The Law of Restitution* (1993) p 150; see also Birks 'Receipt' in Birks and Pretto (eds) *Breach of Trust* (2002) pp 213–240; and Lord Walker (2005) Sydney LR 187). Nevertheless, we emphasised 'should become' because it must be appreciated that most of the cases on recipient liability have operated on the understandable premise that recipient liability has been and remains, for the moment, fault-based as is also the position for 'accessory liability'. It is worth emphasising that the available remedies against the stranger can differ depending on which of the two categories is applicable to the facts of any given case. Where the stranger 'knowingly receives' trust property for its own use and benefit in breach of trust, then the property or substitute assets might be traceable into the stranger's hands. The stranger will then hold the property or its substitute on constructive trust for the beneficiary/principal. This assumes, of course, that the stranger is not a bona fide purchaser for value without notice. But what if the stranger no longer has the property or its substitute? Then the courts may, in the alternative, hold the defendant *personally* liable to account as if a constructive trustee to make restitution to the claimant. On the other hand, where the stranger did not handle or receive trust property, but 'dishonestly assisted' in a breach of trust there is no possibility of a proprietary claim being successful, there being no traceable assets. Instead the court may only impose a personal liability upon the stranger to account in equity for losses to the beneficiary/principal.

In *Barnes v Addy* Lord Selborne was principally concerned to emphasise the practical importance of setting limits to the scope of the remedies, particularly as they might affect agents. As part of the normal process of delegation in trust management, such persons as solicitors or bankers may be temporarily in possession of trust property. But this does not necessarily mean that if their conduct in relation to the trust property is inconsistent with the terms of the trust, they are to be liable as constructive trustees. Heeding Lord Selborne's warning, courts have emphasised the need to protect agents who act honestly within the scope of their agency, even if, by following the trustees' instructions, they participate in some breach of trust. Sachs LJ has pointed out that 'where the agent of the trustee acts honestly and confines himself to the duties of an agent then, though he will not be accountable to the beneficiaries, they will have their remedy against the persons who are the trustees' (*Carl-Zeiss-Stiftung v Herbert Smith & Co (No 2)* [1969] 2 Ch 276 at 299; and see in particular *Mara v Browne* [1896] 1 Ch 199; *Williams-Ashman v Price and Williams* [1942] Ch 219).

On the other hand, and to reiterate the point, a 'stranger' who receives and improperly deals with trust property (as may occur, for instance, when a bank applies trust money to reduce a personal overdraft owing to it: see *Westpac Banking Corpn v Savin* [1985] 2 NZLR 41, NZCA), or who participates in a breach of trust on the part of a trustee or fiduciary, may be subject to a personal liability, under one or other of the two categories just outlined.

The context in which liability is sought to be imposed on third parties is by no means restricted to the trustee-beneficiary relationship. On the contrary the circumstances often involve fraud on the part of other fiduciaries and are commonly linked to complex commercial transactions. The earlier authorities tended to be corporate fraud cases, usually involving a company purchasing its own shares – conduct unlawful initially under the Companies Act 1948, s 54, now replaced by the Companies Act 2006 Part 18 – and the participation of others such as banks who are or claim to be unaware of what is being done. Other cases involve international fraud where the fraudsters may use the services of accountants and lawyers and their nominee companies, especially in offshore tax havens, for money laundering. The amounts involved can be substantial. It is estimated that the financial services sector in the UK, for instance, is losing some £11 billion per year from economic crime including fraud and money laundering (RSM Robson Rhodes Economic Crime Survey 2004). (On money laundering generally see the website of the inter-governmental body, The Financial Action Task Force (FATF), www.fatf-gafi.org; Alldridge *Money Laundering Law* (2003); Millington and Sutherland *The Proceeds of Crime* (2nd edn, 2006) and the EC Third Money Laundering Directive 2005/60/EC implemented in Money Laundering Regulations 2007, SI 2007/2157.)

In such circumstances obtaining a remedy against a third party is often of considerable practical importance for the beneficiary or principal. Primary redress against the trustee or fiduciary may be useless because this person is insolvent or has absconded (or both). The trust property may have been dissipated by the fraud or other breach complained of. Alternatively, it may be untraceable – either in the practical sense (eg where it has been transmitted into money in a numbered Swiss bank account), or in a legal sense (eg where it is beyond the reach of the tracing procedure because it has been transferred to a bona fide purchaser for value who has no notice of the breach). On the other hand, the type of 'strangers' who may be made liable under 'recipient' or 'accessory' liability principles are often solvent, indeed affluent, corporations, such as banks and building societies. They are attractive defendants for aggrieved beneficiaries or principals to have within their sights.

Before proceeding to consider in closer detail the two heads of personal liability to which strangers can be subject, it is appropriate, if somewhat disquieting, to warn the reader against any expectation that the law in this area is in an unambiguous and ordered state. On the contrary, exposition and understanding of the law is hampered by conceptual confusion about the criteria for imposing liability and by prescriptive controversy about the direction that the law should take. Arguments for a reconsideration of the present law, such as those advanced by Lord Nicholls, are not provoked solely by pure conceptualist considerations. Those considerations themselves also reflect to some degree a disquiet at the fact that there exists such a diversity of remedies available for any particular unauthorised disposition of property in breach of trust. Aside from possible actions for knowing receipt and dishonest assistance there may also be the possibility of a *personal* unjust enrichment claim at law on the basis of money had and received, and of successful tracing leading to *proprietary* claims, both at law and in equity, against recipients of the original assets or their substitutes. This plethora of actions is all of course in addition to a personal action in equity against whoever was responsible for the original breach of trust.

In our view it is therefore necessary when seeking to understand the scope and direction of the law on 'recipient' and 'accessory' liability to keep in mind those other possible heads of liability and also the wider vision about the future direction of the law.

(b) Recipient liability and 'knowing receipt'

(1) Introduction

Under this limited category – the 'dishonest assistance' category being much more sweeping – there are three distinct requirements to be met for liability to be imposed. There must be (i) a disposal of assets in breach of trust or fiduciary duty, (ii) *beneficial* receipt by the defendant – not receipt or dealing as, for example, an agent – of the assets or their traceable product and (iii) knowledge that the property received was transferred in breach of trust or fiduciary duty (*El Ajou v Dollar Land Holdings* [1994] 2 All ER 685 at 700 per Hoffmann LJ). This straightforward formula incorporates several distinct and difficult questions. In part these questions spring from there being two categories of strangers in knowing receipt cases, the volunteer and the purchaser. The recurrent theme, however, is that of knowledge. As regards the innocent volunteer, if she still has the trust property or its traceable equivalent, then of course she must return the property or account for its value. But otherwise the central issue is the degree of knowledge required of that person before personal liability for 'knowing receipt' will attach so that the attribute of innocence no longer applies. Unfortunately differences of judicial opinion as to the degree of knowledge required for 'knowing receipt liability' to be imposed have not made that issue a straightforward one. Discussion has until recently focused around a five-fold criterion of knowledge propounded by Peter Gibson J in *Baden Delvaux and Lecuit v Société Générale* [1983] BCLC 325 (see below) whereas latterly notions of 'dishonesty' and 'unconscionability' have been advanced as alternative criteria. The divergence of views as to the appropriate criteria for satisfying the 'knowledge' requirement has inevitably generated a degree of uncertainty in the law although, at the time of writing, in terms of precedent, 'unconscionability' has the recent authority of the Court of Appeal to support it (*BCCI (Overseas) Ltd v Akindele* [2001] Ch 437).

Where the stranger is not a volunteer, but a contracting party, the picture is still more complex. The contracting party – the 'stranger' – may claim it cannot be liable as if a constructive trustee as it is a bona fide purchaser of the property without notice. The issue then posed is what levels of *notice* for the bona fide purchaser defence and of *knowledge* for the knowing receipt personal liability claim are respectively required. In particular, is the same standard applicable to both concepts? Indeed, should knowledge and notice be treated as synonymous? A firm statement of principle against aligning the concepts of knowledge and notice was advanced by Sir Robert Megarry VC in *Re Montagu's Settlement Trusts* [1992] 4 All ER 308. This was premised on his view that the doctrines relating to 'purchaser without notice' and to 'constructive trusteeship for knowing receipt' are concerned with matters that differ in important respects (at 320):

> The [doctrine of purchaser without notice] is concerned with the question whether a person takes property subject to or free from some equity. [Knowing receipt] is concerned with whether or not a person is to have imposed upon him the personal burdens and obligations of trusteeship. I do not see why one of the touchstones for determining the burdens on property should be the same as that for deciding whether to impose a personal obligation on a man. The cold calculus of constructive and imputed notice does not seem to me to be an appropriate instrument for deciding whether a man's conscience is sufficiently affected for it to be right to bind him by the obligations of a constructive trustee.

An inference to be drawn from this approach is that in theory a person may be deemed to have 'notice' for the purposes of a proprietary claim where property is received in breach of trust but may not have the requisite knowledge for the purposes of a knowing receipt claim once the property is dissipated. It should be noted, however, that the 'cold calculus of constructive and imputed notice' is a concept most apparent where the property being transferred consists of legal title to land since there the doctrines of actual and constructive notice have a specific and well-established content. Even if, in relation to land, one accepts the proposition advanced by Megarry it does not necessarily follow that for other assets the degree of 'knowledge' relevant to establishing liability in knowing receipt need differ from the requirement of 'notice' for the purposes of the bona fide purchaser defence. In particular it must not be overlooked that whilst *Re Montagu's Settlement Trust* was concerned with a family trust context – the gratuitous and mistaken transfer of chattels by executors to a legatee – it is in predominantly commercial situations that the controversy over knowing receipt has arisen.

In *Polly Peck International plc v Nadir (No 2)* [1992] 4 All ER 769 a different view was taken of the requirements of knowledge and notice but this time in the context of an alleged international fraud involving transfers and exchanges of currencies. Whilst Scott LJ (with whom the other judges agreed on this point) considered that notice and knowledge were not synonymous terms, he found that 'the degree of knowledge on the part of [the defendant] that PPI must establish for the purpose of its [in personam] constructive trust case is . . . requisite also for the purposes of its equitable [proprietary] tracing claim' (at 782). In contrast to the comments and approach of Megarry VC in *Re Montagu's Settlement Trusts* (see above) Scott LJ equated the requirements of notice necessary for the bona fide purchaser defence to a proprietary claim with the degree of knowledge required for personal liability based on knowing receipt. He justified this by distinguishing the tracing of money from the tracing of land or valuable chattels. Scott LJ considered that in tracing land and valuable chattels actual or constructive *notice* was sufficient. However, he held that in tracing money actual or constructive *knowledge* rather than notice was necessary. Bryan (1993) 109 LQR 368 argues that 'there is little to commend' Scott LJ's distinction and that it runs counter to established authority (see *Re Diplock* and *Re Montagu's Settlement Trusts* [1987] 2 WLR 1192; [1992] 4 All ER 308 per Megarry VC; but cf Fox (1998) 57 CLJ 391; Jaffey (2001) 15(3) TLI 151 at 154–155; and generally Gardner (1996) 112 LQR 56 at 58–70). The outcome of Scott LJ's decision would *seem* to make it easier for a defendant to resist the proprietary claim, ie by apparently increasing the level of knowledge required of the defendant for the proprietary claim to be established, at least where the asset to be traced is money. But this conclusion depends on what Scott LJ means by knowledge, an issue to which we now turn.

(2) Commerce, recipient liability and a 'knowledge' requirement

It is therefore necessary to consider in that commercial context just how rigorous a duty of inquiry should be expected of a stranger who beneficially receives but does not retain trust property transferred in breach of trust. In legal and in policy terms the key question remains: how far should liability be imposed on a person (including a company) not because of what it knows but because of what it ought to know, or because of facts about which it ought to have made inquiries? Although not the final or definitive word on the subject the categorisation of the possible relevant types of knowledge advanced by Peter Gibson J in *Baden Delvaux* still provides a convenient starting-point for analysis ([1983] BCLC 325 at [250]):

What types of knowledge are relevant for the purposes of constructive trusteeship? Mr Price submits that knowledge can comprise any one of five different mental states which he described as follows: (i) actual knowledge; (ii) wilfully shutting one's eyes to the obvious; (iii) wilfully and recklessly failing to make such inquiries as an honest and reasonable man would make; (iv) knowledge of circumstances which would indicate the facts to an honest and reasonable man; (v) knowledge of circumstances which would put an honest and reasonable man on inquiry. More accurately, apart from actual knowledge they are formulations of the circumstances which may lead the court to impute knowledge of the facts to the alleged constructive trustee even though he lacked actual knowledge of those facts. Thus the court will treat a person as having constructive knowledge of the facts if he wilfully shuts his eyes to the relevant facts which would be obvious if he opened his eyes, such constructive knowledge being usually termed (though by a metaphor of historical inaccuracy) 'Nelsonian knowledge'. Similarly the court may treat a person as having constructive knowledge of the facts (type (iv) knowledge) if he has actual knowledge of circumstances which would indicate the facts to an honest and reasonable man.

Which of the five levels of knowledge will result in liability for the recipient of trust property, bearing in mind as we must still do, that the liability has formally at least been fault-based? In particular, when should a person who has not made inquiries be liable for failing to do so?

In *Polly Peck International plc v Nadir (No 2)* Scott LJ accepted that actual knowledge (*Baden* level (i)) and wilfully and recklessly failing to make such inquiries as an honest and reasonable man would have made (*Baden* level (iii)) would meet the knowledge requirements for the personal liability claim against the defendant bank. However, he considered that knowledge of facts that would put an honest and reasonable man on inquiry (*Baden* level (v)) might not be sufficient for liability. Scott LJ was of the opinion, however, that the *Baden* levels of knowledge were not rigid categories but 'may merge imperceptibly into [one] another'. In Scott LJ's view, therefore, the real question was whether the circumstances in which the currency transfers were made – there were 117 of them – should have made the defendant bank suspicious of the propriety of what was being done. The circumstances were that at the time of the transfers of sterling the then head of Polly Peck International and the instigator of the fraudulent transfers, Asil Nadir, was a man of unblemished commercial reputation and integrity, who presided over a group of companies with a massive and increasing annual turnover. Scott LJ considered that although the transfers were large there was no reason that the defendant bank should have suspected impropriety, especially as there were other explanations for the size of the transfers. He stated that the test is 'not satisfied by the inference of no more than curiosity' (at 778).

Another fraud case in which analysis of the degree of knowledge required for knowing receipt was undertaken, this time by Millett J, was *El Ajou v Dollar Land Holdings plc* [1993] 3 All ER 717. As mentioned previously, the investment manager of El Ajou was bribed by three Canadians into buying worthless shares with EA's money. The Canadians channelled the funds through various countries and ultimately used the funds to buy a share in a property development project with DLH. Later DLH bought out the Canadians' share with knowledge that they were being investigated for some form of irregular conduct. EA brought an action against DLH, for personal liability for knowing receipt on the basis that DLH received the money from the Canadians with knowledge that it represented the proceeds of fraud or, alternatively, that at the time DLH bought the Canadians' interest in the project it did so with knowledge of their fraud. In its defence, DLH argued (i) that it had no knowledge of the fraud, and (ii) that in purchasing the Canadians' interest it was a bona fide purchaser for value without notice. Millett J commented on the degree of knowledge necessary to establish the defence as follows (at 739):

> For my own part I agree that even where the plaintiff's claim is a proprietary one, and the defendant raises the defence of bona fide purchaser for value without notice, there is no room for the doctrine of constructive notice in the strict conveyancing sense in a factual situation where it is not the custom and practice to make inquiry. But it does not follow that there is no room for an analogous doctrine in a situation in which any honest and reasonable man would have made inquiry. Vinelott J [in *Eagle Trust plc v SBC Securities Ltd* [1992] 4 All ER 488 at 509–510] held that the knowledge might be inferred if the circumstances were such that an honest and reasonable man would have inferred that the moneys were probably trust moneys and were being misapplied. He left open the question whether a recipient might escape liability if the court was satisfied that, although an honest and reasonable man would have realised this, through foolishness or inexperience [an honest defendant] did not in fact suspect it.
>
> That question does not arise in the present case.

Without deciding the point, Millett J was prepared to presume that, at least in high-level commercial dealings with corporate assets, a person would be personally liable under the category of 'knowing receipt' if he went ahead without further inquiry in circumstances in which an honest and reasonable man would have realised that the money was probably trust money and was being misapplied. However, he considered that 'a recipient is not expected to be unduly suspicious' (at 739). A similar sentiment, although specifically concerning the meaning of constructive notice [sic] in a *proprietary* action to establish priority in ownership of wrongfully transferred shares, was expressed by Millett J in *Macmillan Inc v Bishopsgate Investment Trust Plc* [1995] 3 All ER 747 (at 783): 'Account officers are not detectives. Unless and until they are alerted to the possibility of wrongdoing, they proceed, and are entitled to proceed, on the assumption that they are dealing with honest men.' (See the Epilogue at 782–783 for the factual background prompting the judge's comments; see also in the context of banking Steyn J in *Barclays Bank plc v Quincecare Ltd* [1992] 4 All ER 363 at 377: '[T]rust, not distrust, is also the basis of a bank's dealings with its customers.')

At this point it is tempting to sympathise with the stoical sentiment in Sir Robert Megarry's judgment in *Re Montagu's Settlement Trust* [1992] 4 All ER 308 where he declined to attempt to 'reconcile all the authorities and dicta, for such a task is beyond me; and in this I suspect I am not alone' (at 329). Subsequent decisions have if anything added to the problem of reconciliation. It is nevertheless possible on the basis of the authorities prior to the Court of Appeal decision in *Bank of Credit and Commerce International (Overseas) Limited (BCCI) v Akindele* [2000] 4 All ER 221 to identify four different propositions about the level of knowledge required for 'knowing receipt' liability.

One proposition is that any of the five categories of knowledge identified in *Baden Delvaux* will suffice for the imposition of liability (see eg Millett J in *Agip (Africa) v Jackson* [1990] Ch 265 at 290), against which one can point to the judgment of Megarry VC in *Re Montague's Settlement Trusts* as offering a second proposition. He conceded that knowledge is not confined to actual knowledge and extends to include *Baden Delvaux* categories (ii) and (iii) but added the following reservation: 'Whether knowledge of the Baden types (iv) and (v) suffices . . . is at best doubtful; in my view it does not, for I cannot see that the carelessness involved will normally amount to a want of probity' (ibid). The third proposition, a variant on the Megarry position, specifically alludes to the commercial context and argues that only the first three of the Baden categories are relevant in that context and that, therefore, Baden categories (iv) and (v) can be relevant, if at all, in non-commercial transactions only (*Eagle Trust plc v SBC Securities* [1992] 4 All ER 488; and *Cowan de Groot Properties v Eagle Trust plc* [1992] 4 All ER 700). Against that view it should be noted that there are decisions of Commonwealth courts that have expressed a preference for the view that 'constructive knowledge' can be sufficient to establish liability even in commercial transactions (see eg *Westpac Banking Corpn v Savin* [1985] 2 NZLR 41, CA; *Citadel General Assurance Co v Lloyds Bank Canada* (1997) 152 DLR (4th) 411, a decision of the Supreme Court of Canada). Lastly, it has been contended that the test for 'knowledge' in knowing receipt is and should be the same as that for 'dishonesty' in dishonest assistance (see *Dubai Aluminium Co v Salaam* [2000] 2 Lloyd's Rep 168 at 172, CA; and *Bank of America v Arnell* [1999] Lloyd's Rep Bank 399 at 406).

(3) Commerce, recipient liability and 'unconscionability'

The various criteria and leading authorities were reviewed by the Court of Appeal in *BCCI (Overseas) Ltd v Akindele* [2000] 4 All ER 221 where the conclusion was reached that 'the recipient's state of knowledge must be such as to make it "unconscionable" for him to retain the benefit of the receipt'. In the transaction in question certain directors of BCCI (Overseas) Ltd entered into an artificial loan arrangement with the defendant Akindele (A), the immediate purpose of which, along with other transactions, was to make it appear to the outside world that the bank was better financed than was in fact the case. Under the arrangement (A) paid US$10m to the company in exchange for shares on the understanding that the shares would subsequently be repurchased at a price that would give the defendant a 15% annual return on his investment. The liquidators of the insolvent bank sought to recover A's profit of US$6.679m – A received US$16.679m from the company – alleging both dishonest assistance and knowing receipt on the part of A. Neither claim succeeded in the High Court where Carnwath J proceeded on the assumption that 'dishonesty in one form or another' – and he appeared to equate this with any of the Baden categories (i) to (iii) – was a prerequisite for liability for both 'dishonest assistance' and 'knowing receipt'. Nourse LJ, giving the opinion of the Court of Appeal, disagreed with the application of a 'dishonesty' test for the knowing receipt category, stating that (at 229): 'the judge's omission to distinguish between the questions of knowledge and dishonesty, was incorrect in law. While a knowing recipient will often be found to have acted dishonestly, it has never been a prerequisite of the liability that he should.'

Nourse LJ then proceeded to consider the question 'If not dishonesty what should be the criterion for imposing liability?', identifying the problem in the following way (at 231):

> With the proliferation in the last 20 years or so of cases in which the misapplied assets of companies have come into the hands of third parties, there has been a sustained judicial and extra judicial debate as to the knowledge on the part of the recipient which is required in order to found liability in knowing receipt. Expressed in its simplest terms, the question is whether the recipient must have actual knowledge (or the equivalent) that the assets received are traceable to a breach of trust or whether constructive knowledge is enough. The instinctive approach of most equity judges, especially in this court, has been to assume that constructive knowledge is enough. But there is now a series of decisions of eminent first instance judges who, after considering the question in greater depth, have come to the contrary conclusion, at all events when commercial transactions are in point. In the Commonwealth, on the other hand, the preponderance of authority has been in favour of the view that constructive knowledge is enough.

Nourse LJ reviewed in some detail the conflicting English and Commonwealth authorities and continued (at 235):

> [...] I have grave doubts about the utility [of identifying different states of knowledge] in cases of knowing receipt. Quite apart from its origins in a context of knowing assis-tance ... any categorisation is of little value unless the purpose it is to serve is adequately defined, whether it be fivefold, as in the *Baden* case [1993] 1 WLR 509, or twofold, as in the classical division between actual and constructive knowledge, a division which has itself become blurred in recent authorities.
>
> What then, in the context of knowing receipt, is the purpose to be served by a cate-gorisation of knowledge? It can only be to enable the court to determine whether, in the words of Buckley LJ in *Belmont Finance Corpn Ltd v Williams Furniture Ltd* (No 2) [1980] 1 All ER 393, 405, the recipient can 'conscientiously retain [the] funds against the company'

or, in the words of Sir Robert Megarry VC in *In re Montagu's Settlement Trusts* [1987] Ch 264, 273, '[the recipient's] conscience is sufficiently affected for it to be right to bind him by the obligations of a constructive trustee'. But, if that is the purpose, there is no need for categorisation. All that is necessary is that the recipient's state of knowledge should be such as to make it unconscionable for him to retain the benefit of the receipt.

For these reasons I have come to the view that, just as there is now a single test of dishonesty for knowing assistance, so ought there to be a single test of knowledge for knowing receipt. The recipient's state of knowledge must be such as to make it unconscionable for him to retain the benefit of the receipt. A test in that form, though it cannot, any more than any other, avoid difficulties of application, ought to avoid those of definition and allocation to which the previous categorisations have led. Moreover, it should better enable the courts to give commonsense decisions in the commercial context in which claims in knowing receipt are now frequently made ...

Adopting a test of unconscionability inevitably invites the criticism that whilst it may provide a linguistically precise criterion this is deceptive in that in application it offers no clearer guidance than its predecessors as to when liability for knowing receipt might be imposed (see eg Birks in Birks and Pretto (eds) *Breach of Trust* (2002) ch 7 at 226; see also the doubts expressed by Lord Nicholls below at p 755). This practical consequence is, of course, recognised by Nourse LJ although sceptics may doubt whether invoking the notion of 'commonsense decisions in the commercial context' necessarily provides an adequate response. Nevertheless, two particular points of guidance can, in our view, be inferred from that reference to 'commonsense decisions'. One is that, for all practical purposes, what constitutes knowledge in any given case is a question of fact for the court. The other point is that unconscionability does not depend on the individual moral compass of the recipient; what constitutes knowledge will be inferred from the relevant facts, including the behaviour of the defendant, in the particular commercial context. And therein lies a further problem. In general terms do we expect a particular standard of commercial morality to be applied in such cases and if so what is it? Should the law be standard reflecting or standard setting? More specifically the underlying questions about knowledge and the duty to inquire remain central issues for the law on knowing receipt: should liability be imposed on a person (including a company) not just because of what it knows but because of what it ought to know, or because of facts about which it ought to have made inquiries? Commonsense decisions will explicitly or implicitly have to adopt some benchmark as to the extent of investigation to be expected in commercial arrangements if the participants are to be confident of avoiding recipient liability.

And what of the defendant Chief Akindele? He retained his money. Nourse LJ held that on the facts as found by Carnwath J the defendant's conduct was not unconscionable, adding perhaps significantly for our understanding of unconscionability (at 238, emphasis added): 'Equally ... I would have held that the defendant did not have *actual or constructive knowledge* that his receipt of the US$6.79m [sic] was traceable to a breach or breaches of fiduciary duty by [the employees].'

(4) Commerce, recipient liability and restitution

It is tempting to conclude that these difficulties of determining what constitutes the necessary degree of fault for knowing receipt liability would disappear if, as has been widely argued, recipient liability in equity were to be 'harmonised' with liability at common law under the rubric of the law of restitution. In *El Ajou v Dollar Land Holdings plc* [1993] 3 All ER 717 at 739 Millett J (as he then was), an influential proponent of this view, commented that the 'requirements in respect of knowledge for the common law claim for money had and received, the personal claim for an account in equity against a knowing recipient and the equitable proprietary claim' should not be different, as this would inhibit the development of a 'logical and coherent system of restitution'. He repeated this view in his opinion in *Twinsectra v Yardley* [2002] 2 AC 164 adding (at 194): 'There is powerful academic support for the proposition that the liability of the recipient is the same as in other cases of restitution, that is to say strict but subject to a change of position defence.' These statements do, of course, represent a prescription of what the judge perceives as a desirable outcome rather than a description of the present state of the authorities. Although there are differences of nuance amongst the proponents, the essence of the proposition is that those who receive misappropriated or misapplied trust property should be held strictly accountable subject only to the defences of change of position or, in the case of a proprietary claim only, of bona fide purchaser for value since otherwise they would be unjustly enriched (see eg Birks [1989] LMCLQ 296; 'Receipt' in Birks and Pretto (eds) *Breach of Trust* (2002) ch 7; Millett (1995) 9 TLI 35; *Powell v Thompson* [1991] 1 NZLR 597, discussed by Rickett (1991) 11 OJLS 598 at 602; and see the important essay by Lord Nicholls in Cornish et al (eds) *Restitution: Past, Present and Future* (1998) and the reassertion of his view, obiter, in *Criterion Properties plc v Stratford UK Properties LLC* [2004] 1 WLR 1846 at 1848; but cf the decision of the High Court of Australia in *Farah Constructions Pty Ltd v Say-Dee Pty Ltd* [2007] HCA 22 strongly reaffirming the fault-based liability approach; (2007) 66(3) CLJ 515; Hayton (2007) 21(2) TLI 55; (2008) 124 LQR 26). In fact the approach suggested by Lord Nicholls is more nuanced than that of some proponents of a 'strict liability' approach in that he appears to envisage the possible retention of a fault-based liability for 'knowing receipt' where the recipient is shown to have actual guilty knowledge. But alongside this fault-based liability there could arise strict liability for the innocent or negligent recipient subject to a change of position defence (see also Lord Walker (2005) Sydney LR 187 at 202 endorsing this approach). It is evident, however, that pursuing the path advocated by some of a shift from a 'fault-based' criterion to one of strict liability does not remove considerations of 'fault' from the equation. If, as is certainly the case, a change of position defence requires good faith on the part of the defendant then this will entail elaboration of what constitutes 'good faith'. It is difficult to see why precisely the same type of questions about 'knowledge' and 'notice' that have proved so perplexing for 'knowing receipt' will not reappear in this new context. In *Niru Battery Manufacturing Co v Milestone Trading Ltd (No 1)* [2002] 2 All ER (Comm) 705, for instance, Moore-Bick J concluded that lack of good faith 'is capable of embracing a failure to act in a commercially acceptable way and sharp practice of a kind that falls short of outright dishonesty as well as dishonesty itself' (at [135]; see also *Papamichael v National Westminster Bank Plc* [2003] 1 Lloyd's Rep 341 at 369: 'wilfully and recklessly failing to make such inquiries as an honest and reasonable man would make'). The Court of Appeal in the *Niru* case ([2004] 1 Lloyd's Rep 344) upheld the decision of Moore-Bick J although Clarke and Sedley LJJ both referred to the 'knowing receipt' criteria in *BCCI v Akindele* and controversially concluded that a defendant could not establish the change of position defence in circumstances where it would be 'inequitable or unconscionable, and thus unjust' to do so (at [162] and [192]; see the critical comments of Birks (2004) 120 LQR 373; Burrows (2004) 63(2) CLJ 276 at 280: '[T]akes us back to the dark ages of the subject'; Ellinger (2005) 121 LQR 51).

Even if one were to agree with the suggested realignment of common law and equitable liability in this area it is clear that the underlying issue of 'fault' would remain but relocated so that the burden of proof would have shifted formally from the claimant to the defendant. This was one of the consequences that led Nourse LJ in *BCCI v Akindele* to express reservations about the desirability and practicability of strict liability restitution superseding the present fault-based system in the manner proposed by Lord Nicholls. The following comments of Nourse LJ are strictly obiter, no attempt having been made to argue the case on a strict liability restitutionary basis (at 236):

> While in general it may be possible to sympathise with a tendency to subsume a further part of our law of restitution under the principles of unjust enrichment, I beg leave to doubt whether strict liability coupled with a change of position defence would be preferable to fault-based liability in many commercial transactions, for example where, as here, the receipt is of a company's funds which have been misapplied by its directors. Without having heard argument it is unwise to be dogmatic, but in such a case it would appear to be commercially unworkable ... that, simply on proof of an internal misapplication of the company's funds, the burden should shift to the recipient to defend the receipt either by a change of position or perhaps in some other way.

Whether 'commercial unworkability' is a real obstacle to an acceptance of the 'strict liability approach' is difficult to determine in the absence of detailed argument or indeed empirical evidence as to the compliance cost of the approach. It is though difficult to find flaw with the point made by Lionel Smith that under the strict liability approach 'there is no procedure which a bank, be it ever so honest, can adopt in order to ensure that it is not prima facie liable for the receipt of trust funds' ((2000) 116 LQR 412 at 435). Smith goes on to argue that '[p]rima facie liability implies potentially extended periods of expense and uncertainty when litigation is pending . . . ' (ibid).

In any event, and by way of summary, the decision of the Court of Appeal in *BCCI (Overseas) Ltd v Akindele* has confirmed that liability for knowing receipt remains fault-based and that the single test for liability is 'unconscionability'. Nevertheless the fact that supporters of a strict liability approach include influential judicial voices such as Lords Nicholls and Walker as well as the recently retired Lord Millett means that future reform cannot be ruled out. Indeed the House of Lords may take the opportunity offered by the appeal in *Charter Plc v City Index Ltd and others* [2008] Ch 313 CA to pronounce on the nature of liability for knowing receipt although the central issue in the appeal is the interpretation and application of the Civil Liability (Contribution) Act 1978 (Gardner (2009) 125(1) LQR 20–24).

Consider the following points:

(1) In circumstances *not* involving a transfer of land, would you agree that the requirements of 'notice' and 'knowledge' applicable respectively to the proprietary and personal claims are now in effect synonymous? (Cf Vinelott J in *Eagle Trust plc v SBC Securities Ltd* [1993] 1 WLR 484 at 504–506 and Millett J in *El Ajou* (above but see also *Macmillan Inc v Bishopsgate Investment Trust plc (No 3)* [1995] 1 WLR 978); and see generally Moriarty in Birks (ed) *Laundering and Tracing* (1995); Gardner (1996) 112 LQR 56; and the Canadian Supreme Court decisions in *Gold v Rosenberg* (1997) 152 DLR (4th) 385 and *Citadel General Assurance Co v Lloyds Bank Canada* (1997) 152 DLR (4th) 411).

(2) Should 'carelessness' on the part of a recipient ever be sufficient to justify the imposition of knowing receipt liability on 'the volunteer' or on 'the purchaser'? In the pensions surplus case of *Hillsdown Holdings plc v Pensions Ombudsman* [1997] 1 All ER 862 Knox J reasserted the view that in a case where there was no dishonesty – 'an honest muddle' – then liability for knowing receipt should depend on 'whether the conscience of the recipient is sufficiently affected to justify the imposition of such a trust' (at 903 citing the opinion of Megarry VC in *Re Montagu's Settlement Trusts* [1987] Ch 264 at 285). The case was slightly unusual in that the recipient company was held liable in part because it was the instigator, albeit innocently, of the breach of trust by the pension fund trustees.

(3) In cases where the defendant to a knowing receipt claim is a company, as in *El Ajou,* when should a director's knowledge acquired in another capacity be attributed to the company? (Cf Millett J's analysis [1993] 3 All ER 717 at 740–742 with that of Hoffmann LJ [1994] 2 All ER 685 at 705–706; see also *Meridian Global Funds Management Asia Ltd v Securities Commission* [1995] 2 AC 500, PC; Sealy [1995] CLJ 507; Grantham (1996) 59 MLR 732;

and generally Davies *Gower and Davies' Principles of Modern Company Law* (8th edn, 2008) pp 178–191.)

(4) Should the innocent volunteer who receives trust property beneficially be made strictly liable to account for the value of the property received assuming that the 'change of position' defence adopted in *Lipkin Gorman* were to be adopted? This would have the effect of aligning recipient liability in equity with that applicable to a common law restitutionary action for 'money had and received' and with a modified '*Re Diplock*' personal liability in equity (see above, p 738; and generally Birks in Birks and Pretto (eds) *Breach of Trust* (2002) ch 7; Lord Nicholls 'Knowing Receipt: the Need for a New Landmark' in Cornish et al (eds) *Restitution: Past, Present and Future* (1998) p 231; Martin [1998] Conv 13; but cf Gardner (1996) 112 LQR 56 at 87–93; Smith (2000) 116 LQR 412; and Watt in Cooke (ed) *Modern Studies in Property Law* (Vol III, 2005) ch 5). Aligning or 'harmonising' the law on civil liability so that like cases are treated alike has the merit of achieving order and simplicity in the law. The question here, however, is whether we are dealing with 'like cases'. Smith, a sceptic of the 'strict liability' alignment proposition, has pointed out that 'a beneficiary's interest under a trust does not carry with it the same incidents as legal title' nor, as regards a *Re Diplock* claim, is 'an expectancy in an unadministered estate' a beneficial interest in a trust (op cit at 444). The fact that there are differences such as those alluded to by Smith does not determine whether it is or is not desirable that strict liability should replace knowledge as the basis for recipient liability. It does mean that the perceived advantage of harmonising the law on civil liability is not by itself a sufficient justification for doing so. Regard needs to be had both to the doctrinal consequences identified by Smith and the practical commercial implications referred to by Nourse LJ in *BCCI v Akindele* (see above, p 755).

(5) It may be recalled that in *Barnes v Addy* (1874) 9 Ch App 244 Lord Selborne sought to warn courts against too readily imposing liability 'as a constructive trustee' on those such as agents who receive trust property in a ministerial capacity, even where they have participated in some breach of trust (see above, p 743). Apart from the possibility of 'knowing receipt' liability, agents may become liable 'as constructive trustees' if subsequent to receipt of the trust property they acquire the requisite level of knowledge of breach of trust and then misapply the trust property. This liability, whilst it can be formally distinguished from 'knowing receipt', is clearly a very close relative and there would seem no reason why the same criterion for liability should not apply, be it knowledge in some form or, post-*BCCI v Akindele*, 'unconscionability'. The same considerations would apply to a stranger who receives trust property that has been misapplied but who only subsequently fulfils the criterion for liability, usually by gaining the relevant knowledge of the breach, and then deals with the trust property in a manner inconsistent with the terms of the trust. Here again liability for 'inconsistent dealing' may be imposed.

(c) Accessory liability and 'dishonest assistance'

(1) Introduction

We mentioned above that the decision of the Privy Council in *Royal Brunei Airlines Sdn Bhd v Tan* [1995] 3 All ER 97 and its acceptance by the House of Lords in *Twinsectra v Yardley* [2002] 2 AC 164, has brought about an important shift in the law on 'accessory liability'. In particular the decision has prompted a reappraisal of two of the following four elements identified by Peter Gibson J in *Baden Delvaux and Lecuit v Société Générale* [1983] BCLC 325 as requiring to be satisfied for personal liability to be imposed under this heading whether designated as being 'accountable as if a constructive trustee' or, adopting the formulation of Lord Millett in *Dubai Aluminium Company Ltd v Salaam* [2002] UKHL 48, 'accountable in equity'. The four elements were:

(1) the existence of a trust;
(2) the existence of a dishonest and fraudulent design on the part of the trustee of the trust;
(3) assistance in that design by the person, in the role of 'stranger'; and
(4) 'knowledge' by the stranger.

We might add a fifth almost self-evident element, that there must be some resulting loss for which the claimant seeks compensation (see Elliott and Mitchell (2004) 67(1) MLR 16–47; Ridge (2008) 124 LQR 445–468). Elements (2) and (4) are directly affected by *Royal Brunei* so that (i) just a breach of trust is now sufficient to satisfy the requirement of (2), whilst (ii) dishonesty on the part of the accessory is required under (4). By contrast elements (1) and (3) remain largely unaltered. As regards (1), this category of liability is not restricted to trusts narrowly defined. The existence of a fiduciary relationship between the 'trustee' and the property of another person is sufficient, as with, for example, a company director and the property of the company. Indeed many of the modern cases have involved unauthorised and sometimes illegal transactions instigated by company directors or senior managers. Element (3), whether the stranger has 'assisted', is a question of fact in relation to which the cases give little guidance on the nature or degree of assistance required. Some areas of uncertainty about the interpretation of these two elements will be briefly touched upon after we have considered the more fundamental changes introduced to elements (2) – breach of trust – and (4) – dishonesty.

(2) Breach of trust

Cases subsequent to *Barnes v Addy* had largely followed the dictum of Lord Selborne to the effect that accessory liability could arise only where there was 'some dishonest and fraudulent design on the part of the trustees'. In *Royal Brunei* the plaintiff airline appointed a firm (BLT) to act as its general travel agent for the sale of passenger and cargo transportation. It was agreed that sale proceeds collected by BLT were to be held in trust for the airline and paid to it within 30 days. In breach of the agreement BLT paid the amounts due to the airline into its own current account for its own business use. BLT fell into arrears, the contract was terminated and BLT subsequently became insolvent. The airline sought to recover its losses from Tan, BLT's managing director and principal shareholder, on the basis of 'knowing assistance'. The Brunei Court of Appeal, finding against the plaintiff airline, had held that whilst there had clearly been a breach of trust by BLT in which Tan had assisted, there had not been the requisite element of 'fraud or dishonesty' on the part of BLT.

On appeal by the airline, Lord Nicholls, delivering the opinion of the Privy Council, concluded that all that was required was a breach of trust on the part of the trustee (BLT) and it was immaterial whether this had been committed honestly or fraudulently. Lord Nicholls reviewed the authorities prior to *Barnes v Addy* and concluded that they did not support the view that dishonesty on the part of the trustee was a prerequisite to liability. On the contrary, he suggested that a tendency had developed to interpret and apply the dictum of Lord Selborne too rigidly – 'as though it were a statute' (at 103). To illustrate what he perceived to be the unsatisfactory nature of that development, Lord Nicholls provided, inter alia, a hypothetical example of a trustee (T) who mistakenly but honestly believes he is authorised by the terms of the trust deed to make a payment out of the trust fund to a particular person. He asks a solicitor (S) to carry through the transaction. S knows both that the proposed payment would be a plain breach of trust and that T mistakenly believes otherwise. Dishonestly, S leaves T under that misapprehension and prepares the necessary documentation. Lord Nicholls suggests that if the accessory principle is not to be artificially constricted, it ought to be applicable in such a case. Such improbable hypotheticals aside, in the opinion of Lord Nicholls the shift from 'dishonesty' to 'breach' as a prerequisite for accessory liability rested primarily on a reappraisal of the rationale for the liability (at 102):

[W]hat matters is the state of mind of the third party sought to be made liable, not the state of mind of the trustee. The trustee will be liable in any event for the breach of trust, even if he acted innocently, unless excused by an exemption clause in the trust instrument or relieved by the court. But *his* state of mind is essentially irrelevant to the question whether the *third party* should be made liable to the beneficiaries for the breach of trust. If the liability of the third party is fault-based, what matters is the nature of his fault, not that of the trustee. In this regard dishonesty on the part of the third party would seem to be a sufficient basis for his liability, irrespective of the state of mind of the trustee who is in breach of trust. It is difficult to see why, if the third party dishonestly assisted in a breach, there should be a further prerequisite to his liability, namely, that the trustee also must have been acting dishonestly. The alternative view would mean that a dishonest third party is liable if the trustee is dishonest, but if the trustee did not act dishonestly that of itself would excuse a dishonest third party from liability. That would make no sense.

In practical terms the instances where the accessory will be dishonest and the trustee or fiduciary is not are likely to be rare. Indeed, and paradoxically, in *Royal Brunei* itself the firm (BLT) was dishonest since the dishonest state of mind of its managing director, Tan, was imputed to the company.

(3) Dishonesty
(i) From 'knowledge' to 'dishonesty': the Royal Brunei Airlines case

Prior to *Royal Brunei Airlines Sdn Bhd v Tan* [1995] 3 All ER 97 sharp differences of academic and judicial opinion had arisen over element (4), the nature and degree of knowledge required on the part of the 'stranger'. Indeed it had been claimed, almost in desperation, that 'it is virtually impossible to extract any precedent from a group of cases which consists of first instance decisions and conflicting obiter dicta from the Court of Appeal' (Norman (1992) 12 LS 332). The central problem was to determine whether dishonesty or, alternatively, constructive knowledge of the breach of trust – in effect negligence – on the part of the accessory would suffice to impose liability. In the following discussion it is important to bear in mind that there are both conceptual and practical dimensions to the problem. On the one hand, if equity is perceived as a jurisdiction of conscience, should we not say that the conscience of the stranger will only be affected where there is want of probity or dishonesty? (*Agip (Africa) Ltd v Jackson* [1992] 4 All ER 385 per Millett J; and Birks (1989) 105 LQR 352 at 355.) On the other hand, as a practical matter, should the law reflect the degree to which it is thought that strangers such as banks, solicitors and accountants should be obliged to make inquiries about transactions they undertake for their clients?

Although not directly at issue in *Royal Brunei*, the Privy Council considered what 'state of mind' was required of the accessory for liability to be imposed. Lord Nicholls, emphasising that the liability should be fault-based and drawing an analogy with the economic tort of interference with the performance of a contract, rejected the argument that no liability should ever attach to the accessory: 'beneficiaries are entitled to expect that third parties will refrain from intentionally intruding in the trustee–beneficiary relationship' (at 104). Similarly rejected was the 'other extreme' proposition that there should be strict liability even on an innocent third party: 'everyday business would become impossible'(ibid). What, though, of negligence? Here Lord Nicholls in effect reaffirmed the warning words of Lord Selborne as to the undesirability of imposing accessory liability for negligence on 'the hosts of people who act for trustees in various ways: as advisers, consultants, bankers and agents of many kinds' (at 108). After all they will be liable to *trustees* if they fail to exercise reasonable skill and care. There was, in his view, therefore no compelling reason why they should also owe a duty of care to the beneficiaries.

Rejection of negligence as a criterion led inexorably in the opinion of Lord Nicholls to adopting dishonesty as the test for accessory liability. But what

exactly is dishonesty in this context? Lord Nicholls sought to define it in the
following manner (at 105):

> Whatever may be the position in some criminal or other contexts ... in the context of the
> accessory liability principle acting dishonestly, or with a lack of probity, which is synonymous,
> means simply not acting as an honest person would in the circumstances. This is an objective
> standard. At first sight this may seem surprising. Honesty has a connotation of subjectivity,
> as distinct from the objectivity of negligence. Honesty, indeed, does have a strong subjective
> element in that it is a description of a type of conduct assessed in the light of what a person
> actually knew at the time, as distinct from what a reasonable person would have known
> or appreciated. Further, honesty and its counterpart dishonesty are mostly concerned with
> advertent conduct, not inadvertent conduct. Carelessness is not dishonesty. Thus for the
> most part dishonesty is to be equated with conscious impropriety.
>
> However, these subjective characteristics of honesty do not mean that individuals are
> free to set their own standards of honesty in particular circumstances. The standard of what
> constitutes honest conduct is not subjective. Honesty is not an optional scale, with higher
> or lower values according to the moral standards of each individual. If a person knowingly
> appropriates another's property, he will not escape a finding of dishonesty simply because
> he sees nothing wrong in such behaviour ...

It was open to question at the time just how far forward this characterisation of
dishonesty would take us in clarifying the law. Indeed, despite having substituted
a test of 'dishonesty' in place of reliance on the *Baden-Delvaux* five categories
of knowledge, Lord Nicholls appeared to revert to some notion of knowledge
when he attempted to clarify what he and, by inference, most people understand
by 'dishonesty' (at 389):

> In most situations there is little difficulty in identifying how an honest person would behave.
> Honest people do not intentionally deceive others to their detriment. Honest people do not
> knowingly take others' property. Unless there is a very good and compelling reason, an
> honest person does not participate in a transaction if he knows it involves a misapplication
> of trust assets to the detriment of the beneficiaries. Nor does an honest person in such a
> case deliberately close his eyes and ears, or deliberately not ask questions, lest he learn
> something he would rather not know, and then proceed regardless.

Possibly in recognition of potential pitfalls in interpreting the test of 'dishonesty' Lord Nicholls emphasised an almost contextual dimension to ascertaining
dishonesty, citing (at 107) Knox J's reference to a person who is 'guilty of commercially unacceptable conduct in the particular context involved' (*Cowan de
Groot Properties Ltd v Eagle Trust plc* [1992] 4 All ER 700 at 761). As Lord Millett
in his dissenting opinion in *Twinsectra v Yardley* [2002] 2 AC 164, was to point
out (at 197): 'There is no trace in Lord Nicholls' opinion that the defendant
should have been aware that he was acting contrary to objective standards of

dishonesty.' In Lord Millett's view this meant that Lord Nicholls was using the term 'dishonesty' to characterise the defendant's conduct, not his state of mind.

Despite the best efforts of Lord Nicholls to achieve greater clarity and certainty by adopting a 'dishonesty' test, different interpretations of the test began to emerge in subsequent cases (see eg *Grupo Torras v Al-Sabah* [2001] Lloyd's Rep Bank 36; *Heinl v Jyske Bank (Gibraltar)* [1999] Lloyd's Rep Bank 511; *Walker v Stones* [2000] WTLR 79; and generally Mitchell 'Assistance' in Birks and Pretto (eds) *Breach of Trust* (2002) 139 at pp 204–208).

(ii) Interpreting 'dishonesty': From *Twinsectra v Yardley* to *Barlow Clowes International Ltd v Eurotrust International Ltd*

The matter then came before the House of Lords in *Twinsectra v Yardley* [2002] 2 AC 164 (see Andrews [2003] Conv 398–410; Thompson [2002] Conv 387–399; Yeo and Tijo (2002) 118 LQR 502–508; Rickett (2002) 10 RLR 112–120). The claimants (Twinsectra) agreed to provide a loan for the purchase of property and advanced £1m to the borrower's solicitors Sims (S), who in effect acted as guarantors for the borrower (Yardley), subject to an undertaking in the following terms: 'The loan moneys will be utilised solely for the acquisition of property on behalf of our client and for no other purposes.' It was also agreed that S would retain 'the loan moneys' until they were applied in the acquisition of property on behalf of the borrower. In breach of the undertaking S, who subsequently went bankrupt and were unable to repay the loan, advanced the money to a different solicitor (Leach) who was also acting for Yardley and who then paid the money out as and when instructed by him. Leach took no steps to ensure that the money was applied only in the acquisition of property and, in the event, Yardley used a substantial part of it for other purposes. Twinsectra claimed that the original arrangement between itself, S and Yardley meant that S held the money in *trust* for Twinsectra, but subject to a *power* to apply it by way of loan to Yardley in accordance with the undertaking (see Chapter 15 for a discussion of the type of trust in the case – a *Quistclose* trust). The claimant contended, and the Court of Appeal and the House of Lords agreed, that the payment by S to Leach was in breach of the undertaking and was therefore a breach of trust. But could Leach be held liable for 'dishonestly assisting' in the breach? Carnwath J had concluded, at first instance, that Leach was not dishonest but the judge also found that '[Leach] deliberately shut his eyes to the implications' of his acts. The Court of Appeal thought that the two conclusions were inconsistent, that the judge had overlooked the possibility that 'wilful blindness' could be dishonest and that therefore Leach was liable for dishonest assistance. On appeal the House of Lords, Lord Millett dissenting, restored the decision of Carnwath J on the 'dishonesty' point.

Lord Hutton, giving the principal opinion of the majority in the House, specifically approved the principle stated by Lord Nicholls in *Royal Brunei* that dishonesty was a necessary ingredient of accessory liability. Faced with differing views as to the meaning of dishonesty Lord Hutton proceeded to identify three possible interpretations of what Lord Nicholls had meant by the term. These were a 'subjective' standard, an 'objective' standard and what Lord Hutton described as 'a combined test'. He explained the different standards in the following way (at 172):

> There is a purely subjective standard, whereby a person is only regarded as dishonest if he transgresses his own standard of honesty, even if that standard is contrary to that of reasonable and honest people. This has been termed the 'Robin Hood test' and has been rejected by the courts. [See Sir Christopher Slade in *Walker v Stones* [2001] QB 902 at 939]. . . . Secondly, there is a purely objective standard whereby a person acts dishonestly if his conduct is dishonest by the ordinary standards of reasonable and honest people, even if he does not realise this. Thirdly, there is a standard which combines an objective test and a subjective test, and which requires that before there can be a finding of dishonesty it must be established that the defendant's conduct was dishonest by the ordinary standards of reasonable and honest people and that he himself realised that by those standards his conduct was dishonest.

Lord Hutton concluded that the last of these, the 'combined test', represented the correct interpretation of the dishonesty test adopted by Lord Nicholls in *Royal Brunei*. Reconciling this test with the actual language and approach of Lord Nicholls required some ingenuity and there is more than a suspicion that the majority opinions were influenced by a reluctance to attach the label 'dishonest' to a professional person who had not been 'dishonest' in the criminal law sense: 'A finding by a judge that a defendant has been dishonest is a grave finding, and it is particularly grave against a professional man, such as a solicitor' (at 174 per Lord Hutton).

The Privy Council subsequently revisited the test in *Barlow Clowes International Ltd v Eurotrust International Ltd* [2005] UKPC 37 ((2006) 122 LQR 171 (Yeo); (2006) 65(1) CLJ 18 (Conaglen); [2006] Conv 188 (Ryan)). Lord Hoffmann, who had been one of the majority in *Twinsectra*, sought to clarify an 'element of ambiguity' in the *Twinsectra* interpretation of *Royal Brunei* dishonesty, an ambiguity which had apparently confused academics. The clarification is that '[a defendant's] knowledge of the transaction had to be such as to render his participation contrary to normally acceptable standards of honest conduct. It did not require that he should have had reflections about what those normally acceptable standards were' (para 15). This clarification or reinterpretation can mean only, in effect, that the third limb of Lord Hutton's formulation of the combined test is redundant. But, it may be said, is not this conclusion premature given that *Barlow Clowes* is a Privy Council decision? It should be noted that not only were two members of the Appellate Committee (Lords Hoffmann and Steyn) that sat in *Twinsectra* on the panel but so also was Lord Nicholls. Moreover the Court of Appeal in *Abou-Rahmah v Abacha* [2006] EWCA Civ 1492 unanimously followed *Barlow Clowes*, Arden LJ, for instance, concluding that 'the law as laid down in the Twinsectra case, as interpreted in the Privy

Council in Barlow Clowes, [represents] the law of England and Wales' (at para 69).

These clarifications of *Twinsectra* pose the possibility that the dissenting opinion of Lord Millett in that case, to be discussed next, may provide a more appropriate touchstone for interpreting dishonesty

(iii) Dishonesty and knowledge: 'knowing assistance revisited'

Lord Millett's opinion was that Lord Nicholls had been adopting a purely objective standard of dishonesty and that consequently it was the conduct of the defendant, not his or her state of mind, that was at issue for the purposes of civil liability. In a strong dissenting opinion Lord Millett therefore preferred a formula for civil liability whereby 'it should not be necessary that the defendant realised that his conduct was dishonest; it should be sufficient that it constituted intentional wrongdoing' (at 201, para 127). Moreover Lord Millett clamed that an objective test was in accordance with Lord Selborne's statement in *Barnes v Addy* LR 9 Ch App 244 and traditional doctrine (ibid): 'This taught that a person who knowingly participates in the misdirection of money is liable to compensate the injured party. While negligence is not a sufficient condition of liability, intentional wrongdoing is. Such conduct is culpable and falls below the objective standards of honesty adopted by ordinary people.'

On that basis Lord Millett would have held the defendant Leach liable since he (Leach) knew every detail of the undertaking given to Twinsectra and that the payment to him by the other solicitor (Sims) and his own subsequent disbursement of the money were all in breach of the undertaking. But what of the damage to a defendant's reputation that was a matter of concern for Lord Hutton? Lord Millett commented that '[f]or my own part, I have no difficulty in equating the knowing mishandling of money with dishonest conduct' (at 201–202, para 134). But Lord Millett acknowledged that '[m]any judges would be reluctant to brand a professional man as dishonest where he was unaware that honest people would consider his conduct to be so' (ibid). He therefore concluded that 'if the condition of liability is intentional wrongdoing and not conscious dishonesty as understood in the criminal courts, I think that we should return to the traditional description of this head of equitable liability as arising from "knowing assistance"' (ibid).

Lord Millett was, so to speak, hoist by his own petard in so far as it was an earlier judgment of his own in *Agip (Africa) v Jackson* [1992] 4 All ER 385 that had first paved the way to a replacement of a criterion of 'knowledge' with one of 'dishonesty'.

(iv) 'Dishonest assistance' in practice

Whilst clarification of the test for dishonesty was a paramount issue in *Twinsectra* it is evident that the weight to be attached to findings of fact by the judge at first instance was also an issue. Lord Slynn summed up the dilemma this way (at 167):

Prima facie shutting one's eyes to problems or implications and not following them up may well indicate dishonesty; on the other hand prima facie it needs a strong case to justify the Court of Appeal reversing the finding as to dishonesty of the trial judge who has heard the witness and gone in detail into all the facts.

An illustration of how the assessment of dishonesty might operate in practice can be gleaned from a money laundering case, *Agip (Africa) v Jackson* [1992] 4 All ER 385, that predates *Royal Brunei, Twinsectra* and *Barlow Clowes* but arguably applies, in effect, a dishonesty test. In the case, Millett J (as he then was) sought to clarify the test for 'knowing assistance' by introducing the concept of dishonesty – 'the true distinction is between honesty and dishonesty. It is essentially a jury question' (at 405). Agip explored for oil in Tunisia. Its chief accountant, Z, fraudulently altered cheques signed by Agip's senior officers and made them payable to a puppet company, B, controlled by J, a partner in Jackson & Co, and G, an employee. Jackson & Co were a firm of accountants on the Isle of Man. Agip's bank then paid B. J and G then paid the proceeds of the forged cheques into Jackson & Co's client account and later paid out moneys in accordance with instructions from C, a lawyer resident in France, usually to a jewellery company in France. J and G believed that they were laundering the money to avoid Tunisian exchange controls or to assist the evasion of tax. Millett J went on to hold that J and G were personally liable as constructive trustees because they acted dishonestly: they knew they were laundering money, they were involved in concealing this by the use of a number of companies and they must have realised that at least their clients *might* be involved in a fraud. It was not necessary that J or G 'should have been aware of the precise nature of the fraud or even the identity of its victim. A man who consciously assists others by making arrangements which he knows are calculated to conceal what is happening from a third party takes the risk they are part of a fraud practised on that party' (at 406; see also *Barlow Clowes International Ltd v Eurotrust International Ltd* [2005] UKPC 37: 'Someone can know, and can certainly suspect, that he is assisting in a misappropriation of money without knowing that the money is held on trust or what a trust means' [28]).

Consider the following points:

(1) Does changing the test for liability from 'knowledge' – however interpreted – to 'dishonesty' obscure a more fundamental issue at the borderline of accessory liability: 'To what extent, if at all, in their dealings with trustees should a third party owe a duty of care to beneficiaries "to check that trustees are not misbehaving"?' On this point Lord Nicholls comments that 'as a general proposition . . . beneficiaries cannot reasonably expect that all the world dealing with their trustees should owe them a duty to take care lest the trustees are behaving dishonestly' (at 108). Consider, however, the view of one commentator on the relevance of commercial considerations to the test for accessory liability (Austin (1986) 6 OJLS 444 at 452–453):

> The law should reinforce canons of good commercial practice in appropriate areas, while not attempting to prescribe too widely or absolutely.... The admonition against equitable intervention in commerce is to be taken carefully into account in defining the duty of inquiry (if any) of the particular variety of commercial assistant whose conduct is in question, but it should not be an argument for totally exempting commercial men from the legal consequences of failure to meet prudential standards.

(2) Would basing liability on a stranger's 'unconscionable conduct' (*Powell v Thompson* [1991] 1 NZLR 597 at 613 per Thomas J) enable the court to evaluate the circumstances more fully and thereby 'do justice' more effectively than will reliance on a test of 'dishonesty'? Or would this lead to greater uncertainty about the appropriate standards of commercial conduct for banks and other third parties?

In *Royal Brunei* Lord Nicholls, whilst accepting that 'unconscionable is a word of immediate appeal to an equity lawyer', rejected unconscionable conduct as a test for liability (at 108):

> It must be recognised, however, that unconscionable is not a word in everyday use by non-lawyers. If it is to be used in this context, and if it is to be the touchstone for liability as an accessory, it is essential to be clear on what, in this context, unconscionable means. If unconscionable means no more than dishonesty, then dishonesty is the preferable label. If unconscionable means something different, it must be said that it is not clear what that something different is. Either way, therefore, the term is better avoided in this context.

(3) Any consideration of the ways in which third parties such as solicitors, accountants, banks, etc in practice conduct their dealings with trustees or others subject to fiduciary obligations cannot ignore the impact of developments in criminal law culminating in the Proceeds of Crime Act (PCA) 2002. This statute consolidates existing provisions concerning money laundering whilst also reworking some of the principal offences and expanding the reporting obligations. The combined effect of the provisions broadly speaking is that it is now an offence for any person to provide assistance to a money launderer so as to conceal, disguise, convert or transfer property if that person *knows* or *suspects*, that the property 'constitutes or represents' the proceeds of crime (PCA 2002, ss 327–329, 340(3)). Of at least equal significance for the professional adviser is the disclosure obligation contained in s 330 of the Act. Under this section a person commits an offence if he fails to report 'as soon as practicable' to the appropriate authority that he 'knows or suspects' or 'has reasonable grounds for knowing or suspecting' that another person is engaged in money laundering (s 330(2)–(4)). Moreover if a disclosure is made it will be an offence under s 333 – the 'tipping off' section – to communicate that information to, for

instance, a client if it is 'likely to prejudice any investigation which might be conducted' by the relevant authority. The disclosure obligation in s 330 is subject to the condition that the 'information or other matter' on which a person's knowledge or suspicion is based came to him in the course of business regulated under the Financial Services and Markets Act 2000. Section 330(6)(b) of the PCA 2002 protects legal advisers from the offence of non-disclosure where the information came to them in circumstances where legal privilege applies (see generally on the practical implications of an offshore dimension Antoine *Confidentiality in Offshore Financial Law* (2002)). Significantly these statutory provisions are complemented by the Money Laundering Regulations 2007, SI 2007/2157, which require any firm involved in any of a wide range of activities specified in the Regulations and in the Financial Services and Markets Act 2000 to put in place internal controls, policies and procedures to prevent money laundering (see eg Law Society *Anti-Money Laundering Practice Note* (2008)); and generally Alldridge *Money Laundering Law* (2003); Ulph *Commercial Fraud* (2006); Wadsley (2001) 16(5) JIBL 125 and (2008) 29(3) Comp Law 65–75; Middleton (2008) 11(1) JMLC 34–46). The practical significance of these changes is that many professional firms will be obliged to have in place monitoring systems which require them to be vigilant about the activities of their clients. It is estimated, for instance, that under the s 330 reporting requirements around 10,000 reports were submitted by lawyers in 2005.

A key practical question for the solicitor, accountant or banker is this: should the fact that you have a reasonable suspicion about a client's transactions sufficient to lead you to submit a report under s 330 of PCA 2002 to the relevant authorities such as the National Criminal Intelligence Service mean that you can nevertheless assist in that transaction and still avoid the risk of liability for 'dishonest assistance'? After all suspicion falls some way short of actual knowledge let alone dishonesty (see Stokes and Arora [2004] JBL 332–356; and *Tayeb v HSCB Bank plc* [2004] EWHC 1529). Moreover, if you were to refuse to carry out the transaction you will be limited in the explanation that you can offer the client if you are to avoid committing a 'tipping off' offence under s 333. One practical option is to make an application to the High Court for administration directions under the Civil Procedure Rules 1998, Pt 64. This may forestall an action by the client requiring you to comply with his or her instructions whilst also helping to provide some evidence of 'honesty' should a third party subsequently bring an action for dishonest assistance. It remains uncertain as to the degree of 'suspicion' necessary to justify a refusal to comply with a client's instructions (see *Finers v Miro* [1991] 1 WLR 35; *The Governor and Company of the Bank of Scotland v A Ltd* [2001] 1 WLR 751). Indeed given the current stance of the criminal law on money laundering can we still with full confidence endorse Millett J's maxim in relation to recipient liability that 'a recipient is not expected to be unduly suspicious' (*El Ajou v Dollar Land Holdings plc* [1993] 3 All ER 717 at 739 per Millett J; see also Gardner (1996) 112 LQR 56 at 80–83; McCormack (1995) 9 TLI 102 at 106; Fox (1998) 57(2) CLJ 391–405; and in relation specifically to banks Gleeson in Birks (ed) *Laundering and Tracing* (1995) ch 5; Stokes [2007] JBL 502–526).

(4) In *Royal Brunei* Lord Nicholls states that 'liability as a constructive trustee for "knowing assistance" is a form of secondary liability in the sense that it only arises where there has been a breach of trust' (at 99–100). In *Brown v Bennett* [1998] 2 BCLC 97 Rattee J held that that head of liability could only be invoked against an accessory where there was some breach of trust *affecting property* and could not apply where the breach concerned was a mere breach of fiduciary duty, such as the duty of directors to manage the affairs of a company in the best interests of the company. Is this decision consistent either with a view that 'accessory liability' is fault-based or with a policy to reinforce the integrity of fiduciary relationships? (See comment by Grantham and Rickett (1998) 114 LQR 357.)

(5) 'Dishonest assistance' requires active assistance in the commission of the breach of trust. In *Brinks Ltd v Abu-Saleh (No 3)* (1995) *Times* 23 October one Elcombe, accompanied by his wife, made six trips to Switzerland carrying £3m in cash, part of the laundered proceeds of a £26m bullion robbery. Elcombe had entered into a courier agreement with one of the robbers but believed, as did his wife, that the cash to be laundered was the subject of a tax evasion exercise. The plaintiff company sought to fix Mrs Elcombe with 'accessory liability' on the basis that her presence was intended to cloak what she knew to be an illegal operation with the appearance of a family holiday, thus making it easier to cross borders. Rimer J held, on the facts, that she was not a party to the courier agreement, had not carried out any part of the courier activity and went on the trips in her capacity as Elmore's wife to keep him company; presence did not constitute assistance. This may be thought a narrow interpretation (see Stevens [1996] Conv 447; Birks [1996] LMCLQ 1; Oakley (1996) 10 TLI 53; Berg (1996) 59 MLR 443 at 447–448.)

(6) In the somewhat unusual litigation pleadings in *Dubai Aluminium Co Ltd v Salaam* [2003] 2 AC 366 the House of Lords confirmed that the partners of a person held liable for dishonest assistance can be vicariously liable for the acts of that person provided that the conduct in question can fairly and properly be regarded as having been done either in the ordinary course of the firm's business or with the authority of the co-partners. In reaching this conclusion the House rejected the proposition that the 'wrongful acts' for which a partnership could be vicariously liable under the Partnership Act 1890, s 10 were confined to common law torts only (see also *Balfron Trustees Ltd v Peterson* [2001] IRLR 758 where Laddie J held that a firm of solicitors could be vicariously liable even where the acts of dishonest assistance were committed by an employee who was not a partner (therefore outside the scope of s 10)). The unusual nature of the pleadings in *Dubai Aluminium*

was that the partners in the firm (F) were themselves arguing that they should be vicariously liable for acts carried out by another partner (A). A had acted as solicitor for the defendant S in drafting documents and assisting in the fraud that had resulted in the claimants, Dubai Aluminium (D), being defrauded of some US$50m. F had settled D's claim in the sum of US$10m and sought a contribution from S, who still retained the proceeds of the fraud, under the provisions of the Civil Liability (Contribution) Act 1978. F's claim for contribution – successful to the full extent of the $10m settlement figure – depended on it showing that it was liable, under the Partnership Act 1890, s 10, for the wrongful acts committed by A. In his judgment Lord Millett commented that he saw no 'rational ground for restricting the liability to torts, or for excluding liability in equity, particularly when equitable liability often has its counterpart at common law' (at 395). He then proceeded to pose the following rhetorical questions:

> Why should a firm be vicariously liable if a partner procures or induces a breach of contract but not if he procures or participates in a breach of trust or fiduciary duty? If the risk of wrongdoing is one which can fairly be said to be reasonably incidental to the employer's business, why should it matter that the liability arises in equity and not at common law or by statute?

Whilst the answer may be that it is immaterial for the purposes of vicarious liability whether the wrongdoing has its roots in equity or common law, it does not necessarily follow that accessory liability in equity can be assimilated with the economic tort of inducing breach of contract. Whilst there is certainly academic and judicial support for the proposition that there should be 'a general principle of secondary liability for assisting or procuring the breach of any legal or equitable duty' the courts seem unpersuaded as yet that it is desirable to develop the law in this way (see *Credit Lyonnais Bank Nederland NV v Export Credit Guarantee Department* [2000] 1 AC 486 at 496–497, but cf Harpum (1995) 111 LQR 545 at 546; Birks *Civil Wrongs: A New World* (1991) p 100; Lord Hoffmann 'The Redundancy of Knowing Assistance' in Birks (ed) *The Frontiers of Liability* (1994); Andrews [2003] Conv 398–410; and dicta of Lord Nicholls in *Royal Brunei Airlines Sdn Bhd v Tan* [1995] 2 AC 378 at 387). Whilst there may be an analogy between procuring or inducing breaches of contract and breaches of trust, cases of dishonest assistance often involve just 'assistance' and not 'inducement'. Assimilation would, as matters stand, seemingly require an expansion in tortious liability, a development that is itself contentious (see eg *OBG Ltd v Allan* [2008] 1 AC 1; Carty [2008] 124 LQR 641–674; and the comment by Weir *Economic Torts* (1997) p 31, footnote 31: 'equitable rights, with their property flavour, are rather stronger in some ways than contractual rights, so it would come as no surprise to find them better protected against third parties.')

5. Injunctions

(a) Introduction

In this chapter our emphasis so far has tended to be on ways in which 'beneficiaries' can seek to recover misappropriated property or to obtain either restitution of property or compensation for loss where a proprietary claim is not available or will not 'do the trick'. A preferable option for a beneficiary may be to pre-empt any misappropriation of funds or prevent any breach of trust occurring. Even if prevention cannot be achieved, it may still be important to ensure that fraudsters or their associates cannot conceal assets or remove them from the jurisdiction of the courts before a remedy can be obtained. It is here that injunctive relief in its several forms has an important role to play. As will be evident in the following pages injunctive relief can be awarded in a wide variety of contexts. These go way beyond the immediate concerns of this chapter but, notwithstanding the different contexts, a study of the key cases is necessary for an understanding of the principles and rules governing the award of injunctive relief.

(b) Types of injunction

Injunctions are orders issued by a court that prohibit or reverse some kind of wrongful activity. These are powerful legal tools: to fail to comply with their conditions is to act in contempt of court and can result in imprisonment. Nowadays they are granted under Supreme Court Act 1981, s 37(1), which gives the court a discretionary power to do so 'in all cases in which it appears to the court to be just and convenient'.

   Injunctions can be categorised according to how they achieve their goals. For example, an injunction can be constructed so as to stop some kind of activity. Thus a group of people may be ordered to stop demonstrating on property that belongs to another, or, more pertinently for our purposes, a fiduciary may be ordered to desist from acting in breach of his duty. This type of injunction – a 'prohibitory' injunction – may therefore be characterised as having a 'negative' effect. By contrast, a 'mandatory' injunction is phrased so that it orders some kind of activity to be carried out. For example, in *Redland Bricks v Morris* [1970] AC 652, M ran a market garden on land that sloped down to and adjoined land owned by RB. RB, a brick company, excavated its own land for clay to make its bricks. As a result, M's land began to slip onto RB's land. M successfully sued for damages but was also granted, at first instance, a mandatory injunction that RB should take all necessary steps to restore support to M's land within six months. Mandatory injunctions are more likely to have significant financial consequences and courts are more cautious in granting them. In *Redland Bricks*, for example, the cost of complying with the injunction was estimated at £35,000; the value of that part of the plaintiffs' land on which the support work was required was approximately £1,500 (the House of Lords refused the injunction).

The injunction in *Redland Bricks* was also an example of a further kind of injunction: the *quia timet* injunction. As the language (literally meaning 'because he [the claimant] fears') implies, 'mere vague apprehension is not sufficient to support an action for a quia timet injunction. There must be an immediate threat to do something' (per Lord Buckmaster in *Graigola Merthyr Co Ltd v Swansea Corp* [1929] AC 344 at 352). This is designed to stop a claimant's rights from being infringed where no damage has yet been done; it can be mandatory or prohibitory in form. In *Redland Bricks*, the injunction was requested in order to prevent any *further* slippage; the first instance decision had included a prohibitory injunction preventing any further excavation and awarding damages to compensate for the slippage to date.

Injunctions can also be granted on a permanent as well as a temporary basis. Claims that their rights have been infringed can be resolved by granting a 'perpetual' injunction in claimants' favour. However, there may be cases where the time lag between issuing proceedings and final judgment is lengthy. This creates a 'procedural imbalance' between the parties that favours the defendant. As Zuckerman has put it, 'the longer the lapse of time between the commencement of proceedings and final judgment, the greater the scope that the defendant has for undermining the plaintiff's entitlement' ((1993) 56 MLR 325 at 329). Hence a temporary injunction can be issued at an interim stage, designed to prevent further damage to the claimant's interests, until the matter can be fully tried. This is the subject of the next section.

It can be seen therefore that the injunction is a powerful weapon in the hands of the court, one which defendants disregard at their peril. Breach of an injunction can constitute contempt of court for which the punishment can be extensive damages, seizure ('sequestration') of one's assets and even imprisonment (see the saga of *Shalson v Russo* [2002] WL 1655059 (application for release) where a fraudster on a grand scale was sentenced to two years in prison for around 100 breaches of freezing and search orders).

(c) 'Holding the ring': interlocutory (or 'interim') injunctions

Granting interlocutory injunctions creates a dilemma for a court. The object of civil proceedings is to achieve justice as between parties, usually, one might hope, through the equal treatment of the parties. Where, *pending trial*, one side claims ongoing and irreparable harm to its interests by the other, the court faces the difficulty that if it allows matters to continue as they are, then the claimant may well suffer damage which cannot ultimately be compensated at trial. Whether there is *legally recognised* damage, however, depends on the claimant's claim being substantiated at full trial. Until then, there is the risk that if an injunction is granted, the defendant's rights will instead be infringed. Whatever the court does at this stage, it must of necessity act partially: it must take the side of the claimant or of the defendant, even though matters have not yet been finally adjudicated. A balance must be found between 'on the one hand, the need to reduce the risk of harm to lawful rights pending litigation and, on the other . . . the imperative of impartiality which argues for non-interference prior to final judgement' (Zuckerman op cit at 326).

The approach of the UK courts here has been influenced by their approach to interlocutory procedures generally. For example, the jurisdiction to grant interlocutory injunctions is based in part on the need for a quick decision. This means that hearings are likely to be quickly prepared. Evidence will normally be presented in affidavit form only (Civil Procedure Rules ('CPR'), r 25.3). In addition, the courts proceed on the assumption that the dispute will be litigated in full later. The implications of this are both that it might be inappropriate to go too far in pre-judging the final court's findings at an interlocutory stage, and that any harm done in the meantime can be put right by the final court. In light of these considerations, the approach is to preserve the status quo – the existing position – until trial. In doing so, the courts recognise nevertheless that harm may be done in the meantime to one or other party, depending on the final outcome. They have therefore developed a test that looks to the 'balance of convenience' as between the parties. This involves assessing both the harm that each side is likely to incur, according to whether the injunction is granted or not, and whether that harm can be compensated at trial in money terms. To ensure that this is not a hollow exercise, a cross-undertaking in damages for any loss incurred must be given by the claimant as part of the order (CPR 25, P D 004, r 5.1(1)).

The leading case in the area is *American Cyanamid Co v Ethicon Ltd* [1975] AC 396. The case sets out the dilemma facing the court, and focuses on the extent to which the plaintiff's chances of success at final trial need to be established – relevant to the prospects of injustice and harm to the defendant – before relief will be granted. Before *American Cyanamid*, the courts had held that in order to obtain an interim injunction, the plaintiff had to make out a prima facie case: that at trial, he would have a better than even chance of winning (see eg *Preston v Luck* (1884) 27 Ch D 497; *Fellowes & Son v Fisher* [1976] QB 122). Only in these circumstances would the court consider whether it was in the balance of convenience to grant or withhold the injunction. In *American Cyanamid* the House of Lords appeared to establish a different test.

American Cyanamid Co v Ethicon Ltd [1975] AC 396

The plaintiffs, Cyanamid, owned a patent that covered artificial surgical sutures. Ethicon, who had dominated the market with sutures made from catgut, were about to launch their own artificial suture in Britain. Cyanamid claimed that it breached the terms of their patent. Ethicon resisted Cyanamid's claims on grounds, inter alia, that the patent did not cover their product. At first instance, Cyanamid was granted the injunction it sought, but the Court of Appeal discharged the order on the grounds that no prima facie case of infringement had been made out. Cyanamid appealed to the House of Lords. Lord Diplock pointed to the problems posed by the prima facie rule (at 406):

> In those cases where the legal rights of the parties depend upon facts that are in dispute between them, the evidence available to the court at the hearing of the application for an interlocutory injunction is incomplete. It is given on affidavit and has not been tested by oral cross-examination. The purpose sought to be achieved by giving to the court discretion to grant such injunctions would be stultified if the discretion were clogged by a technical rule forbidding its exercise if upon that incomplete untested evidence the court evaluated the chances of the plaintiff's ultimate success in the action at 50 per cent or less, but permitting its exercise if the court evaluated his chances at more than 50 per cent.

Lord Diplock considered the authorities supporting the 'prima facie case' rule and continued (at 407):

> Your Lordships should in my view take this opportunity of declaring that there is no such rule ... The court no doubt must be satisfied that the claim is not frivolous or vexatious; in other words, that there is a serious question to be tried.
>
> It is no part of the court's function at this stage of the litigation to try to resolve conflicts of evidence on affidavit as to facts on which the claims of either party may ultimately depend nor to decide difficult questions of law which call for detailed argument and mature considerations. These are matters to be dealt with at the trial ... unless the material available to the court at the [interim] hearing ... fails to disclose that the plaintiff has any real prospect of succeeding in his claim for a permanent injunction at the trial, the court should go on to consider whether the balance of convenience lies in favour of granting or refusing the interlocutory relief that is sought.

Lord Diplock emphasised that the governing principle on this point was that the court should first consider whether the plaintiff or defendant would be adequately compensated by damages from the other party whichever one should be successful at trial and continued (at 408):

> It is where there is doubt as to the adequacy of the respective remedies in damages available to either party or to both, that the question of balance of convenience arises ... Where other factors appear to be evenly balanced it is a counsel of prudence to take such measures as are calculated to preserve the status quo. If the defendant is enjoined temporarily from doing something that he has not done before, the only effect of the interlocutory injunction in the event of his succeeding at the trial is to postpone the date at which he is able to embark upon a course of action which he has not previously found it necessary to undertake: whereas to interrupt him in the conduct of an established enterprise would cause much greater inconvenience to him since he would have to start again to establish it in the event of his succeeding at the trial.

The appeal was allowed.

Consider the following points:

(1) Do you agree with the court's approach to the 'prima facie v good arguable case' point? Does the court in *American Cyanamid* adequately address the concerns of 'procedural imbalance' raised above? Zuckerman, for example, has argued that the idea that the purpose of the interlocutory procedure is to preserve the status quo 'obscures' both (i) the (more appropriate) idea of its role to minimise the risk of harm to lawful rights, and (ii) the functional outcome that giving or withholding the interlocutory injunction will often either end the dispute or at least give to one side an advantage that in consequence skews the process ((1993) 56 MLR 325 at 327–328; see also (1994) 14 OJLS 353). In these circumstances, giving an undertaking in damages does not assist.

(2) The most well-known, some might say notorious, illustration of the 'skewing' process occurs with the awarding of interlocutory injunctions in the context of labour disputes. Under the Trade Union and Labour Relations (Consolidation) Act 1992, s 221(2), in considering whether to grant an interlocutory injunction, the court must have regard to the likelihood of the defendant (ie the party taking industrial action) establishing at trial that the action was 'in contemplation of a trade dispute'. Whilst for labour disputes this formally modifies the *American Cyanamid* test, in practice the change does not seem to have affected the outcome whereby interim injunctions are readily awarded. This tends to determine the outcome of the dispute since cases are rarely taken to full trial (see eg Evans (1987) 25 BJIR 419; Auerbach (1988) 17 ILJ 227; Gall and Mackay (1996) 34(4) BJIR 567–582).

(3) The principles set out in *American Cyanamid* have been held in subsequent cases to be guidelines, rather than fixed rules (see *Fellowes v Fisher, Cayne v Global Natural Resources plc* [1984] 1 All ER 225; *Cambridge Nutrition Ltd v BBC* [1990] 3 All ER 523 at 533 per Kerr LJ; *Factortame Ltd v Secretary of State for Transport (No 2)* [1990] AC 85 at 116 per Lord Goff). It has furthermore been acknowledged that courts do *in practice* 'pay regard to the relative strengths of the parties' despite the holding in *Cyanamid*. Whether this is 'legitimate' is another question, but 'it is common knowledge that it happens frequently . . .' (per Laddie J *Series 5 Software Ltd v Clarke* [1996] 1 All ER 853). In *Series 5 Software*, Laddie J held that the panel in *Cyanamid* had not intended to exclude consideration of the strengths of the cases in most cases and that, on the contrary, such consideration would often prove relevant (citing *Hoffmann-La Roche (F) & Co AG v Secretary of State for Trade and Industry* [1975] AC 295, HL, decided a few months before *Cyanamid* by a panel that included Lords Diplock and Cross, both of whom sat in *Cyanamid*). Rather than following a formulaic set of rules to decide whether to grant the remedy, Laddie J indicated a set of factors that should be borne in mind. These included '(a) the extent to which damages are likely to be an adequate remedy for each party and the ability of the other

party to pay, (b) the balance of convenience, (c) the maintenance of the status quo, and (d) any clear view the court may reach as to the relative strengths of the parties' cases' (at 865).

The court, however, acknowledged that it 'should rarely attempt to resolve complex issues of disputed fact or law'; but that 'if...the court is able to come to a view as to the strength of the parties' cases on the credible evidence, then it should do so' (at 865). Whether one views the approach adopted by Laddie J in *Series 5 Software* as 'a first instance rejection of the *Cyanamid* approach' (see *Hayton* at p 885 approving the 'bold' and 'sensible' view adopted by Laddie J) or more modestly as a re-interpretation of it, Laddie J's decision has been praised as reasserting the central role of judicial discretion in the granting of interlocutory relief (see Phillips [1997] JBL 486; Keay (2004) 23 CJQ 133–151). It might even be argued that Laddie J's approach is consistent with the more practical and interventionist approach to case management subsequently adopted by the courts under the Civil Procedure Rules 1998 (SI 3132/1998). These place much greater emphasis on identifying and resolving issues likely to go to a hearing at an early stage so as to reduce the delays between commencing proceedings and trial, a concern of Lord Diplock in *American Cyanamid*.

(4) Both *Cyanamid* and the undertaking in damages are concerned with compensating (interim) damage in financial terms. The courts have, however, recognised that there are other interests that are not easy to assess in such terms, and have developed rules to deal with them. An injunction will therefore not generally be granted to restrain a libel if the defendant states an intention to justify that libel, unless the statement in question was obviously untruthful and libellous and the plea of justification was bound to fail (see *Bonnard v Perryman* [1891] 2 Ch 269; *Greene v Associated Newspapers Ltd* [2005] 3 WLR 281 where the Court of Appeal confirmed that the position is unaffected by s 12(3) of the Human Rights Act 1998 (see below)). The courts are here concerned to avoid the remedy being used simply to 'gag' speech: it is considered important 'in the public interest that the truth should out... There is no wrong done if it is true, or if it is fair comment on a matter of public interest' (per Lord Denning MR *Fraser v Evans* [1969] 1 QB 349, but cf *Gulf Oil (GB) Ltd v Page* [1987] Ch 327 – injunction can be granted where 'sole or dominant purpose' is to injure). Note that an injunction may also be awarded to restrain a breach of confidence. Whilst protection of equitable concepts of confidence (see Chapter 16) tend to outweigh considerations of freedom of speech, a comparable defence of 'public interest' may be sustained (see eg *A-G v Guardian Newspapers Ltd (No 2)* [1990] 1 AC 109; see Jones (1989) CLP 49).

The implementation of the Human Rights Act 1998 has lent added weight to the importance accorded to considerations of freedom of speech in the contexts just described. Where the exercise of the right to freedom of expression, protected by Article 10 of the European Convention on Human Rights, might be affected by the grant of interim injunctive relief regard must be had by the court to the requirements of s 12 of the 1998 Act. Section 12(2) emphasises the importance of seeking to ensure that the respondent receives notification of the application for relief whilst s 12(3) in effect requires a merits-based test to be applied in deciding whether or not to grant relief rather than the lower *American Cyanamid* criterion:

> s12(3) No such relief is to be granted so as to restrain publication before trial unless the court is satisfied that the applicant is likely to establish that publication should not be allowed.

But what did 'likely' mean in this context? In *Cream Holdings Ltd v Banerjee* [2005] 1 AC 253 the House of Lords held that s 12(3) means that interim relief should not generally be granted unless the applicant can show that it would probably, as in 'more likely than not', succeed at trial. The only caveat was that if the potential adverse consequences of publication would be 'particularly grave' then a lesser prospect of success would satisfy the test. A prominent illustration of the possible application of this caveat can be seen in *Douglas v Hello! Ltd* [2005] 3 WLR 881 where the Court of Appeal disapproved a previous decision of a differently constituted CA to lift an interim injunction restraining publication of the wedding photographs of a 'well-known couple' (see also *Mosley v News Group Newspapers Ltd* [2008] EWHC 687; *A v B (a company)* [2002] 2 All ER 545 on the approach to be followed where the competing Convention rights are at issue: respect for private life (Article 8) versus freedom of expression (Article 10)).

(5) As might be expected, injunctions can be awarded to restrain breaches of trust such as selling trust property for a price below that formally offered by a prospective purchaser (see *Buttle v Saunders* [1950] 2 All ER 193). An injunction may also be awarded to prevent a defendant disposing of property where a claimant has an equitable tracing claim (see *Polly Peck International plc v Nadir (No 2)* [1992] 4 All ER 769, discussed at pp 748 and 782).

(d) Securing the assets: 'freezing orders' ('Mareva' injunctions) and 'search orders' ('Anton Piller' orders)

(1) Introduction

During an application for an interlocutory injunction, both parties are likely to be at the hearing, so that each side will have an opportunity to state their case. Compare this with the situation regarding either 'freezing' or 'search' orders, considered below, where applications are generally (and in the case of search orders, necessarily) made ex parte. Note that freezing orders were more commonly known as 'Mareva' injunctions, after *Mareva Cia Naviera SA v International Bulkcarriers SA* [1975] 2 Lloyd's Rep 509, CA, the second case in which this type of relief was granted. Search orders were more commonly known as 'Anton Piller' orders, again after an early case: *Anton Piller KG v Manufacturing*

Processes [1976] Ch 55, CA. The name changes have accompanied the reform of the Civil Procedure Rules (see now CPR 25.1(f) and (h) and 25 PD-003 et seq). We will here use the new terminology although of course the original nomenclature will be found in cases preceding the reforms.

The freezing and search orders have been described as 'law's two "nuclear" weapons' (*Bank Mellat v Nikpour* [1985] FSR 87 at 92 per Donaldson LJ) and as 'the greatest piece of judicial law reform in my time' (Lord Denning *The Closing Chapter* (1983) p 225). The association of two recent emanations of equity with 'nuclear weapons' might seem somewhat contradictory but the metaphor does highlight the powerful potential of the two orders as weapons against, inter alia, fraud (see eg *Re Bank of Credit and Commerce International SA (No 9)* [1994] 3 All ER 764 where a worldwide freezing order was awarded against persons allegedly involved in the fraudulent mismanagement of the collapsed BCCI bank group).

(2) Freezing orders (Mareva injunctions)

Introduction The aims of a freezing order are in principle quite limited: to prevent for a limited time specified assets from being removed from the jurisdiction of the court, in the context of specific legal action and in the face of a risk that this action might, if successful, be frustrated. It works, as its new name suggests, by freezing assets in the hands of a defendant or third parties (such as banks). The jurisdiction can be justified on the basis of necessity: to prevent a defendant from 'taking action designed to ensure that subsequent orders of the court are rendered less effective than would otherwise be the case' (*Derby & Co v Weldon (Nos 3 and 4)* [1990] Ch 65 at 76). There is also a public policy dimension to the jurisdiction: that is, to protect the credibility of court judgments against those who would evade and therefore undermine them and to prevent injustice (see *Iraqi Ministry of Defence v Arcepey Shipping Co SA (Gillespie Bros & Co Ltd intervening) The Angel Bell* [1980] 1 All ER 480 per Goff J at 486).

But awarding a freezing order can result in extensive harm to a defendant, including the loss or disruption of business and business relationships. In addition, contrary to normal rules of natural justice, the order is often made ex parte. We have already seen that interlocutory injunctions can be very powerful tools; this is all the more true of freezing orders, especially in light of the principle that 'the threatened dispersal of assets is not a wrongful act . . . for subject to any special rules relating to insolvency, a person can do what he likes with his own . . .' (*Mercedes Benz v Leiduck* [1996] AC 284 at 303, PC). There are therefore concerns as to whether orders are, in principle as well as practice, too easily obtained (but cf Devonshire [2004] JBL 357–377).

Guidelines for a freezing order There is a three-part test to be satisfied before an order is made. The claimant, applying in support of an existing cause of action (see eg *Veracruz Transportation Inc v VC Shipping Co Inc* [1992] 1 Lloyd's

Rep 353; *Ninemia Maritime Corpn v Trave Schiffahrtsgesellschaft mbH ('The Niedersachsen')* [1984] 1 All ER 398), must establish (i) that he has a good arguable case; (ii) that there are assets to which the order can attach; and (iii) that there is a real risk that those assets will be dissipated (see *Derby & Co Ltd v Weldon* [1990] Ch 48 at 57 per Parker LJ).

As regards the first requirement – 'a good arguable case' – this is considered to be 'in conformity' with that set out in *Cyanamid* but more stringent in application (per Lord Denning *The Pertamina* [1977] 3 All ER 324 at 334; and see *Gee on Commercial Injunctions* (5th edn, 2004) at pp 340–343). The courts thus appear once again to focus on finding a balance between ensuring that such extreme relief is not granted too easily and 'abstaining from expressing any opinion upon the merits of the case until the hearing' (*Derby & Co Ltd v Weldon* [1990] Ch 48 at 57).

Difficulties of principle and practicality can, however, arise. First, as mentioned above, it is in principle difficult to justify such a draconian remedy in any other than cases of clear necessity. If the claimant's case is not a strong one, it is hard to establish such necessity. As regards practicality, it is also difficult to see where the threshold is between a good arguable case and one where there is a serious question to be tried. Prior to *The Niedersachsen*, Mustill J explained that a good arguable case might be one 'which a good advocate can get on its feet' (*Orri v Moundreas* [1981] Com LR 168). In *The Niedersachsen*, he considered several other expressions and concluded eventually that a good arguable case is one 'that was more than barely capable of serious argument, but not necessarily one which the judge considers would have a better than 50 per cent chance of success' (at 404). The test is therefore possibly more stringent than that for obtaining an interlocutory injunction per se, but is far from satisfying critics of the procedure.

The second aspect of the test is the claimant's obligation to establish that the defendant has assets against which an order can be made. Initially, a freezing order could be obtained only against assets within the jurisdiction. There is now, however, the possibility of obtaining 'worldwide' orders, which are discussed below.

The third element of the guidelines is that there must be a 'real risk of dissipation' of the assets. In *The Niedersachsen*, the court held the applicable test was 'whether, on the assumption that the plaintiffs have shown "a good arguable case", the court concludes, on the whole of the evidence then before it, that the refusal of a Mareva injunction would involve a real risk that a judgement or award in favour of the plaintiffs would remain unsatisfied' ([1983] 1 WLR 1412 at 1422).

There are two contrasting points to emphasise about this requirement. On the one hand, the claimant does not have to prove that the defendant is about to remove assets *with the intent* of defeating a judgment debt. As Gee has put it, this 'would have been an extremely difficult test to satisfy, for however unreliable a defendant has been in the past, it is nevertheless far from easy to prove his present state of mind in relation to future dealings with his assets' (*Gee on Commercial Injunctions* (5th edn, 2004) para 12–032). On the other hand, the claimant does need to adduce 'solid evidence', not a mere assertion, that assets will be dissipated. It is doubtful that one can be much more precise than this other than to point out that commercial considerations cannot be ignored. Thus it is not enough that the defendant is abroad: 'no one would wish any reputable foreign company to be plagued with a Mareva injunction simply because it has agreed to London arbitration' (*Third Chandris Shipping Corpn v Unimarine SA* [1979] 2 All ER 972 at 985 per Lord Denning). If a defendant is a foreign company, there must be evidence from which 'the commercial court, like a prudent, sensible commercial man, can infer a danger of default *if* assets are removed' (*The Third Chandris* at 987 per Lawton LJ, emphasis added). This implies that there are two stages to be addressed: that assets may be removed and that, if they are, the defendant will not satisfy any judgment debt against him. On balance it therefore seems that it may be sufficient for the plaintiff to demonstrate that the defendant is unreliable in general – a bad debtor, say, or an unknown quantity in the business world, even after inquiries have been made – rather than establish the 'nefarious intent' of defeating the plaintiff in the particular instance.

Consider the following points:

(1) We have noted that hearings for freezing orders are often held ex parte in order to prevent pre-emptive action by a defendant. Clearly, apart from the procedural unfairness inherent in this situation, there is the potential for abuse, since it is easier for a claimant to establish a good case when the defendant is not there to point out either its weaknesses or any defences to it. In order to counteract this problem, one of the conditions on which the freezing order is granted is that the plaintiff must make 'full and frank disclosure of all matters in his knowledge which are material for the judge to know . . . [and] . . . should give particulars of his claim against the defendant, stating the ground of his claim and the amount thereof, and fairly stating the points made against it by the defendant' (per Lord Denning *Third Chandris Corpn v Unimarine SA* [1979] QB 645 at 668; see *Bank Mellat v Nikpour* [1985] FSR 87 and *Brink's Mat v Elcombe* [1988] 3 All ER 188, where it was held that the plaintiff must disclose all facts known to him as well as any additional facts that he would have known had he made proper inquiries). If it is subsequently discovered that full disclosure has not been made, then the injunction may be discharged (see *Ali & Fahd Shobokshi Group Ltd v Moneim* [1989] 2 All ER 404; *Dubai Bank Ltd v Galadari* [1990] 1 Lloyd's Rep 120, CA). Do you think that this procedural mechanism can in fact overcome the unfairness inherent in the procedure? (See generally Zuckerman (1993) 56 MLR 325 and (1993) 109 LQR 432.)

(2) As with interlocutory injunctions, an applicant must give an undertaking that 'if the court . . . finds that [the Mareva] has caused loss to the Respondent, and decides that the Respondent should be compensated for that loss, the Applicant will comply with any Order the Court may make'. The applicant must also 'cause a written guarantee [of a given amount] to be issued from a bank having a place of business within England and Wales, such guarantee being in respect of any Order' referred to above (see CPR 1999 25PD-005). The fact that a claimant may not be good for the money does not necessarily rule out the possibility that an order will be made (*Allen v Jambo* [1980] 2 All ER 502, where the plaintiff was legally aided; see also Zuckerman (1993) 12 CJQ 268; (1994) 53 CLJ 546).

(3) An order will allow a respondent an allowance for his 'ordinary living expenses', his 'ordinary and proper business expenses' and a 'reasonable sum' for legal advice and representation (*Iraqi Ministry of Defence v Arcepy Shipping Co, The Angel Bell* [1981] QB 65, 70–71, *Polly Peck International plc v Nadir (No 2)* [1992] 4 All ER 769; and CPR 25PD-005 draft order, para 3).

(4) A 'freezing order' grants a form of interim protection to the applicant. It does not of itself confer proprietary protection on him (see *Flightline Limited v Edwards* [2003] 1 WLR 1200 CA). Nor does it impose a duty of care on a third party, such as a bank, with whom the 'frozen assets' are lodged (*Customs and Excise Commissioners v Barclays Bank plc* [2007] 1 AC 181; (2006) 65(3) CLJ 484 (Capper)).

The worldwide freezing order The development of the 'worldwide freezing order' (WFO) took even further what had already been described as 'revolutionary'. In *Derby & Co v Weldon (Nos 3 and 4)* [1990] Ch 65, the Court of Appeal held 'unequivocally' that a court can order a defendant's assets to be frozen even if they are situated outside the jurisdiction (at 92–93). In order to make this step, the court has to deal with two problems. First, as we have seen, a freezing order can only be granted in support of a cause of action that has already been initiated. This means that the court must generally have jurisdiction over that cause of action. This will not always be clear where international parties and business are involved. A court can, however, claim jurisdiction where, for example, the defendant is present in England and served with a writ; or where the cause of action centres on damage sustained in England (CPR Pt 6). In addition, even if the cause of action cannot be heard in England, English courts can sometimes claim jurisdiction to give interim relief (see Civil Jurisdiction and Judgments Act 1982, s 25 and eg *Crédit Suisse Fides Trust SA v Cuoghi* [1997] 3 All ER 724; *Motorola Credit Corporation v Uzan (No 6)* [2003] EWCA Civ 752 CA; see also *Haiti (Republic of) v Duvalier* [1990] 1 QB 202; and Collins (1989) 105 LQR 262).

A second difficulty is that the court must also be able to claim jurisdiction over *assets* that are held overseas. Remember, however, that one of the fundamental characteristics of an equitable remedy is that it operates in personam. Hence, provided that the court can properly claim jurisdiction over an individual, it does not offend against the jurisdiction of another court to make an order against that person (but cf the uncertain position where EC law applies, *Banco Nacional de Comercio Exterior SNC v Empresa de Telecomunicationes de Cuba SA* [2007] EWCA Civ 622; Merrett [2008] LMCLQ 71–87). Whether the order is effective when served against third parties holding the relevant assets is another question altogether. Lord Donaldson addressed this difficulty in *Derby v Weldon (Nos 3 and 4)* and held that an order intended to have worldwide effect should be declared enforceable by the relevant foreign court. Having been registered as such, it may be served and enforced on the third party in the external jurisdiction (at 82–84).

In addition to these jurisdictional difficulties, the courts have stated that worldwide freezing orders will only be granted in 'exceptional' circumstances (see *Derby & Co v Weldon (Nos 3 and 4)* op cit and *Re Bank of Credit and Commerce International SA (No 9)* [1994] 3 All ER 764). It is not always easy, however, to recognise such stringency at work. An example is *United Mizrahi Bank v Doherty* [1998] 2 All ER 230. Here the defendant, D, worked for the plaintiff bank, which alleged that he had wrongfully procured customers who were then persuaded to enter into transactions with the bank, whereby they made payments to third parties, for the benefit of D. It was alleged that D siphoned this money to various offshore entities, as well as his wife (the fifth defendant in the action) and was used to buy properties. An order was made whereby all Mr and Mrs Doherty's assets were frozen in this country and abroad, subject to certain financial limits, pending trial (cf *Re BCCI SA (No 9)* – 'complex international . . . financial dealings' with both defendants claiming not to be resident in the UK considered 'exceptional' by Rattee J). Moreover, the Court of Appeal in *Crédit Suisse Fides Trust v Cuoghi* appeared to suggest that the only relevant question was whether it would be 'inexpedient' to make the order (per Millett LJ at 732).

It should however be noted that an order to freeze 'all' assets is unusual. Not only are defendants granted an income from their assets to cover personal, business and legal expenses, as noted above, but it has been held that the court 'should not go further than necessity dictates . . . in the first instances it should look to assets within the jurisdiction . . . The existence of *sufficient* assets within the jurisdiction is an excellent reason for confining the jurisdiction to such assets but, other considerations apart, the fewer the assets within the jurisdiction the greater the necessity for taking protective measures in relation to those outside it' (*Derby v Weldon (Nos 3 & 4)* per Lord Donaldson at 79).

Lastly, the potentially powerful impact of a worldwide freezing order has led the courts to require safeguards to be put in place to protect defendants. Partly to meet these concerns it became the practice to require the claimant to give an undertaking not to seek to *enforce* the WFO abroad without the permission of the court. That posed the question as to what factors the court should consider before granting the permission. The Court of Appeal in *Dadourian Group International Inc v Simms* [2006] 1 WLR 2499, drawing on the submissions of counsel and previous case law, identified eight 'non-exhaustive' guidelines – unsurprisingly termed the 'Dadourian' guidelines – that courts should consider in deciding whether to grant the permission sought (described in some detail at 2502–2508; see Meisel (2007) 26 CJQ 176–180). The whole tenor of the guidelines, which tend to overlap in places, is understandably to emphasise the role of 'justice and convenience' of granting the permission (guideline 1) and the need to balance the interests of all actual and potential parties to the foreign proceedings (guideline 3) as well as the 'risk of dissipation of the assets' (guideline 7). The guidelines will doubtless assist the court in what nevertheless remains the difficult task of striking the right balance between the interests of a claimant trying to ensure that any victory in the main dispute is not rendered fruitless and those of a defendant who wishes to protect his business worldwide from being severely disrupted, perhaps even destroyed, before trial.

A Polly Peck postscript At several points in this chapter we have had cause to mention the demise of Polly Peck International and the attempts by administrators of the insolvent company to recover some £371m allegedly misappropriated by its founder Asil Nadir. It may be recalled that the administrators had sought to trace funds to an account of the Central Bank of Cyprus, held with a London clearing bank, and also to hold the Central Bank liable as a constructive trustee under a 'knowing receipt' claim. At first instance Millett J had granted a worldwide Mareva injunction against certain of the bank's assets. On appeal the injunction was discharged and replaced by an interlocutory injunction restraining the bank from using a particular sum (representing the value of funds claimed to be traceable to the bank) except in the course of its usual banking business.

Scott LJ recognised that it was possible that if the Mareva injunction was lifted any judgment obtained may turn out to be worthless, because the funds might be transferred back to Northern Cyprus. On the other hand the Mareva injunction would 'seriously interfere with the Central Bank's normal course of business and will, quite possibly destroy the Central Bank. . . . To impose a Mareva injunction that will have that effect in order to protect a cause of action that is no more than speculative is not simply wrong in principle but positively unfair' (*Polly Peck International v Nadir (No 2)* [1992] 4 All ER 769 at 784; see also Lord Donaldson MR (at 786): 'I am not to be taken as saying that a Mareva injunction can never be granted against a bank, but the circumstances would have to be unusual'). It is evident from the judgments that those seeking to recover the proceeds of fraud which have found their way into banks will find it difficult to convince a court that a freezing order (Mareva injunction) should be issued against the assets of the bank itself.

(3) Search orders (Anton Piller orders)

Introduction Search orders were developed to allow a claimant in a current or impending action to enter onto a defendant's premises and search for and preserve property relevant to the action, which would otherwise be destroyed by the defendant. In view of these circumstances, it was recognised that the application must be heard ex parte: if the defendant is such that he is likely to destroy either evidence of wrong-doing or the claimant's property, then any notice he has of a search will give him time to do just that. However, there are serious implications for 'ordinary civil liberties' (*Lock International plc v Beswick* [1989] 1 WLR 1268 at 1279) in both the application procedure and the search itself. As we have seen, a hearing ex parte infringes the principles of natural justice, whereby everyone has a right to be heard in his own defence. In addition, the search involves the potential for trespass on another's property, the humiliation of the individual concerned and the interruption of his family life if the target of the search is his home, or loss of reputation if it is his business. Carrying on that business may well be halted if records and stock in trade are taken. Indeed in *Lock International* itself, a case in which the previously issued and in the view of the court unjustifiable search order was discharged, the claimant's solicitors had removed, inter alia, nearly all the defendants' commercial papers, computer records and prototypes. There is also the danger that the privilege against self-incrimination in criminal proceedings will be infringed if incriminating evidence is found as a result of the search.

Nevertheless, the danger of injustice to the claimant if useful evidence is destroyed is considered sufficient to justify the continuation of the jurisdiction. The courts must therefore once again balance the two sets of considerations. Hoffmann J has put it as follows (*Lock International plc v Beswick*) [1989] 1 WLR 1268 at 1280):

> The more intrusive orders allowing searches of premises or vehicles require a careful balancing of, on the one hand, the plaintiff's right to recover his property or to preserve important evidence against, on the other hand, violation of the privacy of the defendant who has had no opportunity to put his side of the case. It is not merely that the defendant may be innocent. The making of an intrusive order ex parte is contrary to ordinary principles of justice and can only be done where there is a paramount need to prevent a denial of justice to the plaintiff. The absolute extremity of the court's powers is to permit a search of a defendant's dwelling-house, with the humiliation and family distress which that frequently involves.

Guidelines for a search order It is with this sort of consideration in mind that Ormrod LJ set out the following requirements for the granting of a search (Anton Piller) order (*Anton Piller v Manufacturing Processes Ltd* [1976] Ch 55 at 62):

> There are three essential preconditions for the making of such an order . . . First, there must be an extremely strong prima facie case. Secondly, the damage, potential or actual, must be very serious for the applicant. Thirdly, there must be clear evidence that the defendants have in their possession incriminating documents or things, and that there is a real possibility that they may destroy such material before any application inter partes can be made.

Lord Denning MR in the case added that the order should only be made where it would do 'no real harm to the defendant or his case' (at 61). In a report on 'the practical operation of Anton Piller Orders' by a committee appointed by the Judges' Council and chaired by Staughton LJ (Lord Chancellor's Department 1992) this element of the test was further refined. Here it was said that the harm 'likely to be caused by the execution of the Anton Piller order to the respondent and his business affairs must not be excessive or out of proportion to the legitimate object of the order' (at para 2.8).

It is useful to consider Ormrod LJ's third condition in *Anton Piller* as falling into two parts, since it is clear that the fact that the defendant may have relevant documents or records is not sufficient alone to allow an order to be made. Just as for freezing orders there must be evidence of a risk that assets will be dissipated, here there must be evidence of the potential for the destruction of relevant property. However, such evidence may be difficult to find: 'It is seldom that one can get cogent or actual evidence of a threat to destroy materials or documents. So it is necessary for it to be inferred from the material that is before the court' (per Oliver LJ *Dunlop Holdings Ltd v Staravia* [1982] Com LR 3). Bea has argued that search orders accordingly became 'relatively easy' to obtain by the mid-1980s (*Injunctions* (9th edn, 2007) para 8.09 et seq). Subsequent 'miscarriages of justice' prompted Dillon LJ in *Booker McConnell plc v Plascow* [1985] RPC 425 to comment that '[t]he phrase "a real possibility" [of destruction] is to be contrasted with the extravagant fears which seem to afflict all plaintiffs who have complaints of breach of confidence, breach of copyright or passing off. . . .' A court nevertheless has a difficulty here. It may well be unfair to infer from the fact that a defendant is engaged in nefarious activity such as, for example, 'pirating' copyrighted material, that he is generally untrustworthy, especially in view of the serious consequences of granting an order. However, other evidence of the risk of destruction may be elusive and a certain amount of inference is likely to be necessary.

For these reasons, which stem largely from the fact that the application has to be made ex parte, the duties on the applicant and his solicitors are onerous. There is, as for freezing orders, an extensive duty to make full and frank disclosure of all relevant facts, even, for example, to such matters as how the order is to be executed (see *Gee on Commercial Injunctions* (5th edn, 2004) ch 9). The importance of disclosure was emphasised in *Columbia Pictures Inc v Robinson* [1987] Ch 38, the first full trial of matters arising from the issue of a search order. Scott J found a significant failure to disclose material facts and that an order had been wrongfully made in part because of this. He commented, inter alia, that even disclosure was an 'unsatisfactory' procedure, since the plaintiff's solicitor 'cannot be expected to present the available evidence from the respondent's point of view' (at 75). Nevertheless, he held that 'affidavits ought to err on the side of excessive disclosure. In the case of material falling into the grey area of possible relevance, the judge, not the plaintiff's solicitors, should be the judge of relevance' (at 77).

Various further safeguards are now written into the form of the order granted. They include, for example, the provision that the order must specify exactly which premises are to be searched, who is to carry out the search and what materials are to be searched for. No material can be removed unless this is anticipated by the terms of the order; and items taken for copying must not be retained for more than two days (see generally CPR 25-PD-004, paras 7 and 8). In addition, the claimant must give an undertaking to pay damages if the court finds that making the order, carrying it out or a breach in its terms 'has caused loss to the Respondent' (CPR 25PD-007, Sch C (1)).

Consider the following points:

(1) Search orders are of potential difficulty for fiduciaries whose principals are the respondents in an action. For example, if a plaintiff is attempting to trace assets so as to bring a proprietary or personal claim, part of the process may be to serve a search order against a bank holding assets in the defendant's name. If this is the case, then the plaintiff can obtain a 'gagging order' against the bank to prevent it for a limited time from complying with its duty to use its best endeavours as fiduciary to inform its client of the proceedings (see *Robertson v Canadian Bank of Commerce* [1994] 1 WLR 1493; and *Gee* paras 17.016–17.018).

(2) Search orders work by requiring 'any person described in the order' (Civil Procedure Act 1997, s 7(3)) to 'permit' those executing the order to enter the relevant premises. The problem is that if consent is not given, then a trespass takes place. Since these are not police search warrants, but limited and interim measures in civil proceedings, consent is needed. The order therefore requires the defendant to give it. He may if he chooses decline to do so, but he will then be in contempt of court – even if he intends in the meantime to apply for the discharge or variation of the order – and risks being committed to prison (see Dockray and Thomas (1998) 17 CJQ 272 at 277 et seq).

(3) In *Columbia Pictures*, Scott J described the procedures as 'essentially unfair' (at 73, and see also Zuckerman (1994) 14 OJLS 353). Do you agree? Is there a method of achieving the desired ends without introducing any element of unfairness?

(4) For the privilege against self-incrimination, see *IBM United Kingdom Ltd v Prima Data International Ltd* [1994] 1 WLR 719; *Cobra Golf Inc v Rata* (No

2) [1997] 2 WLR 629; *C plc v P* [2006] 3 WLR 273 (evidence of criminal activity); and generally *Gee* para 17.030 et seq; *Bean* para 8.18.

6. Specific performance

As explained in the introduction to this chapter, our coverage of the equitable remedy of specific performance is brief in the extreme. The conceptual and practical explanation is that the remedy is principally concerned with the performance of contractual relations and is conventionally studied in that context. Our purpose here is simply to sketch in some of the outer boundaries and the underlying rationale of specific performance as a preliminary to our coverage of equitable damages which can be awarded in lieu both of injunctions and specific performance.

As with other equitable remedies such as injunctive relief the award of an order for specific performance is formally discretionary although the exercise of the discretion now operates within a reasonably clear structure of principles and rules. It is, for instance, well established that specific performance will not normally be ordered to enforce contracts for personal services, such as employment contracts, whereas the converse is the case for contracts for the sale or lease of land (but cf in the case of contracts of employment where injunctions were issued the somewhat specific factual backgrounds: *Hill v CA Parsons Ltd* [1972] Ch 305; and *Hughes v London Borough of Southwark* [1988] IRLR 55). Also in common with the injunction, an order for specific performance is made personally against a defendant; to ignore it constitutes contempt of court, punishable ultimately by imprisonment.

But when and why should an order for specific performance of a contract be made? The underlying rationale was recently restated by Lord Hoffmann in *Co-operative Insurance Society Ltd v Argyll Stores (Holdings) Ltd* [1997] 3 All ER 297 at 301:

> Specific performance is traditionally regarded in English law as an exceptional remedy, as opposed to the common law damages to which the successful plaintiff is entitled as of right.... [B]y the nineteenth century it was orthodox doctrine that the power to decree specific performance was part of the discretionary jurisdiction of the Court of Chancery to do justice in cases in which the remedies available at common law were inadequate. This is the basis of the general principle that specific performance will not be ordered when damages are an adequate remedy.

There are certain well-established circumstances where it is recognised that an award of damages would not be an adequate remedy. Uniqueness of the property that is the subject-matter of the contract is one common element. Land has conventionally been deemed to be unique and hence, so it is said, 'the damages for the loss of such a bargain ... would constitute a wholly inadequate and unjust remedy for the breach. That is why the normal remedy is by a decree of specific performance' (per Lord Diplock in *Sudbrook Trading Estate Ltd v Eggleton* [1983] 1 AC 444 at 478). By way of contrast most chattels and other personal property are not unique since substitute products can usually be obtained in the marketplace. Nevertheless, specific performance may be ordered where an alternative is not freely available on the market (see eg *Sky Petroleum Ltd v VIP Petroleum Ltd* [1974] 1 All ER 954 where in unusual circumstances no alternative supply of petroleum products was available). In an age of housing estates with properties of similar, often identical, design uniqueness of land is a less evident quality but the underlying rationale – the ready availability of a similar product – still remains as an important consideration in determining whether to exercise the discretion.

'Alternative market' justifications aside, there are numerous categories of contractual relations where specific performance will not usually be ordered. In *Co-operative Insurance Society Ltd v Argyll Stores (Holdings) Ltd*, for instance, the House of Lords confirmed that only in very exceptional circumstances would specific performance be ordered to compel a defendant to carry on a business indefinitely. In the case itself the defendant supermarket (Safeway) – a leaseholder whose premises were the focal point of a shopping centre and subject to a covenant under the lease to keep open during the usual hours of business – had been trading at a loss and wanted to close the store. The House of Lords, reversing the majority opinion of the Court of Appeal ([1996] 3 All ER 934, CA) refused to order specific performance of the covenant (see Jones (1997) 56 CLJ 488; Phang (1998) 61 MLR 421; Luxton [1998] Conv 396, but cf Tettenborn [1998] Conv 23). The formal rationale here is that specific performance will not be ordered where constant supervision might be required by the court. Underpinning this objection is the fact that in the last resort the only means of enforcing an order is by punishment for contempt of court. Aside from a possible lack of effectiveness – the defendant may still refuse to perform – the courts are concerned about the possible unjust consequences. The injustice here lies partly in the way an order for specific performance might impinge unfairly on one of the parties and partly in a broader perception concerning the public interest. Lord Hoffmann in the House of Lords, concurring with the dissenting opinion of Millett LJ in the Court of Appeal ([1996] 3 All ER 934 at 948–950), summarised these twin justifications as follows (at 303–304):

> The loss which the defendant may suffer through having to comply with the order (for example, by running a business at a loss for an indefinite period) may be far greater than the plaintiff would suffer from the contract being broken. It is true that the defendant has, by his own breach of contract, put himself in such an unfortunate position. But the purpose of the law of contract is not to punish wrongdoing but to satisfy the expectations of the party entitled to performance. A remedy which enables him to secure, in money terms, more than the performance due to him is unjust. From a wider perspective, it cannot be in the public interest for the courts to require someone to carry on business at a loss if there

is any plausible alternative by which the other party can be given compensation. It is not only a waste of resources but yokes the parties together in a continuing hostile relationship. The order for specific performance prolongs the battle. If the defendant is ordered to run a business, its conduct becomes the subject of a flow of complaints, solicitors' letters and affidavits. This is wasteful for both parties and the legal system. An award of damages, on the other hand, brings the litigation to an end. The defendant pays damages, the forensic link between them is severed, they go their separate ways and the wounds of conflict can heal.

Here, of course, with this consideration of 'injustice', the original concern of equity resurfaces, as it does with the recognition of various defences available to defendants. Not surprisingly, where a defendant has a right to rescind a contract on grounds, for instance, of misrepresentation by the claimant, specific performance will not be ordered, nor will it where great hardship would be caused to a defendant or third party (see eg the unfortunate family circumstances in *Patel v Ali* [1984] Ch 283; and for more extensive textbook reviews of the whole jurisdiction, see eg *Pettit* ch 29; *Hanbury and Martin* ch 24). There is, moreover, an alternative to an award of specific performance in the form of equitable damages. Admirable though the creativity of the courts of equity may have been in complementing the common law remedy of damages, it came to be recognised, certainly by the nineteenth century, that there was a gap in the procedures of the legal system. Could damages be awarded under the equity jurisdiction or would the plaintiff have to institute separate proceedings in the common law courts? It is to that issue that we turn next.

7. Equitable damages

(a) Introduction

The most common form of remedy at common law is an award of damages: it is this that a claimant will be looking for if knocked down by a negligent driver or faced with a breach of contract. We have also seen that equity can offer further and more sweeping means of redress, which act 'on the body' – in personam – and can provide a remedy where the common law monetary solution would be inadequate. It would appear, therefore, that a right to damages in equity is irrelevant: one nowadays chooses to go to equity precisely because a money award is not adequate to compensate you. The courts do nevertheless have jurisdiction to grant such damages in equity.

The statutory jurisdiction arises under what is now the Supreme Court Act 1981, s 50. This provides that: 'Where the . . . High Court has jurisdiction to entertain an application for an injunction or specific performance, it may award damages in addition to, or in substitution for, an injunction or specific performance.' The original provision was found in the Chancery Amendment Act 1858 (or 'Lord Cairns' Act'), enacted prior to the Judicature Acts 1873–75, in order to deal with the 'complaints... constantly made by the public, that when plaintiffs came into a court of equity for specific performance the court of equity sent them to a court of law in order to recover damages, so that parties were bandied about, as it was said, from one court to the other... The object... of that Act... was to prevent parties from being so sent from one court to the other' (*Ferguson v Wilson* (1866) 2 Ch App 77 at 88).

The Act therefore played a role in preventing procedural anomalies. The jurisdiction was not, however, abandoned after procedural fusion in 1873–75. Relief is still granted under s 50 where common law relief is not available or appropriate and equitable relief in the form of specific performance or injunction is likewise considered inappropriate. It appears that it may also be available where the right that has been infringed arises in equity alone (see *A-G v Observer Ltd* [1990] 1 AC 109 at 286, where Lord Goff refers to the 'remedy of damages, which in cases of breach of confidence is now available, despite the equitable nature of the wrong, through a beneficent interpretation of... Lord Cairns' Act').

We here examine the substance of the jurisdiction in the context of injunctive relief and the difficulties that arise with it.

(b) The jurisdictional question

We have seen that s 50 gives a court the power to award damages in equity where 'it has jurisdiction' to grant, inter alia, an injunction. As with other equitable remedies, the power gives the courts discretion to grant the relief. A preliminary difficulty is distinguishing cases where the court does not have the *power* to make an order (ie it does not have the jurisdiction to do so) from those where the court does have such power, but chooses to exercise its *discretion* so as to turn down the application. A situation where this matters is one where a court decides, in its discretion, not to award an injunction. The question is whether this means that it cannot therefore award damages instead.

This question has been answered by recent authority in the negative (*Jaggard v Sawyer* [1995] 2 All ER 189; earlier authorities had indicated the opposite: eg *Aynsley v Glover* (1874) LR 18 Eq 544). The statutory power to award damages arises where the wrong in question is susceptible of prevention by injunction, even if the court might in its discretion decide against an injunction per se. As Cairns LJ himself put it, the power arises in cases where there are 'all those ingredients which would enable the court, if it thought fit, to exercise its power' to give relief in specie (*Ferguson v Wilson* at 91; and see generally Ingman and Wakefield [1981] Conv 286; Jolowicz (1975) 34 CLJ 224).

(c) Exercising the discretion

Given that the court does have the jurisdiction to award damages, what matters will it take into account when deciding whether to exercise its discretion to do so? The statute gives no guidance on this point, so the courts have developed rules of thumb. In *Shelfer v City of London Electric Co* [1895] 1 Ch 287, a case where the cause of action lay in nuisance, Lindley LJ held that the jurisdiction to award damages instead of an injunction 'ought not to be exercised in such cases except under very exceptional circumstances' (at 316). AL Smith LJ went further (at 322–323):

> In such cases [as this] the well-known rule is not to accede to the application [for the grant of damages] but to grant the injunction sought, for the plaintiff's legal right has been invaded and he is prima facie entitled to an injunction.
>
> There are, however, cases in which this rule may be relaxed... In any instance in which a case for an injunction has been made out, if the plaintiff by his acts or laches has disentitled himself to an injunction the Court may award damages in its place.... In my opinion, it may be stated as a good working rule that –
>
> (1) If the injury to the plaintiff's legal rights is small,
> (2) And is one which is capable of being estimated in money,
> (3) And is one which can be adequately compensated by a small money payment,
> (4) And the case is one in which it would be oppressive to the defendant to grant an injunction:–
>
> then damages in substitution for an injunction may be granted.

It is not clear that the 'working rule' in *Shelfer* takes us very far in determining whether damages ought to be substituted for an injunction. Indeed Smith LJ himself acknowledged in *Shelfer* that it would be 'impossible to lay down any rule as to what, under the differing circumstances of each case, constitutes either a small injury, or one that can be estimated in money, or what is a small money payment, or an adequate compensation, or what would be oppressive to the defendant' (at 323). Moreover there is an element of circularity involved here: an injunction is under consideration because common law damages are not considered adequate; why then consider equitable damages in substitution for the injunction, on the grounds of their adequacy in compensating the plaintiff's injury? (See eg *Spry The Principles of Equitable Remedies* (6th edn, 2001) p 640.) This objection would appear all the more convincing when the measure of damages that is attainable is considered (see below). Nevertheless the approach in *Shelfer* was endorsed by the Court of Appeal in *Jaggard v Sawyer* [1995] 2 All ER 189 although here again emphasis was placed on it as being 'only a working rule' and not 'an exhaustive statement of the circumstances in which damages may be awarded instead of an injunction' (per Millett LJ at 208). Here, the defendant built a house in breach of a restrictive covenant. The plaintiff (a neighbour) objected. The court refused a mandatory injunction, following the *Shelfer* guidelines: the injury was small (traffic increases down the road in question would be small) and could be quantified, the defendant had not acted in disregard of the plaintiff's interests and the plaintiff had failed to obtain interim relief, so taking the risk that by the time the matter came to court, the grant of an injunction would be inequitable.

(d) The measure of damages

A final, vexing, question must briefly be addressed. Having decided that it has both the jurisdiction to consider an award and is minded in its discretion to do so, how much money can the claimant win? We have seen that the award is made in principle when common law damages are not available or adequate, in substitution for an injunction or an award of specific performance. It may appear somewhat paradoxical, therefore, that in *Johnson v Agnew* [1980] AC 367 dicta of Lord Wilberforce indicated that equitable damages could be awarded *only* on the same basis as common law damages: that is, in order to compensate for loss suffered. The point has been the subject of controversy. In *Wrotham Park Estate Co v Parkside Homes Ltd* [1974] 1 WLR 798, houses were built by the defendant in breach of a restrictive covenant (which is enforceable by successors in title only in equity). The houses had been sold to third parties by the time the action came to trial. A mandatory injunction was therefore refused and the court agreed to make an award of damages. The plaintiffs had suffered no financial loss as a result of the breach; substantial damages were assessed instead, under Lord Cairns' Act, on the basis of how much the plaintiffs might hypothetically have been willing to accept to relax the covenant.

In *Surrey County Council v Bredero Homes* [1993] 1 WLR 1361 a case with similar facts to *Wrotham Park*, although with no injunction being sought, a claim was made for common law damages to be assessed on the same basis as that adopted in that case. Notwithstanding the similarities, the claim was rejected by the Court of Appeal. Nominal damages only were awarded, it being questioned whether the measure of compensation in *Wrotham Park* was in line with *Johnson v Agnew* (see Ingman [1994] Conv 110). This matter arose again, however, in the Court of Appeal in *Jaggard v Sawyer* [1995] 2 All ER 189 where what might be described as a robust approach was taken to the question. Having rejected a claim for a mandatory injunction, Sir Thomas Bingham MR held that the measure adopted in *Wrotham Park* was based on compensatory principles, and upheld damages in the instant case for an amount reflecting what the beneficiary of a restrictive covenant would have demanded as a price for waiving compliance with the covenant (see also Millett LJ emphasising, in a sense, the economic significance to the value of the covenant of the ability to claim an injunction (at 212)).

More recently still in *Attorney General (A-G) v Blake* [2001] 1 AC 268 (see further (e) below) *Wrotham Park* was cited with approval – '[shining] rather as a solitary beacon' – in preference to the approach in *Surrey CC v Bredero Homes*. Lord Nicholls, for instance, whilst agreeing that compensation is normally calculated by reference to a claimant's *financial loss*, considered that this did not exclude circumstances where other yardsticks might apply. He summarised the position as follows (at 281):

> The measure of damages awarded in this type of case is often analysed as damages for loss of a bargaining opportunity or, which comes to the same, the price payable for the compulsory acquisition of a right. This analysis is correct.

On this view, the payment of a hypothetical 'reasonable fee' for a lost opportunity to bargain can just about be analysed as an award of compensatory damages for loss (but cf Cunnington (2007) 123 LQR 48; Rotherham [2008] LMCLQ 25–55). It is, however, less obvious that a comparable analysis can be applied to the outcome of the breach of contract issue in *A-G v Blake*, to which we now turn.

(e) Losses, gains and a blurring of boundaries

In *A-G v Blake (Jonathan Cape Ltd, third party)* [2001] 1 AC 268 the House of Lords by 4:1 rejected the prevailing orthodoxy that damages in contract were restricted solely to recoupment of financial loss and instead held that it is now possible in certain rare circumstances for the victim of a breach of contract to be awarded the profits earned by the breaker of the contract (see Edelman [2001] LMCLQ 9). The particular 'rare circumstance' of the case was that an action for breach of a confidentiality clause in his contract of employment was the only practicable remedy available against George Blake, sometime member of the Secret Intelligence Services (SIS) but who had been in effect an agent for the Soviet Union. Blake had been convicted and imprisoned but escaped to Moscow where he continued to live and where he subsequently wrote his autobiography, *No Other Choice*, for which the publisher Jonathan Cape Ltd agreed to pay £150,000. The Attorney-General sought successfully to claim for the Crown the moneys that were otherwise owed to George Blake.

Lord Nicholls, giving the leading opinion, made extensive reference to, inter alia, academic literature generally critical of the rigidity of the prevailing orthodoxy and summarised the issue before the House as follows (at 281): 'The question is whether the court will award substantial damages for an infringement when no financial loss flows from the infringement and, moreover, in a suitable case will assess the damages by reference to the defendant's profit obtained from the infringement.' In deference to a concern that a positive decision might introduce an unacceptable degree of uncertainty into commercial contracts, it was emphasised that the remedy of 'an account of profits' would be available only in exceptional cases, of which the instant case was clearly one, and at the discretion of the court. Lord Nicholls located the jurisdiction firmly within the area occupied by other equitable remedies (at 284):

> When exceptionally, a just response to a breach of contract so requires, the court should be able to grant the discretionary remedy of requiring a defendant to account to the plaintiff for the benefits he has received from his breach of contract. In the same way as a plaintiff's interest in performance of a contract may render it just and equitable for the court to make an order for specific performance or grant an injunction, so the plaintiff's interest in performance may make it just and equitable that the defendant should retain no benefit from his breach of contract.

In a roundabout fashion the eliding of distinctions between the measurement of damages at equity and at common law brings us face to face with contemporary developments in this area of the law whilst returning us to one of the underlying themes of this chapter – 'harmonisation' in the law. It is tempting to conclude that what we are witnessing with equitable damages, as also with 'knowing receipt' and with tracing, is a growing impetus to challenge the existing rationales for some of the historically derived conceptual distinctions in areas of our private law system. There is, however, another theme that has surfaced at several points in this chapter, the more pragmatic one of commercial consequences of legal change. At times this influence may be pleaded in support of assimilating common law and equitable concepts, at others a more sceptical tone may be discernible. Lord Hobhouse, for instance, had this to say in his dissenting opinion in *A-G v Blake* (at 299):

> I must also sound a further note of warning that if some more extensive principle of awarding non-compensatory damages for breach of contract is to be introduced into our commercial law the consequences will be very far-reaching and disruptive. I do not believe that such is the intention of your Lordships but if others are tempted to try to extend the decision of the present exceptional case to commercial situations so as to introduce restitutionary rights beyond those presently recognised by the law of restitution, such a step will require very careful consideration before it is acceded to.

On the specific issue in *A-G v Blake* it is probable that the wholly exceptional facts of the case were central to the decision to deprive Blake of any benefit. Moreover it is likely that 'careful consideration' and probably inconsistency of approach will occur before it becomes clear just how far this extension of the law for gain-based damages for breach of contract will in Lord Steyn's words from the case '[be] hammered out on the anvil of concrete cases' (cf the contrasting views of Leng and Leong [2002] JBL 513–538 and Campbell [2003] JBL 131–144; see also *Experience Hendrix LLC v PPX* [2003] 1 All ER (Comm) 830; Campbell and Wylie (2003) 62(3) CLJ 605–630; Edelman [2003] RLR 101; Graham (2004) 120 LQR 26; *WWF World Wide Fund for Nature v World Wrestling Federation Inc* [2008] 1 WLR 445; and the perceptive and more wide-ranging legal-contextual commentary on this area in Waddams *Dimensions of Private Law – Categories and Concepts in Anglo-American Legal Reasoning* (2003) ch 6). The broader point is that the need for 'careful consideration' is not only applicable to commercial considerations. It is equally relevant to conceptualist-derived arguments for change. The trite conclusion here is simply to emphasise that whilst we may wish to, and arguably should, treat like cases alike we must equally be careful not to confuse similarity with equivalence. It is tempting, along with the late Jimmy Hendrix, to utter the despairing plea: 'There must be some way out of here / Said the joker to the thief / There's too much confusion here / I can't get no relief' (*All Along the Watchtower* © Bob Dylan). But it is somehow reassuring to discover that the path to enlightenment and ultimately to equitable relief follows in the footsteps of a Soviet spy and a 'rock 'n roll' legend.

15

Trusts in commerce III: commerce, credit and the trust

1. Introduction

We have seen in Chapters 11 and 14 how the determination of the courts to protect the interest of the beneficiaries in the event of trustee insolvency or misconduct was manifested in two ways in particular: (i) the separation of trust property from the insolvent's own assets; and (ii) the provision of the process of equitable tracing. Thus, property held by an insolvent or bankrupt person or company in trust for another is, with one exception, not available to the liquidator or trustee in bankruptcy to meet the claims of creditors. The exception is where an insolvent trustee has outlaid its own moneys in satisfaction of the trust's liabilities. A right of indemnity arises against trust assets for such liabilities satisfied on the trust's behalf (eg in running a business of the trust). This gives the trustee a proprietary interest in the trust assets, which may pass to a trustee in bankruptcy or liquidator for the benefit of creditors (see generally *Hayton and Marshall* at pp 693–703). In certain rare circumstances it has been held that property held on trust may be available to the liquidator to cover its costs if the insolvent's other assets are insufficient (see Chapter 14, p 740). The reasoning behind the fundamental principle that the insolvent's property does not include trust property is clear enough: trust property is beneficially owned not by the insolvent or bankrupt trustee, but by the beneficiaries. Furthermore the principle – described as 'the cornerstone of the English law of trusts' (Waters (1983) 21 Alta LR 395 at 402) – is not confined to express trusts but extends also to cases of imputed trusts. The effects of this principle and its close companion, equitable tracing, are graphically summarised in the following extract from the Cork Report.

Report of Review Committee on Insolvency Law and Practice (Cmnd 8558, 1982) para 1045

Where a claimant can establish that he has an interest in property in the hands of or under the control of the insolvent which is impressed with a trust, express, implied or constructive, he is not required to rank as an unsecured creditor, but may call for the return of the trust property to which the general body of creditors have no right to resort. If the insolvent has

> mixed property held on trust with his own property, the claimant will have a charge on the mixed property to the extent of his interest and if, in accordance with the equitable rules of tracing, he can identify the trust property to which he is entitled, he has a right to have it or its proceeds handed over to him. Only if and to the extent that he is unable to identify the trust property will he be left to resort to a claim as an unsecured creditor of the insolvent for the loss sustained by the insolvent's breach of trust.

For those engaged in commerce, the attractiveness of establishing a beneficial interest in money or goods supplied to a company which may become insolvent is the alteration of their legal status: from the lowly (and often unpaid) unsecured creditor to the beneficiary with rights that prevail over all creditors. As the Cork Report indicates, major changes have occurred since the nineteenth century in the methods of finance in commerce and industry. These include a great increase in the use of loans, often secured by means of a floating charge on the whole or a substantial part of a company's undertaking. One consequence is that where a commercial insolvency occurs, a large and increasing proportion of the debtor's assets are claimed by the secured and preferential creditors, frequently leaving unsecured creditors to pick over the bare bones of the carcass. Faced with this unattractive prospect, creditors who would otherwise be unsecured have turned their attention to the privileged status which equity courts developed to protect beneficiaries.

In this chapter we consider three specific commercial contexts in which potential creditors have attempted to make use of (i) the protection afforded by the separation of trust property from that of the insolvent; and/or (ii) the availability of equitable tracing in those circumstances where there exists some fiduciary relationship sufficient to give rise to an equitable right of property.

The application of these equitable doctrines to commercial contexts raises legal and policy questions which we can but briefly touch on. Accordingly the focus is primarily on the effectiveness of these attempts by creditors to obtain some degree of protection and the extent to which the attempts have proven compatible with established equitable principles. However, it is important to note that granting recognition to beneficial interests in property held by an insolvent may conflict with some of the policies underlying insolvency law, for example, maximising the assets within the insolvent's estate so that unsecured creditors are not prejudiced and, where trust principles operate to confer security, ensuring that later lenders have notice of the security.

The contexts we consider are: first, protection of payments made by consumers in advance of delivery of the goods or services purchased (section 2 below); second, provision of security for a loan made by A to B to achieve a particular purpose, the security to be operative only until the money is expended in implementing the purpose (section 3 below); third, the securing, for a supplier of goods, of payment of the price of the goods in the event of the buyer's insolvency (section 4 below).

2. Consumer prepayments and the trust

(a) The prepayment problem

Prepayment is not a term of art but, broadly speaking, refers to any payment in advance made by a consumer to a trader for goods or services which are not to be supplied immediately. Such payments are commonly made to mail-order houses, furniture and electrical goods retailers, travel firms and building contractors for home improvement work.

The problem with prepayment is that if a supplier becomes insolvent, then customers who have made prepayments, but not received goods or services, are almost invariably unsecured creditors under insolvency law. Therefore, they are unlikely to receive all or any substantial proportion of their money back. Usually the prepaying customer cannot identify which of the trader's stock (if any) could be said to belong to the customer so that the customer could claim these goods. This lack of identification or appropriation also prevents a trust being recognised over the goods because there is no identifiable trust property (see *Re Goldcorp Exchange* [1995] 1 AC 74). But amendments to the Sale of Goods Act may give rights to prepaying customers in some circumstances if what they have paid for forms part of an identifiable bulk (see Ulph [1996] JBL 482, 485 and Chapter 4, p 174). The incidence of the problem in practice is uncertain. There are no recent collected statistics of either the total annual volume of consumer prepayments or the proportion of those prepayments that are lost to the consumer.

(b) Remedies

(1) Introduction

Recognition of the problem has resulted in the introduction of a number of special schemes, voluntary and statutory, to protect the public. Some trade associations have voluntarily established compensation schemes (eg Safe Home Ordering Protection Scheme (www.shops-uk.org.uk); see also the Direct Marketing Association, www.dma.org.uk), whilst the Estate Agents Act 1979, s 13 requires a client's money to be held in trust for the client in a separate bank account (for a review of the various schemes see *OFT* paras 3.1–3.13; Scott and Black (eds) *Cranston's Consumers and the Law* (3rd edn, 2000) pp 436–439; and see generally Lowe and Woodroffe *Consumer Law and Practice* (7th edn, 2007)). Such schemes are necessarily limited in coverage and it is therefore no surprise that the attention of consumers' organisations has been drawn towards the feasibility of establishing some form of proprietary claim. It is here that the trust presents possibilities.

(2) The 'Kayford' trust

Strong judicial encouragement for using the trust to protect consumers was forthcoming in *Re Kayford*.

Re Kayford [1975] 1 All ER 604

Kayford Ltd (K) conducted a mail order business, customers paying either a deposit or the full price before receiving the goods they had ordered. K's chief supplier (a company to which K had lent substantial sums of money) got into financial difficulties, and this threatened both K's solvency and its ability to supply goods. An accountant advised K to open a separate 'Customers' Trust Deposit Account' and pay into it money received from customers for goods not yet delivered, withdrawing money only on delivery of the goods. The company accepted the advice but initially paid money into a dormant deposit account in the company's name, only later altering the name of the account. K subsequently went into voluntary liquidation. The judge found sufficient evidence of an intention to create a trust in the discussions of K's managing director, the accountant and the bank manager.

Megarry J: The question for me is whether the money in the bank account . . . is held on trust for those who paid it, or whether it forms part of the general assets of the company.

. . . I may say at the outset that on the facts of the case [counsel for the joint liquidators] was unable to contend that any question of a fraudulent preference arose. If one leaves on one side any case in which an insolvent company seeks to declare a trust in favour of creditors, one is concerned here with the question not of preferring creditors but of preventing those who pay money from becoming creditors, by making them beneficiaries under a trust . . . I feel no doubt that the intention was that there should be a trust. There are no formal difficulties. The property concerned is pure personalty, and so writing, though desirable, is not an essential. There is no doubt about the so-called 'three certainties' of a trust. The subject-matter to be held on trust is clear, and so are the beneficial interests therein, as well as the beneficiaries. As for the requisite certainty of words, it is well settled that a trust can be created without using the words 'trust' or 'confidence' or the like: the question is whether in substance a sufficient intention to create a trust has been manifested.

In *Re Nanwa Gold Mines Ltd* [1955] 3 All ER 219 the money was sent on the faith of a promise to keep it in a separate account, but there is nothing in that case or in any other authority that I know of to suggest that this is essential. I feel no doubt that here a trust was created. From the outset the advice (which was accepted) was to establish a trust account at the bank. The whole purpose of what was done was to ensure that the moneys remained in the beneficial ownership of those who sent them, and a trust is the obvious means of achieving this. No doubt the general rule is that if you send money to a company for goods which are not delivered, you are merely a creditor of the company unless a trust has been created. The sender may create a trust by using appropriate words when he sends the money (though I wonder how many do this, even if they are equity lawyers), or the company may do it by taking suitable steps on or before receiving the money. If either is done, the obligations in respect of the money are transformed from contract to property, from debt to trust. Payment into a separate bank account is a useful (though by no means conclusive) indication of an intention to create a trust, but of course there is nothing to prevent the company from binding itself by a trust even if there are no effective banking arrangements.

The correctness of Megarry J's assertion that no question of *fraudulent* preference arose because the company was not preferring creditors but preventing customers from becoming creditors has been doubted (see Goodhart and Jones (1980) 43 MLR 489 at 496–498 querying whether Kayford's unilateral voluntary declaration of trust contravened the Companies Act 1948, ss 302, 320; and Waters (1983) 21 Alta LR 395 at 416–418; but cf *Re Chelsea Cloisters Ltd* (1980) 41 P & CR 98 (tenants' deposits held in trust by landlord company in liquidation) and *Re Lewis's of Leicester Ltd* [1995] 1 BCLC 428 at 438–439 (payment of the takings of department store concessionaires into separate accounts); see also *OT Computers Ltd (in administration) v First National Tricity Finance Ltd* [2003] EWHC 1010 where payments into a 'customers' trust account' for customers' prepayments for computers were upheld but not payments into a similar account for 'urgent suppliers', as the class of beneficiaries (ie 'urgent suppliers') was too vague. The Insolvency Act (IA) 1986, with its more far-reaching provisions, could possibly be used to invalidate a *Kayford* trust under s 238 (transactions at undervalue) or s 239 (preferences, ie putting a creditor in a better position on insolvency) (see eg McCormack (1990) 134 SJ 216 at 217; and McCartney (1992) 8 Construction LJ 360). However, reliance on these sections was not successful in *Re Lewis's of Leicester Ltd*: Robert Walker J concluded that the payment – 'on the advice of experienced insolvency practitioners' – of 'shop takings' from sales by concessionaires into separate accounts, was undertaken to protect the store's immediate trading position and 'not to prefer' the interests of the concessionaires trading in the store. Moreover, if we assume that in *Re Kayford* (i) the customers intended that the prepayments would belong to Kayford, and (ii) Kayford had the option upon physical receipt of the money to decline the order and return the prepayment, then could it not equally accept the prepayment on the terms that it was trust moneys? (See Goode *Payment Obligations in Commercial and Financial Transactions* (2nd edn, 1989) p 18, n 64.) In *Re Farepak Food & Gifts Ltd (in administration)* [2006] EWHC 3272 (Ch) (discussed later), the preference issue was paramount in avoiding operation of the *Kayford*-type trust. However, the court recognised that for moneys received after the administration commenced a company 'may return or repudiate money which it does not wish to receive and which it had not already received' (para 56). This may imply that creating a *Kayford*-type trust may overcome the preference problem for moneys received after the trust's creation.

To the extent that doubts about *Re Kayford* are based only on the unilateral declaration of trust in that case – the customers were unaware of the company's intention – they do not undermine the proposition that a trust to protect consumers' prepayments can be valid where the trust arrangement is created at the behest of the consumer. Apart from the distinct possibility that the trader may refuse to accept the order on that basis – and of course a valid trust cannot be created if the intended trustee will not act as such – such an individual approach is likely to be of only marginal effect. Many consumers will be unaware of the possibility. Moreover the creation of the trust will protect the prepayment only if paid into a separate account, or, where mixed in an account with non-trust money, if it is possible to trace under the rules described in Chapter 14. If the trust property cannot be traced in this way, the consumer will be left with merely a personal claim against the trader, and thus remain an unsecured creditor.

A situation which provides some insights into potential limitations on the use of the trust in insolvency is *Re Challoner Club Ltd (in liquidation)* (1997) *Times* 4 November. In that case, members of a company (an incorporated club) that was in difficult financial circumstances donated funds to the company to keep it afloat. The company attempted to create a trust over those funds, and the donations were paid into a designated bank account segregated from other moneys belonging to the club. Lloyd J stated:

> If these moneys were to be held on a valid and binding trust it must have been possible to spell out with certainty the circumstances in which the money became available to the Club to be used for its general purposes; and conversely the circumstances failing which there being satisfied the money became repayable to the member who had provided the money.

The trust failed because the court could not identify when the members would receive the money back, because its terms were too uncertain. The money was therefore considered to belong to the company and available to the company's creditors on a winding-up. Thus in devising a consumer prepayments trust a company would be wise expressly to resolve that the beneficiaries of the trust (the prepaying customers) will get their funds back on insolvency.

(3) The limitations of the trust as a universal remedy

The evidentiary and practical limitations for a claimant asserting a *Kayford*-type trust were highlighted in *Re Farepak Food and Gifts Ltd (in admin): Dubey v HM Revenue & Customs* [2006] EWHC 3272 (Ch). This case might be called the case of the 'not so happy Christmas'. Farepak operated a Christmas saving scheme under which customers contributed small amounts of money to 'agents' who passed the contributions on to Farepak. There were approximately 26,000 agents, most of them having no more than six or seven customers. The customers made advance payments to purchase a shopping voucher, hamper or other goods for Christmas. Farepak was insolvent and went into administration on 13 October 2006. However, in the three days leading up to the administration, the directors attempted to establish a *Kayford*-type trust to protect the customers. The Administrators applied for court directions about who was entitled to the money in the alleged *Kayford* trust. The case was brought on quickly so that if the customers were entitled to any funds, they would be able to receive these before Christmas. Unfortunately, the customers were unsuccessful for several reasons. Primarily, the *Kayford*-type trust failed because the court held it involved a preference. The customers paid moneys to the agents, who received those moneys on behalf of Farepak and later forwarded the moneys to Farepak. When Farepak directors declared a trust over moneys in Farepak's bank account, this constituted a preference.

The customers had become Farepak's creditors when the agents received the contributions from the customers. At the point of payment to an agent, the money was 'received' by Farepak. Thus, the trust was void under insolvency law. However, the court recognised that if it was possible to treat any customers as paying the money directly to Farepak, then there might not be a preference 'because they are not creditors at the moment of creation of a trust over their money', presumably because Farepak could decide the terms upon which it would accept such moneys, but 'filtering those customers out may be difficult if not impossible' (para 52). Customers who could claim under a *Kayford*-type trust would need evidence of their direct payment to Farepak. Unfortunately, due to the speed of bringing the case on, no such evidence was available.

Given what we have discussed above, it is not surprising that some attention has been paid towards universalising the protection offered by a *Kayford*-type trust. The desirability of legislation was considered but ultimately rejected by the Cork Committee:

> 1050. We understand the sense of grievance felt by those who have lost money in such circumstances, but we are satisfied that the proposal is impracticable. In many cases, advance payments are an essential part of the trader's working capital. For example, a mail order company often has to purchase and pay for goods which have been ordered by the customer, or for materials from which to manufacture them, before delivery; a tour operator often needs to use the deposits received from his clients in paying a deposit to the foreign hotel . . .

> 1051. . . . Some of those who have given evidence to us, recognising that it is not practical to require a separate account to be maintained, have urged that nevertheless payments in advance for goods or services, should be repaid in full in the event of the trader's insolvency. In effect, this is to call for the creation of a new class of preferential claim.

> 1052. In our view, this attitude is misguided. The customer who pays in advance for goods or services to be supplied later extends credit just as surely as the trader who supplies in advance goods or services to be paid for later. There is no essential difference. Each gives credit; and if the credit is misplaced, each should bear the loss rateably.

> 1053. One of our members on the other hand is of the opinion that a purchaser of future goods should not be expected to provide the working capital and he would therefore recommend that:

> (a) any company dealing direct with the public and accepting payment in advance for goods or services must have sufficient working capital; and
> (b) payments made in advance should become trust money, and placed in a trust account until the goods paid for are delivered;

> but the rest of us do not agree.

> 1054. Of course, any trader is free, by taking the appropriate steps, to create a trust which will prevail in the event of his insolvency.

The Committee welcomed 'the sympathetic attitude to this problem shown by Megarry J' in *Re Kayford.*

The contention (para 1052) that there is no essential difference between prepayment customers and traders supplying goods or services on credit is controversial. It seems unlikely that, subjectively, prepayment customers see themselves as providers of unsecured credit. And the OFT questioned the objective basis of the comparison (*The Protection of Consumer Prepayments: A Discussion Paper* para 5.11):

> [Prepayment customers] do not consciously become creditors, and they have no means of securing the money which they advance. Consumers cannot assess the risk fully, and the Office does not regard it as feasible that consumers should be expected to check on the financial standing of traders (eg by consulting company returns and accounts filed with the Department of Trade and Industry). Major creditors, particularly banks, can secure their loans, and other suppliers of credit have a certain security as a result of informal advice and information from their peers. They may also insure their risks through organisations such as Trade Indemnity. Consumers will always remain the least protected creditors, unless steps are taken to improve their position.

But, as the OFT recognises, even acceptance of the points made in their argument does not lead to a conclusion that a statutory trust account is an appropriate remedy. Administration costs for individual firms (eg extra book-keeping) may increase and effective public monitoring may be difficult and expensive (see *OFT* paras 6.9–6.24). To ensure, for example, that a trader did not transfer a payment from a trust account to a general account before completion of the contract would require close supervision. Furthermore, a study by Ogus and Rowley *Prepayments and Insolvency* (OFT Occasional Paper 1984, para 5.50), suggests that alternative sources of finance would either be unavailable or available only at extremely high rates of interest, and consequently that the growth rate of the national economy 'may well suffer' (for an alternative view see Richardson [1985] JBL 456).

The Cork Committee rejected the remedial approaches of preferred status for unsecured creditors and the compulsory trust account. Instead it opted primarily for a preventative approach by proposing, for example, a tightening of the disqualification provisions for delinquent company directors and the institution of a new concept of wrongful trading which would expose directors to a measure of personal liability when their business failed. The recommendations of the Cork Report have not been fully implemented (see *A Revised Framework for Insolvency Law* (Cmnd 9175, 1984); and IA 1986, ss 214–217). However, under the IA 1986 a company director who 'knew or ought to have concluded that there was no reasonable prospect that the company would avoid going into insolvent liquidation' (s 214(2)(b)), is required to take all possible steps to minimise the potential loss to the company's creditors (s 214(3)). If a court is satisfied that the necessary steps were not taken, it can now order the errant director to contribute personally to the insolvent company's assets (s 214(1)). (For a fuller explanation, see eg Davies *Gower and Davies' Principles of Modern Company Law* (8th edn, 2008) pp 215–219.) Finally, any expectation that a European solution to the general prepayment problem would be forthcoming has been disappointed. Notwithstanding the stimulus of the Single European Market and the associated encouragement of cross-border distance selling, the European Directive on Distance Selling (97/7/EC) contains no measures which would protect consumers against a supplier's insolvency (see Consumer Protection (Distance Selling) Regulations 2000, SI 2000/ 2334).

(c) Conclusion

The rejection of a statutory trust account approach may have effectively sidelined the '*Kayford* trust'. If so, the attempt to use the trust-form will not have foundered on any inherent restrictiveness in trust law (but cf *Re Goldcorp Exchange* [1995] 1 AC 74; and see also the difficulty in establishing the requisite intention in *Holiday Promotions (Europe) Ltd* [1996] 2 BCLC 618; and *Re HB Haina & Associates Inc* (1978) 86 DLR (3d) 262). This could not, however, be so confidently claimed of all the available remedies. If the funds in a mixed bank account were to prove insufficient to meet all claims, and customers were forced to invoke the present equitable tracing rules regulating priorities therein, they would be likely to find them both cumbersome in operation and arbitrary in outcome. For this reason the Cork Report recommended that legislation be introduced to achieve a pari passu distribution among claimants to a fund, thus sidestepping the application of the rules in *Clayton*'s case (1816) 1 Mer 572 and *Re Hallett's Estate* (1880) 13 Ch D 696. But the principal reason for the trust's limited usefulness in this context is simply that a more widespread application is incompatible with contemporary commercial practice. There remains the possibility of individuals exercising freedom of contract, that linchpin of the common law, to stipulate that prepayments to, for instance, mail order houses must be held in a separate trust account until delivery of goods. But the usually inferior bargaining power of the consumer, and the lack of incentive for the trader to agree, suggests this will not be common.

In fundamental terms, however, the application of the trust in this consumer context, whilst perhaps reinforcing our awareness of the flexibility of the formalities required to create an express trust of personalty, presents no challenge to established doctrines of trust law (but cf *Re Multi Guarantee Ltd* [1987] BCLC 257). The same claim cannot so easily be sustained in respect to the next two examples to be discussed.

3. Loans, security and the trust

(a) Protecting the lender's interest

Where a lender, A, lends money to a debtor, B, the latter's obligation is personal, to repay money to A. But what is the status of the transaction if A loans money to B for a specified purpose, eg to pay C, and requires the money to be kept in a separate account until expended on that purpose? Is this a loan arrangement or does B hold the money as trustee? If the latter, for whom is B trustee: A or C or both?

In certain circumstances the courts will in fact permit a trust and loan relationship to co-exist within an overall transaction. Consequently, A may advance money to B on the basis that B holds it on a primary trust to carry out a purpose, and if the purpose is performed, the relationship between A and B is then a pure creditor-debtor relationship. But if for some reason, eg B's insolvency, the purpose cannot be performed, then B holds the money on a secondary trust for the lender. The intention and effect of this now not uncommon commercial arrangement is clear enough: it is to give the lender security interest until the moneys have been spent on the specified purpose (see Stevens (2005) 23 Corp & Sec LJ 325 (Aust)). However, unlike a secured loan made to a company it does not have to be registered and therefore there is no public notice of the transaction. The validity of this device was confirmed by the House of Lords in *Barclays Bank Ltd v Quistclose Investments Ltd* (below) and subsequently reassessed by Lord Millett in *Twinsectra Limited v Yardley* [2002] 2 AC 164.

(b) The *Quistclose* trust

Barclays Bank Ltd v Quistclose Investments Ltd [1970] AC 567

At an annual general meeting on 2 July 1964, Rolls Razor Ltd (RR), although in severe financial difficulties, declared a dividend on its shares to be paid on 24 July. Quistclose (Q) agreed to lend RR £209,719 solely for the purpose of paying the dividend. The loan was paid into a separate account with Barclays Bank, with whom RR was substantially overdrawn. The bank was aware of the arrangement between RR and Q. Before the dividend was paid RR went into voluntary liquidation. The bank claimed to be entitled to set off the money, in its view the beneficial property of RR, against the overdraft. The House of Lords unanimously decided that the money had been received by RR on trust to pay the dividend; and that the primary trust having failed, the money was held on a secondary trust for the respondent Q. As the bank had notice of these trust dispositions, its claim failed.

> **Lord Wilberforce** (giving the unanimous judgment of the House): Two questions arise, both of which must be answered favourably to the respondents if they are to recover the money from the appellants. The first is whether, as between the respondents and Rolls Razor, Ltd, the terms on which the loan was made were such as to impress on the sum of £209,719 8s 6d a trust in their favour in the event of the dividend not being paid. The second is whether, in that event, the appellants had such notice of the trust or of the circumstances giving rise to it as to make the trust binding on them.

It is not difficult to establish precisely on what terms the money was advanced by the respondents to Rolls Razor, Ltd. There is no doubt that the loan was made specifically in order to enable Rolls Razor, Ltd, to pay the dividend. There is equally, in my opinion, no doubt that the loan was made only so as to enable Rolls Razor, Ltd, to pay the dividend and for no other purpose. This follows quite clearly from the terms of the letter of Rolls Razor, Ltd, to the appellants of July 15, 1964, which letter, before transmission to the appellants, was sent to the respondents under open cover in order that the cheque might be (as it was) enclosed in it. The mutual intention of the respondents and of Rolls Razor, Ltd, and the essence of the bargain, was that the sum advanced should not become part of the assets of Rolls Razor, Ltd, but should be used exclusively for payment of a particular class of its creditors, namely, those entitled to the dividend. A necessary consequence from this, by process simply of interpretation, must be that if, for any reason, the dividend could not be paid, the money was to be returned to the respondents; the word 'only' or 'exclusively' can have no other meaning or effect.

That arrangements of this character for the payment of a person's creditors by a third person, give rise to a relationship of a fiduciary character or trust, in favour, as a primary trust, of the creditors, and secondarily, if the primary trust fails, of the third person, has been recognised in a series of cases over some 150 years.

Lord Wilberforce reviewed competing lines of authority and concluded that 'They do not negative the proposition that a trust may exist where the mutual intention is that they should not be included.' He continued:

The second, and main, argument for the appellants was of a more sophisticated character. The transaction, it was said, between the respondents and Rolls Razor, Ltd, was one of loan giving rise to a legal action of debt. This necessarily excluded the implication of any trust, enforceable in equity, in the respondents' favour: a transaction may attract one action or the other, it could not admit of both.

My lords, I must say that I find this argument unattractive. Let us see what it involves. It means that the law does not permit an arrangement to be made by which one person agrees to advance money to another, on terms that the money is to be used exclusively to pay debts of the latter, and if, and so far as not so used, rather than becoming a general asset of the latter available to his creditors at large, is to be returned to the lender. The lender is obliged, in such a case, because he is a lender, to accept, whatever the mutual wishes of lender and borrower may be, that the money he was willing to make available for one purpose only shall be freely available for others of the borrower's creditors for whom he has not the slightest desire to provide.

I should be surprised if an argument of this kind – so conceptualist in character – had ever been accepted. In truth it has plainly been rejected by the eminent judges who from 1819 onwards have permitted arrangements of this type to be enforced, and have approved them as being for the benefit of creditors and all concerned. There is surely no difficulty in recognising the co-existence in one transaction of legal and equitable rights and remedies: when the money is advanced, the lender acquires an equitable right to see that it is applied for the primary designated purpose (see *Re Rogers* where both Lindley and Kay LJJ explicitly recognised this): when the purpose has been carried out (ie, the debt paid) the lender has his remedy against the borrower in debt: if the primary purpose cannot be carried out, the question arises if a secondary purpose (ie, repayment to the lender) has been agreed, expressly or by implication: if it has, the remedies of equity may be invoked to give effect to it, if it has not (and the money is intended to fall within the general fund of the debtor's assets) then there is the appropriate remedy for recovery of a loan. I can appreciate no reason why the flexible interplay of law and equity cannot let in these practical arrangements, and other variations if desired: it would be to the discredit of both systems if they could not. In the present case the intention to create a secondary trust for the benefit of the lenders, to arise if the primary trust, to pay the dividend, could not be carried out, is clear and I can find no reason why the law should not give effect to it.

Goodhart and Jones, in their seminal article on the interrelation of commerce and equitable doctrine ((1980) 43 MLR 489), suggest that on the facts *Quistclose* 'is a just and commendable decision. No creditor had been misled into making a further loan by the existence of the separate dividend account; and there was no doubt that the bank knew of the agreement between the parties' (at 494). But this may not always be so. Indeed one purpose of a *Quistclose*-type transaction may be to create an impression of commercial solidity so as to enable the borrower to continue trading and avoid insolvency, with the consequence that fresh liabilities to creditors will probably be incurred (see *Re Northern Developments (Holdings) Ltd* 6 October 1978, unreported). Whether (in the absence of some form of registration or public notice) such arrangements should then be enforceable and, if so, by whom, is more questionable.

Consider the following points:

(1) Is there any doubt about the mutual intention of Rolls Razor and Quistclose on the facts of the case? Is it right to consider that Lord Wilberforce 'ascribed an intention to *Quistclose* it never actually had'? See Swadling 'Orthodoxy' in Swadling (ed) *The Quistclose Trust: Critical Essays* (2004) p 19.

(2) If a bank loan document provides that the borrower is to use the loan for a specified purpose and that the loan or any part of it that is not used for that purpose is to be held on trust for the bank, does this create a *Quistclose* trust? Does the answer depend on whether the bank deposits the money in a separate bank account from the borrower's other funds? See *R v Common Professional Examination Board, ex p Mealing-McCleod* (2000) *Times* 2 May. In such a circumstance, should the borrower be under an equitable obligation to return the money not properly used for the purpose to the bank?

(3) Do you agree with the view that if English law were to move to a more rational system of registration of security interests, a *Quistclose* trust ought to be registered on a public register before it could be held to be valid so that other lenders and creditors would be aware of it when making decisions to

lend? (See Stephens 'Insolvency' in *Swadling* (ed) p 166, cf Glister [2004] LMCLQ 460.) Or is the reality that *Quistclose* trusts tend to be used where time or circumstances do not allow traditional forms of security to be implemented? (See McKendrick in *Swadling* (ed) pp 150–152.)

(c) The enforceability puzzle: a 'new model' commercial trust?

The *Quistclose* trust has held a fascination for trust lawyers for almost forty years. For some, it is a modern enigma wrapped in a mystery. One problem of legal analysis is to identify the legal basis of the trust: is its enforcement compatible with established trusts law doctrine or are we witnessing the emergence of a 'new model' commercial trust? The point arises not least because several puzzling questions were either not raised in *Quistclose* or were left unanswered by Lord Wilberforce, perhaps deliberately so as not unduly to restrict future development of 'the flexible interplay of law and equity. Thus the exact nature of *Quistclose*'s 'equitable right to see that the loan is applied for the primary designated purpose' is unclear. Heydon and Loughlan (*Cases and Materials on Equity and Trusts* (6th edn, 2002)) comment (at pp 467–468) that: 'This is not the right of a beneficiary, for if the primary purpose is fulfilled the lender becomes a simple creditor. It is unusual to say the least, for a party in a position comparable to that of a settlor to retain a right to supervise the administration of a trust for the benefit of a class of which he is not a member'. Moreover, it may not always be straightforward to identify a precise point at which the primary purpose is fulfilled, the trust 'spent' and the equitable right thereby extinguished (cf *Re EVTR* [1987] BCLC 646). Similar uncertainty surrounds the status of the particular class of creditors for whose benefit the primary trust in *Quistclose* was created, ie the shareholders post declaration of dividend. Are they beneficiaries under a private express trust with associated rights of enforcement? If not, are we presented with an example of a 'purpose trust' infringing the beneficiary principle? Of course, such problems are sidestepped if we disregard Lord Wilberforce's statement that the primary trust is in favour of the creditors and reinterpret the *Quistclose* trust as being a trust where the beneficial interest lies not in the creditors but in the lender as Lord Millett did in *Twinsectra v Yardley* (see below).

The points raised above were not considered in *Quistclose* as it was assumed that the primary trust had failed (see Goodhart and Jones (1980) 43 MLR 489 at 494 n 28 for an explanation of this assumption). Subsequently Sir Robert Megarry VC in *Re Northern Developments (Holdings) Ltd* accepted that those persons intended to benefit, although not beneficiaries, did have enforceable rights. Peter Gibson J seemingly endorsed this view in *Carreras Rothmans Ltd v Freeman Mathews Treasure Ltd* [1985] Ch 207. In that case the plaintiff (CR) employed the defendant company (FMT) to manage its advertising. In doing this FMT contracted as principal with production agencies and advertising media, and paid accounts submitted by them for work done on the plaintiff's advertising. By early 1983 FMT was in financial difficulties, and CR became concerned about the damage to its advertising campaign if FMT should collapse. CR therefore agreed with FMT that CR would pay a monthly sum into a special bank account at FMT's bank, on which the latter could draw for the sole purpose of settling debts with agency and media creditors (the 'third party creditors'). FMT went into liquidation and CR brought proceedings against FMT and the liquidator, claiming that the money in the account was held on trust for the sole purpose of paying the 'third-party creditors' and sought an order that the money should be so applied. The defendants argued that the third-party creditors had no enforceable rights and that the trust was therefore void. The judge reviewed *Northern Developments* and commented as follows (at 222):

> **Peter Gibson LJ:** In that case the eponymous company ('Northern') was the parent company of a group of companies including one ('Kelly') which was in financial straits. Seventeen banks agreed to put up a fund in excess of half a million pounds in an attempt to rescue Kelly. The banks already had other companies in the group as customers. They paid the moneys into an account in Northern's name for the express purpose of providing moneys for Kelly's unsecured creditors and for no other purpose, the amounts advanced being treated as advances to the banks' other customers in the group. The fund was used to sustain Kelly for a time, but then Kelly was put into receivership at a time when a little over half the fund remained unexpended. One of the questions for the court was who was entitled to that balance. Sir Robert Megarry VC held that there was a *Quistclose*-type of trust attaching to the fund, that trust was a purpose trust but enforceable by identifiable individuals, namely the banks as lenders, Kelly, for whose immediate benefit the fund was established, and Kelly's creditors. The reason given by Sir Robert Megarry VC for holding that Kelly's creditors had enforceable rights were [sic] the words of Lord Wilberforce in the *Quistclose* case, describing the *Quistclose*-type of trust as giving rise to a relationship of a fiduciary character or trust in favour of the creditors. However, Sir Robert Megarry VC went on to describe the interests of the creditors in this way:
>
>> 'The fund was established not with the object of vesting the beneficial interest in them, but in order to confer a benefit on Kelly (and so, consequentially, on the rest of the group and the bankers) by ensuring that Kelly's creditors would be paid in an orderly manner. There is perhaps some parallel in the position of a beneficiary entitled to a share of residue under a will. What he has is not a beneficial interest in any asset forming part of residue, but a right to compel the executor to administer the assets of the deceased properly. It seems to me that it is that sort of right which the creditors of Kelly had.'
>
> The interest of the banks was held to be under the secondary trust if the primary trust failed. In the light of that authority I cannot accept the joint submission [in the present case] that the third-party creditors for the payment of whose debts the plaintiff had paid the moneys into the special account had no enforceable rights. In any event I do not comprehend how a trust, which on no footing could the plaintiff revoke unilaterally, and

which was expressed as a trust to pay third parties and was still capable of performance, could nevertheless leave the beneficial interest in the plaintiff which had parted with the moneys. On Sir Robert Megarry VC's analysis the beneficial interest is in suspense until the payment is made.

The trust was upheld and the order granted, although the defendants were successful in a counterclaim.

Sir Robert Megarry VC described the arrangements in *Northern Developments* as giving rise to a trust of the kind recognised in *Re Denley's Trust Deed* [1969] 1 Ch 373 (see Chapter 5). This implies a willingness to accept a trust where the beneficial interest is in suspense, but rights of enforcement are available both to the provider of the trust fund and to those who might benefit from it. This explanation has its adherents (see Rickett (1991) 107 LQR 60) but the conclusion and line of reasoning has been challenged. Lord Millett in *Twinsectra* considered that acknowledging the beneficial interest to be 'in suspense' is unorthodox and fails to understand the role which the resulting trust can play in developing the *Quistclose* trust (at 189). However, in a discretionary trust where the trustee has a power of appointment the beneficial interest may be in suspense until the power of appointment is exercised in favour of a beneficiary. What is so unorthodox about the beneficial interest in a *Quistclose* trust being in suspense? Moreover, Lord Millett rejected the reliance on *Re Denley's Trust Deed* to support the validity of the primary trust because he considered the stated purpose of the relevant trust as too uncertain and unenforceable.

Worthington in *Proprietary Interests in Commercial Transactions* (1996) pp 54–55 argues that Megarry VC's analysis could not be applied today even though the intention of the arrangements in *Carreras Rothmans Limited* was that the funds were never to be the agency's and were to be repaid to Rothmans on insolvency. Worthington argues that the arrangements involved the agency effectively making one of its existing assets (the debt from Rothmans) available exclusively to one class of its creditors (the third parties owed money on Rothmans' account). In Worthington's view this is probably a preference and invalid under IA 1986, ss 239 and 340.

(d) Alternative explanations

Lord Millett (prior to his elevation to the judiciary) advanced a wide-ranging explanation of the types of circumstances where *Quistclose* trusts could arise. He adopted an orthodox approach, constructed around the concept of the lender's intention, to explain the enforceability puzzle posed by the *Quistclose*-type trust ((1985) 101 LQR 269; cf a similar approach outlined by The Hon Mr Justice Priestley in 'The Romalpa Clause and the Quistclose Trust' in Finn (ed) *Equity and Commercial Relationships* (1987) p 237, n 58). In the following summary, it is assumed that A has lent money to B solely for the purpose of paying B's creditors (C).

P Millett (1985) 101 LQR 269 at 290

The following, it is suggested, may be regarded as suitable guidelines by which A's intention may be ascertained:

(1) If A's intention was to benefit C, or his object would be frustrated if he were to retain a power of revocation, the transaction will create an irrevocable trust in favour of C, enforceable by C but not by A. The beneficial interest in the trust property will be in C.

(2) If A's intention was to benefit B (though without vesting a beneficial interest in him), or to benefit himself by furthering some private or commercial interest of his own, and not (except incidentally) to benefit C, then the transaction will create a trust in favour of A alone, and B will hold the trust property in trust to comply with A's directions. The trust will be enforceable by A but not by C. The beneficial interest will remain in A.

(3) Where A's object was to save B from bankruptcy by enabling him to pay his creditors, the prima facie inference is that set out in paragraph 2 above. Wherever that is the correct inference:

  (i) Where A has an interest of his own, separate and distinct from any interest of B, in seeing that the money is applied for the stated purpose, B will be under a positive obligation, enforceable by A, to apply it for that purpose. Where A has no such interest, B will be regarded as having a power, but no duty, to apply it for the stated purpose, and A's remedy will be confined to preventing the misapplication of the money.

  (ii) Prima facie, A's directions will be regarded as revocable by him; but he may contract with B not to revoke them without B's consent.

  (iii) Communication to C of the arrangements prior to A's revocation will effect an assignment of A's equitable interest to C, and convert A's revocable mandate into an irrevocable trust for C.

This analysis by Millett has received judicial acceptance in the New Zealand Court of Appeal (see *General Communications Ltd v Development Finance Corpn New Zealand Ltd* [1990] 3 NZLR 406 at 432–433). When *Twinsectra Ltd v Yardley* [2002] AC 164 came before the House of Lords, Lord Millett effectively adopted point 2 above as the basis for his judgment. That case involved a series of complex commercial dealings between the parties but can be reduced to a fairly simple set of facts. Mr Yardley's companies were involved in three property transactions and for the purchase of one property at Apperley Bridge, Bradford, the relevant company needed finance. Negotiations were begun with Twinsectra for a loan. Before the Twinsectra loan was finalised, Barclays Bank provided the company sufficient finance to undertake the purchase of Apperley Bridge. Prior to Barclays Bank agreeing to provide the moneys, the company's financial adviser had told Twinsectra that it would require the £1 million and that a solicitor's undertaking would be given by Mr Paul Leach, ie an undertaking that the funds would only be used for a purchase of property. Leach refused to give such an undertaking but Yardley obtained a relevant undertaking from another firm of lawyers which was engaged in business dealings with him. That firm was Sims & Roper. Sims & Roper received the money in return for the following undertaking:

(1) The loan moneys would be retained by us until such time as they are applied in the acquisition of property on behalf of our client [Yardley's company].

(2) The loan moneys would be utilised solely for the acquisition of property on behalf of our client and for no other purpose.

(3) We will pay you [Twinsectra] the said sum of £1m together with interest calculated at the rate of £657.53 per day... such repayment to be made [within 4 calendar months after receipt of the loan moneys by us].

Sims & Roper did not retain the money as required under the undertakings and simply paid it to Leach who disbursed it on instructions of Mr Yardley. Twinsectra sought to make Sims & Roper liable for breach of trust. Presented with a variety of different legal interpretations of these arrangements, counsel for Twinsectra, in opening argument before Carnwath J at first instance, referred compendiously to the relevant trust as a 'conceptual grab-bag' being an 'express/implied/constructive/bare trust upon which Sims & Roper held the money'. In closing he relied principally on a resulting trust arising from the terms of the undertaking viewed in the light of the decision of the House of Lords in *Quistclose*. Carnwath J held that no *Quistclose* trust arose because the undertaking was too vague and Twinsectra did not intend to create a trust.

On appeal Potter LJ adopted the following analysis ([2000] WTLR 527):

> However, when a loan is made for a special purpose, equity will interfere in appropriate cases to prevent the borrower from using that money for any other purpose. The purpose imposed at the time of the advance creates an enforceable restriction on the borrower's use of the money. Although the lender's right to enforce the restriction is treated as arising on the basis of a 'trust', the use of that word does not enlarge the lender's interest in the fund. The borrower is entitled to the beneficial use of the money, subject to the lender's right to prevent its misuse; the lender's limited interest in the fund is sufficient to prevent its use for other than the special purpose for which it was advanced.

Potter LJ went on to hold that the release of the money in breach of the undertaking was a breach of the fiduciary obligations owed to Twinsectra created by the undertakings. In the House of Lords, on the issue of whether a trust was created, Lords Slynn and Steyn agreed with Lord Hoffmann. Lord Hoffmann did not give any extensive analysis to the form of the trust, nor did he even refer to it as a *Quistclose* trust but he considered a trust existed. Lord Millett analysed the trust on the basis that it was a form of *Quistclose* trust and gave his interpretation of the nature of the *Quistclose* trust. Lord Hutton agreed with both Lord Hoffmann and Lord Millett that the solicitor's undertaking given by Sims & Roper to Twinsectra created a trust but it cannot be assumed that he agreed with the full analysis of the *Quistclose* trust as provided by Lord Millett.

Lord Hoffmann (at 168): The trial judge (Carnwath J) did not accept that the moneys were 'subject to any form of trust in Sims's and Roper's hands'. I do not imagine the judge could have meant this to be taken literally. Money in a solicitor's client account is held on trust. The only question is the terms of that trust. I should think that what Carnwath J meant was that Sims held the money on trust for Mr Yardley absolutely. That is the way it was put by Mr Oliver, who appeared for Mr Leach. But, like the Court of Appeal, I must respectfully disagree. The terms of the trust upon which Sims held the money must be found in the undertaking which they gave to Twinsectra as a condition of payment. Clauses 1 and 2 of that undertaking made it clear that the money was not to be at the free disposal of Mr Yardley. Sims was not to part with the money to Mr Yardley or any one else except for the purpose of enabling him to acquire property.

In my opinion the effect of the undertaking was to provide that the money in Sims client account should remain Twinsectra's money until such time as it was applied for the acquisition of property in accordance with the undertaking. For example, if Mr Yardley went bankrupt before the money had been so applied, it would not have formed part of his estate, as it would have done if Sims had held it in trust for him absolutely. The undertaking would have ensured that Twinsectra could get it back. It follows that Sims held the money in *trust* for Twinsectra, but subject to a *power* to apply it by way of loan to Mr Yardley in accordance with the undertaking. No doubt Sims also owed fiduciary obligations to Mr Yardley in respect of the exercise of the power, but we need not concern ourselves with those obligations because in fact the money was applied wholly for Mr Yardley's benefit . . .

Lord Hoffmann went on to explain that the undertaking was a very unusual one but it was not void for uncertainty. Lord Millett discussed the undertakings in the context of the *Quistclose* case. Perhaps he was prompted to do so by the arguments of counsel before Carnwath J and due to the Court of Appeal judgment.

Lord Millett (at 184): When money is advanced, the lender requires a right, enforceable in equity, to see that it is applied for the stated purpose, or more accurately to prevent its application for any other purpose. This prevents the borrower from obtaining any beneficial interest in the money, at least while the designated purpose is still capable of being carried out. Once the purpose has been carried out, the lender has his normal remedy in debt. If for any reason the purpose cannot be carried out, the question arises whether the money falls within the general fund of the borrower's assets, in which case it passes to his trustee in bankruptcy in the event of his insolvency and the lender is merely a loan creditor; or whether it is held on a resulting trust for the lender. This depends on the intention of the parties collected from the terms of the arrangement and the circumstance of the case.

. . . (at 185): Arrangements of this kind are not intended to provide security for repayment of the loan, but to prevent the money from being applied otherwise than in accordance with the lender's wishes. If the money is properly applied, the loan is unsecured. This was true of all the decided cases, including the *Quistclose* case itself.

Lord Millett then stated that if Lord Wilberforce's approach is adopted there are two successive trusts, a primary trust for payment to identifiable beneficiaries, such as creditors or shareholders, and a secondary trust in favour of the lender arising on failure of the primary trust. He then identified four potential options for the beneficial interest in the primary trust. It could be located in (i) the lender; (ii) the borrower; (iii) in the contemplated beneficiary; or (iv) in suspense. Lord Millett then concluded (at 192–193):

> I would reject all the alternative analyses, ... and hold the *Quistclose* trust to be an entirely orthodox example of the kind of default trust known as a resulting trust. The lender pays the money to the borrower by way of loan, but does not part with the entire beneficial interest in the money, and insofar as he does not, it is held on resulting trust for lender from the outset. Contrary to the opinion of the Court of Appeal, it is the borrower who has a very limited use of the money, being obliged to apply it for the stated purpose or return it. He has no beneficial interest in the money, which remains throughout in the lender subject to mainly the borrower's power or duty to apply the moneys in accordance with the lender's instructions. When the purpose fails, the money is returnable to the lender, not under some new trust in his favour which comes into being on the failure of the purpose, but because the resulting trust in his favour is no longer subject to any power on the part of the borrower to make use of the money. Whether the borrower is obliged to apply the money for the stated purpose or merely at liberty to do so, and whether the lender can countermand the borrower's mandate while it is still capable of being carried out, must depend on the circumstances of the particular case.

The Court of Appeal in *Twinsectra* had appeared to adopt the view advanced by Chambers that the *Quistclose* trust is a form of a resulting trust (Chambers *Resulting Trusts* (1997) ch 3). Chambers argued that in a *Quistclose* situation, a lender does not intend to confer an unrestricted benefit on the borrower. Accordingly, a resulting trust arises because the lender lacks an intention to benefit the borrower if the purpose of paying creditors fails (pp 68, 84–85). Under this explanation the borrower gets the full beneficial ownership in the moneys subject only to the lender's right to prevent the moneys being used for another purpose. Chambers's focus is on the nature of the obligation where funds are lent for a specific purpose and in his view the cases leading up to *Quistclose* did not justify the approach taken by Lord Wilberforce. The lender's right is seen as a right to enforce the intended purpose. Chambers considers this right imposes a corresponding obligation that is something less than a trust obligation.

Indeed, there are those who would prefer that the obligation be not classified as an equitable or trust obligation, but only as a contract. Thus a return of moneys to the lender is an instance of unjust enrichment in action or the failure or frustration of the contract (Birks in Swadling (ed) *The Quistclose Trust: Critical Essays* (2004) pp 128 et seq). However, there are those who analyse *Quistclose* based on property law concepts. The use of the money for the specified purpose can be seen as a condition precedent for transfer of the beneficial interest from the lender to someone else ie the borrower or the third party that could benefit from the purpose being satisfied (see Klinck (2005) 42 Can Bus LJ 427).

Note that if the beneficial interest in the moneys is in the borrower, with the trust only arising on the borrower's winding up, or on failure of the purpose, the borrower is divested of assets that would be available to creditors on the winding up. Such a situation may be seen as a preference to the lender or otherwise inconsistent with the pari passu insolvency regime (see Stephens in *Swadling* (ed) pp 154–156). Moreover, under the Chambers approach the creditors should not be seen as having a right to enforce the trust and there is no trust in their favour. Where creditors have been given the right to enforce payment to themselves, this is seen as arising from subsequent conduct of either the borrower or the lender. Thus in *Northern Developments* the communication of the details of the arrangement to the creditors gave rise to an equitable interest in their favour enabling them to enforce the obligation, which was co-extensive with the lender's rights to enforce the use of the money for the purpose. In short, the borrower's use or enjoyment of the fund is subject to two equitable interests: 'one in favour of the lender and another in favour of the creditors' (*Resulting Trusts* (1997) at p 82).

Both the resulting trust approach and Lord Millett's extra-judicial view are not without their own difficulties (see Ho and Smart 'Reinterpreting the *Quistclose Trust*: A critique of Chambers' analysis' (2001) 21 O J Ls 267; and Tettenborn 'Resulting Trusts and Insolvency' in Rose (ed) *Restitution and Insolvency* (2000) p 56). Chambers's resulting trust approach seems to treat the borrower as having full title to the moneys, but can this be right when the borrower can only use the moneys for the specified purpose? This contrasts with Lord Millett's resulting trust approach in *Twinsectra* which recognises the beneficial interest as being vested in the lender. Do, for instance, both these explanations fail to recognise the significance of the underlying loan contract between the parties? (See Burns (1992) 18 Monash LR 147.) Moreover do they downplay Lord Wilberforce's requirement of a common intention of the parties that a trust be established? In contrast in *Carreras Rothmans Ltd v Freeman Mathews Treasure Ltd* [1985] Ch 207, Peter Gibson J, responding to counsel's argument that the requirements for an express trust were lacking, commented (at 222): 'I doubt if it is helpful to analyse the *Quistclose* type of case in terms of the constituent parts of a conventional settlement, though it may of course be crucial to ascertain in whose favour the secondary trust operates . . . and who has an enforceable right.'

While to some Lord Millett's analysis in *Twinsectra* is an example of his point in 2 above and is the only basis for the *Quistclose* trust, others recognise that the facts of each case, and identifying A's intention, may lead to other potential explanations of how the trust is intended to operate. Chambers revisited the *Quistclose* trust in the wider context of potential types of restrictions on the use of money in 'Restrictions on the Use of Money' in *Swadling* (ed) p 77.

Chambers recognised that when A pays money to B, to be used only to pay to C, the beneficial ownership of that money could belong in A, B or C or beneficial ownership may be shared by a mixture of A, B and C. It depends on the facts of each case and the intentions of the parties deduced from those facts.

Justice Gummow from Australia, writing extra-judicially post-*Twinsectra*, noted that the Millett explanation effectuated the presumed intention of A, that A retain the balance of the beneficial interest. However, A's intention may not always be a 'presumed intention'. An express trust may exist or be inferred from adequate evidence and accordingly it 'may be open, in a particular case, to find on the true construction of what was said and written, that there had been manifested an express intention that whole of the interest be transferred, with the creation of new interests including a beneficial "default" interest in A' ((2003) 77 ALJ 30 at 38). In any event, whether the trust in favour of A is an express trust or a resulting trust would seem to be a function of the facts of each case. However, judicial analysis of the primary trust seems to be inconsistent and has failed to benefit from the academic writing on this topic (cf *Cooper v PRG Powerhouse Ltd* [2008] EWHC 498 (Ch) – a purpose trust; *Templeton Insurance Ltd v Penningtons Solicitors LLP* [2006] EWHC 685 (Ch) – resulting trust subject to a power to apply the money for a purpose; *Latimer v CIR* [2004] 3 NZLR 157 at 571 (PC) – 'express resulting trust rather than implied resulting trust; see also Turner (2005) Aust Bus .R 392).

Consider the following points:

(1) In *Twinsectra*, Lord Millett rejected the notion that the *Quistclose* trust was a trust for creditors who would have no rights to enforce the trust. Is his argument convincing that the lender's goal would not be to benefit the creditors but rather to protect the ailing company by enabling it to trade out of its difficulties, which would involve payment to creditors while it was so trading?

(2) Which do you consider is a better description of the trust in *Quistclose*: (a) a trust for the lender who may be divested of its beneficial interest by payment of the debt; or (b) an express trust for the shareholder-creditors subject to a condition upon which they might take their beneficial interest (see *Re Australian Elizabethan Theatre Trust* (1991) 102 ALR 681 per Gummow J – the condition in *Quistclose*, which was not satisfied, being that the shareholders retained a right to payment of a dividend); or (c) a non-charitable purpose trust subject to a condition similar to that in (b) above; or (d) a primary trust for the lender with a secondary, resulting trust (*Rowan v Dann* (1991) 64 C & PR 202))?

(3) Club members came to the rescue of their financially imperilled club in *Re Challoner Club Ltd (in liquidation)* (1997) *Times* 4 November by donating funds which the company attempted to set aside under a trust (see above, p 800). Is this case susceptible to a *Quistclose* analysis? Did the club members

and the club have a mutual intention that their donations were for the specific purposes of rescuing the club and if that purpose failed, were to be returned to the members? (See also *Re Gillingham Bus Disaster Fund* [1959] Ch 62 and Birks in *Swadling* (ed) p 121 et seq.)

(e) *Quistclose* and remedial constructive trusts

Rickett ((1991) 107 LQR 60), reviewing the recognition of *Quistclose*-type trusts in England, Australia and New Zealand, considered that judges in different jurisdictions adopted either (i) an orthodox approach applying established trust law principles to *Quistclose* situations, or (ii) viewed the *Quistclose* trust as a form of remedial trust and applied its principles with varying degrees of flexibility. (See generally on the remedial trust point: Scott [1993] LMCLQ 330; Bridge (1992) 12 OJLS 333; Rickett (1991) 107 LQR 608; Paciocco (1989) 68 Can BR 315.) In England several cases before *Twinsectra* indicated the possibility of a more flexible recognition of *Quistclose* trusts, ie recognising *Quistclose* trusts in situations where one or more elements of Lord Wilberforce's exposition are lacking. Taylor LJ in *Tropical Capital Investment Ltd v Stanlake Holdings Ltd* (unreported, noted by Rickett [1992] LMCLQ 3) applied a *Quistclose* analysis where moneys were loaned but the purpose 'was to buy tyres', a general rather than a specific purpose for the loan. This enabled the lender to recover the moneys when they were used for a different, and in fact fraudulent, purpose. In *Twinsectra* the purpose of the borrower was similarly vague, ie to buy property.

In many respects, the flexible use of *Quistclose*-type trusts and the recognition of different options for location of the beneficial ownership, as discussed above, lead to the conclusion that the *Quistclose* trust may not be a genus but merely one species of a type of trust, ie there may not be one form of *Quistclose* trust but potential variants which depend on the facts of the case: the essential ingredient to all being that the borrower's right to the funds is not unrestricted but held on a fiduciary obligation or trust for some of the parties or for purposes.

Consider the following points:

(1) If a person borrows money from a bank by way of a personal loan the bank generally requires the loan to be for a purpose, such as buying a stereo or car or having a holiday. We can compare this to a cash advance which is obtained on a credit card; this is a loan but no purpose is specified to the lender. How specific must a purpose be before Lord Wilberforce's requirements in *Quistclose* will be satisfied? If a general purpose was required rather than a specific purpose would this convert many loans into *Quistclose* trusts?

(2) Even if we can explain a *Quistclose* trust on orthodox lines, should Parliament treat the *Quistclose* trust as an anomaly and restrain its application to debt repayments as suggested in *Re Miles* ((1988) 85 ALR 216 per Pincus J)? (Cf the extension of *Quistclose* to the purchase of machinery (*Re EVTR*

[1987] BCLC 646), to leases granted for use in a proposed joint venture (*Rowan v Dann* (1991) 64 P & CR 202) and in cases of fraud (*Tropical Capital Investment Ltd v Stanlake Holdings Ltd*).)

(3) *Quistclose* trusts tend to be created when the solvency of the borrower is in doubt, and may be part of a corporate survival-salvage plan. Should the courts promote such goals and develop the *Quistclose* trust as part of broader principles aimed at promoting such corporate salvage plans? (See Austin (1986) 6 OJLS 444 and (1988) 11 UNSW LJ 66 at 74.)

(4) Compare the trenchant expression by Lord Mustill of the Privy Council's views in *Re Goldcorp Exchange* [1995] 1 AC 74 with those of the New Zealand Court of Appeal in *Liggett v Kensington* [1993] 1 NZLR 257 regarding the issue of identifying purposes and the creation of trusts (see Chapter 16, p 847 et seq).

4. Reservation of title and the equitable tracing doctrine

(a) Unsecured creditors, freedom of contract and reservation of title clauses

In a commercial insolvency the plight of unsecured commercial creditors, for example, suppliers of materials to a manufacturer, is likely to be no better than that of our hapless consumer discussed previously. Goods supplied by a seller to a trader normally become the latter's property as soon as possession of them has been obtained and before they have been paid for. If the trader becomes insolvent the goods will be part of the assets, available to be sold and the proceeds divided among the creditors. An unpaid supplier with a personal claim based on a debtor-creditor relationship will rank as an unsecured creditor. One way for the unpaid supplier to obtain security for payment of goods supplied is to use a reservation of title clause, stipulating that ownership, by which we mean property in the goods as opposed to possession of them, shall not pass until the buyer makes payment. Unless they have been paid for, the goods do not form part of the assets of the buyer when it becomes insolvent.

The basis for this device lies in the principles of freedom of contract and the law's preference for construing transactions according to their legal form, rather than their effect or substance. Although such freedom is not untrammelled, the Sale of Goods Act 1979 (ss 17, 19) specifically provides parties to a contract for sale of specific goods with the freedom to select the moment when the property in the goods passes from the seller to the buyer. A contract term providing that this is not to take place until the purchase price has been paid in full is known as 'a reservation of title clause'. But reservation of title clauses may adopt a more complex form than what may be termed the 'simple' clause just described. Goods are often supplied on the basis that before payment is made, they will be resold or used in the production of other goods. Sellers have, therefore, attempted to reserve title not only in the original goods but also in their manufactured product and in the proceeds of sale of both. A still more ambitious extension is a 'simple reservation of title' clause which seeks to secure not only the price of the particular goods being supplied, but also payment of all indebtedness, existing or future, of the buyer to the supplier. Notwithstanding that such clauses are more readily considered as forms of security, they were held valid in a Scottish case, *Armour v Thyssen Edelstahlwerke AG* [1990] 3 All ER 481, HL (for a fuller explanation of such clauses see McCormack *Reservation of Title* (2nd edn, 1995) at pp 1–2 and 237–245). Thus there are four potential claims that a seller might seek to make by means of a reservation of title clause: (i) the original goods; (ii) the proceeds from sales of the original goods; (iii) new products created from the original goods; and (iv) the proceeds from sales of such new products.

In *Aluminium Industrie Vaassen BV v Romalpa Aluminium Ltd* [1976] 1 WLR 676 the Court of Appeal engrafted the right to trace in equity on to a commercial sale agreement, including a reservation of title clause. *Romalpa* established that a seller, S, who supplies goods under a reservation of title clause, and authorises the buyer, B, to resell them on condition that B accounts for the proceeds of sale, may, in the event of the buyer's insolvency, have an equitable right to trace those proceeds and prevent them falling within the buyer's assets. The benefit for S is clear: a personal right against the buyer is supplemented by a proprietary right to the proceeds. The court also held that a seller in such circumstances may claim back any goods supplied remaining in the buyer's hands. *Romalpa* gave a considerable impetus to the use of reservation of title clauses in their various forms described above. Indeed the case has been described as having 'a greater impact on commercial law than almost any other case decided this century' (Goode *Proprietary Rights and Insolvency in Sales Transactions* (2nd edn, 1989) p 84).

Doubts have been expressed as to whether the full commercial implications of '*Romalpa* clauses', as reservation of title clauses are now commonly called, were fully appreciated by the Court of Appeal (see Goode p 84; Davies (1985) 129 SJ 3; De Lacy (1995) 24 Anglo-Am LR 327). In subsequent cases a restrictive judicial approach has been adopted towards their interpretation. Unfortunately this area of the law has become 'a maze if not a minefield' (per Staughton J in *Hendy Lennox (Industrial Engines) Ltd v Grahame Puttick Ltd* [1984] 1 WLR 485 at 493), both because of its technicality and because it involves the law relating to, inter alia, agency, bailment, sale of goods, mortgages and charges as well as trusts and equitable tracing principles. Fortunately, it is not necessary for us to chart a path all the way through the minefield, and the subject is more fully dealt with in depth in the context of commercial law texts (see in addition to *McCormack* and *Goode,* Davies *Effective Retention of Title* (1991); and, for a review of developments, see Palmer (1992) 5 J Contract Law 175; Hicks [1993] JBL at 485–490; McCormack [1994] Conv 129; Worthington *Proprietary Interests in Commercial Transactions* (1996) pp 7–42). Here we adopt a more limited perspective, concerning ourselves with two principal themes. (1) How far has the use of equitable tracing in this context required modification of established equitable principles? (2) What has been the influence of commercial considerations on this development? However, some familiarity with other methods of obtaining security for goods supplied is necessary.

(b) The commercial framework

Report of Review Committee on Insolvency Law and Practice (Cmnd 8558, 1982) paras 1596–1598

1596. . . . Goods can be prevented from passing into the ownership of the debtor by way of reservation of title under a contract for the sale of goods, by leasing and by hire purchase. A property interest can be retained by means of a lien, provided that possession of the property has been retained, actually or constructively.

1597. Moreover, and most importantly a security interest can be obtained by means of a mortgage, charge, or other enforceable encumbrance. In this last category there feature, as regards insolvent companies, floating charges which enable the debtor company to carry on business in the ordinary course, dealing with the assets the subject-matter of the charge accordingly, but on the basis that insolvency causes a crystallisation of the charge and withdraws the property the subject-matter of the charge from the unencumbered estate of the insolvent company.

1598. All these methods of improving the position of the creditor from that of an unsecured creditor fall to be considered together. It would, for example, be short-sighted to consider reservation of title without observing the close analogy between its extended form – a purported retention of an interest in goods the subject-matter of a sale and in all property deriving directly or indirectly from those goods by way of security for all sums due from the purchaser to the seller on any account whatsoever – and a floating charge. Where a seller is in a position, vis-à-vis his buyer, to demand reservation of title he may equally be in a position to demand the protection of a charge. A clause purporting to operate by way of reservation may be interpreted by the courts as constituting a charge or as partly reserving title and partly constituting a charge.

Mention must also be made of the Companies Act 2006, s 874, which renders certain charges created by a company, including floating charges, void against the liquidator or any creditor of the company unless duly registered with the Registrar of Companies. The purpose of the statutory requirement is to warn prospective creditors of the existence of such charges. In contrast, no registration of reservation of title clauses is necessary, with the obvious consequence that other prospective creditors of a buyer will be unaware of their existence. This prompted criticisms with regard to the similar provision under the 1985 Companies Act (see *Cork Report* paras 1600–1604) that:

(1) a proliferation of reservation of title clauses would undermine the existing supply of credit. A company's prospective creditors, for example, banks,

could no longer rely on a periodical statement of a company's assets such as stock or work in progress, since a substantial proportion might in law be the property of suppliers;

(2) receivers trying to keep a business operating, while attempting to reorganise it or find a purchaser for it as a going concern, would find it difficult if suppliers of goods could claim stock or work in progress.

The Cork Report did suggest certain reforms and expressed the hope that eventually a comprehensive registration system covering reservation of title clauses could be introduced (paras 1624–1651; see the limited reform introduced in the Insolvency Act 1986, s 15; Wheeler [1987] JBL 180) but all such potential reform seems to have stalled. But the Report also concluded that some of the expressed fears were exaggerated, because the impact of reservation of title clauses had been less than anticipated. First, the balance of bargaining power means that sellers cannot always impose extended reservation of title clauses, particularly where such a clause is likely to prevent the buyer from using the proceeds of sale as part of the cash flow of the business. A second reason for the limited effect of the clauses is the factual difficulty in proving a claim (see Wheeler *Reservation of Title Clauses* (1991) pp 24–28). If the effectiveness of the clause is disputed, the seller may be restrained by an injunction and not be able to repossess the goods (see *Lipe v Leyland DAF Ltd* [1994] 1 BCLC 84). A third reason may be found in judicial decisions restricting the scope of *Romalpa* clauses.

(c) *Romalpa*, unmixed goods and the requirements for an equitable tracing claim

As was seen in Chapter 14, it seemed settled, after *Re Diplock* [1948] Ch 465, that there can be no right to trace in equity unless (i) there is at some stage a fiduciary relationship between the claimant and the defendant or a person from whom the defendant acquires property, and (ii) there is some equitable proprietary interest vested in the claimant (see also *Westdeutsche Landesbank Girozentrale v Islington London Borough Council* [1996] AC 669 per Lord Browne-Wilkinson: 'Your Lordships should not be taken as casting any doubt on the principles of tracing as established in *Re Diplock*' (at 714)). Moreover it also appeared that for the remedy to be available the equitable proprietary interest had to be separate from legal ownership (a view criticised by Maudsley (1959) 75 LQR 234; and Oakley (1975) 28 CLP 64). At first glance *Romalpa* seems difficult to reconcile with either of these requirements. The plaintiff (AIV) had supplied aluminium foil to the defendant company Romalpa under a contract subject to a reservation of title clause (no 13) which provided, inter alia:

[The] ownership of the material to be delivered by AIV will only be transferred to purchaser when he has met all that is owing to AIV, no matter on what grounds.

On the appointment of a receiver, Romalpa owed AIV £122,000 but had in its possession a quantity of unused foil. It was conceded that Romalpa had possessed an implied power to sell unmixed foil and the proceeds of just such a sale, £35,000, were in a separate account. AIV recovered the unused foil over which it had reserved legal title until fully paid. But what of the proceeds of the sales of foil? Had Romalpa's power to sell been exercised on its own account, in which case the £35,000 would form part of its own assets, or on behalf of AIV? The answer to this question depended, in part, on whether Romalpa was an agent for AIV in selling the foil. Romalpa conceded that it was a bailee of the foil until payment and the Court of Appeal construed the contract between Romalpa and AIV to mean that Romalpa was selling the foil as agent for AIV to whom it therefore remained fully accountable for the proceeds of sale. Roskill LJ summarised the position this way ([1976] 1 WLR 676 at 690):

> If an agent lawfully sells his principal's goods, he stands in a fiduciary relationship to his principal for those goods and their proceeds. A bailee is in like position in relation to his bailor's goods.

As Goode has pointed out ((1976) 92 LQR 528 at 550), Roskill LJ was not implying that a bailee is a fiduciary of bailed goods (which in general he is not) but was simply making the point that, on the facts of the case, the terms on which the goods were delivered to the defendant, Romalpa, made it accountable as a fiduciary for the proceeds. Consequently, as Romalpa was an agent, the necessary fiduciary relationship existed to enable AIV to use the equitable tracing process and technically, therefore, *Romalpa* does not infringe the requirement of a fiduciary relationship, although it does involve some stretching of the concept. Furthermore, we should note that no unauthorised transaction occurred in *Romalpa*: the case therefore firmly established that tracing in equity was permitted even into the proceeds of authorised resales by a buyer as part of a continuing business arrangement with the supplier.

What we have not yet considered is whether the plaintiff in *Romalpa* possessed the equitable proprietary interest necessary for equitable tracing. The Court of Appeal allowed AIV to trace, but did not discuss this particular point. Although not a strong authority, *Romalpa* nevertheless suggests that the requirement of an equitable proprietary interest may now be satisfied by the claimant retaining absolute ownership (ie where legal and equitable interests are combined), at least where a fiduciary relationship with respect to the goods supplied is established. This approach is derived from the fiduciary duty of an agent to account for the proceeds of sale to the owner of goods sold. In *Foley v Hill* (1848) 2 HL Cas 28 at 35 it was noted that where an agent sells its principal's goods:

> The goods remain the goods of the owner or principal until the sale takes place, and the moment the money is received the money remains the property of the principal.

The agent holds the legal title to the moneys (or the right to receive the moneys, ie a book debt) whilst the equitable interest in the moneys (or book debt) lies in the principal. Thus the principal can trace from the goods into the moneys or any bank account into which they are deposited. However, the duty to account has its own limits. It may be displaced where the parties agree to operate a running account. Then the agent is only a debtor, and not a trustee, of the moneys. In the present context this is more likely to be the case where the agent makes multiple sales of the principal's goods (see also *Triffit Nurseries v Salads Etcetera Ltd* [2000] 2 Lloyd's Rep 74; see also *E Pfeiffer Weinkellerei-Weineinkauf GmbH & Co v Arbuthnot Factors Ltd* [1988] 1 WLR 150 at 159 where Phillips J considered that this is the more usual assumption when a buyer makes sub-sales). The outcome of the developments outlined above is that the elements necessary to support equitable tracing *may* be satisfied by a *Romalpa* clause. But subsequent decisions, perhaps reflecting scant judicial enthusiasm for the consequences of *Romalpa*, have tended, where ambiguity is present, to construe *Romalpa* clauses as not giving rise either to a fiduciary relationship or to a fiduciary duty to account. The main objections taken to their existence are:

(1) that the facts are inconsistent with a fiduciary relationship, for example, the buyer is permitted to keep part of the profits of a sub-sale and this is not consistent with an agency relationship (Davies *Effective Retention of Title* (1991) pp 60–61); and

(2) whether or not the relationship is generally fiduciary, the particular facts of the case are inconsistent with a fiduciary duty to account, for example, the buyer is permitted a credit period and this is inconsistent with the seller having a beneficial interest in the proceeds of sub-sales, or there is no requirement to keep the proceeds of sale separate or to account for them to the claimant.

For example, in *Re Andrabell Ltd* [1984] 3 All ER 407 the company resold goods – travel bags – supplied by the plaintiffs, paid the proceeds into a general bank account and then went into liquidation without having paid for the bags. The court rejected the claim to the proceeds of sale because, inter alia, (i) there was no requirement in the contract to keep the proceeds of sale separate or to account for them to the plaintiff, and (ii) unlike in *Romalpa*, no fiduciary relationship was admitted (see also *Hendy Lennox (Industrial Engines) Ltd v Grahame Puttick Ltd* [1984] 2 All ER 152). But, theoretically, where a contract of sale expressly prescribes that the relationship is fiduciary and sets out a duty to account for the proceeds of sale and to keep them separate, the courts should accept the existence of a fiduciary obligation on the buyer which will give rise to an equitable right to trace (see Parris *Effective Retention of Title Clauses* (1986); and *Goode* pp 99–100). As Goode notes (pp 100–101):

> where... it is apparent from the construction of the contract that B held the goods as S's bailee and was disposing of them as his agent, then in undertaking to make over the proceeds B is doing no more than agreeing to account for that which in equity belonged to S from the outset as the proceeds of his goods and to which he would anyway have had an equitable tracing claim.

But even in circumstances such as those, English courts at first instance have striven to avoid granting the secured status sought by the claimant. Thus the duty to account has been construed as contractual only, not fiduciary (see *Tatung (UK) Ltd v Galex Telesure Ltd* (1988) 5 BCC 325; and *Compaq Computers Ltd v Abercorn Group Ltd* [1991] BCC 484, cf *Puma Australia Ltd v Sportsman's Australia Ltd* unreported, noted by De Lacy [1993] Conv 375). The lukewarm judicial reception of reservation of title is manifested in *Tatung* and *Compaq Computers* where reservation of title clauses claiming the proceeds of sub-sales (or book debts arising from sub-sales) are considered as unregistered charges over such proceeds and book debts, and are therefore invalid under s 874 of the Companies Act 2006. The legal basis for this outcome is challengeable. Worthington, for instance, argues that there is no charge because charges only exist where rights are conferred by the chargee (ie the buyer), and in the current example the seller's interest in the goods/proceeds is not conferred by the buyer (*Proprietary Interests in Commercial Transactions* (1996) p 39; see also Nolan (2004) 120 LQR 108 at 134–135).

Consider the following points:

(1) Is the logical conclusion of the approach adopted in *Tatung* and *Compaq Computers* that it is impossible for two contracting parties to create a valid fiduciary duty to account? (See de Lacy [1993] Conv 375; Ahdar [1993] LMCLQ 382.)

(2) If the relationship between the seller and buyer is not fiduciary, is an agreement by the buyer to hold the proceeds of sub-sales for the seller, a declaration of trust raising the same issues under the IA 1986 as the *Kayford* trust?

(3) The economic effect of *Romalpa* clauses is to give security to the seller for the purchase price of the goods. However, the validity of such clauses relies on the courts upholding their legal form rather than classifying them according to what they achieve in substance. Should the courts prefer form over substance where the transaction is in effect a security device? (See Bridge [1992] JBL 1; *McEntire v Crossley Bros* [1895] AC 457; *Welsh Development Agency v Export Finance Co Ltd* [1992] BCC 270, CA; cf [1990] BCC 393 (at first instance); and *Re Curtain Dream plc* [1990] BCLC 925).

(4) The unsympathetic treatment given to duties to account in reservation of title cases can be compared with the largely favourable treatment of the duties to set aside and retain moneys on behalf of contractors and

sub-contractors under building contracts (see *Rayack Construction Ltd v Lampeter Meat Co Ltd* (1979) 12 BLR 30; *Re Arthur Sanders Ltd* (1981) 17 BLR 125; *Lovell Construction Ltd v Independent Estates Ltd (in liquidation)* [1994] 1 BCLC 31; Tanner (1987) 3 Construction LJ 94; and McCartney (1992) 8 Construction LJ 360, cf *Mac-Jordan Construction Ltd v Brookmount Erostin Ltd (in receivership)* [1992] BCLC 350). Is there any policy reason justifying different treatment?

(5) In *Re Bond Worth Ltd* [1980] Ch 228 Slade J held a retention of title clause which claimed to give the seller equitable title to the goods sold to be an unregistered and unenforceable charge. Worthington argues that Slade J failed to focus on the rights of the buyer and dismissed the notion of a trust too readily (op cit p 23). A settlor (here the seller) can create a trust for itself within usual trust concepts. Was this what was done implicitly in *Re Bond Worth*? Does this fit within the actual framework of sales of goods or is Roskill LJ's view in *Romalpa* that an agency relationship is intended a more attractive interpretation?

(6) Do you agree with the view in Law Commission CP 164 *Registration of Security Interest: Company Charges and Property other than Land* (2002) that (a) a *Romalpa* clause is functionally similar to security over goods supplied and new goods or proceeds (para 6.21), (b) the question of whether a retention of title clause creates a registrable charge should be left to the courts, and (c) *Romalpa* clauses should be registrable like security interests (paras 5.12 and 7.24; but see Final Report (Law Com No 296, 2005) where the matter has been deferred for further consideration)? (Note that the Australian High Court has held that retention of title clauses can come within a statutory definition of a 'security interest': see *General Motors Acceptance Corporation Australia v Southbank Traders Pty Ltd* [2007] HCA 19; and see also discussion in McCormack [2002] JBL 113 at 133–134 and [2003] LMCLQ 80 at 83.) Should trusts or other fiduciary relationships which effectively confer priority of one creditor over another not be valid unless they are registered like other security devices? Note that in *Armour v Thyssen Edelstahlwerk AG* [1991] 2 AC 339 (a Scottish case) the fact that the retention of title clause covered all moneys owing did not convert it into a registrable charge. See also *Associated Alloys Pty Ltd v ACN 001 452 106 Pty Ltd (in liq)* (2000) 202 CLR 588 (an Australian case) where the High Court of Australia held a trust could be created if the subject trust property was identified to be a proportion of the proceeds received from sales of new goods created from the seller's products (ie a trust of future acquired property, being the proceeds) and such a trust was not a charge.

(d) Reservation of title, mixing of goods and the limits of equitable tracing

In *Romalpa* the aluminium foil had not been mixed with other material, nor processed in any way. Commonly, however, a seller supplies materials that are to be made up into products or, alternatively, consumed in the manufacturing process. We saw in Chapter 14 that tracing ends when identification of property is no longer possible, but we also saw that equity's metaphysical approach allows tracing into a mixed fund. Can a seller then rely on its reservation of title clause to trace into the product resulting from the mixing?

Borden (UK) Ltd v Scottish Timber Products Ltd [1981] Ch 25

Borden supplied STP with resin on terms that legal ownership of the resin was to pass only when payment had been made for that resin and all other goods supplied up to the time of payment. Borden knew that usually within two days of receiving the resin, STP made it up into glue, and then mixed it with wood chippings to make chipboard. The contract contained no provision giving Borden any rights in the finished products or the proceeds of their sale. At the time a receiver was appointed, STP owed Borden £318,321 and Borden claimed a charge on any chipboard made with their resin and on the proceeds of sale of such chipboard.

Judge Rubin ([1979] 2 Lloyd's Rep 168) held that STP was in a fiduciary relationship with Borden, as bailee of the resin, and that Borden was entitled to trace into the product and proceeds. STP appealed. Bridge LJ doubted whether the reservation of title clause created any fiduciary relationship but was prepared to assume that such a relationship did exist up to the moment the resin was used in manufacture. Bridge LJ then considered whether equitable tracing – the tracing remedy as he called it – was possible:

> It is conceded that there is no previous authority which establishes that the tracing remedy can be exercised where there has been an admixture of the goods of A with the goods of B in such a way that they both lose their identity and result in the production of goods of an entirely different kind; but it is urged that the availability of such a remedy is supported by the application by analogy of principles derived from the decided cases. The main authority relied on by the judge in reaching his conclusion, and by counsel in his argument for the sellers is the decision of this court in the case of *Aluminium Industrie Vaassen BV v Romalpa Aluminium Ltd.*

Bridge LJ distinguished *Romalpa* on the facts:

> I come to what, to my mind, is really the heart of the matter: can the tracing remedy here claimed be supported in the application by analogy of the well-known principles of tracing expounded so clearly in the judgment of Jessel MR in *Re Hallett's Estate* (1880) 13 Ch D 696 at 708–711? . . .
>
> What are the salient features of the doctrine that Jessel MR there expounds? First, it will be observed that in all cases the party entitled to trace is referred to as the beneficial owner of the property, be it money or goods, which the 'trustee', in the broad sense in which Jessel MR uses that word, including all fiduciary relationships, has disposed of. In the instant

case, even if I assume that so long as the resin remained resin the beneficial ownership of the resin remained in the sellers, I do not see how the concept of the beneficial ownership remaining in the sellers after use in manufacture can here possibly be reconciled with the liberty which the sellers gave to the buyers to use that resin in the manufacturing process for the buyers' benefit, producing their own chipboard and in the process destroying the very existence of the resin.

Secondly, the doctrine expounded by Jessel MR contemplates the tracing of goods into money and money into goods. In the latter case it matters not that the moneys represent a mixed fund of which a part only is impressed with the relevant trust. The cestui que trust has a charge on the mixed fund or the property into which it has passed for the amount of the trust moneys. It is at the heart of counsel's argument for the sellers to submit that the same applies to a mixture of goods with goods, relying in particular on Jessel MR's illustration of the mixed bag of sovereigns. Now I can well see the force of that argument if the goods mixed are all of a homogeneous character. Supposing I deposit a ton of my corn with a corn factor as bailee, who does not store it separately but mixes it with corn of his own. This, I apprehend, would leave unaffected my rights as bailor, including the right to trace. But a mixture of heterogeneous goods in a manufacturing process wherein the original goods lose their character and what emerges is a wholly new product is in my judgment something entirely different.

Bridge LJ identified a number of practical difficulties with the propositions advanced by the respondent sellers, including that of quantifying the proportion of the value of the manufactured product which the 'tracer' could claim as properly attributable to his ingredient:

In the instant case, a breakdown of the actual coatings of chipboard over a period of seven months to 29 July 1977 has been agreed, attributing 17 per cent of the total cost to the cost of resin, subject to a reservation with respect to wastage and over usage. But one can well see that in many cases where the cost of materials and labour involved in a particular production process were constantly fluctuating it might be quite impossible to assign a proportion of the total cost properly attributable to one particular ingredient with any certainty at all.

The lesson to be learned from these conclusions is a simple one. If a seller of goods to a manufacturer, who knows that his goods are to be used in the manufacturing process before they are paid for, wishes to reserve to himself an effective security for the payment of the price, he cannot rely on a simple reservation of title clause such as that relied on by the sellers. If he wishes to acquire rights over the finished product, he can only do so by express contractual stipulation.

The appeal was unanimously upheld.

Although Bridge LJ recognised the possibility of tracing into a homogeneous mixture, the Court of Appeal was patently unenthusiastic about any extensions of reservation of title into the manufactured product or its proceeds (see Templeman LJ's trenchant judgment (at 44) referring to the task being asked of the court as 'unearthing the unearthable, tracing the untraceable, and calculating the incalculable').

Two principal reasons were advanced for negating Borden's claim. One, distinguishing *Romalpa*, was that no fiduciary relationship existed in respect to the resin. On established principles, in the absence of a fiduciary relationship there is no ability to trace in equity. The other reason was that the scope of equitable tracing would be exceeded. The latter is a troublesome reason as it is not clearly supported by pre-existing tracing principles. Given the metaphysical nature of equitable tracing, the court's conclusions about loss of identifiability of a product or its proceeds is somewhat arbitrary. The resin had unquestionably been physically consumed, but it was conceded that its proportionate value was calculable and was therefore, in accounting terms, identifiable. One hundred and fifty years ago the New York Supreme Court, in *Dunning v Stearns* 9 Barb 630 (1850), had had no difficulty in recognising the ability to trace ash supplied by a seller into a buyer's mixed product, potash, where the contract of sale contained a clause creating a lien over any potash made from the ash. This was held valid on the basis that it was the parties' intention to create a lien until the sellers' claim for the price was satisfied. Thus, had it wished to, the court in *Borden* could have recognised a charge or lien over the manufactured product equal in value to the proportionate value of the resin. Might the approach to equitable tracing adopted in *Borden*, therefore, reflect a degree of conceptual confusion? It is not specific items of property or 'real things' that are traced. Rather, as indicated previously (see Chapter 14, p 717), equitable tracing is a process whereby assets are identified against which a remedy may be given. In other words, it is not 'the thing' acquired by the buyer which is being traced but the 'values inherent' in it. As Birks has argued: 'we might say . . . that value has the capacity to survive independently of both form and substance' ([1992] CLP 69 at 98). Thus the issue is the extent to which the courts are prepared to recognise that the value of the original 'thing' may be transmitted into another 'thing' (cf Rotherham *Proprietary Remedies in Context* (2002) ch 5). The question then is whether, having traced successfully, the claimant can assert a proprietary claim (see also Smith *The Law of Tracing* (1997) p 115 n 213: '[*Borden*] must be seen as [a case] in which, even though tracing was possible, proprietary rights could not be established in the traceable product of the plaintiff's resin, because it was turned into chipboard with the plaintiff's consent').

Accepting the limits placed on equitable tracing in *Borden*, it may still be difficult to identify the precise point at which a seller's goods lose their identity and become a new product in the hands of the buyer (Webb [2000] JBL 513 at 520–525 et seq). On the one hand, relatively minor processing in *Re Peachdart Ltd* [1984] Ch 131 ('leather into handbags') and in *Modelboard Ltd v Outer Box Ltd* [1992] BCC 945 ('cardboard sheet into boxes') was considered to be sufficient for the goods to lose their identity. On the other hand, in

Pongakawa Sawmill Ltd v New Zealand Forest Products Ltd [1992] 3 NZLR 304 sellers successfully reclaimed logs sawn into timber, and in *Armour v Thyssen Edelstahlwerke AG* [1990] 3 All ER 481 steel cut into strips was also successfully reclaimed (see also *CKE Engineering Ltd (in admin)* [2007] LT 3/10/2007 – zinc into lower-grade zinc ingots; *Coleman v Harvey* [1989] 1 NZLR 723 – coins into ingots; and also see *Re Weddel (NZ) Ltd* (1996) 5 NZBLC 104). Whereas in formal terms rationalisation of these decisions is possible, for our purposes it is relevant just to note that it depends on fine distinctions being drawn about manufacturing processes (see Webb [2000] JBL 513; Hicks [1993] JBL 485; and Ahdar [1993] LMCLQ 382) and even abattoir practice (*Chaigley Farms Ltd v Crawford, Kaye and Grayshire Ltd (T/A Leylands)* [1996] BCC 957, noted De Lacy [1998] Conv 52).

However, notwithstanding the decision in *Borden* about the limits of tracing, it may be premature to assume that a court would reach a similar conclusion about those limits where a manufacturer wrongfully, ie without authority, commingled or blended its own materials with those belonging to another – see *Lupton v White* (1808) 15 Ves 432 – or even where the wrongful mixing was of homogeneous goods, namely, lead ore. In *Glencore International v MTI* [2001] Lloyd's Rep 284 at 329–330, where oils were mixed, Moore-Bick J considered that where mixing of products was wrongful, the contributors could claim proportionate shares of the mixed product, or any new product created: any doubts about the contribution by the wrongdoer would not be resolved in the wrongdoer's favour. Moreover, Moore-Bick J distinguished *Borden* because it was a consensual use of product (at 325) and noted that the claimant in *Borden* had conceded title to the new product was vested in the manufacturer (for a discussion of the principles see Phillips (2007) 20(6) Insolv Int 81–84; Bell *The Modern Law of Personal Property* (1990) pp 69–73; McCormack *Reservation of Title* (2nd edn, 1995) pp 54–62; Whittaker [1984] 100 LQR 35; Matthews (1981) 10 Anglo-Am LR 121 and (1981) CLP 159, cf the House of Lords' approach in *Mercer v Craven Grain Storage Ltd* [1994] CLC 328; Smith (1995) 111 LQR 10; Ulph [2001] LMCLQ 447).

It only remains to add that even had Borden expressly stipulated in the contract that it was to acquire an equitable interest in the chipboard or its proceeds, two members of the Court of Appeal (Templeman and Buckley LJJ) would have treated this as a charge created by the buyer. This would then have been void as against the receiver for non-registration under the Companies Act (currently CA 2006, s 874). Subsequent cases have confirmed that where the seller's goods are incorporated by the buyer in new products, it may be extraordinarily difficult to draft a clause effective to retain title in the product or proceeds for the seller. Such clauses seem likely to be construed, however precise their language, as intending to vest legal ownership of the manufactured product in the buyer subject only to a registrable charge in favour of the seller (*Re Peachdart* [1984] Ch 131).

Not all courts would refuse to allow tracing where the supplier's product has been reworked. The High Court in Australia in *Associated Alloys Pty Ltd v ACN 001 452 106 Pty Ltd* (2000) 202 CLR 588 considered a clause which provided that if the purchaser used the seller's product in some manufacturing process then the purchaser 'shall hold such part of the proceeds of such manufacturing or construction process' as relates to the product in trust for the seller. The amount held was to be equal in monetary terms to the amount owing by the purchaser to the seller at the time of receipt of such proceeds. The court held that this retention of title clause operated as an agreement to create a trust over the proceeds of sales of products manufactured by the purchaser using the products supplied by the seller. However, for the seller this was a pyrrhic victory as the court held that the seller had not proved that any proceeds had in fact, been received by the purchaser. Hence, a theoretical right to trace may have existed, but due to absence of proof, all problems about tracing were neatly sidestepped by the court. Also, the court gave an unusually restrictive interpretation to the word 'proceeds' (see Carlen (2002) 30 Aus Bus LR 106; and Ong (2000) 12 Bond LR 148).

Whether *Associated Alloys Pty Ltd* would find favour in England is debatable. Notwithstanding the approach in *Borden* it remains open to seller and buyer to agree which of them is to be the owner of any manufactured product (see the tentative suggestions by both Goff and Oliver LJJ in *Clough Mill Ltd v Martin* [1985] 1 WLR 111 at 115 and 124, CA; *Glencore International v MTI* [2001] 1 Lloyds Rep 284 at 321–322; and see also *Davies* pp 105–113; *McCormack* pp 109–127; McMeel 'Retention of Title' in Rose (ed) *Restitution and Insolvency* (2000)). Thus a seller and buyer may agree that they would be co-owners of any new product (see *Coleman v Harvey* [1989] 1 NZLR 723; and in *Re Stapylton Fletcher Ltd* [1994] 1 WLR 1181 at 1198–1199, cf *ICI New Zealand Ltd v Agnew* [1998] 2 NZLR 129; Webb [2000] JBL 513 at 531 et seq) and that where the buyer then sold the new product with the seller's consent, the buyer would be acting as an agent (Watts [1990] 106 LQR 552). Even if effective this strategy simply takes the debate full circle and back to the point discussed previously, namely, whether the buyer qua agent owes a fiduciary duty to account to the seller for the proceeds of any sale.

(e) Conclusion

What we have been reviewing are attempts by drafters of agreements to combine equitable tracing with the contractual freedom of parties to determine the time when ownership in property passes, in order to create a mechanism that will operate as a security interest which does not require registration.

Rotherham invites us to distinguish the various analyses in such areas to the extent to which they are based on 'principle' or 'policy' (*Rotherham* (2002) p 153). But it has not been our concern to offer a comprehensive account of the present validity or commercial desirability of various forms of reservation of title clauses. As regards validity, it is sufficient to note that as long as goods, or perhaps their proceeds of sale, remain separate and identifiable, a clause reserving title until all the goods delivered under a contract have been paid for will be valid and not registrable. Moreover such validity extends to a clause retaining title until all debts owed to the seller are paid. On the other hand, an attempt to reserve title either in goods which are consumed or lose their separate identity in a manufacturing process, or in the proceeds of sale of the manufactured goods is unlikely to be upheld. The courts, in circumventing such clauses, have argued variously that no fiduciary relationship exists (*Re Andrabell Ltd* [1984] 3 All ER 407), that the purported scope of the clause extends beyond the limits of equitable tracing (*Borden (UK) Ltd v Scottish Timber Products Ltd* [1981] Ch 25) or finally that the clause, rather than recognising a charge that arises by operation of law, has the effect of creating a registrable charge (eg *Re Peachdart Ltd* [1984] Ch 131, but cf *Clough Mill Ltd v Martin* [1985] 1 WLR 111).

As regards the commercial desirability of enforcing such clauses, the effect of a successful *Romalpa* clause is to take the supplier of goods outside the category of unsecured creditors. Equitable tracing and its accompanying proprietary remedies then give the supplier priority over their claims. Indeed, a successful *Romalpa* clause could also override prior floating charges and preferential creditors' claims. Much the same effect is achieved for the supplier of funds under a *Quistclose*-type arrangement. But, as Goodhart and Jones ((1980) 43 MLR 489) have pointed out (at 511): 'such suppliers are, however, de facto if not de jure creditors for money lent or goods supplied.' The conclusion they draw is that: 'it would be more equitable to improve the position of unsecured creditors generally – for example, by limiting the effect of floating charges or by restricting the class of preferred creditors – than to create yet another class of protected "creditors" and leave the general creditors with even less to divide up among themselves'.

If couched in terms of a conflict whereby one class of creditors seeks to obtain an advantage over unprotected creditors, by means of a device undetectable by the latter, the argument for restricting the application of the equitable proprietary remedies in this commercial context seems conclusive at first glance. Moreover these devices may also encourage more lending by the unsecured creditors, to their detriment, because of the apparent solidity of the company (see Belcher and Beljan [1997] JBL 1). There are, however, other factors to consider, one being the operation of insolvency law in practice and another the relationship between contractual freedom and statutory standards. As regards the former, the Cork Committee noted that the invalidity of *Romalpa* clauses does not benefit the unsecured creditor but rather the floating charge holder (para 1634). Moreover there are many undiscoverable claims that operate in an insolvency: liens, rights of set-off, rights of stoppage in transit, as well as *Kayford* and *Quistclose*-type trusts discussed earlier in this chapter. Elias (*Explaining*

Constructive Trusts (1990) pp 135–143) argues that in light of these factors there is no good reason for not recognising other preferential claims such as those of reservation of title holders. An alternative approach, previously mentioned, is for reservation of title clauses to be treated as forms of security and subjected to a registration requirement.

A *Romalpa* clause is part of a commercial contractual relationship between supplier and buyer of goods. Turning then to the relationship between contractual freedom and statutory standards, the question is how far this bargain should be allowed to sustain a proprietary claim, to the likely detriment of third parties, beyond the operation of the terms of the Sale of Goods Act 1979 defining the time that the property in goods passes. But the courts must also weigh a still more remote and intangible consideration (arguably present in *Quistclose* and *Northern Development*), namely the possible gains of corporate rescue as against the risks of incurring further indebtedness. A supplier of goods or funds may know that refusal of further supplies may bring about a rapid collapse of the company seeking supplies, whereas an extension of further supplies may provide the company a lifeline to overcome its trading difficulties, and thus avoid receivership. The argument, as developed by Austin ((1986) 6 OJLS 444) is that 'in the economic interests of the community, the law should provide some simple mechanisms for encouraging suppliers to participate in corporate rescues without thereby being relegated to the lowest division of creditors; and should do so by case law if the means are at hand, without waiting for statutory law reform'. However, to the extent that a *Quistclose* type encourages further credit by another lender it may cause injustice. Arguably, in such circumstances *Quistclose* trusts should be limited to where the lender clearly intended a trust (*Rotherham* (2002) p 163). While there is an issue about the fairness of *Quistclose* trusts given their undiscoverability by lenders, in both the Law Commission's *Consultation Paper, Registration of Security Interests: Company Charges and Property Other than Land* (CP 164) (2002) and its second consultative report, *Company Security Interests* (Law Com No 176, 2004), the Law Commission considered that *Quistclose* trusts should not need to be registered in the same way as charges or other securities and the matter should be left for the courts to determine whether or not a particular *Quistclose* trust is a security interest requiring registration (see generally Glister [2004] LMCLQ 460).

The uneven, indeed uneasy, judicial reception extended to *Romalpa* clauses perhaps reflects a respect for the contractual freedom of parties to make their own bargains tempered by an awareness both of the dilemmas posed to receivers by reservation of title clauses and the consequences of such clauses for the general body of creditors. The outcome is that the courts have muddled through to the compromise position summarised above. The compromise has generally depended upon strained construction of contractual clauses combined with a juggling of equitable concepts. This process is not guaranteed to produce predictability of outcome, a quality of some value in commercial transactions.

It might perhaps be better, as Austin has suggested, for the courts overtly to develop a concept of a 'corporate rescue principle' which, in the absence of comprehensive legislation, or as an alternative to the voluntary administration procedures of the Insolvency Act 1986, would dictate when the equitable proprietary remedies discussed in this chapter could and should be enforced. Whether in practice this would produce greater predictability is itself uncertain.

What, therefore, have been the consequences of this muddling-through for our principal concern, the equitable tracing remedy? Formally, very little. The limit established by *Borden* on the scope of tracing constitutes but one specific instance of loss of identity, derived, we argue, from perceived commercial convenience rather than from equitable principle. More significantly, although the *Re Diplock* prerequisites for equitable tracing – fiduciary relationship and the claimant's equitable proprietary interest – remain formally intact, *Romalpa* appears to weaken substantially their practical significance particularly in the case of the second requirement (see also the discussion in Chapter 14). Indeed, the uncertain ambit of fiduciary relationships is considered further in the next chapter. It may just be that, if proposals requiring registration of reservation of title clauses are ever enacted, *Romalpa* will have had a more lasting effect in the law of trusts than in commercial law. However, change in personal property securities law moves at a glacial pace, and earlier suggestions that the law be changed so that retention of title clauses would be registered to ensure their validity have been shelved for further consideration (cf Law Commission Final Report *Company Security Interests* (Law Com No 296, 2005) with *Company Charges and Property other than Land* (CF 164) (2002) and Law Com No 176 (2004) and, earlier, Diamond *Security over Property other than Land*, DTI Consultation Document (1986)).

16

Trusts in commerce IV: fiduciary relationships, commerce and the trust

1. Introduction

Two previous chapters in this commercial section of the book (Chapters 13 and 15) have focused generally on the conscious use of a trust as a convenient method of achieving specific commercial objectives – thus falling within what was termed in Chapter 1 the 'trust-twisting' aspect of trust usage. The emphasis in this chapter shifts diametrically to the position where those engaged in some form of commercial activity may find themselves subject to fiduciary duties and, if in breach of those duties, may have imposed on them one or more of the equitable remedies, including constructive trusteeship, that the courts can call upon.

Consider the following examples of problems that might be encountered:

(1) Trustees appoint a solicitor, S, who, while carrying out their instructions, acquires confidential information about a company in which the trust fund has a substantial shareholding. Mistakenly believing that she has the trustees' and beneficiaries' consent, S acquires a large shareholding herself, reconstructs the company and makes a substantial profit for herself and the trust shareholding. A disgruntled beneficiary, whose proper consent was not obtained, claims that S's shares are trust property.

(2) A mining company, M, employs a geologist, G, to survey an area and report on any mineral deposits. G returns with relatively little information, but proceeds to stake claims to mineral deposits on her own behalf in the same area. M seeks to establish that the claims are rightfully its property.

(3) An employee of bank A mistakenly overpays a large sum of money to bank B. The mistake is discovered by B which takes no immediate action to rectify the position. B becomes insolvent and is put into liquidation before A discovers the error made by its employee. A wishes to recover the full amount overpaid.

In none of these examples do we find a beneficiary claiming against a trustee. But a feature common to them all is that one of the possible remedies a court may impose, in the interests of what can be loosely called 'justice' or even 'morality', is a constructive trust. Consequently in examples (1) and (2) the 'shares', and the 'mining claims' may both become 'trust property' held by the legal owner now as trustee for those claiming the property. In (3) the amount overpaid, if identifiable, may also become trust property although the correct justification for this result is unclear and indeed contentious.

First, however, we must note a possible further feature common to examples (1) and (2), and, perhaps surprisingly, (3). The court may hold that the solicitor, the employee and the bank respectively are all fiduciaries. It is the existence of a fiduciary relationship that provides the basis for imposing a constructive trust. In Chapter 1 we identified as one of the two most common instances where a constructive trust can be imposed – the heartland of the concept – the situation where some breach of duty arising out of a fiduciary relationship has occurred.

The fiduciary relationship par excellence is that of trustee-beneficiary – the fiduciary element there, in Scott's words, being 'peculiarly intense' (see Chapter 9). How far the standards of conduct derived from that relationship are or should be applied to non-trustees engaged in some form of commercial activity is one concern of this chapter. To assess this it is convenient to identify the following three distinct issues, which are considered separately in section 2 below. First, what relationships are defined as fiduciary? Second, what is the extent of the fiduciary obligations associated with each relationship? The reference to 'peculiarly intense' warns us that the standards applicable to trustee-beneficiary relationships are not necessarily appropriate for all fiduciaries. Third, is the imposition of a constructive trust, a proprietary remedy, appropriate? A duty to account or equitable compensation may, for example, be alternative remedies in some circumstances.

These questions do not obviously explain the tentative mention above of 'morality' nor the purpose of fiduciary relationships. Consider the oft-quoted words of Chief Justice Cardozo advocating a strict deterrent approach in the US courts: 'Many forms of conduct permissible in a workaday world for those acting at arm's length, are forbidden to those bound by fiduciary ties. A trustee is held to something stricter than the morals of the market place. Not honesty alone, but the punctilio of an honor the most sensitive is then the standard of behaviour' (*Meinhard v Salmon* 164 NE 545 at 546 (1928)). A further object of this chapter is therefore to explore the relationship between the pressures of the marketplace and the demands of a fiduciary morality. Thus, we would say that the fiduciary relationship is, to some extent, standard-setting. But it operates in a different context from common law notions of contract and negligence as standard-setting mechanisms. As McLachlin J in the Canadian case *Canson Enterprises Ltd v Broughton & Co* (1991) 85 DLR (4th) 129 at 154 noted, because equity has a different foundation to the common law the basis of fiduciary relationships:

> . . . [is] distinct from the tort of negligence and contract. In negligence and contract the parties are taken to be independent and equal actors, concerned primarily with their own self-interest. Consequently, the law seeks a balance between enforcing obligations

> by awarding compensation and preserving optimum freedom for those involved in the relationship in question, communal or otherwise. The essence of the fiduciary relationship, by contrast, is that one party pledges herself to act in the best interest of the other. The fiduciary relationship has trust, not self-interest, at its core, and when breach occurs, the balance favours the person wronged. The freedom of the fiduciary is diminished by the nature of the obligation he or she has undertaken...

Note that at least one commentator, Conaglen, does not agree that fiduciary duties involve an element of morality or standard-setting (Conaglen (2005) 121 LQR 452 at 472–473). He argues the purpose of fiduciary duties is to increase the likelihood of proper performance of the fiduciary's other (non-fiduciary) duties (cf Lee (2007) 27 OJLS 327 and see Samet (2008) 28(4) LQR 763).

It must not be forgotten that most commercial activity is contract-based and there may be different views as to the desirability of recognising or imposing fiduciary duties in contract-based relationships. Do, therefore, the demands of fiduciary morality impose unwarranted constraints on commercial behaviour or, alternatively, is the fiduciary obligation being itself defined by commercial practice? In considering these issues we must not forget that where a relationship is created by contract, the terms of the contract may potentially modify the fiduciary obligations or duties that would otherwise arise in that relationship.

2. Fiduciary relationships and breach of fiduciary duty

The term 'fiduciary' is an abstract term, but one possessing a 'core' meaning, namely that a person in that position is under a duty of loyalty to some other person or body. This duty is then translated into a fundamental legal principle that a fiduciary should not allow personal interest to conflict with that duty. The principle, and a rationale for it, emerge in the judgment of Lord Herschell in *Bray v Ford* [1896] AC 44 at 51–52:

> It is an inflexible rule of a Court of Equity that a person in a fiduciary position... is not, unless otherwise expressly provided, entitled to make a profit; he is not allowed to put himself in a position where his interest and duty conflict. It does not appear to me that this rule is, as has been said, founded upon principles of morality. I regard it rather as based on the consideration that, human nature being what it is, there is danger, in such circumstances, of the person holding a fiduciary position being swayed by interest rather than by duty, and thus prejudicing those whom he was bound to protect. It has, therefore, been deemed expedient to lay down this positive rule. But I am satisfied that it might be departed from in many cases, without any breach of morality, without any wrong being inflicted, and without any consciousness of wrong-doing.

The principle is applied most rigorously to trustees – although traces of a new flexibility are apparent here – via the various rules relating, for example, to trustee remuneration, both direct and indirect, and to dealings with beneficiaries or with trust property (see Chapter 9). Applying the principle to others who are also in some degree fiduciaries is, however, much less certain than the exhortations about 'inflexible rules' may suggest. Indeed the final sentence in the extract from Lord Herschell's judgment and our reference to 'some degree' both hint at this. The problem is exactly how far are fiduciaries, other than trustees, to be subjected to the full gamut of rules devised to enforce the duty of undivided loyalty? What factors might justify a differential application of the strict standards?

However, before considering these questions there is logically a prior problem to be resolved. Who is a fiduciary, and what is the nature of a relationship that leads the court to attach the 'fiduciary' label? This is a subject which has been said to have 'something of the fascination for equity lawyers . . . that the search for the Holy Grail had for the knights of antiquity' (Waters (1986) Can BR 37 at 56). We would add that the search for understanding has proved equally arduous.

(a) Identifying the 'fiduciary relationship'

(1) The development of the concept
(See generally Glover *Equity, Restitution and Fraud* (2003) ch 2; Finn *Fiduciary Obligations* (1977); Shepherd *The Law of Fiduciaries* (1981); and Bean *Fiduciary Obligations and Joint Ventures* (1995).)

L S Sealy 'Fiduciary Relationships' (1962) CLJ 69 at 69–70

Breach of trust, or confidence, is one of the traditional heads of jurisdiction in Chancery:

These three give place in court of conscience, Fraud, accident, and breach of confidence (quoted in Maitland *Equity* (1932) 2nd edn, p 7n).

From this branch of equity we derive, of course, the whole of our law of trusts; but matters of confidence in earlier times covered a good deal more ground than trusts of property as we know them today. In the reports of eighteenth- and early nineteenth-century cases we find the word used in many different contexts. A was said to have confidence reposed in him by B not only where B had entrusted A with property to hold and deal with on behalf of himself or others – as in the trust strictly so called – but also where A undertook to exercise a power, to conduct a sale, to supervise an estate or business, or in some other way to become B's employee or agent. Confidence was also reposed where B was dependent on A's advice, perhaps because A was a professional adviser or expert, or more familiar with the subject-matter; because A was on the spot and B at a distance; or because A was a trusted servant or friend, or a person of dominant character or position who was able to influence B's decisions. Again, confidence might be induced where A by words or conduct represented to B that he would deal fairly with him. In all these cases the broad general principle applied was that if a confidence is reposed, and that confidence is abused, a court

> of equity shall give relief. (Lord Thurlow in *Gartside v Isherwood* (1783) 1 Bro CC 558 at 560.)
>
> Our ancestors did not mince words: many of these matters of confidence were naturally called 'trusts', whether there was any strict trust of property or not.

Sealy goes on to describe how the trust gradually developed into a fully fledged concept, with the consequence that the word 'trust' acquired its modern technical meaning. This development left in its wake a number of situations similar to although more limited in terms of obligation than trusteeship, but now without even the benefit of a label. The outcome during the nineteenth century was, as Sealy observes, that 'the word fiduciary (which earlier had received very little judicial support) was adopted to describe these situations which fell short of the now strictly-defined trust' (at 71–72). Indeed, it is still sometimes applied in the context of undue influence (*Mahoney v Purnell* [1996] 3 All ER 61 at 90–91) and in the context of confidential information (*A-G v Blake* [2001] 1 AC 268).

To bring the picture up to date, it can be said that there now exists a core of well-established relationships which are *to some extent* fiduciary – company director-company, principal-agent, partner-co-partner, solicitor-client, employer-employee. By saying these relationships are to some extent fiduciary we mean that some of the potential fiduciary duties apply to them: Fletcher-Moulton LJ's warning against any assumption that common standards are applicable to all fiduciaries must always be borne in mind (*Re Coomber* [1911] 1 Ch 723 at 728; see Chapter 9, p 434). An approach which judges commonly use is to compare the relationship in question with the well-established fiduciary relationships to determine whether that relationship is similar to one of the existing categories. In this fashion judges use comparisons and argue by analogy to establish whether or not the particular relationship is fiduciary or, at least, fiduciary in part. This is a status-based approach to determining the issues (see *Bean* p 98). For example, in *Boardman v Phipps* [1967] 2 AC 46 which we discuss later, the main protagonists were considered to be analogous to trustees and agents and hence in a fiduciary relationship. But the courts also can deny the existence of fiduciary relationships by comparison with the existing categories as in *Appleby v Cowley* (1982) *Times* 14 April, in which Megarry VC denied that a fiduciary relationship existed between the head of barristers' chambers and the barristers in those chambers as the head of chambers was not acting as an agent. Using a status-based approach means that courts will focus on similarities between relationships but may not seek out either the underlying characteristics which indicate why the relationship should be considered fiduciary or some meaningful definition for the term 'fiduciary'.

Once we move beyond the core categories the term fiduciary has proved extraordinarily resistant to attempts to devise a 'strict definition'. There have been attempts to devise a uniform test, notably by Canadian academics, in particular Flannigan ((1989) 9 OJLS 285) and Shepherd (*The Law of Fiduciaries* (1981)), but none has been judicially adopted. Indeed there may be different bases for different types of fiduciary relationships. For example, the partner-co-partner fiduciary relationship is one borne out of the mutual trust and confidence (see *Thompson's Trustee v Heaton* [1974] 1 WLR 605 at 613) between parties combining for a common end and who are roughly equal in status. Thus the partnership fiduciary relationship can be considered to be different in nature to the other typical fiduciary relationships, where there is often an unequal status. For that reason we prefer to call it the 'collaborative fiduciary relationship' (see *Bean* ch 7).

That there can be different bases for fiduciary relationships emerges clearly from the judgment of La Forest J in *LAC Minerals v International Corona Ltd* (1989) 61 DLR (4th) 14 at 27 (Supreme Court of Canada) where he identifies three different instances in which the word 'fiduciary' tends to be used: (i) in the traditional categories of fiduciary relationship; (ii) in cases of a specific fiduciary duty arising on the facts; and (iii) in remedial or 'fictional' fiduciary relationships. In considering whether a relationship is 'fiduciary' we must be clear about the sense in which we are using the word, as the underlying basis of the different usages may be different.

(2) Identifying a fiduciary relationship

Notwithstanding the apparent open-ended nature of the fiduciary concept implied in La Forest J's analysis, attempts can be made to identify some underlying principles at work which may be distilled into a general test for recognition of a fiduciary relationship. The Law Commission, for instance, has described the nature of the relationship as being 'one in which a person undertakes to act on behalf of or for the benefit of another, often as an intermediary with a discretion or power which affects the interests of the other who depends on the fiduciary for information and advice' (*Fiduciary Duties and Regulatory Rules*: Law Com No 236 (1995) para 1.3). The courts in Commonwealth countries have also grappled with the issue of determining when a fiduciary relationship exists in recent times and two 'tests' – the *undertaking test* and the *power and discretion test* – have been developed, and elements of both tests appear to be embodied in the Law Commission's description. These tests or guides can give us an indication both of the possible boundaries of the fiduciary relationship and of the possible developments that may occur in our courts.

But how exactly do these tests relate to La Forest J's second category in *LAC Minerals v International Corona*, situations where, on the facts, a fiduciary duty can be established? Fact-based fiduciary status is 'the modern battleground', with the advantages that flow from fiduciary status providing the incentive to argue for recognition of a fiduciary duty or relationship (Worthington *Equity* (2nd edn, 2006) pp 141–142). For example, in *Coleman v Myers* [1997] 2 NZLR 225, CA the New Zealand Court of Appeal recognised a duty owed by directors directly to shareholders (rather than to their company) where the shareholders had placed trust and confidence in particular directors (cf Flannigan [2004] JBL 277 at 295 et seq; *Peskin v Anderson* [2001] 1 BCLC 372, CA). In our view, many instances where the courts have claimed a specific fact-based fiduciary duty exists, can be explained as an application of the undertaking test or a determination that a duty exists using the same factors as exist in the power and discretion test.

'The Undertaking Test' This test or general guide has often been applied in Australian cases. It was originally proposed by Scott in his pioneering article 'The Fiduciary Principle' (1949) 37 Cal LR 539 and was explained by Finn in *Fiduciary Obligations* (1977) in the following way (p 201):

> [A fiduciary] is, simply, someone who undertakes to act for or on behalf of another in some particular matter or matters. That undertaking may be of a general character. It may be specific and limited. It is immaterial whether the undertaking is or is not in the form of a contract. It is immaterial that the undertaking is gratuitous. And the undertaking may be officiously assumed without request.

Put in this form this 'test' appears to be similar to a definition of agency as it emphasises acting on another's behalf or representing another's interests. This 'test' comfortably encompasses the examples of well-established fiduciary relationships outlined above. Lord Browne-Wilkinson appeared to accept this test in *White v Jones* [1995] 2 WLR 187 at 209–210 where he considered that the model for finding a fiduciary relationship exists where 'one party, A, has assumed to act in relation to the property or affairs of another, B. A, having assumed responsibility, pro tanto, for B's affairs is taken to have assumed certain duties in relation to the conduct of those affairs including normally a duty of care. Thus, a trustee assumes responsibility for the management of the property of the beneficiary, a company director for the affairs of the company and an agent for those of his principal. By so assuming to act in B's affairs, A comes under fiduciary duties to B.' But, here we should note that the duty of care that may be imposed on a fiduciary is not recognised as a fiduciary duty, except, it may yet be argued, in the case of trustees.

The undertaking test is of less obvious assistance in some cases which are classified as fiduciary, but which appear to be at the very borderline of the concept.

'The Power and Discretion Test' This test focuses more on the beneficiary. It has often been applied in Canadian cases and was adopted in New Zealand in *DHL International (NZ) Ltd v Richmond Ltd* [1993] 3 NZLR 10 at 22, CA. The test can be seen as comprising the following three elements (*Frame v Smith* (1987) 42 DLR (4th) 81 at 99 per Wilson J):

(1) The fiduciary has scope for the exercise of some discretion or power.
(2) The fiduciary can unilaterally exercise that power or discretion so as to affect the beneficiary's legal or practical interests.
(3) The beneficiary is peculiarly vulnerable to or at the mercy of the fiduciary holding the discretion or power.

This test aims to identify when one person is *obliged* to act in the interests of another and it does not depend on identifying any undertaking so to act. The 'legal and practical interests' of the potential beneficiary are defined generously and thus the test has a potentially wide application to a number of fact situations. However, what constitutes 'vulnerability' for the third part of the test is uncertain – in *LAC Minerals v International Corona Ltd*, for instance, different judges came to different conclusions as to the existence of a fiduciary relationship, based on their views of vulnerability. In Canada, the use of this test has led to a great widening of those who may be potential fiduciaries: in *Norberg v Wynrib* (1992) 92 DLR (4th) 449, for instance, two judges held a doctor to be a fiduciary and liable for compensation in equity for a breach of a fiduciary duty to act in the best interests of the patient (see also *McInerney v MacDonald* (1992) 137 NR 35; cf the Australian approach in *Breen v Williams* (1995) 186 CLR 71 where the High Court expressly rejected an argument that doctors were fiduciaries (see also Bartlett (1997) 5 Med L Rev 193; Nolan (1997) 113 LQR 220)). The Canadian approach has seen fiduciary relationships extend from relationships dealing with commercial and economic interests to personal and private relations (see Joyce [2002] 28 Monash LR 239). The possible consequences of this type of development in fiduciary relationships must not be overlooked. In using wide or easily manipulated tests in order to recognise a fiduciary relationship and give a remedy, are we forcing fiduciary relationships to do the work of other areas of the law, for example, contract and tort? Finn, for instance, suggests that recognising more fiduciary relationships and awarding compensation for breach will lead to 'the development of what is, in effect, a surrogate tort of negligence' (Finn in McKendrick (ed) *Commercial Aspects of Trusts and Fiduciary Obligations* (1992) p 7).

When identifying fiduciary relationships outside the usual core of well-established relationships, it is likely that contract law will play a key role. Most commercial relationships are contract-based and it is the terms of the contract that will establish or negate the fiduciary relationship or a particular fiduciary duty. In the Australian case, *Hospital Products Ltd v United Surgical Corpn* (1984) 156 CLR 41 at 97, Mason J indicated that where a contract provides the basis of the fiduciary relationship that contract regulates the extent of fiduciary liability. Accordingly, 'if it is to exist at all [the fiduciary relationship] must accommodate itself to the terms of the contract so that it is consistent with, and conforms to', the terms of the contract. This has relevance not only for considering potential new fiduciary relationships but also for negating fiduciary duties forming part of the existing recognised fiduciary relationships such as principal–agents, partner–co-partner and solicitor–client, as these fiduciary relationships tend to be based in written contracts. A recent Australian case, *ASIC v Citigroup Global Market Australia Pty Ltd* [2007] FCA 963 illustrates the issues about identifying new contract-based fiduciary relationships. In this case, Citigroup had been engaged to advise Toll Holdings Ltd (Toll) on a proposed takeover for Patrick Corporation Ltd (Patrick). While advising Toll, Citigroup purchased shares in Patrick which, if Citigroup was a fiduciary, would breach the rule against conflict of interest. However, Citigroup's letter of engagement contained an express provision that Citigroup was engaged by Toll as 'an independent contractor and not in any other capacity including as a fiduciary'. The court held that this provision was clear language which excluded a fiduciary relationship (cf Tuch (2005) 29 Melb ULR 478). The court indicated that, but for the engagement letter, the pre-contract dealings between Citigroup and Toll would have pointed strongly towards the existence of a fiduciary relationship in Citigroup's role as an adviser to Toll. The court indicated that in the recognised categories of fiduciary relationship informed consent of the counterparty might be needed to remove the fiduciary relationship. However, where a fiduciary relationship is sought to be recognised outside these categories informed consent is not needed to negate the fiduciary relationship. As noted by Getzler (2008) 124 LQR 15 at 19–20 a policy question arises as to why investment banks and other financial advisers, who wield power over their clients and who are prone to act in conflict with the client's interest, are not also candidates for stronger public policy control through a presumption of initial fiduciary duties.

The court's approach to dealing with exclusion of a fiduciary relationship may be superficially acceptable if the investment bank's counterparty is another large corporation. But, should the same considerations apply where a small investor contracts with an investment bank or other adviser? We can also compare the treatment of Citigroup with other fiduciaries such as solicitors (see p 857). Moreover, the decision in *Citigroup* can be further criticised: was it theoretically acceptable to exclude all potential fiduciary duties by virtue of a general exclusion of a fiduciary relationship? Should not the court have also considered whether, in the absence of a general fiduciary relationship, any specific fiduciary duties arose on the facts?

(3) The scope of the fiduciary relationship

It cannot be reiterated too often nor stressed too strongly that not every act of a fiduciary is necessarily subject to the very onerous fiduciary obligations to the 'beneficiary'. In particular, where a fiduciary relationship is voluntarily created the relationship is usually directed at achieving a particular purpose. For example, a trustee is obliged to invest certain assets, an agent is employed to undertake a certain task and a partner undertakes a specific business. The position was clearly stated by Dixon J in the High Court of Australia over half a century ago (*Birtchnell v Equity Trustee Executors and Agency Co Ltd* (1929) 42 CLR 384 at 408, approved by Lord Wilberforce in

New Zealand Netherlands Society Oranje Inc v Kuys [1973] 2 All ER 1222 at 1226, PC):

> The subject-matter over which the fiduciary obligations extend is determined by the character of the venture or undertaking for which the [relationship] exists, and this is to be ascertained, not merely from the express agreement of the parties, whether embodied in written instrument or not, but also from the course of dealing actually pursued . . . Once the subject-matter of the [relationship] is so determined, it ought not be difficult to apply the clear and inflexible doctrines which determine the accountability of fiduciaries . . .

The subject-matter over which the fiduciary duties extend can be called the 'scope' or 'ambit' of the fiduciary relationship. The point here is that a party to a contract, for instance, can be a fiduciary in relation to part of his activities and not a fiduciary for other parts.

The identification of the scope of the fiduciary relationship can be seen as equivalent to the requirement in trusts law of certainty of trust property. Although a fiduciary relationship may not involve control of property, as a trust does, the res or thing to which the fiduciary's or trustee's duties attach is central to both relationships. Because property is easily identified the scope of the trust relationship is easy to identify. While the res of a fiduciary relationship may be more nebulous it is just as important to define its scope. Only after identifying it can we ask whether a breach has occurred within the scope of the relationship (see Lord Upjohn in *Boardman v Phipps* [1967] 2 AC 46 at 127). For example, a farmer may own several properties and an agent may be employed to manage all the farmer's property or only a particular farm. If the relationship is confined to a particular farm that farm will form the limits of the relationship. This is not to say, however, that matters outside the relationship cannot have an impact on it. Consider the simple example of an agent who manages a farmer's orchard which is dependent on another's irrigation facilities. If the agent purchases the irrigation facility then fiduciary issues are involved because the orchard may be affected, ie the subject-matter of the fiduciary relationship is affected. But if the agent purchases a dairy farm near the orchard, fiduciary issues ought not be involved as the subject-matter (the orchard) is unaffected.

(4) 'Fiduciary': a remedy or a relationship?

The process of determining liability for breach of fiduciary duty has been presented as a series of logical steps. First, identify the particular fiduciary relationship and its scope; second, decide whether breach of some specific duty has occurred; third, implement the appropriate remedy.

This approach was generally endorsed by Megarry VC in *Tito v Waddell (No 2)* [1977] 3 All ER 129 – 'litigation on the grand scale' as he aptly described it in a 241-page judgment. In this case mining rights to phosphate deposits on Ocean Island, a small island in the Pacific Ocean, were acquired by the governments of the UK, Australia and New Zealand. The mining operation was carried on by the British Phosphate Commissioners, in which the Crown had a 42% interest. The rates of royalty on the deposit were, in the absence of agreement, to be fixed by the Crown's resident commissioner. A clause in a 1928 Ordinance stated that the royalties were to be held in trust for the islanders. The islanders subsequently claimed (i) that the rates of royalty were set too low and, inter alia, (ii) that the Crown was accordingly in breach of a fiduciary duty to the islanders in the manner that it carried out its functions. Megarry VC firmly rejected the argument that a fiduciary duty could be imposed merely because there was an obligation to perform certain functions (at 233):

> Furthermore, I cannot see that coupling the job to be performed with self-dealing in the performance of it makes any difference. If there is a fiduciary duty, the equitable rules about self-dealing apply: but self-dealing does not impose the duty. Equity bases its rules about self-dealing on some pre-existing fiduciary duty: it is a disregard of this pre-existing duty that subjects the self-dealer to the consequences of the self-dealing rules. I do not think that one can take a person who is subject to no pre-existing fiduciary duty and then say that because he self-deals he is thereupon subjected to a fiduciary duty.

Notwithstanding Megarry VC's affirmation of the formally logical approach to determining fiduciary accountability, it remains questionable whether that approach can be sustained in what La Forest J called the 'fictional' or 'remedial' fiduciary relationships. It will be recalled (see Chapter 4), that in *Tito v Waddell* Megarry VC defined the relationship as a 'trust in the higher sense' meaning a non-enforceable government obligation. However, in not wholly dissimilar litigation, the Supreme Court of Canada recognised the existence of fiduciary duties on the Crown to protect indigenous or aboriginal people (*Guerin v R* (1984) 13 DLR (4th) 321), although the court was divided on whether the fiduciary duty was sui generis or 'full blown trusteeship' per Wilson J (see also *Delgamuukw v British Columbia* (1991) 79 DLR (4th) 185; Bryant (1993) 27 U Brit Col LR 19; and generally Kulchyski (ed) *Unjust Relations: Aboriginal Rights in Canadian Courts* (1994)). This division in the court may be symptomatic of the underlying reality, that the desire for a remedy may lead to the recognition of a fiduciary relationship (see also *Mabo v State of Queensland (No 2)* (1992) 175 CLR 1, cf Toohey J with Dawson J; Brennan (1992) 15 Syd LR 206 and Gray (2008) 32 Melb ULR 115).

The facts of *Reading v A-G* [1951] AC 507 nicely illustrate the vague character of the term 'fiduciary'. Reading was an army staff-sergeant, stationed in Egypt in 1943–44, who was paid substantial sums by local civilians to ride in uniform in their lorries carrying contraband goods. His presence enabled the lorries to pass civilian police check-points unsearched. He was eventually caught and the British Government confiscated some £19,000 from him. His petition to recover the money failed. One of the grounds applied by the Court of Appeal ([1949] 2 All ER 68), and affirmed by the House of Lords, was that Reading was in a fiduciary relationship to the Crown and was, therefore, under a duty to account for the profit made. But what was the basis of the fiduciary relationship? Asquith LJ recognised that he was using the term 'fiduciary relation' in a 'very loose, or at all events a very comprehensive, sense', but concluded (at 71) that 'such a relation subsisted in this case as to the user of the uniform and the opportunities and facilities attached to it, and that the suppliant obtained the sums claimed by acting in breach of the duties imposed by that relation'. The reasoning in *Reading* suggests that, in the appropriate circumstances – such as preventing ex-Sergeant Reading recovering his 'commission' – the requirement of a fiduciary relationship may be easily satisfied. Suspicion engendered by *Reading* that, just occasionally, a desired outcome is dictating the identification of the supposedly prior requirement, the fiduciary relationship, is reinforced by *Chase Manhattan Bank NA v Israel-British Bank (London) Ltd* [1981] Ch 105.

This was a case of an expensive clerical error. It illustrates the mental gymnastics occasionally demanded to satisfy the requirement that a subsisting fiduciary relationship is a necessary precondition of the equitable right to trace (see generally Chapters 14 and 15). The plaintiff, Chase Manhattan, C, paid $2m to the defendant Israel-British Bank, I-B. Later the same day, as a result of a book-keeping error, C mistakenly repeated the payment. The defendants, I-B, discovered the mistake within two days but did nothing to correct it. I-B became insolvent and went into liquidation some four weeks later. A common law personal action to recover the second payment was available to C but, in view of I-B's insolvency, C would have been unlikely to recover anything like the full $2m. C therefore sought to invoke the equitable doctrine of tracing, and to trace, if possible, the money into I-B's assets so as to assert a proprietary claim against those assets. But C had made a payment in settlement of what it believed to be a commercial debt. Furthermore, prior to that mistaken payment, C had not been in any fiduciary relationship with I-B which was its commercial competitor. Nevertheless Goulding J was able to circumvent these difficulties: he concluded that 'a person who pays money to another under a factual mistake retains an equitable property in it and the conscience of that other is subjected to a fiduciary duty to respect his proprietary right' (at 119). Thus, in what was in substance, of course, a dispute between C and I-B's creditors, C was entitled to trace and I-B required to hold the money, if traceable, on a constructive trust (see (1980) 39 CLJ 272 (Tettenborn) and 275 (Jones) for contemporary conflicting views on the merits of the respective claims). *Chase Manhattan* appeared to indicate that, at least for the purpose of establishing a right to trace, the courts may be willing to stretch the concept of fiduciary relationship to breaking point. A corollary of this reasoning, however, is that any development that removed or attenuated equitable tracing's requirement of a fiduciary relationship, would in turn reduce the perceived need to conjure up the 'fictional' fiduciary. Restitution lawyers have argued for the use of (or the judicial recognition of) the resulting trust as a means of giving the right to trace in equity where there is no fiduciary relationship. The approach of Millett

J at first instance in *El Ajou v Dollar Land Holdings plc* [1993] 3 All ER 717 was thought to be a significant development in this direction; he indicated (at 734) that where there is no existing fiduciary relationship a right to trace in equity may be created or 'exist' by identifying (would imputing be too strong a term?) a resulting trust. Subsequently the same judge frankly admitted to this creative aspect of his judgment in *El Ajou*: 'I was concerned to circumvent the supposed rule that there must be a fiduciary relationship or retained beneficial interest before resort may be had to equitable tracing rules' (*Bristol and West Building Society v Mothew* [1998] Ch 1 at 23). However, both *Chase Manhattan* and those in favour of expanding the recognition of resulting trusts have their critics. Indeed, the decision of the House of Lords in *Westdeutsche Landesbank Girozentral v Islington London Borough Council* [1996] AC 669 may spell an end to both approaches (cf Burrows (2001) 117 LQR 412 at 426, 429; see Chapter 1 at p 28). Lord Browne-Wilkinson criticised the reasoning in *Chase Manhattan* in the *Westdeutsche* case (at 714) but strangely considered the result may be correct given the defendant bank knew of the mistaken payment within two days of it being made and still retained the moneys (cf Lord Millett in Degeling and Edelman (eds) *Equity in Commercial Law* (2005) at 318: '. . . the decision [*Chase Manhattan*] is highly doubtful. I regard it as wrongly decided').

All that one need conclude here is that we should not slip easily into the assumption that the term 'fiduciary' will always be attached at random to a relationship or that some form of trust will be recognised to do 'justice', where there is no alternative remedy or the available remedy seems inadequate. Instead, we should recognise that, whilst the term 'fiduciary' may operate somewhat as a veil, it is one behind which, it can be argued, 'individual rules and principles have been developed' (Finn *Fiduciary Obligations* (1977) p 1). The search for universally applicable statements of principle must therefore give way to consideration of more precise questions such as the specific standards of conduct which the courts expect to be demonstrated in particular professional or commercial relationships. Thus, we need to move from questions concerned with identifying fiduciary relationships to questions focusing on the content of the fiduciary obligations that apply to the person identified as a 'fiduciary'. But before we do so, we need to canvas the possibility of recognising a constructive trust – without there being a fiduciary relationship – as providing an alternative route for claimants to plead and the law to adopt in a case such as *Chase Manhattan*.

(b) Remedial constructive trusts

The usual reason for claiming a fiduciary relationship exists is so that the court can award a constructive trust over some property or interest as a remedy. Surprisingly, in the *Westdeutsche* case, Lord Browne-Wilkinson hinted that the way forward for English law may involve recognising remedial constructive trusts, ie constructive trusts imposed where there is no existing fiduciary relationship (see the extract from his opinion cited in Chapter 1, p 32). It will be recalled that he drew a distinction between a recognised or an 'institutional' constructive trust and a 'remedial' constructive trust, emphasising that the latter 'is a judicial remedy giving rise to an enforceable equitable obligation', the extent to which it operates retrospectively to the prejudice of third parties being within the discretion of the court.

There is a great fear in our law that recognising a remedial constructive trust will give rise to indiscriminate or unjustified variation of existing property rights. Birks has warned against discretionary adjustment of property rights in *The Frontiers of Liability* Vol 2 (1994) p 218. Clearly, the recognition of a remedial constructive trust would require a principled analysis to prevent judges having too free a rein and creating unnecessary uncertainty in law. In Canada, the remedial constructive trust is being developed in a reasonably principled manner by the Supreme Court of Canada to remedy wrongful conduct and to prevent unjust enrichment (see eg *Korkontzilas v Soulos* (1997) 146 DLR (4th) 214; and Wright *The Remedial Constructive Trust* (1998) pp 36–46).

Those claiming a remedial constructive trust would seek to do so on insolvency to gain a priority over other claimants. The glimmer of light for such hopeful claimants indicated by Lord Browne-Wilkinson's comments in *Westdeutsche* was, however, quickly put out by the Court of Appeal in *Re Polly Peck International plc (No 2)* [1998] 3 All ER 812. This case involved, amongst other things, a claim for a remedial constructive trust which would effectively give priority to the claimant over other creditors of the company. In rejecting the award of remedial constructive trust Mummery LJ commented (at 827):

> If the asset is the absolute beneficial property of the company there is no general power in the liquidator, the administrators or the court to amend or modify the statutory scheme so as to transfer that asset or to declare it to be held for the benefit of another person. To do that would be to give a preference to another person who enjoys no preference under the statutory scheme...
>
> [It was] submitted that 'the law moves'. That is true. But it cannot be legitimately moved by a judicial decision down a road signed 'No Entry' by Parliament. The insolvency road is blocked off to remedial constructive trusts, at least when judge driven in a vehicle of discretion.
>
> For those reasons alone, I would refuse leave to the applicants to commence these proceedings. To a trust lawyer, and even more so to an insolvency lawyer, the prospect of a court imposing such a trust is inconceivable and, in my judgement, even the most enthusiastic student of the law of restitution, would be forced to recognise that the scheme imposed by statute for a fair distribution of the assets of an insolvent company precludes the application of the equitable principles manifested in the remedial constructive trust developed by such courts as the Supreme Court of Canada.

This approach creates a Catch-22 for claimants because it is really on insolvency that they would desire a remedial constructive trust. The underlying philosophy of the pari passu distribution on an insolvency is that all such claimants are equal and, therefore, one should not have a preference over the others. This begs the question of whether all claimants are equal and, if they are not, whether a remedial constructive trust should be declared in favour of the more deserving claimant. Some commentators argue that unsecured creditors take the risk that the person they deal with may become insolvent, and that their failure to take security when they gave credit is a ground for treating those unsecured creditors differently to other persons who did not accept the risk of insolvency, usually the claimants arguing for the remedial constructive trust (see *Wright* pp 143–148; Paciocco (1989) 68 Can Bar Rev 315, cf *Re Goldcorp Exchange* [1995] 1 AC 74).

Whether one claimant in an insolvency should be preferred to another by recognising a remedial constructive trust is raised by the facts in the Privy Council decision in *Re Goldcorp Exchange Ltd* [1995] 1 AC 74 on appeal from the New Zealand Court of Appeal.

The Goldcorp case   The New Zealand courts had appeared to recognise remedial constructive trusts (in the absence of fiduciary relationships) ostensibly to remedy behaviour they considered to be 'unconscionable', for example, *Elders Pastoral Ltd v Bank of New Zealand* [1989] 2 NZLR 180. However, in the *Goldcorp* litigation (see below) the NZ Court of Appeal in *Liggett v Kensington* [1993] 1 NZLR 257, rather than recognise a remedial constructive trust, was able to discover a fiduciary relationship between Goldcorp and the plaintiff purchasers, a questionable outcome in the circumstances. If a proprietary remedy was to be awarded to the claimants, it can be argued that a remedial constructive trust may have provided a more intellectually satisfying option.

The case involved the collapse of Goldcorp Exchange Ltd which dealt in gold and other precious metals. Goldcorp's business was primarily with jewellery manufacturers and dealers in jewellery but it actively marketed and sold gold bullion and gold coins to members of the public. Goldcorp was insolvent and the receivers of the company sought court directions as to the ownership of the gold bullion held by the company. The gold bullion was claimed by the Bank of New Zealand under a debenture and also by members of the public who had agreed to purchase gold coins or gold bullion.

There were several different classes of claimant with the largest category being the over 1,500 claimants known as the 'non-allocated purchasers'. These claimants bought gold which was held in an unseparated bulk rather than in separate ingots which were identifiable as being owned by a particular non-allocated purchaser. The non-allocated purchasers' claims far exceeded Goldcorp's gold bullion held at any time. There was no prospect of any payment to any unsecured creditors nor to the non-allocated purchasers if they were not entitled to the gold bullion.

In the New Zealand Court of Appeal the majority, Cooke P and Gault J, exploited the imprecision inherent in the fiduciary concept to hold that a fiduciary relationship existed between Goldcorp and the non-allocated purchasers. This fiduciary relationship was based on Goldcorp's representations and promises that it would store and insure the gold bullion purchased by the non-allocated purchasers and arrange for a leading chartered accounting firm to audit its bullion stocks to ensure accuracy of its holdings. The majority found that the non-allocated purchasers placed trust and reliance in those representations which justified the recognition of a fiduciary relationship. However, the money Goldcorp received from the non-allocated purchasers was deposited in Goldcorp's overdrawn bank account. Thus, technically, even if there were a fiduciary relationship, ordinary tracing rules (see Chapter 14) would mean that there was no asset into which the non-allocated purchasers could trace. Surprisingly, the Court of Appeal held that the non-allocated purchasers could trace into the stocks of gold bullion held by the company at the time of its insolvency. However, as an alternative ground of his judgment, Gault J held that he would have also awarded a remedial constructive trust in favour of non-allocated purchasers ([1993] 1 NZLR 257 at 283).

On appeal, the Privy Council reversed the New Zealand Court of Appeal decision, holding that no fiduciary relationship existed, and no other form of trust arose. Therefore, no rights to trace into the bullion arose. The Privy Council considered that the non-allocated purchasers were merely unsecured creditors who would be treated the same as all of the other unsecured creditors.

The Privy Council (*Re Goldcorp Exchange Ltd* [1995] 1 AC 74) considered the relationship to be nothing more than that of vendor/purchaser and that the obligations under the contracts of sale and the collateral promises, representations and reliance by the purchasers did not give rise to a fiduciary relationship or any form of trust noting that: '. . . [it] is possible without misuse of language to say that the customer has put faith in the company, and that their trust had not been repaid. But the vocabulary is misleading; high expectations do not necessarily lead to equitable remedies.' Moreover, the Privy Council rejected the argument that the court should declare a remedial constructive trust in favour of the non-allocated purchasers concluding that what occurred was merely a breach of contract without creating an equitable interest in the gold. Whilst recognising the possibility of the co-existence of an equitable interest for the non-allocated purchasers and their contractual rights, the Privy Council went on to assert 'it is hard to see how this could co-exist [in the circumstances] with a contract which, so far as anyone knew, might be performed by actual delivery of the goods' (at 104). This assertion is difficult to reconcile with the significant equity jurisprudence involved in *Quistclose* trusts and *Romalpa* clauses discussed in Chapter 15. Further, a remedial constructive trust as usually understood would not require an equitable interest to exist before the trust is recognised. The Privy Council conceded there was an imbalance between the non-allocated purchasers and the bank, but this did not enable the court to intervene to redress the imbalance by imposing a trust that gave the non-allocated purchasers priority over the bank's debenture (at 104).

Goldcorp and the remedial constructive trust The complex issues that require consideration before a remedial constructive trust could be recognised in our law were rather masked by the Privy Council referring to the situation in *Goldcorp* as one of an imbalance of relative positions. If the courts are to recognise remedial constructive trusts they must do so on a principled basis. They must answer three questions. First, what wrongs should give rise to a constructive trust? Second, what would be the extent of the constructive trust in the particular facts (ie to what assets would it attach)? Third, are there any factual or policy reasons in the circumstances which would favour or rule out a constructive trust? Generally, theorists who argue in favour of remedial constructive trusts do so on two bases, known as the 'proprietary interest justification' and the 'acceptance of risk explanation' (Paciocco (1989) 68 Can Bar Rev 315 at 322 et seq). The proprietary interest justification for the remedial constructive trust is that the wrong done to the claimant justifies the recognition of an equitable interest in its favour. However, this begs the question of what factual element of the wrongdoing is so special as to make giving the claimant a proprietary interest appropriate in the first place. In *Re Goldcorp Exchange* the argument would be that Goldcorp's gross breach of contract prevented the non-allocated purchasers from obtaining title to the bullion and, therefore, the non-allocated purchasers should be given an equitable proprietary interest in the bullion.

The 'acceptance risk' explanation provides the basis for arguing that the claimant should get priority over the defendant's *unsecured* creditors. By not taking security over the defendant's assets in their business dealings with the defendant, unsecured creditors have accepted the risk of the defendant becoming insolvent and their not being paid. Conversely, beneficiaries of trusts are not in a position to take security and cannot be said to accept the risk of insolvency. As a result it is appropriate to protect beneficiaries on an insolvency. The acceptance of risk explanation can also apply to 'involuntary creditors' who mistakenly make payments (such as the bank in *Chase Manhattan*) or those who are wrongly compelled to make the payment in question. However, as Wright notes (p 144), arguing that a creditor failed to take security and, therefore, should be treated as accepting that he or she may get nothing on insolvency, does not explain why another person should be a beneficiary of a constructive trust. Rather, acknowledging that one person accepted a risk of insolvency merely removes a prohibition on the courts giving proprietary relief to the other person – it alone does not necessarily justify the rewarding of remedial constructive trust. Moreover, if we delve deeply into this so-called 'explanation', we see it glosses over some realities of commercial life. Some potential constructive trust beneficiaries may have accepted the risk of insolvency of the defendant. The issue is difficult to determine where the potential constructive trust beneficiary has a contractual relationship with the defendant and the reason for the constructive trust is related to the contract, as in *Re Goldcorp Exchange*. Also, as Paciocco notes (at 325) not all unsecured creditors will have accepted the risk of a defendant's insolvency, for example, both victims of the defendant's negligence or other torts (for their damages) and the defendant's employees (for their wages) are unsecured creditors. Further, in reality, small trade creditors are not in a position to take security.

A more refined version of this acceptance of risk explanation may be needed to justify awarding a remedial constructive trust. Scott argues that if the plaintiff was unaware of the risk of insolvency inherent in the transaction which he or she was entering or was unable to protect his or her interests, then these are grounds for distinguishing the plaintiff from other creditors. Determining these issues may involve a detailed analysis of the facts in each case. Perhaps the solution lies in seeing the risk acceptance argument from a different perspective and to recognise, as did Megarry J in *Re Kayford Ltd* [1975] 1 WLR 279 at 282, that different considerations may apply to businesses, consumers and trade creditors (Scott [1993] LMCLQ 330 at 345). Generally, traders are aware of commercial risks they take and may be better able to protect their position but unsophisticated members of the public are not. In *Re Goldcorp Exchange*, the reliance of the non-allocated purchasers on Goldcorp, and their inability to protect themselves from Goldcorp's breach of contract may be a sufficient special situation to justify the recognition of an equitable proprietary interest in their favour, thus giving them priority over other unsecured creditors. However, this leads to the next issue – should this special situation be sufficient to give them priority over the bank, who did take security (a secured creditor) and who cannot be said to have accepted the risk of Goldcorp's insolvency?

In answering this question, we need to focus on two remaining questions: to what assets is the remedial constructive trust to attach, and are there any policy or other reasons which would favour or deny the imposing of the remedial constructive trust? As the non-allocated purchasers had contracted with Goldcorp for bullion, it is easy to make the link to Goldcorp's bullion stocks as the assets over which the constructive trust would attach. This is what the non-allocated purchasers had bargained for. But in other circumstances there may be facts, or even the claimant's own conduct, which indicate the extent of the priority to be granted to the claimant should be limited or even removed entirely. By recognising the remedial constructive trust as a discretionary remedy, equitable defences also would be relevant to whether or not it is granted.

Gault J in the New Zealand Court of Appeal accepted that in situations of conflict between parties such as the unsophisticated non-allocated purchasers and a sophisticated bank, the *moral claim* of those unsophisticated purchasers is greater (at 351) and he may have been sympathetic enough to award a remedial constructive trust. Additional, less moralistic, arguments may be necessary to overcome the reluctance of our courts to impose remedial constructive trusts. A policy justification for non-allocated purchasers being given priority over the bank could have lain in the recognition that the bank, in taking security from Goldcorp, could be in no better position that Goldcorp. Thus, the bank's security over Goldcorp's stocks of gold could be treated as subject to claims by the non-allocated purchasers arising from the methods by which Goldcorp obtained those stocks of gold. Alternatively, as Gault J found, the bank may have had knowledge of Goldcorp's methods of operation which may have raised an equity in favour of the non-allocated purchasers and disabled the bank from taking advantage of the priority of its debenture (at 283). Early in the twentieth century, Maitland considered that equity judges cared too much about beneficiaries and too little about creditors but, to develop further, the law needs to balance the interests of both and make explicit policy choices about the merits of both beneficiaries' and creditors' claims. Resolution of such issues seems to raise unresolvable problems about which claimants are to be preferred over others. No wonder the courts defer to Parliament on such issues and avoid imputing trusts.

Consider the following questions:

(1) Do you agree with Finn in Cornish et al (eds) *Restitution: Past, Present and Future* (1998) p 264 that *Re Goldcorp Exchange* [1995] 1 AC 74 is a case which should have involved the imposing of a remedial constructive trust or equitable lien to do justice to the investors in that case? In our discussion of *Re Kayford* in Chapter 15 we identified that the trust declared by the company in that case could potentially be open to challenge as constituting a preference on insolvency. If this happened, would a remedial constructive trust imposed over the consumer's prepayment be a just result given the policy arguments aired in favour of the trust in *Re Kayford*?

(2) Rickett and Grantham discuss the remedial constructive trust in a wryly entitled article 'Towards a More Constructive Classification of Trusts' (1999) LMCLQ 111. They argue that trusts should be seen as the law's response to certain types of 'events'. What 'events' could give rise to a remedial constructive trust as a response to an injustice caused by some factual state of affairs? For example, one might say that breach of a fiduciary duty is an event giving rise to a constructive trust. Could not other wrongs such as defamation, theft (see Lord Browne-Wilkinson in *Westdeutsche* at 716; *Australian Postal Corpn v Lutak* (1991) 21 NSWLR 584 at 589) and fraudulent misrepresentation (cf *Box v Barclays Bank plc* [1998] All ER (D) 108) be treated as similar 'events' as justifying at least a remedial constructive trust? (Cf Watts (1996) 112 LQR 219.)

(c) Fiduciaries, breach of confidence and undue influence

To conclude this section, reference must be made to the companion equitable jurisdictions of breaches of confidence (which can also be described as breach of a duty of confidentiality) and undue influence (as a ground whereby gifts or bargains may be set aside or 'rescinded'). Their relationship with the duties that may be imposed on fiduciaries is discussed below.

Duties of confidentiality In a commercial context, the protection of confidential information is vital to many business enterprises and the courts have long protected trade secrets and other forms of confidential information. Protection of confidential information arose out of equity's protection of confidences. The duty is said to be based on the requirement that a person who receives information in confidence, should not take an unfair advantage of it to the detriment of the disclosing party (see *Seager v Copydex Ltd* [1967] 2 All ER 415 at 417 per Lord Denning; Jones (1970) 86 LQR 46).

Megarry J considered that the duty, as it applies in a commercial context, is for a person not to use the confidential information disclosed without paying a reasonable sum for it (see *Coco v AN Clark (Engineers) Ltd* [1969] RPC 41 at 48). This approach appears different to that which would arise if the duty was a fiduciary duty. If the duty is a fiduciary one then it would protect the secrecy of the information and should absolutely forbid the unauthorised use or disclosure of the information by the person who is said to be the fiduciary. However, a duty to keep information confidential may also be seen as protecting the time and effort that went into creating the information rather than merely protecting its secrecy. Moreover, some formulations of the duty require the person who has received the information not to use it to the detriment of the other. If detrimental use is a necessary requirement of a duty of confidentiality, this would place that duty in a different category to fiduciary relationships which do not require any detriment to the principal/beneficiary (see Klinck (1998) 33 McGill LJ 600; and *Boardman v Phipps* (below, p 864).

In some respects, protection of confidential information and fiduciary obligations are very similar and overlap (see *LAC Minerals Ltd v International Corona Resources Ltd* (1989) 61 DLR (4th) 14). If a person trusts another so as to provide the other with confidential information, and the person receiving the information abuses that trust, equity can intervene to prevent the abuse. This is similar to the rationale for recognition of fiduciary relationships, which is to prevent abuse of trust placed by one party in another. However, various underlying bases have been cited in the past as the basis for protection of confidential information and these include contract and property as well as equity (see generally Gurry *Breach of Confidence* (1984); Bean (1993) 11 Journal of Energy & Natural Resources Law 75; Meagher et al *Equity: Doctrines and Remedies* (4th edn, 2002) ch 41; and also Law Commission Working Paper No 58, proposing a new tort of breach of confidence). A duty of confidentiality can be considered to be a fiduciary duty or can be considered to be an independent equitable doctrine, and it may be unwise to be categorical on this point given that the law relating to the duty of confidentiality is still developing.

The Law Commission in *Fiduciary Duties and Regulatory Rules* (1995) Law Com No 236 recognised that fiduciaries are subject to a duty of confidentiality so that they may only use information obtained in confidence *from* the principal/beneficiary *for* the benefit of the principal/beneficiary and must not use it for the fiduciary's own advantage, or for the benefit of any other person (at p 2). But what this really recognises is that a fiduciary is likely to come into contact with confidential information in performing his or her role. The circumstances giving rise to an action for a breach of confidence may also give rise to a breach of fiduciary duty because the fiduciary is misusing confidential information in committing a breach of a fiduciary duty. As La Forest J noted in *LAC Minerals* (at 35–36) the concept of duties of confidentiality is not necessarily parasitic upon fiduciary concepts and can have its own independent life, but the two duties may overlap and be intertwined in the same fact scenario. We must, however, recognise that this is not always the case. A duty of confidentiality can have a wider sphere of operation than the protection of commercially sensitive information and can be used to protect disclosure of government secrets and personal or private information (see *Argyll v Argyll* [1967] Ch 302; *Stephens v Avery* [1988] 2 All ER 477; *Campbell v MGN Ltd* [2004] 2 AC 457; *Douglas v Hello! Ltd (No 6)* [2005] 3 WLR 88). The implementation of the Human Rights Act 1998 may result in personal or private information, such as personal secrets, developing into a distinct right of privacy (Wu (2003) 23 LS 135 at 144; Phillipson (2003) 66(5) MLR 726). Thus, we consider the duty of confidentiality to be related to fiduciary duties but having its own independent sphere of life and, probably, being best analysed as a separate head of liability from fiduciary duties, at least in a modern context.

Undue influence   Undue influence does not usually manifest itself in commercial transactions (except in the cases of guarantors being procured for business transactions, as a result of their personal relationship with debtors: see generally Fehlberg *Sexually Transmitted Debt* (1997); Burns (2003) 23 LS 21). But the notions of 'influence' and 'confidence' associated with fiduciaries are, as Sealy demonstrates (see above, p 836) closely intertwined. However, the juristic basis of the doctrine of undue influence is uncertain. As Lord Nicholls noted in *Royal Bank of Scotland plc v Etridge (No 2)* [2002] 2 AC 773:

> There is no single touchstone for determining whether the principle is applicable. Several expressions have been used in an endeavour to encapsulate the essence: trust and confidence, reliance, dependence or vulnerability on the one hand and ascendancy, domination or control on the other. None of these descriptions is perfect. None is all embracing. Each has its proper place.

Indeed, a person exercising undue influence over another is often labelled a fiduciary but the underlying basis of the relationship appears to be different to the traditional categories of fiduciary relationship. The solicitor/client relationship is one of the core categories of fiduciary relationships and also gives rise to a presumption of undue influence by the solicitor against the client in any transaction between them. But, presumptions of undue influence apply in many other categories of relationship which are unrelated to the core fiduciary relationships, for example, religious and spiritual advisers and their followers, guardians and their wards, doctors and their patients (but not superior officers and other ranks: see *R v HM A-G for England and Wales* [2003] UKPC (PC)). These relationships tend not to be relationships involving commercial and economic interest or management of property which are generally at the heart of fiduciary relationships. The underlying basis of the court's jurisdiction to set aside gifts and contracts which are tainted with undue influence is 'to prevent taking surreptitious advantage of the weakness and necessity of another: which knowingly to do is equally against the conscience as to take advantage of its ignorance . . .' (*Earl of Chesterfield v Janssen* (1751) 2 Ves Sen 125 per Lord Hardwicke LC). In the modern context undue influence can be set out as a series of categories as the House of Lords did in *Barclays Bank plc v O'Brien* [1994] 1 AC 180 at 189–190:

> A person who has been induced to enter into a transaction by the undue influence of another (the wrongdoer) is entitled to set that transaction aside as against the wrongdoer. Such undue influence is either actual or presumed . . .
>
> Class 1: Actual undue influence. In these cases it is necessary for the claimant to prove affirmatively that the wrongdoer exerted undue influence on the complainant to enter into the particular transaction which is impugned.
>
> Class 2: Presumed undue influence. In these cases the complainant only has to show, in the first instance, that there was a relationship of trust and confidence between the complainant and the wrongdoer of such a nature that it is fair to presume that the wrongdoer abused that relationship in procuring the complainant to enter into the impugned transaction.
>
> In Class 2 cases, therefore, there is no need to prove evidence that actual undue influence was exerted in relation to the particular transaction impugned: once a confidential relationship has been proved, the burden then shifts to the wrongdoer to prove that the complainant entered into the impugned transaction freely, for example by showing that the complainant had independent advice.

Flannigan ((1989) 9 OJLS 285 at 309) argues that the person who exerts undue influence over another person has control of that person and hence control over his or her property. Thus the dominant party is analogous to other fiduciaries who control the property of another (ie trustees, agents and directors). A similar conclusion but one derived from a different basis has been advanced by Duggan who adopts an economics-based analysis of the relationship between undue influence and fiduciary law ('Undue Influence' in Parkinson (ed) *The Principles of Equity* (2nd edn, 2003) pp 428–431). Duggan concludes that undue influence and fiduciary law have the same function, that of preventing a person from exploiting an opportunity to take advantage of or cheat the principal/beneficiary where the opportunity arises out of the principal's/beneficiary's inability to bargain for effective contractual sanctions against such cheating.

Despite the similarities, it appeared, prior to *Barclays Bank plc v O'Brien* and *CIBC Mortgages plc v Pitt* [1994] 1 AC 200, that the law relating to undue influence was moving in a different direction from that of other fiduciary relationships by requiring manifest disadvantage from a transaction before the court would intervene. In *Etridge (No 2)* the House of Lords dispensed with manifest disadvantage as a requirement and replaced it with a test requiring the transaction to be one which 'calls for explanation' or is not readily explicable by the relationship of the parties for undue influence to be proved. Even if the concept of manifest disadvantage is dispensed with, it appears to us that there may be different motivating forces in dealing with cases of undue influence than in those of breach of fiduciary duties. Some even suggest that the doctrine of undue influence should be merged into equity's jurisdiction to provide relief against unconscionable bargains because of these doctrines' 'shared values and assumptions' (Capper (1998) 114 LQR 479). Thus while those exercising undue influence are often categorised as fiduciaries, this may be an inappropriate use of terminology. (On the doctrine of undue influence generally see *Goff and Jones* (7th edn, 2007) ch 11; Birks and Chin 'On the Nature of Undue Influence' in Beatson and Friedmann (eds) *Good Faith and Fault in Contract Law* (1995) cf Chen-Wishart 'Undue Influence: Beyond Impaired Consent and Wrongdoing towards a Relational Analysis' in Burrows and Rodger (eds) *Mapping the Law* (2006) ch 11).

(d) Defining the content of fiduciary duties: conflicts of interest and the 'secret profits' rule

To identify a fiduciary relationship is only the start of the process. As Frankfurter J stated in the US Supreme Court (*SEC v Chenery Corpn* 318 US 80 (1943) at 85–86):

> To state that a man is a fiduciary only begins analysis; it gives direction to further inquiry. To whom is he a fiduciary? What obligations does he owe as a fiduciary? In what respect has he failed to discharge these obligations? And what are the consequences of his deviation from duty?

The purpose of this section is to introduce the obligations or duties that a person may owe as a fiduciary. The primary duty is that a fiduciary may not have a conflict between his personal interest and that of his principal (ie the person to whom he stands in a fiduciary relationship). This is the 'no conflict rule', the emphasis of which is to prevent a fiduciary from putting his own interests, or those of another, ahead of the principal's interests.

As a corollary of that principle, the courts have developed the rule that the fiduciary will be liable to account to the 'principal' for any unauthorised profit made by virtue of his position as fiduciary or through use of the principal's property (cf McLean 'The Theoretical Basis of the Trustee's Duty of Loyalty' (1969) 7 Alta LR 218). This is the 'no secret profits' rule or, better put, the 'no unauthorised profits' rule. Each of these rules will be considered in turn.

(1) The 'no conflict of interest' rule

The clearest expression of the no conflict of interest rule, which applies to trustees and other fiduciaries, is from Lord Cranworth LC in *Aberdeen Rly v Blaikie Bros* ((1854) 1 Macq 461 at 471):

> ...it is a rule of universal application, that no one, having such duties to discharge, shall be allowed to enter into engagements in which he has, or can have, a personal interest conflicting, or which possibly may conflict, with the interests of those whom he is bound to protect.

The case involved a director of a company who was also a partner in a partnership that sold goods to the company. There was a clear conflict between the director's duty to the company (to obtain the goods at the lowest price) and his interest as a partner (to sell the goods at the highest price).

Historically the courts adopted an approach to such cases based heavily on a concern with deterrence (see Chapter 9, p 435). As will be seen shortly, much contemporary debate centres on how strictly the no conflict rule should be interpreted. Closely associated with this concern is the view that a strict approach was, some might say still is, necessary so as to maintain strict standards of behaviour for trustees and other fiduciaries.

The deterrent approach is also manifested in a variant of the 'no conflict' rule, that is where trustees are the trustees of more than one trust. Here the trustees are obliged not to have a conflict between the duties that they owe to the beneficiaries of the different trusts. This problem also arises where other fiduciaries have more than one principal or client. This aspect of the 'no conflict' rule has been called the fiduciary's 'duty of undivided loyalty' (Law Commission *Fiduciary Duties and Regulatory Rules* (Law Com No 236) para 1.4). This perennial problem has become increasingly significant of late in the context of mergers of firms of solicitors, and also in the financial services arena where a financial institution may have different sections specialising in different financial services. These sections may be involved in several aspects of the same transaction for different clients; for example, a bank providing finance to the bidder for the take-over, may advise the target on the merits of defending the take-over bid, and provide broking services to shareholders wishing to buy or sell shares of the target company. The law does not view each division separately, but as a part of the same legal entity. Is there a potential conflict of interest if the target company is also a client of the bank? Or if the bank advises the bidder of information about the target company which was provided to the bank by the target company for a different purpose? However, a fiduciary can act for different principals with potentially opposing interests, but only with the informed consent of such principals. But where such consent is given, how does fiduciary law enforce the duty of loyalty where there is more than one master? (see Conaglen (2009) 125 LQR 111 at 127 et seq).

The types of conflicts that can arise in practice have been categorised by Finn (in *McKendrick* (ed) p 22) in the following way: (1) 'same matter' conflicts, ie where two parts of a firm act for opposing sides to a deal or lawsuit or on opposite sides of a transaction; (2) 'former-client' conflicts, ie where a firm now represents a person against its former client (where the risk is that confidential information about the former client will be abused); (3) 'use of information' conflicts (called by Finn 'separate matter conflicts'), ie where the fiduciary may be tempted to use information gathered from, or for, one client for the benefit of another (see below regarding *Boardman v Phipps* at p 860); and (4) 'fair dealing' conflicts where the fiduciary is dealing with its beneficiary/principal (discussed in Chapter 9; see also Simpson 'Conflict' in Birks and Pretto (eds) *Breach of Trust* (2002)).

An example – solicitors and conflicts of interest How should such conflicts of interest (or between duties owed to different principals) be dealt with? Is the strict approach as exemplified in *Aberdeen Rly v Blaikie Bros* always necessary or, indeed, feasible in this type of contemporary context? The Law Society, for example, prohibited solicitors from acting for a client where the possibility of a conflict of duties to different clients may arise, subject to limited exceptions applicable to conveyancing and where informed consent is obtained (see the Law Society's *Solicitors' Code of Conduct* (2007) Rule 3).

Modern legal practice has seen mergers of law firms, lawyers frequently moving from one firm to another and growth of very large law firms (Lee (1992) 19 J Law and Society 31; Paterson (1996) 3 IJLP 137; and Flood (1996) 3 IJLP 169). This gives rise to particular problems especially when firms merge but they act for competing clients. A modification to the strict approach, the use of so-called 'Chinese Walls', has been suggested as an answer to the prohibition of a fiduciary being involved in a 'same matter' conflict (eg in the case of mergers of solicitors' firms; see *Solicitors' Code of Conduct* Rules 3 and 4 and Guidance Notes. Where a Chinese Wall is employed, the different sections of the company or firm that are acting for clients whose interests are opposed are 'kept apart' from each other, and internal procedures are adopted so that neither part can have access to the information held by the other. There may even be physical or geographical separation of the different sections or procedures to ensure 'adversarial dealings' between the different sections (see generally Midgley (1992) 55 MLR 822; Rider (1978) 42 Conv (NS) 114; and ch 5 'Conflicts of Interest and the Chinese Wall' in *The Regulation of the British Securities Industry* (1979); Herzel and Collins 'The Chinese Wall Revisited' (1983) 4 Co Law 14; Griffiths-Baker *Serving Two Masters* (2002) ch 6).

The courts, however, have expressed doubts as to the effectiveness of Chinese Walls because of the problems of ensuring confidentiality for each client (*Prince Jefri Bolkiah v KPMG* [1999] 2 WLR 215 at 227–229; *Supasave Retail Ltd v Coward Chance* [1991] 1 All ER 668; *Re a Firm of Solicitors* [1992] 1 All ER 353; Reynolds (1991) 107 LQR 536). In *Marks & Spencer plc v Freshfields*

Bruckhaus Deringer [2004] EWCA Crim 741, Freshfields was prevented by an injunction from acting for a consortium seeking to take over Marks & Spencer. Marks & Spencer was an existing Freshfields client, and the Court of Appeal rejected Freshfields' argument that engagement by the consortium was in respect of an unrelated matter to the existing Marks & Spencer engagements. In any event, Freshfields argued it had proposed elaborate Chinese Wall procedures to prevent information about Marks & Spencer leaking to solicitors working for the consortium, but the court also rejected this argument. The Law Society's rules in the *Solicitors' Code of Conduct* emphasise both client consent and protection of a client's confidential information as requirements for solicitors acting where a conflict exists.

A comparable problem can arise with 'former client conflicts'. A lawyer may cease to act for a client for a number of reasons, for example, the client may seek other advisers or the lawyer may move to a different firm. When should the former client be able to restrain the lawyer from acting against that client's interests? If the relationship between the lawyer and the client has ended, there may be no conflict of interest where the lawyer acts against the former client. However, there may be a duty of confidentiality that remains to prevent the lawyer from acting unless the court is satisfied that there is no risk of disclosure or misuse of the confidential information (see *Re A Firm of Solicitors* [1997] Ch 1 at 9–10; affirmed in *Prince Jefri Bolkiah v KPMG* [1999] 2 WLR 215 at 229 per Lord Millett; *McDonald Estate v Martin* (1990) 77 DLR (4th) 249; and, generally, Hollander and Salzedo *Conflicts of Interest and Chinese Walls* (2nd edn, 2004); Goubran (2006) 30 Melb ULR 88; Waller (2001) 117 LQR 335; Galanter and Palay 'Large Law Firms and Professional Responsibility' in Cranston (ed) *Legal Ethics and Professional Responsibility* (1995)). Here also, the adoption of a strict approach – 'no risk' – marks a move away from an earlier standard requiring 'a real probability of real mischief' (*Rakusen v Ellis, Munday & Clarke* [1912] 1 Ch 831).

The strict approach of avoiding conflicts between the interests of different principals can be sidestepped where the solicitor acts for different clients in the same transaction. To do this the scope of the relationship with one of the clients must be limited in some way so that effectively there is no conflict as in *Clark Boyce v Mouat* [1993] 3 WLR 1021, PC. In that case the defendant solicitor firm agreed to act for a mother (the plaintiff) and son in mortgaging her house as security for a loan to the son, the latter's own solicitor having declined to act for both parties. Unfortunately the son defaulted. The defendant firm had fully explained to the mother the nature of the transaction and the risk that she was running. Moreover the mother had declined three invitations to take independent legal advice.

There was, though, a very different outcome in *Hilton v Barker Booth & Eastwood* [2005] 1 All ER 651, where Lord Walker referred to the facts as 'particularly shocking'. The case involved solicitors acting for a vendor and a purchaser in a transaction and whether an implied contract term removed the usual fiduciary duty to avoid a conflict of duties owed to different clients. This case also raised the issue of whether, by informed consent from both clients, a solicitor's duties could be narrowed. While acting for the vendor (H), his solicitors (BBE) also acted for the purchaser (B), a convicted fraudster and a bankrupt. BBE knew of B's past but did not disclose this to H. Further, BBE had provided the deposit moneys to the purchaser, thereby also having a personal interest in the transaction and creating a conflict between duty and personal interest. The judge at first instance held that BBE had breached its fiduciary duty by acting for both parties but ultimately H's loss was not caused by BBE's breach. The Court of Appeal affirmed the decision but held that the contract between H and BBE contained an implied term excusing BBE from disclosing to H 'confidential' information about B. Getzler (2006) 122 LQR 1 at 5 notes that prior to *Hilton*, the Court of Appeal had been influenced by the position developed in the courts in the wake of the mortgage loss cases in the 1990s; solicitors were sued for poor assessment of the value of securities or the creditworthiness of debtors and solicitors who had acted for both sides of transactions during the housing boom period were particularly at risk. However, the House of Lords put paid to this watering down of fiduciary duties, holding that BBE had breached its fiduciary duties and that no implied term existed.

The implied term approach derived from the treatment of a real estate agent in *Kelly v Cooper Associates* [1993] AC 205 (see below, p 876). Lord Walker, giving the leading judgment, noted that the solicitor–client relationship is primarily contractual and thus depends on the express and implied terms of its retainer but also that the relationship between solicitor and client is fiduciary. Whilst acknowledging the decision in *Kelly v Cooper*, Lord Walker considered that neither express nor implied contractual terms in the retainer between H and BBE reduced or limited the fiduciary duties owed by BBE (see Turner (2005) 79 Aus. LJ 488 for criticism of Lord Walker's approach on express and implied terms). Further, Lord Walker considered that the breach by BBE (ie failure to tell H that BBE could not act for him and that he should seek other advice) should not be used to exonerate BBE for another breach of duty (failure to tell H facts about B that would have saved H from ruin) as this was against both common sense and justice.

Getzler suggests that the result in *Hilton* indicates that *Kelly v Cooper Associates* does not provide a charter for reducing fiduciary duties in commercial contexts through implied consent and that the decision in *Hilton* 'sets the equilibrium of legal and business trust at a higher rather than a lower level, at a time when there is much institutional pressure abroad to relax [fiduciary] standards' (at 7; see also Langbein (2005) 114 Yale LJ 99 and Tamar Frankel *Trust and Honesty: America's Business Culture at a Crossroad* (2005)).

Consider the following issues:

(1) Do Chinese Walls prevent conflicts between duties owed to clients or do they merely provide a means for managing such conflicts? Can Chinese Walls be made effective (bear in mind that there must be some senior

managers of the company or firm who will be overseeing the sections who are on either side of the Wall)?

(2) What justifications are there for relaxing the prohibition on fiduciaries having 'same matters' conflicts? Is there a public interest in maintaining the sanctity of certain relationships (eg solicitor–client, trustee–beneficiary, investment adviser–client) that requires the strict prevention of 'same matter' conflicts (cf *Clark Boyce v Mouat* [1993] 3 WLR 1021, PC)? Are there any unique features to the solicitor–client relationship which require it to be treated differently from other fiduciaries such as real estate agents (see *Kelly v Cooper Associates* [1993] AC 205)?

(3) Lawyers are also officers of the court and Gubran notes this 'serves to distinguish a lawyer from the ordinary fiduciary. The distinction is reflected in the importance courts attached to the legal profession's propriety. High standards of the propriety enhance public confidence in the administration of justice' (2006) 30 Melb ULR 88 at 106. Do you agree that special, possibly higher, standards should apply to lawyers to bolster the administration of justice? In an Australian case, *Spincode Pty Ltd v Look Software Pty Ltd* (2001) 4 VR 501, Brooking JA criticised the House of Lords approach in *Prince Jefri Bolkiah v KPMG* [1999] 2 WLR 215, suggesting that the fiduciary duty of loyalty and the proper administration of justice were, along with protection of confidential information, equal bases for restraining a lawyer from acting. Does it make sense for fiduciary obligations to have an effect beyond the termination of the client's retainer (*Spincode* at p 522; see also Goubran (2006) 30 Melb ULR 88)?

Ongoing business relationships – a complex problem   How does the duty to avoid a conflict of interest play out where the adviser and the person advised have an ongoing relationship or a relationship covering different areas of business? For example, a large corporation may engage an auditor to investigate its financial statements and advise if its accounts represent a true and fair view of its financial position. The firm that provides the auditing service may also have other divisions which provide services to the same corporation, for example, tax consultancy services, providing financial advice or even advice in relation to information technology and business systems. Do these multiple relationships lead to a conflict of interest in that the adviser may be tempted to put its ongoing business relationships with the company ahead of its duty to advise the company correctly, where such advice may anger the management of the company who may terminate the business relationship?

One end of the spectrum is the Australian case, *Pilmer v The Duke Group (in liq)* (2001) 207 CLR 165, where an offeror company engaged an accounting firm during a take-over bid for a target company. The accounting firm was instructed to advise on whether the price offered for the target was fair. The accounting firm's report was negligently prepared. However, as well as seeking remedies for negligence, the offeror company (now in liquidation) alleged breach of a fiduciary duty by the accounting firm. A good summary is provided by Duggan ((2003) 24 Aust Bar Rev 150 at 157) which we adopt. The company's fiduciary claim was that the accounting firm as an adviser was in a fiduciary relationship with the company and therefore the accounting firm had a duty to avoid conflicts of interest. However, the accounting firm had a conflict of interest because of its ongoing association with members of the board of the company and because it had an interest in reporting favourably so it would get more work from the company in the future. The High Court of Australia rejected this claim for breach of fiduciary duty, first, because technically the accounting firm gave no advice (it merely gave an opinion) and, second, because proof of past dealings between an accounting firm and a client does not itself establish a conflict of interest. Moreover, the expectation or hope of future business is not in itself a conflict. Most professional advisers would hope that the proper performance of the task at hand would lead the client to retain them again ((2001) 207 CLR 165 at 183). Kirby J dissented and considered that the accounting firm was not able to provide an independent and impartial report on the value of the target company.

Duggan points out that Kirby J's judgment 'suggested there may be a conflict of interest in any case where an accounting firm [professional adviser] has an ongoing relationship with the company's board. The logical extension is the company could not safely use the same auditors from one year to the next. There would always be the risk of one year's report being coloured by the firm's expectation of re-engagement for the next year's audit' (at 158). Obviously, such regular changing of advisers would lead to increased costs for companies but might it not lead to advisers who may be less likely to 'pull their punches' when it comes to advising wayward management?

At the other end of the spectrum is the collapse of Enron Corporation, which led to the disintegration of the international consulting firm, Arthur Andersen (AA). AA falsely certified that Enron's financial statements fairly represented its financial position. Unlike the accountants in *Pilmer*, AA supplied various services to Enron other than merely auditing and these services were a major source of revenue for AA. This lack of independence between AA and Enron tempted AA to do what management wanted (ie falsely certify the accounts) rather than disclose the company's true adverse position. Duggan considers that it can plausibly be said that the cross-selling of other services by an accounting firm providing auditing services gives rise to a conflict of interest in relation to those auditing services. The ability of the company to threaten to withhold future non-audit work if the accounting firm's audit is not to the management's liking, can operate as a disincentive to the audit division's acting properly (Gordon (2002) 69 U Chi LR 1233 at 1237–1238). Rather than rely on fiduciary law, the US response to the Enron collapse is the well-known Sarbanes-Oxley Act of 2002 which amended the US Securities Exchange Act to prohibit an accounting firm which provides auditing services from providing other services to the same corporation, with very limited exemptions.

(2) The origins of the 'no secret profits' rule

An initially surprising starting-point for study of the 'no secret profits' rule is *Keech v Sandford*, an 'obscurely reported' case concerning the renewal of a lease by a trustee (see Cretney (1969) 83 Conv 161 at 162 and see Getzler 'Rumford Market and the Genesis of Fiduciary Obligations' in Burrows and Rodger *Mapping the Law* (2006) ch 31).

Keech v Sandford (1726) Sel Cas Ch 61   The defendant held a lease of the profits of a market on trust for the plaintiff, a minor. The lessor, concerned about difficulties of enforcement against a minor, refused to renew the lease in favour of the trust, whereupon the trustee renewed the lease for his own benefit. The plaintiff sought an account of profits made since the renewal of the lease and to have the lease assigned to him.

> **Lord King LC:** I must consider this as a trust for the infant; for I very well see, if a trustee, on the refusal to renew, might have a lease to himself, few trust estates would be renewed to cestui que use; though I do not say there is a fraud in this case, yet he should rather have let it run out, than to have had the lease to himself. This may seem hard, that the trustee is the only person of all mankind who might not have the lease: but it is very proper that rule should be strictly pursued, and not in the least relaxed; for it is very obvious what would be the consequence of letting trustees have the lease, on refusal to renew to cestui que use. So decreed, that the lease should be assigned to the infant, and that the trustee should be indemnified from any covenants comprised in the lease, and an account of the profits made since the renewal.

It made no difference to the outcome that the trust could not obtain the lease and that the trustee was, it seems, acting in good faith. The decision appeared to reflect a scepticism – similar to that later demonstrated by Lord Eldon LC in *Ex p James* (1803) 8 Ves 337, a trustee self-dealing case (see above, p 452) – about the ability of a court to assess a trustee's true motivation. Two distinct consequences – one specific, one general – have flowed from *Keech v Sandford*. The specific consequence, which is not considered here, is the further development of rules concerning renewal of a lease for a fiduciary's – not just a trustee's – own benefit, and 'the associated question of whether a fiduciary may purchase the freehold reversion of property of which his principal is lessee' (Oakley *Constructive Trusts* (3rd edn, 1997) p 65 and generally pp 65–69; see also Cretney (1969) 33 Conv 161). The general consequence is the broad 'no secret profits' rule. This was not an inevitable development as *Keech v Sandford* can be seen as a straightforward conflict of interest case. Moreover, the outcome might have been just one rule – the 'no conflicts' rule – rather than two rules each with a potential for independent operation. Be that as it may, the rigorous standard imposed on the trustee in *Keech v Sandford* has spread from this narrow base to include a diverse variety of circumstances where profits might be made, and to entrap a wide range of fiduciaries, including company directors, partners, and agents. It is the liability of fiduciaries in such relationships that primarily concerns us here.

(3) Subsequent development of the 'no secret profits' rule

The extensive influence, and the strictness, of *Keech v Sandford* are exemplified by the House of Lords' decision in *Regal (Hastings) Ltd v Gulliver* [1942] 1 All ER 378, [1967] 2 AC 134n which did not appear in the official law reports until after it had been extensively cited in *Boardman v Phipps* (see below). The appellant company, RH, owned a cinema in Hastings. A subsidiary company, A Ltd, with an authorised share capital of 5,000 £1 ordinary shares, was formed to acquire the leases on two other local cinemas. The owner of the cinemas would lease them only if the share capital was fully subscribed. RH had resources to put only £2,000 into the subsidiary. Accordingly the directors financed the transaction by personally taking up most of the balance of 3,000 shares (some were also taken up by outsiders). Shortly afterwards the shares in the combined concern (RH and A Ltd) were sold. The directors derived a profit of £2 16s 1d per share from the sale of their shares in A Ltd. The new controllers of RH successfully brought an action to recover the profits from the now ex-directors of RH. In finding in favour of RH, Lord Russell, who delivered the principal judgment, was explicit (at 149): 'The equitable rule in *Keech v Sandford* . . . applies to the directors in full force.'

It was immaterial that the directors acted bona fide, that RH could not afford to purchase the shares in A, and that the purchasers of RH obtained a windfall profit – in effect paying less for shares in A than they had expected to. Thus a strict deterrent rule was applied, the implications of which were clearly spelt out by Lord Russell (at 144–145):

> The rule of equity which insists on those, who by use of a fiduciary position make a profit, being liable to account for that profit, in no way depends on fraud, or absence of bona fides; or upon such questions or considerations as whether the profit would or should otherwise have gone to the plaintiff, or whether the profiteer was under a duty to obtain the source of the profit for the plaintiff, or whether he took a risk or acted as he did for the benefit of the plaintiff, or whether the plaintiff has in fact been damaged or benefited by his action.
>
> The liability arises from the mere fact of a profit having, in the stated circumstances, been made. The profiteer, however honest and well-intentioned, cannot escape the risk of being called upon to account.

The test to be applied to determine liability, not only for directors but for fiduciaries generally, was formulated in the shape of a question by Lord Wright (at 154):

> That question can be briefly stated to be whether an agent, a director, a trustee or other person in an analogous fiduciary position, when a demand is made upon him by the person to whom he stands in the fiduciary relationship to account for profits acquired by him by

> reason of his fiduciary position, and by reason of the opportunity and the knowledge, or
> either, resulting from it, is entitled to defeat the claim upon any ground save that he made
> profits with the knowledge and assent of the other person.

The answer was clear, and in the absence of such assent the directors were held accountable for the profits they had made out of the shares.

This unbending approach, with its rationale of deterrence, was subsequently adopted in *Boardman v Phipps* as applying to agents, or those analogous to agents, by a bare majority in the House of Lords. Paradoxically the judgments also open up prospects for mitigating the penalty for breach of duty and circumventing the scope of the strict rule.

Boardman v Phipps [1967] 2 AC 46

A testator, who died in 1944, left his residuary estate, which included 8,000 shares, about 27% of the total issued shares in a private company Lester and Harris Ltd (LH), upon trust for his widow for life and, after her death, for his four children. The trustees were his widow (who by 1955 was senile and took no part in the affairs of the trust), his daughter, Mrs Noble (N), and an accountant Fox (F). John Phipps, the respondent, was a son of the testator, and one of the beneficiaries. The two appellants were his brother Tom, another beneficiary, and Boardman who acted as solicitor to the trust and to the testator's children (other than John Phipps).

By 1956 the appellants had become dissatisfied with the state of the company's affairs. During the following six years (a period grouped by the court into the three phases described below) the appellants purchased for themselves the remaining shares in the company, thus obtaining control of it. They then sold LH's plants in Australia and Coventry, and re-organised the remainder of the company.

Consequently they were able to distribute a substantial capital profit to the shareholders, without reducing the value of the shares. The trust shareholding benefited by about £47,000 while Boardman and Tom Phipps made a profit of about £75,000.

Phase 1 (December 1955–April 1957) The appellants attended the annual general meeting of LH as proxies of the two active trustees, F and N, and obtained valuable information about the company. Shortly afterwards with the consent of F and N (the testator's widow was not consulted) the appellants bid, albeit unsuccessfully, in their own names for the remainder of the shares. The trustees themselves had no power to purchase further shares in the company without the consent of the court, and F, the managing trustee, said he would not even consider seeking this.

Phase 2 (April 1957–August 1958) Negotiations continued between Boardman and the directors of LH but proved abortive. Boardman, however, still purportedly acting on behalf of trustees, obtained further information about the value of the company's assets.

Phase 3 (August 1958–61) The widow died in November 1958 and Boardman wrote to the remaining beneficiaries, including the respondent, asking whether they objected to himself and Phipps taking a controlling interest in LH. None did so but the court subsequently held that Boardman had not disclosed sufficient information to be able to establish the defence of consent. In March 1959, Boardman and Phipps signed a conditional agreement to purchase the remaining shares which they did shortly afterwards.

LH was then reorganised and the capital distribution made. The respondent became dissatisfied and issued a writ claiming (i) an account of the profits made on the shares purchased by the appellants; and (ii) that the appellants held five-eighteenths of the shares as constructive trustees for him. Wilberforce J granted the relief sought ([1964] 1 WLR 993); the decision was affirmed by the Court of Appeal ([1965] Ch 992) and by a 3:2 majority in the House of Lords ([1967] 2 AC 46 – Viscount Dilhorne and Lord Upjohn dissenting):

> **Lord Cohen:** Wilberforce J and, in the Court of Appeal, both Lord Denning MR and Pearson LJ based their decision in favour of the respondent on the decision of your lordships' House in *Regal (Hastings) Ltd v Gulliver*

Lord Cohen referred to the passages in the speeches of Lords Russell and Wright, quoted above at p 863, and rejected an argument that the present case was distinguishable:

> [The argument] does not seem to me to give due weight to the fact that the appellants obtained both the information which satisfied them that the purchase of the shares would be a good investment and the opportunity of acquiring them as a result of acting for certain purposes on behalf of the trustees. Information is, of course, not property in the strict sense of that word and, as I have already stated, it does not necessarily follow that because an agent acquired information and opportunity while acting in a fiduciary capacity he is accountable to his principals for any profit that comes his way as the result of the use he makes of that information and opportunity. His liability to account must depend on the facts of the case. In the present case much of the information came the appellants' way when Mr Boardman was acting on behalf of the trustees on the instructions of Mr Fox and the opportunity of bidding for the shares came because he purported for all purposes except for making the bid to be acting on behalf of the owners of the 8,000 shares in the company. In these circumstances it seems to me that the principle of the *Regal* case applies and that the courts below came to the right conclusion.
>
> That is enough to dispose of the case but I would add that an agent is, in my opinion, liable to account for profits he makes out of trust property if there is a possibility of conflict between his interest and his duty to his principal. Mr Boardman and Tom Phipps were not general agents of the trustees but they were their agents for certain limited purposes. The

information they had obtained and the opportunity to purchase the 21,986 shares afforded them by their relations with the directors of the company – an opportunity they got as the result of their introduction to the directors by Mr Fox – were not property in the strict sense but that information and that opportunity they owed to their representing themselves as agents for the holders of the 8,000 shares held by the trustees. In these circumstances they could not, I think, use that information and that opportunity to purchase the shares for themselves if there was any possibility that the trustees might wish to acquire them for the trust. Mr Boardman was the solicitor whom the trustees were in the habit of consulting if they wanted legal advice. Granted that he would not be bound to advise on any point unless he is consulted, he would still be the person they would consult if they wanted advice. He would clearly have advised them that they had no power to invest in shares of the company without the sanction of the court. In the first phase he would also have had to advise on the evidence then available that the court would be unlikely to give such sanction: but the appellants learnt much more during the second phase. It may well be that even in the third phase the answer of the court would have been the same but, in my opinion, Mr Boardman would not have been able to give unprejudiced advice if he had been consulted by the trustees and was at the same time negotiating for the purchase of the shares on behalf of himself and Tom Phipps. In other words, there was, in my opinion, at the crucial date (March, 1959), a possibility of a conflict between his interest and his duty . . .

I desire to repeat that the integrity of the appellants is not in doubt. They acted with complete honesty throughout and the respondent is a fortunate man in that the rigour of equity enables him to participate in the profits which have accrued as the result of the action taken by the appellants in March, 1959, in purchasing the shares at their own risk. As the last paragraph of his judgment clearly shows, the trial judge evidently shared this view. He directed an inquiry as to what sum is proper to be allowed to the appellants or either of them in respect of his work and skill in obtaining the said shares and the profits in respect thereof. The trial judge concluded by expressing the opinion that payment should be on a liberal scale. With that observation I respectfully agree.

Lord Upjohn (dissenting): Rules of equity have to be applied to such a great diversity of circumstances that they can be stated only in the most general terms and applied with particular attention to the exact circumstances of each case. The relevant rule for the decision of this case is the fundamental rule of equity that a person in a fiduciary capacity must not make a profit out of a trust which is part of the wider rule that a trustee must not place himself in a position where his duty and his interest may conflict.

Lord Upjohn then strongly endorsed Lord Herschell's statement of the applicable rule from *Bray v Ford* – see above, p 835 – and quoted from Cranworth LC in *Aberdeen Rly v Blaikie Bros* – see above, p 856.

The phrase 'possibly may conflict' requires consideration. In my view it means that the reasonable man looking at the relevant facts and circumstances of the particular case would think that there was a real sensible possibility of conflict; not that you could imagine some situation arising which might, in some conceivable possibility in events not contemplated as real sensible possibilities by any reasonable person, result in a conflict . . .

My Lords, the judgments of Wilberforce J and Lord Denning MR and Pearson LJ proceeded upon the footing that by acting as self-appointed agents the appellants placed themselves in a fiduciary capacity to the trustees and became accountable accordingly. That they were never in fact agents has been demonstrated by Lord Denning in his judgment and I desire to add nothing thereto except to say I agree with him. But as I have already pointed out it seems to me that this question whether this assumption of office leads to the conclusion that the appellants were accountable requires a closer analysis than it has received in the lower courts.

This analysis requires detailed consideration:

1 The facts and circumstances must be carefully examined to see whether in fact a purported agent and even a confidential agent is in a fiduciary relationship to his principal. It does not necessarily follow that he is in such a position (see *Re Coomber* [1911] 1 Ch 723).

2 Once it is established that there is such a relationship, that relationship must be examined to see what duties are thereby imposed upon the agent, to see what is the scope and ambit of the duties charged upon him.

3 Having defined the scope of those duties one must see whether he has committed some breach thereof and by placing himself within the scope and ambit of those duties in a position where his duty and interest may possibly conflict. It is only at this stage that any question of accountability arises.

4 Finally, having established accountability it only goes so far as to render the agent accountable for profits made within the scope and ambit of his duty.

Lord Upjohn considered and rejected as 'untenable' the following proposition put forward by Russell LJ in the Court of Appeal ([1965] Ch 992 at 1031): 'The substantial trust shareholding was an asset of which one aspect was its potential use as a means of acquiring knowledge of the company's affairs, or of negotiating allocations of the company's assets, or of inducing other shareholders to part with their shares. That aspect was part of the trust assets.' Lord Upjohn contended that 'In general, information is not property at all. It is normally open to all who have eyes to read and ears to hear'. After reviewing the facts of the case in some detail, he concluded:

I have dealt with the problems that arise in this case at considerable length but it could, in my opinion, be dealt with quite shortly.

In *Barnes v Addy* (1874) 9 Ch App 244 at 251 Lord Selborne LC said:

'It is equally important to maintain the doctrine of trusts which is established in this court, and not to strain it by unreasonable construction beyond its due and proper limits. There would be no better method of undermining the sound doctrines of equity than to make unreasonable and inequitable applications of them.'

> That, in my judgement, is applicable to this case.
>
> The trustees were not willing to buy more shares in the company. The active trustees were very willing that the appellants should do so themselves for the benefit of their large minority holding. The trustees, so to speak, lent their name to the appellants in the course of prolonged and difficult negotiations and, of course, the appellants thereby learnt much which would have otherwise been denied to them. The negotiations were in the end brilliantly successful.
>
> And how successful Tom was in his reorganisation of the company is apparent to all. They ought to be very grateful.
>
> In the long run the appellants have bought for themselves at entirely their own risk with their own money shares which the trustees never contemplated buying and they did so in circumstances fully known and approved of by the trustees.
>
> To extend the doctrines of equity to make the appellants accountable in such circumstances is, in my judgement, to make unreasonable and inequitable application of such doctrines.

Notwithstanding the recommendation that the appellants should be awarded remuneration on a liberal scale (cf the discussion of court-ordered remuneration for trustees in Chapter 9), the majority judgments in *Boardman v Phipps* clearly reaffirm a commitment to a strict standard of fiduciary obligation. Lord Hodson, for example, in specifically endorsing Lord Wright's formulation of the 'secret profits' principle in *Regal* states (at 105) 'it is obviously important to . . . do nothing to whittle away the scope [of the obligation] or the absolute responsibility which it imposes'. Unfortunately, however, it is not easy to determine what the precise standard is. Indeed it has even been claimed that *Boardman v Phipps* 'seems to provide support for virtually any position in the area of fiduciaries any subsequent court wishes to take' (Shepherd *The Law of Fiduciaries* (1981) p 7).

Consider the following points:

(1) In *Aas v Benham* [1891] 2 Ch 244, a partnership case about the scope of the fiduciary relationship, Lindley LJ, responding to a claim that a partner had used for his own benefit information obtained while acting on partnership business, maintained (at 256) that 'there is no principle or authority which entitles a firm to benefits derived by a partner from the use of information for purposes which are wholly without the scope of the firm's business'. Is it not the source of the information, but the use to which it is applied, that is important in such matters?

(2) What was the scope of the fiduciary relationship in *Boardman v Phipps*? What did Boardman and Phipps undertake to do for the trustees in the various stages of the operation? Did their roles change, and, if so, did the scope of the fiduciary relationship between the trustees and Boardman change? When the scope of the relationship is narrowly defined, the area within which fiduciary duties may operate is decreased: as an example see *Clark Boyce v Mouat* [1993] 3 WLR 1021.

(3) Both Lords Hodson and Guest classified the information obtained by the appellants as trust property. Does Lord Cohen's judgment endorse this conclusion? If a fiduciary has used trust property to make a profit for himself is any consideration of conflict of interest even necessary? Is there not an immediate and obvious conflict between his duty (to use trust property to benefit the beneficiary) and his interests (using it to make a profit for himself)?

Information does not come neatly marked for fiduciaries so that the fiduciary instinctively knows to whom the information 'belongs' and in what capacity it is received. A fiduciary may acquire information (i) by mere receipt, ie it is given to him without any indication that it is for his principal, (ii) by receipt with an indication that it is for the principal, (iii) by the principal disclosing the information to the fiduciary, (iv) by actively seeking the information without using the principal's resources, ie money or property, or (v) by actively seeking or creating the information *using* the principal's resources (of money or property). If we consider that information is property belonging in equity to the principal then an unauthorised use of the information by a fiduciary is a misuse of a principal's asset. Where the information is created using the principal's resources or paid for by the principal, then it is easy to treat the information as belonging to the principal and it can be dealt with as the misappropriation of an asset. Alternatively, we may consider that information has a special character and while it may have some of the characteristics of property, it is not truly property. This approach would require us to consider more fully which particular competing interests should be protected. Indeed, the application of the notion of property to the circumstances in 'information' or 'opportunity' cases has also been strongly criticised by Weinrib ((1975) 25 U Toronto LJ 1 at 10):

> Property is itself merely the label for that crystallized bundle of economic interests which the law deems worthy of protection. When intangibles such as information and opportunity are at stake, affixing the label of property constitutes a conclusion, not a reason. The difficulty is not to supply a label but to identify the protected interest.

It may in any event be that the property basis for liability in *Boardman* is something of a 'red herring', particularly as it is not the sole or, arguably, the principal basis for the decision. In contrast with at least two of the majority judgments, Lord Upjohn held that information was not property as such, although he recognised that information may be protected under the equitable duty of confidentiality. As we noted earlier the duty of confidence may be analysed as being a fiduciary duty but it is not necessarily dependent upon fiduciary concepts and can have its own independent sphere of operation (eg cf Sopinka J and La Forest J in *LAC Minerals Ltd v International Corona Resources Ltd* (1989) 61 DLR (4th) 14; Davies [1990] Lloyd's MCLQ

4). In the circumstances Boardman and Phipps may have owed a duty of confidence to Lester & Harris Ltd (rather than to the trustees) because the company disclosed the information to them, but that was not in issue in the case.

(4) Uncertainty about the basis for imposing liability in *Boardman v Phipps* may pose difficulties for fiduciaries (eg corporate trustees, solicitors, merchant bankers), who have multiple clients, and who in the course of their business for one client learn confidential information which may be of advantage to other clients. As an exercise we suggest that you draft a memo to a hypothetical manager of a bank's trustee department, indicating the practice to be followed in such circumstances. You should take into account (i) the possibility of the confidential information being acquired by the bank's corporate finance department which advises companies on such matters as take-overs, share issues and mergers (see our discussion of Chinese Walls above, p 857 and (ii) the use of non-confidential information that was produced and paid for by different clients.

(5) It is possible to distil from the judgments in *Boardman* application of both the 'no conflict' and 'no secret profit' rules. As regards the former there is disagreement as to the degree of likelihood of conflict necessary (cf the formulations of Lords Cohen and Upjohn). Furthermore, can it be argued that Lord Upjohn subordinates the 'no secret profit' rule to the 'no conflict of interest' rule? If so, does this mean that the scope of the fiduciary relationship is itself determined by the likelihood of conflict? Or does it mean that the scope of the fiduciary relationship determines whether a conflict of interest is possible? Would you agree that Lord Upjohn 'dissented on the facts but not on the law'?

(6) Do you agree with the unanimous view of the judges that Boardman's enterprise should be generously rewarded? Before answering, consider the case from the perspective of (i) those LH shareholders without access to confidential information about the value of the company's assets, and (ii) the employees of LH (see Rider (1978) 42 Conv 114 at 122). Note that the House of Lords considered Boardman was acting honestly; see also *Guinness plc v Saunders* [1990] 2 AC 663; cf the approach to the dishonest fiduciary in *Murad v Al-Saraj* [2005] EWCA Civ 959. Although strictly obiter all three judges in *Murad* were attracted by the idea of softening the strict *Boardman v Phipps* approach to liability to account in a way that would permit the court to form a view whether, for instance, a principal would nevertheless have proceeded with a transaction had full disclosure been made by an 'innocent' fiduciary (cf the different views of McInnes (2006) 122 LQR 11 and Conaglen (2006) 65(2) CLJ 278; see also Samet (2008) 28(4) LQR 763; Langbein 'Questioning the Trust Law Duty of Loyalty: Sole Interest or Best Interest?' (2005) 114 Yale LJ 929).

(7) Where profit is made by reason of a fiduciary position an escape route for the fiduciary is to establish that the fully informed consent of the principal was

obtained. In *Boardman*, for example, the appellants obtained the consent of the two active trustees, but not of the inactive trustee and life-tenant, the widow, nor, after her death, the fully informed consent of the respondent. But in *Boardman* were the appellants in a fiduciary relationship with the trustees or the beneficiaries or both?

(4) Contemporary application: the standard modified?

Boardman v Phipps stands seemingly like a rock, firmly supporting the imposition of liability on a fiduciary wherever equity's strict standards are infringed (analogously see Berg (2001) 117 LQR 366). In criticising the decision ((1968) 84 LQR 472 at 474), Jones emphasised that this is so 'even though [the fiduciary] acted honestly and in his principal's best interest, even though his principal benefited as well as he from his conduct, even though his principal could not otherwise have obtained the benefit and even though the benefit was obtained through the use of the fiduciary's own assets and in consequence of his personal skill and judgement'. Some contend that such rocks block our view and stop us making further inquiries about what is best for beneficiaries (see Langbein (2005) 114 Yale LJ 929 who argues that a trustee should be able to have a personal conflicting interest in a transaction as long as it can prove that the transaction was prudently undertaken in the best interest of the beneficiaries).

However, rocks can be eroded, and even the House of Lords majority, at the very moment of upholding the formally strict standard, mitigated its rigours by approving Wilberforce J's decision that Boardman should be remunerated on a liberal scale in respect of the work and skill employed. Subsequent cases present an inconsistent picture, with some Commonwealth cases seemingly adopting a more liberal approach than English decisions.

Two 'information' and 'opportunity' cases involving company directors illustrate the trend.

In *Industrial Development Consultants Ltd v Cooley* [1972] 2 All ER 162, [1972] 1 WLR 443 (both references are provided as, unusually, there are significant differences between the two reports), the one-time managing director of the plaintiff company was held liable to it as constructive trustee of a contract he had personally obtained from the Eastern Gas Board and to account for profits he had made thereby (see Prentice (1972) 50 Can BR 623; Rajak (1972) 35 MLR 655). While the managing director, Cooley had negotiated with the Board for the purpose of obtaining work for the plaintiff, but the negotiations came to nothing. A representative of the Board subsequently informed Cooley that it would not deal with his company but that he would have a good chance of obtaining the contract for himself if he left the company. Cooley obtained a release from his contract by falsely representing that he was ill, and then entered into a contract with the Gas Board to do work substantially similar to that he had unsuccessfully sought for the plaintiff. In Roskill J's view it was immaterial both that the information came to Cooley in his private capacity – it was information relevant to the plaintiff which should have been passed on – and that the chance of IDC obtaining the contract was rated at no greater than 10%. The decision as to the allocation of the contract was that of the Gas Board not Cooley. What then was the basis of liability? The fact that the information was of commercial value to IDC meant, in Roskill J's view, that Cooley by preparing to bid for the contract 'was putting himself into the position in which the duty to his employers, the plaintiffs, and his own private interests conflicted and conflicted grievously' ([1972] 2 All ER 162 at 175; cf *Peso-Silver Mines Ltd v Cropper* (1966) 58 DLR (2d) 1 (SCC), criticised by Beck (1971) 48 Can BR 80; Prentice (1967) 30 MLR 450). Cooley was held liable to account to IDC for the profits he had made. *Boardman v Phipps* is referred to as authority, but surprisingly the only judgment Roskill J cites is that of Lord Upjohn, with reference to 'real sensible possibility of conflict' (see also Koh (2003) 66(6) MLR 894).

Erosion more clearly occurs with the decision in *Queensland Mines v Hudson* (1978) 52 ALJR 399, where the benign attitude manifested by the Privy Council towards the activities of a company director is scarcely reconcilable with *Regal* (but see also *Island Export Finance Ltd v Umunna* [1986] BCLC 460); *Balston Ltd v Headline Filters Ltd* [1990] FSR 385; *Framlington Group plc v Anderson* [1995] 1 BCLC 475 and the discussion in Lowry and Edmunds [2000] JBL 122). Hudson was the managing director of Queensland Mines, QM. In 1961, Hudson, 'using the resources and good name of the company' (at 401), was about to obtain mining exploration licences for the company. QM encountered major financial difficulties and could not proceed with the project. Hudson then resigned as managing director (although he remained a director until 1971), took the licences in his own name, but acknowledged that he held them for QM. At a 1962 board meeting Hudson gave a candid appraisal of the likely risks and benefits of exploiting the licences. The Board decided not to pursue the matter further. Eventually Hudson was able to finance the mining operation, and from 1966 onwards received substantial royalties. QM sought to hold Hudson accountable for the profit. The Privy Council rejected the claim and held: (1) that on the date of the board meeting QM had given Hudson its fully informed consent to exploit the licences, and (2) that the rejection of the licences took the project outside the scope of Hudson's fiduciary duties to the company. Accordingly, in the opinion of the court, applying Lord Upjohn's test from *Boardman*, there was no real, sensible possibility of a conflict between Hudson and QM *after* the board meeting.

As to ground (1) of this decision, the consent of the board has not normally been considered adequate in such a situation: it is the consent of shareholders in a general meeting which has been required (see Sullivan (1979) 42 MLR 711; but see now the statutory modification in Companies Act 2006, s 175(5)). Ground (2) is sharply criticised by Sullivan (at 714):

> Clearly, as Lord Scarman emphasised, decisions relating to licences fell within the managerial competence of the board, (1978) 52 ALJR 399 at 404, and undeniably the directors could have disposed of [QM's] interest in the licences to Hudson if acting in good faith and at

> arm's length and receiving value. But merely for a board to decide on behalf of the company that a venture is unsuitable or non-feasible should not of itself release it for exploitation by the directors. Hitherto, fiduciaries have not been permitted to exploit opportunities which have arisen in the course and execution of their office even when those with the requisite authority have turned down the venture on behalf of the principal [see *Regal* and *Boardman*] . . .
>
> The orthodoxy is that the directors' legal powers of management are subject to the equitable obligations imposed by their fiduciary role: [*Queensland Mines*] stands this on its head in allowing a managerial decision to delineate the scope of a fiduciary obligation.

What is to be made of the seemingly conflicting outcomes just described? It appeared, for instance, that after *Queensland Mines* and *Island Export Finance Ltd v Umunna* that a new test for assessing breach of duty was emerging. Under the 'maturing business opportunity' test, as it became known, directors would be disqualified from obtaining for themselves a maturing business opportunity only where the company was actively pursuing it. Were we therefore witnessing a shift from a concentration on the status of the relationship between the parties to a consideration simply of the circumstances of particular transactions? If so this would mark a sharp break with the strict standards forged by *Regal* and *Boardman*. *Queensland Mines* may have been influenced by the considerations that Hudson had made full disclosure and that QM waited a full 11 years – and until the profits had been safely garnered in at no risk to itself – before issuing a writ (cf Cooley's active deceit of IDC). The tension between the differing emphases in *IDC v Cooley* and *Queensland Mines* has not disappeared. In England the Court of Appeal in *Bhullar v Bhullar* [2003] BCLC 241 has recently rejected the 'maturing business opportunity' test and instead reasserted the centrality of a disclosure obligation and the relevance of a strict, status-based interpretation of what constitutes a 'corporate opportunity' (see Prentice and Payne (2004) 120 LQR 198; Armour (2004) 63(1) CLJ 33; *Item Software (UK) Ltd v Fassihi* [2005] 2 BCLC 91 (note the Court of Appeal's reference to the often suggested, but incorrect, duty on the errant fiduciary to disclose his or her wrongdoing; cf Ho and Lee (2007) 66(2) CLJ 348); see also Companies Act 2006, s 175; and Scott (2003) 66 MLR 852 for a comparison with US law).

Perhaps the appropriate, if trite, conclusion is that fiduciary rules can be stated at a level of generality only. Alternatively, we may postulate that there is tension when applying fiduciary rules applicable to trustees to directors, and when moulding those rules for company directors. The application of fiduciary rules in marginal cases to any given set of facts will involve questions of fine judgement and narrow distinctions. If so, one must simply be aware of the present methodology applied by the courts in deciding these cases, and of the leeway for imposing or avoiding liability. In *Swain v Law Society* [1982] 1 WLR 17, Oliver LJ summarised the situation as follows (at 37):

> What one has to do is ascertain first of all whether there was a fiduciary relationship and, if there was, from what it arose and what, if there was any, was the trust property; and then to inquire whether that of which an account is claimed either arose, directly or indirectly, from the trust property itself or was acquired not only in the course of, but by reason of, the fiduciary relationship.

The opportunities for exercising discretion arise at three stages: (i) identifying a fiduciary relationship; (ii) defining the scope of the obligation arising out of the relationship; and (iii) establishing a defence of fully informed consent. A central question to be asked, therefore, is what factors, including those of policy, are likely to influence the court's exercise of these discretions.

(e) Fiduciary duties: some policy considerations

(1) The appropriate standard

For purposes of comparison three distinct approaches to imposing liability on fiduciaries can be adopted. These can be called strict deterrence, modified deterrence and retrospective assessment. Strict deterrence is represented by the approach that emerges from the line of decisions starting with *Keech v Sandford* and culminating in the majority judgments in *Boardman v Phipps*. Modified deterrence, we suggest, is best reflected by a requirement that liability should be imposed only if there exists a real, sensible possibility of conflict of interest and duty. Under this approach it would still be immaterial whether, *in fact* the fiduciary had pursued his own interest: the real possibility of such a conflict existing would be sufficient. Retrospective assessment, as its name implies, requires the court to assess whether any advantage was actually taken by the fiduciary and to decide on liability accordingly (see generally the influential article by Jones (1968) 84 LQR 472, advocating the application of the doctrine of 'unjust enrichment').

But selecting between these formulations should, we suggest, involve a consideration of the policy objectives to be pursued. A conclusion as to the appropriate standard may differ as between one category of fiduciary and another. There are indeed good reasons why courts should not, for example, automatically apply the same criteria to company directors as to trustees, especially given their role as entrepreneurs (cf Sealy 'The Director as Trustee' [1967] CLJ 83). Indeed, the commercial environment in which directors operate may influence judicial treatment of them as fiduciaries. Evidence for this is (a) the permission for directors to be on boards of competing companies without triggering an automatic conflict of interest (*In Plus Group Ltd v Pyke* [2002] 2 BCLC 201 (CA); note Flannigan [2003] JBL 277 at 291), (b) the trend in Australia toward lenient treatment of directors who are appointees or nominees of shareholders (*Re 2GB Pty Ltd* [1964–65] NSWR 1648; *Harkness v Commonwealth Bank* (1993) 32 NSWLR 543) and (c) the trend to categorise the director's duty of care and skill as a negligence-based duty rather than a fiduciary duty (see Heydon 'Are the Duties of Company Directors to Exercise Care and Skill Fiduciary?' in *Degeling and Edelman* ch 9; and in relation to acting in the best interests of the company see Flannigan (2006) 122 LQR 449). Also, in the future, the courts may modify fiduciary duties of directors of government-owned companies or statutory authorities because of the different contextual setting and stakeholders involved (see generally Whincop (2002) 25 NSWLJ 379).

'Information' and 'opportunity' cases in the corporate arena provide a useful context for examining sharply differing views as to the appropriate standard to be applied. One consideration advanced by Weinrib ((1975) 25 U Toronto LJ 1), is that: 'the fiduciary obligation is ... one thread in the net thrown up by the common law for the protection of business structures ... [In] the course of protecting the plaintiff's organisation, the fiduciary concept simultaneously performs the subordinate function of maintaining the integrity of the marketplace.' But the achievement of protection and integrity is not synonymous with any one particular approach. Sealy, for example (*Company Law and Commercial Reality* (1984) pp 38–39), has suggested that it was simply problems of proof which initially justified the adoption of a strict standard (see eg *Keech v Sandford*). He therefore argues against 'the slavish perpetuation' of the trust rules to company directors, on the ground that evidential problems are minimal for modern courts, which can go into the details of a case and weigh up whether there has been a conflict of interest and duty. In contrast it has been argued by Norris JA, dissenting in *Peso-Silver Mines v Cropper* (1965) 56 DLR (2d) 117 at 139 that the strict standard, as applied to directors in *Regal*, should be maintained because of the difficulty of monitoring abuse, a sentiment of some attraction post-Enron (see also Sullivan (1979) 42 MLR 711):

> ... the complexities of modern business are a very good reason why the rule should be enforced strictly in order that such complexities may not be used as a smoke screen or shield behind which fraud may be perpetrated ... In order that people may be assured of their protection against improper acts of trustees [sic] it is necessary that their activities be circumscribed within rigid limits ... No great hardship is imposed on directors by the enforcement of the rule as a very simple course *is* available to them which they may follow [ie obtain the shareholders' consent].

There is, however, a second and countervailing consideration to be set against protection of corporate structures, namely the need not to discourage business enterprise. The argument here is that the automatic application of strict, deterrent standards does not make commercial sense – it inhibits enterprise – because it prevents the court from ever assessing whether any real conflict of interest and duty exists and it thereby widens the scope of potentially prohibited activity (see Jones (1968) 84 LQR 472; but cf Bishop and Prentice (1983) MLR 289 at 302–303 on company directors). Moreover, the recognition or imposition of fiduciary duties can add to the cost of a transaction; indeed, the fees and costing of a transaction may have been calculated on the basis that no fiduciary duty was present (eg see Clarke and Farrar [1982] U Illinois LR 229 at 234 n 21, 235, 244).

As stated earlier, one way of using the leeway provided by the generality of the rules is to say that a person may be a fiduciary for part of his activities but not for other parts (see *Queensland Mines v Hudson* (1978) 52 ALJR 399; *New Zealand Netherlands Society Oranje Inc v Kuys* [1973] 1 WLR 1126; *Aas v Benham* [1891] 2 Ch 244). Alternatively, leeway may be provided by recognising that the structure of the trust or fiduciary relationship *as created* involves an inherent conflict of interest. Thus the way potential fiduciary duties operate in that context must be modified, as in *Sargeant v National Westminster Bank plc* (1990) 61 P&CR 518, CA or recognised as not existing in that specific context. A good example is the Privy Council decision in *Kelly v Cooper Associates* [1993] AC 205. Here, real estate agents acted for the vendors of adjoining properties. A prospective purchaser made an offer for each property. The real estate agents did not tell the plaintiff that the purchaser wished to buy both properties, and if they had, the plaintiff may have been able to secure a higher price. The plaintiff brought an action for breach of fiduciary duty on the basis that the real estate agents had not disclosed relevant information and that they had put themselves in a position where their duty to the plaintiff vendor conflicted with their personal interests in obtaining commissions on sales of both properties. The Privy Council considered that the high standards that might apply to trustees and others should not apply to real estate agents because of the context in which they operate. Given that real estate agents often act for more than one vendor in a neighbourhood it would be unrealistic to impose a constraint on them that would effectively require them to put the interest of one vendor ahead of all others. The underlying policy is that real estate agents should be free to act for several competing principals, and given this policy, strict adherence to prevention of conflict of interests would not serve society well. The Privy Council emphasised that customers of real estate agents know that agents do act for multiple vendors and thus it must be an implied term of the agency contract that the real estate agents are entitled to act for other vendors selling competing properties. Thus they can keep secret information obtained from different vendors in connection with the sale of their properties. This contextual approach depends heavily on the Privy Council's interpretation of the market within which real estate agents operate and the appropriate policy to be followed. The Privy Council's approach has been criticised on a number of grounds by Reynolds [1994] JBL 144 and Brown (1993) 109 LQR 206.

(2) Policy and commercial contracts

Our reference above to commercial sense, with its emphasis on the practical limitations of the fiduciary concept, brings us full circle to our initial question: in what circumstances, and to what extent, should one party be held to be in a fiduciary relationship with another? The line of reasoning here initially seems straightforward. Commerce is contract-dominated and is based on the premise that self-interested behaviour in the market will lead to the common good. Where parties are self-interested then fiduciary duties are less likely to be created as these duties require a party to act in another's interest. But commerce and trust are not so easily separated. Some social scientists suggest that trust, in its layman's sense, is 'an unavoidable dimension of social interaction' and is both present and necessary in all complex economic systems (see Gambetta (ed) *Trust* (1988) Foreword; but cf Hayek *The Three Sources of Human Values* (1978)). But how far will (or can) such trust be translated by the courts into enforced commercial standards? The co-existence of contractual duties and fiduciary duties has long been established in the elementary commercial relationships of partnership and agency. However, the recognition of the co-existence of contractual duties and fiduciary duties in new commercial transactions and relationships can be seen as equity *penetrating* or *infiltrating* commercial law. It is newer types of business arrangement such as franchising and joint ventures which are providing a forum, particularly in the Commonwealth courts, for marking out the boundaries of the fiduciary relation. In such circumstances these boundaries run hard up against those of the contractual nexus between commercial entities bargaining at arm's length.

The 'intrusion' of equity into commercial law has often been criticised by judges, not least by that firm advocate of laissez-faire Bramwell LJ who stated in *New Zealand and Australian Land Co v Watson* (1881) 7 QBD 374 at 382:

> Now, I do not desire to find fault with the various intricacies and doctrines connected with trusts, but I should be very sorry to see them introduced into commercial transactions, and an agent in a commercial transaction turned into *a* trustee with all the troubles that attend that relation.

(See also Lord Selborne LC in *Barnes v Addy* (1874) 9 Ch App 244 at 251 and Lindley LJ in *Manchester Trust v Furness* [1895] 2 QB 539 at 545; but see Mr Justice Kennedy 'Equity in a Commercial Context' in Finn (ed) *Equity and Commercial Relationships* (1987) p 104.)

The appropriateness of equity and its proprietary remedies in regulating commercial relationships is therefore a significant undercurrent in the different views as to the basis for fiduciary relationships. Those who interpret the *recognition* of fiduciary relationships as the *imposition* of fiduciary relationships see the policy issue in the following terms: is it appropriate for equity to 'regulate the conduct of parties dealing at arm's length in commercial transactions who have made (or who are at the least capable of making) extensive contractual provisions as to their respective rights and obligations'?

It does appear that the courts will not readily classify such relationships, entered into by two business organisations, as fiduciary at least where the parties' interests in performing the contract are seen, at least in some important respects, as opposed to one another (see eg *Jirna v Mister Donut of Canada* (1973) 40 DLR (3d) 303; *Hospital Products International v United States Surgical Corpn* (1984) 58 ALJR 587). On the other hand, where there is a joint or common interest the courts may be more willing to find a collaborative fiduciary relationship in so far as is necessary to protect the common interest (see *United Dominions Corpn Ltd v Brian Pty Ltd* (1985) 60 ALR 741; *John v James* [1991] FSR 397; *Global Container Lines v Bonyad Shipping Co* [1998] 1 Lloyd's Rep 528; *Bean* (1995); Lehane 'Fiduciaries in a Commercial Context' in Finn (ed) *Essays in Equity* (1985)). This may even extend to pre-contractual relationships: see *Bean* (1995) pp 269–272; cf the approach in *Banner Homes Group plc v Luff Developments* [2000] Ch 372.

Given that a contract will usually form the basis of commercial parties' relationships, it is open to them to include terms in the contract which affect how fiduciary duties could regulate their relationship. Commercial parties could include terms which modify the operation of a fiduciary duty (ie by imposing a lesser standard of behaviour) or by removing a fiduciary duty entirely (eg *Hayim v Citibank NA* [1987] AC 730 and *ASIC v Citigroup Global Markets Pty Ltd* [2007] FCA 963) or by seeking to exclude liability for breach of a duty (on the basis of *Armitage v Nurse* [1997] 2 All ER 705). Even if the parties attempt to exclude fiduciary duties from regulating their behaviour, the courts may develop other standards, possibly based on a trustee's duty of fair dealing with a beneficiary or obligations of good faith, as a means of regulating behaviour in commercial relationships.

It is doubtful, however, that we can adequately explain the present state of the law in this area solely by reference to the categories of commercial undertakings. There is a wider picture to consider. We have previously suggested (see p 834) that the idea of 'morality' might be claimed to be integral to a duty of loyalty and instrumental in keeping the conduct of fiduciaries 'at a level higher than that trodden by the crowd'. Finn, commenting on the increasing tendency in Commonwealth jurisdictions to recognise fiduciary duties in contractual or commercial relationships, argues that the courts are indeed trying to secure heightened standards of behaviour between commercial parties (see [1989] 12 UNSWLJ 76; (1989) 17 Melb ULR 87; and 'The Fiduciary Principle' in Youdan (ed) *Equity, Fiduciaries and Trusts* (1989)). He doubts whether the adoption of a fiduciary standard is the most appropriate means, but if his analysis is correct, this indicates a judicial concern that runs wider than the contractual nexus between two parties. This could even be interpreted as a reassertion of a much earlier approach which recognised that a failure of equity to intervene and set appropriate standards could lead to abuse (see Lord Langdale MR in *Gillett v Peppercorne* (1840) 3 Beav 78 at 84).

But the idea of a fiduciary morality has still wider implications than just discouraging self-serving conduct. In corporate affairs, for instance, it can be argued that, in providing a control mechanism against abuse of managerial power, the fiduciary duty of loyalty also helps to legitimise corporate man-agerial power (see eg Stokes 'Company Law and Legal Theory' in Twining (ed) *Legal Theory and Common Law* (1986); and generally Hopt and Teubner (eds) *Corporate Governance and Directors' Liabilities* (1984)). Yet this argument encounters problems. The fiduciary rules failed, for example, to counter certain manifestations of self-serving behaviour – such as maintaining an interest in a contract with one's company – which are now regulated by statute (see Companies Act 2006, Pt 10; statutory provisions of this nature are sometimes viewed as essential where fiduciary duties binding directors at general law are commonly excluded or watered down by provisions in the company's articles). Also this control mechanism is limited by the courts' reluctance to interfere in managerial decisions (see Tunc (1986) 102 LQR 549; Bean [1993] JBL 24). Moreover, an assumption is that directors' managerial decisions are constrained within boundaries set by the fiduciary nature of their relationship to the company. This view does not sit comfortably, however, with the decision about the scope of fiduciary obligation in *Queensland Mines v Hudson*, which appears to reverse the relationship, or the recent push to treat the director's duty of care as a non-fiduciary duty. Indeed, if widely applied, the approach in *Queensland Mines* would contribute to fiduciary rules becoming merely 'standard reflecting', in the sense of complying with business practice, rather than 'standard setting' as the legitimation function requires (see also Duggan (1997) 113 LQR 601 at 619–626). The legitimation may ultimately be more symbolic than real (cf Beck (1971) 48 Can BR 80).

(3) Fiduciary law in a regulatory context

Certain fiduciaries have duties imposed on them by statute or under rules made by professional bodies which regulate the conduct of their activities, eg solicitors are subject to the Law Society's rules on professional conduct. Under the Financial Services and Markets Act 2000 financial intermediaries are governed by rules made by self-regulatory organisations. These financial intermediaries are usually agents of one form or another and therefore would generally be subject to fiduciary duties. However, the rules made usually overlap with the applicable fiduciary duties and may even conflict with them. The role of fiduciary law and its appropriateness in the context of such public law regulation and self-regulatory regimes was discussed in the Law Commission's Consultation Paper *Fiduciary Duties and Regulatory Rules* (No 124, 1992) and its report of the same title in 1995, Law Com No 236. In the Consultation Paper, the Law Commission provisionally concluded that where a fiduciary 'is subject to public law regulation . . . the classic formulation of fiduciary obligations needs to take account of the way modern commercial organisations are organised and regulated' (para 7.18). Thus the Law Commission considered that if a regulator had been given express power to modify private law rights then modification of fiduciary duties was acceptable, but where the regulator had not been given such power the Law Commission favoured the courts taking into account 'reasonable regulatory rules' in determining whether a breach of a fiduciary duty had occurred. The effect of this approach would be that, 'where a court considers that a regulatory rule is reasonable, it would be taken into account in determining the content of the fiduciary obligation. Thus, non-compliance with a reasonable rule may tend to indicate that conduct falls below the required standard, while compliance with such a rule will tend to indicate that there has been no breach of duty' (para 7.22).

In its final report, Law Com No 236 (1995), the Law Commission indicated that if there was a mismatch between what fiduciary duties required in a regulatory context and what is required or permitted by regulatory rules, the court would probably take account of the regulatory rules in determining the content of the fiduciary duty (para 14.20). The Law Commission also accepted that where the entity (which was subject to regulation) contracted with its principal/beneficiary, the terms of the contract could modify the operation of those fiduciary duties. Thus, the terms of the contract could deal with any mismatch between what was permitted by the regulatory rules and what was required by fiduciary duties. However, the Law Commission considered that judicial views on Chinese Walls, as a method of dealing with conflicts of interest or conflicts of duty owed to different principals, still posed a potential problem. The Law Commission recommended legislation to protect entities using properly constructed Chinese Walls.

Consider the following questions:

(1) What policy arguments can be mounted against recognition of fiduciary relationships or fiduciary duties in commercial or contractual relationships? Are these sufficient to outweigh the need for standards of commercial morality?

(2) Should equity be allowed to regulate what would otherwise be contractual and tortious relations by use of the fiduciary relationship? Alternatively, should tortious liability be widened to apply to trustees' breaches of trust? (See Williams and Hepple *Foundations of the Law of Tort* (1976) p 18, cf *Wickstead v Browne* (1992) 30 NSWLR 1 (note Kirby P in dissent); and see more generally on these classification issues and their implications Cane *The Anatomy of Tort Law* (1997) pp 186–196; and Birks (1996) 26 U West Australia LR 1.)

(3) The Law Commission saw the aim of the law as 'adequate protection of customers, the facilitation of the efficient functioning of the market and clarity as to customers' rights and firms' duties'. How far does fiduciary law with its emphasis on protection of vulnerable parties conflict with the other specified goals? Should the fiduciary relationship apply only to otherwise unregulated relationships?

(4) Is there any conflict of interest involved if regulatory rules are made by self-regulating bodies which are largely composed of members of the profession or business they regulate?

(5) Should the courts take into account whether a fiduciary is subject to a 'reasonable regulatory rule' which offers 'adequate customer protection' and, if so, what factors should a court take into account? How is a court to assess these factors in practice? Should the courts in determining reasonableness favour a modified deterrence approach or one of strict deterrence?

(6) If fiduciary law is about standard-setting, does it have a wider role to play, perhaps encompassing governmental functions? (Cf *Tito v Waddell (No 2)* [1977] 3 All ER 129 with *Guerin v R* (1984) 13 DLR (4th) 321.) Are there any policy reasons why fiduciary obligations should not be imposed on the Crown or different levels of government? (Cf *Bromley London Borough Council v Greater London Council* [1982] 1 All ER 129; *Westminster City Council v Porter* [2003] Ch 436, noted Barratt (2004) 63 CLJ(3) 540; and see Cooper (1997) 6 Social and Legal Studies (2) 235.)

3. Remedies

Where there has been a breach of a fiduciary duty the full range of equitable remedies is available to a court and there may also be advantages in terms of limitation periods for actions when compared to common law remedies (cf Mather [2008] JBL 344). These remedies include injunctions, avoiding a term of a contract (*United Dominions Corpn Ltd v Brian Pty Ltd* (1985) 60 ALR 741), equitable compensation for a loss incurred (*Nocton v Lord Ashburton* [1914] AC 932 especially at 946 and 956–957), equitable lien and a personal liability to account for a profit made (see generally Chapter 14). Perhaps the most important remedy, where a fiduciary has profited from a breach of duty, is to declare the fiduciary a constructive trustee of the profits and liable to account for those profits to his principal (see eg *Boardman v Phipps*; *Industrial Developments Corpn v Cooley*). As was seen in Chapter 14 there is a distinction between a *personal* liability to account and the *proprietary* remedy of constructive trust. It does seem, however, that the courts frequently use the term 'accountable' even when imposing a constructive trust on the fiduciary. It also seems that the courts impose constructive trusteeship almost automatically, and irrespective of whether the fiduciary has deliberately infringed his duty, or whether the fiduciary was honest and the breach of duty occurred accidentally. This potentially has the proprietary implications – for example, as regards 'tracing' the relevant property – outlined in Chapter 14 (at p 717). It can be argued, however, that the court should exercise a discretion to award other less onerous proprietary remedies (such as a lien) in lieu of a constructive trust (see Youdan 'The Fiduciary Principle: The Applicability of Proprietary Remedies' in Youdan (ed) *Equity, Fiduciaries and Trusts* (1989) ch 3; Evans (2001) 23 Syd LR 463).

(a) The problem of bribes

A surprising exception to imposing a constructive trust was provided by a much criticised decision, *Lister v Stubbs* (1890) 45 Ch D 1, and a line of cases that followed it (see Maudsley (1959) 75 LQR 234; Goff and Jones *The Law of Restitution* (7th edn, 2007) pp 752–755; Rotherham (1992) 2 Auck LR 84; Rotherham *Proprietary Remedies in Context* (2002) ch 8). *Lister v Stubbs* must now be considered in light of the Privy Council decision in *A-G for Hong Kong v Reid* [1994] 1 All ER 1, which may now be accepted as orthodoxy (see *Daraydan*

Holdings Ltd v Solland International Ltd [2004] EWHC 6222 (Ch); *Tesco Stores Ltd v Pook* [2003] EWHC 823 (Ch)).

In *Lister v Stubbs*, Stubbs was employed by Lister as a purchasing agent, and was bribed to channel business to a third party. Lister sought to have Stubbs declared a constructive trustee of the bribe so that the money could be followed into its produce, namely investments that Stubbs had purchased with the bribe. Lister would thus have obtained the benefit of any increase in value and his claim would have been secured even had Stubbs become a bankrupt. The Court of Appeal held, however, that Stubbs was liable only to pay over the sum he had received: 'the relation between them is that of debtor and creditor: it is not trustee and cestui que trust' (per Lindley MR at 15). *Lister v Stubbs* thus drew a fine distinction between use of a fiduciary position and use of property subject to the fiduciary relationship.

In *A-G for Hong Kong v Reid*, criminals paid bribes to Reid to obstruct their prosecutions. Reid was employed as a Crown Counsel in Hong Kong, and invested the bribes, totalling NZ$540,000, in land which increased in value to NZ$2.4m. For the Crown the A-G (Hong Kong) claimed Reid was a fiduciary, that *Lister v Stubbs* was wrongly decided, and therefore that Reid held any land purchased using bribes on constructive trust for the Crown. The Privy Council agreed, emphasising that *Lister* itself was inconsistent with earlier authority not cited in that case and preferring the views of Lai Kew Chai J in *Sumitomo Bank Ltd v Thahir* [1993] 1 SLR 735 at 810 (Singapore) and Lord Millett (extra-judicially) in 'Bribes and Secret Commissions' [1993] Restitution LR 7. The Privy Council noting that 'Bribery is an evil practice which threatens the foundations of civilised society' ([1994] 1 All ER 1 at 4), equated the taking of bribes with a fiduciary profiting from his position, thus theoretically bringing it within the no secret profits rule. The Privy Council, in a stance consistent with *Boardman v Phipps*, therefore concluded that as a fiduciary must account for the bribe to his principal/beneficiary and must not profit from a breach of trust, the bribe and any profit made from it must be held on trust for the principal/beneficiary. Unfortunately, the Privy Council relied in part on the maxim that 'equity regards as done that which ought to be done' (see Chapter 4 at p 119). It did so to hold that the bribe was a debt that belonged to the principal and, therefore, would be held on trust for the principal. This aspect of the judgment (together with the constructive trust as the outcome) has been the subject of much criticism (eg McKendrick (1994) 110 LQR 509 at 513; Sealy (1995) 9 J Contract L 37 at 50; Crilley [1994] Restitution LR 57; Oakley [1994] CLJ 31; cf Hayton 'Unique Rules for the Unique Institution, the Trust' in *Degeling and Edelman* at pp 284–286).

The decision, clearly intended by the court to be fully applicable to English cases, removes the apparent anomaly of *Lister v Stubbs*. But not all would agree that a satisfactory outcome has yet been achieved. It may be argued, for instance, that the courts in this area should distinguish between the honest and the dishonest fiduciary making an unauthorised or secret profit. The constructive trust should be reserved as a drastic sanction for the latter (see eg Jones (1968)

84 LQR 472) even though, formally, the secret profit rules draw no distinction between the honest and the dishonest. If this approach were to be followed, *A-G for Hong Kong v Reid* would have the same result but the imposition of only a personal remedy against the seemingly dishonest agent in *Lister v Stubbs* and the imposition of a constructive trust of the shares held by the honest solicitor in *Boardman v Phipps* would both be seen as misguided. As an alternative to recovery against the fiduciary the principal may seek redress from the briber (see *Fyffes Group Ltd v Templeman* [2000] 2 Lloyd's Rep 643).

A further complication is that sometimes third-party interests are involved. In particular, if the fiduciary goes bankrupt, the persons who will chiefly suffer from the imposition of a constructive trust instead of a purely personal remedy are the general creditors. In *A-G for Hong Kong v Reid*, however, the Privy Council was in no doubt as to the fairness of this outcome: in principle the fiduciary held the bribe on trust from the moment of *receipt*, and since the unsecured creditors 'cannot be in a better position than their debtor' (at 5), they cannot take any benefit from the bribe either. But would this be fair to them where, as illustrated in *Boardman v Phipps*, the breach of fiduciary duty giving rise to the constructive trust did not harm the principals in any way, but actually enriched them? Thus, should the principal be entitled, in the bankruptcy of the fiduciary, to extract from the available assets the full value of the relevant secret profit, wholly as a windfall, whereas the general creditors, most of whom will have given valuable consideration for their debts, must be left to scramble for the 'crumbs' left over? It may be premature and therefore unwise to assume, however, that we have only a choice between the poles of personal liability to account and a full-blown proprietary constructive trust.

There are other possibilities. Goode, for example, has proposed what he calls an ad rem remedy, which would not give the principal absolute priority in insolvency (see Goode in both *McKendrick* (ed) pp 146–148 and in Burrows (ed) *Essays on the Law of Restitution* (1991) pp 221–222; and its adoption by McLachlin J in *Korkontzilas v Soulos* (1997) 146 DLR (4th) 214 at 230, but cf Birks (1992) 45 CLP 69 at 80–94). Another alternative would be to award an equitable lien rather than a constructive trust (eg *Lord Napier and Ettrick v Kershaw* [1993] AC 713 – here protecting a right to subrogation). This too can be seen as a compromise solution, as it offers priority against only the unsecured creditors on insolvency and allows the secured creditors to keep their priority on an insolvency.

Concurrent remedies being claimed may also be relevant to questions of fairness. For example, the award of a generous allowance in *Boardman v Phipps*, arguably in recognition of Boardman's honesty as well as his effort and entrepreneurial flair, mitigated substantially the impact of the constructive trust. Indeed, in effect it created a form of 'profit-sharing agreement' between the protagonists, an approach also evident in *O'Sullivan v Management Agency Music Ltd* [1985] 3 All ER 351 (see Bishop and Prentice (1983) 46 MLR 289 at 295–304; (1986) 49 MLR 118; see also *Re Badfinger* (2002) EMLR 2). However, uncertainty surrounds the circumstances in which the court will exercise its inherent jurisdiction to award remuneration (see generally Chapter 9). In *O'Sullivan*, for example, even though the contracts between a singer and his manager were unfair and set aside on the grounds of undue influence and breach of fiduciary duty, the manager was awarded remuneration because he had contributed significantly to the singer's success. On the other hand, the House of Lords in *Guinness plc v Saunders* [1990] 2 AC 663 refused to award remuneration to a director who, it was assumed, had acted bona fide although in circumstances involving a stark conflict of interest and duty. Formally, the basis for the decision was that the board of directors had the power to award remuneration and the court therefore should not interfere (at 689 per Lord Templeman and at 701–702 per Lord Goff; see Davies *Gower and Davies' Principles of Modern Company Law* (8th edn, 2008) p 540). By way of guidance Lord Goff indicated, somewhat puzzlingly in the light of *O'Sullivan*, that the jurisdiction should be restricted to cases where it could not have the effect of encouraging 'trustees' to put themselves in a position of conflict of interest and duty.

Australian law seems to be headed in a more flexible direction. In *Warman International v Dwyer* (1995) 182 CLR 544, a case involving a senior manager usurping a business opportunity, the High Court of Australia awarded an account of profits in circumstances where *Boardman v Phipps* would have indicated that a constructive trust may have been the appropriate remedy. In *Warman International*, the dishonest senior manager resigned not to acquire a specific asset, but to acquire an import business currently carried on by his employer under a licence from a foreign exporter. He also developed other business activities in conjunction with the exporter. The High Court recognised that in certain circumstances a court has the discretion not to award a remedy: a remedy including a constructive trust could be defeated by equitable defences such as estoppel, laches, acquiescence and delay, and it could be defeated by the plaintiff's own inequitable conduct. Moreover it was considered generally inappropriate to award a constructive trust where the errant fiduciary acquired a business rather than some specific asset. Whether English law will recognise such judicial flexibility or continue with the liberal allowance approach for use of a fiduciary's skill remains open given the clamour of both the supporters of *A-G for Hong Kong v Reid* and its critics.

(b) Equitable compensation

We have dealt with the situation of a fiduciary making a profit from a breach of trust. But what is equity's remedy where the breach causes the principal or beneficiary a loss? In these circumstances equity awards compensation, a remedy somewhat akin to damages but not quite the same as damages because of equity's unique approach. (See generally Rickett 'Where are we Going with Equitable Compensation' in Oakley (ed) *Trends in Contemporary Trust Law* (1996) p 177; Getzler 'Equitable Compensation and the Regulation of the

Fiduciary Relationship' in Birks and Rose (eds) *Restitution and Equity* Vol 1 (2000) p 235; Conaglen (2003) 119 LQR 246.)

In the case of a trustee in breach of trust the rule is simple: he or she is obliged to restore the trust fund to the state it was in at the time of the breach and causation is usually irrelevant because the loss flows from the breach. How can this be applied to other fiduciaries where there is no trust fund? In grappling with this conundrum the House of Lords in *Target Holdings v Redferns* [1996] AC 421 has recognised that such fiduciaries should make good a loss suffered by the beneficiary and which, using hindsight and common sense, can be said to have been caused by the breach. These matters of causation and compensation were considered in detail in Chapter 11 (see p 573 et seq). We would simply reiterate here that perhaps a distinction needs to be made between equitable compensation being a restoration of a trust fund paid away in breach of trust, and equitable compensation for loss caused by other breaches of fiduciary duty or by misadministration of the trust (cf the High Court of Australia in *Youyang Ltd v Minter Ellison* (2003); Elliott and Edelman (2003) 119 LQR 545). Fairness comes into play because it would be unfair to require the fiduciary to compensate the beneficiary for losses which the fiduciary did not cause, where no trust property has been paid away (see *Hulbert v Avens* [2003] EWHC 76 and also Getzler 'Am I My Beneficiary's Keeper? Fusion and Loss-Based Fiduciary Remedies' in *Degeling and Edelman* ch 10).

Consider the following:

(1) Watts suggests that desire to strip profits from an errant fiduciary ceases to have a point where the fiduciary is insolvent. Such profit-stripping only penalises a fiduciary's creditors (Watts (1994) 110 LQR 178 at 180). Is he right? Or are there good policy reasons for preventing a windfall to the fiduciary's creditors?

(2) Can the flexibility to award an allowance to an honest fiduciary be seen as a means of recognising a crude form of causation, ie that the gains were not wholly caused by the breach of trust but were partly caused by the fiduciary's use of his or her skills?

(3) The Australian High Court has held that if a principal seeks rescission of a contract made with a fiduciary in breach of fiduciary duty, the court can impose conditions on the grant of rescission (see *Maguire v Makaronis* (1997) 71 ALJR 781). If the terms upon which the contract is rescinded are favourable to the errant fiduciary, does this undermine the operation of the rigour of the fiduciary standard? (See Moriarty (1998) 114 LQR 9 at 12.)

4. A postscript

In this chapter there are several references to cases from Commonwealth jurisdictions and, in particular, readers will have noted the different approaches that different Commonwealth jurisdictions have adopted. We agree with Finn's view to the effect that a notable feature of judge-made law in England, Canada, New Zealand and Australia of the last two decades has been a greater willingness to protect persons in vulnerable positions from misuse of power that others possess over them, and that this has been especially so in equity in its supervision of private, professional and commercial relationships and dealings ('Equitable Doctrine and Discretion in Remedies' in Cornish et al (eds) *Restitution: Past, Present and Future* (1998) pp 256–257).

Human society being what it is, it appears to us that similar legal problems arise in each jurisdiction. However, the flexibility of equity enables each jurisdiction to solve those problems differently, albeit that the principles used originally came from the same source – preventing breach of confidence placed by one person in another. Why is this so? We have alluded to the flexibility of the current state of the law in determining whether a fiduciary relationships exists is one part of the answer. For example, the readiness of the Canadian courts to recognise the existence of fiduciary relationships enables those courts to solve problems in a different way than in England or Australia. Other parts of the answer depend on the interaction of the law applying to fiduciaries and trusts with local legislation and judicial temperament. Australian courts have not gone down the Canadian path but have been developing the equitable doctrine of unconscionability based on equity's jurisdiction to prevent unconscionable transactions (*Commercial Bank v Amadio* (1983) 151 CLR 447; *Garcia v National Australia Bank* (1998) 155 ALR 164). This doctrine has been used to provide remedies to vulnerable parties where one person takes advantage of that vulnerability. In some ways, this reduces the need for recognition of a fictitious or even a real fiduciary relationship to allow a remedy to be given to the vulnerable.

At this point there seems no movement in our courts to follow the Canadian approach of increasing the recognition of fiduciary relationships outside the core categories or adopting the Australian revitalisation of the unconscionability doctrine (cf *Credit Lyonnais Bank Nederland v Burch* [1997] 1 All ER 144 at 151 and *Boustany v Pigott* (1993) 69 P&CR 298 at 304, PC). Yet Lord Browne-Wilkinson's comments in *Westdeutsche* (see above, p 32) may ultimately open the door in the long term for some form of remedial constructive trust. While the English courts have made innovative decisions in other areas of equity, in cases such as *Lord Napier and Ettrick v Hunter* [1993] AC 713 and *Barclays Bank v O'Brien* [1994] 1 AC 180, there has also been a marked reluctance to embrace the potential innovative use of trust concepts in cases such as *Polly Peck plc, Westdeutsche* and by the Privy Council in *Re Goldcorp Exchange Ltd*. Innovative developments in the Commonwealth are possible indicators of how our law will develop. But students of trust law should realise that the local contexts in which these decisions arise may explain our courts' readiness (or lack thereof) to adopt these approaches.

17

Trust, contract and unincorporated associations

1. Trusts within the rules of an association

It will be seen in Chapters 18–20 that the trust has come to play an important part in the context of not-for-profit activity that the law regards as charitable. But the trust also has an important role to play, alongside other legal concepts such as contract, in non-charitable not-for-profit activity. Numerous not-for-profit organisations are formed not as companies or any other kind of corporate body, but as unincorporated associations. In *Conservative and Unionist Central Office v Burrell* [1982] 1 WLR 522 Lawton LJ suggested that an unincorporated association will have the following features:

   (i) two or more persons bound together for one or more common purposes (not being business purposes);
  (ii) having mutual rights and duties arising from a contract between them;
 (iii) in an organisation with rules to determine who controls it and its funds and on what terms; and
  (iv) which members must be able to join or leave at will.

This last named requirement is contentious unless it means that membership is voluntary, since many unincorporated associations are likely to have rules which impose some restrictions on membership (see also *Underhill and Hayton* p 163 for a similar criticism).

   The trust concept is invoked when the rules make provision – as they do commonly, but not in every case – for the property collectively owned by the association's members to be vested in the names of trustees. This is particularly likely to be done where the property includes land, or an interest in land (such as a lease), or shares, or any other property of which the legal title cannot be put – either for legal reasons, or on practical grounds – into the names of all the members of the association (for a hypothetical example, see example 8 in Chapter 1, p 10).

   The presupposition underlying this analysis should be noted. It is that an unincorporated association, unlike a limited company, is not a legal entity separate from its members. One cannot, in law, speak of property being owned by an unincorporated association. The property must instead be owned by its members or, as just suggested, by some persons holding title to the property on their behalf. The status of these persons as trustees is often spelt out expressly in the rules: if it is not, a court may be prepared to impute a trust.

The types of non-profit association which are unincorporated and which commonly designate trustees to hold property on their behalf are many and varied. The purposes may be 'inward-turning' – that is, devoted to the benefit of the members alone, as in the case of a private golf club – or 'outward-turning' – that is, devoted towards some aim, such as a political cause, in which the members have no personal material interest – or a mixture of the two.

The following passage from a case in 1979 elaborates some of these general points and offers an explanation of the nature of the trust which may appear within the rules of an unincorporated non-profit association:

Re Bucks Constabulary Widows' and Orphans' Fund (No 2) [1979] 1 All ER 623 at 626–627

Walton J: . . . If a number of persons associate together, for whatever purpose, if that purpose is one which involves the acquisition of cash or property of any magnitude, then, for practical purposes, some one or more persons have to act in the capacity of treasurers or holders of the property. In any sophisticated association there will accordingly be one or more trustees in whom the property that is acquired by the association will be vested. These trustees will of course not hold such property on their own behalf. Usually there will be a committee of some description which will run the affairs of the association; though of course in a small association the committee may well comprise all the members; and the normal course of events will be that the trustee, if there is a formal trustee, will declare that he holds the property of the association in his hands on trust to deal with it as directed by the committee. If the trust deed is a shade more sophisticated it may add that the trustee holds the assets on trust for the members in accordance with the rules of the association. Now in all such cases it appears to me quite clear that, unless under the rules governing the association the property thereof has been wholly devoted to charity, or unless and to the extent to which the other trusts have validly been declared of such property, the persons, and the only persons, interested therein are the members. Save by way of a valid declaration of trust in their favour, there is no scope for any other person acquiring any rights in the property of the association, although of course it may well be that third parties may obtain contractual or proprietary rights, such as a mortgage, over those assets as the result of a valid contract with the trustees or members of the committee as representing the association.

I can see no reason for thinking that this analysis is any different whether the purpose for which the members of the association associate are [sic] a social club, a sporting club, to establish a widows' and orphans' fund, to obtain a separate Parliament for Cornwall, or to further the advance of alchemy. It matters not. All the assets of the association are held in trust for its members (of course subject to the contractual claims of anybody having a valid contract with the association) save and except to the extent to which valid trusts have otherwise been declared of its property.

Walton J's explanation does not address all the questions that might be asked about the nature of the trust involved in an unincorporated association. When, for instance, Walton J speaks of the assets of an association being 'held on trust for its members', to which category or categories of members is he referring? Does he mean all the persons who become members at any time during the existence of the association, or only those persons who are members at the time when the trust is created? If the former, how are the beneficial interests under the trust altered when a member dies or leaves the association, or a new member is admitted? In the case of the resignation of a member, are the provisions of s 53(1)(c) of the Law of Property Act (LPA) 1925 applicable and, if so, are they commonly satisfied? It has been suggested (see *Parker and Mellows* p 90) that a signed acceptance by each member of the rules drafted in an appropriate form might satisfy s 53(1)(c) although it must be doubtful how far in practice this is actually done.

The legal and practical issues posed by these and other related questions have proved particularly problematic in two contexts: (i) the validity of bequests to an association; and (ii) the ownership of an association's funds when it is dissolved or becomes moribund. It is to these issues that we therefore now turn.

2. Bequests to an association

(a) The problems outlined

The question of the validity or invalidity of bequests to a non-charitable unincorporated association has received extended treatment in the case law. At first sight, it might seem strange that this question should be problematic, seeing that inter vivos transfers of money or property to such associations generally encounter no difficulties. Nobody seems ever to suggest, for instance, that the payment of a member's subscription to an unincorporated darts club, or the inter vivos gift of a holding of shares to a (non-charitable) society devoted to proving that the earth is flat, should not take effect according to the parties' intentions. But the following factors conspire to create doubts as to the validity of bequests to non-charitable associations:

(1) If, on its proper interpretation, the bequest creates a trust for the purposes of the association, the trust is open to attack on the ground, already discussed in Chapter 5, that trusts for non-charitable purposes are void. Such trusts are likely to infringe one or more of the following principles: the principle of certainty of objects, the beneficiary principle and, where the bequest is intended to be of endowment capital, the rule against perpetual duration of trusts unless restricted to an appropriate perpetuity period (Perpetuities and Accumulations Act 1964, s 15(4)).

(2) Because a bequest forms part of a will, under which the legal title to the whole of the deceased's estate is vested, initially at least, in the executor, it is natural to conclude that some form of trust is created expressly or impliedly by the bequest.

(3) Unlike companies or other corporate bodies, the unincorporated association named in the bequest cannot claim that 'it' is the beneficiary under the trust so created. This is because, in law, 'it' has no separate legal existence apart from its members.

(4) The alternative contention that the true beneficiaries are the members of the association encounters the following problems:

(i) it does not seem to reflect the testator's true intentions, particularly when the association has been formed to pursue some 'outward-turning' purpose, in which the members have no material interest; and

(ii) if it is argued that the future as well as the present members make up the class of beneficiaries, conflict with the common law rule against remoteness of vesting may arise. A gift to present and future members is a class gift, ie to persons identified by a description. Under the common law rule the whole gift would fail if, at the outset, it was possible – and it almost always was – that *even one* person might become a member of the class outside the perpetuity period. However, after the Perpetuities and Accumulations Act 1964 the trust will be valid since we can 'wait and see' until the end of the period (ss 3(1), (4), (5), 4(4)). At that point the class closes and the beneficial interest vests in those who are then members of the association. This point appears occasionally to have been overlooked (see eg *Re Grant's Will Trusts* [1979] 3 All ER 359 at 366).

(5) A consideration of practical importance is that, unlike inter vivos gifts, bequests of doubtful validity are often challenged. This is because there often exist one or more persons – usually residuary beneficiaries or the next of kin of the testator – who have the interest and motivation to mount a legal challenge. If a widow finds, for instance, that a large proportion of her deceased husband's estate is left in his will to some outlandish group – for example, the Flat Earth Society – to which he has formed an attraction in his declining years, she is highly likely to listen eagerly to any lawyer who suggests that the bequest may be set aside on technical legal grounds. There is normally no such motivated claimant in the case of an inter vivos gift, except where the donor – to whom the property generally reverts if the gift is set aside – changes his or her mind.

These propositions highlight the advantages to be gained by an 'outward-turning' unincorporated association through framing its purposes as charitable. As will be seen in Chapter 18, bequests made to a charitable association are not threatened by invalidity on the grounds just outlined.

(b) The relevant authorities

It must be emphasised at the outset that, following the leading case of *Leahy v A-G for New South Wales* in 1959 ([1959] AC 457, PC), the courts have developed three principal ways of construing gifts to unincorporated associations, all of which in varying degrees present practical difficulties in their application to the language in which gifts and bequests are often couched. The methods are: (i) gift to the individual persons who are members of the association at the date of the gift as tenants in common or joint tenants; (ii) a gift by way of endowment for the association, which must necessarily be held on trust; and (iii) a gift to members but subject to their respective contractual rights and liabilities towards each other. The last named is a mode of construction developed by the courts partly in response to the perceived difficulties posed by constructions (i) and (ii). For reasons that will be explored below it remains questionable whether any of these ways of construing gifts or bequests provides a satisfactory legal mechanism for implementing what the donor or testator probably intended. Our approach to the authorities is broadly chronological reflecting a gradual if at times inconsistent move on the part of the courts from a restrictive to a more pragmatic assessment of donors' and testators' intentions.

(1) A restrictive approach

A Privy Council case in 1959, *Leahy v A-G for New South Wales* (below), illustrates well how a court may feel compelled to interpret a seemingly straightforward disposition to a non-charitable association as a trust for non-charitable purposes, and therefore void. Intriguingly the approach adopted is to assume that prima facie the bequest is to be interpreted as a gift to the individual members at the date of the gift (as in (i) above) but then to test this assumption against the language of the bequest. Paradoxically this seemingly sympathetic approach is likely to result in the bequest failing since option (i) would only very rarely fit the language employed or the specific intention of the testator.

Leahy v A-G for New South Wales [1959] AC 457, PC

By clause 3 of his will the testator, Francis George Leahy, provided as follows:

> 3. As to my property known as 'Elmslea' situated at Bungendore aforesaid and the whole of the lands comprising the same and the whole of the furniture contained in the homestead thereon upon trust for such order of nuns of the Catholic Church or the Christian Brothers as my executors and trustees shall select and I again direct that the selection of the order of nuns or Brothers as the case may be to benefit under this clause of my will shall be in the sole and absolute discretion of my said executors and trustees.

The appellants, the widow and children of the testator, challenged the validity of the disposition. The evidence showed that some orders of nuns included in the clause were contemplative orders and therefore non-charitable (see Chapter 19, p 986), while others were charitable.

Viscount Simonds

. . . The question . . . appears to be whether, even if the gift to a selected Order of Nuns is prima facie a gift to the individual members of that Order, there are other considerations arising out of the terms of the will, or the nature of the society, its organisation and rules, or the subject-matter of the gift which should lead the court to conclude that, though prima facie the gift is an absolute one (absolute both in quality of estate and in freedom from restriction) to individual nuns, yet it is invalid because it is in the nature of an endowment and tends to a perpetuity or for any other reason. This raises a problem which is not easy to solve, as the divergent opinions in the High Court indicate.

The prima facie validity of such a gift (by which term their Lordships intend a bequest or demise [sic]) is a convenient starting point for the examination of the relevant law . . .

Viscount Simonds referred to the following passage from the judgment of Lord Hanworth, MR in *Re Macaulay's Estate*, reported only in a footnote to *Re Price* [1943] Ch 422 at 435:

'The problem may be stated in this way. If the gift is in truth to the present members of the society described by their society name so that they have the beneficial use of the property and can, if they please, alienate and put the proceeds in their own pocket, then there is a present gift to individuals which is good: but if the gift is intended for the good not only of the present but of future members so that the present members are in the position of trustees and have no right to appropriate the property or its proceeds for their personal benefit then the gift is invalid. It may be invalid by reason of there being a trust created, or it may be by reason of the terms that the period allowed by the rule against perpetuities would be exceeded.'

It is not very clear what is intended by the dichotomy suggested in the last sentence of the citation, but the penultimate sentence goes to the root of the matter. At the risk of repetition their Lordships would point out that, if a gift is made to individuals, whether under their own names or in the name of their society, and the conclusion is reached that they are not intended to take beneficially, then they take as trustees. If so, it must be ascertained who are the beneficiaries. If at the death of the testator the class of beneficiaries is fixed and ascertained or ascertainable within the limit of the rule against perpetuities, all is well. If it is not so fixed and not so ascertainable the trust must fail. Of such a trust no better example could be found than a gift to an Order for the benefit of a community of nuns, once it is established that the community is not confined to living and ascertained persons. A wider question is opened if it appears that the trust is not for persons but for a non-charitable purpose. As has been pointed out, no one can enforce such a trust. . . .

It must now be asked, then, whether in the present case there are sufficient indications to displace the prima facie conclusion that the gift made by clause 3 of the will is to the individual members of the selected Order of Nuns at the date of the testator's death so that they can together dispose of it as they think fit. It appears to their Lordships that such indications are ample.

In the first place, it is not altogether irrelevant that the gift is in terms upon trust for a selected Order. It is true that this can in law be regarded as a trust in favour of each and every member of the Order. But at least the form of the gift is not to the members, and it may be questioned whether the testator understood the niceties of the law. In the second place, the members of the selected Order may be numerous, very numerous perhaps, and they may be spread over the world. If the gift is to the individuals it is to all the members who were living at the death of the testator, but only to them. It is not easy to believe that the testator intended an 'immediate beneficial legacy' (to use the words of Lord Buckmaster) to such a body of beneficiaries. In the third place, the subject-matter of the gift cannot be ignored. It appears from the evidence filed in the suit that Elmslea is a grazing property of about 730 acres, with a furnished homestead containing 20 rooms and a number of outbuildings. With the greatest respect to those judges who have taken a different view, their Lordships do not find it possible to regard all the individual members of an Order as intended to become the beneficial owners of such a property. Little or no evidence has been given about the organisation and rules of the several Orders but it is at least permissible to doubt whether it is a common feature of them, that all their members regard themselves or are to be regarded as having the capacity of (say) the Corps of Commissionaires (see *Re Clarke* [1901] 2 Ch 110) to put an end to their association and distribute its assets. On the contrary, it seems reasonably clear that, however little the testator understood the effect in law of a gift to an unincorporated body of persons by their society name, his intention was to create a trust, not merely for the benefit of the existing members of the selected Order, but for its benefit as a continuing society and for the furtherance of its work . . .

The gift in clause 3 was then held to be void at general law, but under a NSW statutory provision, s 370 of the Conveyancing Act 1919, it survived to the extent of covering Orders of Nuns which were charitable.

In *Bacon v Pianta* (1966) 114 CLR 634, the High Court of Australia applied the decision in *Leahy*'s case so as to hold invalid a bequest of a testator's residuary estate (comprising only personal property) to the Communist Party of Australia 'for its sole use and benefit'. The party was an unincorporated association. In ruling that the bequest was 'to the members, both present and future, in trust for the purposes of the party', and was therefore void because the party's purposes were political, not charitable, the court took particular account of the following matters:

(1) the form of the bequest, especially the use of the phrase 'for its sole use and benefit';
(2) the size of the party (over 5,000 members);

(3) the geographical spread of the members, through all the Australian States and the Northern Territory;

(4) the degree of fluctuation in the membership (in the two years following the testator's death, 420 people ceased to be members and 776 joined the party); and

(5) the apparent lack of legal or practical capacity on the part of the members to terminate the association and divide its assets.

(2) Broadening the analysis

Some decisions in England since *Leahy*'s case have developed an approach whereby the choice no longer lies simply between interpreting a bequest to an unincorporated association as (i) an outright gift to the members individually, to be divided in equal shares, which is usually not in accordance with the testator's intention; or (ii) a trust for the association's purposes, which will be void unless the purposes are charitable. The following is a good example of this line of authority, first espoused by Cross J in *Neville Estates v Madden* [1962] Ch 832.

Re Recher's Will Trusts [1972] Ch 526

By her will dated 23 May 1957 Mrs Recher (R) gave a share of her residuary estate to what the judge construed as 'The London and Provincial Anti-Vivisection Society'. The society had ceased to exist on 1 January 1957. R died in 1962 and Brightman J considered first whether the gift would have been valid if the unincorporated association had still existed then.

Brightman J: Having reached the conclusion that the gift in question is not a gift to the members of the London and Provincial society at the date of death, as joint tenants or tenants in common, so as to entitle a member as of right to a distributive share, nor an attempted gift to present and future members beneficially, and is not a gift in trust for the purposes of the society, I must now consider how otherwise, if at all, it is capable of taking effect.

As I have already mentioned, the rules of the London and Provincial society do not purport to create any trusts except in so far as the honorary trustees are not beneficial owners of the assets of the society, but are trustees upon trust to deal with such assets according to the directions of the committee.

A trust for non-charitable purposes, as distinct from a trust for individuals, is clearly void because there is no beneficiary. It does not, however, follow that persons cannot band themselves together as an association or society, pay subscriptions and validly devote their funds in pursuit of some lawful non-charitable purpose. An obvious example is a members' social club. But it is not essential that the members should only intend to secure direct personal advantages to themselves. The association may be one in which personal advantages to the members are combined with the pursuit of some outside purpose. Or the association may be one which offers no personal benefit at all to the members, the funds of the association being applied exclusively to the pursuit of some outside purpose.

Such an association of persons is bound, I would think, to have some sort of constitution; that is to say, the rights and liabilities of the members of the association will inevitably depend on some form of contract inter se, usually evidenced by a set of rules. In the present case it appears to me clear that the life members, the ordinary members and the associate members of the London and Provincial society were bound together by a contract inter se. Any such member was entitled to the rights and subject to the liabilities defined by the rules. If the committee acted contrary to the rules, an individual member would be entitled to take proceedings in the courts to compel observance of the rules or to recover damages for any loss he had suffered as a result of the breach of contract. As and when a member paid his subscription to the association, he would be subjecting his money to the disposition and expenditure thereof laid down by the rules. That is to say, the member would be bound to permit, and entitled to require, the honorary trustees and other members of the society to deal with that subscription in accordance with the lawful directions of the committee. Those directions would include the expenditure of that subscription, as part of the general funds of the association, in furthering the objects of the association. The resultant situation, on analysis, is that the London and Provincial society represented an organisation of individuals bound together by a contract under which their subscriptions became, as it were, mandated towards a certain type of expenditure as adumbrated in rule 1. Just as the two parties to a bi-partite bargain can vary or terminate their contract by mutual assent, so it must follow that the life members, ordinary members and associate members of the London and Provincial society could, at any moment of time, by unanimous agreement (or by majority vote, if the rules so prescribe), vary or terminate their multi-partite contract. There would be no limit to the type of variation or termination to which all might agree. There is no private trust or trust for charitable purposes or other trust to hinder the process. It follows that if all members agreed, they could decide to wind up the London and Provincial society and divide the net assets among themselves beneficially. No one would have any locus standi to stop them so doing. The contract is the same as any other contract and concerns only those who are parties to it, that is to say, the members of the society.

The funds of such an association may, of course, be derived not only from the subscriptions of the contracting parties but also from donations from non-contracting parties and legacies from persons who have died. In the case of a donation which is not accompanied by any words which purport to impose a trust, it seems to me that the gift takes effect in favour of the existing members of the association as an accretion to the funds which are the subject-matter of the contract which such members have made inter se, and falls to be dealt with in precisely the same way as the funds which the members themselves have subscribed. So, in the case of a legacy. In the absence of words which purport to impose a trust, the legacy is a gift to the members beneficially, not as joint tenants or as tenants in common so as to entitle each member to an immediate distributive share, but as an accretion to the funds which are the subject-matter of the contract which the members have made inter se.

In my judgment the legacy in the present case to the London and Provincial society ought to be construed as a legacy of that type, that is to say, a legacy to the members beneficially as an accretion to the funds subject to the contract which they have made inter se. Of course,

> the testatrix did not intend the members of the society to divide her bounty between themselves, and doubtless she was ignorant of that remote but theoretical possibility. Her knowledge or absence of knowledge of the true legal analysis of the gift is irrelevant. The legacy is accordingly in my view valid, subject only to the effect of the events of January 1, 1957.

His lordship held, however, that the gift lapsed owing to the dissolution of the association in 1957.

The liberality of this approach to construing a bequest was taken a stage further in *Re Lipinski's Will Trusts* [1976] Ch 235. There a bequest was made on trust '. . . for the Hull Judeans (Maccabi) Association in memory of my late wife to be used solely in the work of constructing the new buildings for the Association and/or improvements to the said buildings'. Oliver J acknowledged that there appeared to be a difficulty in construing the gift as being one to members of the Association subject to their contractual rights inter se where there is a specific direction – 'to be used solely . . .' – seemingly limiting the manner of dealing with the gift. Notwithstanding the seemingly mandatory nature of that phrase Oliver J was willing to construe the bequest as an absolute gift to the current members, along the lines indicated in *Re Recher*, ie 'as an accretion to the funds which are the subject-matter of the contract which the members have made inter se' (at 248):

> If a valid gift may be made to an unincorporated body as a simple accretion to the funds which are the subject matter of the contract which the members have made inter se . . . I do not really see why such a gift, which specifies a purpose which is within the powers of the association and of which the members of the association are the beneficiaries, should fail. Why are not the beneficiaries able to enforce the trust or, indeed, in the exercise of their contractual rights, to terminate the trust for their own benefit? Where the donee association is itself the beneficiary of the prescribed purpose, there seems to me to be the strongest argument in common sense for saying that the gift should be construed as an absolute one [ie a simple accretion to the funds which are the subject matter of the contract between the members] – the more so where, if the purpose is carried out, the members can by appropriate action vest the resulting property in themselves, for here the trustees and the beneficiaries are the same persons.

Alternatively the judge also seemed prepared to uphold the disposition by applying the principle of *Re Denley* [1969] 1 Ch 373 (see Chapter 5, p 258). On that basis Oliver J appeared to treat the gift as specifying a particular purpose for the benefit of ascertained beneficiaries, namely, the members of the Association for the time being thereby in his view circumventing any perpetuity problem (but cf Hackney [1976] ASCL 419; Rickett (1980) 39 CLJ 88). The decision arrived at by the judge was that 'whether one treats the gift as a "purpose" trust or as an absolute gift with a superadded direction . . . all roads lead to the same conclusion' (at 250). It might be thought unusual to find that the facts can support what might seem to be alternative rather than complementary legal conclusions – absolute gift and purpose trust. Also Oliver J seems to envisage that even under the *Re Denley* 'purpose trust' analysis the members of the Association would be able to terminate the trust. If so, this tends to limit the efficacy of the purpose element from *Re Denley* when applied to the context of a members' association.

On the other hand, in *Re Grant's Will Trusts* [1979] 3 All ER 359 the court held that it could not apply the interpretation relied on in *Re Recher*. The judgment (criticised by Green (1980) 43 MLR 459) does not cast doubt on the contract-holding approach but serves to emphasise that questions of construction can still be decisive in determining the nature and validity of a bequest. The case concerned a bequest of residuary estate to 'the Labour Party Property Committee for the benefit of the Chertsey Headquarters of the Chertsey and Walton Constituency Labour Party'. Vinelott J held that this bequest could not be interpreted as an outright gift to the members individually, nor as a gift to the members beneficially on the footing that the property given should be dealt with in accordance with the rules of the association whereby the members were contractually bound. Instead, it was a gift on trust for the purposes of the Chertsey Headquarters of the Constituency Labour Party (the 'CLP') and therefore void. His Lordship explained this conclusion as follows (at 371–372):

> I base this conclusion on two grounds. First, the members of the Chertsey and Walton CLP do not control the property, given by subscription or otherwise, to the CLP. The rules which govern the CLP are capable of being altered by an outside body which could direct an alteration under which the general committee of the CLP would be bound to transfer any property for the time being held for the benefit of the CLP to the national Labour Party for national purposes. The members of the Chertsey and Walton CLP could not alter the rules so as to make the property bequeathed by the testator applicable for some purpose other than that provided by the rules; nor could they direct that property to be divided amongst themselves beneficially . . . The first ground is of itself conclusive, but there is another ground which reinforces this conclusion. The gift is not in terms a gift to the Chertsey and Walton CLP, but to the Labour Party Property Committee, who are to hold the property for the benefit of, that is in trust for, the Chertsey headquarters of the Chertsey and Walton CLP. The fact that a gift is a gift to trustees and not in terms to an unincorporated association militates against construing it as a gift to the members of the association at a date when the gift takes effect, and against construing the words indicating the purposes for which the property is to be used as expressing the testator's intention or motive in making the gift and not as imposing any trust. This was, indeed, one of the considerations which led the Privy Council in *Leahy*'s case to hold that the gift '. . . upon trust for such Order of Nuns of the Catholic Church or the Christian Brothers as my Executors and Trustees should select' would, apart from the Australian equivalent of the Charitable Trusts (Validation) Act 1954, have been invalid.

(3) Conceptual confusion

Academic commentators (see eg Green (1980) 34 MLR 459) have in general welcomed the result achieved by what may be called the 'property subject to contract' or 'contract-holding' approach, adopted in *Recher*, whilst expressing reservations about its theoretical correctness. In addition to the point concerning formalities (LPA 1925, s 53(1)(c)) mentioned previously, the chief theoretical criticism is that the approach seems to assume that the contract contained in the rules of the relevant association can, in some way, 'bind' the property being given. It is argued that, whilst trust obligations may bind and 'run with' property, contractual obligations cannot. If, however, this line of reasoning is pressed too far, it suggests that inter vivos transfers of property to an unincorporated association might be vulnerable to claims by individual members for their proportionate share of the property, even though the property is transferred to trustees, or a treasurer or other proper officer(s) of the association authorised under the rules to receive, and give receipts for, such property. This conclusion would substantially undermine the basis on which unincorporated associations operate, even though contractual remedies would in theory presumably be available against the members who would be in breach of their contractual obligations. The problem here is that the law seems compelled to adopt the terminology and notions of 'contract' to provide a means of acquiring and, as importantly, enforcing a form of communitarian property ownership. What this mode of ownership in a group or association requires is a system of 'internal regulations allocating use-privileges and control-powers between members' whilst removing any vesting of a transmissible property right or power in an individual member of the group or association (see generally the discussion in Harris 'What is Non-Private Property?' in Harris (ed) *Property Problems: From Genes to Pension Funds* (1997) p 175 at pp 178–180). It should therefore not surprise us if the solution offered by contract to this problem of property presents some conceptual difficulties.

Recognition of the theoretical difficulties that accompany the contract-holding theory of members' ownership is not new. Maitland observed that 'the "ownership in equity" that the member of a club has in land, buildings, books etc is of a very strange kind', and concluded that '[we] have to suppose numerous tacit contracts which no one knows that he is making, for after every election there must be a fresh contract between the new member and all the old members. But every judge on the bench is a member of at least one club, and we know that, if a thousand tacit contracts have to be discovered, a tolerable result will be obtained' ('Trust and Corporation' in Fisher (ed) *Collected Papers, Vol III* (1911) pp 377–378).

How much weight, therefore, should be attached to contemporary criticism that the contract-holding theory is inconsistent with aspects of classical contractual analysis? After all, much contractual doctrine derives from a schema which is premised upon individual autonomy and consent and is intended to facilitate market transactions. By contrast the type of contractual arrangement associated with clubs, societies, trade unions and even some political parties is one that is concerned primarily with collective self-government. Although formulated in the very different context of analysing collective labour agreements, Selznick's claim that 'the idea of contract . . . runs up against the idea of association' is equally apposite here (Selznick *Law, Society and Industrial Justice* (1969) p 150). Perhaps we should just pragmatically accept, as the courts implicitly appear to have done, that the contractual relation binding unincorporated associations is *sui generis*. Unfortunately, even the adoption of such a convenient conclusion does not resolve all the troublesome questions that bedevil debate about beneficial ownership of the assets of unincorporated associations. Where, for instance, entitlement to the assets of a dissolved or moribund association is in issue, there remains room for argument about the scope and interpretation of the mutual contract. Indeed it cannot be assumed that the contract-holding approach will necessarily provide the most convenient or legally defensible solution in those circumstances (see section 3 below).

Consider the following points:

(1) In the light of later decisions, such as *Re Recher*, how relevant nowadays (if at all relevant) are the specific factual circumstances relied on in *Leahy* and *Bacon v Pianta* for holding the dispositions in those cases to be void?

(2) Vinelott J states as the second reason for his decision in *Re Grant* that *where* a gift is to trustees '[that] militates against construing it as a gift to the members of the association . . . and against construing the words indicating the purposes . . . as expressing the testator's intention or motive in making the gift and not as imposing any trust'. Does this suggest that a non-charitable association which designates trustees to hold its property, in the manner described in *Re Bucks Constabulary* (above, p 888), thereby heightens the risk that a bequest to the association will be construed as a purpose trust and held to be void? If so, is this a satisfactory position for the law to adopt?

(3) Vinelott J treats *Re Denley* as if it were a case of a discretionary trust for persons only (see also Chapter 5, p 260). Acceptance of this analysis would exclude the possibility of validating a legacy to an unincorporated association as a trust for purposes directly or indirectly benefiting present members (and future members assuming a suitable perpetuity period has been adopted). Depending on one's analysis of *Re Lipinski* Vinelott J's interpretation appears to conflict with the decision in that case (see Rickett (1980) 39 CLJ 88 at 105; (1982) 12 VUWLR 1; cf McKay (1977) 9 VUWLR 1). However, even if *Re Denley* is accepted as circumventing the enforceability problem posed by the beneficiary principle, this may not have assisted Mr Grant. At best *Re Denley* recognises as valid only those trusts where the benefit for ascertained individuals is not too indirect or intangible. Would,

for instance, the benefit accruing to party members in *Re Grant* be considered too abstract? Indeed, can *Re Denley* be applied at all to an association whose purposes are 'outward-turning'? Lastly, the trust in *Re Grant* may have had to satisfy the rule against inalienability, and failed to do so (see Rickett (1980) 39 CLJ 88 at 101–104, but cf Green (1980) 44 MLR 459 at 460, and Maudsley *The Modern Law of Perpetuities* (1979) pp 177–178).

(4) In *Smith & Dormer v Packhurst* (1742) 3 Atk 135, a case in which the validity of a key clause in strict settlements (the 'trust to preserve contingent remainders': see Chapter 2) was confirmed by the House of Lords despite compelling arguments to the contrary, Willes CJ said (at 139): 'Surely, it is a much less evil to make a construction, even contrary to the common rules of law . . . than to overthrow one may say 100,000 settlements; for it is a maxim in law, as well as reason, *communis error facit jus*' (a common error becomes the law). In the light of your reading, is this maxim relevant in the present context?

(c) Conclusion

We have concentrated on the validity of bequests to unincorporated associations but what of inter vivos gifts or subscriptions? As Brightman J observed in *Re Recher* [1972] Ch 526 at 536, 'it would astonish a layman to be told that there was a difficulty in his giving a legacy to an unincorporated non-charitable society which he had, or could have, supported without trouble during his lifetime'. But how then could subscriptions be effectuated to a constituency Labour Party? Vinelott J's response in *Re Grant* is to invoke a resulting trust explanation – the original subscribers retain an 'ultimate proprietary right' so that in the event of dissolution of the constituency party the remaining funds would be held on resulting trust for them. Subsequently in *Conservative and Unionist Central Office v Burrell* [1982] 1 WLR 522 – where it was held that the Conservative Party was *not* an unincorporated association and again therefore no recourse could be had to the contract-holding analysis of *Re Recher* to explain beneficial ownership of party funds – an alternative explanation, or perhaps rationalisation, was advanced obiter in the Court of Appeal by Brightman LJ. He suggests that a contributor is simply giving the treasurer a mandate, probably via a contract of agency, whereby the latter is permitted to add the contribution to the general funds of the party. Once that is achieved the mandate becomes irrevocable although the contributor would be able to sue the treasurer (and his successors?) to prevent misapplication of party funds, at least until on ordinary accounting principles the contribution had been spent. Brightman LJ made no comment on an alternative suggestion advanced by Vinelott J at first instance ([1980] 3 All ER 42) that the treasurer would come under a special equitable obligation similar to that of an executor (see Rickett (1980) 39 CLJ 88; (1982) 12 VUWLR 1).

Whilst Brightman LJ's analysis may explain how inter vivos contributions are valid, it does not appear to resolve the problems posed by bequests, since no contract of agency can be set up at the moment of death. His Lordship recognised the problem, observed that 'I think the answer is not difficult to find' but then keeps us guessing – 'I do not wish to prejudge it' (at 530). To date no one has managed to tender a satisfactory explanation. As far as the Conservative Party is concerned, any difficulties were circumvented as early as 1949 by the use of eight offshore limited companies named after English rivers although how potential donors are alerted to their existence remains unclear (see eg *Guardian* 13 March 1993, p 5 and generally Davies *We, The Nation* (1995) citing Lord Woolton: 'our lawyers have given us a very ingenious solution' (at p 180)). As far as unincorporated associations are concerned Brightman LJ's evasion is not necessarily a difficulty since, in the course of his judgment, he firmly endorsed the contract-holding theory for such associations. However, as the luckless Mr Grant's attempted bequest shows, questions of construction of a testator's intention may still rule out the theory's application in some cases.

Of course there may arise the straightforward case where the donor positively intends to benefit the current members so that they may claim their individual shares of the gift (cf on the matter of intention here Matthews [1995] Conv 302 and Gardner [1998] 62 Conv 8). But once we move beyond that rarity we encounter, as one persuasive critic has observed (Hackney *Understanding Equity and Trusts* (1987) p 81), the recurring problem that in this context 'we are not looking at what the donor intends, but trying to fit his intentions into a legal framework that works, whether or not it approximates to the category he has in mind'. (See Figure 17.1 for an illustration of the process by which social fact can be transmuted into legal category by interpreting the intention of a donor.) The source of the problem resides in the limits imposed by the available legal tools. In particular the combination of the beneficiary principle and the refusal to give effect to trust purposes as mere powers (see Chapter 5, p 264), has forced the courts to search for contrived explanations of property holding in non-charitable associations. The outcome is unsatisfactory. On the one hand 'courts are allowing purposes to be effectuated under the cloak of contractual apparatus, which they would strike down if they came honestly out into the open as purpose trusts' (*Hackney* p 82). On the other hand, some other courts, applying techniques of construction more strictly, may invalidate similar dispositions. Perhaps only legislation can remedy the present confusion (see eg Succession Act (Queensland) 1981, s 63; Lee 'Trusts and Trust-Like Obligations with Respect to Unincorporated Associations' in Finn (ed) *Essays in Equity* (1985)).

The matters of construction discussed above are also relevant to the next issue to be considered: determining the distribution of assets of an unincorporated association where it becomes moribund or is dissolved.

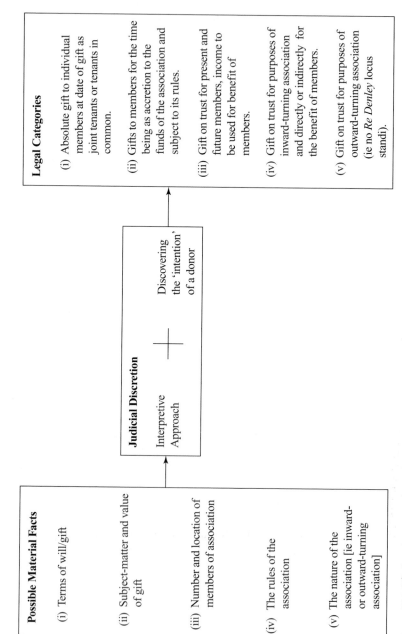

Possible Material Facts

(i) Terms of will/gift

(ii) Subject-matter and value of gift

(iii) Number and location of members of association

(iv) The rules of the association

(v) The nature of the association [ie inward- or outward-turning association]

Judicial Discretion

Interpretive Approach

$+$

Discovering the 'intention' of a donor

Legal Categories

(i) Absolute gift to individual members at date of gift as joint tenants or tenants in common.

(ii) Gifts to members for the time being as accretion to the funds of the association and subject to its rules.

(iii) Gift on trust for present and future members, income to be used for benefit of members.

(iv) Gift on trust for purposes of inward-turning association and directly or indirectly for the benefit of members.

(v) Gift on trust for purposes of outward-turning association (ie no *Re Denley* locus standi).

Figure 17.1 Gifts to unincorporated associations

3. Destination of assets on the dissolution of an unincorporated association

One might assume that at least in principle the distribution of an association's assets on its dissolution would be straightforward, namely that it would be determined by the way the property was beneficially owned prior to dissolution. Subject to any specific provision in the association's rules the members for the time being might be expected to be entitled to the assets. This would be consistent with the contract-holding approach as analysed in *Re Recher* which, despite the reservations about its theoretical basis discussed above, now seems firmly established as the principal explanation of how property is beneficially owned within unincorporated associations. Certainly the early view (see *Re Printers and Transferrers Amalgamated Trades Protection Society* [1899] 2 Ch 184) that the entitlement of members past and present to the assets, at least as regards their own contributions, is founded on a resulting trust basis, taking account of contributions paid and, where relevant, benefits received, has not been followed in recent cases (see most recently *Re Bucks Constabulary Fund Friendly Society (No 2)* [1979] 1 All ER 623 and *Re GKN Bolts and Nuts Ltd Sports and Social Club* [1982] 1 WLR 774).

It would be premature to conclude, however, that the question has now decamped completely to the realms of contract law. Practical considerations and legal argument may combine to limit the universal application of our initial assumption. Thus it will be seen below that two additional methods of distributing surplus funds have been canvassed in the cases: namely that the assets should either (i) where no person can establish title to them, be treated as bona vacantia and pass to the Crown, or (ii) where the funds have been provided by donors external to the association, should revert to them under a resulting trust. One point to consider in evaluating these alternative approaches is that surplus funds can arise in several distinct contexts. Caution is therefore advisable in assessing whether cases governing the destination of surplus funds in oversubscribed or failed public appeals or in instances of pension fund closure or even failure of private express trusts should necessarily apply to the dissolution of an unincorporated association.

The bona vacantia solution will most obviously be applicable where the association has become moribund as, for instance, where all the members or perhaps even all the members bar one have died. The reasoning behind this conclusion is apparent in the following dicta of Walton J in *Re Bucks Constabulary Fund Friendly Society (No 2)* [1979] 1 All ER 623 at 629:

> Before I turn to a consideration of the authorities, it is I think pertinent to observe that all unincorporated societies rest in contract to this extent, that there is an implied contract between all of the members inter se governed by the rules of the society. In default of any rule to the contrary, and it will seldom if ever be that there is such a rule, when a member

> ceases to be a member of the association he ipso facto ceases to have any interest in its funds... As membership always ceases on death, past members or the estates of deceased members therefore have no interest in the assets. Further, unless expressly so provided by the rules, unincorporated societies are not really tontine societies, intended to provide benefits for the longest liver of the members. Therefore, although it is difficult to say in any given case precisely when a society becomes moribund, it is quite clear that if a society is reduced to a single member neither he, still less his personal representatives on his behalf, can say he is or was the society and therefore entitled solely to its fund. It may be that it will be sufficient for the society's continued existence if there are two members, but if there is only one the society as such must cease to exist. There is no association, since one can hardly associate with oneself or enjoy one's own society. And so indeed the assets have become ownerless.

More contentiously both the bona vacantia and resulting trust solutions have been applied in at least one modern case concerning the destination of surplus assets of a benefit fund with members still living. In *Re West Sussex Constabulary's Benevolent Fund* [1970] 2 WLR 848, subsequently distinguished by Walton J in the *Bucks* case (see below), the assets of a fund originally set up in 1930 to provide for dependants of deceased members of the force, had come from four sources: (1) contributions of past and present members; (2) proceeds of entertainments, raffles and sweepstakes; (3) anonymous contributions to collecting boxes; and (4) other donations and legacies. As regards funds derived from external sources (2) and (3) Goff J decided that a bona vacantia solution was appropriate. This was (i) because the funds from (2) were the result of contract under which 'the purchaser pays his money as the price of what is offered and that he receives' (at 853), and (ii) because of the presumed intention of contributors to collecting boxes that they would not want their money back in any circumstances. It is apparent that to achieve a convenient solution the court is here imputing an intention to contributors, since the perceived alternative of resulting trust is seen as impractical. In contrast funds provided under category (4) were to be held on resulting trust, the equally artificial rationale being that named donors could be presumed to expect to get their money back in the event of a surplus arising (cf the analysis of the relationship between intention and resulting trust in *Westdeutsche Landesbank Girozentrale v Islington London Borough Council* [1996] AC 669 per Lord Browne-Wilkinson). Lastly, as regards the contributions of past and present members, Goff J reverted to a contractual basis, holding that resulting trust had no role to play here. The outcome, however, was that funds derived from contributions also passed to the Crown as bona vacantia because (at 851):

> those persons who remained members until their deaths are in any event excluded because they have had all they contracted for, either because their widows and dependants have received or are in receipt of prescribed benefits, or because they did not have a widow or dependants.

But how is this judgment to be reconciled with our expectation derived from the contract-holding approach that, whatever their origin, the assets would belong to the members? One simple answer is that Goff J did not accept that a 'pensions or dependant relatives' fund whereby only third parties could benefit, such as that in *West Sussex*, was analogous to a members' club. Subsequently in *Re Bucks* Walton J has cast doubt both on the validity of this distinction and on the resulting mode of distribution arrived at in *West Sussex*.

Re Bucks Constabulary Widows' and Orphans' Fund Friendly Society (No 2) [1979] 1 All ER 623

The Bucks Constabulary Widows' and Orphans' Fund Friendly society was established primarily to provide relief for the widows and orphans of deceased members of the Bucks Constabulary. In 1968 the Constabulary was amalgamated and it was resolved that the society should be wound up. The society, which was an unincorporated association registered under the Friendly Societies Act 1896, had no rules providing for the distribution of its assets in these circumstances. The question for the court was whether the surplus assets should pass bona vacantia to the Crown or whether they should be distributed amongst the members of the society at the date of its dissolution. Walton J commented as follows on the decision in *West Sussex*, the facts of which in the words of the judge 'present remarkable parallels to the facts in the present case':

Walton J: It will be observed that the first reason given by the judge for his decision is that he could not accept the principle of the members' clubs as applicable... If all that Goff J meant was that the purposes of the fund before him were totally different from those of a members' club then of course one must agree, but if he meant to imply that there was some totally different principle of law applicable one must ask why that should be. His second reason is that in all the cases where the surviving members had taken, the organisation existed for the benefit of the members for the time being exclusively. This may be so, so far as actual decisions go, but what is the principle? Why are the members not in control, complete control, save as to any existing contractual rights, of the assets belonging to their organisation? One could understand the position being different if valid trusts had been declared of the assets in favour of third parties, for example charities, but that this was emphatically not the case was demonstrated by the fact that Goff J recognised that the members could have altered the rules prior to dissolution and put the assets into their own pockets. If there was no obstacle to their doing this, it shows in my judgement quite clearly that the money was theirs all the time. Finally he purports to follow *Cunnack v Edwards* [1896] 2 Ch 679 and it will be seen from the analysis which I have already made of that case that it was extremely special in its facts, resting on a curious provision of the 1829 Act which is no longer applicable. As I have already indicated, in the light of s 49(1) of the 1896 Act the case before Goff J is readily distinguishable, but I regret that, quite apart from that, I am wholly unable to square it with the relevant principles of law applicable.

> The conclusion therefore is that, as on dissolution there were members of the society here in question in existence, its assets are held on trust for such members to the total exclusion of any claim on behalf of the Crown.

Whereas *West Sussex* can be distinguished from *Re Bucks* on the narrow basis that, unlike the latter, it was a simple unincorporated association unaffected by the Friendly Societies Act 1896, it is clear that Walton J's decision rests not on this point but on a more fundamental proposition, ie that the nature of the association is immaterial to questions of beneficial ownership. On this view the contract-holding approach applies to all the assets of an unincorporated association both prior to and post-dissolution. Thus the assets should be divided amongst the members irrespective of whether the society is 'inward-turning' or 'outward-turning'. It therefore follows that Walton J would have decided that a different distribution of those assets derived from members, from entertainments and from anonymous donors was appropriate in *West Sussex*, namely in favour of the members rather than the Crown. Moreover it can be inferred from Walton J's endorsement of the contract-holding approach that, had he been deciding the question, the assets derived from donations and legacies would also have been divisible amongst the members on a contractual basis rather than held on resulting trust for the donors.

The judgment in *Re Bucks*, having persuasively assigned the ownership question to the realm of contract, appeared to leave the law in this area firmly settled. Unfortunately dicta in two cases (*Davis v Richards and Wallington Industries Ltd* [1990] 1 WLR 1511 and *Air Jamaica Ltd v Charlton* [1999] 1 WLR 1399) concerning the destination of surplus funds in occupational pension schemes have reintroduced an element of uncertainty and suggest that there may yet be 'life in the old dog' of resulting trust.

The case of *Davis v Richards and Wallington Industries Ltd* concerned the almost commonplace circumstance (see Chapter 13) of dispute about entitlement to a pension fund surplus where the parent company was insolvent. In fact allocation was determined by the terms of the trust deed, but Scott J went on to consider obiter the position had the deed been invalid. The surplus derived from three sources: (i) employer's contributions; (ii) employees' contributions; and (iii) funds transferred from pension schemes of other companies. The judge accepted that in the circumstances of a surplus where the trust deed was not definitive, an analogy could be drawn with the unincorporated association cases. The premise that a pension scheme can be viewed even by analogy as a species of unincorporated association is questionable, but more significant for present purposes is that the judge did not accept an argument that in such a context contract and resulting trust are mutually exclusive. On the contrary he preferred an approach whereby a resulting trust would be imputed in favour of the provider of the funds unless it was 'absolutely clear' that a resulting trust was to be excluded (at 1541):

> In my opinion, a resulting trust will be excluded not only by an express provision but also if its exclusion is to be implied. If the intention of the contributor that a resulting trust should not apply is the proper conclusion, it would not be right, in my opinion, for the law to contradict that intention. In my judgment, therefore, the fact that a payment to a fund has been made under contract and that the payer has obtained all that he or she bargained for under the contract is not necessarily a decisive argument against resulting trust.

The outcome, had Scott J been forced to decide the case on this basis, would have been that the surplus attributable to employer's contributions would have been held on resulting trust, whilst that attributable to employees and transferred funds would pass as bona vacantia. The discovery of a 'clear intention' on behalf of employee contributors that there should be no resulting trust in their favour is contentious and seems based on a combination of the 'bargain' issue, notwithstanding the 'not necessarily a decisive argument' observation, and on the judge's perception of the practicalities of finding otherwise. The dictum of Scott J needs, however, to be treated with caution, not least because the judge appears to treat the options available to him as being *either* bona vacantia *or* resulting trust. The possibility of members' ownership along the lines of *Re Bucks* is simply not addressed, although this may be because, as Gardner suggests, 'it appears somewhat as though Scott J did not realise he was departing from the usual treatment, so we do not have the benefit of his own account of the distinctions to be drawn' ('New Angles on Unincorporated Associations' [1992] Conv 41 at 44; see also Martin [1991] Conv 366).

A further reason for treating the views of Scott J with caution is that dicta in the recent Privy Council case of *Air Jamaica Ltd v Charlton* [1999] 1 WLR 1399 has cast doubt on his analysis and on the appropriateness of a bona vacantia solution. In the case there was a partial failure of the trusts in the pension scheme with the consequence that there was a $400m surplus. By the time the litigation reached the Privy Council there were three claimants: the pension scheme members, the employer and the Crown claiming the surplus as bona vacantia. Under the terms of the scheme both airline and the employees had made matching contributions. The Privy Council concluded that the surplus was held on resulting trust in equal shares for the members and the airline. As regards the members' claim, the Privy Council, obiter, specifically rejected the proposition that if members had received all that they had bargained for they would have no expectation of receiving any return of excess contributions. It consequently disapproved as incorrect the approach of Scott J to the imputation of intention. These comments were obiter because in fact the members had not received all that they bargained for. As for the airline's claim a clause in a pension trust deed stating that 'no moneys which at any time have been contributed by the Company . . . shall in any circumstances be repayable to the Company' did not prevent the Privy Council from holding that a resulting trust should be imposed rather than the funds pass to the Crown as bona vacantia. The purpose of the clause, as Lord Millett saw it, was to prevent the airline amending the scheme so as to obtain any repayment and was 'not a pre-emptive but misguided attempt to rebut a resulting trust which would arise dehors the scheme' (at 1412).

Quite what conclusions can be drawn from these cases is uncertain. We have two pensions surplus cases in neither of which are the facts or the social contexts analogous to those surrounding the dissolution of unincorporated associations. Moreover any legal guidance is necessarily qualified by the fact that we are faced with obiter piled on obiter. Perhaps the most that can be hazarded is that *Air Jamaica* has reasserted the position that only as the last of last resorts should property devolve to the Crown as bona vacantia.

Consider the following points:

(1) The endorsement of the contract-holding approach in *Re Bucks*, following *Re Recher*, appears to leave no room for the imposition of a resulting trust solution where the funds represent the subscriptions of members or the proceeds of entertainments or collecting boxes. This would also appear to be the position for gifts or bequests generally, with the possible exception of purpose trusts. As regards such trusts, on the assumption that a gift or bequest to an 'inward-turning' unincorporated association for its purposes can be valid as a *Denley*-type purpose trust (but cf *Re Grant*), then on dissolution the destination of the money should in principle be determined by the law of trusts, ie on resulting trust for the donor or her estate, or as a gift over if one is indicated.

(2) Even where it is decided that surplus assets should belong to the members, there remain the questions of which members and in what proportions. The simple and correct answer is distribution according to the association's rules, but what if there are no rules? In *Re Bucks* Walton J was firmly of the opinion that division should be in equal shares amongst the members at the date of dissolution (at 637):

> Prima facie there can be no doubt at all but that the distribution is on the basis of equality, because, as between a number of people contractually interested in a fund, there is no other method of distribution if no other method is provided by the terms of the contract, and it is not for one moment suggested here that there is any other method of distribution provided by the contract . . .
>
> An ingenious argument has been put by counsel for the third and fifth defendants: the members of the society are entitled in equity to the surplus funds which are distributable among them, therefore they are to be distributed among them according to equitable principles and those principles should, like all equitable principles, be moulded to fit the circumstances of the case, and in one case it would therefore be equitable to distribute in equal shares, in another case it might be equitable to distribute in proportion to the subscription that they have paid, and I suppose that in another case it might be equitable to distribute according to the length of their

> respective feet, following a very well-known equitable precedent. Well, I completely deny the basic premise. The members are not entitled in equity to the fund; they are entitled at law. It is a matter, so far as the members are concerned, of pure contract, and, being a matter of pure contract, it is, in my judgement, as far as distribution is concerned, completely divorced from all questions of equitable doctrines. It is a matter of simple entitlement, and that entitlement must be, and can only be, in equal shares.

A difficulty in this type of case is that there are likely to be different classes of members. The question then is to what extent, if at all, should the distribution of surplus assets take account of such considerations as length of membership or type of membership (eg full, associate, temporary)? In *Re Sick and Funeral Society of St John's Sunday School* [1973] Ch 51 the surplus was distributed in proportion to contributions in circumstances where some members had contributed at a full rate whilst others had made half rate contributions only. By contrast in *GKN Bolts and Nuts Sports and Social Club* [1982] 1 WLR 774 a social club formed for the benefit of employees had ceased to exist in 1975 and, following financial difficulties, it resolved to sell its sports ground and distribute the proceeds of sale, some £240,000. In ordering equal distribution amongst full members at the date of dissolution Sir Robert Megarry VC, with commendable candour, summarised what he saw as the approach of the courts in these cases (at 776):

> As is common in club cases, there are many obscurities and uncertainties, and some difficulty in the law. In such cases, the court usually has to take a broad sword to the problems, and eschew an unduly meticulous examination of the rules and regulations...I think that the courts have to be ready to allow general concepts of reasonableness, fairness and common sense to be given more than their usual weight when confronted by claims to the contrary which appear to be based on any strict interpretation and rigid application of the letter of the rules.

These words and a similar practical approach were adopted by Collins J in *Re Horley Town Football Club* [2006] EWHC 2386 where the categories of membership extended to include associate members who enjoyed the same rights as full members except as regarded voting. The judge accepted the proposition that a mere inequality in voting rights would not mean that a category of members should necessarily be excluded altogether from any entitlement to surplus assets of an association upon its dissolution. But he noted that in this case associate membership had been granted merely to ensure compliance with the licensing laws and therefore that 'it would be wholly unrealistic to treat the introduction of associate members by amendment of the Rules as a transfer of the Club's property to them' (at para 127). He concluded that the assets of the club were held on a bare trust for the full members who were entitled to share the assets on a per capita basis (see Luxton [2007] Conv 274).

(3) Gardner ([1992] Conv 41) has pointed out that there appears to be a fundamental difference between the approach in *Re Bucks* and that manifested in, for example, *West Sussex* and *Davis v Richards and Wallington Industries Ltd.* In the former the fate of money on dissolution follows logically from an analysis of the way in which money is originally paid in and, we would argue, beneficially owned, whereas in the latter 'the question of disposing of the money on dissolution . . . [owes] nothing to the intentions with which it was given to begin with' (Gardner at 49). In short it is directed more towards achieving a preferred outcome. In contrast, the contract-holding approach appears to offer an internally consistent legal analysis rooted in a firm foundation of respect for the wishes of donors and members. But this foundation is shaky since at times, in order to validate gifts or bequests under the contract-holding approach, the courts are imputing non-existent intentions to donors (see above, p 904 and Gardner op cit). Thus from this standpoint both approaches can be seen as incorporating a measure of result orientation, under the guise of interpreting people's real intentions.

(4) It will be recalled that central to the approach of Walton J in *Re Bucks* was the conviction, at least for the purposes of determining the ownership of assets, that no distinction should be drawn between different types of unincorporated associations: common legal principles apply to all. In reality, however, unincorporated associations are many and various in both their aims and structures. Where a donation or bequest is genuinely intended to be for the benefit of the members, the contract-holding approach provides a satisfactory outcome for the interested parties, donors and members alike. But consider the perhaps improbable instance of an association receiving a large gift or bequest to further its purposes whereupon the members accede to temptation and purport to dissolve the association and share out the proceeds. As Hackney has observed about a comparable hypothetical example '[the] equal division amongst survivors' doctrine has not yet shown itself capable of inventing rules to meet this situation; formulating the implied term will need some ingenuity' (*Understanding Equity and Trusts* (1987) at p 158). There is no evidence that the situation has arisen in modern times but, were it ever to occur, might not the courts be receptive to any tenable argument that would prevent the members sharing the proceeds even where permitted by the rules of the association? After all, even if, as Green has suggested in relation to gifts and bequests, 'for the donor, the price of validity is unenforceability' ((1980) 43 MLR 460), the courts may baulk at allowing unenforceability to be transmuted into unconscionability. Aside from implying terms into a contract, the courts might even have recourse to the notions of mandate or equitable lien canvassed in *Conservative and Unionist Central Office v Burrell* [1982] 2 All ER 1. The broader conclusion drawn by Hackney is that what he terms a 'remedial resulting trust' solution

is to be preferred in the dissolution cases since 'the resulting trust cases have shown flexibility according to circumstance' (at p 158). Would such a solution (i) grant excessive discretion to the courts in place of clear rules and predictability of outcome, and (ii) constitute a substantial intrusion by the state into the internal affairs of private associations?

(5) Assume that the Law Reform Commission is soliciting opinion on the reform of the law in this area. Draft a memorandum to the Commission commenting, in particular, on the following questions:

(a) Should the courts be given a statutory power to direct a disposal of surplus assets in some manner which the court thinks just?

(b) Should the courts be given the authority to decide that surplus assets should be transferred to 'any association or corporation having amongst its objects any object similar to anything within the objects of the association being dissolved'?

(c) Which, if any, of the following persons or groups should be able to seek an order from the court:

(i) a member or former member of the association;

(ii) any person who has given property or services for the benefit of the association

(iii) an association or corporation such as that named in (b) above; or

(iv) any person who might derive a benefit from the pursuit of the association's objects?

(6) The practical difficulties that can accompany a resulting trust solution to a surplus fund problem are graphically illustrated by *Re Gillingham Bus Disaster Fund* [1958] 1 All ER 37. The case concerned an appeal to establish a memorial fund on behalf of a squad of Royal Marine cadets killed or injured in a road accident. There was a surplus fund of £7,300 and, not being a members' club case, the question was whether the surplus should be held on resulting trust for the donors or go to the Crown as bona vacantia. Harman J decided that the surplus should be held on resulting trust for the donors, and paid into court while an inquiry was conducted to identify the subscribers. He explained his conclusion in terms of legal presumptions about a donor's intention (at 41):

> The reasoning behind this is that the settlor or donor did not part with his money absolutely out and out but only sub modo to the intent that his wishes as declared by the declaration of trust should be carried into effect. When, therefore, this has been done any surplus still belongs to him. This doctrine does not, in my judgment, rest on any evidence of the state of mind of the settlor, for in the vast majority of cases no doubt he does not expect to see his money back: he has created a trust which so far as he can see will absorb the whole of it. The resulting trust arises where that expectation is for some unforeseen reason cheated of fruition, and is an inference of law based on after-knowledge of the event.

However, as was recognised by Goff J in *Re West Sussex Constabulary's Benevolent Fund Trusts* [1970] 1 All ER 544, where sources such as street collections are involved, the inconvenience of being required to trace subscribers is very evident, nowhere more so than in the aftermath of *Re Gillingham* itself. It appears that the donors were never traced and the money languished in the Treasury, uninvested, until in December 1993 it was distributed to 17 survivors of the original accident. They received £400 each (*Guardian* 4 December 1993). Consequently, the courts now appear to favour the opposite presumption about intention, namely that donors who put their money into collecting boxes should be regarded as 'intending to part with their money out and out, absolutely, in all circumstances' (per Goff J at 550). Thus, whereas other donations and legacies will be held on resulting trust, unused money from collections is likely to pass as bona vacantia along with unused proceeds of entertainments and raffles, etc. In the two last-named instances the relationship is one of contract – the entertainment will have been enjoyed, the gamble won or lost – and this leaves no scope for a resulting trust.

(7) As a postscript to the surplus fund problem, it should be noted that in some cases, usually involving a fund for a very small number of beneficiaries, the courts have applied the 'purpose as a motive' reasoning adopted in *Re Sanderson* [1857] 3 K & J 497 as an alternative to a resulting trust solution (see Chapter 5 at p 260). That case itself and others such as *Re Andrew's Trust* [1905] 2 Ch 48 and *Re Abbot Fund Trusts* [1900] 2 Ch 326 have tended principally to be concerned with the destination of surplus moneys where a specified purpose had been completed. The latter two cases involved funds that had been subscribed respectively for the education of the children of a deceased clergyman and for the support of two deaf and dumb ladies. When the respective purposes could no longer be carried out – in *Re Andrew's Trust* the children having completed their education and in *Re Abbot Fund Trusts* the two ladies having died – the alternatives were seen as either a resulting trust to subscribers or a *Re Sanderson* solution. The latter was applied in *Re Andrew's Trust* whereas the resulting trust to subscribers was adopted in *Re Abbot Fund Trusts*. There is little point in attempting to reconcile the decisions in the cases, the different outcomes being convenient not least because the *Re Andrew's Trust* beneficiaries were still living. The cases can be dismissed as turning on their facts as indeed the Court of Appeal acknowledged in the more recent case of *Re Osoba* [1979] 1 WLR 247.

18

An introduction to the law of charity

1. Introduction

Charity is a deep-rooted element in human behaviour. To provide emotional, spiritual or material comfort to those in need is an instinctive aspect of social behaviour, and is reinforced by religious and ethical precepts extolling it as one of the most ennobling forms of conduct (see generally Chesterman *Charities, Trusts and Social Welfare* (1979) ch 1). In the words of a standard legal text (*Tudor on Charities* (9th edn, 2003) p 1) elaborating on the words of Sir William Grant MR in *Morice v Bishop of Durham* (1805)): 'in its widest sense, the word "charity" denotes "all the good affections that men ought to bear towards each other".' And at its best, charity invokes a warm response. There is a touching depth of pity and sympathy shown by the following message sent with a donation in 1966 to the Aberfan Disaster Trust Fund: 'Please use this small amount in any way you wish. I was saving it up for a new coat, O God, I wish I had save [sic] more. Yours sincerely, A Mother' (Nightingale *Charities* (1973) p 178). The Bob Geldof-inspired Band Aid Trust appeared to strike a similar chord when remarkably raising £69m in 1985 in aid of famine relief. And the fund-raising antics displayed on 'Red Nose Day' commonly raise in the region of £50m for Comic Relief to be used for a wide range of charitable purposes. Most striking of all in recent times was the public response to the Disasters Emergency Committee (DEC) Tsunami Appeal in January 2005. Close to £390m was raised via some 2.8–3 million telephone, text, online and postal donations (see www.dec.org.uk).

But there is another aspect to charity: it has never been wholly free from moral ambiguity. Even among primitive tribes, the act of giving has been found to represent an assertion of power over the recipients, who are obliged, unless they can repay, to show some form of deference or obedience to the giver. This is not merely because they may then be more likely to receive a further gift, but because receipt, if not accompanied by a counter-gift or repayment, in some way acknowledges inferiority (see Mauss *Essai sur le Don* (trans Cunnison, 1966)). And we can but wonder about the feelings underlying some charitable gifts that have occurred in our own society: 'A lady is buried in St Bartholomew's churchyard, West Smithfield, who left a fund to be distributed amongst aged women every Good Friday; but she added the puerile and cruel requirement that these infirm crones should pick up their sixpences from the surface of her grave' (Kenny *The True Principles of Legislation with Regard to Property Given for Charitable and Other Public Uses* (1880) p 17).

In medieval times, charity received particular emphasis as a Christian duty. Fulfilment might confer material rewards in this world, whereas neglect was bound to incur hell-fire and damnation in the next. Emphasis of this nature on the element of duty in charity and on the attendant rewards and punishments further blurs its moral quality, for in these terms it appears more like enlightened self-interest than true charity.

Irrespective of its moral implications, charity is also one of the principal means whereby society dispenses material benefits and services among the poor, the destitute, the sick, the aged, the ill-educated and other citizens whom it deems to be in need in some way or other. Philanthropy – being a synonym for the word 'charity' in its popular sense – is defined in Chambers Dictionary as 'charitable regard for one's fellow human beings, especially in the form of benevolence to those in need'. It is not the only social mechanism by which welfare needs are catered for: support within the family, obligations within guilds, clubs and other forms of fraternity, mutual insurance, services provided in the commercial marketplace and the social security benefits and social services provided by the modern welfare state are all other forms of social welfare provision. Moreover, as will be seen later, the distinctions drawn between provision of services by the market, by the state and by the voluntary sector have recently tended to become increasingly blurred (see eg Ware (ed) *Charities and Government* (1989) chs 2 and 4; Hanvey and Philpot (eds) *Sweet Charity* (1996) chs 1 and 3; Dunn (ed) *The Voluntary Sector, the State and the Law* (2000); and generally on current trends and government policy *Partnership in Public Services: An Action Plan for Third Sector Involvement* (Office of the Third Sector, 2006)). But even in its simplest and most direct form – the giving of alms (as it used to be called) or a 'hand-out' (as it is often now called) to a beggar – philanthropy not only has moral implications for the philanthropist but a broader social relevance as a contribution to the welfare requirements of the community.

In the smallest, simplest communities, philanthropic welfare provision can frequently take this simple form of direct almsgiving. In more sophisticated societies, intermediary institutions appear, not simply when philanthropists make gifts posthumously, but also when the scale of their giving or the particular purpose which they wish to achieve is such that straightforward gifts to the objects of their benevolence are impossible or inappropriate. Such an institution is necessary for a whole range of reasons when, for example, a rich philanthropist wishes to bequeath £100,000 to found a laboratory for cancer research. The underlying motivation may be similar to that of simple almsgiving, but because (i) it is a posthumous gift, (ii) it comprises a large sum of money, and (iii) it contemplates specific welfare purposes for which premises, equipment, trained staff, etc, are required, some institutional structure must be established to implement it.

This section of the book is chiefly concerned with the law's role at the conjuncture just identified – ie where philanthropic giving in the interests of social welfare requires some sort of institutional structure to carry out its purposes. A practical explanation why this subject – one apparently more appropriate to a text on welfare provision – appears in this book is simply that within English law the trust is the legal form most widely adopted to provide that institutional structure. But to achieve this prominence the charitable trust had to be substantially modified and in the process has been made the recipient of especially favourable rules by the courts (see section 4(a) below) – illustrating in yet another sphere of social activity the adaptability of the trust device.

The trust has certain strengths in facilitating institutional philanthropy. It fulfils the philanthropist's desire to transfer his property to other persons with some assurance that they or their successors will be bound to apply it in the manner specified in the trust instrument. The creation of a charitable trust by will can also ensure that in some measure the name and the repute of the philanthropist live on after his death: in short, it may indulge a dynastic as well as a philanthropic motivation (cf Friedman (1964) 73 Yale LJ 547 at 547–551). Furthermore, as the example drawn from *Kenny* (above) suggests, the trust-form allows the founder to stamp markedly individualistic desires on the manner in which the property is applied (see also the precise and 'unusual' requirements expressed in *Re Gwyon* [1930] 1 Ch 255 and generally the examples in *Chesterman* (1979) pp 193–197). Indeed where the proclivities of donors are concerned Warburton has sagely noted that '[I]t is unrealistic to expect pure altruism.' The fact that the 'objects of a charitable trust can be tailored closely to the wishes of the donor and protected from amendment' can therefore still be an advantage today when trying to encourage 'those who have been termed "the newly rich" to donate to charity' ('Charitable Trusts: Still Going Strong 400 Years after the Statute of Charitable Uses' in Hayton (ed) *Extending the Boundaries of Trusts and Similar Ring-fenced Funds* (2002) p 174). Of course, not all trusts exemplify eccentric individualism. Many charitable trusts created by individual donors and testators have broadly defined purposes, giving the trustees and those concerned in the administration of the trust considerable leeway in deciding how the trust property can be most usefully applied to meet current needs. Yet despite these strengths the trust-form fails in two major respects to meet the demands which philanthropy may put on it.

In the first place, the theoretical presupposition that a trust is enforced by its beneficiaries is inappropriate because in order to have the range and flexibility which philanthropic endeavour requires a trust in the context of philanthropy must be expressed in terms of purposes. There are therefore no individual beneficiaries who can instigate legal proceedings to enforce the trust. To overcome this weakness, the courts have had to develop a special exemption from the normal principles of trusts law concerning purpose trusts (see section 4(a) below), and there has had to be specified an official 'guardian' of charitable trusts. In theory this is the monarch, in the role of a benevolent 'father of the community', but in practice it is the Crown's first law officer, the Attorney-General. Also it has proved necessary to establish a supervisory agency, the Charity Commission, in the form of a non-ministerial government department accountable to the Home Secretary to oversee the proper administration and enforcement of charitable trusts (see Chapter 20). The powers and responsibilities of the Commission are now to be found primarily in the Charities Act 1993, a consolidating measure (the consolidated legislation being principally the Charities Act 1960 and Pt 1 of the Charities Act 1992). This statutory regulatory framework has been extended and strengthened by the Charities Act 2006, principally by amendment to the 1993 Act.

The second deficiency of the trust-form is that a charitable trust by itself is ill-adapted for 'associated philanthropy'. Consequently two governing legal forms other than the trust are also commonly used nowadays: the unincorporated association and the company limited by guarantee. In contrast to the trust, they are most commonly used in situations where:

(1) a founding group, rather than an individual, both determines the range of activities to be undertaken initially and provides at least part of the original funding;

(2) control of the organisation and its funds is to be vested in a management committee or a board of directors or some such body elected democratically from time to time, rather than in trustees nominated for an indefinite period by the individual founders; and

(3) it is presupposed that both the objectives laid down in the constitution and the broad policies adopted by the controlling body may change from time to time in accordance with the wishes of a changing membership, rather than being marked out by the individual founder for an indefinite period and with the degree of specificity that he chooses.

To this list can be added the consideration that where the charity is likely to be involved in large commercial contracts the limited liability associated with the corporate form has clear advantages as compared with the personal liability of trusteeship (see generally Hill (1993/4) 2 CL & PR at 133–147).

An unincorporated association, as was seen in the previous chapter, is in its legal essence a contract between its members, whereby rules are formulated with regard to its purposes, its management structure, the rights and liabilities of its members inter se, and so on (see generally Warburton *Unincorporated Associations: Law and Practice* (2nd edn, 1992)). In addition, the constitution frequently but not necessarily contains an express declaration that the association's property is to be held on trust for its purposes by designated trustees. A company limited by guarantee (and, indeed, other corporate structures, such as the chartered corporation, which occasionally are specially created for charitable organisations) makes no express use of the trust concept at all, though by operation of law the property may be deemed, in some respects at least, to be held on 'trust' for the corporation's purposes (see *Von Ernst et Cie SA v Inland Revenue Comrs* [1980] 1 WLR 468; Warburton [1984] Conv 112; Picarda *The Law and Practice Relating to Charities* (3rd edn, 1999) pp 407–410; Luxton *The Law of Charities* (2001) pp 489–492). This reinsertion of the trust presents a source of potential confusion for charities that adopt the corporate legal form. It is unclear exactly how duties imposed on directors by company law mesh with duties imposed on trustees by charity law (see Luxton, op cit, pp 16–22). There are also other ways, such as the burden of dual registration with the obligation to submit accounts both to the Registrar of Companies and to the Charity Commission, in which the current corporate forms do not 'fit' the needs of charities. Dissatisfaction with these arrangements prompted the Department of Trade and Industry in its review of company law to suggest a new legal form should be made available to charities (*Modern Company Law for a Competitive Economy: Final Report* (2001) para 4.63 et seq). This recommendation, adopted by the Government, was implemented in the Charities Act 2006, s 34 and Sch 7 of which provide the basic framework for a new legal form of incorporation designed specifically for charities, the Charitable Incorporated Organisation (CIO). Its principal purpose is to enable charities to enjoy the benefits of incorporation such as reduced risk of personal liability without the burden of the dual registration requirement referred to above. In future CIOs will need to register only with the Charity Commission who will in turn oversee their regulation (see Cross [2008] JBL 662–687).

Because governing legal forms other than the trust are thus used by institutions applying property to charitable purposes, the word 'charities' is more accurate than 'charitable trusts' to describe the whole range of such institutions.

Whatever descriptive term is applied, it must be emphasised that 'charitable' has a technical legal meaning quite distinct from its popular meaning. Opinion surveys have consistently shown that public understanding about what is and what is not legally charitable is imperfect, tending towards both over- and under-inclusiveness: commonly cited examples are respectively Amnesty International and Eton College, a mere 7% of respondents to a survey commissioned by the Charity Commission believing Eton to be a charity (see Report of findings of a survey of public trust and confidence in charities (Opinion Leader Research, 2005); see also Brindle in *Society Guardian* 12 February 2003, p 4 citing the findings of an ICM research poll commissioned by the NCVO (National Council for Voluntary Organisations)). Indeed it has been judicially claimed that 'the legal meaning and the popular meaning of the word "charitable" are so far apart that it is necessary almost to dismiss the popular meaning from the mind as misleading before setting out to determine whether a gift is charitable within the legal meaning' (per Lord Wrenbury in *Verge v Somerville* [1924] AC 496 at 502). Despite this somewhat hyperbolic claim, 'charitable' is the nearest equivalent in English law to popular notions such as 'philanthropic' or 'benevolent' or (in the vernacular sense) 'charitable', but it is by no means synonymous with these or indeed with social welfare. The types of purpose which the law has accepted as 'charitable' in this technical sense are too numerous and heterogeneous to summarise in a brief description and we consider this important issue in detail in Chapter 19. It is sufficient to note for the present that until recently charitable purposes were authoritatively classified under four headings: relief of poverty, advancement of education, advancement of religion and other purposes beneficial to the community (*Income Tax Special Purposes Comrs v Pemsel* (1891)) (see below, p 926). This classification gives an impression of logic and clarity, but in reality 'charity' within the law has, as will be seen, taken on a somewhat eccentric life of its own. To a considerable extent this eccentricity remains unaffected by the enactment of a statutory definition of charitable purposes in the Charities Act 2006, ss 1–3. In effect the statutory definition amounts, in our view, to little more than an explicit statement of the categories developed through the extensive case law, albeit with the benefit of some clarification and a modest extension of recognised charitable purposes. Moreover, as will be seen in Chapter 19, the provisions in the Act intended to facilitate further evolution in what the law recognises as charitable purposes largely replicate the approach developed through the case law.

To complete this introductory section it is necessary to refer again to the favourable treatment bestowed upon charities by the law. A significant concession has been the provision by the legislature of fiscal advantages to all charities whatever their legal structure (see section 4(b) below). An important outcome of *Pemsel* was that a majority of the House of Lords rejected the Revenue's argument that a limited definition of 'charitable' should be adopted under tax statutes. Nowadays, the same definition of 'charitable' applies in trusts law (where it chiefly originated), tax law and indeed administrative law (in so far as the registration and supervision of charities by the Charity Commission falls under this branch of the law). The contribution of this merging of the two separate streams of trusts and tax law to the eccentric definition of 'charitable' is considered in Chapter 19.

From what has been said so far it will be apparent that a study of charity law cannot be restricted to trusts law, even as modified by those rules which directly and specifically relate to charitable trusts. It must also take account of the fiscal implications of charitable status, and, venturing clearly into the realm of public administration, include those rules which define the supervisory and regulatory jurisdiction of the Charity Commission and control the granting of subsidies to charities by other government agencies. Yet, notwithstanding these fiscal and public administration considerations, the dominant legal structure remains the trust with the consequence that charity law is left, in Hackney's words, 'looking distinctly like a public law wolf in private law sheep's clothing' ([1981] CLP 113 at 119; and see Freedland 'Charity Law and the Public/Private Distinction' in Mitchell and Moody (eds) *Foundations of Charity* (2000)).

There are two further ways in which a public dimension to charity law and to the activities of some charities can entail legal consequences, both deriving from the Human Rights Act (HRA) 1998 and the incorporation into UK law of the European Convention on Human Rights with effect from 2 October 2000. Under the HRA 1998, s 6(1) it is unlawful for a public authority to act in a way which is incompatible with a Convention right; 'a public authority' includes 'a court or tribunal' (s 6(3)(a)) and 'any person certain of whose functions are functions of a public nature' (s 6(3)(b)). In some circumstances charities themselves may be thought to be exercising 'functions of a public nature' such as providing residential care facilities for the mentally handicapped via a contractual relationship with local authorities. In those circumstances do the acts or omissions of the charity itself come within the scope of the statute? Unsurprisingly the courts are demonstrating considerable caution in determining whether a function is 'of a public nature'. In *Aston Cantlow and Wilmcote v Wallbank* [2003] UKHL 37 Lord Nicholls stated that there was no single test of universal application to be applied in deciding the point: 'Factors to be taken into account included the extent to which in carrying out the relevant function the body was publicly funded or was exercising statutory powers, or was taking the place of central government or local authorities, or was providing a public service' (at [12]; cf *Poplar Housing v Donoghue* [2001] 4 All ER 604 ('public function') and *R v Leonard Cheshire Foundation* [2002] 2 All ER 936 ('private function')). Unfortunately a later decision of the House of Lords in *YL v Birmingham City Council* [2007] UKHL 27 has not resolved the matter ((2007) 66(3) CLJ 485). By a bare 3:2 majority their Lordships held that a private for-profit company providing care home services under a contractual relationship with a resident was not within the scope of s 6(3)(b) even though the funding of the contract was provided by the Council in pursuance of a duty under the National Assistance Act 1948. The majority placed most significance on the contractual and hence private law aspect of the arrangement between the resident and the company whereas the dissenting judges adopted an approach that concentrated more on a consideration of the sort of 'factors' referred to by Lord Nicholls in *Aston Cantlow*. The applicability of s 6(3)(b) to charities or other not-for-profit bodies providing public services under a contractual relationship with a public authority therefore remains uncertain (see generally Craig (2002) 118 LQR 551; Cane (2004) 120 LQR 41; Oliver [2004] PL 329; and Palmer (2007) 66(3) CLJ 559).

Aside from charities themselves exercising public functions, a more obvious manifestation of the influence of the HRA 1998 concerns the interpretation of charity law by the courts and the Charity Commission. Whatever debate there may be about which institutions fall within the definition of 'public authority' in s 6(3)(b) it is clear that the criteria encompass a public body such as the Charity Commission. One practical implication of the HRA 1998 for the role of the Commission and, of course, the courts is that in deciding, for instance, whether a particular purpose is charitable in law under the Charities Act 2006 the Commission or the courts must act in a way that is not incompatible with a Convention right. In particular they must have regard to the implications of relevant Articles of the European Convention, such as Articles 9 (Freedom of thought, conscience and religion) and 10 (Freedom of expression). As these issues are primarily concerned with the definition of charitable purposes they are therefore considered in detail at the appropriate points in Chapter 19.

The rest of this chapter presents background material concerning the history and functions of charities and charity law as well as examining the current significance of legal charitable status for an organisation.

2. Charity, the state and charity law: a background

Gareth Jones has observed that 'Few branches of English law have responded so significantly to social, religious and economic pressures as the law of charity' ((1974) 33 CLJ 63; see also *Chesterman* chs 2–5; Jones *History of the Law of Charity 1532–1827* (1969); Owen *English Philanthropy 1660–1960* (1965); and on charity more generally Davis Smith 'The Voluntary Tradition' in Davis Smith et al (eds) *An Introduction to the Voluntary Sector* (1995) pp 9–39). Plainly the interrelationship of these factors cannot be fully explored here: all that can be attempted is to provide a thumb-nail sketch of the principal developments with particular reference to the role of the state as, simultaneously, supporter and regulator of charitable activity and, eventually, main supplier of welfare provision.

(a) The late Middle Ages to the late eighteenth century

As previously suggested religious precepts, though frequently disregarded in practice, have been influential in prompting philanthropic acts. In the late Middle Ages the most significant social welfare institution was the Roman Catholic Church, with the state, centrally and locally, playing a secondary role. The contributions of wealthy private individuals towards social welfare were therefore chiefly, though not wholly, channelled through ecclesiastical institutions. Furthermore, a philanthropic disposition in a will, whether in specific terms or by means of a clause in general terms (eg that property be applied for 'pious causes'), would be recognised and implemented by the ecclesiastical courts. In a rudimentary way, these courts conferred on such bequests privileges similar to those now enjoyed by charitable trusts: for example, a bequest 'for pious causes' would not fail for uncertainty, and if it were not possible to fulfil the precise purposes stipulated by the testator, a bequest would be applied to similar ones, under what is now called the principle of cy-près. This was thought essential in order to preserve the value inherent in the testator's pious intentions.

By the end of the reign of Elizabeth I three important historical developments – the decline of the Church's influence (in part attributable to corruption and inefficiency), economic dislocation arising principally from agrarian change, and the establishment of a wealthy merchant class – had contributed to a major change in social welfare provision. Both private philanthropy and the state's role were affected.

Tudor philanthropy, strongly influenced by the new merchant class, was marked above all by a substantial trend towards secularisation. The proportion of money and property given or bequeathed to secular welfare purposes such as education or poor relief increased substantially at the expense of gifts and bequests to ecclesiastical institutions. The result was that 'the real volume of money devoted to socially useful purposes increased, since so much of pre-Reformation charity was devoted to such non-utilitarian purposes as church embellishment and masses for the dead' (Stone (1959) *History* vol 44, p 260).

The state, for its part, could not remain indifferent to the vagrancy and threats to social order created by economic dislocation. A wide range of measures bearing upon the living conditions of the poor was adopted. In particular statutory provision for the poor, to be administered by the parish and paid for out of local rates, was introduced in 1572, in the process drawing a distinction between relief for the 'deserving' and correction of the 'undeserving' poor (see Slack *Poverty and Policy in Tudor and Stuart England* (1988)). But this parish responsibility was intended to be residual only. Private philanthropy was expected to meet most of the expense of dealing with the unemployed poor. The Tudor state in its various emanations was therefore eager to facilitate and encourage private philanthropy.

This eagerness manifested itself in a number of ways. The Court of Chancery recognised and enforced the charitable use along with its attendant privileges, helping it to become the predominant legal mechanism for effectuating philanthropic purposes. But a system of Chancery enforcement had its weaknesses (*Jones* pp 19–21). Even though the Attorney-General came to be recognised as a 'representative plaintiff' to enforce charitable trusts, the need for administrative machinery to police them became apparent. A policy of reliance on private philanthropy would have been seriously undermined if misuse or misappropriation of charity property could not be detected or remedied. Accordingly, when comprehensive poor law codes were enacted in 1597 and 1601 in response to severe economic crises and the resulting fears of social upheaval, there was included in each of them a statute entitled the Statute of Charitable Uses, providing for commissioners to be appointed to investigate a wide range of issues relating to charity administration, particularly misappropriations of charity property. The system appears to have been successful for some time, but it fell into disuse by the late eighteenth century because of both the reduced importance attached to charities and the emergence of an alternative Chancery enforcement procedure – the action brought by the Attorney-General at the instance of a private citizen, called a 'relator' (see *Chesterman* pp 37–39).

The 1601 statute was to be of major importance in the law of charities for another reason. The preamble listed certain 'charitable and godlie uses' which marked the limits of the statute's operation and came in due course to form the basis of the modern legal definition of 'charitable purpose'. The preamble is as follows:

> Whereas lands . . . chattels, money . . . have been . . . given . . . by sundry . . . well disposed persons: Some for relief of aged, impotent, and poor people, some for maintenance of sick and maimed soldiers and mariners, schools of learning, free schools, and scholars in universities; some for repair of bridges, ports, havens, causeways, churches, seabanks and highways; some for education and preferment of orphans; some for or towards relief, stock or maintenance for houses of correction; some for marriages of poor maids; some for supportation, aid and help of young tradesmen, handicraftsmen, and persons decayed; and others for relief or redemption of prisoners or captives, and for aid or ease of any poor inhabitants concerning payment of fifteens, setting out of soldiers and other taxes; which lands [etc] . . . have not been employed according to the charitable intent of the givers . . . by reason of frauds, breaches of trust, and negligence . . .

This list includes a wide variety of purposes of which some are obviously closely integrated with the new poor law – 'relief of aged . . . and poor people', 'education . . . of orphans' – whereas others are less apparently related to this – 'maintenance of . . . schools of learning . . . and scholars in universities', 'repair of bridges, ports . . . churches . . . and highways'. Yet a distinguished Chancery lawyer of the time, Francis Moore, argued that whatever the literal wording of the preamble, it was intended to be almost wholly confined to purposes which would operate to the benefit of the public as a whole – in particular, the parish ratepayer – by alleviating poverty and thereby reducing the burden of poor rates. In short 'public benefit was the key to the statute and poverty its principal manifestation' (*Jones* p 27).

During the seventeenth and much of the eighteenth century, although philanthropy continued to bear the brunt of poor relief, state support for charity was less evident. We have already mentioned the deterioration in enforcement procedures that occurred in the eighteenth century. A further manifestation of reduced legislative enthusiasm for charity, at least when confronted with a conflict between the claims of charity and those of family interest in land, is to be found in the Mortmain and Charitable Uses Act of 1736 which attempted to limit the devising of land to charitable purposes by specifying elaborate formal requirements (see Stebbings (1991) 12 J Legal History 7). Whether the Act actually prejudiced charities is uncertain (see *Owen* p 72). It did, however, have an important indirect effect on the legal definition of charity because several somewhat anti-clerical decisions under the Act broadened the concept of 'charitable' (see below).

(b) From the Industrial Revolution to the emerging welfare state

The next major developments in the law and practice of charity were prompted by the social dislocation brought about by the rise of industrial capitalism in the late eighteenth and nineteenth centuries. Tawney has argued that early in this new age of economic expansion it seemed to many, influenced by the economic doctrine of laissez-faire and the Malthusian theory of population, 'that the greatest of evils is idleness, that the poor are the victims not of circumstances but of their own "idle, irregular and wicked courses", that the truest charity is not to enervate them by relief, but so to reform their character that relief may be unnecessary' (*Religion and the Rise of Capitalism* (1926) p 238, cited in the *Report of the Committee on the Law and Practice Relating to Charitable Trusts* (Nathan Report) (Cmnd 8710, 1952) para 40). From this moralistic base there re-emerged in the nineteenth century a welfare system premised on distinguishing 'the deserving' from the 'undeserving' poor.

The enactment of the Poor Law Amendment Act 1834 re-established a deterrent system of state poor law, imposing harsh conditions on those who sought relief. (See generally Checkland and Checkland (eds) *The Poor Law Report of 1834* (1974); Fraser (ed) *The New Poor Law in the Nineteenth Century* (1976).) But the role of the state as a provider of poor relief was intended to be subsidiary only. The mutual aid provided by the many working men's Friendly and Co-operative Societies that flourished around the middle of the century was one important source of support. Important though these organisations were they tended to involve and benefit predominantly members of the skilled working class. To philanthropy was left the task of meeting the social welfare needs of others of the 'deserving' poor. The Victorian social conscience responded to the call. Charities proliferated and the resources applied to philanthropy significantly exceeded state expenditure under the poor law. But a strong moralistic element persisted, reflected in the existence of charities specifically directed to encouraging such virtues as self-reliance, sobriety and frugality, and in the campaign to discourage indiscriminate relief giving by charities (see eg Roberts 'Head versus Heart?' in Cunningham and Innes (eds) *Charity, Philanthropy and Reform* (1998) ch 3; and Daunton (ed) *Progress and Poverty* (1995)). The latter was part of a broader campaign in which the Charity Organisation Society (COS), a famous voluntary organisation established in 1869, took the lead. The campaign's objects were to uphold the separation of the two spheres, state and private philanthropy, and, furthermore, vigorously to oppose the statutory inroads into social welfare that occurred in the late nineteenth and early twentieth centuries.

The sort of activities just described, with their attendant strain of moral and social indoctrination, lend weight to a thesis that social control was a potent driving force behind philanthropic activity. But both in terms of methods and purposes Victorian philanthropy was much more than a tale of moralism and social control. (See *Owen* chs 4–18, but cf Harrison 'Philanthropy and the Victorians' (1966) Victorian Studies vol 9 at 353; Prochaska 'Philanthropy' in Thompson (ed) *The Cambridge Social History of Britain 1750–1950* (1990) vol 3; on the social control controversy see Thompson 'Social Control in Victorian Britain' (1989) Economic History Review 189–208, Rozin *The Rich and Poor: Jewish Philanthropy and Social Control in Nineteenth-Century London* (1999); Donajgrodski (ed) *Social Control in Nineteenth Century Britain* (1977); and a critical review by Weiner (1978) 12 J Social History 314–320.) Campaigning and lobbying for all manner of causes, some such as anti-slavery being highly contentious, became a significant feature of voluntary activity (see eg Jones in Daunton (ed) *Charity, Self-Interest and Welfare in the English Past* (1996) ch 3). Also the range and scale of giving was huge and nineteenth-century philanthropy contributed massively, for instance, to the establishment and upkeep of voluntary hospitals and (notably towards the end of the century) medical research. Indeed many of today's most prominent charities were founded in this period (eg YMCA (1844); Dr Barnardo's Homes (1866); NSPCC (1884); National Trust (1895)). But despite the volume of giving, organised philanthropy proved inadequate to resolve the enormous social welfare problems of large and growing industrial cities and towns, although Owen suggests that 'both by its successes and abysmal failures, philanthropy helped to reveal the real outlines of the problem' (*Owen* p 597).

In the nineteenth century two important developments also occurred in the definition of charity, although neither appears to have been strongly influenced by prevailing social policy considerations. First, the legal definition of charitable purpose, based upon the 1601 preamble, became firmly entrenched within the law of trusts. In *Morice v Bishop of Durham* (1804) 9 Ves 399 (see also Chapter 5) a testatrix bequeathed her residuary personalty on trust to her executor, the Bishop of Durham, 'for such objects of benevolence and liberality as [he], in his own discretion, should most approve of'. The court ruled that these purposes were not charitable because they were not specifically listed in the preamble nor 'by analogies deemed within its spirit and intendment' (at 405; affd (1805) 10 Ves 522 at 541). In so far as any policy considerations underlay the curtailment of the concept of 'charitable' effected by *Morice v Bishop of Durham* they derived from contemporary judicial hostility to bequests for charitable purposes which threatened to deprive the testator's family of their 'rightful due'.

Paradoxically, however, this narrowing of the definition contrasted with the decisions under the Mortmain and Charitable Uses Act 1736 which invalidated certain dispositions of land to charities by widening the 'public benefit' element in the definition. Important cases in which gifts were struck down under the Act by virtue of a broad interpretation of 'charitable' include *Townley v Bedwell* (1801) 6 Ves 194 (devise to establish botanical gardens), *Thornton v Howe* (1862) 31 Beav 14 (a key decision on 'advancement of religion') and *Tatham v Drummond* (1864) 4 De GJ & Sm 484 (a key decision on animal charities).

It would seem also that the cases based on the 1736 Act assisted in distorting significantly the preamble's definition of 'charitable' in its transmission to the charity law of the nineteenth century and of modern times. This distortion affected the concept of 'public benefit'. It was argued earlier (see p 922) that, according to the intentions of the Elizabethan legislature and the authoritative contemporary interpretation, the 1601 preamble's concept of 'charitable' contained a 'public benefit' requirement calling for benefit to the poor, or at least to rich and poor alike. Without this, the Act's objective of lightening the burden of parish poor relief and other parochial obligations on ratepayers would not be achieved. But this aspect of 'public benefit' does not appear in a number of cases under the Mortmain Act, which virtually equated 'charitable' with 'public' purposes. For example, in *Trustees of the British Museum v White* (1826) 2 Sim & St 594 at 596, Leach VC specifically rejected the argument that because charity involved 'something in the nature of a relief' the Museum was not charitable. It accordingly became possible in cases decided with reference to the preamble to maintain that 'public benefit' existed where any section of the community, not specifically the poor or the rich and the poor together, derived benefit.

The implications of this interpretation of 'public benefit' became apparent as early as 1827 in *A-G v Lord Lonsdale* (1827) 1 Sim 105. A bequest of personalty upon trust to establish a school for educating 'the sons of gentlemen' (whether or not fees were to be paid is not stated in the report) was held charitable and entitled to cy-près application on the simple reasoning that advancement of education was one of the categories of purpose listed in the preamble. Despite an earlier decision that the preamble covered free schools only (*A-G v Hewer* (1700) 2 Vern 387), Leach VC simply said: 'The institution of a school for the sons of gentlemen is not, in popular language, a charity; but in the view of the statute of Elizabeth, all schools are so to be considered . . .' ((1827) 1 Sim 105 at 109).

The second development came in 1891 with the 4:2 majority decision in *Pemsel's* case to endorse the general law definition of charitable purposes first advanced in *Morice v Bishop of Durham* and extend it into a new arena – that of central government taxation. All charities had enjoyed relief from income taxation since the tax was introduced in 1799. In 1863 William Gladstone fiercely attacked the scope of the relief, seeking unsuccessfully to restrict it to hospitals, colleges and almshouses ((1863) 3 *Hansard* 170 at 200–247; see also Owen *English Philanthropy 1660–1960* (1965) pp 331–332). Notwithstanding the parliamentary setback the Inland Revenue sought to reduce the scope of the tax exemptions by removing them from religious and educational trusts, an approach supported in some degree in Scotland by the Court of Session in *Baird's Trustees v Lord Advocate* (1888) 15 Sess Cas (4th series) 682. This Inland Revenue initiative not only ultimately triggered the *Pemsel* litigation but also prompted a protest from *The Times* that the Commissioners were usurping a function of Parliament (see *Owen* p 334). This sentiment was to find an echo in the judgment of Lord Macnaghten in *Pemsel* (see below). What is most striking, however, is that although the judgments in *Pemsel* are long and learned, and include two dissents, the implications of the decision in terms of fiscal policy were scarcely discussed (see *Chesterman* pp 58–62; Paterson (1974) 1 Br J Law and Society 118 at 122). The *Pemsel* decision is much more than a historical curiosity. It entrenched in the law a symbiosis of charitable status and tax relief. That relationship, as will be seen in Chapter 19, continues to provoke academic debate and some judicial disagreement about the influence that the entitlement to tax reliefs has had and should have on the development of charity law. It is also at the heart of political controversy over the granting of charitable status with its accompanying tax advantages to certain private schools and hospitals.

Income Tax Special Purposes Comrs v Pemsel [1891] AC 531

Under a trust deed executed in 1813, land in Middlesex was conveyed to trustees on trust, inter alia, to pay one-half of the rents and profits 'for the general purposes of maintaining, supporting and advancing the missionary establishments among heathen nations of the Protestant Episcopal Church, known as Unitas Fratrum, or United Brethren'.

Until 1886, the Income Tax Commissioners granted tax exemptions to the trustees in respect of this trust, under an exemption provision in the Income Tax Act 1842 applying to the rents and profits of lands vested in trustees for 'charitable purposes', so far as the same were applied to charitable purposes. In 1886, the Commissioners withdrew the exemption. The trustees then sought a writ of mandamus to compel the Commissioners to grant it. They failed at first instance, but succeeded in the Court of Appeal. The appeal of the Commissioners to the House of Lords was dismissed by a majority of 4:2.

Lord Macnaghten: . . . That according to the law of England a technical meaning is attached to the word 'charity', and to the word 'charitable' in such expressions as 'charitable uses', 'charitable trusts', or 'charitable purposes', cannot, I think, be denied. The Court of Chancery has always regarded with peculiar favour those trusts of a public nature which, according to the doctrine of the Court derived from the piety of early times, are considered to be charitable . . .

Of all words in the English language bearing a popular as well as a legal signification I am not sure that there is one which more unmistakably has a technical meaning in the strictest sense of the term, that is a meaning clear and distinct, peculiar to the law as understood and administered in this country, and not depending upon or coterminous with the popular or vulgar use of the word . . .

How far then, it may be asked, does the popular meaning of the word 'charity' correspond with its legal meaning? 'Charity' in its legal sense comprises four principal divisions: trusts for the relief of poverty; trusts for the advancement of education; trusts for the advancement of religion; and trusts for other purposes beneficial to the community, not falling under any of the preceding heads. The trusts last referred to are not the less charitable in the eye of the law, because incidentally they benefit the rich as well as the poor, as indeed, every charity that deserves the name must do either directly or indirectly. It seems to me that a person of education, at any rate, if he were speaking as the Act is speaking with reference to endowed charities, would include in the category educational and religious charities, as well as charities for the relief of the poor. Roughly speaking, I think he would exclude the fourth division. Even there it is difficult to draw the line. A layman would probably be amused if he were told that a gift to the Chancellor of the Exchequer for the benefit of the nation was a charity. Many people, I think, would consider a gift for the support of a lifeboat a charitable gift, though its object is not the advancement of religion, or the advancement of education, or the relief of the poor. And even a layman might take the same favourable view of a gratuitous supply of pure water for the benefit of a crowded neighbourhood. But after all, this is rather an academical discussion. If a gentleman of education, without legal training, were asked what is the meaning of 'a trust for charitable purposes', I think he would most probably reply, 'That sounds like a legal phrase. You had better ask a lawyer' . . .

With the policy of taxing charities I have nothing to do. It may be right, or it may be wrong; but speaking for myself, I am not sorry to be compelled to give my voice for the respondent. To my mind it is rather startling to find the established practice of so many years suddenly set aside by an administrative department of their own motion, and after something like an assurance given to Parliament that no change would be made without the interposition of the Legislature. In 1865 the Treasury communicated to Parliament the fact that they had come to the conclusion that the subject was 'one which should be reserved to be dealt with by the Legislature, and that in the meantime the practice which has hitherto prevailed should be followed'. For such a conclusion, even if the claim of the Crown had been originally well-founded, there would be much to be said. The Legislature declaring the law can at the same time grant immunity for the past; but a change of practice, established by judicial decision only, would leave the bulk of the charitable foundations in this country exposed to liabilities appalling in amount.

I am, therefore, glad to find that the claim of the Crown is based on what seems to me to be a very superficial view of the meaning of the Legislature, and my opinion is that the appeal should be dismissed with costs.

Lords Watson and Herschell delivered concurring speeches. Lord Morris agreed.

Lord Bramwell (dissenting): The question that remains is whether lands with a trust to apply income for the purpose of 'maintaining, supporting and advancing the missionary establishment among heathen nations of the Protestant Episcopal Church known by the name of Unitas Fratrum or United Brethren', are 'for charitable purposes' within 5 & 6 Vict c 35, s 61. It is said that they are on two grounds; first, that the natural meaning of the words 'charitable purposes' includes such a trust; secondly, that, whether it does or not, 'charitable purposes' have a technical meaning, and include everything that would have been administered in Chancery under 43 Eliz c 4, or which had been administered, as I understand it, by the Court of Chancery, upon the same principle, before the passing of that Act.

It is somewhat remarkable that some of the opinions in favour of the respondent are so on the first ground, and think the other wrong; whilst others are in their favour on the second ground and not on the first. Some are against them on both my Lord Chancellor, Lord Coleridge, the Scotch Judges in *Baird's* case (15 Sess Cas 4th Series, 682), and I must add myself.

I hold that the conversion of heathens and heathen nations to Christianity or any other religion is not a charitable purpose. That it is benevolent, I admit. The provider of funds for such a purpose doubtless thinks that the conversion will make the converts better and happier during this life, with better hope hereafter. I dare say this donor did so. So did those who provided the faggots and racks which were used as instruments of conversion in times gone by. I am far from suggesting that the donor would have given funds for such a purpose as torture; but if the mere good intent makes the purpose charitable, then I say the intent is the same in the one case as in the other. And I believe in all cases of propagandism there is mixed up a wish for the prevalence of those opinions we entertain, because they are ours.

But what is a *charitable* purpose? Whatever definition is given, if it is right as far as it goes, in my opinion this trust is not within it. I will attempt one. I think a charitable purpose is where assistance is given to the bringing up, feeding, clothing, lodging, and education of those who from poverty, or comparative poverty, stand in need of such assistance: see per Lord Coleridge (22 QBD 301). That a temporal benefit is meant, being money, or having a money value. This definition is probably insufficient. It very likely would not include some charitable purposes, though I cannot think what, and include some not charitable, though also I cannot think what; but I think it substantially correct, and that no well-founded amendment of it would include the purposes to which this fund is dedicated . . .

Lord Bramwell then rejected the view that 'charitable purposes' had an artificial meaning, and concluded that not every purpose listed in the preamble was a 'charitable purpose'.

. . . some cases within the 43 Eliz could not, according to any reasonable definition of the words, be said to be 'charitable purposes'. I take, for example, 'schools of learning' not limited to the poor, 'repair of sea-banks', 'relief, & c, for houses of correction', which is in aid of rates not paid by the poor. So, also, a bequest for keeping chimes in repair has been held to be within the statute (*Turner v Ogden*) perhaps because causing a lessening of church rates, if, indeed, they could have been applied to such a purpose, which I do not know. So, also, a bequest upon trust to pay, divide or dispose thereof for the benefit or advancement of societies, subscriptions or purposes having regard to the glory of God in the spiritual welfare of his creatures: *Townsend v Carus*. So, also, a school for the sons of gentlemen: *A-G v Lord Lonsdale*. Let it not be supposed that I find any fault with Courts of Equity for calling every trust within the statute of Elizabeth a charity. It was not strictly accurate, but was concise, and saved a circumlocution . . .

Lord Halsbury LC also delivered a dissenting speech.

Public policy considerations were more explicitly to the fore where charity supervision was involved. In view of the role accorded to charity, it is hardly surprising that eighteenth-century apathy with regard to supervision gave way to pressures for a significant degree of state intervention. A Royal Commission, chaired by a Whig reformer, Lord Brougham, amassed a vast amount of evidence between 1819 and 1840 to the effect that a large proportion of the country's many charitable endowments were of little or no practical use. This was partly a result of fraud, but mostly of mismanagement in the investment and application of funds. Brougham's report provided the factual basis for the enactment of the Charitable Trusts Acts 1853, 1855 and 1860. These established for the first time a central and permanent, although understaffed, Charity Commission, charged with supervising the administration of charitable endowments (see generally *Owen* pp 183–208; Thompson *The Charity Commission and the Age of Reform* (1978)). But no political unanimity existed about the desirability or extent of state supervision and the legislation contained three important limitations. First, only endowed charities were covered. Second, in response to Tory objections based on the need to preserve trustee autonomy, the Commissioners could not intervene without the consent of a majority of trustees where a charity's annual income from property exceeded £50. Third, charities subject to the jurisdiction could generally not be 'modernised' by a cy-près scheme unless there was a wholesale 'failure' – the original purposes had to be impossible or wholly impracticable – and even then only a minor re-diverting of the original aims was usually possible. In short, the Commissioners' powers were at their strongest in the matter of 'tidying up' the innumerable small trusts which were of little or no use. When all the limitations affecting the Commissioners' exercise of powers under the Charitable Trusts Acts are considered in conjunction, their overall impact on the use of charity resources in the country was inevitably slight.

The nineteenth century, therefore, handed on to the age which followed it a structure of charity law having the following key features:

(1) rules of equity whereby express charitable trusts enjoyed certain privileges (as to certainty of objects, enforcement by a state functionary, perpetuity and alteration of objects in case of 'failure') when compared with non-charitable trusts;

(2) a permanent Charity Commission empowered, subject to significant limitations, to supervise the management of charitable trusts and to remodel their purposes when they proved impossible or impracticable;

(3) an important fiscal exemption for *all* charitable organisations (not merely charitable trusts) – ie the exemption from income tax; and

(4) a definition of 'charitable' which was based on the 1601 preamble (though differing significantly from the Elizabethan interpretation of 'public benefit') and was applicable to each of the three specific issues referred to in (1), (2) and (3).

This framework of charity law emerged in the late nineteenth century against a background of far-reaching changes in the mechanisms of social welfare within British society. As already stated, the funds and energies of private philanthropists and charity workers proved inadequate, particularly in the larger cities, to deal with the massive incidence of poverty, disease and homelessness, so graphically captured by Sara Wise in *The Blackest Streets: The Life and Death of a Victorian Slum* (2008). By the First World War, the state had taken major steps towards assuming the predominant role in welfare provision, thereby relegating philanthropy to the position of 'junior partner in the welfare firm' (see *Owen* ch 19).

3. Charity in a welfare state

(a) New roles for philanthropic organisations

After 1914 the most important single factor affecting the activities of private philanthropy in England was the massive growth in state welfare. In major fields of welfare provision, such as income maintenance, education, housing and medical care, the process of state take-over which had begun in the late nineteenth and early twentieth centuries continued more or less unchecked until the mid-1970s. The implementation of major social welfare changes immediately after the Second World War (eg Education Act 1944, National Health Service Act 1946, National Assistance Act 1948) confirmed philanthropy's role as 'junior partner' in all major areas of welfare provision. When the growing effect of employer-sponsored welfare provision, what Richard Titmuss called occupational welfare (*Essays on 'The Welfare State'* (1958)), is included it is not surprising that institutionalised private philanthropy became relegated to a subsidiary role in welfare provision. A renewal of official interest in voluntary action and voluntary organisations, prompted initially in the mid-1970s by the economic pressures to restrict public expenditure, especially spending on social welfare, has yet to alter this balance significantly, at least as regards *financing* of provision. A different picture is emerging as regards the *delivery* of services.

These social and economic developments have prompted numerous reassessments during the last 60 years of the tasks which private philanthropy should be fulfilling. Two important studies following the Second World War (Beveridge *Voluntary Action* (1948); *Report of the Committee on the Law and Practice Relating to Charitable Trusts* (the Nathan Report) (Cmd 8710, 1952)) defined these tasks as follows: pioneering new areas of welfare provision, collaborating in various ways with state agencies of social welfare and acting in appropriate circumstances as a critic of state welfare. Particular emphasis was laid on this last activity in the Nathan Report:

Para 5.5. Some of the most valuable activities of voluntary societies consist, however, in the fact that they are able to stand aside from and criticise state action, or inaction, in the interests of the inarticulate man-in-the-street. This may take the form of helping individuals to know and obtain their rights. It also consists in a more general activity of collecting data about some point where the shoe seems to pinch or a need remains unmet. The general machinery of democratic agitation, deputations, letters to the Press, questions in the House, conferences and the rest of it, may then be put into operation in order to convince a wider public that action is necessary.

In fact for the first decade and a half of the welfare state private philanthropy seemed 'to [be] marking time' (Wolfenden Committee *The Future of Voluntary Organisations* (1978) p 20). But in the 1960s and 1970s new forms of voluntary organisation sprang up, with a significantly different emphasis to existing activity.

M Brenton *The Voluntary Sector in British Social Services* (1985) p 36

The alternative organisations, groups and movements that grew up in the 1960s and 1970s were in many ways the by-product of the public sector welfare system. They were as much a reaction of frustration to the deficiencies, size and inaccessibility of the state welfare apparatus as they were the result of pressures to participate and protest thrown up by a wider process of social and cultural change. They also reflected the emergence and recognition of new social need, such as that produced by the disintegrating effects of slum clearance policies, or the rising rates of divorce and growing numbers of single-parent families. Many of the pressure-group activities that evolved were aimed at forcing change directly in public policies [eg Child Poverty Action Group (1965); Shelter (1966)]; many advice and information services were developed to help people find their way around the welfare state; many of the mutual aid and self-help activities that emerged were a signal of gaps in state provision [eg Gingerbread (1970) for single parents].

These new or, perhaps more accurately, resurrected roles (cf the nineteenth-century tradition of mutual aid and the campaigning activities of the Charity Organisation Society) were reflected in the analysis of the Wolfenden Report, a large-scale study of the work of voluntary organisations. This summarised their relationship to state welfare as follows (*The Future of Voluntary Organisations* (1978) p 43):

A voluntary organisation can act in the following ways in relation to the statutory system:

As a pressure group seeking changes in the policy and provision of other organisations.

As the pioneer of new services with the intention that if successful they should be adopted more widely either by statutory or by voluntary agencies.

As the provider of services complementary or additional or alternative to statutory services.

As the sole provider of services.

The Report itself did not advocate any fundamental change in the role of the state although 'in a sense it asks the state to move over and give more space to voluntary endeavour' (*Brenton* p 49; see generally Gladstone *Voluntary Action in a Changing World* (1979); Hadley and Hatch *Social Welfare and the Failure of the State* (1982)). But it can be seen with the benefit of hindsight that the Wolfenden Committee was operating in 1978 within a political agenda that was in the process of being transformed. Indeed, after Wolfenden the emergent shift in the economic and, as importantly, the ideological climate became more pronounced. In particular the taken-for-granted role of the state was challenged by a strong reaffirmation of a view from the 'Radical Right' that this role should be minimised both for individualist philosophical reasons and for economic considerations (see *Brenton* pp 139–46; Lawrence (1982) 2 Critical Social Policy at 14; Le Grand and Robinson (eds) *Privatisation and the Welfare State* (1984); Johnson *Reconstructing the Welfare State: A Decade of Change 1980–1990* (1990); Pierson *Dismantling the Welfare State? Reagan, Thatcher and the Politics of Retrenchment* (1994)). It was argued that social welfare needs should primarily be met by the family, by the market, and by voluntary organisations, with the state reverting to the role of gap-filler. In short what appeared to be envisaged under this approach was a shift away from a modern or social democratic welfare state towards a residual welfare state, ie state provision as a safety net only (see eg Abrahamson *Social Policy in Europe Towards 2000* (1991)). Apart from ideological justifications it may be argued that voluntary welfare is cheaper than state welfare because it is less bureaucratic and relies on volunteer or low-paid workers (particularly women).

The shift in the role of the state became most evident with the changes, less apocalyptic than initially envisaged, introduced during the third Thatcher administration (1987 onwards). In practice the state moved more towards being a purchaser of services from the private and voluntary sectors in a quasi-market system rather than being a sole provider (see eg Deakin in Davis Smith et al (eds) *An Introduction to the Voluntary Sector* (1995) ch 2; Taylor (1996) 8 Social Policy Review 40 at 40–62; Rhodes (1996) 44 Political Studies 652 and Lewis (1999) 10(3) Voluntas 255).

The terminology deployed to justify an enhanced role of this nature for the voluntary sector has altered slightly under subsequent Labour governments but arguably this reflects a change of emphasis; the underlying economic, ideological and political rationales remain largely intact. These rationales can loosely be summarised as those of economic efficiency, social cohesion and the enhancement of a participative democracy. One practical consequence of this almost consensual political understanding about the role of the voluntary sector is that charities remain a preferred vehicle for the delivery of many social services whether alone or in partnership with the public sector. Indeed the significant development to date has been the accentuation of the division mentioned previously between *financing* and *delivery* of services (see generally Tony Blair *The Third Way: New Politics for the New Century* (1998); *The Role of the Voluntary and Community Sector in Service Delivery: A Cross Cutting Review* (HM Treasury, September 2002); *Partnership in Public Services: An Action Plan for Third Sector Involvement* (Office of the Third Sector, 2006); *The Future Role of the Third Sector in Social and Economic Regeneration: Final Report* (HM Treasury and the Cabinet Office, Cm 7189, 2007)).

Advocacy of the increasing involvement of charities in the delivery of activities such as training provision and various social services is not solely a matter of economics in the sense of offering, in the opinion of its proponents, a perceived more efficient delivery of services and a corresponding reduction of public expenditure. There is a supporting theme, articulated with increasing frequency, to the effect that creating 'a space' for involvement of the voluntary sector in this way has broader benefits for civil society. The notion of a 'space' for the voluntary sector to operate within a model of civil society comprising the state, the market and the informal (or personal and family) sectors was adopted by a 1996 Report from a Commission on the Future of the Voluntary Sector chaired by Professor Deakin (*Meeting the Challenge of Change: Voluntary Action into the 21st Century* (1996); and see Evers (1995) 6(2) Voluntas 159–182). The notion of the voluntary sector as an essential element in a pluralist society had also been a significant feature of the Wolfenden Committee analysis. Indeed Mulgan and Landry, drawing an analogy with Adam Smith's use of the invisible hand metaphor of economic theory, argued in an influential 1995 publication that voluntary action with its potential to enhance social inclusion was one of the facets of human activity that helped to constitute 'the other invisible hand' without which a free society cannot function successfully (*The Other Invisible Hand: Remaking Charity for the 21st Century* (Demos 1995, Paper 15) at pp 14–21; see also O'Halloran *Charity Law and Social Inclusion* (2007) ch 2). These ideas or themes were clearly articulated in the Deakin Report, whose broad brief was 'to provide a clear vision of the role of the voluntary sector in England over the next decade'. The Report summarised the role of voluntary organisations in civil society in the following way:

> 1.3.32 Civil Society . . . is made up of the state, the market and the informal sector (the world of personal and family relations), each with a distinctive set of rationales and values. Within this triangular 'force field' there is a public space, inside which voluntary organisations exist and work.
>
>   1.3.33 This model presents the voluntary sector as performing a positive, active role, not simply doing whatever doesn't fit into any other sector. . . .
>
>   1.3.35 . . . The essence is that the actions taken by voluntary and community organisations are contributions made neither commercially (for their economic value) nor compulsorily (by conscription or taxation). In order for the space for voluntary activity to be as substantial and productive as possible, society must esteem both the values associated with these contributions and what is achieved through them – the public benefit, to adopt a term from charity law. And in this process of change, voluntary organisations can also function as the essential cohesive element (the glue, if you like) that helps to hold society more tightly together.

Emphasis on this notion of social cohesion finds a clear echo within many contemporary policy statements of the government. In the *Compact on Relations between Government and the Voluntary and Community Sector in England* (Cm 4100, 1998), for instance, the contribution of the voluntary and community sector is described as 'fundamental to the development of a democratic, socially inclusive society' (at para 5).

The renewed emphasis in contemporary social policy debates on mutual aid and on the voluntary sector, the adoption of a more prominent role for that sector both as critic of inadequacies in state welfare provision and increasingly as contractual partner in providing services, the shifts of philanthropic activity into new areas all pose questions for legal regulation. To an extent the Charities Act 2006 addresses some matters such as making more explicit and accessible to the layperson the definition of charitable purposes (see Chapter 19) and modernising the regulatory powers of the Charity Commission (see Chapter 20). Other issues such as the appropriateness of the same definition of 'charitable' continuing to apply in tax law as well as in charity law have been left unaltered and remain a matter of controversy. Aside from the still divisive position of fee-charging private schools and hospitals enjoying the tax reliefs accompanying charitable status, the fiscal question is particularly pertinent where a charity is competing with commercial organisations to deliver a contracted-out public service: does the charity's favoured fiscal status give it an unfair competitive advantage? Another contentious aspect of charity law left unresolved by the Charities Act 2006 is how far charities should be able to campaign for legal and social change without endangering their charitable status. These are questions that have generated wide-ranging analyses and critiques, and to which we return in the next two chapters.

To complete our picture of philanthropic activity in the welfare state we need to consider next the size of the charitable sector and the sources of its finance. First, however, a cautionary note of explanation about terminology is apposite here. 'Voluntary sector', 'not-for-profit sector', 'third sector' and 'charity' are *not* synonyms. Nevertheless a large proportion of voluntary sector organisations, but by no means all, are charitable at law. As will be seen in Chapter 19 the dividing line can be contentious, particularly where organisations fall outside the ambit of charity because their purposes are deemed too political or because they are viewed as mutual benefit organisations.

(b) The demography of charity

(1) The size of the charity sector

The relegation of philanthropic activity to a subsidiary role did not and has not had the effect of stifling the voluntary spirit. At the present time, charities are abundant and on the increase. In 1952, the Nathan Report noted (para 103) that there were about 110,000 charitable trusts known to the Charity Commissioners and the Ministry of Education. As at 31 March 2008 the number of 'charities' (this term includes both charitable trusts and charitable organisations established otherwise than as trusts) registered with the Charity Commission had grown to 190,387 of which 21,054 were subsidiaries or branches of other charities. This means that there are 169,333 'main' charities on the Register (www.charity-commission.gov.uk/registeredcharities/factfigures/). In addition there are a substantial but uncertain number of unregistered charities, estimated to number at least 40,000 (see Hedley in Davis Smith et al *An Introduction to the Voluntary Sector* (1995) ch 17, but cf a 1987 estimate of 110,000 (Home Office and HM Treasury *Efficiency Scrutiny of the Supervision of Charities* (1987) Annex E)). At present some 5,000–6,000 charities are newly registered each year, although by no means all of these would be newly formed. Indeed the increase in total registration since 1992 largely reflects the fact that as from 1993 most charities with an annual income amounting to more than £1,000 were required to register. The Charities Act 2006, s 3A(2)(d) has increased this figure to £5,000, thereby relieving more small charities from this requirement. The number of recorded cases of charities being removed from the register in each year has also increased (5,073 in 2007) as the Charity Commission becomes more successful in identifying charities which have ceased to operate or been wound up. By way of comparison only about 3,500 charities in total were removed from the register between 1961 and 1985.

These figures provide an overall snapshot view, and do not reveal one by-now quite long-standing trend: that is the relative decrease in the number of charities devoted to poverty, accompanied by an increase in those devoted to social welfare and culture and to children and young people. The recent Annual Reports of the Charity Commissioners confirm that much new charitable activity has reflected contemporary social concerns (eg victim support schemes, rehabilitation of drug addicts, relief for youth unemployment, environmental conservation, support for physical recreation, promotion of urban and rural regeneration). However, data about the number of charities tells us little about the proportion of total charitable resources devoted to the various charitable objects. According to research conducted by the Charities Aid Foundation (CAF) the most popular causes amongst individual donors are medical research and religious causes (17% and 16% respectively of donations) although children/young people, hospices/hospitals and overseas relief all receive approximately 10% each of total donations from this source (see CAF *UK Giving* (2007) pp 19–20).

In fact there have been considerable difficulties in obtaining reliable general financial statistics for charities. This is partly because until 1998 there was no uniform and rigorously enforced set of rules requiring charities to disclose their income and partly because charity income is so unevenly distributed as to make accurate sample surveys difficult. A survey by the Office of National Statistics based on a sample frame of 120,000 general registered charities in 1994–95 estimated their total income then to be £11,776m (Ward et al, *Economic Trends* (1996) 517, November). By contrast the Charity Commission estimated the total income of all registered charities in 1997 to be £18,400m (Annual Report 1997, para 61). By the end of March 2008 this particular estimate of the total income of 'main' charities had risen to £45,910m. In general economic terms the income of charities constitutes 3–4% of Gross Domestic Product. Moreover 'main' charities now employ around 600,000 workers, representing the equivalent of 488,000 full-time equivalent jobs or 2.2% of the total UK workforce (NCVO *The UK Voluntary Sector Almanac* (2006)). The same survey estimates the capital value of the total assets of registered charities as being approximately £65,000m.

One striking feature of the data when disaggregated is that the distribution of the income is extremely skewed. The vast majority of charities are very small. In 2008 some 55.6% of registered main charities had an annual income of less than £10,000 accounting for only about 0.6% of the total income of all charities. In contrast in the same year around 90% of that total income was attributable to just over 8% of registered charities, the largest 706 of those (approximately 0.4% of all registered charities and all with an income of £10m or more) receiving 51% of charitable income (www.charity-commission.gov.uk/registeredcharities/factfigures.asp). In short a very small minority of the total charity population has substantial resources and a large majority comparatively little.

A further significant feature of charity finance is that approximately 65–70% of income is now derived from fees and charges, other commercial activity and grants from statutory bodies. Any notion that the voluntary sector as a whole is financed to any great extent from sources of voluntary income would be misconceived. It is this change in the source and type of finance and its implications that we consider next.

(2) New patterns of finance for philanthropic organisations

Sources of finance for philanthropic organisations can be classified under the following headings:

(i) Voluntary giving from individuals – legacies and other donations.
(ii) Voluntary giving from institutions – donations, grants or other donations from companies; grants from charitable trusts.
(iii) Investment income.
(iv) Grants from central or local government and government-funded agencies (eg Arts Council, Sports Council).
(v) Fees and charges paid by recipients of services or by statutory bodies.
(vi) Commercial activity.

The two most significant trends in the composition of charity income over the last half-century are (a) the decline in importance of individual giving compared with other sources of income (see generally *Chesterman* pp 92–99; the Wolfenden Report, App 6A and 6C; and the Deakin Report, *Meeting the Challenge of Change: Voluntary Action into the 21st Century* (1996)); and (b) the increasing importance of fees and charges and funding by governmental and other statutory bodies. The pattern of charitable giving is broadly similar from year to year, with around three-fifths (55–60%) of the UK adult population giving to charity each month, producing an overall average figure of £16 for every UK adult, donors and non-donors. Women are more likely to give than men (60% versus 49% per cent), although less (£25 per month) than men (£29 per month). While people on higher incomes tend to give more to charity and more frequently, they give less than any other group as a proportion of their income. Overall in 2006–07 the estimated amount donated by individuals to charity was £9.5 billion, 3% less than in the previous year (*UK Civil Society Almanac*, 2008; CAF *UK Giving* (2007)).

Care is needed in translating these sorts of figures into any general proposition about the level of commitment to charitable giving. It should not be overlooked that a small group of donors (fewer than one in ten) gave more than £100 per month although this group contributed over 50% of the total amount donated by individuals. It is therefore not surprising to discover that cash donations such as street collections and 'door to door' collections remain the most common methods of giving (48% of donors) but also that the amounts given by these methods are relatively modest (18% of total donations) (see CAF *UK Giving* (2007) Table 4 and Figure 11).

The figures on corporate giving to charity for the post-1990 period are elusive and more contentious although it has been estimated that the level of corporate giving is quite stable, consistently amounting to around 0.2% of pre-tax profits (see eg Pharoah (ed) *Dimensions of the Voluntary Sector 1997* p 126). The effect of tax changes introduced in the Finance Act 2000 (see section 4 below) makes the data on corporate giving even more difficult to interpret. There is, though, some evidence that since the changes were introduced the level of corporate financial support may have dropped, albeit possibly for technical reasons associated with the substitution of covenanted giving by the Gift Aid scheme (see CAF Research Briefing Paper, May 2003).

The overall effect of the changes described here is that as traditional forms of finance decline in importance the charity sector is coming to rely more heavily on non-voluntary sources of income. A particularly significant change is the increasing reliance on state funding. According to data contained in the *2004 Voluntary Sector Almanac* the percentage of income from central and local government agencies in 2001–02 had risen in a decade to 37% as compared with 27% in 1991 (see also Smith and Whittington *Charity: The Spectre of Over-regulation and State Dependency* (2006)). Income from state sources appears to have stabilised around the higher figure, with research from the National Council for Voluntary Organisations (NCVO) showing that government funding to the voluntary sector has only increased by 1.5% since 2001 (*Voluntary Sector Almanac* 2007 p 59). That global figure conceals a trend in the type of financing whereby Government is moving away from grant funding towards awarding contracts to charities for delivering public services. Grants made up 52% of state funding to charities in 2001–02 but just 38% in 2004–05 with the contractual share increasing from 48% to 62% and with larger organisations benefiting the most.

One more recent addition to the sources of income referred to above is the funding from the National Lottery. Initially there were six separate funds benefiting from the proceeds of the National Lottery, the Community Fund (formerly the National Lottery Charities Board) being the one most closely linked to the funding of charities. It was empowered to support 'charitable, benevolent and philanthropic organisations', a definition that included organisations whose purposes are predominantly charitable but which have some purposes that fall outside the legal definition of charitable purposes. By the end of 2003 the Community Fund had committed funds to the value of £2,458m to some 53,998 projects. Total lottery funding of 'good causes' by all the six separate funds since its introduction amounted to £15 billion, a proportion of which was distributed to charities over and above that allocated by the Community Fund (see eg Smerdon in Pharoah (ed) *Dimensions of the Voluntary Sector 1997* pp 23–28 where it is estimated that in 1995 and 1996 charities received approximately £1.3 billion of *all* Lottery funding). The structure of the disbursement of lottery funding was changed in 2004 with the amalgamation of the separate funds into a single fund – the Big Lottery Fund (BLF) – subsequently formalised in the National Lottery Act 2006. Since 1 June 2004, the start of the BLF, awards of more than £1,275 million have been made to the voluntary sector (74% of the total grant awards), the amount received by charities in 2005–06 being estimated at £0.6 billion (Big Lottery Fund Annual Report 2008; *Civil Society Almanac* 2008).

The impact of the Lottery on the charity sector remains uncertain for two reasons, one concerning the impact on donors' propensity to give to charity and the other concerning allocation of funding. As regards the former, a study by Banks and Tanner suggested that the introduction of the Lottery did not have a 'significant effect' on individual charitable giving ('The State of Donation 1974–96' *IFS Commentary 62* (1997)). On the other hand, many charities for whom their own lotteries and 'scratch cards' have been important sources of revenue claim that sales of these were affected detrimentally (see eg *The Times* 5 November 1998). Also one study comparing the donations of National Lottery players with non-lottery players suggests that donations for the latter group are significantly higher and that the introduction of the Lottery can account for individual donations being 12% lower than might have been expected based on pre-Lottery trends (see Charities Aid Foundation *Donations Foresight* (2001) pp 9–10).

Where distribution of lottery funding is concerned, the introduction of the new legal framework in the National Lottery Act 2006 prompted some concern that governments might be tempted to direct lottery funding towards specific policy areas and thereby reduce the funds previously available to the

Community Fund and 'good causes'. In response, the BLF Board publicly undertook that between 60% and 70% of all its funding would go to the voluntary
and community sector (VCS). The National Lottery Act 2006 makes no reference to this undertaking but during debate on the National Lottery Bill
(21 March 2006) Lord Davies of Oldham said: 'I am this evening prepared to
place on the record that the Government will act as the guarantor of Big Lottery
Fund's undertaking that 60 per cent to 70 per cent of its funding will go to the
voluntary and community sectors.' One other related consideration is whether
the funding policy of the BLF will differ from that of its predecessor, the Community Fund, which had displayed a willingness to fund unpopular causes, eg
through the controversial grant of £336,261 in August 2002 to the National
Coalition of Anti-Deportation Campaigns (cf the total of £285m distributed
by the fund in 2002, of which £7m was designated to assist asylum seekers;
and see generally on the hostile campaign conducted in the media, Snoddy and
Ashworth *It Could Be You: The Untold Story of the UK National Lottery* (2000)
pp 170–174).

Aggregated figures for charity income conceal significant variations in the
sources of funding for different types of charity. Thus there are two categories of
charity (advancement of religion and medical research) which have historically
relied on donations as their major source of revenue (see eg Posnett *Charity
Statistics* (1983–84) p 58, Table 4). Then there are those charities, the largest
in terms of income, which generate fee revenue. Ninety-four per cent of the
income of charities whose main object is 'social welfare' is derived from fees paid
predominantly by central and local government. Other prominent examples of
charities reliant on fee income are independent schools (see generally Lee (ed)
Sources of Charity Finance (1989)). In sharp contrast the dominant charity type
in numerical terms is that group, frequently empowered to support a wide
range of objects, which relies primarily on income from the investment of
capital endowment. In terms of total income, however, this type of charity is by
far the smallest, although dominating this sector are a number of substantial
grant-making trusts.

One conclusion to be drawn from our discussion of the demography of
charity is that there is not a single, homogeneous charity sector. Instead there
are several distinct sectors, and within each one there exist wide variations
in resources. This has three significant implications for the accountability of
charities which we consider further in Chapter 20. First, as many charities
come increasingly to depend on grants or fees from statutory bodies, is there
emerging a system of state administrative regulation and accountability – be it
by monitoring of contracts or otherwise – separate from the statutory regulatory
role of the Charity Commission? Second, will the reformed statutory framework
in the now revised Charities Act 1993 be robust enough to deal with the shifts in
charitable activity and finance that we have described? Lastly, does charity law
ensure that the resources of the large number of very small charities are used
effectively?

4. 'Privileges' of charitable status

In this section we examine the privileges applicable to charitable trusts only –
'trusts law privileges' – and those applicable to all charities – 'fiscal privileges' –
and assess their importance.

(a) Privileges of charitable trusts under trusts law

The idea that charitable trusts should enjoy especially favourable treatment can
be traced right back to the enforcement of 'pious uses'. It crystallised fully in the
early nineteenth century, with the decision in *Morice v Bishop of Durham* (see
above, p 924).

A charitable trust is exempt from the operation of the following rules of
trusts law: (i) the rule that, in order to be valid, a trust must specify with
adequate certainty one or more human beneficiaries ('certainty of objects');
(ii) the rules against perpetual duration and, to a limited degree, undue remoteness of vesting ('perpetuities'); and (iii) (subject to some exceptions) the doctrine of lapse, whereby if fulfilment of a trust disposition is initially ineffective
or subsequently fails, the trust property is held on trust for those expressed to
be entitled in default, or in the absence of any such person(s), upon resulting
trust for the settlor or his next of kin (see Chapter 5). We shall consider each of
these in turn.

(1) Certainty of objects

A charitable trust, whether it is expressed wholly in terms of purposes or whether
alongside its charitable purposes it expressly or impliedly designates those individuals intended to benefit from the implementation of the purpose, is still a
valid trust. Thus there is no requirement that the objects of the trust must be
certain, at least not in the manner required by the certainty of objects test for
private express trusts. To obtain this privilege the purposes, other than purely
ancillary purposes, must be 'wholly' or 'exclusively' charitable. The trust will fail
if it is possible for the funds subject to the gift to be devoted to non-charitable
purposes. To that extent, therefore, the trust purposes must be expressed with
sufficient clarity at least to exclude application of the funds to non-charitable
purposes. Here small drafting errors – use of 'or' rather than 'and' can have
drastic consequences. For example, in *Chichester Diocesan Fund v Simpson*
[1944] AC 341 a will contained a trust 'for such charitable . . . institutions or
other benevolent objects . . . as my . . . executors . . . may . . . select'. The House
of Lords held that 'or' should be construed disjunctively, that following *Morice
v Bishop of Durham* (1805) 'benevolent' was a term of wider import than 'charitable', that it was therefore possible for all the trust funds to be applied to
non-charitable (ie 'benevolent') objects, and that the trust was therefore void
(see also *A-G of the Cayman Islands v Wahr-Hansen* [2001] 1 AC 75, PC, where
the phrase 'or any organizations or institutions operating for the public good'

was held to be capable of permitting applications of money to purposes that were not exclusively charitable). On the other hand, to give but one example, 'charitable *and* benevolent' was upheld as valid and exclusively charitable in *Re Best* [1904] 2 Ch 354 (see also *Re Carapiet* [2002] EWHC 1304 – 'education and advancement in life' construed conjunctively – and generally *Picarda* pp 145–147; and Warburton (ed) *Tudor on Charities* (9th edn, 2003) pp 222–225 on 'and/or' cases). Unfortunately even the presence of the conjunction 'and' may not be decisive. The phrase 'to such religious, charitable and philanthropic objects' as might be selected was construed disjunctively by Sargant J in *Re Eades* [1920] 2 Ch 353. Dicta in that case to the effect that the greater the number of qualifications or characteristics enumerated, the more probable it is that a disjunctive construction be adopted was approved by the Privy Council in *A-G of the Bahamas v Royal Trust Co* [1986] 1 WLR 1001 ('any purposes for and/or connected with the education and welfare of Bahamian children and young people' construed disjunctively leading to the failure of a residuary bequest). But as Lord Oliver, giving the judgment of the Board, emphasised, it is a matter of construction of the particular disposition – previous cases are only guidelines and of limited assistance. The fact remains that the 'exclusively charitable' requirement remains in full force but is qualified in respect of some pre-1952 trust instruments by the Charitable Trusts (Validation) Act 1954 (see Cullity (1967) 16 ICLQ 464; Maurice (1954) 18 Conv 532; Sheridan (1993/94) CL & PR 1).

The privileged position of charitable purposes under the rules governing certainty of objects is illustrated also in the particular context of unincorporated associations. As explained in Chapter 17, clauses purporting to vest the property of unincorporated associations in trustees and bequests of property to unincorporated associations are both vulnerable to legal challenge if the association's purposes are non-charitable. No such problems arise where the association is a charitable one.

Finally, the law's acceptance of purpose trusts provided that they fall within the legal definition of 'charitable' results in charity enjoying a favoured position in two further respects. First, in accordance with long-established rules, the funds and energies of a public official, the Attorney-General, are devoted to the enforcement and protection of charitable trusts (see Chapter 20). Second, in cases where the purposes are so broad (eg 'for charitable purposes in England') that the trustees do not know what specific objects they should pursue, the law provides procedures whereby they may obtain official guidance. Both the court and the Charity Commissioners have jurisdiction (Charities Act 1993, s 16(1)) to establish 'a scheme of administration' under which specific projects are determined.

(2) Perpetuities

Charitable trusts are not subject to the general rule of trusts law that a trust drafted wholly or partly in terms of purposes cannot be expressed to last indefinitely (the rule against inalienability). They also enjoy a limited exemption from the rule against remoteness of vesting (see Chapter 6, p 318 for a brief outline of these rules).

Charitable trusts may expressly state that they are intended to last for ever or, as is more commonly the case, they may simply omit any mention of the period for which they are intended to last. This does not mean that the settlors can direct trustees to accumulate charity income for any period they may wish: charitable trusts have been subject to the same statutory restrictions on accumulation of income as other trusts (see Chapter 6, p 319). In 1998 the Law Commission proposed that these restrictions be largely abolished but not for charitable trusts (Report No 251 *The Rules Against Perpetuities and Excessive Accumulations* (HC 579, 1998) para 10.15). For the latter any duty or power conferred on trustees to accumulate income would cease to have effect at the end of a proposed statutory period of 21 years. The Law Commission's Report reasoned that in the absence of any restriction on the accumulation of income by charities, the only restraint would be provided by the fiduciary obligation of the trustees to exercise the power of accumulation in the best interests of the trust. Subject to this, in theory a charity could accumulate indefinitely with the consequence that there would be no effective mechanism for control over the dead hand of the settlor: 'a settlor [could] direct long-term accumulations of income for the fulfilment of some charitable purpose of a grandiose kind that will not come about for many years' (para 10.19). The Law Commission view was endorsed in a Consultation Paper published by the then Lord Chancellor's Department subject, however, to a proposal that the Charity Commission should be given a general power to authorise a derogation from this principle where it considers it 'would be expedient in the interests of [a] charity in the furtherance of its objects' (*The Rule against Excessive Accumulations* (September 2002) paras 23–28 at 28). These proposals are now contained in Clause 14 of the Perpetuities and Accumulations Bill 2009 (see further pp 316–317). Assuming implementation, the consequence will be that the privilege of perpetual or indefinite duration will continue to apply only to the charity's capital endowment, subject to the possibility that the trust's purposes may be altered under a cy-près scheme (see Chapter 20).

The one exemption from the rule against remoteness of vesting is that a gift over from one charity to another charity is valid even if it takes place outside the permitted perpetuity periods (*Christ's Hospital v Grainger* (1849) 1 Mac & G 460). Thus, for example, a gift on trust for the relief of poverty in England until 3000 AD, then on trust for the advancement of education in England thereafter, is wholly valid. The reasoning here is that since the law allows property to be devoted to charity for ever, it need have no concern to ensure that the second charitable purpose replaces the first within the perpetuity period.

Paradoxically this particular legal privilege of charitable status can be exploited by conveyancers to produce, in effect, a perpetual non-charitable trust. If, for example, a testator T bequeaths property to the trustees of charity X on trust for X's purposes until they fail to maintain T's tomb, and thereafter to charity Y, the gift over to Y is valid notwithstanding that it may vest outside the perpetuity period (*Re Tyler* [1891] 3 Ch 252). The trustees of X thus have to maintain the tomb if they want to retain the funds for X. 'This is not', Hanbury and Martin wryly suggest (at p 403), 'a satisfactory use of charity privilege'.

In contrast a gift over from a non-charity to a charity or from a charity to a non-charity must vest within one of the perpetuity periods, subject now to the normal rules regarding 'wait and see' (*Re Bowen* [1893] 2 Ch 491; Perpetuities and Accumulations Act 1964, s 3). Suggestions that *any* gift to a charity should be exempt from the rule against remoteness of vesting were firmly rejected by the Law Commission in the 1998 Report. It is evident that its decision was influenced by the possibility of more extensive 'abuse' of the privilege, as where A leaves property to B on condition that if B or B's successors attempt to dispose of the property to any person not a descendant of A, the property should pass to charity X. As the Commission points out, this would enable a settlor to create, in effect, a perpetual trust in favour of his or her family (para 7.37). Notwithstanding the scepticism evident here and the possibilities of exploitation described in the previous paragraph, the Commission nevertheless recommended no change to the 'privilege' permitting gifts over from one charity to another at any future time (paras 7.34 and 7.37; see Perpetuities and Accumulations Bill 2009, cl 2(2)).

(3) Lapse and the cy-près doctrine

Where a private trust fails – or 'lapses' – the equitable ownership in the property held by trustees is returned to or 'results back' to the settlor or to the residuary estate if the settlor is deceased. But if fulfilment of a charitable gift or bequest fails so that under normal trusts law principles a lapse would occur, the cy-près doctrine may, but not necessarily will, 'rescue' the property for charity. That is to say, in some instances the Chancery Division or the Charity Commission may establish a cy-près scheme whereby the originally stipulated purposes which have 'failed' are replaced by new purposes which are charitable in law and similar to those originally stipulated. It is important here not to confuse a cy-près scheme and its accompanying alteration of the terms of the gift with a scheme of administration (described in section 4(a)(1) above). As regards the latter, in some circumstances the court or the Charity Commission may be able to interpret the gift in a way that circumvents failure and enables a scheme of administration to be made, 'clarifying' the stated purposes of the gift. This negates the need for recourse to the cy-près doctrine. As might be suspected, the distinction between circumstances where there is no failure and 'clarification' is permissible and those where failure of the gift is found and alteration under a cy-près scheme is required, whilst conceptually sound, can be difficult to draw. Predictability is not helped in that the application of certain rules of construction or lines of reasoning can transform what may look initially to us like 'failure' of the gift into a situation where there is no failure at all. Unfortunately these distinctions can be important as in circumstances of what is termed 'initial failure', to be discussed shortly, it is necessary to be able to establish the presence of a 'general charitable intention' before the cy-près doctrine can operate. That requirement is forestalled if the court or Commission can conclude that there is no failure. The cy-près doctrine and the making of a scheme under it therefore operates in some sense as a last resort to rescue a gift that would otherwise fail. The relevant rules implementing the doctrine were given statutory form in 1960 and are now to be found in the Charities Act 1993.

A cy-près scheme can be made, or 'settled', both where a gift fails at the outset ('initial failure') and where it fails after having vested ('subsequent failure'). A key distinction between the two categories is that in cases of initial failure, but not subsequent failure, a cy-près scheme cannot be made unless a 'general charitable intention', referred to above, can be discerned, for instance, in the will (see further below, p 947). Most litigation has tended to occur over gifts in wills where the claims of charity are opposed by those entitled should the gift fail. In this context, assuming that there is no subsequent gift over to a non-charitable object, it is important to keep in mind that once a charitable gift has taken effect in the will – ie on the death of the testator or testatrix – the property is dedicated to charity in perpetuity. In *Re Slevin* [1891] 2 Ch 236, for instance, a testator had bequeathed £200 to an orphanage still in existence at the date of his death but which closed soon after and *before* the legacy had been paid over. The Court of Appeal held that 'the legacy became the property of the charity' on the death of the testator irrespective of whether or not it was ever paid to the charity. In short *Re Slevin* is a case of subsequent failure and the property could therefore be applied cy-près without the need to establish a general charitable intention.

Before considering the 'rescue function' of cy-près, in which the keynote is that property is preserved for application within the realm of charity, we must stress it is not the only task performed in cy-près proceedings. Since the late nineteenth century, cy-près has been urged as a mechanism whereby the purposes of all types of charitable organisations – trusts or otherwise – might be 'varied' or modernised (see *Nathan Report* paras 92–109; Sheridan and Delaney *The Cy-Près Doctrine* (1959); Mulheron *The Modern Cy-près Doctrine* (2006)). Apart from rare cases such as *Re Slevin* (and see *Re Wright* [1954] Ch 347 as to vesting date) the category of 'subsequent failure' is almost congruent with the 'modernisation' aspect of cy-près. The use of the term 'modernisation', however, more appropriately encapsulates the contemporary legal and policy issues surrounding this application of the cy-près doctrine. This 'modernisation' function for cy-près, which we examine in Chapter 20, must be distinguished from the 'rescue' function because (i) the existence of a general charitable intention does not have to be separately established for the former, and (ii) the much more extensively used modernisation function is in practice exercised almost exclusively by the Charity Commission which has the same jurisdiction and powers as the Chancery Division for this purpose (Charities Act 1993, s 16(1)). By contrast the relatively infrequent 'rescue' cases will usually come before the court because more often than not they involve special questions of law or fact, or are otherwise contentious, and the Commission's jurisdiction is curtailed in these circumstances (Charities Act 1993, s 16(3), (10)).

The substantive law governing the rescue function has three key principles. The first is self-evident – some charitable purpose or institution must be designated. Next there must be a failure of purposes, and, to reiterate the point, in cases of initial failure a general charitable intention must be present.

Failure   Before 1960 'failure' permitting cy-près application occurred only where it was 'impossible' or 'impracticable' to carry out the purposes of a trust. An obvious example of 'impossibility' is where the gift is to a named charitable institution which has ceased to exist by the time the gift comes into force, or indeed appears never to have existed (*Re Harwood* [1936] Ch 285). On the other hand, the mere fact that the institution has been incorrectly described does not constitute 'failure' and therefore does not affect the validity of the gift (eg *Re Spence's Will Trusts* [1978] 3 All ER 92 – 'The Blind Home, Scott Street, Keighley' instead of 'Keighley and District Home for the Blind'). Failure can equally occur where there is a gift for a specifically identified purpose; examples of 'impracticability' here would be where the available funds are inadequate (eg *Re Beck* (1926) 42 TLR 245 – funds insufficient to build lifeboats) or a suitable site cannot be found (eg *Biscoe v Jackson* (1887) 35 Ch D 460 – no land available to build a soup kitchen and cottage hospital in Shoreditch).

Nowadays s 13(1) of the Charities Act 1993, restating and also extending the existing principles (*Re Lepton's Charity* [1972] Ch 276 at 284), sets out a composite and exhaustive catalogue of the circumstances constituting 'failure' for the purposes of both the 'rescue' and 'modernisation' functions. These two aspects of cy-près are mixed together in s 13(1). But one can isolate the following provisions as bearing substantially although not exclusively on 'rescue':

(1)   . . . the circumstances in which the original purposes of a charitable gift can be altered to allow the property given or part of it to be applied cy-près shall be as follows:

   (a) where the original purposes, in whole or in part,
      (i)   have been as far as may be fulfilled, or
      (ii) cannot be carried out, or not according to the directions given and to the spirit of the gift; or
   (b) where the original purposes provide a use for part only of the property available by virtue of the gift; or . . .
   (c) where the original purposes, in whole or in part, have since they were laid down –
      (i)   been adequately provided for by other means, or
      (ii) ceased, as being useless or harmful to the community or for other reasons to be in law charitable; . . .

> (2) Subsection (1) shall not affect the conditions which must be satisfied in order that property given for charitable purposes may be applied cy-près except in so far as those conditions require a failure of the original purposes.

Note that s 13(2) confirms that subsection (1) is concerned solely with a categorisation of failure. It does not affect the requirement that in a case of initial failure the gift will lapse unless a general charitable intention can be discerned.

Before examining the matter of general charitable intention it is important to re-emphasise that there can be circumstances where what appears to be a total failure of a charitable bequest may be held not to be a failure at all. Amongst the cases to confirm this are several that concern bequests to voluntary hospitals taken over by the state under the National Health Service scheme between the date of the will and the date of death. At first sight such bequests would appear to fail on the ground that the intended named beneficiary institution ceased to exist before the bequest came into force. But the cases show the courts developing one or other of two lines of reasoning to establish that there is, after all, no failure.

In some instances (*Re Morgan* [1950] Ch 637; and see generally *Re Faraker* [1912] 2 Ch 488) they have held that the dissolved hospital or other charitable organisation, together with its property, may be 'traced' into some new organisation which has replaced it or with which it has amalgamated (which may, for instance, be a larger public hospital made up of the merger of several voluntary hospitals). Alternatively they have interpreted the bequest as a trust for the purposes of the dissolved organisation as distinct from an out-and-out gift to it, have ruled that these charitable purposes survived the ending of the specific organisation and thus have reached the conclusion that the trust itself did not fail (see *Re Lucas* [1948] 2 All ER 22 – considered in *Re Spence's Will Trusts* [1978] 3 All ER 92 – and the 'liberal' approach to construction applied in *Re Broadbent (dec'd)* [2001] EWCA Civ 714). The line of reasoning supporting 'validity' rather than 'failure' is relatively easy to maintain when the dissolved organisation was an unincorporated association because, as we have seen in Chapter 17, in this type of charity the property is commonly vested in trustees on an express trust for the charity's purposes (see *Re Finger's Will Trusts* [1972] Ch 286). It is less likely to apply where the organisation was a company or other corporate body (*Re Stemson* [1970] Ch 16; *Re Finger's Will Trusts*; and see Warburton [1984] Conv 112) because prima facie such organisations do not hold their property on trust for the purposes contained in their objects clauses. Buckley J put the proposition in the following way (*Re Vernon's Will Trusts* [1972] Ch 300n at 303): 'the natural construction . . . is that the bequest is made to the corporate body as part of its general funds, that is to say, beneficially and without the imposition of any trust. That the testator's motive in making the bequest may have undoubtedly been to assist the work of the incorporated body would be insufficient to create a trust.' To put it simply, the purposes die with the company.

These presumptions as to each type of organisation are not irrebuttable. It is possible (i) to construe a gift to an unincorporated association as wholly dependent on the continuance of the specific association, not merely as a trust for its purposes in abstract terms (*Re Vernon's Will Trusts* [1972] Ch 300n), and (ii) to construe a gift to a company as a gift on trust for its purposes rather than an out-and-out gift (*Re Meyers* [1951] Ch 534). But they are strong presumptions (see generally Hutton (1969) 32 MLR 283; Cotterell (1972) 36 Conv 198; Martin (1974) 38 Conv 187; Rickett (1980) 39 CLJ 88). They are also presumptions that have been criticised as leading to anomalous results (see eg Goff J in *Re Finger's Will Trusts*). Support for the doubts expressed by Goff J can be found in Australian authorities. There it has been held that there should be a presumption that in either case the gift – whether to a company or to an unincorporated association – is made for the purposes of the institution (see *Sir Moses Montefiore Jewish Home v Howell & Co* [1984] 2 NSWLR 406; and in similar vein see *Re Christian Brothers of Ireland in Canada* (2000) 47 OR (3d) 674 (Ontario Court of Appeal)). If the policy objective is to save charitable gifts and so far as possible to apply them to the purposes intended by the donor, then the approach taken in these cases has much to commend it.

The position in English law, however, remains that stated in *Re Vernon* and reiterated in *Re ARMS (Multiple Sclerosis Research) Ltd* [1997] 1 WLR 877. In the latter case several testators made testamentary gifts valued at £117,208 to an incorporated charity, ARMS (Multiple Sclerosis) Ltd, which went into insolvent liquidation *after* the wills were made but *before* the deaths of the testators. At the dates of the various deaths the company had not been formally dissolved and therefore, following *Re Vernon*, would take the property beneficially unless there was sufficient evidence to show that the company was intended to take as trustee for its purposes. The point at issue was that if the gifts did form part of the company's assets, then in accordance with the Insolvency Act 1986, s 143(1) they would be available for distribution amongst its creditors. Neuberger J recognised that there was a 'very strong suspicion' that the testators could not have intended that outcome but held that '[the suspicion] is insufficient to justify a plain departure from the plain words of a will' (at 882). He consequently held that even though the main beneficiaries of the gifts would be the creditors of the company the gifts could not be construed as being for the charitable purposes of the company but were rather gifts to the company itself.

It must be emphasised that if the court adopts one or other of the two 'very refined' (*Re Roberts* [1963] 1 All ER 674 at 681) lines of reasoning described above – those of 'amalgamation or tracing' and 'gifts for purposes not institutions' – the need to rely on the cy-près doctrine is forestalled. No failure means no cy-près scheme. As importantly there is therefore no necessity to consider whether a 'general' or 'paramount' charitable intention is present.

'General charitable intention' As previously stated, in cases of initial failure, but not subsequent failure, a cy-près scheme cannot be made unless the gift manifests a 'general charitable intention'. If no such intention is present in a case of initial failure, the gift lapses. This restriction on the scope of cy-près derives from late eighteenth and early nineteenth-century decisions in which the courts were particularly concerned to protect the expectations of heirs against charitable dispositions (see *Jones* pp 138–156). It is by no means easy to determine in any individual case whether the donor's or testator's charitable intention will be labelled 'general' or 'particular'. There are many judicial statements attempting to clarify the approach to be adopted, including this formulation by Buckley J in *Re Lysaght* [1966] Ch 191 at 202:

> A general charitable intention... may be said to be a paramount intention on the part of a donor to effect some charitable purpose which the court can find a method of putting into operation, notwithstanding that it is impracticable to give effect to some direction by the donor which is not an essential part of his true intention – not, that is to say, part of his paramount intention.
>
> In contrast, a particular charitable intention exists where the donor means his charitable disposition to take effect if, but only if, it can be carried into effect in a particular specified way, for example, in connection with a particular school to be established at a particular place (*Re Wilson* [1913] 1 Ch 314), or by establishing a home in a particular house (*Re Packe* [1918] 1 Ch 437).

This formulation is similar to that advocated in some other jurisdictions. In *A-G for New South Wales v Perpetual Trustee Co Ltd* (1940) 63 CLR 209 Dixon and Evatt JJ identified the distinction as being one (at 225, emphasis added):

> Between on the one hand, cases in which every element in the description of the trust is *indispensable* to the validity and operation of the disposition and, on the other hand, cases where a further and more general purpose is disclosed as the true and substantial object of the trust, which may therefore be carried into effect at the expense of some part of the particular direction given by the trust instrument.

The 'indispensability' test has found support in New Zealand (*Alacoque v Roache* [1998] 2 NZLR 250 at 254 per Somers J) but, notwithstanding these attempts to formulate a workable test, a decision on this issue is in practice often very artificial: 'To search for such a paramount... charitable... intention is in many cases to follow a will-o'-the-wisp' (per Vinelott J in *Re Woodhams* [1981] 1 All ER 202 at 210). The court has to rely on very slight indications in the terms of the gift or bequest itself and any other disposition (eg legacies, residuary bequests) with which it is associated in the same document.

Two closely connected situations – mentioned above in the context of initial failure – in which the issue of general charitable intention is finely balanced are where a testator has left property to an institution which was charitable and (a) the institution has ceased to exist between the time of execution of the will and the testator's death or (b) it has never existed. In category (a) there is prima facie no general charitable intention because the testator has indicated precisely that it is the particular institution and nothing else that he wishes to benefit (eg *Re Harwood* [1936] Ch 285; *Re Spence* [1978] 3 All ER 92; *Re Rymer* [1895] 1 Ch 19, but cf *A-G for New South Wales v Public Trustee* (1987) 8 NSWLR 550). This presumption may, however, be rebutted by appropriate indications in the will, such as the presence of other gifts of a charitable nature, sometimes termed as 'charity by association'. In *Re Spence*, which contains a thorough review of the leading cases, Megarry VC stated that 'the doctrine [charity by association] depends, at least to some extent, on the detection of "kindred objects" in the charities to which the shares of residue are given; in this respect the charities must in some degree be ejusdem generis'. In *Re Satterthwaite's Will Trusts* [1966] 1 WLR 277, for instance, a testatrix, who had made quite explicit her hatred for the human race, left her residuary estate to what she believed to be nine animal charities apparently selected from the pages of the London telephone directories. One of the named charitable institutions had ceased to operate by the time the will took effect and therefore that gift failed. But could the property be applied cy-près on the basis that the will exhibited a general charitable intention? The Court of Appeal held that it could: 'I have no doubt from the nature of the other dispositions by this testatrix that a general intention can be discerned in favour of charity through the medium of kindness to animals' (at 286 per Russell LJ). More contentiously, in *Re Finger's Will Trusts* [1972] Ch 286 Goff J was able to discover a general charitable intention and thereby order a cy-près scheme to be settled in respect of a failed bequest to a defunct incorporated charity, the National Council for Maternity and Child Welfare. Goff J treated as significant in discovering a general charitable intention (i) the fact that with minor exceptions the whole estate was devoted to charity (there were 11 named charities although it would be difficult to maintain that they were ejusdem generis); (ii) the Council was mainly a co-ordinating body; and (iii) the evidence that the testatrix mistakenly regarded herself as having no relatives.

The decision on this point in the case can be contrasted with the more restrictive approaches evident in *Re Spence* and *Re Harwood*. Goff J specifically distinguished the latter case, commenting that 'Farwell J did not say that it was impossible to find a general charitable intention where there is a gift to an identifiable body which has ceased to exist but only that it would be very difficult' (at 299). The facts identified by Goff J as evidence of a general charitable intention were in his view sufficient to overcome 'the difficulty' despite the apparent absence of 'kindred objects'. Perhaps all that can be said here is that a significant degree of discretion rests with the court in interpreting the factual matrix in any given case.

The difficulty of identifying a 'general charitable intention' has doubtless constituted an inducement for the courts to develop, as we have previously seen, various 'refined' principles for establishing that the institution in question, or at least its purposes, still subsists in some form and that there has therefore been no 'failure' after all.

In category (b) – gift to an institution that never existed (eg *Re Harwood* [1936] Ch 285 – bequest to non-existent 'Peace Society of Belfast') – the prima facie response of the courts is to say that the testatrix had a general charitable intention. Since by hypothesis she never had a particular institution in mind she is deemed to have been thinking in general terms of the type of charitable purpose indicated by the name by which she sought to describe the intended beneficiary. This rather artificial presumption may also be rebutted, where, for example, there is a residuary charitable gift into which the property contained in the specific gift will fall in the event of lapse (*Re Goldschmidt* [1957] 1 All ER 513).

Charitable appeals In one special class of initial failure, principally concerning contributions to public appeal funds where the fund proves insufficient for the designated purpose, statutory provision is made for application of property cy-près, regardless of the particular intention (Charities Act 1993, s 14). The object of the section is to remove the need to undertake extensive inquiries where donors cannot be easily identified or traced, or where contributions have been made, for example, to street collections. In fact, the section may be superfluous particularly in light of *Re West Sussex Constabulary's Benevolent Fund Trusts* [1970] 1 All ER 544 (see below and Chapter 17, p 904; see also Wilson [1983] Conv 40; though cf the Australian case of *Beggs v Kirkpatrick* [1961] VR 764). The section did not, however, apply where there was a known donor or testator with the consequence that a resulting trust would still arise in favour of that person. The Charities Act 2006 in effect reverses that presumption. Under a new rather convoluted s 14A inserted in the 1993 Act those making an appeal will be able to specify that property given in response to it will, if the appeal fails, be applied cy-près 'as if given for charitable purposes generally' unless donors indicate otherwise by making a 'relevant declaration' at the time of making the gift that in those circumstances they wish to be given the opportunity of requesting its return.

Where a charitable appeal has a surplus after fulfilling the stipulated purposes or fails subsequently in some other way, the cy-près doctrine is automatically available, assuming these cases are to be treated as instances of 'subsequent failure'. Notwithstanding the apparent reliance in *Re North Devon and West Somerset Relief Fund Trusts* [1953] 1 WLR 1260 (oversubscribed flood relief fund) on the donors having a general charitable intention, it is generally accepted that there is no need to establish any such intention (see eg *Re Wokingham Fire Brigade Trusts* [1951] Ch 373, approved obiter in *Re Ulverston and District New Hospital Building Trusts* [1956] Ch 622 at 636; Picarda *The Law and Practice Relating to Charities* (3rd edn, 1999) ch 28, but cf Luxton [1983] Conv 107 for an alternative view).

The advantages of charitable status in this context are apparent when compared with the problems that can arise if an over-subscribed public appeal turns out not to be charitable. Where, for instance, no indication is given in the appeal as to the destination of any surplus, the two possibilities are that it should either be returned to the donors or be paid to the Crown as bona vacantia. In *Re Gillingham Bus Disaster Fund* [1958] Ch 300, Harman J decided that a surplus fund of £7,300 should be held on resulting trust, even for donors whose identity would be difficult to discover, and paid into court while an inquiry was conducted to try and identify them. He explained his reasoning by reference to the intentions of donors: 'I see no reason myself to suppose that the small giver who is anonymous has any wider intention than the large giver who is named' (at 314). Whilst the reasoning is arguably sound in principle the inconvenience of being required to trace such donors is apparent where, for instance, street collections are involved. Indeed, as was seen in Chapter 17, the donors were never traced and the money remained undistributed until 1993 (see p 907). Consequently, the courts now appear to favour the opposite presumption about intention, namely that donors who put their money into collecting boxes should be regarded as 'intending to part with their money out and out, absolutely, in all circumstances' (per Goff J in *Re West Sussex Constabulary's Benevolent Fund Trusts* [1970] 1 All ER 544 at 550).

In an attempt to prevent these difficulties arising with surplus or indeed under-subscribed funds the Attorney-General prepared guidelines for both charitable and non-charitable appeals (eg recommending that a clear indication as to the destination of any surplus be given in any appeal), and circulated these to bodies such as local authorities, the Law Society and the major banks (see Charity Commission Guidance Note CC 40 (July 2002)). In practice non-charitable status has often been chosen (see Suddards *Administration of Appeal Funds* (1991)).

(4) The declining importance of the privileges

In certain important respects the extent to which charitable trusts are 'privileged' – or, to express this in another way, the gap between the law's treatment of charitable trusts and its treatment of non-charitable trusts – has been reduced by virtue of relaxation in the rules governing the validity of non-charitable trusts. First and foremost, and notwithstanding the restrictive decision on 'administrative unworkability' in *R v District Auditor ex parte West Yorkshire MCC* [1986] RVR 24, these trusts are now governed by less stringent rules as regards certainty of objects (see Chapter 5). In both *Re Denley* [1969] 1 Ch 373 and *McPhail v Doulton* [1971] AC 424, the decisions primarily responsible for liberalisation of the relevant rules, a trust for the welfare of a company's employees was created; in the latter case, relations of the testator were also to be benefited. But for rules defining a section of the public under charity law (see Chapter 19), these trusts could fairly easily have been framed as charitable trusts. As it was, they were set up as private trusts, with, in *Denley*, the purposive element of recreation made quite explicit. Second, as explained in Chapter 17, a similar liberalising effect is identifiable in some recent decisions regarding gifts and bequests on trust for non-charitable unincorporated associations.

Whereas in these two respects the gap between charitable and non-charitable trusts has narrowed, the privileges of the former class are still important. The founders of charitable trusts are still free (i) to express their wishes wholly in terms of purposes, (ii) to rely on the Attorney-General to enforce them and the Charity Commission to establish schemes of administration if a specific mode of use of the property must be determined, and (iii) to express a desire that their wishes be observed for ever. They also have the assurance of knowing that unforeseen events threatening to destroy their charitable trust may result in no more than a re-orientation of their purposes under a cy-près scheme. Lastly, the members of unincorporated charitable associations and those people who wish to leave money or property by will to such associations have the assurance of knowing that the validity of any clause purporting to vest the association's property in trustees, or of any bequest to the association, cannot be challenged on the ground that the trust so created is a purpose trust.

(b) The fiscal privileges of charities

(1) The development of the privileges

Without doubt the most important twentieth-century developments with regard to the privileges which the magic label 'charitable' evokes in English law occurred in the field of taxation. In the new century the significance of the fiscal privileges has taken on an added impetus. One hundred years ago, it would have been thought absurd to describe charity law as a sub-branch of tax law; nowadays, this description, while not wholly apt, has an element of truth. Two developments in taxation have brought about this change.

First, the range of fiscal liabilities from which charities have been declared wholly or partly exempt has grown. By the time of *Pemsel* in 1891, charities were exempt from tax on their income, whether this was received by way of dividend, interest or other annual or periodic payments. They also received some measure of discretionary relief from local rates. On the other hand, there was no favourable tax treatment for donors. Extension of the range of these exemptions has occurred in two ways in particular. First, existing taxes have had wholesale or partial exemptions for charities or dispositions to charity carved out of them, as with the creation in 1972 of a substantial exemption for charitable bequests from estate duty, an exemption that has been carried over into inheritance tax. This trend has intensified since 1979 with the introduction of further reliefs for both individual and corporate donors to charity. Second, on the introduction of new taxes charities have been declared wholly or partly exempt from them: such was the case with capital gains tax (introduced in 1965).

The second development in taxation is that the importance of the exemptions for individual charities or donors has been increased on account of variations in the rates at which some of the relevant taxes are levied. Logically, if somewhat perversely, the higher the tax rates the greater is the value of the exemption and, of course, vice versa. Changes in tax rates therefore have an impact on the theoretical value of the privileges and, in the case of covenanted income and its successor Gift Aid, on the actual amount repaid by HMRC to charity.

These developments have not always been the outcome of conscious policy decisions. The provision of statutory rate relief crystallised following lengthy official discussion, embodied in a committee report (*Report of the Pritchard Committee on the Rating of Charities and Kindred Bodies* (Cmnd 831, 1959); Waters (1960) 23 MLR 68). But tax relief on covenanted income emerged almost by accident (see *Owen* pp 336–338; *Final Report of the Radcliffe Commission on the Taxation of Profits and Income* (Cmd 9474, 1955) paras 144–152, 176–181; Stopforth [1986] BTR 101). Some other exemptions – for example, under capital gains tax (CGT) or income tax (IT) – were consciously created, in line with a general policy assumption, but were not exhaustively discussed. Furthermore, the policy of exempting charities has not been consistent. Despite considerable lobbying, charities have not succeeded in obtaining any general exemption from Value Added Tax (VAT).

Extension of the range and value of charity's tax privileges has thus been a general trend, but by no means an inexorable one. The consequence is that the current position is complex and lacks coherence. In 1997, partly in response to requests from charities, the Treasury initiated a review of the taxation of charities to see if it is possible to create a more coherent and simpler system 'receptive to the needs of today's charities'. The review culminated in a 1999 consultation document *Review of Charity Taxation* (and see Alexander [1999] BTR 221). The Review contained the following clear statement of government policy:

> Our responsibility is to help create a culture of giving. That requires a tax system that will encourage more people to give more; a tax system that offers effective incentives and is as simple as possible for donors and charities to operate.

Whether, in fact, greater emphasis on the availability of fiscal reliefs for donors and charities was or is likely to help create a 'culture of giving' is uncertain. Leaving to one side the intriguing moral position that acts of altruism need to be 'incentivised' by tax reliefs, it must not be overlooked that the tax relief merely reduces but does not remove the economic cost to the donor of making a gift. If you wish to give to your favourite charity £10 after deduction of income tax the fact that HMRC will add to the value of the gift the income tax already paid by you (£2.50 on the grossed-up amount of £12.50 at 2008–09 rates of income tax) does not alter the fact that you must first be prepared to reduce your disposable income by that £10. Notwithstanding the extension of tax reliefs to individual and corporate donors there is scant empirical evidence to suggest that in the UK we are 'incentivised' to increase our donations to charity. Research commissioned by Charities Aid Foundation to coincide with

National Giving Week in October 2004 suggested that for most people donating more to charity would be a low priority if they had extra disposable income (CAF News, October 2004; see also Edwards *A Bit Rich? What the Wealthy Think about Giving* (Institute for Public Policy Research, 2002); Walker and Pharoah *A Lot to Give – Trends in Charitable Giving for the 21st Century* (2002)). Even the response to disaster appeals can give a misleading impression. Based on data from the Disasters Emergency Committee, it is estimated that for each £1m given to disaster appeals overall giving increases by just £0.2m, so that £0.8m simply replaces other giving (see Abdy et al *Donations Foresight: Project Summary* (2001) p 10).

Nevertheless, following the 1999 Treasury review a package of measures designed to stimulate charitable giving and also to simplify the rules on trading by charities was introduced in the Finance Act 2000 and is summarised below together with details of the other currently applicable fiscal reliefs. One important practical change to emphasise is that with effect from April 2000 the system of providing tax relief where payments were made to a charity under a four-year covenant ceased to have effect. In its place tax relief for donors is now given under the more straightforward Gift Aid regime (see below). It does seem that this simplified system has led to an increase in the proportion of donations for which tax relief can be claimed back by charities from the tax authorities (Charities Aid Foundation *UK Giving* (2007) 21–24).

(2) Fiscal privileges presently accorded to charities and donors

The array of exemptions and reliefs attached to the legal concept of charity breaks down into two groups: those for the charity itself and those for the donor. The following brief outline adopts this classification. It is necessary to note however that the relative straightforwardness of this position has recently been slightly undermined by the implementation of the work of the Tax Law Rewrite programme which has resulted in separate legislative frameworks for charitable trusts on the one hand and unincorporated charities and charitable companies on the other. (See generally HM Revenue and Customs website for full details: www.hmrc.gov.uk/charities/index.htm.)

Exemptions and reliefs for charities   A charitable trust established in the UK is exempt from income tax on property income and on investment income broadly defined (Income Tax Act (ITA) 2007, ss 531 and 532), and a charitable company or unincorporated association enjoys similar exemption from corporation tax (Income and Corporation Taxes Act (ICTA) 1988, s 505(1)). In both categories of exemption there is an important additional requirement: the income must have been applied for charitable purposes only. HMRC therefore potentially has a role in policing the proper use of charity money (see *IRC v Educational Grants Association Ltd* [1967] Ch 993; and Chapter 19, p 1014). The temptation for some donors to exploit these provisions for their own benefit has led to the introduction of anti-avoidance measures where there is a 'substantial donor transaction', substantial being a donation of £25,000 or more in any twelve-month period (ITA 2007, ss 549–552).

Where a charity undertakes any form of trade the profits are in principle liable to income tax unless the charity can bring the activity within one of the limited statutory exemptions or extra-statutory concessions. As regards the former, profits from trading will be exempt only where the profits are used solely for the purposes of the charity and where the trade satisfies one of three conditions. One is that the trade must be exercised in the course of the actual carrying out of a primary purpose of the charity (ITA 2007, s 525(1)(a)); examples would be profits from courses run by an educational charity or from an exhibition held by an art gallery or museum. The second condition is where the work in connection with the trade is mainly carried out by beneficiaries of the charity, for example, selling items made by disabled people who are themselves beneficiaries (ITA 2007, s 525(1)(b)). The third condition, introduced by the Finance Act 2000 and now in ITA 2007, s 526 is where the charity can bring itself within a 'small scale' trading exemption. Under this provision where the annual turnover falls below certain limits the profits will be exempt from income tax. The current annual turnover limit is £5,000, or if the turnover is greater than £5,000, 25% of the charity's gross income, subject to a cap of £50,000. To reiterate, if a trade does not satisfy one of the above conditions, the profits of the trade will *in principle* not be exempt from tax regardless of whether or not they are used for the purposes of the charity.

In practice, however, these limitations on the availability of tax exemption for trading activity are more apparent than real for three reasons. First, it is evident that trading activity which is ancillary to the carrying out of a primary purpose of the charity will also be exempted. The provision by a university of a crèche for the children of students or the sale of refreshments to visitors to a museum are amongst the examples cited by HMRC (see generally Kessler (1995–96) 3 CL & PR 3 at 149–156). Second, as an extra-statutory concession, HMRC does not charge tax in respect of profits made from 'incidental' fund-raising activities provided that the activities would qualify for exemption from Value Added Tax (VAT), an exemption covering events such as sponsored walks, bazaars, jumble sales and, perhaps more saliently nowadays, car boot sales (ITA 2007, s 529 and VAT Act 1994, Schedule 9, Group 12).

The third and most important reason why the limitations are more apparent than real lies in the use of subsidiary trading companies. Where trading is carried on that is not within one of the exemptions, most charities form a subsidiary company to run the trade. Companies owned by charities are liable to pay tax on trading profits in the same way as other companies. But, like other companies, they can get tax relief for donations to charity. By donating all of their taxable profits to charity under the Gift Aid scheme the company can get a tax deduction in its corporation tax computation equal to the amount of the profits. Thus the profits of the company are kept effectively at zero thereby avoiding paying corporation tax (see ICTA 1988, s 339, as amended by Finance

Act 2000, s 40; Finance Act 1997, s 64; and [1997] BTR 4 at 218–221). In the hands of the charity the donation will not be regarded as trading income, so that it will be exempted from tax (provided, of course, the donation is used for charitable purposes). Under the Gift Aid scheme the company itself gets relief for the actual payment it makes to the charity and because the company has not deducted tax from the payment the charity no longer has to make a claim to HMRC. Whilst this system has the merit of simplicity it does depend on companies ensuring that they pay over to the charity the full amount they wish to give, remembering that the charity will not be receiving an additional amount back in tax from HMRC, as was the position prior to 1 April 2000. There is some evidence that at least initially this was not happening (CAF Research *Briefing Paper* March 2003).

As regards capital assets of a charity, no CGT is payable where a gain accrues to a charity, again provided the gain is applied for charitable purposes, and no stamp duty is payable on the transfer of assets to a charity (Taxation of Chargeable Gains Act (TCGA) 1992, s 256).

Charities are entitled to an 80% reduction in non-domestic rates on properties which they occupy and are used 'wholly or mainly for charitable purposes' and a local authority has discretion to waive the whole or any part of the balance (Local Government Finance Act (LGFA) 1988, ss 43(5) and (6), 47). This applies equally to buildings occupied for administrative purposes and to 'charity shops' (LGFA 1988, s 64(10)).

As previously indicated, there is no general exemption for charities from VAT, a tax levied on all goods and services supplied in the course of a business. Whilst VAT may be chargeable on goods and services supplied by *some* charities (see Warburton (1994–95) 3 CL & PR at 37–46) almost all charities will have to bear VAT on goods and services which they purchase – the 'input' tax (but see Value Added Tax Act 1994, Sch 8, Groups 4, 5, 6, 8, 12 and 15 and Sch 9, Groups 6, 7, 10, 12 and 13 for reliefs in the zero-rate and for exempt schedules respectively). Charities can benefit from zero-rating in two ways. One is that if the particular goods or services supplied to the charity are within those specified in Sch 8 then VAT will not be added to the cost to the charity. The second benefit accrues where a charity makes zero-rated 'supplies' to its beneficiaries or to others. Then not only will no VAT be chargeable to the beneficiary but also the charity will be able to recover 'input' VAT charged in respect of that supply. The sale of stray cats and dogs by an animal rescue charity, for instance, is zero-rated under Sch 8. These particular benefits do not significantly mitigate the position concerning irrecoverable VAT currently paid by charities, estimated at £460m a year (HM Treasury *Review of Charity Taxation* (1999) para 5.10; see also the government decision that 'no fundamental changes' should be made to the VAT system to permit recovery of this money by charities: HM Treasury *The Role of the Voluntary and Community Sector in Service Delivery: A Cross Cutting Review* (2002) p 27; Warburton [2007] BTR 1, 73–86).

Exemptions and reliefs for donors   There is no charge to inheritance tax on gifts to charities by individuals during lifetime or on death (IHTA 1984, s 23), or if made by way of payment from a pre-existing trust (s 76). There is also no charge to CGT where property is disposed of to a charity (TCGA 1992, s 241). As a result of a number of changes since 1990, in computing their income for higher rates of income taxpayers can now deduct any payment made to charity under Gift Aid (ITA 2007, s 414). Moreover, as indicated above, a charity receiving a qualifying donation under Gift Aid is treated as receiving the payment net of basic rate tax and can accordingly reclaim the tax from HMRC. If, for example, the taxpayer gives a total of £400 to various charities then under Gift Aid this sum is treated as a gift made net of basic rate tax (ie after tax has been taken off at the basic rate). With the basic rate in 2008–09 at 20%, the charities reclaim £100 (£400 x 20/80) and the taxpayer's gross gift becomes worth £500 (£400 + £100) to the charities. One limitation to be noted on the Gift Aid scheme is that a gift will not be a qualifying donation if the donor receives benefits in return for the gift that are, broadly speaking, more than 25% of the value of the gift (ITA 2007, s 418; and see *St Dunstan's v Major* [1997] STC 212). Certain admission rights, such as those admitting National Trust members to the Trust's properties free of charge, are disregarded for this purpose (ITA 2007, s 420). As well as giving money through Gift Aid an individual donor can also get income tax relief for gifts to charity of certain shares and securities (ITA 2007, s 431). Also, as indicated in the previous section, Gift Aid donations by a company are deductible from its taxable profits for corporation tax purposes.

Lastly, to complete the picture, there has been in force since 1987 a 'payroll deduction scheme', also known as Give as You Earn (GAYE). Under the terms of the scheme, as widened by the Finance Act 2000, employers may, if they wish, operate an arrangement whereby employees can obtain tax relief on donations to charity deducted from their wages (Income Tax (Earnings and Pensions) Act 2003, ss 713–715; see Morris [1989] Conv 175 and [1991] 5(1) TLI 3).

(3) The value of the privileges

The precise value of these exemptions and reliefs is uncertain. Whereas the approximate value of VAT and local authority rate relief and a more precise figure on tax repaid to charities in respect of Gift Aid are known, no exact information is available about the cost of exempting charities from tax on income which they receive without deduction of tax. HMRC has estimated that the total value of the reliefs for charities for the tax year 2007–08 is £2,190m (*HMRC Statistics 2007–08* Table 10.2). To this amount can be added the sum of £770m attributable to the various reliefs given to individual donors themselves. This figure does not include any of the reliefs available to corporate donors for whom data is not available. One way of interpreting the amount of the known tax relief is that the figure is equivalent to approximately 3.0p on the standard rate of income tax.

(4) Fiscal 'privilege': a misnomer?

Our adoption of the term 'privilege' for the tax reliefs and exemptions described above assumes the validity of a particular principle for evaluating the effects of a tax system. The Royal Commission on the Taxation of Profits and Income put the point clearly in their 1955 Report: 'Accepting the view that all parts of the national income are prima facie subject to a tax on income, the system does amount in effect to a grant of public moneys towards the furtherance of such causes as come within the legal category of charity' ((Cmd 9474, 1955) para 164). From this standpoint it is a short step to the position that tax reliefs should be equated with other forms of government expenditure for the purposes of justifiability and control and this concept of 'tax expenditures' (as the reliefs are then called) has received official recognition (HM Treasury *Public Expenditure White Paper* (Cmnd 7439, 1979); see generally Surrey and McDaniel *Tax Expenditures* (1985); Willis and Hardwick *Tax Expenditures in the United Kingdom* (1978); and Hogwood 'The Hidden Face of Public Expenditure' (1989) 17(2) Policy and Politics at 111). Description can easily slide into prescription here. Consider therefore the strong note of dissent registered by Kristol about the adoption of such language and the implication that, in the interests of efficient budgetary control, tax reliefs should be replaced by a system of direct subsidies ('Taxes, Poverty and Equality' (1974) 37 The Public Interest 3 at 15):

> Whereas a subsidy used to mean a governmental expenditure for a certain purpose, it now acquires quite another meaning – ie a generous decision by government not to take your money.
>
> When a man makes a tax-deductible gift to charity, whose money has he given away? Traditionally, it has been thought that he gives away his own money, and that the tax deduction exists only to encourage him to give away his own money for such a purpose. Today, however, one hears it commonly said that he has only in part given away his own money – in actuality he has also given away some 'public' money . . . It is then said – indeed, it is now a cliché – that the object of his philanthropy (a museum, say) is *'in effect'* being subsidised by public monies.
>
> What we are talking about here is no slight terminological quibble. At issue is a basic principle of social and political philosophy – the principle that used to be called 'private property'. The conversion of tax incentives into 'tax subsidies' or 'tax expenditures' means that 'in effect' a substantial part of everyone's income really belongs to the government – only the government, when it generously or foolishly refrains from taxing it away, tolerates our possession and use of it.

Whether or not such terms as 'subsidy' or 'expenditure' or indeed 'privilege' are appropriate, it is *not* a necessary corollary of their adoption that the existing system of tax reliefs should be replaced by direct state subsidies. It would be equally plausible to retain a system of reliefs but one available, for instance, to a more restricted category of charities. The use of terms such as 'privilege' does, however, imply that the favoured tax treatment at present potentially available to all charities should be justifiable. We review this issue in more detail in Chapter 19 after we have examined more closely the definition of charity.

It is convenient to mention here a further strand of criticism of the tax 'privileges' that is directed principally at their perceived beneficial consequences for the trading and contracting activities of some charities. The most obvious manifestation of this phenomenon is the large number of charity shops to be found in our shopping centres. The expansion of this commercial activity has prompted complaints, particularly from small businesses, that tax reliefs give charities (or their trading subsidiaries) an unfair competitive advantage in selling to the public (see eg *The Deakin Report* (1996) pp 91–92; Beer [1995] BTR at 156–172).

Finally, it must be noted that the term 'privilege' can be misleading in another way. Some of the exemptions and reliefs granted to charities and donors are also available to non-charitable institutions and people who give to them. The inheritance tax legislation, for example, contains partial exemption for gifts to political parties (IHTA 1984, s 24), and friendly societies, whether or not charitable, enjoy exemptions from taxation on both capital gains and income (ICTA 1988, s 459) provided that their income does not exceed certain statutory limits. Some 5,180 sports clubs which are registered (as at 2 March 2009) with HMRC under the Community Amateur Sports Club (CASC) scheme established under the Finance Act 2002 receive tax and rate reliefs very similar to those available to comparable charitable sporting bodies.

(c) Charities and discrimination

Although not normally considered as a 'privilege' of charitable status, it is in our view appropriate to mention in this context the special provision applicable to charities in current anti-discrimination legislation. By virtue of the Sex Discrimination Act (SDA) 1975, the Race Relations Act (RRA) 1976, the Disability Discrimination Act (DDA) 1995 and the Equality Act (EA) 2006, it is unlawful to discriminate in a wide range of prescribed circumstances on grounds of sex, colour, race, nationality or ethnic or national origins or disability or religion. In a number of general capacities – for example, as employers or owners of property – charities are bound by these Acts to the same extent as other individuals or organisations. There is an exception from this proscription for charities who provide employment opportunities for particular categories of disabled persons. Under DDA 1995, s 10 it is not unlawful for such charities to treat those categories of persons more favourably than other disabled persons. Were this not so, the Royal National Institute for the Blind, for example, would not be able to offer employment to visually handicapped people in preference to people with other kinds of disability.

When it comes to conferral of benefits on persons charities enjoy a general immunity from the Acts, subject to the one exception under the RRA 1976 described below. Under SDA 1975, s 43(2), where a 'charitable instrument' contains a provision for conferring benefits on persons of one sex only, this provision is not invalidated by the Act. Thus single-sex charities such as the YMCA or Girl Guides are quite lawful (see also *Hugh-Jones v St John's College, Cambridge* [1979] ICR 848 – single-sex research fellowship lawful). Similarly under RRA 1976 s 34(2), (3), and EA 2006, s 58 the general position is that provisions for conferring benefits on persons of a class defined by reference to race, nationality or ethnic or national origins or religion or belief are exempt from the Acts. In short, it is lawful to discriminate in favour of, but not against, such groups although distinguishing the positive from the negative provides fertile ground for imaginative draftsmanship (see the decision of the Charity Commission in 2007 to reject the application for registration from the English Ethnic Trust and Ironside Community Trust: www.charity-commission.gov.uk/Library/registration/pdfs/eetrustdecision.pdf). The same effect is achieved with regard to disabled persons by DDA 1995, s 19(5)(k). The one exception, however, is that in a provision defining a beneficial class by reference to colour, the colour qualification is void (s 34(1)) and must be disregarded by the charity trustees. Thus a trust 'to educate white children in Coventry' would become a trust 'to educate children in Coventry' (see also *In the Estate of Winsome Joy Harding* [2007] EWHC 3, 'Black community of Hackney, Haringey, Islington and Tower Hamlets' where the colour restriction is disregarded).

This privileged status emphasises the autonomy enjoyed by charitable donors. It also leaves scope for charitable organisations to pursue 'affirmative action' for minorities at a disadvantage in the community – which is indeed one of charity's primary functions (see also the decision of the Charity Commissioners on the charitable status of community associations for the benefit of ethnic minorities (*Decisions of the Charity Commissioners* vol 4 (1995) 17)). It is noteworthy, however, that apparently lawful discriminatory provisions may still be subject to removal under the cy-près doctrine (see *Re Lysaght* [1966] Ch 191; *Re Dominion Students' Hall Trust* [1947] Ch 183 where a 'colour bar' was removed from the constitution of a London hall of residence for Commonwealth and American students; and Watkin [1981] Conv 131 where s 34(1) is severely criticised). It only remains to add that the excision in *Re Lysaght* of a religious discrimination condition on the grounds that it was not an essential part of the true paramount charitable intention of the testatrix reflects a liberal application of the cy-près doctrine (see also *Re Woodhams* [1981] 1 All ER 202; and the still more explicit decision of the Ontario Court of Appeal in *Re Canada Trust Co and Ontario Human Rights Commission* (1990) 69 DLR (4th) 321). The exercise of the doctrine in this fashion suggests that our perception of cy-près as a privilege needs on occasion to be adjusted to incorporate the notion of control. It also suggests that interpretation of the cy-près doctrine in this manner forestalls any need to address jurisdictional difficulties that recourse to the non-discrimination provisions of the Human Rights Act 1998 might pose.

5. Conclusion

We have described in this chapter the importance of legal privileges for charitable trusts and of fiscal privileges for all charities. Charitable status also has a more indirect significance in relation to fund-raising. Whereas it is rarely a requirement of access to central or local government grant support, smaller organisations are 'nevertheless often dependent on gaining charitable status, as such status is almost always the prerequisite for grant-aid from charitable trusts' (Goodman Committee Report *Charity Law and Voluntary Organisations* (1976) para 7). The reason is simple enough: the grant-giving trust, in order that it may itself have the benefits of charitable status, will usually be bound by its own constitution to confine its grant-making activities to organisations of a charitable nature. There are some notable exceptions (eg Gulbenkian Foundation) but a very high proportion of the considerable resources which are locked up in the very large and well-known grant-making trusts – Wellcome, Nuffield, Cadbury, Rowntree and so on – as well as in numerous other smaller but still very affluent ones, are held upon charitable trusts. The consequence is that any grant-seeking organisation wishing to obtain even only a minute share of the resources of any one of them must itself be a charity. If the trustees of the grant-making trust ignore this requirement they violate their own duties as trustees. The importance of charitable status for access to funding has been slightly reduced with the advent of the National Lottery. The BLF is empowered to make grants 'for charitable, benevolent or philanthropic purposes' (see National Lottery etc Act 1993, s 44(1)). This form of wording sidesteps the problem highlighted in charity law by the 'and/or' cases discussed earlier in this chapter (see p 940).

One possible further indirect advantage of charitable status in the fund-raising context is that it may be treated by donors as a mark of respectability, responsibility and proven worth, perhaps even encouraging them to give without closely investigating the value of the activity being carried out. A study by Ipsos Mori on behalf of the Charity Commission suggests there is a high level of trust and confidence in charities, apparently higher, for instance, than that shown for central or local government, private companies or banks (see *Public Trust and Confidence in Charities* (Charity Commission, 2008); cf the ambiguous attitudes to charitable giving revealed in a report: Edwards *A Bit Rich? What the Wealthy Think about Giving* (Institute for Public Policy Research, 2002)).

A generally positive view of the benefits of charitable status for fund-raising today should not blind us to the possibility that perceptions of donors can change. We have seen in this chapter that income donated to charity by individuals appears to be somewhat static in real terms. In fact this outcome reflects the effect of two opposing trends: the number of households giving is declining whilst the amount donated per household is increasing (see Banks and Tanner *The State of Donation: Household Gifts to Charity 1974–1996* IFS Commentary 62 (1997)). Significantly the greatest proportionate decline is amongst young households in their twenties and thirties. Moreover these households are less likely to give than were today's middle-aged households when they were young. The cause for this shift remains to be determined but Pharoah and Tanner, reviewing the evidence, suggest that the decline may plausibly be linked to 'wider social and economic changes, such as increasing income inequality and uncertainty, and *changes in the role of charitable organisations*' (emphasis added) ((1997) 18(4) Fiscal Studies 441). In so far as this role is associated with delivery of public services there is evidence that public opinion is divided over this matter with, according to one recent survey, 30% being in favour, 32% being opposed and 38% not sure. Of concern from the standpoint of donations one in four of those surveyed stated that they would be less likely to donate to charities which receive income from government to provide services (*Charity Awareness Monitor*, February 2007, www.nfpsynergy.net).

These practical consequences of charitable status and of contemporary charity activity, and indeed the legal and fiscal privileges described earlier, do not have any necessary connection with those aspects of charity law concerning the definition of charitable purposes and the supervision of charities to be considered in Chapters 19 and 20 respectively. Yet implicit in our previous suggestion that charity law can, with an element of truth, be described as a sub-branch of fiscal law, is a premise that a link exists between the two which extends beyond merely recognising that charitable status can have legal and fiscal consequences. To be specific, in our study of present charity law in the next two chapters, we need to consider how far charity law concerning definition and supervision of charities has been and is influenced both by the alteration in fiscal privileges and the changes in the relationship between philanthropic activity and state welfare that we have outlined. As regards the definition of charity it can be argued that the fiscal consequences accompanying the label 'charitable' have directly influenced judicial decisions, particularly as regards the 'public benefit' requirement, with the result that a more stringent definition has emerged (see in particular Cross (1956) 72 LQR 187 at 204–206). This argument is considered further in Chapter 19, whilst in Chapter 20 we consider the price that the law now imposes on charities in terms of subjection to official supervision, principally in the Charities Act 1993, in return for the privileges it grants and the more extensive role being bestowed upon charities by the state.

Consider the following points:

(1) The following proposition is advanced by Newby in 'The Deferential Dialectic' (1975) 17 Comparative Studies in Society and History 139 at 161:

> Clearly one does not wish to deny the conscious validity of the philanthropic and Christian motivations to charity, but charity has long been, *in effect,* an integral part of the legitimation of social subordination, not only through its status-enhancing properties but because it has been used discriminatingly in favour of the 'deserving' (ie deferential) poor.

Do you agree?

(2) How would you have decided the issues in *Pemsel*?

(3) Under the cy-près doctrine, is too much significance attached to the 'intention of the donor' in deciding whether there is (i) an 'initial failure' or (ii) a general charitable intention?

(4) Five children, aged between two and ten, are orphaned following a motorway accident. The mayor of their home town wishes to appeal for funds 'to help them'. Draft the appeal for her.

(5) Does the current system of tax and business rate reliefs granted to charities unfairly advantage them with regard to the commercial operators, often small businesses, with whom they compete? See, for example, Beer [1995] BTR 156–172; Rose-Ackerman (1982) 34 Stan LR 1017; Hansmann (1989) 75 Vir LR 605.

19

A legal definition of 'charity'

1. Introduction

(a) An agenda for change

In the previous chapter we observed that the nineteenth century had handed on a definition of charity based on the preamble to the Statute of Charitable Uses 1601 but encrusted with a luxuriant growth of case law. Despite several official and unofficial proposals during the twentieth century to reform and/or clarify the definition the legislature had until recently taken no major steps in this direction (see Colwyn Commission (Cmd 615, 1920) Pt III, s xiv; Nathan Report (Cmd 8710, 1952) paras 123–140; Report of the Radcliffe Commission on the Taxation of Profits and Income (Cmd 9474, 1955) ch 7; Goodman Committee Report *Charity Law and Voluntary Organisations* (1976) para 23 and App I). There had been an obvious opportunity for reform at the time of the Charities Act 1960 but this statute, while repealing the 1601 preamble, left the definition itself untouched. The matter appeared to have been settled by the Conservative government in its 1989 review of the regulatory framework provided by charity law (*Charities: A Framework For the Future* (Cm 694, 1989). The opinion expressed in the Review was that any reformulation or attempt to give the definition statutory effect was undesirable: 'There would appear to be few advantages in attempting a wholesale redefinition of charitable status – and many real dangers in doing so' (para 2.17). One of those dangers was perceived to be that a statutory definition would put at risk a valuable feature of the common law definition, its flexibility. The legislation that ensued (Charities Acts 1992 and 1993) was predominantly concerned with matters of regulation and accountability (see Chapter 20) and left the definition untouched.

The settlement adopted in the early 1990s did not still debate on the subject of charity law. Indeed quite the contrary was the case and the debate gained added impetus in the next decade as a series of reports from think-tanks, pressure groups and committees all contributed to the maelstrom (see eg Knight *CENTRIS Report: Voluntary Action in the 1990s* (1993); Mulgan and Landry *The Other Invisible Hand* (1996 Demos)). The critique developed in the Demos study, its authors intriguingly including Geoffrey Mulgan, later to become head of the Downing Street Policy Innovation Unit, was particularly acerbic: 'The [voluntary] sector remains defined legally by a rag bag of outdated rules and definitions, by tax privileges that are often inappropriate, and by rules of governance that are at best ill-defined and at worst paternalistic' (at p 11). A more restrained contribution was to emerge in the same year from a Commission, the Deakin Commission, set up under the auspices of a co-ordinating pressure group for the voluntary sector, the National Council for Voluntary Organisations, to report on the role for the voluntary sector in general (NCVO *The Report of the Commission on the Future of the Voluntary Sector* (1996)). Amongst its many recommendations was that there should be a single umbrella definition, the Report itself appearing to favour a formulation along the lines of 'purposes beneficial to the community' although it recommended that the matter should be referred to the Law Commission. This did not happen but in 1998 the Charity Commission of its own volition initiated a review 'to consider the scope of charitable status within the current law and in the light of changing social and economic circumstances'. In particular the review was to consider 'whether there is scope to develop further the boundaries of charitable status by the flexible use of our powers to apply and interpret the law' (RR1 *The Review of the Register of Charities* (October 2001) para 2). Some review papers sought to clarify what the Commission viewed as general principles such as Public Benefit (see RR8 *The Public Character of Charities* (2001)) whilst others give guidance on the approach of the Commissioners to the 'flexible use of powers' in incrementally extending the boundaries of charitable status (see eg ranging from RR2 *Promotion of Urban and Rural Regeneration* (1999) to RR11 *Charitable Status and Sport* (2003) and more recently RR12 *Promotion of Human Rights* (2005)).

The review process was to a large extent overtaken by events when in July 2001 the Prime Minister referred the whole matter of the legal context within which charity and the voluntary sector in general operate to the Cabinet Office Strategy Unit. This initiative can be seen as part of the overall government strategy to enhance the economic and social contribution of charities and the wider not-for-profit sector (see generally Chapter 18). The Strategy Unit report recommended a diverse range of reforms to the legal framework, many concerned with accountability (see Chapter 20), but also proposing the adoption of a statutory definition of charitable purposes (*Private Action, Public Benefit. A Review of Charities and the Wider Not-For-Profit Sector* (2002)). The recommendation as regards definition was accepted by the government subject only to minor modifications (Home Office *Charities and Not-for-Profits: A Modern Legal Framework* (July 2003)) and a draft Charities Bill was published in May 2004 for pre-legislative scrutiny by a Joint Committee of both Houses of Parliament (Report *The Draft Charities Bill* HL 167 / HC 660 (September 2004)). A slightly revised version of the Charities Bill was introduced in the House of Lords in December 2004. The General Election of 2005 intervened but there was a broad measure of cross-party support for the legislation, which was reintroduced and finally reached the statute book as the Charities Act (CA) 2006.

(b) The Charities Act 2006

Whilst the CA 2006 is predominantly concerned with the modernisation of the regulatory framework within which the Charity Commission and charities must operate (see Chapter 20) it also sets out a statutory definition of 'charity'. As was the position under the CA 1960, charity is stated to mean 'an institution which is established for charitable purposes only' and which is subject to the control of the High Court (CA 2006, s 1(1)). A charitable purpose is then defined in s 2(1) as one which (a) 'falls within subsection 2' (see below) and (b) 'is for the public benefit'. In short the intention is that all the purposes listed in s 2(2) are only *potentially* charitable; 'potentially' because to be granted charitable status the purpose must also be 'for the public benefit' (s 2(1)(b) and s 3). The purposes listed in s 2(2) are as follows:

(a) the prevention or relief of poverty,
(b) the advancement of education;
(c) the advancement of religion;
(d) the advancement of health or the saving of lives;
(e) the advancement of citizenship or community development;
(f) the advancement of the arts, culture, heritage or science;
(g) the advancement of amateur sport;
(h) the advancement of human rights, conflict resolution or reconciliation or the promotion of religious or racial harmony or equality and diversity;
(i) the advancement of environmental protection or improvement;
(j) the relief of those in need by reason of youth, age, ill-health, disability, financial hardship or other disadvantage;
(k) the advancement of animal welfare;
(l) the promotion of the efficiency of the armed forces of the Crown, or of the efficiency of the police, fire and rescue services or ambulance services;
(m) any other purposes within subsection (4).

Subsection 4 in effect retains the 'other purposes beneficial to the community' category, the fourth of the categories of charitable purposes set out by Lord Macnaghten in *Income Tax Special Purposes Commissioners v Pemsel* [1891] AC 531.

Before examining the present definition in more detail a number of general observations are in order. First, subject to two minor caveats the thirteen 'heads' or 'categories' of charity are clearly derived from and largely reflect the existing types of charitable purposes established by case law. Indeed the government specifically indicated that the new statutory list would not exclude any purposes that are currently charitable (Home Office *Charities and Not-for-Profits:*

A Modern Legal Framework (July 2003) para 3.13). Arguably the advancement of amateur sport as a specific purpose goes further than the present law which has tended to regard sport as charitable only where it is a means to the achievement of some other charitable purpose such as encouraging participation in healthy recreation (see below, p 994). Also the advancement of 'conflict resolution or reconciliation' might be argued to represent a modest extension in the current law although it would appear to have been foreshadowed by dicta in *Southwood v Attorney-General* [2000] WTLR 1199 (see below, p 1001). In both these instances the government accepted the view, almost as if for the avoidance of doubt, that the purposes should be confirmed as charitable in the interests of greater certainty (para 3.12). The decision, in a sense, to 'codify' the existing common law definition in a more detailed and explicit form seems based on the premise that 'the definition is largely inaccessible to the lay person because of its foundation in the common law' (para 3.12). Whether accessibility will be improved by incorporating in a statute a list of purposes almost identical to those that the Charity Commission or any informed adviser could previously provide remains to be seen. In short it can be argued that the proposed statutory definition of charitable purposes is concerned with image and accessibility rather than any change of real substance.

A second general point to note concerns a presumption of public benefit believed to have applied to the first three categories set out by Lord Macnaghten in *Pemsel*, namely (i) relief of poverty, (ii) advancement of education and (iii) advancement of religion (but cf Hackney (2008) 124 LQR 347 challenging the assumption of a 'presumption'). The government accepted the recommendation that the presumption should be removed (para 3.17) and this is achieved by s 3(2): 'it is not to be presumed that a purpose of a particular description is for the public benefit'. Beyond that modification the government indicated that it did not intend to move to a statutory definition of public benefit and that the common law tests should remain, an intention reflected in s 3(3): 'any reference to the public benefit is a reference to the public benefit as that term is understood for the purposes of the law relating to charities in England and Wales' (see further below, p 1002). The reasons for retaining the non-statutory common law approach to a definition of public benefit are stated to be 'flexibility, certainty and its capacity to accommodate the diversity of the sector' (Home Office *Charities and Not-for-Profits: A Modern Legal Framework* (July 2003) para 3.17).

A further point concerns those matters of 'flexibility, certainty and diversity'. One test of the success of a statutory definition is whether it can adequately accommodate any changing emphasis of philanthropic activity in the future. The retention of the 'any other purposes' catch-all category in s 2(2)(m), which appears potentially to provide the greatest scope for recognising new developments, sends out a positive signal in this regard. There is no reason to think that either the courts or the Charity Commission will resile from the sentiment of Lord Wilberforce, commenting on the scope of that *Pemsel* 'any other purposes' category in a leading case, *Scottish Burial Reform and Cremation Society v Glasgow City Corpn* [1968] AC 138, 'that the law of charity is a moving subject which may well have evolved even since 1891' (at 154).

Lastly, reform is clearly in the air as concern at the appropriateness of the common law definition based on the Macnaghten guidelines from *Pemsel* has been expressed in other Commonwealth jurisdictions. A preference for a statutory definition based predominantly on existing charitable purposes has been recommended in Australia, New Zealand and, closer to home, the Republic of Ireland. (See *The Report of the Inquiry into the Definition of Charities and Related Organisations* (2001), www.cde.gov.au (Australia); Working Party on Registration *Reporting and Monitoring of Charities* (2002), www.treasury.gov.nz/charities (New Zealand); the Law Reform Committee of the Law Society of Ireland *Charity Law: The Case for Reform* (2002); and see generally Picarda (2002) 8 CL & PR 1.) A comparable reform has been introduced in the Scottish legal system under the Charity and Trustee Investment (Scotland) Act 2005 (see Ford (2005) 16 KCLJ 1; www.oscr.org.uk).

(c) Summary

In light of the changes outlined above it is appropriate here to indicate the overall framework into which the legal definition has become crystallised and now encapsulated in statutory form. In order to be charitable in law the purposes of a trust or other institution must satisfy the following criteria:

(1) They must fall within one or more of the statutory categories referred to above. Alternatively, the purposes may be one of those set out in s 1 of the Recreational Charities Act 1958. Frequently an organisation's purposes belong to two or more of the categories (as eg would occur in the case of a trust 'to educate the poor children of Willesden').

(2) The purposes must also satisfy the requirement of being for the 'public benefit'. This requirement comprises two distinct, though closely related, principles that can be phrased as follows. Principle 1: there must be an identifiable benefit or benefits; Principle 2: the benefit must be available to the public at large or to a sufficient section of the public.

As indicated above, CA 2006, s 3(2) removes the presumption that compliance with Principle 1 was satisfied, assuming the presumption was not rebutted, once it was shown that a particular purpose was for the relief of poverty or the advancement of education or, less certainly, the advancement of religion. Removing a presumption, even one whose effect could be sidestepped or marginalised by appropriate evidence or interpretation of the meaning of a concept such as education, potentially opens up to scrutiny a number of troublesome legal and policy issues. We know from the case law that benefit can take different forms; it can be tangible or intangible, direct or indirect. But what criteria can we apply in determining whether an organisation's stated purpose or its advancement provides sufficient benefit to qualify as being charitable? It seems unlikely, for instance, that any special evidence would be required nowadays to demonstrate that providing emergency aid to the victims of a natural disaster would be beneficial. But opinions may differ sharply when matters of religious belief or educational benefit or artistic merit or promotion of animal welfare as against animal experimentation for medical research are concerned. As regards the evidence, three basic points can be made at this preliminary stage. First, the subjective opinion of the donor or founder of the organisation that the particular purpose claimed is of public benefit does not determine the outcome. Second, in circumstances where benefit is not self-evident, unlike our disaster relief example, it is well established that whether there is a benefit 'is a question to be answered by the court on forming an opinion on the evidence before it' (Russell J in *Re Hummeltenberg* [1923] 1 Ch 237 at 242 – a case concerning the training of mediums). The court or more commonly the Charity Commission will therefore, where appropriate, have regard to expert opinion and seek to arrive at an objective assessment of benefit, and this will include balancing benefits against possible detriments or harm. Third, assessment of public benefit is not a popularity test based on public opinion, although the Charity Commission suggests that 'public attitudes and opinion . . . can enable us to shape the legal understanding of what is charitable in a way that is relevant for today's society' (*Charities and Public Benefit* (2008) para D8). This last observation is likely to be most relevant where the 'some other purpose' category is concerned. It is not fruitful to go beyond these general observations at this stage and the interpretation of Principle 1 is in our view best explored by considering it in the context of the specific heads of charitable purposes.

Principle 2 – the 'section of the public' requirement – poses problems of a different order. Under the pre-CA 2006 law several distinct tests were developed by the courts, a development difficult to pigeonhole under specific categories of charitable purpose. Indeed, notwithstanding the Government's claim that the common law approach to interpretation of public benefit offered 'certainty', the law developed in a way that resulted in some confusion, in particular as to the appropriate test(s) to be applied to the 'other beneficial purposes' Macnaghten category in *Pemsel*. In our view discussion of this principle in contrast to Principle 1 is therefore best undertaken as an entity for several reasons. One quite simply is that the rationale(s) for the various tests are more easily understood if studied in this way. A second reason is that interpretation and application of Principle 2 cuts across distinct boundaries of the charitable purposes listed in CA 2006, s 2(2), particularly where the charitable status of fee-charging institutions such as private schools, hospitals or care homes is at issue. Lastly, this is an aspect of charity law where the fiscal privileges discussed in Chapter 18 may have exercised a significant legal and policy influence.

(3) Although not always expressed as separate requirements a trust or other organisation may fail to qualify for charitable status if its purposes (a) are substantially political, or (b) involve profit distribution.

(4) The purposes, unless purely ancillary to the main objects, must be exclusively charitable. This long-standing requirement (see Chapter 18 at p 000) is reflected in s 1(1)(a): '. . . "charity" means an institution which – (a) is established for charitable purposes *only*' (emphasis added).

Before examining these criteria and their implementation in more detail there are two general observations that must be made about the ways in which the law has been and is being developed.

One observation represents more a warning to the reader when considering decided cases and assessing possible future developments. In different eras fluctuations in judicial attitudes to charity have been in evidence. For example, where there exists an ambiguity in language that might threaten the validity of a charitable gift Lord Loreburn could comment in 1908 that 'there is no better rule than that a benignant construction will be placed upon charitable bequests' (*Weir v Crum-Brown* [1908] AC 162 at 167). Subsequently there emerged a more restrictive attitude towards charity, possibly in response to the increase in its fiscal privileges. This attitude was particularly apparent in decisions affecting both aspects of the public benefit requirement. Thus there has been a hardening of a principle that it is for the court, not the founder of a purported charity, to say whether the purposes stipulated confer a tangible benefit. A dictum in the opposite sense in *Re Foveaux* [1895] 2 Ch 501 per Chitty J has been firmly disapproved of in several later decisions (eg *National Anti-Vivisection Society v IRC* [1948] AC 31 at 44, 66–67; *Re Pinion* [1965] Ch 85 at 106). Similar pressures would appear to have encouraged the courts to develop stricter tests as regards the second limb – the 'section of the public' requirement – notably as we shall see in a number of decisions reached in the immediate post-Second World War period (eg in particular *Re Compton* [1945] Ch 123; *Oppenheim v Tobacco Securities Trust Co Ltd* [1951] AC 297; *IRC v Baddeley* [1955] AC 572).

More recently Lord Hailsham, reaffirming Lord Loreburn's dictum, has said that: 'In construing trust deeds the intention of which is to set up a charitable trust, and in others too, where it can be claimed there is an ambiguity, a benignant construction should be given if possible' (*IRC v McMullen* [1981] AC 1 at 14, endorsed in *Guild v IRC* [1992] 2 All ER 10, HL). Yet neither hostility nor favouritism has ever been unalloyed. A benign construction where the question, for example, is one of uncertainty, or where a gift is capable of two constructions one of which would make it void and the other effectual, is not necessarily inconsistent with the adoption of a restrictive approach in other circumstances. A court might therefore still adopt such a restrictive approach in applying the criteria of public benefit if faced with a trust or other organisation whose purposes it does not consider sufficiently beneficial to merit the accolade of charity and the fiscal privileges that accompany it. Indeed it has been argued that the courts may at times have adopted a stricter approach in cases where the Inland Revenue (now Her Majesty's Revenue and Customs (HMRC)) is a party to the litigation than in those cases where trust validity involves only intra-family disputes (see G (later Lord) Cross (1956) 72 LQR 187 at 204–205). There is, however, little evidence that this approach currently finds favour with the courts (see *Guild v IRC* [1992] 2 All ER 10 at 18).

Our second general observation is that it would be a mistake to assume that courts are frequently making such judgments on charitable status. This is not so: the courts make only a handful of such decisions. A trust or other organisation seeking to avail itself of the favours the law bestows on charities must first attain official recognition as a charity (Charities Act (CA) 1993, s 3 and 3A; see section 2 below). This process of official recognition of charitable status can best be illustrated by use of the iceberg metaphor. At the tip of the iceberg is the occasional decision of the courts, whereas the hidden mass of the iceberg is made up of the 5,000 plus administrative decisions of the Charity Commission each year. Of course many of these decisions involve straightforward application of the established case law but the continuing expansion in the range of philanthropic activity, particularly when of a pioneering nature, means that the Charity Commission can be called upon to determine charitable status relatively free from the constraint of established precedents. In such cases it has a significant degree of discretion, and its decisions are in many instances a better guide to the boundaries of 'charitable purpose' than older decisions of the courts.

In the rest of this chapter our approach to examining the definition of charity is as follows: the purposes listed in CA 2006, s 2(2) and the statutory category under the Recreational Charities Act 1958 are each considered in turn. We then consider separately the second limb of public benefit – 'the section of the public' requirement – because it is of such key importance to the definition, and its development and present limits are best understood if presented this way. Finally we consider two particularly contentious aspects of charitable status – 'fee-charging institutions' and 'politics' – and conclude with some comments about reform.

First, however, in the next section we briefly outline the procedures governing official recognition as a charity, with particular reference to the role of the Charity Commission.

2. Procedure governing registration as a charity

For the first 60 years of the twentieth century the function of determining charitable status was shared between the courts, the Inland Revenue and the Charity Commission. Then, in 1960 an almost universally mandatory system of registration with the Charity Commission was instituted and subsequently expanded in the Charities Act 1993. The CA 2006 substitutes three new sections – 3, 3A and 3B – for the previous s 3 of the 1993 Act although the new ss 3 and 3B in effect reproduce in a different structure the previous provision. Section 3A, by contrast, introduces new requirements for the registration of charities, making different provision for different categories of charity.

Under s 3(1)–(3), the Commission is required to establish and maintain a register of 'charities', in which particulars to be specified by them are to be entered with regard to every charity not specifically excused by s 3A(2) from the obligation to register. Charities excused include (i) 'exempt charities' (s 3A(2)(a) and Sch 2) which are those broadly speaking subject to some alternative form of supervisory control (eg universities, trustees of various national art galleries and museums, further education corporations); (ii) charities excepted by order of the Charity Commission or regulations made by the Secretary of State and whose gross annual income does not exceed £100,000 (s 3A(2)(b)(c)) and (iii) largely on grounds of administrative convenience, small charities (s 3A(2)(d)), ie those whose income from all sources does not amount to more than £5,000 a year. It is anticipated that the effect of raising the income threshold for registration from £1,000 to £5,000 will release several thousand small charities from the obligation to register. Whether this will result in small charities deciding not to register is uncertain since many take the view that the cachet of being a registered charity outweighs the potential administrative disadvantages of registration. The mandatory obligation on the Commission to register all 'charities' not specifically excused is reinforced by s 3B(1)(a) under which the 'charity trustees' are under a duty to apply for registration and to supply to the Charity Commission copies (or where no document is extant, particulars) of the 'trusts' of the charity and such other documents and information as the Commission may require. It constitutes an offence to provide false or misleading information to the Commission (CA 1993, s 11). The Register, which is now computerised, is open to public inspection. In cases of doubt or difficulty about the charitable nature of an organisation applying for registration the Commission is empowered (s 10) to consult with HMRC, and will usually do so, not least because the latter is the most likely appellant against a contentious decision to register.

Any impression that the Charity Commission is simply a 'rubber-stamping' administrative authority would be misleading for two reasons both of which provide it with a degree of discretion. First, there are the ambiguities and gaps within the definition that have already been mentioned. Second, there is an investigative element in the registration process.

As regards the latter, the Commission observed in its 1966 Annual Report that 'we are bound by the decision of the courts to base our decision whether an institution is a charity upon the words used in its constitution or other instrument of government' (para 34; see also *McGovern v A-G* [1982] Ch 321 at 346 to the effect that it should not be inferred that trustees will use unlawful means in carrying out their charitable purposes). This observation appears to negate any suggestion of discretion. In the same report, however (paras 37–40), the Commission demonstrates a readiness to probe into the activities of an organisation and the intention of trustees if faced with *draft documents* that (para 37) 'attempt to dress up the purposes of the proposed institution in words which it is hoped will be accepted as charitable even though the purposes, as phrased, are quite remote from the true intentions of the promoters'. By 1996 this approach is confirmed and arguably broadened into a more general practice whereby consideration of any applicant organisa-tion's purposes is stated to involve 'looking at both its objects and its activities' (Annual Report para 79). Whether this practice of the Commission is correct as a matter of law is contentious, although recent judicial dicta could be construed as supporting the Commission's position. In *Southwood v Attorney-General* [2000] WTLR 1199 Chadwick LJ comments that 'the declaration of trust, like any other written instrument, must be construed with a proper regard to the circumstances in which it came to be executed. . . . [I]t is necessary to look at the material emanating from [the trustees] in advance of the execution of the declaration of trust' (see also Mitchell 'Reviewing the Register' in Mitchell and Moody (eds) *Foundations of Charity* (2000) p 175 at pp 184–6; and note the decision of the government to decline to clarify in statute the circumstances in which the Commission can employ an 'activities test', Home Office, *Charities and Not-for-Profits: A Modern Legal Framework* (2003) paras 6.9–6.11). The consequence is that in practice most organisations are likely to comply with 'invitations', 'suggestions' or 'strong advice' from the Commission to amend their documentation and procedures, if that is the price to pay for registration (see eg *Decisions of the Charity Commissioners* vol 4 (1995) pp 1–7, The Fairtrade Foundation). In addition the Commission can require a charity to change its name if its proposed title is 'likely to mislead' the public as to the purposes or activities of the charity (Charities Act 1993, s 6).

The importance of the registration procedure is enhanced by s 4(1) which states: 'An institution shall for all purposes other than rectification of the register be conclusively presumed to be or have been a charity at any time when it is or was on the register.' The significant point here is that the fiscal authorities are bound by the entry on the register subject only to an appeal to the new Charity Tribunal introduced by the CA 2006, s 8 and Sch 4 (see below and Chapter 20), although tax relief may subsequently be disallowed if funds are not used 'for charitable purposes only' (see *IRC v Educational Grants Association Ltd* [1967] Ch 993, discussed below at p 1014). Thus it is the interaction of s 3, making registration mandatory for most charities, and s 4, making it conclusive of charitable status for virtually all purposes, that elevates the registration procedure to its primary position within the institutional structure for official recognition of charitable status.

Given the importance of registration what remedy is there for an aggrieved applicant? Although the Commission operated an informal procedure of inter-nal review and appeal the fact that this process had no external or indepen-dent element had long been a source of criticism. The Strategy Unit Report recommended, and the government agreed, that an independent tribunal should be introduced to hear appeals against the decisions of the Commission as registrar and regulator (*Private Action, Public Benefit* (2002) paras 7.69–7.79). The newly constituted Charity Tribunal has the power to quash the decisions of the Commission and where appropriate either to remit the matter to the Commission for reconsideration or direct the Commission to rectify the register. In effect the tribunal will operate as a 'court of first instance' for appeals against certain decisions of the Charity Commission.

The absence of an independent tribunal did not mean that decisions were unreviewable in the courts. An appeal could be taken to the High Court against any decision of the Commission to grant or refuse registration (or, for that matter, deregistration). The infrequency with which the procedure was invoked – only six appeals between 1961 and 1986, for instance – did not mean that everyone was content with the decisions of the Commission but rather that appeals to the High Court are expensive. Given the relatively scanty resources of the majority of new philanthropic organisations, it is no surprise that appeals were scarcely ever fought to a conclusion. It remains to be seen whether the introduction of the new tribunal will significantly alter this position.

The overall outcome of the establishment of the compulsory registration procedure is that the Commission has developed its own substratum of law and practice regarding what is or is not a charity and has applied this, along with the binding principles established by the courts and more than a smattering of precedents from HMRC, within a framework of administrative rather than judicial procedures.

3. The categories of charity

(a) Prevention and relief of poverty

The 'relief of poverty' constituted the first of the Macnaghten categories in *Pemsel* and can trace its legal origins to the phrase 'the relief of aged, impotent and poor people' in the preamble of 1601. Relief of the aged and relief of the 'impotent' (ie those suffering from sickness or other physical disabilities) now find their home elsewhere in CA 2006, s 2 whilst the poverty heading has been expanded to incorporate 'prevention of poverty'. It is clear that 'relief' and 'prevention' are to be read disjunctively so that a charity can now be set up to deal solely with the issue of preventing poverty. Giving debt or money management advice, thereby helping people in danger of falling into poverty, is cited by the Charity Commission as a potential method of preventing property. Where 'relief of poverty' is concerned the notion has been very broadly interpreted. The prolific case law indicates that whereas purposes drafted in terms of 'poverty' or 'poor people' are, naturally, within the category, these terms are not the only possible ones. Synonyms such as 'of limited means' and 'needy' (*Re Gardom* [1914] 1 Ch 662; *Re Payne's Estate* (1954) 11 WWRNS 424 respectively) are permissible alternatives. They confirm that poverty is not limited to absolute destitution. Moreover, a requirement that poverty is intended to be a prerequisite to obtaining benefit can be inferred without the word 'poverty' or any of the normally accepted synonyms being present. In *Re Niyazi's Will Trusts* [1978] 1 WLR 910, Megarry J held a gift of residue of about £15,000 to help establish a working men's hostel in Cyprus to be for the relief of poverty, notwithstanding that in *Re Sanders* [1954] Ch 265 Harman J had rejected this characterisation for a trust to provide dwellings 'for the working classes and their families', working classes not constituting a section of the poor. A combination of the size of the gift, the nature of the accommodation ('working men's hostel') and evidence of the acute housing shortage in the proposed location provided sufficient connotations of 'lower income' to distinguish *Re Sanders* and make the gift charitable, although it was 'desperately near the borderline' (at 915). A well-known contemporary example of an organisation coming within this category is the Fairtrade Foundation whose purpose – the promotion of a 'fair trade mark' – was accepted by the Commission as a means of relieving poverty.

The Fairtrade Foundation example and, notwithstanding their different outcomes, cases such as *Re Sanders* and *Re Niyazi* are all indirectly confronting a contentious political issue: whether poverty should be defined in absolute or relative terms (see Alcock *Understanding Poverty* (3rd edn, 2006) for a comprehensive and critical survey of the topic). In practice it is probably a mistake to assume that there are just two polar opposite definitions, the 'absolute' and the 'relative'. Few, if any, adherents of an absolute standard would disagree that the 'actual needs of the poor' are different in 2009 to those defined in the pioneering studies of Booth (*The Life and Labour of the People* (1889)) and Rowntree (*Poverty: A Study of Town Life* (1901)). An absolute standard is therefore usually seen as one that is itself 'relative' at least in terms of historical period and, we might add, geographical location (it costs more to keep warm in mid-winter in Moscow than in Marbella). In short there is a tendency even with an absolute definition for the minimum level to rise as living standards generally improve.

The decision of the Charity Commissioners in *Garfield Poverty Trust* is consistent with that type of approach to defining poverty. The Commissioners decided that members of a religious group who had insufficient means themselves to take out mortgages could be termed 'poor' and that the provision of low-interest or interest-free loans to enable them to purchase accommodation was therefore charitable (*Decisions of the Charity Commissioners* vol 3 (1995) p 7).

There is one further dimension to the question of whether poverty should be defined in absolute or relative terms. Should the social positions and prior economic circumstances of individuals be relevant to whether they are defined as poor? In fact the case law is ambivalent. On the one hand, a circumspect attitude is evident in a case such as *Re Cohen* [1973] 1 All ER 889 ('in special need'). Templeman J held that the trust was for the relief of poverty but only after declaring himself satisfied, on all the evidence, that only those who were 'genuinely' poor would benefit, ie by implication, 'poor' in some absolute sense. On the other hand, the concluding words of the following frequently cited dictum of Evershed MR in *Re Coulthurst* [1951] Ch 661 at 666 display sympathy for the notion that poverty should be a relative matter in the sense that an individual's prior circumstances be taken into account:

> It is quite clearly established that poverty does not mean destitution: it is a word of wide and somewhat indefinite import; it may not unfairly be paraphrased for present purposes as meaning persons who have to 'go short' in the ordinary acceptation of that term, due regard being had to their status in life, and so forth.

In conformity with this dictum gifts for 'distressed gentlefolk' (*Re Young* [1951] Ch 344), and even 'any of my fellow members [of the Savage Club, 1 Carlton House Terrace, London SW 1] . . . who have fallen on evil days' (*Re Young* [1955] 1 WLR 1269) have been held charitable. The recent case of *Re Segelman* [1996] Ch 171 appears more in tune with this 'individual relativist' and flexible approach to defining the meaning of 'going short'. The court accepted that whilst most members of the class of beneficiaries ('poor and needy' relatives) were 'comfortably off . . . but not affluent' they may 'need a helping hand from time to time in order to overcome an unforeseen crisis: the failure of a business venture, urgent repairs to a dwelling house or expenses brought on by reason of failing health' (at 190). The restricted nature of the beneficial class in *Segelman* raises a particular problem in relation to the section of the public requirement and we therefore consider the case and some of the implications in more detail at p 1006.

There is one further conundrum posed by a charitable heading of 'prevention and relief of poverty' where the relief element might be thought nowadays to be the duty of the state. The bare essentials of life are, in theory at least, provided by social security benefits, with the right to means-tested benefits constituting a subsistence 'safety-net' for those not catered for adequately or at all by, for instance, the Jobseeker's Allowance. Local authority social services in addition confer a number of benefits in kind on their poor residents – furniture, bedding, domestic assistance and so on. For poverty charities to adopt the same income level entitlement criterion as, say, Income Support or to provide equivalent forms of material assistance would be substantially to duplicate the operations of the state.

The problem has most obviously and frequently arisen in the context of cy-près schemes to modernise some of the many, very old poverty charities (see Chapter 20). The Commission has on several occasions emphasised that charity funds should not be used simply to relieve central and local government departments of their statutory responsibilities (see Annual Reports 1967 paras 17–20 and 1975 para 29). The Commission has also on several occasions listed examples of provision for the poor to 'top up' what the state furnishes but which still represents relief of poverty. Its most recent guidance contains, inter alia, the following illustrations (The Prevention or Relief of Poverty for the Public Benefit (December 2008) Annex A):

> **Grants of money**...[These are principally to be directed towards meeting immediate, non-recurring needs, eg payments to assist in meeting electricity and gas bills, or payments of television licence fees.]
>
> **The provision of items** [either outright or, if expensive and appropriate, on loan, such as] –
>
> • furniture, bedding, clothing, food, fuel, heating appliances;
> • washing machines and fridges;
>
> **The provision of facilities** [such as]:
>
> • the supply of tools or books;
> • payment of fees for instruction or examinations or of expenses connected with vocational training or with language, literacy, numerical or technical skills;
> • travelling expenses to help the recipients to earn their living; or
> • equipment and funds for recreational pursuits or training intended to bring the quality of life of the beneficiaries to a reasonable standard.

Put shortly, the Commission envisages a stratum of individual resources above the poverty line to which the state adheres, but does not attempt to define it by reference to any kind of rigid means test. Instead the guidance suggests that 'anyone who does not have the resources to provide themselves, either on a short- or long-term basis, with the normal things of life which most people take for granted' would probably qualify for help (p 9).

The new guidance omits what has been a constant presence in previous guidance, namely the warning that trustees should not use charitable funds 'simply to replace state benefits' as to do this would mean that 'in effect the charity would be relieving the State, not the beneficiary' (CC4 replaced by the December 2008 guidance). It is to be hoped that this does not mean that the Charity Commission now regards it as acceptable for charities to take over the role of providing payments to meet social security claimants' 'exceptional needs' (ie those not adequately provided for by regular weekly benefit payments) that are supposed to be met from a discretionary 'Social Fund'. A potential loophole in the scheme is that scheme officers from the social security arm of the Department of Work and Pensions (DWP), in determining whether to approve a payment or, more commonly, a loan 'shall have regard to', inter alia, 'the possibility that some other person or body may wholly or partly meet it' (Social Security Contributions and Benefits Act 1992, s 140(1)(c); see *Reform of Social Security* (Cmnd 9691, 1985) pp 36–45). It is simply not known how far the DWP officials who now administer the fund do have regard to the possibility of a charity providing assistance rather than the state. A difficulty for them is that the government provides each DWP district with an annual budget (Social

Security Administration Act 1992, s 168). The DWP officials are directed to manage the budget so that, as far as possible, high priority applications can be met but without exceeding their cash-limited budgets (CPAG *National Welfare Benefits Handbook 2007–08* pp 482–483). Whether an applicant receives a payment can therefore depend on when they apply and the amount available in the budget. DWP and National Audit Office (NAO) statistics tend to confirm that around 45% of applications for grants and around 25% of applications for loans are rejected annually, in the case of loan applications most commonly because the applicant is deemed unlikely to be able to repay in view of other debts outstanding (NAO *Helping Those in Financial Hardship: The Running of the Social Fund* HC 179 Session 2004–05). One consequence is to increase the demands on charities to provide resources that might previously have been met by the state (see Leat *Trusts in Transition* (1992); Bennett *Out of Pocket – Failure of the Social Fund* (1995); National Association of Citizens Advice Bureaux *Unfair and Underfunded* (2002); and generally the strongly critical Third Report of the Social Security Committee, Session 2000–01 (HC 232); Buck *The Social Fund: Law and Practice* (3rd edn, 2007)). This practice does not mean that charities are replacing aid that the state *is* giving, since by definition the state has ceased to provide that support. It may, however, be thought to be blurring in substance if not in form the boundaries between state and voluntary action.

(b) Advancement of education

(1) The boundaries of the category

The educational purposes specified in the preamble are relatively specific, with references to 'the maintenance of schools of learning, free schools and scholars in universities . . . education and preferment of orphans'. The process of reasoning by analogy has taken us a long way from this position and 'advancement of education' now constitutes a very wide category of charitable purposes indeed. What added to the breadth of the category was the extension to include cultural fields, such as music, dance, drama and the fine arts (eg *Re Shakespeare Memorial Trust* [1923] 2 Ch 398; *Royal Choral Society v IRC* [1943] 2 All ER 101). These have been hived off and now appear as a distinct category in CA 2006, s 2(2)(f) and are therefore discussed under their own heading.

In *IRC v McMullen* [1980] 1 All ER 884 Lord Hailsham emphasised the dynamic nature of the concept of education (at 890):

> What has to be remembered . . . is that both the legal conception of charity, and within it the educated man's ideas about education are not static, but moving and changing. Both change with changes in ideas about social values. Both have evolved with the years. In particular in applying the law to contemporary circumstances it is extremely dangerous to forget that thoughts concerning the scope and width of education differed in the past greatly from those which are now generally accepted.

Included under the category of advancement of education are purposes which are defined in very broad terms and transcend national boundaries ('for the benefit, advancement and propagation of education and learning in every part of the world' (*Whicker v Hume* (1858) 7 HL Cas 124), as well as specific projects such as the establishment or maintenance of a single library or museum or institution of learning (eg *British Museum Trustees v White* (1826) 2 Sim & St 594), or even a teaching post or scholarship therein (*Yates v University College London* (1875) LR 7 HL 438). It takes in institutions and activities catering for people of all ages, ranging from day nurseries for children between three and five (Annual Report 1966 App A, para 3), to elite societies established for the benefit of eminent scholars, such as the Royal Society (*Royal Society of London v Thompson* (1881) 17 Ch D 407). Since advancement of education, like the other remaining categories of charitable purposes to be discussed, is distinct from prevention and relief of poverty, there is no restriction in terms of means or social class on the persons who may be entitled to benefit, nor is charging of fees prohibited (see p 1017).

By way of further illustration of the width of the concept of education, it includes not merely the areas of knowledge with which orthodox syllabuses within the traditional educational hierarchy are concerned, but also industrial and technical training and the encouraging of craftsmanship (*Re Koettgen* [1954] Ch 252; *Construction Industry Training Board v A-G* [1973] Ch 173; *IRC v White* [1980] TR 155). Moreover, as some of the above examples illustrate, this category of charitable purpose does not presuppose the establishment or prior existence of an educational institution. Accordingly, to quote one random example the publication of law reports (*Incorporated Council of Law Reporting for England and Wales v A-G* [1971] 3 All ER 1029) has been held to advance education. The last-named case also illustrates a further point: 'One must not confuse the results flowing from the achievement of a purpose with the purpose itself, any more than one should have regard to the motives of those who set that purpose in motion' (at 1040 per Sachs LJ). The consequence that members of the legal profession use the knowledge acquired from the law reports to earn their living is therefore incidental, and does not detract from the Council's broad educational object.

In like fashion, the fact that membership of a professional society may confer some benefit on the members does not prevent it from being a charity, unless the main object of the society is the promotion of the status or welfare of its members (*Royal College of Surgeons v National Bank Ltd* [1952] AC 631; cf *General Nursing Council for England and Wales v St Marylebone Borough Council* [1959] AC 540). The distinction drawn between a 'consequence', in the shape of incidental benefits, and a 'purpose' is plain enough in concept, but it does emphasise the importance of careful drafting of constitutions and trust deeds alike. Nowhere is this more evident than in the decision of the New Zealand Court of Appeal to uphold by a 3:2 majority the charitable status of the Medical Council of New Zealand (*Commissioner of Inland Revenue v Medical Council of New Zealand* [1997] 2 NZLR 297). The majority held that the council was exclusively established for the purpose of 'the protection and benefit of the public', any benefit to registered practitioners being incidental and consequential. Whilst the case is not directly concerned with the advancement of education the reasoning emphasising the distinction between 'purpose' and 'consequence' is equally applicable. In similar vein the Charity Commission in 2001 agreed to register the General Medical Council (GMC) as a charity ([2001] Ch Com Dec, 2 April). The decision of the Commission is a further illustration of the quasi-judicial function that they perform in that it was necessary to distinguish a decision of the Court of Appeal in 1928 that held the GMC to be non-charitable as a body that predominantly benefited medical practitioners (*General Medical Council v Inland Revenue Comrs* [1928] 1 All ER 252). The Commission accepted the proposition that changes in circumstances since 1928, including changes made to the constitution of the GMC, pointed to the conclusion that the GMC was now established to serve the public interest in promoting the health of the community.

For a particular educational activity to be charitable there must be some way of showing that the public will benefit from it or, to put the point differently, that education will be 'advanced'. Consequently there has on occasion been uncertainty about the charitable status of research. In *Re Shaw* [1957] 1 WLR 729 (where George Bernard Shaw had bequeathed funds for pursuing inquiries into the feasibility of introducing a new 40-letter alphabet and the advantages to be gained from its use) Harman J cast doubt on the charitable nature of research: 'if the object be merely the increase of knowledge, that is not in itself a charitable object unless it be combined with teaching or education' (at 737). Subsequently however in *Re Hopkins' Will Trusts* [1965] Ch 669, Wilberforce J displayed a more sympathetic approach to 'research'. *Re Hopkins'* concerned a testamentary gift to the 'Francis Bacon Society Inc', 'to be earmarked and applied towards finding the Bacon–Shakespeare manuscripts'. The general purposes of the society were to encourage the study of Francis Bacon and of the evidence in favour of the view that Bacon was the author of 'the plays commonly ascribed to Shakespeare'. Wilberforce J held that the trust was for the advancement of education. He was satisfied that if the search for the Bacon-Shakespeare manuscripts were successful, the results would certainly be promulgated to the world at large, though not necessarily by formal teaching. In his view, the appropriate rule was as follows (at 680):

In order to be charitable, research must either be of educational value to the researcher or must be so directed as to lead to something which will pass into the store of educational material, or so as to improve the sum of communicable knowledge in an area which education may cover – education in this last context extending to the formation of literary taste and appreciation.

There now seems little doubt that research in a useful subject of study will be charitable provided the results of the research are to be disseminated, and 'the court will be readily inclined to construe a trust for research as importing subsequent dissemination of the results thereof' (*McGovern v A-G* [1982] Ch 321 at 352 per Slade J, quoting his own unreported judgment in *Re Besterman* (1980) *Times* 21 January – trust for completing research on Voltaire and Rousseau held valid). Although not necessarily inconsistent with this approach the cautionary words of Iacobucci J in the Canadian Supreme Court should be noted: 'Simply providing an opportunity for people to educate themselves such as by making available materials with which this might be accomplished but need not be, is not enough' (*Vancouver Society of Immigrant and Visible Minority Women v Minister of National Revenue* (1999) 169 DLR (4th) 34 at 113).

Lastly, purposes thought to be properly or traditionally associated with formal education (notably at school) may fall within the educational umbrella even though they are not per se educational or otherwise charitable. On this basis, games played at schools, school outings, the pursuits of boy scouts and girl guides and athletic, social and cultural activities organised within a students' union have been held to constitute a sufficient contribution to the educational aims of schools or universities to fall within the educational category (see eg *London Hospital Medical College v IRC* [1976] 2 All ER 113). The House of Lords decision in *IRC v McMullen* [1980] 1 All ER 884 both confirmed the inclusion of these activities as being for the 'advancement of education' and further extended the scope of the category. A trust established by the Football Association 'to provide . . . facilities which will enable or encourage pupils of Schools and Universities . . . to play Association Football or other games or sports . . .' was held charitable despite the absence of any direct link to a particular educational institution (see also Annual Report 1991 para 74 (Cliff Richard Tennis Development Trust)). Lord Hailsham emphasised the last point with some vehemence: 'I reject any idea which would cramp the education of the young within the school or university syllabus, confine it within the school or university campus, limit it to formal instruction, or render it devoid of pleasure in the exercise of skill' (at 893).

(2) Limiting the category

The removal of the presumption of 'public benefit' from advancement of education means that in principle, as discussed previously, benefit must be capable of proof through factual and positive evidence if possible. But the practical significance of the change wrought by the removal of the presumption remains to be seen. The fact, for instance, that a charity-founder believes that an organisation's purposes are educational was not decisive even when the presumption applied. There was clear authority that the court or the Charity Commission, assisted where appropriate by expert evidence, were the final arbiters particularly where there existed divergences of opinion as to educational merit. In fact two key cases on this issue have involved matters of artistic evaluation and are therefore considered in that context (see below, p 993) but the approach adopted is equally applicable to the advancement of education.

More troublesome is the scope for subjective evaluation on the part of the courts or the Commission where a trust fails because it is deemed to be too propagandist. A significant reason for the failure of the trust in *Re Shaw* [1957] 1 WLR 729 – the 40-letter alphabet case – was because of a propaganda element in the trust which tended merely 'to persuade the public that the adoption of the new script would be a "good thing" and that, in my view, is not education' (at 738).

But this judgment of Harman J should be contrasted with the unreported decision of Whitford J in *Re Women's Service Trust* (27 February 1976). The objects of the trust, which was established in 1926, were defined as 'promoting the equality of women with men in political and economic opportunity'. Whitford J concluded that 'the promulgation of the principles believed in by the founder must lead to an advancement in thinking and on education in ideas of general benefit to the community, whatever the result of the promulgation might be . . .' (Annual Report 1977 para 36). A judge less inclined to accept the merits of the feminist cause could easily have used the label 'propagandist' as a stick with which to beat a trust of this nature. Moreover, it is also questionable whether George Bernard Shaw's trust was any more propagandist than that in *Re Hopkins*, yet the propagandist element in the latter passed without comment.

Nevertheless it has been confirmed in a number of other decisions of the courts and the Charity Commission that 'mere propaganda' is not education (eg *Re Bushnell* [1975] 1 WLR 1596). These decisions generally relate to propaganda of a political nature, for example, propaganda in support of a political party, or of a campaign to change or preserve the law in a particular respect, and are best considered in that context (see below, p 1024).

(c) Advancement of religion

There are two provisions of the CA 2006 that impinge on this heading, a generic one being the removal in s 3(3) of the public benefit presumption, whilst a specific one in s 2(3)(a) effects some limited clarification on the meaning of 'religion' in charity law. In determining the current scope of this heading it would be unwise to assume that the two provisions just mentioned will bring about any significant change in a pre-2006 position that evinced a predominantly liberal approach to the granting of charitable status.

(1) An emergent liberal approach

Trusts or other organisations which serve to promote virtually any form of religion, Christian or non-Christian, in virtually any sort of way, have been brought within the category of 'advancement of religion'. Subject to one important exception, the law was liberal as to the range of faiths that may be 'advanced'. The exception, arguably a diminished one, is that the Roman Catholic faith, and other faiths in which emphasis may on occasion be placed on purely spiritual activity rather than 'good works' or proselytising, suffered from an interpretation of the public benefit requirement which has been claimed to have preserved an anti-Catholicism of former times (see Blakeney (1981) 2 J Legal History 207, but cf Rickett [1990] Conv 34 and Ware (ed) *Charity and Government* (1989) pp 222–247).

Indeed, liberality as to the range of faiths that may be advanced is a comparatively recent development (Crowther *Religious Trusts* (1954) ch 4). Over a long period, stretching from before the preamble to at least the mid-nineteenth century, the charitable status of religious trusts was intimately bound up with the question of religious toleration. The case which is generally taken to be the *fons et origo* of the law's present-day willingness to accept virtually any genuinely theistic sect, no matter how small or obscure or eccentric, as a 'religion', is *Thornton v Howe* (1862) 31 Beav 14. Here Romilly MR held charitable a devise of land to promote the publication of what he called the 'foolish' works of Johanna Southcote, a self-styled mother of the second Messiah. Eccentric Southcote may have been, but with her savage attacks on the established clergy – 'Lovers and Adulterers' – and with what E P Thompson has described as 'apocalyptic fervour' she attracted a large following, particularly among the poor (see *The Making of the English Working Class* (1968) pp 420–428; and J Rogers *Mr Wroe's Virgins* (1992)). However, the immediate consequence of a judgment which was to have such a liberalising effect, was to invalidate the gift under the Mortmain and Charitable Uses Act 1736, so that the decision itself was not as tolerant as it appears at first sight. Nevertheless, its interpretation of the circumstances when an ostensibly religious purpose might fail to be granted charitable status pervades modern decisions (*Re Watson* [1973] 1 WLR 1472, noted (1974) 90 LQR 4; and see also *Holmes v A-G* Annual Report 1981 paras 22–30). In *Re Watson*, for instance, Plowman J followed *Thornton v Howe* in holding charitable a testamentary trust to publish the religious commentaries of a recently retired builder, despite expert evidence that they were of no intrinsic worth and would serve little purpose other than to confirm the fundamentalist, Calvinist and pacifist beliefs of the small religious group to which the writer belonged.

(2) The meaning of religion

Prior to the CA 2006 the benchmark case in clarifying the interpretation of religion in charity law was *Re South Place Ethical Society* [1980] 1 WLR 1565 where Dillon J stressed that 'two of the essential attributes of religion are faith and worship; faith in a God and worship of that God' (at 1572). Accordingly, organisations which seek to foster ethical and moral standards, but which do so on a wholly humanistic or, indeed, expressly atheistic footing, will not be held to advance religion (South Place Ethical Society was, however, held charitable under the second and fourth *Pemsel* categories: see Hoffer (1981) 131 NLJ 761; St J Robilliard [1981] Conv 150–154). Whilst there was no judicial decision directly on the point (save as regards Judaism, which was accepted to be a religion, eg in *Neville Estates Ltd v Madden* [1962] Ch 832), it was generally assumed that non-Christian religions fell within the category. Thus, regulations excepting various types of religious organisation from obligations under the Charities

Act 1993 (SI 1963/2074) explicitly included reference to 'provision for public religious worship . . . whether or not of the Christian religion' and other organisations connected with non-Christians prominent among ethnic minorities in the UK – Sikhs, Hindus and Muslims, for example – have been registered and are referred to in the Charity Commission's reports (see eg Annual Report 1976 paras 109–112; and also *Varsani v Jesani* [1998] 3 All ER 273 where it was assumed without comment that promoting the faith of a particular Hindu sect was charitable). The Strategy Unit recommended that a statutory definition should make clear that faiths that are multi-deity (such as Hinduism) or non-deity (such as some types of Buddhism) qualify for charitable status (*Private Action, Public Benefit* (2002) paras 4.32–4.34).

The CA 2006 eschews any definition of religion providing instead in s 2(3)(a) merely that 'religion' *includes*:

(i) a religion which involves belief in more than one god, and
(ii) a religion which does not involve belief in a god.

The question then is whether this form of words does any more than implement the limited widening of the interpretation of religion recommended by the Strategy Unit and thereby provides in effect a statutory seal of approval to the Charity Commission's previous practice referred to above. If it does then the clearest guide to that practice is to be found in the 1999 decision of the Charity Commission to reject the application of the Church of Scientology (CoS) to be registered as a charity for the advancement of religion ([1999] Ch Com Dec, 17 November). The inspiration behind the Church, which numbers several well-known Hollywood 'stars' amongst its followers (eg John Travolta, Tom Cruise, Shirley Maclaine, Juliette Lewis), is an American science fiction writer, L Ron Hubbard (1911–1986), who developed a set of beliefs – 'Dianetics' – about the workings of the human mind and spirit which he expounded in numerous publications during the 1950s. The Court of Appeal in *R v Registrar General, ex p Segerdal* [1970] 2 QB 697 cast doubt on the claim of Scientology to be a religion rather than a philosophy. The litigation was not directly concerned with charitable status but whether a 'chapel' was a place of religious worship. Lord Denning commented obiter that the beliefs of Scientology appeared to be 'more a philosophy of the existence of man or of life rather than a religion' and that 'there was nothing in it of reverence for God or a deity' (at 707). Having considered the decision in *Segerdal* and dicta from other authorities as well as the opinion of Dillon J the Charity Commission concluded that the definition of religion in English charity law was characterised by a 'belief in a supreme being' and 'an expression of that belief through worship'. This arguably slight extension of the criteria set out by Dillon J from a theistic belief in a God to belief in a supreme being did not assist the CoS. Whilst the Commission accepted the proposition that Scientology believes in a supreme being, it did not accept that there was evidence of worship: 'The core practices of Scientology, being auditing and training, do not constitute worship as they do not display the essential characteristic of reverence or veneration for a supreme being' (op cit pp 25–26).

By contrast in Australia the Church of Scientology has been recognised as a 'religious institution' and therefore exempt from liability to a payroll tax in Victoria. The High Court of Australia rejected Dillon J's test as too narrow (*Church of the New Faith v Comrs for Pay-Roll Tax* (1982) 154 CLR 120, noted (1984) 14 Melb ULR 539 and [1984] Conv 449). Although the judgments contain differing approaches to the question of what is a religion, a feature distinguishing the Commonwealth approach appears to be the absence of a requirement that there must be belief in a deity.

Unsurprisingly, in view of the differing Commonwealth interpretations of criteria appropriate to define religion, the CoS argued in the alternative that the definition of religion applied by a public body such as the Charity Commission must be compatible with the European Convention on Human Rights (Human Rights Act 1998, s 6; and see Quint and Spring (1999) 5(3) CL & PR 153; Harding (2008) 71(2) MLR 159–182). The gist of the proposition is that the failure to grant charitable status means that tax reliefs are not available to CoS and that as a consequence the ability of the Church to teach and pass on its beliefs is materially affected. This outcome, it is argued, therefore results in an infringement of Article 9 – 'freedom of thought, conscience and religion'. In addition the CoS sought to argue that the Article 14 protection against religious discrimination in the enjoyment of Convention rights (such as that in Article 9) was also infringed by the definition of religion. The Commission did not accept these arguments concluding that the definition as interpreted by the courts and applied by the Commission satisfied the requirement developed by the European Court of Human Rights of 'objectivity' and 'reasonable justification' (see Edge and Loughrey 'Religious Charities and the Juridification of the Charity Commission' (2001) 21 LS 36–64 for a contrary view).

(3) A public benefit limitation

Prima facie, purposes within the category of 'advancement of religion' have been recognised as conferring a tangible benefit on the community at large. In *Funnell v Stewart* [1996] 1 WLR 288, for instance, the court held that the work of faith-healing was charitable under this heading provided only that there was sufficient religious element present (see Fletcher (1996) 112 LQR 557). Notwithstanding a dictum to the contrary in an earlier case (*Re Hummeltenberg* [1923] 1 Ch 237 at 241 per Russell J), the judge decided that it was not necessary to prove that the healing actually worked and that 'sufficient element of public benefit is assumed' unless there is contrary evidence. The presumption of benefit could therefore be rebutted but to do so it has generally been necessary since *Thornton v Howe* to prove that the particular doctrines or practices are 'adverse to the foundations of all religion and . . . subversive of all morality' (per Plowman J in *Re Watson* [1973] 1 WLR 1472 at 1482–1483, following Romilly MR in *Thornton v Howe* (1862) 31 Beav 14 at 19). The extreme liberality of this test needs, however, to be viewed both in the light of a more restrictive element in the case law and in consideration of the difference, if any, to be made by the statutory removal of the presumption.

The restrictive element emerges from the leading modern decision *Gilmour v Coats* (below) on the rule that 'benefit to the public must be tangible'. This case concerned a trust by will for the purposes of a Roman Catholic community of cloistered nuns. The nuns did not carry out religious work outside the convent, but maintained a life of pious retreat, meditating, fasting and holding private religious services in which they engaged in intercessory prayer. The Roman Catholic Archbishop of Westminster tendered evidence to the effect that members of the public derived spiritual benefit from this, in so far as their souls were the subject of the nuns' intercessory prayers and also that they were edified and inspired by the example of the nuns' piety, self-denial and religious devotion. Although relying to some extent on previous authority to the effect that cloistered religious communities were not charitable, the House of Lords also held that these alleged benefits were not such as would be recognised by the law ([1949] AC 426 at 446):

> **Lord Simonds:** My Lords, I would speak with all respect and reverence of those who spend their lives in cloistered piety, and in this House of Lords Spiritual and Temporal, which daily commences its proceedings with intercessory prayers, how can I deny that the Divine Being may in His wisdom think fit to answer them? But, my Lords, whether I affirm or deny, whether I believe or disbelieve, what has that to do with the proof which the court demands that a particular purpose satisfies the test of benefit to the community? Here is something which is manifestly not susceptible of proof. But, then it is said, this is a matter not of proof but of belief: for the value of intercessory prayer is a tenet of the Catholic faith, therefore in such prayer there is benefit to the community. But it is just at this 'therefore' that I must pause. It is, no doubt, true that the advancement of religion is, generally speaking, one of the heads of charity. But it does not follow from this that the court must accept as proved whatever a particular church believes. The faithful must embrace their faith believing where they cannot prove: the court can act only on proof. A gift to two or ten or a hundred cloistered nuns in the belief that their prayers will benefit the world at large does not from that belief alone derive validity any more than does the belief of any other donor for any other purpose.
>
> I turn to the second of the alleged elements of public benefit, edification by example. And I think that this argument can be dealt with very shortly. It is in my opinion sufficient to say that this is something too vague and intangible to satisfy the prescribed test. The test of public benefit has, I think, been developed in the last two centuries. To-day it is beyond doubt that that element must be present. No court would be rash enough to attempt to define precisely or exhaustively what its content must be. But it would assume a burden which it could not discharge if now for the first time it admitted into the category of public benefit something so indirect, remote, imponderable and, I would add, controversial as the benefit which may be derived by others from the example of pious lives.

Notwithstanding this decision it was held subsequently, in *Neville Estates Ltd v Madden* [1962] Ch 832 at 853 that the ruling on 'edification by example' should not be applied to restricted religious groups, such as a Jewish synagogue, when the members did live in the everyday world, because 'the court is . . . entitled to assume that some benefit accrues to the public from the attendance at places of worship of persons who live in this world and mix with their fellow citizens' (but cf *Re Warre* [1953] 1 WLR 725). The strictness of *Gilmour v Coats* is striking and there is an unresolved clash between this strictness and the liberality of decisions on 'fringe' sects such as *Thornton v Howe* (1862) and *Re Watson* (1973). The cases can be tenuously reconciled on the basis that *Gilmour v Coats* merely requires an element of proselytising of the particular belief or at least some degree of contact with the outside world. The distinction, unsatisfactory though it may be, was relied on in *Re Hetherington* [1989] 2 All ER 129 where Browne-Wilkinson VC held charitable a gift of '£2,000 to the Roman Catholic Bishop of Westminster for masses for the repose of the souls of my husband and my parents and my sisters and also myself when I die'. *Gilmour v Coats* had cast doubt on the charitable status of such gifts but the Vice-Chancellor upheld the gift, distinguishing (at 135) between 'the celebration of a religious rite in public' which does confer a sufficient public benefit, and the same act in private which does not 'since any benefit by prayer or example is incapable of proof in the legal sense, and any element of edification is limited to a private, not public, class of those present at the celebration' (see Rickett [1990] Conv 34; Sherrin (1990) 32 Malaya LR 114).

A liberalising approach is also evident in the decision of the Charity Commission to recognise as charitable the Society of the Precious Blood, an enclosed contemplative Community of Anglican Nuns at Burnham Abbey devoted to perpetual intercession, whose members are bound by vows of chastity, poverty and obedience.

The Constitution of the Society provided, inter alia, that:

> (2) The first work of the Sisters is their intercessory prayer, of which the Eucharist is the centre. . . . This life of prayer finds an outward expression in caring for guests who come for a period of rest or retreat, or for counsel or other help which the Community can give.

The Inland Revenue contended that the purpose of the Society was contemplation and devotion to perpetual intercession and that any outward expression of that purpose (eg counselling etc) was merely incidental. Accordingly it was argued that under the principle established in *Gilmour v Coats* there was no public benefit.

Given the way and the extent to which the Society's purposes were actually carried out and the absence of strict rules excluding the public, the Commission concluded that the charitable activities were the outward and visible object of the Society and as such the Society could be regarded as charitable at law (The

Society of the Precious Blood (1989); *Decisions of the Charity Commissioners* vol 3 (1995) p 16).

The capacity to sidestep the restrictive aspects of *Gilmour v Coats* (as in *Neville Estates v Madden* and *Society of the Precious Blood*), the adoption of a benign approach to construction (*Re Hetherington*) and the re-affirmation in *Re Watson* of the unchallenged status of *Thornton v Howe* all tended to facilitate a liberalising approach to what is deemed charitable for the advancement of religion. The overall outcome was that the restrictive element in *Gilmour v Coats*, perhaps redolent of a particular era in charity law, was gradually being eroded.

One corollary of a liberalising approach is that there has appeared to be scant scope under charity law to challenge the proliferating numbers of novel and/or obscure religious sects about which official concern has at times been expressed (see eg Annual Report 1982 Appendix C; Picarda (1981) 131 NLJ, 23 April, 436–437; and generally the 1989 White Paper *Charities: A Framework for the Future*, paras 2.18–2.36). There is evidence that the courts were prepared to consider whether a particular doctrine might be contrary to the public interest where for example it can be shown that it 'causes dissension in, and a break-up of, family life' (Annual Report 1976 para 131; and see *Holmes v A-G* Annual Report 1981 paras 28–29). This is plainly a rather limited restriction in that it looks only to negative detrimental impact rather than requiring positive beneficial effect.

Will then the statutory removal of the presumption of public benefit lead to a more restrictive approach? Should the Charity Commission or the courts require charities for the advancement of religion to establish, in cases of doubt, that they provide some positive public benefit? It has, for instance, been suggested that 'it is surely legitimate to ask whether a sufficiently substantial number of people will be benefited by a particular religious trust' and 'benefit ought not to be assumed in the case of religious writings of a foolish or incoherent nature' (*Picarda* pp 115–116 and see Hackney (1973) ASCL 464 criticising *Re Watson*). The Commission has issued supplementary guidance in which it comments, perhaps with *Re Watson* in mind, that a religion must have 'a certain level of cogency, coherence, seriousness and importance; as opposed to a self-promoting organisation set up to promote one or two persons' (*The Advancement of Religion for the Public Benefit* (December 2008; Annex A). It is open to question whether going much beyond this limited sort of appraisal could be achieved without involving the courts or the Commission in matters of religious controversy in a way which the present law is claimed to avoid. The Commission may be on more secure territory where it emphasises that detrimental effects of an organisation's activities can be taken into account. The Commission refers to activities that may be damaging to mental or physical health or that promote hatred of others or that unlawfully restrict a person's freedom. These disqualifying criteria can be argued to represent a modern manifestation of the approach in *Thornton v Howe*. In their decision on the Church of Scientology (CoS) application, for example, the Commission concluded that even had CoS qualified as a religion charitable status would be withheld because the presumption of public benefit was rebutted *in part* by the evidence of public and judicial concern about the activities of the organisation. The Commission refer to receipt by them 'of a number of unsolicited objections' about Scientology generally, to adverse press coverage and to unfavourable judicial comment. As regards the latter the Commission concedes that this occurred in cases where the issues were not 'fully argued nor evidence about Scientology and the Church made fully available to the court' ([1999] Ch Com Dec, 17 November, pp 47–48). A more objective assessment than this may be required if the Commission is to avoid its decisions being challenged on human rights grounds (see eg *Hoffman v Austria* (1994) 17 EHRR 293 on the requirement of 'objective public criteria').

Moreover, although not specifically directed at the public benefit proposition, there is a challenge to its apparent rationality in the somewhat acerbic observation of Murdoch J in the High Court of Australia, commenting on the criteria alleged to negate religion as set out by the Supreme Court of Victoria (*Church of the New Faith v Comr for Pay-Roll Tax* (1983) 49 ALR 65 at 94):

> Christianity claims to have begun with a founder and twelve adherents. It had no written constitution, and no permanent meeting place. It borrowed heavily from the teachings of the Jewish religion, but had no complete and absolute moral code. Its founder exhorted people to love one another and taught by example. Outsiders regarded his teachings, especially about the nature of divinity, as ambiguous, obscure and contradictory, as well as blasphemous and illegal. On the criteria used in this case by the Supreme Court of Victoria early Christianity would not have been considered religious.

There remains a more fundamental question concerning public benefit left untouched by the above discussion. Given the secularisation of much of charity law since its early religious origins does the phenomenon of religious worship itself still merit charitable status with its accompanying legal and fiscal privileges? The rationale for this has not been discussed in the English case law, it simply being assumed that 'any religion is at least likely to be better than none'. The importance of antiquity should not be underestimated but in a more positive vein the 1989 White Paper claimed that 'trusts for the advancement of religion have contributed much to the spiritual welfare of generations of individuals and to the sound development of our society' (para 2.22). Similar sentiments were expressed in the Strategy Unit Report (*Private Action, Public Benefit* (2002) paras 4.32–4.34). It is also the case that the obligation of charity is seen as a fundamental tenet of most religions. Whether these or other arguments justify the continuation of the legal and fiscal privileges of charitable status is a matter we return to at the end of this chapter.

(4) Means of advancement

It is not proposed to elaborate in great detail here on the whole range of methods by which religion may be 'advanced' (see generally Charity Commission *The Advancement of Religion for the Public Benefit* (December 2008; Annex B). 'Advancement' may be achieved by provision for virtually any aspect of religious activity. This can include contribution to general spiritual well-being, the provision of public rituals and ceremonies and more obvious examples such as the general furtherance of the work of long-established or newly founded churches, denominations and sects; erection, maintenance and repair of churches and other places of worship (eg *A-G v Day* [1900] 1 Ch 31); upkeep and religious education of clergy and other church officials (eg *Re Randell* (1888) 38 Ch D 213); and perhaps obscurely the provision of prizes at a Sunday school (*Re Strickland* [1936] 3 All ER 1027), and even exorcism (Annual Report 1976 paras 65–68).

Within the cases establishing this list of instances, which is not exhaustive, some fine lines are drawn. To give one example, the 'parish work' of a local vicar is not wholly religious (*Farley v Westminster Bank* [1939] AC 430), so that trusts in aid of this work will be non-charitable if not confined to its religious aspect, yet a gift to a vicar 'for his work in the parish' has been held to contain such a restriction by implication (Re *Simson* [1946] Ch 299).

(d) The advancement of health or the saving of lives

As noted previously the origins of this category can be traced to the 1601 Preamble with its reference to 'relief of the impotent' (ie those suffering from sickness or other physical disabilities rather than the modern sexual dysfunction meaning of the term). Section 2(3)(a) of the 2006 Act makes explicit that this category includes 'prevention or relief of sickness, disease or human suffering'. The obvious manifestations of this category are those such as medical research and the provision of facilities to ease suffering. The latter extends to incorporate the provision of 'complementary, alternative or holistic' methods provided that there is sufficient evidence that the methods can be effective (see eg the House of Lords, 6th Report of the Select Committee on Science and Technology, 'Complementary and Alternative Medicine' Session 1999–2000). Consistent with this approach the Commission has recognised as charitable the National Federation of Spiritual Healers whose approved purposes are: 'to promote public health by the promotion of spiritual healing for the benefit of the public by educating and training healers and by ensuring proper standards in the practice of spiritual healing' (Decisions of the Charity Commission, 2002). Trusts and other organisations for the relief of distress from natural disasters and other such calamities, where not restricted to relief of poverty amongst victims, are also likely to come within this category (*Re North Devon and West Somerset Relief Fund Trusts* [1953] 1 WLR 1260). Other examples are the establishment and maintenance of mountain rescue facilities and, with an eye on prevention, the promotion of road safety.

It should be noted that hospitals and clinics are not ipso facto non-charitable merely because they charge sufficient fees to cover their costs, nor need they be confined to the poor. If, however, they are run with a view to profit or are expressly confined to the rich they will not qualify as charitable. The charging of fees by private hospitals and whether fee levels should be restricted if the hospitals are to have charitable status is a contentious issue. This directly concerns the 'section of the public' requirement and is therefore considered further at p 1018.

(e) The advancement of citizenship or community development

This category is almost emblematic of one of the principal objectives underpinning government policy towards the voluntary sector in that it includes 'the promotion of civic responsibility, volunteering, the voluntary sector or the effectiveness or efficiency of charities' (CA 2006, s 2(3)(c)(ii) and see Charity Commission Register Review papers RR 13 *Promotion of the Voluntary Sector* (2004) and RR 14 *Promoting the Efficiency and Effectiveness of Charities and the Effective Use of Charitable Resources* (2004)). A recent illustration of the approach of the Commission was the decision to register as a charity the Charity Bank Ltd, a not-for-profit bank whose raison d'être is to provide loans, guarantees etc to charities on beneficial terms ([2002] Ch Com Dec 17 April).

The specific inclusion in the 2006 Act of 'rural or urban regeneration' (s 2(3)(c)(i)) reflected the earlier decision of the Charity Commission to recognise 'the promotion of urban and rural regeneration for public benefit in areas of social and economic deprivation' as a charitable purpose in its own right (see RR 2 *Promotion of Urban and Rural Regeneration* (1999)). The Charity Commission states that organisations who seek charitable status under this heading must include amongst their objects 'the maintenance or improvement of the physical, social and economic infrastructure' and 'assisting people who are at a disadvantage because of their social and economic circumstances'. There are many ways of achieving these objects but amongst those recognised by the Commission are activites as diverse as 'helping to improve housing standards generally . . . where poor housing is a problem' and 'providing . . . advice to new or existing businesses or where it would lead to training and employment opportunities for unemployed people'.

There is a potential difficulty lurking here, however, in that fulfilment of the purpose may directly or indirectly benefit *specific* individuals or businesses and not just the community as a whole. In *IRC v Oldham Training and Enterprise Council* [1996] STC 1218, in essence a test case about the charitable status of all TECs, Lightman J reaffirmed that 'merely incidental benefit' to individuals will not infringe charitable status. The problem of course lies in determining when a benefit is incidental. One of the main objects of Oldham TEC, a government-funded company limited by guarantee, was 'to promote industry, commerce and enterprise . . .' for the benefit of the public of Oldham. A subsidiary object was 'to provide . . . support services and advice to and for local businesses'. Lightman J concluded that taken together the objects would allow Oldham TEC to confer benefits on individuals, apparently in a more than incidental way, and that any consequential benefit for the community – improving business and employment in Oldham – was 'too remote' (at 1235, but cf *IRC v White* (1980) 55 TC 651; and the critical note by Roycroft [1997] BTR 1 at 59–62). The decision that TECs were therefore not charitable was fortuitous since by the date of the hearing Oldham TEC had purported to merge with its local non-charitable Chamber of Commerce and it was no longer in the TEC's interest to be a charity (see *Financial Times* 12 April 1996). Conversely, in the case of ViRSA Educational Trust, the Commission decided that registration could proceed. This organisation was established inter alia 'to provide training and guidance to rural communities on establishing and maintaining [retail and other services] and to promote trades and crafts connected with the rural economy as a whole'. The organisation was charitable because it provided support to rural communities generally as compared with promoting particular village shops which would confer too high a degree of private benefit on the proprietors to be charitable.

The limitations that the drawing of quite fine distinctions between public and private benefit in this area might have imposed on community-focused business activity have been significantly ameliorated by developments outside of the charity sector. Although the topic goes beyond the concerns of this book it should be noted that the Strategy Unit Report cast its net more widely than just the charity sector. Its remit extended to developing a modern legal framework for the not-for-profit sector in general including what have become known as 'social enterprises' (*Private Action, Public Benefit* (2002) chapter 5; DTI *Enterprise for Communities: Proposals for a Community Interest Company* (2003); and see Dunn and Riley (2004) 67(4) MLR 632–657; generally Jacobs in Ware (ed) *Charities and Government* (1989) ch 4). Subsequently a new corporate legal form – the Community Interest Company (CIC) – has been introduced for these non-charitable social enterprises in Pt II of the Companies (Audit, Investigations and Community Enterprise) Act 2004). The CIC is a 'not for profit' limited by guarantee company with a statutory asset lock in its memorandum and articles of association. This means that statutory legal protection is provided against demutualisation and 'windfall profits' being paid to its members and directors. This new legal model can accommodate co-operative, not for profit, voluntary or commercial models as long as all its activities contribute to providing benefit to the community (see generally www.cicregulator.gov.uk). There are, though, no CIC specific tax reliefs or exemptions available, the CIC being treated for tax purposes like any other company.

(f) The advancement of the arts, culture, heritage or science

Prior to the new categorisation introduced in CA 2006, purposes for the advancement of the arts, culture etc had long been considered charitable as one element in the advancement of education category. Amongst the many examples are a trust to promote the works of Shakespeare (*Re Shakespeare*

Memorial Trust [1923] 2 Ch 398) and the Royal Choral Society whose principal purpose was 'to form and maintain a choir in order to promote the practice and performance of choral works' (*Royal Choral Society v IRC* [1943] 2 All ER 101). Furthermore, in common with the advancement of education, this category of charitable purpose does not presuppose the establishment or prior existence of an artistic institution. Accordingly 'the bringing of masterpieces of fine art within the reach of the people of Ireland' (*Re Shaw's Will Trusts* [1952] Ch 163) has been held to be charitable.

As indicated previously in the context of advancement of education, divergences of opinion are clearly possible where artistic evaluations are involved. A comparison of two cases illustrates the point. In *Re Delius* [1957] Ch 299 a trust established by the will of the widow of the composer Frederick Delius 'for or towards the advancement . . . of the musical works of my late husband' was held educational and charitable, it being assumed by Roxburgh J on the basis of appropriate evidence that this composer was 'one whose music is worth appreciating' (at 307). On the other hand, in *Re Pinion* [1965] Ch 85 an artist and prolific collector of paintings, furniture and all sorts of *objets d'art*, Harry Pinion, purported to bequeath his studio and its contents on trust to be maintained as a museum open to the public. On hearing expert evidence that his own pictures in the studio were 'atrociously bad' and that very few of the *objets d'art* collected by him were of any aesthetic merit – one expert even expressed surprise that 'so voracious a collector should not by hazard have picked up even one meritorious object' (at 107) – the Court of Appeal held the trust void. Harman LJ commented (at 107): 'I can conceive of no useful object to be served in foisting upon the public this mass of junk. It has neither public utility nor educative value.'

One can perhaps have little quarrel with the results in these two cases, although the trust in *Re Pinion* had been upheld at first instance by Wilberforce J ([1963] 2 All ER 1049). On the other hand, in a post-modern era where relativist judgements challenge the accepted canons of the arts how will courts or the Charity Commission react to possibly conflicting 'expert opinion' on the educational value of popular culture? It remains to be seen whether a trust 'for the advancement of the musical works of Bob Dylan' or even of the Sex Pistols would be viewed as favourably as the musical works of Delius. Roxburgh J deftly sidestepped a comparable issue in *Delius*, commenting that 'it was not necessary to consider what the position might be if the trusts were for the promotion of the works of some inadequate composer' (at 307).

(g) The advancement of amateur sport

Unfortunately for those who look back with fond memories to the educational and recreational benefits of teenage years spent wielding a snooker cue, the advancement of amateur sport is subject to the qualification that '"sport" means sports or games which promote health by involving mental skill or exertion' (CA 2006, s 2(3)(d); and see generally RR 11 *Charitable Status and Sport* (2003)). This has the effect, in the view of the Charity Commission, of excluding from this category of charitable purposes recreational activities such as angling, shooting and also various motor sports. In fact recognition of the advancement of amateur sport as a charitable purpose is an illustration of the process of incremental change operated by the Commission. An obstacle to recognition was perceived to be the comments of members of the Court of Appeal in *Re Nottage* [1895] 2 Ch 649 to the effect that the promotion of sport was not charitable irrespective of any accompanying health benefits (per Lindley LJ at 655 and Lopes LJ at 656). The restriction in *Re Nottage* on the promotion of sporting activity began to look increasingly out of step 'in the light of the role of sport in modern social conditions' (North Tawton Rugby Union Football Club, *Decisions of the Charity Commissioners* vol 5 (1997) p 13). The conditions identified included the decreasing availability of sports activities in schools and the increased acceptance of the value of people of all ages partaking in healthy exercise (see generally Smith (1998) 5(2) CL & PR 135–142). The Commission has subsequently sought to distinguish the comments in *Re Nottage* as being obiter, as the case was concerned with whether the promotion of a particular sport, yacht racing, was charitable (cf the decision of the Canadian Supreme Court in *Amateur Youth Soccer Association v Canada Revenue* [2007] 3 SCR 217 reaffirming the common law position; see McInnes (2008) 124 LQR 202). On the other hand it is quite possible for an organisation supplying a particular type of sporting activity, such as horse riding, to attain charitable status under, for instance, s 2(2)(j) with the provision of riding for the disabled, there being 513 such organisations registered with the Commission. Here again, however, the requirement of public benefit must not be overlooked. A club that operates restrictions on its membership, other than those strictly necessary to enable the club to operate effectively, would not satisfy a public benefit test since it could not claim to be encouraging community participation. In practice it seems likely that many amateur sports clubs that might wish to take advantage of the more liberal approach to attaining charitable status will nevertheless need to make changes to their constitutions if they are to qualify as such. Their position will be similar should they opt to follow the alternative route to gaining tax relief offered under Sch 18 to the Finance Act 2002 by registering as a Community Amateur Sports Club with HMRC (see Quint and Nurse (2002) 7(3) CL & PR 201–207; Lloyd [2003] PCB 4 at 261–269).

(h) The advancement of human rights, conflict resolution or reconciliation or the promotion of religious or racial harmony or equality and diversity

The specific recognition of the advancement of human rights as a charitable purpose marks a change in the law since the 1982 decision of the High Court in *McGovern v A-G* [1982] Ch 321. Then certain of the objects of Amnesty International Trust including 'procuring the abolition of torture or inhumane or degrading treatment or punishment' were held to be non-charitable. The reason for this initially surprising conclusion was that their attainment would require a change in law or in the policy of governments and that the purposes were therefore political and not charitable purposes (see below, p 1019 on charity and politics). The enactment of the Human Rights Act (HRA) 1998 with its 'incorporation' of the European Convention on Human Rights enabled the Charity Commission to adopt a fresh approach. The reasoning is that acceptance of the HRA 1998 by the various political parties means that the question of whether it would be beneficial to the public to recognise and enforce European Convention rights is no longer a political one under charity law. It was not difficult to find an appropriate analogy, the promotion of mental and moral improvement being a clear contender (*Re South Place Ethical Society* [1980] 1 WLR 1565; and see Charity Commission RR 12 *The Promotion of Human Rights* (2005) for detailed guidance on the various ways in which a charity may promote human rights).

The advancement of conflict resolution is yet another of the categories specified in the Act that had already been recognised by the Charity Commission under the 'other beneficial purposes' head. In 2003 the Restorative Justice Consortium was entered on the Register, the Commission accepting that it was charitable to promote a purpose where, inter alia, 'all the parties with a stake in a particular conflict or offence come together to resolve collectively how to deal with its aftermath and its implications for the future'. The search for an analogy was unproblematic, the Commission citing such established purposes as 'the promotion of the sound administration of the law' and 'the protection of life and property'.

(i) The advancement of environmental protection or improvement

This now constitutes a major species of charitable purpose, stemming originally from an important phrase in the 1601 preamble referring to the provision of public amenities. Whereas the preamble mentioned the 'repair of bridges, ports, havens, causeways, sea-banks, and highways', virtually all of which is now wholly within state responsibility, the modern equivalent within charity law is the protection or improvement of the environment including, for example, preservation of the countryside and of the country's architectural heritage as by the National Trust (*Re Verrall* [1916] 1 Ch 100; Annual Report 1968 paras 67–72). The Charity Commission emphasises that charities concerned with environmental protection or improvement may need to produce independent expert evidence, that is authoritative and objective, to show that the particular species, land or habitat to be conserved is worthy of conservation (see RR 9 *Preservation and Conservation* (2001)). Recent decisions of the Commission confirm that this category also extends to include purposes such as promoting sustainable development or the promotion of recycling of goods ([2003] Ch Com Dec, 9 May (*Environment Foundation*); [2002] Ch Com Dec, April

(*Recycling in Ottery* – provision of a scrapyard where the public could bring items for recycling)). Protection of the environment has increasingly involved a strong campaigning element. This can pose problems for charity law and public understanding of the law. Where the campaign is interpreted as having primarily a political purpose, as political is understood under charity law, an organisation such as Greenpeace will not be recognised as charitable even though some 60% of the public believe it to be a charity (see Ipsos/MORI research conducted for the Charity Commission *Public Trust and Confidence in Charities* (2008) p 25).

(j) Relief of those in need by reason of youth, age, ill-health, disability, financial hardship or other disadvantage

By way of elaboration of this category s 2(3)(e) states that it includes 'relief given by the provision of accommodation or care to the persons mentioned' in the category. It is evident that there is something of an overlap here with the 'relief of poverty' category and there are doubtless many charitable institutions whose purposes fall under both heads. The emphasis here remains, as it always has, that some element of relief must be present. This was defined in the following manner by Peter Gibson J in *Joseph Rowntree Memorial Trust Housing Association Ltd v A-G* [1983] 2 WLR 284 at 292:

> The word 'relief' implies that the persons in question have a need attributable to their condition as aged, impotent or poor persons which requires alleviating, and which those persons could not alleviate, or would find difficulty in alleviating, themselves from their own resources. The word 'relief' is not synonymous with 'benefit'.... Thus a gift of money to the aged millionaires of Mayfair would not relieve a need of theirs as aged persons.

The provision of special housing for the aged is an increasingly prominent aspect of activity under this category, and it is seemingly no objection that full-cost fees are charged. As with hospitals and clinics if housing provision is run with a view to profit or is expressly confined to the rich it will not qualify as charitable.

Subject to the proviso concerning relief virtually any activity in aid of the groups mentioned falls within this category. It also encompasses much contemporary social welfare or social rehabilitation charitable activity (eg NSPCC, Barnardos). Among the many examples cited in the Annual Reports of the Commission are: rehabilitation of drug addicts; crime victim support schemes; family conciliation services; provision for 'latch-key' children. Specificity of purposes remains important in this area because phrases such as 'general benefit and welfare' may be considered too wide. If unaccompanied by any clarification of the methods to be adopted, they may be construed as permitting the application of funds to non-charitable purposes and hence infringe the requirement that purposes be exclusively charitable (see *Re Cole* [1958] 3 All ER 102; *A-G of the Bahamas v Royal Trust Co* [1986] 1 WLR 1001; and *A-G of the Cayman Islands v Wahr-Hansen* [2001] 1 AC 75, PC).

(k) The advancement of animal welfare

Animal charities nowadays are numerous and wealthy, representing perhaps the most extreme instance of charity's drift towards matters peripheral to social welfare (see eg RSPCA and RSPB with incomes in 2007 of £114m and £103m respectively). The 1601 preamble makes no mention of animals and the charitable status of gifts for the welfare of animals was originally restricted to those animals useful to man (*London University v Yarrow* (1857) 1 De G & J 72). Subsequently the category widened appreciably and the justification for the promotion of animal welfare generally was found in notions of moral elevation of humans. This received fulsome expression from Swinfen Eady LJ in *Re Wedgwood* [1915] 1 Ch 113 at 122, which concerned a trust for the benefit and protection of animals, with particular reference, once again, to improving methods for slaughtering them (being kind, as one might say, to the last drop of blood):

> A gift for the benefit and protection of animals tends to promote and encourage kindness towards them, to discourage cruelty, and to ameliorate the condition of the brute creation, and thus to stimulate humane and generous sentiments in man towards the lower animals, and by these means promote feelings of humanity and morality generally, repress brutality, and thus elevate the human race.

A less sentimental approach was adopted by a Court of Appeal, apparently determined to restrict any further extension of this category, in *Re Grove-Grady* [1929] 1 Ch 557, where a trust to set up an animal refuge safe from human interference was held not charitable. In the opinion of the court the public derived no benefit from such a refuge: 'The one characteristic of the refuge is that it is free from the molestation of man, while all the fauna within it are to be free to molest and harry one another' (per Lord Hanworth MR at 574; cf Charity Commission RR 9 *Preservation and Conservation* (2001) where it is suggested that alternative means of access 'such as video cameras' are acceptable in appropriate circumstances). One way of limiting the effect of that decision would be to accept that many purposes connected with animals should be charitable as being for the protection of the environment. In *A-G (NSW) v Sawtell* [1978] 2 NSWLR 200, for instance, the testatrix directed that her residuary estate should be 'devoted to the preservation of my native wild life (both flora and fauna)'. The executors had received advice, apparently relying heavily on the decision in *Re Grove-Grady*, that the gift was invalid. The court held that the bequest constituted a valid charitable trust. Holland J accepted the evidence before the court that public benefit was to be derived from 'the preservation of wild life, native or exotic'. He emphasised that (at 211) 'the evidence was to the effect that there has developed over the last few decades a greatly intensified public interest in wild life, its preservation and the opportunity to observe it in the wild [both in Australia and worldwide]'. Specific statutory recognition in s 2(2)(k) of the advancement of animal welfare as a freestanding charitable purpose suggests that it is time for English law to dispense with applying the convoluted criteria of *Re Wedgwood* that requires some other recognised public benefit to be present (see eg Animal Abuse, Injustice and Defence Society in *Decisions of the Charity Commissioners* vol 2 (1994) pp 1–4). It only remains to add that where the welfare of mankind and of animals come into conflict the former generally takes precedence in the law of charity. In *National Anti-Vivisection Society v IRC* [1948] AC 31 the House of Lords held, inter alia, that the public benefit emanating from the contributions of experimental vivisection to medicine outweighed the detriment arising from the cruelties perpetrated upon the animal victims.

(l) The promotion of the efficiency of the armed forces of the Crown, or of the efficiency of the police, fire and rescue services or ambulance services

This set of purposes, all more or less to do with supporting the efficiency of essential services, is the only one added to the Act during its passage through the parliamentary stages. None of the purposes represent any extension of the charitable purpose category as all were well established under the 'other beneficial purposes head'. Little would be gained by listing the old authorities here. It is, however, important to note the emphasis on efficiency. Distinguishing between on the one hand the provision of some facility to promote efficiency of a particular police force and, on the other hand, the provision of some similar facility whose principal purpose is to provide private benefit to the members with enhanced efficiency being a possible side-effect is not straightforward (*IRC v City of Glasgow Police Athletic Association* [1953] AC 38; cf *London Hospital Medical College v IRC* [1976] 1 WLR 613).

4. Recognising new charitable purposes under CA 2006, s 2(2)(m)

The CA 2006 sought to avoid the risk latent in any list-based definition that it would be so overly prescriptive that in time it would become an anachronism with the possibility of demands for a new definition surfacing in 2015 and 2025. This was to be achieved by in effect retaining in clause 2(2)(m) and 2(4) the catch-all category of 'other purposes beneficial to the community':

2(2)

(l) any other purposes within subsection (4)

2(4) The purposes within this subsection . . . are –

(a) any purposes not within paragraphs (a) to (l) of subsection (2) but recognised as charitable purposes under existing charity law or by virtue of section 1 of the Recreational Charities Act 1958;

(b) any purposes that may reasonably be regarded as analogous to, or within the spirit of, any purposes falling within any of those paragraphs or paragraph (a) above; and

> (c) any purposes that may reasonably be regarded as analogous to, or within the spirit of, any purposes which have been recognised under charity law as falling within paragraph (b) above or this paragraph.

It must be emphasised that nothing in the Act alters the fundamental proposition that not every benevolent purpose is charitable. This position emerges clearly enough from the judgment of Viscount Cave LC in *A-G v National Provincial Bank* [1924] AC 262 at 265:

> Lord Macnaghten did not mean that all trusts beneficial to the community are charitable, but that there were certain beneficial trusts which fall within that category: and accordingly to argue that because a trust is for a purpose beneficial to the community it is therefore a charitable trust is to turn round his sentence and to give it a different meaning. So here it is not enough to say that the trust in question is, for public purposes beneficial to the community or is for the public welfare; you must also show it to be a charitable trust.

Thus it is clear law that this category is limited to purposes which are (i) beneficial to the community, (ii) not within any of the preceding categories, *and* (iii) recognised by the law as charitable by a process of reasoning by analogy or being within the spirit of some other charitable purpose. The reference to 'the spirit of some other charitable purpose' can be viewed as a twenty-first century incarnation of the somewhat mystical requirement 'that a trust is not charitable and entitled to the privileges which charity confers unless it is within the spirit and intendment of the preamble' (per Lord Simonds in *Williams' Trustees v IRC* [1947] AC 447 at 455). The process of reasoning by analogy was graphically described by Lord Reid in *Scottish Burial Reform and Cremation Society Ltd v Glasgow City Corpn* [1968] AC 138 at 146–147:

> The courts appear to have proceeded first by seeking some analogy between an object mentioned in the preamble and the object with regard to which they had to reach a decision. And then they appear to have gone further and to have been satisfied if they could find an analogy between an object already held to be charitable and the new object claimed to be charitable. And this gradual extension has proceeded so far that there are few modern reported cases where a bequest or donation was made or an institution was being carried on for a clearly specified object which was for the benefit of the public at large and not of individuals, and yet the object was held not to be within the spirit and intendment of the Statute of Elizabeth I.

The apparently liberalising nature of the process described by Lord Reid was extended further in *Incorporated Council of Law Reporting for England and Wales v A-G* [1972] Ch 73 where Russell LJ, with whom Sachs LJ agreed, proposed a new approach (at 88):

> ... when considering ... 'other purposes beneficial to the community' ... the courts in consistently saying that not all such are necessarily charitable in law, are in substance accepting that if a purpose is shown to be so beneficial or of such utility it is prima facie charitable in law, but have left open a line of retreat based on the equity of the statute in case they are faced with a purpose (eg a political purpose) which could not have been within the contemplation of the statute even if the then legislators had been endowed with the gift of foresight into the circumstances of later centuries.
>
> In a case such as the present, in which in my view the object cannot be thought otherwise than beneficial to the community and of general public utility, I believe the proper question to ask is whether there are any grounds for holding it to be outside the equity of the statute.

In short, proof of public benefit raised a presumption (though still only a presumption) that the purpose was charitable. Subsequently in *Re South Place Ethical Society* [1980] 1 WLR 1565 Dillon J doubted whether this formally more generous approach was consistent with earlier House of Lords' decisions, such as *Williams' Trustees v IRC* (cf Lord Browne-Wilkinson's comment obiter in *A-G of the Cayman Islands v Wahr-Hansen* [2001] 1 AC 75 that Russell LJ 's approach 'has much to commend it' (at 82)). Moreover the CA 2006 explicitly reasserts the status of the reasoning by analogy process.

An important consideration therefore is whether this test will *in practice* prevent organisations involved in novel or pioneering philanthropic activity from obtaining charitable status. It is here that the approach of the Charity Commission (see below) acquires significance because, in the absence of regular appeals from their decisions, the development of this category will remain largely with the Commission.

Charity Commission: *Recognising Charitable Purposes* (RR1a, 2001) paras 23–24

> 23. ...
>
> The Commission will take a constructive approach in adapting the concept of charity to meet constantly evolving social needs and new ideas through which those needs can be met. Acting within the legal framework which governs the recognition of new charitable purposes, we would aim to act constructively and imaginatively.
>
> In considering new purposes as charitable we will look closely at those purposes which have already been recognised as charitable ... We will also look at contemporary needs of society and relevant legislation passed by Parliament and, where Convention rights are in issue, to the European Convention on Human Rights and decisions of the European Court of Human Rights and the European Commission of Human Rights.
>
> In identifying a new purpose as charitable we will, following the legal framework, need to be clear that there exists a sufficient correlation between those new purposes and purposes already accepted as charitable. While in most cases a sufficiently close analogy

may be found, in others an analogy may be found by following the broad principles which may be derived... from decided cases of the court or the Commission.

In addition we will need to be clear that the purpose is not a political purpose as understood in charity law and that the purposes are expressed with clarity and certainty to facilitate monitoring by us and any subsequent control by the court should that be necessary.

24. In effect, our view is that we will look for a suitable analogy in order to confirm whether or not the way in which a purpose will benefit the public is charitable. We also believe it will nearly always be possible to find an analogy, if the nature of the benefit is really of a kind that ought to be recognised as charitable.

Illustrations of how this approach is applied in practice can be gleaned from the Annual Reports of the Commission, as in the following extract:

We have... decided that providing advice and facilities concerning contraception can be a good charitable purpose by analogy with the preservation and protection of good health; and that family conciliation services formed to persuade the parties to settle differences relating to custody of children, property and other matters by negotiation before judicial hearing instead of burdening the courts with detailed dispute between the parties, were by analogy directed to the administration of the law directly affecting the social well-being of the public and families. Similarly we decided that the promotion of good community relations is, within the context of modern multi-racial and multi-cultural society, a valid charitable purpose by analogy with decided cases concerning the preservation of public order and the prevention of breaches of the peace [*IRC v City of Glasgow Police Athletic Association* [1953] AC 380], or the mental and moral improvement of man [eg *Re South Place Ethical Society* [1980] 1 WLR 1565]. (Annual Report 1985 para 5)

The last example given by the Commission also illustrates a procedural aspect of its role in developing the scope of charity: it is free to decide in principle on the charitable nature of a particular purpose even though no specific application is under consideration. Accordingly in 1983 the Commission decided to reverse its previous policy on the charitable status of 'the promotion of racial harmony'. It had considered itself bound by *Re Strakosch* [1949] Ch 529 in which it was held that the appeasement of racial feelings (between the Dutch- and English-speaking sections of the South African Community) was a political purpose and therefore not charitable. The policy reversal was explained in the following way (Annual Report 1983, paras 18–20):

18.... We took the view that *Re Strakosch* did not freeze the appeasement of racial feeling as a political purpose for all time. In England and Wales the question of whether it would be beneficial to the public to appease racial feeling appeared to be no longer a political one as legislation had been passed in an attempt to enforce good race relations and it is unlikely that any substantial body of opinion in England and Wales would not consider the promotion of good race relations to be a purpose beneficial to the community.

19. We considered that the promotion of racial harmony was undoubtedly for the benefit of the public; but the question to be answered was whether it was also charitable in law. We took the view that the promotion of racial harmony or good race relations is analogous to purposes which the Courts have held to be charitable . . . [see above extract from Annual Report 1985].

Discussion of general principles takes one little further than this. An indication of contemporary application has been given and, as the Commission has acknowledged on several occasions, its decisions will inevitably move further and further away from cases decided by the court. The present more creative approach of the Commission appears to be little impeded by the analogy requirement.

If a more creative approach is being applied, two particular considerations arise. First, earlier cases become less reliable authorities (cf *Re Strakosch*). Second, there is the possibility that the application of a liberal process of analogy is tantamount to continuing to apply a prima facie test. It is therefore necessary to consider what factors might prevent an application being considered in the eyes of the court or the Commission 'suitable for registration'. The principal areas of concern are that the purposes do not benefit a sufficient section of the public (section 8 below) or are too 'political' in certain specific senses (section 9 below). These considerations apart, it is tempting to suggest that reasoning by analogy imposes few constraints on fertile imaginations. It remains to be seen whether our courts and the Commission will feel able or willing to match the ingenuity of the Canadian Federal Court of Appeal in recognising as a charitable purpose analogous to 'the repair of highways' the provision of free access to the information highway (*Re Vancouver Regional Free Net Association and Minister of National Revenue* (1996) 137 DLR (4th) 206, but cf the dissenting judgment of Décarry J disapproving 'the potentially misleading use of analogies' (at 220–221)).

It only remains to add that the Charity Commission register provides plentiful examples of purposes that fall under this 'other beneficial purposes' head such as the promotion of industry or of agriculture, the provision of war memorials and the promotion of the moral or spiritual welfare or improvement of the community. It is this last purpose which can reduce the significance of 'humanist' organisations failing to be recognised as religions even under the extended criteria of CA 2006, s 2(3)(a), as was and remains the case with *Re South Place Ethical Society* ([1980] 1 WLR 1565 at 1575–1576). Indeed this possibility was specifically referred to by the government during the passage of the Bill: '[it] allows non-religious belief systems, such as those promoting moral and spiritual welfare to be charitable by another route' (Lord Bassam HL debates 12 October 2005, cols 292–298). That criterion has also provided one of the analogies for recognising as charitable Public Concern at Work, an organisation whose general purposes are to encourage ethical standards at work and provide advice and assistance to 'whistleblowers' (*Decisions of the Charity Commissioners* vol 2 (1994) pp 5–10).

5. State/charity relations: a comment

We saw in Chapter 18 how statutory income has become an increasingly important element in the funding of many charities. But the financial flow is not just in one direction and an underlying tension about the role of charity vis-à-vis that of the state, discussed briefly under relief of poverty, has recently taken on a sharper edge. This is most apparent in relation to the National Health Service. Following the introduction of the NHS in 1948 reliance on charitable funds was rendered almost obsolete on grounds, it was said, both of principle and efficiency (Bevan *In Place of Fear* (1953)). This did not stop people donating money to hospitals, but charitable appeals for hospitals only re-emerged on any significant scale after 1980 (see now National Health Service Act 2006, s 222). It has been estimated, for instance, that currently at least 10% of NHS spending in London is provided by charitable funds (see eg (2000) 321 BMJ 982; and generally Lattimer and Holly *Charity and NHS Reform* (1992)). Of course, in so far as the funds are 'supplementary' to what is provided directly or indirectly by the Department of Health, the distinction between 'state' and 'charity' is maintained but when the figure approaches 10% is this becoming a distinction without a difference?

The above illustration does not involve a charity in directly supplying services such as those that a local authority, for instance, may have a statutory duty to provide. In a landmark decision in 2004 the Commission registered as charities the Trafford Community Leisure Trust and the Wigan Leisure and Culture Trust ([2004] Ch Com Dec, 21 April). In both instances the organisations were set up specifically to enter into contracts with their respective local government authorities to deliver services that the authorities had either a discretionary power or a statutory duty to provide. The Commission decided that provided an organisation was independent with exclusively charitable purposes operating for the public benefit, it could have as its charitable purpose the discharging of 'a function or service that a governmental authority had a responsibility to provide'. The Commission found legal support for its decision in a series of mid-nineteenth century decisions where it was accepted as a good charitable purpose 'to relieve the community from general or local taxation provided that such purpose was applied for the benefit of a sufficient section of the community' (para 6.1.5, citing *Att-Gen v Bushby* (1857) 24 Beav 299; *Thellusson v Woodford* (1799) 4 Ves 227; and *Nightingale v Goulbourn* (1848) 2 PH 594). Such authorities long predate the emergence of the modern state and the decision marks a step change away from the previously expressed view of the Commission about state/charity relations.

6. Recreational purposes and the Recreational Charities Act 1958

As mentioned previously the decision of the Court of Appeal in *Re Nottage* [1895] 2 Ch 649 was understood to mean that promotion of games-playing per se was not charitable. Promotion of specific sports, however, is distinguished from the promotion of recreation generally, whereby people are enabled to play any game or undertake any relaxing activity that they may choose. At general law, it was and remains a charitable purpose to promote facilities for recreation in the course of establishing or maintaining public parks (*Re Hadden* [1932] 1 Ch 133; *Re Morgan* [1955] 2 All ER 632). By analogy with these authorities the Charity Commission upheld the provision of a public ice rink as charitable (Annual Report 1984 paras 19–25).

Until 1955, it was assumed that these and other common law authorities went far enough to confirm the charitable status of recreation generally, but *IRC v Baddeley* [1955] AC 572 cast serious doubt on this assumption. By a majority of 4:1 (Lord Reid dissenting) the House of Lords held that a trust's purposes aiming to promote 'the moral, social and physical well-being of persons resident . . . in West Ham and Leyton' were not exclusively charitable because of the inclusion of 'social' purposes.

In order to resolve these doubts and to confirm the charitable status of various long-established charities such as the National Playing Fields Association, the Recreational Charities Act 1958 was enacted. The following extract incorporates amendments introduced by CA 2006, s 5 that modernise some of the terminology but, more significantly, to ensure compliance with the European Convention on Human Rights, remove the potentially discriminatory impact of a gender requirement that meant that whilst women's institutes could be registered men's institutes could not. In s 1 a category of recreational charitable purposes is defined in the following terms:

> (1) ... it shall be and be deemed always to have been charitable to provide, or assist in the provision of, facilities for recreational or other leisure-time occupation, if the facilities are provided in the interests of social welfare...
>
> (2) The requirement in subsection (1) that the facilities are provided in the interests of social welfare cannot be satisfied if the basic conditions are not met.
>
> (2A) The basic conditions are –
>
> > (a) that the facilities are provided with the object of improving the conditions of life for the persons for whom the facilities are primarily intended: and
> >
> > (b) that either –
> >
> > > (i) those persons have need of the facilities by reason of their youth, age, infirmity or disability, poverty or social and economic circumstances; or
> > >
> > > (ii) the facilities are to be available to the members of the public at large or to male, or to female members of the public at large.

Under these provisions, the Commission has registered numerous organisations such as recreational centres open to the public or to a disabled group such as the blind, day nurseries for the under-fives (these are also educational) and women's institutes.

The somewhat curious drafting of the statute with its importation of a 'social welfare' requirement (s 1(1) and (2)) has posed problems of interpretation not least in a sporting context. In particular, decisions at first instance [1978] 1 WLR 664 and Court of Appeal [1979] 1 WLR 130 in *IRC v McMullen* raised doubts as to the scope of the Act. At first sight, setting up facilities for football and other games at schools and universities appears to be recreational within sub-s 1(1), being designed to 'improve the conditions of life' of pupils within sub-s (2A)(a) and aimed at persons who have 'need of such facilities ... by virtue of their youth' within sub-s (2A)(b). Walton J and the majority in the Court of Appeal held, however, that the key phrase 'social welfare', particularly when amplified by the 'improving the conditions of life' requirement, denoted an element of deprivation, though not necessarily financial deprivation. In contrast Bridge LJ (dissenting) disagreed that social welfare could be limited to the deprived: 'Hyde Park improves the conditions of life for residents in Mayfair as much as for those in Pimlico or the Portobello Road' (at 143). The more liberal approach of Bridge LJ was subsequently endorsed by the House of Lords in *Guild v IRC* [1992] 2 All ER 10. A bequest for use 'in connection with the Sports Centre in North Berwick or some similar purpose in connection with sport' was upheld. Lord Keith, giving the sole opinion of the House, rejected the argument that s 1(1) imported into s 1(2)(a) a 'deprivation' requirement: 'It suffices if [the facilities] are provided with the object of improving the conditions of life for the members of the community generally' (at 18).

The decision in *Guild* has unfortunately not resolved all doubts as to the meaning of social welfare in s 1(1) and (2). Lord Keith, apparently accepting that s 1(2A) states the 'essential elements' of social welfare rather than providing a definition as such, nevertheless commented: 'it is difficult to envisage a case where, although these essential elements are present, yet the facilities are not provided in the interests of social welfare' (at 17). The Charity Commission has subsequently taken the view, however, that an institution can meet the express requirements of s 1(2) but still fail to satisfy the overriding 'social welfare' requirement of s 1(1). In a test case application to clarify the charitable status of amateur sports clubs with open memberships the Commission considered the interpretation of the expression 'social welfare' under other legislation and concluded that it included the following two characteristics: (i) an ethical element – 'meeting needs which, morally speaking, ought to be met by society'; and (ii) an altruistic element – 'seeking to improve the conditions of life of others rather than of oneself' (*North Tawton Rugby Union Football Club*, Decisions of the Charity Commissioners vol 5 (1997) at p 11). Consequently the Commission rejected the application principally on the grounds of an absence of altruism – 'on balance the facilities were provided by the members for themselves' (see also the refusal to register Birchfield Harriers Athletic Club, Annual Report 1989 paras 54–55). More recent guidance issued by the Charity Commission demonstrates a continuing wariness in the direction: 'It may also be difficult to accept that the provision of facilities for a single sport meets the social obligation aspect of the social welfare requirement, particularly if they can only be used by people who have acquired a given level of skill' (Charity Commission RR4 The Recreational Charities Act 1958 (2000) A 25).

The fact that a facility can satisfy the requirement of being provided in the interests of social welfare still leaves one further obstacle to surmount, namely the second limb of the public benefit test, a topic considered at p 1016).

7. Charities: an international postscript

To the modern student of charity law the following statement may seem superfluous but it should be noted for the avoidance of doubt that it is no longer necessary to establish positively that the purpose of a charity to be carried out overseas must benefit, albeit indirectly, the public within the UK. It has long been accepted that the relief of poverty, the advancement of religion and the advancement of education are charitable in whatever part of the world they are carried out by a UK charity. Doubt had been expressed about the charitable status of some purposes carried on outside the UK. Lord Evershed MR in *Camille and Henry Dreyfus Foundation Inc v IRC* [1954] Ch 672 stated that he saw 'formidable difficulties, where the objects of the trust were, say, the setting out of soldiers or the repair of bridges or causeways in a foreign country. To such cases the argument of public policy (meaning United Kingdom public policy) might be the answer' (at 684). In 1993 the Charity Commissioners reassessed their approach and concluded that 'one should first consider whether [institutions operating abroad] would be regarded as charities if their operations are confined to the United Kingdom'. If they would, then they should be presumed also to be charitable even though operating abroad 'unless it would be contrary to public policy to recognise them' (*Decisions of the Charity Commissioners* vol 1 (1993) pp 16–17). This approach self-confessedly takes as its raison d'être the comments of Evershed MR on public policy and it has subsequently been approved by Jacob J in *Re Carapiet's Trust* [2002] EWHC 1304.

8. Public benefit

(a) Introduction

In this section we examine the requirement, referred to by the Charity Commission as Principle 2, that the class of persons eligible to derive benefit must constitute the public as a whole 'or an appreciably important class of the community' (per Lord Westbury in *Verge v Somerville* [1924] AC 496 at 499). A number of preliminary points must be made. First, one obvious object of the requirement is to prevent private classes of individuals from benefiting from the privileges associated with charitable status. The problem, as will be seen, lies in devising a test or tests that can distinguish the 'private' from the 'public'. Second, it is important to bear in mind that the 'section of the public' requirement emphasises eligibility for benefit; it does not insist that each and every person eligible should actually derive benefit from the purposes in question. This has particular significance for educational charities (see p 1008). Third, the requirement has been developed by the courts in a manner that differs from category to category, having been minimal for poverty charities and of doubtful relevance for religious charities, but increasingly substantial for educational and some other charitable purposes. Reconciling the disparate authorities is not easy not least because, as Lord Simonds observed on this point, 'the law of charity . . . has been built up, not logically, but empirically' (*Gilmour v Coats* [1949] AC 426 at 448). The fourth and final point is to reiterate that the emergence of a more restrictive approach to this requirement coincided both with the post-1945 increases in personal taxation which added to the significance of the fiscal privileges, and with the strong influence of Lord Simonds on this area of law (see Stevens *Law and Politics* (1978) pp 346–347; Paterson *The Law Lords* (1982) pp 118–121; Jones (1974) 33 CLJ 63). As we shall see, whether or not fiscal privileges should be a determining factor in granting charitable status has prompted disagreement amongst the Law Lords.

At first glance the CA 2006 offers no greater degree of clarity. Section 2 states that a charitable purpose is one that falls within the statutory list of categories and 'is for the public benefit'. The requirement of public benefit, it will be recalled, is then 'defined' in s 3(2) and (3) as follows:

(2) In determining whether that requirement is satisfied in relation to any such purpose, it is not to be presumed that a purpose of a particular description is for the public benefit.

(3) In this Part any reference to the public benefit is a reference to the public benefit as that term is understood for the purposes of the law relating to charities in England and Wales.

This formulation prompted considerable disagreement amongst lawyers, politicians and the Charity Commission as to its meaning and application, particularly in the context of fee-charging institutions such as private schools and hospitals (see eg Joint Committee on the Draft Charities Bill – First Report *The Draft Charities Bill* HL 167/HC 660 (September 2004) paras 70–102). At the core of the legal debate is what effect if any the removal of the presumption of public benefit would have on the section of the public requirement given that clause 3(3) appears specifically to retain the existing public benefit tests as decided through the cases. In this regard the Commission appears to accept that whilst it will try as part of its function to derive principles from the rather small number of key cases, the law will apply 'differently in respect of different charitable purposes' (*Charities and Public Benefit* (2008) para H 1). With those cautionary comments in mind our approach is therefore first to review those key cases and any principles that might be drawn from them and then to assess some possible implications of the new legal framework with particular reference to the issue of fee-charging and charitable status.

(b) A 'personal nexus test' and the advancement of education

Positive examples abound of groups who satisfy the 'section of the public' requirement under the advancement of education category (eg residents of a sizeable locality, those following a common calling or profession). Nevertheless, when it came to providing a definitive test, cases in this area generated rather more negative than positive guidance, a personal nexus test being the outcome.

The starting-point in the modern law of attempts to define an 'appreciably important class of the community' is *Re Compton* [1945] Ch 123 where the Court of Appeal held a perpetual trust 'for the education of Compton and Powell and Montague children' to be non-charitable and therefore invalid because the class thus defined did not constitute a section of the public. Six years later, in *Oppenheim v Tobacco Securities Trust Co Ltd* [1951] AC 297, the House of Lords (Lord MacDermott dissenting) ruled that a trust to provide as the trustees thought fit 'for the education of children of employees or former employees of the British-American Tobacco Co Ltd . . . or any of its subsidiary or allied companies' should suffer the same fate for the same reasons, even though the number of employees of the company and their subsidiary and allied companies was in excess of 110,000. The feature common to both these cases emerges most clearly in the judgment of Lord Simonds in *Oppenheim* (at 305):

> These words 'section of the community' have no special sanctity, but they conveniently indicate (1) that the possible (I emphasise the word 'possible') beneficiaries must not be numerically negligible, and (2) that the quality which distinguishes them from other members of the community, so that they form by themselves a section of it, must be a quality which does not depend on their relationship to a particular individual. It is for this reason that a trust for the education of members of a family or, as in *Re Compton*, of a number of families cannot be regarded as charitable. A group of persons may be numerous, but, if the nexus between them is their personal relationship to a single *propositus* or to several *propositi*, they are neither the community nor a section of the community for charitable purposes.
>
> I come, then, to the present case where the class of beneficiaries is numerous but the difficulty arises in regard to their common and distinguishing quality. That quality is being children of employees of one or other of a group of companies. I can make no distinction between children of employees and the employees themselves. In both cases the common quality is found in employment by particular employers . . .
>
> It appears to me that it would be an extension [of the legal definition of charity], for which there is no justification in principle or authority, to regard common employment as a quality which constitutes those employed a section of the community. It must not, I think,

be forgotten that charitable institutions enjoy rare and increasing privileges, and that the claim to come within that privileged class should be clearly established. . . .

Learned counsel for the appellant sought to fortify his case by pointing to the anomalies that would ensue from the rejection of his argument. For, he said, admittedly those who follow a profession or calling - clergymen, lawyers, colliers, tobacco-workers and so on - are a section of the public; how strange then it would be if, as in the case of railwaymen, those who follow a particular calling are all employed by one employer. Would a trust for the education of railwaymen be charitable, but a trust for the education of men employed on the railways by the Transport Board not be charitable? And what of service of the Crown, whether in civil service or the armed forces? Is there a difference between soldiers and soldiers of the King? My Lords, I am not impressed by this sort of argument and will consider on its merits, if the occasion should arise, the case where the description of the occupation and the employment is in effect the same, where in a word, if you know what a man does, you know who employs him to do it.

Lord MacDermott in his dissenting judgment laid stress on the very anomalies that left Lord Simonds unimpressed, concluding that the *Compton* test was 'a very arbitrary and artificial rule', and that therefore a more appropriate test was 'to treat the matter very much as a question of degree'. As will be seen shortly, his views on the appropriate test subsequently received strong support from dicta of Lord Cross in *Dingle v Turner* [1972] AC 601, a 'leapfrog appeal' under the Administration of Justice Act 1969, ss 12 and 13 from the decision of the High Court.

(c) A relief of poverty anomaly: 'poor relatives' and 'poor employees'

'The requirement of public benefit has been reduced, in the field of poverty, almost to vanishing point' (*Hanbury and Martin* p 433): that is to say, it has not been necessary to show that the class of persons eligible to benefit constitutes the public, or a section thereof. This concession derives from a line of eighteenth- and nineteenth-century cases known as the 'poor relations' cases (see *Picarda* pp 40–43) which all involved devises or bequests to 'my poor relations' or some similarly defined class of beneficiaries. This line of authorities, which had extended to include trusts for 'poor members' of societies and 'poor employees of a company', appeared increasingly anomalous in the twentieth century due to the emerging stringency in the requirement of public benefit under the other heads and seemed clearly incompatible with any personal nexus test. But in *Dingle v Turner* [1972] AC 601, a case involving a trust to pay pensions to 'poor employees of E Dingle & Co Ltd', the House of Lords endorsed the poverty exception. It held that innumerable trusts had been established in reliance on the old 'poor relations' cases and it was unwise to 'cast doubt on decisions of respectable antiquity in order to introduce a greater harmony into the law of charity as a whole' (per Lord Cross at 622, quoting Lord Simonds in *Oppenheim v Tobacco Securities Trust Co Ltd* [1951] AC 297 at 309). As to other restricted categories, the House of Lords decided it would be illogical to draw distinctions between 'poor relations' and, for example, 'poor employees', and therefore all poverty charities should be treated alike.

The 'vanishing point' referred to above has, however, not quite been reached. It is still necessary, if difficult, to draw a line between charitable trusts for the relief of poverty and private trusts in favour of individuals who happen to be poor. The test to be applied, and one approved in *Dingle v Turner*, was stated by Jenkins LJ in *Re Scarisbrick* [1951] Ch 622 at 655 as follows:

> I think the true question in each case has really been whether the gift was for the relief of poverty amongst a class of persons, or . . . a particular description of poor people or was merely a gift to individuals, albeit with relief of poverty amongst those individuals as the motive of the gift, or with a selective preference for the poor or poorest amongst those individuals.

This formulation is easier to state than to apply to borderline cases, but the relevant circumstances are likely to include the number of potential beneficiaries, their relationship to the trust founder and the amount of money involved (see the facts of *Re Cohen* [1973] 1 WLR 415). In *Re Segelman* [1996] Ch 171 the residuary estate worth some £8m was to be held on trust for 21 years for the benefit of 'poor and needy' members of a beneficial class. There was provision for any surplus at the end of the period to be distributed at the trustees' discretion to charities after the proper claims of the poor and needy members of the family had been satisfied. The class of possible beneficiaries at the date of the testator's death comprised merely 26 persons but was likely to be increased over the following 21 years by the birth of further members who would be unknown to the testator. This factor appeared to influence Chadwick J in deciding that although close to the borderline the gift to 'poor and needy' members of the class constituted a charitable 'poor relations' trust. The court was prepared to assume that at the end of the 21-year period there 'would or might be a substantial surplus' (at 193) to be distributed to other charitable purposes. The combination in *Re Segelman* of a sizeable fund (on which no inheritance tax or income tax would be chargeable) and a relatively small beneficial class allied to a flexible 'relativist' interpretation of 'poor and needy' (see p 976) suggests that the time is ripe for a reconsideration of the 'poor relations cases'. The anomaly is difficult to defend on any policy ground and the Charity Commission is of the opinion that the new statutory framework gives it the authority to review their status although it appears to harbour fewer reservations about the merits of charitable status for 'poor employee benevolent funds' (*The Prevention or Relief of Poverty for the Public Benefit* (December 2008) para E3).

(d) A flexible approach and a 'question of degree test'

It was beyond doubt after the decision in *Oppenheim* that the personal nexus test applied to the advancement of education category. In addition there was ample authority that in at least some circumstances a trust under the 'other beneficial purposes' Macnaghten category would not be charitable if the eligible beneficiaries were confined to persons defined by reference to a personal nexus with a named propositus (eg *Re Hobourn Aero Components Ltd's Air Raid Distress Fund* [1946] Ch 194 – distress fund limited to employees but with no poverty requirement held non-charitable). This test was specifically invoked in *Re Mead* [1961] 1 WLR 1244 in holding that the members of a trade union, being the class to whom benefit under a trust to establish a sanatorium for consumptive patients and a convalescent home was limited, did not constitute a section of the public.

But the scope of the test and its rationale came under critical scrutiny in the following wide-ranging dicta of Lord Cross in *Dingle v Turner* [1972] AC 601 at 624–625:

> The *Oppenheim* case was a case of an educational trust and although the majority evidently agreed with the view expressed by the Court of Appeal in the *Hobourn Aero* case [1946] Ch 194, that the *Compton* rule was of universal application outside the field of poverty, it would no doubt be open to this House without overruling *Oppenheim* to hold that the scope of the rule was more limited. If ever I should be called on to pronounce on this question – which does not arise in this appeal – I would as at present advised be inclined to draw a distinction between the practical merits of the *Compton* rule and the reasoning by which Lord Greene MR sought to justify it. That reasoning – based on the distinction between personal and impersonal relationships – has never seemed to me very satisfactory and I have always – if I may say so – felt the force of the criticism to which my noble and learned friend Lord MacDermott subjected it in his dissenting speech in the *Oppenheim* case. For my part I would prefer to approach the problem on far broader lines. The phrase 'a section of the public' is in truth a phrase which may mean different things to different people. In the law of charity judges have sought to elucidate its meaning by contrasting it with another phrase 'a fluctuating body of private individuals'. But I get little help from the supposed contrast for as I see it one and the same aggregate of persons may well be describable both as a section of the public and as a fluctuating body of private individuals. The ratepayers in the Royal Borough of Kensington and Chelsea, for example, certainly constitute a section of the public; but would it be a misuse of language to describe them as a 'fluctuating body of private individuals'? After all, every part of the public is composed of individuals and being susceptible of increase or decrease is fluctuating. So at the end of the day one is left where one started with the bare contrast between 'public' and 'private'. No doubt some classes are more naturally describable as sections of the public than as private classes while other classes are more naturally describable as private classes than as sections of the public. The blind, for example, can naturally be described as a section of the public; but what they have

in common – their blindness – does not join them together in such a way that they could be called a private class. On the other hand, the descendants of Mr Gladstone might more reasonably be described as a 'private class' than as a section of the public, and in the field of common employment the same might well be said of the employees in some fairly small firm. But if one turns to large companies employing many thousands of men and women most of whom are quite unknown to one another and to the directors the answer is by no means so clear. One might say that in such a case the distinction between a section of the public and a private class is not applicable at all or even that the employees in such concerns as ICI or GEC are just as much a 'section of the public' as the residents in some geographical area. In truth the question whether or not the potential beneficiaries of a trust can fairly be said to constitute a section of the public is a question of degree and cannot be by itself decisive of the question whether the trust is a charity. Much must depend on the purpose of the trust. It may well be that, on the one hand, a trust to promote some purpose, *prima facie* charitable, will constitute a charity even though the class of potential beneficiaries might fairly be called a private class and that, on the other hand, a trust to promote another purpose, also *prima facie* charitable, will not constitute a charity even though the class of potential beneficiaries might seem to some people fairly describable as a section of the public.

In answering the question whether any given trust is a charitable trust the courts – as I see it – cannot avoid having regard to the fiscal privileges accorded to charities. As counsel for the Attorney-General remarked in the course of the argument the law of charity is bedevilled by the fact that charitable trusts enjoy two quite different sorts of privilege. On the one hand, they enjoy immunity from the rules against perpetuity and uncertainty and although individual potential beneficiaries cannot sue to enforce them the public interest arising under them is protected by the Attorney-General. If this was all there would be no reason for the courts not to look favourably on the claim of any 'purpose' trust to be considered as a charity if it seemed calculated to confer some real benefit on those intended to benefit by it whoever they might be and if it would fail if not held to be a charity. But that is not all. Charities automatically enjoy fiscal privileges which with the increased burden of taxation have become more and more important and in deciding that such and such a trust is a charitable trust the court is endowing it with a substantial annual subsidy at the expense of the taxpayer. Indeed, claims of trusts to rank as charities are just as often challenged by the Revenue as by those who would take the fund if the trust was invalid. It is, of course, unfortunate that the recognition of any trust as a valid charitable trust should automatically attract fiscal privileges, for the question whether a trust to further some purpose is so little likely to benefit the public that it ought to be declared invalid and the question whether it is likely to confer such great benefits on the public that it should enjoy fiscal immunity are really two quite different questions. The logical solution would be to separate them and to say – as the Radcliffe Commission proposed – that only some charities should enjoy fiscal privileges. But as things are, validity and fiscal immunity march hand in hand and the decisions in the *Compton* and *Oppenheim* cases were pretty obviously influenced by the consideration that if such trusts as were there in question were held valid they would enjoy an undeserved fiscal immunity. To establish a trust for the education of the children of employees in a company in which you are interested is no doubt a meritorious act; but however numerous the employees may be the purpose which you are seeking to achieve is not a public purpose. It is a company purpose and there is no reason why your fellow taxpayers should contribute to a scheme which by providing 'fringe benefits' for your employees will benefit the company by making their conditions of employment more attractive. The temptation to enlist the assistance of the law of charity in private endeavours of this sort is considerable – witness the recent case of the Metal Box scholarships – *IRC v Educational Grants Association Ltd* [1967] Ch 993 – and the courts must do what they can to discourage such attempts. In the field of poverty the danger is not so great as in the field of education – for while people are keenly alive to the need to give their children a good education and to the expense of doing so, they are generally optimistic enough not to entertain serious fears of falling on evil days much before they fall on them. Consequently the existence of company 'benevolent funds', the income of which is free of tax does not constitute a very attractive 'fringe benefit'. This is a practical justification – although not, of course, the historical explanation – for the special treatment accorded to poverty trusts in charity law. For the same sort of reason a trust to promote some religion among the employees of a company might perhaps safely be held to be charitable provided that it was clear that the benefits were to be purely spiritual. On the other hand, many 'purpose' trusts falling under Lord Macnaghten's fourth head if confined to a class of employees would clearly be open to the same sort of objection as educational trusts. As I see it, it is on these broad lines rather than for the reasons actually given by Lord Greene MR that the *Compton* rule can best be justified.

The *Oppenheim* and *Dingle v Turner* cases leave unresolved a number of difficult theoretical and practical problems.

Consider in particular the following points:

(1) Lord Cross did not purport to overrule either *Compton* or *Oppenheim*. Nevertheless, with the exception of the point as to fiscal privileges, all the other Law Lords appeared to endorse the dicta of Lord Cross. Thus the continued standing of the *Compton* test, at least outside the category of education, is uncertain.

(2) It has been argued that Lord Cross uses the word 'purpose' ambiguously (see Watkin [1978] Conv 277). Is he proposing that 'purposes' in the sense *either* of motives for creating a trust *or* of 'consequences' of its creation should be taken into account when assessing 'public benefit'?

(3) In *Dingle v Turner* the House of Lords disagreed whether fiscal considerations were relevant to the question of public benefit. Lord Simon briefly concurred with Lord Cross's judgment whereas Lords Dilhorne, Hodson and MacDermott all expressed reservations about this. Lord MacDermott confusingly added, however, that: 'this subject [ie fiscal privileges] may be material on the question whether what is alleged to be a charity is sufficiently altruistic in nature to qualify as such but beyond that, and without

wishing to express any final view on the matter, I doubt if these consequential privileges have much relevance to the primary question whether
a given trust or purpose should be held charitable in law.' Is Lord Mac-
Dermott suggesting here that fiscal privileges should not be relevant in
deciding whether a specified purpose is prima facie charitable but may be
relevant to determining whether that purpose satisfies the section of the
public requirement, applying a 'question of degree' test? If this is a correct
interpretation of Lord MacDermott's words, then the gap between himself
and Lord Cross on the relevance of fiscal privileges is much narrower than
is generally supposed.

(4) In *Oppenheim* it is stated that 'no evidence was given of any connexion
of the grantors [ie those who established the trust] with the company
except that John Phillips was a large stockholder' (at 299). The existence or
otherwise of any personal or commercial link between the trust founder(s)
and the class to be benefited is immaterial under the 'personal nexus'
test.

(5) The apparent certainty provided by the *Compton* 'bright line' test as restated
by Lord Simonds in *Oppenheim* is somewhat illusory for two reasons.

First, it refers to one or 'several' propositi (or points of reference) but
does not indicate what number the propositi must reach (eg what about
HSBC *and* Shell *and* IBM, etc) before it can be said that the *Compton* test
can no longer be sensibly applied (*Davies v Perpetual Trustee Co Ltd* [1959]
AC 439).

Second, the weakness of a test which looks to form rather than substance
is exposed in a case where a charity is established in favour of the public
but is de facto administered in favour of a narrow class. In *IRC v Educational Grants Association Ltd* (EGA) ([1967] Ch 123; affd 993) members of
the management of Metal Box Ltd established EGA, a company limited by
guarantee, whose principal objects were defined in general terms for the
advancement of education. EGA was funded by covenanted payments from
Metal Box and donations from the chairman and his brother. Between 1958
and 1962 the proportion of income paid to children of Metal Box employees varied annually between 76% and 85%. The Inland Revenue, while
conceding the charitable status of EGA, disallowed a claim for repayment
of tax on covenanted income for that period. Pennycuick J and the Court
of Appeal held that the tax was not recoverable. The principal ground
adopted by all the judges was that since, in accordance with *Oppenheim*,
the 'Metal Box Children' were not a 'section of the public', the payments
in their favour were made by way of 'private' as opposed to 'public' benefit
and therefore the income had not been applied 'to charitable purposes
only' (ICTA 1988, s 505(1)). This decision, however, leaves several loose
ends.

First, there was judicial disagreement about whether the charitable status
of EGA should have been conceded. Second, it is not clear at what point

(eg 49%, 25%, 5%) the application of funds would cease to be by way of 'private benefit'. A 'straw in the wind' as regards the approach of HMRC may lie in the Income Tax (Earnings and Pensions) Act 2003, s 213. Under this section scholarships awarded to children (of higher paid employees) out of a trust fund (whether charitable or not) established by the employer will be treated as taxable income of the employees unless *not more than* 25% of the total annual value of scholarships are awarded to employees (ie 75% or more must be made available to the community at large if the charge to income tax is to be avoided; cf also Inland Revenue treatment of recip-rocal benefits under gifts to charity, Ghosh and Robson [1993] BTR 496). Third, Pennycuick J expressed considerable doubt about *Re Koettgen* [1954] Ch 252, a case relied on by EGA, where an educational trust in favour of a broad primary class but with a direction that preference be given to the families of employees up to a maximum of 75% of the income, had been held charitable. Its validity had already been doubted by the Privy Council in *Caffoor v Income Tax Comr, Colombo* [1961] AC 584 – 'it edges very near to being inconsistent with *Oppenheim*' (at 604) – and it is clear that if there is an absolute right in favour of a private group, rather than simply a pref-erence, then the trust cannot be charitable (see *Re Martin* (1977) 121 Sol Jo 828). The Charity Commission followed *Re Koettgen* in three reported cases (the relevant percentages being 65% and 75%) but with a warning that the 'application of too large a proportion' of the income would consti-tute an application for non-charitable purposes (Annual Report 1978 paras 86–89). However, if *Re Koettgen* remains good authority, there would seem to be a loophole in the law. Private or company purposes can be furthered in the guise of charity and with (in some measure) the privileges attached to charitable status.

(6) Where the advancement of religion category is concerned it is questionable whether a separate section of the public test is even applicable. In *Gilmour v Coats* [1949] AC 426 Lord Simonds acknowledged that there was 'a speciously logical appearance' to the argument that because membership of the order of cloistered nuns was 'open to any woman in the wide world who has the necessary vocation' (at 448) in the same way as a scholarship is open to anyone who wishes to compete, the persons eligible to derive what was undoubtedly, for them, a tangible benefit did constitute a section of the public. Lord Simonds rejected the argument and refused to accept that on this issue an analogy could be drawn between educational and religious trusts. How then, in *Neville Estates v Madden* [1962] Ch 832, could a trust for the advancement of religion among the members of Catford Synagogue – 'no more a section of the public than the members for the time being of a Carmelite priory' (at 853) – be held charitable? Cross J was able to reconcile the two cases but only, as we have seen (p 983), by saying that the public as a whole derived a tangible benefit from the fact that members of the synagogue went out after their worship there and made contact with their

fellow citizens. This appears to blur the two limbs of public benefit and suggests that the public benefit requirement in religious charities will be satisfied merely by the existence of some tangible benefit, however indirect and tenuous, to the public as a whole. It may be added that the applicability of the *Compton–Oppenheim* test to religious trusts has never been resolved in the courts.

(e) A 'class within a class' test

The 'personal nexus' and 'question of degree' tests are not, unfortunately, the only competitors jostling for position in providing a benchmark for interpreting the 'section of the public' requirement.

A further possible test emerged from some cases decided under the 'other beneficial purposes' category. The consequence is that there may in certain circumstances be a still more restrictive section of the public requirement applicable to some purposes previously gathered under that heading. It will be recalled that the ratio of the majority decision in *IRC v Baddeley* [1955] AC 572 (above, p 1004) was that the proposed purposes were not exclusively charitable, but in addition Lords Simonds and Somervell expressed the view that the persons eligible to benefit – Methodists resident in West Ham and Leyton – were not a 'section of the public' (Lord Reid dissented and Lords Porter and Tucker expressly left the point open). The proposed beneficial class constituted instead 'a class within a class' and the limitation of benefit to persons of a particular creed did not follow naturally or logically from the broadly defined purposes of the trust. It is difficult to predict the circumstances in which this aspect of the 'public benefit' requirement is likely to emerge, although it seems to constitute a technique whereby a court may hold non-charitable a trust under what was the 'other beneficial purposes' category with eccentric or quirky or arbitrary limitations on the range of eligible beneficiaries (cf *Davies v Perpetual Trustee Co Ltd* [1959] AC 439). It did not, for instance, prevent a bequest 'to found a home for old Presbyterian persons' being held charitable, seemingly on the basis of indirect benefit to the public at large from having at least some of the elderly housed (*Re Dunlop* [1984] NI 408). It is noteworthy that in *Re Dunlop* no conclusion was expressed as to the test to be applied other than that the relief of poverty exception in *Dingle v Turner* did not apply to trusts to relieve 'aged and impotent' persons (see Dawson [1987] Conv 114). There is also evidence that the Charity Commission is attempting to adopt a more generous approach to the public benefit requirement under the RCA 1958, s 1(1). The Commission has indicated that it will be prepared to recognise as charitable community associations or recreational organisations established primarily for ethnic minority groups, technically 'a class within a class'. The view of the Commission is that, at least for the purposes of the statute, the intention of Parliament was to relax the common law rule prohibiting a class within a class (*Decisions of the Charity Commissioners* vol 4 (1995) pp 17–21).

(f) 'Section of the public': an interim conclusion

The legal conundrum remains: which section of the public test is appropri-ate for what purpose and in what circumstances? The answer to the conun-drum may depend on at least two connected considerations. One is how far the scope of the personal nexus and the 'class within a class' tests described above should now be reassessed in light of the support expressed by Lord Cross in *Dingle v Turner* for a 'question of degree' test for public benefit, one that takes account of the purpose of the trust. The second consider-ation refers to the implications of s 3 of the CA 2006 and its interpreta-tion and implementation by the Charity Commission for all the competing tests.

In its present analysis of the legal rules concerning public benefit the Charity Commission specifically endorses the approach of Lord Cross and the question of degree test as representing 'a proper basis for considering what constitutes a sufficent section of the public' (*Charities and Public Benefit: Analysis of the Law* (2008) para 3.14). Moreover, noting that a 'class within a class test' has not been generally endorsed by the courts, the Commission goes beyond its position outlined in (e) above and indicates that it does not consider the test to be a good basis for analysis in this area. The scepticism expressed by the Commission with regard to the 'poor relations' anomaly has already been noted. As regards the personal nexus test the Commission recognises that the test has value as a means of denying charitable status to *Compton* and *Oppenheim* type trusts or organisations but intends to be 'both cautious and flexible' in the application of the test (para 3.45).

There remains, however, one further and particularly contentious area of the public benefit requirement to examine: the application of that requirement to fee-charging institutions.

(g) Charging fees and distributing profits

It is clear that institutions whose governing instrument allows for profits to be distributed to persons other than beneficiaries or charities are not themselves charities (*Re Girls' Public Day School Trust Ltd* [1951] Ch 400). It is equally clear that the mere charging of fees will not render an otherwise charitable institution non-charitable, not even apparently where the bargained arrangement might provide an incidental profit for the beneficiary (*Joseph Rowntree Memorial Trust Housing Association v A-G* [1983] Ch 159 criticised by Nobles (1983) 46 MLR 782). There remains the question as to whether the public benefit requirement imposes any constraint on those fee-charging organisations with charitable status such as many private hospitals, nursing homes and private schools. The point arose for consideration by the Privy Council in relation to private hospitals in *Re Resch*.

Re Resch's Will Trusts [1969] 1 AC 514

Edmund Resch bequeathed two-thirds of the net income of his residuary estate (valued at A$8m) to the Sisters of Charity for the general purposes of St Vincent's Private Hospital. The private hospital (which had 82 beds) was close to a public hospital (which had 500 beds) also run by the Sisters of Charity. It was argued on behalf of the next of kin (1) that a gift which in effect excluded the poor was not charitable; (2) following Lord Simonds' judgment in *IRC v Baddeley*, a hospital open not to the sick as a whole but only to the sick who are able to pay could not be charitable because it was not a form of relief accorded to the whole community yet by its very nature advantageous only to the few but 'a form of relief accorded to a selected few out of a larger number equally willing and able to take advantage of it (ie "a class within a class")'. The gift was held to be charitable.

Lord Wilberforce: [The appellants] appealed to some well known authorities. In *Jones v Williams* (1767) Amb 651 Mr Ambler attributes to Lord Camden LC (at p 652) a definition of charity as a 'gift to a general public use, which extends to the poor as well as to the rich' – the gift there was to provide a supply of water, and if that should fail to the Foundling and Lying-in Hospitals. Then in *Re Macduff* [1896] 2 Ch 451 in a general discussion of such expressions as 'charitable' or 'philanthropic', Lindley LJ said (at p 464) 'I am quite aware that a trust may be charitable, and yet not confined to the poor but I doubt very much whether a trust would be declared to be charitable which excluded the poor'.... Their lordships accept the correctness of what has been said in those cases, but they must be rightly understood. It would be a wrong conclusion from them to state that a trust for the provision of medical facilities would necessarily fail to be charitable merely because by reason of expense they could only be made use of by persons of some means. To provide, in response to public need, medical treatment otherwise inaccessible but in its nature expensive, without any profit motive, might well be charitable: on the other hand to limit admission to a nursing home to the rich would not be so. The test is essentially one of public benefit, and indirect as well as direct benefit enters into the account. In the present case, the element of public benefit is strongly present. It is not disputed that a need exists to provide accommodation and medical treatment in conditions of greater privacy and relaxation than would be possible in a general hospital and as a supplement to the facilities of a general hospital. This is what the private hospital does and it does so at, approximately, cost price. The service is needed by all, not only by the well-to-do. So far as its nature permits it is open to all: the charges are not low, but the evidence shows that it cannot be said that the poor are excluded: such exclusion as there is, is of some of the poor – namely those who have (a) not contributed sufficiently to a medical benefit scheme or (b) need to stay longer in the hospital than their benefit will cover or (c) cannot get a reduction of or exemption from the charges. The general benefit to the community of such facilities results from the relief to the beds and medical staff of the general hospital, the availability of a particular type of nursing and treatment which supplements that provided by the general hospital and the benefit to the standard of medical care in the general hospital which arises from the juxtaposition of the two institutions.

The judgment confirms that the mere charging of fees will not render an otherwise charitable purpose non-charitable but is elliptical on the 'section of the public' requirement. Its broader significance for this requirement is therefore more difficult to determine. Lord Wilberforce does not, for instance, directly address the very full argument advanced by counsel for the next of kin invoking *Baddeley* and the 'class within a class' test (see [1969] 1 AC 514 at 520–526 and 530–532). Surprisingly the case is not even mentioned in his opinion. Moreover the introduction of considerations of indirect benefit appears to blur the distinction we suggest can be drawn between the two limbs of public benefit (see also Watkin [1976] Conv 277 at 285–290) unless it can be inferred that the Privy Council was adopting the pragmatic 'question of degree' test. Indeed one of the attributes claimed for this test by Lord MacDermott in *Oppenheim* was that it allowed indirect benefit to be considered ([1951] AC 297 at 318).

The adoption of such a test in preference to the more precise formulae favoured by Lord Simonds in *Oppenheim* and *IRC v Baddeley* does however potentially expose a number of issues to closer scrutiny.

Consider in particular the following points:

(1) Whether the public as a whole derives an 'indirect' or 'tangible' benefit from the provision of private health facilities is economically, socially and philosophically contentious. The specific and general factual contexts of *Re Resch* should therefore not be overlooked. The private and public hospitals in *Re Resch* were adjacent to each other, and the private insurance-based system of financing health care provision then operating in Australia was significantly different to the tax-funded system applicable in the UK. That is still largely the position although there has been an expansion in the number of non-NHS acute treatment hospitals in the UK providing health care services to predominantly private fee-paying patients. Somewhat surprisingly the Charity Commission is currently unable to provide precise details of the numbers of fee-charging hospitals registered as charities, although an estimate from the sector itself puts the number at 84 in 2007 (see Morris (2007) 18 KLJ 455 at 456). The largest of the charitable not-for-profit providers is Nuffield Health with, in 2008, 39 hospitals and an annual income of £549m. Whether the provision of private health care facilities represents additional resources depends significantly in the UK context on an assumption that there is no consequential diminution of NHS provision or staffing levels. It is partly because of concern about these issues that the Government's decision in 2003 to commission a number of independent sector treatment centres (ISTCs) to treat NHS patients who required relatively straightforward elective or diagnostic procedures provoked controversy (see generally the House of Commons Health Committee report on ISTCs, 4th Report Session 2005–06 HC 934-1: 'The ISTC programme is intended eventually to provide about half a million procedures per year at a cost of over £5 billion in total. . . . This could clearly affect the viability of

many existing NHS providers over the next five years and possibly beyond';
Pollock (2008) 336 BMJ 421–424.)

Whereas these considerations may be susceptible to some degree of quantification, there is much less agreement about the long-term consequences
of private provision on levels of state funding and scope of public provision
(see eg Le Grand and Robinson (eds) *Privatisation and the Welfare State*
(1984) chs 6 and 7; Lattimer *The Gift of Health* (1996); Pierson *Beyond the
Welfare State?* (3rd edn, 2006); and classically Titmuss *The Gift Relationship*
(1970) ch 14, and comment by Glazer (1971) 24 Public Interest 86–94).
Bright-line tests such as those propounded by the majority in *Oppenheim*
and by Lords Simonds and Somervell in *Baddeley* rescue the courts from
overt consideration of all these issues.

(2) Does the approach to 'public benefit' adopted in *Re Resch* with its reference
to 'indirect benefit' require 'self-help' cases such as *Re Mead* (above, p 1006)
to be reassessed?

(3) The CA 2006, s 7 sets out a series of objectives for the Charity Commission,
one of which is 'to promote awareness and understanding of the operation of the public benefit requirement'. In furtherance of that objective s
4(1) of the Act states that the Commission 'must issue guidance' although
that guidance is not legally binding on charity trustees or on anyone else,
although the trustees 'must have regard to any such guidance' (s 4(6)) when
exercising any powers or duties to which the guidance is relevant.

With regard to fee-charging charities the draft guidance published by the
Commission in January 2005 drew extensively on the decision of the Privy
Council in *Re Resch*. When considering the extent to which the charging
of fees by a charity may affect its ability to demonstrate public benefit
the Charity Commission stated that the following broad principles apply
(*Public Benefit: The Legal Principles* (2005) para 34):

> • Both direct and indirect benefits to the public, or a sufficient section of the public,
> may be taken into account in deciding whether an organisation is set up and
> operates for the benefit of the public;
> • The fact that the charitable facilities or services will be charged for, and will be
> provided mainly to people who can afford to pay the charges, does not necessarily
> mean that the organisation is not set up for and does not operate for the benefit
> of the public;
> • However, an organisation which wholly excluded less well off people from any
> benefits, direct or indirect, would not be set up and operate for the benefit of the
> public and therefore would not be a charity.

The guidance outlines various ways (para 36) in which the test might
be satisfied, all of which draw heavily on the reasoning and illustrations
employed by Lord Wilberforce in *Re Resch*. As suggested above this approach

is tantamount to applying the 'question of degree' test favoured by Lord Cross in *Dingle v Turner* (see p 1011). It is therefore arguable that the Charity Commission is purporting to develop the test on public benefit in a direction that significantly extends the scope of the decision in *Re Resch*, a case which, as also suggested above, was reached in a particular context and where certain key arguments were not addressed by Lord Wilberforce in his opinion. On the other hand the Commission appears to be adopting a narrower view of the type of indirect benefit that can be relevant. It would not, in its view, satisfy the public benefit requirement 'if the only benefits available to people who are unable to pay the fees are wider benefits such as those which, it can be argued, the public in general receives where a service provided by a charity relieves public funds' (*Charities and Public Benefit* (2008) para F10-4). The decision of the Charity Commission in 2007 to refuse registration to Odstock Private Care Limited is the sole occasion on which the criteria referred to above have been applied in the context of health care provision. The scale of charges – examples quoted were £661 and £8,063 for colonoscopy and knee replacement respectively – were held to be such that poor people would not be able to afford them. Moreover on the evidence presented the cost of medical insurance had not been shown to be affordable by poor people. Lastly, as regards indirect benefit, the degree of complementarity between private and public provision claimed to exist in *Re Resch* was not present in the case.

(h) Conclusion: public benefit, 'section of the public' and altruism

In Chapter 18 we noted that the majority decision in *Pemsel* imported into tax law a generous notion of 'public benefit'. The subsequent emergence of the 'section of the public' requirement can be interpreted as an attempt, in response to this liberality, to restrict the availability of the consequential fiscal privileges because of their increasing value. But the rules as formulated, for example, in the 'personal nexus' test, were not specifically directed to this objective. Rather, such issues are decided under the guise of distinguishing a 'section of the public' from 'a fluctuating body of private individuals' or by reference to 'personal' and 'impersonal' qualities. These formulae can be criticised for their arbitrariness but there is a more fundamental objection. Whereas they undoubtedly provide a basis whereby some types of self-seeking organisation (notably, employees' educational trusts) can be denied the privileges of charitable status, they have diverted attention away from the theoretically distinct issue of altruism. One consequence is that other organisations such as fee-charging schools and hospitals which, it can be argued, also lack altruism have been allowed to enjoy charitable status because they are in theory open to the public as a whole. The point is not whether those institutions should retain their charitable status and the accompanying fiscal privileges, but that the formulations of principle in charity law have tended to mask the real policy issues at stake (see *Chesterman* ch 14; Gladstone *Charity, Law and Social Justice* (1982) pp 60–74; Moffat in Ware (ed) *Charities and Government* (1989) ch 8).

It might have been anticipated that this much-debated issue would have been directly addressed in the Charities Act 2006. Instead of this happening the legislature has presented the Charity Commission with unfortunate legal and policy dilemmas. It is evident that one minimalist objective of government policy was to ensure that some greater degree of access would be made available to the public by fee-charging institutions. The Strategy Unit Report argued that the removal of the presumption of public benefit would mean that 'for example, to maintain their charitable status, independent schools which charge high fees have to make significant provision for those who cannot pay full fees . . .' (*Private Action, Public Benefit* (2002) para 4.26). The legal difficulty is that whilst, as has been seen previously, CA 2006, s 3(2) purports to remove the assumed presumption of public benefit, s 3(3) retains the interpretation of public benefit established by the case law. Consequently, so it may be argued, the charitable status of fee-charging schools is firmly established under that case law so that, whatever may have been the legislative intention, nothing in the Act requires those institutions to take any additional measures to retain their charitable status (see Luxton in Dixon and Griffiths (eds) *Contemporary Perspectives on Property, Equity and Trust Law* (2007) ch 10). After all if the personal nexus test is the sole one applicable to the advancement of education category there is no doubt that most private schools could satisfy its requirements, there being no prior contractual nexus amongst pupils or parents and the numbers of potential beneficiaries are not negligible. On the other hand it is possible to argue that the scope of the personal nexus test and the decisions in *Compton* and *Oppenheim* should be confined just to those cases where there are family or business relationships and that a different test such as that in *Re Resch* should apply. This appears to be the position adopted by the Charity Commission even though there is no direct legal authority to support such a proposition, hence the legal dilemma.

The failure to address directly the public benefit issue in the context of private schools and hospitals was raised by critics at various points during the passage of the Charities Act 2006. Indeed the Joint Committee of the Commons and the Lords that scrutinised the original draft Bill in 2004 went so far as to suggest that the best solution might lie in removing charitable status from them whilst leaving open the possibility of comparable tax benefits being granted where sufficient public benefit could be demonstrated (Report of the Joint Committee on the Draft Charities Bill (HL 167 – 1/ HC 660 – 1). The Government rejected the recommendation. Whether their reasoning is based on analysis of the likely legal effects of s 3 or resides in a political calculation is unknown. It is though not difficult to have sympathy with the view expressed in the Second Reading of the Bill in the Lords by a leading charity lawyer and cross-bench peer, Lord Phillips of Sudbury, 'that [the Government] want the appearance of a change without the substance and that they want to satisfy critics of the status quo without arousing the middle classes. In short they want the credits without any opprobrium' (HL Debates 20 January 2005, col 907).

The Charity Commission has deftly attempted to sidestep the broader arguments about the charitable status and public benefit of private schools or hospitals in general by emphasising that its function is 'to decide whether a particular organisation is or is not a charity. It is not about assessing whether a particular group of charities, or a section of the charitable sector as a whole, is for the public benefit' (*Charities and Public Benefit* (2008) para D3). It is though questionable whether matters of legal and political controversy are so easily avoided. How exactly is the Commission to decide what level of means-tested scholarships should be made available or how extensive must be the interaction between a private school and local state schools to justify charitable status and the accompanying tax reliefs? In making such a decision should the Commission take into account the detrimental consequence for the local state school that, so it is argued, can result from 'creaming off' its most able pupils?

Paradoxically, opting for a more universal implementation of the supposedly more rational 'question of degree' test advanced by Lord Cross in *Dingle v Turner* may, as Gareth Jones shrewdly observed, 'create more problems than it solves' ((1974) 33 CLJ 63 at 66). Indeed, Gardner points out that one virtue of a rule-based system of defining public benefit is that it limits the 'need for value judgements' from the courts and Commission (*An Introduction to the Law of Trusts* (2nd edn, 2003) p 114). This justification reaches its strongest, yet most contentious, pitch at the point where charity and politics overtly collide, the topic we consider next.

9. Charities and political activity

(a) The scope of the principle

There is a sharp theoretical dividing line in the modern law of charities between charitable and political purposes: the former exclude the latter. In 1978 the Charity Commission refused to register Amnesty International Trust whose objects, among otherwise admittedly charitable purposes, included (1) attempting to secure the release of prisoners of conscience, and (2) procuring the abolition of torture or inhumane or degrading treatment or punishment. The Trust appealed and in *McGovern v A-G* [1982] Ch 321 Slade J recognised that 'Amnesty International . . . is performing a function which many will regard as being of great value to humanity' but upheld the Commission's decision because the disputed purposes were 'substantially political', not 'charitable' (Watkin [1982] Conv 387; Weiss (1983) 46 MLR 385; Nobles (1982) 45 MLR 704).

This initially puzzling conclusion reflects a position whereby politics has a specific meaning in the context of charity law. Not surprisingly the promotion of the cause of a political party is not charitable (*Bonar Law Memorial Trust v IRC* (1933) 49 TLR 220 (Conservative); *Re Ogden* [1933] Ch 678 (Liberal); *Re Hopkinson* [1949] 1 All ER 346 (Socialist)). Neither, it would seem, is the promulgation of a general political doctrine (*Re Bushnell* [1975] 1 All ER 721, 'furthering socialised medicine in a socialist state'), nor the fostering of a particular attitude towards potentially contentious issues which edge into the arena of political debate, such as promoting international peace and understanding (*Re Strakosch* [1949] Ch 529, but cf *Re Koeppler Will Trusts* [1985] 2 All ER 869; and see also the discussion of 'propaganda', above, p 982). There is one further and important dimension to the concept 'political'. Earlier in this chapter we referred to the House of Lords' decision in *National Anti-Vivisection Society v IRC* that the public benefit from experimental vivisection outweighed the detriment of cruelty to animals. An alternative reason for holding the National Anti-Vivisection Society non-charitable was (Lord Porter dissenting) that the total abolition of vivisection required a change in the law and that this was therefore a political purpose.

National Anti-Vivisection Society v IRC [1948] AC 31

Lord Simonds referred to a passage from Lord Parker's speech in *Bowman v Secular Society Ltd* [1917] AC 406 at 442 '. . . a trust for the attainment of political objects has always been held invalid, not because it is illegal . . . but because the court has no means of judging whether a proposed change in the law will or will not be for the public benefit', and commented as follows (at 62):

> My Lords, I see no reason for supposing that Lord Parker . . . used the expression 'political objects' in any narrow sense or was confining it to objects of acute political controversy. On the contrary, he was, I think, propounding familiar doctrine, nowhere better stated than in a textbook which has long been regarded as of high authority, but appears not to have been cited for this purpose to the courts below (as it certainly was not to your Lordships), *Tyssen on Charitable Bequests*. The passage (1st ed, 1898, p 176) is worth repeating at length: 'It is a common practice for a number of individuals amongst us to form an association for promoting some change in the law . . . It is clear that such an association is not of a charitable nature. However desirable the change may really be, the law could not stultify itself by holding that it was for the public benefit that the law itself should be changed. Each court in deciding on the validity of a gift must decide on the principle that the law is right as it stands. On the other hand, such a gift could not be held void for illegality.'
>
> Lord Parker uses slightly different language, but means the same thing, when he says that the court has no means of judging whether a proposed change in the law will or will not be for the public benefit. It is not for the court to judge and the court has no means of judging. The same question may be looked at from a slightly different angle. One of the tests, and a crucial test, whether a trust is charitable lies in the competence of the court to control and reform it. I would remind your Lordships that it is the King as *parens patriae* who is the guardian of charity, and that it is the right and duty of his Attorney-General to intervene and inform the court if the trustees of a charitable trust fall short of their duty.

> So too it is his duty to assist the court, if need be, in the formulation of a scheme for the execution of a charitable trust. But, my Lords, is it for a moment to be supposed that it is the function of the Attorney-General, on behalf of the Crown, to intervene and demand that a trust shall be established and administered by the court, the object of which is to alter the law in a manner highly prejudicial, as he and His Majesty's Government may think, to the welfare of the state?... There is undoubtedly, a paucity of judicial authority on this point. It may fairly be said that *De Themmines v De Bonneval* (1828) 5 Russ 288, to which Lord Parker referred in *Bowman's* case, turned on the fact that the trust there in question was held to be against public policy. In *IRC v Temperance Council* (1926) 136 LT 27 the principle was clearly recognised by Rowlatt J as it was in *Re Hood* [1931] 1 Ch 240. But in truth the reason of the thing appears to me so clear that I neither expect nor require much authority. I conclude upon this part of the case that a main object of the society is political and for that reason the society is not established for charitable purposes only.

This case confirmed the transformation of the narrow principle that activity contrary to public policy could not be charitable into a much broader principle that endeavours to change the law were 'political' and therefore not charitable.

In *McGovern v A-G* [1982] Ch 321, the Amnesty case, Slade J further extended the political restriction to encompass purposes intended to procure a reversal of government policy or of particular administrative decisions, whether at home or abroad. Since that decision the passage into law of the Human Rights Act 1998 has led to a shift in the legal position vis-à-vis the status of purposes to advance human rights. The pursuit of such a purpose is now consistent with UK law and policy and is, of course, specifically recognised as being so in the CA 2006 (see above, p 994).

Whether the Act has a broader significance for the political purpose disqualification is uncertain. Can it, for instance, be said that the rule preventing charitable status being granted to purposes advocating a change in the law or in government policy is itself an infringement of the Convention rights in Article 10 (freedom of expression) and Article 14 (non-discrimination)? The bare bones of the proposition are similar to those discussed previously in the context of Article 9 (freedom of conscience) and advancement of religion (see above, p 981). Put simply the proposition is that a refusal to grant charitable status with its access to fiscal benefits may prevent or severely restrict an organisation in expressing its views. As with Article 9, Article 10 offers a qualified protection only so that even if the Article 10 infringement premise is accepted the state may be able to defend its restriction on the basis of those various defences in Article 10(2) 'necessary in a democratic society . . . for the protection of the reputation or rights of others . . . , or for maintaining the authority and impartiality of the judiciary' (see generally on this topic Morris (1999) 5 CL & PR 3 at 219; Santow J [1999] CLP 255; Chesterman in Mitchell and Moody (eds) *Foundations of Charity* (2000) p 249 at pp 261–269; Moffat (2002) 13 KCLJ 1).

(b) The principle in practice

The effect of the principle is more limited in practice than at first glance may appear. It was emphasised in the *National Anti-Vivisection Society* case that where the promotion of change in the law is only ancillary to the main charitable objects, the organisation will not cease to be 'exclusively charitable' for that reason alone and therefore charitable status is not automatically lost: 'it is a question of degree of a sort well known to the courts' (per Lord Normand at 77; on ancillary activity in general, see Cullity (1967) 6 Melb ULR 35; Gravells [1978] Conv 92). It is also partly a question of construction of documents to distinguish 'ends' from 'means', a question susceptible to fine distinctions (see *Re Koeppler Will Trusts* [1984] 2 All ER 111; revsd [1985] 2 All ER 869 where the adoption in the Court of Appeal of a 'benignant construction' was a decisive factor; Watkin [1985] Conv 56; De Cruz [1986] NLJ Charities Review 12). A means-ends distinction which places a premium on careful drafting does not quite exhaust the problem posed by ancillary activity in this context. It cannot be assumed that otherwise non-charitable political activity will automatically become acceptable provided it is ancillary to some designated charitable purpose.

The problem arises most clearly with campaigning and lobbying activity. We noted in Chapter 18 that many new and already established organisations operating in traditional charitable spheres were undertaking such activity, and indeed that a perceived function of voluntary activity in the welfare state is to act as critic of state action or inaction. In the aftermath of the Amnesty International litigation the Charity Commissioners published a set of guidelines for trustees on permissible ancillary political activity (1981 Annual Report paras 53–56). The guidelines have subsequently been refined on several occasions. The most recent version (CC 9 – *Campaigning and Political Activities by Charities* (2008)) reflects the recommendation from the Strategy Unit that the tone of the advice should be less cautionary and should put greater emphasis on 'the campaigning and other non-party political activities that charities can undertake' as opposed to emphasising the restrictions (*Private Action, Public Benefit* (2002) p 46). The revised guidelines therefore offer more flexibility to charities provided that (i) the campaigning and political activity is undertaken as a means of furthering the purposes of the charity and is reasonably likely to do so; (ii) the methods used are lawful and an efficient use of charitable resources, and (iii) any emotive material is factually accurate with a well-founded evidence base (see paras D1; G2–3). Within these general guidelines a charity may, inter alia:

> D1. comment publicly on social, economic and political issues [related to its purposes or its work].
>
> D7. provide and publish comments on possible or proposed changes in the law or government policy.
>
>   support or oppose the passage of a Parliamentary Bill if this can reasonably be expected to support the delivery of its charitable purposes.

D9. seek to influence government, local authority or public opinion...
E3. provide information to its supporters or the public on how individual Members of Parliament, local councillors or parties have voted on an issue...
G6. work with and affiliate to a campaigning alliance [even if the alliance includes non-charitable organisations], if there is a reasonable expectation that the arrangement will help to further the charity's purposes.
G9. petition...parliament or national or local government.

By comparison with previous versions the tone of the guidance is much less directive, leaving the judgement as to what is appropriate for the organisation to the charity itself. Indeed in what is a marked change from previous Commission views, the guidance states that 'a charity may choose to focus most, or all, of its resources on political activity for a period. The key issue for charity trustees is the need to ensure that this activity is not, and does not become, the reason for the charity's existence' (para D8). On the other hand, a paternalist concern is still evident in one theme in the new guidelines. That theme is the emphasis placed on a version of 'risk assessment' in the sense of advising the charity to balance the gains to be achieved through political campaigning against the risk of 'damaging the charity's reputation and compromising its independence' (see eg para F1). Unsurprisingly the guidelines reaffirm that charities must not support a political party and whilst 'it may express support for particular policies which will contribute to the delivery of its own charitable purposes' (para E1) it must not seek to persuade people to vote for or against candidates or parties in an election (para E4). The revised guidelines go a considerable way towards clarifying what is acceptable. They also appear more liberal in this regard than previous formulations not least because the strong emphasis on 'style' – being restrained rather than strident in advocacy – is no longer a feature of the guidance.

If a campaigning organisation still perceives these guidelines to be too restrictive it can hive off its charitable activities, as Amnesty International did with its Amnesty International British Section Charitable Trust, although there are associated practical administrative and fund-raising disadvantages. Where such 'organisational fission' has not occurred, there are potentially severe sanctions for undertaking political activity which is not merely ancillary. They include action for breach of trust, withdrawal of tax relief and even as a final resort deregistration of the charity. The potential effectiveness and practical impact of such sanctions are difficult to discern. The Charity Commission has tended in the past to go little further than investigating complaints about political activity and then warning the charity trustees where this is thought necessary. However, the instigation in 1990 of an inquiry into the campaigning activities of Oxfam constituted a warning to other charities and, although no sanctions were applied, appeared to indicate a more interventionist approach: 'We shall continue to monitor closely the activities of OXFAM and other campaigning charities to ensure that their campaigns are within their powers and the limitations imposed by charity law' (Annual Report 1991 para 118; and see Burnell (1992) 3 Voluntas 3 at 311–334; see also the report of an inquiry conducted by the Charity Commission under s 8 of the Charities Act 1993 into the Smith Institute (July 2008)).

A more formidable deterrent for a campaigning charity could be a threat from central or local government to remove direct funding or not to renew a contract, a threat of some potential magnitude because of the growing and substantial reliance on direct and indirect state funding (see Chapter 18). Despite some early signs of an apparent willingness on the part of the state to intervene (see generally Brenton *The Voluntary Sector in British Social Services* (1985) pp 93–96) the current climate appears to favour non-intervention. This is reflected in the adoption in November 1998 of a 'Compact' between government and the voluntary sector which, inter alia, recognises that charities have the right 'to campaign, to comment on government policy and to challenge that policy irrespective of any funding relationship that may exist' (*Compact on Relations between Government and the Voluntary and Community Sector in England* (Cm 4100, 1998) para 9.1). Whilst the Compact is not legally binding the expectation is that the parties will respect the published codes such as the 2005 Funding and Procurement Code (see generally Blackmore *Standing Apart, Working Together* (2004); and the office of the Compact Commissioner www.thecompact.org.uk).

(c) The principle assessed

'A trust for the attainment of political objects', said Lord Parker in *Bowman v Secular Society Ltd* [1917] AC 406 at 442, 'has *always* been held invalid' (our emphasis), and in *National Anti-Vivisection Society v IRC* [1948] AC 31 at 63, Lord Simonds proclaimed that 'the reason of the thing appears to me so clear that I neither expect nor require much authority'. The legal dividing-line between charity and politics is thus portrayed as both long-standing and self-evident. But each of these propositions and the judicially stated reasons for the principle merit close scrutiny.

Consider in particular the following points:

(1) The proposition that the dividing-line in its present form is long-standing is difficult to sustain either on the basis of judicial authority (see *National Anti-Vivisection Society* above and Lord Porter's dissenting speech in that case) or in the light of overtly political activity by charities in the nineteenth century (see Chapter 18). Several of these early activist charities – for example, the Anti-Slavery Society – are still on the register. Their charitable status was confirmed before the political 'disqualification' clearly existed.

(2) Lord Simonds advances three independent reasons for the principle that political purposes are not charitable. We can label these 'evidentiary incapability of the courts', 'constitutional impartiality of the judiciary' and

'political inappropriateness of Attorney-General enforcement'. Is there any contradiction between the proposition that it is for the court objectively to determine 'public benefit' under the 'other purposes beneficial to the community' head of charity and the claim that the 'court has no sufficient means of judging as a matter of evidence whether the proposed change [in law or policy] will or will not be for the public benefit'? Can it be argued that the decision in *National Anti-Vivisection Society* is wholly schizophrenic on this issue?

In *Gilmour v Coats* [1949] 1 All ER 848 Lord Reid emphasised that the law adopts a position of neutrality on the claims of different religions: 'where a particular belief is accepted by one religion and rejected by another, the law can neither accept nor reject it. The law must accept the position that it is right that different religions should each be supported, irrespective of whether or not all its beliefs are true' (at 862). By parity of reasoning could not the courts recognise as charitable a trust one of whose objects is to change the law without this recognition being construed as agreement or disagreement that the change would be for the public benefit? Would such an approach conflict with any of the reasons advanced by Lord Simonds? There is some evidence that Commonwealth courts may move towards a less restrictive approach on these matters (see the 'sympathetic' dicta of Hammond J in *Re Collier (Deceased)* [1998] 1 NZLR 81 at 90; and also Santow J in *Public Trustee v A-G (NSW)* [1997] 42 NSWLR 600 at 607–608 and, writing extra-judicially, [1999] CLP 255). On the other hand, the Court of Appeal in *Southwood v Attorney-General* [2000] WTLR 1199 in effect applied the '*Bowman* test' in confirming that the purposes of the 'Project on Demilitarisation' – including 'to fundamentally question the new forms of militarism arising in the West' and 'to propose alternative policies to achieve disarmament and a conversion of resources from military to civilian purposes' – were political purposes (Garton (2000) 14(4) TLI 233). Chadwick LJ summarised the position as follows:

> There are differing views as to how best to secure peace and avoid war. To give two obvious examples: on the one hand it can be contended that war is best avoided by 'bargaining through strength'; on the other hand it can be argued, with equal passion, that peace is best secured by disarmament – if necessary, by unilateral disarmament. The court is in no position to determine that promotion of the one view rather than the other is for the public benefit. Not only does the court have no material on which to make that choice; to attempt to do so would be to usurp the role of government.

(3) Other possible explanations, not commonly appearing in the judgments (but cf Lord Wright in *National Anti-Vivisection Society* at 52), for the growth and judicial affirmation of the principle in the twentieth century are

that the judiciary do not wish to have to rule on whether 'public benefit' can accrue from, or fiscal privileges are appropriate for, controversial political activity such as advocating higher social security payments or 'providing for the acquisition of practical expertise required to transform the institutions and economies' of countries (Annual Report 1991 App D (The Margaret Thatcher Foundation)).

(4) The concern with the fiscal privileges received specific mention in the Conservative government 1989 White Paper: 'It would be wrong if tax-payers . . . were to find themselves unwittingly distorting the democratic process by subsidising bodies whose true purpose was to campaign not so much for the beneficiaries as for some political end. Nor do the Government believe that the public would for long continue to display their generosity if charities were to ally themselves to causes with which individual donors might well differ strongly on political grounds' (*Charities: A Framework for the Future* (Cm 694, 1989) para 2.41). The tone of the Strategy Unit Report was less admonitory but suggests that the advantages of political campaigning should be balanced against 'the fact that maintaining levels of trust and confidence depends crucially on preserving the charity "brand"' (*Private Action, Public Benefit* (2002) para 4.53).

Consider by way of comparison the following extract from the Report of an Inquiry into Oxfam:

> Essentially the trustees' justification of their campaigning is that certain changes in government or commercial policies based on careful research and their own experience over the years can reduce poverty, distress and suffering amongst their beneficiaries, . . . that it is ancillary to the achievement of their charitable objects, that it generates support for the charity's work, assists fund-raising and helps recruit dedicated staff and volunteers ((1991) p 17).

Should trustees be left to decide whether the activities of the charity will discourage donors? As noted above, whilst the current Charity Commission guidance places considerable emphasis on the need to take account of the possible response of donors to political engagement it appears to accept that the individual charity is best placed to make the final decision. Is the proposition cited above from *Charities: A Framework for the Future* consistent with the position whereby gifts and legacies to political parties are exempt from Inheritance Tax?

(5) The occasional attempts by students' unions to spend union funds on political activities have provoked controversy. The courts have consistently held that such unions are charitable and therefore that expenditure on political purposes would be unlawful (*Baldry v Feintuck* [1972] 2 All ER 81; *A-G v Ross* [1986] 1 WLR 252; *Webb v O'Doherty* (1991) *Times* 11 February; and on the rationale for charitable status see *London Hospital*

Medical College v IRC [1976] 2 All ER 113; and see Education Act 1994, s 20 for a definition of 'students' union'). Seen from the perspective of the union, charitable status can therefore be seen as much as a means of control as a privilege. But what of ancillary activity? The latest guidelines issued by the Department of Education and Science (*Students' Unions: A Guide* (2001)) emphasise that the touchstone remains that 'expenditure of union funds is likely to be permitted only if it furthers the interests of the students in a way that assists in the educational aims of the university or college'. Whilst encouraging political debate and supporting student political societies seems well within this guideline, paying for coaches to transport students to demonstrations on the Iraq War would not. On the other hand, funding trips to demonstrations on such vexatious topics as tuition fees may well withstand scrutiny.

(6) The definition of the term 'political' adopted in *McGovern v A-G* has subsequently been applied outside the context of charity law by the Broadcasting Authority, the body responsible for regulating independent radio services. Applying the Broadcasting Act 1990, s 92(2)(a)(i) the Authority prohibited the broadcast of advertisements by Amnesty International (British Section) on the basis that it was a body 'wholly or mainly of a political nature'. The Court of Appeal confirmed that the Authority was entitled to apply the *McGovern* test. (See *R v Radio Authority, ex p Bull* [1997] 2 All ER 561; *R v S of S for Culture, Media and Sport* [2008] UKHL 15; and Stevens and Feldman [1997] PL 615; and generally on political advertising see Communications Act 2003, s 321(2) and (3); Scott (2003) 66(2) MLR 224–44.)

(7) Kramer, commenting on contemporary shifts away from state provision of social welfare, suggests that 'using voluntary agencies as service providers . . . has considerable ideological appeal because it can be presented as a form of privatisation and the promotion of voluntarism, both of which are highly valued in Britain' ([1991] Voluntas 33 at 55). Not all would agree that any ideological appeal of privatisation and of voluntarism necessarily march hand-in-hand but the general proposition that charity has an ideological dimension has long been advanced (see Chapter 18, p 919; and see Tonkiss and Passey 'Trust, Voluntary Association and Civil Society' in Tonkiss and Passey (eds) *Trust and Civil Society* (2000) pp 31–51 for an overview of recent thinking on this issue). It has also been suggested that there is a political *function* attached to the use of charities as service providers in so far as it can work to reduce the accountability of the state to erstwhile critics: 'Sir Patrick Nairne, ex-Permanent Secretary at the DHSS, discussing the growth in the use of charities as a conduit for public money, remarked: "the advantage for government is that people can't ask questions in the House [of Commons]"' (quoted in Lattimer (1990) *Trust Monitor*, February).

Thus, a wider criticism of the present law which we cannot explore fully here is the allegation that the antithesis between charity and politics wholly ignores certain politically conservative implications of charitable welfare provision (see generally *Chesterman* ch 15; and consider also in this context Sugden 'Voluntary Organisations and the Welfare State' in Le Grand and Robinson (eds) *Privatisation and the Welfare State* ch 5; Moffat 'Charity, Politics and Ideology: A Journey from Bowman to Brecht?' in Fan Sin (ed) *Legal Explorations* (2003) ch 3; Dunn (2006) 26 LS 500–523; Conservative Party *A Stronger Society: Voluntary Action in the 21st Century* (2008)). The fact that the definition of 'political' is constrained within orthodox boundaries is argued by some as buttressing this effect. Consider therefore whether the following proposition can be justified:

> . . . while not all charitable activities are political in the same ways and in the same degrees, any assertion that there is a hard-and-fast dividing-line between the two forms of activity, even in theory, is itself a political affirmation rather than a statement of abiding truth (*Chesterman* p 368).

Alternatively, does the proposition render the term 'political' devoid of any useful meaning in the present context?

10. Reform and the definition of 'charity'

One feature of the long-running debate about charity law reform was criticism of the unsatisfactory legacy created by the decision in *Pemsel* (1891) to inextricably link charitable status and fiscal privileges to the same definition of 'charitable purposes' (see eg Cross (1956) 72 LQR 187 at 206; and Lord Cross in *Dingle v Turner* [1972] AC 601 at 624–625; Gravells (1977) 40 MLR 397; Bright [1989] Conv 28). On the other hand, this was not the view of the Deakin Report (*Meeting the Challenge of Change* (1996) para 3.2.4) and it is clear that a severing of the tax–charitable status link is most emphatically not a step favoured by recent governments of whatever political persuasion. Nevertheless the fact that there exists a party political consensus supporting the status quo should not deter us from continuing to consider the problem bequeathed to us by *Pemsel*.

There are two possible ways of addressing that problem. One is to sever completely the connection between tax and charitable status so that the granting of fiscal reliefs to voluntary organisations would depend upon a set of criteria with no necessary connection to charitable status. The other way, more a modification than a breaking of the link, would be to confine the fiscal privileges to a narrower range of charitable purposes than those which attract the trusts law privileges.

For advocates of a modification strategy fiscal privileges would cease to be available to a range of organisations which are on the periphery of 'charity' and do not really deserve them. Amongst those organisations sometimes cited as endangered species are 'poor employees/relations' trusts, minority religious sects and animal welfare charities. A more radical point of view, well represented in the forceful minority report of Ben Whitaker in the Goodman Committee Report (*Charity Law and Voluntary Organisations* (1976) paras 6–10), is that 'charitable' should be substantially confined to relief of the deprived and the disadvantaged, thereby excluding independent schools, private hospitals and universities (cf the dissenters in *Pemsel* see Chapter 18, p 923; and see the reaffirmation of a redistributional agenda for charity law in Chesterman (1999) 62 MLR 333; and for an overview of the issues see Mitchell (1999) 13 TLI 21). It should be noted, though, that some of the above proposals do not sit comfortably with an analysis that fiscal relief for some charitable activity is simply a logical extension of existing general tax laws. Ashworth, for example, has argued that tax exemption is not a concession where a charity acts merely as a conduit for income to benefit those who are or would themselves be exempt from various taxes (*Charity Statistics 1983/4* pp 62–69; for extensive analyses see Bittker and Rahdert (1976) 85 Yale LJ 299–358, and Gergen (1988) 74 Vand LR 1393). Nevertheless, as Ashworth recognises, this argument cannot itself justify reliefs for those many charities 'either benefiting taxable persons, perhaps some educational and religious charities, or those benefiting non-humans' (p 69). Consider also, for instance, the position where local authorities purchase care and accommodation for the elderly via competitive tendering and a charity wishes to bid for the contract. Should the charity be allowed to draw on the resources of volunteers and use its own income, each being in effect a form of subsidy, to keep costs low and its bid competitive? If so, should it also be allowed the benefits of fiscal privileges that are not available to a commercial competitor?

The proposals for change reviewed above mostly assume that fiscal reliefs should be retained and automatically accrue in some degree to any organisation that satisfies the relevant criteria, however they might be defined. That proposition too can be challenged. Thus it has been argued variously (i) that automatic fiscal reliefs should be wholly abolished and replaced by a system of discriminatory cash subsidies (see, classically, Surrey *Pathways to Tax Reform* (1973) pp 223–232); or, in contrast, (ii) that the relief should be granted to all genuinely non-profit-distributing organisations; or, more radically still, (iii) that tax relief should be available *only* to non-profit organisations operating publicly funded contracts, and then only if annual performance targets were met (Knight *CENTRIS Report: Voluntary Action in the 1990s* (1993)). The last-mentioned proposal recommended that all other organisations should lose tax reliefs, but be free to perform the innovative and radical roles of charity and be financed voluntarily, and campaign if they so chose. The hostile reception accorded by both government and charities to this proposal quickly led to its being sidelined, despite its origins in the Home Office (see eg *Financial Times* 12 and 20 October 1993, but cf Milner *Unravelling the Maze* (CENTRIS 2003) for an updated critique: see www.centris.org.uk).

Underpinning criticisms such as those in the CENTRIS report lies a recognition that a numerically small but financially very substantial part of the charitable sector occupies an increasingly prominent role in service provision with significant implications for both its internal arrangements and external activities (see Morris *Charities and the Contract Culture: Partners or Contractors?* (The Charity Law Unit, University of Liverpool, 1999) and 'Paying the Piper' in Dunn (ed) *The Voluntary Sector, the State and the Law* (2000) ch 9; Nicholls (1997) 17 Critical Social Policy 101; Paxton et al *The Voluntary Sector Delivering Public Services: Transfer or Transformation?* (2005)). It is this very development which leads some to doubt whether a charity can simultaneously win contracts and undertake service provision yet continue to fulfil one of its important functions, that of advocacy: 'The likely price of requiring organisations originally founded on altruism to provide more goods and services for those in need is to reduce their effectiveness in signalling changes in people's needs' (Ware 'Meeting Needs through Voluntary Action: Does Market Society Corrode Altruism?' in Ware and Goodin (eds) *Needs and Welfare* (1990); Seddon *Who Cares? How State Funding and Political Activism Change Charity* (Civitas, 2007)). But the potential sources of tension go significantly wider than the practical dimension of whether advocacy may be at risk. One argument advanced to support the notion of a 'space' in the economy and society within which the voluntary sector can operate is that this arrangement can help contribute to a sense of social cohesion which in turn can moderate the effects of marketisation and individualism in civil society (see eg the review essays by Passey and Tonkiss, Halfpenny and Fenton in Tonkiss and Passey (eds) *Trust and Civil Society* (2000) chs 2, 7 and 8 respectively). Yet is this social cohesion function itself at risk of being subverted by a situation in which the state seeks to engage charity as a supplier of goods and services? Contracting with the state, even though undertaken by only a minority of charities, is altering the public perception of charities (see generally Dunn (2008) 71(2) MLR 247–270; Eikenberry and Kluver (2004) 64(2) Public Administration Review 132–140). This is reflected in survey results that found public opinion to be very divided over whether charities should deliver more public services, with only 30% being in favour (see Chapter 18 at p 962). In short, will charity fall victim to commerce? It is, for instance, open to question whether adopting the rubric of 'charity brand' as a descriptor in the manner adopted in the Strategy Unit Report helps or hinders the notion of charity as a force for social cohesion. If charity comes to be viewed more as a 'third sector' of economic activity, it is doubtful whether fiscal privileges could be kept indefinitely off a new reformist agenda.

Ultimately, however, decisions about the availability and scope of fiscal privileges could even lie outside domestic jurisdiction. Directorate General XXIII of the European Commission has for several years been seeking to remove obstacles to cross-border activity within the voluntary sector. It is still uncertain how far, if at all, these efforts will bring about a degree of regulatory convergence. The Charity Commission, commenting in its 1992 Report on a Proposed EC White Paper on the voluntary sector, suggests that 'the mere publication of the facts will emphasise the desirability of some convergence of the fiscal treatment of the sector...' (para 109). The very diversity of voluntary activity between and within Member States suggests, however, that rapid change is unlikely (see eg the non-binding Communication on Promoting the Role of Voluntary Organisations and Foundations in Europe COM (97) 241; and generally Kendall and Anheier 'The Third Sector and the European Union Policy Process: An Initial Evaluation' (1999) 6(2) European Public Policy 283–307; Evers and Laville (eds) *The Third Sector in Europe* (2004); Dunn in Phillips and Rathgeb Smith (eds) *Between Governments and Regulation: International Trends in Government–Non-Profit Relationships* (2008); see also Waddington (1998) 25 Legal Issues of European Integration 60–92 on the implications for the voluntary sector of EU state aid rules).

20

The regulation of charities

1. Introduction

In Chapter 18 we noted that the Charitable Trusts Acts 1853–1860 established, for the first time, a central permanent Charity Commission empowered to supervise the management of charitable trusts and to remodel their purposes when they proved impracticable or impossible. But its role was severely constrained in three particular respects: (1) its jurisdiction, which extended to certain charitable endowments only and not to 'collecting' charities; (2) its freedom to act of its own motion, which was limited by the degree of autonomy preserved for trustees; and (3) the circumstances in which the Charity Commissioners (or the court) could make cy-près schemes.

Since then two trends in the legal and administrative framework regulating charity have become apparent. On the one hand, charities have been favoured more, notably in financial respects. On the other hand, an attempt has been made to extract a higher price from charities in return for these favours by extending and strengthening the supervisory framework, initially via the Charities Act 1960. This statute enacted most of the recommendations for reform contained in the Nathan Report (*Committee on the Law and Practice Relating to Charitable Trusts* (Cmd 8710, 1952)). Notwithstanding these changes, concern about the efficiency of charities and the effectiveness of supervision over them grew apace, culminating in a series of critical reports in the late 1980s (see *An Efficiency Scrutiny of the Supervision of Charities* (Woodfield Report) (1987); National Audit Office (NAO) *Monitoring and Control of Charities in England and Wales* (HC Paper no 380 (1986–87) and HC Paper no 13 (1990–91)); Public Accounts Committee (HC Paper no 116 (1987–88) and HC Paper no 85 (1991)). In particular it was evident both that there was a widespread lack of compliance with the obligation to submit accounts to the Commission and that additional statutory powers of enforcement were necessary. Subsequently the supervisory framework was strengthened both legally by the Charities Act 1992 and administratively by the allocation of more resources to the Commission. Most of the 1992 Act (other than Pts II and III, principally concerned with fund-raising) was then consolidated along with earlier legislation into the Charities Act (CA) 1993.

The specific objectives behind the revised legal framework were identified as being 'to equip the Charity Commission for a more active role, narrow the scope for abuse, encourage trustees to shoulder their responsibilities, and ensure continuing public confidence in the sector' (*Charities: A Framework for the Future* (Cm 694, 1989) para 1.18). In short the framework was to incorporate an enhanced regulatory role while devolving greater responsibility to trustees. The broader policy imperative, however, was to strike an appropriate balance between control and accountability on the one hand, and 'the freedom . . . of individual organisations to develop and do business' (ibid).

Just over a decade later similar themes can be identified in the Strategy Unit Report (*Private Action, Public Benefit* (2002)). Again emphasis is placed upon building 'public trust and confidence' in the voluntary sector. It is possible to identify five strands to this latest reform strategy as implemented in the Charities Act (CA) 2006. The strand relating to the definition of charity and changes in the range of legal forms available to charities has already been discussed in Chapters 18 and 19. A second strand relates to what might be described as a modernisation agenda. The emphasis here is on initiatives to reduce or remove restrictions on making the most effective use of charity funds, for instance, by facilitating mergers amongst charities. A third strand is concerned with transparency and public accountability. Here a number of modifications to the 1993 Act have been introduced to require charities to provide more and better qualitative information about their performance. A fourth strand focuses more on strengthening controls on fund-raising, an area believed to be of major concern to the public. Lastly, the role of the Charity Commission as the regulator of the charity sector has been strengthened in a number of ways. A key test for the new regime, as for the previous one, is whether it can prove sufficiently flexible to cope with what is a very diverse sector.

It will be recalled that the charitable sector includes a multiplicity of organisations, ranging from those such as the National Trust and Oxfam with annual incomes in excess of £100m down to modest parent–teacher associations with income just sufficient to come within the registration requirements. How far the regulatory framework proves suitable and effective for both types of organisation will be a measure of its success, as will its capacity not to deter willing volunteers from taking on the increased responsibilities and duties of trusteeship that are a corollary of the demands for greater accountability.

In this chapter we therefore consider the appropriateness of the revised regulatory framework, taking account also of the supplemental powers of the court and other state agencies such as Her Majesty's Revenue and Customs (HMRC). Our approach is to divide the subject-matter broadly into two topics: modernisation and accountability. Under the rubric of modernisation we include current policy encouraging mergers of charities as well as the alteration of charitable purposes through official intervention in order that they may better serve the current welfare needs of society. Accountability is principally concerned with supervision of the way charitable purposes are carried out in order to ensure transparency, honesty and efficiency.

Before looking at these specific topics it is necessary to understand the revised structure of the Charity Commission and the general functions imposed on it by the 1993 Act, as amended by the CA 2006.

2. The Charity Commission

(a) Structure and functions: an outline

The CA 2006 has introduced significant formal and, in some degree, substantive changes to the structure and role of the Charity Commission. For the first time since its establishment in 1853 the Commission has legal existence in the form of a body corporate – the functions of the Commission were previously held by the Charity Commissioners on a personal basis. Under the new legal structure the Commission consists of a chairman and 'at least four but not more than eight' other members, of whom two must have legal qualifications of seven years' standing (CA 1993, Sch 1A, para 1), assisted by a complement of staff numbering around 450. The members of the Commission are civil servants appointed by the Secretary of State, to whom they must submit an annual report, but otherwise they act independently of his department. Whilst the Commission is required as part of its functions to comply 'so far as is reasonably practicable' (CA 1993, s 1C(4)) with any request from a Minister of the Crown for information or advice on any matter relating to the functions of the Commission (see below) no Minister has any authority to direct or guide the Commission (s 1A(4)). To that extent the formal division of responsibilities between the government of the day and the Charity Commission remains unaltered by the 2006 Act. This bare statement of the formal position is accurate as regards day-to-day decisions but can give a misleading position about the autonomy of the Commission. The Commission can be and is held publicly accountable for its overall performance through audit procedures and the parliamentary select committee structure. In addition to the pre-1993 scrutiny already mentioned, the Commission has been the subject of further examinations by the National Audit Office (*Regulation and Support of Charities* HC Paper no 2; the Committee of Public Accounts (*Twenty Eighth Report* (1997–98) HC no 408); the Comptroller and Auditor General *Giving Confidently* HC Paper no 234 (2001–02); and again the Committee of Public Accounts *Thirty Ninth Report* (2001–02)).

A major part of the Commission's work involves record-keeping – maintaining a register of charities (now computerised and accessible via the internet) – and exercising the quasi-judicial function of determining charitable status (see Chapter 19). In addition to these specific tasks the principal general functions of the Commission are defined by s 1C(2) as 'encouraging and facilitating the better administration of charities', 'identifying and investigating' misconduct or mismanagement in the administration of charities and 'taking remedial or protective action'; and, a new function, 'determining whether public collection certificates should be issued and remain in force'.

In addition to the specification of the Commission's functions the 2006 Act contains a list of five objectives, arguably making explicit what has been implicit in the strategy of the Commission. In addition to the 'public benefit' objective discussed in Chapter 19 (see p 1020), the Commission's objectives are stated to be 'to increase public trust and confidence in charities', 'to promote the effective use of charitable resources', 'to enhance the accountability of charities' and 'to increase compliance by charity trustees with their legal obligations' (CA 2006, s 1B(3)). The term 'charity trustees' has a special definition: it means 'the persons having the general control and management of the administration of a charity' (CA 1993, s 97(1)). It therefore includes not only trustees in the familiar sense but also, for instance, a management committee or a board of directors of an incorporated charity.

In furthering these objectives and carrying out its functions the Commission has the potential use of a wide range of powers. Those relating directly to modernisation and supervision are discussed later in the chapter, but the powers described briefly below are also important for the day-to-day administration of charities. It should be noted that one particular feature of the regulatory regime remains unaltered by the 2006 Act. The Commission has no authority to exercise the functions of a trustee in relation to any charity nor in any other way to become directly involved in its administration (CA 1993, s 1E(2)).

Any assessment of how effectively the Commission is able to perform its several functions must take account of the resources made available to it. Historically the Commission was under-resourced but criticisms of its effectiveness that emerged during the 1980s prompted an increase in staffing levels to the extent that the numbers more than doubled from 346 in 1988 to a peak of 706 in 1993, falling back to 596 in 1998 and to around 500 today (NAO (1997–98) para 1.7; Committee of Public Accounts *Thirty Ninth Report* (2001–02) para 2; Annual Report 2007–08). Notwithstanding the CA 2006 seemingly expanding the Commission's functions, under the Comprehensive Spending Review Settlement for 2008–11 its budget (£33.5m in 2007–08) is to be reduced by 5% in real terms for each of the years covered by the settlement. The Commission has indicated that in deploying its resources it will prioritise its compliance work.

(1) Giving advice

Under CA 1993, s 29(1), a charity trustee may apply in writing to the Commission for its opinion or advice in relation to any matter 'affecting the performance of his duties' as trustee or 'relating to the proper administration of the charity'. A trustee acting upon the advice is deemed to have acted in accordance with the trust and is thus protected from complaints that he or she has acted in breach of trust (s 29(2)). Section 29 is amended by the 2006 Act so as to confirm formally that the Commission can decide on its own initiative to give advice to charities generally or to any particular class of charity or even to an individual charity (s 29(5)). The giving of advice, both formal and informal, is a prominent feature of the Commission's work, is done free of charge and thus provides an inexpensive alternative to seeking the directions of the court. What if the advice is flawed? No action can be brought against the Commission for common law negligence, primarily it seems because the accuracy of the Commission's opinion or advice can be challenged under the appeal procedures in CA 1993, s 33 (*Mills v Winchester Diocesan Board of Finance* [1989] Ch 428). As intimated above advice is also given on a more general level via a wide range of informative leaflets, all now available on the internet. In addition the Commission instituted (as from 1 April 1996) a system whereby a 'registration pack', containing, for instance, draft constitutions and advice on the registration process, is issued to anyone inquiring about charity registration. It is evident from the Annual Reports of the Commission and from the parliamentary scrutiny that extensive demands are made on the advice services (see eg Report by the Comptroller and Auditor General, op cit, at p 2: 'up from 26,000 in 1996–97 to over 35,000 in 2000–01'). Section 85 of the 1993 Act gives the Secretary of State wide powers to introduce regulations allowing fees to be charged but, despite recommendations to the contrary, there appears to be no intention at present to charge fees for the advice-giving function (cf NAO *Monitoring and Control of Charities* (HC Paper no 380 (1986–87))).

(2) Holding charity property

Under CA 1993, ss 2, 21 and 22 there is established an 'Official Custodian for Charities', to be appointed from the Commission staff. A function of the office is to hold as custodian trustee for a charity – ie with no discretionary powers of management – any land transferred to him by that charity (see Guidance Note CC13 (September 2004)). The practical advantage for trustees who use this facility is that it obviates the need to alter title whenever there is a change of trustee. As regards investments other than land the role of the Official Custodian is limited just to custodianship of property vested in him by the Commission acting under CA 1993, s 18 for the protection of charities (see below, p 1062). The value of property held by the Official Custodian under that jurisdiction is modest indeed (see Annual Report of the Charity Commission 2007–08 Part II).

(3) Facilitating investment

Without statutory authority it would not be possible for trustees to combine funds of different charities for investment purposes. Under CA 1993, s 24 the Commission or the court may establish 'common investment funds' (CIFs) for charities by way of a scheme under which property transferred to such a fund is invested by trustees appointed to manage it (see *Re University of London Charitable Trusts* [1964] Ch 282). The participating charities receive returns of income and capital proportionate to the value of the property contributed. Such a scheme is potentially attractive for the many charities with extremely small trust funds and a scheme may be established on the application of any two or more charities (s 24(2); see also s 25 authorising the creation of 'common deposit' schemes whereby money can be deposited at interest rather than invested more riskily).

As at July 2008 some 46 CIFs had been approved with total assets under management of around £8 billion (see Charity Commission *Common Investment Funds* (2008); and generally Marlow 'Common Investment Funds' (1996–97) 4 CL & PR 1 at 21). CIF funds are regulated by the Commission and are exempt from the supervisory regime of the Financial Services Authority (FSA), although as a matter of policy the Commission mirrors as far as possible FSA requirements.

As part of its general advisory function the Charity Commission issues general guidance to trustees on the investment of charity funds (CC14 *Investment of Charitable Funds* (2004); and see generally on trustee investment Chapter 10).

(4) Sanctioning transactions prima facie outside the charity trustees' powers

Charity trustees may be impelled by administrative considerations to ask for the consent of the Commission or the court to specific transactions. This occurs where, for instance, the administrative powers conferred on the charity trustees by the governing instrument neither permit nor expressly forbid the transaction to be carried out. Under CA 1993, s 26(1) the Commission is empowered to sanction 'any action proposed or contemplated in the administration of a charity' if it appears to them to be 'expedient in the interests of the charity'. The jurisdiction is analogous to that provided under s 57 of the Trustee Act 1925 (see Chapter 7).

In addition to this general authority, the Commission has been empowered to authorise charity trustees to make ex gratia payments outside the terms of the charitable trusts. Until the case of *Re Snowden* [1970] Ch 700 decided to the contrary, it was thought that there was no jurisdiction even for the court or the Attorney-General to authorise such ex gratia payments. In *Re Snowden* Cross J held that the court and the Attorney-General had power to give authority to the trustees to make ex gratia payments out of funds held on charitable trusts. He emphasised that the power to give this authority was to be exercised only in cases where it could be said that if the charity was an individual it would be morally wrong for him to refuse to make the payment (see Annual Reports 1969 paras 26–29 and 1976 paras 113–116). Section 27 of the Charities Act 1993 now extends to the Charity Commission the power to authorise charity trustees to make payments outside the terms of the charitable trusts, but only where the trustees 'regard themselves as under a moral obligation to do so' (s 27(1)(b)(ii); see Charity Commission CC7 *Ex Gratia Payments by Charities* (2001)). The s 27 power cannot, however, be employed to override an express statutory prohibition on disposal of charity assets (see eg *Attorney General v Trustees of the British Museum* [2005] Ch 397 applying British Museum Act 1963, s 3(4)).

Prior to 1 January 1993, the Commission had still more extensive powers: no land held by or in trust for a charity could be disposed of without an order of the court or the Commission. These powers are now much reduced and those of trustees correspondingly increased. The pre-1993 requirement is still retained (CA 1993, s 36(1)) but applies only where a disposition is made either to a 'connected person' (s 36(2)(a) and Sch 5) or where the requirements of s 36(3) or (5) have not been met. These are that the charity trustees *must* before entering into an agreement for the sale, lease or other disposition of land: (a) obtain and consider a written report on the proposed disposition from a qualified surveyor; (b) advertise the disposition in the manner advised by the surveyor; and (c) be satisfied that the terms are the best 'that can reasonably be obtained' for the charity (s 36(3), but cf s 36(5) for the less stringent requirements in the case of a lease for seven years or less). The outcome is that trustees can now dispose of charity property without consent provided the statutory procedures are followed (see *Bayoumi v Women's Total Abstinence Educational Union Ltd* [2004] Ch 46).

This seemingly innocuous shift in authority ran counter to the frequently expressed views of the Commission, as reflected in the following extract from the Annual Report 1983:

> 75. The control exercised by us protects not only the permanent endowment of charities, but property occupied for the purposes of charities. It is a safeguard to beneficiaries and trustees, and prevents abuse by the trustees, and abuse of the trustees by prospective purchasers, local authorities and developers. Repeal would remove control over the use of proceeds of sale; and we should lose a valuable means by which the administration and affairs of charities are brought to our attention. The control also enables us to prevent the unnecessary bringing to an end of useful charitable purposes promoted on functional land; and to identify the need for schemes to apply proceeds of sale. In addition, year by year our supervision of the sales of charity property has resulted in monetary benefit in excess of the costs of the exercise of our control.

These arguments were rejected by the Woodfield Report and by the Conservative government (*Charities: A Framework for the Future* ch 7) in favour of (i) fostering among trustees a greater awareness of their own responsibilities, and (ii) thereby incidentally releasing more resources within the Commission to enhance its supervisory role. This, though, is an area where the increases in the monetary value of charity land can render decisions less than straightforward. (Cf Annual Report 1988 paras 56–62 (*Hampton Fuel Allotments Charity*) – land in use as a nursery and garden centre producing an annual income of £5,500 eventually sold for development of a supermarket for £21m, but only after the Commission had withheld approval of a substantially lower offer.) In such circumstances the automatic requirement of Commission consent may have acted as an effective safeguard of the money value of charity property. The same might be claimed of the use value of what can be called 'functional land', ie land held on trusts that stipulate that it is to be used for the purposes of the charity. Here, there are additional restrictions on trustees, principally concerned with public notification and receipt of representations (CA 1993, s 36(5), (6)), before such land can be disposed of. There must be some doubt as to how adequately the new provisions ensure that the interests of the users of the charity land will be considered (but cf *Oldham Borough Council v A-G* [1993] 2 All ER 432; see generally Dennis [2006] Conv 219–244; Charity Commission CC28 *Disposing of Charity Land* (2007)).

(5) Charity Tribunal

A feature of the new legal framework whose impact on the Charity Commission and on charities themselves it is impossible to estimate with any degree of certainty is the introduction of a Charity Tribunal. As mentioned in Chapter 19, the Tribunal provides an independent forum, usually but not necessarily comprising a legal member and two lay members, to hear appeals against decisions by the Commission on registration matters. But the jurisdiction is more far-reaching, extending to include appeals against a very wide range of 'decisions, directions or orders' made by the Commission in furtherance of many of the powers discussed in this chapter (see CA 2006, s 8 and Schs 3 and 4; Charity Commission OG 95 *The Charity Tribunal* (2008)). There is provision for an appeal on a point of law to the High Court against a decision of the Tribunal. The Tribunal, operative from 1 April 2008, stands separate from the Charity Commission, being part of the general Tribunals Service. With one exception the Charity Tribunal, as with other tribunals in the legal system, can consider afresh any 'decision, direction or order' of the Commission and take account of fresh evidence. The exception concerns those matters referred to in section (4) above where the Commission's sanction for certain actions is required and also any decision by the Commission to institute a s 8 inquiry. For any of these 'reviewable matters' the Charity Tribunal is to apply the principles that would be applied by the High Court in judicial review proceedings (Sch 4, paras 3 and 4).

The uncertainty referred to above is evident in the estimates in the Charity Bill's Regulatory Impact Assessment concerning the possible number of appeals to the Tribunal. It was pointed out that the estimated numbers vary from 35 to 2,500 although for the purposes of calculating costings a figure of 75 appeals was adopted (Final Regulatory Impact Assessment, ch 2). Only two appeals were lodged with the Tribunal in the first twelve months of its existence (see www.charity.tribunals.gov.uk). Its Scottish counterpart is to be abolished after hearing only one case in the two years since its creation in April 2006.

3. Cy-près and matching charitable purposes to social needs

(a) Introduction

One limitation on the ability of the courts or the Charity Commission to modernise charitable trusts was, until 1960, the requirement that 'failure' occurred only where the original purposes became impracticable or impossible (see

Chapter 18, p 941). Yet even before the CA 1960, the courts in some cases had begun to reflect a more liberal construction of this requirement, the most striking example of this tendency being *Re Dominion Students' Hall Trust* [1947] Ch 183. One of the objects of the charity, a company limited by guarantee, was to promote community of citizenship, culture and tradition among all members of the British Commonwealth of nations. The charity maintained a students' hall of residence, but restricted to students 'of European origin only'. The charity was permitted to delete the 'colour bar' from its constitution, even though its implementation was then neither absolutely impracticable nor indeed illegal (see now Race Relations Act 1976, s 34 and Chapter 18, p 960). Evershed J agreed that 'to retain the condition, so far from furthering the charity's main object might defeat it and might be liable to antagonise those students both white and coloured, whose support and goodwill it is the purpose of the charity to sustain' (at 186).

Such examples of liberalism notwithstanding, the Nathan Committee observed in 1952 that 'hundreds, perhaps thousands of trusts need revision, and to an extent that goes beyond anything that could be achieved under present cy-près doctrine' (para 104). The Committee therefore saw its task as (para 60) 'devising appropriate methods which will enable charitable trusts to keep abreast of current needs while preserving the "spirit of the intention of the founders"'.

The two principal methods that the CA 1960 envisaged for achieving this aim were to encourage the co-ordination of activities of local charities and to enlarge the concept of 'failure' for the purposes of cy-près. Both were retained unamended in the CA 1993. Yet despite the innovations there remained in existence a large number of small charities of doubtful effectiveness. The House of Lords Select Committee on the Parochial Charities Bill and the Small Charities Bill (HL Paper no 293.1 (1984–85)) reported on this matter in 1984 and proposed minor reforms. These were implemented in the Charities Act 1985 which provided, in effect, for a form of 'do-it-yourself' cy-près. This statute was in its turn replaced by CA 1993, ss 74 and 75 which further increased the scope for trustees of small charities to apply trust property in what they perceive as a more appropriate and effective fashion, a development continued and extended by the amendments to these sections introduced in the Charities Act 2006, ss 40–44 (see below, p 1052). The changes were intended to remove a number of technical barriers identified in the Strategy Unit Report as inhibiting charities that want to change their objects or even merge (see *Private Action, Public Benefit* (2002) pp 46–47 and the background discussion paper published simultaneously 'Providing Flexibility for Charities to Evolve and Merge'; see also Morris *Legal Issues in Charity Mergers* (The Charity Law Unit, University of Liverpool, 2001).

The three methods of modernising charitable purposes outlined above will be considered in turn. First, however, note that not all 'schemes' altering trusts and made by the courts or the Charity Commission involve the application of property cy-près. A distinction is drawn between 'schemes', which involve, for example, merely a change in the administrative machinery of a trust, and cy-près schemes which involve a modification of the charity's purposes. The significance of the distinction is that administrative changes need only be 'expedient' whereas the more rigorous requirements of CA 1993, s 13 must be satisfied for a cy-près scheme. In *Re J W Laing Trust* [1984] 1 All ER 50 in 1922 Sir John (then plain Mr J W) Laing had set up a trust for 'charitable purposes' with shares in J W Laing Ltd valued at some £15,000. A requirement of the trust was that the whole of the capital and income should be distributed within ten years of the settlor's death. As Peter Gibson J noted no one had foreseen that the settlor would reach the age of 98 before he died in 1978 nor that the value of the shares would increase to the extent that in 1982 the capital value of the fund was £24m with an annual income of around £1.2m. There was evidence that the settlor himself had wanted the trustees to disregard the distribution requirement. Moreover it was agreed that the objects of the charity – individuals and bodies furthering Christian evangelical causes – were considered unsuitable to receive large capital sums. The court held that the requirement was 'inexpedient', that it was administrative in character and not part of the purposes of the trust and could therefore be deleted under the court's inherent jurisdiction. The need to fall within s 13 was thereby avoided.

(b) Co-ordination of activities

Sections 76–78 of the Charities Act 1993 are intended to encourage co-operation and partnership between charity trustees and local authorities, the object being to maximise the effectiveness of charitable resources. Section 76 authorises a local authority to maintain a public index of charities within its administrative area, based on data from the central register. These are 'local charities' (s 96(1)).

The key sections are 77 and 78. Section 77 authorises but does not require local authorities to conduct reviews of the working of these charities, to report to the Commission and to make recommendations to them. But a review can extend only to those charities whose trustees consent (s 77(3)). A trustee of a dole charity told one review organiser that its money 'had been spent on bread since 1735 and "over my dead body will it be distributed in any other way"' (Nightingale *Charities* (1973) p 23).

Although such examples of outright hostility, as compared with inertia or lack of enthusiasm, are perhaps rare, the review system seems to have met with only partial success, not least because local authorities have increasingly felt unable to devote resources to implementing new reviews (see generally *Goodman Committee* paras 174–185; Annual Report 1980 para 154; *Charities: A Framework for the Future* para 6.1).

Under s 78(1) a local authority is empowered to make arrangements for co-ordinating its activities with those of local charities 'in the interests of persons who may benefit' from the service of either. But here again no obligation is put on charity trustees to co-operate and progress therefore depends on mutual agreement between the parties. The powers granted to trustees of small charities by CA 1993, ss 74 and 75 to modify their objects or amalgamate with another charity have further reduced the incentive to conduct local reviews (see below, p 1052).

(c) Modernisation under the cy-près doctrine

(1) Scope of Charities Act 1993, s 13

Failure redefined Modernisation under the cy-près doctrine is now possible by virtue of the enlarged statutory concept of failure. The relevant provisions are set out below (see also Chapter 18, p 941 for an account of the cy-près doctrine at general law and for further provisions in s 13(1) defining initial failure):

> (1) ... the circumstances in which the original purposes of a charitable gift can be altered to allow the property given or part of it to be applied cy-près shall be as follows –
> ...
> (c) where the property available by virtue of the gift and other property applicable for similar purposes can be more effectively used in conjunction, and to that end can suitably, regard being had to [the appropriate considerations], be made applicable to common purposes; or
> (d) where the original purposes were laid down by reference to an area which then was but has since ceased to be a unit for some other purpose, or by reference to a class of persons or to an area which has for any reason since ceased to be suitable, regard being had to [the appropriate considerations], or to be practical in administering the gift; or
> (e) where the original purposes, in whole or in part, have, since they were laid down –
>   (i) been adequately provided for by other means, or
>   (ii) ceased, as being useless or harmful to the community or for other reasons, to be in law charitable, or
>   (iii) ceased in any other way to provide a suitable and effective method of using the property available by virtue of the gift, regard being had to [the appropriate considerations].

The words 'the appropriate considerations' in square brackets in s 13(1) above were added by the Charities Act 2006, s 15 in substitution for the phrase 'the spirit of the gift' although that phrase itself is retained as one element of the 'appropriate considerations' defined in a new s 13(1A) as meaning:

> (a) (on the one hand) the spirit of the gift concerned, and
> (b) (on the other hand) the social and economic circumstances prevailing at the time of the proposed alteration of the original purposes.

The purpose of the change is to relax the requirements that have to be satisfied before a 'cy-près occasion' can be said to exist. Before considering whether s 13, as amended, provides a satisfactory framework for modernising charitable trusts either with outdated objects or where it is thought that the funds can be used more effectively, there are two preliminary points to note. First, as we are concerned with 'subsequent failure' of a pre-existing charitable purpose, no question of identifying a paramount charitable intention should arise – unlike the position with initial failure (see Chapter 18) – at least not in the usual case of an outright gift in perpetuity (but cf Peter Gibson J in *Re J W Laing Trust* [1984] 1 All ER 50 at 53, criticised by Warburton [1984] Conv 319). Second, it should be noted that s 13 is concerned solely with modifying the purposes of a charity. If, therefore, the existing purpose is sufficiently flexible to allow an alternative use of the funds or property, then an application to the court or the Charity Commission under s 13 is unnecessary. The distinction is clear, its practical application sometimes less so.

Consider, for instance, the case of land conveyed in 1962 by Ira Clayton to, inter alia, Oldham Borough Council 'upon trust to preserve and manage the same at all times hereafter as playing fields – to be known as "The Clayton Playing Fields" – for the benefit and enjoyment of the inhabitants of Oldham, Chatterton and Royton'. The council subsequently proposed to sell the land to developers 'for a very large price'. With part of the proceeds the council planned to acquire a new site for playing fields which would have better facilities, in the way of changing rooms and car parking etc, than the existing site. But was the purpose of the original gift that the particular land conveyed should be used forever as playing fields, or alternatively, as contended by the Council, that the purpose was to provide playing fields for the benefit and enjoyment of the inhabitants, the particular site being immaterial? If the former, then it was agreed by all parties that the original purpose was still useful and wholly practicable with the consequence that none of the criteria in s 13 would have been applicable. (See *Observer*, 2 May 1993 citing a residents' campaign group strongly opposed to the sale and which identified 26 different contemporary uses of the land, ranging from football to picnics for the disabled.) The Court of Appeal ([1993] Ch 210), reversing a High Court judgment, concluded that the interpretation favoured by the Council was correct. The consequence was that the local authority could sell the land for supermarket development and provide an alternative recreation site, subject only to obtaining the consent of the Commissioners to the transaction under CA 1960, s 29 (now repealed; see CA 1993, s 36(6), (7)). Had the Court of Appeal upheld the conclusion reached by the High Court, the land could not have been sold as to do so would have been in breach of the purposes of the trust. Notwithstanding the outcome, the case serves to emphasise that the mere fact that trustees identify some more 'socially useful purpose' for charity property does not necessarily mean that a scheme can be made under s 13(1).

Turning then to the scope of s 13(1), potentially the most significant expansion over the pre-1960 definition of failure is offered by s 13(1)(e)(iii) – 'ceased in any other way to provide a suitable and effective method of using the property available by virtue of the gift, regard being had to [the appropriate considerations]'. Confirmation of the widened jurisdiction in the 1960 Act was provided by the Court of Appeal in *Varsani v Jesani* [1998] 3 All ER 273, a case arising out of a schism between majority and minority groups of a particular Hindu sect and resulting in a dispute about control over the property of the sect. Each group contended that it and not the other group was the true professor of the faith for which the charity had been established. The court accepted that under the law as it stood before 1960 it could not have made a scheme: 'It could not be said that it was either impossible or impractical to carry out the purposes of the charity so long as either or both of the groups professed the faith . . . If either group continued to profess that faith then there would be no jurisdiction to make a cy-près scheme' (per Morritt LJ at 282). However, the Court of Appeal approved a scheme under s 13(1)(e)(iii) whereby the funds were divided between the majority and minority groups. Chadwick LJ summarised the position (at 288): 'The original purposes specified in the declaration of trust . . . are no longer a suitable and effective method of using the property . . . because the community is now divided and cannot worship together. Nothing that the court may decide will alter that. To appropriate the use of the property to the one group to the exclusion of the other would be contrary to the spirit in which the gift was made.'

The invocation there of the 'spirit in which the gift was made' refers to the then statutory requirement in s 13(1)(c), (d) and (e)(iii) that in making judgements about failure the courts and the Charity Commission are to have regard to 'the spirit of the gift'. In *Varsani v Jesani* Morritt LJ commented on the phrase 'spirit of the gift' as follows (at 284): ' . . . the concept is clear enough, namely, the basic intention underlying the gift or the substance of the gift rather than the form of words used to express it or the conditions imposed to effect it. It is noteworthy that the phrase is used in s 13(1) only in contexts which require the court to make a value judgement. Thus it does not appear in paras (a)(i), (b), (e)(i) or (ii).' In *Re Lepton's Charity* [1972] Ch 276 and in *Varsani v Jesani* itself this involved construing documents in the light of the available evidence. In *Peggs v Lamb* [1994] Ch 172 the process was taken one step further by Morritt J: 'I do not think that the absence of any founding document precludes the existence of any "spirit of the gift". Accordingly such spirit must likewise be inferred' (at 197). This last comment tends, in our view, to confirm that we are dealing with a somewhat metaphysical construct and that the judicial formulae espoused in the above cases are susceptible to either a liberal or restrictive interpretation (see generally Warburton (1995–96) 3 CL & PR 1 at 1–10). The propensity towards a liberal interpretation is likely to be further encouraged by the change of wording from 'spirit of the gift' to 'appropriate considerations' although, as indicated above, 'spirit of the gift' is retained but as one element only of the 'appropriate considerations'. On the other hand, given the liberal approach of the courts in the recent cases, it is a nice question whether the statutory change is in some degree merely conferring a statutory imprimatur on current practice.

Implementation of s 13(1)   Where s 13(1) does apply the Commission has the same power as the court for establishing a scheme (s 16(1)). In practice the Commission makes the vast majority of modernisation schemes. How effective has the jurisdiction provided by s 13(1) been? The issue of effectiveness shifts the focus on to the new purposes that are substituted for the original purposes. Here also the 2006 Act has introduced changes intended formally to relax the previous criteria within which the Commission operated. Under the general doctrine of cy-près the property made subject to the scheme was required to be applied to purposes as close as is reasonably practicable to the original ones. A new s14B has been added to the Charities Act 1993 stating that the Commission may apply the property for such purposes as it considers appropriate having regard to the following matters:

> (3) The matters are –
>
> (a) the spirit of the original gift,
> (b) the desirability of securing that the property is applied for charitable purposes which are close to the original purposes, and
> (c) the need for the relevant charity to have purposes which are suitable and effective in the light of current social and economic circumstances.

As with the possible interpretation of the 'appropriate considerations' under a revised s 13, a key question is whether the criteria are at all at odds with current Charity Commission practice. It is certainly the case that, notwithstanding a more activist cy-près policy on the part of the Commission after 1960 the manner in which the provisions of s 13(1), in particular sub-s (1)(e)(iii), were applied was criticised for being both inconsistent in interpretation and unduly restrictive (see *Woodfield Report* paras 83–85; *Charities: A Framework for the Future* paras 6.17–6.19; Luxton (1987) NLJ Annual Charities Review, 24 April, p 34). The restrictiveness was considered to spring in part from what critics suggested was an overly restrictive interpretation of the 'spirit of the gift' requirement discussed above.

The response to the criticism was twofold. In 1989 the Government and the Commission agreed that no change in the cy-près doctrine – 'which has an in-built flexibility' – was necessary, but, on the other hand, that 'a flexible and imaginative approach, consistent with due regard to the donor's wishes' should be adopted (*Charities: A Framework for the Future* para 6.18). In its 1989 report the Commission set out guidelines which indicated a more flexible application of the s 13 criteria. In particular it accepted that in preparing a scheme:

> Para 73...To choose a purpose which may be the nearest practicable purpose to the original purposes of the charity, but which is already adequately provided for, or which cannot provide a suitable and effective method of using the charity's property, would be to impose purposes which have already failed within the circumstances laid down in [s 13].

Thus cy-près, in its common law sense of 'as near as possible', appeared to be firmly subordinated to the overriding requirement that new purposes were to be 'suitable and effective'. Moreover the Commission also rejected the notion that 'certain elements of a trust are sacrosanct, for instance . . . religious qualifications in essentially secular charities, sex qualifications particularly in relation to schools' (para 76). Thus, as the Commission put it, 'no part of a charity's trusts is unalterable'.

The outcome of this approach could not be assessed without an exhaustive review of the Commission's current practice (see the Annual Reports for prominent examples, eg Annual Report 1992 paras 46–49 (Bridge House Estates); and see also *Peggs v Lamb* [1994] Ch 172). But consider: (i) whether the following example drawn from the 1983 Report illustrates a restrictive or a flexible approach to the cy-près doctrine; (ii) whether the later approach of the Commission might have resulted in a different scheme to the one created; and (iii) what difference, if any, might the application of the criteria in s 14B(3) have made to the outcome?

> (B) The Royal Star and Garter Homes for Disabled Sailors, Soldiers and Airmen
>
> 50. The object of this large and well-known charity is to provide a home for sailors, soldiers and airmen of Her Majesty's Forces totally paralysed or incapacitated by war or by accident or disease in times of peace. The Governors had never accepted into the Home at Richmond women who had served in Her Majesty's Forces but they now wished to do so and argued that the phrase soldiers etc, included female members of the Armed Forces.
>
> 51. Charities are excepted from the general provisions of the Sex Discrimination Act 1975 and as the charity was founded in 1916 and its appeal literature referred to ex-servicemen we had to advise the Governors that women could not be admitted to the Home. We explained, however, that if they were having difficulty in finding sufficient male beneficiaries this would constitute partial failure of the existing trusts and that in these circumstances we would gladly amend the objects of the charity to include women. The three Governors were reluctant to accept our view that the existing objects of the charity prevented women from becoming beneficiaries but in the course of our discussions with them it became clear that some 25 beds at the Home were vacant, not because there were insufficient male beneficiaries, but because the charity had insufficient funds to keep them

in use. The Governors had been promised a substantial donation to a separate women's fund if women could be admitted to the Home to take up this unused accommodation.

52. We agreed to make a scheme providing that in so far as the Governors were unable, through lack of finance or through lack of applicants, to fill all their accommodation with male beneficiaries they may admit disabled ex-service women nominated by the trustees of the fund to which the substantial donation was to be made, provided that this separate women's fund bore the cost of maintaining them.

Lastly it should be noted that under CA 1993, s 64(2)(A)–(2B) an incorporated charity that wishes to alter its memorandum of association so as to change its objects from one charitable purpose to another must obtain the prior written consent of the Commission (see Charity Commission OG47 (2008)). Otherwise the alteration will be ineffective: a fortiori where a company seeks to amend its memorandum and articles to apply existing charitable funds to non-charitable purposes (CA 1993, s 64(1)).

(2) Instigation of cy-près proceedings

Just identifying the scope of the statutory cy-près doctrine leaves out of account one important question. Who has the duty, or at least the power, to instigate cy-près proceedings before the Charity Commission when the existing purposes of a charity require modernisation?

Section 13(5), in conformity with a prior dictum of Lord Simonds in *National Anti-Vivisection Society v IRC* [1948] AC 31 at 74, imposes a statutory duty on trustees 'where the case permits and requires the property . . . to be applied cy-près, to secure its effective use for charity by taking steps to enable it to be so applied'. The trustees' decision need not be unanimous since, unlike a private trust, a majority of charitable trustees have the power to bind the minority (*Re Whiteley* [1910] 1 Ch 600 at 608). But what if the trustees are unaware of this duty or prefer to ignore it? The difficulty then is that the Commission has only limited powers itself to initiate a scheme. The 1993 Act provides in s 16(4) that the Commission is not to exercise its jurisdiction except in the following circumstances:

(i) On an application by the charity (s 16(4)(a)), or on a reference by the court (s 16(4)(b)).

(ii) Where the Commission is satisfied that charity trustees 'ought in the interests of the charity to apply for a scheme, but have unreasonably refused or neglected to do so', it may, after giving the trustees an opportunity to make representations, proceed of its own volition to make a scheme (s 16(6)). This subsection is subject to the important proviso that the charity must have been in existence for at least 40 years. The procedure, which prior to 1993 required the consent of the Home Secretary, does not appear ever to have been directly invoked although its very existence may enable the Commission to exert some influence on recalcitrant trustees.

> (iii) Where the charity's income from property is below £500, a scheme may be sought under s 16(5) by 'any one or more of the charity trustees' (para (a)), or by 'any person interested in the charity' (para (b)), or 'any two or more inhabitants of the area of the charity, if it is a local charity' (para (c)).

The only circumstances, therefore, in which the Commission can itself set cy-près schemes in train are those specified in (ii) above. The Charity Commission very much sees its role as a facilitator, encouraging charities to consider joint working, up to and including merger in appropriate cases, where they can increase efficiency and provide better service to charity users or beneficiaries (see Charity Commission RS4 *Collaborative Working and Mergers* (2003)).

(d) 'Small' charities

The CA 1993, ss 74 and 75 introduced a procedure, simplifying and widening a jurisdiction previously available under the Charities Act 1985, whereby trustees of small charities could seek to make more effective use of their income. The Charities Act 2006 has further extended this jurisdiction by means of amendment to the 1993 provisions. Under a revised s 74 trustees of an unincorporated charity (A) having a gross income of £10,000 or less during its last financial year and not holding any land on trust to be used for the purposes of the charity may, if at least two-thirds of those trustees voting on a resolution agree, transfer the property of A to another charity (B) to be applied as B's property (s 74(1), (2)(a)). Alternatively the trustees may resolve that the property should be divided between two or more other charities (s 74(2)(b)). The trustees of A must be satisfied both that 'it is expedient in the interests of furthering' the purposes for which the property was held by A and that the purposes of the recipient charity (B) are 'substantially similar' to the purposes of A (s 74(4)). A further option, subject to the same conditions as to 'expediency', is that the trustees of A, again provided that at least two-thirds of those voting agree, can by resolution replace all or any of its purposes with other charitable purposes, so long as the new purposes are 'as similar in character' to those being replaced as is 'reasonably practicable' (s 74C). Note that in neither instance is there any longer a requirement to have regard to 'the spirit of the gift'; the language of expediency, practicability and effectiveness has taken precedence. Moreover the increase in the income threshold from £5,000 to £10,000 in the 2006 Act means that some two-thirds of all registered charities now come within the scope of a jurisdiction that has expanded significantly since its origins in 1984. Then the income limit was £200! In effect the majority of small charities have now been provided with a system of DIY cy-près or merger subject only to the caveat that in both of the above instances the Commission must be notified of the resolution and has the power to object to it, either on procedural grounds or on its merits, and can ultimately prevent the resolution being implemented (s 74A).

In contrast s 75 establishes a small but growing breach in a large principle. Where a charity, other than a corporate charity, has a permanent endowment (which does not include land) and a gross annual income of £1,000 or less and the market value of the endowment does not exceed £10,000, trustees, again if at least two-thirds of those voting on a resolution agree, are empowered to spend the capital (s 75(3)) thereby effectively bringing the charity to an end. The trustees must be satisfied that the purposes for which the fund is established 'could be carried out more effectively' by spending some or all of the capital (s 75(4)). Two modifications introduced by the 2006 Act are that the concurrence of the Commission is no longer required and the trustees need not consider whether there is 'any reasonable possibility' of transferring the property under s 74, as was previously required. A further extension of the discretion conferred on trustees in this area has been introduced in s 75A of the 1993 Act. This section applies to certain larger endowment funds where the fund capital exceeds the financial limits applicable to the s 74 power. Section 75A provides the same power as s 74 in relation to the fund but subject to safeguards because of the larger sums involved. The concurrence of the Charity Commission is required and the Commission must take account of the wishes of the donor(s) as well as any changes in the charity's circumstances, 'including, in particular, its financial position, the needs of its beneficiaries and the social, economic and legal environment in which it operates' (s 75A(8)).

The measures just described seek to eschew compulsion. The role of the Commission remains largely restricted to informing and advising trustees about the jurisdiction and approving changes where appropriate and necessary. The view from the Commission though has certainly been positive. In the 1995 Report, for instance, it is asserted that 'extensive use' has been made of the new powers by trustees, citing the fact that in that year alone the Commission concurred with 1,889 resolutions (Annual Report 1995 para 16). On the other hand, it is difficult to predict just how much impact the revised statutory provisions will have on merger activity or on the practice of collaboration between charities. A survey by the Charity Commission estimated that over one-fifth (22%) of all charities currently work collaboratively. Conversely, 78% of charities, particularly smaller charities, do not have any collaborative working arrangements with other charities. The trend here is very evident. Charities that work collaboratively are more likely to be larger charities – income between £250,000 and £1m – and are more commonly grant or contract funded (Charity Commission RS4A *Collaborative Working and Mergers* (2003)). A similar picture can be seen with merger activity, 13% of large charities having either merged or actively considered a merger in the last ten years. There is seemingly much less interest in mergers amongst the smaller charities.

(e) Conclusion

The legal provisions described above represent a significant element in the state's supervision of charitable activity. It is noteworthy, however, that the provisions of the Charities Act 1993 which aim at co-ordination and review of charitable activity at a local level, and at the reorientation of outmoded purposes, still defer in a number of important respects to the autonomy of both charity trustees and the founders of charities. The co-operation of charity trustees in schemes of co-ordination, local reviews and cy-près proceedings is only in this last-named context required as a duty; otherwise, they have the option not to be involved. Moreover under the cy-près doctrine, even allowing for a more flexible interpretation of the terms of s 13(1), the founder's original wishes command respect when a scheme is under consideration (see generally Mulheron *The Modern Cy-près Doctrine* (2006) 128–139).

It is by no means certain that the changes introduced in CA 2006 will significantly alter this outcome. In part this is because the adoption of the cautious approach in the Strategy Unit Report towards mergers is reflected in what is still essentially a facilitative legislative regime. Moreover such an approach is understandable for several reasons, even apart from the wish to sustain a degree of diversity amongst charities and autonomy for trustees. Evidence on the effectiveness of mergers is at best mixed (see Strategy Unit Background Discussion Paper *Providing Flexibility for Charities to Evolve and Merge* (2002); and on the questionable effectiveness of mergers in the commercial sector see KPMG *Mergers and Acquisitions: A Global Research Report* (1999)). Apart from this pragmatic consideration there are long-standing ideological-cum-practical reservations about adopting a more overt interventionist stance towards the channelling of charitable funds. Thus a fundamental objection to further change, encapsulated in the opinion of one witness to the House of Commons Expenditure Committee, is that insufficient account might be taken of the possible economic consequences: '[donors] are sensitive customers, and if they feel someone else is going to apply their property in some quite different way which they would not like, they are apt not to give at all' (HC Paper no 495 (1974–75) para 63 per Chief Chancery Master Ball). This sentiment is not to be lightly dismissed but subsequently, as we have seen, a less restrictive approach has been adopted to these matters. Indeed in *Varsani v Jesani* [1998] 3 All ER 273 Morritt LJ, whilst recognising that potential donors should not be deterred by a belief that their intentions will be overridden by too ready a use of the cy-près jurisdiction, concluded (at 285):

> . . . [that] problem has to be set beside the equal but opposite problem that, in circumstances unforeseen by the donor, his or her bounty may not achieve all that was intended or was reasonably feasible. The balance between those two considerations has to be struck and was struck by Parliament . . . when . . . it enacted s 13 of the Charities Act 1960. Since then it has been the duty of the court fairly to apply the provisions of that section to the circumstances of each case without any predilection either to making or to refusing to make a scheme altering the original purposes of the charity.

It remains to be seen whether the broadening of the criteria in CA 2006, s 14B(3), in particular to have regard to 'current social and economic circumstances' when devising a scheme, will encourage the adoption of a more expansive approach in this regard. There remain, however, two other difficulties associated with the definition of charity that any sharp shift towards a 'socialisation' of charity would encounter (see also Garton (2007) 21(3) TLI 134–149 on cy-près as a 'vehicle for the redistribution of wealth'). First, the present definition delineates a broad spectrum of purposes within which the trust founder has power to select, specifying the purposes and method of implementation in some detail. Indeed this has been claimed to be one of the virtues of the present structure of charity law. Second, the Commission has no discretion to refuse registration on the grounds, for example, that the organisation is or will be engaged in an area of welfare provision already adequately catered for by state agencies and/or existing charities. The issue is therefore clear: if reform is ever proposed to go beyond simply encouraging the most effective use of the present rules, it is difficult to see how it could avoid having to confront the issue of Charity Commission powers and jurisdiction over the initial registration of a charity.

4. Honesty and efficiency in charity management

(a) Introduction

This section completes the survey of official supervision of charities by investigating the operation of the Charity Commission and other government agencies in endeavouring to ensure that charities act efficiently and honestly. The importance of maintaining and, if possible, increasing public trust and confidence in charities is a consistent theme in recent reports on the charitable and not-for-profit sector, the Strategy Unit Report being no exception (see *Private Action, Public Benefit* (2002) ch 6). The concern is understandable since whilst there may be a sense of goodwill towards the notion of charity there are equally concerns about aspects of their operation and regulation. A Survey of Public Attitudes conducted by Ipsos/MORI for the Charity Commission in 2008 found that 59% were worried about high administration costs and money spent on salaries. Also the public tended to have a negative view of fund-raising practices, both the methods employed and the volume of appeals, with some 50% of those surveyed inclined to agree that charities were using 'more dubious fundraising techniques' (*Public Trust and Confidence in Charities* (2008) p 15; NCVO 'Blurred Vision' (1998) Research Quarterly 1, January). Irrespective of whether or not such perceptions are well founded it is understandable that the opportunity was taken in the CA 2006 to strengthen the regulatory framework. The broad structure, however, remains that first introduced in the Charities Act 1992, now mostly consolidated in the CA 1993 and which extended the Commission's powers and increased trustees' obligations.

The principal agency concerned with maintaining standards of efficiency and honesty therefore remains the Charity Commission, assisted and monitored by the courts, although as will be seen below (p 1067), HMRC also has an important supervisory role. A further measure of control is exercisable by public authorities that may demand detailed particulars of management structure, membership resources, financial planning, accounts, proposed activities and so on as a condition of awarding contracts or granting discretionary financial assistance to a charity (see generally National Audit Office *Working with the Third Sector* (HC 75, Session 2005–06); Public Accounts Select Committee Thirty Second Report *Working with the Voluntary Sector* (HC 717, Session 2005–06)). The supervisory regime of CA 1993 has been extended by CA 2006, s 12 to bring 'exempt charities' (see Chapter 19) within its scope to a greater extent, although they will also be answerable in most instances to alternative supervisory agencies.

The principal impact of official supervision is still directed at the activity of a charity as a going concern, but an initial opportunity to exercise a degree of control occurs when a charity is first established or registered. We reviewed in Chapter 19 the extent to which the Commission can in theory and does in practice seek to use the registration process as an adjunct to its supervisory role. The limited powers that the Commission can exercise at registration were in some respects increased under CA 1993.

The Commission has been given certain powers in relation to charity names and charity trustees. It can now require a charity to change its name if its proposed title is 'likely to mislead' the public as to the purposes or activities of the charity (CA 1993, s 6; see Registered Charity Names, *Decisions of the Charity Commissioners* vol 4 (1995) p 22 where the Commission sets out in some detail the criteria to be applied in interpreting s 6). A proliferation of organisations with similar names is not only confusing but can undermine the value of one of a charity's important assets – its name (see eg *British Diabetic Association v Diabetic Society Ltd* [1995] 4 All ER 812, a 'passing off' action incurring costs over some four years estimated at £500,000; Morris (1996–97) 4 CL & PR 1 at 1–19; Inglis (1996) 18(3) EIPR 166). Note that there are also statutory prohibitions on the use of the words 'charity' or 'charitable' in the names of non-charitable companies or businesses, unless the consent of the Charity Commission has first been obtained (see Companies Act 1985, s 26(2); Business Names Act 1985, s 2(1); and *Decisions of the Charity Commissioners* vol 5 (1997) pp 4–6).

As regards trustees, in view of the key role that they play in the administration of charity it became accepted that some form of monitoring of trustees should be introduced at the time of registration (see Woodfield Report (1987) para 74; White Paper (Cm 694, 1989) paras 5.3–5.6). Under CA 1993, s 72 certain classes of persons are disqualified from being charity trustees. Those disqualified include undischarged bankrupts, any person convicted of an offence involving dishonesty or deception, and any person previously removed from charity trusteeship on grounds of misconduct or mismanagement (s 72(1)). In addition the Commission is required (s 72(6)) to maintain a register open to the public of all people removed from trusteeship either by the Commission itself or by the High Court. Finally, anyone acting as a trustee while disqualified under s 72 is committing a criminal offence (s 73).

But these various controls still operate within a narrow compass. Registration is not a seal of approval: it simply reflects the legal position whereby an organisation whose stated objects are charitable is entitled to be registered under the mandatory provisions of the statute. It would, however, be an error to assume that the registration process comprises merely a few rather modest technical hurdles to be overcome with no other linkage to the regulation of charities. Following criticism of the Commission in a 1997 Report from the National Audit Office (*Regulation and Support of Charities* HC Paper no 2 (1997–98)) and in a subsequent Report from the Public Accounts Committee (28th Report, HC Paper no 408 (1997–98)) the Commission began a new initiative to carry out a risk assessment on organisations seeking registration (see NAO Report Appendix 7 for the criteria). The object is to identify charities likely to be at risk so that the post-registration monitoring and investigation resources can, in effect, be targeted to best effect. To help them in that task the Commission is likely to ask for information such as promotional literature, independent assessments from experts, business plans and so on (see generally CC21 *Registering as a Charity* (2008)). There is therefore a clearer link being established between registration and the continuing regulatory processes.

In describing the process of administrative and financial supervision we shall look first at measures relating to the detection of maladministration, followed by an examination of the remedies available to the supervisory agencies.

(b) Detecting and preventing maladministration

(1) Receiving and checking charity accounts

Historically a major cause of criticism of the supervisory system was the low level of compliance by trustees with the obligation to submit accounts, exacerbated by the corresponding failure of the Commission to monitor and enforce the obligation (see eg NAO (1987) paras 1.13–1.17; and Public Accounts Committee (7th Report, HC Paper no 85 (1990–91) para 3). These failings ultimately engendered both statutory and administrative responses. The CA 1993, Pt VI provided the framework for a revised regulatory regime whilst on the administrative side the number of 'staff years' allocated to monitoring and investigation increased from 11.5 (1987) to 98.5 (1997) with, significantly, the number of qualified accountants rising from zero to nine (NAO (1997–98) paras 1.16, 4.4).

The outline statutory framework in Pt VI has since been both amplified and modified, most recently by the CA 2006. The amplification now takes the form of detailed regulations (currently Charities (Accounts and Reports) Regulations 2008, SI 2008/629) and a Statement of Recommended Practice (SORP 2005) published by the Charity Commission. One purpose of SORP 2005 is to try and ensure some measure of consistency in the ways in which charities present their accounts and thereby, it is thought, to provide a more appropriate basis for comparing the finances of different charities. Apart from setting out in considerable detail what the accounts should include and the manner of their presentation, the Regulations (reg 40(2)(b)) also require as a minimum a brief summary of the main activities and achievements of the charity during the year in relation to the charity's objects, with a more extensive report demanded of an 'auditable charity' (see below). This reporting requirement is elaborated on by the Commission in *Charity Reporting and Accountability* (CC15a) where it is suggested that the annual report offers the chance 'to take stock of how the year compared to the trustees' plans and aspirations, ... and to reflect on difficulties and challenges [and] ... an opportunity to highlight the main activities or significant activities undertaken in order to carry out the charity's purposes for the public benefit' (para D4). It remains to be seen whether increased compliance with these requirements will still criticism of a lack of transparency and of the difficulty in comparing the performance of different charities (see eg Report by Comptroller General *Giving Confidently* Session 2001–02 (HC 234) paras 17–21; and Public Accounts Committee (39th Report (Session 2001–02)) paras 6–11: 'Whilst some charities' annual reports provided helpful information on their activities, others did not permit comparison of planned with actual performance or comparison of performance over time' (para 6)).

Whilst accountability and transparency are important virtues it is recognised that in such a diverse sector of economic activity practicality and cost of compliance are also relevant considerations. Concern about an excessive regulatory burden being imposed on small charities (defined as having annual income or expenditure of less than £25,000) has therefore resulted in the auditing and reporting obligations applicable to them being modified (Deregulation and Contracting Out Act 1994, ss 28–30). A similar sentiment about excessive regulatory burden lies behind the provision in CA 2006, s 28 to raise the threshold at which accounts must have a full professional audit from an income level of £250,000 to £500,000 and to introduce as an alternative an asset value threshold of £2.8m (before liabilities) where the income level is between £100,000 and £500,000.

The CA 2006 simplifies the rules as to when a professional audit is required, and eliminates the differences in the thresholds for company and non-company charities. The overall position is that charity trustees now have three primary duties regarding accounts: (i) to keep proper accounting records, which must be preserved for at least six years (CA 1993, s 41(1), (2)); (ii) to prepare and retain, also for at least six years, a statement of accounts for each financial year complying with requirements prescribed by statutory regulation (s 42(1), (2)); and (iii) where the gross income or expenditure of the charity exceeds £25,000 in any financial year, to submit, within ten months of its end, an annual report on the activities of the charity together with the statement of accounts and the report of an auditor or independent examiner as the case may be (s 45). As regards this last requirement, an audit by a professional auditor (as defined by s 43(2)) is required only where, in the relevant financial year, the gross income and asset value provisions referred to in the previous paragraph apply (s 43(1)). Otherwise, ie where the annual gross income or expenditure is between £25,000 and £500,000, the requirement is satisfied if the accounts have been examined by a competent independent examiner (s 43(3)). It should be noted that the requirements of the statement of accounts are also less stringent where the gross income of the charity does not exceed £25,000 in the financial year (s 42(3)). The annual report and accompanying documents are open to public inspection (s 47).

Differences in the accounting, reporting and auditing regimes of company and non-company charities have been largely eliminated by recent legislation. The Companies Act 2006, s 386, for instance, in effect harmonises the accounting and independent examination regimes for company and non-company charities. In particular, small charitable companies and groups, as defined by the Companies Act 2006, are subject to the external scrutiny provisions of the 1993 Act. Also the Charities Act 2006, s 32 provides for audit thresholds for charitable companies that will produce greater consistencey between both types of charity.

The Commission retains a residual authority under CA 1993, s 69 to appoint and pay an auditor to conduct an independent investigation into the condition and the accounts of any corporate charity. There is one other group of charities, exempt charities, for whom special provision is made. Consistent with the overall legislative approach towards exempt charities, they are not subject to the obligations described above, although they too are required (i) to keep, and retain for at least six years, proper books of accounts; and (ii) to prepare consecutive statements of account relating to a period of not more than 15 months and a balance sheet relating to the end of that period (s 46). There is one additional obligation with which every *registered* charity with a gross annual income or expenditure in excess of £25,000 must comply. Unless the Commission dispenses with the requirement, they must submit an annual return containing prescribed information (s 48). The purpose of the annual return is to enable the Commission to keep the register up to date and also to enable it to monitor charities effectively.

To summarise, we can say that the accounting and reporting framework covers five interlinked areas: (i) the maintenance of accounting records; (ii) the preparation of annual statements of accounts and reports; (iii) an annual audit or examination of accounts; (iv) the submission of the accounts, the annual report and an annual return to the Charity Commission; and (v) the provision of public access to any of the above. To this catalogue can be added the subject of sanctions. Where charities fail to comply with the requirements described here, penalties can now be invoked. Thus persistent failure to submit the annual report or the annual return, or to make accounts available on request (s 47(2)), constitutes an offence (s 49). But more important from the standpoint of accountability is that a failure to comply with the statutory obligations might be expected to prompt a response from the Commission. Indeed it is evident that the accounting requirements are intended to be a key element in its monitoring strategy. To this end, as part of an agreement on 'key performance indicators' agreed with the Treasury, the Commission sets various submission rate targets, currently between 75% and 97.5% depending on the income of the charity and information to be submitted (see Annual Report 2008 p 23 where it would appear that the Commission is largely meeting its targets; cf Annual Report 1986, para 42 where it was conceded that accounts were received from fewer than 10% of registered charities).

(2) Other sources of information

The repeal of CA 1960, s 29 (consent to sales of charity land) deprived the Commission of one source of information about possible maladministration, but in its stead a more general strategy of monitoring registered charities has been implemented. In particular emphasis is being placed (i) on eliciting information at the time of registration as a means of indicating those aspects of a charity which may give rise to concern, and (ii) on identifying categories or types of charity which may be thought particularly susceptible to abuse. But it is apparent that in detecting maladministration the Commission places considerable reliance on complaints and information reported in the media, or received from the police, the public or from disaffected members, employees or trustees of a charity.

To this list of sources can formally be added HMRC, which itself, as a matter of practice, requires accounts and other supporting documents if appropriate to be submitted in any dealings with a charity over tax relief. Indeed some 6,000–7,000 charity accounts are reviewed by HMRC each year as part of its own monitoring exercise (National Audit Office *The Monitoring and Control of Tax Exemptions for Charities* HC Paper no 575 (1997–98) p 12). Under CA 1993, s 10(2) if HMRC suspects, for instance, a misapplication of charity funds by any existing charity, whether registered or not, HMRC is empowered to ignore otherwise binding restrictions on confidentiality and disclose information to the Charity Commission. Information is scarce on the extent of co-operation but in 1997–98, for instance, there were 66 specific referrals of cases to the Commissioners by FICO (Financial Intermediaries and Claims Office), the section of HMRC which administers the exemptions enjoyed by charities. Despite this evidence the Committee of Public Accounts has specifically recommended that greater efforts should be made by both organisations to work together 'to detect non-compliance' (*Inland Revenue: The Monitoring and Control of Tax Exemptions for Charities* 55th Report, HC no 728 (1997–98)).

There is one further potentially important source of information on malpractice or maladministration available to the Charity Commission. CA 1993, s 44A(2) imposes on the auditor or on the independent examiner of accounts a duty to communicate to the Commission in writing any matter relating to the activities or affairs of the charity which he has reasonable cause to believe is, or is likely to be, of material significance for the exercise in relation to the charity of the Commission's functions under s 8 (inquiries) or s 18 (protective powers) of the 1993 Act. In addition both independent examiners and auditors have a discretionary power to inform the Charity Commission in writing of any matter of which they become aware and which they have 'reasonable cause to believe is likely to be relevant' to the exercise by the Charity Commission of any of its functions (CA 1993, s 44A(5)). Under these 'whistle blowing' provisions the persons concerned are released from any duty of confidentiality to the trustees concerning the information or opinion given to the Commission (CA 1993, s 44A(5)).

(3) Inquiries and investigations

Receipt of accounts and annual reports and returns does not necessarily mean that an effective monitoring process will occur. This will depend on what further legal powers are available to the Commission and also to some extent on how effectively their resources are deployed on investigation duties.

A key legal resource is the provision of broad powers of inquiry to the Commission under s 8 of the CA 1993:

> (1) The Commission may from time to time institute inquiries with regard to charities or a particular charity or class of charities, either generally or for particular purposes, but no such inquiry shall extend to any exempt charity [except where this has been requested by its principal regulator].
> (2) The Commission may either conduct such an inquiry itself or appoint a person to conduct it and make a report to it.

The phrase in square brackets in s 8(1) was added by the CA 2006, s 12, Sch 5 as part of the general extension of the Charity Commission's regulatory powers over exempt charities. Most investigations begin with a preliminary evaluation to decide whether there is enough substance in a complaint or expression of concern received to warrant an inquiry. If a decision to proceed is taken, then, in conducting an inquiry the Commission or its appointee may require any person to attend and give evidence on oath, to supply answers (in the form of a statutory declaration, if so ordered) to written questions put to him, or to produce or deliver accounts and other documents (sub-ss (3), (4)). If the Commission so wishes, it may publish a report on the results of its investigations (sub-s (6)). Even where no inquiry is instituted, s 9 of the 1993 Act gives the Commission extensive powers, inter alia, to require any person to provide 'any information in his possession which relates to any charity', and to scrutinise and copy any documents relating to the affairs of a charity, including any exempt charity. The powers that the Commission has under s 9 have been added to by the insertion into the 1993 Act of a new section, s 31A, which in effect provides the Commission with a statutory 'search order' authority. Section 31A gives the Commission power to enter premises and take possession of documents that could be required to be produced under s 9 except that in this instance a s 8 inquiry must have been instituted. Moreover the exercise of the power is subject to obtaining authority from a justice of the peace and there must be reasonable grounds for believing either that a s 9 order would not be complied with or that the relevant documents would be 'removed, tampered with, concealed or destroyed' (s 31A(2)).

As might be anticipated, given the substantial increase in staff devoted to monitoring activity, the Commission now makes extensive use of its powers. It now carries out somewhere between 45 and 75 inquiries each year. Whilst this marks a considerable reduction from the figures in the 1990s when 200–250 inquiries each year tended to be the norm, this possibly reflects a more targeted approach. The Commission strategy appears to be one where emphasis is placed on reserving statutory inquiries only for the most serious cases and seeking to resolve most compliance issues by providing trustees with 'timely advice, guidance and supervision' (Annual Report 2008). In the previous Annual Report the Commission confirmed that its intention is 'to ensure that . . . regulatory engagement with charities is more proportional and focused on risk' (at p 3). Whilst this 'light touch' approach seems consistent with the broad policy aim of reducing the regulatory burden on charities it is less easy to reconcile with the view of the Committee of Public Accounts in its last report on the regulatory role of the Commission: 'In utilising the extra resources earmarked for investigation work, the Commission should . . . increase the number of investigations where justified by the potential abuses identified' and 'make more extensive use of the statutory powers granted by Parliament to help expedite its investigations' (Public Accounts Committee, 39th Report (Session 2001–02) para 5).

Where the Commission identifies what it believes to be a 'cause for concern' there are a range of measures that can be taken to protect charity assets.

(4) Action to protect charity property

The Commission has considerable powers where maladministration or abuse of charity funds is revealed. Thus CA 1993, s 16(1) gives the Commission the same statutory powers as are exercised by the courts for appointing and removing trustees (see generally Chapter 11) and for vesting or transfer of property, subject to the limitations mentioned in the earlier discussion of cy-près schemes (s 16(4), (5); and see above, p 1051). Furthermore, statutory powers to remove or appoint trustees, analogous to those enjoyed by the court under its inherent jurisdiction (see Chapter 11), are conferred on the Commission alone under s 18(4) and (5).

Of greater immediate significance for our purposes, s 18 of the Act also provides far-reaching powers to protect the property of any charity from fraud or mismanagement on the part of those in control of it. There are though two features to emphasise about this jurisdiction. One is that it does not extend to exempt charities. The second feature is that the most important of the powers under s 18, those in s 18(1) and (2), are exercisable only after an inquiry has been instituted under s 8 of the 1993 Act.

Charities Act 1993, s 18(1)

> (1) Where, at any time after it has instituted an inquiry under section 8 . . . with respect to any charity, the Commission is satisfied –
>
> (a) that there is or has been any misconduct or mismanagement in the administration of the charity; or
> (b) that it is necessary or desirable to act for the purpose of protecting the property of the charity or securing a proper application for the purposes of the charity of that property or of property coming to the charity;
>
> the Commission may of its own motion do one or more of the following things
>
> . . .

Those, briefly summarised, are as follows:

(i) suspend for up to 12 months any trustee, officer, agent or employee of the charity, pending consideration of that person's removal (s 18(1)(i) and (11)); and also suspend that person from membership of the charity (s 18A(2)) or terminate their membership (s 18A(3)).
(ii) appoint additional trustees (s 18(1)(ii));
(iii) transfer charity property to the Official Custodian (s 18(1)(iii));
(iv) restrict any dealings in charity property (s 18(1)(iv), (vi));
(v) order any debtor of the charity not to make any payments to it without the Commission's consent (s 18(1)(v));
(vi) appoint a receiver or manager of the charity (ss 18(1)(vii) and 19).

To this list can be added additional powers conferred on the Commission by s 19A and 19B. Under s 19A the Commission is empowered to direct, where the requirements of s 18(1) are satisfied, any trustee or officer or employee of the charity 'to take any action . . . which the Commission considers to be expedient in the interests of the charity'. The discretion is not completely untrammelled as s 19A(3) prevents the Commission from directing a person to do something expressly prohibited by the charity's constitution or by an Act of Parliament or which would be inconsistent with its purposes. On the other hand the Commission is permitted to direct a person to do something which would not otherwise be authorised under the charity's constitution. Under s 19B, where the Commission is satisfied that charity property is not being properly applied for the purposes of the charity it can, if it thinks it 'necessary or desirable', make an order requiring the person who is in possession or control of the property to apply it in a manner specified by the Commission. Conditions similar to those just described in relation to s 19A apply although the institution of a s 8 inquiry is not a prerequisite. As regards the misconduct and mismanagement referred to in s 18(1)(a), note that these concepts extend to include the payment of remuneration to persons acting in the affairs of the charity which is 'excessive in relation to the property which is applied or likely to be applied' for the purposes of the charity (s 18(3)).

An important distinction is drawn in Charities Act 1993, s 18 between two aspects of the powers available to the Commission. Under s 18(2), where the Commission is satisfied that there is or has been 'mismanagement or misconduct' (s 18(2)(a)) *and* that it is necessary or desirable to act to protect property (s 18(2)(b)) then it may (a) establish a scheme for the administration of the charity or (b) order the removal of any of the class of persons mentioned in (i) above who have been responsible for, privy to, contributed to or facilitated misconduct or mismanagement. The more extensive requirement to be satisfied in s 18(2) than in s 18(1) – '*and*' rather than 'or' – reflects a distinction between respectively 'permanent and remedial powers' and 'temporary and protective powers' (*Charities: A Framework for the Future* (1989) paras 5.14–5.16). Thus the powers under s 18(1) can be invoked promptly, whereas use of the powers under s 18(2) is subject to notice requirements to those who may be affected (ss 18(12) and 20) whilst for both subsections there is a right of appeal to the Charity Tribunal (CA 1993, Schedule 1C). It is the facility given under s 18(1) to the Commission to act promptly in the use of its powers, allied to the increased resources applied to monitoring, that the Commission hopes will enable it to achieve its aim of 'giving the public confidence in the integrity of charity' (Annual Report 1997 p 2).

These powers are sweeping and potentially very effective. Unfortunately from the perspective of the researcher the Annual Reports of the Commission no longer provide such detailed statistics as was once the case but a flavour of the range of remedies can be gleaned from the following edited extracts from the Annual Report 1997:

> Para 86. During 1997, five receivers and managers were appointed by our *support staff* to protect charity property which, for a variety of reasons was considered to be at risk.
>
> [Other statutory powers used by the support staff were as follows: Orders restricting transactions 2; Orders and Directions requiring information or documents 7; Trustees removed 2; Trustees appointed 35.]
>
> 110. [Analysis of protective powers exercised by *investigating staff*:
>
> Bank accounts frozen 41; Orders restricting transactions 50; Orders and Directions requiring information or documents 236; Receivers and managers appointed 1; Trustees removed 26; Trustees suspended 13; Trustees appointed 24; Directions to attend meetings 12; Other Orders 11.]

(5) Imposing liability on trustees

Prima facie, normal principles of trusts law determine whether charity trustees are in breach of trust, although in some situations the particular nature of charitable trusts demands some modification in the substantive content of the rules (see eg Charity Commission Guidance Note CC3 (2008) on their requirements, in place of the unattainable informed consent of beneficiaries, for permitting provision of goods or services to a charity by a trustee). Subject to this qualification and to the consideration that the CA 1993 itself imposes specific duties on trustees, such as the duties to register the charity and to file accounts, a breach of charitable trust is identified according to the same criteria as a breach of a private trust. The remedies which can be asserted against the defaulting trustee – injunction, liability to account, restitution of money or property misappropriated etc – are also generally the same (see Chapters 11 and 14).

The panoply of powers available to the Commission also extends to the granting of relief to trustees, and to auditors or independent examiners of accounts, for breach of trust or breach of duty. The jurisdiction, conferred on the Commission by s 73D of the 1993 Act, is analogous to that exercised by the court under Trustee Act (TA) 1925, s 61 and thus the Commission can relieve a person wholly or partly from liability where it considers that the person 'has acted honestly and reasonably and ought fairly to be excused for the breach of trust or duty' (see p 595 for discussion of these criteria in the context of TA 1925, s 61). An important practical distinction from the law of private trusts arises in the instigation of proceedings. To lend weight to the enhanced role of the Charity Commission, CA 1993, s 32 confers on it a power to bring of its own motion legal proceedings with regard to charities. The exercise of this power is subject only to it obtaining the formal agreement of the Attorney-General, who historically, of course, acted as nominal claimant representing the interests of those who stand to benefit from fulfilment of the charitable purposes. The need to provide the Commission with some 'forensic threat' was one reason for the change: 'All too often ... defaulters, or their advisers, use ... negotiations simply as a delaying tactic, in the knowledge that the Commissioners cannot themselves take legal action' (*Charities: A Framework for the Future* (Cm 694, 1989) para 5.28). Picarda has suggested that a supporting reason 'was to relieve the direct workload on the Attorney General' (*The Law and Practice Relating to Charities* (3rd edn, 1999) p 596).

The granting of this power does not completely rule out the possibility of litigation by some party other than the Commission. Under s 33(1) locus standi is extended to other individuals, so long as the proceedings in question are 'charity proceedings' (s 33(8)), ie proceedings relating to the administration of the charity and not, for instance, about the creation of a valid charitable trust (see *Re Belling* [1967] Ch 425; *Hauxwell v Barton-upon-Humber UDC* [1974] Ch 432 at 450).

---

s 33(1) Charity proceedings may be taken with reference to a charity either by the charity, or by any of the charity trustees, or by any person interested in the charity, or by any two or more inhabitants of the area of the charity, if it is a local charity, but not by any other person.

The apparent breadth of this section is qualified by the screening device that, subject to an appeal to the court, the consent of the Commission must be obtained and this should not be given if it can deal with the case itself (s 33(2)–(5)). Furthermore there is considerable uncertainty about the meaning of the term 'person interested in the charity'. Whereas it seems that, at least in certain circumstances, a donor or settlor may qualify (*Brooks v Richardson* [1986] 1 All ER 952, but cf Robert Walker J's doubts on this point in *Scott v National Trust* [1998] 2 All ER 705 at 715), mere public-spiritedness or modest financial support apparently will not suffice (*Re Hampton Fuel Allotment Charity* [1989] Ch 484, CA). Nor, it seems, will a person with a claim adverse to a charity – for example, arising out of a commercial relationship – be a 'person interested' (*Haslemere Estates Ltd v Baker* [1982] 3 All ER 525 at 536–537, but cf *Gunning v Buckfast Abbey Trustees* (1994) *Times* 9 June – fee-paying parents were 'persons interested'). On the other hand, in a membership charity, members of the organisation would usually be recognised as 'persons interested' (see *Muman v Nagasena* [2000] 1 WLR 299 – members of a religious group; and see generally Warburton [1997] Conv 106–118). It is difficult to disagree with the opinion of Nicholls LJ in *Re Hampton Fuel Allotment Charity* that no precise definition could be attempted: 'charitable trusts vary so widely that to seek a definition here is, we believe, to search for a will-o'-the-wisp' (at 494). However, in light of the Attorney-General's role as nominal plaintiff, he concluded that 'to qualify as a plaintiff in his own right a person generally needs to have an interest materially greater than or different from that possessed by ordinary members of the public' (see also Megarry VC in *Haslemere Estates Ltd v Baker* [1982] 3 All ER 525 at 537 – 'some good reason for seeking to enforce the trusts of a charity or secure its due administration', cited with approval by Nicholls LJ). The interposition of the bureaucratic procedure that the Commission's approval be obtained reduces the practical impact of this uncertainty, since any person may complain to the Commission and try to persuade it to take administrative or other action where breach of trust is suspected. It only remains to add that the courts have shown no enthusiasm for permitting judicial review to be employed as an alternative to s 33(1) jurisdiction (see *Scott v National Trust* [1998] 2 All ER 705, 715; *R v National Trust ex parte Scott* [1998] 1 WLR 226, 229; Garton (2006) 20(3) TLI 160–179).

The case of *Muman v Nagasena* [2001] 1 WLR 299 suggests that in some circumstances not only must the authorisation of the Charity Commission be obtained under s 33 – it had not – but also a resort to mediation will be required before legal proceedings can be pursued. The Court of Appeal refused to lift a stay on proceedings in litigation on which 'very substantial sums of money have been spent' until authorisation from the Commission was obtained *and* 'all efforts have been made to secure a mediation of this dispute' (at 305). Mummery LJ made explicit reference to a combined mediation service for charities established by the Centre for Dispute Resolution jointly with the National Council for Voluntary Organisations: 'The purpose of the scheme is to achieve, by voluntary action confidentially conducted, a healing process under which disputes within a charity can be resolved at a modest fee and without diminishing the funds which have been raised for charitable purposes.'

In conclusion, it must not be overlooked that there is in CA 1993 an extensive range of criminal offences for breach of which trustees may be held liable (see Quint (1992–93) 1 CL & PR pp 101–111).

(6) Withdrawal of tax privileges

In Chapter 18 we saw that there is a wide range of valuable tax reliefs available to charities and to donors. Where there are tax reliefs there are also temptations to exploit their availability. One sanction is that where trustees apply their funds in breach of trust, relief for income tax and capital gains tax may be withheld by HMRC on the grounds that the funds in question are not being applied for 'charitable purposes only' (see the *Metal Box* case, discussed in Chapter 19, p 1014). This potentially important form of indirect sanction against fraud or mismanagement is by the adoption of specific anti-avoidance measures to counter abuse of charitable status by means of certain, often complex, tax avoidance schemes (see Finance Act 1986, ss 31 and 33; Income Tax Act 2007, ss 549–552; Annual Report 1986 App F; [1986] BTR 400–407; NAO (1987) para 2.13 for details of HMRC investigations).

The effectiveness of HMRC's systems of monitoring has been subjected to critical scrutiny by the National Audit Office and the Committee of Public Accounts (55th Report *Inland Revenue: The Monitoring and Control of Tax Exemptions for Charities* HC Paper no 728 (1997–98)). The general view expressed by the Committee was that whilst in 1996–97 some £6m in tax revenues had been recovered by compliance activities, those activities lacked sufficient focus. It appears from the Report that HMRC is in the process of adopting a more targeted strategy based on a system of risk assessment. In this respect the response of HMRC is similar to that of the Charity Commission to that same Committee. That response seems to be that 'we are working hard at improving our monitoring systems and you should judge us when they are in place and fully operative'.

It is likely that at some point the Committee of Public Accounts will wish to return to these matters of monitoring and compliance as regards HMRC.

(7) Fund-raising

In 1982 an experienced charity fund-raiser, Alan Clements, founded a charity, Children with Cancer (CwC), with himself, his wife, his cousin and an accountant as trustees. The named beneficiaries included the Great Ormond Street Hospital for Sick Children. CwC was registered in December 1982. Within a month, Clements resigned his trusteeship and contracted on favourable commission terms to become a professional fund-raiser for CwC. Between January and September 1983 Clements, trading as AC Publicity, raised on behalf of CwC £212,399, but received in return commission amounting to £160,888 (ie 75.75%). Similar contracts entered into with other fund-raisers produced approximately £205,000, of which some £167,000 was returned to them as commission. Clements and others were unsuccessfully prosecuted for allegedly conspiring to obtain money by deception, namely by falsely representing that 'CwC was a genuine and honestly conducted charitable trust'. In fact CwC's comparatively meagre share of the money collected had been properly and effectively administered (see *Sunday Times* 28 August 1983; [1985] Voluntary Action, July, pp 12–13).

Concern at the inadequate control exercisable over such fund-raising activities was expressed in the Woodfield Report (Pt 12) and reflected in the Government's 1989 White Paper (*Charities: A Framework for the Future* ch 10; see also NCVO *Malpractice in Fundraising for Charity* (1986)). Subsequently the CA 1992 introduced a new regime to control public fund-raising (Pt II) and public charitable collections (Pt III). The 1992 Act broadly aimed to protect the interests of charities and donors. In fact Pt III of the Act was never brought into force, the deferral seemingly being due to concerns about its detailed operation. In its stead the previous legislation governing public collections remained in place. The CA 2006 has now introduced a new scheme to replace Part III with the emphasis being on a unified local authority licensing scheme for public collections (see below).

The introduction of the new scheme in Pt 3 of the 2006 Act and the accompanying minor modifications to Pt II of the 1992 Act reflect the consideration that, despite the previous changes to the statutory framework, the public perception of fund-raising activities is not very positive. Two continuing areas of public concern appear to be fund-raising costs and some of the methods employed in face-to-face fund-raising in urban centres, often where members of the public are encouraged to donate by means of completing direct debits – so-called 'chugging'. Many people assume, often incorrectly, that such fund-raisers are unpaid volunteers whereas they are commonly employed by professional fund-raising organisations. As regards fund-raising costs ratios these can vary widely; one study in 2001 of charities raising over £100,000 per year suggested that the average cost ratio was 27% – ie 27 pence spent to raise £1. However, 22% of the charities surveyed had a costs ratio in excess of 40% (see generally the Strategy Unit Background Paper *Private Action, Public Benefit: The Regulation of Fundraising* (2002); and for a comparative perspective Morris (2004) 24(4) LS 599–620). Whether a costs ratio of that order is a matter of concern may depend on one's perspective. It is conceivable that an organisation may feel it is justified if it enables it to raise larger sums than would be achieved by employing cheaper methods. Nevertheless it is evident that there is public concern over matters such as those just described. The response of the Government has been twofold. One aspect of the approach has been to introduce the statutory changes referred to above. The other aspect is that the Government accepted the recommendation of the Strategy Unit that self-regulation should be the first resort in improving fundraising standards and practices (see the Code of Conduct and Codes of Fundraising Practice prepared by the Institute of Fundraising www.institute-of-fundraising.org.uk/bestpractice/codes). On the other hand a new s 64A is inserted into the 1992 Act conferring on the Secretary of State the power to make regulations to control charity fund-raising should self-regulation prove to be ineffective.

The revised statutory framework is now to be found in the Charities Act 1992 Part II and the Charities Act 2006 Part 3. Given that other aspects of regulation are to be found in the Charities Act 1993, it is to be hoped that parliamentary time might soon be found for a consolidating statute.

Charities Act 1992, Pt II (ss 58-64) These provisions are directed at controlling the activities of 'professional fund-raisers' and 'commercial participators'. There are several key points to emphasise about this very detailed jurisdiction (see generally Luxton *The Law of Charities* (2001) ch 21).

First, the definitions employed are widely drawn. Thus a professional fund-raiser (defined in s 58(1)–(3)) is any person who carries on a fund-raising business or who, for reward, solicits money or other property for the benefit of a 'charitable institution'. The latter includes both charities strictly defined, and any institution established 'for charitable, benevolent or philanthropic purposes' (s 58(1)). One point is clear. This definition extends beyond what is defined as 'charitable' under the law of charities and is conceivably intended to prevent the gap between lay and legal understandings of what is charitable being exploited. Also, as the definition of 'professional fund-raiser' stands, it would cover a wealth of activities and persons including celebrities making television appeals. Consequently to guard against the net being cast too wide and inhibiting fund-raising, s 58(2) excludes certain categories such as persons making a television or radio appeal in the course of a fund-raising venture undertaken by a charitable institution or a company connected with it. There is also a de minimis exception, so that a person receiving a payment of no more than £5 per day or £500 per year is excluded from the definition of professional fund-raiser (s 58(3)). The aim here is to exclude persons such as volunteers who receive a small honorarium (see Earl Ferrers in Report of the Committee on the Charities Bill, HL, col 219 (11 December 1991)).

A 'commercial participator' is a person who carries on a business other than fund-raising, but who engages in a promotional venture 'in the course of which it is represented that a charitable contribution' will be made to or applied for the benefit of a charitable institution (see Hill (1995–96) 3 CL & PR 17). This definition therefore includes a manufacturer or retailer who, in marketing products, represents that a proportion of the purchase price will be donated to a charitable institution. It also includes credit card companies who issue affinity cards under which a particular charity is to benefit each time the card is used. Not only is the category again widely drawn – 'any person' and 'any promotional venture' – but its scope is reinforced by the way in which 'represents' is defined very broadly in 58(6) – '"represent"... means... represent... in any manner whatever, whether expressly or impliedly'.

The second point to emphasise about this jurisdiction is that written agreements and disclosure of information are central to the process of regulation. Thus the Act makes it unlawful (s 59(1)) for either a professional fund-raiser or a commercial participator to undertake the activities referred to above unless they have entered into a written agreement with the relevant charitable institution, satisfying requirements prescribed by the Charitable Institutions (Fund-raising) Regulations 1994, SI 1994/3024. Any written agreement must contain, for instance, details as to 'the amount by way of remuneration or expenses which the professional fund-raiser is to be entitled to receive' (reg 2(c)).

However, only the institution can enforce compliance with this requirement and then only by means of injunction (s 59(3)). As regards disclosure, the professional fund-raiser and commercial participator must ensure that any solicitation or representation is accompanied by a statement as to who is to benefit and, in general terms, how the fund-raiser is to be remunerated and what proportion of the proceeds of any promotional venture will benefit the designated institution(s) (s 60). Section 60(3A) of the Act now requires either the actual amount of the remuneration to be stated or, if not known, the estimated amount 'calculated as accurately as is reasonably possible'. Previously it had been deemed sufficient just to specify in general terms the method by which remuneration would be determined. To give a seasonal example, the purchaser of charity Christmas cards could expect to know what proportion of the purchase price would be going to the charity. Failure to comply with the disclosure requirement will constitute an offence (s 60(7), (8)).

The third key element to emphasise is the protection afforded to donors and to charitable institutions. Thus s 61 introduces a cooling-off period: in designated circumstances, notably radio and television appeals, donors can within seven days claim repayment of any donation that exceeds £50. Under s 62, charitable institutions are given the right to prevent unauthorised fund-raising on their behalf by seeking an injunction (cf CwC above). But what should the reaction of the charitable institution be if subsequently offered funds raised in this manner? Should it 'take the money and run'? Perhaps so, but the Charity Commission suggests that caution should be the watchword in the interests both of the particular institution and of charity generally:

Annual Report of Charity Commission 1996

Para 202. . . . We recommend that before accepting such donations, trustees should try to vet the fund-raiser and to satisfy themselves that both the methods of fund-raising used and the proportion of funds collected which have been absorbed in commission and administration are reasonable. If this is not done, there is a danger that not only the reputation of their charity, but also that of the sector generally, will be damaged.

These strictures are also reflected in the general guidance on fund-raising published by the Charity Commission (CC20 *Charities and fund-raising* (2008)) at para 57: 'A charity's name is precious. It is the means by which a charity is known and by which its reputation will be judged.' The Commission warns trustees, for instance, that they should be careful how they allow the charity's name to be used by commercial participators in promotional ventures.

Charities Act 2006 Pt 3 (ss 45–66) Part 3 is concerned with public charitable collections, charitable again including 'benevolent or philanthropic purposes' (s 45(2)(b)), and builds on the approach of the CA 1992 Pt III legislation. The main aim is to harmonise and modernise laws regulating charitable appeals made door-to-door or in a public place. The Act provides (s 48) that no collection in a public place (other than narrowly defined exempt local short-term collections (s 50)) can be undertaken unless the promoter of the collection (a) holds a public collections certificate issued by the Charity Commission (s 52) *and* (b) has obtained a permit from the local authority in whose area the collection is to be conducted (s 59). The issuing of a certificate enables the local authority to exercise some degree of control over the number of collections in a public place at any one time. Similar restrictions apply to door-to-door collections save that a permit is not required from the local authority although notification must be given to that authority (s 49(1)(b)). The Act specifies the circumstances under which the Charity Commission can refuse an application for a public collections certificate (s 53) or withdraw or vary a certificate (s 56). Amongst the grounds on which the Commission may refuse an application are those invoking what might be termed a cost–benefit analysis (see eg s 53(1)(f) concerning 'excessive amount by way of remuneration'). As with other aspects of the regulatory powers of the Commission, an appeal against its decision can be made to the Charity Tribunal (s 57). The Act also specifies the circumstances under which a local authority can refuse permits (s 60), eg undue inconvenience to members of the public (s 60(1)(a)), or, indeed, withdraw one previously issued (s 61). There is a right of appeal to the magistrates' courts against local authority decisions (s 62).

Criminal liability A feature of the regulatory framework introduced by the CA 1992 is the creation of a number of criminal offences associated with unlawful fund-raising activities. Amongst the most significant of these offences, in addition to those referred to above concerning disclosure, are (i) soliciting money for an institution that is falsely represented to be a charity (CA 1992, s 63), and (ii) professional fund-raisers or commercial participators failing to transmit money or other property promptly to the relevant charitable institution (Charitable Institutions (Fund-Raising) Regulations 1994, reg 6(2)). It is also an offence for a promoter to conduct a public charitable collection in breach of the requirements of the 2006 Act outlined above (see CA 2006, ss 48(3), 49(5) and also ss 64 and 65).

This statutory framework does not of course exclude the possibility of other forms of criminal liability being imposed on those engaged in fund-raising, illustrations of which can be found in the Annual Reports of the Charity Commission. In 1993, for instance, the Commissioners carried out a joint investigation with the Merseyside Fraud Squad into an organisation called Leukaemia and Cancer Society Fund (commonly known as 'Lu-Can'), which had been established for the purpose of providing grants to local hospitals and cancer and leukaemia sufferers. The inquiry established that over £300,000 had been collected over a three-year period, but only £8,500 had been used for charitable purposes. The rest had been swallowed up in expenses. The promoters of the Fund were found guilty of having conspired together to obtain moneys by deception and received prison sentences ranging from 15 months to two years (Annual Report 1993, but cf *Lewis v Lethbridge* [1987] Crim LR 59 and (1988) 51 MLR 115).

(8) Advertising

Given the need for charities to raise funds it is scarcely surprising that modern marketing techniques, particularly the use of advertising, hold out certain attractions. After all, it might be asked, why should not charities be allowed the freedom of the marketplace to advertise for funds to the same extent as commercial organisations can advertise their products? What may therefore be surprising is that it was not until 4 September 1989 that the restriction on paid-for charity advertising on independent television and radio was lifted. Prior to then charity advertising had either been limited to newspaper and journal outlets or had been permitted use of free appeals ranging from *The Week's Good Cause* on Sunday morning radio to large-scale general appeals such as BBC Children in Need. There is now a plethora of codes and regulations that cover charity advertising most of which are designed, in common with those applicable to commercial organisations, to ensure that advertisements by or for charities are legal, decent, honest and truthful (see Morris 'The Media and the Message' (1995–96) 3 CL & PR 3 at 157–177; *Picarda* pp 635–644; Luxton *The Law of Charities* (2001) ch 23; the *Code of Advertising Practice* at www.asa.org.uk/asa/codes/ and generally www.ofcom.org.uk).

It is evident though that charity advertising raises issues of propriety and ethics more extensive than those associated with advertising detergents. Three issues in particular deserve mention.

First, the financial cost of advertising in popular media outlets can be considerable. It was reported by Morris that in the first six months of 1994, for instance, 52 charities spent a total of £32.5m on agency-placed advertisements alone. It remains to be seen what effect this might have in the medium to long term on the fund-raising activities of the overwhelming majority of charities unable to afford such expenditure. We simply do not yet know whether advertising will stimulate a greater level of giving or merely in effect reallocate existing donations to the larger charities.

The second issue meriting consideration concerns the form that charitable appeals may adopt. Charity advertisers, it is claimed, seek to appeal to five main emotions in their advertising: love, guilt, fear, anger and sex (see McIntosh and McIntosh *Marketing: A Handbook for Charities* (1984); and generally Carter et al *The Charitable Behaviour of the British People* (1987)). How far should charity advertising be permitted to 'exploit' an emotional appeal? Should it be permissible, for example, to use advertisements comparable to that used by the RSPCA in a 1999 newspaper advertisement (to oppose lawful mink farming) displaying several rows of dead, skinned mink under the slogan 'Welcome to the Spring Collection'? The CAP Television Advertising Code, for instance, states, inter alia, that advertisements should 'not exaggerate the scale or nature of any social problem' nor 'suggest that anyone will lack proper feeling or fail in any responsibility through not supporting a charity' and 'treat with care and discretion any issues likely to arouse strong emotions' (para 11.3.4). On the other hand, research carried out at the University of Loughborough between 1991 and 1993 discovered that whereas emotional appeals were generally regarded as suspect, the public also recognised that this type of advertising was most likely to catch their attention and stimulate them to contribute.

The third issue concerns the relationship between advertising and the interests and attitudes of user groups. The CAP Code states that advertisements must 'respect the dignity of those on whose behalf an appeal is being made'. But there are trade-offs and a long-standing tension here. Sir Brian Rix, the then chairman of Mencap, commented in 1984 on the tension between the need to produce an image which will attract financial support yet one which will not undermine the campaign for equal rights and dignity for the mentally handicapped:

> On the one hand, we must present a positive image of mentally handicapped people, to persuade the public to accept them as friends and neighbours. On the other [hand], we must encourage the view that extra resources in the form of state funds and voluntary donations should be made available to meet their special needs ('How to Influence Public Attitudes' *Parents Voice* Autumn 1984, cited in Morris (1995–96) 3 CL & PR no 3, 157 at 174).

Whilst it is clear that the regulatory framework is somewhat diffuse and might benefit from greater co-ordination there appears to be no demand or need at present to move from the considerable emphasis currently placed on codes of practice. Indeed in one area at least it may be argued that a removal of regulation should be considered. One of the most contentious aspects of the definition of charity, the prohibition on pursuing political purposes, has reappeared in the context of controls on advertising. The Broadcasting Act 1990, s 92(2)(a) – replaced by the Communications Act 2003, s 321(2)(a)(b) – prohibited the broadcast of 'any advertisement which is inserted by or on behalf of any body whose objects are wholly or mainly of a political nature' or 'which is directed towards any political end'. In *R v Radio Authority, ex p Bull* [1997] 3 WLR 1094 the Court of Appeal in an application for judicial review held that the Radio Authority had been entitled to adopt the definition of the term 'political' applied in charity law. The court therefore upheld the decision of the Authority to prohibit the broadcast of Amnesty International advertisements seeking to publicise the plight of refugees in Rwanda and Burundi (see the critical comment by Stevens and Feldman [1997] PL 615–622; and on charity and politics generally Chapter 19). Even if we assume the rationale(s) for the 'political purposes' restrictions in charity law are supportable, it is difficult to see why they should carry such weight in an advertising context (see generally on political advertising Scott (2003) 66(2) MLR 224–244; and in relation to the Human Rights Act 1998 *R v S of S for Culture, Media and Sport* [2008] 2 WLR 781)).

(c) The limits of the supervisory framework

The courts and the Charity Commission are thus equipped with a seemingly powerful battery of supervisory rules. As with any other supervisory body or agency the effectiveness of the supervision exercised by the Commission cannot be assessed by considering merely the rules under which it operates. The peculiar position of the Commission must not be overlooked, for it is charged in CA 1993, s 1C with a number of potentially incompatible functions. Its supervisory and investigative role, for instance, does not necessarily sit too comfortably alongside a role of 'friend' in the sense of 'encouraging...the better administration of charities' (s 1C(2)). Indeed, seemingly almost to reassure trustees that their independence would not be threatened by seeking the assistance of the Commission, the revisions to the 1993 Act do not alter the position whereby the Commission is not authorised 'to be directly involved in the administration of a charity' (CA 1993, s 1E(2)(b)). On the other hand, whereas it could once be said that the approach adopted by the Commission evinced almost an 'ideology of non-intervention', there has been a reorientation as a consequence of the legal changes brought in by the 1993 and 2006 Acts. The Commission has acknowledged that the CA 1993 'changes the focus' of its work: 'The Commission's responsibility under the strengthened legislation is to add active supervision to the general accountability of charities...Our monitoring programme helps us to get "the balance right between flexibility and safeguarding charitable money" which the National Audit Office pointed out was the "key to all the Charity Commission's work"' (Annual Report 1997 para 16). When the emphasis of the recent changes to the 1993 Act is borne in mind it is evident that the Commission is now looking more like 'watchdog' than 'guide-dog' (see also [1993] Conv 177). Indeed the Commission may need to exercise some caution in carrying out its extended regulatory functions under the legal framework, lest it be argued that, although even a few instances of abuse may be injurious to the general reputation of charity, the formal regulatory role is so onerous as to constrain the efficiency of the sector (cf Sealey *Company Law and Commercial Reality* (1984) ch 2 criticising aspects of company law reporting requirements; see also Freedman and Godwin [1993] JBL 105 in relation to auditing). The Reports of the Committee of Public Accounts, the parliamentary watchdog of the Charity Commission, have been notable for their strong criticisms of the effectiveness of the Commission as regulator. In its 28th Report in the 1997–98 session, echoing a theme from previous reports, the Committee stated that 'the Commission is paying too little attention to enforcing the accountability of charities, and to the importance of promoting public confidence in the charitable sector' (HC Paper no 408 (1997–98) para 6). The riposte of Richard Fries, the then Chief Charity Commissioner, to the publication of the 1997–98 Report reflected a different emphasis about the perceived role of the Commission as a regulator: 'Okay, call us a regulator, but it has got to be a regulator of a distinctive sort. Before that point is reached, we have to work with the charity's trustees rather than override their decisions. That empowerment of trustees is a fundamental principle' (*Guardian*, 8 April 1998, p 26). The later report of the Committee in session 2001–02 commented that: 'The Commission has increased the effectiveness of its investigations into potential abuses of charitable status by increasing resources devoted to this important role, and by greater transparency through publication of the results of its work' (39th Report *Giving Confidently* (3 July 2002) para 4). Since the last review the Commission has concentrated still further on enhancing its role as regulator. It recognises that as a regulator it does not have the capacity to eliminate or control all risks and would not wish to do so as this would place an unacceptable regulatory burden on charities. Instead the Commission subscribes to a 'risk and proportionality-based' approach whereby it focuses its resources on concerns of greatest risk – zero-tolerance issues – such as criminality, sham charities and, since 2001, terrorism (Risk and Proportionality (2008); Counter Terrorism Strategy (2008) www.charity-commission.gov.uk/investigations/riskprop.asp).

Consider the following points:

(1) Many of the measures described in this chapter are directed at detecting and remedying abuse that occurs within already-registered charities. An additional possibility is that the Commission should be empowered to refuse to register any charity if it is satisfied, for instance, that it is 'not established in good faith' or 'not likely to be properly administered' or 'that an excessive proportion of the total funds obtained by the charity is likely to be received or retained by any person as remuneration or reward'. Under the post-1993 registration procedures certain categories of persons are disqualified from trusteeship and the Commission can intervene over the choice of name for a charity (see p 1056). Moreover the Commission now operates a system of risk assessment on organisations seeking registration with a view to enhancing the effectiveness of post-registration monitoring and investigation. Nevertheless the fact remains that registration is not a seal of approval: it simply reflects the legal position whereby an organisation whose stated objects are charitable is entitled to be registered under the mandatory provisions of the statute. The question remains whether any further changes should be made to the registration procedures or to the discretionary powers of the Commission. Would it be feasible for the Commission to make a judgement about the good faith of the trustees or, bearing in mind that pioneering or

experimental activity is said to be a useful function of modern charity, about the likely efficiency and effectiveness of a charity in fulfilling its objectives? Indeed the whole question of how to measure 'efficiency' and 'effectiveness' is a tendentious topic. Whilst the introduction of an annual Standard Information Return as part of their Report and Accounts has been supported by charities, there is concern that the quantitative information on such matters as administrative cost as a proportion of income etc will be used to produce 'misleading performance league tables'. Indeed a proposal for performance checks of this nature has been made (see *Guardian* 20 November 2007 and www.philanthropycapital.org; cf Home Office *Charities and Not-for-Profits: A Modern Legal Framework* (July 2003) paras 5.1–5.7).

(2) The introduction of a discretion over registration would pose questions fundamental to charity law. The Commission has powers to intervene in instances of improper or ineffective administration. Can a clear line be drawn between such cases and those where at inception the resources to be committed to the proposed charitable purposes are manifestly inadequate or where there are already numerous other charities doing comparable work? Would a logical development, therefore, be a move to a fully discretionary registration process, raising all the attendant problems considered previously in the context of cy-près (see above, p 1054)? Such an extension of state supervision is scarcely compatible with the various freedoms ideologically associated with charity and the voluntary spirit – freedom to stipulate charitable purposes for the property that one is giving 'on trust', and to give time and energy in aid of such purposes, whether as a trustee, an administrator or a worker.

(3) A declared aim of the changes introduced in the CA 1993 was to place more responsibility for managing a charity's affairs squarely on the shoulders of trustees. Consequently many charity trustees are likely to face increasing commercial and managerialist responsibilities, although under the Trustee Act 2000, s 11(3) trustees can delegate certain of their functions to agents, including those of fund-raising and investment of the charity's assets (see also Charity Commission CC 42 *Appointing Nominees and Custodians: Guidance under s.19(4) of the Trustee Act 2000* (February 2001)). The increasing responsibilities have brought to the fore the question of whether the time has come to allow either the appointment of paid corporate trustees or the remuneration of individual trustees. In the case of private trusts the position has been modified to a considerable extent by the Trustee Act 2000, s 29 (see Chapter 9). This provision expressly excludes from its remit trustees of charitable trusts (s 29(1)(b) and (2)(b)). It was accepted by the Law Commission that whilst there might be circumstances where remuneration could be appropriate for charity trustees, it should not be adopted as a general practice. Instead s 30 of the Trustee Act confers a power on the Secretary of State to make regulations for the remuneration of trust corporations or professional trustees. No such regulations have been

made and it is to the policy of the Charity Commission that we still have to look for guidance.

This abstentionist approach is understandable given the perceived social value attaching to volunteering. The Charity Commission estimates that there are over 900,000 charity trustees in England and Wales, 'and the overwhelming majority embody this spirit of volunteering by acting without payment of any kind, or with only their basic expenses covered' (CC11 *Trustee Expenses and Payments* (2008)). Indeed historically the Commission insisted as a prerequisite to registration that trustees (in the 'strict' sense) and members of management committees of unincorporated associations and directors of companies – these are trustees in a statutory sense under CA 1993, s 97 – be expressly debarred from receiving remuneration. Nevertheless there is a tension between adhering to the notion that persons administering charities must act altruistically and not for their own benefit, and yet acknowledging that they must be able to devote time to running them and possess the appropriate skills and abilities.

In 1994 the Commission modified its approach so as to authorise remuneration where it was 'necessary and reasonable in the interests of the charity'. It is though uncertain just how much of a practical problem the remuneration issue is. The Deakin Committee, for instance, was 'surprised to find the issue of payment of trustees not to be as vital a concern in the sector as we expected' (*Meeting the Challenge of Change: Voluntary Action into the 21st Century* (NCVO 1996) para 3.5.7). This may be due partly to a lack of evidence that charities were finding it hard to recruit enough unpaid trustees of sufficient calibre. Moreover the Committee was not convinced that 'substantial new resources of energy, experience and skill would be unearthed by the lure of payment' (ibid). The Committee concluded on this issue 'that the existing requirement that each body of trustees must decide what are reasonable expenses without specific guidance is the most workable' (para 3.5.10).

Since then the Commission has further elaborated on its approach which, whilst incorporating a degree of flexibility, emphasises that the interests of the charity must be the watchword: 'any departure from [a non-remuneration] position is only likely to occur in exceptional circumstances and needs to be fully justified by trustee boards as being clearly in the interests of their charity' (see CC 11 *Trustee Expenses and Payments* (2008) para F2). The Commission emphasis is that trustees cannot lawfully make such payments unless their governing document specifically allows it, or unless they have authority from the Commission or the court. The Commission will only normally give its consent 'where a charity's complexity of operation has led to an unusually high burden of trusteeship'. It is understood that only about 50 charities currently pay any of their trustees (Filou, *Third Sector* 28 November 2007). The CA 2006, s 36 has introduced one modification to the previous arrangements. Trustees can be paid for providing services (and, in some cases, goods) to the charities for which they are trustees subject to a set of conditions that trustee boards must follow in deciding when payment is appropriate (CA 1993, s 73A–C) In particular trustee boards need to ensure that they are not paying more than the 'going rate' for particular good or services and must be satisfied that the arrangement 'would be in the best interests of the charity' and that the payment is not prohibited by any terms of the trust deed.

Do you agree that trusteeship should remain unremunerated, even if, to ask a loaded question, it were to result in trusteeship being overwhelmingly 'white, male, middle-class and professional'? (See generally Harrow and Palmer 'Reassessing Charity Trusteeship in Britain' (1998) 9 Voluntas no 2 at 171–185.)

(4) Assuming that widespread remuneration of trustees seems unlikely to become the norm, a further issue has been whether to allow charities to purchase personal liability insurance for their trustees (see Baxter [1996] Conv 12). Here again the CA 2006 has modified the previous legal position. Section 39 inserts new section 73F into the 1993 Act and provides trustees with a statutory power to purchase such insurance out of the charity's funds subject to certain limitations. The trustees must be satisfied that the purchase is in the best interests of the charity (s 73F(4)–(5)) and the indemnity will apply only for acts either properly undertaken in the administration of a charity or undertaken in breach of trust or breach of duty. The protection will not apply if the liability arises out of conduct which the trustee either knew or should reasonably be assumed to have known 'was not in the interests of the charity' or if he 'did not care whether or not it was in the best interests of the charity or not' (s 73F (2); see generally CC49 *Charities and Insurance* (2007) paras 56–61).

(5) We have concentrated on financial and administrative accountability, but as a postscript raise a more intangible issue. Under a traditional model of charity trusteeship trustees are not democratically elected or removable; they are not answerable to identifiable constituencies nor to consumers. This may be unexceptionable while charities play a subordinate role in the welfare state. Increasingly, however, with responsibility for the delivery of significant parts of social welfare provision being transferred to the voluntary sector, pressure for democratic accountability may become hard to resist (see Brenton *The Voluntary Sector in British Social Services* (1985) pp 195–198). Care is needed with our terminology here; accountability and democracy are not synonyms. As Diana Leat has emphasised: 'Voluntary organisations may (or may not) be accountable to specified groups, but this does not imply that they are internally democratic' ('Are Voluntary Organisations Accountable?' in Billis and Harris (eds) *Voluntary Agencies: Challenges of Organisation and Management* (1996) 61 at 65). In the context of 'user involvement', as it is called, this issue was specifically commented upon by the Deakin Report (1996):

4.6.1 User involvement is a key issue for the future. The recognition that users are generally the best judge of their own needs does not sit comfortably with concepts of 'charity', 'philanthropy' and 'benevolence' and the sector has been strongly criticised by users for being remote and paternalistic.

The Charity Commission has responded positively on this issue. Whilst 'effective management' and 'positive impact on service delivery' are identified as important qualifying criteria for determining whether involvement of users as trustees is appropriate, the tone of the Commission's guidance is supportive. (See CC24 *Users on Board* (May 2000): '. . . trusteeship can restore a sense of ownership and empowerment to users, . . . reduce inequality and discrimination, . . . and increase support for the charity among other users' (at paras 10–11).)

Compare then the comments of Lord Oliver on a comparable issue but in the context of a different type of organisation:

The National Trust: Report on the Workings of the Constitution (1993)

Para 43. Democracy, in fact and in law, is not a concept which fits easily with the fiduciary duties imposed by the law upon those charged with the administration of a trust, whether public or private, for it would be quite wrong for those having responsibility for ordering the affairs of a trust to permit their considered judgment of what would best serve the fiduciary object or the interests of beneficiaries to be overborne by demands of a group of subscribers, however numerous and however well-intentioned.

It is essential to treat any generalised statements in this area with caution as organisations can differ significantly in the type of service to be delivered and in their organisational structures. Thus organisations with a large and active membership such as the National Trust may need to be differentiated from those which are more specifically dedicated to delivery of services, whilst both are very different from that epitome of individual philanthropy, the charitable foundation.

The National Trust was one of several organisations with large memberships that became a site for conflict between competing views over, inter alia, animal rights issues, particularly stag hunting and fox hunting (see Lansley (1996) 7(3) Voluntas 221–240; and generally Warburton [2006] Conv 330–352). Another such organisation was the RSPCA where the conflict took the form of a dispute about the membership rules, in particular whether the Society had the power to exclude from membership those people whose membership the Society believed would be damaging to its interests. The court upheld the Society's right to do this provided it was acting in good faith in the best interests of the Society, although on those grounds it disapproved the particular method of refusing applications and/or removing members (*RSPCA v Attorney-General* [2001] 3 All ER 530).

It would be inappropriate to end a chapter, one of whose key actors is the Charity Commission, with the focus on the decision-making of the High Court. The Commission has a key procedural role to play even there in that proceedings such as those in the *RSPCA* case are charity proceedings under the Charities Act 1993, s 33(8) and therefore require its consent. Moreover, the role of the Commission can be more extensive than this in certain situations of membership conflict. Whilst it is the case that the Commission cannot act in the administration of a charity where the trustees have acted within the scope of their powers and duties and in good faith, it does have the authority to intervene where, for instance, the administration of the charity has broken down to such an extent that the charity is not working effectively or where there is a clear danger of the name of the charity being brought into disrepute (see eg Charity Commission RS7 *Membership Charities* (March 2004)). Then the Commission can have recourse to the various stratagems described in this chapter such as opening an inquiry under s 8 of the Act, or making an Order under s 26 or even providing a scheme setting out new governance provisions. The last word must be left to the CA 2006. Section 25 has strengthened the armoury of the Commission by inserting a new s 29A into the CA 1993 which gives it power to determine the membership of a charity either on the application of the charity itself or at any time after the Commission has instituted a s 8 inquiry with respect to the charity (s 29A(1)). This is potentially a significant yet largely unheralded area of Charity Commission jurisdiction. Membership charities are becoming increasingly common, with just over half of the charities surveyed for a Commission report having a membership structure of some description. Moreover in 44% of those surveyed members can vote in order to influence the charity's governance and, therefore, influence the decisions that affect them.

Index